Essentials of Electrical and Computer Engineering

DAVID V. KERNS, JR.
Olin College

J. DAVID IRWIN
Auburn University

UPPER SADDLE RIVER, NJ 07458

Library of Congress Cataloging-in-Publication Data
Kerns, David V.
Essentials of electrical and computer engineering / David V. Kerns, Jr., J. David Irwin.
p. cm.
ISBN 0-13-923970-7
1. Electric engineering. 2. Computer engineering. I. Irwin, J. David II. Title.

TK146.K43 2004
621.3—dc22 2003023688

Vice President and Editorial Director, ECS: *Marcia J. Horton*
Vice President and Director of Production and Manufacturing, ESM: *David W. Riccardi*
Executive Managing Editor: *Vince O'Brien*
Managing Editor: *David A. George*
Production Editor: *Patty Donovan*
Art Director: *Jayne Conte*
Cover Designer: *Bruce Kenselaar*
Managing Editor, AV Management and Production: *Patricia Burns*
Art Editor: *Xiaohong Zhu*
Manufacturing Manager: *Trudy Pisciotti*
Manufacturing Buyer: *Lynda Castillo*
Marketing Manager: *Holly Stark*

Pearson Prentice Hall
Pearson Education, Inc.
Upper Saddle River, NJ 07458

Printed in the United States of America

10 9 8 7 6 5 4

ISBN 0-13-923970-7

Pearson Education Ltd., London
Pearson Education Australia Pty. Ltd., *Sydney*
Pearson Education Singapore, Pte. Ltd.
Pearson Education North Asia Ltd., *Hong Kong*
Pearson Education Canada, Inc., *Toronto*
Pearson Educación de Mexico, S.A. de C.V.
Pearson Education—Japan, Tokyo
Pearson Education Malaysia, Pte. Ltd.
Pearson Education, Inc., Upper Saddle River, New Jersey

To our parents,
David and Dorothea Kerns
Arthur and Virginia Irwin

Contents

13 Digital Logic Circuits 500

14 Digital Electronic Logic Gates 544

Preface

P.1 Purpose

This book is intended to serve as a text or guidebook for an introductory course or course sequence in electrical engineering or electrical and computer engineering. It is unique in that it is concise; it is highly concentrated and focused on the essential elements of understanding required for all engineering students and for successfully passing the electrical engineering portion of the Fundamentals of Engineering (FE) exam.

The strength of the text is its clear presentation of fundamentals in the context of various applications from all engineering fields. It introduces the latest technologies such as MEMS (Microelectromechanical Systems) to illustrate how modern technologies are interdisciplinary and often require knowledge of several engineering fields.

There is constant attention to providing a learning environment accessible to those with little electrical or computer engineering background. This is achieved through abundant use of analogies, such as mechanical, fluidic, and chemical, and a large number of worked examples, drill exercises, and homework problems crafted to illustrate key principles and with a range of difficulty levels. The summaries at the end of each chapter are extensive and provide an excellent review of important material. When possible, examples that address instrumentation systems and other generally useful applications are highlighted. The optional use of MATLAB as a computing tool allows the course to focus on electrical engineering, instead of linear algebra or differential equations.

The addition of removable *Just-in-Time* Reference Cards provides a powerful tool for student study by summarizing key concepts and equations. The *Just-in-Time* Reference Cards also can be used by the instructor with exams or tests to simulate the environment of the FE examination, in which limited reference material is made available.

The basic understanding and knowledge of electrical and computer engineering provided by this text will serve students well throughout their engineering careers. The focus is on fundamentals that will not change, illustrated through the latest applications. This book will serve well as a reference book on the field of electrical engineering in their future work as practicing engineers.

This text is also suitable for the reader who wishes to use a self-study approach to learn the fundamentals of electrical and computer engineering. The many worked examples, drill problems, and careful explanations within each chapter test the student's understanding, clarify key points, and provide necessary feedback for rich learning.

P.2 Features

For the Student

The presentation is clear and concise. The selection of topics is highly concentrated and focused on elements that are central to electrical and computer engineering. No attempt has been made to cover a wide range of ancillary topics that, while interesting, dilute the focus and effort on essential elements. Extraneous material that would serve only to confuse the beginning student is omitted.

There is an expanded Chapter Summary at the end of each chapter, which provides a clear review of important material. The removable *Just-in-Time* Reference Cards may be used to guide focused self-study, and, with the instructor's permission, can be used as reference material during certain examinations to practice for the FE exam.

The book is an important aid to students who take the FE exam. Some of the examples and end-of-chapter problems are specifically chosen to mimic those found on the electrical portion of the FE exam. Appendix C provides a detailed description of the FE examination and how this text can be used to prepare for it.

The book provides a solid foundation for further study as well as a quick reference to a vast array of fundamental elements. There is sufficient depth in the book to support a later study of advanced topics and the organization, presentation, and index make the text a viable reference.

The hallmark of the book is the manner in which complicated topics are made simple through a presentation that combines analogies, examples, drill problems, and end-of-chapter problems. This text is student-oriented, aimed at presenting the topics in a way that is easy to grasp.

Many nonelectrical majors employ MATLAB in their own curriculum. This important technique is also employed to solve circuit problems, thus placing the solution of circuits in a familiar setting for the student.

For the Instructor

The book offers the instructor maximum flexibility in the design of their course. Many chapters can be skipped or the order of presentation changed, enabling the organization of a coherent presentation tailored to the instructor's specifications. The modular design of the text provides this flexibility. It is assumed most classes would begin with Chapters 1 and 2, completing the material through dc circuits. At this point the instructor has many options including continuing with Chapter 3 (Transient Analysis) or branching to Chapter 9 (Op Amps) or Chapter 4 (AC Circuits). The material can be easily packaged in a sequence that matches the particular needs of a specific audience.

The plethora of examples and drill exercises, the margin notes, the expanded chapter summaries, and the *Just-in-Time* Reference Cards support various modes of student learning and provide the instructor with a rich menu of materials for assistance in teaching. The large number of end-of-chapter problems permits the instructor to select problems of appropriate difficulty and change homework assignments each term with ease.

P.3 System of Units

The system of units used in this text is the international system of units, the Systéme International des Unités, which is normally referred to as the SI standard system. This system, which is composed of the basic units meter (m), kilogram (kg), second (s), ampere (A), degree Kelvin (K), and candela (cd), is defined in all modern physics texts and therefore will not be defined here; we will, however, discuss the units in some detail as we encounter them in our subsequent analyses.

TABLE P.1 Standard Abbreviations and Symbols

Abbreviation	Meaning
ac	Alternating current
A	Ampere
C	Coulomb
db	Decibel
dc	Direct current
F	Farad
H	Henry
Hz	Hertz
J	Joule
m	Meter
N	Newton
N-m	Newton-meter
Ω	Ohm
PF	Power factor
rad	Radian
RLC	Resistance-inductance-capacitance
rms	Root-mean-square
s	Second
S	Siemens
V	Volt
VA	Voltampere
W	Watt

The abbreviations and symbols used to represent the various quantities studied in this text follow standard practice. Table P.1 may be a useful reference if you encounter unfamiliar symbols.

The standard prefixes that are employed in SI are shown in Figure P.1. Note the decimal relationship between these prefixes. These standard prefixes are employed throughout our study of electrical engineering.

Only a few decades ago, a millisecond, 10^{-3}s, was considered to be a short time in the analysis of electric circuits and devices. Advances in technology, however, have led to a state in which we now perform calculations in picoseconds. The remarkable increases in speed and functional performance have been accompanied by phenomenal decreases in the physical size of electronic systems. Miniaturized integrated circuits are commonplace in calcula-

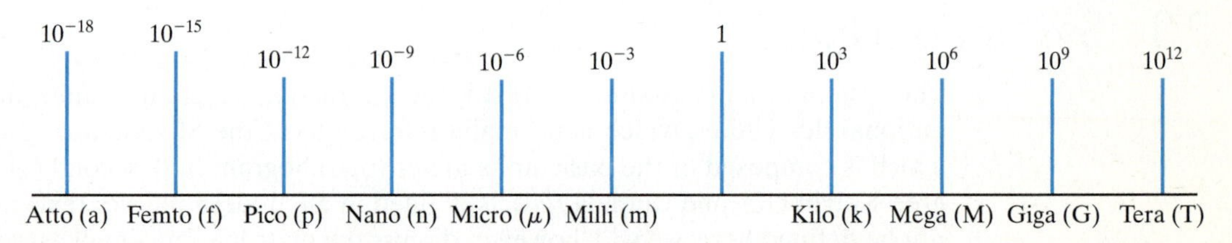

FIGURE P.1 Standard SI multiplier prefixes.

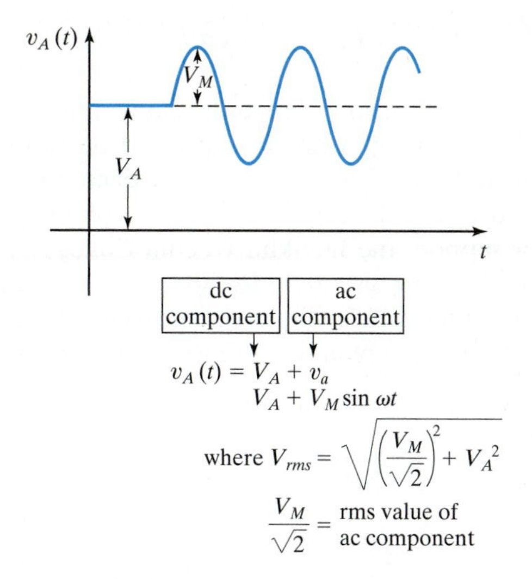

FIGURE P.2 Notation for voltage and current.

tors, computers, and other electronic equipment. A single such chip (typically about 1 cm on each side) can contain millions of devices, while the size of each device or circuit element on the chip is measured in fractions of a micron (1 micron = 10^{-6}m).

P.4 Notation

Two of the most commonly used symbols in the study of electrical engineering are those for voltage (V) and current (I). The use of lowercase or uppercase letters and the particular subscript used with the letter provide information about the voltage or current, as illustrated in the following example:

V, V_1, or V_A = a dc (direct current) value. The use of a capital V or I with a number or capital subscript following indicates a constant, dc value.

$v(t)$, $v_1(t)$, $v_a(t)$, or v_A = the instantaneous value. The use of lowercase v or i with "(t)," or with a capital subscript, indicates the total instantaneous value "as a function of time."

V_M, V_m, I_M, or I_m = the amplitude or maximum value of a sinusoidally varying voltage or current.

V_{rms} or I_{rms} = the RMS or root-mean-square value of a sinusoidally varying voltage or current.

v_a or v_1 = the instantaneous value of the time-varying component (zero average).

The use of these quantities is illustrated graphically in Figure P.2.

DAVID V. KERNS, JR.
Olin College

J. DAVID IRWIN
Auburn University

ACKNOWLEDGMENT

We gratefully acknowledge the many individuals who have assisted us in the writing of this book; we have personally expressed our appreciation to each. We thank our families for their understanding, patience, and encouragement—the commitment of personal time required to complete a project of this scope is large. We also recognize our institutions for their support, the Franklin W. Olin College of Engineering and Auburn University. Finally, we express our gratitude to those who will read and learn from this text. We hope that our presentation will facilitate your learning. If errors are detected, we encourage you to notify the authors by email so these can be corrected in future editions.

About the Authors

David V. Kerns, Jr., is currently Provost and Franklin and Mary Olin Distinguished Professor of Electrical and Computer Engineering at the Franklin W. Olin College of Engineering, Needham, MA. He has served in this position since 1999 as a member of the founding leadership team to establish a new engineering college dedicated to innovation in engineering education. For the prior 13 years he served at Vanderbilt University as Chair of the Electrical Engineering Department and Associate Dean of Engineering. He has also served on the faculties of Florida State University, Auburn University, and Bucknell University, and has taught introductory electrical and computer engineering courses for over 25 years. He also served in industry at Bell Telephone Laboratories and as an entrepreneur in founding two electronics companies. Dr. Kerns has over 100 publications in the areas of microelectronics research and engineering education. He currently serves as President of the IEEE Education Society and is a fellow of the IEEE (Institute for Electrical and Electronic Engineering). He is the coauthor with J. David Irwin of a very successful text, *Introduction to Electrical Engineering,* published by Prentice Hall in 1995.

J. David Irwin is currently Earle C. Williams Eminent Scholar and Head of the Electrical and Computer Engineering Department at Auburn University. Following graduate school in 1967, he joined Bell Telephone Laboratories, Holmdel, New Jersey as a Member of the Technical Staff and was later promoted to Supervisor. He joined Auburn University as an Assistant Professor in 1969 and became Head of the department in 1973. He is the author or co-author of 16 textbooks and the Editor-in-Chief of a large handbook. His circuit's book entitled *Basic Engineering Circuit Analysis,* published by John Wiley and Sons, Inc., is entering its 8th edition. He has served the Institute of Electrical and Electronic Engineers, Inc. (IEEE) and the American Society for Engineering Education (ASEE) in a variety of capacities. He is the past president of both the IEEE Education and Industrial Electronics Societies, and former editor of the IEEE Transactions on Industrial Electronics. He continues to serve the IEEE at both the Institute and Society levels in a number of areas, including award and administrative committees, as well as the management of international conferences. He is a fellow of both the ASEE and the IEEE and has received numerous education-related awards.

1

1-1 Overview

In today's world, many technological problems are so complex that their scope spans a number of engineering and scientific disciplines. Teams of individuals are required to address the seemingly endless number of issues that impact the solution. As a result, many engineers find themselves working on teams with individuals whose technical specialties are quite diverse and it becomes increasingly important to have some working knowledge of engineering disciplines outside our own.

Electrical engineering involves the conception, design, development, and production of the electrical or electronic products and systems needed by our technological society. Electrical engineers play an essential role in creating and advancing this high-technology world of computers, lasers, robots, space exploration, communications, energy, and many other applications of electronic devices and systems.

Many engineering students take the Fundamentals of Engineering (FE) exam administered by the National Council of Examiners for Engineering and Surveying. Successfully passing this exam is one of the first steps to becoming professionally licensed—an important consideration if you ever plan to offer your engineering services to the public. The same FE exam is taken by engineers from all disciplines. There is currently a portion of that exam dealing with electrical engineering, and one of the objectives of this book is to prepare you well for that exam.

In almost every aspect of our everyday lives, we see electrical or electronic functions replacing older technologies. Automobiles have electronic dashboards and electronic ignitions; surveying is done with lasers and electronic range finders; manufacturing processes and other industrial processes in every field, from chemical refining facilities to metal foundries to waste water treatment, all utilize electronic sensors to detect information about the processes; electronic instrumentation systems to gather that information; computer control systems to process the incoming information, make decisions about the process flow, and send out electronic commands to actuators within the facility to correct and control the operation.

The material in this text will give you insight into the knowledge and tools required to understand how these systems operate and to be able to communicate effectively with experts in the field. It is intended to provide you with the vocabulary and the skills to assist you in specifying and purchasing electronic systems or equipment, setting it up in a laboratory or manufacturing area, and effectively utilizing this equipment or instrumentation to accomplish your intended goals. This knowledge will greatly enhance your ability to do your job, whether it be in engineering, management, or any related field.

1-2 Basic Concepts

1.2.1 Charge

Electrical engineers deal primarily with charge, its motion, and the effects of that motion. *Electricity* is a word most often used in a nontechnical context to describe the presence of charge; the term *electricity* is used both to describe charge in motion (for example, through a wire as an *electric current*) and stationary charge, *static electricity.*

Charge is a fundamental property of matter and is said to be conserved—that is, it can neither be created nor destroyed. This means that if the charge moves away from one location, it must appear at another. There are two types of charge, positive charge and negative charge. Charge is the substance of which electric currents are made.

Charges near each other will attract each other or repel from each other according to the following rule: Like charges repel each other; opposite charges attract each other.

The basic structure of an atom is held together by the attractive force between unlike charges. Recall that an atom of hydrogen, with a positively charged nucleus, has an electron with a negative charge that is held in an orbit around the nucleus by the constant attraction between these unlike charges. You've probably done experiments where you rubbed a wool sweater (or a cat) on a hard rubber comb and created static electricity. The comb was originally neutral, containing an equal balance of positive and negative charges. The rubbing action strips charge off the wool and the comb in an unequal way so that there is no longer a balance; one contains more positive charge and less negative charge than the other. The unequal charges attract each other and the charged comb can be used to attract little bits of paper in order to demonstrate the attractive force between unequal charges. In this example the charge once placed on the comb doesn't move easily, and hence the designation static electricity. In case you're wondering, in the above experiment, the comb picks up extra electrons and becomes negatively charged.

Electric charge defined

Charge is designated by the symbol q, and is measured in units of coulombs (C). The negative charge carried by a single individual electron is -1.602×10^{-19} coulombs, and this is the smallest unit of charge that exists. Therefore, charge is quantized in blocks, the magnitude of the charge on a single electron.

1.2.2 The Force Between Two Charges

The force between two small clusters of charge (each one small enough to be considered a point) has been found to be described by the following equation:

$$F = k\frac{q_1 q_2}{d^2} \tag{1.1}$$

where q_1 is the charge at position 1 in coulombs, q_2 is the charge at position 2 in coulombs, d is the distance between the charges in meters, and k is a constant of 8.99×10^9 newton meter^2/C^2.

Example 1.1

If $q_1 = 0.50$ coulombs and $q_2 = -0.03$ coulombs, let us calculate the separation between these two charges if they are attracted together by a force of one newton.

From Eq. (1.1) we find that

$$d = \sqrt{k\frac{q_1 q_2}{F}}$$

and hence

$$d = \sqrt{(8.99 \times 10^9)\frac{0.50 \times 0.03}{1}} = 11{,}612 \textit{ meters}$$

Note: In these calculations, the square root will always be applied to a positive number; if the charges are of opposite sign, the force, F, will be negative (indicating attraction).

Example 1.2

Two electrons drifting through space have come to a position where they are separated by a distance of one micron, that is, 1×10^{-6} meters. We wish to calculate the force between these two electrons and determine if it is attractive or repulsive.

Applying Eq. (1.1) we find that the force $F = 2.3 \times 10^{-16}$ newtons; since the two electrons each have a negative charge, they repel each other.

Drill Exercise

D1.1. A point charge of 1 C creates an attractive force of 0.2 N when placed at a distance of 0.1 m from a second charged object. Find the charge on the second object.

Ans: -2.23×10^{-13}C.

1.2.3 Conductors and Insulators

Conductors and insulators defined

In order to put charge in motion so that it becomes an electric current, we must provide a path through which it can flow easily. In the vast majority of applications, charge will be carried by moving electrons along a path through which they can move easily. Materials through which charge flows readily are called *conductors.* Most metals, such as copper, are excellent conductors and therefore are used for fabrication of electrical wires and the conductive paths on electronic circuit boards.

TABLE 1.1

Conductors	Semiconductors	Insulators
Silver	Silicon	Glass
Gold	Germanium	Plastic
Copper	Gallium Arsenide	Ceramics
Aluminum		Rubber

Insulators are materials that do not allow charge to move easily. Therefore, electric current cannot be made to flow through an insulator. Charge placed on an insulating material, such as the rubber comb, just stays there as static electricity; charge has great difficulty moving through it. Insulating materials are often wrapped around the center conducting core of a wire to prevent the charge from flowing off to some undesired place if the wire inadvertently touches some other object.

Resistance will be defined quantitatively later; however, qualitatively a conductor has a low resistance to the flow of charge, and an insulator has a very high resistance to the flow of charge. There is a wide range of charge conducting abilities of various materials; the resistance to charge movement of copper is about 10^{25} times lower than that of a comparable single piece of quartz. *Semiconductors* fall in the middle between conductors and insulators, and have a moderate resistance to the flow of charge. Table 1.1 lists some common conductors, semiconductors, and insulators.

Example 1.3

Based on our experience, let us classify the following materials as insulators or conductors, that is, selecting the one that fits best: iron, paper, wood, and salt water.

Using either experience or intuition, we select as conductors iron and salt water, and as insulators paper and wood.

1.2.4 Current and Voltage

This section defines two of the most commonly used terms in electrical engineering: *current* (measured in amperes) and *voltage* (measured in volts).

Electric current and its units—or—The current–charge connection

Charge in Motion. Electric *current* implies "charge in motion"; the term *current* is simply a measure of how much charge is moved per unit of time. Current is measured in *amperes*, frequently called the amp and abbreviated as A; one ampere is defined as the transfer of one coulomb in one second. Imagine, for example, a wire carrying four amperes of current. Now imagine a cross-section cut through this wire; in one second of time, four coulombs of charge pass through the plane of that cross-section. Therefore, one ampere is equal to one coulomb/second and four amperes is equal to four coulombs/second.

Example 1.4

Let us determine the number of electrons that pass through a cross-section of a wire carrying one ampere in one second of time.

Recall the charge on a single electron is -1.6×10^{-19} coulombs. Therefore, the number of electrons in one coulomb is

$$\frac{1}{1.6 \times 10^{-19}} = 6.25 \times 10^{18} \textit{ electrons}$$

Example 1.5

A lightning bolt carries 1,000 amperes of current and lasts 38 microseconds. Let us calculate the charge that is deposited on a golf cart hit by the lightning strike.

If we let Q be the total charge deposited on the cart,

$$Q = \frac{\Delta q}{\Delta t} \times \Delta t = \textit{current} \times \textit{time interval}$$

and hence

$$Q = (1000 \textit{ amperes}) \times (38\ \ 10^{-6} \textit{ seconds}) = 0.38 \textit{ coulombs}$$

As illustrated in the above example, the *average* current over a time interval is defined as the total charge transferred divided by the total time interval; we will use the symbol I to represent the average current.

$$I = \frac{\Delta q}{\Delta t} \tag{1.2}$$

where Δq is the change in charge, and Δt is the time interval over which that change occurs.

The instantaneous current, i, is defined as the time rate of change of the charge transfer at any particular instant and is defined by

$$i = \frac{dq}{dt} \tag{1.3}$$

The letter "i" is used to represent current in most texts; the letter "C" was already taken for "coulomb."

Drill Exercise

D1.2. How long does it take a 20A battery charger to deliver a charge of 10^4C?

Ans. 500*s*.

Charge can be transported by various mechanisms. As mentioned, the most common is the movement of electrons through a conductor; however, positive ions flowing the opposite direction can transfer charge, as is the case in electrochemical reactions in batteries or in electroplating. In addition, solid state electronic devices use semiconductor materials in which charge can be moved by electrons carrying negative charge, and "holes" carrying positive charge. The total current through any particular plane is the total net charge transferred divided by the time interval.

$$i = \frac{dq}{dt} = \frac{dq^+ + dq^-}{dt} \tag{1.3a}$$

where dq^+ is the incremental positive charge transferred and dq^- is the incremental negative charge transferred.

Current, a scalar quantity, requires a sign convention; if we assume that the direction we call "positive current" flow is the direction positive charge moves (which is what we will assume in this text), then Eq. (1.3a) reveals that the total current is the sum of the rate of flow of positive charge in one direction and negative charge in the opposite direction.

The sign convention for current

The *sign convention,* which we will adopt here, is the following: Positive current will be defined as the net rate of flow of positive charge. Therefore, a wire conducting electrons to the left will be described as having a positive current to the right.

In our world we encounter currents over many orders of magnitude. Lightning strikes consist of bursts of current that can be tens of thousands of amperes, while at the other end of the scale, the current in a nerve pulse may be only picoamperes. In between is a wide range of currents. For example, typical household appliances require from 0.5 to 10 amperes; individual electronic circuits may require microamperes to milliamperes, and large industrial motors may require hundreds of amperes. A chart showing the range of commonly encountered currents is shown in Figure 1.1.

Fluid Analogy. In beginning the study of electrical engineering, it is often helpful to have an easily understood analogy for some of the concepts. We will use such analogies throughout this book. Consider water flowing in a pipe as analogous to current flowing in a wire. We measure the quantity of water, let's say in gallons; the quantity of electricity is the charge, measured in coulombs. The flow rate of water, the amount of water flowing through a cross-section of pipe per unit time, will be measured in gallons per second; the amount of electric current is the flow rate of charge measured in coulombs per second, which we have given the special name ampere.

Note that current is always a measure of the flow through a conducting path, measured at a particular cross-section through the path, just as flow rate of water is measured at a particular point along the pipe. In the top half of Figure 1.2, we can see that if the conducting path, be it a wire or a pipe, has no branches or alternate paths, the flow rate at any point along the pipe must be the same.

If conducting branches merge into a single path, as illustrated in the lower half of Figure 1.2, the sum of the flow rates in the entering branches must equal the flow rate of the outgoing branch. This is illustrated in the figure with two branches, but it could be any number. Put simply, this is an illustration of the concept "what goes in must come out" (if there's no storage device). This is an illustration of Kirchhoff's current law, which will be explained in more detail in Chapter 2.

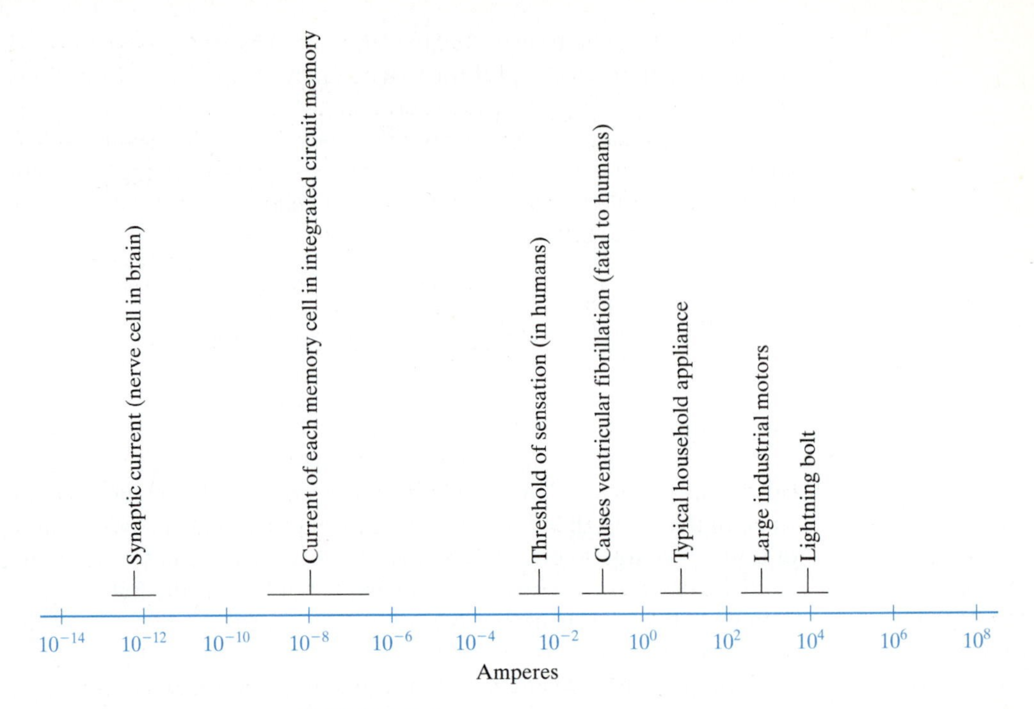

FIGURE 1.1 The range of currents.

Voltage and Energy. Continuing for a moment with the analogy of water flowing in a pipe, imagine that this pipe connects to the input of a turbine, as shown in Figure 1.3(a). The water enters the turbine and pushes against the blades on a shaft, rotating the shaft and doing work. The water is collected at the bottom of the turbine and exits through another pipe. The water entering the turbine has a higher potential energy than that exiting; the potential energy is converted in the turbine to useful work (as energy delivered to the rotation of the shaft), and then exits at a lower potential energy. In the case of water, this potential energy is measured by the pressure. The water pressure entering the turbine is higher than that leaving and

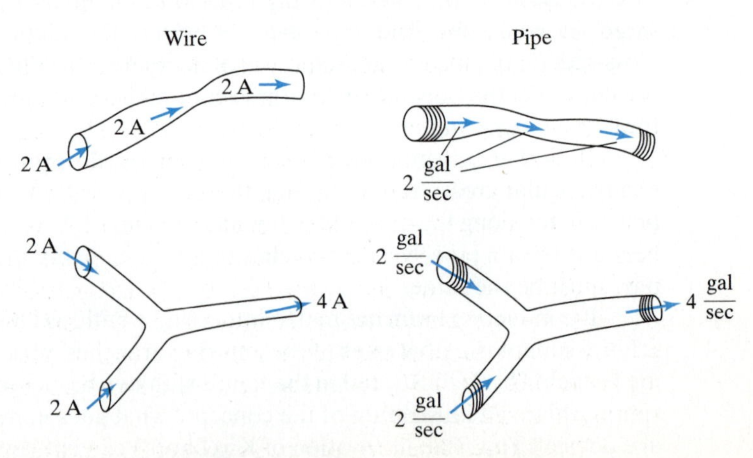

FIGURE 1.2 Flow rate analogy.

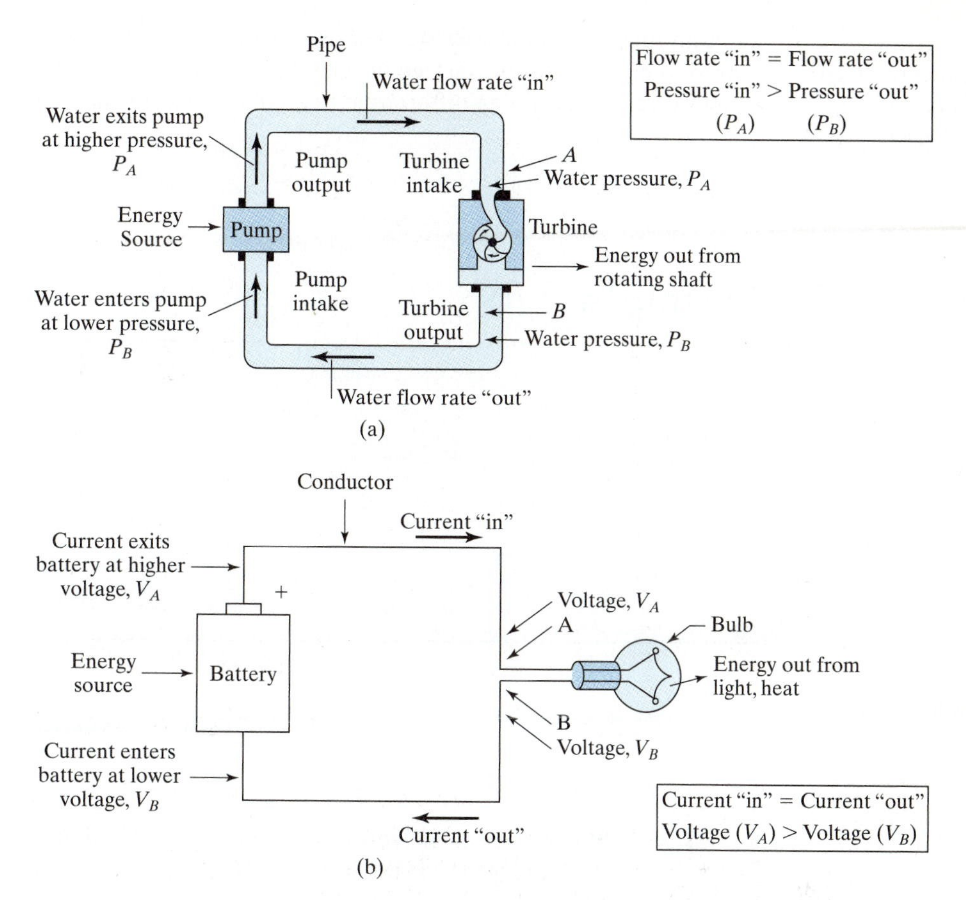

FIGURE 1.3 Simple fluid and electric circuit.

this pressure difference forces the water through the turbine. If the water pressure were the same at the entry point of the turbine as at the exit, then there would be no push or force to drive the water through the turbine. Thus, it is the pressure difference across the turbine that forces the water through it.

The fluid collected at the output of the turbine is at a lower pressure. If this output fluid is to be cycled through again to continue the process, it must be increased in pressure so that it will have the potential energy necessary to drive through the turbine again. This is accomplished by routing the collected water to a pump. The pump provides a source of energy that forces the fluid around in the closed loop.

Now consider an electric current flowing through an electric light bulb, as illustrated in Figure 1.3(b). The "force" or "pressure" that pushes the charge through the light bulb is the voltage difference supplied by the battery. The charge that flows through the light bulb does work, that is, w joules of energy for generating heat and light, and then the charge emerges at the other terminal of the bulb at a lower voltage or potential. There is a *voltage difference* across the bulb, $V_A - V_B$, that moves charge through the bulb; if the voltages were the same, no charge would move.

The voltage value represents potential energy, and the potential difference or voltage difference across the bulb reveals the energy-transfer capability of the charge flow. Voltage is mea-

Voltage and its units—or—The voltage–energy connection

sured in joules per coulomb, defined as the volt, V, and one volt is the energy in joules required to move a positive charge of one coulomb (C) through an element.

Therefore, assuming differential amounts of charge and energy:

$$v = \frac{dw}{dq} \tag{1.4}$$

Example 1.6

If the battery, connected as shown in Figure 1.3(b), supplies a voltage difference of 1.5 volts, such as a flashlight battery, let us calculate the amount of energy used to transfer 0.5 coulombs of charge through the bulb.

From Eq. (1.4)

$$dw = v\,dq$$

Integrating, we obtain

$$w = \int dw = v \int dq = vq = (1.5\text{ V})\,(0.5\text{ C}) = 0.75\ \textit{joules}$$

Drill Exercise

D1.3. A 20-volt battery delivers 0.1 J of energy. (a) How much charge was delivered by the battery? (b) If the process in (a) occurred in 1 μs, what was the current?

Ans: (a) 5×10^{-3} C, (b) 5×10^{3} A.

We encounter a wide range of voltages in everyday experiences. Figure 1.4 shows some examples of voltages ranging from the extremely large voltage differences between clouds and earth that can produce lightning, to the very small voltage differences between locations on the human scalp resulting from electrical activity in the brain. Recordings of the latter are called electroencephalograms (EEGs) and are a common medical diagnostic tool for neurological brain disorders.

Circuit Analogy. Figures 1.3(a) and (b) both show single-loop "circuits," the first utilizing a fluid flow, and the second a current flow.

In Figure 1.3(a), notice that the fluid exits the pump at a high pressure. If the pipe is sufficiently short or is large enough and of good design, we can assume that there is no pressure loss from the exit of the pump to the entry point of the turbine. We make the analogous assumption in our study of electric circuits as illustrated in Figure 1.3(b). The conductor paths, represented by solid lines in the circuit drawing, are assumed ideal and conduct electric charge perfectly, that is, with no loss in voltage. Therefore, the voltage at the plus terminal of the battery is the same as the voltage, V_A, at the top of the bulb; this same voltage would be measured

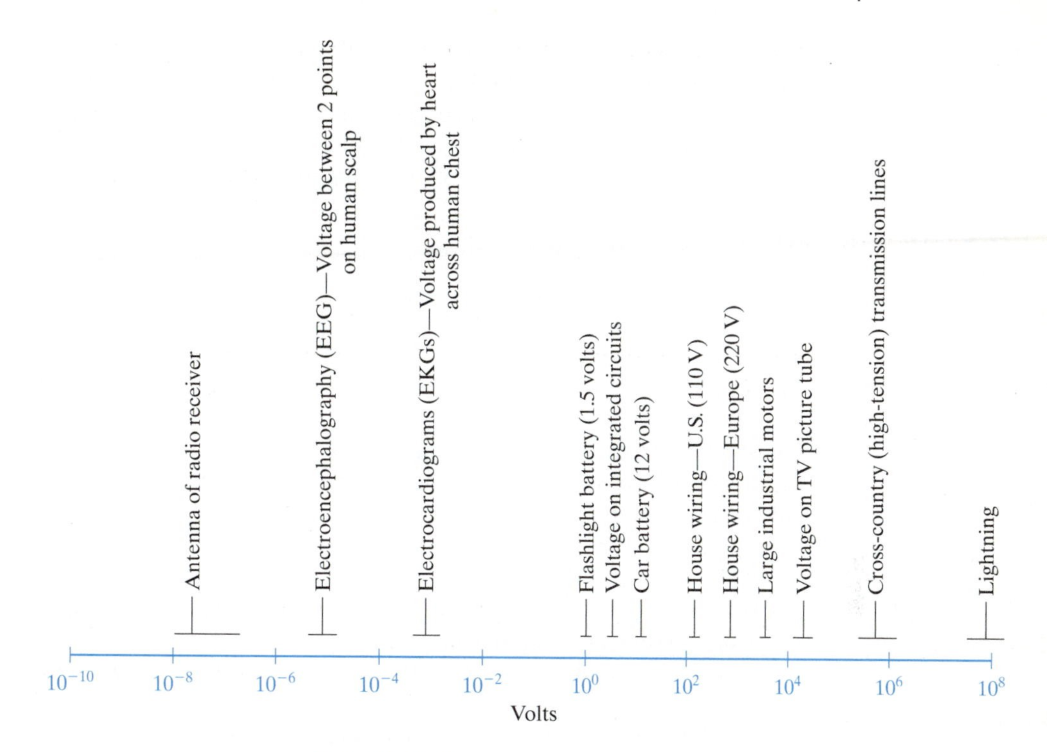

FIGURE 1.4 The range of voltages.

at any point along that conductor between those two points. Similarly, the voltage at the bottom of the bulb is the same anywhere along the lower conducting path to the negative terminal of the battery.

The circuit drawing in Figure 1.3(b) represents, therefore, an idealized "model" of the actual physical circuit. We construct models making certain simplifying assumptions about the various parts of the circuit that will enable us to easily apply mathematical techniques and predict the circuit's performance. If our predicted values agree with those actually measured in real circuits, then the validity of these simplifying assumptions is justified. In a later section in this chapter we will discuss modeling in more detail.

Unless the turbine in Figure 1.3(a) contains some magical storage capacity, in the steady state, that is, after the system has been operating for a while, the flow rate "out" must be the same as the flow rate "in." That is, there can be no net accumulation of water in the turbine that occurs for an unlimited time. It's difficult to imagine more water flowing out than flowing in because there is no source for the extra water; and, the only way less water could flow out than flows in is if it is diverted to some other path or storage area within the turbine. This might happen initially when the system is first turned on—as the reservoir in the bottom of the turbine fills. However, in steady state, the amount of water flowing in during a given amount of time must equal the amount of water flowing out in the same amount of time, that is, their flow rates must be equal.

The analogous situation holds in the electric circuit of Figure 1.3(b). When the circuit is first energized, there may be a brief period of time when the current in does not equal the current out due to establishing an equilibrium charge on various components within the circuit. This "transient" behavior will be studied in Chapter 3. However, after the battery has been connected in the circuit, as shown in Figure 1.3(b), for some time, the current "in" will exactly equal the current "out." The steady state behavior of dc circuits will be examined in Chapter 2 and the steady state behavior of ac circuits will be examined in Chapter 4.

In single-loop circuits such as that illustrated in Figures 1.3(a) and 1.3(b), the flow rate, or current in the electric circuit, is the same at any point around the entire loop.

1.2.5 DC, AC, Frequency, and Spectra

Batteries are sources of electric power that derive their energy from a chemical reaction within the battery. Rechargeable batteries, such as the battery in your car, allow the chemical reaction to be reversed so that electric energy can be stored in the battery and then extracted at a later time.

Power generated in large power generation facilities is carried across many miles by high-voltage transmission lines, where it is distributed at various substations to the users of the power. This power is used for heating, generation of electric light, driving various types of electric motors, and many other applications. Electric power is classified as either dc or ac, direct current or alternating current, respectively.

The abbreviation "dc" stands for direct current, and refers to current that is flowing in a wire continuously in one direction at a specified value. On the other hand, "ac" means alternating current, in which the current goes back and forth, reversing its direction many times per second. The number of times the direction changes (and changes back) per second is called the *frequency, f,* and is expressed by the number of cycles per second, a unit called the Hertz (Hz). An illustration of dc and ac current is shown in Figure 1.5

The difference between dc and ac current

Alternating current (ac) often follows a sinusoidal variation as a function of time. The positive and negative swing of the sine function in the previous figure represents the current first flowing one way and then the other—completing one entire "cycle" in time, *T,* the period.

At dc, and low-frequency ac (up to several hundred Hz), the electric and magnetic interactions remain relatively localized around the current-carrying wire. As frequency is increased, however, a wonderful thing happens. Energy begins to radiate from the wire and propagate through the atmosphere as electromagnetic waves. These are the waves that make possible radio communications, television, satellite communications, radar, and all related forms of wireless communications. These are the same electromagnetic waves that are beamed into a chicken in your microwave oven to transfer energy for cooking. An alternating current applied to a conducting structure tailored to be effective in radiating the energy into the at-

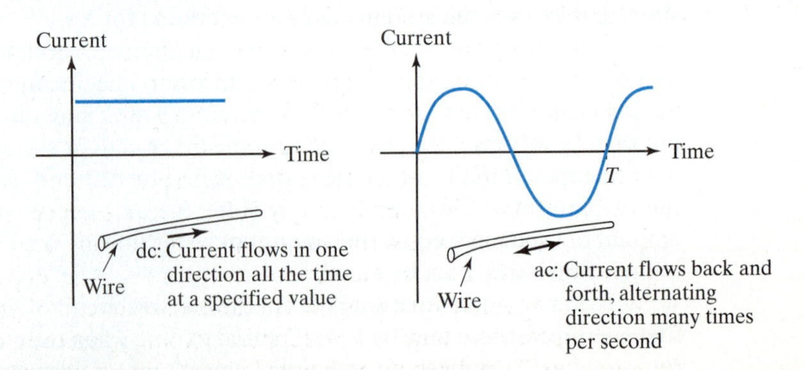

FIGURE 1.5 dc and ac.

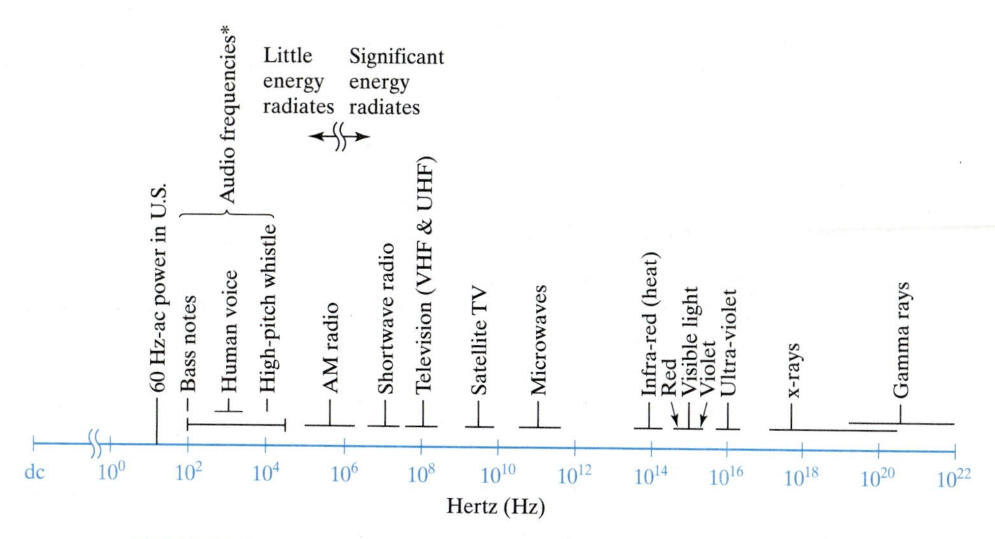

FIGURE 1.6 Frequency spectrum. *Note: We hear sounds by acoustical waves at these frequencies.

mosphere can transmit electromagnetic waves around the world and beyond. Such a structure is called an antenna.

Electromagnetic waves propagating through space travel at the speed of light, c, which is 186,000 miles per second, or 3×10^8 meters per second. Light is an electromagnetic wave within a particular range of frequencies; the exact frequency determines the color.

The frequency of an electromagnetic wave affects many of its characteristics, including the way it propagates through the atmosphere. Figure 1.6 shows the electromagnetic spectrum, with frequency plotted horizontally and the common usage of various parts of this spectrum indicated.

1.2.6 Reference Directions and Polarities

In solving problems involving mechanical systems, we generally set up a coordinate system that defines what we will assume is the positive direction; then when we calculate velocity, for example, and if the answer is a positive number, we know the motion is in the same direction as our assumed positive direction. If, on the other hand, we compute a negative velocity, then the actual motion is in the opposite direction.

We must set up an analogous reference direction or polarity in the solution of electric circuit problems. It is extremely important that the variables that are used to represent voltage between two points be defined in such a way that the solution will let us interpret which point is at the higher potential with respect to the other.

In Figure 1.7(a), the variable that represents the voltage between points A and B has been defined as V_1. The + and − signs define a reference direction for V_1. Since V_1 has a positive value (+2 volts), the terminal with the + reference (terminal A) is at a higher potential than terminal B by 2 volts. If a unit positive charge is moved from point A through the circuit to point B, it will give up energy to the circuit and have 2J less energy when it reaches point B. If a unit positive charge is moved from point B to point A, extra energy must be added in the amount of 2J, and hence the charge will end up with 2J more energy at point A than it started with at point B.

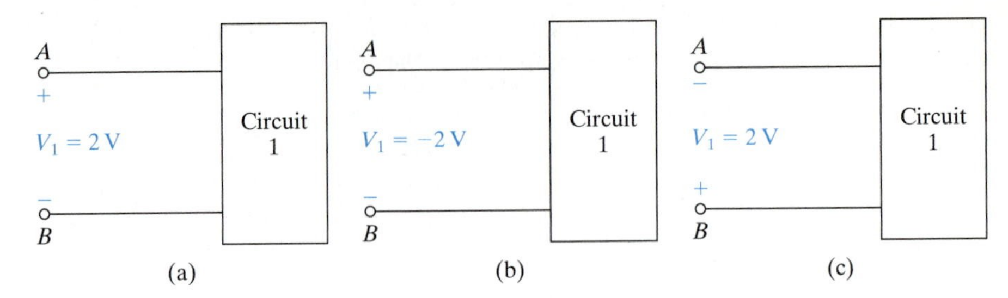

FIGURE 1.7 Voltage polarity relationships.

If, on the other hand, V_1 had a negative sign (like $V_1 = -2$ volts), then it would imply that terminal B was at a higher potential than terminal A, and the situation above would be reversed. This is illustrated in Figure 1.7(b); this figure tells us that terminals A and B have a potential difference (voltage difference) of 2 volts, and that terminal B is more positive than terminal A.

The same situation as that described in Figure 1.7(b) is presented in a fully equivalent way in Figure 1.7(c). Here the reference direction (the + and − signs) are reversed, but the polarity of V_1 is also reversed, so it still conveys the fact that terminal B is more positive than terminal A.

As you can see, it is absolutely necessary to specify both magnitude and direction for voltage and current. It is incomplete to say that the voltage between two points is 10 volts or the current in a line is 2 amperes, since only the magnitude has been given. A figure or schematic circuit drawing with a reference direction shown for each voltage and current is the most commonly used way to show the reference polarities.

The convention used for energy being absorbed or supplied

Energy is another important term in circuit analysis, and the direction of energy transfer is defined by the way the signs of the voltage and current are presented. In Figure 1.8(a), energy is being *supplied to* the element by whatever is attached to the terminals. Note that 2 A, that is, 2 C of positive charge, is moving from point A to point B through the element each second. Each coulomb loses 3J of energy as it passes through the element from A to B. Therefore, the element is absorbing 6J of energy per second. Note that *when the element is absorbing energy, a positive current enters the positive terminal.* In Figure 1.8(b), energy is being *supplied by* the element to whatever is connected to terminals $A - B$. In this case, note that

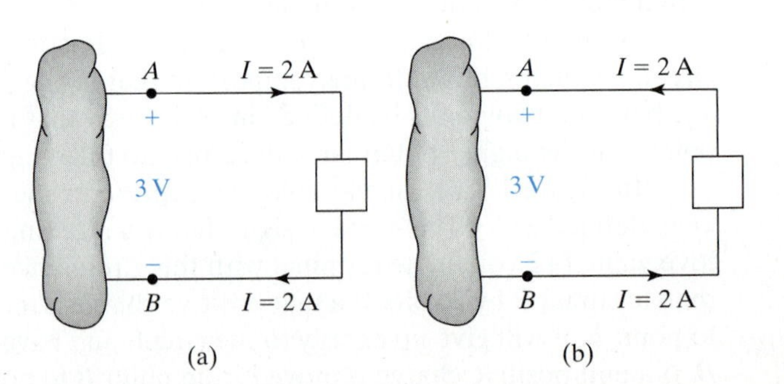

FIGURE 1.8 Voltage—current relationships for (a) energy absorbed and (b) energy supplied

when the element is supplying energy, a positive current enters the negative terminal and leaves via the positive terminal.

1.2.7 Power

Power is defined as the time rate at which energy, w, is produced or consumed, depending on whether the element is a source of power or a user of power, respectively. That is,

$$p = \frac{dw}{dt} \tag{1.5}$$

which can be rewritten as

The electric power–energy relationship

$$p = \frac{dw}{dt} = \left[\frac{dw}{dq}\right]\left[\frac{dq}{dt}\right] = v\,i \tag{1.6}$$

The above equation shows that power can be computed by the product of the voltage across a circuit element and the current through it. Since both voltage and current can vary with time, the power, p, is also a time varying quantity, and can be expressed as $p(t)$.

Therefore, the change in energy from time t_1 to time t_2 can be found by integrating Eq. (1.6), that is

$$w = \int_{t_1}^{t_2} p\,dt = \int_{t_1}^{t_2} vi\,dt$$

Calculation of power requires the use of a consistent sign convention. To determine the sign of any of the quantities involved, the variables for the current and voltage should be arranged as shown in Figure 1.9. The variable for the voltage $v(t)$ is defined as the voltage across the element with the positive reference at the same terminal that the current variable $i(t)$ is entering. This convention is called the *passive sign convention* and will be so noted in the remainder of this book. The product of v and i, with their attendant signs, will determine the magnitude and sign of the power. If the sign of the power is positive, power is being absorbed by the element; if the sign is negative, power is being supplied by the element.

The passive sign convention defined

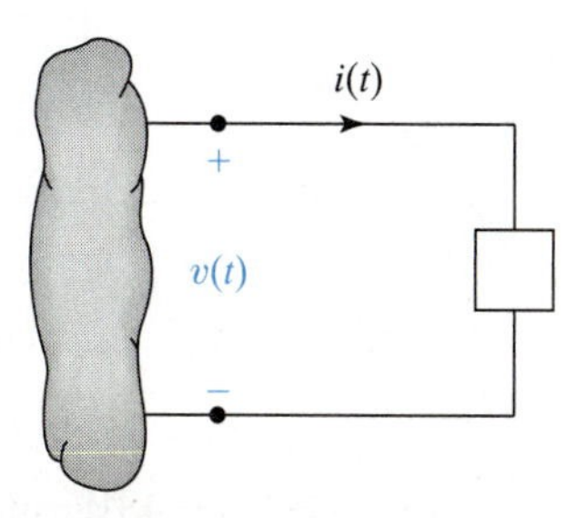

FIGURE 1.9 Sign convention for power.

Example 1.7

We wish to determine the power absorbed, or supplied, by the elements in Figure 1.8.

In Figure 1.8(a), $P = VI = (3\text{ V})\ (2\text{ A}) = 6$ watts (W) is absorbed by the element. In Figure 1.8(b), $P = VI = (3\text{ V})\ (-2\text{ A}) = -6W$ is absorbed by the element, or $+6W$ is supplied by the element.

Example 1.8

Given the two diagrams shown in Figure 1.10, let us determine whether the element is absorbing or supplying power and how much.

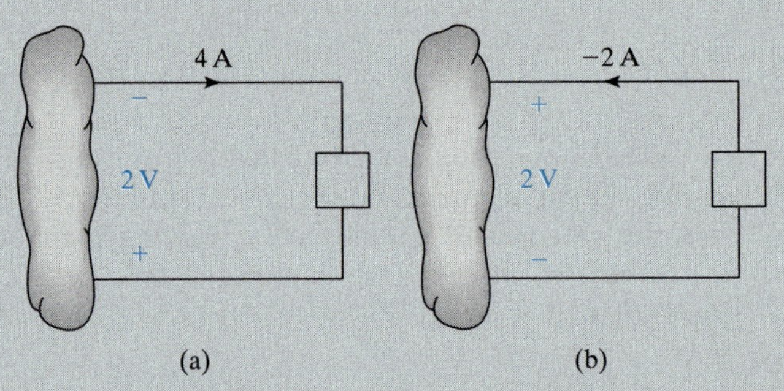

FIGURE 1.10 Elements for Example 1.8.

In Figure 1.10(a), the power is $P = (2\text{ V})\ (-4\text{ A}) = -8W$. Therefore, the element is supplying power. In Figure 1.10(b), the power is $P = (2\text{ V})\ (2\text{ A}) = 4W$. Therefore, the element is absorbing power.

Drill Exercise

D1.4. Determine the amount of power absorbed or supplied by the elements of Figure D1.4.

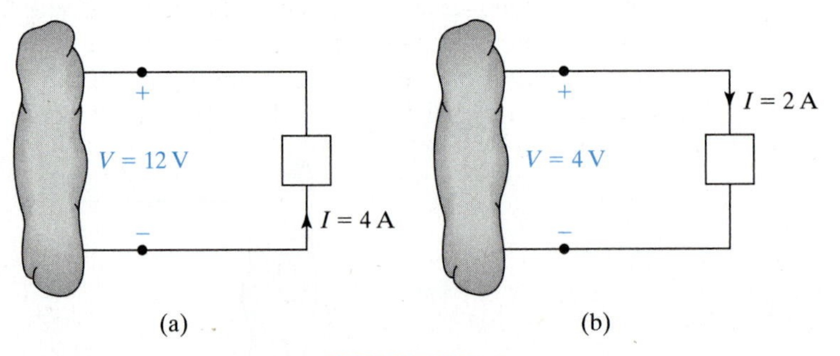

FIGURE D1.4

Ans: (a) $P = -48W$; supplied (b) $P = 8W$; absorbed.

1.2.8 Modeling

Modeling is the process of representing a real physical system with a representation of that system that under some assumptions allows us to solve for its behavior using the analytical tools we have available. Generally, we choose assumptions that make things simpler by disregarding unimportant features. We will apply various mathematical techniques to the model of our system to arrive at solutions. A "predictive model" is one that represents the actual system sufficiently well that we can impose different sets of assumptions and conditions, and accurately predict, by our calculations using the model, the expected behavior of the real physical system.

In our study of electric circuits we make a number of simplifying assumptions. First, we assume that the important characteristics of the circuit can be grouped together in "lumps" or separate blocks, connected together by ideal conductors. This approach is called "lumped element circuit modeling" and is used in electrical and electronic circuit analysis up to microwave frequencies. We will use this approach in this text.

The single-loop electric circuit of Figure 1.3(b) could be described or represented by a single loop of ideal conductors connecting a rectangular block on the left representing the battery with a rectangular block on the right representing the light bulb, as shown in Figure 1.11.

Two terminal circuit elements are classified as either *active* or *passive* based simply on whether they supply energy to the circuit or absorb energy.

Batteries and generators are typically modeled by active elements since they supply energy to a circuit. There are three fundamental passive circuit elements: resistors, capacitors, and inductors.

1.2.9 Ideal Circuit Elements

To make the analysis of electrical circuits simpler, we have defined some idealized circuit elements. These elements can be completely described by knowing the mathematical relation between the voltage across and the current through the element. Idealized active elements consist of independent sources and dependent sources. Each of these comes in two types, the voltage source and the current source.

The common passive circuit elements

There are three circuit elements that normally are assumed as single-valued in circuit analysis, and as such, they are called ideal passive circuit elements: the resistor, the inductor, and the capacitor. All of these will be discussed in detail in later chapters; however, a brief introduction is provided here. These three passive circuit elements differ electrically in the way in which the voltage across is related to the current through each of the elements. As you will see, if v is the voltage across each element and i is the current through each element, the relationships and the commonly used symbols are given in Figure 1.12. The constants, R, L, and C, are known as the resistance (in ohms, Ω), inductance (in henries, H) and capacitance (in farads, F), respectively.

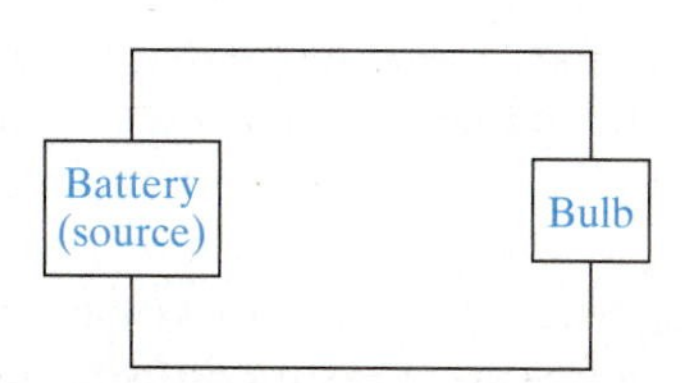

FIGURE 1.11 A simple circuit.

	Resistor	Inductor	Capacitor
Symbol:			
Relationship:	$v = i R$	$v = L\dfrac{di}{dt}$	$v = \dfrac{1}{C}\int i\,dt$
		or	
	$i = \dfrac{1}{R} v$	$i = \dfrac{1}{L}\int v\,dt$	$i = C\dfrac{dv}{dt}$
	(a)	(b)	(c)

FIGURE 1.12 Passive circuit elements.

The resistor represents the part of a circuit component in which energy entering the element by the flow of current through it is transformed to heat. Light can be emitted also if the resistive element becomes hot enough to glow.

The inductor represents a two-terminal electric element in which energy is stored in a magnetic field. Coils of wire such as those used to make an electromagnet, or the windings of wire in an electric motor, must be modeled using inductances.

The third passive circuit element, the capacitor, stores energy in an electric field. The capacitor is often fabricated by two parallel conducting plates separated by an insulating layer.

These three circuit elements, combined with the active elements (sources), can be used to represent, model, and study a wide range of electrical and electronic systems. The next chapter describes the first of these passive elements, the resistor, in more detail.

1.2.10 Sources

Again consider the analogy of fluid flow in the "circuit" of Figure 1.3(a). The pump is the source of energy that powers the flow of fluid—it forces or "pushes" the fluid by providing fluid pressure at the exit of the pump that is higher than that at the intake of the pump.

We might imagine the pump acting in one of two ways. First, we might construct an image of a pump that increases the pressure of the fluid a predefined amount. That is, the pressure at the output of the pump is a fixed number of pressure units larger than that at the input; the pump would provide this pressure difference irrespective of the amount of fluid flowing through the pump. Now, imagine what happens if suddenly the diameter of the pipe and the turbine could somehow magically be increased, so that much more fluid could flow. In order to maintain the same pressure differential as before, the pump would have to quickly work much harder and move much more water per unit time. Conversely, if the flow around the loop were suddenly restricted so that it was more difficult to force as much volume of fluid per unit time around the circuit, the flow rate through the pump would have to quickly decrease; otherwise, there would be a sudden increase in pressure.

The second type of pump would be one that maintains a predefined flow rate through it independent of the pressure differential across it. In this situation if the loop of pipe somehow developed a restriction to flow, the pump would continue to force the same number of gallons per minute around the loop; however, in order to do this it would have to increase the pressure differential across it.

We will use these analogies in the next section.

Independent active circuit elements

Independent Sources. There are electrical sources with direct analogies to the situations described above. An ideal independent voltage source maintains a specified voltage across its terminals independent of the current through it.

This source corresponds to the first type of pump described in the previous section. The voltage between the terminals of the ideal voltage source is determined by the value of the voltage source, regardless of the current passing through it, and regardless of any other circuit parameters.

The specified value of voltage could be a constant value, V_1, in which case we represent this source by the symbol shown in Figure 1.13(a), which would closely model a typical battery. If the specified voltage is a predescribed function of time, $v_1(t)$, we represent this source with the symbol shown in Figure 1.13(b).

In both of these sources the figure shows an additional and very important piece of information, the "reference polarity" or "sign" of the source. In the case of a constant voltage source, that is, a dc source, the "long-bar" end of the symbol is defined to be the positive reference side, and the "+" designates the positive reference side in the other symbol. This designation is equivalent to establishing the positive direction in a coordinate system. It does not mean that the voltage is always more positive at the "+" terminal. It means that if the value of $v(t)$ is positive, then the "+" terminal will be more positive than the other terminal.

The corresponding electrical analogy to the second type of pump described in the previous section is the ideal current source. An ideal independent current source maintains a specified current through it, independent of the voltage developed across its terminals.

The symbol for the ideal independent current source is shown in Figure 1.14. The direction of the arrow indicates the chosen reference direction for "positive" current flow. If the value of $i(t)$ becomes negative, then at that time, positive current would actually be flowing in the opposite direction of the arrow.

The same symbol can be used to represent a dc current source by letting $i(t)$ be a constant, I.

It is important that we pause here to inject a comment concerning the application of circuit models. In general, mathematical models approximate actual physical systems only under a certain range of conditions. Rarely does a model accurately represent a physical system under every set of conditions. To illustrate this point, consider the model for the voltage source in Figure 1.13(b). We assume that the voltage source produces $v(t)$ volts, regardless of what is connected to its terminals. Theoretically, we could adjust the external circuit so that an infinite amount of current would flow, and therefore the voltage source would deliver an infi-

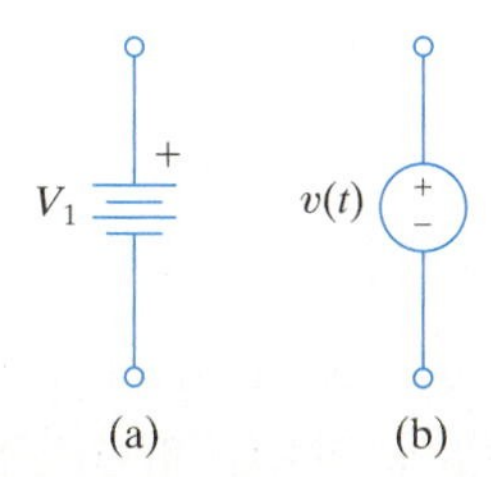

FIGURE 1.13 Independent voltage sources.

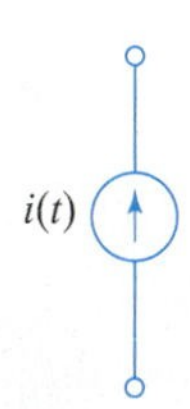

FIGURE 1.14 Independent current source.

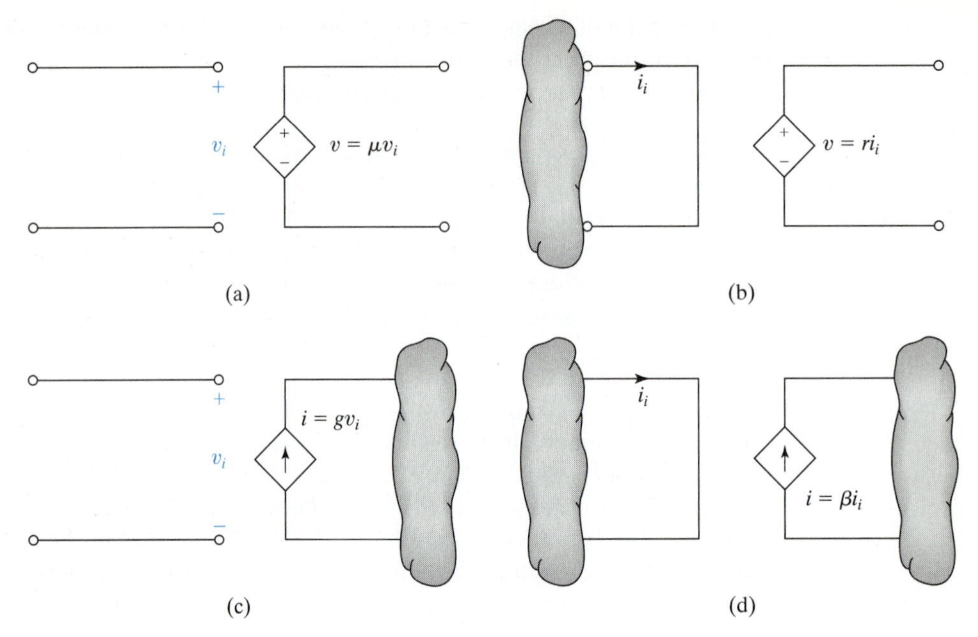

FIGURE 1.15 Dependent sources.

nite amount of power. This is, of course, physically impossible. Hence, the reader is cautioned to keep in mind that models have limitations and are valid representations of physical systems only under certain conditions.

The common dependent active circuit elements

Dependent Sources. In contrast to the independent sources, which produce a particular voltage or current completely unaffected by what is happening in the remainder of the circuit, dependent sources generate a voltage or current that is determined by a voltage or current at a specified location elsewhere in the circuit. These sources are important because they are an integral part of the circuit models used to describe the behavior of many electronic circuit elements, such as transistors.

In contrast to the circle used to represent independent sources, a diamond is used to represent a dependent or controlled source. Figure 1.15 illustrates the four types of dependent sources. The "input" terminals on the left represent the voltage or current that *controls* the dependent source, and the "output" terminals on the right represent the output current or voltage of the controlled source. Note that in Figures 1.15(a) and (d) the quantities μ and β are dimensionless constants because we are transforming voltage to voltage and current to current, respectively. This is not the case in Figures 1.15(b) and (c); hence, when we employ these elements in a later section, we will define the units of the factors, r and g.

Example 1.9

Given the circuits shown in Figure 1.16, we wish to determine the outputs.

In the first circuit, Figure 1.16(a), the output voltage is $V = \mu V_i$ or $V = (20)(2\text{ V}) = 40\text{ V}$. Note that the output voltage has been "amplified" from 2 V at the input port to 40 V at the output port; that is, the circuit has an amplification factor or gain of 20.

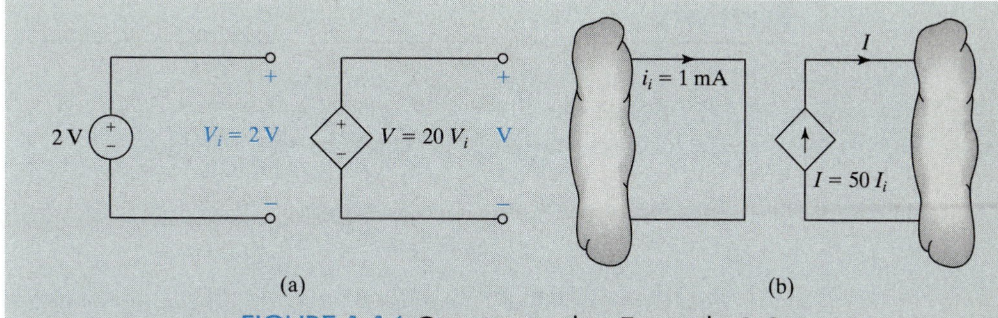

FIGURE 1.16 Circuits used in Example 1.9.

In the circuit of Figure 1.16(b), the output current is $I = \beta I_i = (50)\ (1\text{ mA}) = 50\text{ mA}$; that is, the circuit has a current gain of 50. The output current is 50 times greater than the input current.

1.2.11 Ideal Circuit Model

We can now construct an idealized circuit model of the battery and bulb shown in Figure 1.3(b).

The battery, if ideal, would be represented as an active element, an independent constant voltage source. We could utilize either of the symbols in Figure 1.13, the symbol for a battery, or the more general "circle" symbol for a voltage source where we let the value of the source, $v(t)$, be a constant, V_1. A real battery would likely have some internal resistance that would have to be added to the model, but we will postpone that consideration until later.

The bulb principally changes the flow of electric current into heat and light, and therefore is best modeled by a resistor, which has a symbol as shown in Figure 1.12(a).

Therefore, the real circuit of Figure 1.3(b) can be represented by an idealized lumped element model as shown in Figure 1.17. This drawing is often called a circuit schematic drawing and shows the individual circuit elements connected by lines that represent ideal conductors.

Later in Figure 1.24 we will summarize the types of circuit elements used in the analysis of electric circuits. Note that the branches in this figure under "current sources" have the same format as those under "voltage sources."

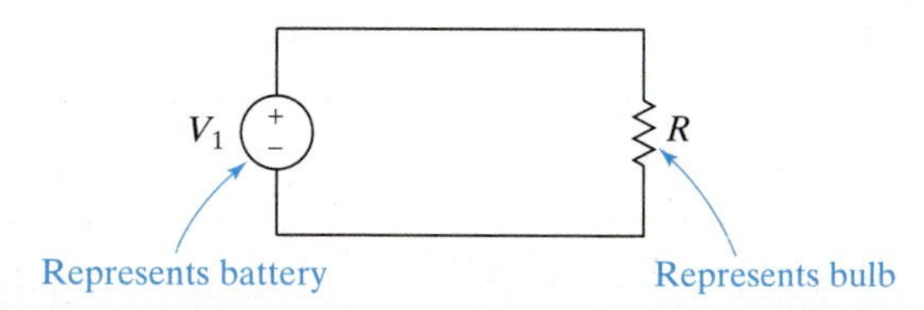

FIGURE 1.17 Ideal circuit model of simple circuit.

Summary

- Like charges repel each other; opposite charges attract.
- The force (in Newtons) between two point charges is

$$F = k\frac{q_1 q_2}{d^2}$$

where k = constant = 8.99×10^9 $N\text{-}m^2/C^2$, q_1 and q_2 are the charges in coulombs, and d is the separation between the charges in meters.
- Current is the time rate of flow of charge, that is,

$$i = \frac{dq}{dt}$$

where i = the current in amperes, dq is the incremental value of charge crossing a plane in an incremental time, dt.
- Positive current is assumed to be in the direction of positive charge movement.
- Direct current (dc) describes charge flow in one direction all the time; alternating current (ac) repeatedly reverses direction. A cycle is defined as one direction reversal and return to the original direction. The number of times per second that an ac current completes a full cycle is defined as the frequency in hertz (Hz). Figure 1.18 illustrates these concepts.

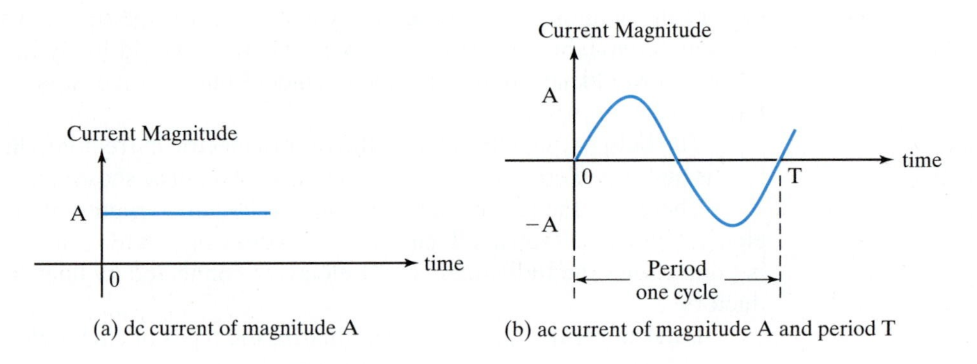

FIGURE 1.18 An illustration of direct current and alternating current.

- Voltage difference is analogous to pressure difference and is defined by

$$v = \frac{dw}{dq}$$

where dw is the incremental energy required to move an incremental charge dq through a voltage difference of v.

- Reference directions must be assigned to voltages across and currents through elements. Figure 1.19 illustrates the magnitude and direction assignments for current and voltage.

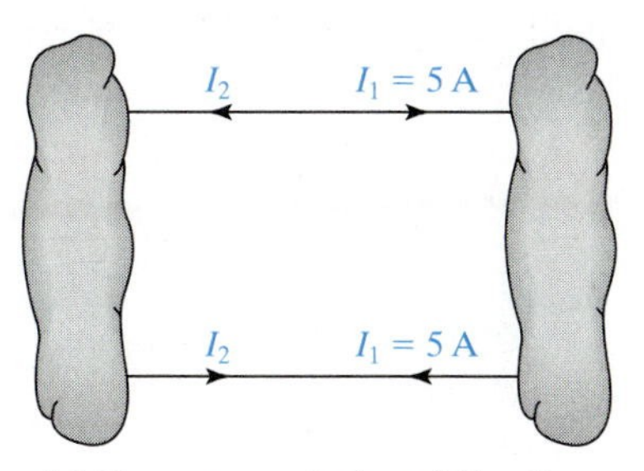

(a) Current magnitude and direction. $I_1 = 5$ A and therefore $I_2 = -5$ A

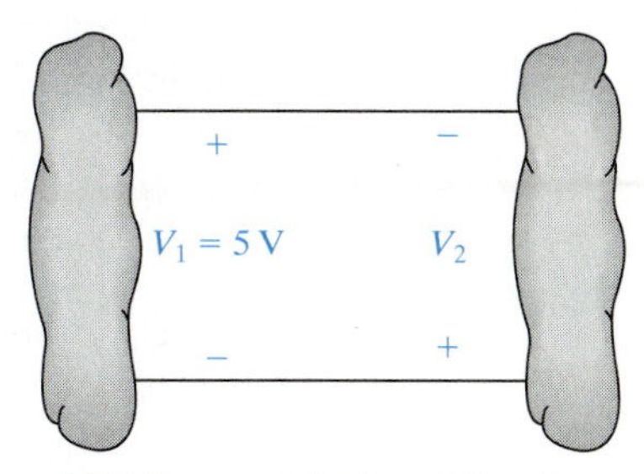

(b) Voltage magnitude and direction. $V_1 = +5$ V and therefore $V_2 = -5$ V

FIGURE 1.19 Magnitude and direction assignments for current and voltage.

- Power, p in watts, is the time rate at which energy, w, is produced or consumed; thus

$$p = \frac{dw}{dt} = vi$$

where v = the voltage across an element, and i = the current through the same element.

- Power is assumed positive if power is being absorbed by an element, and negative if power is being supplied, as illustrated in Figure 1.20.

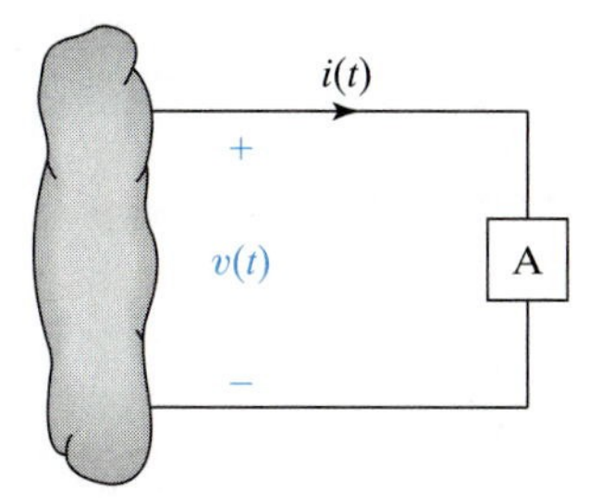

(a) The sign convention for power

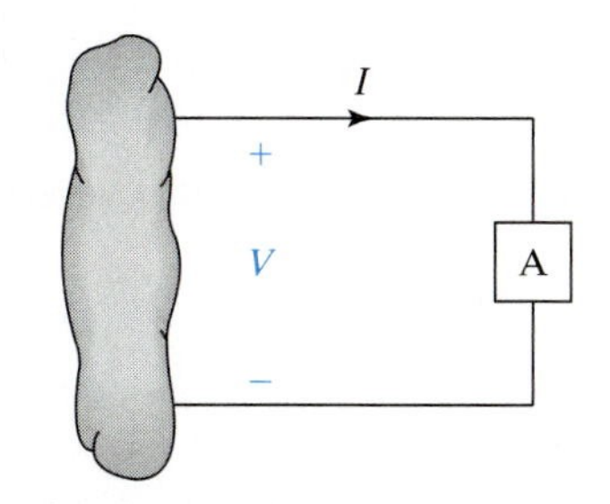

(b) Power is being absorbed by element A, $P = VI$, that is, the circuit within the cloud is supplying energy to element A

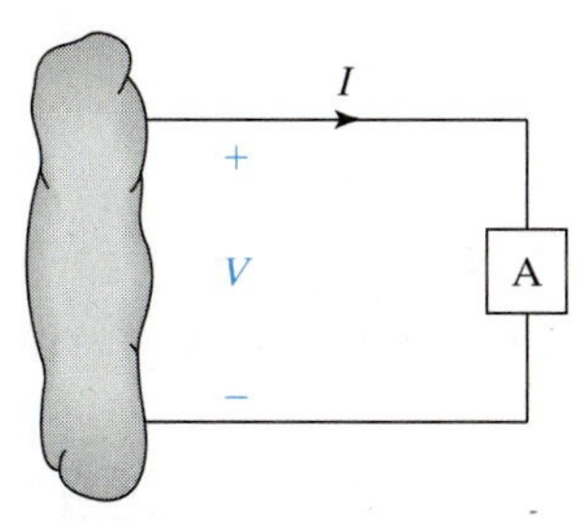

(c) Power is being supplied by element A, $P = V(-I) = -VI$, that is, the cloud is absorbing energy supplied by element A

FIGURE 1.20 An illustration of power relationships.

- Ideal active circuit elements include both current and voltage sources; each can be one of two types: (1) independent or (2) dependent.
- Current sources maintain a prescribed current independent of terminal voltage; voltage sources maintain a prescribed voltage independent of current. These concepts are illustrated in Figure 1.21.

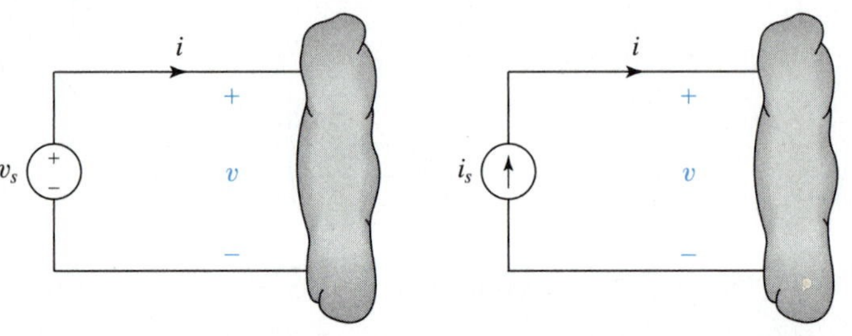

(a) The voltage $v = v_s$, but i could *theoretically* be any value and must be determined from the elements in the cloud

(b) The current $i = i_s$, but the voltage v could *theoretically* be any value and must be determined from the elements in the cloud

FIGURE 1.21 Definitions of independent sources.

- While independent sources have a value that does not depend on any other variable in the circuit, dependent sources are a function of a circuit variable, for example, a current or voltage in another part of the circuit, as shown in Figure 1.22.

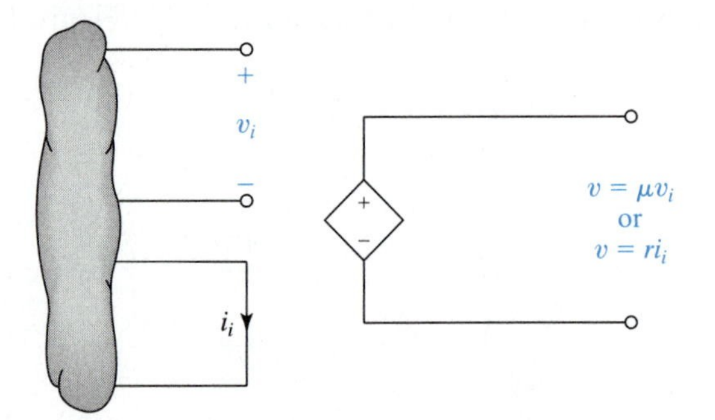

(a) A current or voltage-controlled voltage source

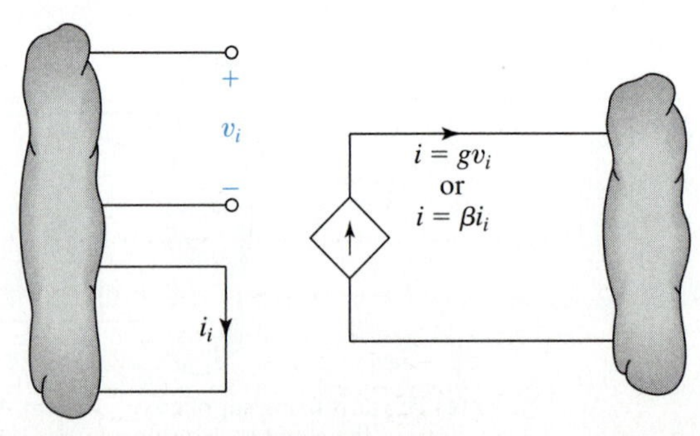

(b) A current or voltage-controlled current source

FIGURE 1.22 Dependent source operations.

- The current/voltage relationships for the passive circuit elements, that is, the resistor, inductor, and capacitor, are shown in Figure 1.23.

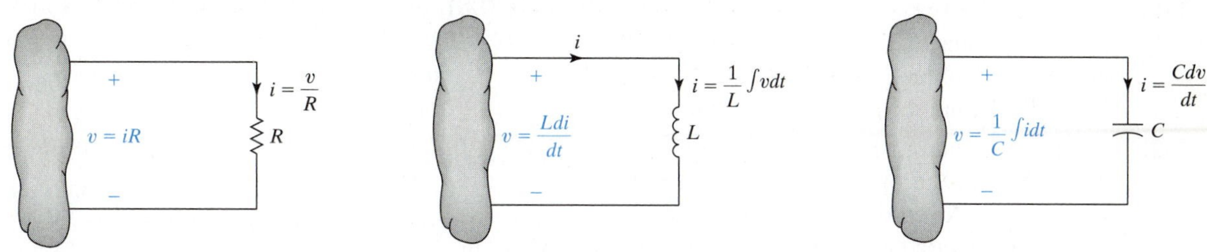

(a) Current/voltage relationships for a resistor. Its value is measured in Ohms.
(b) Current/voltage relationship for an inductor. Its value is measured in Henrys.
(c) Current/voltage relationships for a capacitor. Its value is measured in Farads.

FIGURE 1.23 The defining current/voltage equations for the passive circuit elements R, L, and C.

- A summary of the circuit element designations is shown in Figure 1.24.

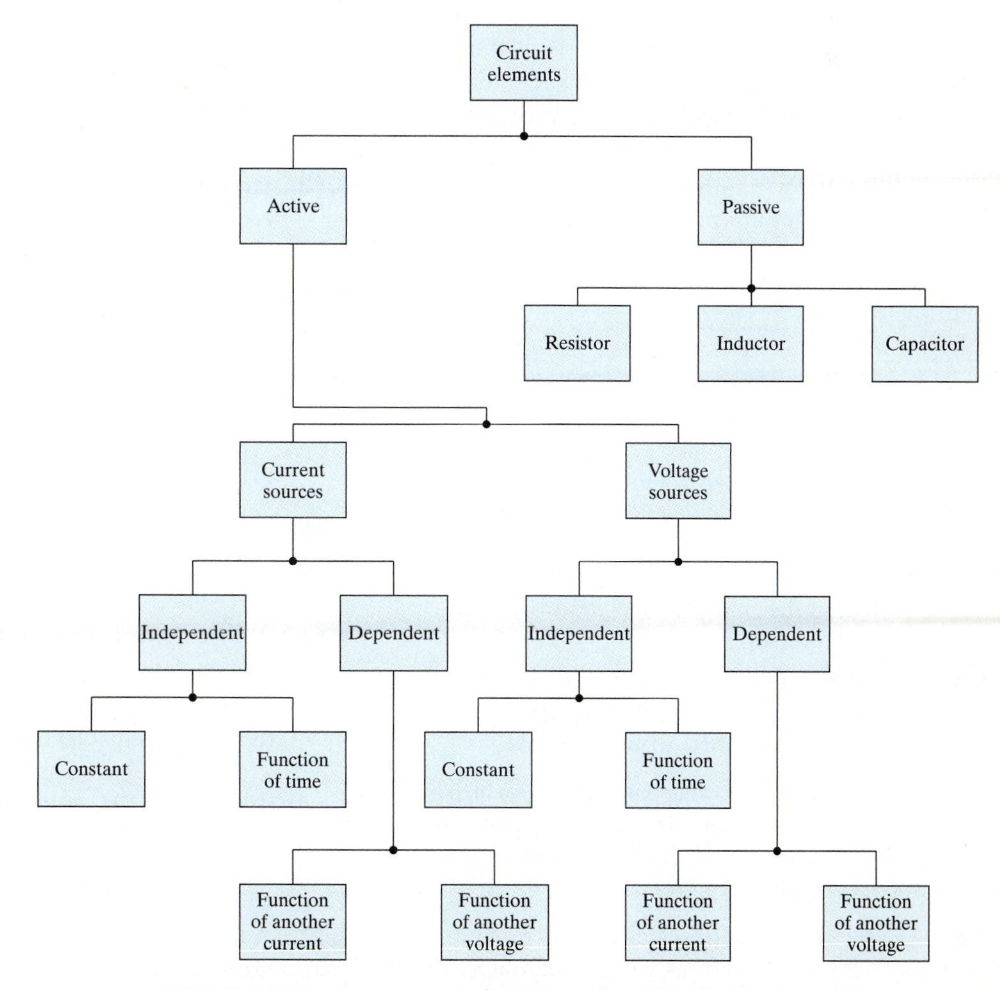

FIGURE 1.24 Summary of circuit element designations.

Problems

1.1. What is the charge, q_1, on an object that is attracted by a force of 3×10^{-3} newtons, to a second charged object with a charge of $q_2 = +1.6 \times 10^{-6}$ C, and separated by one millimeter?

1.2. A micromachined insulating cantilever beam has a charge at the tip of the beam of 6.5 pC. The substrate located 4 microns (1 micron = $1\mu = 1 \times 10^{-6}$ meter) under the beam has a mirror charge of −6.5 pC. What is the magnitude of the force pulling down on the tip of the beam?

1.3. Two identical point charges each of magnitude 0.03 μC separated by a distance of 1 cm experience what magnitude of force between them? Is this force attractive or repulsive?

1.4. Assume the radius of a hydrogen atom is 5.3×10^{-9} cm. Calculate the force between the nucleus of the hydrogen atom and an electron at this radius.

1.5. Three charges are placed in a straight line as shown in Figure P1.5.

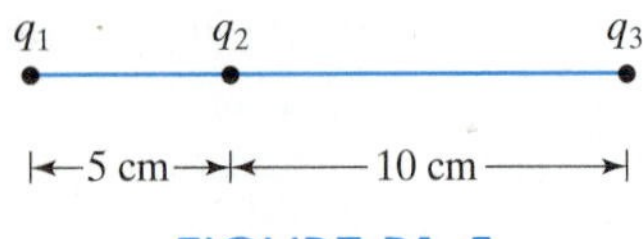

FIGURE P1.5

(a) If $q_1 = -2$ mC, $q_2 = 4$ mC, and $q_3 = 10$ mC, find the magnitude and direction of the resultant force on q_1, q_2, and q_3.
(b) If $q_1 = -3$ mC, find the magnitude and sign of the charge q_3 such that the resultant force on q_2 is zero.

1.6. Classify the following as insulators or conductors: iron, glass, rubber, gold, salt water, silver, ceramics, plastic, brass, wood, copper.

1.7. For each of the following pairs, identify which is the better electrical conductor: (a) wet aluminum or wet wood, (b) salt water or pure water, (c) copper or iron.

1.8. An electric heater operated from a dc source has 8.2×10^{21} electrons pass through it in 10 seconds. How much current (in amperes) is flowing through the heater?

1.9. If an automobile battery delivers 120 A when the car is being started, and the starting process takes 6 seconds, how many electrons flow out of the battery?

1.10. If 3×10^{19} electrons flow uniformly through the cross-section of a wire in 5 *s*, what is the current flowing through the wire?

1.11. Three wires join at a common point or node. The first wire is conducting 3 A into the node and the second wire is conducting 1 A away from the node. What is the magnitude of the current in the third wire, and its direction?

1.12. Two identical automobile headlamps are connected across a 12 V battery. If the total current from the battery is measured to be 6.5 A, what is the current through each headlamp?

1.13. How many electrons are flowing through the cross-section of a wire per second if a current of 0.2 A flows through it?

1.14. What is the typical current range for the following:
(a) Large industrial motor
(b) Household appliances
(c) Lightning bolt
(d) Memory cell of an integrated circuit memory

1.15. If a battery supplies 3 joule of energy in transferring 0.25 coulombs of charge through an element, what is the voltage across the battery?

1.16. A 12 V lantern battery provides 0.5 A to operate an electric bulb. During the time of operation of one-half hour,
(a) How many electrons pass through the bulb?
(b) What is the amount of power delivered to the bulb?
(c) How much energy is provided by the battery?

1.17. A CRT (cathode ray tube) is used for most television and computer video displays. In the back of a CRT is an electron gun emitting a beam of electrons toward a phosphor-coated display screen; the beam makes a visible spot where it impacts the screen. Assuming the electron gun is made 25kV more negative than the screen, how much energy is transferred to a single electron by the time it reaches the screen?

1.18. One electron-volt (1 eV) is defined as the amount of energy gained by an electron moving through a voltage difference of 1 volt. What is this energy expressed in joules?

1.19. A 12V car battery delivers 150 A of current during startup. If it takes one second to start the car, how much energy is supplied by the battery during ignition?

1.20. Categorize the following sources of electric power as either ac or dc.

1. automobile battery
2. solar cell
3. residential power outlet
4. watch battery
5. commercial power generating station
6. fuel cell

1.21. What is the approximate frequency (in Hz) near the center of the portion of the electromagnetic spectrum corresponding to:

1. infrared
2. shortwave radio
3. gamma rays

1.22. What is the approximate frequency (in Hz) near the center of the portion of the electromagnetic spectrum corresponding to (a) television, (b) ultraviolet light, (c) x-rays?

1.23. Assign values to V and I in element B so that it is equivalent to element A (see Figure P1.23).

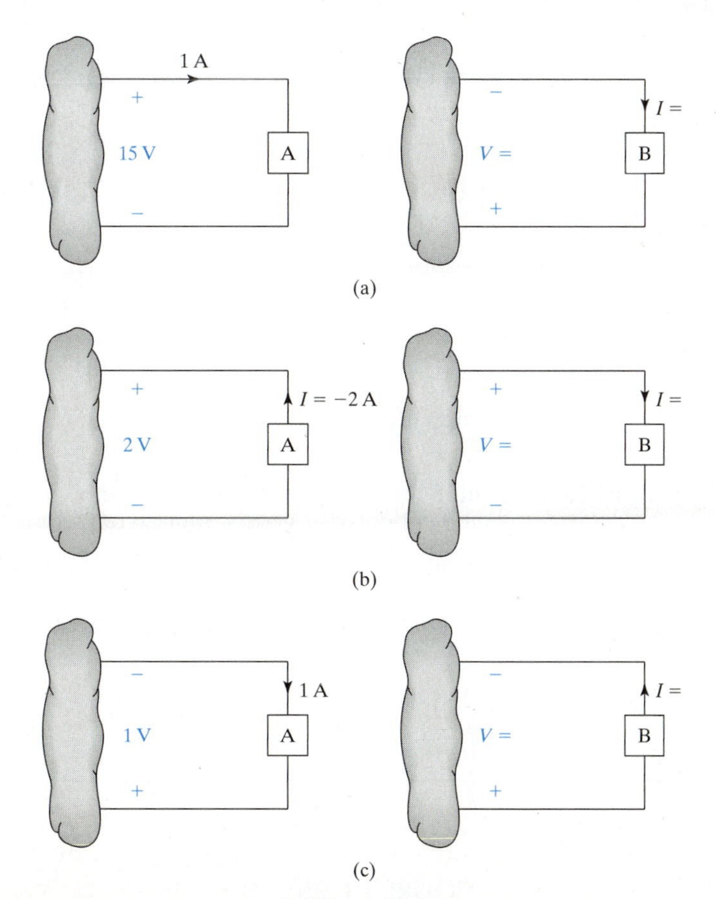

FIGURE P1.23

1.24. Assign directions to currents and polarities to voltages in element B so it is equivalent to element A (see Figure P1.24).

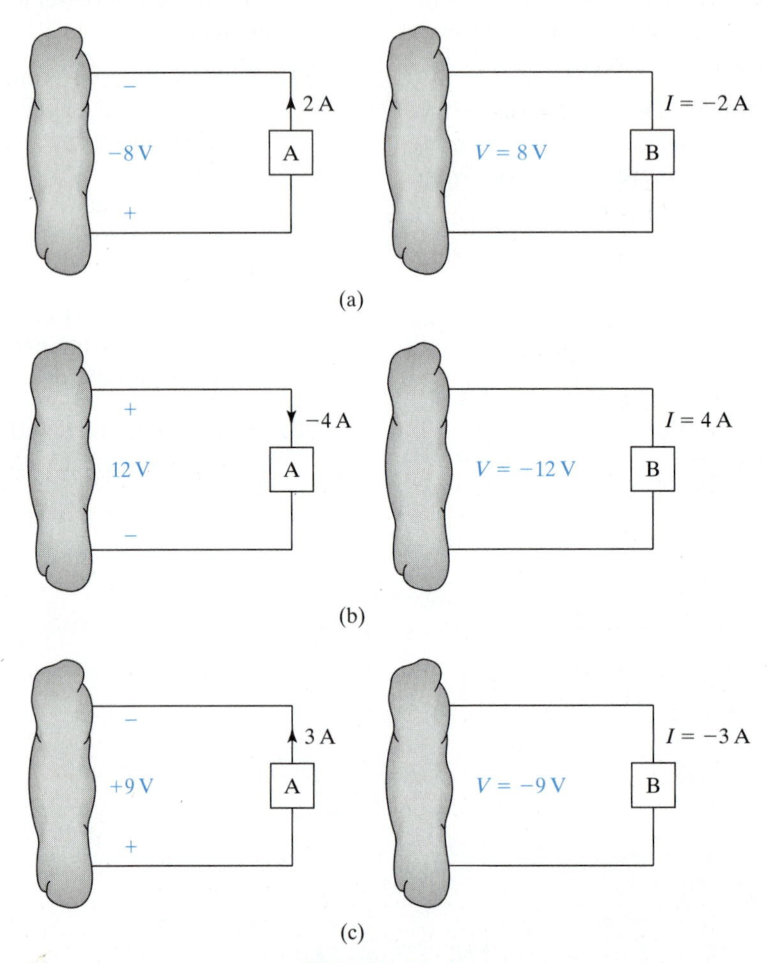

FIGURE P1.24

1.25. In the elements of Figure P1.25, determine for each if they are supplying power or absorbing power and the magnitude of the power being transferred.

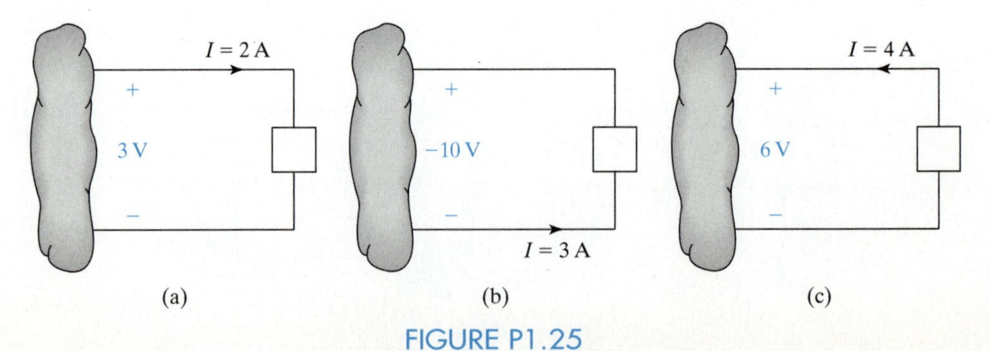

FIGURE P1.25

1.26. In Figure P1.26 determine for each element whether it is supplying or absorbing power. If all the energy absorbed is dissipated as heat, determine the heat dissipated (in joules) over a period of one hour for each of the circuits shown.

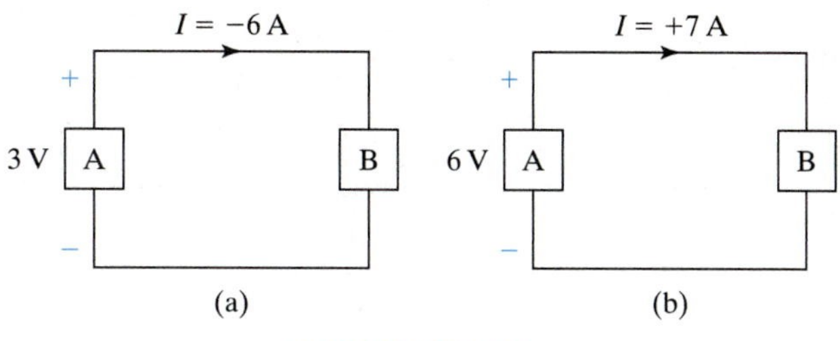

FIGURE P1.26

1.27. A dependent voltage source shown in Figure 1.15(a) has $\mu = 25$. (a) What is the voltage between the terminals on the right, if $v_i = 4.3$ V? (b) If $v_i = 30$ V?

1.28. A current-dependent current source has $\beta = 30$ and produces an output current of 2 mA. What current is flowing through its input terminals?

1.29. What voltage appears at the output of a voltage-dependent voltage source, if $\mu = 10^3$ and the voltage applied to the input terminals is 3×10^{-4} V?

1.30. In the circuit of Figure P1.30, if $\mu = 48$, calculate the value of V_o.

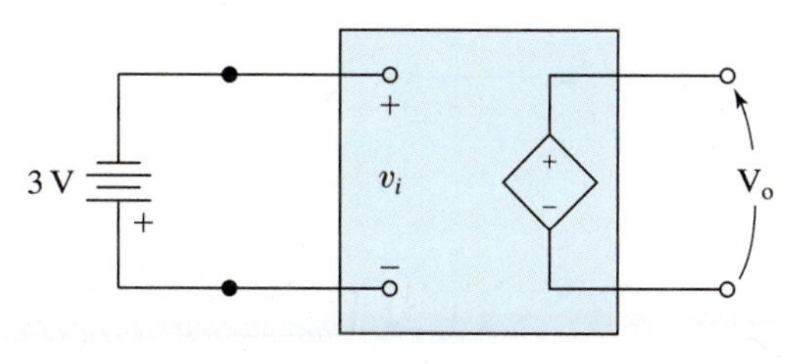

FIGURE P1.30

1.31. In the circuit of Figure P1.31, the output voltage, V_o, is measured to be 30 volts. Calculate the value of μ.

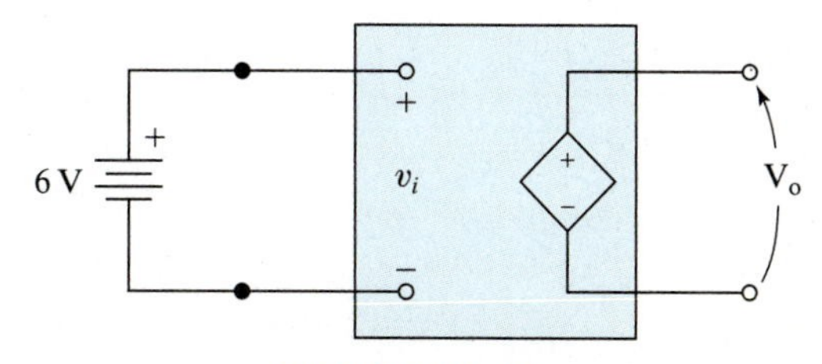

FIGURE P1.31

1.32. In the circuit of Figure P1.32, plot the output voltage, $v_o(t)$, as a function of time. Carefully label the axes.

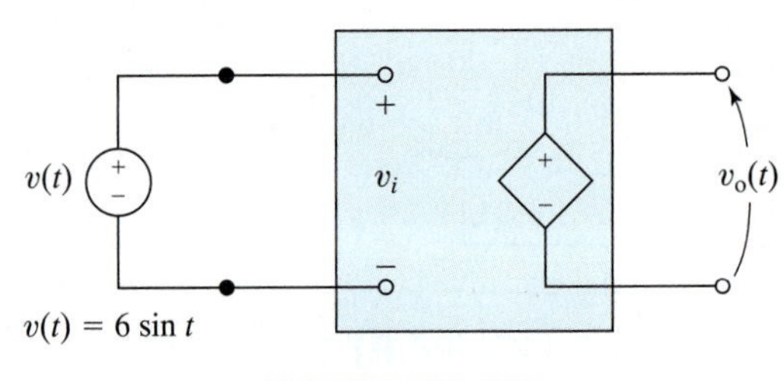

FIGURE P1.32

1.33. In the circuits of Figure P1.33, a voltage-dependent current source with $g = 10^{-3}$ (assume units of volts divided by amperes, or siemens) produces what current through the resistor, R?

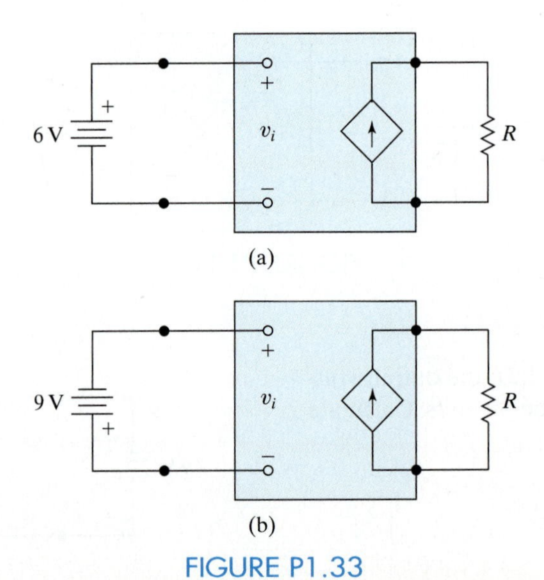

FIGURE P1.33

1.34. In the circuits of Figure P1.34, a current-dependent current source with $\beta = 25$ produces what current through the resistor, R?

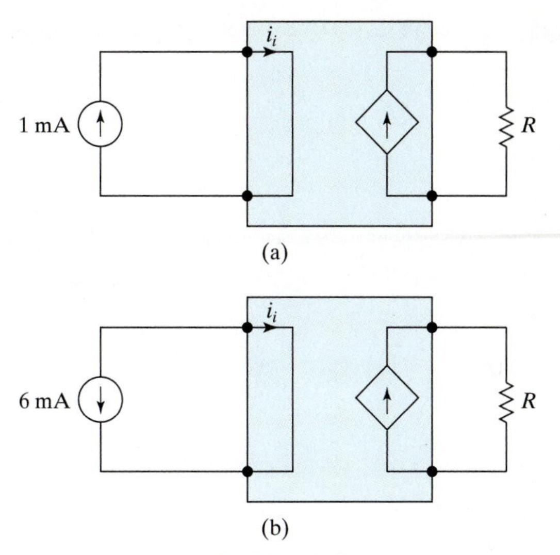

FIGURE P1.34

Circuits

2-1 Introduction

In this chapter we will introduce some of the basic concepts and laws that are fundamental to circuit analysis. We will also illustrate the utility of some of these concepts in practical situations.

The basic laws, such as Ohm's law and Kirchhoff's laws, are presented, along with a number of network theorems that sometimes help simplify and often provide additional insight into our analysis of electric circuits. This material forms the basis for most of the topics contained within the book.

2-2 Ohm's Law

Ohm's law is named for the German physicist Georg Simon Ohm, who is credited with establishing the voltage–current relationship for resistance.

One of three key laws governing circuit analysis

Ohm's law states that *the voltage across a resistance is directly proportional to the current flowing through it.* The resistance, measured in ohms, is the constant of proportionality between the voltage and current.

The resistor is a fundamental circuit element

A circuit element whose electrical characteristic is primarily resistive is called a resistor and is represented by the symbol shown in Figure 2.1(a). A resistor is a physical device that can be fabricated in many ways. Certain standard values of discrete resistors can be purchased in an electronic parts store. These resistors, which find wide use in a variety of electrical applications, are normally carbon composition or wirewound, some typical examples of which are shown in Figure 2.1(b).

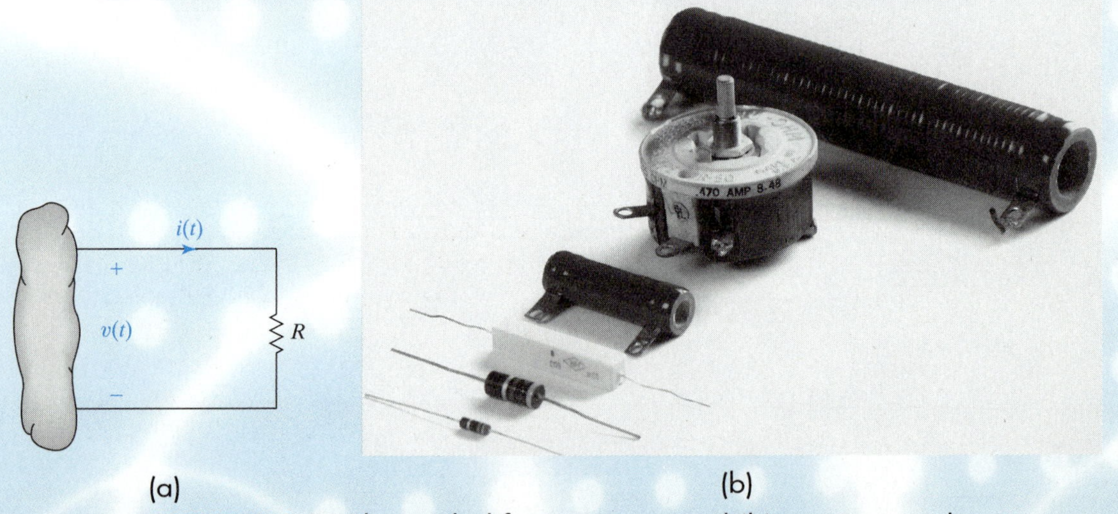

FIGURE 2.1 (a) The symbol for a resistor, and (b) some examples of typical carbon or wirewound resistors.

In addition, resistors can be fabricated using thick or thin films for use in hybrid circuits or they can be fabricated in a semiconductor integrated circuit.

The mathematical relationship of Ohm's law is illustrated by the equation

The equation for Ohm's law

$$v(t) = Ri(t) \text{ where } R \geq 0 \tag{2.1}$$

Note carefully the relationship between the polarity of the voltage and the direction of the current. In addition, note that we have tacitly assumed that the resistor has a constant value and therefore that the voltage–current characteristic is linear.

The symbol Ω is used to represent *ohms,* and therefore

$$1\ \Omega = 1\ \text{V/A}$$

Although we will assume here that the resistors are linear, it is important for readers to realize that some very useful and practical elements do exist that exhibit a nonlinear resistance characteristic. Diodes, which are used extensively in electric circuits, are examples of nonlinear resistors. These elements are discussed in a later chapter.

Since a resistor is a passive element, the proper current–voltage relationship is illustrated in Figure 2.1. The power supplied to the terminals is absorbed by the resistor. Note that the charge moves from the higher (+) to the lower (−) potential as it passes through the resistor and the energy absorbed is dissipated by the resistor in the form of heat. The rate of energy dissipation is the instantaneous power, and therefore

$$p(t) = v(t)i(t) \tag{2.2}$$

which, using Eq. (2.1), can be written as

$$p(t) = Ri^2(t) = \frac{v^2(t)}{R} \tag{2.3}$$

The power relationship for resistors

This equation illustrates that the power dissipated in a resistor is a nonlinear function of either current or voltage and that it is always a positive quantity.

Conductance defined

Conductance, represented by the symbol *G,* is another quantity with wide application in circuit analysis. By definition, conductance is the reciprocal of resistance, that is,

$$G = \frac{1}{R} \tag{2.4}$$

The unit of conductance is the *siemens,* and the relationship between units is

$$1\ S = 1\ A/V$$

Using Eq. (2.4), we can write two additional expressions

$$i(t) = Gv(t) \tag{2.5}$$

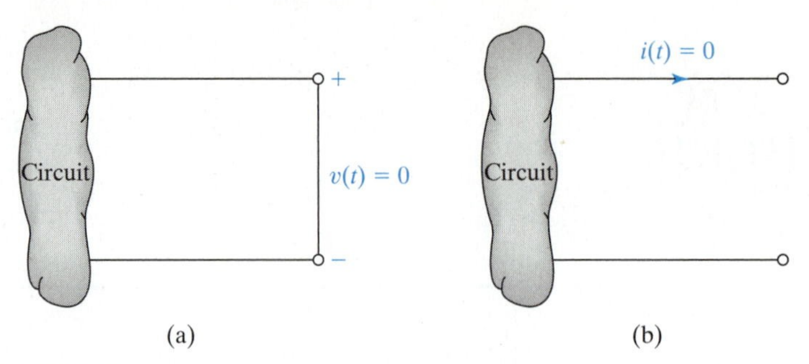

FIGURE 2.2 Diagrams illustrating a short circuit (R = 0) and an open circuit ($R = \infty$).

and

$$p(t) = \frac{i^2(t)}{G} = Gv^2(t) \tag{2.6}$$

Equation (2.5) is another expression of Ohm's law.

Open-circuit and short-circuit definitions

Two specific values of resistance, and therefore conductance, are very important: $R = 0$ ($G = \infty$) and $R = \infty$ ($G = 0$). If the resistance $R = 0$, we have what is called a *short circuit,* illustrated in Figure 2.2a. From Ohm's law

$$\begin{aligned} v(t) &= Ri(t) \\ &= 0 \end{aligned}$$

Therefore, $v(t) = 0$, although the current could theoretically be any value. If the resistance $R = \infty$, as would be the case with a broken wire, we have what is called an *open circuit,* illustrated in Figure 2.2b, and from Ohm's law

$$\begin{aligned} i(t) &= \frac{v(t)}{R} \\ &= 0 \end{aligned}$$

Therefore, the current is zero, regardless of the value of the voltage across the open terminals.

Example 2.1

In the circuit shown in Figure 2.3, determine the current and the power absorbed by the resistor.

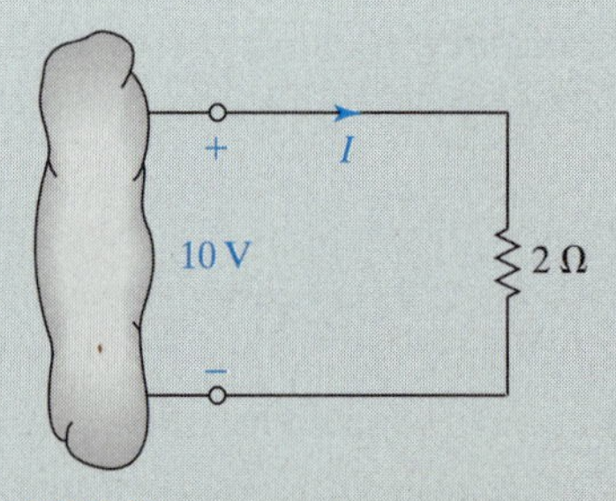

FIGURE 2.3 Circuit for Example 2.1.

Using Eq. (2.1), we find the current to be

$$I = \frac{V}{R} = \frac{10}{2} = 5\ A$$

and from Eq. (2.2) or (2.3), the power absorbed by the resistor is

$$P = VI = (10)(5) = 50\ W$$
$$= RI^2 = (2)(5)^2 = 50\ W$$
$$= \frac{V^2}{R} = \frac{(10)^2}{2} = 50W$$

Drill Exercise

D2.1. Assume a small lamp is modeled as a resistor. Measurements indicate that the voltage across the lamp is 12 V and the current through the lamp is 92.3 mA. Determine the lamp's resistance.

Ans: $R_{\text{Lamp}} = 130\ \Omega$.

D2.2. A heater element draws 2.0 A when connected to a 120 V source. Calculate both the resistance of the element and the power absorbed in the form of heat.

Ans: $R = 60\ \Omega$, $P = 240$ W.

D2.3. A speaker is a device that converts electrical energy into sound energy. Assume the internal resistance of a speaker is typically 8 Ω. The speaker's power rating is the maximum power that can be delivered to it without damage. Therefore, determine the maximum safe current that can be delivered to a stereo speaker with internal resistance of 8 Ω and a power rating of 200 watts.

Ans: $I_{\max} = 5.0$ A.

2-3 Kirchhoff's Laws

The previous circuits that we have considered have all contained a single resistor and were analyzed using Ohm's law. At this point we begin to expand our capabilities to handle more complicated networks, which result from an interconnection of two or more of these simple elements. We will assume that the interconnection is performed by electrical conductors (wires) that have zero resistance, that is, perfect conductors.

Critical circuit definitions

To aid us in our discussion, we will define a number of terms that will be employed throughout our analysis. As will be our approach throughout this text, we will use examples to illustrate the concepts and define the appropriate terms. For example, the circuit shown in Figure 2.4(a) will be used to describe the terms *node, loop, mesh,* and *branch*. A *node* is simply a point of connection of two or more circuit elements. The nodes in the circuit in Figure 2.4(a) are exaggerated in Figure 2.4(b) for clarity. The reader is cautioned to compare the two

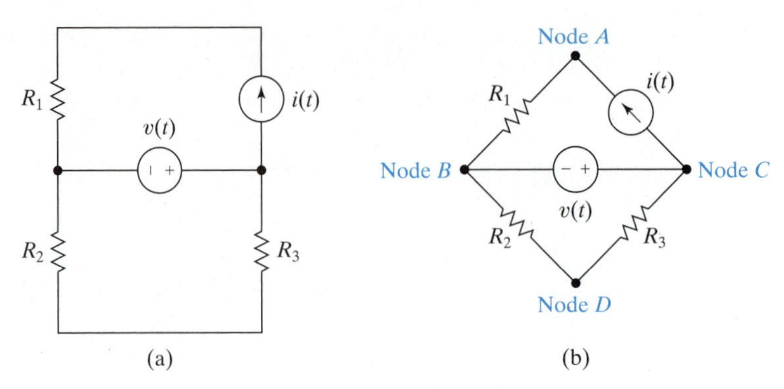

FIGURE 2.4 Circuits used to illustrate terms.

figures carefully and note that although one node can be spread out with perfect conductors, it is still only one node.

A *loop* is simply any closed path through the circuit in which no node is crossed more than once. For example, the paths defined by the nodes *ACBA, BCDB,* and *ACDBA* are all loops. A *mesh* is any loop that does not contain within it another loop. Therefore, the first two paths are meshes; however, the third is not. Finally, a *branch* is a portion of a circuit containing only a single element and the nodes at each end of the element. The circuit in Figure 2.4 contains five branches.

The second of three key laws governing circuit analysis

Given the previous definitions, we are now in a position to consider Kirchhoff's laws, named after the German scientist Gustav Robert Kirchhoff. These two laws are quite simple but extremely important. The first law is *Kirchhoff's current law,* which states that *the algebraic sum of the currents entering any node is zero*. In mathematical form the law appears as

$$\sum_{j=1}^{N} i_j(t) = 0 \tag{2.7}$$

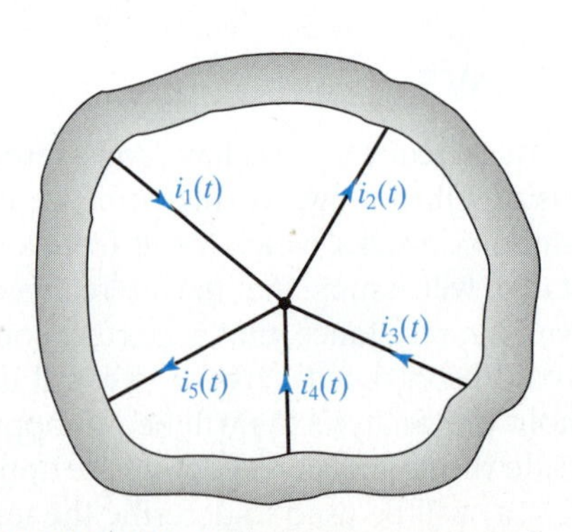

FIGURE 2.5 Currents at a node.

where $i_j(t)$ is the jth current entering the node through branch j and N is the number of branches connected to the node. To understand the use of this law, consider the node shown in Figure 2.5. Applying Kirchhoff's current law to this node yields

$$i_1(t) + [-i_2(t)] + i_3(t) + i_4(t) + [-i_5(t)] = 0$$

We have assumed that the algebraic signs of the currents entering the node are positive and therefore that the signs of the currents leaving the node are negative.

If we multiply the foregoing equation by -1, we obtain the expression

$$-i_1(t) + i_2(t) - i_3(t) - i_4(t) + i_5(t) = 0$$

which simply states that *the algebraic sum of the currents leaving a node is zero*. Alternatively, we can write the equation as

$$i_1(t) + i_3(t) + i_4(t) = i_2(t) + i_5(t)$$

which states that *the sum of the currents entering a node is equal to the sum of the currents leaving the node.* These expressions are alternative forms of Kirchhoff's current law.

Example 2.2

In Figure 2.6, we wish to determine the currents I_1 and I_2.

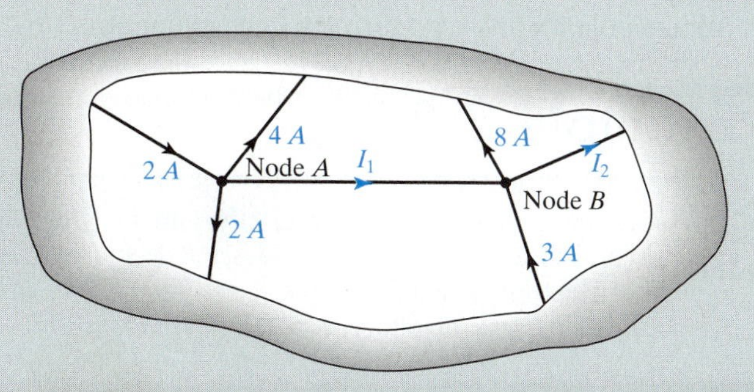

FIGURE 2.6 Illustration nodes for Kirchhoff's current law.

The equations for Kirchhoff's current law at nodes A and B, respectively, are

$$2 - 4 - 2 - I_1 = 0$$

$$I_1 - 8 + 3 - I_2 = 0$$

From the first equation, $I_1 = -4$ A. Since it was assumed that I_1 was leaving node 1, the negative sign illustrates that positive current is actually entering node 1. Using this value of I_1 in the second equation, we find that $I_2 = -9$ A.

Drill Exercise

D2.4. Find the currents I_1 and I_2 in the network in Figure D2.4.

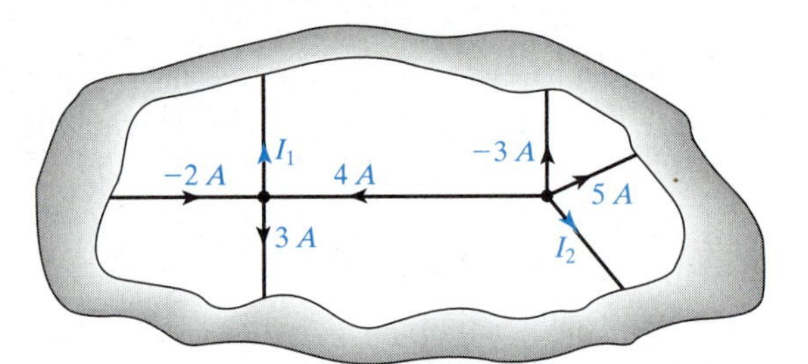

FIGURE D2.4

Ans: $I_1 = -1$ A, $I_2 = -6$ A.

The third of three key laws governing circuit analysis

Kirchhoff's second law, called *Kirchhoff's voltage law,* states that *the algebraic sum of the voltages around any loop is zero.*

Recall that in Kirchhoff's current law, the algebraic sign was required to keep track of whether the currents were entering or leaving a node. In Kirchhoff's voltage law, the algebraic sign is used to keep track of the voltage polarity. In other words, as we traverse the circuit, it is necessary to sum to zero the (− to +) increases and (+ to −) decreases in potential energy level as represented by the voltage. Therefore, it is important that we keep track of the voltage polarity as we go through each element.

Example 2.3

Consider the circuit shown in Figure 2.7(a). In applying Kirchhoff's voltage law, we must traverse the circuit and sum to zero the increases and decreases in energy level. We can traverse the path in either a clockwise or counterclockwise direction, and we can consider an increase in voltage as positive and a decrease in voltage as negative, or vice versa.

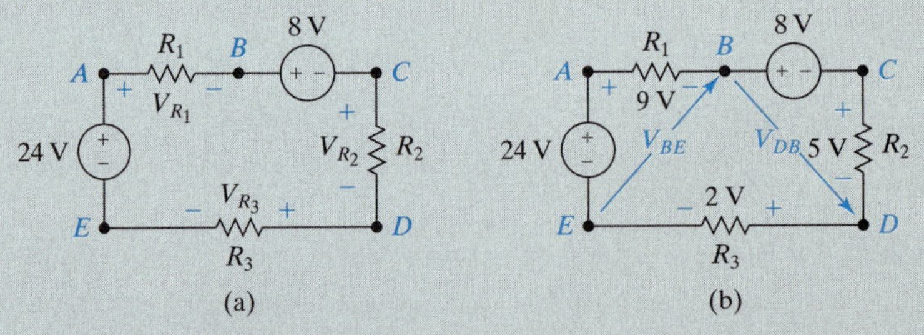

FIGURE 2.7 Circuits used to illustrate Kirchhoff's voltage law.

Assuming that an increase in voltage is positive, starting at node *A* and traversing the circuit in a clockwise direction, we obtain

$$-V_{R1} - 8 - V_{R2} - V_{R3} + 24 = 0$$

Assuming that an increase in voltage is negative, using the same starting point and direction yields

$$V_{R1} + 8 + V_{R2} + V_{R3} - 24 = 0$$

Note that these two equations are identical. Furthermore, we would have obtained the same result if we had started at any node and traversed the network in a counterclockwise direction.

Now suppose that V_{R1} and V_{R2} are known to be 9 V and 5 V, respectively. Then either equation can be used to find $V_{R3} = 2$ V. The circuit with all known voltages labeled is shown in Figure 2.7(b). This network is also used to illustrate the notation V_{AB}, which denotes the voltage of point A with respect to point B. Since the potential is measured between two points, it is convenient to use an arrow between two points with the head of the arrow located at the positive reference. Note that the double subscript notation, the + and − notation, and the single-headed arrow notation are all the same if the head of the arrow is pointing toward the positive terminal and the first subscript in the double subscript notation. If we apply this notation to the network in Figure 2.7(b), we find, for example, that $V_{AE} = +24$ V, $V_{EA} = -24$ V, $V_{CD} = +5$ V, and $V_{DC} = -5$ V. Furthermore, we can apply Kirchhoff's voltage law to the circuit to determine the voltage between any two points. For example, suppose we want to determine the voltage V_{BE}. Note that we have a choice of two paths: one is $BCDEB$ and the other is $BEAB$. For the first path we obtain

$$-8 - 5 - 2 + V_{BE} = 0$$
$$V_{BE} = 15 \text{ V}$$

For the second path the equation is

$$-V_{BE} + 24 - 9 = 0$$
$$V_{BE} = 15 \text{ V}$$

In a similar manner, we can show that

$$V_{DB} = -13 \text{ V}$$

In general, the mathematical representation of Kirchhoff's voltage law is

$$\sum_{j=1}^{N} v_j(t) = 0 \qquad (2.8)$$

where $v_j(t)$ is the voltage across the jth branch (with the proper reference direction) in a loop containing N voltages. This expression is analogous to Eq. (2.7) for Kirchhoff's current law.

Drill Exercise

D2.5. In the network in Figure D2.5, V_{R1} is known to be 4 V. Find V_{R2} and V_{bd}.

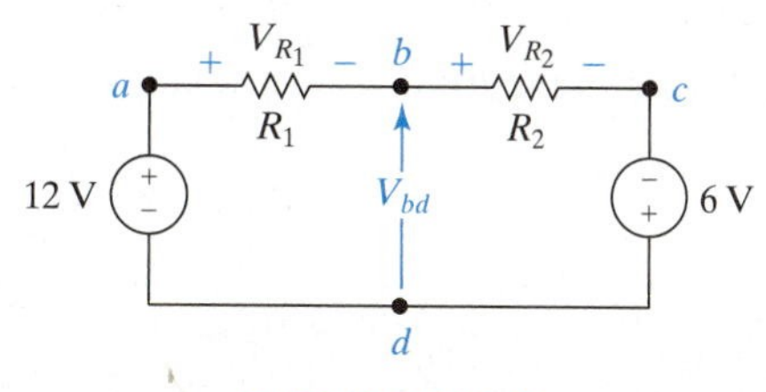

FIGURE D2.5

Ans: $V_{R2} = 14$ V, $V_{bd} = 8$ V.

D2.6. In the network in Figure D2.6, find V_{R4}, V_{bf}, and V_{ec}.

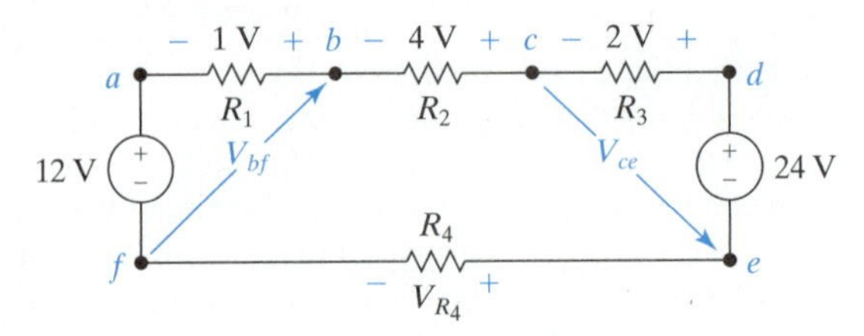

FIGURE D2.6

Ans: $V_{R4} = -5$ V, $V_{bf} = 13$ V, $V_{ec} = -22$ V.

2-4 Single-Loop Circuits

At this point we can begin to apply the laws we presented earlier to the analysis of simple circuits. To begin, we examine what is perhaps the simplest circuit—a single closed path, or loop, of elements. The elements of a single loop carry the same current and therefore are said to be in series. We will now apply Kirchhoff's voltage law and Ohm's law to the circuit to determine various quantities in it.

The circuit shown in Figure 2.8 will serve as a basis for discussion. This circuit consists of a number of independent voltage sources in series with several resistors. We have assumed the current to be in a clockwise direction. If this assumption is correct, the solution of the equations that yields the current will produce a positive value. If the current is actually in the opposite direction, the value of the current variable will simply be negative, indicating that the current is in a direction opposite to that assumed.

Rationale for voltage polarity assignments

Note carefully that we have made voltage polarity assignments for the voltage across each of the resistors in the network in Figure 2.8(a). These assignments are based upon Ohm's law and our choice for the direction of $i_1(t)$ as illustrated in Figure 2.1. In other words, once we have assumed the direction of the current, the terminal the current enters is labeled as the positive terminal. Let us demonstrate that the resultant current is independent of the direction assumed. Applying Kirchhoff's voltage law to the network in Figure 2.8(a) yields

$$-v_{R1} - v_{R2} - v_{R3} - v_2(t) - v_{R4} + v_1(t) = 0$$

or

$$-v_2(t) + v_1(t) = v_{R1} + v_{R2} + v_{R3} + v_{R4}$$

As illustrated in Figure 2.1, Ohm's law specifies that

$$v_{Rj} = i_1(t)\, R_j$$

Therefore,

$$\begin{aligned} v_1(t) - v_2(t) &= i_1(t)\, R_1 + i_1(t)\, R_2 + i_1(t)\, R_3 + i_1(t)\, R_4 \\ &= i_1(t)\, [R_1 + R_2 + R_3 + R_4] \end{aligned}$$

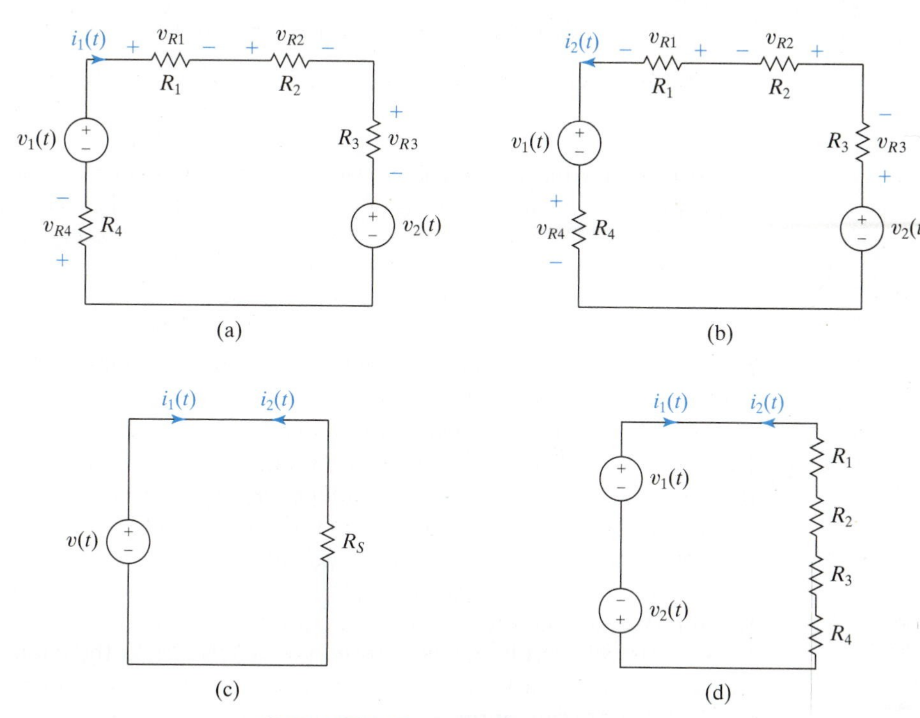

FIGURE 2.8 A single loop circuit.

which can be written as

$$v(t) = i_1(t)\, R_s \tag{2.9}$$

where

$$v(t) = v_1(t) - v_2(t) \tag{2.10}$$

$$R_s = R_1 + R_2 + R_3 + R_4$$

Now let us apply Kirchhoff's voltage law to the circuit in Figure 2.8(b) using $i_2(t)$, which is assumed to be in the opposite direction to that of $i_1(t)$ in Figure 2.8(a). Using the same convention that was used to write the equations for the network in Figure 2.8(a), we obtain

$$-v_1(t) - v_{R4} + v_2(t) - v_{R3} - v_{R2} - v_{R1} = 0$$

or

$$-v_1(t) + v_2(t) = v_{R1} + v_{R2} + v_{R3} + v_{R4}$$

which can be written as

$$-[v_1(t) - v_2(t)] = i_2(t)\,(R_1 + R_2 + R_3 + R_4)$$

or

$$[v_1(t) - v_2(t)] = -i_2(t)\,(R_1 + R_2 + R_3 + R_4)$$

If we compare these results with those for the network in Figure 2.8(a), we find that

$$i_2(t) = -i_1(t)$$

or

$$i_1(t) = -i_2(t)$$

Clearly, the magnitudes of the two currents are the same, but they are negatives of one another since the direction of one is opposite to that of the other. Therefore, the two equations

$$v(t) = i_1(t)\, R_s$$

$$-v(t) = i_2(t)\, R_s$$

that apply to the equivalent circuit in Figure 2.8(c) represent the networks in Figure 2.8(a) and (b) under the conditions in Eq. (2.10).

Furthermore, the network in Figure 2.8(d) is equivalent to each of the networks in Figures 2.8(a), (b), and (c) under the condition stated in Eq. (2.10), that is, we can rearrange the components within the loop without changing the value of the currents $i_1(t)$ and $i_2(t)$. In other words, several voltage sources in series ($v_1(t)$ and $v_2(t)$ in this case) can be replaced by one source, $v(t)$, whose value is the algebraic sum of the individual sources. In addition, the resistors R_1, R_2, R_3, and R_4 can be replaced by a single resistor R_s, which is the sum of the four resistors. We say that the resistor R_s is *equivalent* to the sum of the four resistors since it has the same terminal voltage and current characteristics as the combination. What is demonstrated here is true in general, that is, *the equivalent resistance of any number of resistors in series is simply the sum of the individual resistors.*

Equivalent resistance of resistors connected in series

Example 2.4

Given the network in Figure 2.9, (a) find I, V_{BE}, V_{FD} and the power absorbed by the 3 Ω resistor, and (b) repeat part (a) if the 12 V source is changed to 72 V.

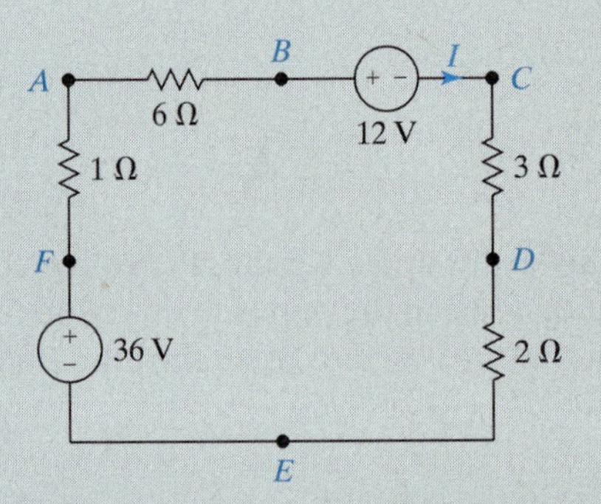

FIGURE 2.9 Circuit used in Example 2.4.

(a) starting at node A and traversing the network in a clockwise direction writing Kirchhoff's voltage law, we obtain

$$-6I - 12 - 3I - 2I + 36 - I = 0$$

or

$$I = 2\text{A}$$

Kirchhoff's voltage law for the path *ABEFA* is

$$-6I - V_{BE} + 36 - 1I = 0$$

Since $I = 2$ A, $V_{BE} = 22$ V. In a similar manner, using the path *FDEF* we find that

$$-V_{FD} - 2I + 36 = 0$$

or

$$V_{FD} = 32 \text{ V}$$

The power dissipated in the 3 Ω resistor is

$$P_{3\Omega} = I^2(3) = 12 \text{ W}$$

(b) Kirchhoff's voltage law for the network in this case is

$$-6I - 72 - 3I - 2I + 36 - 1I = 0$$

or

$$I = -3 \text{ A}$$

Once again, employing Kirchhoff's voltage law for the paths *ABEFA* and *FDEF*, we obtain

$$-6I - V_{BE} + 36 - 1I = 0$$

or $V_{BE} = 57$ V and

$$-V_{FD} - 2I + 36 = 0$$

or $V_{FD} = 42$ V. Finally, $P_{3\Omega} = I^2(3) = 27$ W.

Example 2.5

Light emitting diodes, or LEDs, are used as indicator lamps in a wide variety of electric equipment such as stereos, computers, and cameras. The operation of a standard LED is such that as long as there is a current through the LED, the voltage drop across the LED is approximately constant at 2 V. In the circuit shown in Figure 2.10, determine the value of the resistor *R* so that the current in the LED does not exceed 20 mA.

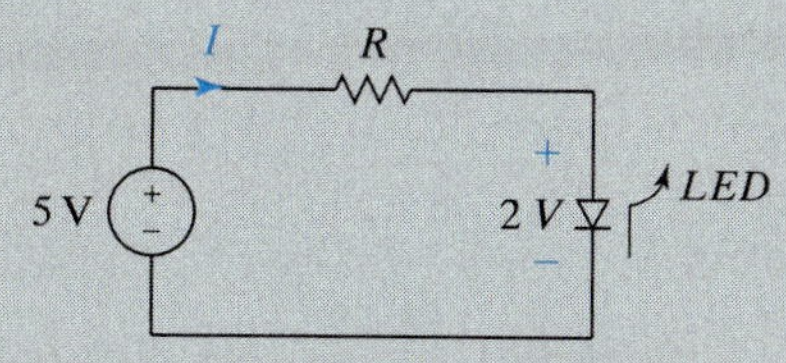

FIGURE 2.10 A simple LED circuit.

Applying Kirchhoff's voltage law to the circuit in Figure 2.10 yields

$$+5 - IR - 2 = 0$$

and if $I = 20$ mA

$$R = 150 \ \Omega$$

Example 2.6

An industrial load is served by a power company generator as shown in Figure 2.11. The transmission line is 100 miles long and has a line resistance of 0.1 Ω/mile. The load absorbs 1.2 megawatts. Determine the amount of power that must be supplied by the generator if the line voltage at the load is (a) 12 kV or (b) 120 kV.

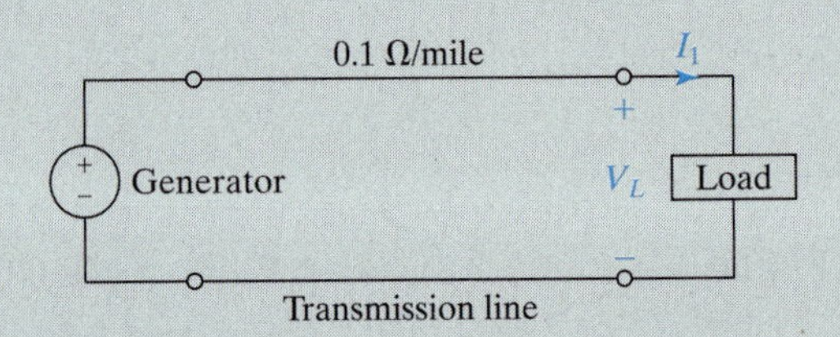

FIGURE 2.11 Circuit used in Example 2.6.

(a) If $V_L = 12$ kV and $P_L = 1.2$ MW, then the line current I_L is

$$I_L = \frac{1.2 \times 10^6}{12 \times 10^3} = 100 \text{ A}$$

The line losses are then

$$\begin{aligned} P_{Line} &= I_L^2 R_{Line} \\ &= (100)^2 (100)(2)(0.1) \\ &= 0.2 \text{ MW} \end{aligned}$$

Therefore, the power that must be supplied by the generator is

$$\begin{aligned} P_{Gen} &= P_L + P_{Line} \\ &= 1.4 \text{ MW} \end{aligned}$$

(b) If $V_L = 120$ kV, then

$$I_L = \frac{1.2 \times 10^6}{120 \times 10^3} = 10 \text{ A}$$

The line losses are then

$$\begin{aligned} P_{Line} &= (10)^2 (100)(2)(0.1) \\ &= 2 \text{ kW} \end{aligned}$$

Therefore, the power that must be supplied by the generator is

$$\begin{aligned} P_{Gen} &= P_L + P_{Line} \\ &= 1.202 \text{ MW} \end{aligned}$$

JUST IN TIME

REFERENCE CARD: CIRCUITS

INDEPENDENT VOLTAGE SOURCE:

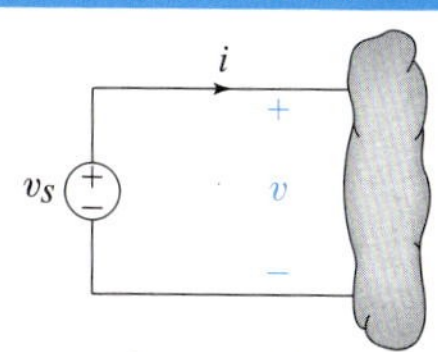

The voltage $v = v_S$, but i could *theoretically be* any value and must be determined from the elements in the cloud.

INDEPENDENT CURRENT SOURCE:

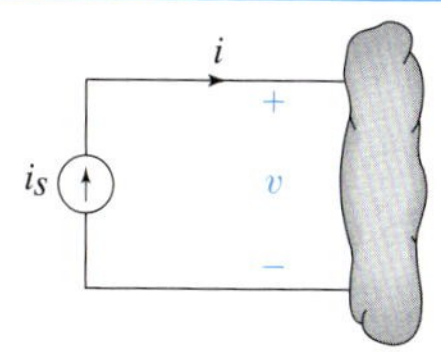

The current $i = i_S$, but the voltage v could *theoretically* be any value and must be determined from the elements in the cloud.

DEPENDENT VOLTAGE SOURCE:

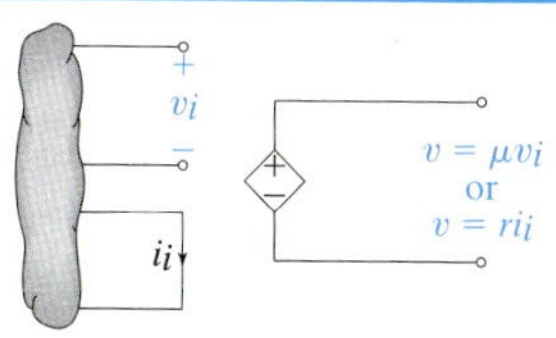

A current or voltage-controlled voltage source.

DEPENDENT CURRENT SOURCE:

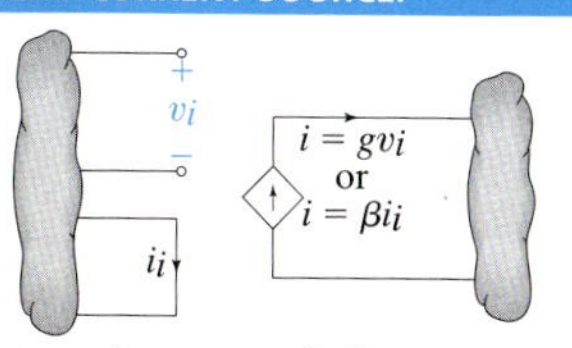

A current or voltage-controlled current source.

DEFINITIONS:

Current	Voltage	Power
$i = \dfrac{dq}{dt}$	$v = \dfrac{dw}{dq}$	$P = \dfrac{dw}{dt} = vi$

Ohm's Law $\quad v(t) = i(t)R$

$$P(t) = v(t)i(t) = i^2(t) \quad R = \frac{v^2(t)}{R}$$

$$G = \frac{1}{R}$$

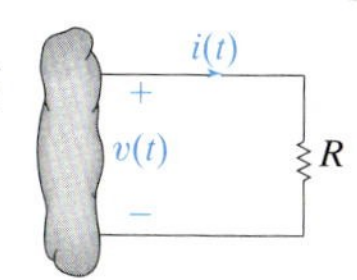

Short circuit $R = 0$

Open circuit $R = \infty$

KCL: Algebraic sum of the currents entering any node is zero.

KVL: Algebraic sum of the voltages around any loop is zero.

RESISTER RELATIONSHIPS:

Series: $R_s = R_1 + R_2 + R_3 + \cdots$

Parallel: $\dfrac{1}{R_p} = \dfrac{1}{R_1} + \dfrac{1}{R_2} + \dfrac{1}{R_3} + \cdots$

VOLTAGE/CURRENT DIVISION

Y⇄Δ Transformations:

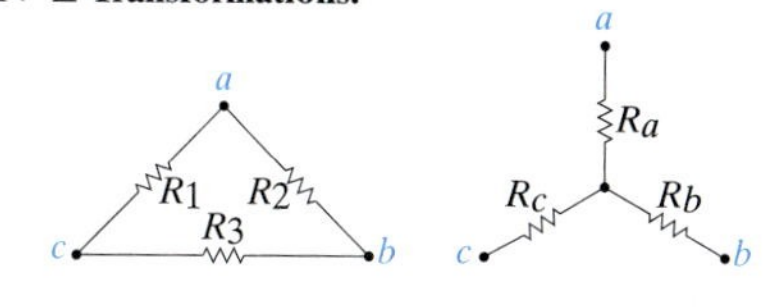

$$R_a = \frac{R_1R_2}{D},\ R_b = \frac{R_2R_3}{D},\ R_c = \frac{R_1R_3}{D},\ D = R_1+R_2+R_3$$

$$R_1 = \frac{N}{R_b},\ R_2 = \frac{N}{R_c},\ R_3 = \frac{N}{R_a},\ N = R_aR_b+R_aR_c+R_bR_c$$

Voltage division:

$$v_{R_1}(t) = \frac{R_1}{R_1 + R_2}v(t)$$

$$v_{R_2}(t) = \frac{R_2}{R_1 + R_2}v(t)$$

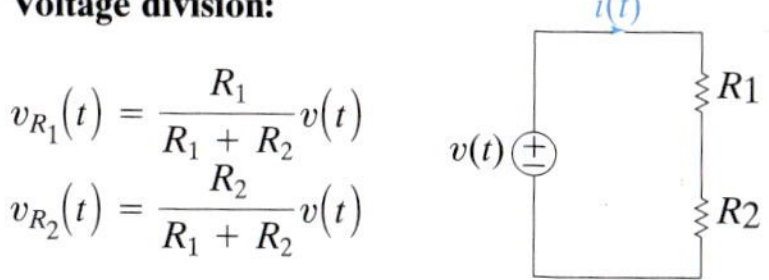

Current division:

$$i_1(t) = \frac{R_2}{R_1 + R_2}i(t)$$

$$i_2(t) = \frac{R_1}{R_1 + R_2}i(t)$$

<u>Node Analysis:</u> Uses KCL to derive a set of linearly independent equations in which the unknown variables are the non-reference node voltages.

<u>Loop Analysis:</u> Uses KVL to derive a set of linearly independent equations in which the unknown variables are the loop currents.

<u>Superposition:</u> The current or voltage at some point in a network containing multiple sources can be calculated as the Algebraic sum of the individual contributions of each source acting alone.

<u>Source Exchange</u>:The series (R, v) connection can be exchanged for the parallel (R, i) connection and vice versa, where $v = iR$.

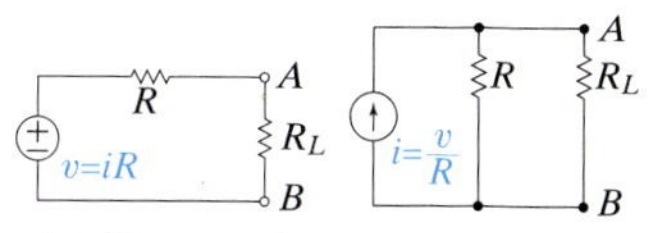

<u>Thevenin's/Norton's Theorem</u>

Thevenin's Theorem states that the network in (a) can be replaced by the network in (b) where V_{oc} is the open-circuit voltage in (c) and $R_{TH} = {}^{V_{OC}}/_{I_{SC}}$ where I_{sc} is the short-circuit current in (d). Norton's Theorem states that the network in (a) can be replaced by the network in (e).

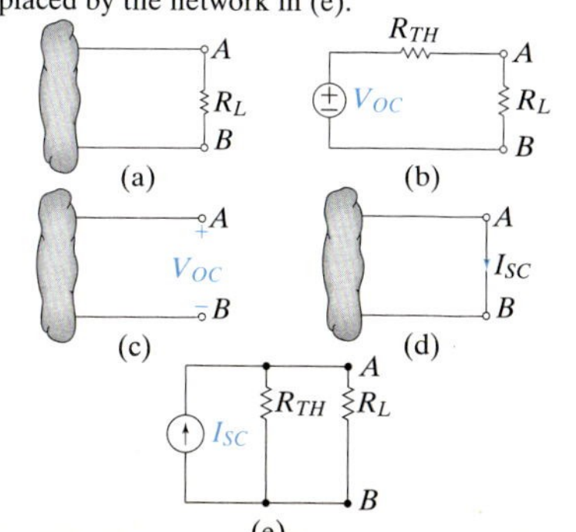

CAPACITOR RELATIONSHIPS:

$$i(t) = C\frac{dv(t)}{dt}, v(t) = \frac{1}{C}\int_{t_o}^{t} i(x)dx + v(t_o), w_C(t) = \frac{1}{2}Cv^2(t)$$

Series $\quad \dfrac{1}{C_s} = \dfrac{1}{C_1} + \dfrac{1}{C_2} + \dfrac{1}{C_3} + \cdots$

Parallel $\quad C_p = C_1 + C_2 + C_3 + \cdots$

INDUCTOR RELATIONSHIPS:

$$v(t) = L\frac{di(t)}{dt}, i(t) = \frac{1}{L}\int_{t}^{t} v(x)dx + i(t_o), w_L(t) = \frac{1}{2}Li^2(t)$$

Series $\quad L_s = L_1 + L_2 + L_3 + \cdots$

Parallel $\quad \dfrac{1}{L_p} = \dfrac{1}{L_1} + \dfrac{1}{L_2} + \dfrac{1}{L_3} + \cdots$

TRANSIENT CIRCUITS—GENERAL SOLUTIONS FOR $x(t) = v(t)$ or $i(t)$:

<u>First</u>-order $\quad x(t) = k_1 + k_2 e^{-t/\tau}$

k_1 is the steady-state solution

τ is the time constant $-\tau$ = RC for an RC network, $\tau = \dfrac{L}{R}$ for a RL network.

<u>Second</u>-order

Case-1 overdamped

$$x(t) = k_1 e^{-(\alpha-\sqrt{\alpha^2-\omega_0^2})} + k_2 e^{-(\alpha+\sqrt{\alpha^2-\omega_0^2})t}$$

Case-2 underdamped

$$x(t) = e^{-\alpha t}\left(A_1 \operatorname{Cos}\sqrt{\omega_0^2-\alpha^2}\, t + A_2 \operatorname{Sin}\sqrt{\omega_0^2 - \alpha^2}\, t\right)$$

Case-3 critically damped $x(t) = \beta_1 e^{-\alpha t} + \beta_2 t e^{-\alpha t}$

where α = exponential damping coefficient and ω_o = undamped natural frequency.

AC STEADY-STATE ANALYSIS:

$x(t) = A \operatorname{Sin}(\omega t + \theta)$ where A is the amplitude or maximum value, ω is the radian or angular frequency and θ is the phase angle in radians $\omega = 2\pi f = {}^{2\pi}/_T$, f is the frequency in hertz and T is the period in seconds. If $y(t) = \beta \operatorname{Sin}(\omega t + \phi)$, $x(t)$ <u>leads</u> $y(t)$ by $\theta - \phi$ radians and $y(t)$ <u>lags</u> $x(t)$ by $\theta - \phi$ radians. If $\theta \neq \phi$, $x(t)$ and $y(t)$ are out of phase.

<u>Phasor</u> – A complex number $A\angle\theta$, A is the magnitude, θ is the phase angle.

Phasor relationship for the passive elements

$$\mathbf{V} = R\mathbf{I}, \quad \mathbf{V} = j\omega L\mathbf{I}, \quad \mathbf{I} = \frac{\mathbf{V}}{j\omega C}$$

<u>Impedance</u> $\mathbf{Z} = \dfrac{\mathbf{V}}{\mathbf{I}}$ and impedances combine like resistors. KCL, KVL, node equations, loop equations, superposition, etc. are all valid in a frequency domain (phasor) analysis.

Average Power $P = \dfrac{1}{2}V_M I_M \operatorname{Cos}(\theta_v - \theta_i)$. For a pure resistive network $P = \dfrac{1}{2}V_M I_M$. For a pure reactive network $P = 0$.

The root-mean-square (rms) or effective value of a periodic signal $i(t)$ is labeled I_{rms} and

$$I_{rms} = \left[\frac{1}{T}\int_{t_o}^{t_o+T} i^2(t)dt\right]^{\frac{1}{2}}$$

where T is the period of the waveform. If $i(t)$ is a current, then $P = I_{rms}^2 R$.

Power Relationships are specified in the diagram:

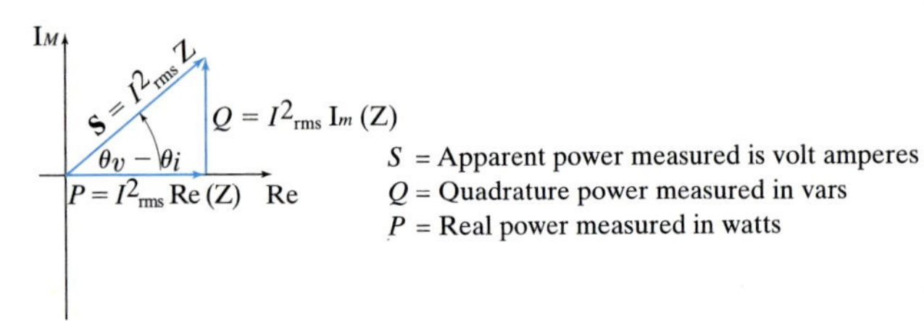

$$\text{PF} = \text{Power factor} = \cos(\theta_v - \theta_i) = \frac{P}{V_{rms} I_{rms}} \text{ and } \theta_v - \theta_i = \text{Power factor angle.}$$

In a RL network
- –The current lags the voltage
- –The power factor is lagging

In a RC network
- –The current leads the voltage
- –The power factor is leading

Power factor correction can typically be accomplished by connecting a bank of capacitors in parallel with the load.

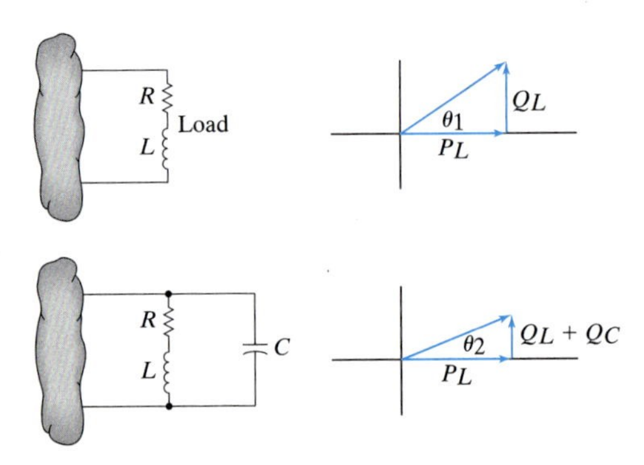

By adding Q_C to Q_L, $\theta_2 < \theta_1$ and since PF = cos θ, the PF is raised by adding the capacitor bank.

In balanced three-phase circuit analysis always think *Y*, i.e., convert to a *Y-Y* system and analyze a single phase. Then shift the results by 120° and 240° for the two remaining phases.

In a balanced *Y-Y* system $V_{\text{Line}} = \sqrt{3}\, V_{\text{Phase}}$ and $I_{\text{Line}} = I_{\text{Phase}}$.

For a Δ-connected load, $V_{\text{Line}} = V_{\text{Phase}}$ = and $I_{\text{Line}} = \sqrt{3}\, I_{\text{Phase}}$.

For a Δ-connected source, the equivalent *Y* source is $V_{\text{Phase}} = V_{\text{Line}}/\sqrt{3}$.

The three-phase power relationships are $S_{1\varphi} = V_p I_p \angle\theta_z = \dfrac{V_L I_L}{\sqrt{3}} \angle\theta_z$ and $|S_T| = \sqrt{3}\, V_L, I_L$.

MAGNETIC CIRCUITS:

For naturally coupled coils, the assignments for voltage and current are similar to those for Ohm's Law, i.e., the assignments for *V* and *I* require that the dots are positive and currents are into the dots. For example, the equations for the following network are

$$\boldsymbol{V}_1 = j\omega L_1 \boldsymbol{I}_1 + j\omega M \boldsymbol{I}_2$$

$$\boldsymbol{V}_2 = j\omega L_2 \boldsymbol{I}_2 + j\omega M \boldsymbol{I}_1$$

The equations for the following ideal transformer are

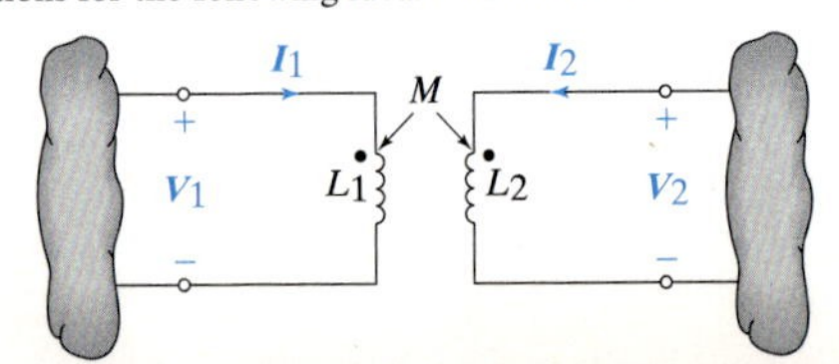

$$\frac{\boldsymbol{V}_1}{\boldsymbol{V}_2} = \frac{N_1}{N_2}$$

$$\frac{\boldsymbol{I}_1}{\boldsymbol{I}_2} = \frac{N_2}{N_1}$$

$$S_1 = S_2$$

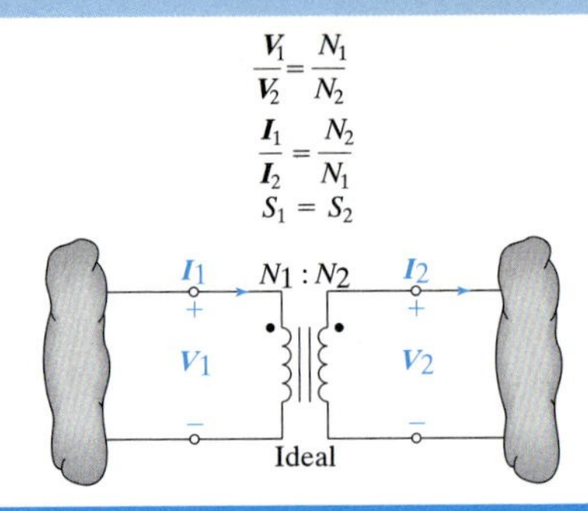

PASSIVE FILTER NETWORKS:

First-Order:

Low Pass

$G_v(j\omega)$ — Ideal characteristic — Typical characteristic — 1, $\frac{1}{\sqrt{2}}$, 0, ω_0, ω

(a)

High Pass

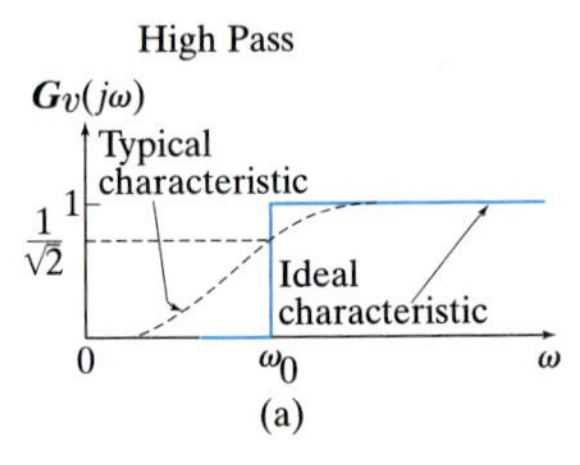

(a)

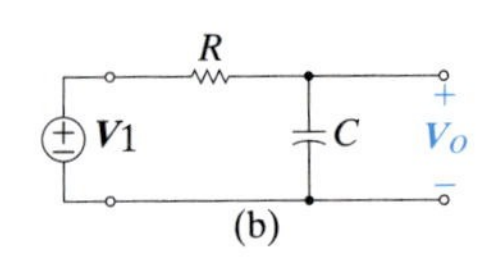

(b)

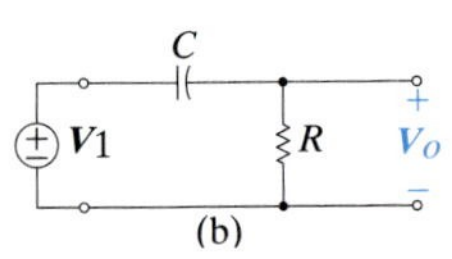

(b)

ω_0 = Break Frequency = Cutoff Frequency = Half Power Frequency

Second-Order:

Band Pass

$G_v(j\omega)$ — 1, $\frac{1}{\sqrt{2}}$, ω_{LO}, ω_0, ω_{H1}, ω

(a)

Band Rejection

$G_v(j\omega)$ — 1, $\frac{1}{\sqrt{2}}$, ω_{LO}, ω_0, ω_{H1}, ω

(b)

V1, L, C, R, Vo

(c)

V1, R, C, L, Vo

(d)

Bandwidth (BW) = $\omega_{HI} - \omega_{LO}$

ω_{HI} = Upper cutoff frequency

ω_{LO} = Lower cutoff frequency

ω_0 = Center frequency

At the resonant frequency ω_o

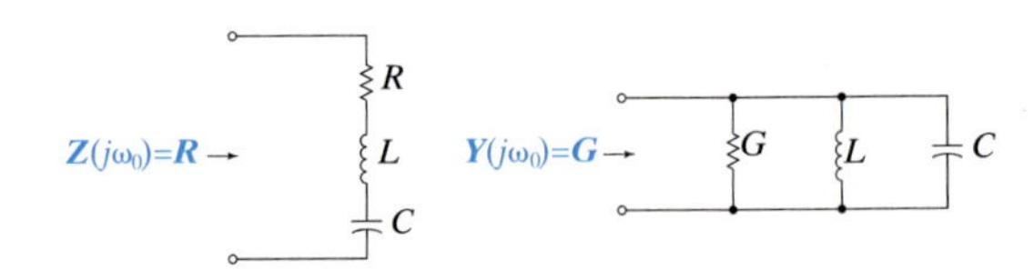

$$\text{BW} = \frac{\omega_o}{Q} = \omega_{HI} - \omega_{LO}$$

$$Q = \frac{\omega_o L}{R} \qquad \omega_o = \frac{1}{\sqrt{LC}} \qquad Q = \omega_o RC$$

Note that the efficiency, that is, the ratio of output power to input power, is quite different. In the first case, the efficiency is 86%, while in the second case, the efficiency is 99.8%. Transmitting at high voltage and low current minimizes the I^2R losses, and therefore, the utilities operate in this mode. The issue is much more complicated than indicated in this simple approach, since as the voltage goes up, so does the cost of insulation and switchgear. Furthermore, broader right-of-ways and higher towers are needed for transmission.

2.4.1 Voltage Division

We introduce this topic using the network shown in Figure 2.12. Applying Kirchhoff's voltage law to this network yields

$$v(t) = R_1 i(t) + R_2 i(t)$$

Solving the equation for $i(t)$ yields

$$i(t) = \frac{v(t)}{R_1 + R_2} \tag{2.11}$$

Knowing the current, we can now apply Ohm's law to determine the voltage across each resistor:

$$\begin{aligned} v_{R1} &= R_1 i(t) \\ &= \frac{R_1}{R_1 + R_2} v(t) \end{aligned} \tag{2.12}$$

Similarly,

$$v_{R2} = \frac{R_2}{R_1 + R_2} v(t) \tag{2.13}$$

Note that the equations satisfy Kirchhoff's voltage law, since

$$+v(t) - \frac{R_1}{R_1 + R_2} v(t) - \frac{R_2}{R_1 + R_2} v(t) = 0$$

Although simple, Eqs. (2.12) and (2.13) are very important because they describe the operation of what is called a voltage divider. In other words, the voltage of *the source $v(t)$ is divided between the resistors R_1 and R_2 in direct proportion to the total $R_1 + R_2$*

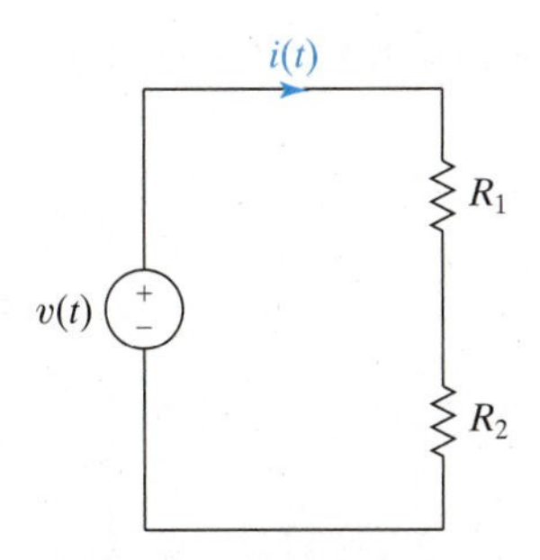

FIGURE 2.12 Two single-loop circuits.

Furthermore, if a voltage $v(t)$ exists across three resistors R_1, R_2, and R_3 in series, then we know that

The voltage division rule

$$v_{R1} = \frac{R_1}{R_1 + R_2 + R_3} v(t)$$

Example 2.7

The volume control circuit for a radio or TV is shown in Figure 2.13(a). A portion of the receiver circuit applies a small fixed voltage to the variable resistance R, which is the volume control potentiometer (pot). This is a resistor with a sliding contact that can be placed anywhere along the resistor. The volume control circuit is actually a voltage divider between V_{in} and V_{out}, as shown in Figure 2.13(b). The voltage V_{out} is amplified by a fixed amount to drive the speaker.

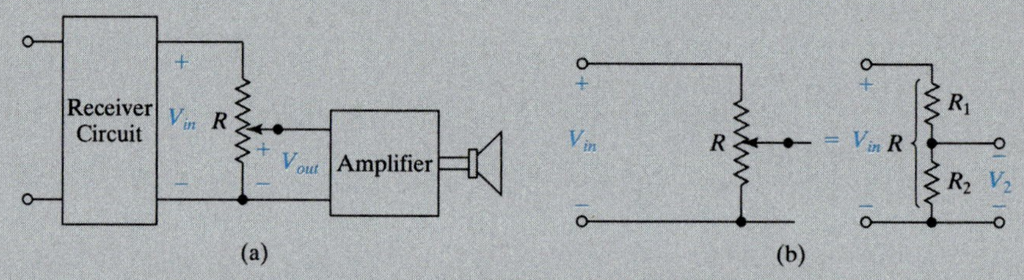

FIGURE 2.13 Volume control circuit.

Now suppose that $V_{in} = 1.6$ V, $R = 24$ kΩ, $R_1 = 12$ kΩ, and $R_2 = 12$ kΩ. Under these conditions, let us find V_{out}.

The voltage divider output is

$$V_{out} = V_{in}\left(\frac{R_2}{R_1 + R_2}\right) = V_{in}\left(\frac{R_2}{R}\right)$$

$$= \frac{1.6}{24000}(12000)$$

$$= 0.8 \text{ V}$$

Drill Exercise

D2.7. Find I and V_0 in the network in Figure D2.7.

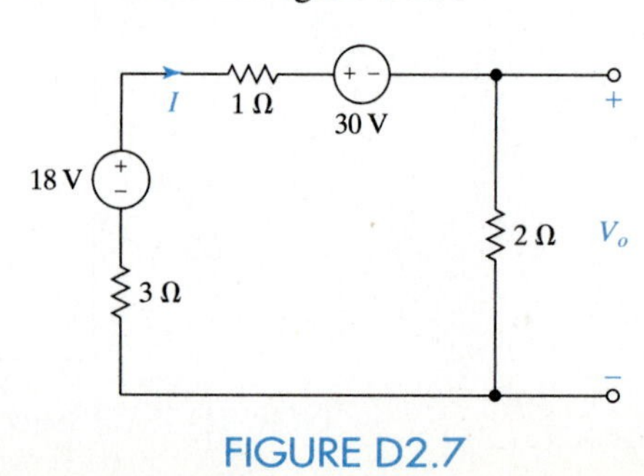

FIGURE D2.7

Ans: $I = -2$ A, $V_0 = -4$ V.

D2.8. Find I, V_{AC}, V_{CB}, and $P_{6\Omega}$ in the network in Figure D2.8.

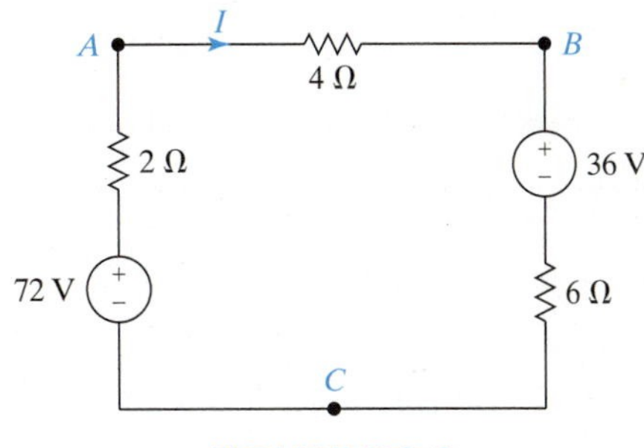

FIGURE D2.8

Ans: $I = 3$ A, $V_{AC} = 66$ V, $V_{CB} = -54$ V, $P_{6\Omega} = 54$ W.

2-5 Single-Node-Pair Circuits

An important circuit is the single-node-pair circuit, an example of which is shown in Figure 2.14(a). In this case the elements have the same voltage across them, and therefore are in parallel. Kirchhoff's current law and Ohm's law will be used to determine the various unknown quantities in these networks.

With reference to the network shown in Figure 2.14(a), we have assumed that the upper node is $v(t)$ volts positive with respect to the lower node. Applying Kirchhoff's current law to the upper node yields

$$i_A(t) - i_1(t) + i_B(t) - i_2(t) - i_C(t) - i_3(t) - i_4(t) = 0$$

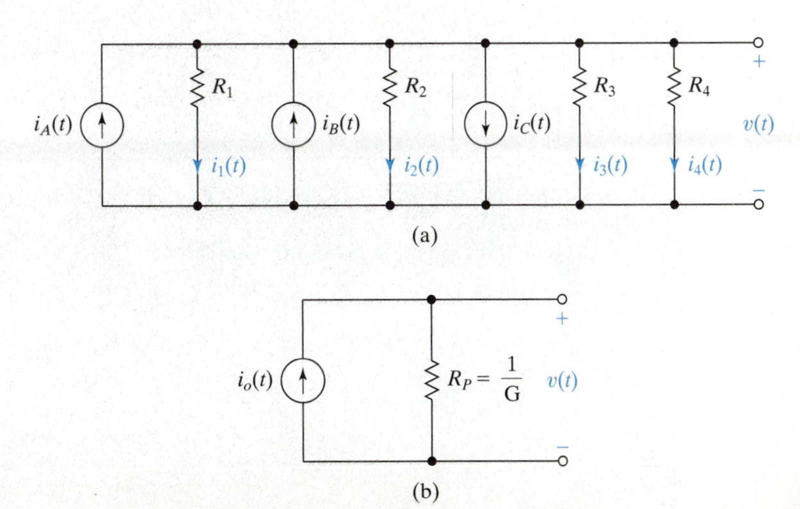

FIGURE 2.14 Equivalent circuits.

or

$$i_A(t) + i_B(t) - i_C(t) = i_i(t) + i_2(t) + i_3(t) + i_4(t)$$

However, from Ohm's law we know that

$$i_j(t) = \frac{v(t)}{R_j}$$

Therefore,

$$i_A(t) + i_B(t) - i_C(t) = \frac{v(t)}{R_1} + \frac{v(t)}{R_2} + \frac{v(t)}{R_3} + \frac{v(t)}{R_4}$$

$$= v(t)\left[\frac{1}{R_1} + \frac{1}{R_2} + \frac{1}{R_3} + \frac{1}{R_4}\right] = v(t)[G_1 + G_2 + G_3 + G_4]$$

This equation can be written as

$$i_o(t) = \frac{v(t)}{R_p} = G_p v(t)$$

where

$$i_o(t) = i_A(t) + i_B(t) - i_c(t)$$

$$\frac{1}{R_p} = \frac{1}{R_1} + \frac{1}{R_2} + \frac{1}{R_3} + \frac{1}{R_4}$$

and

$$G_p = G_1 + G_2 + G_3 + G_4$$

Equivalent conductance of resistors connected in parallel

Under the definitions above, the network in Figure 2.14(a) is equivalent to that in Figure 2.14(b). In other words, several current sources in parallel can be replaced by one source whose value is the *algebraic* sum of the individual sources. Furthermore, *the equivalent conductance of any number of resistors in parallel is simply the sum of the individual conductances.*

Example 2.8

Given the network in Figure 2.15, (a) find V, I_1, I_2, I_3, $P_{4\Omega}$, and (b) repeat part (a) if the 2 A source is changed to 20 A.

(a) Kirchhoff's current law for the network is

$$8 - I_1 - 2 - I_2 - I_3 = 0$$

$$6 = I_1 + I_2 + I_3$$

$$6 = V\left[\frac{1}{12} + \frac{1}{6} + \frac{1}{4}\right]$$

or

$$V = 12 \text{ V}$$

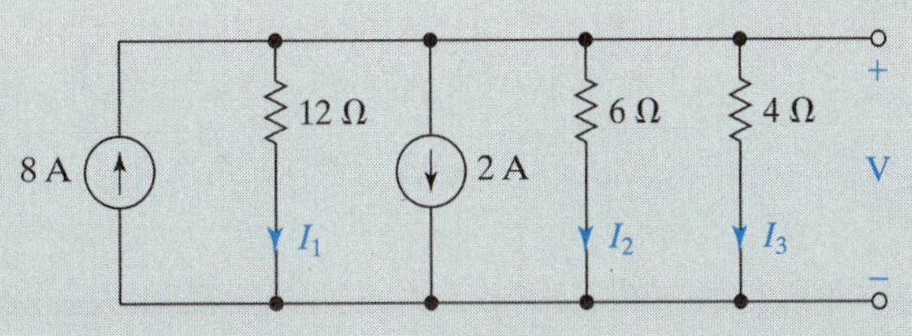

FIGURE 2.15 Circuit used in Example 2.8.

Then using Ohm's law, $I_1 = 1$ A, $I_2 = 2$ A, and $I_3 = 3$ A. In addition,

$$P_{4\Omega} = (I_3)^2(4) = \frac{V^2}{4} = 36 \text{ W}$$

(b) Kirchhoff's current law for the network in this case is

$$8 - I_1 - 20 - I_2 - I_3 = 0$$

or

$$-12 = V\left[\frac{1}{12} + \frac{1}{6} + \frac{1}{4}\right]$$

and hence

$$V = -24 \text{ V}$$

From Ohm's law we obtain $I_1 = -2$ A, $I_2 = -4$ A, and $I_3 = -6$ A. Finally,

$$P_{4\Omega} = (I_3)^2(4) = \frac{V^2}{4} = 144 \text{ W}.$$

Consider the circuit shown in Figure 2.16.

$$\begin{aligned} i(t) &= \frac{v(t)}{R_1} + \frac{v(t)}{R_2} \\ &= \left(\frac{1}{R_1} + \frac{1}{R_2}\right)v(t) \\ &= \frac{v(t)}{R_p} \end{aligned}$$

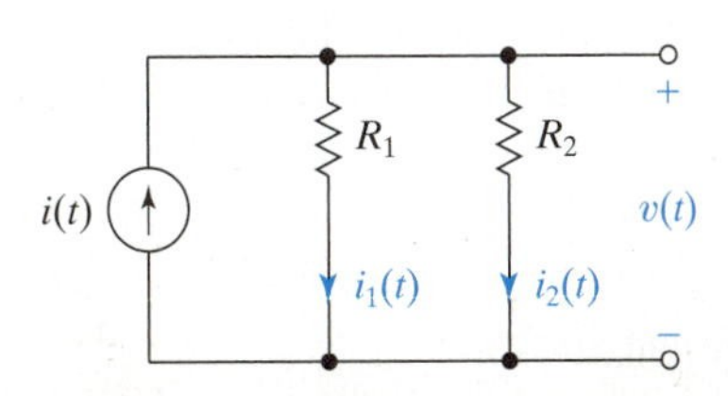

FIGURE 2.16 A circuit used to illustrate current division.

where

$$\frac{1}{R_p} = \frac{1}{R_1} + \frac{1}{R_2} \tag{2.14}$$

and

$$R_p = \frac{R_1 R_2}{R_1 + R_2} \tag{2.15}$$

Therefore, the equivalent resistance of two resistors connected in parallel is equal to the product of their resistances divided by their sum. Note also that this equivalent resistance R_p is always less than either R_1 or R_2. Hence, by connecting resistors in parallel we reduce the overall resistance. In the special case when $R_1 = R_2$, the equivalent resistance is equal to half of the value of the individual resistors.

2.5.1 Current Division

In a manner similar to the way in which voltage divides among series resistors, current divides among resistors connected in parallel. Consider once again the circuit in Figure 2.16 and the relationships in Equations (2.14) and (2.15). As indicated earlier,

$$\begin{aligned} v(t) &= R_p i(t) \\ &= \frac{R_1 R_2}{R_1 + R_2} i(t) \end{aligned} \tag{2.16}$$

Then

$$\begin{aligned} i_1(t) &= \frac{v(t)}{R_1} \\ &= \frac{R_2}{R_1 + R_2} i(t) \end{aligned} \tag{2.17}$$

and

$$\begin{aligned} i_2(t) &= \frac{v(t)}{R_2} \\ &= \frac{R_1}{R_1 + R_2} i(t) \end{aligned} \tag{2.18}$$

Equations (2.17) and (2.18) are mathematical statements of the current-division rule.

The current division rule

Therefore, the current divides in inverse proportion to the resistances. In other words, to determine the current in the branch containing R_1, we multiply the incoming current $i(t)$ by the opposite resistance R_2 and divide that product by the sum of the two resistors. Note that this description applies to the special case of two resistors in parallel.

However, if there are N resistors in parallel so that

$$\frac{1}{R_p} = \frac{1}{R_1} + \frac{1}{R_2} + \cdots + \frac{1}{R_n}$$

and as shown above

$$v(t) = R_p i(t)$$

then the current in the jth branch, that is, R_j, is

$$i_j(t) = \frac{v(t)}{R_j}$$

combining the last two equations yields

$$i_j(t) = \frac{R_p i(t)}{R_j}$$

which is a general expression for current division.

Example 2.9

Consider the circuit shown in Figure 2.17(a). The equivalent circuit is shown in Figure 2.17(b). Given the information specified in the circuit, we wish to determine the currents and equivalent resistance.

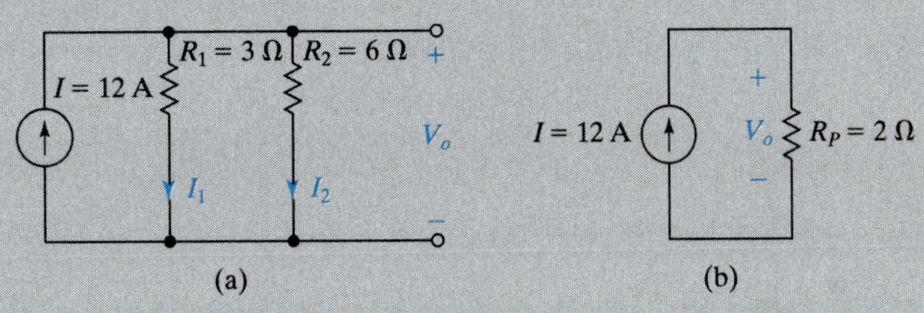

FIGURE 2.17 Example of a parallel circuit.

We can apply current division to determine I_1 and I_2. For example,

$$\begin{aligned} I_1 &= \frac{R_2}{R_1 + R_2} I = \frac{6}{3 + 6}(12) \\ &= 8 \text{ A} \end{aligned}$$

and

$$I_2 = \frac{3}{3 + 6}(12) = 4 \text{ A}$$

Note that the larger current is through the smaller resistor, and vice versa. In addition, one should note that if R_1 and R_2 are equal, the current will divide equally between them.

Note that these currents satisfy Kirchhoff's current law at both the upper and lower nodes.

$$\begin{aligned} I &= I_1 + I_2 \\ 12 \text{ A} &= 8 \text{ A} + 4 \text{ A} \end{aligned}$$

The equivalent resistance for the circuit is

$$\begin{aligned} R_p &= \frac{R_1 R_2}{R_1 + R_2} \\ &= \frac{(3)(6)}{3 + 6} \\ &= 2\ \Omega \end{aligned}$$

Now V_o can be calculated as

$$V_o = R_p I$$
$$= (2)(12)$$
$$= 24 \text{ V}$$

Once the voltage V_0 is known, Ohm's law can also be used to calculate the currents I_1 and I_2.

$$I_1 = \frac{V_o}{R_1}$$
$$= \frac{24}{3}$$
$$= 8 \text{ A}$$

and

$$I_2 = \frac{V_o}{R_2}$$
$$= \frac{24}{6}$$
$$= 4 \text{ A}$$

Drill Exercises

D2.9. Find I_1 and I_2 in the circuit in Figure D2.9 using current division.

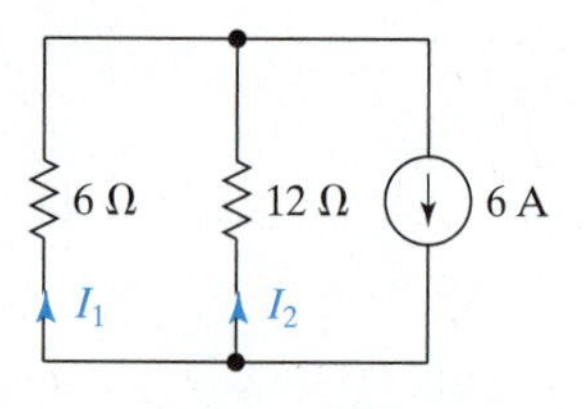

FIGURE D2.9

Ans: $I = 4$ A and $I = 2$ A.

D2.10. Find V, I_1, I_2, and $P_{6\Omega}$ in the network in Figure D2.10.

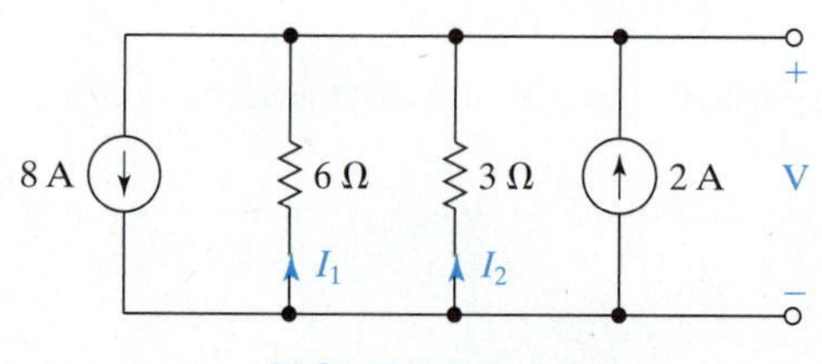

FIGURE D2.10

Ans: $V = -12$ V, $I_1 = -2$ A, $I_2 = 4$ A, and $P_{6\Omega} = 24$ W.

2-6 Resistor Combinations

In the section on single-loop circuits, we demonstrated that the equivalent resistance of N resistors in series is

$$R_S = R_1 + R_2 + \cdots + R_n$$

and in the section on single-node-pair circuits, we illustrated that the equivalent resistance of N resistors in parallel is determined by the expression

$$\frac{1}{R_P} = \frac{1}{R_1} + \frac{1}{R_2} + \cdots + \frac{1}{R_n}$$

Summary of resistor combination rules

The equivalent resistance, in each case, is a single resistance that has the same relation between voltage and current at its terminals as the series or parallel combination does at its designated terminals.

Let us now examine a combination of these two cases.

Example 2.10

Let us determine the resistance at terminals A–B of the network shown in Figure 2.18(a). To determine the equivalent resistance at A–B, we begin at the opposite end of the network and combine resistors as we progress toward terminals A–B. The 8, 1, and 3-Ω resistors connected in series are equivalent to one 12 Ω resistor, which in turn is in parallel with the 6 Ω resistor. This parallel combination is equivalent to one 4 Ω resistor, as shown in Figure 2.18(b). The two 7 Ω resistors and the 4 Ω resistor are in series, and this combination is in parallel with the 9 Ω resistor. Combining these resistors reduces the network to that shown in Figure 2.18(c). Therefore, the resistance at terminals A–B is 18 Ω, as shown in Figure 2.18(d).

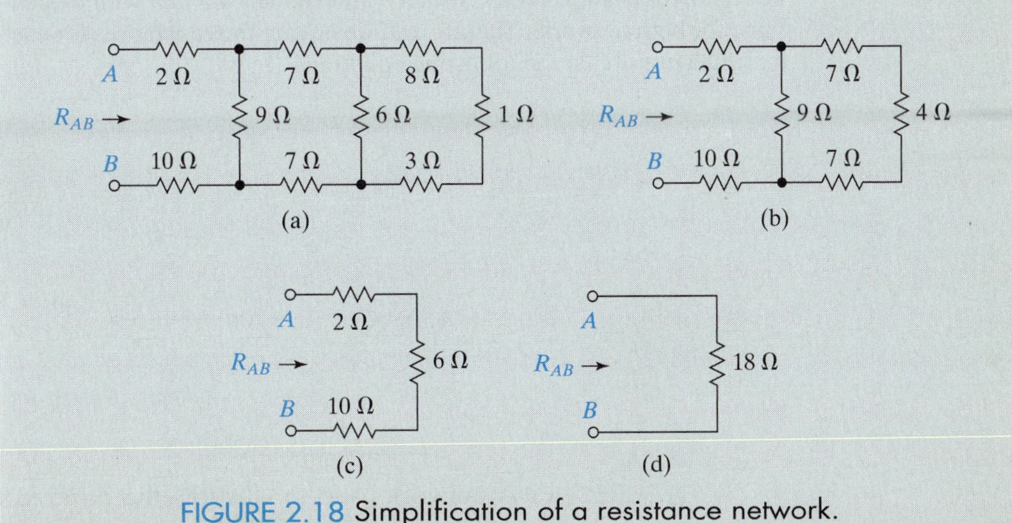

FIGURE 2.18 Simplification of a resistance network.

Drill Exercise

D2.11. Find the equivalent resistance at the terminals A–B in the network in Figure D2.11.

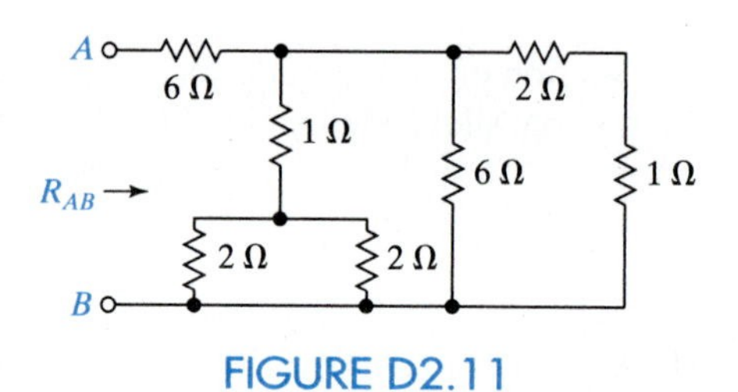

FIGURE D2.11

Ans: $R_{AB} = 7\ \Omega$.

Consider now the circuit in Figure 2.19. Note that when we attempt to reduce the circuit to an equivalent resistor R, we find that nowhere is a resistor in series or parallel with another. Therefore, we cannot attack the problem directly using the techniques we have learned thus far. We can, however, replace one portion of the network with an equivalent circuit and this conversion will permit us to reduce the combination of resistors to a single equivalent resistance with ease. This conversion is called the Y to Δ or Δ to Y transformation.

Note that the resistors in Figure 2.20(a) form a Δ and the resistors in Figure 2.20(b) form a Y. The transformation that relates the resistances R_1, R_2, and R_3 to the resistances R_a, R_b, and R_c is derived as follows. In order for the two networks to be equivalent at each corresponding pair of terminals, it is necessary that the resistance at the corresponding terminals be equal; for example, the resistance at terminals a and b with c open-circuited must be the same for both networks. Therefore, if we equate the resistances for each corresponding set of terminals, we obtain the following equations.

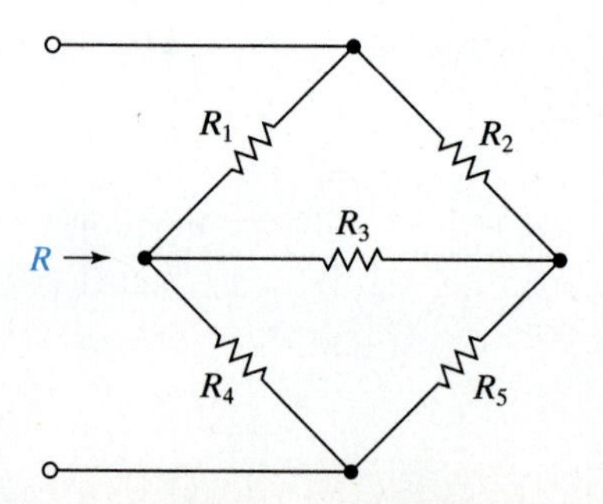

FIGURE 2.19 A network used to illustrate the need for the $Y \rightleftarrows \Delta$ transformation.

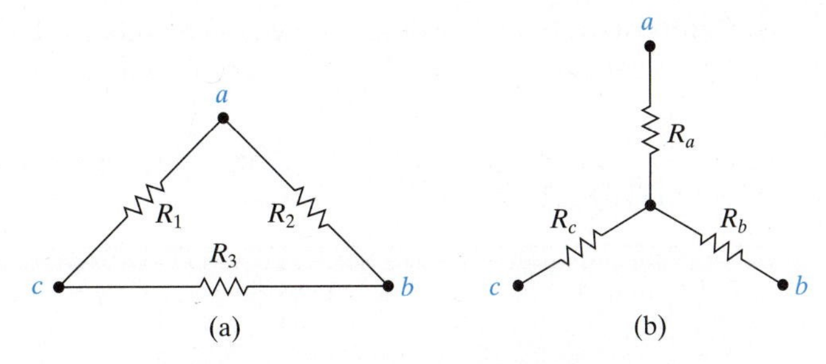

FIGURE 2.20 Δ and *Y* resistance networks.

$$R_{ab} = R_a + R_b = \frac{R_2 (R_1 + R_3)}{R_2 + R_1 + R_3}$$

$$R_{bc} = R_b + R_c = \frac{R_3 (R_1 + R_2)}{R_3 + R_1 + R_2} \tag{2.19}$$

$$R_{ca} = R_c + R_a = \frac{R_1 (R_2 + R_3)}{R_1 + R_2 + R_3}$$

Solving this set of equations for R_a, R_b, and R_c yields

$$R_a = \frac{R_1 R_2}{R_1 + R_2 + R_3}$$

$$R_b = \frac{R_2 R_3}{R_1 + R_2 + R_3} \tag{2.20}$$

$$R_c = \frac{R_1 R_3}{R_1 + R_2 + R_3}$$

The wye/delta conversion formulas

Similarly, if we solve Eq. (2.19) for R_1, R_2, and R_3, we obtain

$$R_1 = \frac{R_a R_b + R_b R_c + R_a R_c}{R_b}$$

$$R_2 = \frac{R_a R_b + R_b R_c + R_a R_c}{R_c} \tag{2.21}$$

$$R_3 = \frac{R_a R_b + R_b R_c + R_a R_c}{R_a}$$

Equations (2.20) and (2.21) are general relationships and apply to any set of resistances connected in a *Y* or Δ. For the balanced case where $R_a = R_b = R_c$ and $R_1 = R_2 = R_3$, the equations above reduce to

$$R_Y = \frac{1}{3} R_\Delta \tag{2.22}$$

Wye/delta conversion for the balanced case

and

$$R_\Delta = 3\, R_Y \tag{2.23}$$

It is important to note that it is easy to remember the formulas since there are definite geometrical patterns associated with the conversion equations.

Example 2.11

Let us find the equivalent resistance of the network in Figure 2.21(a) at the terminals.

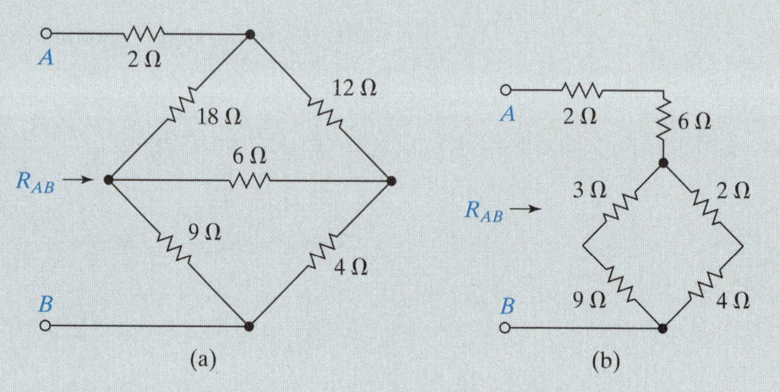

FIGURE 2.21 Circuits used in Example 2.11.

Applying the Δ to Y transformation reduces the network in Figure 2.21(a) to that in Figure 2.21(b). Note that the 3 Ω and 9 Ω resistors are in series and they are in parallel with the series combination of the 2 Ω and 4 Ω resistors. This total combination yields a 4 Ω resistor, which is in series with the 2 Ω and 6 Ω resistors, and thus the resistance at the terminals is 12 Ω.

Drill Exercise

D2.12. Find the resistance at the terminals A–B in the network in Figure D2.12.

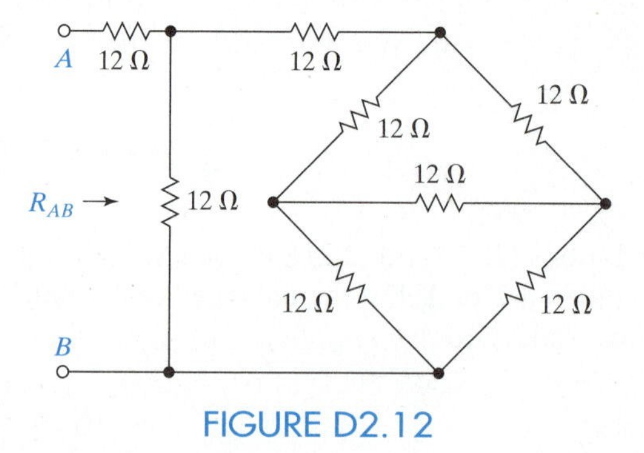

FIGURE D2.12

Ans: $R_{AB} = 20\ \Omega$.

2-7 Nodal Analysis

In order to perform a nodal analysis on a multiple-node circuit, we first select one node, which we refer to as the *reference node*, and measure the voltage at every other node with respect to this reference node. Thus, when we refer to the node voltage at some specific node, we mean the voltage at that node with respect to the reference node.

Reference node defined

Quite often the reference node is the one to which the largest number of branches are connected. It is commonly called *ground* because it is said to be at ground-zero potential and it sometimes represents the chassis or ground line in a practical circuit.

A nodal analysis is based on Kirchhoff's current law (KCL) and the variables in the circuit are selected to be the node voltages.

We will select our variables as being positive with respect to the reference node. If one or more of the node voltages is actually negative with respect to the reference node, the analysis will indicate it.

Suppose for a moment that we know all the node voltages in a given network. Then with reference to Figure 2.22, we can use Ohm's law, that is,

$$i = \frac{V_m - V_n}{R} \tag{2.24}$$

to calculate the current through any resistive element. In this manner we can determine every voltage and every current in the circuit.

In a double-node circuit (i.e., one containing two nodes, one of which is the reference node), a single equation is required to solve for the unknown node voltage. In the case of an N-node circuit, $N - 1$ linearly independent simultaneous equations are required to determine the $N - 1$ unknown node voltages. These equations are written by employing KCL at $N - 1$ of the N nodes.

The following procedure outlines the manner in which the nodal analysis is performed.

The nodal analysis technique

1. Identify and label one node in the network as the reference (ground) node. All non-reference node voltages will be measured with respect to this node.
2. Label the remaining non-reference nodes with an unknown voltage variable, such as V_1, V_2, and so on.
3. The node equation at each non-reference node is obtained by applying Kirchhoff's current law, that is, setting the algebraic sum of the currents leaving the node equal to zero.
4. Solve the resulting set of simultaneous equations for the unknown voltage variables.

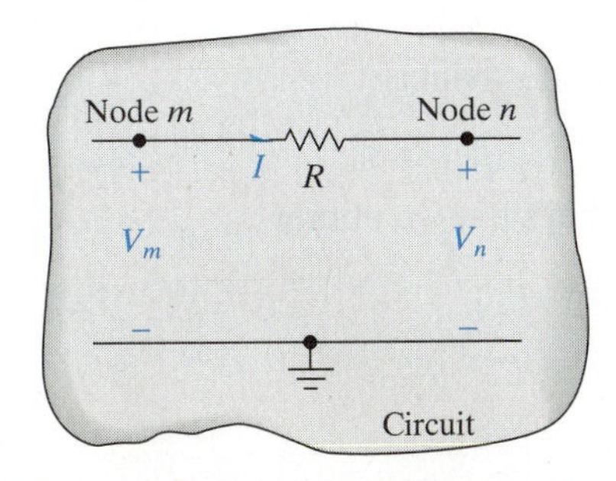

FIGURE 2.22 Circuit used to illustrate Ohm's law in a multiple-node network.

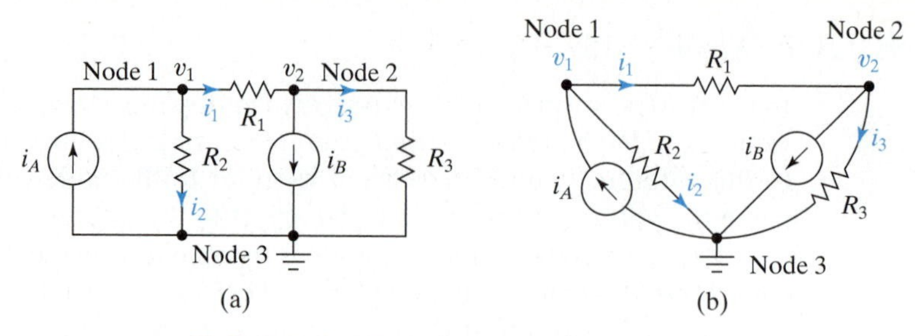

FIGURE 2.23 A three-node network.

There are a number of techniques that can be employed to solve the equation set, for example, Cramer's rule, matrices, and MATLAB. We will illustrate the solution within the text by Cramer's rule. In addition, we will provide an appendix outlining the procedure for employing this technique.

Consider, for example, the circuit shown in Figure 2.23(a). This circuit has three nodes. The node at the bottom is selected as the reference node and is so labeled using the ground symbol, ⏚. This reference node is assumed to be at zero potential and the node voltages v_1 and v_2 are defined with respect to this node.

The circuit is redrawn in Figure 2.23(b) to indicate the nodes clearly. The branch currents are assumed to flow in the directions indicated in the figures. If one or more of the branch currents are actually flowing in a direction opposite to that assumed, the analysis will simply produce a branch current that is negative.

Applying KCL at node 1 yields

$$i_A - i_1 - i_2 = 0$$

Using Ohm's law and noting that the reference node is at zero potential, we obtain

$$i_A - \frac{v_1 - v_2}{R_1} - \frac{v_1 - 0}{R_2} = 0$$

or

$$v_1\left(\frac{1}{R_1} + \frac{1}{R_2}\right) - v_2\left(\frac{1}{R_1}\right) = i_A$$

which could also be written in the form

$$v_1(G_1 + G_2) - v_2(G_1) = i_A$$

KCL at node 2 yields

$$i_1 - i_B - i_3 = 0$$

Using Ohm's law we obtain

$$\frac{v_1 - v_2}{R_1} - i_B - \frac{v_2 - 0}{R_3} = 0$$

or

$$-v_1\left(\frac{1}{R_1}\right) + v_2\left(\frac{1}{R_1} + \frac{1}{R_3}\right) = -i_B$$

which can also be expressed as

$$v_1(G_1) + v_2(G_2 + G_3) = -\,i_B$$

Therefore, the two equations, which when solved yield the node voltages, are

$$v_1\left(\frac{1}{R_1} + \frac{1}{R_2}\right) - v_2\left(\frac{1}{R_1}\right) = i_A$$

$$-\,v_1\left(\frac{1}{R_1}\right) + v_2\left(\frac{1}{R_1} + \frac{1}{R_3}\right) = -i_B$$

Note that the analysis has produced two simultaneous equations in the unknowns v_1 and v_2. They can be solved using any convenient technique, for example, Gaussian elimination, determinants, matrices, or other methods.

Note that a nodal analysis employs KCL in conjunction with Ohm's law. Once the direction of the branch currents has been assumed, then Ohm's law, as illustrated by Figure 2.22 and expressed by Eq. (2.24), is used to express the branch currents in terms of the unknown node voltages. We can assume the currents to be in any direction. However, once we assume a particular direction, we must be very careful to write the currents correctly in terms of the node voltages using Ohm's law.

Example 2.12

Let us use nodal analysis to determine all the currents in the network in Figure 2.24(a). The node voltages and branch currents are labeled as shown in Figure 2.24(b). KCL for the two nodes with node voltages V_1 and V_2 are

$$-\,I_1 - 4 - I_2 - I_3 = 0$$

$$I_3 + 10 - I_4 = 0$$

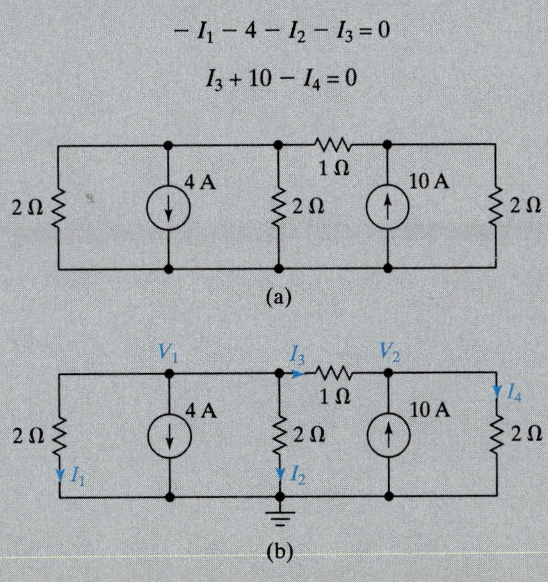

FIGURE 2.24 Circuits used in Example 2.12.

Using Ohm's law these equations can be written as

$$-\frac{V_1 - 0}{2} - 4 - \frac{V_1 - 0}{2} - \frac{V_1 - V_2}{1} = 0$$

$$\frac{V_1 - V_2}{1} + 10 - \frac{V_2 - 0}{2} = 0$$

Simplifying the equations yields

$$2V_1 - V_2 = -4$$

$$-V_1 + (3/2)V_2 = 10$$

Solving the equations by Cramer's Rule (see Appendix B), we first compute the determinant as

$$\begin{aligned} det &= \begin{vmatrix} 2 & -1 \\ -1 & 3/2 \end{vmatrix} \\ &= 2(3/2) - (-1)(-1) \\ &= 2 \end{aligned}$$

The node voltage V_1 is then

$$\begin{aligned} V_1 &= \frac{\begin{vmatrix} -4 & -1 \\ 10 & 3/2 \end{vmatrix}}{det} \\ &= \frac{-4(3/2) - (-1)(10)}{2} \\ &= \frac{-6 + 10}{2} \\ &= 2 \text{ V} \end{aligned}$$

and V_2 is

$$\begin{aligned} V_2 &= \frac{\begin{vmatrix} 2 & -4 \\ -1 & 10 \end{vmatrix}}{2} \\ &= \frac{20 - 4}{2} \\ &= 8 \text{ V} \end{aligned}$$

Therefore $I_1 = 1$ A, $I_2 = 1$ A, $I_3 = -6$ A, and $I_4 = 4$ A. Note that KCL is satisfied at all the nodes in the network.

The MATLAB software package provides us with another convenient technique for solving these nodal equations. To employ this method, we simply write the equations in a matrix format as follows. For example, if the equations are

The MATLAB solution procedure

$$AV1 + BV2 = -I1$$

$$CV1 - DV2 = I2$$

Then the equations can be expressed in matrix form as

$$\mathbf{G}^{*}\mathbf{V} = \mathbf{I}$$

Where the * indicates multiplication, **G** is a 2 × 2 matrix (2 rows and 2 columns), and **V** and **I** are 2 × 1 vectors (2 rows and 1 column).

$$\mathbf{G} = \begin{bmatrix} A & B \\ C & -D \end{bmatrix}, \mathbf{V} = \begin{bmatrix} V1 \\ V2 \end{bmatrix} \text{ and } \mathbf{I} = \begin{bmatrix} -I1 \\ I2 \end{bmatrix}$$

Then the matrix solution of the equations is

$$\mathbf{V} = \mathbf{G}^{-1}\mathbf{I}$$

Where $\mathbf{G}^{-1}$ represents the inverse of the matrix **G.**

MATLAB employs this same format and therefore when the equations are placed in the form

$$\mathbf{G}^{*}\mathbf{V} = \mathbf{I}$$

The solution equation is

$$\mathbf{V} = \text{inv}(\mathbf{G})^{*}\mathbf{I}$$

The MATLAB software uses a prompt of the form ». At this prompt, the rows of the matrix **G** or the vector **I** are entered. Brackets are used to denote both matrices and vectors, semi-colons are used to separate rows, and spaces separate columns. Once **G** and **I** have been defined, the solution equation typed at the prompt », will yield the unknown voltages defined by **V.**

Example 2.13

Let us use MATLAB to determine the node voltages in the previous example.

The computer screen containing the input data consisting of the matrix **G,** the vector **I,** and the solution equation **V** = inv(**G**)***I** is listed below.

```
EDU» G=[2 -1; -1 1.5]
G =
          2.0000  -1.0000
         -1.0000   1.5000
EDU» I=[-4 ;10]
I =
         -4
         10
EDU» V=inv (G) *I
V =
         2
         8
```

Example 2.14

We wish to find all the currents in the network in Figure 2.25 using nodal analysis.

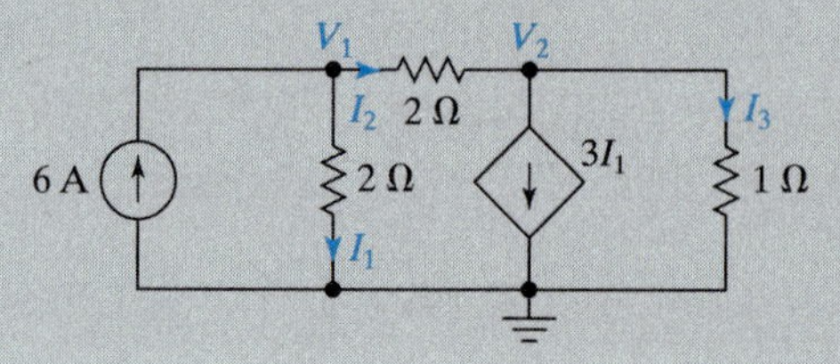

FIGURE 2.25 Circuit used in Example 2.14.

Applying KCL we obtain

$$6 - I_1 - I_2 = 0$$

$$I_2 - 3I_1 - I_3 = 0$$

Using Ohm's law the equations become

$$6 - \frac{V_1}{2} - \frac{V_1 - V_2}{2} = 0$$

$$\frac{V_1 - V_2}{2} - 3\left(\frac{V_1}{2}\right) - \frac{V_2}{1} = 0$$

or

$$V_1 - \frac{1}{2}V_2 = 6$$

$$V_1 + \frac{3}{2}V_2 = 0$$

Solving these equations yields $V_1 = 4.5$ V and $V_2 = -3$ V. Therefore, $I_1 = 2.25$A, $I_2 = 3.75$ A, and $I_3 = -3$ A. Note that KCL is satisfied at every node.

MATLAB can also be employed to determine the node voltages. The computer screen containing the necessary equations, as well as the solution, is listed below.

```
EDU» G=[1 -0.5;1 1.5]
G =
        1.0000 -0.5000
        1.0000 1.5000
EDU» I = [6;0]
I =
        6
        0
EDU» V=inv (G)*I
V =
        4.5000
       -3.0000
```

Drill Exercise

D2.13. Use nodal analysis to find all the currents in the network in Figure D2.13.

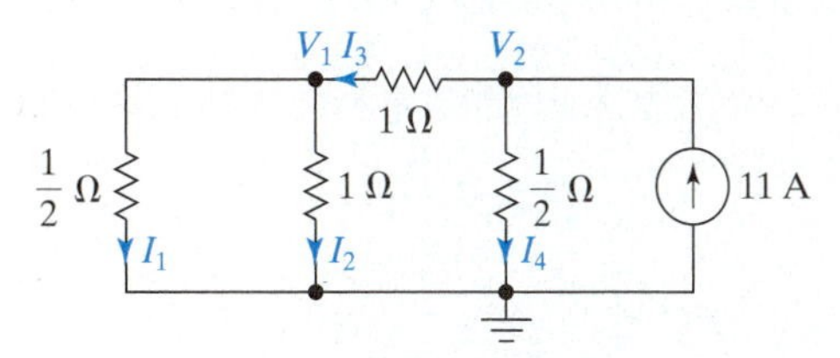

FIGURE D2.13

Ans: $I_1 = 2$ A, $I_2 = 1$ A, $I_3 = 3$ A, and $I_4 = 8$ A.

D2.14. Find all the currents in the network in Fig. D2.14 using nodal analysis.

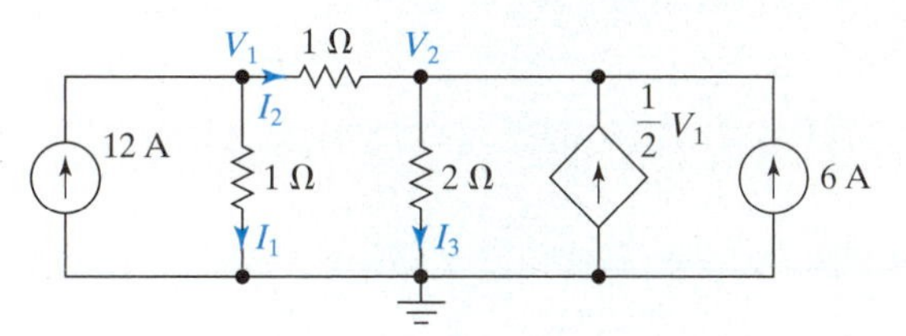

FIGURE D2.14

Ans: $I_1 = 16$ A, $I_2 = -4$ A, $I_3 = 10$ A.

The supernode technique

Consider now the network in Figure 2.26(a). If we attempt to perform a nodal analysis on this circuit to determine the unknown node voltages V_1 and V_2, we quickly find that we cannot express the branch current in the voltage source as a function of V_1 and V_2. However, we can form what is called a *supernode*, which includes the voltage source and the two nodes labeled V_1 and V_2 as shown by the dashed line in Figure 2.26(b). KCL must hold for this supernode, that is, the algebraic sum of the currents entering or leaving the supernode must be zero. Therefore, one valid equation for the network is

$$I_1 - I_A + I_2 + I_B = 0$$

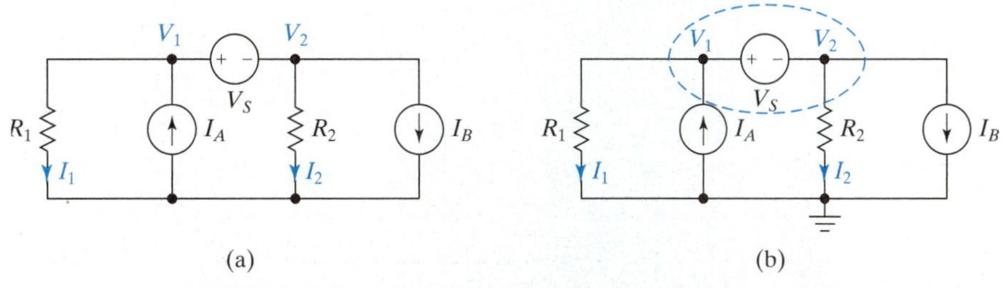

FIGURE 2.26 Circuits illustrating a supernode.

or

$$\frac{V_1}{R_1} + \frac{V_2}{R_2} = I_A - I_B \tag{2.25}$$

Since this is an $N = 3$ node network, we need $N - 1 = 2$ linearly independent equations to determine the node voltages. The second equation is derived from the supernode where the difference in potential between the two node voltages V_1 and V_2 is *constrained* by the voltage source, that is

$$V_1 - V_2 = V_S \tag{2.26}$$

Equations (2.25) and (2.26) will yield the node voltages, which, in turn, can be used to determine all the currents.

Example 2.15

Given the network in Figure 2.27(a), let us find the current in each resistor.

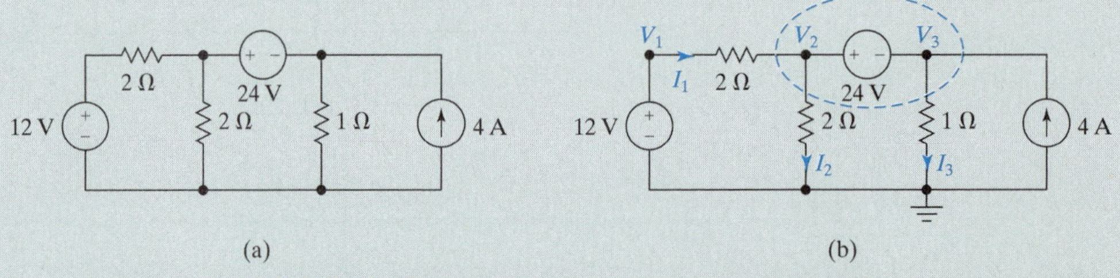

FIGURE 2.27 Circuits used in Example 2.15.

The network is redrawn in Figure 2.27(b). Note that a supernode exists around the 24V source and $V_1 = 12$ V. KCL for the supernode is

$$I_1 - I_2 - I_3 + 4 = 0$$

or

$$\frac{12 - V_2}{2} - \frac{V_2}{2} - \frac{V_3}{1} + 4 = 0$$

which reduces to

$$V_2 + V_3 = 10$$

This equation together with the supernode constraint equation

$$V_2 - V_3 = 24$$

yields $V_2 = 17$ V and $V_3 = -7$ V. The currents in the resistors are then $I_1 = -2.5$ A, $I_2 = 8.5$ A, and $I_3 = -7$ A.

Example 2.16

As a final example in this section, consider the more difficult circuit shown in Figure 2.28(a). Because this circuit is somewhat complex, we will employ MATLAB to solve for the unknown node voltages.

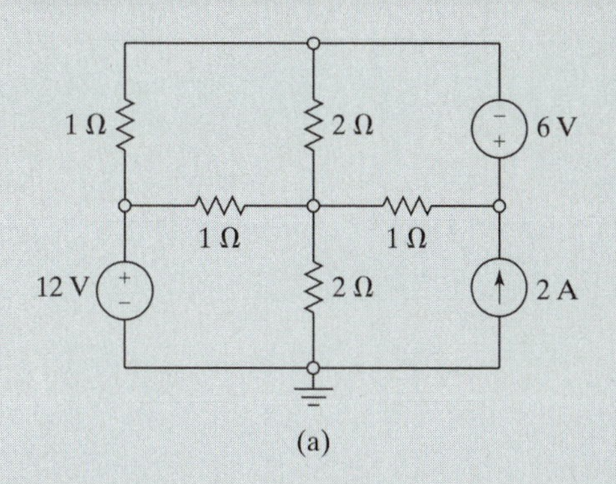

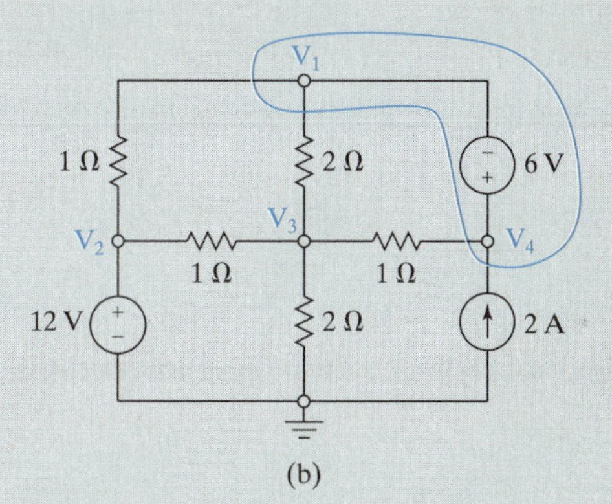

FIGURE 2.28 (a) Circuit used in Example 2.16 and (b) the redrawn circuit illustrating the supernode.

A careful examination of the circuit indicates that one of the node voltages is known to be 12 V, and there exists a supernode between two other nodes. The network is redrawn in Figure 2.28(b) to clearly indicate the presence of the supernode. Since V_2 is constrained to be 12 V and the difference between V_4 and V_1 is constrained to be 6 V, two of the four node equations necessary to solve the network are

$$V_2 = 12$$

$$V_4 - V_1 = 6$$

The two remaining equations are obtained by applying KCL at the supernode and node V_3. These equations are

$$\frac{V_1 - V_2}{1} + \frac{V_1 - V_3}{2} + \frac{V_4 - V_3}{1} = 2$$

$$\frac{V_3 - V_1}{2} + \frac{V_3 - V_2}{1} + \frac{V_3}{2} + \frac{V_3 - V_4}{1} = 0$$

Simplifying the algebra, we obtain

$$\begin{aligned}
\frac{3}{2}V_1 \quad -V_2 \quad -\frac{3}{2}V_3 \quad + V_4 &= 2 \\
V_1 \quad\quad\quad\quad\quad\quad - V_4 &= -6 \\
V_2 &= 12 \\
-\frac{1}{2}V_1 \quad - V_2 \quad + 3V_3 \quad - V_4 &= 0
\end{aligned}$$

The equations expressed in matrix form are

$$\begin{bmatrix} \frac{3}{2} & -1 & -\frac{3}{2} & 1 \\ 1 & 0 & 0 & -1 \\ 0 & 1 & 0 & 0 \\ -\frac{1}{2} & -1 & 3 & -1 \end{bmatrix} \begin{bmatrix} V_1 \\ V_2 \\ V_3 \\ V_4 \end{bmatrix} = \begin{bmatrix} 2 \\ -6 \\ 12 \\ 0 \end{bmatrix}$$

The MATLAB solution that yields the unknown node voltages is as follows.

```
EDU» G=[1.5 -1 -1.5 1;1 0 0 -1;0 1 0 0;-0.5 -1 3 -1]

G =
    1.5000       -1.0000       -1.5000        1.0000
    1.0000             0             0       -1.0000
         0        1.0000             0             0
   -0.5000       -1.0000        3.0000       -1.0000

EDU» I = [2; -6; 12; 0]

I =

     2
    -6
    12
     0

EDU» V=inv (G)*I

V =

    9.7143
   12.0000
   10.8571
   15.7143
```

Drill Exercise

D2.15. Find I_1, I_2, and I_3 in the network in Figure D2.15.

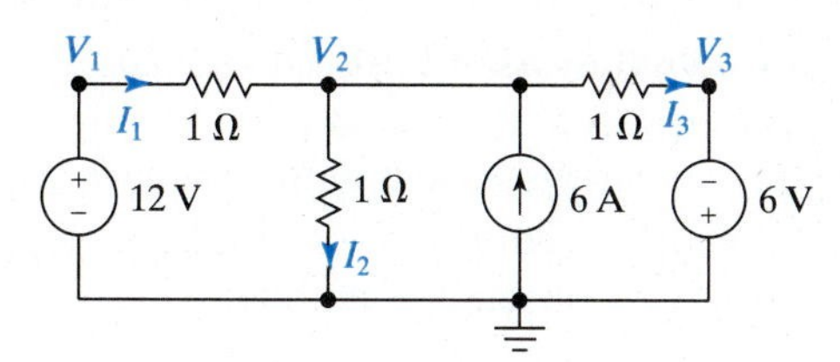

FIGURE D2.15

Ans: $I_1 = 8$ A, $I_2 = 4$ A, and $I_3 = 10$ A.

2-8 Loop and Mesh Analysis

In a nodal analysis the unknown parameters are the node voltages, and KCL is employed to determine them. In contrast to this approach, a loop or mesh analysis uses KVL to determine currents in the circuit. Once the currents are known, Ohm's law can be used to calculate the voltages. We have found that a single equation was sufficient to determine the current in a circuit containing a single loop. If the circuit contains N independent loops, N independent simultaneous equations will be required to describe the network.

The following procedure outlines the manner in which the loop analysis is performed. The networks in Figure 2.29, where we have simply isolated a portion of a circuit, are used to supplement the discussion.

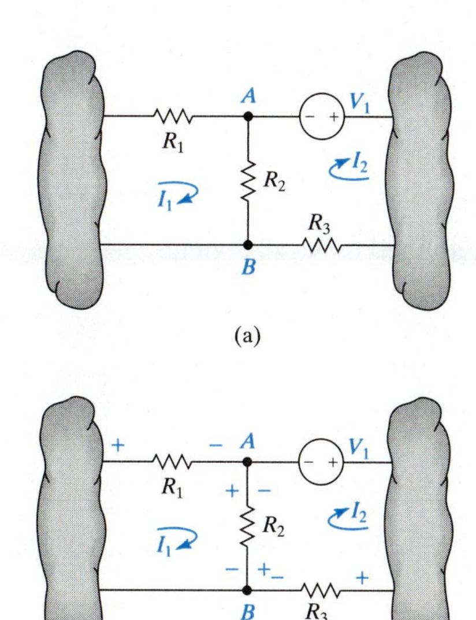

FIGURE 2.29 An isolated portion of a network.

The loop analysis technique

1. Assign an unknown current variable in each loop by drawing a clockwise arrow and labeling the currents as I_1 and I_2, as shown in Figure 2.29(a).
2. Indicate the polarity of the voltages on each resistor by placing a + sign on the end where the assigned current enters, as shown in Figure 2.29(b). Note carefully the two sets of +/− signs on R_2. They indicate that the current in R_2 from A to B is $I_1 - I_2$ and the current in R_2 from B to A is $I_2 - I_1$.
3. The equation for each loop is obtained by applying Kirchhoff's voltage law, that is, setting the algebraic sum of the voltages around each loop equal to zero.
4. Solve the resulting set of simultaneous equations for the unknown current variables using any convenient method.

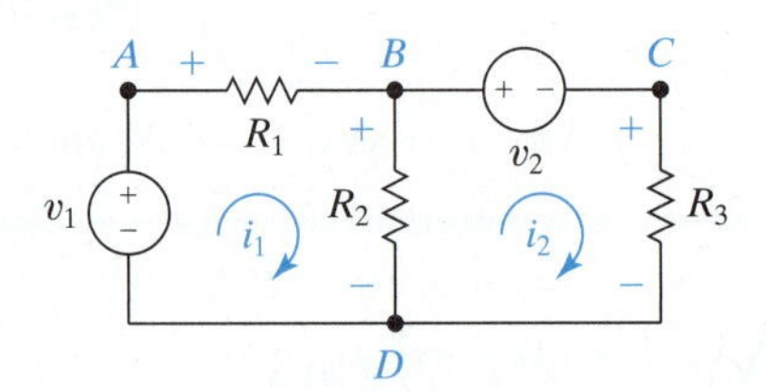

FIGURE 2.30 Two-mesh circuit.

Consider the circuit shown in Figure 2.30. Let us identify two meshes, $A—B—D—A$ and $B—C—D—B$. Let us assume that currents i_1 in the first mesh and i_2 in the second mesh flow clockwise. Then the branch current from B to D through R_2 is $i_1 - i_2$. The directions of the currents have been assumed arbitrarily. As was the case in the nodal analysis, if the actual currents are not in the direction indicated, the values calculated will be negative. Applying KVL to the first mesh yields

$$-i_1R_1 - (i_1 - i_2)R_2 + v_1 = 0$$

or

$$i_1(R_1 + R_2) - i_2R_2 = v_1$$

KVL applied to Mesh 2 yields

$$-v_2 - i_2R_3 + (i_1 - i_2)R_2 = 0$$

or

$$-i_1R_2 + i_2(R_2 + R_3) = -v_2$$

Therefore, the two simultaneous equations required to solve this two-mesh circuit are

$$i_1(R_1 + R_2) - i_2(R_2) = v_1$$

$$-i_1(R_2) + i_2(R_2 + R_3) = -v_2$$

Example 2.17

Let us compute the mesh currents in the circuit in Figure 2.31. The KVL equations for the two meshes are

$$-1I_1 - 2(I_1 - I_2) - 4 - 1I_1 + 12 = 0$$

$$-1I_2 + 20 + 4 - 2(I_2 - I_1) = 0$$

or

$$4I_1 - 2I_2 = 8$$

$$-2I_1 + 3I_2 = 24$$

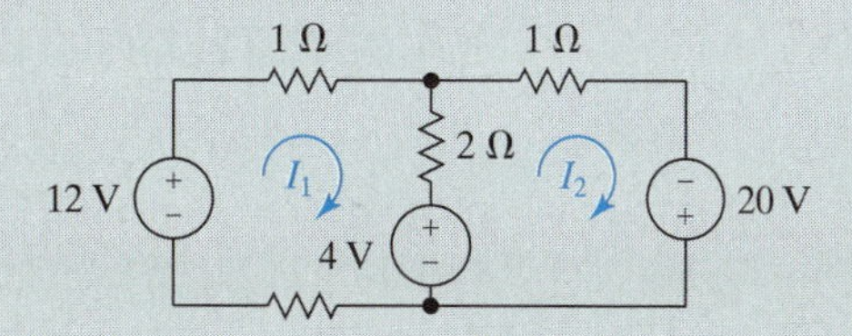

FIGURE 2.31 Circuit used in Example 2.17.

Solving these equations using Cramer's Rule, as illustrated earlier and in Appendix B, will yield $I_1 = 9$ A and $I_2 = 14$ A.

MATLAB can also be used to solve for the loop currents. The MATLAB solution for circuit is outlined below.

```
EDU» G=[4 -2; -2 3]

G =

    4   -2
   -2    3

EDU» V = [8; 24]

V =

    8
   24

EDU» I = inv (G) *V

I =

    9
   14
```

Example 2.18

Let us determine V_0 in the network in Figure 2.32. Note that as we attempt to write the mesh equations using KVL, we find that we cannot express the voltage across the current source in terms of the mesh currents. The current source does, however, *constrain* the mesh currents by the equation

$$I_1 - I_2 = 4$$

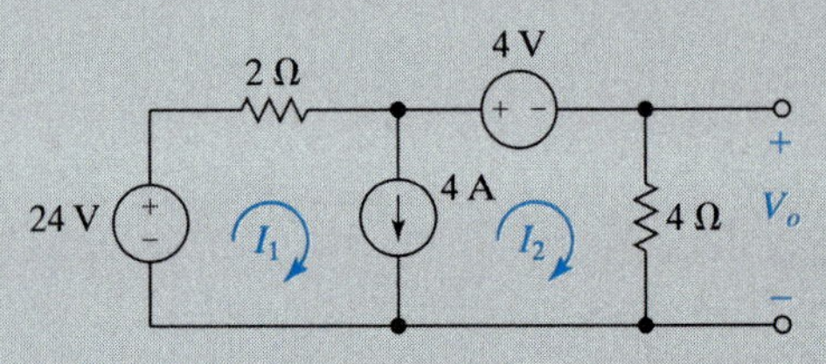

FIGURE 2.32 Circuit used in Example 2.18

This constraint equation is one of the two linearly independent equations needed to find the mesh currents. The other equation can be obtained by applying KVL to the outer loop, that is,

$$+24 - 2I_1 - 4 - 4I_2 = 0$$

Hence, the two equations for the network are

$$I_1 - I_2 = 4$$

$$2I_1 + 4I_2 = 20$$

Using Cramer's Rule to solve these equations yields $I_2 = 2$ A, and therefore, $V_0 = 8$ V.

However, once again we can employ MATLAB to determine the loop currents, as illustrated below.

```
EDU» G = [1 -1;2 4]

G =

     1        -1
     2         4

EDU» V = [4; 20]

V =

     4
    20

EDU» I = inv (G) *V

I =

      6.0000

      2.0000
```

Example 2.19

As a final example in this section, let us revisit the circuit in Figure 2.28. We will use MATLAB to determine the loop currents. The circuit is redrawn in Figure 2.33 where the loop currents are identified. The four loop equations are

$$\begin{aligned} 4I_1 \quad -2I_2 \quad -I_3 \qquad\qquad &= 0 \\ -2I_1 + 3I_2 \qquad\qquad -I_4 &= 6 \\ -I_1 \qquad\qquad + 3I_3 \quad -2I_4 &= 12 \\ I_4 &= -2 \end{aligned}$$

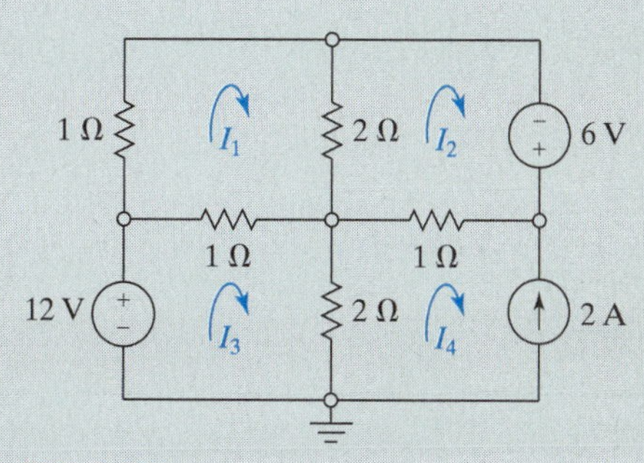

FIGURE 2.33 Circuit used in Example 2.19

Expressing the equations in matrix form yields

$$\begin{bmatrix} 4 & -2 & -1 & 0 \\ -2 & 3 & 0 & -1 \\ -1 & 0 & 3 & -2 \\ 0 & 0 & 0 & 1 \end{bmatrix} \begin{bmatrix} I_1 \\ I_2 \\ I_3 \\ I_4 \end{bmatrix} = \begin{bmatrix} 0 \\ 6 \\ 12 \\ -2 \end{bmatrix}$$

The MATLAB solution that yields the unknown loop currents is as follows.

```
EDU» G = [4 -2 -1 0; -2 3 0 -1; -1 0 3 -2; 0 0 0 1]

G =

     4    -2    -1     0
    -2     3     0    -1
    -1     0     3    -2
     0     0     0     1

EDU» V = [0; 6; 12; -2]

V =

     0
     6
    12
    -2
```

```
EDU » I = inv (G) *V

I =

    2.2857
    2.8571
    3.4286
   -2.0000
```

Given that we know the node voltages and loop currents for the network in Figure 2.28, we can make several checks to ensure that our analyses are correct. For example, the loop current I_1 should be equal to the difference in potential between nodes V_2 and V_1 divided by the 1 Ω resistor connecting the nodes, that is,

$$
\begin{aligned}
I_1 &= \frac{V_2 - V_1}{1} \\
&= \frac{12 - 9.7143}{1} \\
&= 2.2857 \text{ A}
\end{aligned}
$$

This simple check indicates our analyses are correct.

Drill Exercise

D2.16. Use mesh analysis to find V_0 in the network in Figure D2.16.

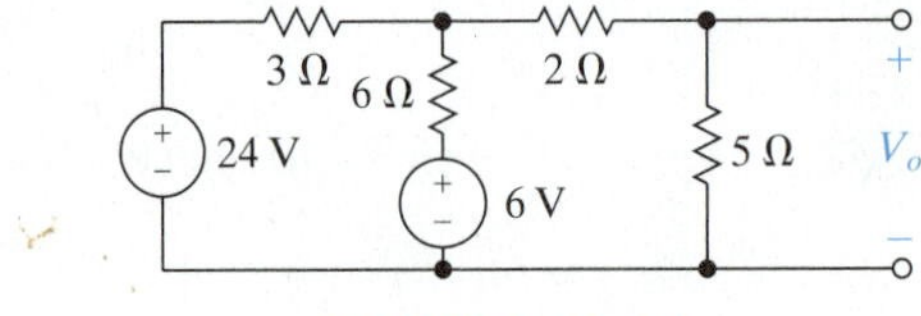

FIGURE D2.16

Ans: $V_0 = 10$ V.

D2.17. Repeat problem D2.16 for the network in Figure D2.17.

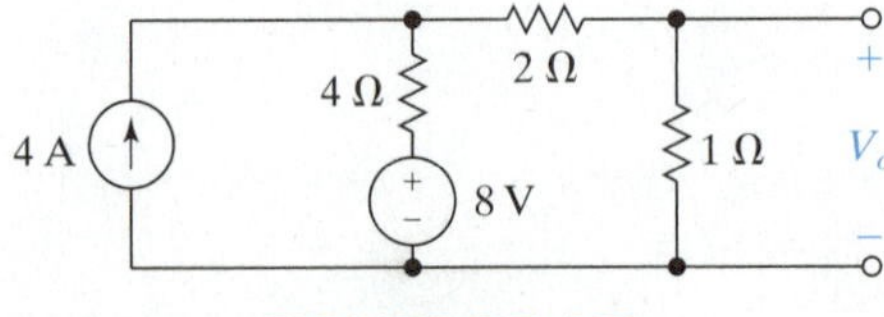

FIGURE D2.17

Ans: $V_0 = 3.43$ V.

2-9 Superposition

The essence of this technique can be stated as follows: in a linear circuit, if two or more sources are present, the net voltage or current at some location is the algebraic sum of the results of each source operating alone. In order for one source to operate alone in the network, all other sources must be made zero. To accomplish this we replace voltage sources with short circuits since the voltage across a short circuit is zero and we replace current sources with open circuits since the current in an open circuit is zero. Since, in this procedure, only one source is operational at a time, each circuit containing only a single source is generally easier to analyze. The following example will serve to illustrate the procedure.

Example 2.20

Consider the network in Figure 2.34(a). We wish to find the voltage $v_o(t)$. Although we could use node equations or loop equations to find $v_o(t)$, only one node equation is required. Using KCL at the node labeled $v_o(t)$ yields

$$\frac{v_A(t) - v_o(t)}{2} + i_A(t) - \frac{v_o(t)}{1} = 0$$

or

$$v_o(t) = \frac{1}{3}v_A(t) + \frac{2}{3}i_A(t)$$

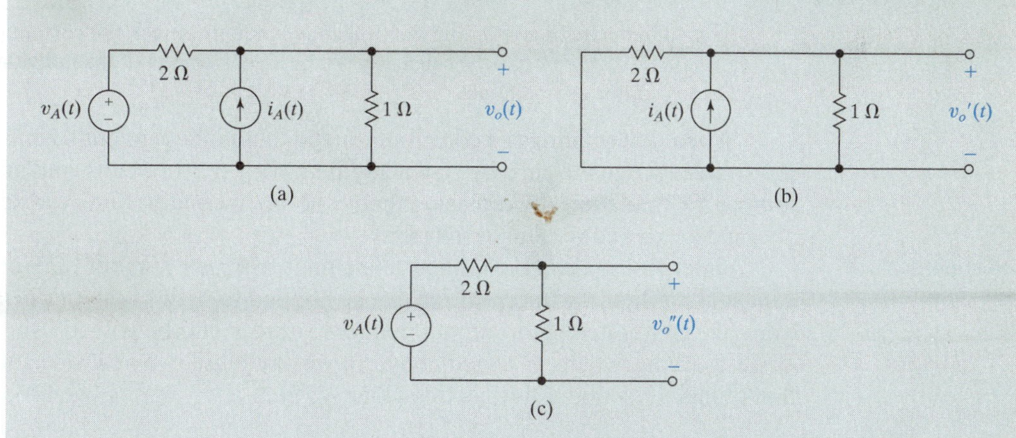

FIGURE 2.34 Circuits used in Example 2.20.

In other words, the voltage $v_o(t)$ has a component due to $v_A(t)$ and a component due to $i_A(t)$. In view of the fact that $v_o(t)$ has two components, one due to each independent source, it would be interesting to examine what each source acting alone would contribute to $v_o(t)$. For $i_A(t)$ to act alone, $v_A(t)$ must be zero. As illustrated in Figure 2.2, $v_A(t) = 0$ means that the source $v_A(t)$ is replaced with a short circuit. Therefore, to determine the value of $v_o(t)$ due to $i_A(t)$ only, we employ the circuit in Figure 2.34(b) and refer to this value of $v_o(t)$ as $v_o'(t)$.

$$v_o'(t) = \frac{(1)(2)}{1+2} i_A(t)$$
$$= \frac{2}{3} i_A(t)$$

Let us now determine the value of $v_o(t)$ due to $v_A(t)$ acting alone and refer to this value as $v_o''(t)$. We employ the circuit shown in Figure 2.34(c) and compute this value as

$$v_o''(t) = \frac{v_A(t)}{2+1}(1)$$
$$= \frac{v_A(t)}{3}$$

Now if we add the values $v_o'(t)$ and $v_o''(t)$, we obtain the value computed directly:

$$v_o(t) = v_o'(t) + v_o''(t)$$
$$= \frac{2}{3} i_A(t) + \frac{v_A(t)}{3}$$

Note that we have superposed the value of $v_o'(t)$ on $v_o''(t)$, or vice versa, to determine the total value of the unknown current.

What we have demonstrated in Example 2.20 is true in general for linear circuits. Linearity requires both additivity and homogeneity (scaling), and since the voltage/current relationship for all the circuits presented in part I of this text satisfies these two conditions, the circuits are linear. *The principle of superposition states that*

> In any linear circuit containing multiple independent sources, the current or voltage at any point in the network may be calculated as the algebraic sum of the individual contributions of each source acting alone.

When determining the contribution due to an independent source, any remaining voltage sources are made zero by replacing them with short circuits, and any remaining current sources are made zero by replacing them with open circuits: however, dependent sources are not made zero and remain in the circuit.

The superposition technique

Superposition can be applied to a circuit with any number of dependent and independent sources. In fact, superposition can be applied to such a network in a variety of ways. For example, a circuit with three independent sources can be solved using each source acting alone, as we have demonstrated above, or we could use two at a time and sum the result with that obtained from the third acting alone.

Example 2.21

Let us use superposition to solve Example 2.18. The network for this example is redrawn in Figure 2.35(a). As stated above, we can determine the output due to the two voltage sources and add that to the output caused by the current source. The output generated by the two voltage sources is obtained from the network in Figure 2.35(b) where the current source has been replaced by an open circuit.

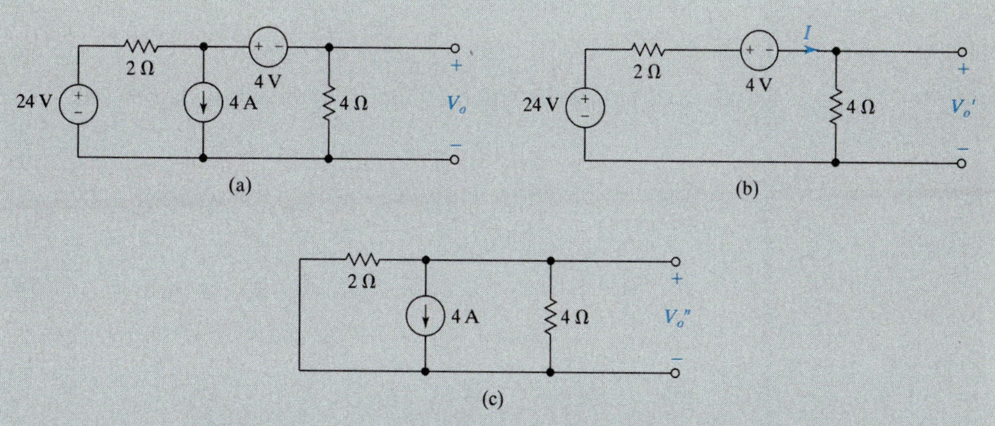

FIGURE 2.35 Circuits used in Example 2.21.

$$I = \frac{24 - 4}{2 + 4} = \frac{20}{6}\text{A}$$

then

$$V_o' = \left(\frac{20}{6}\right)(4) = \frac{80}{6}\text{V}$$

The output generated by the current source is obtained from the network in Figure 2.35(c) where the voltage sources have been replaced by short circuits. Since all the elements are in parallel

$$V_o'' = -4\left[\frac{(2)(4)}{2 + 4}\right]$$

$$= \frac{-32}{6}\text{V}$$

Then using superposition

$$V_o = V_o' + V_o''$$

$$= \frac{80}{6} - \frac{32}{6}$$

$$= 8\text{ V}$$

which is identical to that obtained in Example 2.18

Drill Exercise

D2.18. Use superposition to find V_o in the network in Figure D2.18.

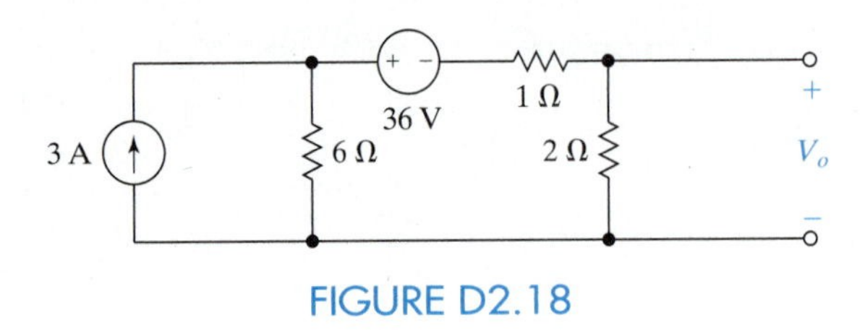

FIGURE D2.18

Ans: $V_o = -4$ V.

2-10 Source Exchange

We introduce this topic by considering the two circuits shown in Figure 2.36. In one case, a voltage source in series with a resistor R_v is connected to the load R_L, and in the other case, a current source in parallel with a resistor R_i is connected to load R_L. We now ask if it is possible to *exchange* the series combination of v and R_v for the parallel combination of i and R_i, and vice versa. The answer is we can, provided that each produces exactly the same voltage and current for any load R_L.

In order to determine the conditions under which the series connection of v and R_v is equivalent to the parallel connection of i and R_i, let us examine the terminal conditions of each. For the network in Figure 2.36(a)

$$i = i_L + \frac{v_L}{R_i}$$

or

$$iR_i = R_i i_L + v_L$$

For the network in Figure 2.36(b)

$$v = i_L R_v + v_L$$

For the two networks to be equivalent, their terminal characteristics must be identical; therefore, equating like terms in the above equations.

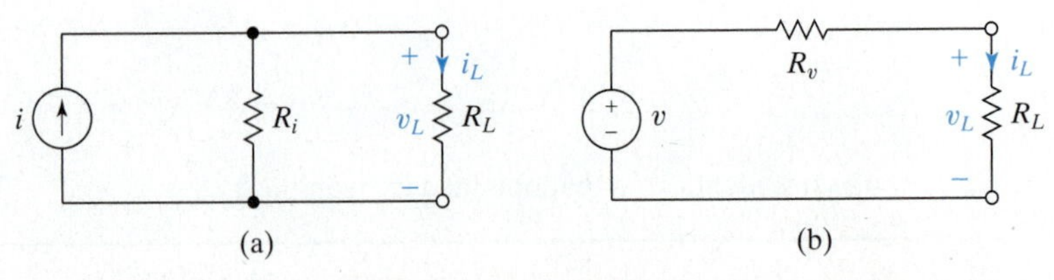

FIGURE 2.36 Circuits used to determine conditions for a source exchange.

$$v = iR_i \quad \text{and} \quad R_i = R_v \tag{2.27}$$

The relationships specified in Eq. (2.27) and Figure 2.36 are extremely important and the reader should not fail to grasp their significance. What these relationships tell us is that if we have embedded within a network a current source i in parallel with a resistor R, we can replace this combination with a voltage source of value $v = iR$ in series with the resistor R. The reverse is also true; that is, a voltage source v in series with a resistor R can be replaced with a current source of value $i = v/R$ in parallel with the resistor R. Parameters within the circuit (e.g., an output voltage) are unchanged under these transformations.

The source transformation/exchange technique

The following example will demonstrate the utility of a *source exchange*. The reader is cautioned to keep the polarity of the voltage source and the direction of the current source in agreement, as shown in Figure 2.36.

Example 2.22

Consider the network in Figure 2.37(a). We wish to compute the current I_o. Note that since node voltages V_1 and V_3 are known, one KCL equation at the center node will yield V_2 and therefore I_o. However, two mesh equations are required to find I_o and two separate circuits must be analyzed to determine I_o using superposition.

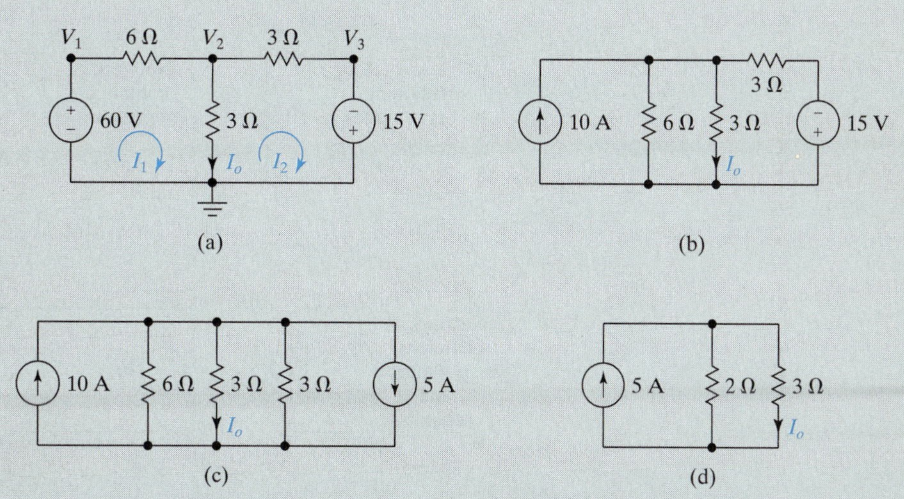

FIGURE 2.37 Circuits employed in Example 2.22.

To solve the problem using source transformation. We first transform the 60 V source and 6 Ω resistor into a 10 A current source in parallel with the 6 Ω resistor, as shown in Figure 2.37(b). Next, the 3 Ω resistor in series with the 15 V source are transformed into a 5 A current source in parallel with the 3 Ω resistor, as shown in Figure 2.37(c). Combining the resistors and current sources yields the network in Figure 2.37(d). Now employing current division, we obtain $I_o = 2$ A.

Drill Exercise

D2.19. Solve problem D2.18 using source transformation.

2-11 Thevenin's and Norton's Theorems

Thus far we have presented a number of techniques for circuit analysis. At this point we will add two theorems to our collection of tools that will prove to be extremely useful. The theorems are named after their authors, M.L. Thevenin, a French engineer, and E.L. Norton, a scientist formerly with Bell Telephone Laboratories.

Suppose that we are given a circuit and that we wish to find the current, voltage, or power that is delivered to some resistor of the network, which we will call the load. *Thevenin's theorem* tells us that we can replace the entire network, exclusive of the load, by an equivalent circuit that contains only an independent voltage source in series with a resistor in such a way that the current–voltage relationship at the load is unchanged. *Norton's theorem* is identical to the statement above except that the equivalent circuit is an independent current source in parallel with a resistor.

Consider the circuit in Figure 2.38(a). This network, exclusive of the load, R_L, can be replaced by the series combination of a voltage source V_{OC} and a resistance R_{TH} where V_{OC} is

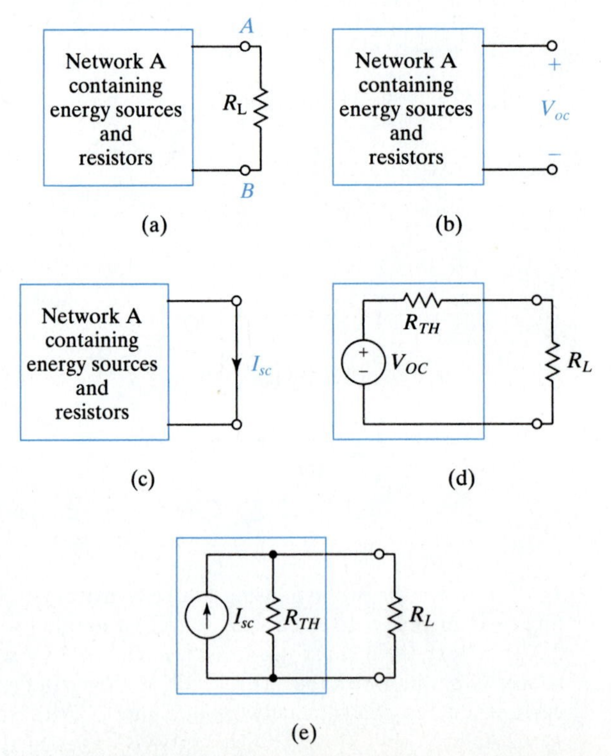

FIGURE 2.38 Concepts used to develop Thevenin's theorem.

the open-circuit voltage at the terminals A-B in Figure 2.38(b) and R_{TH} is the ratio of V_{OC} to the short-circuit current shown in Figure 2.38(c), for example,

$$R_{TH} = \frac{V_{OC}}{I_{SC}} \tag{2.28}$$

Two important theorems for circuit analysis

The *Thevenin equivalent circuit* is then shown in Figure 2.38(d). If the network contains only independent sources, R_{TH} can be found by looking into the open-circuit terminals A-B in Figure 2.38(b) and determining the resistance at those terminals with all voltage sources replaced by short circuits and all current sources replaced with open circuits. However, if dependent sources are present in the network, R_{TH} must be derived from the ratio of V_{OC} to I_{SC}. The *Norton equivalent circuit* is shown in Figure 2.38(e).

Example 2.23

Consider the network in Figure 2.39(a), which corresponds to the network in Fig. 2.38(a). We wish to find V_0 using both Thevenin's and Norton's theorems. We can break the network at either A-B or C-D. If we break the network at A-B, the open circuit voltage shown in Figure 2.39(b), which corresponds to Figure 2.38(b), is obtained as follows:

$$I_1 = \frac{36}{3+6} = 4 \text{ A}$$

$$V_{OC} = (4)(6) = 24 \text{ V}$$

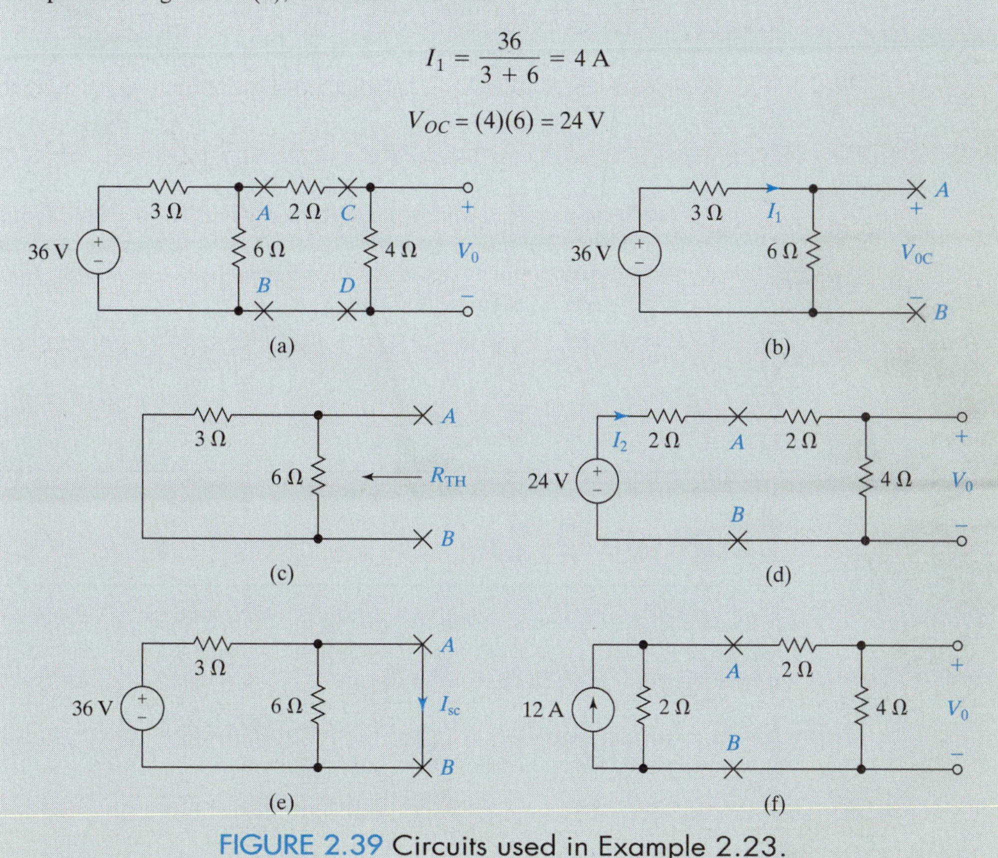

FIGURE 2.39 Circuits used in Example 2.23.

Replacing the 36V source with a short circuit and looking into terminals A and B we find, as shown in Figure 2.39(c), that

$$R_{TH} = \frac{(3)(6)}{3 + 6} = 2\Omega$$

If the Thevenin equivalent circuit is connected to the terminals A-B, the original circuit becomes that shown in Figure 2.39(d), which corresponds to Figure 2.38(d). Then

$$I_2 = \frac{24}{2 + 2 + 4} = 3\text{ A}$$

$$V_o = (3)(4) = 12\text{ V}$$

It is important to note that if we had broken the network at C-D, the open circuit voltage would still be 24 V, since there would be no current in the 2 Ω resistor and therefore no voltage across it. R_{TH} in this case would be 4 Ω, but when this new Thevenin equivalent circuit is reconnected to the 4 Ω load, the final answer would be the same.

We could also determine V_0 using Norton's theorem. Once again, the network is broken at terminals A-B. The short-circuit current is shown in Figure 2.39(e), which corresponds to Figure 2.38(c). Since no current will flow in the 6 Ω resistor in parallel with the short circuit,

$$I_{SC} = \frac{36}{3} = 12\text{ A}$$

The Thevenin equivalent resistance was computed in Figure 2.39(c) to be $R_{TH} = 2\ \Omega$. As stated earlier, note that R_{TH} can also be computed at the terminals A-B using the expression

$$R_{TH} = \frac{V_{OC}}{I_{SC}} = \frac{24}{12} = 2\Omega$$

If the Norton equivalent circuit consisting of the short-circuit current source in parallel with the Thevenin equivalent resistance is now attached to the remainder of the original network at terminals A-B, the resultant network is shown in Figure 2.39(f), which corresponds to Figure 2.38(e).

Using current division, we find that

$$V_0 = 12\left(\frac{2}{2 + 2 + 4}\right)(4)$$

$$= 12\text{ V}$$

Example 2.24

We wish to use Thevenin's theorem to solve Example 2.18. The network in Figure 2.32 is redrawn in Figure 2.40(a). If we break the network at the 4 load, the open-circuit voltage can be computed from the network in Figure 2.40(b). Note that $I_1 = 4$ A. Then, using KVL,

$$V_{CS} = 24 - 2(4) = 16\text{ V}$$

Applying KVL again, we find that

$$V_{OC} = V_{CS} - 4$$

$$= 12\text{ V}$$

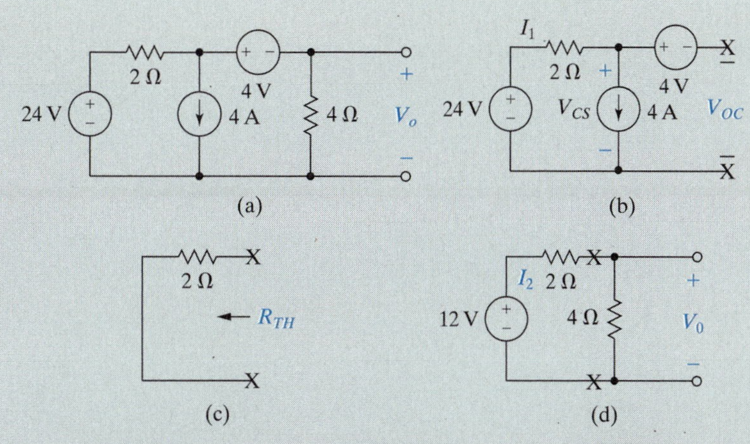

FIGURE 2.40 Circuits used in Example 2.24.

R_{TH} is found by replacing the voltage sources with short circuits and the current source with an open circuit and, as shown in Figure 2.40(c), $R_{TH} = 2\Omega$. Finally, if the Thevenin equivalent circuit is reconnected to the 4 Ω load, as shown in Figure 2.40(d),

$$I_2 = \frac{12}{2 + 4} = 2\text{ A}$$

and

$$V_o = (2)(4) = 8\text{ V}$$

Drill Exercise

D2.20. Solve problem D2.16 using Thevenin's theorem.

D2.21. Solve problem D2.17 using Thevenin's theorem.

Finally, let us consider one example that we will examine in a variety of ways.

Example 2.25

Let us determine the power absorbed in the 2 Ω resistor in the circuit in Figure 2.41(a). We will solve this problem using nodal analysis, mesh analysis, superposition, source exchange, Thevenin's theorem, and Norton's theorem.

The node equations for the network shown in Figure 2.41(a) are

$$V_1 = 24$$
$$V_2 = 12$$
$$\frac{V_o - V_1}{3} + \frac{V_o - V_2}{6} + \frac{V_o}{2} = 0$$

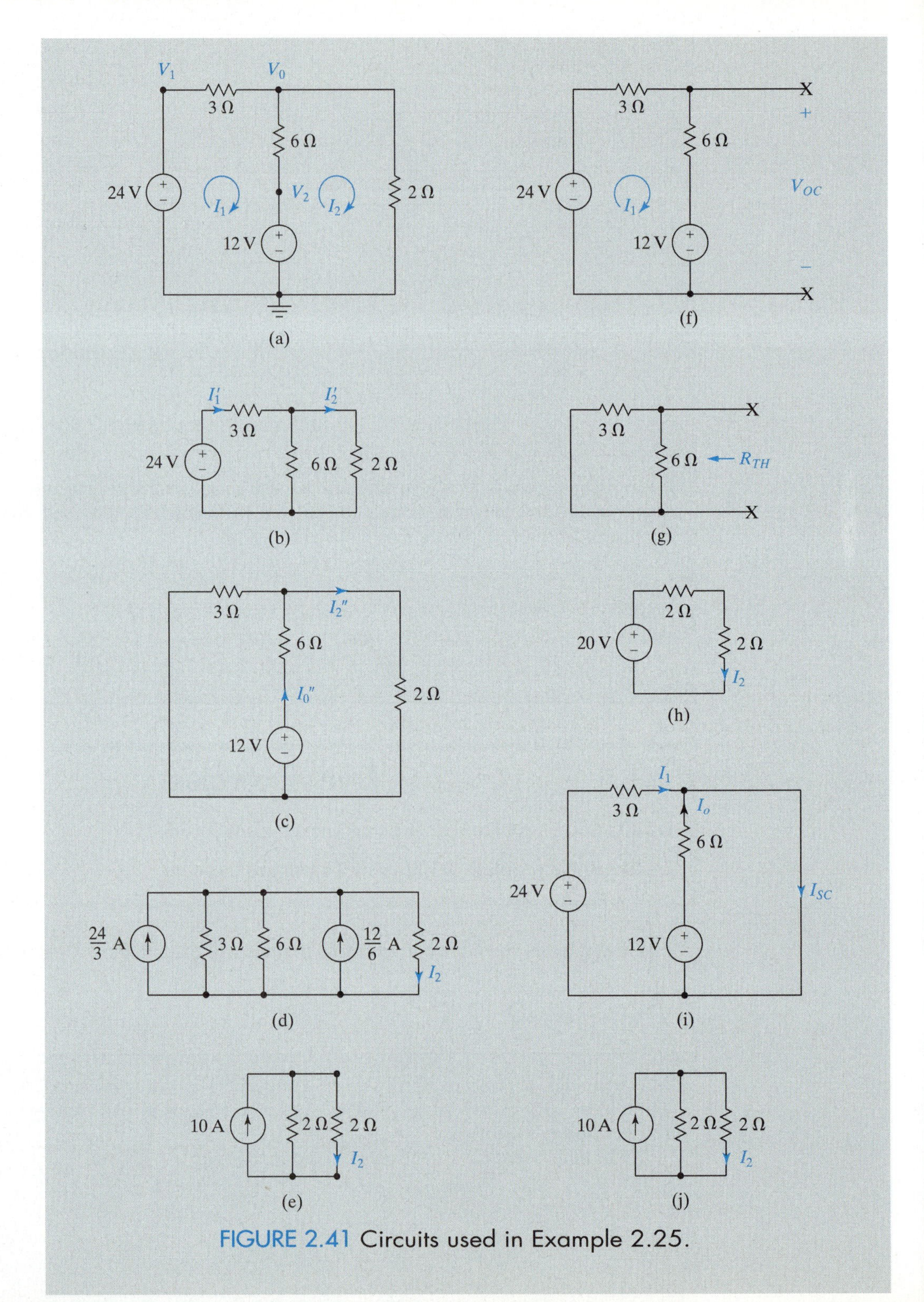

FIGURE 2.41 Circuits used in Example 2.25.

These equations yield

$$V_o = 10\text{ V}$$

Therefore, the current in the 2 Ω resistor is

$$I_{2\Omega} = \frac{10}{2} = 5\text{ A}$$

and

$$P_{2\Omega} = (5)^2(2) = 50\text{ W}$$

The mesh equations for the network shown in Figure 2.41(a) are

$$+24 - 3I_1 - 6(I_1 - I_2) - 12 = 0$$
$$+12 - 6(I_2 - I_1) - 2I_2 = 0$$

or

$$9I_1 - 6I_2 = 12$$
$$-6I_1 + 8I_2 = 12$$

Solving these equations for I_2 yields

$$I_2 = 5\text{ A}$$

Therefore, the power absorbed by the 2 Ω resistor is 50 W.

In the application of superposition, we first consider the 24 V source acting alone as shown in Fig. 2.41(b). The equivalent resistance seen by the 24 V source is 3 Ω + 6 Ω in parallel with 2 Ω, that is

$$Req_1 = 3 + \frac{(6)(2)}{6 + 2}$$

and hence

$$I_1' = \frac{24}{3 + \frac{12}{8}}$$

I'_2 can be obtained by current division as

$$I_2' = \frac{I_1'(6)}{6 + 2}$$

Solving for I'_2 yields

$$I'_2 = 4\text{ A}$$

The component of I_2 caused by the 12 V source is derived from Figure 2.41(c). Following an identical approach to that used to determine I_1', we find that

$$Req_2 = 6 + \frac{(3)(2)}{3 + 2}$$

and hence

$$I_o'' = \frac{12}{6 + 6/5}$$

Once again, using current division

$$I_2'' = I_o''\left(\frac{3}{2+3}\right)$$

Solving for I_2'' we obtain

$$I_2'' = 1\,A$$

Therefore, using superposition

$$I_2 = I_2' + I_2''$$
$$= 5\text{A}$$

and then the power absorbed by the 2 Ω resistor is 50 W.

In applying source transformation to the network in Figure 2.41(a), we transform the 24 V source in series with the 3 Ω resistor into an 8 A source in parallel with the 3 Ω resistor. The 12 V source and 6 Ω resistor are transformed in a similar manner. The resulting network is shown in Figure 2.41(d). Combining the two current sources and the 3 Ω and 6 Ω resistors yields the circuit in Figure 2.41(e). Applying current division to this network yields $I_2 = 5$ A.

Using Thevenin's theorem, we break the network at the 2 Ω load, as shown in Figure 2.41(f). KVL around the closed path yields

$$+24 - 3I - 6I - 12 = 0$$

Hence

$$I = \frac{4}{3}\text{A}$$

KVL applied once again to the right-hand loop including V_{OC} yields

$$+12 + 6\left(\frac{4}{3}\right) - V_{OC} = 0$$

or

$$V_{OC} = 20\text{ V}$$

R_{TH} is derived from the network in Figure 2.41(g) as

$$R_{TH} = \frac{(3)(6)}{3+6} = 2\Omega$$

Replacing the network in Figure 2.41(f) with its Thevenin equivalent and connecting it to the 2 Ω resistor yields the circuit in Figure 2.41(h). Obviously, the current I_2 in this network is 5 A.

The short circuit current required for the Norton equivalent is computed from the network in Figure 2.41(i).

$$I_{SC} = I_1 + I_o$$
$$= \frac{24}{3} + \frac{12}{6} = 10\text{ A}$$

R_{TH} has already been calculated. Connecting the Norton equivalent circuit to the 2 Ω resistor produces the network in Figure 2.41(j). Using current division, I_2 is found to be 5 A.

As a final point, note that when we perform a source exchange we are simply replacing a Thevenin equivalent circuit with a Norton equivalent circuit, and vice versa.

2-12 Measurements and the Wheatstone Bridge

A relatively simple dc circuit is commonly used to measure a wide variety of physical parameters such as strain, force, flow rate, and so on. The circuit is called a Wheatstone Bridge and consists of four resistive elements in a "diamond" topology. Typically, a dc voltage, V_{dc}, is applied using a battery or dc power source between the "top" and "bottom" of the bridge, and the output voltage is measured between the two mid-points, labeled a and b in Figure 2.42.

First, convince yourself that if all four resistors had exactly the same resistance value, the output voltage, $V_0 = V_{ab}$, would be zero volts. (Each side of the bridge acts as a voltage divider, and for this case, $V_a = V_b = \frac{1}{2} V_{dc}$; therefore, $V_0 = V_a - V_b = 0$ V.) Notice, however, that $R3$ in this circuit has an arrow through it indicating it can change in value; $R3$ is the sensor element that changes resistance in relation to a physical variable we wish to measure.

A very common measurement is that of strain, $\varepsilon = \Delta L/L$, or the ratio of the change in length to the length of a physical structure. Strain gauges are simply resistors that change resistance value in proportion to the strain applied. Therefore, if we glue a strain gauge to the top of a cantilever beam, and the beam is deflected downward, the top of the beam extends (tension) and experiences a positive strain. The strain gauge experiences the same strain, and its resistance value increases an incremental amount in proportion to the applied strain. If R_3 in the above figure was a strain gauge, then

$$R_3 = R_o + \Delta R = R_o\,(1 + \Delta R/R_o)$$

where R_o is the unstrained resistance value.

A common bridge circuit used in electrical measurements

A drawing of a cantilever beam with a strain gauge attached in a bridge circuit is shown in Figure 2.43.

To calculate the actual value of R_3, one must know the unstrained value of the strain gauge, R_o, and the gauge factor, G. G is defined as $\Delta R/R_o$ per unit of strain, and is a calibration factor generally provided by the strain gauge manufacturer.

Therefore, we now can state a relation between the value of R_3 and the applied strain, ε.

$$R_3 = R_o\,(1 + \Delta R/R_o) = R_o\,(1 + G\varepsilon)$$

Now, to calculate the output voltage, V_o,

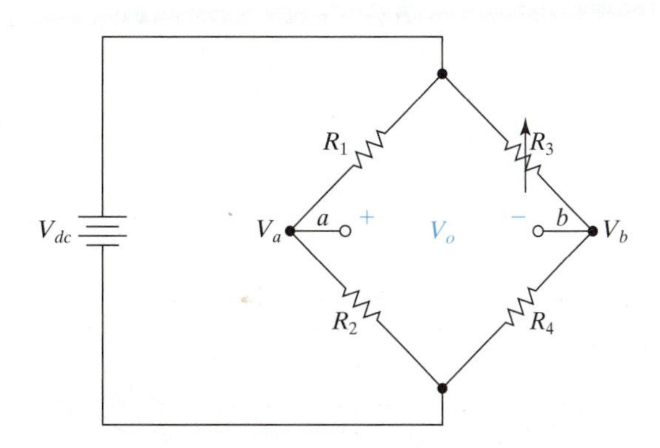

FIGURE 2.42 Basic Wheatstone Bridge.

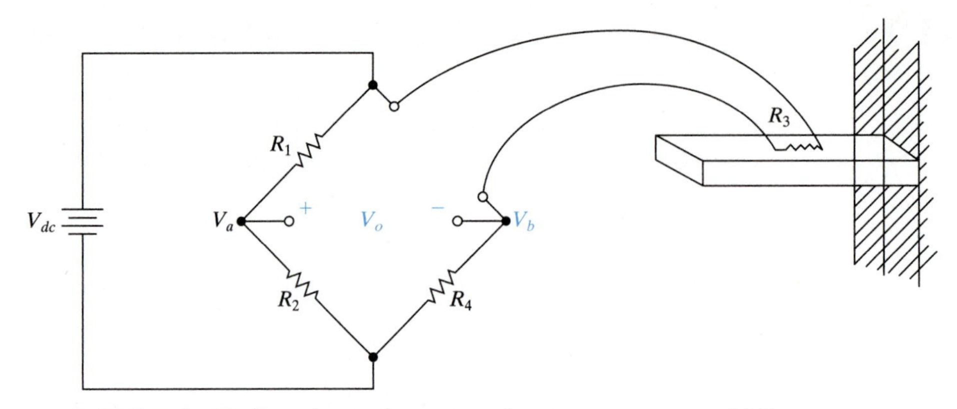

FIGURE 2.43 Cantilever beam with strain gauge in Wheatstone Bridge circuit.

$$V_o = V_a - V_b$$

$$V_a = V_{dc}\left(\frac{R_2}{R_1 + R_2}\right)$$

$$V_b = V_{dc}\left(\frac{R_4}{R_3 + R_4}\right)$$

Therefore,

$$V_o = V_{dc}\left[\frac{R_2}{R_1 + R_2} - \frac{R_4}{R_3 + R_4}\right] = V_{dc}\left[\frac{R_2}{R_1 + R_2} - \frac{R_4}{R_o\,(1 + G\varepsilon) + R_4}\right]$$

Example 2.26

A strain gauge (with gauge factor $G = 2.7$, and $R_o = 1\ \text{k}\Omega$) is placed 1 cm from the anchor on the top of a cantilever beam 10 cm long, 1 cm wide, and a height of 0.2 cm. The strain gauge is connected in a Wheatstone Bridge circuit with the other resistor values all equal to 1 kΩ; a 12 V battery is used as a power source.

(a) What is the value of V_o if the beam is not deflected?

(b) What is the value of V_o if the strain gauge experiences a strain of 1E-4?

a) If $\varepsilon = 0$, $V_o = V_{dc}\left[\dfrac{R_2}{R_1 + R_2} - \dfrac{R_4}{R_0 + R_4}\right] = 12\left[\dfrac{1\text{k}}{2\text{k}} - \dfrac{1\text{k}}{2\text{k}}\right] = 0\ \text{V}$

b) If $\varepsilon = 10^{-4}$, $V_o = V_{dc}\left[\dfrac{R_2}{R_1 + R_2} - \dfrac{R_4}{R_0\,(1 + G\varepsilon) + R_4}\right]$

$$V_o = 12\left\{\frac{1\text{k}}{2\text{k}} - \frac{1\text{k}}{1\text{k}[1 + 2.7(10^{-4})] + 1\text{k}}\right\} = 8.0 \times 10^{-4}\ \text{V}$$

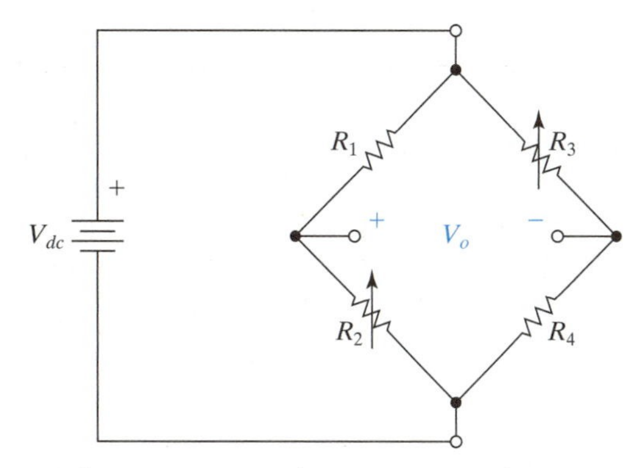

FIGURE 2.44 Wheatstone Bridge circuit with two strain gauges.

Often, several gauges are used in the same bridge circuit to increase the sensitivity of the measurement. For example, in the previous illustration, if two strain gauges were placed on top of the beam, and these gauges were placed in *opposite* positions in the bridge circuit, as the resistance of both increase in value, Vo changes by twice as much as in the original example. (See Figure 2.44.) One could obtain further sensitivity by placing two strain gauges on top of the beam (where they experience tension in a downward beam deflection) and two strain gauges on the bottom of the beam (where they experience compression in a downward beam deflection). For this case the two gauges on top increase in resistance and the two on the bottom decrease in resistance by the same amount. The output voltage of the bridge circuit is four times that of the original circuit. In practice, there is a tradeoff between purchasing and installing multiple strain gauges and the increased sensitivity of measurement obtained.

For measuring flow rate of liquids and gases, a "hot-wire anemometer" is often used. In this case a resistive wire is heated by the current flowing through it, and placed in the stream of gas flow. The resistance of the wire changes with temperature, and the higher the gas flow rate, the more the wire is cooled. Therefore, there is a relationship between flow rate and the resistance of the wire. The heated wire is placed in a Wheatstone bridge circuit, and the bridge output voltage is a function of gas flow rate. (See Figure 2.45.)

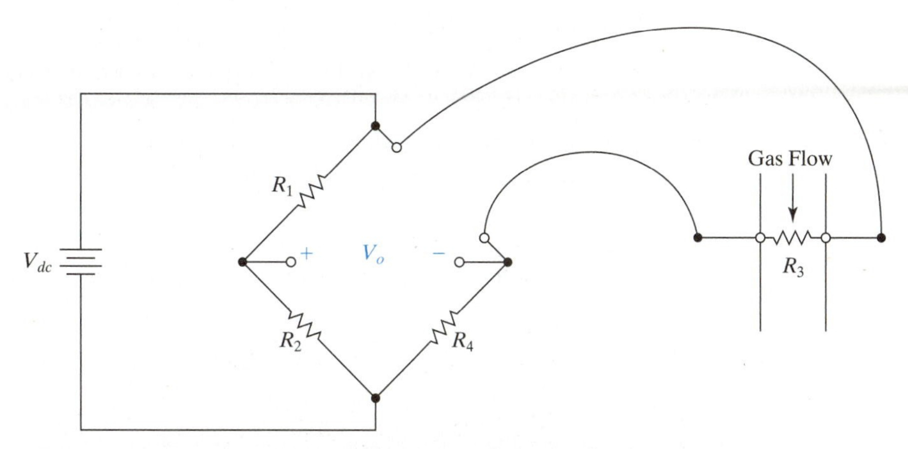

FIGURE 2.45 Hot-wire anemometer for gas flow rate measurement in Wheatstone Bridge circuit.

Summary

- Ohm's law states that the voltage V across a resistance R is directly proportional to the current I through it, that is, $V = IR$, where V is in volts, I is in amperes, and R is in ohms. The relationships are demonstrated in Figure 2.46.

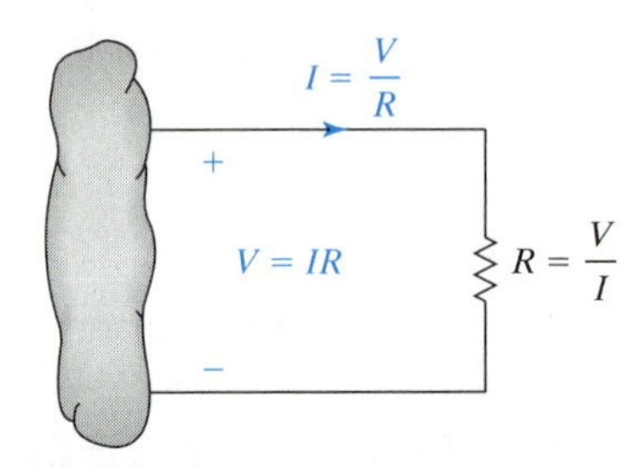

FIGURE 2.46 Ohm's law relationships.

- Conductance G, in siemens, is the reciprocal of resistance, that is, $G = \frac{1}{R}$.
- Node, loop, mesh, and branch are four common terms employed in circuit analysis and are defined using Figure 2.47.

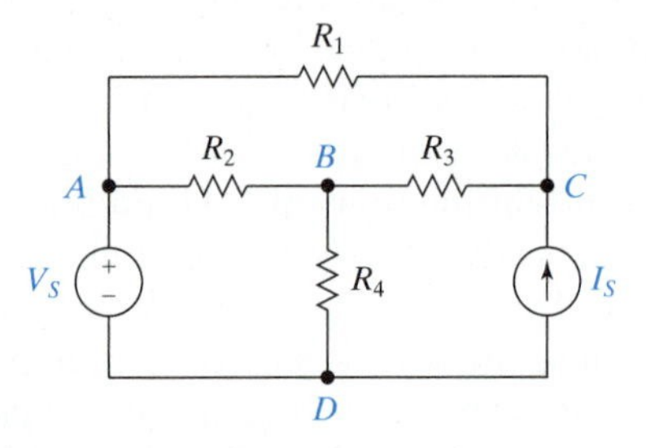

The connection points A, B, C, and D are nodes.
The path A-B-D-A is a mesh.
The path A-B-C-D-A is a loop, but not a mesh.
Each element connected between two nodes is a branch.

FIGURE 2.47 Circuit element definitions.

- Short circuit is a branch in which $R = 0$ and therefore, $V = 0$ for any I. Open circuit is a branch in which $R = \infty$ and therefore, $I = 0$ for any V. The circuits are illustrated in Figure 2.48.

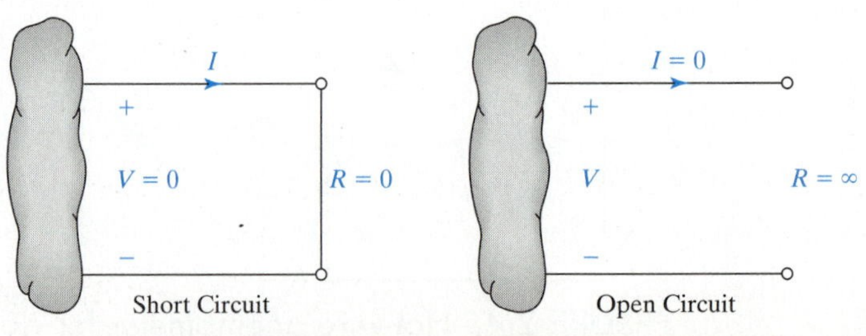

FIGURE 2.48 Short/open circuit illustrations.

- KCL states that the algebraic sum of the currents entering any node is zero. Assuming the currents entering the node in Figure 2.49 to be positive, $i_1 + i_2 - i_3 = 0$ or $i_1 + i_2 = i_3$

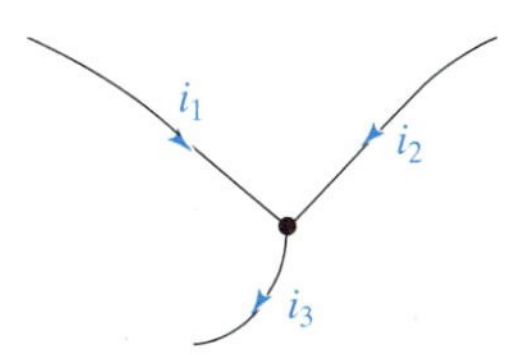

FIGURE 2.49 KCL demonstration.

- KVL states that the algebraic sum of the voltages around any loop is zero. For the circuit shown in Figure 2.50, the KVL equation is $\pm V_{S1} \mp V_{R_1} \mp V_{S2} \mp V_{R_2} = 0$.

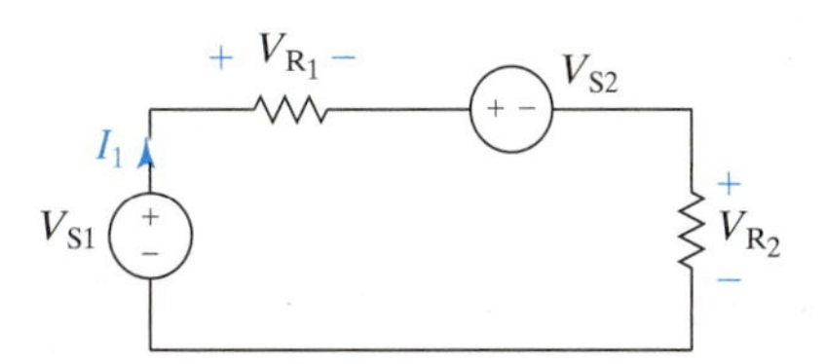

FIGURE 2.50 KVL demonstration circuit.

- Resistances in series add as $R_{total} = R_1 + R_2 + R_3 + \cdots$. For example, R_T for the network in Figure 2.51 is $R_T = 2k + 4k + 6k = 12k\Omega$

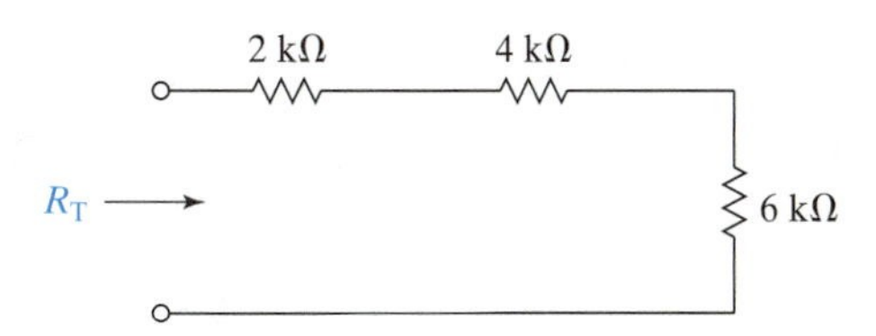

FIGURE 2.51 Resistors in series.

- Conductances in parallel add as $G_{total} = G_1 + G_2 + G_3 + \cdots$. For example, G_T for the network in Figure 2.52 is $G_T = 0.1 + 0.2 + 0.4 = 0.7\text{S}$.

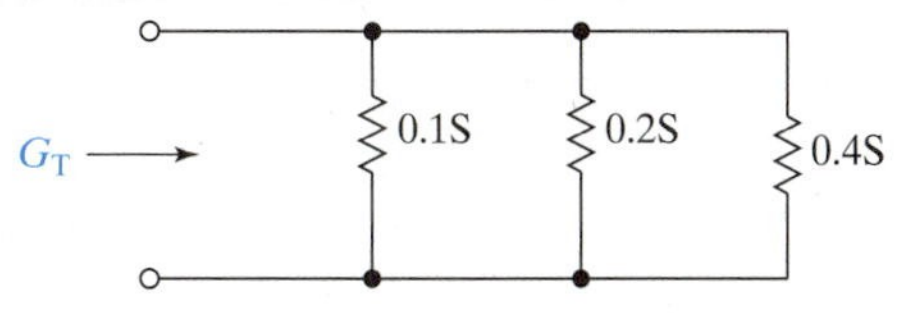

FIGURE 2.52 Conductances in parallel.

- In current division a current I is divided between parallel resistors R_1 and R_2 as

$$I_{R1} = \left(\frac{R_2}{R_1 + R_2}\right)I$$

For example, in the circuit in Figure 2.53,

$$I_1 = \frac{12}{k}\left(\frac{4k}{6k}\right) = 8mA \text{ and } I_2 = \frac{12}{k}\left(\frac{2k}{6k}\right) = 4mA$$

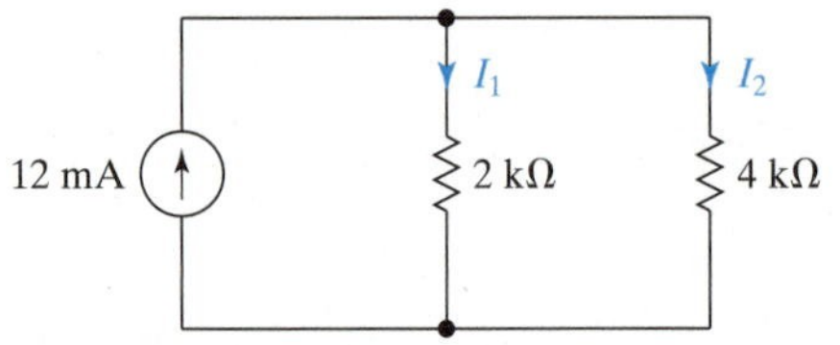

FIGURE 2.53 Current division demonstration network.

- In voltage division a voltage V is divided between series resistors R_1 and R_2 in direct proportion to their resistance, that is,

$$V_{R1} = \left(\frac{R_1}{R_1 + R_2}\right)V$$

For example, in the network in Figure 2.54,

$$V_1 = 12\left(\frac{2k}{6k}\right) = 4V \text{ and } V_2 = 12\left(\frac{4k}{6k}\right) = 8V$$

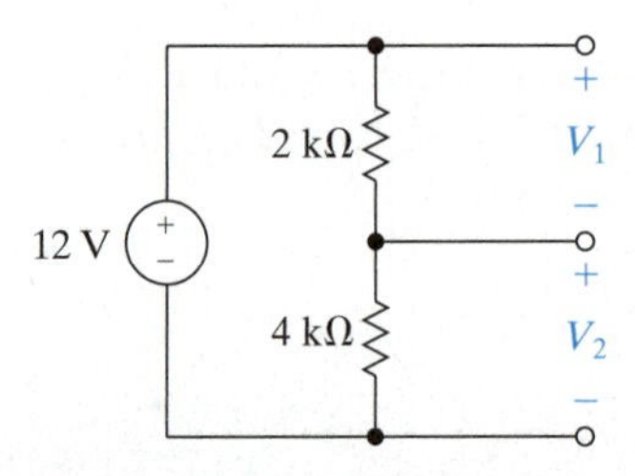

FIGURE 2.54 Voltage division demonstration network.

- The delta-wye transformation permits the conversion of a set of resistors connected in delta to a set of resistors connected in wye, and vice versa. Example calculations for the 1.5 kΩ and 12 kΩ resistors shown in Figure 2.55 are

$$1.5k\Omega = \frac{(6k)(6k)}{6k + 6k + 12k}\Omega \text{ and } 12k\Omega = \frac{(3k)(1.5k) + (3k)(1.5k) + (3k)(3\Omega)}{1.5k}\Omega$$

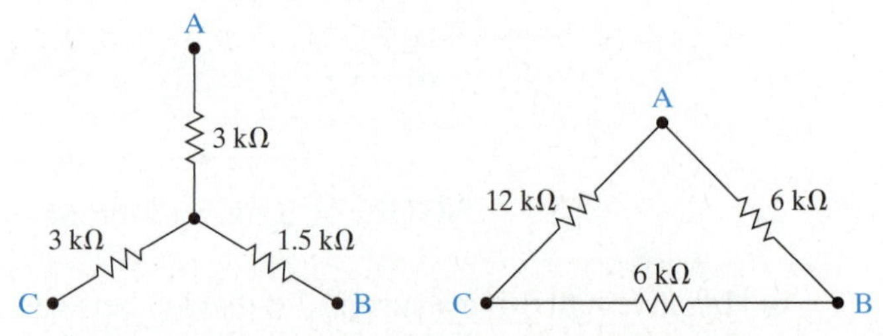

FIGURE 2.55 Wye and delta equivalent circuits.

- In a nodal analysis, $N - 1$ linearly independent simultaneous equations are required to find the $N - 1$ unknown node voltages in a N-node circuit. The network in Figure 2.56

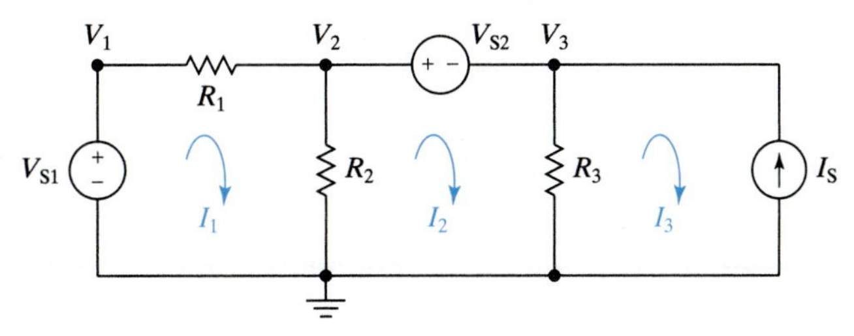

FIGURE 2.56 An example circuit.

has four nodes and hence three linearly independent KCL equations at the nodes labeled V_1, V_2, and V_3 are sufficient for a nodal analysis.

- In a loop analysis, N linearly independent simultaneous equations are required to find the N unknown loop currents in a N-loop network. The network in Figure 2.56 has three loops and therefore, three linearly independent loop equations for the loops labeled I_1, I_2, and I_3 are sufficient for a loop analysis.
- In linear network analysis, we can use:
  - Superposition, which permits us to determine the effect of multiple independent sources as the sum of the effects of the individual sources acting one at a time.
  - Source exchange, which permits us to replace a voltage source V and resistance R in series with a parallel combination of a current source $I = V/R$ and the resistance R, and vice versa.
  - Thevenin's theorem permits us to replace a network of sources and resistors at a pair of terminals with a series combination of a source and resistor, that is, the open-circuit voltage and the Thevenin equivalent resistance at the terminals.
  - Norton's theorem is equivalent to Thevenin's theorem, except that the network is replaced by a parallel combination of a current source and resistor, that is, the short-circuit current and the Thevenin equivalent resistance at the terminals.

The networks in Figure 2.57 can be used to demonstrate these techniques. We will employ each method to determine I_0 in the circuit in Figure 2.57(a). Using superposition, we obtain $I_0 = I_0' + I_0'' = \frac{4}{3k} + \frac{2}{k} = \frac{10}{3}\text{mA}$ from the circuits in Figure 2.57(b) and (c). Using source exchange, we convert the $12V$ source and series 6 kΩ resistor to a current source in parallel with the 6 kΩ resistor, as shown in Figure 2.57(d). Then using current division, $I_0 = \left(\frac{2}{k} + \frac{3}{k}\right)\left(\frac{6k}{6k + 3k}\right) = \frac{10}{3}\text{mA}$. In the application of Thevenin's theorem, the open-circuit voltage, obtained from the network in Figure 2.57(e), is $V_{OC} = 12 + \left(\frac{3}{k}\right)(6k) = 30$ V, and the $R_{TH} = 6$ kΩ, as shown in Figure 2.57(f). Applying the Thevenin equivalent circuit to the load, as shown in Fig. 2.57(g), yields $I_0 = \frac{10}{3}\text{mA}$. Using Norton's theorem, the short-circuit current, obtained from the network in Figure 2.57(h), is $I_{SC} = \frac{12}{6k} + \frac{3}{k} = 5$ mA. The Thevenin equivalent resistance is known to be 6 kΩ. Applying the Norton equivalent circuit to the load, as shown in Figure 2.57(i), yields $I_0 = \frac{5}{k}\left(\frac{6k}{9k}\right) = \frac{10}{3}\text{mA}$.

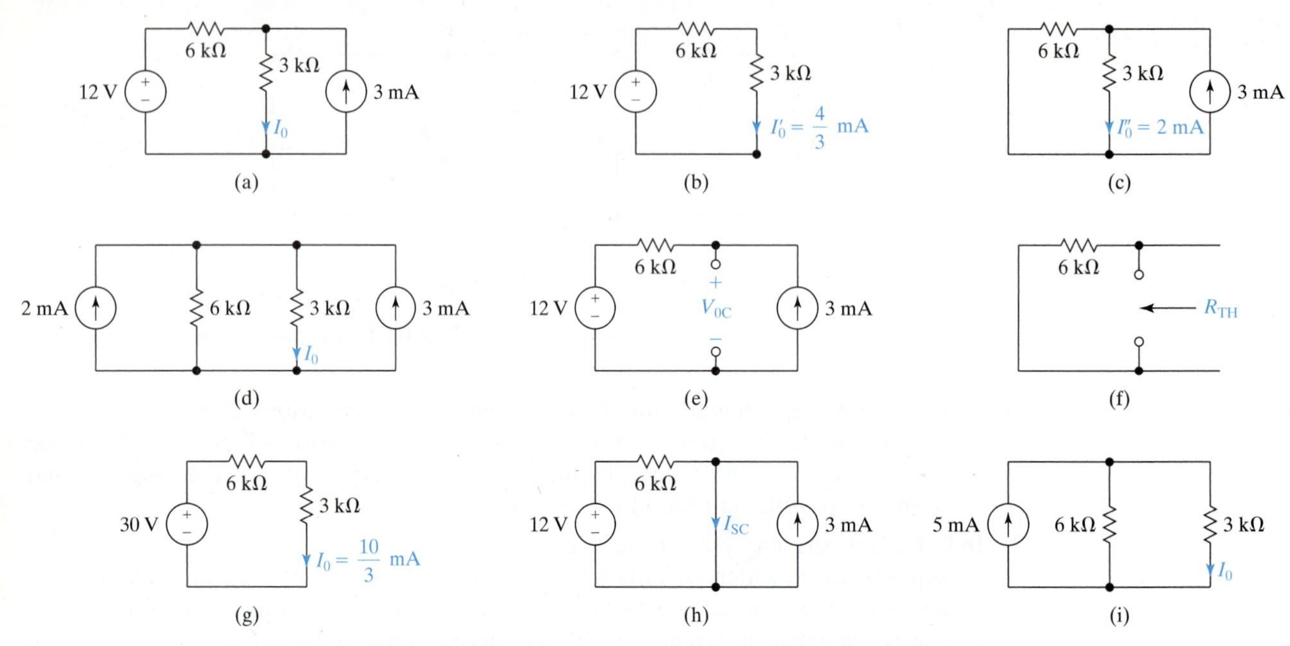

FIGURE 2.57 Circuits used to explain network analysis techniques.

- An important and versatile circuit for measuring a wide variety of physical parameters is the Wheatstone Bridge. The bridge is shown in Figure 2.58 and is used to convert a resistance change to a voltage change. It consists of two voltage dividers, and the output voltage is the difference between them.

$$V_0 = V_S\left(\frac{R_1}{R_1 + R_2} - \frac{R_3}{R_3 + R_4}\right)$$

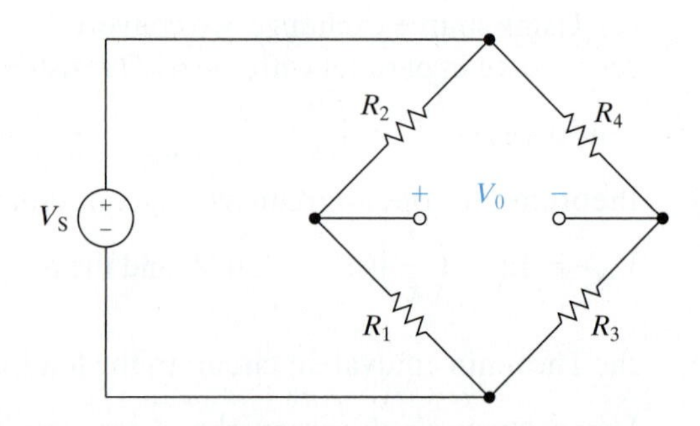

FIGURE 2.58 A Wheatstone Bridge circuit.

Problems

2.1. Find I_1 in the circuit in Figure P2.1.

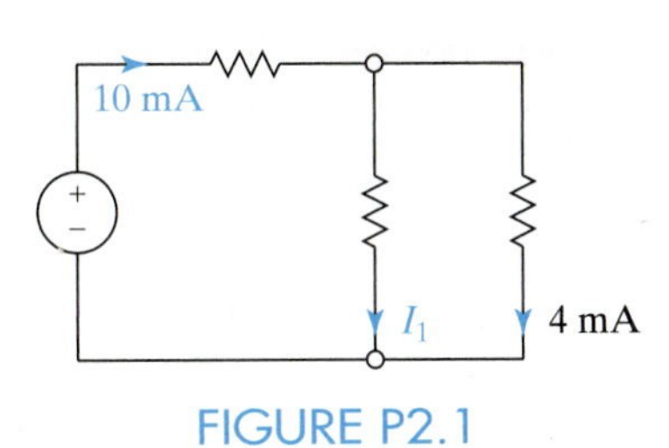

FIGURE P2.1

2.2. If $I_3 = 4$ mA, $I_4 = 8$ mA, and $I_5 = 6$ mA, find I_1, I_2, and I_6 in the network in Figure P2.2.

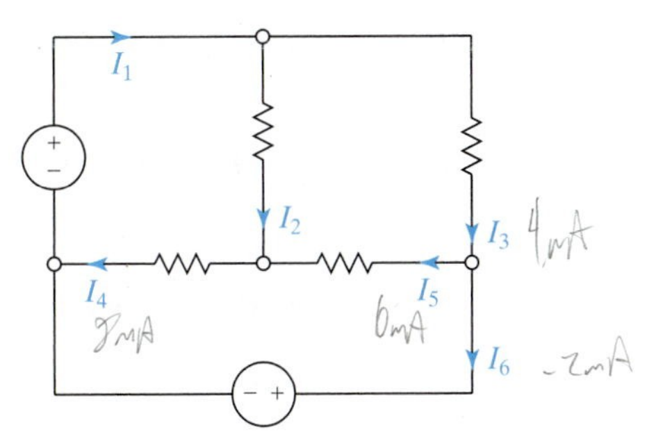

FIGURE P2.2

2.3. If $I_2 = 2$ mA, $I_4 = 4$ mA, and $I_6 = 6$ mA, find I_1, I_3, and I_5 in the network in Figure P2.3.

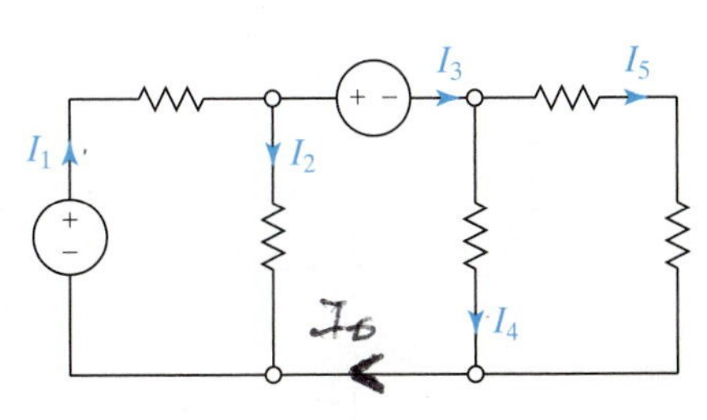

FIGURE P2.3

2.4. If $I_4 = 2$ mA, $I_6 = 3$ mA, and $I_7 = 5$ mA, find I_1, I_2, I_3, and I_5 in the circuit in Figure P2.4.

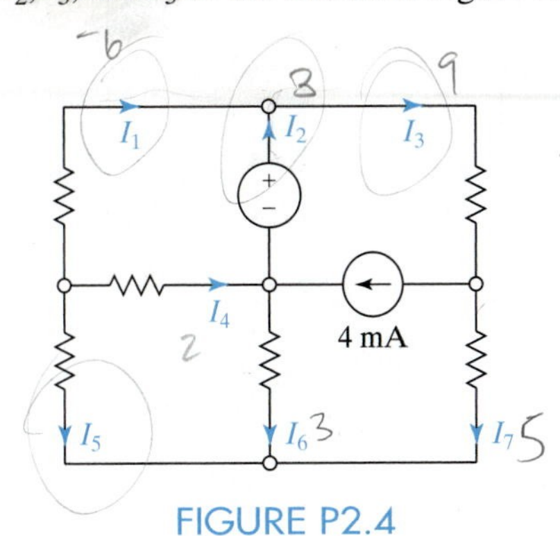

FIGURE P2.4

2.5. If $V_2 = 10$V in the network in Figure P2.5, find V_1 and V_{bd}.

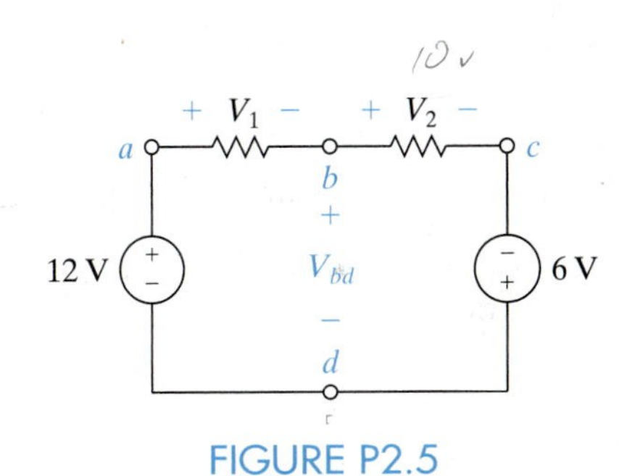

FIGURE P2.5

2.6. In the circuit in Figure P2.6, $V_2 = V_3 = 2$V. Find V_1, V_{bc}, and V_{da}.

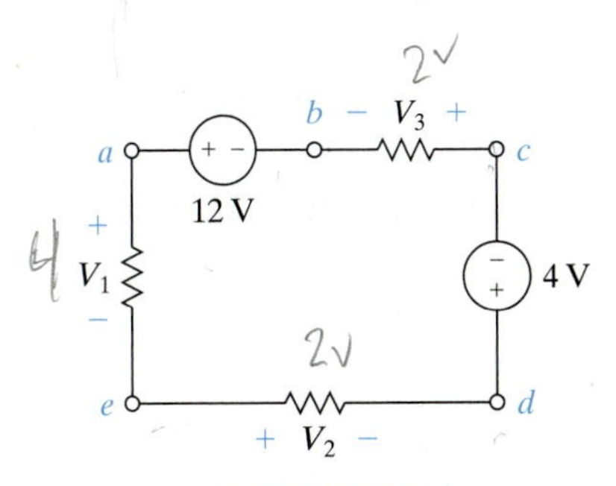

FIGURE P2.6

2.7. Find V_1, V_2, and V_3 in the circuit in Figure P2.7.

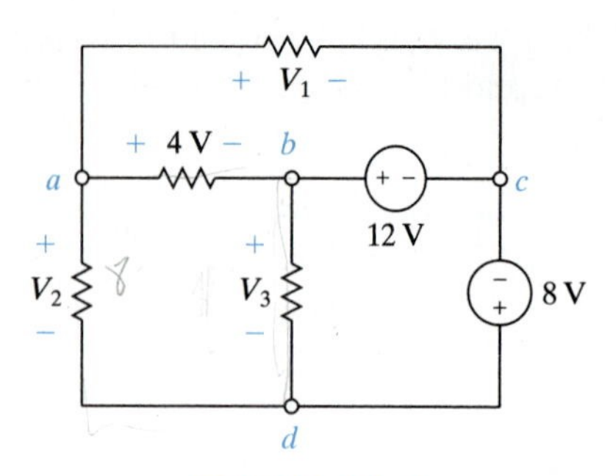

FIGURE P2.7

2.8. In the network in Figure P2.8, $V_4 = 6$V. Find V_1, V_2, V_3, and V_5.

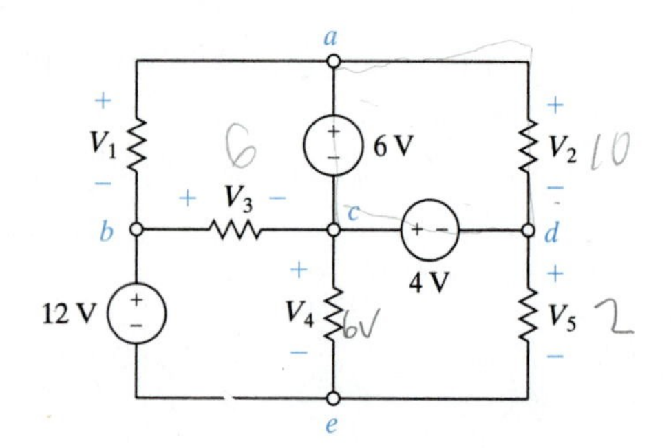

FIGURE P2.8

2.9. Find I in the circuit in Figure P2.9.

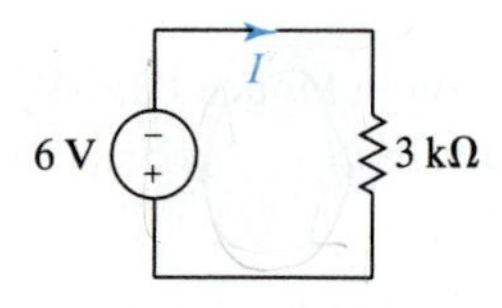

FIGURE P2.9

2.10. In the circuit in Figure P2.10, find R.

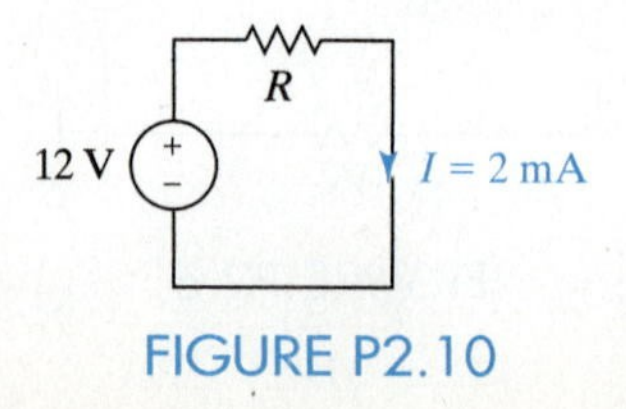

FIGURE P2.10

2.11. In the network in Figure P2.11, the power absorbed by the resistor is 8mW. Find V_S.

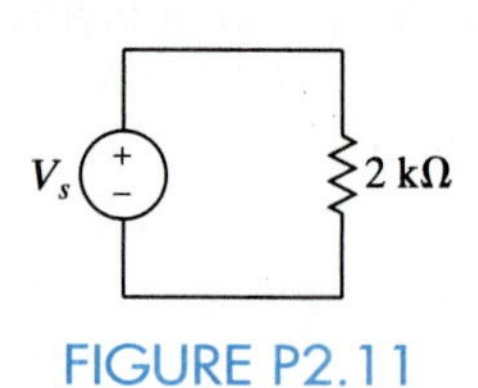

FIGURE P2.11

2.12. Find I and V_0 in the circuit in Figure P2.12.

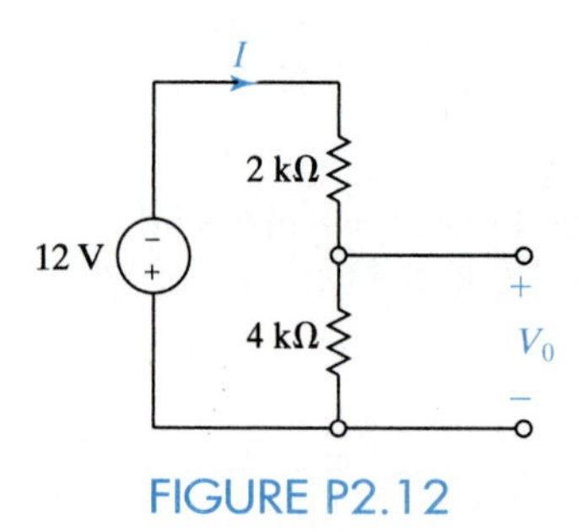

FIGURE P2.12

2.13. Find I_1, V_1, and V_2 in the network in Figure P2.13.

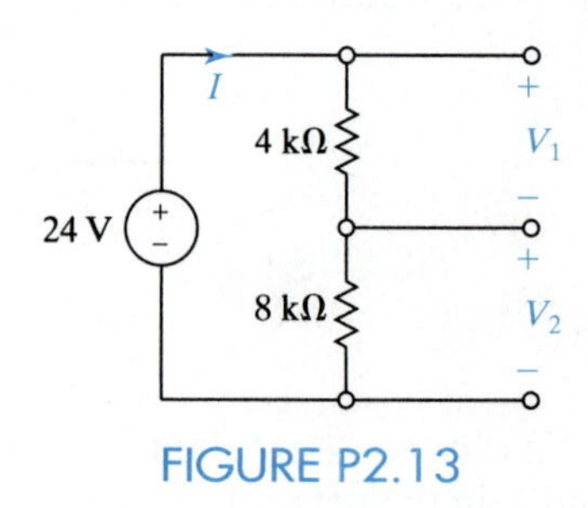

FIGURE P2.13

2.14. Find V_S and V_0 in the network in Figure P2.14.

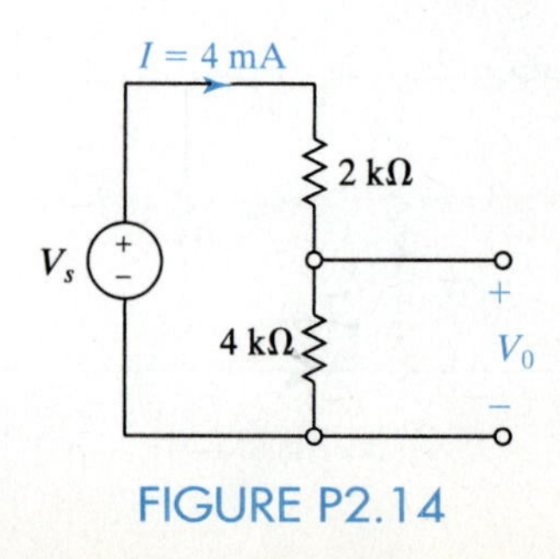

FIGURE P2.14

2.15. Find V_S and I in the circuit in Figure P2.15.

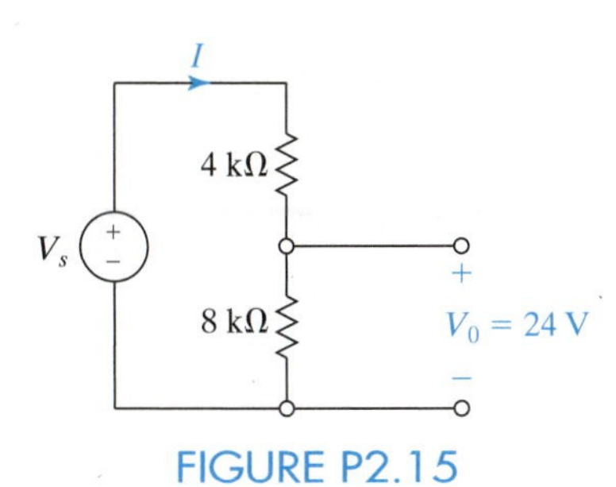

FIGURE P2.15

2.16. Find V_S in the network in Figure P2.16.

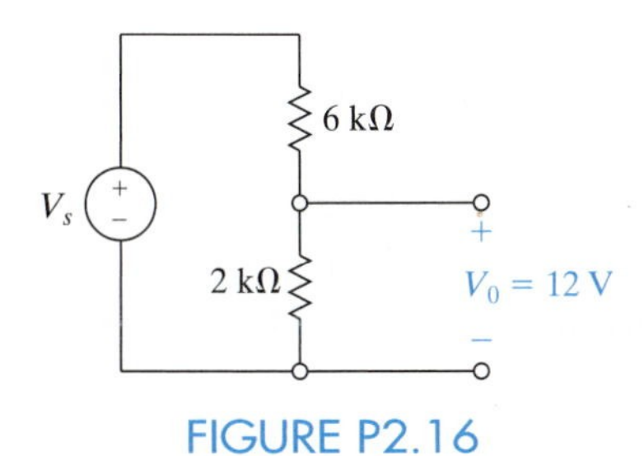

FIGURE P2.16

2.17. Use voltage division to find V_0 in the network in Figure P2.17.

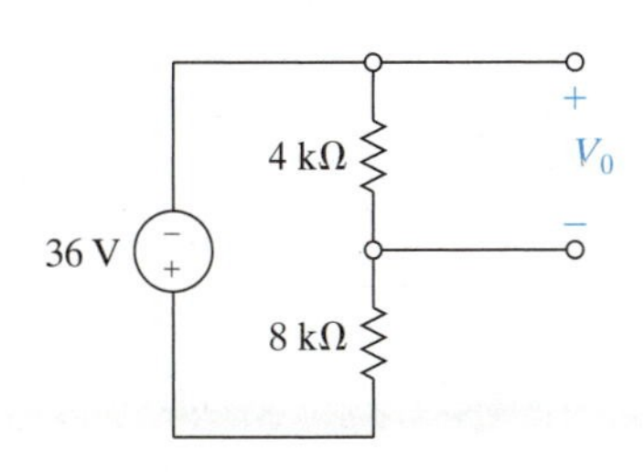

FIGURE P2.17

2.18. Use voltage division to find V_0 in the circuit in Figure P2.18.

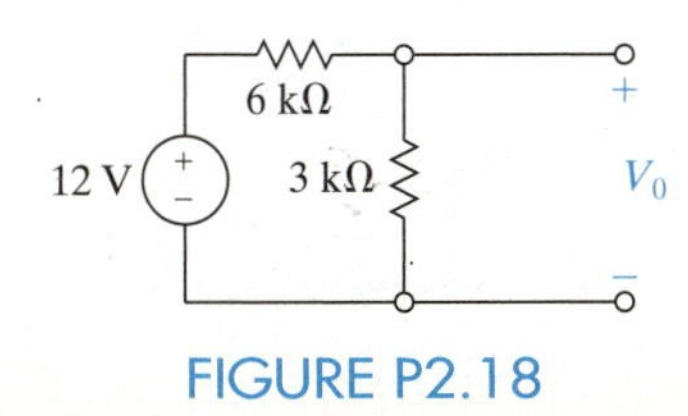

FIGURE P2.18

2.19. Use voltage division to find V_0 in the circuit in Figure P2.19.

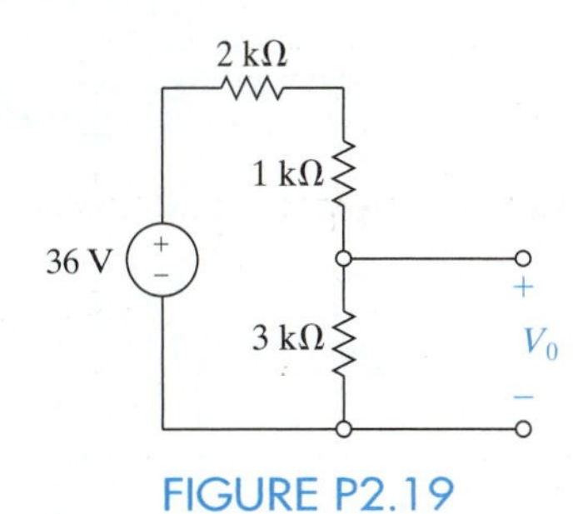

FIGURE P2.19

2.20. Use voltage division to find V_S in the network in Figure P2.20.

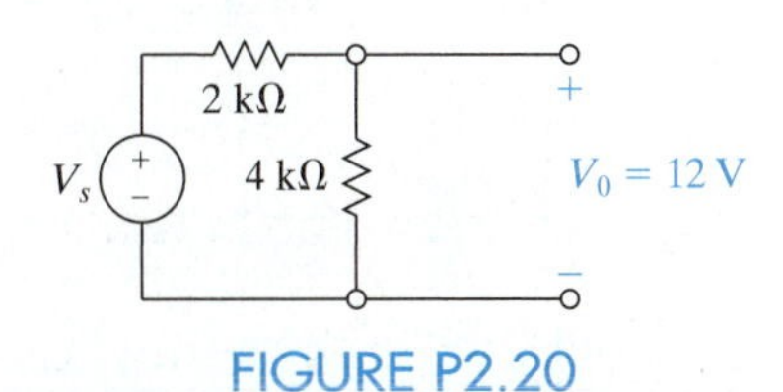

FIGURE P2.20

2.21. Use voltage division to find V_S in the network in Figure P2.21.

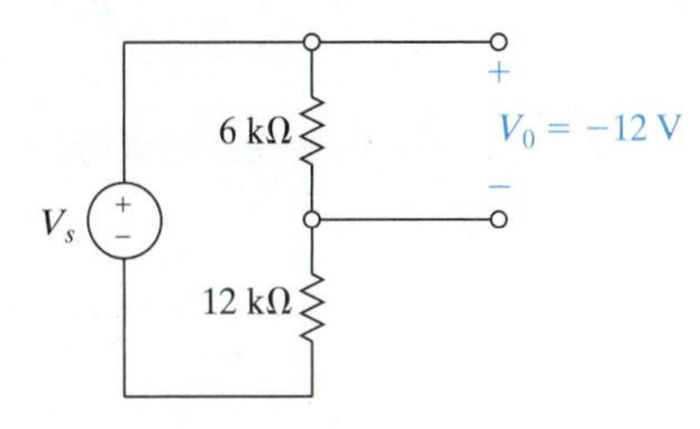

FIGURE P2.21

2.22. Use voltage division to find V_S in the circuit in Figure P2.22.

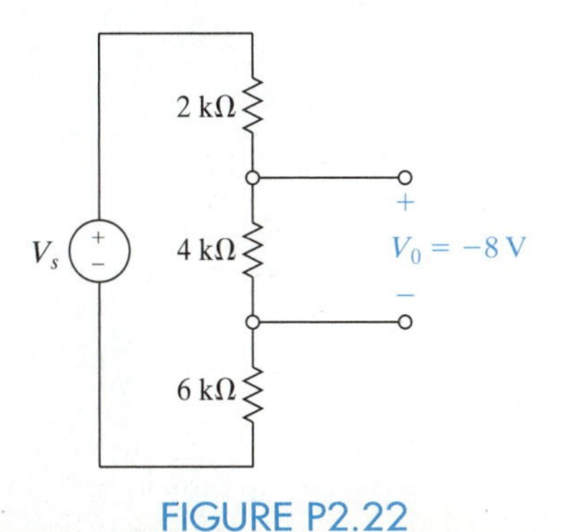

FIGURE P2.22

2.23. Use voltage division to find V_S in the network in Figure P2.23.

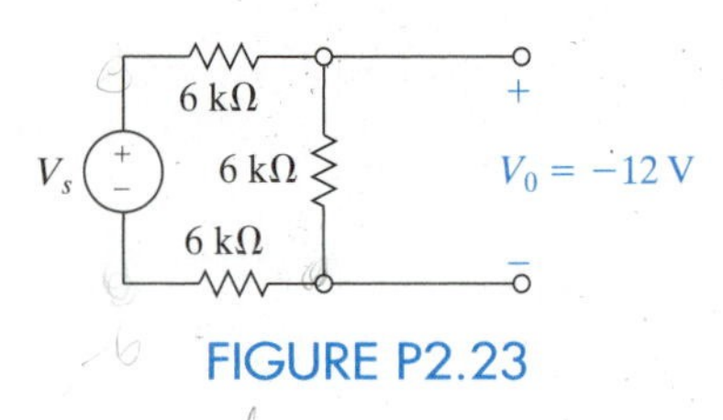

FIGURE P2.23

2.24. Find V_0 in the circuit in Figure P2.24.

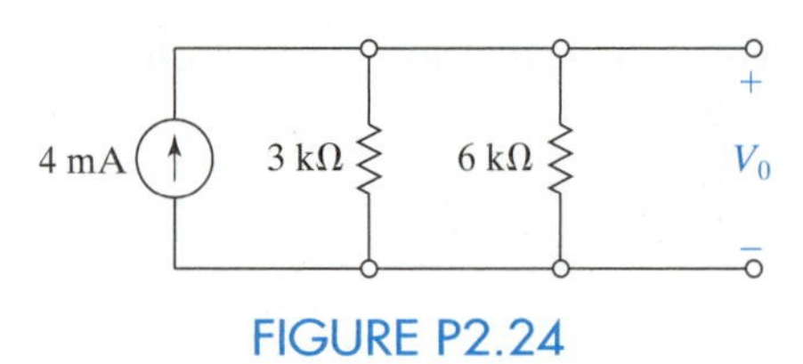

FIGURE P2.24

2.25. Find V_0 and I_1 in the network in Figure P2.25.

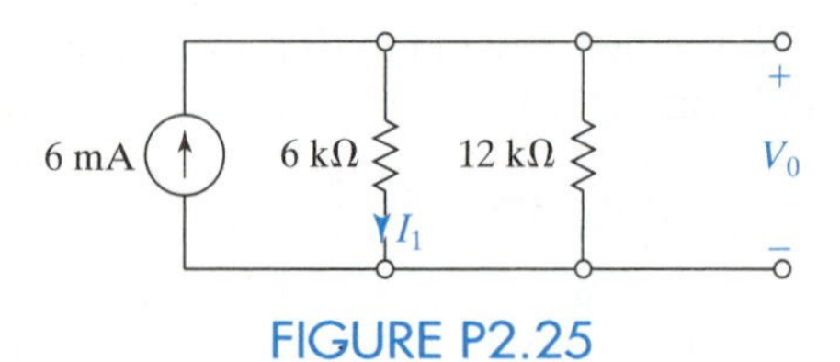

FIGURE P2.25

2.26. Find I_1 and I_2 in the circuit in Figure P2.26.

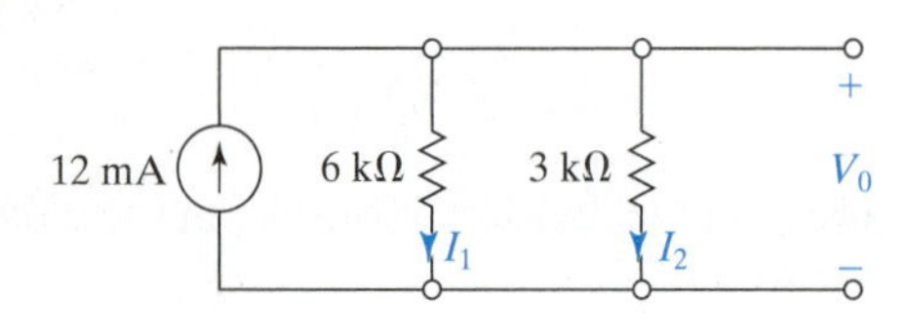

FIGURE P2.26

2.27. Use current division to find I_1 and I_2 in the network in Figure P2.27.

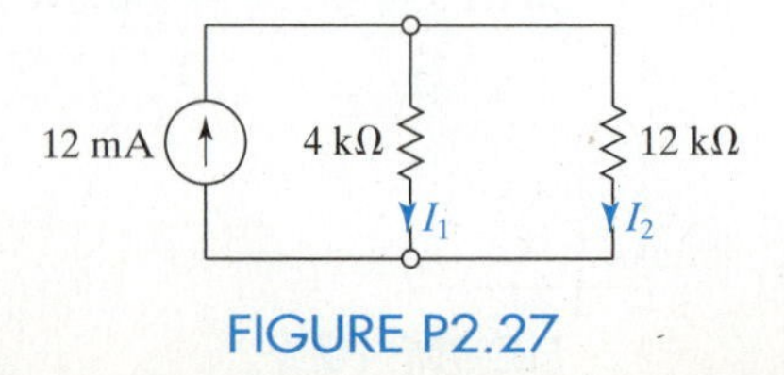

FIGURE P2.27

2.28. Use current division to find I_1 in the network in Figure P2.28.

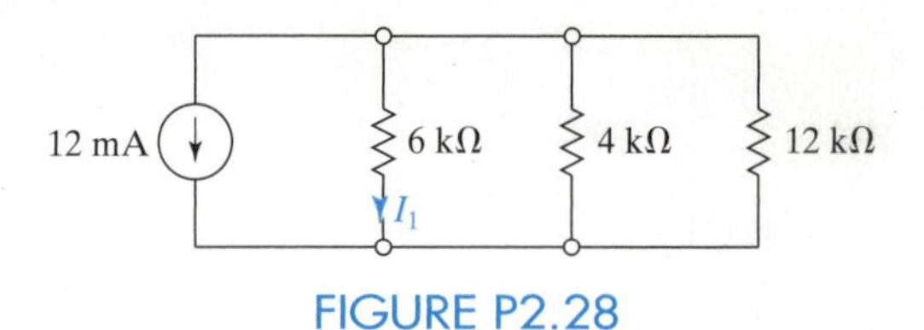

FIGURE P2.28

2.29. Use current division to find I_0 in the circuit in Figure P2.29.

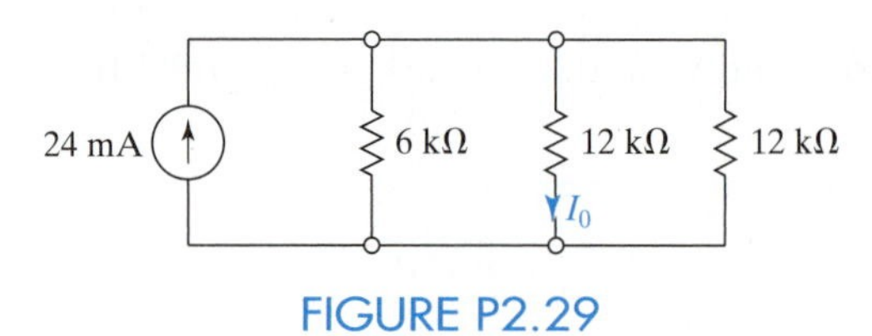

FIGURE P2.29

2.30. Find I_S in the network in Figure P2.30 using current division.

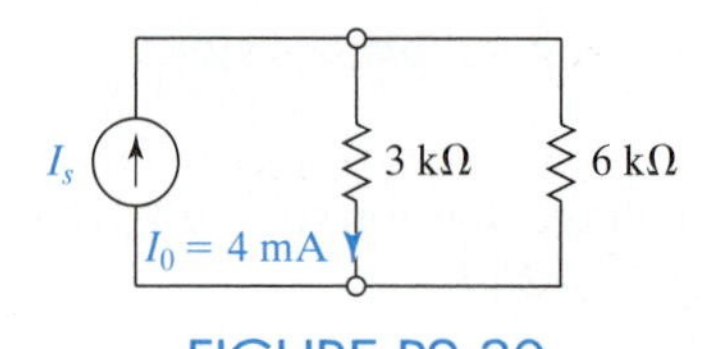

FIGURE P2.30

2.31. Find I_S in the circuit in Figure P2.31 using current division.

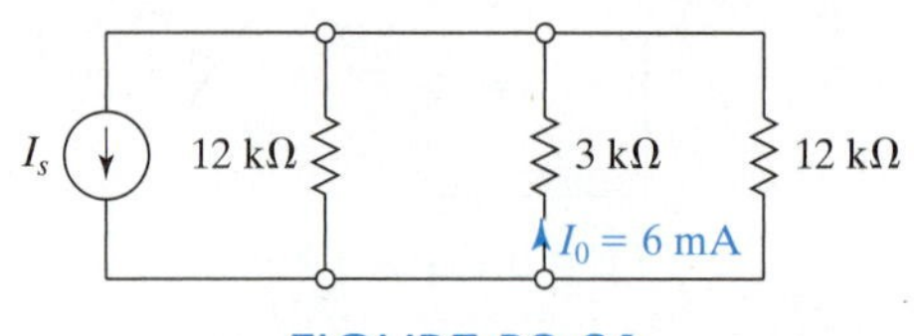

FIGURE P2.31

2.32. Find V_0 in the circuit in Figure P2.32.

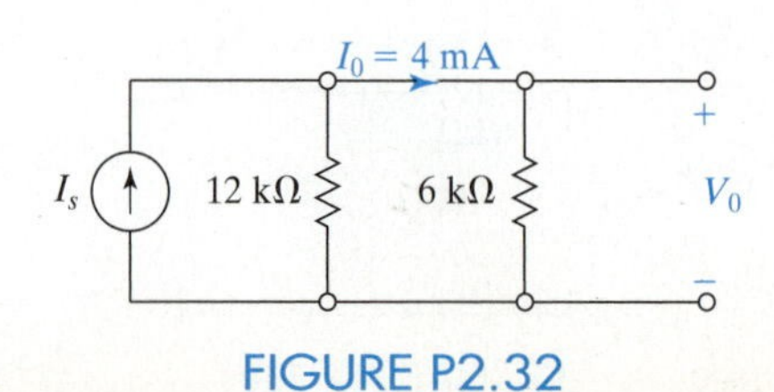

FIGURE P2.32

2.33. In the network in Figure P2.33, $I_1 = 3$ mA. Find V_0.

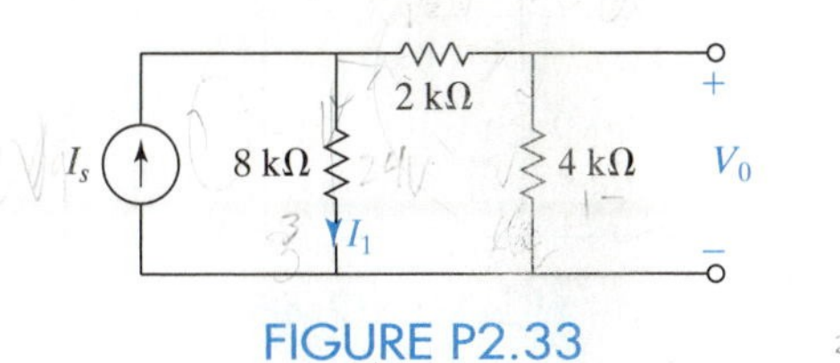

FIGURE P2.33

2.34. In the circuit in Figure P2.34, $I_2 = 4$ mA. Find I_1 and V_0.

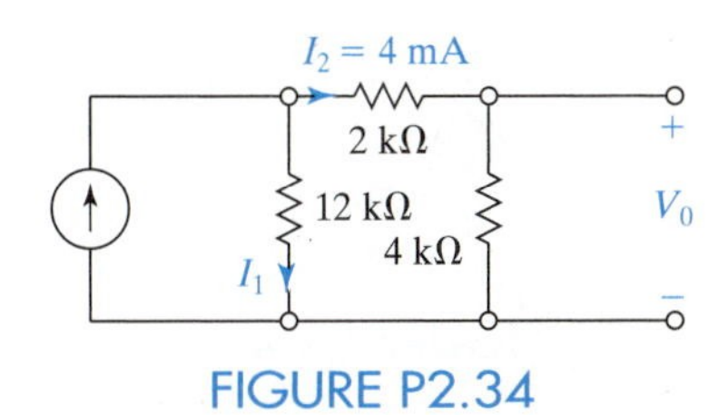

FIGURE P2.34

2.35. Find V_0 in the network in Figure P2.35.

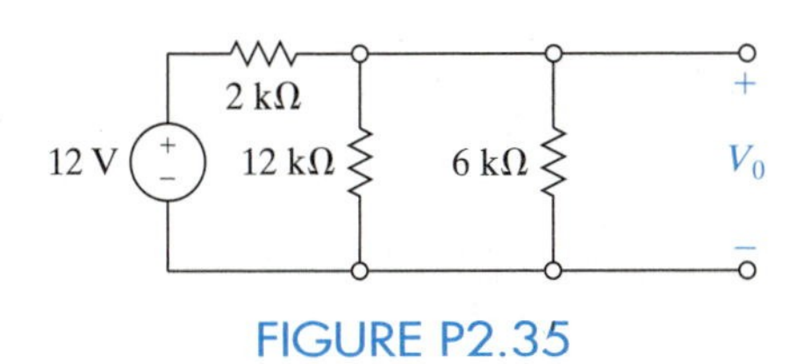

FIGURE P2.35

2.36. If $I_1 = 2$ mA, find V_S in the circuit in Figure P2.36.

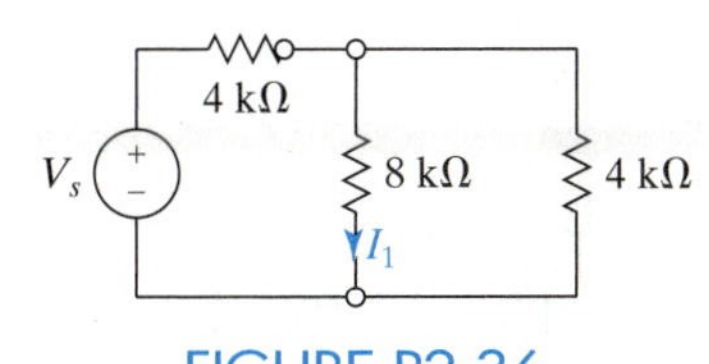

FIGURE P2.36

2.37. Find I_S in the network in Figure P2.37.

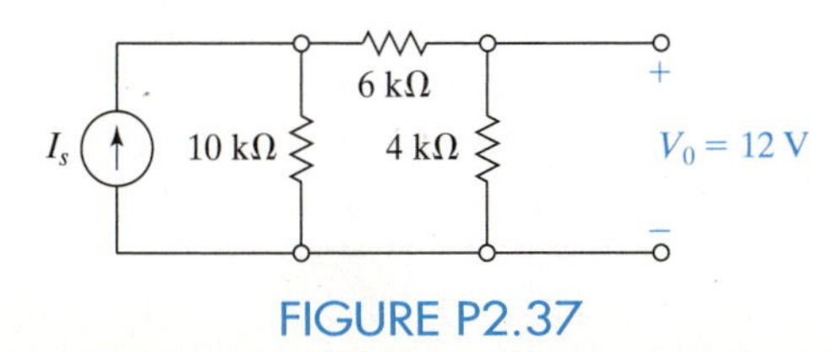

FIGURE P2.37

2.38. Find R_{AB} in the network in Figure P2.38.

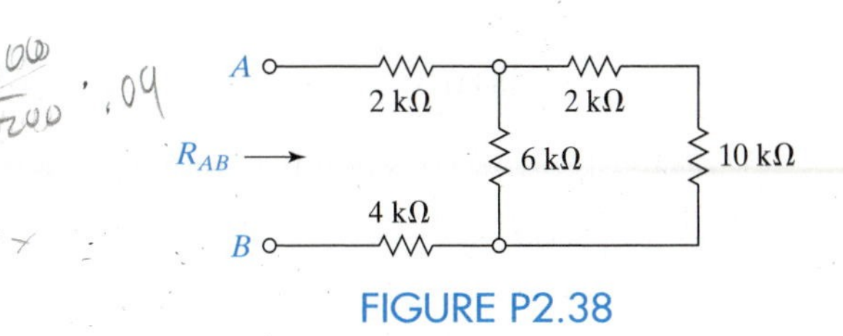

FIGURE P2.38

2.39. Find R_{AB} in the circuit in Figure P2.39.

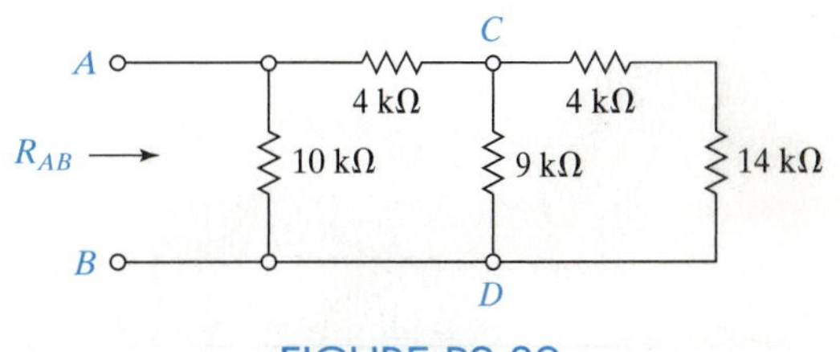

FIGURE P2.39

2.40. Find R_{AB} in the circuit in Figure P2.40.

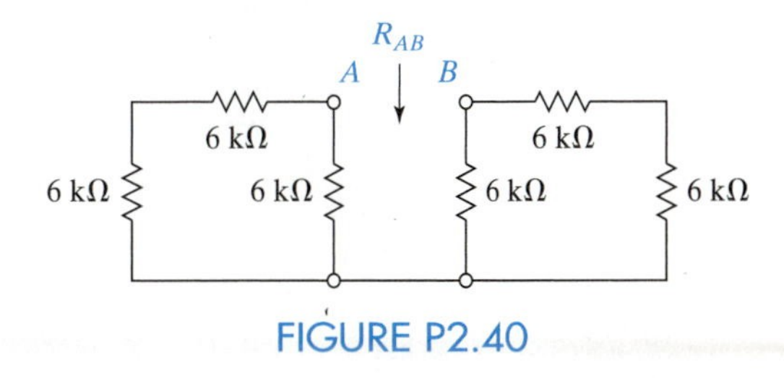

FIGURE P2.40

2.41. Find R_{AB} in the network in Figure P2.41.

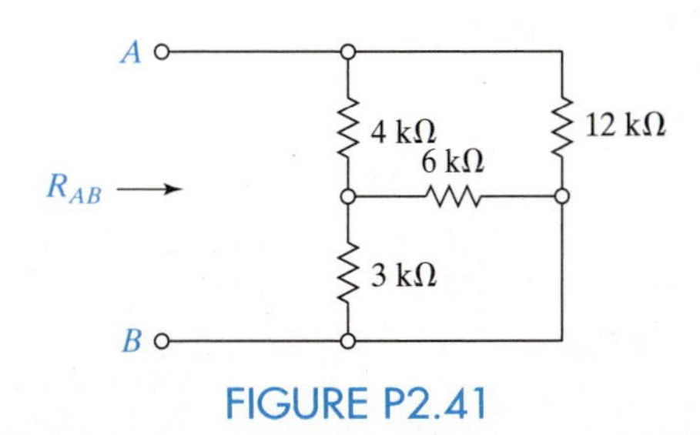

FIGURE P2.41

2.42. Find R_{AB} in the network in Figure P2.42.

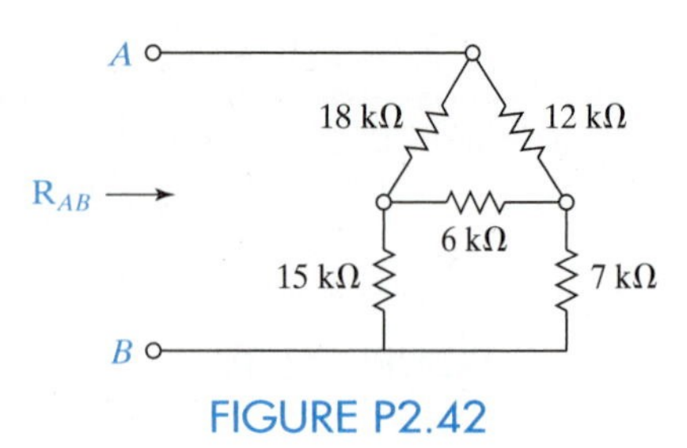

FIGURE P2.42

2.43. Find R_{AB} in the circuit in Figure P2.43.

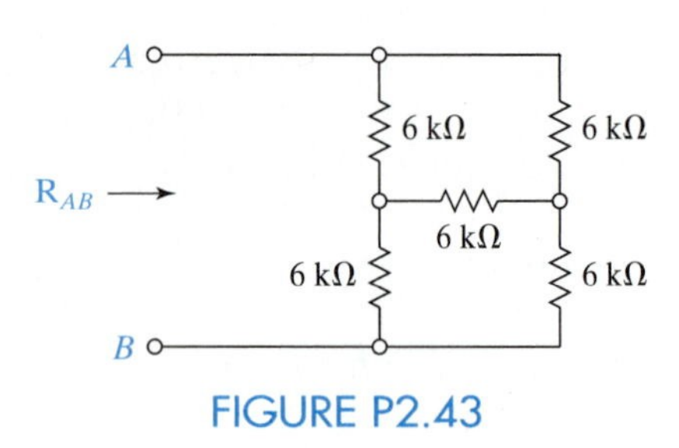

FIGURE P2.43

2.44. Find R_{AB} in the network in Figure P2.44.

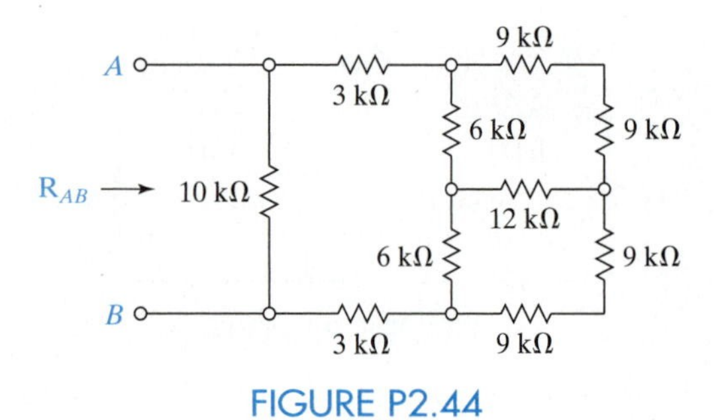

FIGURE P2.44

2.45. Use nodal analysis to find I_0 in the network in Figure P2.45.

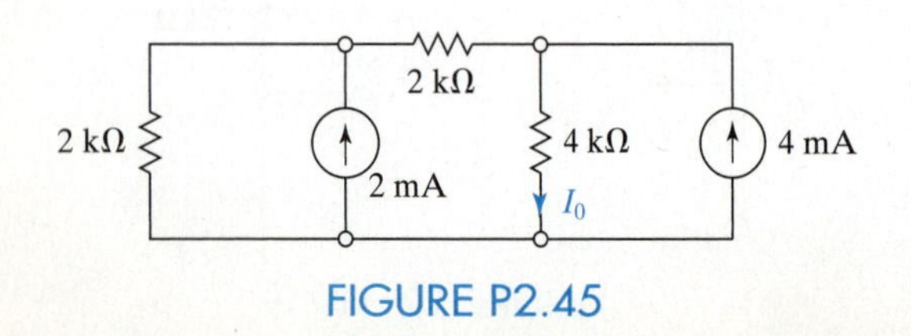

FIGURE P2.45

2.46. Find I_0 in the circuit in Figure P2.46.

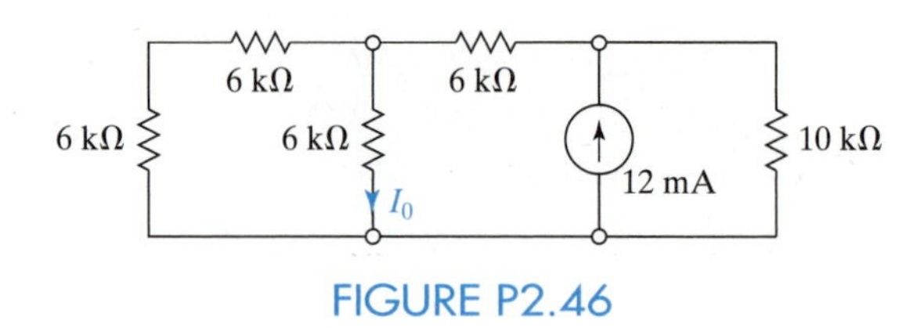

FIGURE P2.46

2.47. Find I_0 in the circuit in Figure P2.47 using nodal analysis.

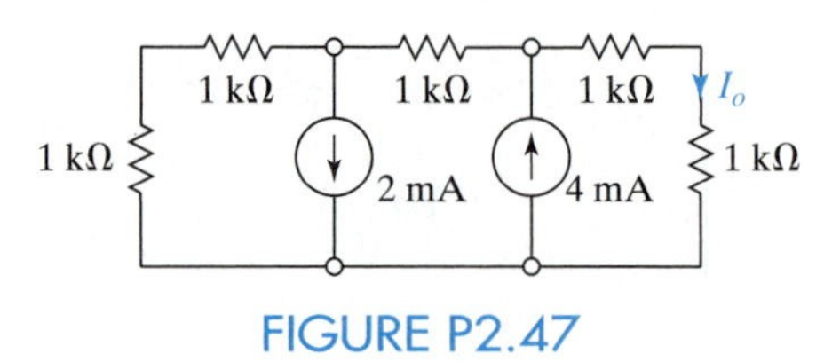

FIGURE P2.47

2.48. Find I_0 in the network in Figure P2.48.

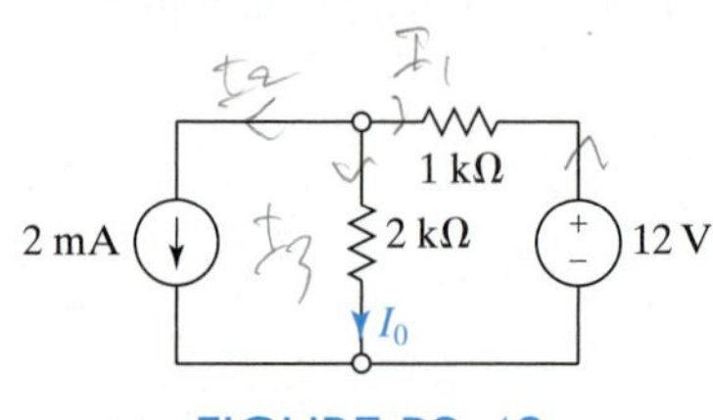

FIGURE P2.48

2.49. Find I_0 in the circuit in Figure P2.49.

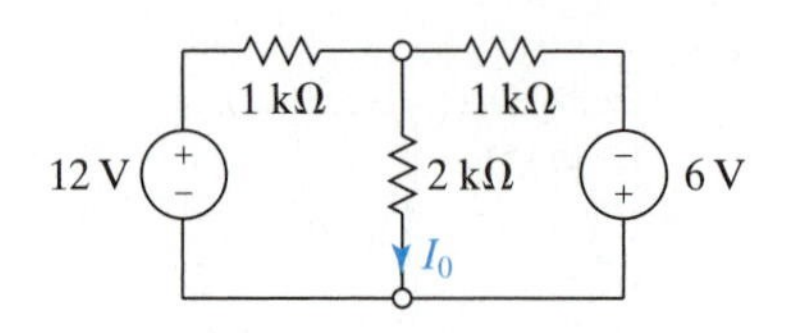

FIGURE P2.49

2.50. Find I_0 in the network in Figure P2.50.

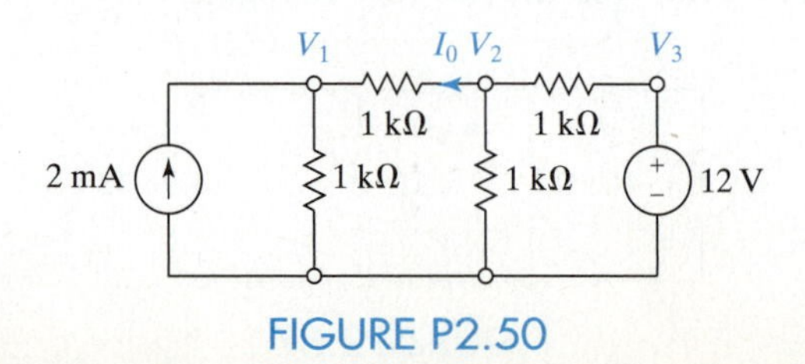

FIGURE P2.50

2.51. Find V_0 in the circuit in Figure P2.51.

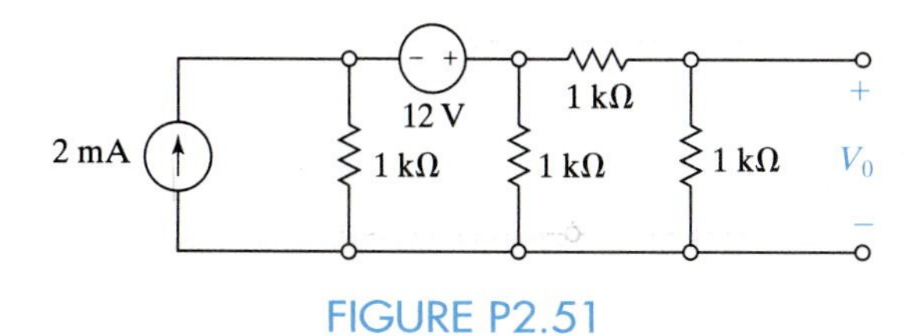

FIGURE P2.51

2.52. Find the node voltages in the circuit in Figure P2.52.

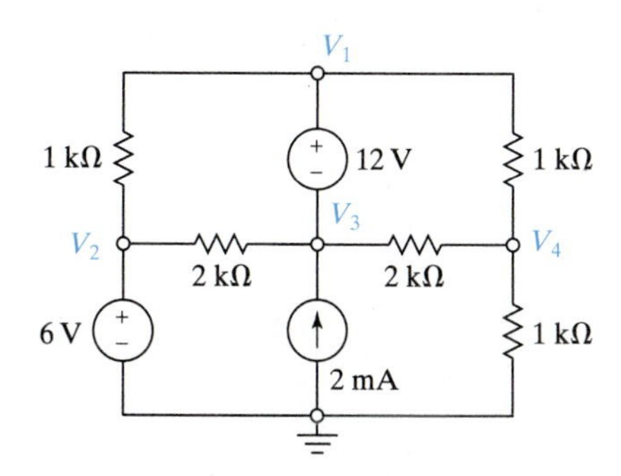

FIGURE P2.52

2.53. Solve problem 2.51 using MATLAB.

2.54. Solve problem 2.52 using MATLAB.

2.55. Use loop analysis to find I_1, I_2, and V_0 in the circuit in Figure P2.55.

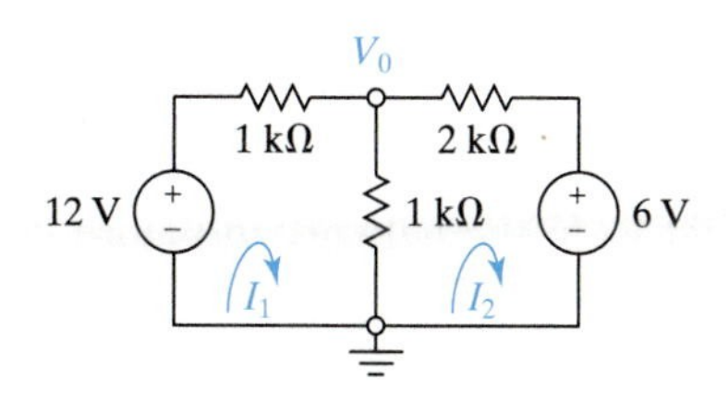

FIGURE P2.55

2.56. Find V_0 in the network in Figure P2.56.

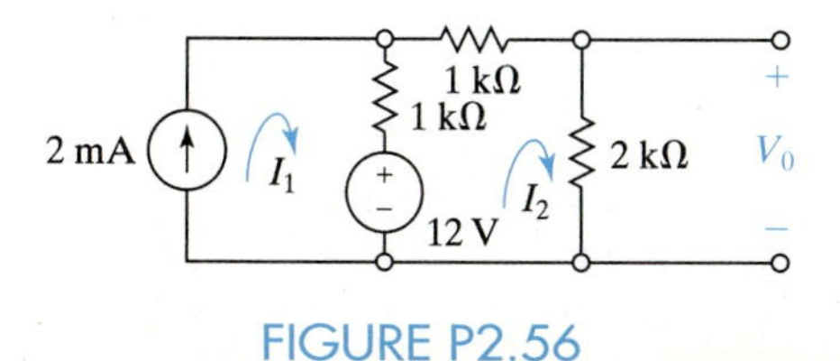

FIGURE P2.56

2.57. Find V_0 in the circuit in Figure P2.57.

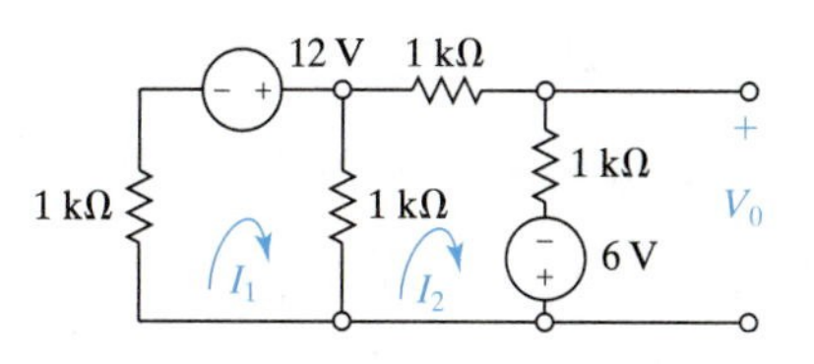

FIGURE P2.57

2.58. Find I_0 in the network in Figure P2.58 using loop analysis.

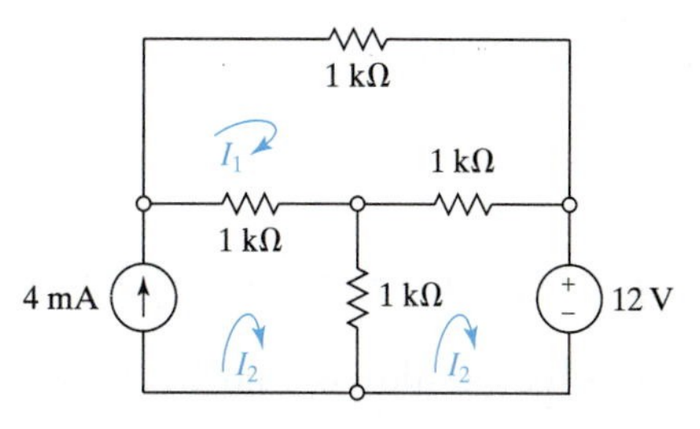

FIGURE P2.58

2.59. Use loop analysis to find V_0 in the circuit in Figure P2.59.

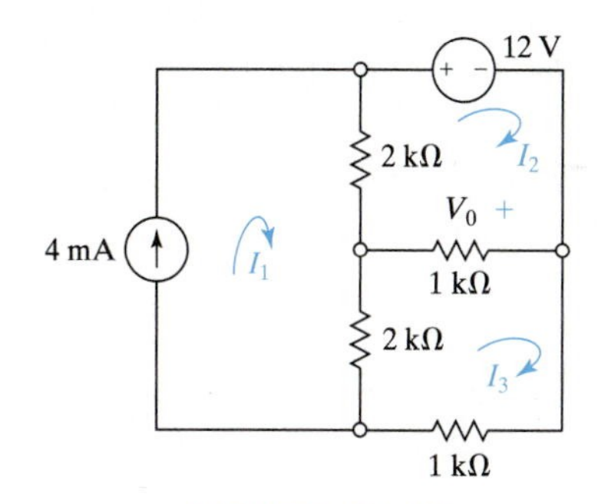

FIGURE P2.59

2.60. Find all loop currents in the network in Figure P2.60.

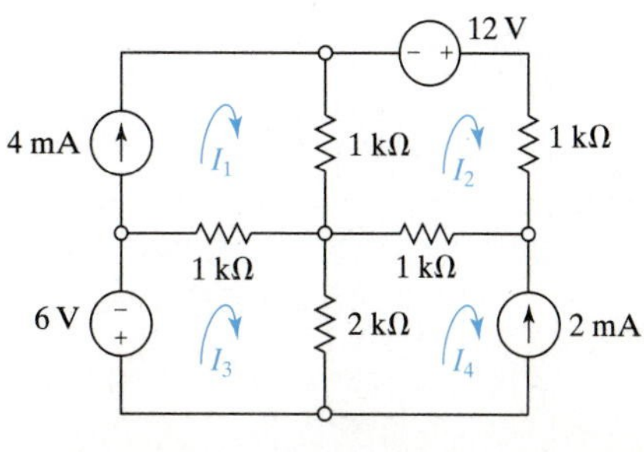

FIGURE P2.60

2.61. Solve problem 2.59 using MATLAB.

2.62. Solve problem 2.60 using MATLAB.

2.63. Find I_0 in the circuit in Figure P2.63 using superposition.

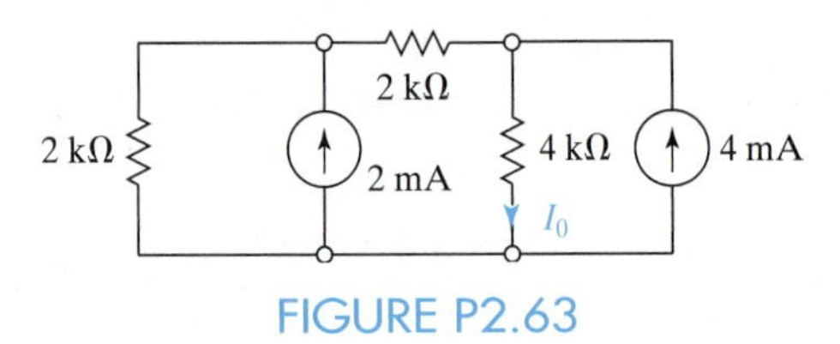

FIGURE P2.63

2.64. Solve problem 2.49 using superposition.

2.65. Use superposition to find V_0 in the circuit in Figure P2.65.

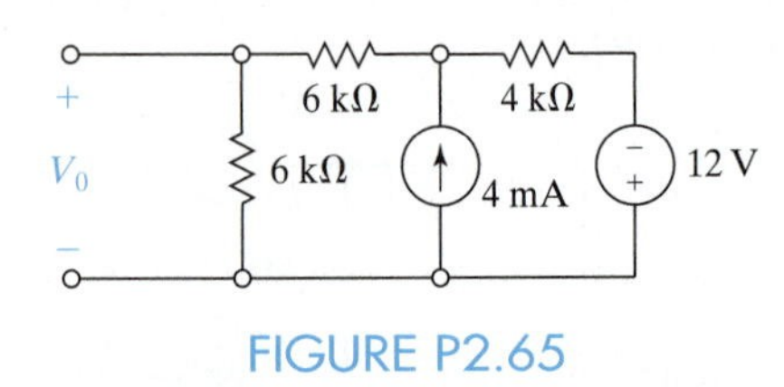

FIGURE P2.65

2.66. Find I_0 in the network in Figure P2.66 using superposition.

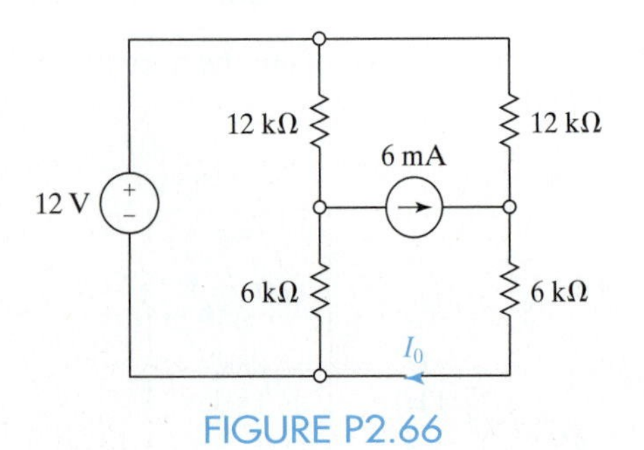

FIGURE P2.66

2.67. Use superposition to find V_0 in the circuit in Figure P2.67.

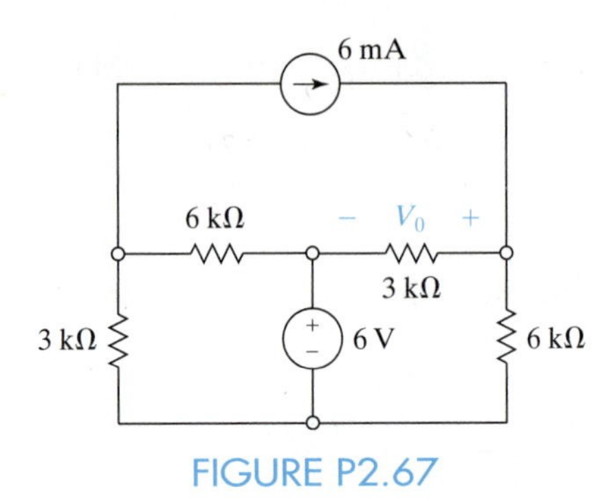

FIGURE P2.67

2.68. Solve problem 2.49 using source transformation.

2.69. Solve problem 2.51 using source transformation.

2.70. Use source transformation to find V_0 in the circuit in Figure P2.70.

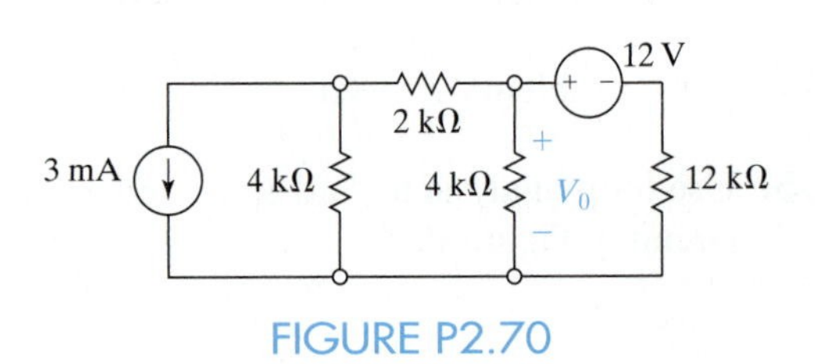

FIGURE P2.70

2.71. Find V_0 in the network in Figure P2.71 using source transformation.

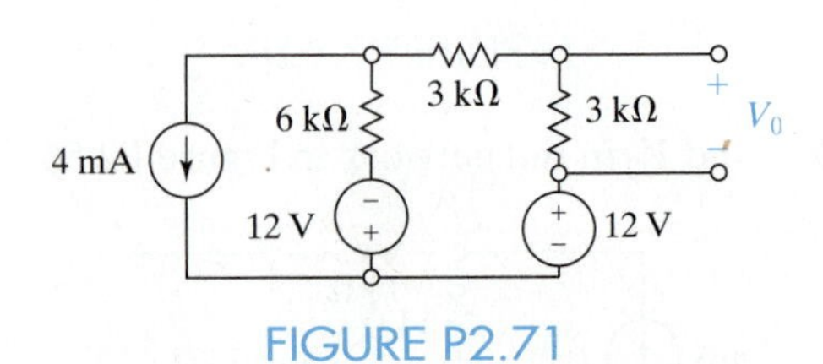

FIGURE P2.71

2.72. Use source transformation to find I_0 in the circuit in Figure P2.72.

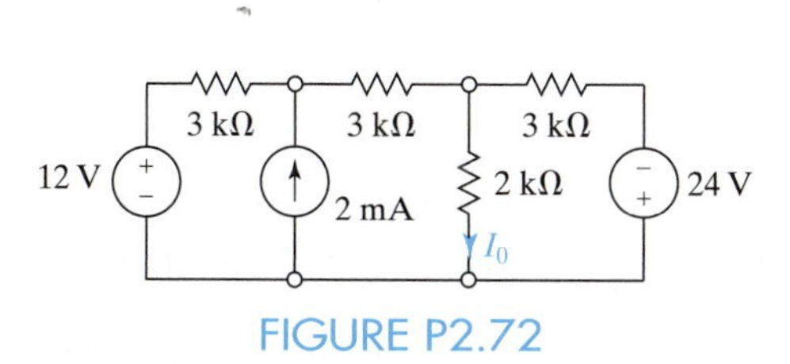

FIGURE P2.72

2.73. Use Thevenin's theorem to find I_0 in the network in Figure P2.73.

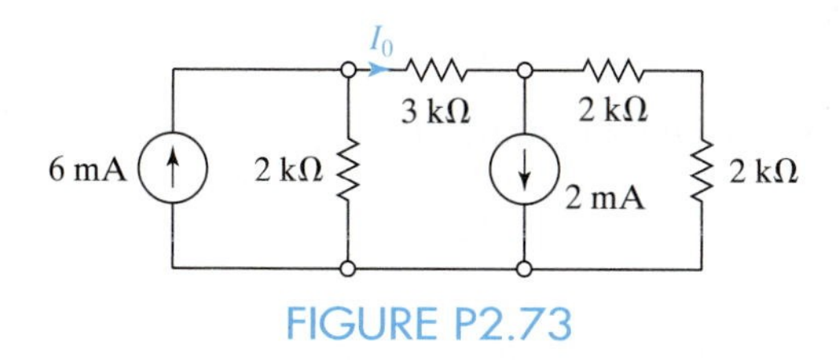

FIGURE P2.73

2.74. Solve problem 2.49 using Thevenin's theorem.

2.75. Use Thevenin's theorem to find V_0 in the network in Figure P2.75.

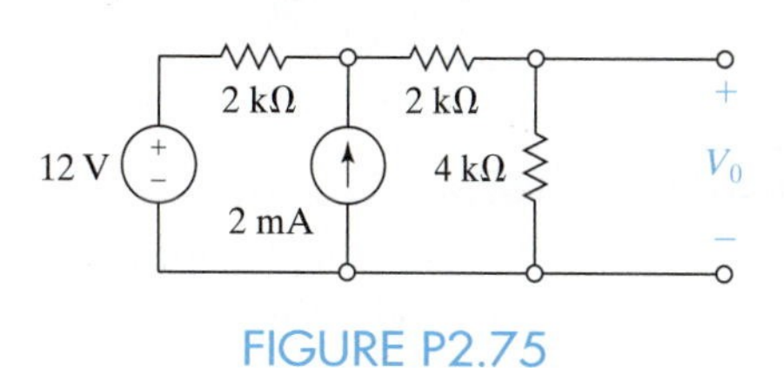

FIGURE P2.75

2.76. Solve problem 2.67 using Thevenin's theorem.

2.77. Solve problem 2.71 using Thevenin's theorem.

2.78. Solve problem 2.63 using Norton's theorem.

2.79. Find I_0 in the circuit in Figure P2.79 using Norton's theorem.

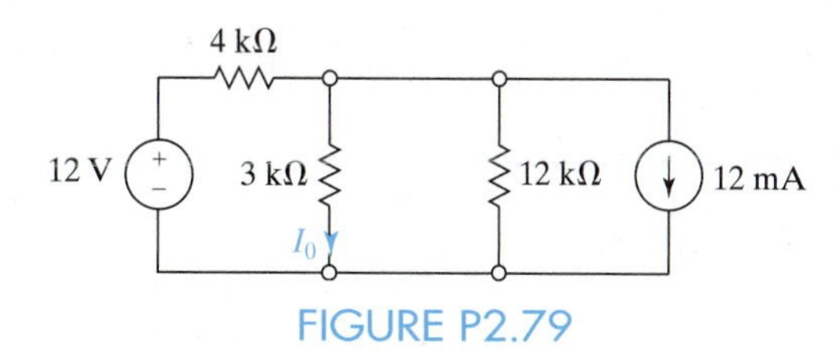

FIGURE P2.79

2.80. Solve problem 2.70 using Norton's theorem.

3-1 Introduction

In this chapter we will perform what is commonly known as a transient analysis. In this type of analysis we examine the behavior of a network as a function of time after a sudden change in the network occurs due to switches opening or closing.

Before proceeding with our study of transient analysis, and an introduction of two new passive elements, we wish to reiterate, for comparison purposes, the properties of a resistor. Ohm's law, that is,

$$v(t) = i(t)R$$

Equivalent resistor combinations

holds for all time including transient voltages and currents. In addition, the equivalent resistance of N resistors connected in series is

$$R_S = R_1 + R_2 + R_3 + \cdots + R_N$$

and the equivalent resistance of N resistors connected in parallel is

$$\frac{1}{R_P} = \frac{1}{R_1} + \frac{1}{R_2} + \frac{1}{R_3} + \cdots + \frac{1}{R_N}$$

The two new passive elements we wish to introduce in this chapter are the capacitor and the inductor. Both these elements possess several important features: they are linear elements, their terminal characteristics are described by linear differential equations, and like a mechanical spring, they are capable of storing energy.

Techniques for the analysis of first-order networks, that is, networks that contain a single storage element, will be presented first, and the time constant of a network will be introduced. The analysis procedures will then be extended to second-order circuits, for example, those in which an inductor and capacitor are present simultaneously.

3-2 Capacitors and Inductors

3.2.1 Capacitors

Capacitors consist of two conducting surfaces separated by a nonconducting, or dielectric, material. A simplified capacitor and its electrical symbol are shown in Figure 3.1. If a voltage V exists across the capacitor, positive charges will be transferred to one plate and negative charges to the other. The charge on the capacitor is proportional to the voltage across it as defined by the relationship

$$q = CV \tag{3.1}$$

The capacitor and its units

where since q is in coulombs and V is in volts, the constant of proportionality C has units of coulombs per volt, or "Farads" (F) after the famous English physicist Michael Faraday.

Capacitors may be fixed or variable and typically range from thousands of microfarads (μF) to picofarads (pf).

Some typical capacitors that could be purchased in an electronic parts store are shown in Figure 3.2. These devices find wide application in radios, TVs, high-voltage power systems, and a host of other applications.

3.2.2 Energy Stored in a Capacitor

As shown in Figure 3.1, the parallel plates of the capacitor are separated by a dielectric—for example, air—and therefore the conduction current in the wires cannot flow internally between the plates. *Therefore, if the voltage across a capacitor is a constant, the current is zero and the capacitor looks like an open circuit,* a fact we will use extensively later in this chapter. However, if the voltage across the capacitor changes with time, so will the charge, and thus

$$q(t) = Cv(t) \tag{3.2}$$

The time rate of change of charge is current. Hence

$$i(t) = \frac{dq(t)}{dt} \tag{3.3}$$

The current–voltage–energy interrelationships for a capacitor

From Eqs. (3.2) and (3.3), we find that the terminal characteristics of a capacitor are defined by the linear differential equation

$$i(t) = C\frac{dv(t)}{dt} \tag{3.4}$$

If the current/voltage relationship for the capacitor defined by Eq. (3.4) is integrated, we obtain the equation

$$v(t) = \frac{1}{C}\int_{-\infty}^{t} i(x)\,dx \tag{3.5}$$

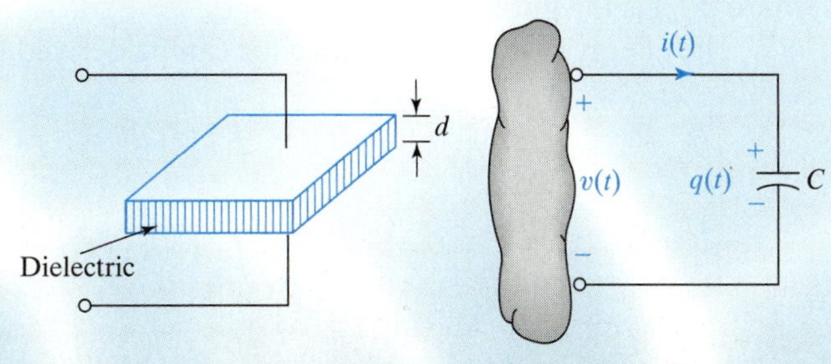

FIGURE 3.1 Capacitor and its electrical symbol.

FIGURE 3.2 Some examples of practical capacitors.

which can be expressed in the form

$$\begin{aligned} v(t) &= \frac{1}{C}\int_{-\infty}^{t_o} i(x)\,dx + \frac{1}{C}\int_{t_o}^{t} i(x)\,dx \\ &= v(t_o) + \frac{1}{C}\int_{t_o}^{t} i(x)\,dx \end{aligned} \tag{3.6}$$

where $v(t_o)$ is the initial capacitor voltage.

The energy stored in the capacitor can be derived from the power delivered to it.

$$\begin{aligned} w_c(t) &= \int p(t)\,dt \\ &= \int_{-\infty}^{t} [v(x)]\left[C\frac{dv(x)}{dx}\right] dx \\ &= \frac{1}{2}Cv^2(t)\ joules \end{aligned} \tag{3.7}$$

Although we have modeled the capacitor as an ideal device, practical capacitors normally have some very large leakage resistance, which provides a parallel conduction path between the plates. In addition, it is important to note that an instantaneous jump in the voltage across a capacitor is not physically realizable since such a jump would require moving a finite amount of charge in zero time, producing an infinite current. This latter point is another fact we will use extensively later in this chapter in transient analysis.

Example 3.1

If the voltage across a 5-μF capacitor is as shown Figure 3.3(a), let us determine the waveform for the current in the capacitor and the energy stored in the electric field of the capacitor at $t = 6$ ms.

The equations for the line segments of the waveform within the given time intervals are

$$
\begin{aligned}
v(t) &= \frac{24}{6 \times 10^{-3}} t && 0 \leq t \leq 6 \text{ ms} \\
&= \frac{-24}{2 \times 10^{-3}} t + 96 && 6 \leq t \leq 8 \text{ ms} \\
&= 0 && 8 \text{ ms} \leq t
\end{aligned}
$$

Using Eq. (3.4),

$$
\begin{aligned}
i(t) &= C \frac{dv(t)}{dt} \\
&= (5 \times 10^{-6})(4 \times 10^{5}) && 0 \leq t \leq 6 \text{ ms} \\
&= 20 \text{ mA} && 0 \leq t \leq 6 \text{ ms} \\
i(t) &= (5 \times 10^{-6})(-12 \times 10^{3}) && 6 \leq t \leq 8 \text{ ms} \\
&= -60 \text{ mA} && 6 \leq t \leq 8 \text{ ms} \\
i(t) &= 0 && 8 \text{ ms} \leq t
\end{aligned}
$$

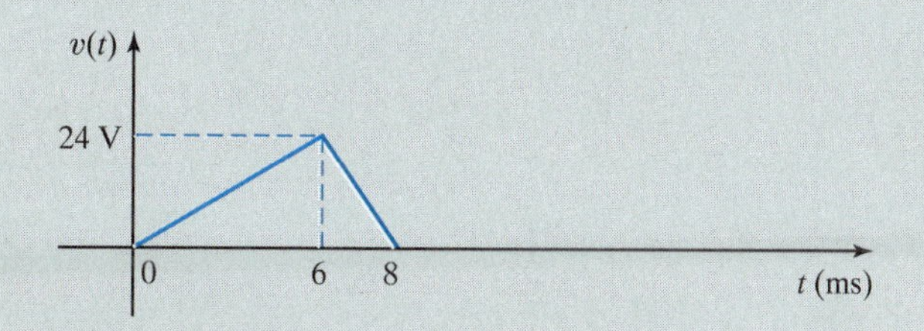

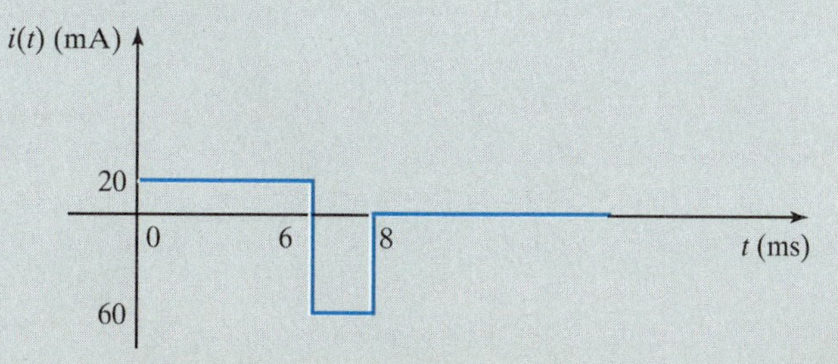

FIGURE 3.3 Voltage and current waveforms for Example 3.1.

The current waveform is shown in Figure 3.3(b).

The energy stored in the electric field of the capacitor at $t = 6$ ms is

$$w_c(t) = \frac{1}{2}Cv^2(t)$$

$$w_c(6\text{ ms}) = \frac{1}{2}(5 \times 10^{-6})(24)^2$$

$$= 1440\ \mu\text{J}$$

3.2.3 Capacitor Combinations

Just as resistors can be combined in series and parallel combinations, interconnected capacitors can be combined to yield a single equivalent capacitance. Using Kirchhoff's voltage law, we can show that if N capacitors are connected in series, their equivalent capacitance is

$$\frac{1}{C_s} = \frac{1}{C_1} + \frac{1}{C_2} + \cdots + \frac{1}{C_N} \tag{3.8}$$

Combining capacitors in series or parallel

Using Kirchhoff's current law we can show that if N capacitors are connected in parallel, their equivalent capacitance is

$$C_p = C_1 + C_2 + \cdots + C_N \tag{3.9}$$

Note that capacitors in series combine like resistors in parallel and capacitors in parallel combine like resistors in series.

Example 3.2

Let us find the total capacitance C_T at the terminals A-B of the network shown in Figure 3.4(a).

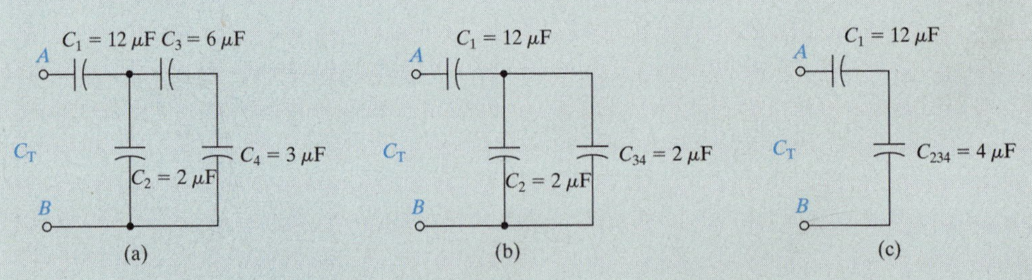

FIGURE 3.4 Circuits used in Example 3.2.

C_3 and C_4 are in series and therefore,

$$\frac{1}{C_{34}} = \frac{1}{C_3} + \frac{1}{C_4} = \frac{1}{6\ \mu\text{F}} + \frac{1}{3\ \mu\text{F}}$$

$$C_{34} = 2\ \mu\text{F}$$

Then C_2 and C_{34} are in parallel as shown in Figure 3.3(b) and hence

$$\begin{aligned} C_{234} &= C_2 + C_{34} \\ &= 4\ \mu\text{F} \end{aligned}$$

Finally, C_1 and C_{234} are in series as shown in Figure 3.3(c) and hence the total capacitance is

$$\frac{1}{C_T} = \frac{1}{C_1} + \frac{1}{C_{234}}$$

$$C_T = 3\ \mu\text{F}$$

Drill Exercise

D3.1. Find the total capacitance of the network in Figure D3.1.

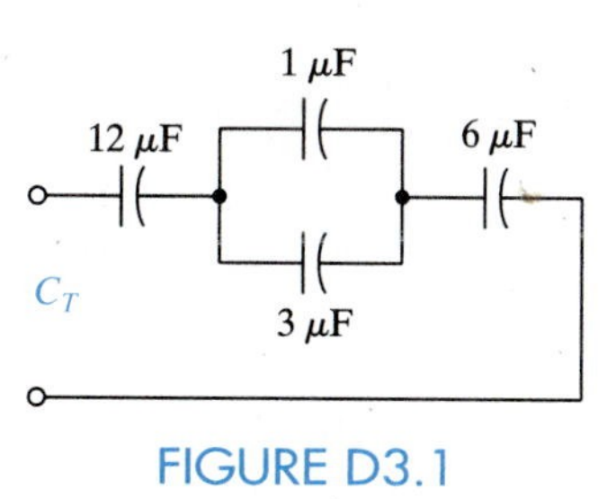

FIGURE D3.1

Ans: 2 μF.

3.2.4 Inductors

The ideal *inductor* is a circuit element that consists of a conducting wire that is wound around a core. The core material may range from some nonmagnetic material to a ferro-magnetic material. These elements are employed in a variety of electric equipment and form the basis for large power transformers.

Two typical inductors and their electrical symbol are shown in Figure 3.5. The flux lines for nonmagnetic core inductors, shown in Figure 3.5(a), extend beyond the inductor itself. In contrast, a magnetic core confines the flux, as shown in Figure 3.5(b).

Some typical inductors that could be purchased in an electronic parts store are shown in Figure 3.6

The inductor and its units

The American inventor Joseph Henry discovered that the voltage/current relationship for an inductor is

$$v(t) = L\frac{di(t)}{dt} \tag{3.10}$$

where the constant of proportionality L is called the inductance, and is measured in the unit "Henry." Practical inductors typically range from a few microhenrys to tens of henries. Equa-

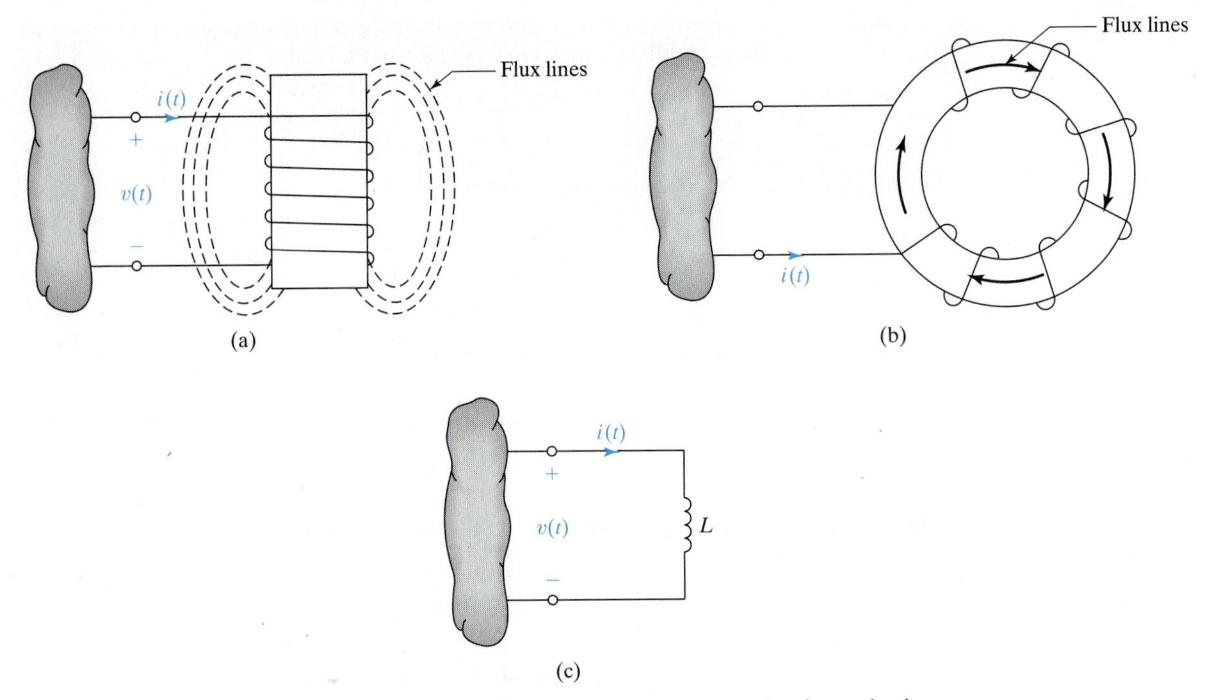

FIGURE 3.5 Inductors and their electrical symbol.

tion (3.10) indicates that 1 henry is dimensionally equal to 1 volt-second per ampere. The relationship described by Eq. (3.10) indicates that a voltage that is produced by a changing magnetic field is proportional to the time rate of change of the current that generates the magnetic field. Note, however, if the current is constant, the voltage across the inductor is zero, that is, $di/dt = 0$.

FIGURE 3.6 Some examples of practical inductors.

The current–voltage–energy interrelationships for an inductor

Therefore, in a situation analogous to the capacitor *if the current in an inductor is constant, the voltage across the inductor is zero and the inductor acts like a short circuit,* a fact we will use extensively later in the chapter.

3.2.5 Energy Stored in an Inductor

Following an identical development of the equations for a capacitor, the current in an inductor can be written as

$$i(t) = \frac{1}{L}\int_{-\infty}^{t} v(x)\,dx \tag{3.11}$$

or

$$i(t) = i(t_o) + \frac{1}{L}\int_{t_o}^{t} v(x)\,dx \tag{3.12}$$

The power delivered to an inductor is

$$\begin{aligned} p(t) &= v(t)i(t) \\ &= \left[L\frac{di(t)}{dt}\right]i(t) \end{aligned} \tag{3.13}$$

By integrating the power we find the energy stored in the magnetic field is

$$w_L(t) = \int_{-\infty}^{t}\left[L\frac{di(x)}{dx}\right]i(x)\,dx$$

or

$$w_L(t) = \frac{1}{2}Li^2(t) \qquad \textit{joules} \tag{3.14}$$

A practical inductor cannot store energy as well as a practical capacitor because there is always some winding resistance in the coil, which quickly dissipates energy. In addition, just as the voltage across a capacitor cannot change instantaneously, the current in an inductor cannot change instantaneously. This point is very useful in transient analysis and we will apply it there.

Example 3.3

If the current in a 10mH inductor has the waveform shown in Figure 3.7(a), let us determine the waveform for the voltage.

The equations that describe the waveform within the time intervals are

$$\begin{aligned} i(t) &= \frac{(20 \times 10^{-3})t}{2 \times 10^{-3}} & 0 \le t \le 2\text{ ms} \\ &= \frac{-(20 \times 10^{-3})t}{2 \times 10^{-3}} + 40 \times 10^{-3} & 2 \le t \le 4\text{ ms} \\ &= 0 & 4\text{ ms} \le t \end{aligned}$$

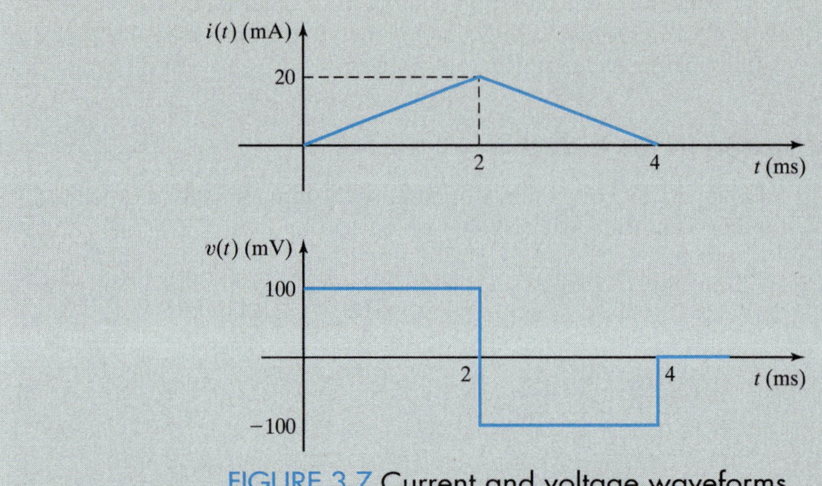

FIGURE 3.7 Current and voltage waveforms for a 10 mH inductor.

Using Eq. (3.10) we obtain

$$v(t) = (10 \times 10^{-3})\frac{20 \times 10^{-3}}{2 \times 10^{-3}} \qquad 0 \le t \le 2 \text{ ms}$$

$$= 100 \text{ mV}$$

and

$$v(t) = (10 \times 10^{-3})\left(\frac{-20 \times 10^{-3}}{2 \times 10^{-3}}\right) \qquad 2 \le t \le 4 \text{ ms}$$

$$= -100 \text{ mV}$$

and

$$v(t) = 0 \qquad 4 \text{ ms} \le t$$

Hence, the voltage waveform is shown in Figure 3.7(b).

3.2.6 Inductor Combinations

Inductors combine in exactly the same manner as resistors. For example, using Kirchhoff's voltage law we can show that if N inductors are connected in series, their equivalent inductance is

$$L_s = L_1 + L_2 + \cdots + L_N \tag{3.15}$$

Combining inductors in series or parallel

Furthermore, using Kirchhoff's current law we can show that if N inductors are connected in parallel, their equivalent inductance is

$$\frac{1}{L_p} = \frac{1}{L_1} + \frac{1}{L_2} + \cdots + \frac{1}{L_N} \tag{3.16}$$

Example 3.4

We wish to determine the total inductance L_T at the terminals A-B of the circuit shown in Figure 3.8(a).

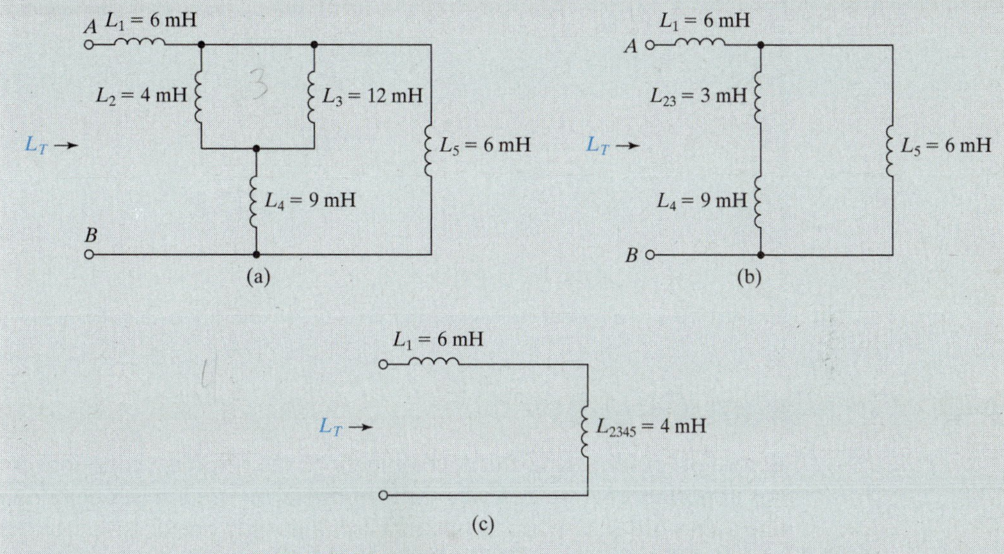

FIGURE 3.8 Circuits used in Example 3.4.

Note that L_5 cannot be combined with L_3 or L_4. However, L_2 and L_3 are in parallel, and hence

$$\frac{1}{L_{23}} = \frac{1}{L_2} + \frac{1}{L_3} = \frac{1}{4\text{ mH}} + \frac{1}{12\text{ mH}}$$

$$L_{23} = 3\text{ mH}$$

As shown in Figure 3.8(b), L_{23} and L_4 are in series, and hence

$$L_{234} = L_{23} + L_4$$
$$= 12\text{ mH}$$

L_{234} and L_5 are in parallel and therefore,

$$\frac{1}{L_{2345}} = \frac{1}{L_{234}} + \frac{1}{L_5}$$

$$L_{2345} = 4\text{ mH}$$

Then, from Figure 3.8(c)

$$L_T = L_1 + L_{2345}$$
$$= 10\text{ mH}$$

Drill Exercise

D3.2. Find the total inductance in the network in Figure D3.2.

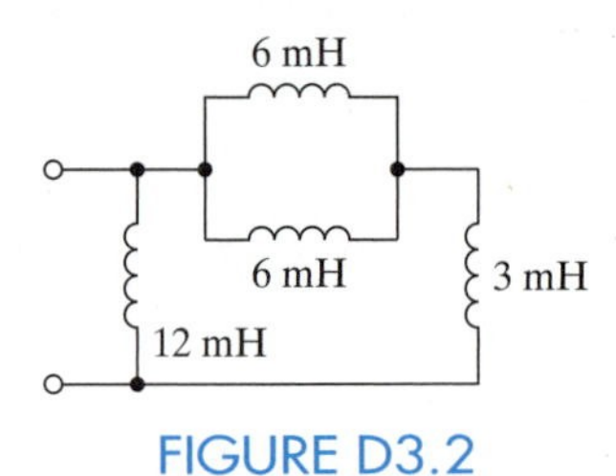

FIGURE D3.2

Ans: $L_T = 4$ mH.

3-3 First-Order Circuits

Before proceeding with the development of the response equations for first-order networks it is important that we describe some of the terms used in this development. To begin, we define a first-order network as one that contains only one passive storage element, that is, a capacitor or an inductor. The transient analysis we will perform examines the transition of voltages and currents in the network that take place as a result of opening or closing a switch during the time interval between two steady-state conditions. These steady-state conditions exist when the network is in a quiescent state and all voltages and currents have maintained their values for a very long period of time.

Consider now the two networks, each with a single passive storage element, shown in Figure 3.9. In each case, at time $t = 0$, a switch is closed and we wish to determine the equation that describes the operation of the network for time $t > 0$. In the capacitive circuit, our approach is to use KCL to describe the capacitor voltage, and in the inductive circuit we use KVL to describe the inductor current.

By employing KCL at the node between the resistor and capacitor in the RC network we obtain the equation that describes the capacitor voltage for $t > 0$ as

$$C\frac{dv(t)}{dt} = \frac{v(t) - V_S}{R} = 0$$

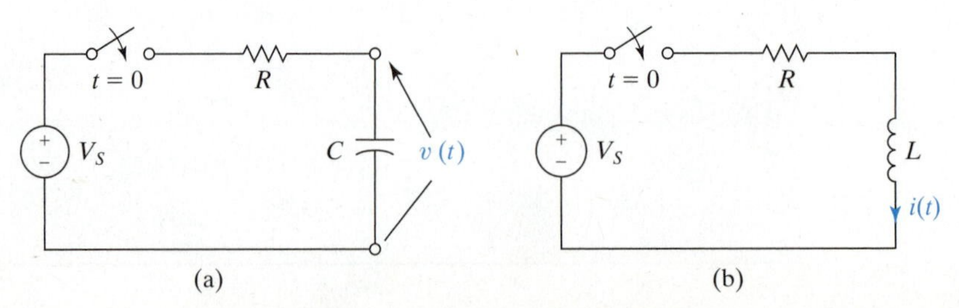

FIGURE 3.9 RC and RL circuits.

or

$$\frac{dv(t)}{dt} + \frac{v(t)}{RC} = \frac{V_S}{RC} \tag{3.17}$$

In a similar manner, the KVL equation that describes the inductor current for $t > 0$ is

$$L\frac{di(t)}{dt} + Ri(t) = V_S$$

or

$$\frac{di(t)}{dt} + \frac{R}{L}i(t) = \frac{V_S}{L} \tag{3.18}$$

Thus, we find that a network with only a single storage element can be described by a differential equation of the form

$$\frac{dx(t)}{dt} + \alpha\, x(t) = A \tag{3.19}$$

where $x(t)$ represents $v(t)$ or $i(t)$. The general solution of this equation is

$$x(t) = K_1 + K_2 e^{-t/\tau} \tag{3.20}$$

The general equation for first-order transient circuits

where K_1, K_2, and τ are constant terms. The term K_1 is known as the steady-state solution since after a very long period of time, that is, $t \to \infty$, the term $K_2 e^{-t/\tau} \to 0$. The term τ is called the time constant of the network and we will show that $\tau = RC$ for an RC network and L/R for an RL network.

3.3.1 Series *RC* Network Solution

The differential equation that describes the RC network shown in Figure 3.9(a) was found to be

$$\frac{dv(t)}{dt} + \frac{v(t)}{RC} = \frac{V_S}{RC}$$

Substituting the general solution in Equation (3.20) into the differential equation yields

$$\frac{-K_2}{\tau}e^{-t/\tau} + \frac{K_1}{RC} + \frac{K_2}{RC}e^{-t/\tau} = \frac{V_S}{RC}$$

Equating the constant and exponential terms, we obtain

$$K_1 = V_S$$

$$\tau = RC$$

Therefore, the solution of the differential equation can be expressed as

$$v(t) = V_S + K_2 e^{-t/RC}$$

where, as indicated earlier, V_S is the steady-state value and RC is the network's time constant. The only unknown in the equation, K_2, can be determined by the initial condition on the capacitor. If the capacitor voltage is zero at $t = 0$, then

$$0 = V_S + K_2$$

or

$$K_2 = -V_S$$

Hence, the complete solution for $v(t)$ is

$$v(t) = V_s - V_s e^{-t/RC}$$

3.3.2 Series *RL* Network Solution

The differential equation that describes the *RL* network shown in Figure 3.9(b) was found to be

$$\frac{di(t)}{dt} + \frac{R}{L} i(t) = \frac{V_s}{L}$$

Once again, substituting Equation (3.20) into this differential equation and equating constant and exponential terms yields

$$i(t) = \frac{V_S}{R} + K_2 e^{-(\frac{R}{L})t}$$

where V_S/R is the steady-state value and L/R is the time constant. If the inductor current is zero at $t = 0$, then

$$0 = \frac{V_s}{R} + K_2$$

or

$$K_2 = -\frac{V_s}{R}$$

Therefore,

$$i(t) = \frac{V_S}{R} - \frac{V_S}{R} e^{-(\frac{R}{L})t}$$

3.3.3 The Network Time Constant

Some properties of the time constant are illustrated in Figure 3.10. Figure 3.10(a) illustrates that the value of $x_c(t) = K_2 e^{-t/\tau}$ is $0.368K_2$ at $t = \tau$, $0.135K_2$ at $t = 2\tau$, and so on. In other words, in one time constant the value of the function drops by 63.2%. In five time constants $x_c(t) = .0067K_2$, which is less than 1% of its original value.

The time constant and its impact

Figure 3.10(b) illustrates the difference between a large time constant, that is, slow response, and a small time constant, that is, fast response. If the time constant is large, a long time is required for the network to settle down to its steady-state value. However, if the time constant is small, steady state is reached quickly. Air conditioning systems have relatively slow time constants. If the thermostat in a room is moved from 75°F to 70°F, several minutes will be required to cool the area to the desired temperature, and thus on a plot of temperature versus time, the curve would be relatively flat. In contrast, the switching time for transistors on a very large-scale integrated circuit is typically measured in nanoseconds to picoseconds.

Finally, it is very important to note that, although the two networks in Figure 3.9—upon which our analysis thus far has been based—are quite simple, by using Thevenin's theorem we can reduce more complicated networks to these two forms.

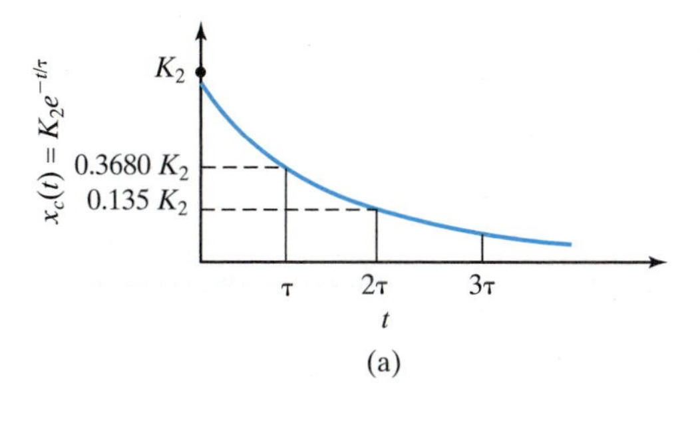

(a)

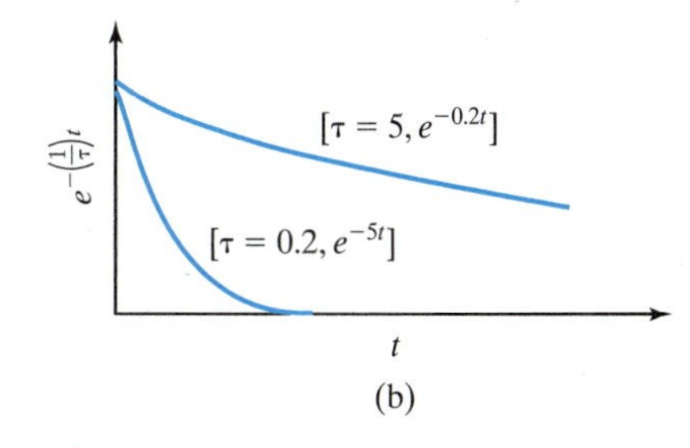

(b)

FIGURE 3.10 Time constant properties.

3.3.4 The Analysis Procedure

As we begin the analysis procedure and illustrate it through a number of examples, it is important to recall two key assumptions that are employed throughout the analysis

- In a steady-state condition, the capacitor voltage is constant, its current is zero, and therefore the capacitor looks like an open circuit.
- In a steady-state condition, the inductor current is constant, its voltage is zero, and the inductor looks like a short circuit.

The following examples illustrate our approach to transient analysis.

Example 3.5

For the circuit in Figure 3.11(a), the switch opens at $t = 0$. We wish to find $v_o(t)$ for $t > 0$.

We begin our analysis by assuming that the network in Figure 3.11(a) is in steady state prior to opening the switch. Under this condition, the capacitor can be replaced by an open circuit because the source voltage is constant and therefore the current in the capacitor is $C\frac{dv_c(t)}{dt} = 0$. The resulting network in Figure 3.11(b) is a simple voltage divider and thus $v_c(0)$, the initial capacitor voltage, is 8 V. Now that the initial condition on the capacitor is known, we examine the circuit that results from opening the switch.

The network for $t > 0$ is shown in Figure 3.11(c). At this point we write an equation in terms of the voltage across the capacitor. Applying KCL to this circuit yields

$$C\frac{dv_c(t)}{dt} + \frac{v_c(t)}{R_2} = 0$$

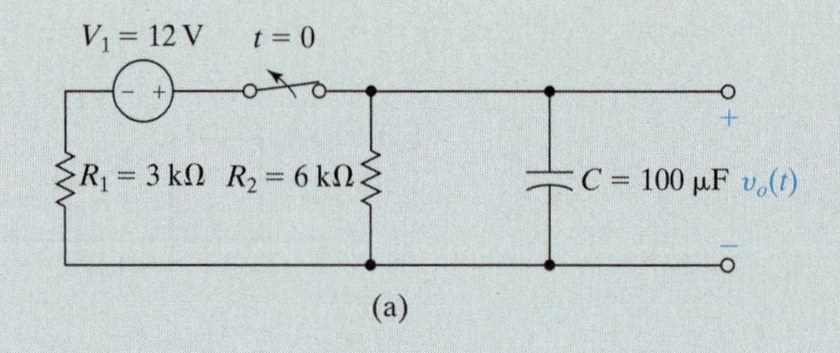

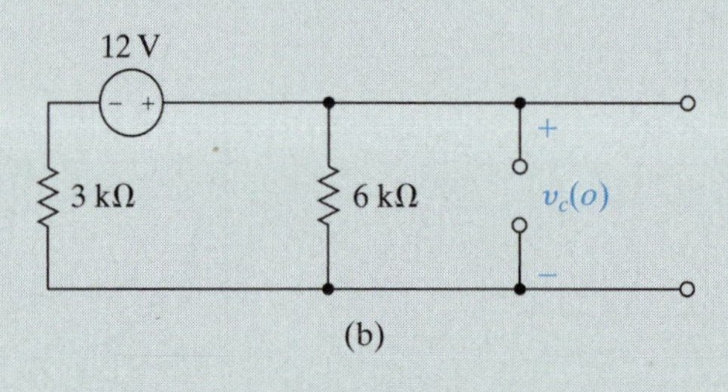

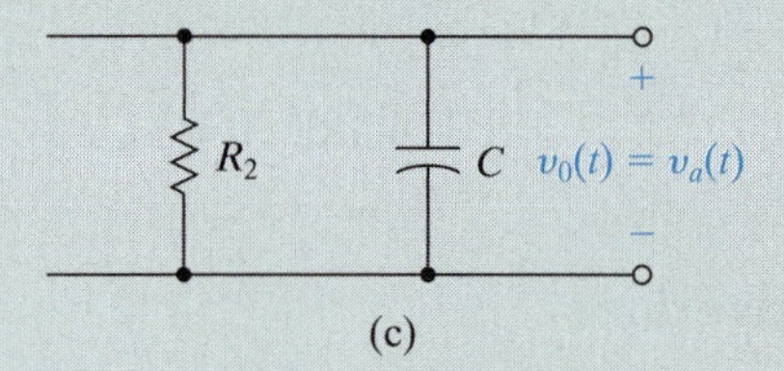

FIGURE 3.11 Circuits used in Example 3.5.

or

$$\frac{dv_c(t)}{dt} + \frac{v_c(t)}{R_2C} = 0$$

As indicated earlier, if we assume the solution is of the form

$$v_c(t) = K_2e^{-t/\tau}$$

then substituting this expression into the differential equation yields

$$\frac{-K_2e^{-t/\tau}}{\tau} + \frac{K_2e^{-t/\tau}}{R_2C} = 0$$

and the time constant for the circuit is

$$\tau = R_2C$$

Therefore,

$$v_c(t) = K_2e^{-t/R_2C}$$

However, from the initial condition we know that

$$v_c(0) = 8$$

Hence, the complete solution is

$$v_c(t) = 8e^{-t/R_2C}$$
$$= 8e^{-t/0.6} \text{ volts}$$

where, as shown in Figure 3.11(a), $v_o(t) = v_c(t)$. A plot of this function is shown in Figure 3.12.

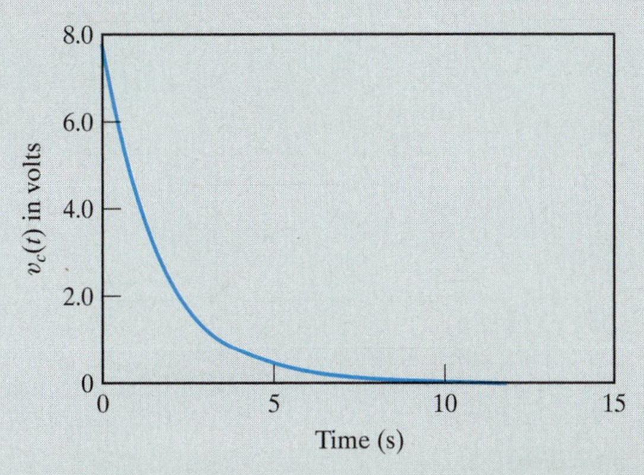

FIGURE 3.12 A plot of $v_c(t)$ as a function of t.

Example 3.6

In the network in Figure 3.13(a), the switch closes at $t = 0$. We wish to find $v_o(t)$ for $t > 0$.

Assuming the network in Figure 3.13(a) is in steady state prior to closing the switch, the inductor can be replaced by a short circuit because the voltage source is constant, therefore the current in the inductor is constant, and hence $v_L(t) = Ldi_2(t)/dt = 0$. The resulting network in Figure 3.13(b) illustrates that $i_L(0) = 2\text{A}$. Now that the initial condition on the inductor is known, we examine the circuits that result from closing the switch.

The network for $t > 0$ is shown in Figure 3.13(c). At this point we write an equation in terms of the current through the inductor. Applying KVL to this circuit yields

$$L\frac{di_L(t)}{dt} + R_2 i_L(t) = 0$$

or

$$\frac{di_L(t)}{dt} + \frac{R_2}{L}i_L(t) = 0$$

Again, we assume a solution of the form

$$i_L(t) = K_2 e^{-t/\tau}$$

Following a development identical to that illustrated in Example 3.5 we find that

$$\tau = \frac{L}{R_2}$$

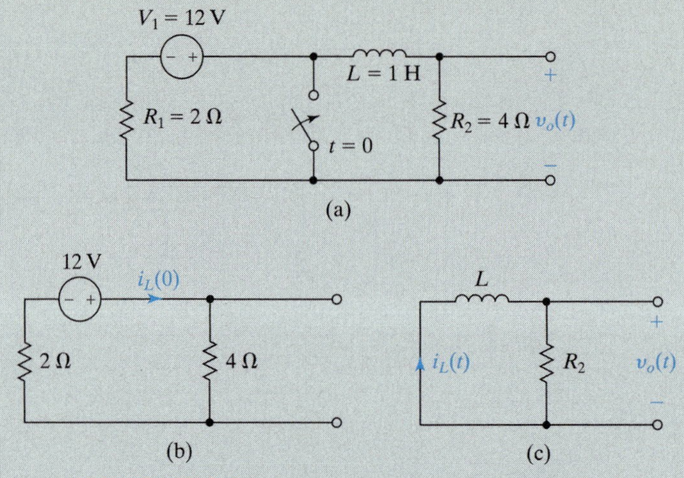

FIGURE 3.13 Circuits used in Example 3.6.

and hence

$$i_L(t) = K_2 e^{-\frac{R_2 t}{L}}$$

Employing the initial condition

$$i_L(0) = 2 = K_2$$

Therefore,

$$i_L(t) = 2e^{-4t} \text{ A}$$

Then

$$\begin{aligned} v_o(t) &= R_2 i_L(t) \\ &= 8e^{-4t} \text{ V} \end{aligned}$$

A plot of this function is shown in Figure 3.14.

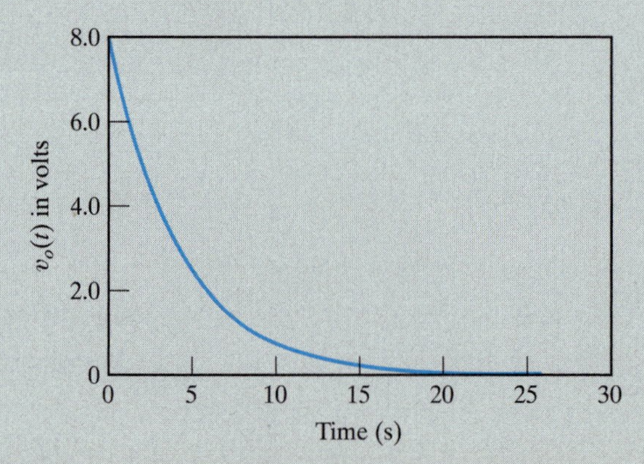

FIGURE 3.14 A plot of $v_o(t)$ as a function of t.

Example 3.7

We wish to find both $v_c(t)$ and $v_o(t)$ for $t > 0$ in the network in Figure 3.15(a).

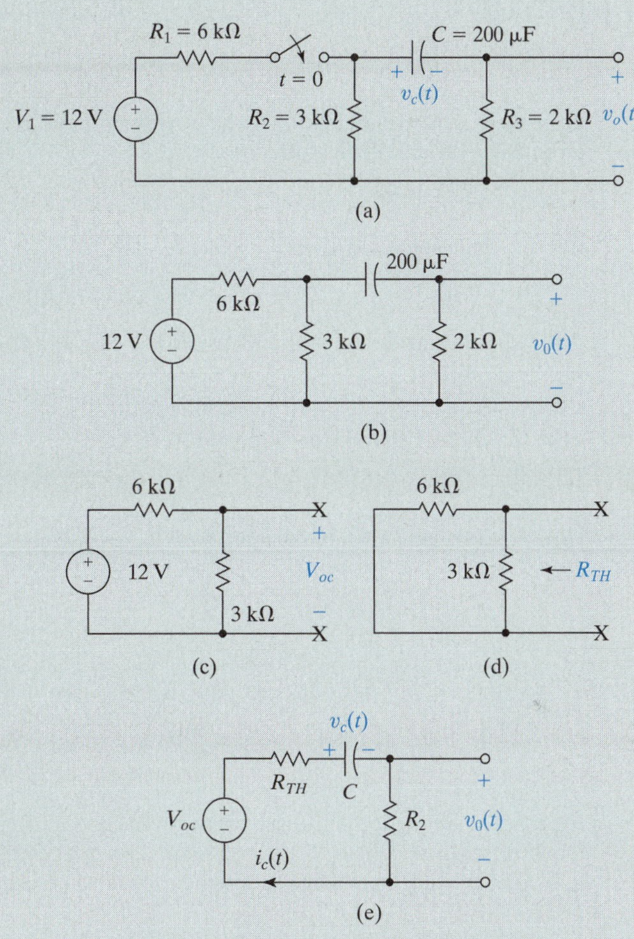

FIGURE 3.15 Circuits used in Example 3.7.

Assuming the network is in steady state prior to closing the switch, we find that the initial voltage on the capacitor is 0 since the voltage source is not yet connected to the remainder of the circuit.

The network for $t > 0$ is shown in Figure 3.15(b). This network can be simplified by replacing V_1, R_1, and R_2 with its Thevenin equivalent. The open-circuit voltage derived from Figure 3.15(c) is $V_{oc} = 4$ V and the Thevenin equivalent resistance determined from the circuit in Figure 3.15(d) is $R_{TH} = 2$ kΩ. Hence, the circuit in Figure 3.15(b) reduces to that shown in Figure 3.15(e). The voltage across the capacitor in Figure 3.15(e) can be expressed as

$$C\frac{dv_c(t)}{dt} = i_c(t)$$

Applying KVL to the circuit yields the equation

$$V_{oc} = R_{TH}i_c(t) + v_c(t) + R_2 i_c(t)$$

Combining the last two equations yields the expression

$$\frac{dv_c(t)}{dt} + \frac{v_c(t)}{(R_{TH} + R_2)C} = \frac{V_{oc}}{(R_{TH} + R_1)C}$$

Since there is a constant forcing function present in the equation, the solution of this first-order differential equation will be of the form

$$v_c(t) = K_1 + K_2 e^{-t/\tau}$$

where as indicated earlier

$$\tau = (R_{TH} + R_2)C$$

Since in steady state the capacitor looks like an open circuit, $v_c(t = \infty) = V_{oc}$. Therefore,

$$v_c(\infty) = V_{oc} = K_1 + 0$$

since the exponential approaches 0 as $t \to \infty$. Then

$$v_c(t) = V_{oc} + K_2 e^{-t/\tau}$$

However, employing the initial condition

$$v_c(0) = 0 = V_{oc} + K_2$$

or

$$K_2 = -V_{oc}$$

Therefore, using the circuit parameters the expression for $v_c(t)$ becomes

$$v_c(t) = 4 - 4e^{-t/0.8}\text{ V}$$

Note that this equation satisfies both the initial and final values of the function $v_c(t)$. A plot of this function is shown in Figure 3.16. Recall, however, that we also wish to find the output voltage, $v_o(t)$, for $t > 0$. Knowing the voltage across the capacitor, we can compute the current via the equation

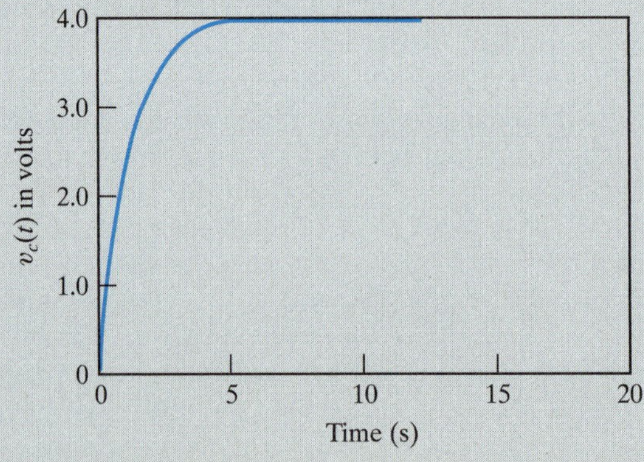

FIGURE 3.16 A plot of $v_c(t)$ as a function of t.

$$i_c(t) = C\frac{dv_c(t)}{dt}$$

and using this result we can determine the voltage $v_o(t)$ from the expression

$$v_o(t) = R_2 i_c(t)$$

Performing the operation indicated by the two equations above yields

$$v_o(t) = 2e^{-t/0.8}\ V$$

Before proceeding further, it is instructive to summarize the approach that is being employed to perform a transient analysis. In a systematic fashion we have first used the original circuit prior to switch action to determine the initial capacitor voltage $v_c(0)$ or inductor current $i_L(0)$. Second, for the network that exists after switch action we have derived an expression for the capacitor voltage, $v_c(t)$, or inductor current, $i_L(t)$. This expression yields the time constant of the network, τ. Third, the initial and final conditions are used to determine the constraints in the equation for either the capacitor voltage, $v_c(t)$, or inductor current, $i_L(t)$. Finally, if the unknown is neither the capacitor voltage nor inductor current, equations that describe the network are used in conjunction with $v_c(t)$ or $i_L(t)$ to determine the desired quantity.

Let us consider now an example in which the forcing function is not a constant. In this case, as stated earlier, the particular integral solution will consist of functional forms of the forcing function and its first derivative.

Example 3.8

We wish to determine $v_o(t)$ for $t > 0$ in the network in Figure 3.17(a).

In the steady state prior to closing the switch the current in the inductor is zero and hence $i(0) = 0$.

For $t > 0$, KVL for the network yields

$$L\frac{di(t)}{dt} + Ri(t) = v_S(t)$$

or

$$\frac{di(t)}{dt} + \frac{R}{L}i(t) = \frac{v_S(t)}{L}$$

Using the known parameters the equation becomes

$$\frac{di(t)}{dt} + 2i(t) = 6e^{-4t} \qquad t > 0$$

The complementary solution is derived from the equation

$$\frac{di_c(t)}{dt} + 2i_c(t) = 0 \qquad t > 0$$

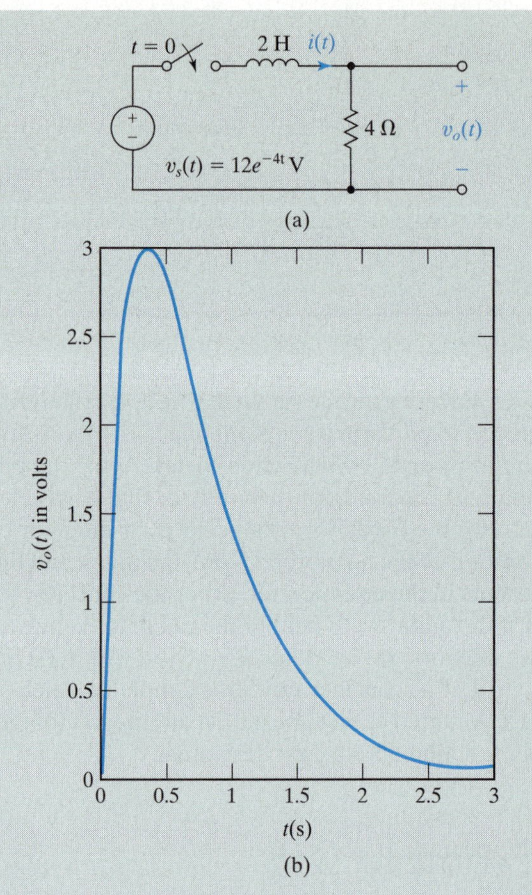

FIGURE 3.17 A circuit and its transient response.

and hence

$$i_c(t) = K_2 e^{-2t}$$

The particular solution is obtained from the equation

$$\frac{di_p(t)}{dt} + 2i_p(t) = 6e^{-4t} \qquad t > 0$$

Assuming that $i_p(t)$ is of the form of the input and its derivatives, we select $i_p(t) = K_1 e^{-4t}$. Then

$$\frac{d}{dt}(K_1 e^{-4t}) + 2K_1 e^{-4t} = 6e^{-4t}$$

or

$$-4K_1 + 2K_1 = 6$$

$$K_1 = -3$$

Hence

$$i(t) = i_c(t) + i_p(t)$$
$$= K_2e^{-2t} - 3e^{-4t}$$

However, $i(0) = 0$, and therefore,

$$0 = K_2 - 3$$

or

$$K_2 = 3$$

then

$$i(t) = 3[e^{-2t} - e^{-4t}] \text{ A}$$

and

$$v_o(t) = 12[e^{-2t} - e^{-4t}] \text{ V}$$

This voltage is shown plotted in Figure 3.17(b).

Drill Exercises

D3.3. Find $i_o(t)$ and $v_o(t)$ for $t > 0$ in the network in Figure D3.3.

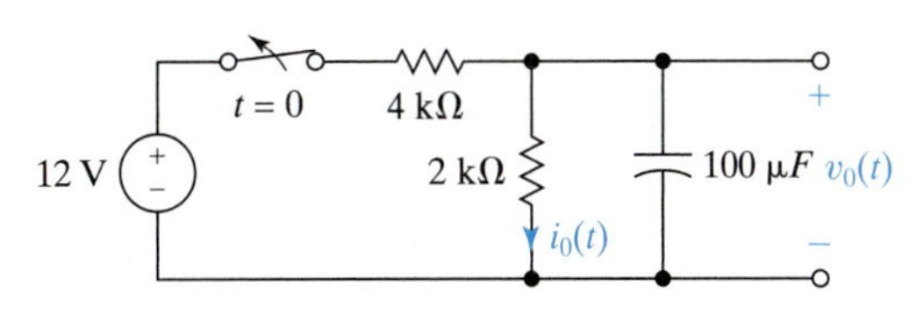

FIGURE D3.3

Ans: $v_o(t) = 4e^{-t/0.2}$ V and $i_o(t) = 2e^{-t/0.2}$ mA.

D3.4. Find $v_o(t)$ for $t > 0$ in the network in Figure D3.4.

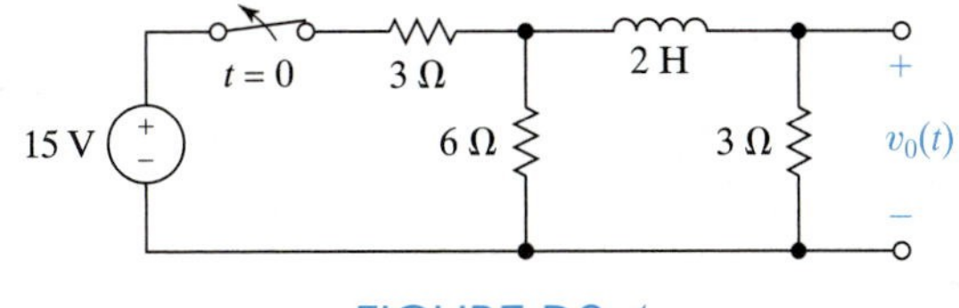

FIGURE D3.4

Ans: $v_o(t) = 6e^{-4.5t}$ V.

D3.5. Find $i(t)$ for $t > 0$ in the network in Figure D3.5.

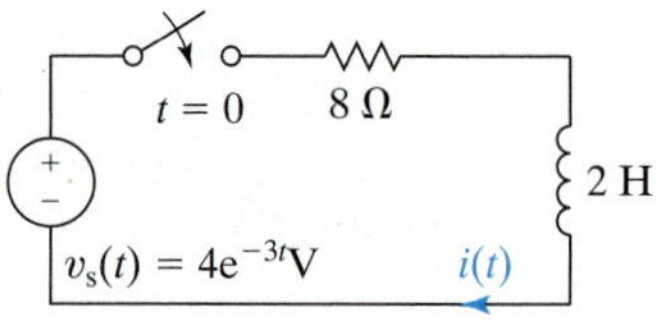

$t = 0$ $8\ \Omega$ $2\ \mathrm{H}$

$v_s(t) = 4e^{-3t}\mathrm{V}$ $i(t)$

FIGURE D3.5

Ans: $i(t) = 2[e^{-3t} - e^{-4t}]$ A.

3-4 Second-Order Circuits

Let us now extend our analysis to the case where a capacitor and inductor are present in the network simultaneously. Consider, for example, the two basic RLC circuits shown in Figure 3.18.

If we follow the procedure outlined for first-order circuits and write the KCL equation for the network in Figure 3.18(a) and the KVL equation for the network in Figure 3.18(b) and differentiate the resulting equations with respect to time, we obtain

$$\begin{aligned} \frac{d^2v(t)}{dt^2} + \frac{1}{RC}\frac{dv(t)}{dt} + \frac{1}{LC}v(t) &= 0 \\ \frac{d^2i(t)}{dt^2} + \frac{R}{L}\frac{di(t)}{dt} + \frac{1}{LC}i(t) &= 0 \end{aligned} \tag{3.21}$$

Note that both circuits lead to second-order differential equations with constant coefficients. These equations can be expressed in a more general form as

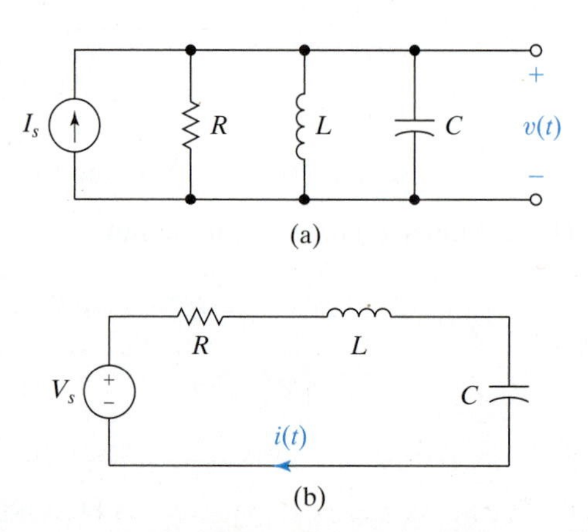

FIGURE 3.18 Parallel and series RLC circuits.

$$\frac{d^2x(t)}{dt^2} + 2\alpha\frac{dx(t)}{dt} + \omega_0^2\,x(t) = 0 \tag{3.22}$$

where again $x(t)$ represents either $v(t)$ or $i(t)$.

An important equation that is related to this differential equation is called the *characteristic equation*. This equation is expressed in the form

$$s^2 + 2\,\alpha s + \omega_0^2 = 0 \tag{3.23}$$

Three critically important terms for second-order transient circuits

where s is simply a convenient variable. The terms α and ω_0 are important factors: α is known as the exponential *damping coefficient* and ω_0 is called the *undamped natural frequency*. The roots of the characteristic equation, which can be obtained using the quadratic formula, can be expressed as

$$\begin{aligned} s_1 &= -\alpha + \sqrt{\alpha^2 - \omega_0^2} \\ s_2 &= -\alpha - \sqrt{\alpha^2 - \omega_0^2} \end{aligned} \tag{3.24}$$

s_1 and s_2 are called *natural frequencies* because they determine the natural, that is, unforced, response of the network.

By unforced response we mean the manner in which the network responds to an initial voltage on a capacitor or an initial current through an inductor. The natural (unforced) response will be in one of three forms depending upon the values of α and ω_0.

The three cases of damping

Case 1, $\alpha > \omega_0$. This is commonly called *overdamped*. The natural frequencies s_1 and s_2 are real and unequal, and therefore the natural response is of the form

$$x_c(t) = K_1 e^{-(\alpha - \sqrt{\alpha^2 - \omega_0^2})t} + K_2 e^{-(\alpha + \sqrt{\alpha^2 - \omega_0^2})t} \tag{3.25}$$

where K_1 and K_2 are found from the initial conditions. This indicates that the natural response is the sum of two decaying exponentials.

Case 2, $\alpha < \omega_0$. This case is called *underdamped*. Since $\omega_0 > \alpha$, we can employ Euler's identities to show that the response can be written as

$$x_c(t) = e^{-\alpha t}\left(A_1 \cos\sqrt{\omega_0^2 - \alpha^2}\,t + A_2 \sin\sqrt{\omega_0^2 - \alpha^2}\,t\right) \tag{3.26}$$

where A_1 and A_2, like K_1 and K_2, are constants, which are evaluated using the initial conditions $x(0)$ and $dx(0)/dt$. The natural response in this case is an exponentially damped oscillation.

Case 3, $\alpha = \omega_0$. This case, called *critically damped,* results in

$$s_1 = s_2 = -\alpha$$

In the case where the characteristic equation has repeated roots, we can show that the general solution can be written as

$$x_c\,(t) = B_1 e^{-\alpha t} + B_2\,t e^{-\alpha t} \tag{3.27}$$

where B_1 and B_2 are constants derived from the initial conditions.

The results we have just presented are summarized in Table 3.1.

TABLE 3.1 Homogeneous Network Equation $\frac{d^2x(t)}{dt^2} + 2\alpha\frac{dx(t)}{dt} + \omega_0^2 x(t) = 0$

Damping Condition	Natural (Unforced) Response Equation	Type of Response
$\alpha > \omega_0$	$x(t) = K_1 e^{-(\alpha - \sqrt{\alpha^2 - \omega_0^2})t} + K_2 e^{-(\alpha + \sqrt{\alpha^2 - \omega_0^2})t}$	Overdamped
$\alpha < \omega_0$	$x(t) = e^{-\alpha t}[K_1 \cos \sqrt{\omega_0^2 - \alpha^2}t + K_2 \sin \sqrt{\omega_0^2 - \alpha^2}t]$	Underdamped
$\alpha = \omega_0$	$x(t) = K_1 e^{-\alpha t} + K_2 te^{-\alpha t}$	Critically damped

Drill Exercises

D3.6. A parallel RLC circuit has the following circuit parameters: $R = 1\ \Omega$, $L = 2$ H, and $C = 2$ F. Using Eq. (3.28) and (3.32), compute the damping ratio and the undamped natural frequency of this network.

Ans: $\alpha = 0.25$, $\omega_o = 0.5$ rad/s.

D3.7. A series RLC circuit consists of $R = 2\ \Omega$, $L = 1$ H, and a capacitor. Determine the type of response exhibited by the network if (a) $C = 1/2$ F, (b) $C = 1$ F, and (c) $C = 2$ F.

Ans: (a) underdamped, (b) critically damped, (c) overdamped.

3.4.1 The Analysis Procedure

We now analyze some simple RLC circuits that contain both nonzero initial conditions and constant forcing functions.

Example 3.9

Consider the network in Figure 3.19. The circuit parameters are $R = 2\ \Omega$, $L = 5$ H. $C = 1/5$ F, $i_L(0) = -1$ A, and $v_c(0) = 4$ V. We wish to determine the equation for the voltage $v(t)$.

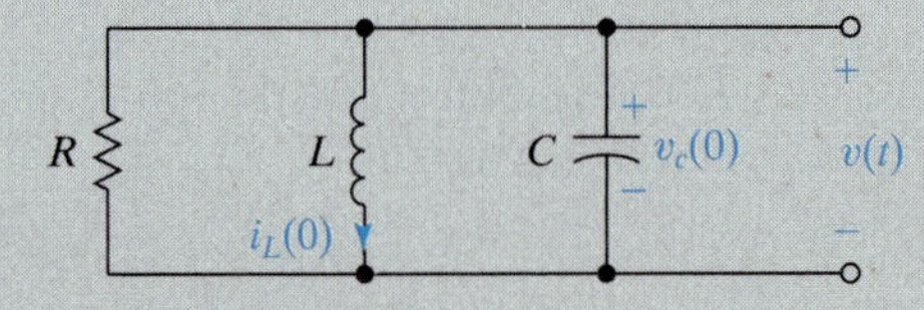

FIGURE 3.19 A parallel RLC circuit with initial conditions.

We know from Eq. (3.21) that the general form of the second-order differential equation that describes the voltage $v(t)$ is

$$\frac{d^2v(t)}{dt^2} + \frac{1}{RC}\frac{dv(t)}{dt} + \frac{1}{LC}v(t) = 0$$

With the given parameter values the equation becomes

$$\frac{d^2v(t)}{dt^2} + 2.5\frac{dv(t)}{dt} + v(t) = 0$$

The characteristic equation for the network is

$$s^2 + 2.5s + 1 = 0$$

and the roots are

$$s_1 = -2$$

$$s_2 = -0.5$$

Since the roots are real and unequal, the circuit is overdamped, and $v(t)$ is of the form

$$v(t) = K_1e^{-2t} + K_2e^{-0.5t}$$

The initial conditions are now employed to determine the constants K_1 and K_2. Since $v(t) = v_c(t)$

$$v_c(0) = v(0) = 4 = K_1 + K_2$$

The second equation needed to determine K_1 and K_2 is normally obtained from the expression

$$\frac{dv(t)}{dt} = -2K_1e^{-2t} - 0.5K_2e^{-0.5t}$$

However, the second initial condition is not given as $dv(0)/dt$; we were given $i_L(0)$. We can, however, circumvent this problem by noting that the node equation for the circuit can be written as

$$C\frac{dv(t)}{dt} + \frac{v(t)}{R} + i_L(t) = 0$$

or

$$\frac{dv(t)}{dt} = \frac{-1}{RC}v(t) - \frac{i_L(t)}{C}$$

At $t = 0$

$$\frac{dv(0)}{dt} = \frac{-1}{RC}v(0) - \frac{1}{C}i_L(0)$$

$$= -2.5(4) - 5(-1)$$

$$= -5$$

But since

$$\frac{dv(t)}{dt} = -2K_1e^{-2t} - 0.5K_2e^{-0.5t}$$

then when $t = 0$

$$-5 = -2K_1 - 0.5K_2$$

This equation together with the equation

$$4 = K_1 + K_2$$

produces the constants $K_1 = 2$ and $K_2 = 2$. Therefore, the final equation for the voltage is

$$v(t) = 2e^{-2t} + 2e^{-0.5t}\text{ V}$$

In addition, note that in comparison with the *RL* and *RC* circuits analyzed earlier, the response of this circuit is controlled by two time constants.

Example 3.10

Let us determine the equation for $v(t), t > 0$ in the network in Figure 3.20 if the network parameters are as follows: $R = 2\Omega$, $L = 4\text{H}$ and $C = \frac{4}{17}\text{F}$. The initial conditions are zero, that is, $i_L(0) = 0$ and $v_c(0) = 0$.

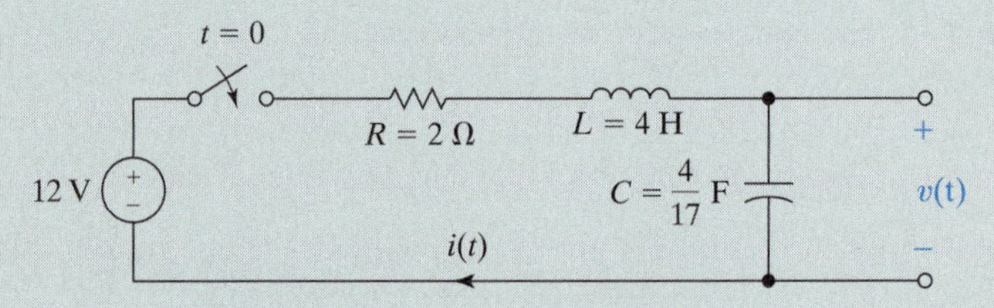

FIGURE 3.20 A series RLC circuit.

For $t > 0$, the KVL equation for the network is

$$Ri(t) + L\frac{di(t)}{dt} + v(t) = 12$$

where

$$i(t) = C\frac{dv(t)}{dt}$$

Combining these two equations yields

$$RC\frac{dv(t)}{dt} + LC\frac{d^2v(t)}{dt^2} + v(t) = 12$$

or

$$\frac{d^2v(t)}{dt^2} + \frac{R}{L}\frac{dv(t)}{dt} + \frac{1}{LC}v(t) = \frac{12}{LC}$$

which, given the network parameters, is

$$\frac{d^2v(t)}{dt^2} + \frac{1}{2}\frac{dv(t)}{dt} + \frac{17}{16}v(t) = \frac{51}{4}$$

The characteristic equation is

$$s^2 + \frac{1}{2}s + \frac{17}{16} = 0$$

and the roots are

$$s_1 = -\frac{1}{4} + j\frac{\sqrt{17}}{4}$$

$$s_2 = -\frac{1}{4} - j\frac{\sqrt{17}}{4}$$

Since the roots are complex, the circuit is underdamped. In addition, a constant forcing function is present, that is, the 12 volt source. Hence, the solution will be of the form

$$v(t) = K_1 e^{-t/4} \cos\frac{\sqrt{17}}{4}t + K_2 e^{-t/4} \sin\frac{\sqrt{17}}{4}t + K_3$$

Once again, we recall that in the steady state, the inductor looks like a short circuit and the capacitor looks like an open circuit. Therefore,

$$v(\infty) = v_c(\infty) = 12 = K_3$$

Thus

$$v(t) = K_1 e^{-t/4} \cos\frac{\sqrt{17}}{4}t + K_2 e^{-t/4} \sin\frac{\sqrt{17}}{4}t + 12$$

In addition,

$$v(0) = v_c(0) = 0 = K_1 + 12$$

or

$$K_1 = -12$$

then

$$v(t) = -12 e^{-t/4} \cos\frac{\sqrt{17}}{4}t + K_2 e^{-t/4} \sin\frac{\sqrt{17}}{4}t + 12$$

The initial condition on the inductor can be employed using the expression

$$i(t) = C\frac{dv(t)}{dt}$$

Therefore,

$$\begin{aligned}\frac{dv(t)}{dt} &= 3e^{-t/4}\cos\frac{\sqrt{17}}{4}t + 12\left(\frac{\sqrt{17}}{4}\right)e^{-t/4}\sin\frac{\sqrt{17}}{4}t - \frac{K_2}{4}e^{-t/4}\sin\frac{\sqrt{17}}{4}t + \frac{\sqrt{17}}{4}K_2 e^{-t/4}\cos\frac{\sqrt{17}}{4}t \\ &= \left[3 + \frac{\sqrt{17}}{4}K_2\right]e^{-t/4}\cos\frac{\sqrt{17}}{4}t + \left[12\left(\frac{\sqrt{17}}{4}\right) - \frac{K_2}{4}\right]e^{-t/4}\sin\frac{\sqrt{17}}{4}t\end{aligned}$$

then

$$i_L(0) = i(0) = 0 = 3 + \frac{\sqrt{17}}{4}K_2$$

$$K_2 = -\frac{12}{\sqrt{17}}$$

and as a result

$$v(t) = -12e^{-t/4}\cos\frac{\sqrt{17}}{4}t - \frac{12}{\sqrt{17}}e^{-t/4}\sin\frac{\sqrt{17}}{4}t + 12$$

Note that this equation satisfies the initial condition $v(0) = 0$. In addition, as $t \to \infty$ (the steady-state condition), the inductor acts like a short circuit and the capacitor acts like an open circuit so that 12 V appears at the output. The equation also satisfies this final condition, that is, $v(\infty) = 12$ V. A plot of this function is shown in Figure 3.21.

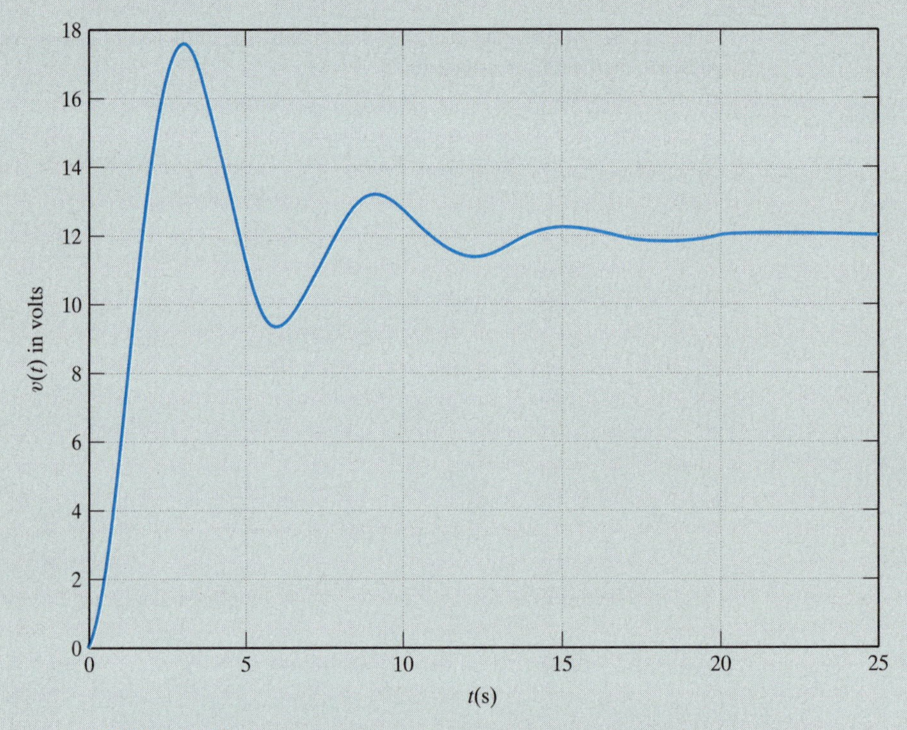

FIGURE 3.21 A plot of the output voltage in Example 3.10.

Drill Exercises

D3.8. The switch in the network in Figure D3.8 moves from position 1 to position 2 at $t = 0$. Find $v(t)$ for $t > 0$.

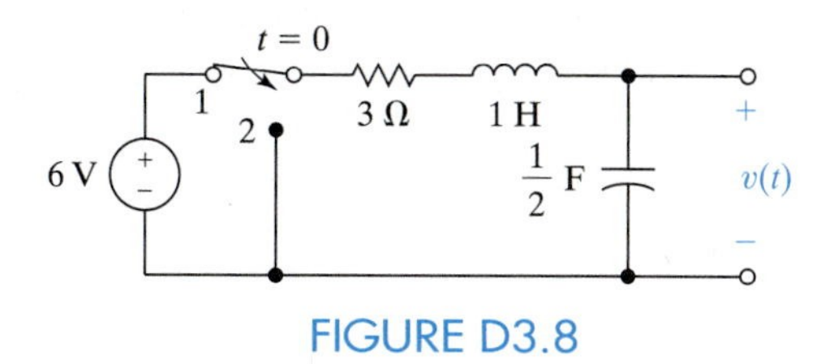

FIGURE D3.8

Ans: $v(t) = 12e^{-t} - 6e^{-2t}$ V.

D3.9. The switch in the network in Figure D3.9 moves from position 1 to position 2 at $t = 0$. Find $v(t)$ for $t > 0$.

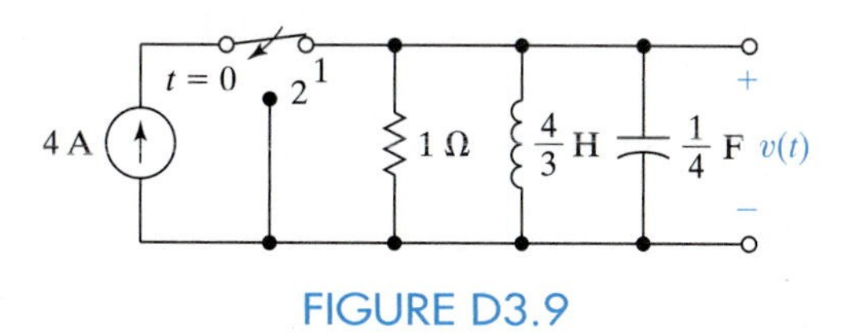

FIGURE D3.9

Ans: $v(t) = -8e^{-t} + 8e^{-3t}$ V.

Summary

- The capacitor equations are outlined in Figure 3.22.

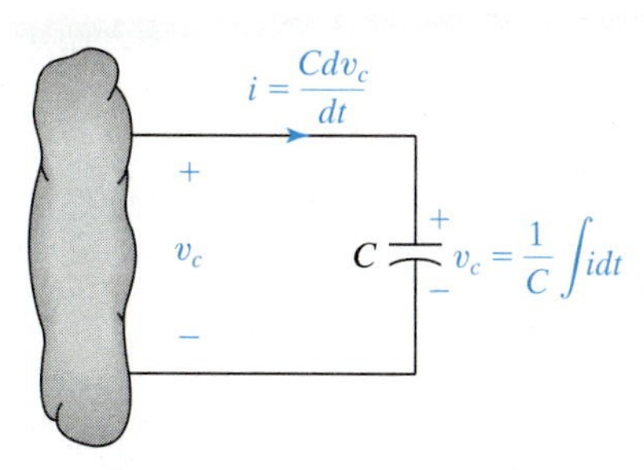

FIGURE 3.22 Capacitor-defining equations.

The energy stored in the capacitor is $W_C = \frac{1}{2}Cv_C^2$.

- Capacitors in series combine like resistors in parallel.

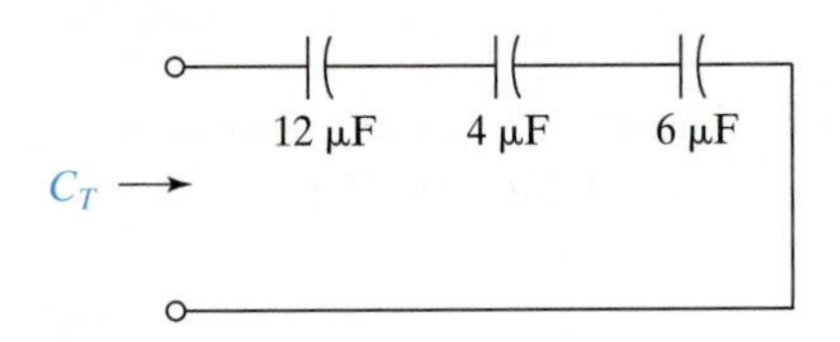

FIGURE 3.23 Capacitors in series.

$$\frac{1}{C_T} = \frac{1}{12\ \mu} + \frac{1}{4\ \mu} + \frac{1}{6\ \mu} \text{ and hence } C_T = 2\ \mu F$$

- Capacitors in parallel combine like resistors in series.

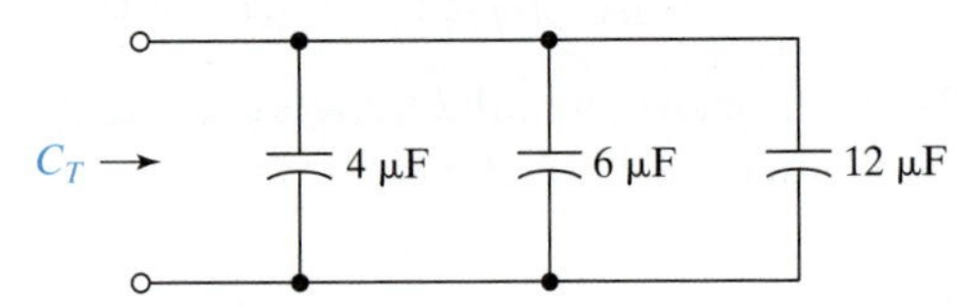

FIGURE 3.24 Capacitors in parallel.

$$C_T = 4\ \mu + 6\ \mu + 12\ \mu = 22\ \mu F$$

- The inductor equations are outlined in Figure 3.25.

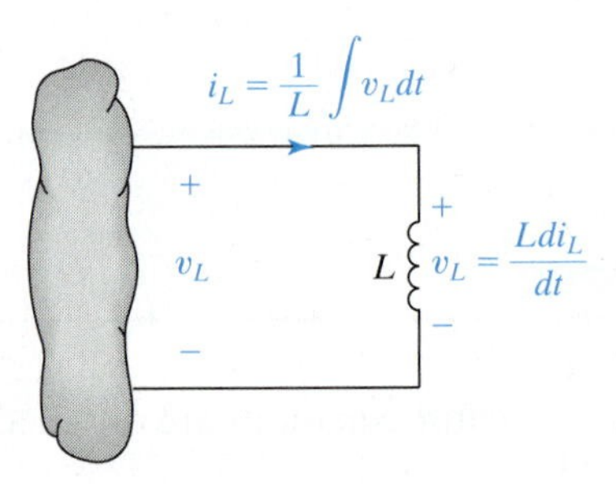

FIGURE 3.25 Inductor-defining equations.

The energy stored in the inductor is $W_L = \frac{1}{2}Li_L^2$.

- Inductors in series combine like resistors in series.

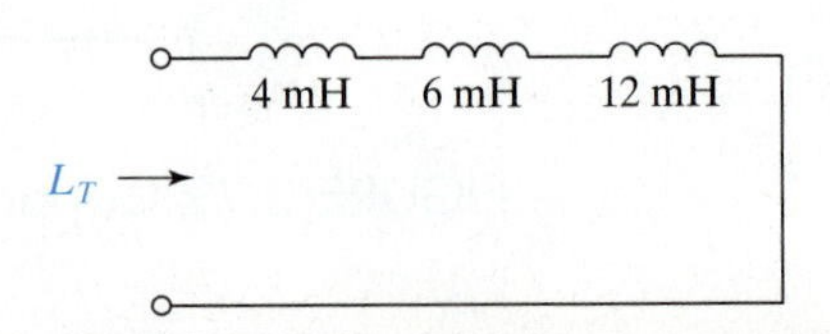

FIGURE 3.26 Inductors in series.

$$L_T = 4 \text{ m} + 6 \text{ m} + 12 \text{ m} = 22 \text{ mH}$$

- Inductors in parallel combine like resistors in parallel.

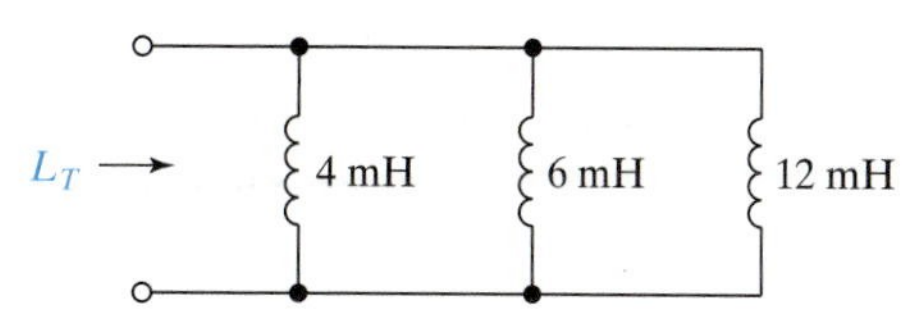

FIGURE 3.27 Inductors in parallel.

$$\frac{1}{L_T} = \frac{1}{4 \text{ m}} + \frac{1}{6 \text{ m}} + \frac{1}{12 \text{ m}} \text{ and hence } L_T = 2 \text{ mH}$$

- The forced response of a circuit is that due to external energy sources. The natural response of a circuit is that due to energy storage elements within the network, that is, inductors and capacitors. For example, for the network in Figure 3.28 the forced response is due to $v_S(t)$ and the natural response is due to $i_L(0)$ and $v_C(0)$.

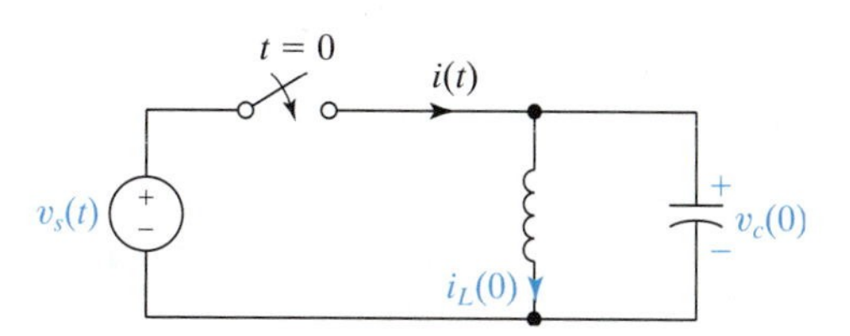

FIGURE 3.28 A transient network.

- The transient response of a first-order network is of the form $x(t) = K_1 + K_2 e^{-t/\tau}$ where $x(t)$ is any current or voltage in the network, K_1 is the steady-state response, and τ is the time constant of the network. The time constant τ is either $\tau = R_{TH}C$ or $\tau = \dfrac{L}{R_{TH}}$.
- The procedure for determining the transient behavior of a first-order network is
  - For the network that exists prior to switch action, determine the initial capacitor voltage or inductor current.
  - For the network that exists after switch action, derive an expression for the capacitor voltage or inductor current, which will yield the time constant of the network.
  - Use the initial and final conditions to determine the constants in the equation for the capacitor voltage or inductor current.
  - If the desired quantity is not the capacitor voltage or inductor current, use equations that describe the network to find the desired quantity.
- The transient response of a second-order network is determined by the roots of the network's characteristic equation.

$$\frac{d^2x}{dt^2} + 2\alpha\frac{dx}{dt} + \omega_0^2 x = 0$$

For roots of the form a and b, the response is overdamped and

$$x(t) = k_1 e^{-at} + k_2 e^{-bt}.$$

For roots of the form $a \pm jb$, the response is underdamped and

$$x(t) = k_1 e^{-at} \cos bt + k_2 e^{-at} \sin bt.$$

For a double root of the form a, the response is critically damped and

$$x(t) = k_1 e^{-at} + tk_2 e^{-at}.$$

Problems

3.1. The voltage across a 10 μF capacitor is given by the waveform in Figure P3.1. Compute the current waveform.

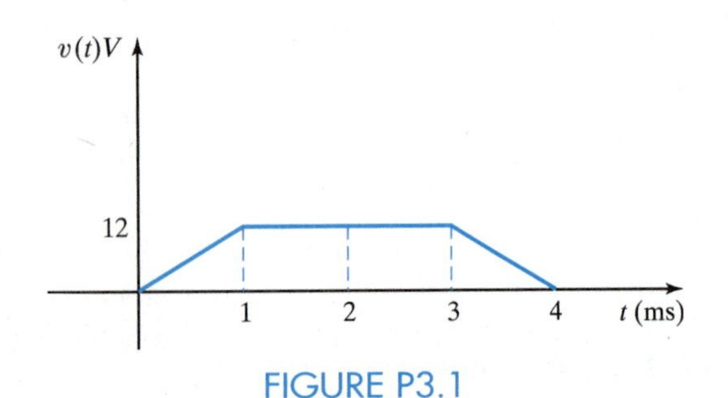

FIGURE P3.1

3.2. The voltage waveform across a 5 μF capacitor is shown in Figure P3.2. Determine the waveform for the current.

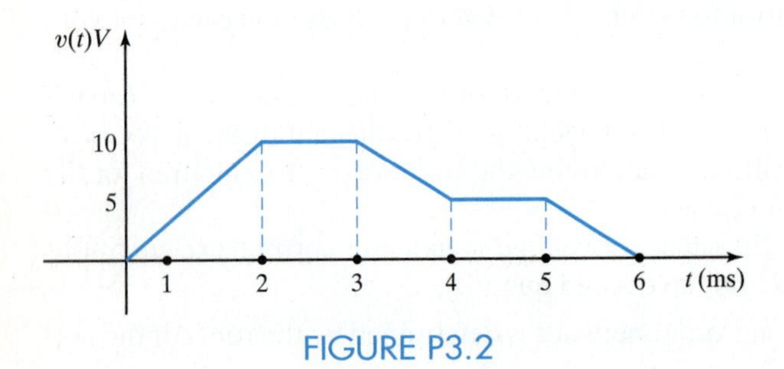

FIGURE P3.2

3.3. The voltage across a 10 μF capacitor is shown in Figure P3.3. Determine the current waveform.

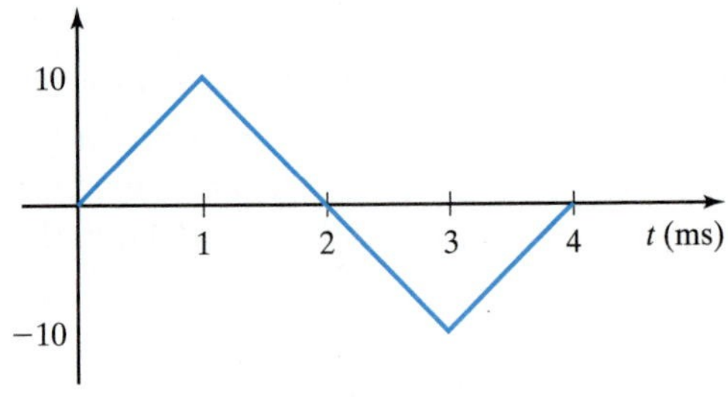

FIGURE P3.3

3.4. The voltage waveform across a 20 μF capacitor is shown in Figure P3.4. Compute the waveform of the capacitor current.

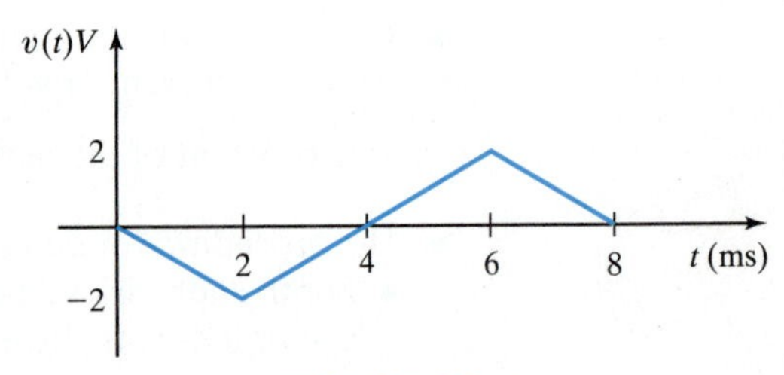

FIGURE P3.4

3.5. Find the equivalent capacitance at the terminals A-B in the network in Figure P3.5.

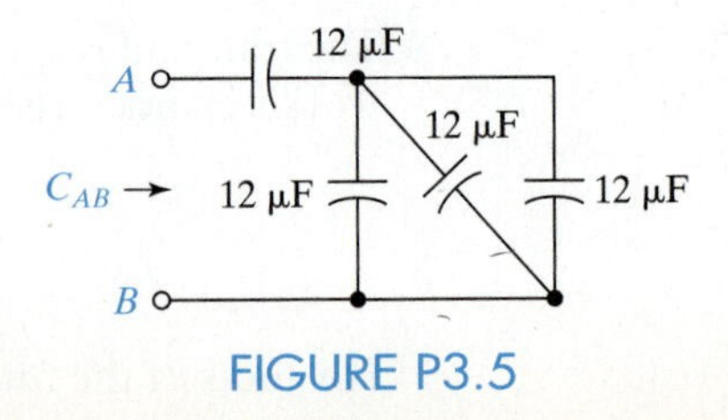

FIGURE P3.5

3.6. Find C_{AB} at the terminals of the circuit in Figure P3.6.

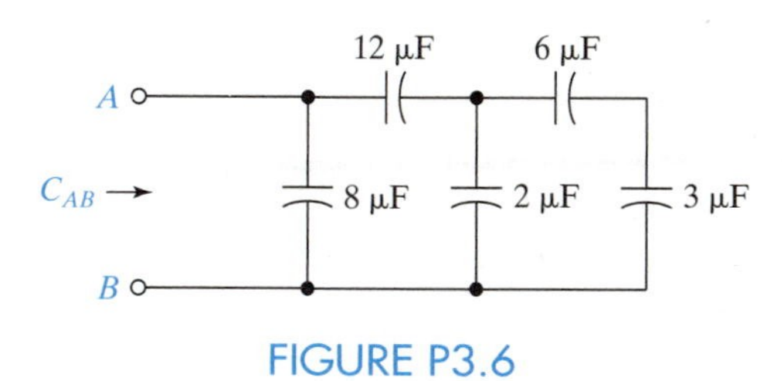

FIGURE P3.6

3.7. Find C_{AB} in the network in Figure P3.7.

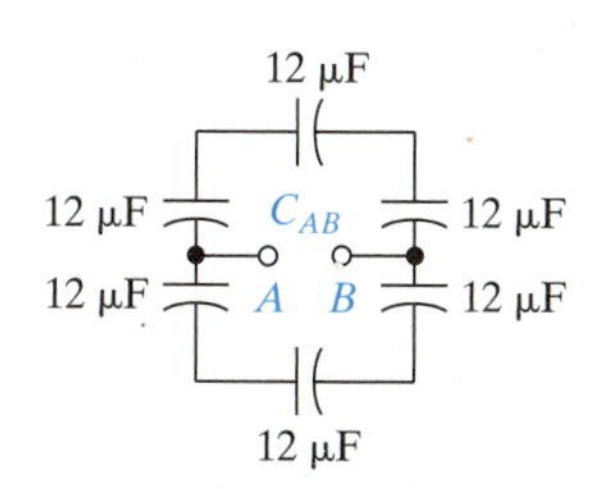

FIGURE P3.7

3.8. Find the equivalent capacitance C_{AB} in the network in Figure P3.8.

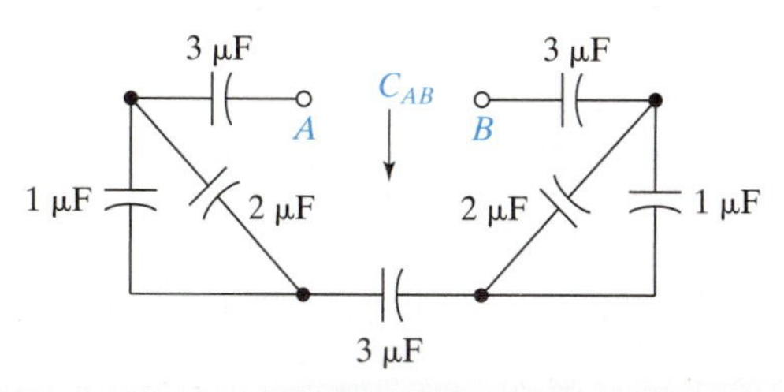

FIGURE P3.8

3.9. Find C_{AB} in the circuit in Figure P3.9. All capacitor values are in micro farads.

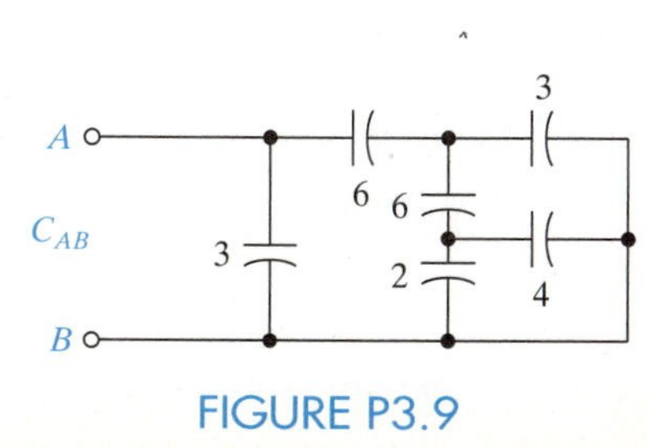

FIGURE P3.9

3.10. The current in a 20 mH inductor is given by the waveform in Figure P3.10. Compute the waveform for the inductor voltage.

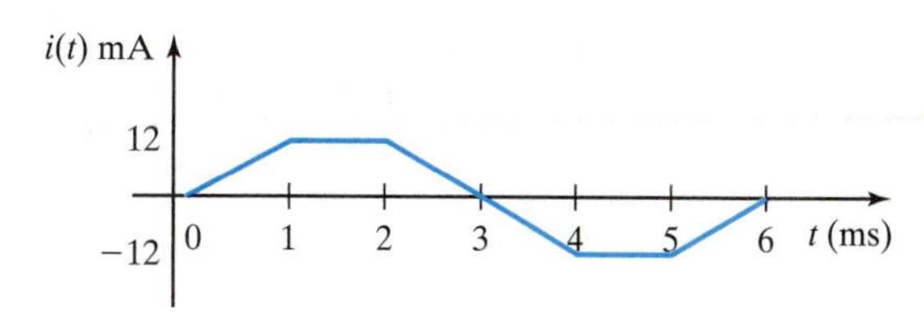

FIGURE P3.10

3.11. The current in a 10 mH inductor has the waveform shown in Figure P3.11. Determine the waveform of the inductor voltage.

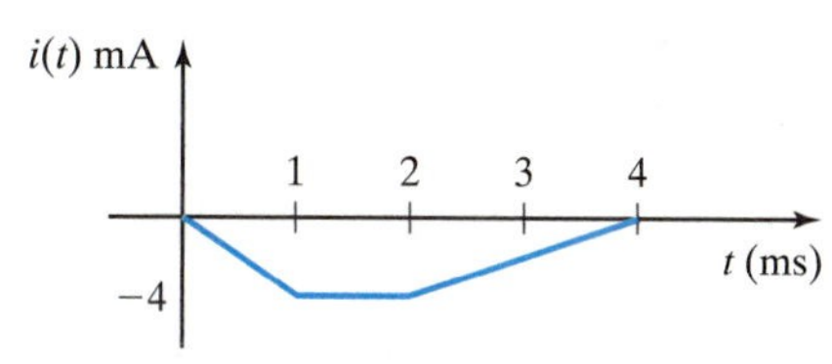

FIGURE P3.11

3.12. The waveform of the current in a 40 mH inductor is shown in Figure P3.12. Determine the waveform of the inductor voltage.

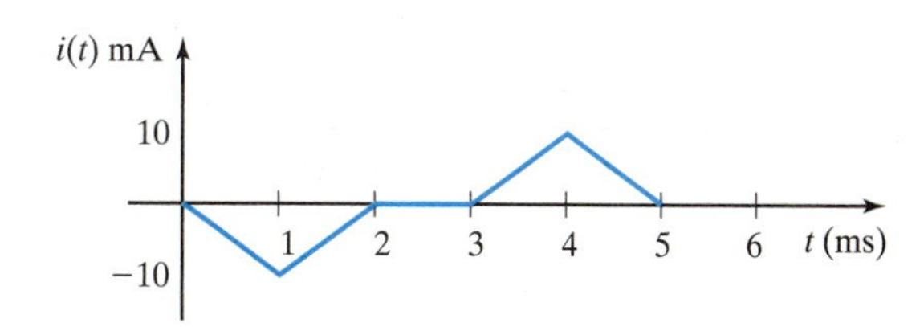

FIGURE P3.12

3.13. The current in a 6 mH inductor is shown in Figure P3.13. Determine the waveform of the inductor voltage.

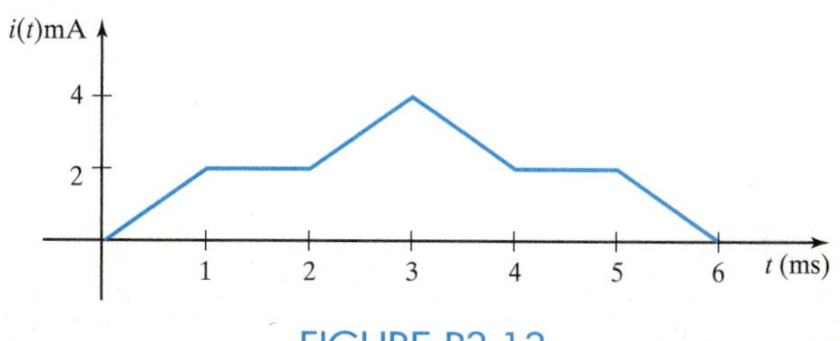

FIGURE P3.13

3.14. Find the equivalent inductance at the terminals A-B in the circuit in Figure P3.14.

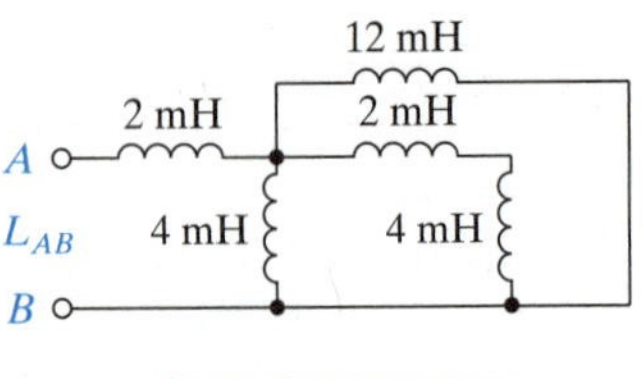

FIGURE P3.14

3.15. Find L_{AB} in the network in Figure P3.15. All inductors are 12mH.

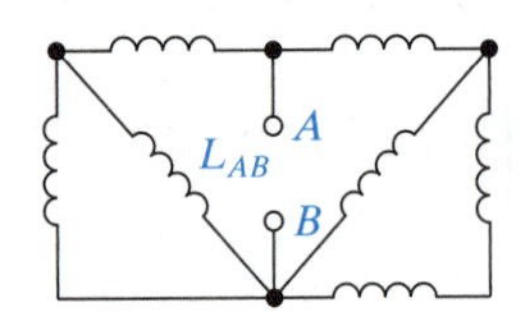

FIGURE P3.15

3.16. Find L_{AB} in the circuit shown in Figure P3.16.

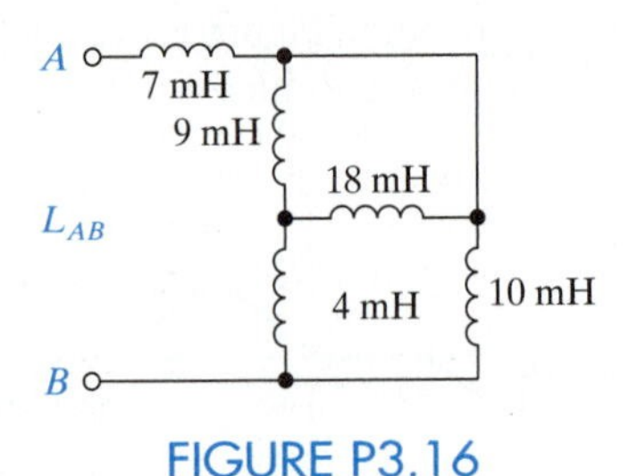

FIGURE P3.16

3.17. Find the equivalent inductance of the network shown in Figure P3.17 at the terminals A-B. All inductors are 8 mH.

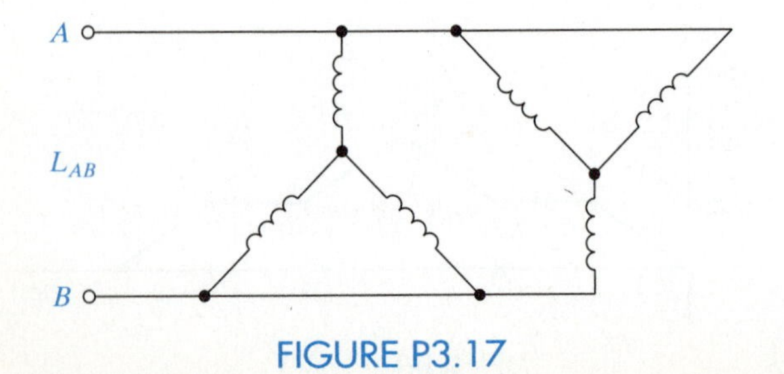

FIGURE P3.17

3.18. Determine the inductance at the terminals A-B of the circuit shown in Figure P3.18.

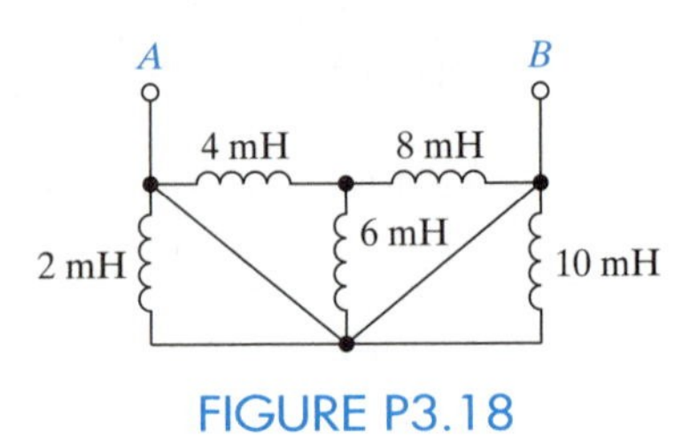

FIGURE P3.18

3.19. Find the inductance labeled L_{AB} in the network in Figure P3.19.

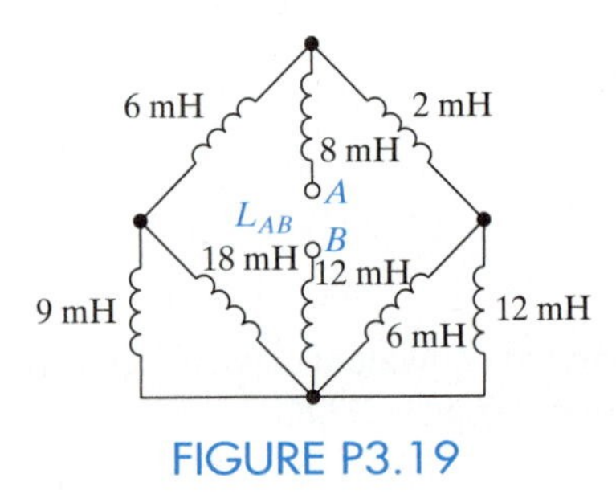

FIGURE P3.19

3.20. A flash bulb circuit for a camera is shown in Figure P3.20. Initially both switches are open. Switch 1 closes to charge the capacitor. Once the capacitor is charged, switch 1 opens. When switch 2 closes, the energy stored in the capacitor is discharged through the light bulb represented by the 0.2 Ω resistor. Find the equation of the current that causes the bulb to flash.

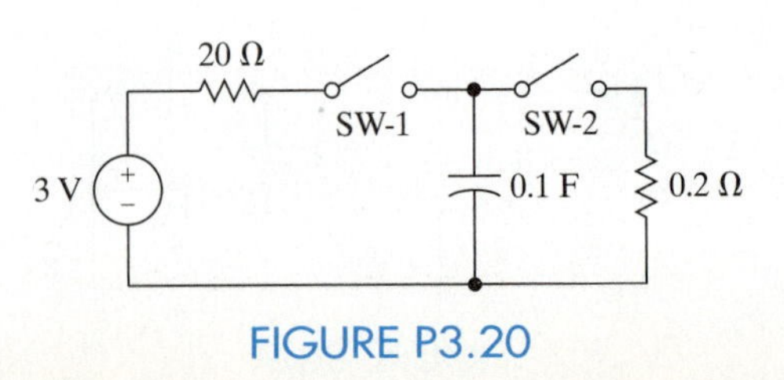

FIGURE P3.20

3.21. Given the network in Figure P.3.21, assume the switch has been in position 1 for a long time and moves to position 2 at $t = 0$. Calculate the voltage $v_0(t)$ for $t > 0$.

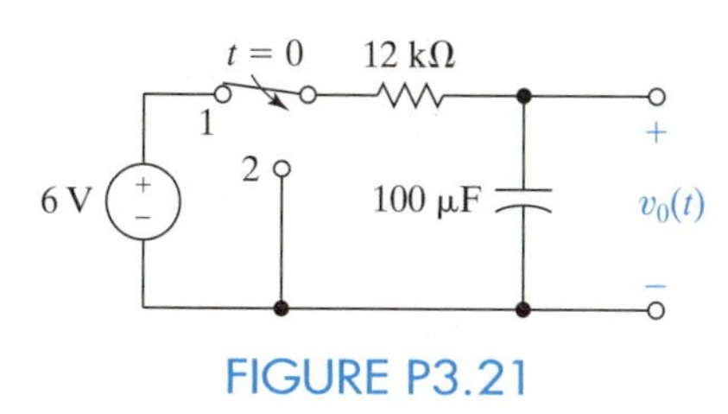

FIGURE P3.21

3.22. The switch in the network in Figure P3.22 closes at $t = 0$. Calculate $v_0(t)$ for $t > 0$.

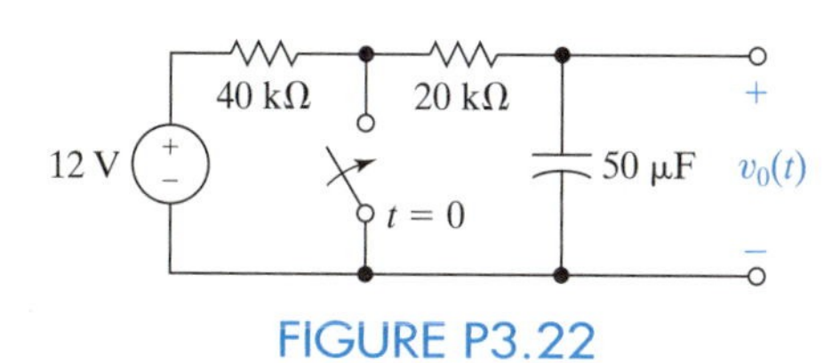

FIGURE P3.22

3.23. Consider the circuit shown in Figure P3.23. Assuming that the switch has been in position 1 for a long time, at time $t = 0$ the switch is moved to position 2. Calculate the current $i(t)$ for $t > 0$.

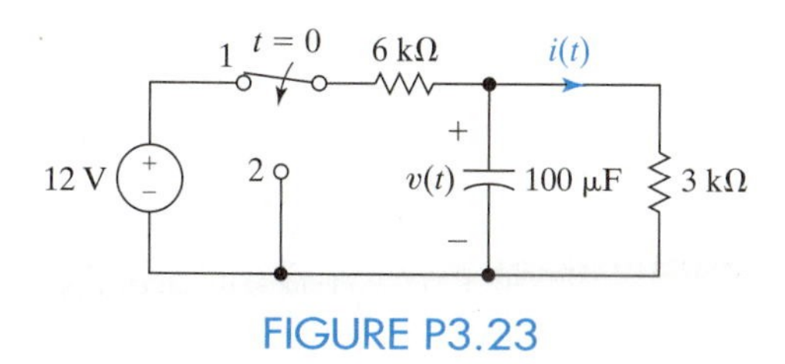

FIGURE P3.23

3.24. In the circuit in Figure P3.24 find $i_0(t)$ for $t > 0$.

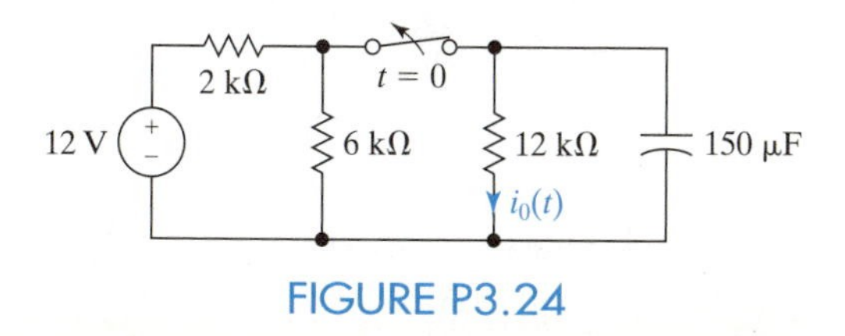

FIGURE P3.24

3.25. Find $v_c(t)$ for $t > 0$ in the circuit shown in Figure P3.25.

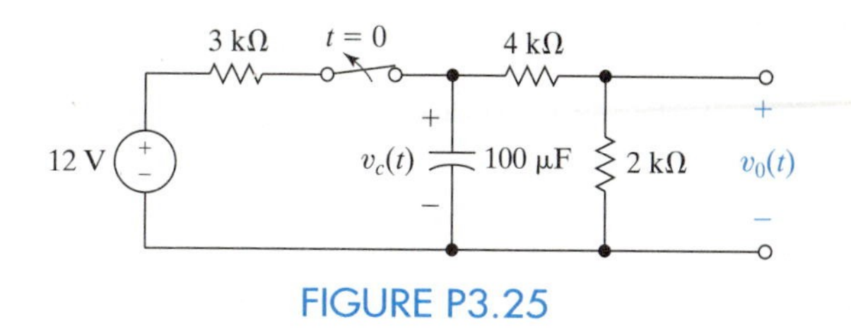

FIGURE P3.25

3.26. Find $i_0(t)$ for $t > 0$ in the circuit in Figure P3.26.

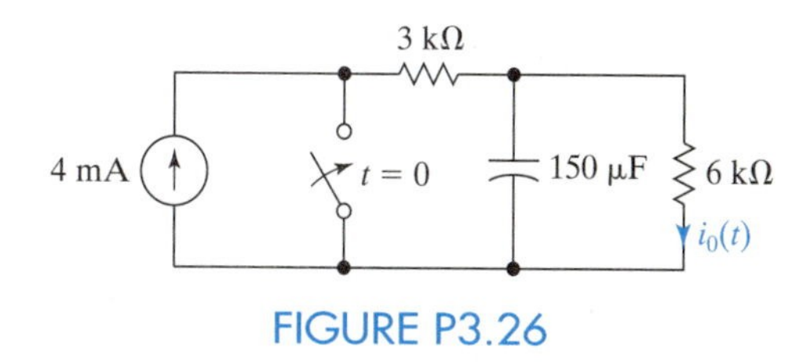

FIGURE P3.26

3.27. Consider the network in Figure P3.27. At $t = 0$, the switch opens. Find $v_0(t)$ for $t > 0$.

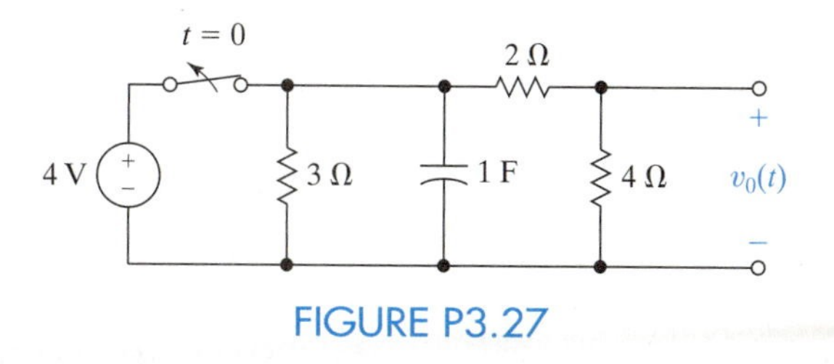

FIGURE P3.27

3.28. Find $v_c(t)$ for $t > 0$ in the network in Figure P3.28.

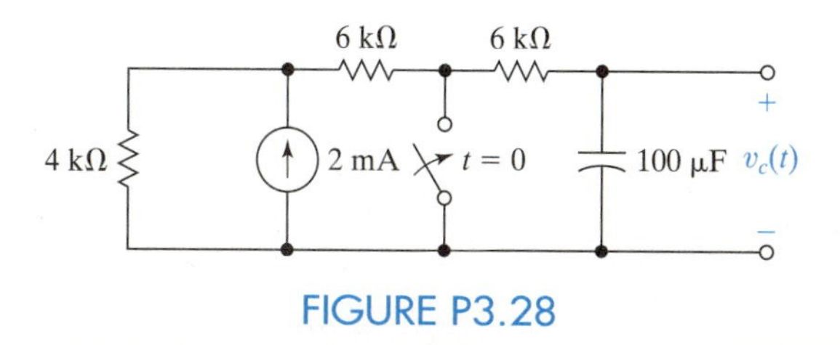

FIGURE P3.28

3.29. Consider the network in Figure P3.29. The switch closes at $t = 0$. Find $v_0(t)$ for $t > 0$.

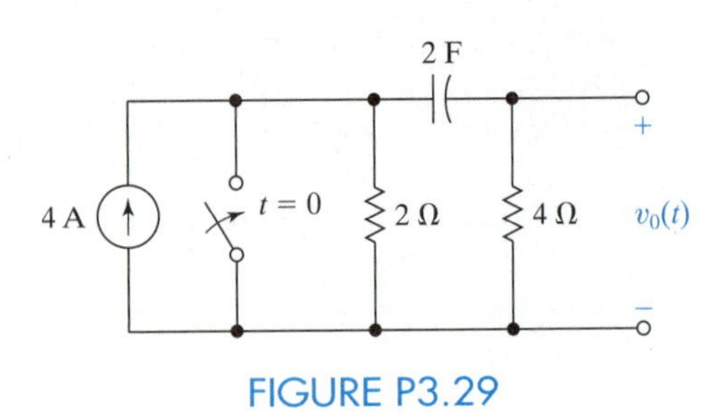

FIGURE P3.29

3.30. Find $i_0(t)$ for $t > 0$ in Figure P3.30.

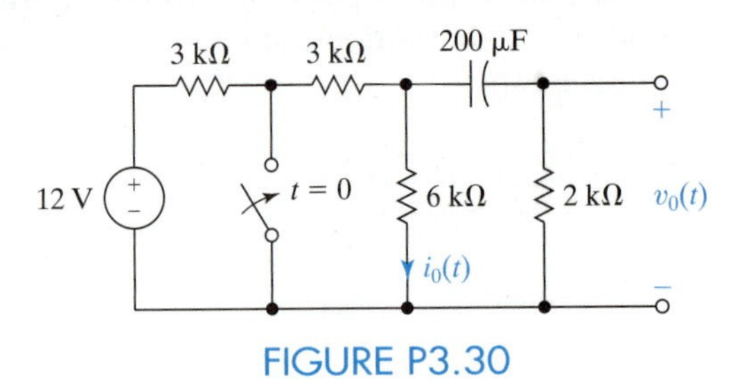

FIGURE P3.30

3.31. Find $v_c(t)$ for $t > 0$ in the circuit in Figure P3.31.

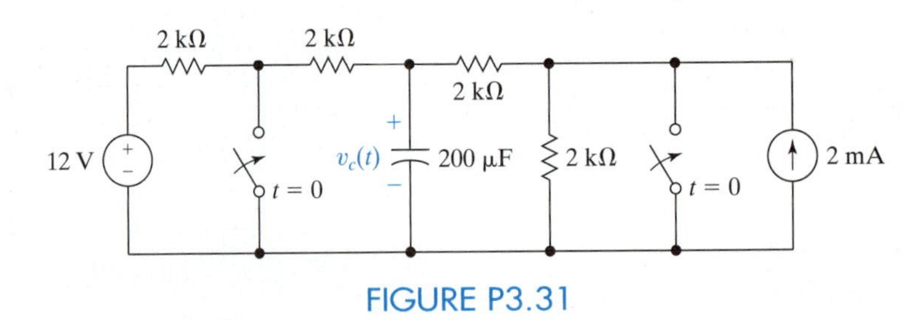

FIGURE P3.31

3.32. Find $i_0(t)$ for $t > 0$ in Figure P3.32.

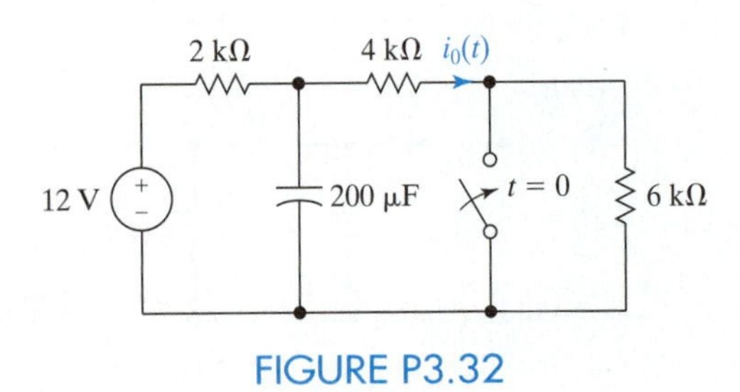

FIGURE P3.32

3.33. Consider the circuit shown in Figure P3.33. The circuit is steady state prior to time $t = 0$, when the switch is closed. Calculate the current $i(t)$ for $t > 0$.

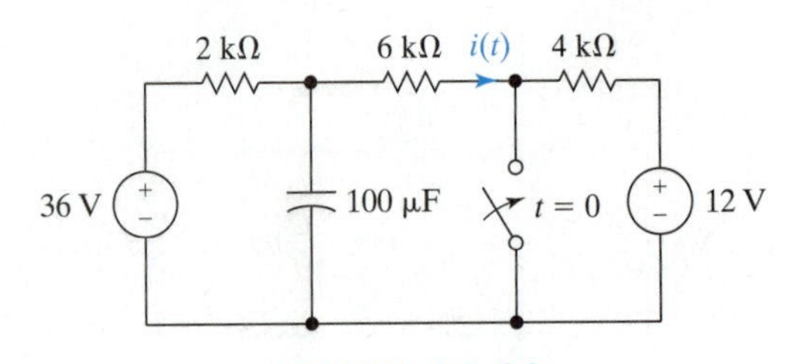

FIGURE P3.33

3.34. In the circuit in Figure P3.34 find $v_c(t)$ for $t > 0$.

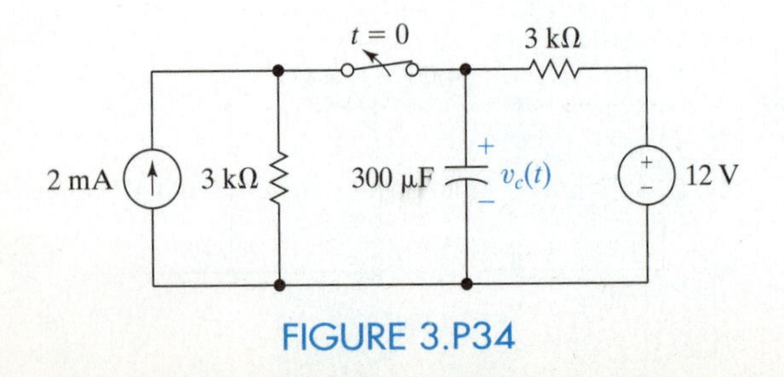

FIGURE 3.P34

3.35. In the network in Figure P3.35, find $i_L(t)$ for $t > 0$.

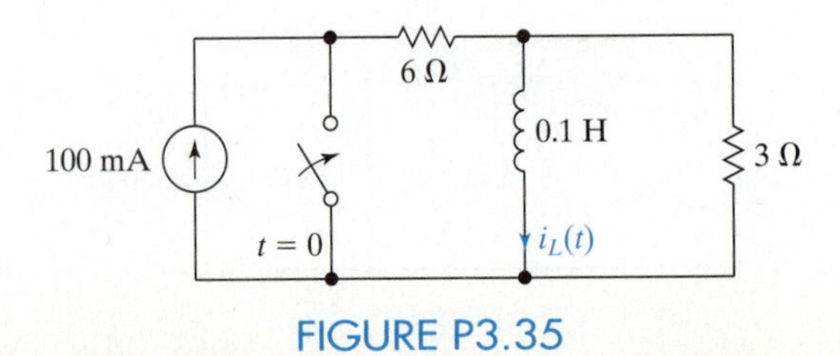

FIGURE P3.35

3.36. Given the circuit shown in Figure P3.36, at $t = 0$ the switch is opened. Calculate the current $i(t)$ for $t > 0$.

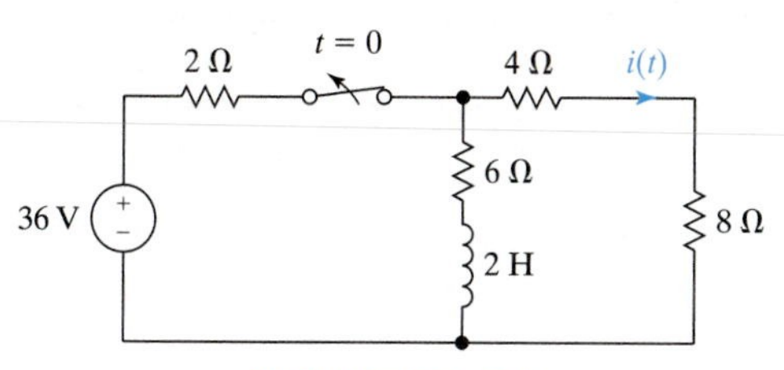

FIGURE P3.36

3.37. Find $v_0(t)$ for $t > 0$ in the circuit in Figure P3.37.

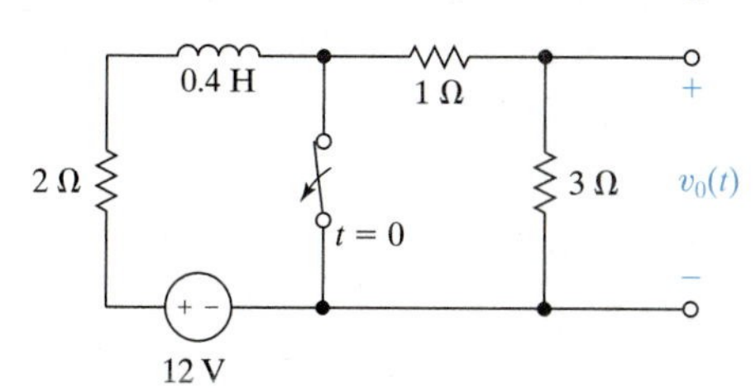

FIGURE P3.37

3.38. In the circuit shown in Figure P3.38, the switch opens at $t = 0$. Find $i_1(t)$ for $t > 0$.

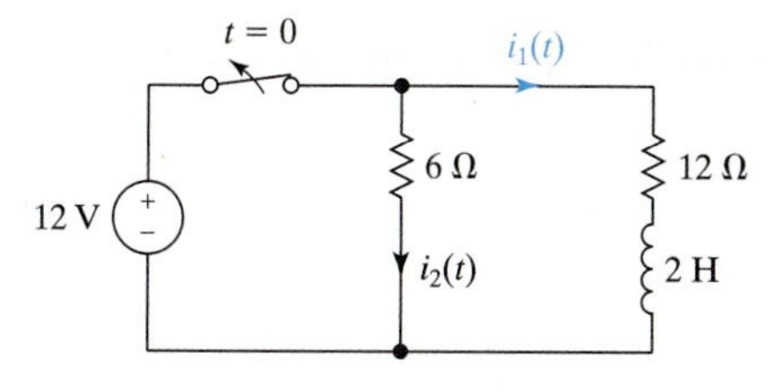

FIGURE P3.38

3.39. Consider the network shown in Figure P3.39. If the switch opens at $t = 0$, find the output voltage $v_0(t)$ for $t > 0$.

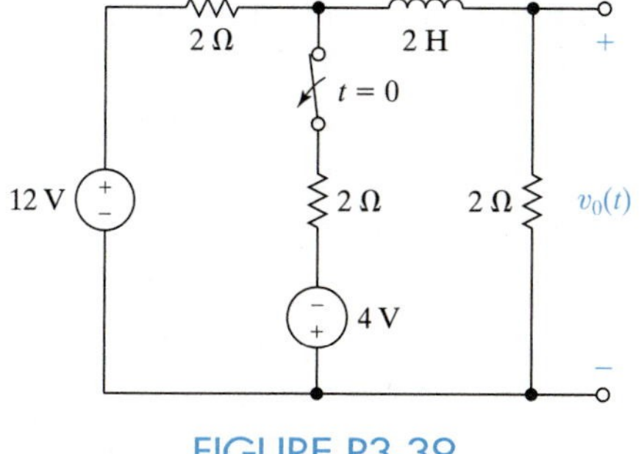

FIGURE P3.39

3.40. Find $v_0(t)$ for $t > 0$ in the circuit in Figure P3.40.

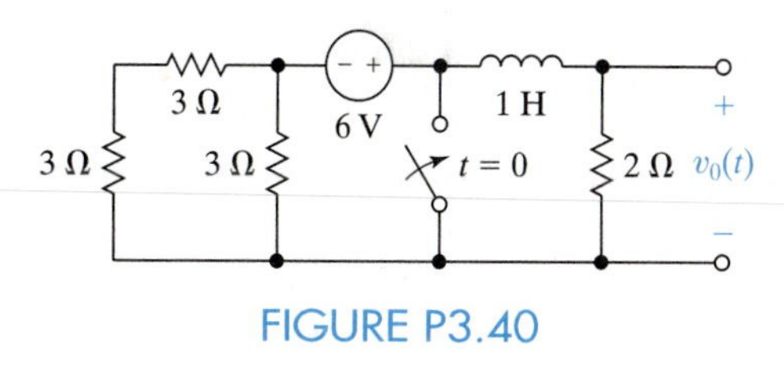

FIGURE P3.40

3.41. The switch in the network in Figure P3.41 closes at $t = 0$. Find $i_0(t)$ for $t > 0$.

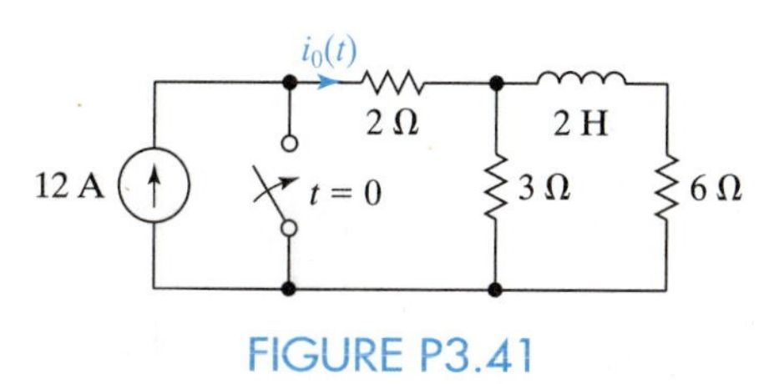

FIGURE P3.41

3.42. The switch in the network in Figure P3.42 opens at $t = 0$. Find $v_0(t)$ for $t > 0$.

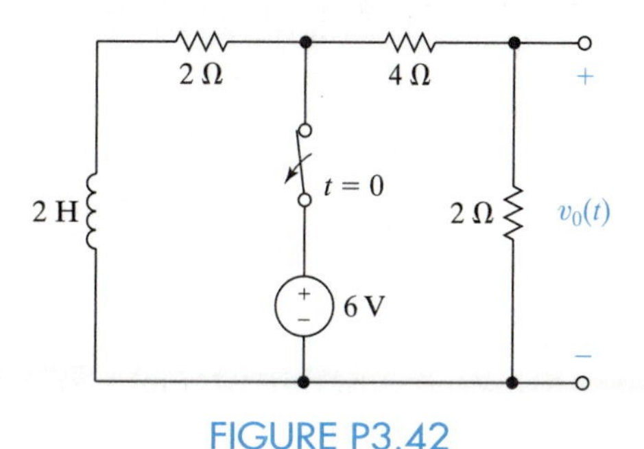

FIGURE P3.42

3.43. Find $v_0(t)$ for $t > 0$ in the circuit in Figure P3.43.

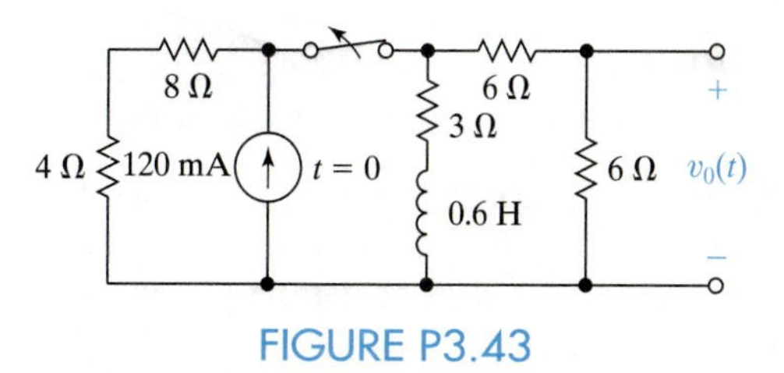

FIGURE P3.43

3.44. Determine $i_0(t)$ for $t > 0$ in Figure P3.44.

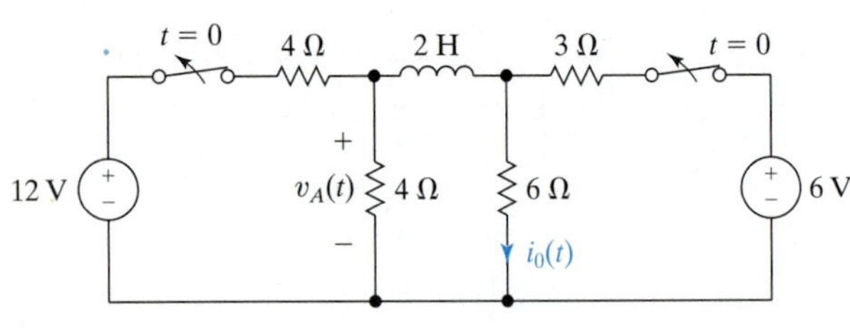

FIGURE P3.44

3.45. In the network in Figure P3.45, find $i_L(t)$ for $t > 0$.

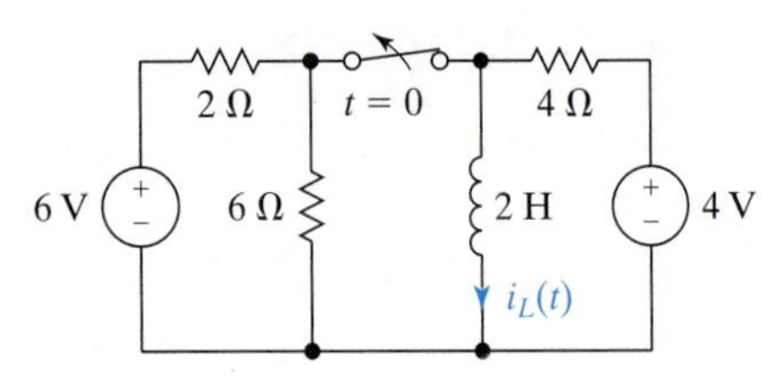

FIGURE P3.45

3.46. Given the series circuit in Figure P3.46 with the following network parameters $R = 2\Omega$, $L = \frac{1}{4}H$, and $C = \frac{1}{9}F$, determine the type of damping the network will exhibit.

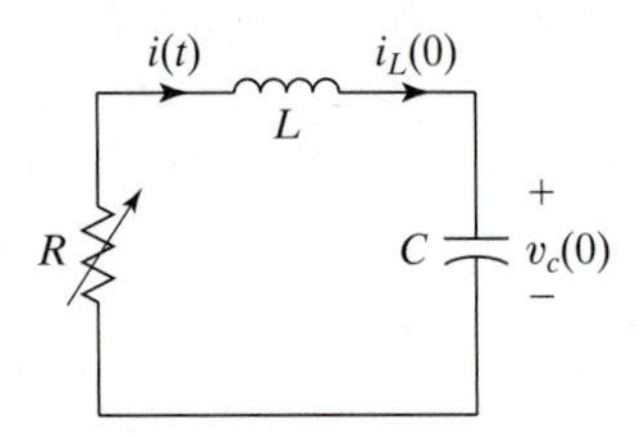

FIGURE P3.46

3.47. The resistor in the network in problem 3.46 is changed to $R = 3\Omega$. What impact does this change have on the circuit damping?

3.48. If the resistor in the circuit in problem 3.46 is changed to $R = 4\Omega$, will this change have any effect on the circuit's damping? If so, what, and if not, why not?

3.49. The parameters for the parallel RLC circuit in Figure P3.49 are $R = 1\Omega$, $L = 1H$, and $C = \frac{1}{4}F$. Determine the type of damping exhibited by the circuit.

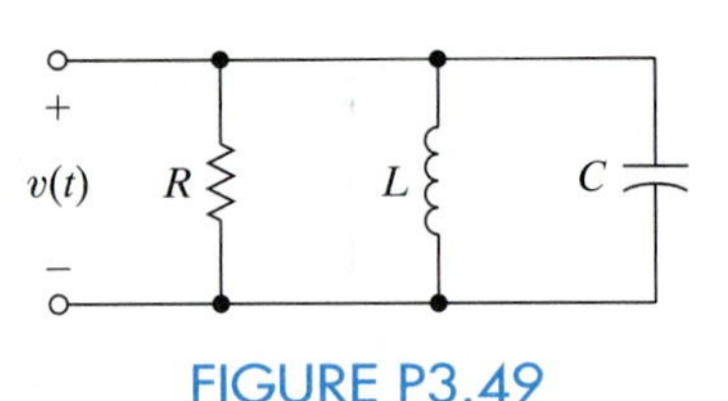

FIGURE P3.49

3.50. If the inductance in the network in problem 3.49 is decreased by a factor of 2, determine the impact on the network's damping characteristics.

3.51. If the inductance in the circuit in problem 3.49 is changed to $L = \frac{4}{3}H$, determine the effect of this change on the network's damping characteristics.

3.52. The series RLC circuit shown in Figure P3.52 has the following parameters: $C = 0.04$ F, $L = 1$ H, $R = 6\Omega$, $i_L(0) = 4\,A$, and $v_c(0) = -4$ V. Find the equation for the current $i(t)$.

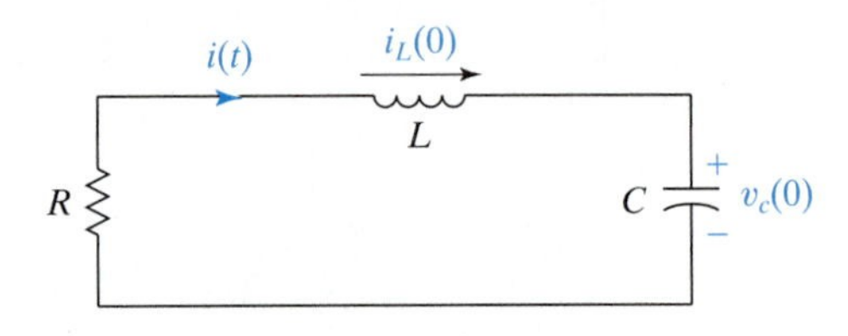

FIGURE P3.52

3.53. For the underdamped circuit shown in Figure P3.53, determine the voltage $v(t)$ if the initial conditions on the storage elements are $i_L(0) = 1$ A and $v_c(0) = 10$ V.

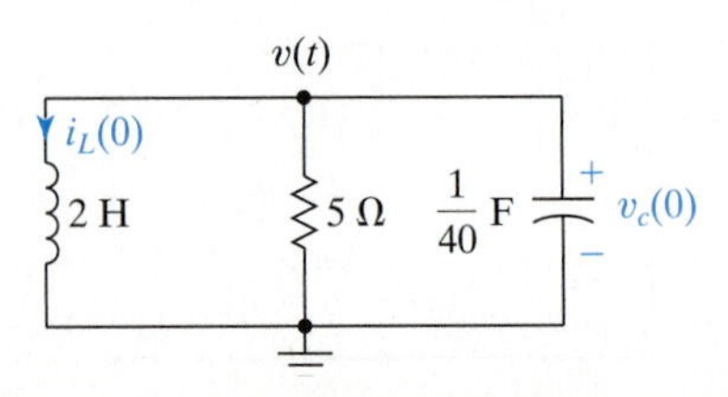

FIGURE P3.53

3.54. Determine the equation for the current $i(t)$, $t > 0$, in the circuit shown in Figure P3.54.

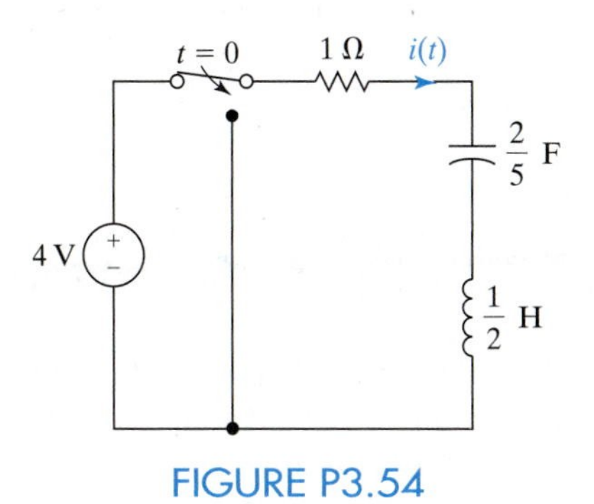

FIGURE P3.54

3.55. In the circuit shown in Figure P3.55, find $v(t)$, $t > 0$.

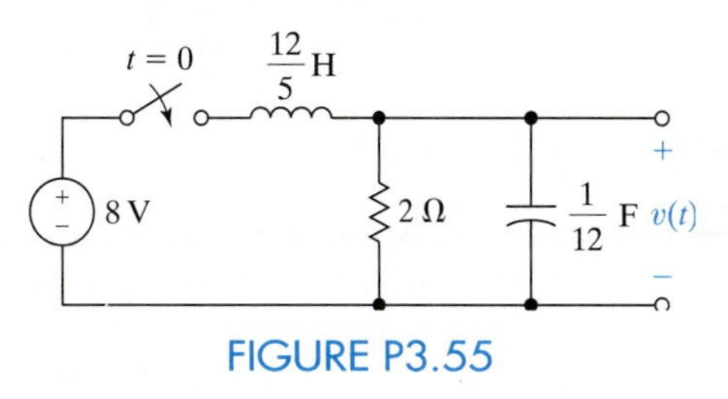

FIGURE P3.55

4-1 Introduction

At this point in our analysis of linear circuits we have learned how to determine both their natural and forced responses. We found that the natural response is simply a characteristic of the network.

In this chapter we concentrate on the steady-state forced response of circuits with alternating current (ac) inputs. In ac circuits the forcing function is sinusoidal in nature, that is, the waveform of the input looks like a sine or cosine function. In this *steady-state analysis* we ignore the transient nature of the response since it will vanish prior to the steady state.

It is interesting to note that although Thomas Edison originally used direct current (dc), ac became the dominant waveform because it can be easily generated with rotating machines and can be stepped up and down with transformers (topics that will be discussed in later chapters). Furthermore, the ac waveform is used throughout the world in the electric power industry and therefore is present, for example, at the ac outlets in our home, office, and laboratory.

4-2 Sinusoidal Functions

We begin our discussion of these functions by considering both sine and cosine waves of the form

$$\begin{aligned} x(\omega t) &= X_M \sin \omega t \\ y(\omega t) &= Y_M \cos \omega t \end{aligned} \tag{4.1}$$

where $x(\omega t)$ and $y(\omega t)$ could represent any voltage or current. In Eq. (4.1), X_M and Y_M are the *amplitudes* or *maximum values,* ω is the *radian* or *angular frequency,* and ωt is the *argument.* Two plots of these equations as a function of their arguments are shown in Figure 4.1. Note that the functions in Figure 4.1(a) are periodic and repeat after 2π radians. The functions in Figure 4.1(b) are periodic with a *period* of T seconds. Each function repeats itself after one period. Periodicity can be expressed in general for a function $p(t)$ with period T as

Sinusoidal component definitions

$$p(t + nT) = p(t) \qquad n = 1, 2, 3 \tag{4.2}$$

The *frequency* in Hertz (cycles per second) is related to the period by the equation

$$f = \frac{1}{T} \tag{4.3}$$

For the functions shown in Figure 4.1(a)

$$\omega T = 2\pi$$

and therefore

$$\omega = \frac{2\pi}{T} = 2\pi f \tag{4.4}$$

Equation (4.4) is the general relationship among period in seconds, frequency in Hertz and radian frequency.

Although, as indicated above, in our discussions of sinusoidal functions we mean either sine or cosine function of time, we now consider a more general expression for a sinusoidal function of the form

$$x(t) = X_M \sin(\omega t + \theta) \tag{4.5}$$

where θ is called the *phase angle*. For comparison, Eqs. (4.1) and (4.5) are plotted in Figure 4.2. Since any point on the waveform $X_M \sin(\omega t + \theta)$ occurs θ radians earlier in time than the corresponding point on the waveform $X_M \sin\omega t$, $X_M \sin\omega t$ lags $X_M \sin(\omega t + \theta)$ by θ radians. In general, if

$$x_1(t) = X_{M1} \sin(\omega t + \theta)$$

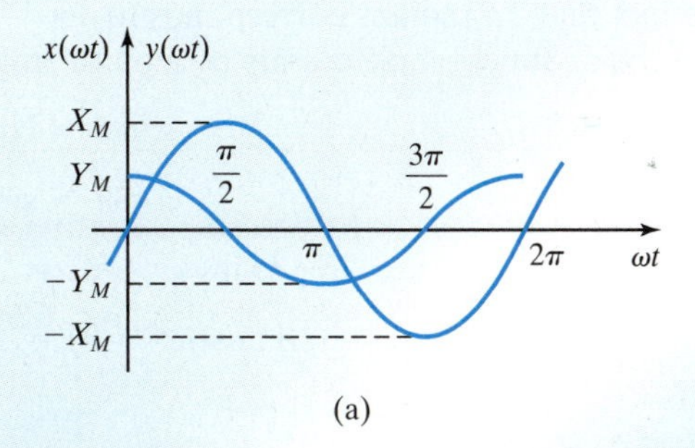

(a)

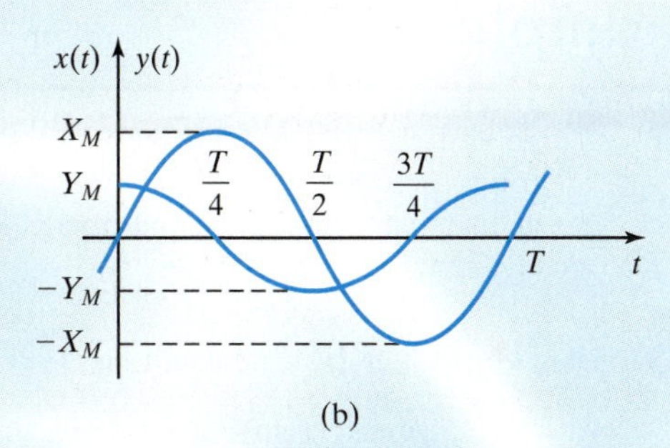

(b)

FIGURE 4.1 Plots of sine and cosine waves as a function of both ωt and t.

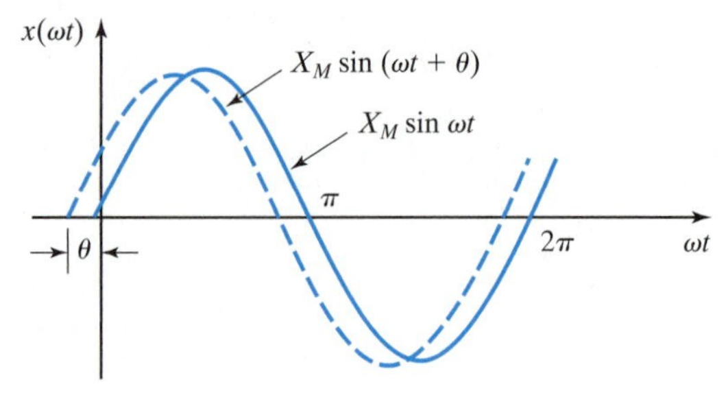

FIGURE 4.2 Graphical illustration of $X_M \sin(\omega t + \theta)$ leading $X_M \sin \omega t$ by θ radians.

and

$$x_2(t) = X_{M2} \sin(\omega t + \phi)$$

Then $x_1(t)$ *leads* $x_2(t)$ by $\theta - \phi$ radians and $x_2(t)$ *lags* $x_1(t)$ by $\theta - \phi$ radians. If $\theta = \phi$, the waveforms are *in phase*, and if $\theta \neq \phi$, the waveforms are *out of phase*. It is important to note that when comparing sinusoidal functions *of the same frequency* to determine the phase difference, both functions should be expressed as sines or cosines with positive amplitudes.

Leading and lagging phase angles defined

In the equations above, ωt, ϕ, and θ are expressed in radians, and since they are added to form the total argument of the trigonometric function, they all must be in the same units. However, in practice the phase angle is normally expressed in degrees. Therefore, throughout this text we will express phase angles in degrees and convert ωt from radians to degrees using the fact that 2π radians corresponds to 360°. The following equations illustrate that the sine and cosine function differ only by a phase angle

$$\begin{aligned} \sin\omega t &= \cos(\omega t - 90^\circ) \\ \cos\omega t &= \sin(\omega t + 90^\circ) \end{aligned} \tag{4.6}$$

$$\begin{aligned} -A\sin(\omega t + \theta) &= A\sin(\omega t + \theta \pm 180^\circ) \\ -A\cos(\omega t + \theta) &= A\cos(\omega t + \theta \pm 180^\circ) \end{aligned} \tag{4.7}$$

Example 4.1

Let us compute the phase angle between the two voltages $v_1(t) = 12\sin(\omega t + 60^\circ)$V and $v_2(t) = -6\cos(\omega t + 30^\circ)$V.

Since the minus sign corresponds to a phase angle of ±180°, $v_2(t)$ can be expressed as

$$v_2(t) = -6\cos(\omega t + 30^\circ) = 6\cos(\omega t + 210^\circ)\text{V}$$

Then using Eq. (4.7), $v_2(t)$ can be written as

$$v_2(t) = 6\sin(\omega t + 300^\circ)\text{V}$$

Now that both voltages of the same frequency are expressed as sine waves with positive amplitudes, the phase difference can be determined. $v_1(t)$ leads $v_2(t)$ by $60^\circ - 300^\circ = -240^\circ = +120^\circ$ and $v_2(t)$ lags $v_1(t)$ by $+120^\circ$.

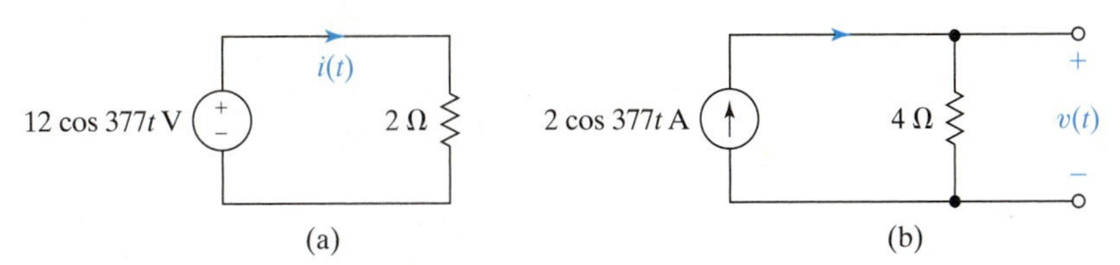

FIGURE 4.3 ac circuits with sinusoidal forcing functions.

Our interest in understanding the properties of these sinusoidal functions is their use as forcing functions in ac circuits. Although we could use either sine or cosine functions as forcing functions, in our subsequent analyses we will generally use only the cosine function.

Consider, for example, the two circuits in Figure 4.3.

Note that both forcing functions, that is, a voltage source in Figure 4.3(a) and a current source in Fig. 4.3(b), are cosine waves with a frequency of 60 Hz. Recall from Eq. (2.1) that the mathematical statement of Ohm's law is

$$v(t) = Ri(t), \quad R \geq 0$$

therefore, as indicated in the network in Figure 4.3(a),

$$i(t) = \frac{12 \cos 377t}{2}$$

$$= 6 \cos 377t \text{ A}$$

and from the circuit in Figure 4.3(b),

$$v(t) = (2 \cos 377t)(4)$$

$$= 8 \cos 377t \text{ V}$$

Note that in each case the voltage and current are in phase, that is, there is no phase angle between them. While this is always true for resistors, it is not the case for capacitors and inductors, as we will demonstrate later.

Drill Exercises

D4.1. Given the voltage $v(t) = 120 \cos\left(314t + \frac{\pi}{4}\right)$ V, determine the frequency of the voltage in Hertz and the phase angle in degrees.

Ans: $f = 50$ Hz and $\theta = 45°$.

D4.2. Given the two branch currents $i_1(t) = 2 \sin(377t + 45°)$ and $i_2(t) = -4 \sin(377t + 60°)$ A, determine the phase angle by which $i_1(t)$ leads $i_2(t)$.

Ans: $i_1(t)$ leads $i_2(t)$ by $-195°$.

4-3 The Sinusoidal Function/Complex Number Connection

If we apply a sinusoidal forcing function to a linear network, the steady-state voltages and currents in the network will also be sinusoidal. For example, KVL would dictate that if one branch voltage is a sinusoid of some frequency, the other branch voltages must be sinusoids of the same frequency.

Consider for a moment a series circuit consisting of a resistor, inductor, and a voltage source of value $V_M \cos\omega t$ as shown in Figure 4.4.

The current $i(t)$ leaving the positive terminal of the source is described by the KVL equation

$$L\frac{di(t)}{dt} + Ri(t) = V_M \cos \omega t \tag{4.8}$$

Since the input voltage is $V_M \cos\omega t$, we must ask ourselves what is the proper form of the current, that is, what function $i(t)$ when multiplied by R and added to its derivative multiplied by L will yield a cosine function $V_M \cos\omega t$. Since the derivative of the cosine function is just a sine function, which can be expressed as a cosine function with a phase angle, a logical choice is

$$i(t) = I_M \cos(\omega t + \phi) \tag{4.9}$$

If we substitute Eq. (4.9) into Eq. (4.8) and solve for the two unknowns I_M and ϕ, it is straightforward but tedious to show that

$$I_M = \frac{V_M}{\sqrt{R^2 + \omega^2 L^2}}$$

and

$$\phi = -\tan^{-1}\frac{\omega L}{R}$$

therefore,

$$i(t) = \frac{V_M}{\sqrt{R^2 + \omega^2 L^2}} \cos\left(\omega t - \tan^{-1}\frac{\omega L}{R}\right) \tag{4.10}$$

Since the solution to this very simple problem is quite laborious, as we imagine trying to attack a more complicated network we are prompted to ask if there isn't a better way! There is indeed a better way, and it involves establishing a correspondence between sinu-

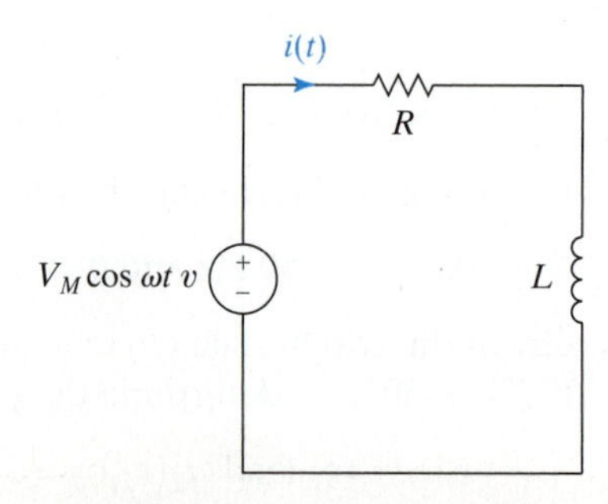

FIGURE 4.4 An RL circuit.

soidal time functions and complex numbers. This correspondence will lead to a set of algebraic equations for the loop currents or node voltages in which the coefficients of these variables are complex numbers.

The vehicle we will employ to establish a relationship between time-varying sinusoidal functions and complex numbers is Euler's equation, which for our purposes is written as

$$e^{j\omega t} = \cos\omega t + j\sin\omega t \tag{4.11}$$

This complex function, which is in essence a polar to rectangular conversion, has a real part and an imaginary part:

$$\begin{aligned} \mathrm{Re}(e^{j\omega t}) &= \cos\omega t \\ \mathrm{Im}(e^{j\omega t}) &= \sin\omega t \end{aligned} \tag{4.12}$$

where *Re* $(-)$ and *Im* $(-)$ represent the real part and the imaginary part, respectively, of the function in the parentheses.

The function $e^{j\omega t}$ can also be viewed as a vector that rotates counter-clockwise as a function of time and its projection along the x axis is the $\cos\omega t$ and its projection along the y axis is $\sin\omega t$, as shown in Figure 4.5.

Now suppose that we select as our forcing function the nonrealizable voltage

$$v(t) = V_M e^{j\omega t} \tag{4.13}$$

which because of Euler's identity can be written as

$$v(t) = V_M\cos\omega t + jV_M\sin\omega t \tag{4.14}$$

The real and imaginary parts of this function are each realizable. We think of this complex forcing function as two forcing functions, a real one and an imaginary one, and as a consequence

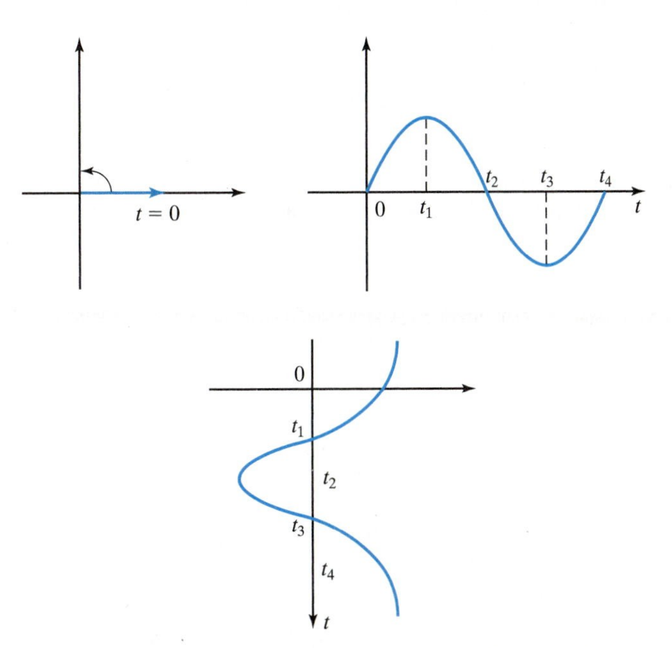

FIGURE 4.5 A rotating vector with its real and imaginary components.

of linearity, the principle of superposition applies and thus the current response can be written as

$$i(t) = I_M\cos(\omega t + \phi) + jI_M\sin(\omega t + \phi) \tag{4.15}$$

Where $I_M\cos(\omega t + \phi)$ is the response due to $V_M\cos\omega t$ and $jI_M\sin(\omega t + \phi)$ is the response due to $jV_M \sin \omega t$. This expression for the current containing both a real term and an imaginary term can be written via Euler's equation as

$$i(t) = I_M e^{j(\omega t+\phi)} \tag{4.16}$$

Because of the relationships above we find that rather than applying the forcing function $V_M\cos\omega t$ and calculating the response $I_M\cos(\omega t + \phi)$, we can apply the complex forcing function $V_M e^{j\omega t}$ and calculate the response $I_M e^{j(\omega t+\phi)}$, the real part of which is the desired response $I_M\cos(\omega t + \phi)$. Although this procedure may initially appear to be more complicated, it is not. It is via this technique that we will convert the differential equation to an algebraic equation, which is much easier to solve.

Once again, let us determine the current in the RL circuit described by Eq. (4.8). However, rather than applying $V_M\cos\omega t$, we will apply $V_M e^{j\omega t}$. The forced response will be of the form

$$i(t) = I_M e^{j(\omega t-\phi)}$$

where only I_M and ϕ are unknown. Substituting $v(t)$ and $i(t)$ into the differential equation for the circuit, we obtain

$$RI_M e^{j(\omega t+\phi)} + L\frac{d}{dt}(I_M e^{j(\omega t+\phi)}) = V_M e^{j\omega t}$$

Taking the indicated derivative, we obtain

$$RI_M e^{j(\omega t+\phi)} + j\omega L I_M e^{j(\omega t+\phi)} = V_M e^{j\omega t}$$

Dividing each term of the equation by the common factor $e^{j\omega t}$ yields

$$RI_M e^{j\phi} + j\omega L I_M e^{j\phi} = V_M$$

which is an algebraic equation with complex coefficients. This equation can be written as

$$I_M e^{j\phi} = \frac{V_M}{R + j\omega L}$$

Converting the right-hand side of the equation to exponential or polar form produces the equation

$$I_M e^{j\phi} = \frac{V_M}{\sqrt{R^2 + \omega^2 L^2}} e^{j(-\tan^{-1}(\frac{\omega L}{R}))}$$

(A quick refresher on complex numbers is given in Appendix A for readers who need to sharpen their skills in this area.) The form above clearly indicates that the magnitude and phase of the resulting current are

$$I_M = \frac{V_M}{\sqrt{R^2 + \omega^2 L^2}}$$

and

$$\phi = -\tan^{-1}\frac{\omega L}{R}$$

However, since our actual forcing function was $V_M\cos\omega t$ rather than $V_M e^{j\omega t}$, our actual response is the real part of the complex response:

$$\begin{aligned} i(t) &= I_M\cos(\omega t + \phi) \\ &= \frac{V_M}{\sqrt{R^2 + \omega^2 L^2}}\cos\left(\omega t - \tan^{-1}\frac{\omega L}{R}\right) \end{aligned}$$

Note that this is identical to the response obtained by solving the differential equation for the current $i(t)$.

The relationship between sinusoidal time functions and complex numbers

In summary, our correspondence between sinusoidal time functions and complex numbers is based upon Euler's equation, which permits us to express a voltage or current in the form

$$\begin{aligned} x(t) &= X_M\cos(\omega t + \theta) \\ &= R_e[X_M e^{j(\omega t+\theta)}] \end{aligned}$$

where $x(t)$ is a current $i(t)$ or a voltage $v(t)$. This latter equation can be expressed as

$$x(t) = R_e[(X_M e^{j\theta})e^{j\omega t}]$$

4.3.1 Phasors

As the previous analysis indicates, the term $e^{j\omega t}$ is a common factor in the defining equations for a network and therefore is simply implicit in the analysis. It is the remaining terms, that is, X_M and θ, that completely describe the magnitude and phase angle of the unknown current or voltage. We define the complex representation, $X_M e^{j\theta}$, as a *phasor*. Thus, a phasor is a complex number, expressed in polar form, consisting of two terms: X_M, which represents the *magnitude* of the sinusoidal signal, and θ, which represents the *phase angle* of the sinusoidal signal, which is measured with respect to a cosine signal. As a distinguishing feature, phasors will be written in boldface type.

Phasors consist of a magnitude and phase angle

If we now employ phasors in the analysis of the *RL* circuit, Eq. (4.8) becomes

$$L\frac{d}{dt}(\mathbf{I}e^{j\omega t}) + R\mathbf{I}e^{j\omega t} = \mathbf{V}e^{j\omega t}$$

where $\mathbf{I} = I_M\angle\phi$ and $\mathbf{V} = V_M\angle 0^\circ$. Performing the indicated derivative and eliminating the common factor $e^{j\omega t}$ yields the phasor equation

$$j\omega L\mathbf{I} + R\mathbf{I} = \mathbf{V}$$

Therefore,

$$\mathbf{I} = \frac{\mathbf{V}}{R + j\omega L} = I_M\angle\phi = \frac{V_M}{\sqrt{R^2 + \omega^2 L^2}}\angle -\tan^{-1}\frac{\omega L}{R}$$

Thus

$$i(t) = \frac{V_M}{\sqrt{R^2 + \omega^2 L^2}}\cos\left(\omega t - \tan^{-1}\frac{\omega L}{R}\right)$$

which, once again, is the function we obtained earlier.

We refer to a phasor analysis as a *frequency domain* analysis. Thus, we have transformed a set of differential equations with sinusoidal forcing functions in the time domain to a set of algebraic equations containing complex numbers in the frequency domain. In effect, we are now faced with solving a set of algebraic equations for the unknown phasors. The phasors are then simply transformed back to the time domain to yield the solution of the original set of differential equations. In addition, as indicated earlier, we have tacitly assumed that sinusoidal functions would be represented as phasors with a phase angle based on a cosine function. Therefore, in both the transformation between the time domain and the frequency domain, as well as the reverse transformation

The transformation between the frequency domain and the time domain

$$A\cos(\omega t \pm \theta) \leftrightarrow A\,\underline{/\pm\theta}$$
$$A\sin(\omega t \pm \theta) \leftrightarrow A\,\underline{/\pm\theta - 90^\circ} \qquad (4.17)$$

Example 4.2

Convert the time functions $v(t) = 24\cos(377t - 45^\circ)$ and $i(t) = 12\sin(377t + 120^\circ)$ to phasors.

Using the phasor transformation shown above, we have

$$\mathbf{V} = 24\underline{/-45^\circ}$$
$$\mathbf{I} = 12\underline{/120^\circ - 90^\circ} = 12\underline{/30^\circ}$$

Example 4.3

Convert the phasors $\mathbf{V} = 16\underline{/20^\circ}$ and $\mathbf{I} = 10\underline{/-75^\circ}$ from the frequency domain to the time domain if the frequency is 60 Hz.

Employing the reverse transformation for phasors, we find that

$$v(t) = 16\cos(377t + 20^\circ)$$
$$i(t) = 10\cos(377t - 75^\circ)$$

Drill Exercises

D4.3. Convert the following voltage functions to phasors.

$$v_1(t) = 12\cos(377t - 425^\circ)\text{ V}$$
$$v_2(t) = 18\sin(2513t + 4.2^\circ)\text{ V}$$

Ans: $\mathbf{V_1} = 12\underline{/-425^\circ}\text{V}$, $\mathbf{V_2} = 18\underline{/-85.8^\circ}\text{V}$.

D4.4. Convert the following phasors to the time domain if the frequency is 400 Hz.

$$\mathbf{V}_1 = 10\underline{/20^\circ}$$
$$\mathbf{V}_2 = 12\underline{/-60^\circ}$$

Ans: $v_1(t) = 10\cos(800\pi t + 20^\circ)\text{V}$, $v_2(t) = 12\cos(800\pi t - 60^\circ)$ V.

4-4 Phasor Relationships for Circuit Elements

The next step in our development of the phasor analysis technique is the establishment of the phasor relationships between voltage and current for the passive elements R, L, and C.

4.4.1 Resistor

For a resistor, the voltage–current relationship is

$$v(t) = R\,i(t) \tag{4.18}$$

Applying $v(t) = V_M e^{j(\omega t + \theta_v)}$ yields $i(t) = I_M e^{j(\omega t + \theta_i)}$ and therefore,

$$V_M e^{j(\omega t + \theta_v)} = R I_M e^{j(\omega t + \theta_i)}$$

which can be written in phasor form as

$$\mathbf{V} = R\mathbf{I} \tag{4.19}$$

where $\mathbf{V} = V_M e^{j\theta_v} = V_M \underline{/\theta_v}$ and $\mathbf{I} = I_M e^{j\theta_i} = I_M \underline{/\theta_i}$. In this case $\theta_v = \theta_i$ and the current and voltage are *in phase*.

4.4.2 Inductor

The voltage–current relationship for an inductor is

Phasor relationships for the common passive elements

$$v(t) = L\frac{di(t)}{dt} \tag{4.20}$$

The same arguments that lead to the development of Eq. (4.19) yield the relationship

$$\mathbf{V} = j\omega L\mathbf{I} \tag{4.21}$$

The imaginary operator $j = 1e^{j90^\circ} = 1\underline{/90^\circ} = \sqrt{-1}$. Therefore, in an inductor, the voltage leads the current by 90°or the current lags the voltage by 90°.

4.4.3 Capacitor

For a capacitor the voltage–current relationship is

$$i(t) = C\frac{dv(t)}{dt} \tag{4.22}$$

which can be written in phasor form as

$$\mathbf{I} = j\omega C\mathbf{V} \tag{4.23}$$

Hence, in a capacitor, the current leads the voltage by 90°or the voltage lags the current by 90°.

Since phasors are complex numbers, they can be graphically represented as line segments on a *phasor diagram*. This diagram illustrates the relative magnitude of one phasor with another, the angle between them, and their relative position with respect to one another. Figure 4.6 illustrates the voltage–current relationship, the sinusoidal waveforms, and the phasor diagrams for the three passive elements.

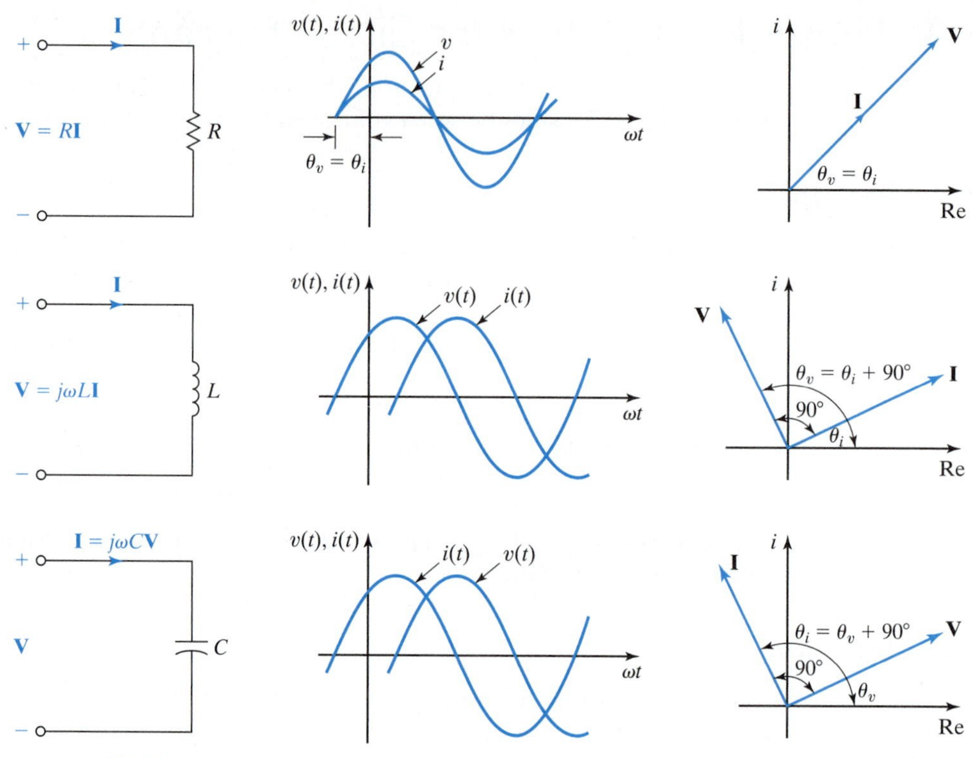

FIGURE 4.6 Characteristics of the passive elements *R, L*, and *C*.

4–5 Impedance and Admittance

Having examined each of the passive circuit elements in the frequency domain, we now define the *Impedance* **Z** in exactly the same manner in which we defined resistance earlier.

Impedance (resistance and reactance) defined

Impedance is defined as the ratio of the phasor voltage **V** to the phasor current **I**:

$$\mathbf{Z} = \frac{\mathbf{V}}{\mathbf{I}} \tag{4.24}$$

at the two terminals of the element related to one another by the passive sign convention, as illustrated in Figure 4.7. Equation (4.24) can be written in the form

$$\mathbf{Z} = \frac{V_M\angle\theta_v}{I_M\angle\theta_i} = \frac{V_M}{I_M}\angle\theta_v - \theta_i = Z\angle\theta_z \tag{4.25}$$

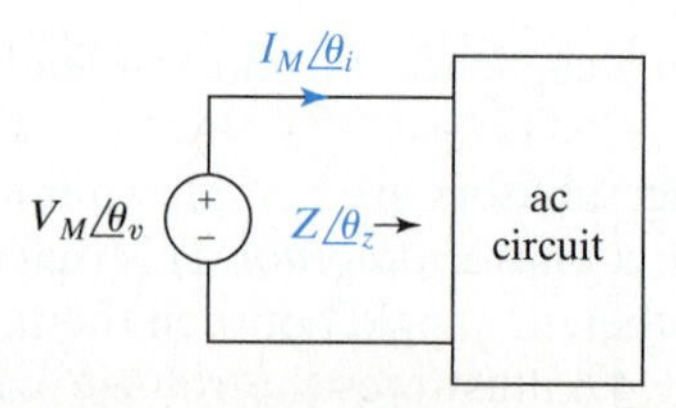

FIGURE 4.7 General impedance relationship.

Since **Z** is the ratio of **V** to **I**, the units of **Z** are ohms. Thus, impedance in an ac circuit is analogous to resistance in a dc circuit. In rectangular form, impedance is expressed as

$$\mathbf{Z}(j\omega) = R(\omega) + jX(\omega) \tag{4.26}$$

where $R(\omega)$ is the *real, or resistive, component* and $X(\omega)$ is the *imaginary, or reactive, component.*

This latter component, that is, reactance, is the imaginary component of the impedance and its units are the same as those of the resistive component—Ohms.

Equation (4.26) clearly indicates that **Z**, which is frequency dependent, is a complex number; however, it is not a phasor. Recall that the phasors **V** and **I** correspond to time-domain, steady-state signals. However, the impedance, **Z**, has no meaning in the time domain

Equations (4.25) and (4.26) indicate that

$$Z\angle\theta_z = R + jX$$

Therefore,

$$Z = \sqrt{R^2 + X^2} \tag{4.27}$$

$$\theta_z = \tan^{-1}\frac{X}{R} \tag{4.28}$$

where

$$R = Z\cos\theta_z$$
$$X = Z\sin\theta_z$$

For the three passive elements, R, L, and C, the impedance of each when viewed as individual components is

$$Z_R = R$$
$$Z_L = j\omega L$$
$$Z_C = 1/j\omega C$$

Just as it was advantageous to know how to determine the equivalent resistance of a series and/or parallel combination of resistors in a dc circuit, we now want to learn how to determine the equivalent impedance in an ac circuit when the passive elements are interconnected. The determination of equivalent impedance is based on Kirchhoff's current law (KCL) and Kirchhoff's voltage law (KVL). Therefore, we must see if these laws are valid in the frequency domain. Suppose, for example, that a circuit is driven by voltage sources of the form $V_{M_m}\cos(\omega t + \theta_m)$. Then, since the network is linear, every steady-state current in the network will be of the form $I_{M_k}\cos(\omega t + \phi_k)$. At any node in the circuit. KCL, written in the time domain, is

$$i_1(t) + i_2(t) + \cdots i_n(t) = 0$$

$$I_{M_1}\cos(\omega t + \phi_1) + I_{M_2}\cos(\omega t + \phi_2) + \cdots + I_{M_n}\cos(\omega t + \phi_n) = 0$$

From our previous work we can immediately apply the phasor transformation to the equation above to obtain

$$\mathbf{I}_1 + \mathbf{I}_2 + \ldots \mathbf{I}_n = 0$$

However, this equation is simply KCL in the frequency domain. In a similar manner we can show that KVL applies in the frequency domain. Using the fact that KCL and KVL are valid

Combining impedances in series and parallel

in the frequency domain, we can show, as was done in Chapter 2 for resistors, that impedances can be combined using the same rules that we established for resistor combinations, that is, if $\mathbf{Z}_1, \mathbf{Z}_2, \mathbf{Z}_3, \ldots, \mathbf{Z}_n$ are connected in series, the equivalent impedance $\mathbf{Z}_s$ is

$$\mathbf{Z}_s = \mathbf{Z}_1 + \mathbf{Z}_2 + \mathbf{Z}_3 + \ldots + \mathbf{Z}_n \tag{4.29}$$

and if $\mathbf{Z}_1, \mathbf{Z}_2, \mathbf{Z}_3, \ldots, \mathbf{Z}_n$ are connected in parallel, the equivalent impedance is

$$\frac{\mathbf{1}}{\mathbf{Z}_p} = \frac{\mathbf{1}}{\mathbf{Z}_1} + \frac{\mathbf{1}}{\mathbf{Z}_2} + \frac{\mathbf{1}}{\mathbf{Z}_3} + \cdots + \frac{\mathbf{1}}{\mathbf{Z}_n} \tag{4.30}$$

Example 4.4

In a farmhouse, the wiring circuit for the basement area uses a 25 A circuit breaker. The circuit breaker will open if the current in it exceeds 25 A. The basement circuit is modeled as shown in Figure 4.8. Given this network, we wish to know (a) if all the lamps and the dryer can be turned on at the same time, and (b) if the space heater can be used if everything else in the circuit is on.

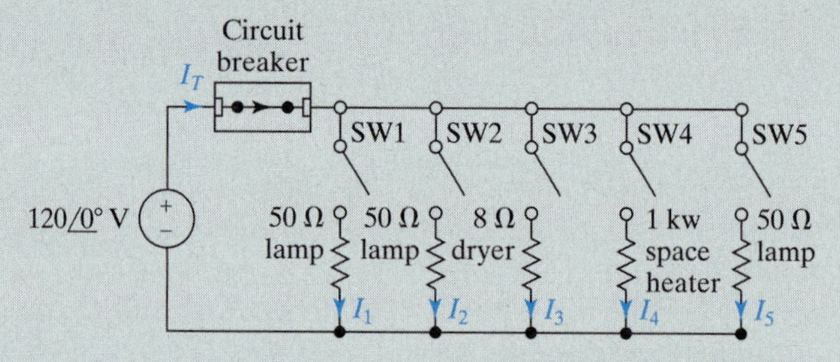

FIGURE 4.8 Circuit used in Example 4.4.

(a) If all lamps and the dryer are on, that is, switches *sw*1, *sw*2, *sw*3, and *sw*5 are closed, then

$$\mathbf{I}_1 = \mathbf{I}_2 = \mathbf{I}_5 = \frac{120\angle 0^\circ}{50}$$
$$= 2.4\angle 0^\circ \text{ A}$$

and

$$\mathbf{I}_3 = \frac{120\angle 0^\circ}{8}$$
$$= 15\angle 0^\circ \text{ A}$$

Therefore, the total current

$$\mathbf{I}_T = \mathbf{I}_1 + \mathbf{I}_2 + \mathbf{I}_3 + \mathbf{I}_5$$
$$= 22.2\angle 0^\circ \text{ A}$$

Since this has a magnitude less than 25 A, the circuit breaker will permit this current in the circuit.

(b) The 1 kW space heater will draw a current of

$$\mathbf{I}_4 = \frac{1000}{120}\angle 0^\circ$$
$$= 8.33\angle 0^\circ \text{A}$$

If the space heater is turned on while everything else is on, the total current will be

$$\mathbf{I}_T = \mathbf{I}_1 + \mathbf{I}_2 + \mathbf{I}_3 + \mathbf{I}_4 + \mathbf{I}_5$$
$$= 30.53 \angle 0^\circ \text{ A}$$

and the circuit breaker will open, interrupting the circuit.

Example 4.5

Determine the equivalent impedance of the network shown in Figure 4.9 if the frequency is $f = 60$ Hz. Then compute the current $i(t)$ if the voltage source is $v(t) = 50 \cos(\omega t + 30^\circ)$ V. Finally, calculate the equivalent impedance if the frequency is that used in aircraft, that is, $f = 400$ Hz.

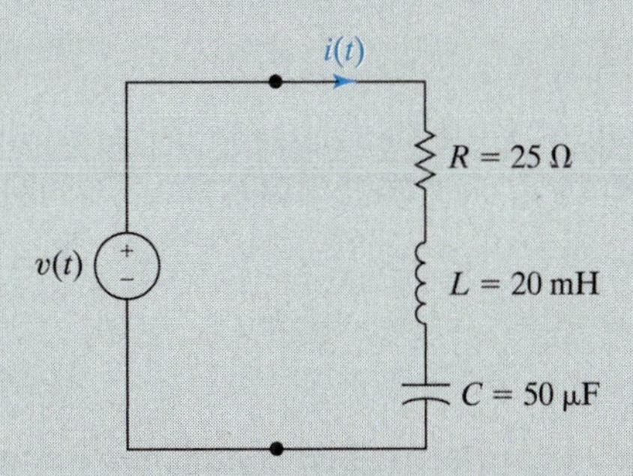

FIGURE 4.9 Series ac circuit.

The impedances of the individual elements at 60 Hz are

$$\mathbf{Z}_R = 25\ \Omega$$

$$\mathbf{Z}_L = j\omega\mathbf{L} = j(2\pi \times 60)(20 \times 10^{-3}) = j7.54\ \Omega$$

$$\mathbf{Z}_C = \frac{-j}{\omega C} = \frac{-j}{(2\pi \times 60)(50 \times 10^{-6})} = -j53.05\ \Omega$$

Since the elements are in series

$$\mathbf{Z} = \mathbf{Z}_R + \mathbf{Z}_L + \mathbf{Z}_C$$
$$= 25 - j45.51\ \Omega$$

the current in the circuit is given by

$$\mathbf{I} = \frac{\mathbf{V}}{\mathbf{Z}} = \frac{50\angle 30^\circ}{25 - j45.51} = \frac{50\angle 30^\circ}{51.92\angle -61.22^\circ} = 0.96\angle 91.22^\circ \text{A}$$

or in the time domain, $i(t) = 0.96 \cos(377t + 91.22^\circ)$ A.

If the frequency is 400 Hz, the impedance of each element is

$$\mathbf{Z}_R = 25\ \Omega$$

$$\mathbf{Z}_L = j\omega L = j50.27\ \Omega$$

$$\mathbf{Z}_c = \frac{-j}{\omega C} = -j7.96\ \Omega$$

The total impedance is then

$$\mathbf{Z} = 25 + j42.31 = 49.14\underline{/59.42°}\ \Omega$$

It is important to note that at the frequency $f = 60$ Hz, the reactance of the circuit is capacitive, that is, if the impedance is written as $R + jX$, $X < 0$; however, at $f = 400$ Hz the reactance is inductive since $X > 0$.

Another quantity that is very useful in the analysis of ac circuits is *admittance,* which is the reciprocal of impedance, that is,

$$\mathbf{Y} = \frac{1}{\mathbf{Z}} = \frac{\mathbf{I}}{\mathbf{V}} \tag{4.31}$$

The units of **Y** are Siemens, and this quantity is analogous to conductance in resistive dc circuits. Since **Z** is a complex number, **Y** is also a complex number

$$\mathbf{Y} = Y_M\underline{/\theta_Y} \tag{4.32}$$

Admittance (conductance and susceptance) defined

which is written in rectangular form as

$$\mathbf{Y} = G + jB \tag{4.33}$$

where G and B are called *conductance* and *susceptance,* respectively. Because of the relationship between **Y** and **Z**, we can express the components of one quantity as a function of the components of the other

$$G + jB = \frac{1}{R + jX} \tag{4.34}$$

Rationalizing the right-hand side of this equation yields

$$G + jB = \frac{R - jX}{R^2 + X^2}$$

and therefore,

$$G = \frac{R}{R^2 + X^2} \qquad B = \frac{-X}{R^2 + X^2} \tag{4.35}$$

In a similar manner we can show that

$$R = \frac{G}{G^2 + B^2} \tag{4.36}$$

$$X = \frac{-B}{G^2 + B^2} \tag{4.37}$$

It is very important to note that in general R and G are not reciprocals of one another. The same is true for X and B. The purely resistive case is an exception. In the purely reactive case the quantities are negative reciprocals of one another.

The admittance of the individual passive elements is

$$\begin{aligned} \mathbf{Y}_R &= \frac{1}{R} = G \\ \mathbf{Y}_L &= \frac{1}{j\omega L} = \frac{1}{\omega L}\angle -90^\circ \\ \mathbf{Y}_C &= j\omega C = \omega C \angle 90^\circ \end{aligned} \tag{4.38}$$

Once again, since KCL and KVL are valid in the frequency domain, we can show, using the same approach outlined in Chapter 2 for conductance in resistive circuits, that the rules for combining admittances are the same as those for combining conductances; that is, if $\mathbf{Y}_1, \mathbf{Y}_2, \mathbf{Y}_3, \ldots, \mathbf{Y}_n$ are connected in parallel, the equivalent admittance is

Combining admittances in series and parallel

$$\mathbf{Y}_p = \mathbf{Y}_1 + \mathbf{Y}_2 + \ldots + \mathbf{Y}_n \tag{4.39}$$

and if $\mathbf{Y}_1, \mathbf{Y}_2, \ldots, \mathbf{Y}_n$ are connected in series, the equivalent admittance is

$$\frac{1}{\mathbf{Y}_s} = \frac{1}{\mathbf{Y}_1} + \frac{1}{\mathbf{Y}_2} + \cdots + \frac{1}{\mathbf{Y}_n} \tag{4.40}$$

Example 4.6

Let us compute the impedance $\mathbf{Z}_T$ at the terminals of the network shown in Figure 4.10(a). We will first determine $\mathbf{Z}_T$ using only impedances and then we will solve the problem using a combination of impedance and admittance.

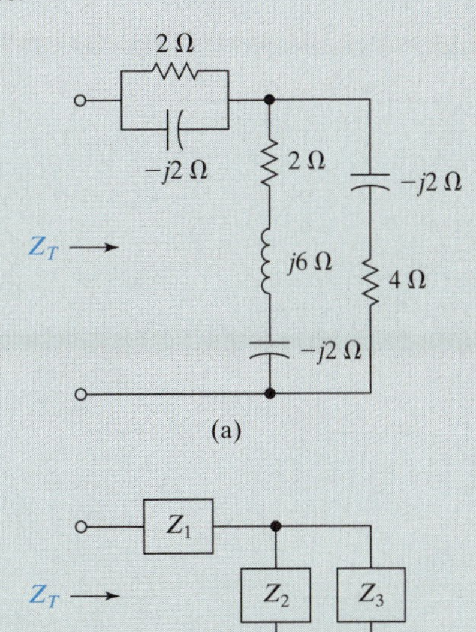

FIGURE 4.10 Circuits used in Example 4.6.

The circuit is redrawn as shown in Figure 4.10(b). From that network we find that

$$\mathbf{Z}_{23} = \frac{\mathbf{Z}_2\mathbf{Z}_3}{\mathbf{Z}_2 + \mathbf{Z}_3}$$

$$= \frac{(2 + j4)(4 - j2)}{2 + j4 + 4 - j2}$$

$$= 3 + j1\ \Omega$$

Furthermore,

$$\mathbf{Z}_1 = \frac{(2)(-j2)}{2 - j2}$$

$$= 1 - j1\ \Omega$$

Therefore,

$$\mathbf{Z}_T = \mathbf{Z}_1 + \mathbf{Z}_{23}$$

$$= 4\ \Omega$$

Using admittances we find that

$$\mathbf{Y}_3 = \frac{1}{\mathbf{Z}_3} = \frac{1}{4 - j2} = 0.20 + j0.10\ S$$

And

$$\mathbf{Y}_2 = \frac{1}{\mathbf{Z}_2} = \frac{1}{2 + j4} = 0.10 - j0.20\ S$$

Hence

$$\mathbf{Y}_{23} = \mathbf{Y}_2 + \mathbf{Y}_3 = 0.30 - j0.10\ S$$

And

$$\mathbf{Z}_{23} = \frac{1}{\mathbf{Y}_{23}} = \frac{1}{0.30 - j0.10} = 3 + j1\ \Omega$$

Now since

$$\mathbf{Y}_1 = \frac{1}{2} + \frac{1}{-j2} = 0.5 + j0.5\ S$$

Then

$$\mathbf{Z}_1 = \frac{1}{\mathbf{Y}_1} = \frac{1}{0.5 + j0.5} = 1 - j1\ \Omega$$

And therefore,

$$\mathbf{Z}_T = \mathbf{Z}_1 + \mathbf{Z}_{23} = 4\ \Omega$$

which, of course, is identical to that obtained above.

Drill Exercise

D4.5. Compute the impedance $\mathbf{Z}_T$ in the network in Figure D4.5.

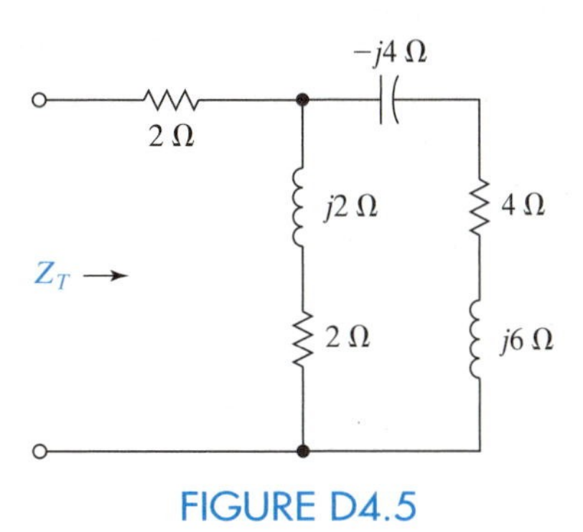

FIGURE D4.5

Ans: $\mathbf{Z}_T = 3.38 + j1.08\ \Omega$.

4-6 Y ⇆ Δ Transformations

Wye/delta transformations for impedance

The wye-to-delta and delta-to-wye transformations presented earlier for resistance are also valid for impedance in the frequency domain. Therefore, the impedances shown in Figure 4.11 are related by the following equations:

$$\mathbf{Z}_a = \frac{\mathbf{Z}_1\mathbf{Z}_2}{\mathbf{Z}_1 + \mathbf{Z}_2 + \mathbf{Z}_3}$$

$$\mathbf{Z}_b = \frac{\mathbf{Z}_1\mathbf{Z}_3}{\mathbf{Z}_1 + \mathbf{Z}_2 + \mathbf{Z}_3} \qquad (4.41)$$

$$\mathbf{Z}_c = \frac{\mathbf{Z}_2\mathbf{Z}_3}{\mathbf{Z}_1 + \mathbf{Z}_2 + \mathbf{Z}_3}$$

and

$$\mathbf{Z}_1 = \frac{\mathbf{Z}_a\mathbf{Z}_b + \mathbf{Z}_b\mathbf{Z}_c + \mathbf{Z}_c\mathbf{Z}_a}{\mathbf{Z}_c}$$

$$\mathbf{Z}_2 = \frac{\mathbf{Z}_a\mathbf{Z}_b + \mathbf{Z}_b\mathbf{Z}_c + \mathbf{Z}_c\mathbf{Z}_a}{\mathbf{Z}_b} \qquad (4.42)$$

$$\mathbf{Z}_3 = \frac{\mathbf{Z}_a\mathbf{Z}_b + \mathbf{Z}_b\mathbf{Z}_c + \mathbf{Z}_c\mathbf{Z}_a}{\mathbf{Z}_a}$$

These equations are general relationships and therefore apply to any set of impedances connected in a wye or delta configuration.

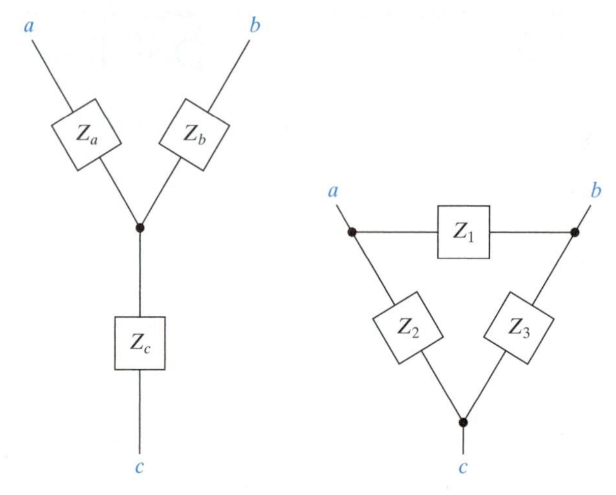

FIGURE 4.11 Wye and delta network configurations.

Example 4.7

Let us determine the impedance Z_{eq} at the terminals $A - B$ of the network in Figure 4.12(a). To simplify the network we must convert one of the back-to-back deltas into a wye.

If we select the delta defined by the points C, D, and E, the impedances of the corresponding wye are calculated from Eq. (4.41) as

$$\frac{(2)(-j2 + j4)}{2 - j2 + j4 + 1 + j1} = \frac{2(j2)}{3 + j3} = 0.66 + j0.66\ \Omega$$

$$\frac{(2)(1 + j1)}{3 + j3} = 0.67\ \Omega$$

$$\frac{(-j2 + j4)(1 + j1)}{3 + j3} = j0.67\ \Omega$$

and shown in Figure 4.12(b). If we now combine the two impedances in parallel, we obtain

$$\frac{(0.67 - j1)(2 + j0.67)}{0.67 - j1 + 2 + j0.67} = 0.81 - j0.48\ \Omega$$

which reduces the network to that shown in Figure 4.12(c). Hence, the equivalent impedance is

$$\mathbf{Z}_{eq} = 2 + 0.66 + j0.66 + 0.81 - j0.48$$

$$= 3.47 + j0.18\ \Omega$$

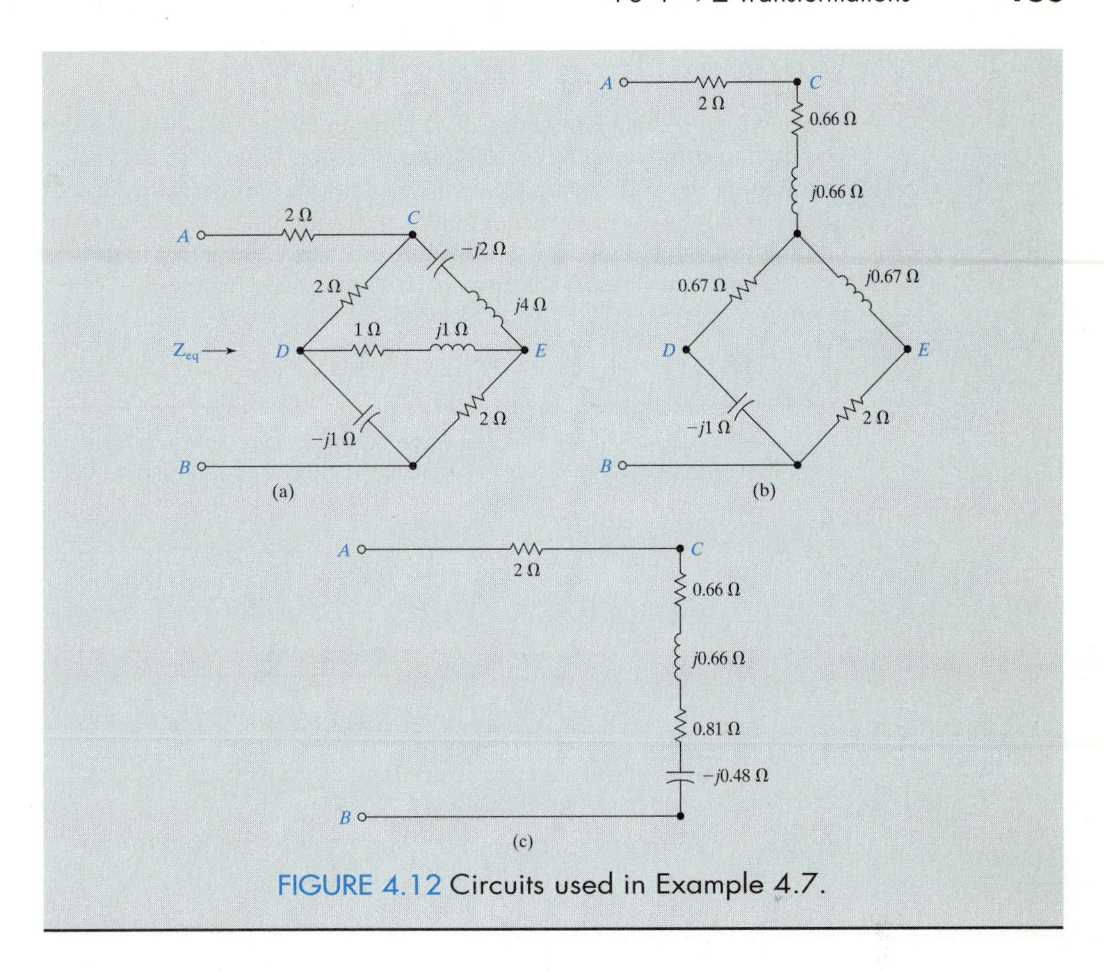

FIGURE 4.12 Circuits used in Example 4.7.

Drill Exercise

D4.6. Determine $\mathbf{Z}_{eq}$ at the terminals $A - B$ of the network shown in Figure D4.6.

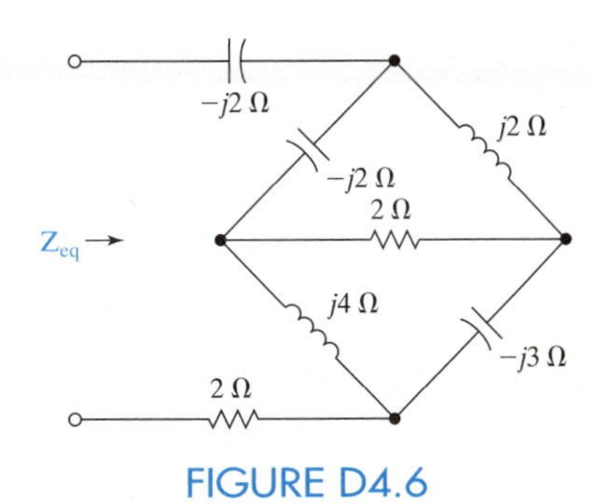

FIGURE D4.6

Ans: $\mathbf{Z}_{eq} = 4 - j4\ \Omega$.

4-7 Basic Analysis Using Kirchhoff's Laws

We have shown that Kirchhoff's laws apply in the frequency domain, and therefore they can be used to compute steady-state voltages and currents in ac circuits. This approach involves expressing the voltages and currents as phasors, and once this is done, the ac steady-state analysis employing phasor equations is performed in an identical fashion to that used in the dc analysis of resistive circuits—the only difference being that in steady-state ac circuit analysis the algebraic phasor equations have complex coefficients.

Example 4.8

We wish to calculate the voltages and currents in the circuit shown in Figure 4.13. Our approach will be as follows. We will calculate the total impedance seen by the source $\mathbf{V}_s$.

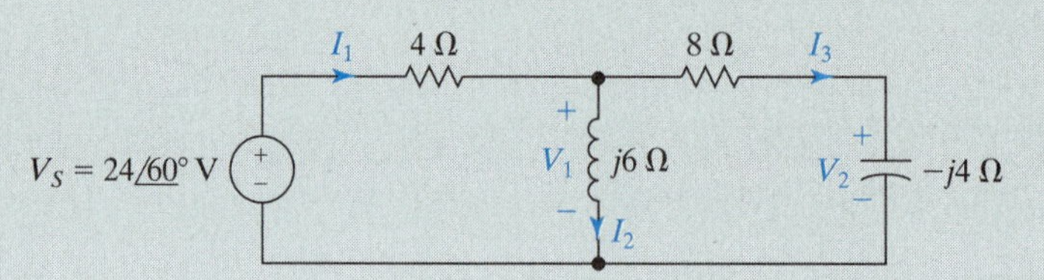

FIGURE 4.13 Example of an ac circuit.

Then we will use this to determine $\mathbf{I}_1$. Knowing $\mathbf{I}_1$, we can compute $\mathbf{V}_1$ using KVL. Knowing $\mathbf{V}_1$, we can compute $\mathbf{I}_2$ and $\mathbf{I}_3$, and so on.

$$\mathbf{Z}_{eq} = 4 + \frac{(j6)(8 - j4)}{j6 + 8 - j4}$$

$$= 4 + \frac{24 + j48}{8 + j2}$$

$$= 4 + 4.24 + j4.94$$

$$= 9.61\underline{/30.94^\circ}\ \Omega$$

Then

$$\mathbf{I}_1 = \frac{\mathbf{V}_s}{\mathbf{Z}_{eq}} = \frac{24\underline{/60^\circ}}{9.61\underline{/30.94^\circ}}$$

$$= 2.5\underline{/29.06^\circ}\ \text{A}$$

$\mathbf{V}_1$ can be determined using KVL:

$$\mathbf{V}_1 = \mathbf{V}_s - 4\mathbf{I}_1$$

$$= 24\underline{/60^\circ} - 10\underline{/29.06^\circ}$$

$$= 3.26 + j15.92 = 16.25\underline{/78.43^\circ}\mathbf{V}$$

Note that $\mathbf{V}_1$ could also be computed via voltage division:

$$\mathbf{V}_1 = \frac{\mathbf{V}_s \dfrac{(j6)(8 - j4)}{j6 + 8 - j4}}{4 + \dfrac{(j6)(8 - j4)}{j6 + 8 - j4}}\ \text{V}$$

which from our previous calculation is

$$\mathbf{V}_1 = \frac{(24\underline{/60^\circ})(6.5\underline{/49.30^\circ})}{9.61\underline{/30.49^\circ}}$$
$$= 16.25\underline{/78.43^\circ}\text{ V}$$

Knowing $\mathbf{V}_1$, we can calculate both $\mathbf{I}_2$ and $\mathbf{I}_3$:

$$\mathbf{I}_2 = \frac{\mathbf{V}_1}{j6} = \frac{16.25\underline{/78.43^\circ}}{6\underline{/90^\circ}}$$
$$= 2.71\underline{/-11.56^\circ}\text{ A}$$

and

$$\mathbf{I}_3 = \frac{\mathbf{V}_1}{8 - j4}$$
$$= 1.82\underline{/105^\circ}\text{ A}$$

$\mathbf{I}_2$ and $\mathbf{I}_3$ could have been calculated by current division. For example, $\mathbf{I}_2$ could be determined by

$$\mathbf{I}_2 = \frac{\mathbf{I}_1(8 - j4)}{8 - j4 + j6}$$
$$= \frac{(2.5\underline{/29.06^\circ})(8.94\underline{/-26.57^\circ})}{8 + j2}$$
$$= 2.71\underline{/-11.56^\circ}\text{ A}$$

Finally, $\mathbf{V}_2$ can be computed as

$$\mathbf{V}_2 = \mathbf{I}_3(-j4)$$
$$= 7.28\underline{/15^\circ}\text{ V}$$

This value could also have been computed by voltage division.

Once the voltages and currents have been calculated we can display them in a graphical fashion using what is called a phasor diagram. In this diagram we simply plot the various phasors of interest and, in so doing, we can immediately see the relationship among them. For example, the phasor diagram for the three currents in this example is shown in Figure 4.14 and represents a graphical illustration of KCL.

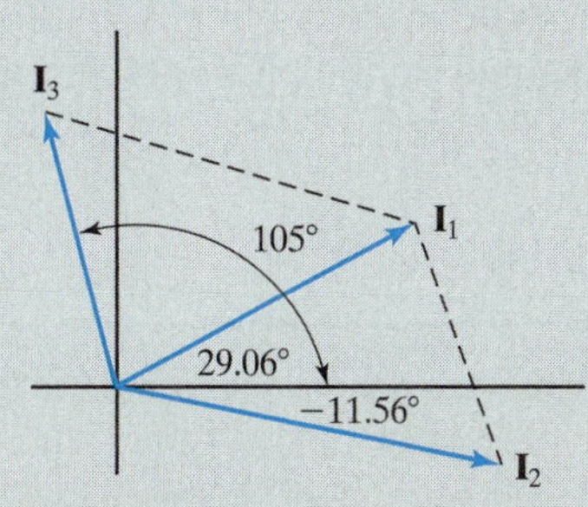

FIGURE 4.14 Phasor diagram for the currents in Example 4.8.

We have demonstrated the use of KCL, KVL, and the relationship $\mathbf{V} = \mathbf{IZ}$ in the solution of ac steady-state circuit problems. Since the passive circuit elements R, L, and C are linear components, the circuit analysis tools used in dc circuit analysis are applicable in ac steady-state analysis also. The primary difference between these two analyses is that in the ac case, the use of phasors, impedance, and admittance lead to equations involving complex numbers.

Drill Exercise

D4.7. Given the network in Figure D4.7, find the voltages $\mathbf{V}_L$, $\mathbf{V}_R$, and $\mathbf{V}_C$ and plot them on a phasor diagram.

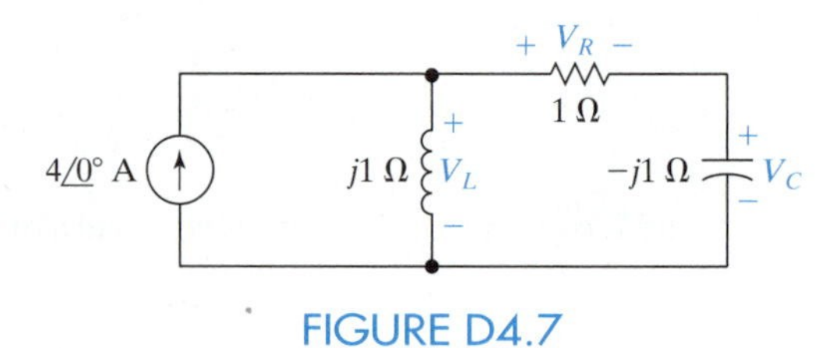

FIGURE D4.7

Ans: $\mathbf{V}_L = 4\sqrt{2}\,\underline{/45^\circ}$ V, $\mathbf{V}_R = 4\,\underline{/90^\circ}$ V, $\mathbf{V}_C = 4\,\underline{/0^\circ}$ V, and the phasor diagram is as shown below.

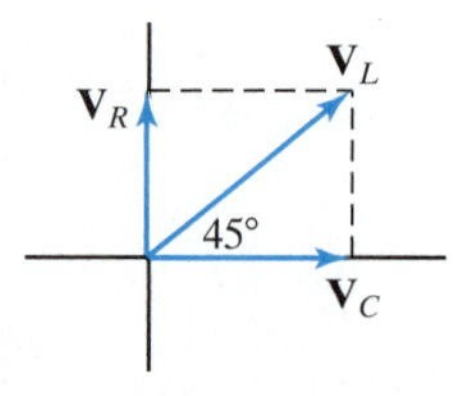

4-8 Nodal Analysis

Nodal analysis can be used in the frequency domain

The following example illustrates that *nodal analysis* is performed in exactly the same manner as it was in dc resistive circuits. In this section nodal analysis will be employed in the frequency domain using the phasor technique.

Example 4.9

Let us compute the node voltages and use them to find $\mathbf{I}_0$ in the circuit shown in Figure 4.15. There are four nodes and, therefore, three equations are needed to solve the circuit.

Note that $\mathbf{V}_0 = 12\,\underline{/0^\circ}$ V and, therefore, is known. KCL applied to the remaining nodes yields the equations

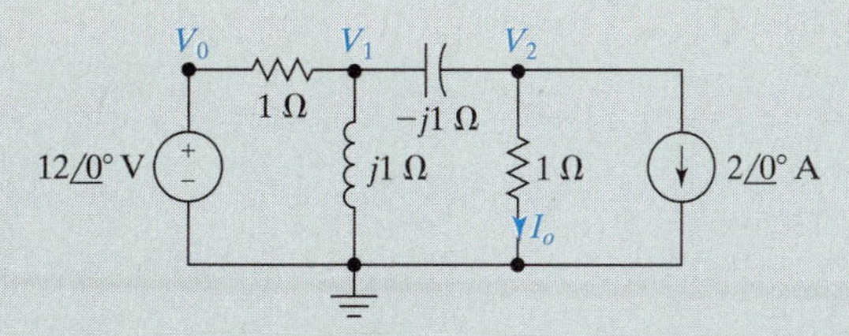

FIGURE 4.15 Circuit analyzed in Example 4.9.

$$\frac{\mathbf{V}_1 - \mathbf{V}_0}{1} + \frac{\mathbf{V}_1}{j1} + \frac{\mathbf{V}_1 - \mathbf{V}_2}{-j1} = 0$$

$$\frac{\mathbf{V}_2 - \mathbf{V}_1}{-j1} + \frac{\mathbf{V}_2}{1} + 2\underline{/0^\circ} = 0$$

which when simplified become

$$1\mathbf{V}_1 - j1\mathbf{V}_2 = 12\underline{/0^\circ}$$

$$-j1\mathbf{V}_1 + (1 + j)\mathbf{V}_2 = -2\underline{/0^\circ}$$

Solving the equations by Cramer's rule, we first compute the determinant as

$$\begin{aligned} det &= \begin{vmatrix} 1 & -j1 \\ -j1 & 1 + j \end{vmatrix} \\ &= 1(1 + j) - (-j)(-j) \\ &= 2 + j \end{aligned}$$

The node voltage $\mathbf{V}_1$ is then

$$\begin{aligned} \mathbf{V}_1 &= \frac{\begin{vmatrix} 12\underline{/0^\circ} & -j1 \\ -2\underline{/0^\circ} & 1 + j \end{vmatrix}}{2 + j} \\ &= \frac{12(1 + j) - (-2)(-j1)}{2 + j} \\ &= \frac{12 + j10}{2 + j} \\ &= \frac{34}{5} + j\frac{8}{5}\text{V} \end{aligned}$$

and the node voltage $\mathbf{V}_2$ is

$$\begin{aligned} \mathbf{V}_2 &= \frac{\begin{vmatrix} 1 & 12\underline{/0^\circ} \\ -j & -2\underline{/0^\circ} \end{vmatrix}}{2 + j} \\ &= \frac{-2 + j12}{2 + j} \\ &= \frac{8}{5} + j\frac{26}{5}\text{V} \end{aligned}$$

Then

$$\mathbf{I}_0 = \frac{\mathbf{V}_2}{1}$$

$$= \frac{8}{5} + j\frac{26}{5}\text{A}$$

The use of MATLAB in the frequency domain

The node voltages could also be computed using MATLAB. In this ac case, a complex number $x + jy$ is listed as $x + j * y$ (although MATLAB typically uses i instead of j). The node equation to be solved is **Y*V** = **I** and the solution is **V** = inv(**Y**)***I**. The MATLAB solution is listed as follows.

```
EDU»  Y = [1 -j*1; -j*1 1 + j*1]

Y =

    1.0000                  0 - 1.0000i
         0 - 1.0000i 1.0000 + 1.0000i

EDU»   I = [12; -2]

I =

    12
    -2

EDU» V = inv (Y) *I

V =

    6.8000 + 1.6000i
    1.6000 + 5.2000i
```

Drill Exercise

D4.8. Use nodal analysis to find $\mathbf{I}_0$ in the circuit in Figure D4.8.

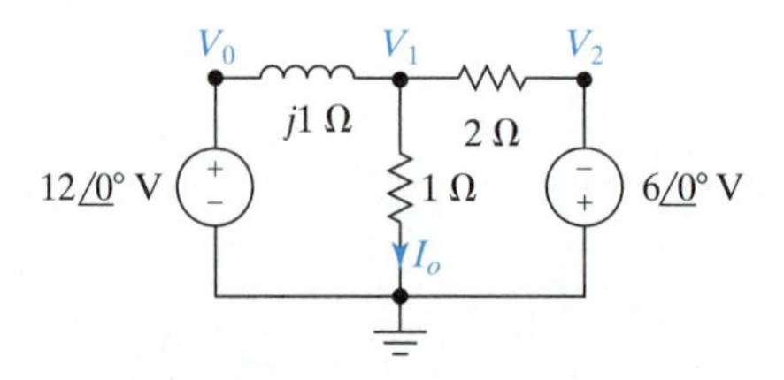

FIGURE D4.8

Ans: $\mathbf{I}_0 = \left(\frac{30}{13} - j\frac{84}{13}\right)$ A.

4-9 Mesh and Loop Analysis

Loop analysis is applicable in the frequency domain

The following example will illustrate the use of *mesh* and *loop analyses* in ac steady-state circuits. For comparison we will use the circuit in Example 4.9.

Example 4.10

Consider the network in Figure 4.16 in which the mesh currents are labeled. Note that since the mesh current $\mathbf{I}_3$ goes through the current source, $\mathbf{I}_3 = 2\angle 0°$ A. The KVL equations for the two remaining meshes are

$$(1 + j)\mathbf{I}_1 - j1\mathbf{I}_2 = 12\angle 0°$$

$$-j1\mathbf{I}_1 + (j1 - j1 + 1)\mathbf{I}_2 - 1\mathbf{I}_3 = 0$$

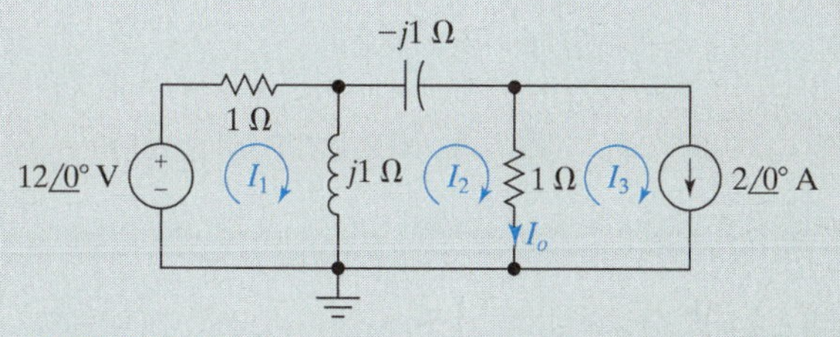

FIGURE 4.16 Circuit used in Example 4.10.

Simplifying the equations yields

$$(1 + j)\mathbf{I}_1 - j\mathbf{I}_2 = 12\angle 0°$$

$$-j\mathbf{I}_1 + \mathbf{I}_2 = 2\angle 0°$$

The determinant for the equation is

$$det = \begin{vmatrix} 1 + j & -j \\ -j & 1 \end{vmatrix}$$

$$= (1 + j)(1) - (-j)(-j)$$

$$= 2 + j$$

The current $\mathbf{I}_1$ is then

$$\mathbf{I}_1 = \frac{\begin{vmatrix} 12\angle 0° & -j \\ 2\angle 0° & 1 \end{vmatrix}}{2 + j}$$

$$= \frac{12 + 2j}{2 + j}$$

$$= \left(\frac{26}{5} - j\frac{8}{5}\right) \text{A}$$

and the current $\mathbf{I}_2$ is

$$\mathbf{I}_2 = \frac{\begin{vmatrix} 1+j & 12\angle 0^\circ \\ -j & 2\angle 0^\circ \end{vmatrix}}{2+j}$$

$$= \frac{2(1+j)+12j}{2+j}$$

$$= \left(\frac{18}{5} + j\frac{26}{5}\right) \text{A}$$

The MATLAB solution to this problem involves solving the equation $\mathbf{Z} * \mathbf{I} = \mathbf{V}$. The input data, as well as the solution expression $\mathbf{I} = \text{inv}(\mathbf{Z}) * \mathbf{V}$, is listed below.

```
EDU» Z=[1 + j*1 -j*1; -j*1 1]

Z =

   1.0000 + 1.0000i       0 - 1.0000i
        0 - 1.0000i 1.0000

EDU» V=[12; 2]

V =

   12
    2

EDU» I=inv(Z)*V

I =

   5.2000 - 1.6000i
   3.6000 + 5.2000i
```

Then, as shown in Figure 4.16, $\mathbf{I}_0$ is

$$\mathbf{I}_0 = \mathbf{I}_2 - \mathbf{I}_3$$

$$= \frac{18}{5} + j\frac{26}{5} - 2$$

$$= \left(\frac{8}{5} + j\frac{26}{5}\right) \text{A}$$

which is of course identical to that obtained in Example 4.9.

Drill Exercise

D4.9. Use mesh equations to find $\mathbf{V}_0$ in the network in Figure D4.9.

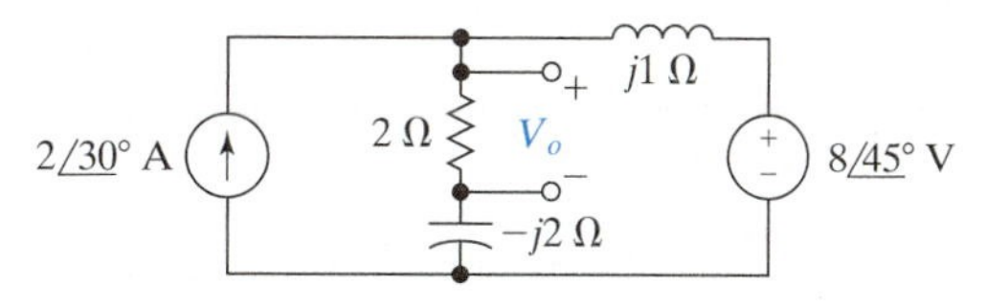

FIGURE D4.9

Ans: $\mathbf{V}_0 = 0.76 + j7.76$ V.

Example 4.11

Finally, let us demonstrate the use of MATLAB in the solution of a network that would be difficult to solve by hand. Furthermore, we will employ both node and loop analyses in obtaining a solution. The network is shown in Figure 4.17 where both loop currents and node voltages have been identified.

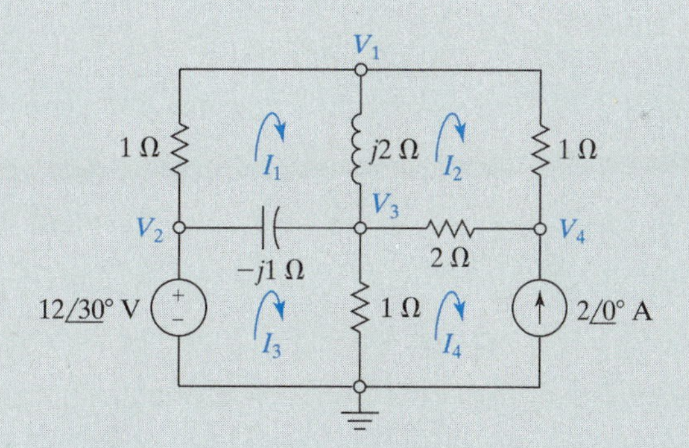

FIGURE 4.17 Circuit used in Example 4.11

The node equations for the network are

$$\frac{\mathbf{V}_1 - \mathbf{V}_2}{1} + \frac{\mathbf{V}_1 - \mathbf{V}_3}{j2} + \frac{\mathbf{V}_1 - \mathbf{V}_4}{1} = 0$$

$$\mathbf{V}_2 = 12\angle 30^\circ$$

$$\frac{\mathbf{V}_3 - \mathbf{V}_1}{j2} + \frac{\mathbf{V}_3 - \mathbf{V}_2}{-j1} + \frac{\mathbf{V}_3}{1} + \frac{\mathbf{V}_3 - \mathbf{V}_4}{2} = 0$$

$$\frac{\mathbf{V}_4 - \mathbf{V}_1}{1} + \frac{\mathbf{V}_4 - \mathbf{V}_3}{2} = 2\angle 0^\circ$$

Simplifying the equations we obtain

$$\begin{aligned}
(2 - j0.5)\mathbf{V}_1 \quad -\mathbf{V}_2 \quad + j0.5\mathbf{V}_3 \quad -\mathbf{V}_4 &= 0 \\
\mathbf{V}_2 &= 12\angle 30^\circ \\
j0.5\mathbf{V}_1 \quad -j\mathbf{V}_2 \quad (1.5 + j0.5)\mathbf{V}_3 \quad -0.5\mathbf{V}_4 &= 0 \\
-\mathbf{V}_1 \quad -0.5\mathbf{V}_3 \quad 1.5\mathbf{V}_4 &= 2
\end{aligned}$$

which in matrix form is

$$\begin{bmatrix} 2 - j0.5 & -1 & j0.5 & -1 \\ 0 & 1 & 0 & 0 \\ j0.5 & -j & 1.5 + j0.5 & -0.5 \\ -1 & 0 & -0.5 & 1.5 \end{bmatrix} \begin{bmatrix} \mathbf{V}_1 \\ \mathbf{V}_2 \\ \mathbf{V}_3 \\ \mathbf{V}_4 \end{bmatrix} = \begin{bmatrix} 0 \\ 12\angle 30^\circ \\ 0 \\ 2 \end{bmatrix}$$

Since complex sources are expressed in rectangular form, we use the fact that 2 pi radians is equivalent to 360 degrees and thus

$$\mathbf{V}_1 = 12\angle 30^\circ = x + j * y$$

where

$$x = 12 * \cos(30 * 2 * \text{pi}/360) = 10.3923$$

$$y = 12 * \sin(30 * 2 * \text{pi}/360) = 6.0000$$

Given this data, the MATLAB solution for the node voltages is listed as follows.

```
EDU» x = 12 * cos (30 * 2 * pi/360)

x =

       10.3923

EDU» y = 12 * sin (30 * 2 * pi/360)

y =

       6.0000

EDU» V1 = x + j * y

V1 =

     10.3923 + 6.0000i

EDU» Y = [2 - j * 0.5 -1 j * 0.5 -1; 0 1 0 0; j * 0.5 -j * 1 1.5 +
        j * 0.5 -0.5; -1 0 -0.5 1.5]

Y =

   2.0000 - 0.5000i  -1.0000                    0 + 0.5000i -1.0000
        0             1.0000                    0                 0
        0 + 0.5000i        0 - 1.0000i  1.5000 + 0.5000i -0.5000
  -1.0000                  0           -0.5000            1.5000

EDU» I = [0; V1; 0; 2]

I =

        0
  10.3923 + 6.0000i
        0
   2.0000
```

```
EDU» V = inv (Y) * I

V =

   8.6244 + 7.9010i
  10.3923 + 6.0000i
   3.1296 + 5.3617i
   8.1261 + 7.0546i
```

With reference to Figure 4.17, the loop equations for the network are

$$(1 + j2 - j1)\mathbf{I}_1 - j2\mathbf{I}_2 - (-j1)\mathbf{I}_3 = 0$$

$$-j2\mathbf{I}_1 + (1 + 2 + j2)\mathbf{I}_2 - 2\mathbf{I}_4 = 0$$

$$-(-j1)\mathbf{I}_1 + (1 - j1)\mathbf{I}_3 - 1\mathbf{I}_4 = 12\angle 30^\circ$$

$$I_4 = -2\angle 0^\circ$$

or in matrix form,

$$\begin{bmatrix} 1 + j1 & -j2 & j1 & 0 \\ -j2 & 3 + j2 & 0 & -2 \\ j1 & 0 & 1 - j1 & -1 \\ 0 & 0 & 0 & 1 \end{bmatrix} \begin{bmatrix} \mathbf{I}_1 \\ \mathbf{I}_2 \\ \mathbf{I}_3 \\ \mathbf{I}_4 \end{bmatrix} = \begin{bmatrix} 0 \\ 0 \\ 12\angle 30^\circ \\ -2 \end{bmatrix}$$

The MATLAB solution for the loop equations is listed below.

```
EDU» Z = [1+j*1 -j*2 j*1 0; -j*2 3+j*2 0 -2; j*1 0 1-j*1 -1; 0 0 0 1]

Z =

   1.0000 + 1.0000i        0 - 2.0000i        0 + 1.0000i        0
        0 - 2.0000i   3.0000 + 2.0000i        0            -2.0000
        0 + 1.0000i        0             1.0000 - 1.0000i -1.0000
        0                  0                  0             1.0000

EDU» x=12*cos (30*2*pi/360)

x =

   10.3923

EDU» y=12*sin (30*2*pi/360)

Y =

    6.0000

EDU» V1 = x+j*y

V1 =

   10.3923 + 6.0000i

EDU» V = [0; 0; V1; -2]

V =

        0
        0
   10.3923 + 6.0000i
   -2.0000
```

```
EDU» I=inv (Z) *V.

I =

    1.7679 - 1.9010i
    0.4983 + 0.8464i
    1.1296 + 5.3617i
   -2.0000
```

Since we now have both the node voltages and the loop currents, we can make a number of checks to see if the solutions are correct. For example,

$$\begin{aligned}\mathbf{I}_1 &= \frac{\mathbf{V}_2 - \mathbf{V}_1}{1}\\ &= \frac{10.3923 + j6.0000 - (8.6244 + j7.9010)}{1}\\ &= 1.7679 - j1.9010 \text{ A}\end{aligned}$$

which indicates to us that both solutions agree.

4–10 Superposition

Superposition can be applied in the frequency domain

The *principle of superposition* will be illustrated by considering, once again, the circuit analyzed in Example 4.9.

Example 4.12

We wish to find $\mathbf{I}_0$ in the network in Figure 4.18(a). First, we begin making the current source zero by replacing it with an open circuit and deriving the component of $\mathbf{I}_0$ caused by the voltage source acting alone. We call this component $\mathbf{I}_0'$ and obtain it from the network in Figure 4.18(b). The current $\mathbf{I}_v$ is equal to the voltage source value divided by the total impedance seen by the source or

$$\mathbf{I}_v = \frac{12\angle 0^\circ}{1 + \dfrac{(1-j)(j)}{1-j+j}}$$

Then, using current division

$$\begin{aligned}\mathbf{I}_0' &= \mathbf{I}_v\left(\frac{j}{j+1-j}\right)\\ &= \frac{12}{1+j+1}(j)\\ &= \frac{12j}{2+j}\text{A}\end{aligned}$$

Next, the component of $\mathbf{I}_0$ caused by the current source acting alone, that is, $\mathbf{I}_0''$, is obtained from the network in Figure 4.18(c), where the voltage source has been replaced with a short circuit.

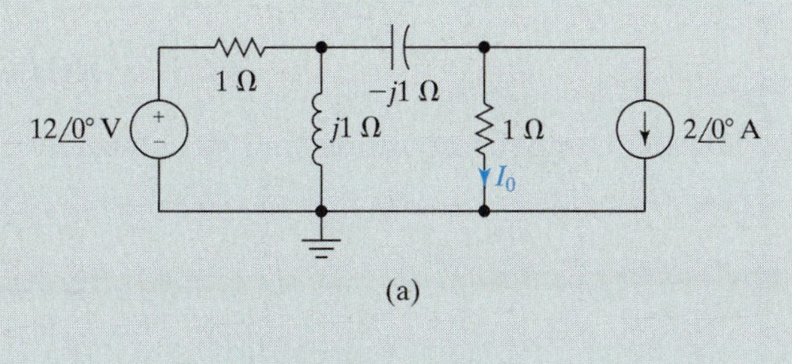

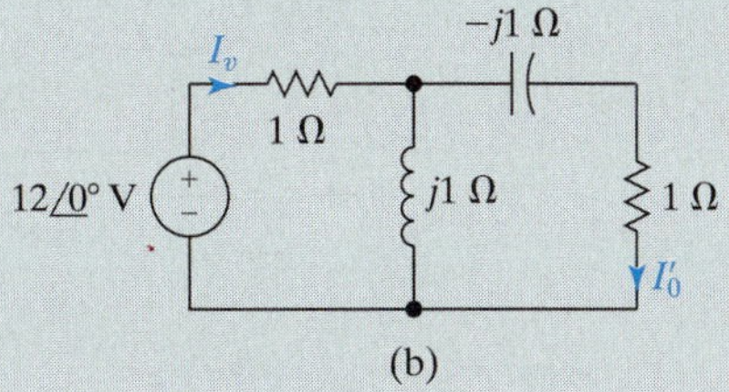

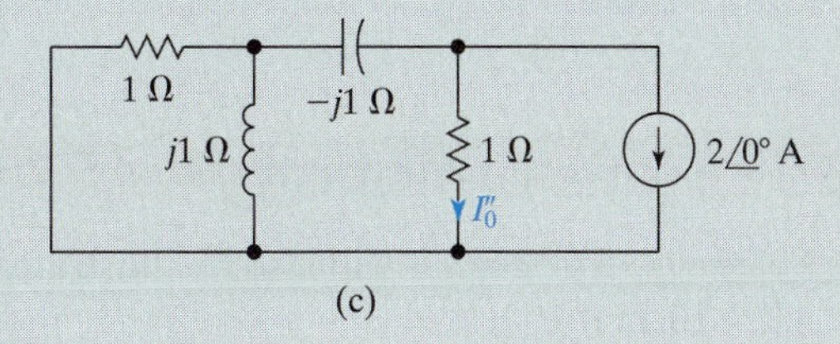

FIGURE 4.18 Circuits used in Example 4.12.

Using current division we find that

$$\mathbf{I}_0'' = -2\angle 0^\circ \frac{-j + \dfrac{(1)(j)}{1+j}}{1 - j + \dfrac{(1)(j)}{1+j}}$$

$$= \frac{-2}{1 + j + 1}$$

$$= \frac{-2}{2 + j}\text{A}$$

Therefore,

$$\mathbf{I}_0 = \mathbf{I}_0' + \mathbf{I}_0''$$

$$= \frac{12j}{2+j} + \frac{-2}{2+j}$$

$$= \frac{-2 + j12}{2 + j}$$

$$= \left(\frac{8}{5} + j\frac{26}{5}\right)\text{A}$$

which is identical to that obtained earlier.

Drill Exercise

D4.10. Using superposition, find $\mathbf{V}_0$ in the network in Figure D4.10.

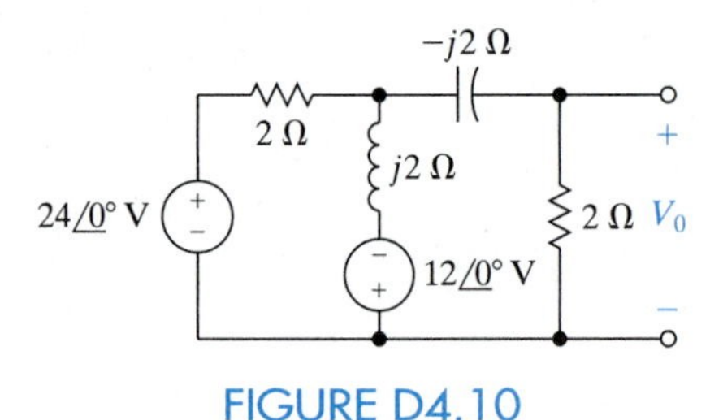

FIGURE D4.10

Ans: $\mathbf{V}_0 = 12\angle 90°$ V.

4-11 Source Transformation

Source transformation/exchange is applicable in the frequency domain

Source transformation will also be illustrated by solving the network examined in Examples 4.9, 4.10, and 4.11.

Example 4.13

The original network examined in the previous three examples is shown in Figure 4.19(a). Let us employ source transformation to find $\mathbf{I}_0$ in this network.

We begin the network simplification by transforming the $12\angle 0°$ V source in series with the 1-ohm resistor into a $12\angle 0°$ A current source in parallel with the 1-ohm resistor as shown in Figure 4.19(b). The parallel combination of the 1-ohm resistor and the $j1$-ohm inductor is

$$\mathbf{Z}_p = \frac{(1)(j)}{1 + j}$$

$$= \frac{1}{2} + j\frac{1}{2}\,\Omega$$

If we now transform this impedance, $\mathbf{Z}_p$, which is in parallel with the $12\angle 0°$ A current source, into a voltage source in series with the impedance $\mathbf{Z}_p$, we obtain the circuit shown in Figure 4.19(c). Note carefully that with each successive transformation we are absorbing circuit elements, and thus simplifying the network, as we reduce the network around the unknown $\mathbf{I}_0$. The impedance in series with the $6(1 + j)$ V source is

$$\mathbf{Z}_s = \frac{1}{2} + j\frac{1}{2} - j$$

$$= \frac{1}{2} - j\frac{1}{2}\,\Omega$$

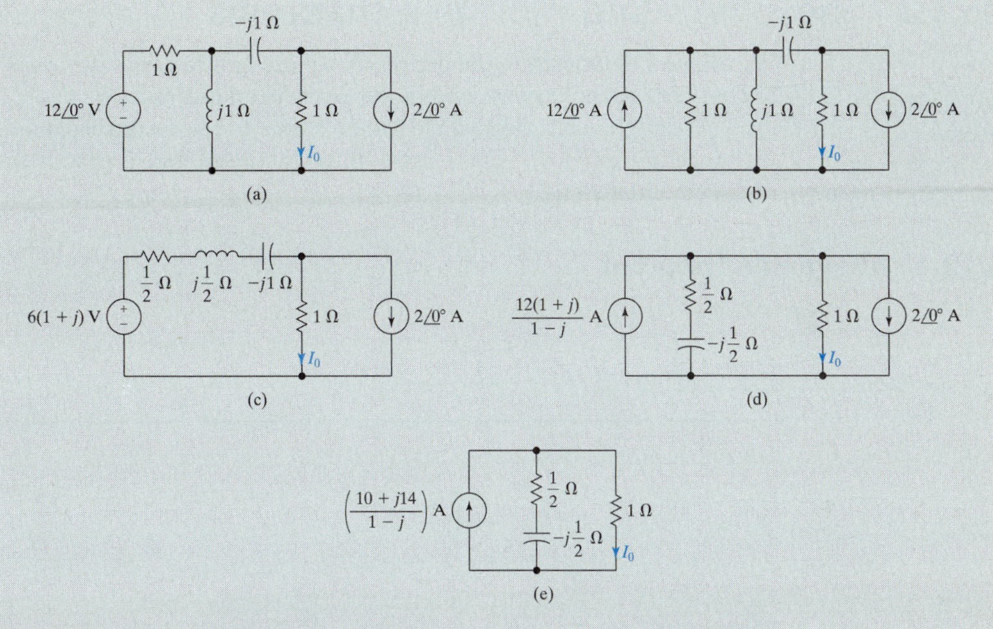

FIGURE 4.19 Circuits used in Example 4.13.

Thus, transforming the $6(1 + j)$ V source in series with the impedance $\mathbf{Z}_s$ into a current source in parallel with this impedance yields the circuit in Figure 4.19(d). At this point we note that the two current sources in the network in Figure 4.19(d) are in parallel and therefore can be added to produce one resultant source, which is

$$\mathbf{I}_T = \frac{12(1 + j)}{1 - j} - 2$$

$$= \left(\frac{10 + j14}{1 - j}\right) \text{A}$$

Thus, the network in Figure 4.19(d) has been simplified to that in Figure 4.19(e). Employing current division yields the current $\mathbf{I}_0$

$$\mathbf{I}_0 = \left(\frac{10 + j14}{1 - j}\right)\left(\frac{\frac{1}{2} - j\frac{1}{2}}{\frac{1}{2} - j\frac{1}{2} + 1}\right)$$

$$= \left(\frac{8}{5} + j\frac{26}{5}\right) \text{A}$$

Drill Exercise

D4.11. Find $\mathbf{V}_0$ in problem D4.10 using source transformation.

4–12 Thevenin's and Norton's Theorems

Two useful theorems applicable in the frequency domain

We will now demonstrate the use of *Thevenin's and Norton's theorems* by using them to solve the network we have examined in the last several examples.

At this point it is worthwhile for the reader to review the explanation in Section 2.11 since the procedure employed in the use of these theorems here is exactly the same as that outlined for dc circuit analysis.

4.12.1 Thevenins Theorem

Example 4.14

Once again, let us find the current $\mathbf{I}_0$ in the circuit in Figure 4.20(a).

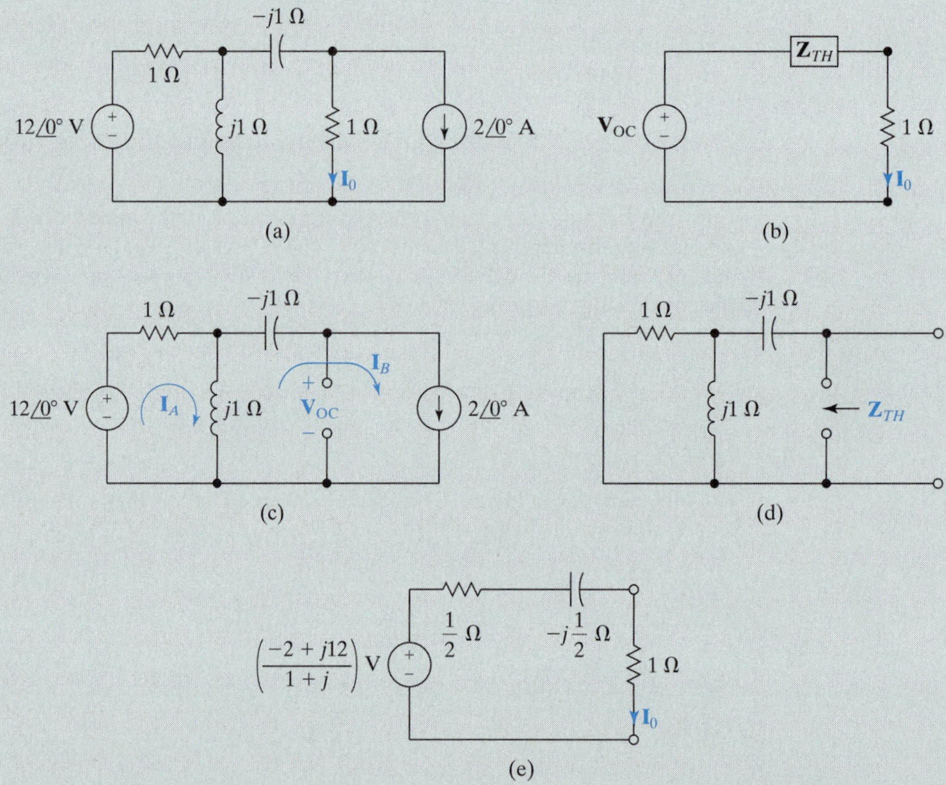

FIGURE 4.20 Circuits used to illustrate Thevenin's theorem.

We will analyze this circuit by removing the 1 Ω resistor and then developing an equivalent circuit for the remainder of the network.

This equivalent circuit will consist of a voltage source whose value is the open circuit voltage determined at the terminals where the 1Ω resistor was connected, and this source is placed in series with the Thevenin equivalent impedance, which is the impedance seen looking into the terminals where the 1Ω resistor was connected with all independent sources made zero. Finally, we will recombine the 1Ω resistor with this equivalent circuit, as shown in Figure 4.20(b).

The open circuit voltage at the resistor containing $\mathbf{I}_0$ is shown in Figure 4.20(c). Note that the voltage $\mathbf{V}_{OC}$ is the voltage across the current source. However, recall that although we know the voltage across a voltage source, we have to use the rest of the circuit to compute the current in the voltage source. In a similar manner, although we know the current in a current source, we have to use the balance of the network to find the voltage across it. Therefore, we have shown in Figure 4.20(c) two mesh currents I_A and I_B. The equation for the first mesh is

$$\mathbf{V}_{oc}\, 12\angle 0^\circ - 1\mathbf{I}_A - j(\mathbf{I}_A - \mathbf{I}_B) = 0$$

and since $\mathbf{I}_B$ passes directly through the current source,

$$\mathbf{I}_B = 2\angle 0^\circ$$

Solving the two equations for $\mathbf{I}_A$ yields

$$\mathbf{I}_A = \left(\frac{12 + j2}{1 + j}\right) \text{A}$$

Now KVL for the closed path containing the voltage source and the open circuit voltage is

$$12\angle 0^\circ - 1\mathbf{I}_A - (-j)\mathbf{I}_B - \mathbf{V}_{oc} = 0$$

which yields

$$\mathbf{V}_{oc} = \left(\frac{-2 + j12}{1 + j}\right) V$$

The Thevenin equivalent impedance, $\mathbf{Z}_{TH}$, is derived from the network in Figure 4.20(d) where the voltage source has been replaced with a short circuit and the current source replaced with an open circuit. This impedance is

$$\mathbf{Z}_{TH} = -j + \frac{(1)(j)}{1 + j}$$

$$= \frac{1}{2} - j\frac{1}{2}, \Omega$$

Now the Thevenin equivalent circuit consisting of the open circuit voltage in series with the Thevenin equivalent impedance is used to replace the entire network exclusive of the 1-ohm resistor containing the current $\mathbf{I}_0$. This network is shown in Figure 4.20(e). The current $\mathbf{I}_0$ is then

$$\mathbf{I}_0 = \frac{\dfrac{-2 + j12}{1 + j}}{\dfrac{1}{2} - j\dfrac{1}{2} + 1}$$

$$= \left(\frac{8}{5} + j\frac{26}{5}\right) A$$

4.12.2 Norton's Theorem

Example 4.15

We will now solve the problem in Example 14.13 using Norton's theorem. In this case, the equivalent circuit for the network that remains after the 1Ω resistor has been removed consists of a current source, which is equal to the short-circuit current at the terminals of the 1Ω resistor, in parallel with the Thevenin equivalent impedance, as shown in Figure 4.21(a).

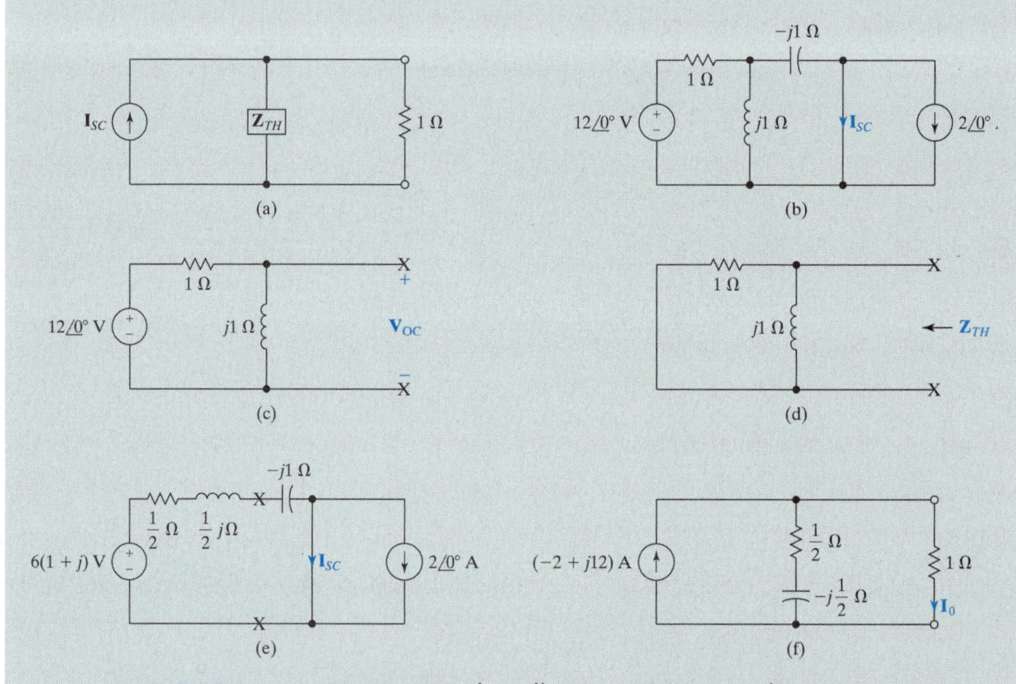

FIGURE 4.21 Circuits used to illustrate Norton's theorem.

To begin, the 1-ohm resistor containing $\mathbf{I}_0$ is replaced with a short circuit as shown in Figure 4.21(b). The current in this short circuit, $\mathbf{I}_{SC}$, will consist of two components: one due to the $12\angle 0°$ V source and one due to the $2\angle 0°$ A source. It is important to note at this point that current emanating from the current source will simply return through the short circuit since this is the path of least resistance. Furthermore, the current generated by the voltage source that flows in the capacitor will all flow through the short circuit. Sometimes it is easier to understand these points if we redraw the circuit in Figure 4.21(b) by collapsing the short circuit to a single point.

The network in Figure 4.21(b) is just another network and therefore all the techniques we have learned for finding voltages and currents apply to it also. Therefore, we will demonstrate the use of Thevenin's theorem to provide some simplification. Let us find the Thevenin equivalent circuit for the portion of the network to the left of the capacitor. Thus, we break the network at that point and find the open circuit voltage shown in Figure 4.21(c). Using voltage division,

$$\mathbf{V}_{OC} = 12\angle 0^\circ\left(\frac{j}{1+j}\right)$$

$$= \frac{12j}{1+j}$$

$$= 6(1+j)\text{ V}$$

The Thevenin equivalent impedance derived from Figure 4.21(d) is

$$\mathbf{Z}_{TH} = \frac{(1)(j)}{1+j}$$

$$= \frac{1}{2} + j\frac{1}{2}\,\Omega$$

If we connect the Thevenin equivalent circuit to the original network, we obtain the circuit shown in Figure 4.21(e). Compare this network to that shown in Figure 4.19(c). From the network in Figure 4.21(e) we find that

$$\mathbf{I}_{sc} = \frac{6(1+j)}{\frac{1}{2} - j\frac{1}{2}} - 2\angle 0^\circ$$

$$= (-2 + j12)\text{ A}$$

The Thevenin equivalent impedance was found earlier to be

$$\mathbf{Z}_{TH} = \frac{1}{2} - j\frac{1}{2}\,\Omega$$

Now, if the Norton equivalent, consisting of the short-circuit current source in parallel with the Thevenin equivalent impedance, is connected to the 1-ohm resistor as shown in Figure 4.21(f), we find that the current $\mathbf{I}_0$ is obtained by current division as

$$\mathbf{I}_0 = (-2 + \text{j}12)\left[\frac{\left(\frac{1}{2} - \text{j}\frac{1}{2}\right)}{\frac{1}{2} - \text{j}\frac{1}{2} + 1}\right]$$

$$= \left(\frac{8}{5} + \text{j}\frac{26}{5}\right)\text{A}$$

Drill Exercise

D4.12. Use Thevenin's theorem to find $\mathbf{V}_0$ in problem D4.10.

4-13 Nonsinusoidal Steady-State Response

Thus far the signals we have considered have either been a dc or an ac sinusoidal signal with a specific frequency. However, in electrical engineering we encounter a variety of periodic signals, many of which are nonsinusoidal.

In general, a periodic signal is one that satisfies the relationship

$$f(t) = f(t + nT) \quad n = \pm 1, \pm 2, \pm 3, \cdots$$

for every value of t where T is the period. For example, the pulse train shown in Figure 4.22(a) is used as a timing marker in digital systems, and the saw tooth waveform shown in Figure 4.22(b) is used to drive the beam across the cathode ray tube in an oscilloscope.

Expressing a periodic time function as a Fourier series

At this point, if we could somehow decompose a nonsinusoidal periodic signal into a set of sinusoidal periodic signals of different frequencies, our background would permit us to determine the steady-state response. The vehicle we will employ to accomplish this is the *Fourier Series*, which is based upon the work of Jean Baptiste Joseph Fourier (1768–1830). Although our analysis will be confined to electric circuits, it is important to point out that the techniques are applicable to a wide range of engineering problems. In fact, it was Fourier's work in heat flow that led to the techniques that will be presented here.

In his work, Fourier demonstrated that a periodic function $f(t)$ could be expressed as a sum of sinusoidal functions. Therefore, given this result and the fact that if a periodic function is expressed as a sum of linearly independent functions, and each function in the sum is periodic with the same period, then the function $f(t)$ can be expressed in the form

$$f(t) = a_0 + \sum_{n=1}^{\infty} D_n \cos(n\omega_0 t + \theta_n) \tag{4.43}$$

where $\omega_0 = 2\pi/T$ and a_0 is the average value of the waveform. An examination of this expression illustrates that all sinusoidal waveforms that are periodic with period T have been included. For example, for $n = 1$, one cycle covers T seconds and $D_1 \cos(\omega_0 t + \theta_1)$ is called

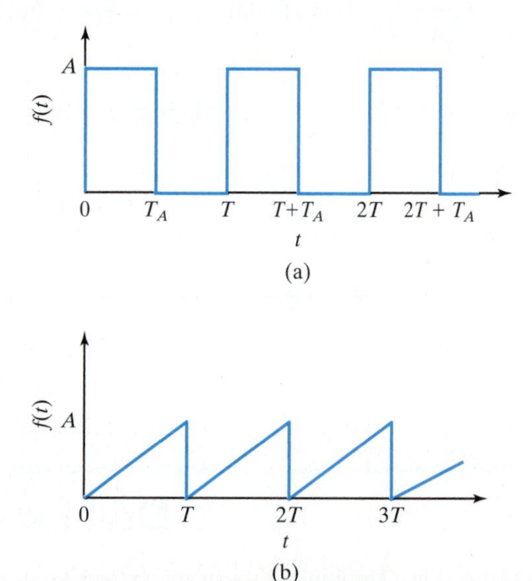

FIGURE 4.22 Nonsinusoidal periodic waveforms.

the fundamental. For $n = 2$, two cycles fall within T seconds and the term $D_2 \cos(2\omega_0 t + \theta_2)$ is called the second harmonic. In general, for $n = k$, k cycles fall within T seconds, $D_k \cos(k\omega_0 t + \theta_k)$ is the kth harmonic term, and $D_k \angle \theta_k$ is the *phasor* for this term.

Since the function $\cos(n\omega_0 t + \theta_n)$ can be written in exponential form using Euler's identity or as a sum of cosine and sine terms of the form $\cos n\omega_0 t$ and $\sin n\omega_0 t$, the series in Eq. (4.43) can be written as

$$f(t) = a_0 + \sum_{\substack{n=-\infty \\ n \neq 0}}^{\infty} \mathbf{c}_n e^{jn\omega_0 t} = \sum_{n=-\infty}^{\infty} \mathbf{c}_n e^{jn\omega_0 t} \tag{4.44}$$

$$= a_0 + \sum_{n=1}^{\infty} (a_n \cos n\omega_0 t + b_n \sin n\omega_0 t) \tag{4.45}$$

The approach we will take will be to represent a nonsinusoidal periodic input by a sum of complex exponential functions, which because of Euler's identity is equivalent to a sum of sines and cosines. We will then use (1) the superposition property of linear systems and (2) our knowledge that the steady state response of a time-invariant linear system to a sinusoidal input of frequency ω_0 is a sinusoidal function of the same frequency to determine the response of such a system.

In order to illustrate the manner in which a nonsinusoidal periodic signal can be represented by a Fourier series, consider the periodic function terms shown in Figure 4.23(a). In Figure 4.23 we can see the impact of using a specific number of te in the series to represent the original function. Note that the series more closely represents the original function as we employ more and more terms.

4.13.1 Exponential Fourier Series

Any physically realizable periodic signal may be represented over the interval $t_1 < t < t_1 + T$ by the *exponential Fourier series*

$$f(t) = \sum_{n=-\infty}^{\infty} \mathbf{c}_n e^{jn\omega_0 t} \tag{4.46}$$

where the $\mathbf{c}_n$ are the complex (phasor) Fourier coefficients. These coefficients are derived as follows. Multiplying both sides of Eq. (4.46) by $e^{-jk\omega_0 t}$ and integrating over the interval t_1 to $t_1 + T$, we obtain

$$\int_{t_1}^{t_1+T} f(t) e^{-jk\omega_0 t}\, dt = \int_{t_1}^{t_1+T} \left(\sum_{n=-\infty}^{\infty} \mathbf{c}_n e^{jn\omega_0 t} \right) e^{-jk\omega_0 t}\, dt$$

since

$$\int_{t_1}^{t_1-T} e^{j(n-k)\omega_0 t}\, dt = \begin{cases} 0 & \text{for } n \neq k \\ T & \text{for } n = k \end{cases}$$

Therefore, the Fourier coefficients are defined by the equation

$$\mathbf{c}_n = \frac{1}{T_0} \int_{t_1}^{t_1+T} f(t) e^{-jn\omega_0 t}\, dt \tag{4.47}$$

The following example illustrates the manner in which we can represent a periodic signal by an exponential Fourier series.

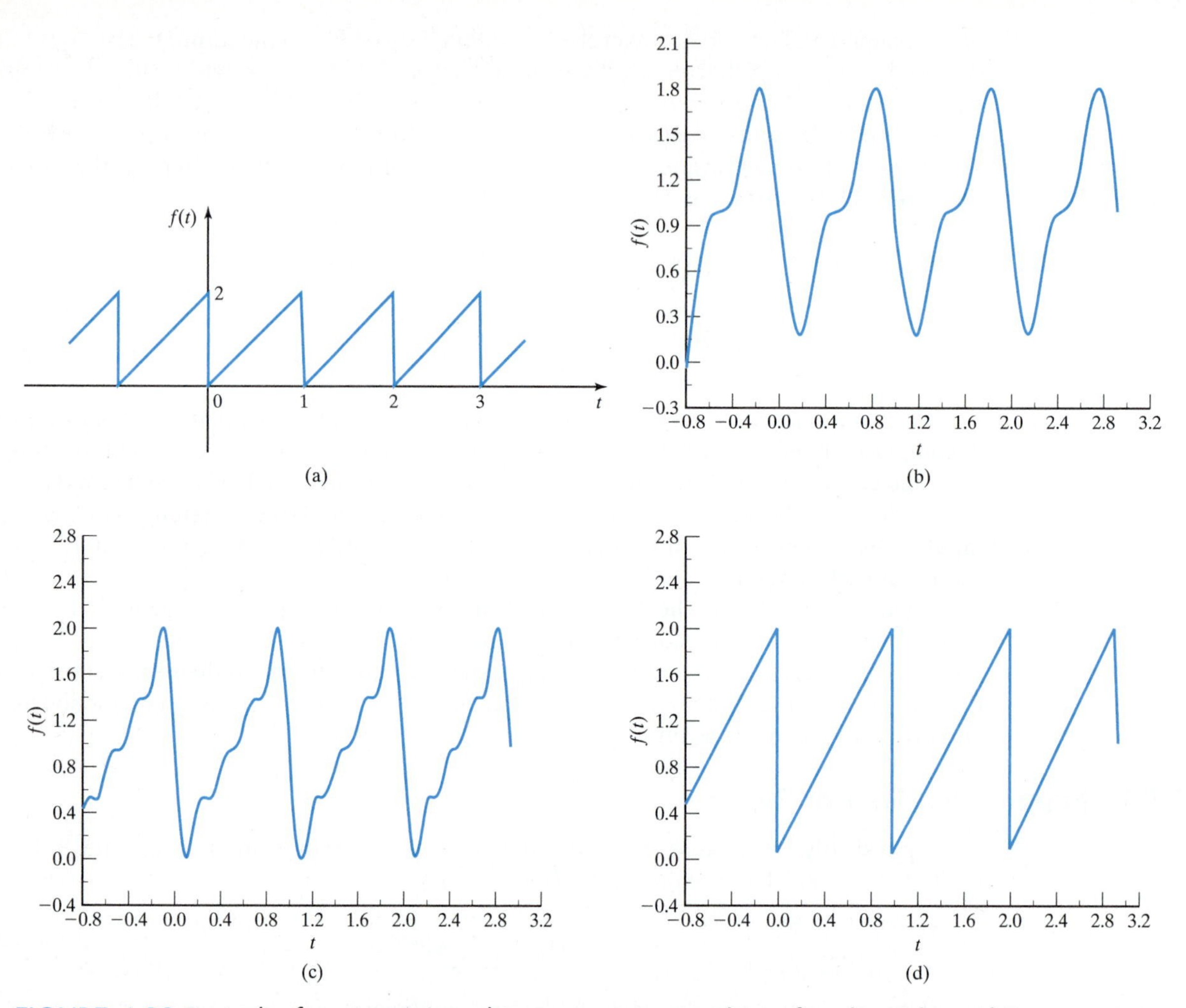

FIGURE 4.23 Periodic function (a) and its representation by a fixed number of Fourier series terms: (b) 2 terms; (c) 4 terms; (d) 100 terms.

Example 4.16

We wish to determine the exponential Fourier series for the periodic voltage waveform shown in Figure 4.24.

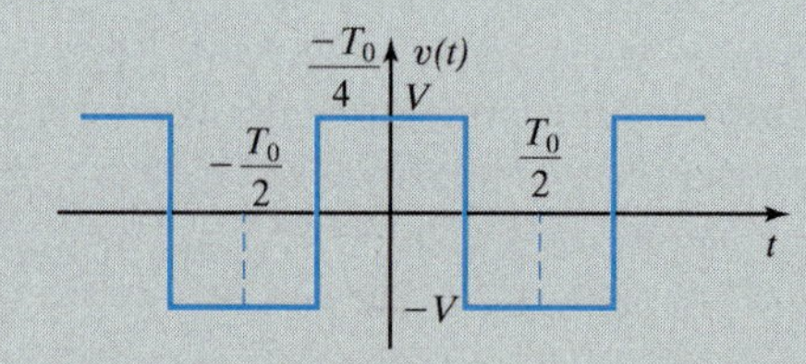

FIGURE 4.24 Periodic voltage waveform.

The Fourier coefficients are determined using Eq. (4.47) by integrating over one complete period of the waveform.

$$\mathbf{c}_n = \frac{1}{T_0}\int_{-T/2}^{T/2} f(t)e^{-jn\omega_0 t}\,dt$$

$$= \frac{1}{T_0}\int_{-T/2}^{-T/4} - Ve^{-jn\omega_0 t}\,dt + \int_{-T/4}^{T/4} Ve^{-jn\omega_0 t}\,dt + \int_{T/4}^{T/2} - Ve^{-jn\omega_0 t}$$

$$= \frac{V}{jn\omega_0 T}\left[+e^{-jn\omega_0 t}\Big|_{-T/2}^{-T/4} - e^{-jn\omega_0 t}\Big|_{-T/4}^{T/4} + e^{jn\omega_0 t}\Big|_{T/4}^{T/2}\right]$$

$$= \frac{V}{jn\omega_0 T}(2e^{jn\pi/2} - 2e^{-jn\pi/2} + e^{-jn\pi} - e^{+jn\pi})$$

$$= \frac{V}{n\omega_0 T}\left[4\sin\frac{n\pi}{2} - 2\sin(n\pi)\right]$$

$$= 0 \qquad \text{for } n \text{ even}$$

$$= \frac{2V}{n\pi}\sin\frac{n\pi}{2} \qquad \text{for } n \text{ odd}$$

Since $\mathbf{c}_0$ corresponds to the average value of the waveform $\mathbf{c}_0 = 0$, this term can also be evaluated using the original equation for $\mathbf{c}_n$. Therefore,

$$v(t) = \sum_{\substack{n=-\infty\\ n\neq 0\\ n \text{ odd}}}^{\infty} \frac{2V}{n\pi}\sin\frac{n\pi}{2}e^{jn\omega_0 t}$$

This equation can be written as

$$v(t) = \sum_{\substack{n=1\\ n \text{ odd}}}^{\infty} \frac{2V}{n\pi}\sin\frac{n\pi}{2}e^{jn\omega_0 t} + \sum_{\substack{n=-1\\ n \text{ odd}}}^{-\infty} \frac{2V}{n\pi}\sin\frac{n\pi}{2}e^{jn\omega_0 t}$$

$$= \sum_{\substack{n=1\\ n \text{ odd}}}^{\infty} \left(\frac{2V}{n\pi}\sin\frac{n\pi}{2}\right)e^{jn\omega_0 t} + \left(\frac{2V}{n\pi}\sin\frac{n\pi}{2}\right)^{*} e^{-jn\omega_0 t}$$

Since a number plus its complex conjugate is equal to two times the real part of the number, $v(t)$ can be written as

$$v(t) = \sum_{\substack{n=1\\ n \text{ odd}}}^{\infty} 2Re\left(\frac{2V}{n\pi}\sin\frac{n\pi}{2}e^{jn\omega_0 t}\right)$$

or

$$v(t) = \sum_{\substack{n=1\\ n \text{ odd}}}^{\infty} \frac{4V}{n\pi}\sin\frac{n\pi}{2}\cos n\omega_0 t$$

Note that this same result could have been obtained by integrating over the interval $-T/4$ to $3T/4$ or any other one-period interval.

D4.13. Find the Fourier coefficients for the waveform in Figure D4.13.

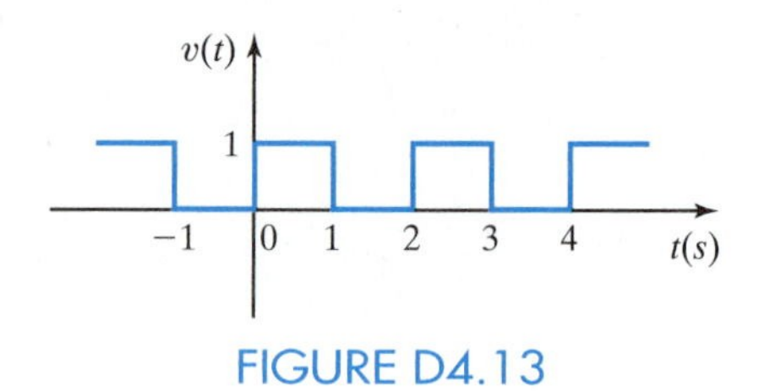

FIGURE D4.13

Ans: $\mathbf{c}_n = \dfrac{1 - e^{-jn\pi}}{j2\pi n}$

A short listing of the Fourier series for a number of common waveforms is shown in Table 4.1. These series can be derived using the approach illustrated in Example 4.16.

4.13.2 Network Response

The circuit response to a periodic input signal

If a periodic signal is applied to a network, the steady-state voltage or current response at some point in the circuit can be found in the following manner. First, we represent the periodic forcing function by a Fourier series. If the input forcing function for a network is a voltage, the input can be expressed in the form

$$v(t) = v_0 + v_1(t) + v_2(t) + \cdots$$

and therefore represented in the time domain as shown in Figure 4.25. Each source has its own amplitude and frequency. Next we determine the response due to each component of the

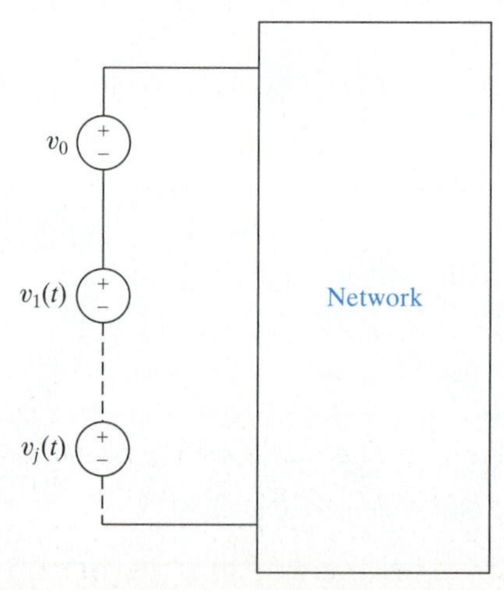

FIGURE 4.25 Network with a periodic voltage forcing function.

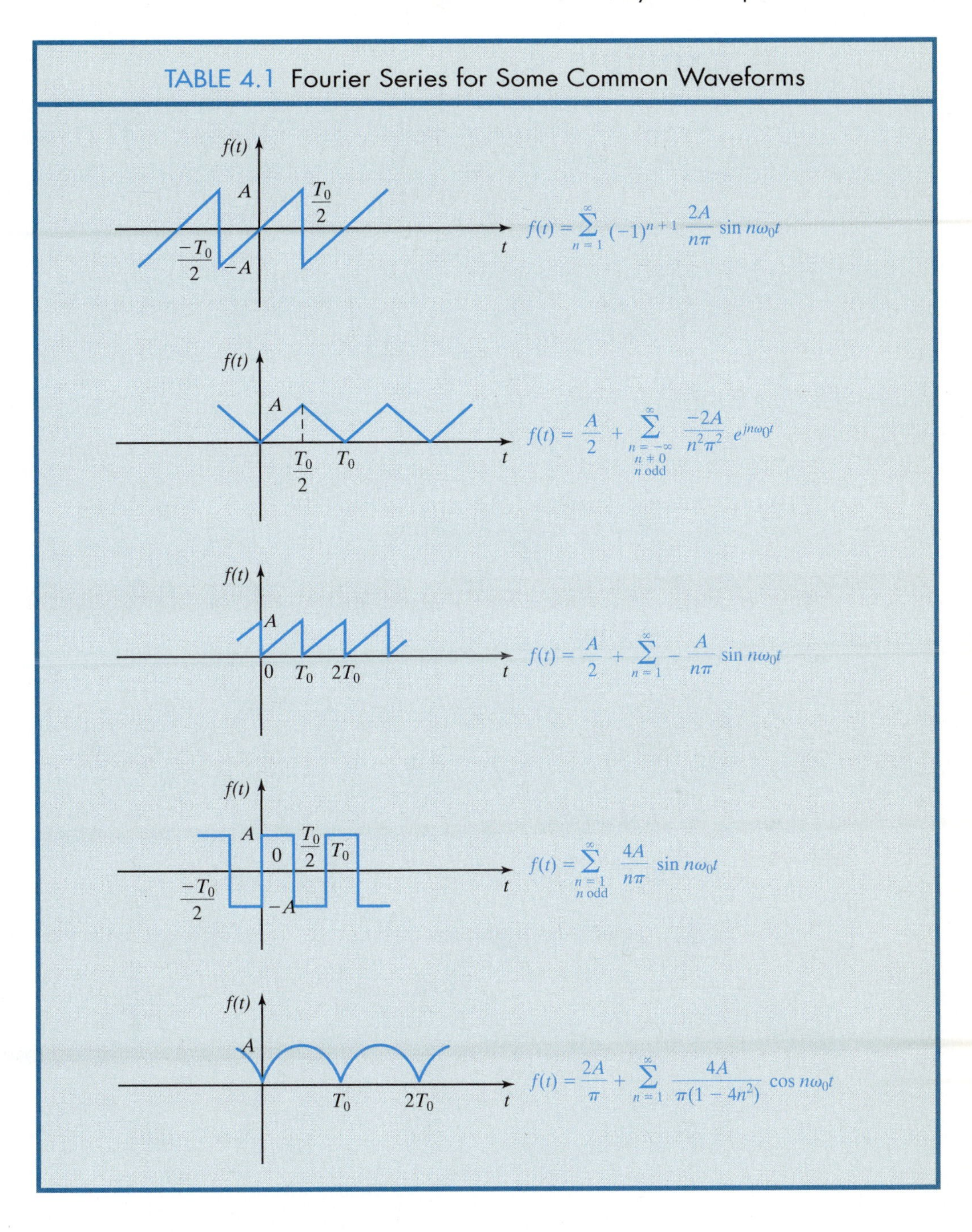

input Fourier series; that is, we use phasor analysis in the frequency domain to determine the network response due to each source. The network response due to each source in the frequency domain is then transformed to the time domain. Finally, we add the time domain solutions due to each source using the principle of superposition to obtain the Fourier series for the total **steady-state** network response.

Example 4.17

We wish to determine the steady-state voltage $v_0(t)$ in Figure 4.26 if the input voltage $v(t)$ is given by the expression

$$v(t) = 7.5\cos(2t - 122°) + 2.2\cos(6t - 102°) + 1.3\cos(10t - 97°) + 0.91\cos(14t - 95°) + \cdots$$

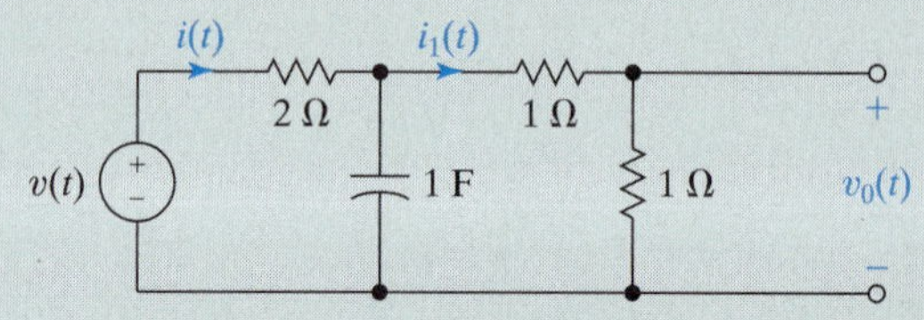

FIGURE 4.26 *RC* circuit employed in Example 4.15.

Note that this source has no constant term, and therefore its dc value is zero.

From the network we find that

$$\mathbf{I} = \frac{\mathbf{V}}{2 + \dfrac{2/j\omega}{2 + 1/j\omega}} = \frac{\mathbf{V}(1 + 2j\omega)}{4 + 4j\omega}$$

$$\mathbf{I}_1 = \frac{\mathbf{I}(1/j\omega)}{2 + 1/j\omega} = \frac{\mathbf{I}}{1 + 2j\omega}$$

$$\mathbf{V}_0 = (1)\mathbf{I}_1 = 1 \cdot \frac{\mathbf{V}(1 + 2j\omega)}{4 + 4j\omega}\,\frac{1}{1 + 2j\omega} = \frac{\mathbf{V}}{4 + 4j\omega}$$

Therefore, since $\omega_0 = 2$

$$\mathbf{V}_0(n) = \frac{\mathbf{V}(n)}{4 + j8n}$$

The individual components of the output due to the components of the input source are then

$$\mathbf{V}_0(\omega_0) = \frac{7.5\angle -122°}{4 + j8} = 0.84\angle -185.4° \text{ V}$$

$$\mathbf{V}_0(3\omega_0) = \frac{2.2\angle -102°}{4 + j24} = 0.09\angle -182.5° \text{ V}$$

$$\mathbf{V}_0(5\omega_0) = \frac{1.3\angle -97°}{4 + j40} = 0.03\angle -181.3° \text{ V}$$

$$\mathbf{V}_0(7\omega_0) = \frac{0.91\angle -95°}{4 + j56} = 0.016\angle -181° \text{ V}$$

Hence, the steady-state output voltage $v_0(t)$ can be written as

$$v_0(t) = 0.84\cos(2t - 185.4°) + 0.09\cos(6t - 182.5°) + 0.03\cos(10t - 181.3°) + 0.016\cos(14t - 181°) + \cdots \text{V}$$

Drill Exercise

D4.14. Determine the expression for the steady-state current $i(t)$ in Figure D4.14 if the input voltage $v_s(t)$ is given by the expression

$$v_s(t) = 10 + 8\cos(2t) + 6\cos(4t - 60°) + 4\cos(6t - 45°)\text{ V}$$

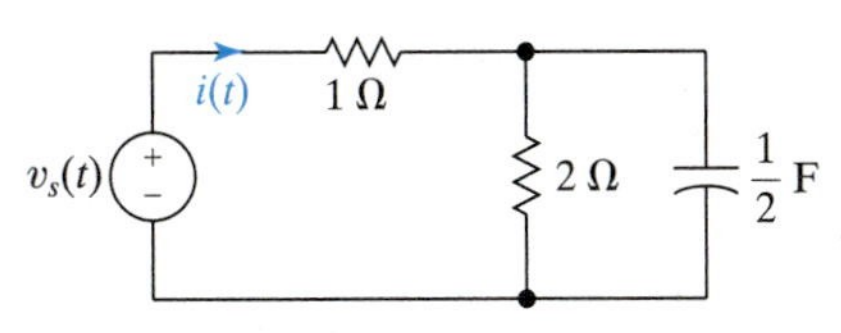

FIGURE D4.14

Ans:
$i(t) = 3.33 + 4.96\cos(2t + 29.74°) + 4.96\cos(4t - 37.17°) + 3.63\cos(6t - 27.89°) + \cdots\text{ A}$

Summary

- The frequency of the U.S. and Canadian power grid is 60 Hz.
- Two sinusoidal functions, $x(t) = A\sin(\omega t + \theta)$ and $y(t) = B\sin(\omega t + \phi)$, are said to be in phase if $\theta = \phi$, and out of phase if $\theta \neq \phi$. The functions are illustrated in Figure 4.27.
- A sinusoidal time function $x(t) = A\cos(\omega t + \theta)$ can be represented as a phasor, $\mathbf{X} = A\angle\theta$, which consists of a magnitude A and a phase angle θ. The phasor is measured with respect to a cosine signal and written in boldface type. The function is shown in Figure 4.28.
- Phasor manipulation is performed in complex algebra, and phasor analysis is called a frequency domain analysis. If $\mathbf{X} = X\angle\theta = a + jb$ and $\mathbf{Y} = Y\angle\phi = c + jd$, then

  Addition: $\mathbf{X} + \mathbf{Y} = (a + c) + j(b + d)$

  Subtraction: $\mathbf{X} - \mathbf{Y} = (a - c) + j(b - d)$

  Multiplication: $(\mathbf{X})(\mathbf{Y}) = XY\angle\theta + \phi$

  Division: $\dfrac{\mathbf{X}}{\mathbf{Y}} = \dfrac{X}{Y}\angle\theta - \phi$
- The phasor relationship for a resistor, capacitor, and inductor are $\mathbf{V} = R\mathbf{I}$, $\mathbf{I} = j\omega C\mathbf{V}$, and $\mathbf{V} = j\omega L\mathbf{I}$. The relationships are shown in Figure 4.29.
- Impedance is defined as the ratio of the phasor voltage to the phasor current. Admittance is the reciprocal of impedance. The defining equations are $\mathbf{Z} = \dfrac{\mathbf{V}}{\mathbf{I}}$ and $\mathbf{Y} = \dfrac{\mathbf{I}}{\mathbf{V}} = \dfrac{1}{\mathbf{Z}}$.

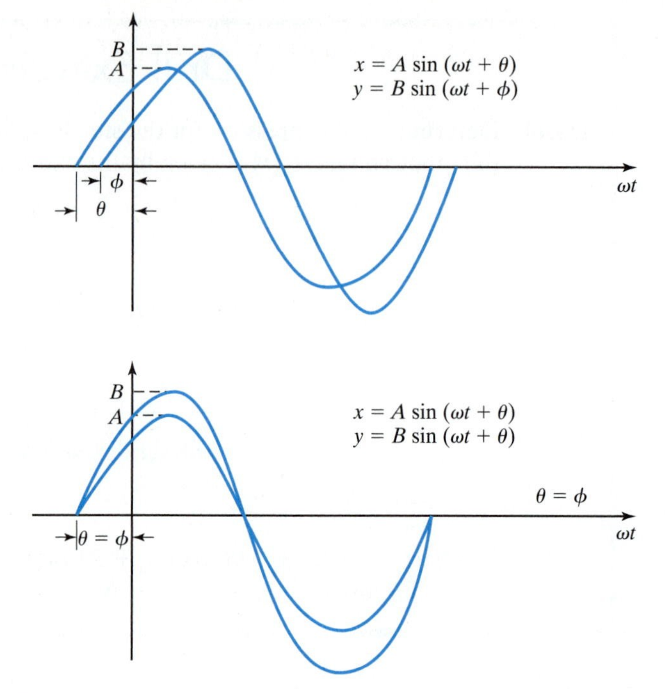

FIGURE 4.27 Sinusoidal functions in and out of phase.

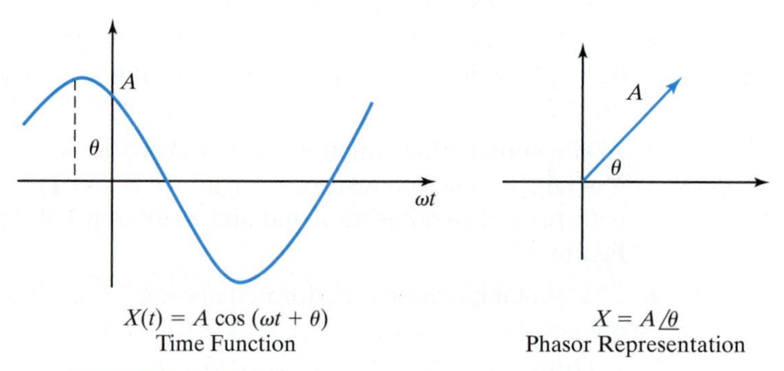

FIGURE 4.28 Time and phasor representations.

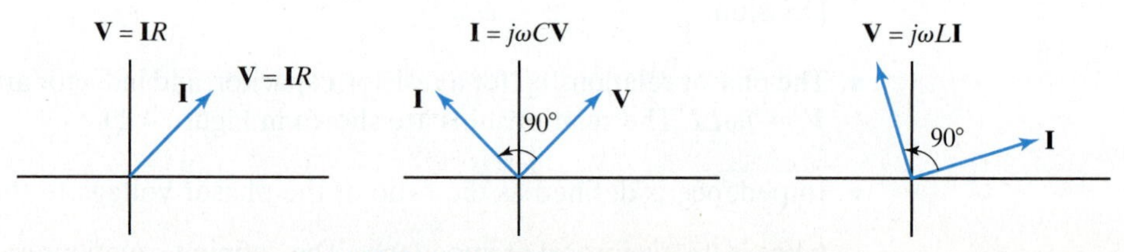

FIGURE 4.29 Phasor relationships.

- Kirchhoff's laws hold in the frequency domain as illustrated in Figure 4.30.

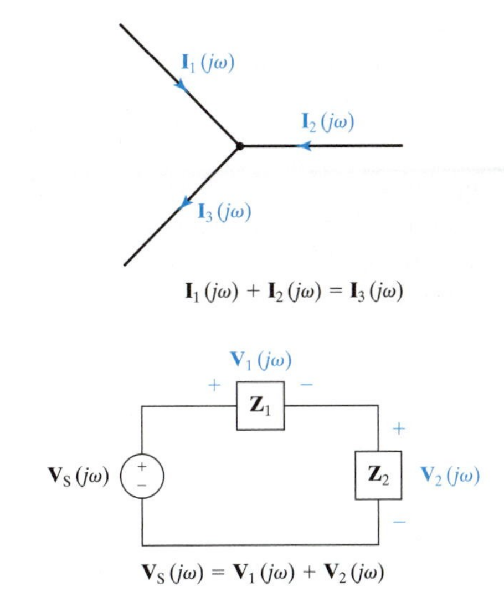

FIGURE 4.30 An illustration of *KCL* and *KVL*.

- The wye-delta transformation is applicable in the frequency domain.

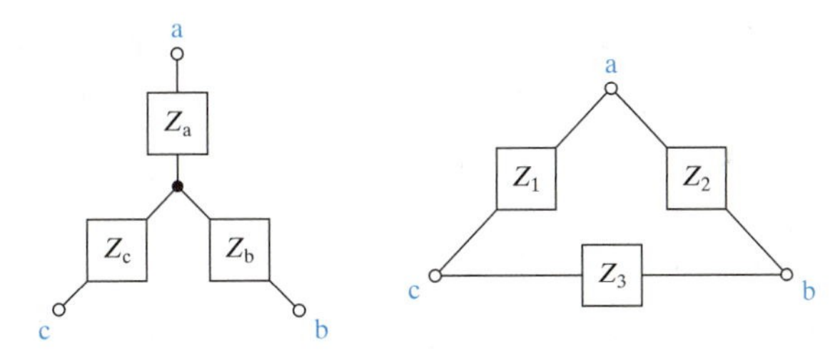

FIGURE 4.31 *Y* and Δ configurations.

The relationships among the impedances shown in Figure 4.31 are

$$Z_a = \frac{Z_1 Z_2}{D} \qquad Z_1 = \frac{N}{Z_b}$$

$$Z_b = \frac{Z_2 Z_3}{D} \qquad Z_2 = \frac{N}{Z_c}$$

$$Z_c = \frac{Z_1 Z_3}{D} \qquad Z_3 = \frac{N}{Z_a}$$

where $D = Z_1 + Z_2 + Z_3$ and $N = Z_a Z_b + Z_a Z_c + Z_b Z_c$.

- The following analysis techniques are used in the frequency domain:
  Nodal analysis
  Loop analysis
  Superposition

Source exchange
Thevenin's theorem
Norton's theorem

- A periodic nonsinusoidal function can be expressed as a sum of sinusoidal functions called a Fourier series, that is, $f(t) = a_0 + \sum_{n=1}^{\infty} a_n \cos n\omega_0 t + b_n \sin n\omega_0 t$.
- Superposition can be used to determine the response of a network to a nonsinusoidal input function. As shown in Figure 4.32, if the input is a periodic nonsinusoidal signal of the form $v_S(t) = v_{S0} + v_{S1}(t) + v_{S2}(t) + --$ then the response, determined via superposition, is $v_0(t) = v_{00} + v_{01}(t) + v_{02}(t) + --$

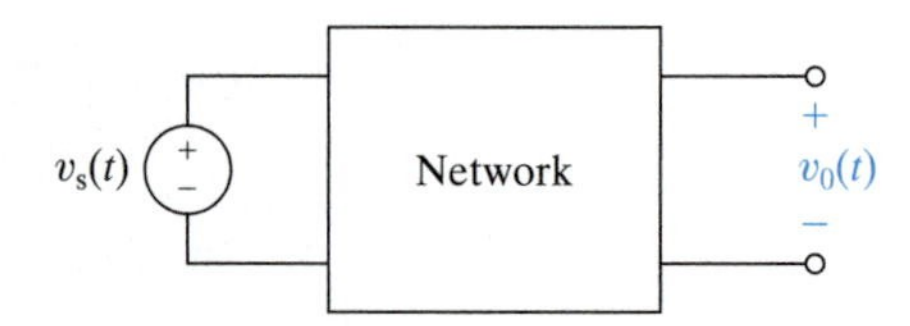

FIGURE 4.32 Network input/output relationship.

Problems

4.1. Determine the frequency of the following two currents and the phase angle between them.

$$i_1(t) = 4\cos(754t - 60°)\ \text{A}$$

$$i_2(t) = 3\cos(754t + 20°)\ \text{A}$$

4.2. Determine the frequency of the following voltages and the phase angle between them.

$$v_1(t) = 100\sin(377t + 25°)\ \text{V}$$

$$v_2(t) = 60\cos(377t - 40°)\ \text{V}$$

4.3. Find $\mathbf{V}_1$ in the network in Figure P4.3.

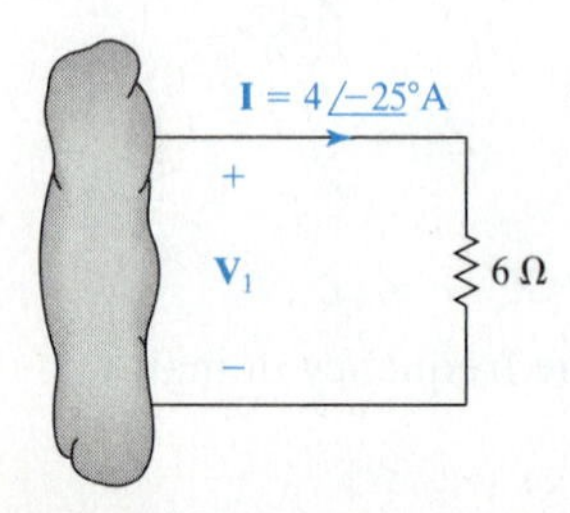

FIGURE P4.3

4.4. In the circuit in Figure P4.4, $v_1(t) = 12\cos(377t + 20°)$ V. Find I.

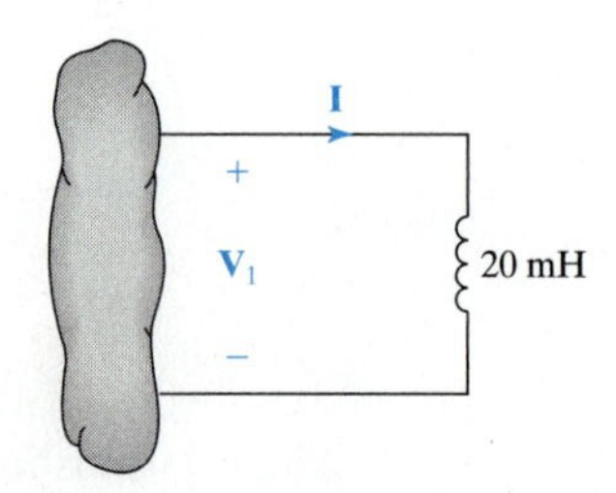

FIGURE P4.4

4.5. In the circuit in Figure P4.5, $i(t) = 2\cos(377t + 60°)$ A. Find $\mathbf{V}_1$.

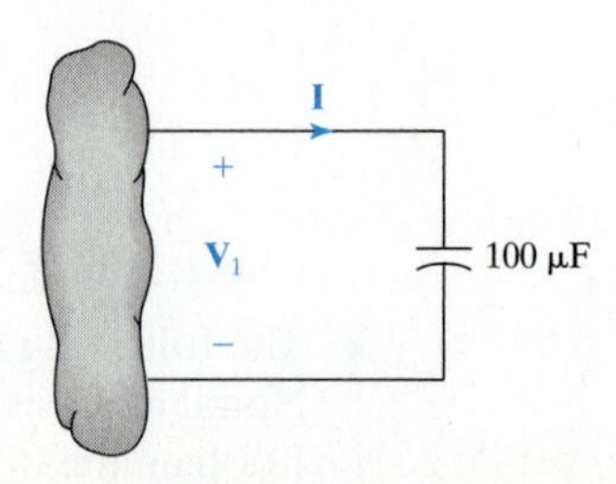

FIGURE P4.5

4.6. Find the impedance $\mathbf{Z}$ shown in Figure P4.6. $\omega = 377$ r/s.

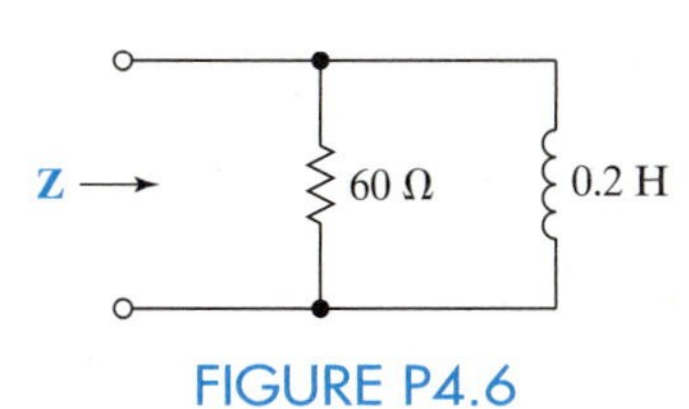

FIGURE P4.6

4.7. Determine the impedance $\mathbf{Z}$ shown in Figure P4.7. $f = 60$ Hz.

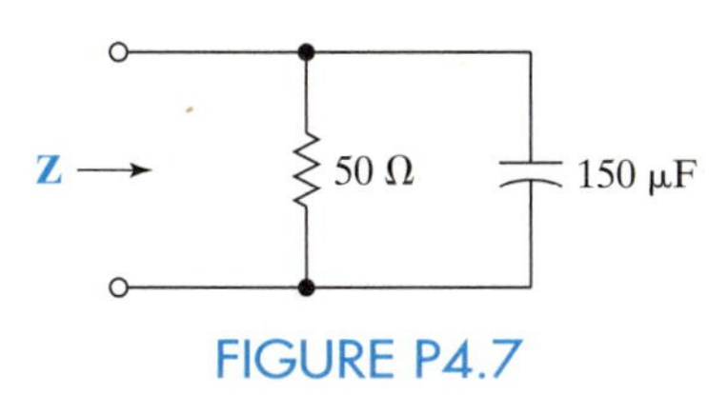

FIGURE P4.7

4.8. Find $\mathbf{Z}$ in Figure P4.8 if $\omega = 10$ r/s.

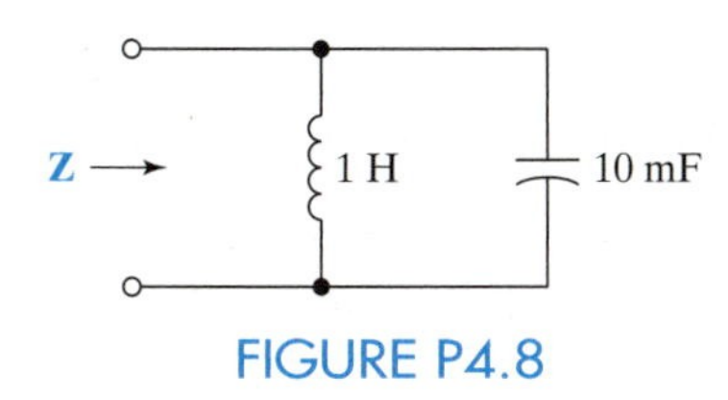

FIGURE P4.8

4.9. Calculate the equivalent impedance at terminals *A*-*B* in the circuit shown in Figure P4.9.

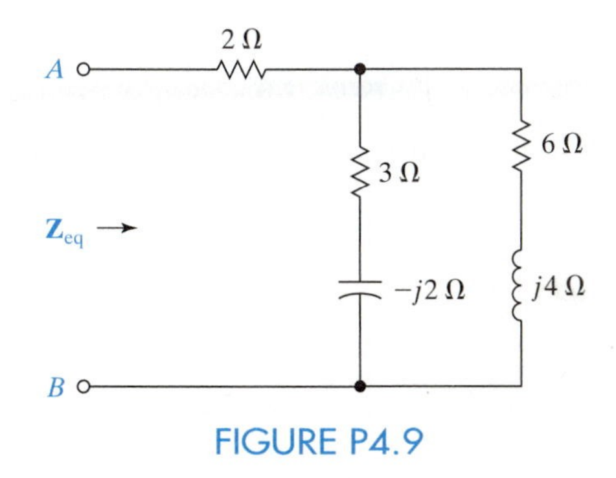

FIGURE P4.9

4.10. Determine the impedance $\mathbf{Z}$ shown in the circuit in Figure P4.10.

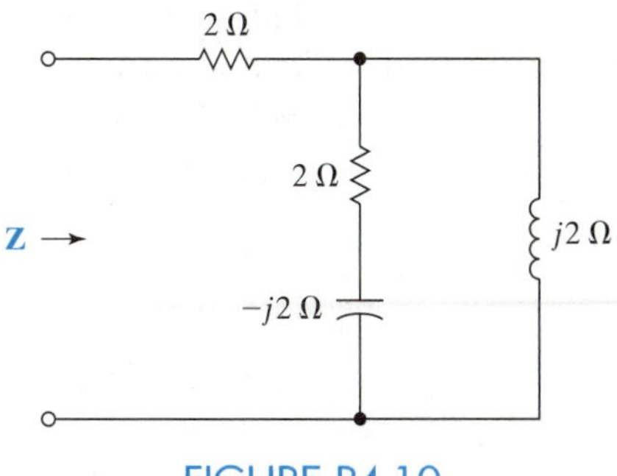

FIGURE P4.10

4.11. Find the equivalent impedance $\mathbf{Z}$ shown in the circuit in Figure P4.11.

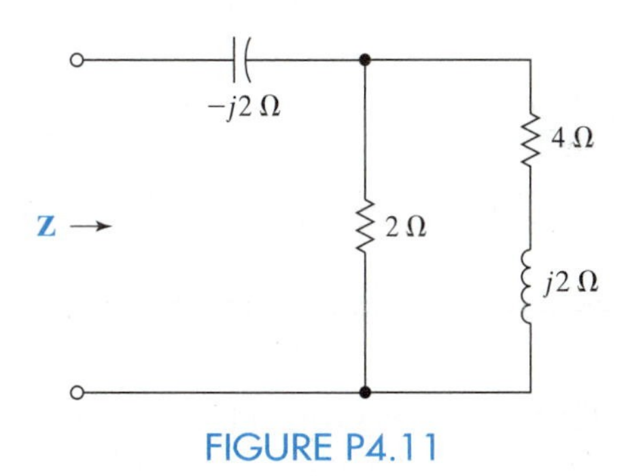

FIGURE P4.11

4.12. Calculate $\mathbf{Y}_{eq}$ as shown in Figure P4.12.

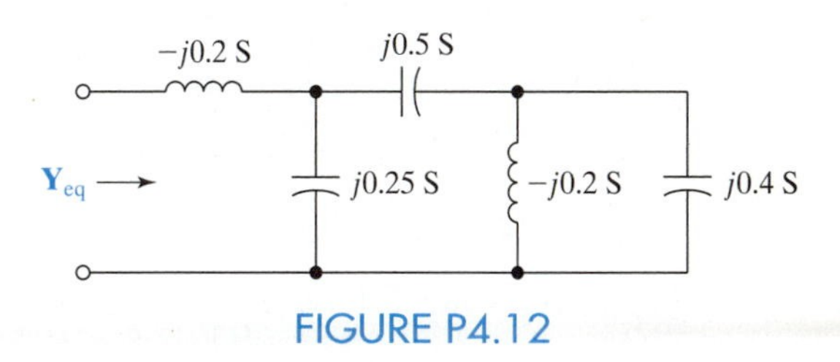

FIGURE P4.12

4.13. Calculate the equivalent admittance $\mathbf{Y}_p$ for the network in Figure P4.13 and use it to determine the current I if $\mathbf{V}_S = 60\angle 45°$ V.

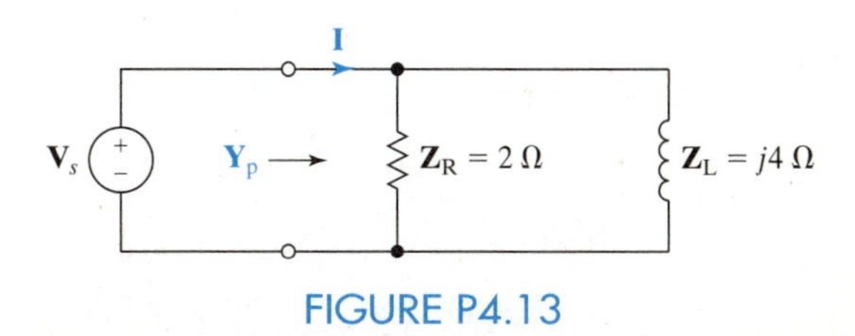

FIGURE P4.13

4.14. Determine the equivalent impedance **Z** shown in the network in Figure P4.14.

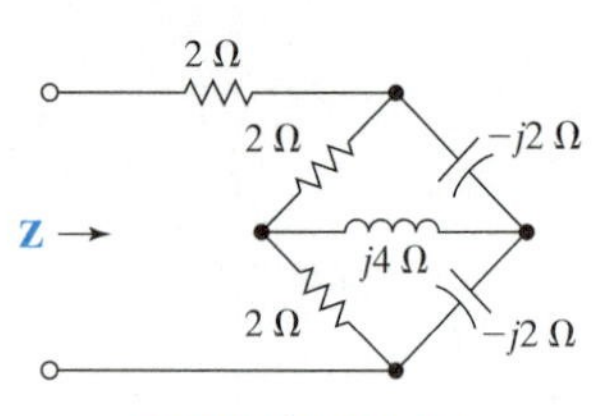

FIGURE P4.14

4.15. Calculate the impedance $\mathbf{Z}_{AB}$ at the terminals *A*-*B* in the network in Figure P4.15.

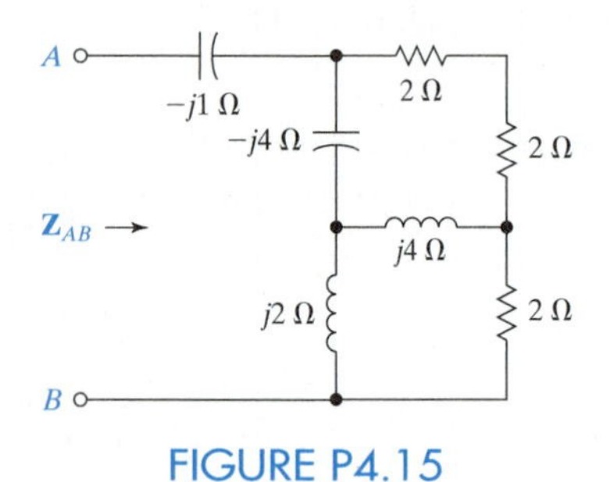

FIGURE P4.15

4.16. Find $\mathbf{V}_0$ in the circuit in Figure P4.16.

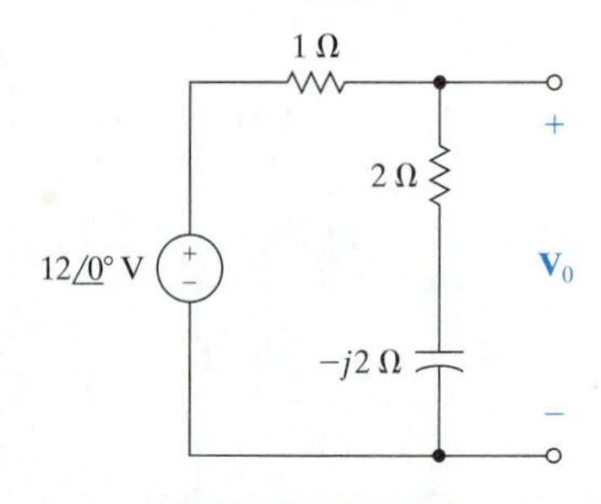

FIGURE P4.16

4.17. Calculate $\mathbf{V}_0$ in the network in Figure P4.17.

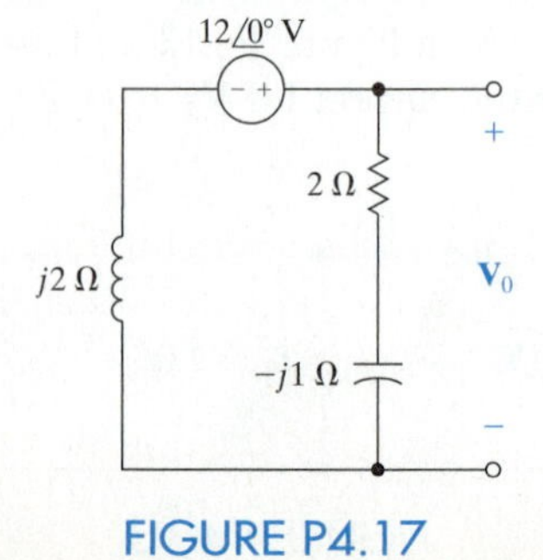

FIGURE P4.17

4.18. Find $\mathbf{V}_0$ in the network in Figure P4.18.

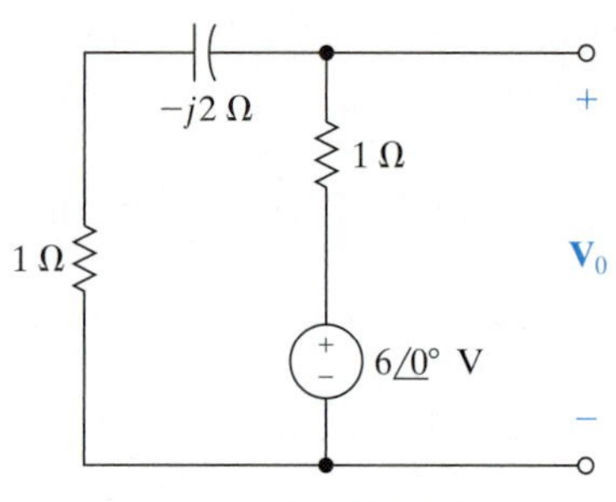

FIGURE P4.18

4.19. Find $\mathbf{V}_0$ in the circuit in Figure P4.19.

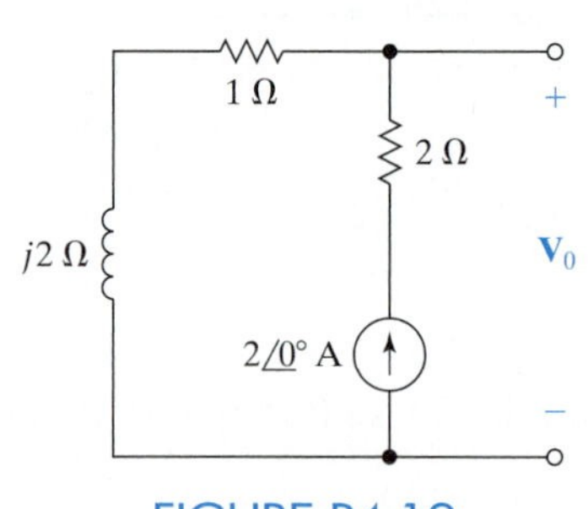

FIGURE P4.19

4.20. In the circuit in Figure P4.20, find $\mathbf{V}_0$.

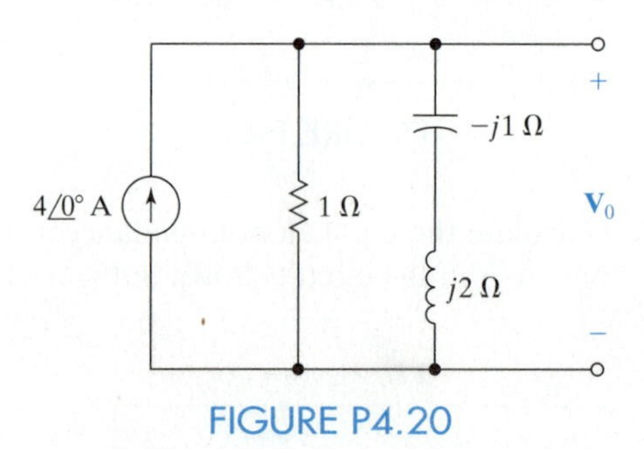

FIGURE P4.20

4.21. Find $\mathbf{V}_0$ in the network in Figure P4.21.

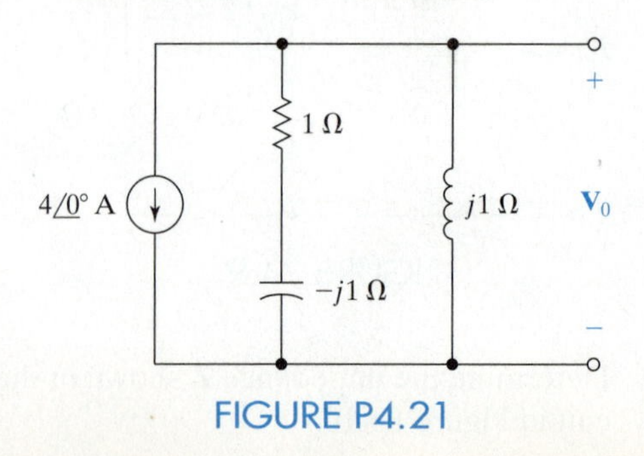

FIGURE P4.21

4.22. Calculate $\mathbf{I}_0$ in the circuit in Figure P4.22.

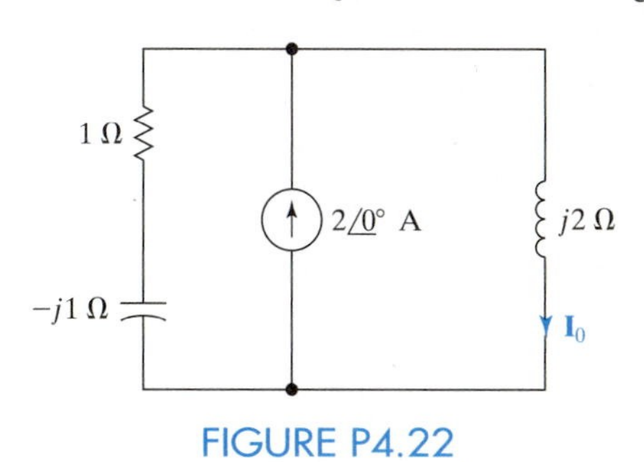

FIGURE P4.22

4.23. Find $\mathbf{I}_0$ in the network in Figure P4.23.

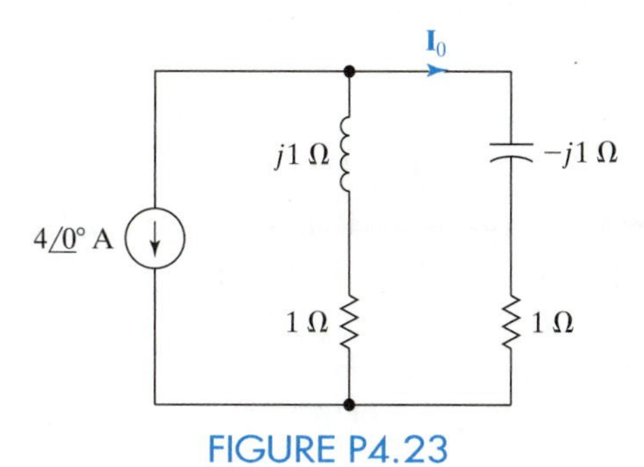

FIGURE P4.23

4.24. Determine the voltage across the current source in the network in Figure P4.24.

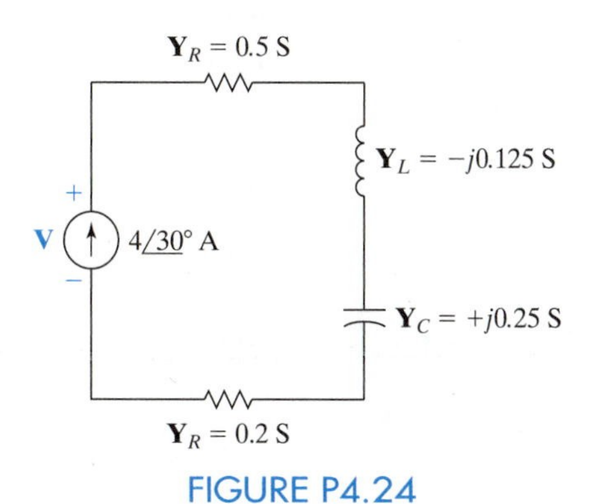

FIGURE P4.24

4.25. Find the current **I** in the network in Figure P4.25.

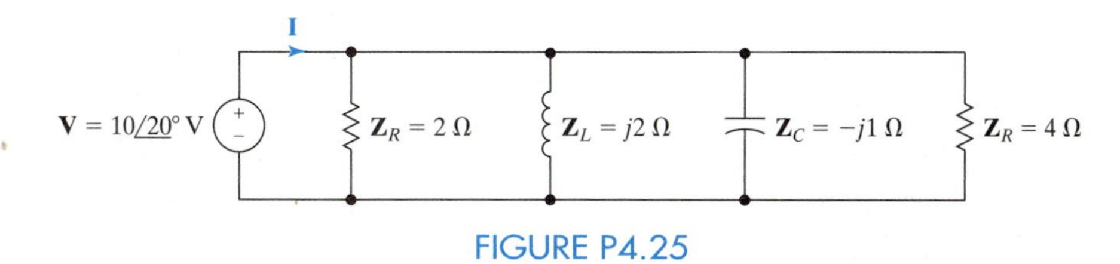

FIGURE P4.25

4.26. Find the currents $\mathbf{I}_1$, $\mathbf{I}_2$, and $\mathbf{I}_3$ in the network in Figure P4.26.

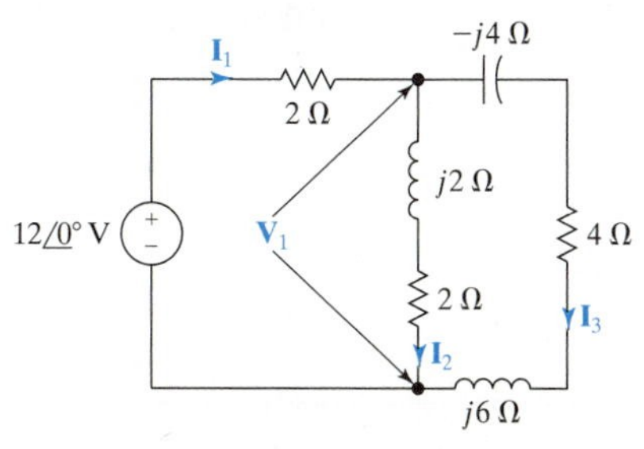

FIGURE P4.26

4.27. Find $\mathbf{I}_0$ in the network in Figure P4.27.

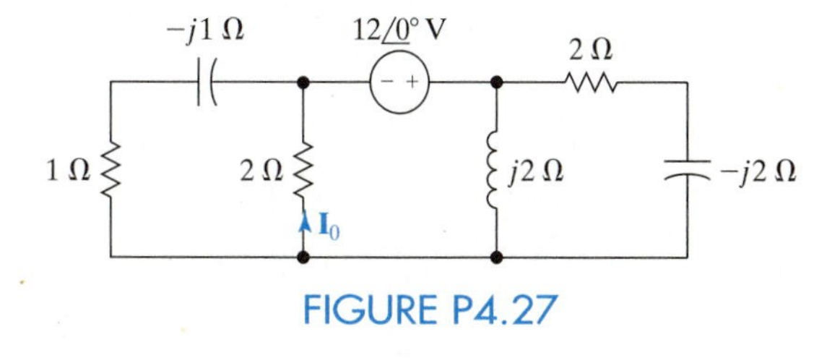

FIGURE P4.27

4.28. Draw a phasor diagram illustrating all currents and voltages for the network in Figure P4.28.

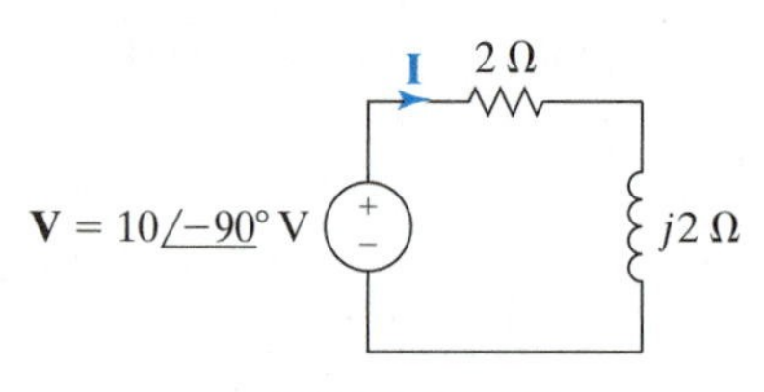

FIGURE P4.28

4.29. Draw a phasor diagram illustrating all currents and voltages for the network in Figure P4.29.

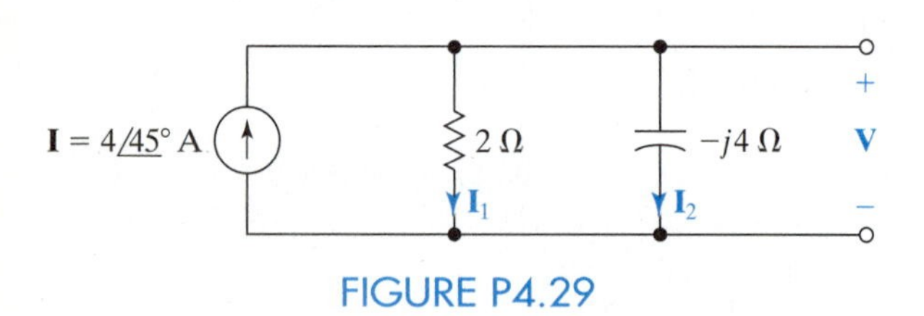

FIGURE P4.29

4.30. In the network in Figure P4.30, $\mathbf{V}_0$ is known to be $8\angle 45°$ V. Compute $\mathbf{V}_S$.

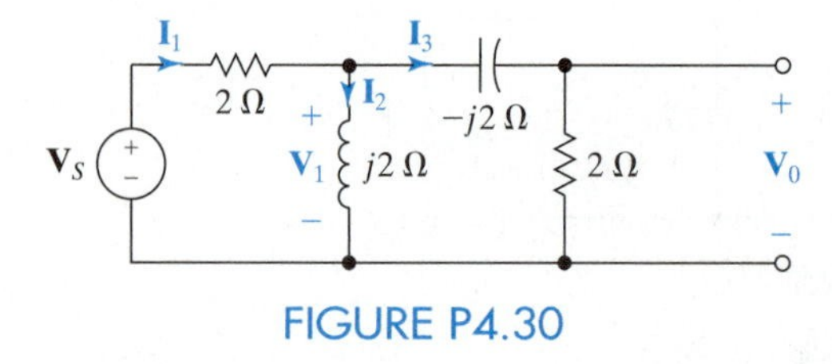

FIGURE P4.30

4.31. Use nodal analysis to find $\mathbf{V}_1$ and $\mathbf{V}_2$ in the circuit in Figure P4.31.

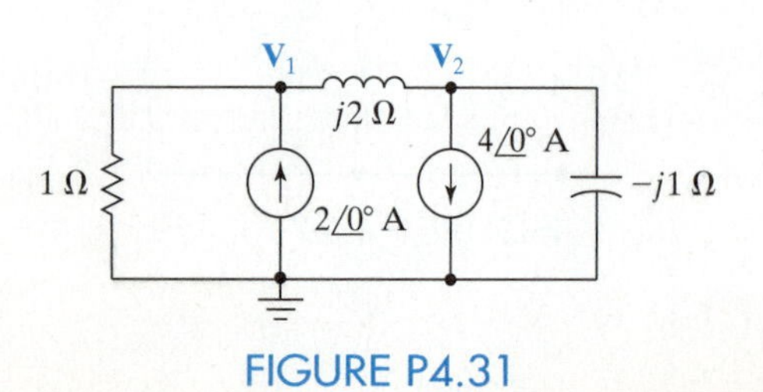

FIGURE P4.31

4.32. Use nodal analysis to find $\mathbf{I}_0$ in the circuit in Figure P4.32.

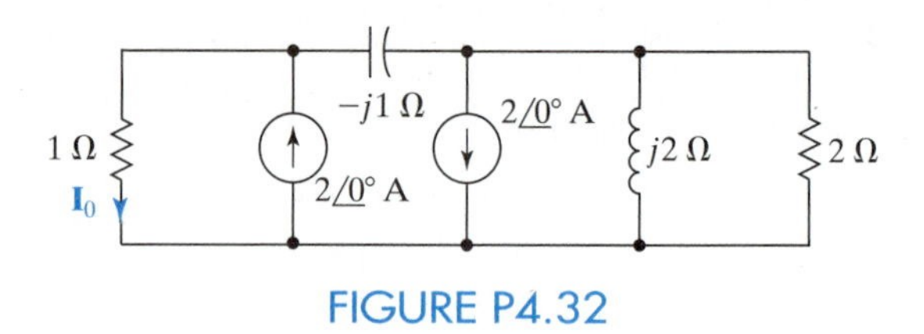

FIGURE P4.32

4.33. Use nodal equations to find the current in the inductor in the circuit shown in Figure P4.33.

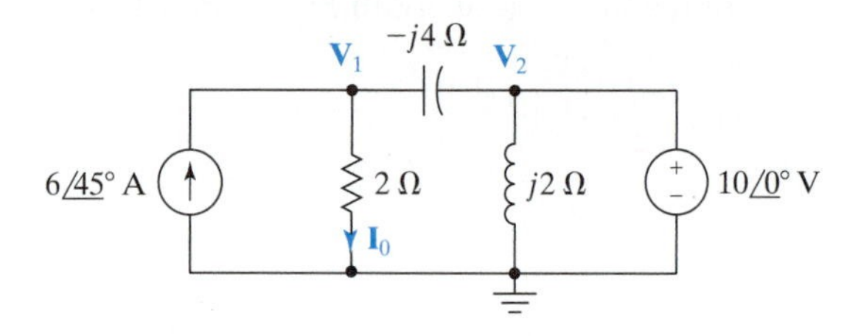

FIGURE P4.33

4.34. Determine $\mathbf{I}_0$ in the circuit shown in Figure P4.34 using nodal analysis.

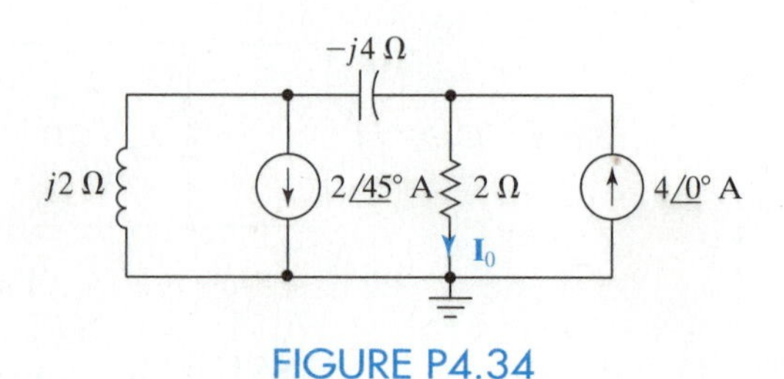

FIGURE P4.34

4.35. Determine $\mathbf{V}_0$ in the circuit shown in Figure P4.35.

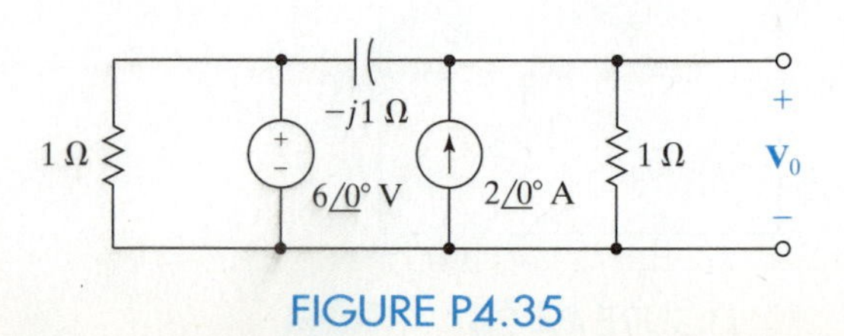

FIGURE P4.35

4.36. Find $\mathbf{I}_0$ in the circuit in Figure P4.36.

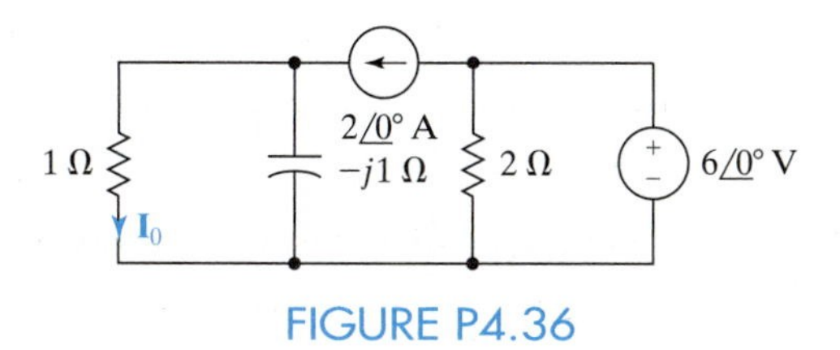

FIGURE P4.36

4.37. Use mesh analysis to find $\mathbf{V}_0$ in the circuit shown in Figure P4.37.

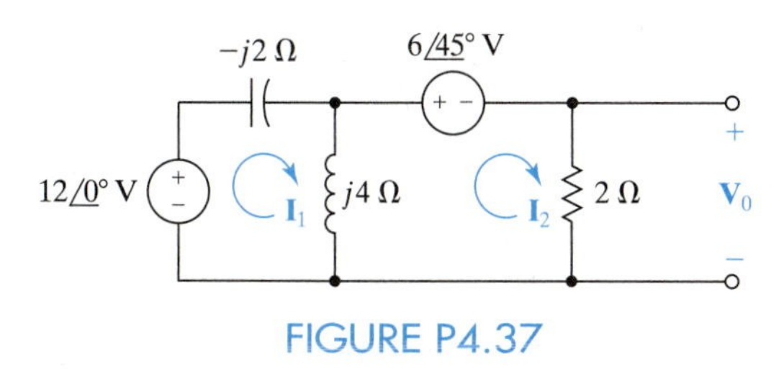

FIGURE P4.37

4.38. Find the currents $\mathbf{I}_1$ and $\mathbf{I}_2$ in the circuit in Figure P4.38.

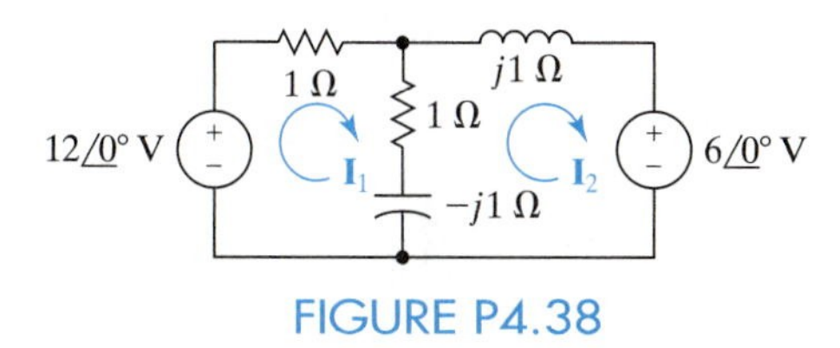

FIGURE P4.38

4.39. Find $\mathbf{V}_0$ in the network in Figure P4.39 using loop analysis.

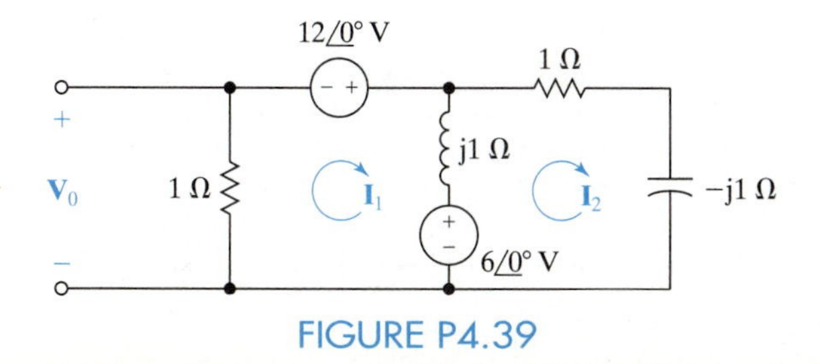

FIGURE P4.39

4.40. Use loop analysis to find $\mathbf{I}_0$ in the circuit in Figure P4.40.

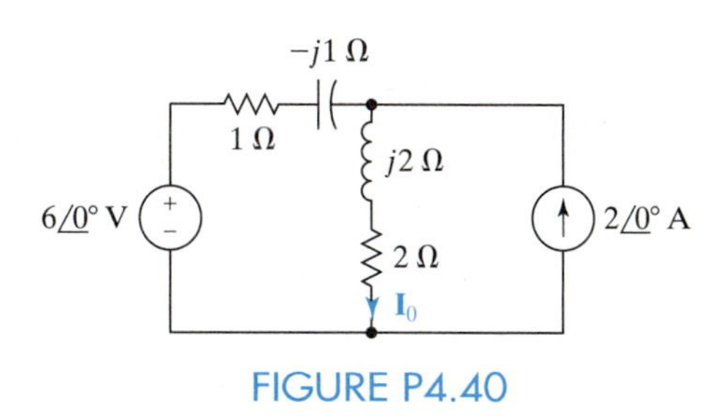

FIGURE P4.40

4.41. Find $\mathbf{V}_0$ in the network in Figure P4.41 using loop analysis.

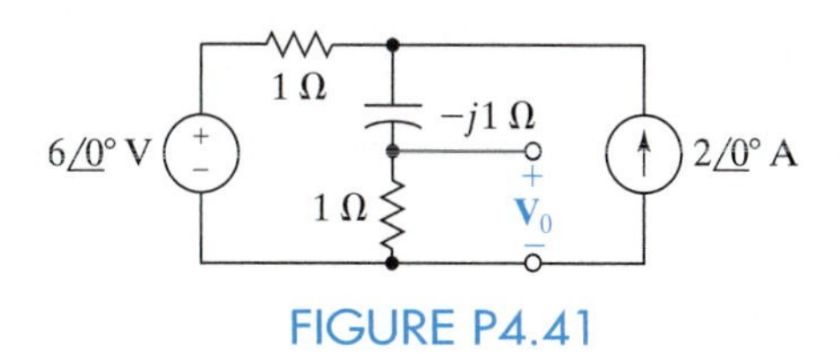

FIGURE P4.41

4.42. Solve problem 4.31 using MATLAB.

4.43. Solve problem 4.32 using MATLAB.

4.44. Solve problem 4.38 using MATLAB.

4.45. Solve problem 4.39 using MATLAB.

4.46. Find $\mathbf{V}_0$ in the circuit in Figure P4.46 using superposition.

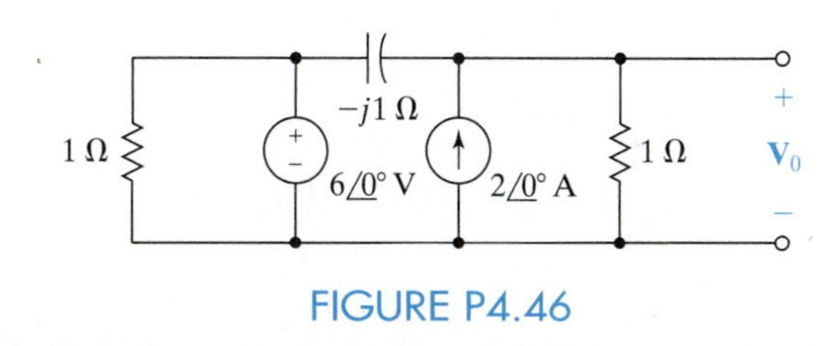

FIGURE P4.46

4.47. Use superposition to find $\mathbf{I}_0$ in the network in Figure P4.47.

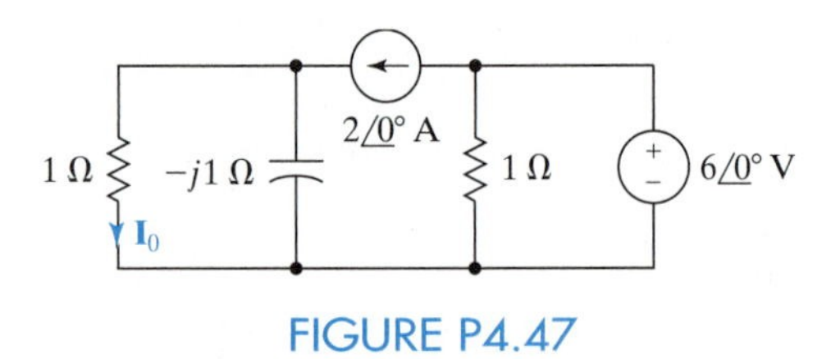

FIGURE P4.47

4.48. Solve problem 4.37 using superposition.

4.49. Use superposition to find $\mathbf{V}_0$ in the circuit in Figure P4.49.

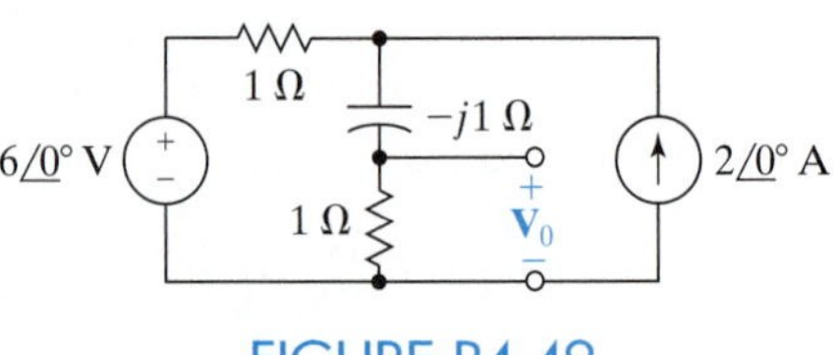

FIGURE P4.49

4.50. Find $\mathbf{I}_0$ in the network in Figure P4.50 using superposition.

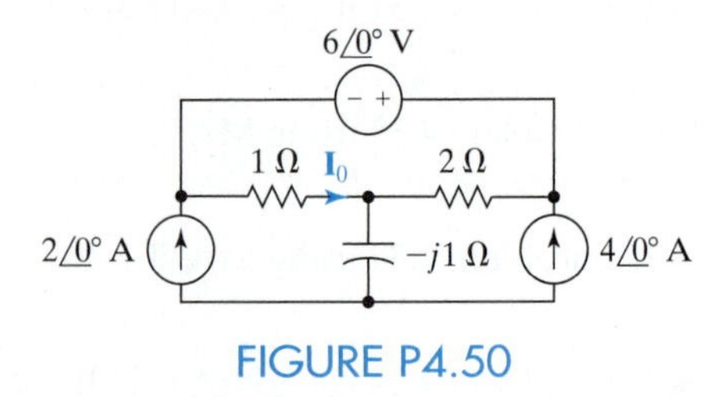

FIGURE P4.50

4.51. Use superposition to find $\mathbf{V}_0$ in the circuit in Figure P4.51.

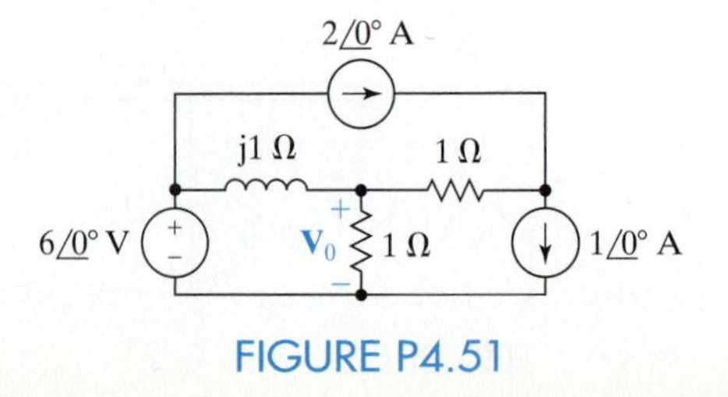

FIGURE P4.51

4.52. Use source transformation to find $\mathbf{I}_0$ in the network in Figure P4.52.

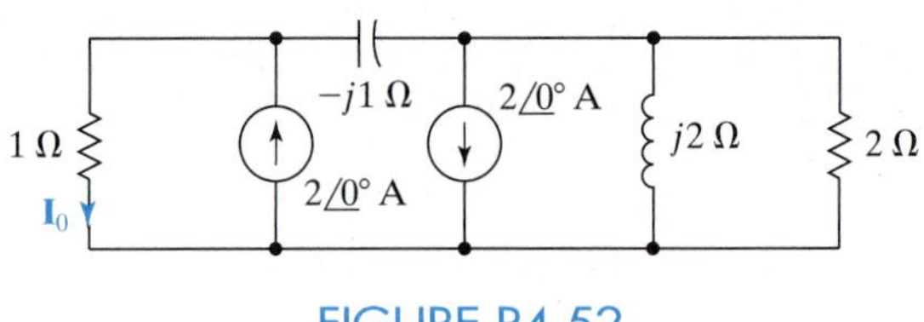

FIGURE P4.52

4.53. Find $\mathbf{V}_0$ in the network in Figure P4.53 using source transformation.

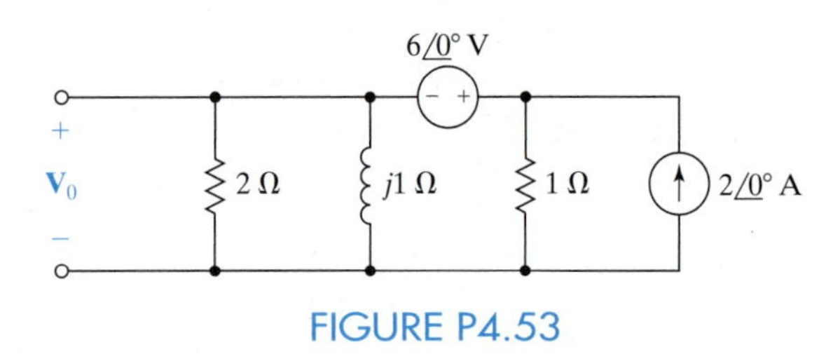

FIGURE P4.53

4.54. Use source transformation to find $\mathbf{I}_0$ in the circuit in Figure P4.54.

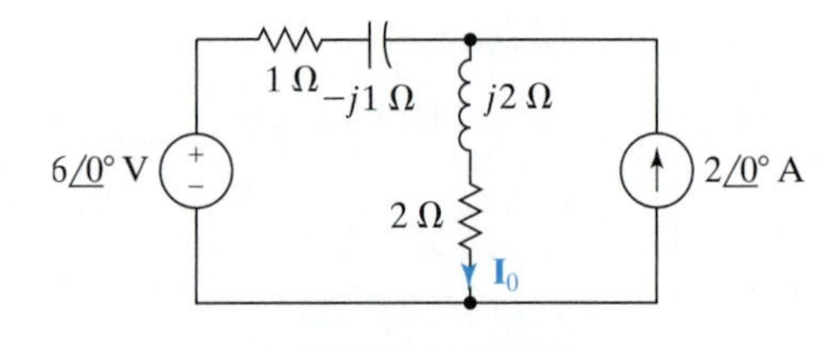

FIGURE P4.54

4.55. Use source transformation to find $\mathbf{V}_0$ in the network in Figure P4.55.

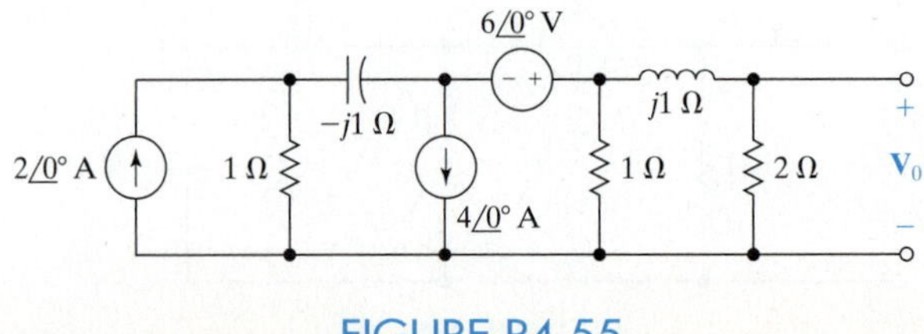

FIGURE P4.55

4.56. Solve problem 4.41 using Thevenin's theorem.

4.57. Solve problem 4.40 using Thevenin's theorem.

4.58. Solve problem 4.39 using Thevenin's theorem.

4.59. Solve problem 4.51 using Thevenin's theorem.

4.60. Find $\mathbf{I}_0$ in the network in Figure P4.60 using Thevenin's theorem.

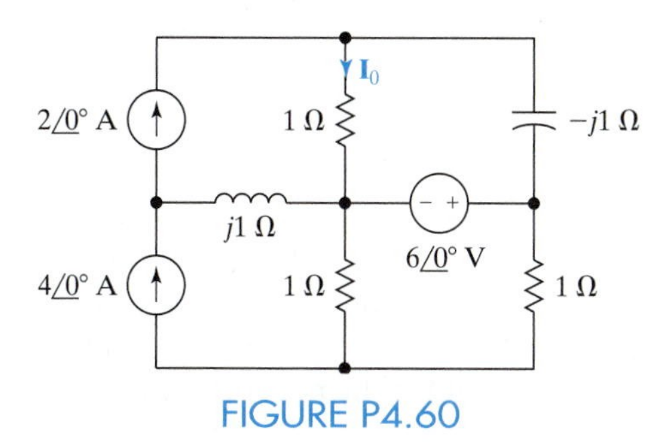

FIGURE P4.60

4.61. Solve problem 4.32 using Norton's theorem.

4.62. Solve problem 4.40 using Norton's theorem.

4.63. Use Norton's theorem to find $\mathbf{V}_0$ in the circuit in Figure P4.63.

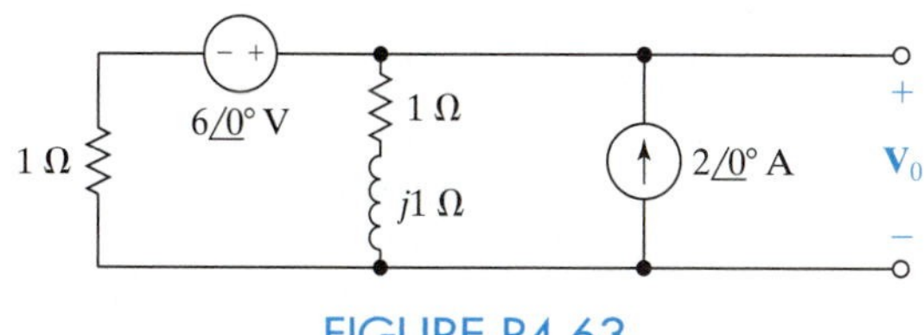

FIGURE P4.63

4.64. Find the exponential Fourier series for the periodic function shown in Figure P4.64.

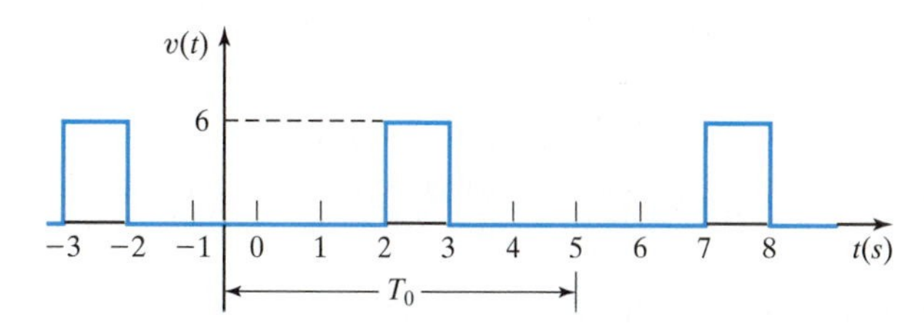

FIGURE P4.64

4.65. Find the Fourier coefficients for the waveform in Figure P4.65.

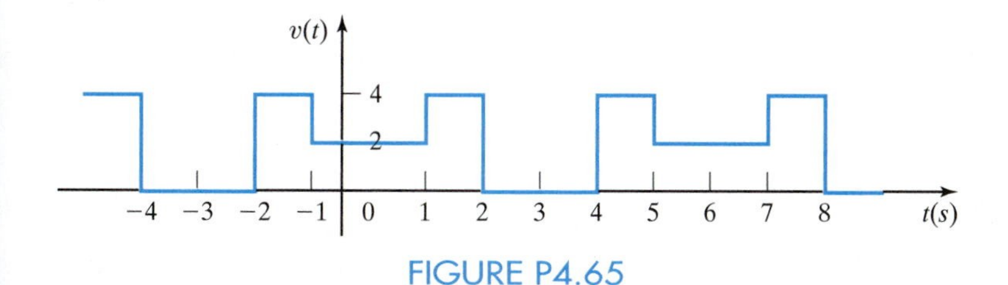

FIGURE P4.65

4.66. If the input voltage in Figure P4.66 is $v_s(t) = 1 - \frac{2}{\pi}\sum_{n=1}^{\infty}\frac{1}{n}\sin 0.2\,\pi nt$ V, find the expression for the steady-state current $i_0(t)$.

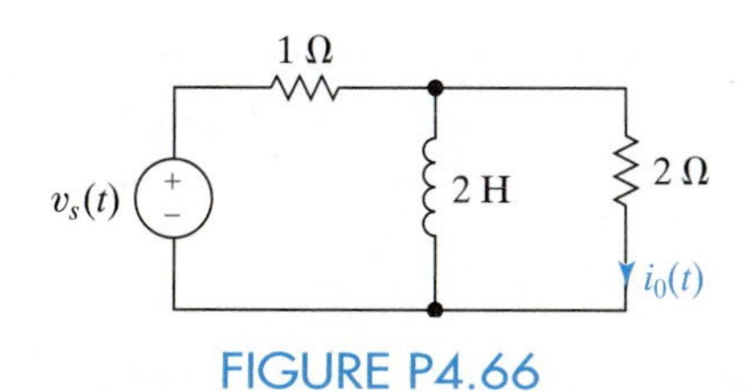

FIGURE P4.66

4.67. Determine the first three terms of the steady-state voltage $v_0(t)$ in Figure P4.67 if the input voltage is a periodic signal of the form.

$$v(t) = \frac{1}{2} + \sum_{n=1}^{\infty}\frac{1}{n\pi}(\cos n\pi - 1)\sin nt \text{ V}$$

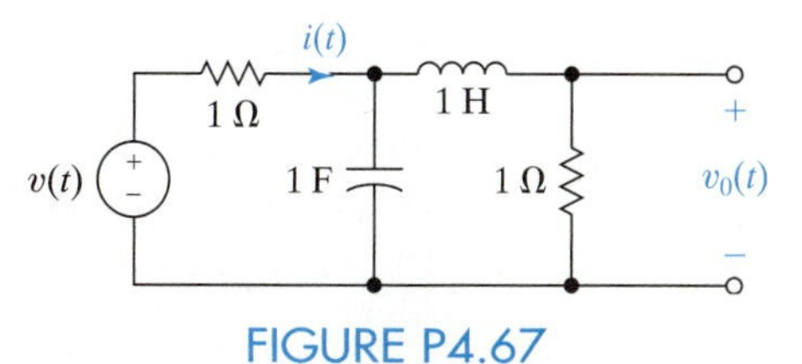

FIGURE P4.67

5

5-1 Introduction

In the preceding chapters, we were primarily concerned with determining the voltage or current at some point in a network. Of equal importance to us in many situations is the power that is supplied or absorbed by some element. Therefore, in this chapter we explore the many ramifications of power in ac circuits. We will first treat the single phase case, that is, the types of networks we have examined thus far. Then we will investigate three-phase circuits, which are typically employed in high-power applications.

5-2 Instantaneous Power

By employing the sign convention adopted in the earlier chapters, we can compute the *instantaneous power* supplied or absorbed by any device as the product of the instantaneous voltage across the device and the instantaneous current through it. Consider the circuit shown in Figure 5.1. In general, the steady-state voltage and current for the network can be written as

$$v(t) = V_M \cos(\omega t + \theta_v) \tag{5.1}$$

$$i(t) = I_M \cos(\omega t + \theta_i) \tag{5.2}$$

The instantaneous power is then

$$\begin{aligned} p(t) &= v(t)i(t) \\ &= V_M I_M \cos(\omega t + \theta_v)\cos(\omega t + \theta_i) \end{aligned} \tag{5.3}$$

Employing the following trigonometric identity

$$\cos\phi_1 \cos\phi_2 = \tfrac{1}{2}[\cos(\phi_1 - \phi_2) + \cos(\phi_1 + \phi_2)] \tag{5.4}$$

the instantaneous power can be written as

$$p(t) = \frac{V_M I_M}{2}[\cos(\theta_v - \theta_i) + \cos(2\omega t + \theta_v + \theta_i)] \tag{5.5}$$

The expression for instantaneous power

Note that the instantaneous power consists of two terms. The first term is a constant (i.e., it is time independent); and the second term is a cosine wave of twice the excitation frequency. We examine this equation in more detail in the next section.

Example 5.1

The circuit in Figure 5.1 has the following parameters: $v(t) = 4\cos(\omega t + 60°)$ V and $\mathbf{Z} = 2\angle 30°\ \Omega$. We wish to determine equations for the current and the instantaneous power as a function of time, and plot these functions with the voltage on a single graph for comparison.

Since

Steady-State Power Analysis

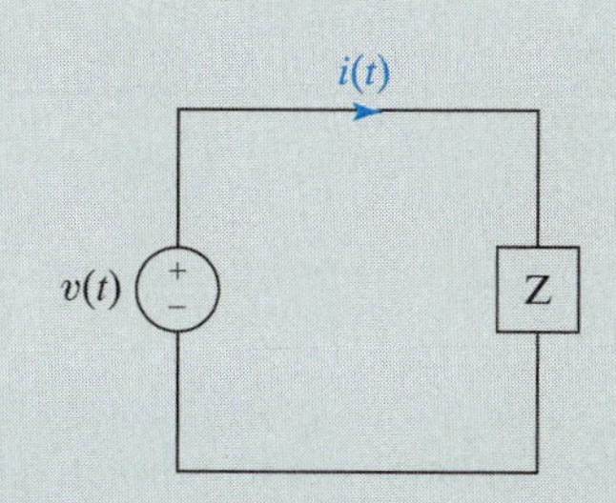

FIGURE 5.1 Simple ac network.

$$\mathbf{I} = \frac{4\angle 60^\circ}{2\angle 30^\circ}$$

$$= 2\angle 30^\circ \text{ A}$$

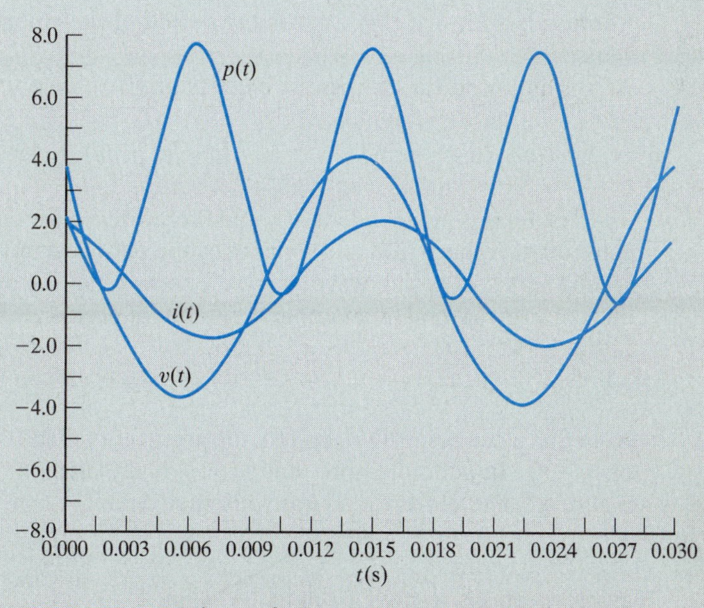

FIGURE 5.2 Plots of $v(t)$, $i(t)$, and $p(t)$ for the circuit in Example 5.1 using $f = 60$ Hz.

then

$$i(t) = 2\cos(\omega t + 30^\circ) \text{ A}$$

From Eq. (5.5)

$$\begin{aligned} p(t) &= 4[\cos(30^\circ) + \cos(2\omega t + 90^\circ)] \\ &= 3.46 + 4\cos(2\omega t + 90^\circ) \text{ W} \end{aligned}$$

A plot of this function, together with plots of the voltage and current, are shown in Figure 5.2. As can be seen in the figure, the instantaneous power has an average value, and the frequency is twice that of the voltage or current.

5-3 Average Power

The average value of any periodic waveform (e.g., a sinusoidal function) can be computed by integrating the function over a complete period and dividing this result by the period. Therefore, if the voltage and current are given by Eqs. (5.1) and (5.2), respectively, the *average power* is

$$\begin{aligned} P &= \frac{1}{T}\int_{t_0}^{t_0+T} p(t)\,dt \\ &= \frac{1}{T}\int_{t_0}^{t_0+T} V_M I_M \cos(\omega t + \theta_v)\cos(\omega t + \theta_i)\,dt \end{aligned} \tag{5.6}$$

where t_0 is arbitrary, $T = 2\pi/\omega$ is the period of the voltage or current, and P is measured in watts.

Employing Eq. (5.5) in the expression (5.6), we obtain

$$P = \frac{1}{T}\int_{t_0}^{t_0+T} \frac{V_M I_M}{2}[\cos(\theta_v - \theta_i) + \cos(2\omega t + \theta_v + \theta_i)]\,dt \tag{5.7}$$

The first term is independent of t, and therefore a constant in the integration. Integrating the constant over the period and dividing by the period simply results in the original constant. The second term is a cosine wave. It is well known that the average value of a cosine wave over one complete period or an integral number of periods is zero. Therefore, Eq. (5.7) reduces to

The general equation for average power

$$P = \tfrac{1}{2} V_M I_M \cos(\theta_v - \theta_i) \tag{5.8}$$

Note that since $\cos(-\theta) = \cos(\theta)$, the argument for the cosine function can be either $\theta_v - \theta_i$ or $\theta_i - \theta_v$. In addition, note that $\theta_v - \theta_i$ is the angle of the circuit impedance as shown in Figure 5.1. Therefore, for a purely resistive circuit,

$$P = \tfrac{1}{2} V_M I_M \tag{5.9}$$

and for a purely reactive circuit,

$$\begin{aligned} P &= \tfrac{1}{2} V_M I_M \cos(90^\circ) \\ &= 0 \end{aligned}$$

Because purely reactive impedances absorb no average power, they are often called lossless elements. The purely reactive network operates in a mode in which it stores energy over one part of the period and releases it over another.

Example 5.2

For the circuit shown in Figure 5.3 we wish to determine both the total average power absorbed and the total average power supplied. From the figure we note that

$$\mathbf{I}_1 = \frac{12\angle 45^\circ}{4} = 3\angle 45^\circ \text{ A}$$

$$\mathbf{I}_2 = \frac{12\angle 45^\circ}{2 - j1} = \frac{12\angle 45^\circ}{2.24\angle -26.57^\circ} = 5.37\angle 71.57^\circ \text{ A}$$

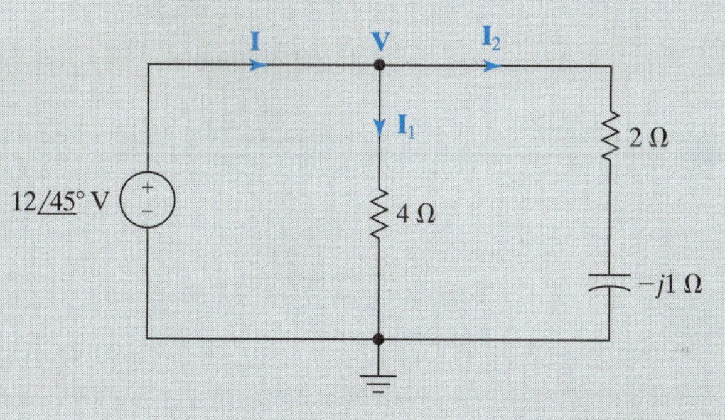

FIGURE 5.3 Example circuit for illustrating a power balance.

and therefore,

$$\begin{aligned} \mathbf{I} &= \mathbf{I}_1 + \mathbf{I}_2 \\ &= 3\angle 45^\circ + 5.37\angle 71.57^\circ \\ &= 8.16\angle 62.08^\circ \text{ A} \end{aligned}$$

The average power absorbed in the 4 Ω resistor is

$$P_{4\Omega} = \tfrac{1}{2} V_M I_M = \tfrac{1}{2}(12)(3) = 18 \text{ W}$$

The average power absorbed in the 2 Ω resistor is

$$P_{2\Omega} = \tfrac{1}{2} I_M^2 R = \tfrac{1}{2}(5.37)^2(2) = 28.8 \text{ W}$$

Therefore, the total average power absorbed is

$$P_A = 18 + 28.8 = 46.8 \text{ W}$$

Note that we could have calculated the power absorbed in the 2 Ω resistor using $\tfrac{1}{2}V_M^2/R$ if we had first calculated the voltage across the 2 Ω resistor.

The total average power supplied by the source is

$$\begin{aligned} P_s &= +\tfrac{1}{2}V_M I_M \cos(\theta_v - \theta_i) \\ &= +\tfrac{1}{2}(12)(8.16)\cos(45^\circ - 62.08^\circ) \\ &= +46.8 \text{ W} \end{aligned}$$

Thus, the total average power supplied is, of course, equal to the total average power absorbed.

Drill Exercise

D5.1. Find the average power absorbed by each resistor in the network in Figure D5.1.

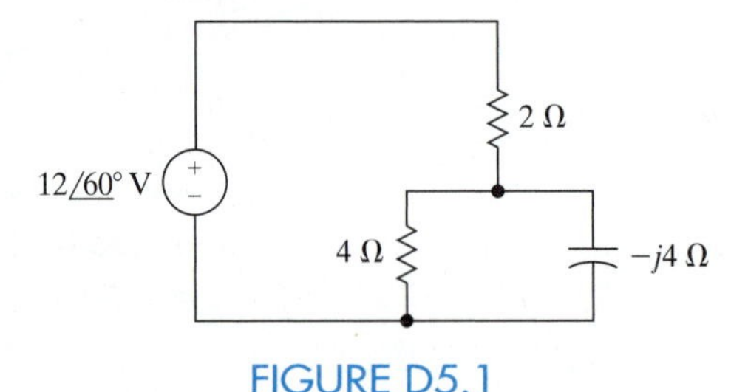

FIGURE D5.1

Ans: $P_{2\Omega} = 7.18$ W, $P_{4\Omega} = 7.14$ W.

D5.2. Given the network in Figure D5.2, find the average power absorbed by each passive circuit element and the total average power supplied by the current source.

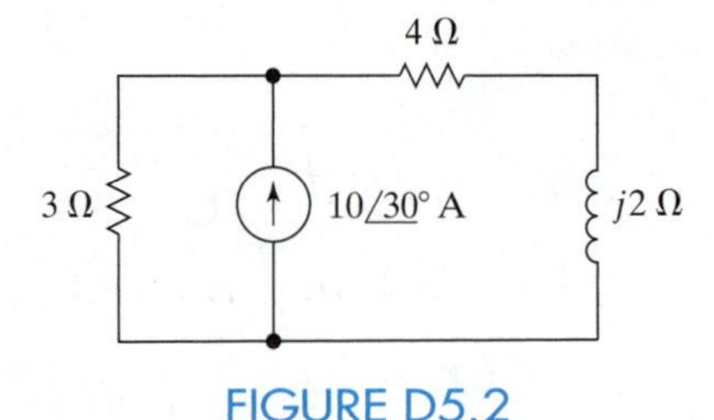

FIGURE D5.2

Ans: $P_{3\Omega} = 56.62$ W, $P_{4\Omega} = 33.95$ W, $P_L = 0$, $P_{cs} = -90.50$ W.

5-4 Effective or RMS Values

In the preceding sections of this chapter we have shown that the average power absorbed by a resistive load is directly dependent on the type, or types, of sources that are delivering power to the load. For example, if the source was dc, the average power absorbed was I^2R; and if the source was sinusoidal, the average power was $\frac{1}{2}I_M^2R$. Although these two types of waveforms are extremely important, they are by no means the only waveforms we will encounter in circuit analysis. Therefore, a technique by which we can compare the effectiveness of different sources in delivering power to a resistive load would be quite useful.

In order to accomplish this comparison, we define what is called the *effective value of a periodic waveform.* We define the effective value of a periodic current as a constant, or dc value, which delivers the same average power to a resistor R. Let us call the constant current I_{eff}. Then the average power delivered to a resistor as a result of this current is

$$P = I_{eff}^2 R$$

Similarly, the average power delivered to a resistor by a periodic current $i(t)$ is

$$P = \frac{1}{T}\int_{t_0}^{t_0+T} i^2(t)R\,dt \tag{5.10}$$

Equating these two expressions, we find that

$$I_{eff} = \sqrt{\frac{1}{T}\int_{t_0}^{t_0+T} i^2(t)\,dt} \tag{5.11}$$

The general equation for the rms value of a periodic signal

Note that this effective value is found by first determining the square of the current, then computing the average or mean value, and finally taking the square root. Thus, in "reading" the mathematical Eq. (5.11), we are determining the *root-mean-square,* which we abbreviate as *rms,* and therefore I_{eff} is called I_{rms}.

Example 5.3

The waveform for the current in a 5 Ω resistor is shown in Figure 5.4. We wish to find the average power absorbed by the resistor.

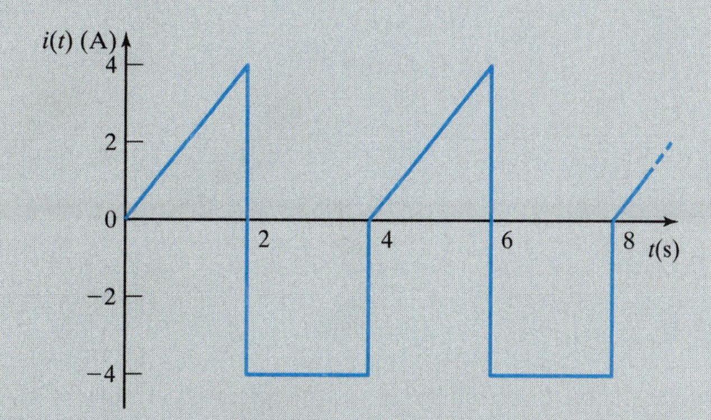

FIGURE 5.4 Waveform used in Example 5.3.

The equations for the current within the time interval $0 \le t \le 4$ seconds are

$$i(t) = \begin{cases} 2t & 0 \le t \le 2 \text{ sec} \\ -4 & 2 \le t \le 4 \text{ sec} \end{cases}$$

Therefore, the rms value of the current is

$$I_{rms} = \left[\frac{1}{4}\left(\int_0^2 (2t)^2\,dt + \int_2^4 (-4)^2\,dt\right)\right]^{1/2}$$

$$= \left[\frac{1}{4}\left(\frac{4t^3}{3}\bigg|_0^2 + 16t\bigg|_2^4\right)\right]^{1/2}$$

$$= 3.27 \text{ A rms}$$

Then the average power absorbed by the 5 Ω resistor is

$$P = I_{rms}^2(R)$$

$$= (3.27)^2(5)$$

$$= 53.3 \text{ W}$$

Example 5.4

We wish to compute the rms value of the waveform $i(t) = I_M \cos(\omega t - \theta)$, which has a period of $T = 2\pi/\omega$.
Substituting these expressions into Eq. (5.11) yields

$$I_{rms} = \left[\frac{1}{T}\int_0^T I_M^2 \cos^2(\omega t - \theta)\,dt\right]^{1/2}$$

Using the trigonometric identity

$$\cos^2\phi = \tfrac{1}{2} + \tfrac{1}{2}\cos 2\phi$$

the equation above can be expressed as

$$I_{rms} = I_M\left[\frac{\omega}{2\pi}\int_0^{2\pi/\omega} [\tfrac{1}{2} + \tfrac{1}{2}\cos(2\omega t - 2\theta)]\,dt\right]^{1/2}$$

Since we know that the average or mean value of a cosine wave is zero,

$$I_{rms} = I_M\left[\frac{\omega}{2\pi}\int_0^{2\pi/\omega} \frac{1}{2}dt\right]^{1/2}$$

$$= I_M\left[\frac{\omega}{2\pi}\left(\frac{t}{2}\right)\bigg|_0^{2\pi/\omega}\right]^{1/2} = \frac{I_M}{\sqrt{2}}$$

The rms value of a sinusoidal function

Therefore, the rms value of a sinusoid is equal to the maximum value divided by the $\sqrt{2}$. Hence, a sinusoidal current with a maximum value of I_M delivers the same average power to a resistor R as a dc current with a value of $I_M/\sqrt{2}$.

Using the rms values for voltage and current, the average power can be written in general as

$$P = V_{rms} I_{rms} \cos(\theta_v - \theta_i) \quad (5.12)$$

The power absorbed by a resistor R is

$$P = I_{\text{rms}}^2 R = \frac{V_{\text{rms}}^2}{R} \tag{5.13}$$

Comparison of average, maximum, and rms values for a sinusoidal function

In dealing with voltages and currents in numerous electrical applications, it is important to know whether the values quoted are the maximum, average, or rms. For example, the normal 120 V ac electrical outlets have an rms value of 120 V, an average value of 0 V, and a maximum value, or amplitude, of $120\sqrt{2}$ V.

Drill Exercises

D5.3. Compute the rms value of the voltage waveform shown in Figure D5.3.

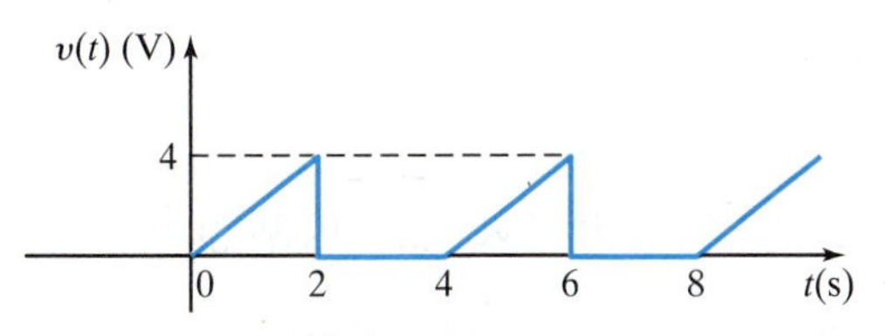

FIGURE D5.3

Ans: $V_{\text{rms}} = 1.633$ V rms.

D5.4. The current waveform in Figure D5.4 is flowing through a 10 Ω resistor. Determine the average power delivered to the resistor.

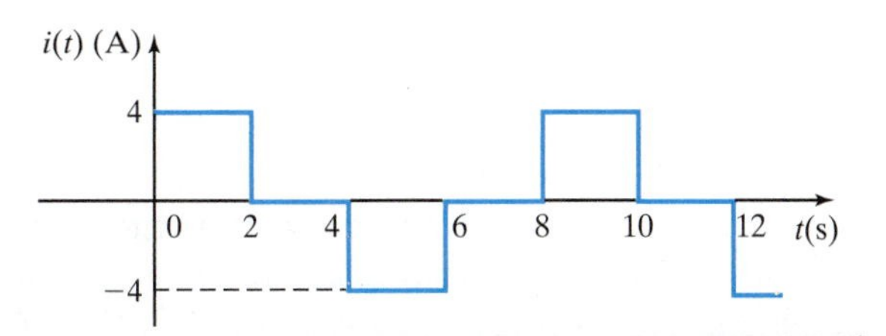

FIGURE D5.4

Ans: $P = 80$ W.

5-5 The Power Factor

The power factor is a very important quantity. Its importance stems in part from the economic impact it has on industrial users of large amounts of power. In this section we carefully define this term and then illustrate its significance via some practical examples. Earlier we showed that a load operating in the ac steady state is delivering an average power of

$$P = V_{rms} I_{rms} \cos(\theta_v - \theta_i)$$

We will now further define the terms in this important equation. The product $V_{rms} I_{rms}$ is referred to as the *apparent power.* Although the term $\cos(\theta_v - \theta_i)$ is a dimensionless quantity, and the units of P are watts, apparent power is normally stated in volt-amperes (VA) or kilovolt-amperes (kVA) in order to distinguish it from average power. We now define the *power factor* (PF) as the ratio of the average power to the apparent power, that is,

Power factor defined

$$PF = \frac{P}{V_{rms} I_{rms}} = \cos(\theta_v - \theta_i) \tag{5.14}$$

where

$$\cos(\theta_v - \theta_i) = \cos \theta_{ZL} \tag{5.15}$$

The angle $\theta_v - \theta_i = \theta_{ZL}$ is the phase angle of the load impedance and is often referred to as the *power factor angle.* The extreme positions for this angle correspond to a purely resistive load where $\theta_{ZL} = 0$, the PF is 1, and the purely reactive load where $\theta_{ZL} = \pm 90°$ and the PF is 0. It is, of course, possible to have a unity PF for a load containing R, L, and C elements if the values of the circuit elements are such that a zero phase angle is obtained at the particular operating frequency.

There is, of course, a whole range of power factor angles between $\pm$ 90° and 0°. If the load is an equivalent RC combination, then the PF angle lies between the limits $-90° < \theta_{ZL} < 0°$. On the other hand, if the load is an equivalent RL combination, then the PF angle lies between the limits $0 < \theta_{ZL} < 90°$. Obviously, confusion in identifying the type of load could result, due to the fact that $\cos(+\theta_{ZL}) = \cos(-\theta_{ZL})$. To circumvent this problem, the PF is said to be either *leading* or *lagging,* where these two terms refer to the phase of the current with respect to the voltage. Since the current leads the voltage in an RC load, the load has a *leading* PF. In a similar manner, an RL load has a *lagging* PF; therefore, load impedances of $\mathbf{Z}_L = 1 - j1$ and $\mathbf{Z}_L = 2 + j1$ have power factors of $\cos(-45°) = 0.707$ leading and $\cos(26.59°) = 0.894$ lagging, respectively.

Leading and lagging power factors

Example 5.5

An industrial load consumes 88 kW at a PF of 0.707 lagging from a 480 V rms line. The transmission line resistance from the power company's transformer to the plant is 0.08 Ω. Let us determine the power that must be supplied by the power company (a) under present conditions, and (b) if the PF is somehow changed to 0.90 lagging.

(a) The equivalent circuit for these conditions is shown in Figure 5.5. Using Eq. (5.14), the magnitude of the rms current into the plant is

$$\begin{aligned} I_{rms} &= \frac{P_L}{(PF)(V_{rms})} \\ &= \frac{(88)(10^3)}{(0.707)(480)} \\ &= 259.3 \text{ A rms} \end{aligned}$$

The power that must be supplied by the power company is

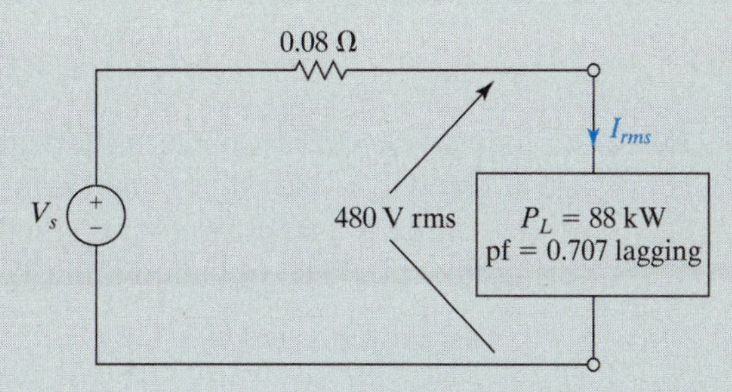

FIGURE 5.5 Example circuit for examining the supply of power.

$$
\begin{aligned}
P_s &= P_L + (0.08)I_{\text{rms}}^2 \\
&= 88{,}000 + (0.08)(259.3)^2 \\
&= 93.38 \text{ kW}
\end{aligned}
$$

(b) Suppose now that the PF is somehow changed to 0.90 lagging but the voltage remains constant at 480 V. The rms load current for this condition is

$$
\begin{aligned}
I_{\text{rms}} &= \frac{P_L}{(\text{PF})(V_{\text{rms}})} \\
&= \frac{(88)(10^3)}{(0.90)(480)} \\
&= 203.7 \text{ A rms}
\end{aligned}
$$

Under these conditions, the power company must generate

$$
\begin{aligned}
P_s &= P_L + (0.08)I_{\text{rms}}^2 \\
&= 88{,}000 + (0.08)(203.7)^2 \\
&= 91.32 \text{ kW}
\end{aligned}
$$

Note carefully the difference between the two cases. A simple change in the PF of the load from 0.707 lagging to 0.90 lagging has had an interesting effect. Note that in the first case the power company must generate 93.38 kW in order to supply the plant with 88 kW of power because the low power factor means that the line losses will be high—5.38 kW. However, in the second case the power company need only generate 91.32 kW in order to supply the plant with its required power, and the corresponding line losses are only 3.32 kW.

The example clearly indicates the economic impact of the load's power factor. A low power factor at the load means that the utility generators must be capable of carrying more current at constant voltage, and they must also supply power for higher $I_{\text{rms}}^2 R$ line losses than would be required if the load's power factor were high. Since line losses represent energy expended in heat and benefit no one, the utility will insist that a plant maintain a high PF, typically 0.90 lagging or better, and adjust their rate schedule to penalize plants that do not conform to this requirement. In the next section we will demonstrate a simple and economical technique for achieving this power factor correction.

Drill Exercise

D5.5. An industrial load consumes 100 kW at 0.707 PF lagging. The 60 Hz line voltage at the load is $480\underline{/0°}$ V rms. The transmission line resistance between the power company's transformer and the load is 0.1 Ω. Determine the power savings that could be obtained if the PF is changed to 0.94 lagging.

Ans: Power saved is 3.771 kW.

5-6 Complex Power

In our study of ac steady-state power, it is convenient to introduce another quantity, which is commonly called *complex power.* To develop the relationship between this quantity and others we have presented in the preceding sections, consider the circuit shown in Figure 5.6. The complex power is defined to be

$$\mathbf{S} = \mathbf{V}_{\text{rms}} \mathbf{I}^*_{\text{rms}} \tag{5.16}$$

where $\mathbf{I}^*_{\text{rms}}$ refers to the complex conjugate of $\mathbf{I}_{\text{rms}}$; that is, if $\mathbf{I}_{\text{rms}} = \mathbf{I}_{\text{rms}}\underline{/\theta_i} = I_r + jI_i$, then $\mathbf{I}^*_{\text{rms}} = \mathbf{I}_{\text{rms}}\underline{/-\theta_i} = I_r - jI_i$. Complex power is then

$$\mathbf{S} = V_{\text{rms}}\underline{/\theta_v}\, I_{\text{rms}}\underline{/-\theta_i} = V_{\text{rms}} I_{\text{rms}}\underline{/\theta_v - \theta_i} \tag{5.17}$$

or

Relationship among complex power, average power, and reactive power

$$\mathbf{S} = V_{\text{rms}} I_{\text{rms}} \cos(\theta_v - \theta_i) + jV_{\text{rms}} I_{\text{rms}} \sin(\theta_v - \theta_i) \tag{5.18}$$

where, of course, $\theta_v - \theta_i = \theta_z$. We note from Eq. (5.18) that the real part of the complex power is simply the *real* or *average power.* The imaginary part of $\mathbf{S}$ we call the *reactive* or *quadrature power.* Therefore, complex power can be expressed in the form

$$\mathbf{S} = P + jQ \tag{5.19}$$

where

$$P = Re(\mathbf{S}) = V_{\text{rms}} I_{\text{rms}} \cos(\theta_v - \theta_i) \tag{5.20}$$

$$Q = Im(\mathbf{S}) = V_{\text{rms}} I_{\text{rms}} \sin(\theta_v - \theta_i) \tag{5.21}$$

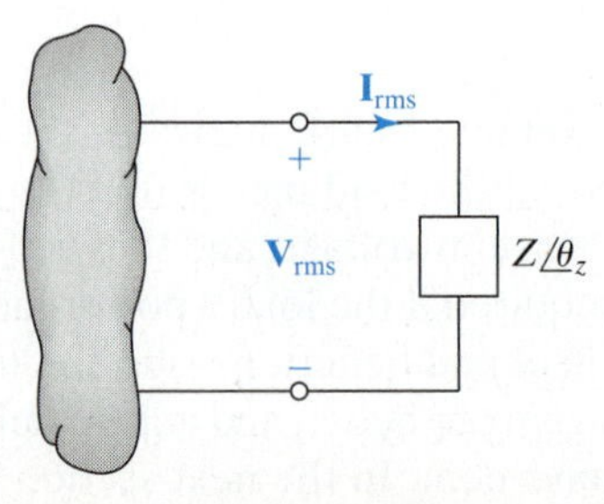

FIGURE 5.6 Circuit used to explain power relationships.

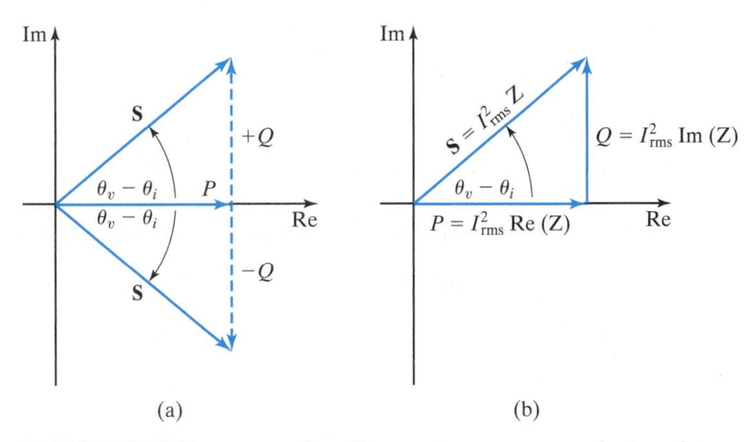

FIGURE 5.7 Diagram for illustrating power relationships.

and as shown in Eq. (5.18), the magnitude of the complex power is what we have called the *apparent power,* and the phase angle for complex power is simply the *power factor angle.* Complex power, like apparent power, is measured in volt-amperes, real power is measured in watts, and in order to distinguish Q from other quantities, which in fact have the same dimensions, it is measured in volt-amperes reactive, or var.

Equations (5.20) and (5.21) can be written as

$$P = I^2_{rms}Re(\mathbf{Z}) \tag{5.22}$$

$$Q = I^2_{rms}Im(\mathbf{Z}) \tag{5.23}$$

and therefore, Eq. (5.19) can be expressed as

$$\mathbf{S} = I^2_{rms}\mathbf{Z} \tag{5.24}$$

The relationships among **S,** P, and Q can be expressed via the diagrams shown in Figures 5.7(a) and (b). In Figure 5.7(a) we note the following conditions. If Q is positive, the load is inductive, the power factor is lagging, and the complex number **S** lies in the first quadrant. If Q is negative, the load is capacitive, the power factor is leading, and the complex number **S** lies in the fourth quadrant. If Q is zero, the load is resistive, the power factor is unity, and the complex number **S** lies along the positive real axis. Figure 5.7(b) illustrates the relationships expressed by Eqs. (5.22) to (5.24) for an inductive load.

Example 5.6

A small manufacturing plant is located one mile down a transmission line that has a resistance of 0.1 Ω/mile. The line reactance is negligible. At the plant the line voltage is 480 $\angle 0°$ V rms, and the plant consumes 120 kW at 0.85 PF lagging. We wish to determine the voltage and power factor at the input of the transmission line using (a) a complex power approach, and (b) a circuit analysis approach.

(a) The problem is modeled as shown in Figure 5.8(a). At the load, $P_L = 120$ kW and the power factor angle is

$$\theta_{ZL} = \cos^{-1} 0.85$$
$$= 31.79°$$

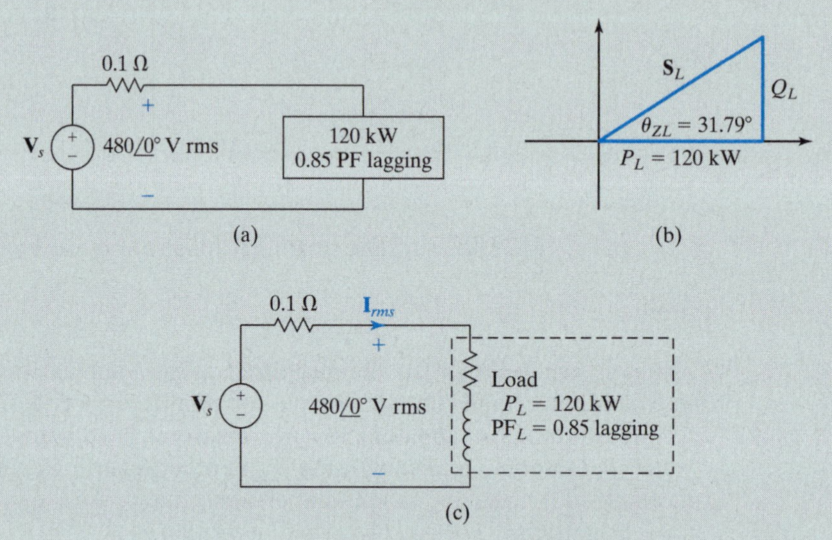

FIGURE 5.8 Diagrams used in Example 5.6.

The power triangle for the load is shown in Figure 5.8(b). The trigonometric relationship among the parameters permits us to determine the unknowns S_L and Q_L, for example,

$$\tan 31.79° = \frac{Q_L}{P_L}$$

and hence

$$Q_L = 74.364 \text{ kvar}$$

then

$$\mathbf{S}_L = P_L + jQ_L$$
$$= 141.180\angle 31.79° \text{ kVA}$$

The magnitude of the current is

$$I_{\text{rms}} = \frac{S_L}{V_{\text{rms}}}$$
$$= \frac{141{,}180}{480}$$
$$= 294.13 \text{ A rms}$$

The real power losses in the line are

$$P_{Line} = (294.13)^2\,(0.1)$$
$$= 8651.24 \text{ W}$$

Then the real power that must be supplied is

$$P_S = P_L + P_{Line}$$
$$= 128{,}651.24 \text{ W}$$

Therefore,

$$\mathbf{S}_s = P_s + jQ_s$$
$$= 128{,}651.24 + j74{,}364$$
$$= 148{,}597.26\underline{/30.03^\circ} \text{ VA}$$

Hence, the input voltage is

$$V_s = \frac{S_s}{I_{\text{rms}}}$$
$$= 505.22 \text{ V rms}$$

and the power factor at the input is

$$\text{PF}_s = \cos 30.03^\circ$$
$$= 0.866 \text{ lagging}$$

(b) From the previous analysis we know that

$$\mathbf{S}_L = 141.180\underline{/31.79^\circ} \text{ kVA}$$

and since

$$\mathbf{S}_L = \mathbf{V}_{\text{rms}} \mathbf{I}^*_{\text{rms}}$$

the line current is

$$\mathbf{I}_{\text{rms}} = 294.13\underline{/-31.79^\circ} \text{ A rms}$$

Although the information is not needed for the solution, it is interesting to note that the equivalent impedance at the load is

$$\mathbf{Z}_L = \frac{480\underline{/0^\circ}}{294.13\underline{/-31.79^\circ}}$$
$$= 1.39 + j0.86\ \Omega$$

and the relationships

$$P_L = I^2_{\text{rms}} Re(\mathbf{Z}_L)$$
$$Q_L = I^2_{\text{rms}} Im(\mathbf{Z}_L)$$

are satisfied. The circuit diagram is shown in Figure 5.8(c).
Applying KVL

$$\mathbf{V}_s = R_{Line}\mathbf{I}_{\text{rms}} + \mathbf{V}_L$$
$$= (0.1)(294.13\underline{/-31.79^\circ}) + 480\underline{/0^\circ}$$
$$= 505.22\underline{/-1.76^\circ} \text{ V rms}$$

and

$$\text{PF}_s = \cos 30.03^\circ$$
$$= 0.866 \text{ lagging}$$

Drill Exercise

D5.6. An industrial load operates at 20 kW, 0.8 PF lagging with a line voltage of $220\angle 0^\circ$ V rms. Construct the power triangle for the load.

Ans:

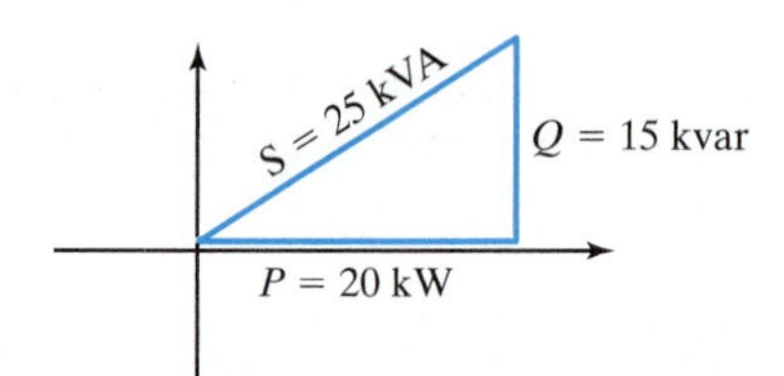

FIGURE D5.6

5-7 Power Factor Correction

Industrial plants that require large amounts of power have a wide variety of loads. However, by nature the loads normally have a lagging power factor. In view of the results obtained in Example 5.5, we are naturally led to ask if there is any convenient technique for raising the power factor of a load. Since a typical load may be a bank of induction motors or other expensive machinery, the technique for raising the PF should be an economical one in order to be feasible.

To answer the question we pose, let us examine the circuit shown in Figure 5.9. The circuit illustrates a typical industrial load. In parallel with this load we have placed a capacitor. The original complex power for the load $\mathbf{Z}_L$, which we will denote as $\mathbf{S}_{old}$, is

$$\mathbf{S}_{old} = P_{old} + jQ_{old} = |\mathbf{S}_{old}|\angle\theta_{old}$$

The new complex power that results from adding a capacitor is

$$\mathbf{S}_{new} = P_{old} + jQ_{new} = |\mathbf{S}_{new}|\angle\theta_{new}$$

where θ_{new} is specified by the required power factor. The difference between the new and old complex powers is caused by the addition of the capacitor. Hence

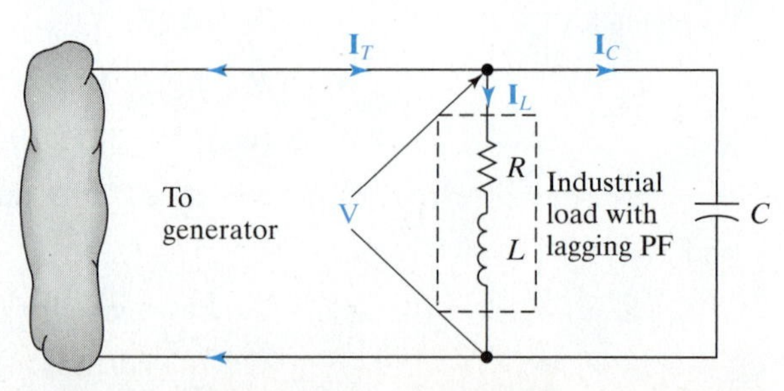

FIGURE 5.9 Circuit for power factor correction.

$$\mathbf{S}_{cap} = \mathbf{S}_{new} - \mathbf{S}_{old} \tag{5.25}$$

and since the capacitor is purely reactive,

$$\mathbf{S}_{cap} = +jQ_{cap} = -j\omega CV_{\text{rms}}^2 \tag{5.26}$$

The use of capacitors in power factor correction

Equation (5.26) can be used to find the required value of C in order to achieve the new specified power factor. In general, we want the power factor to be large, and therefore the power factor angle must be small, i.e., the larger the desired power factor, the smaller the angle $\theta_{new} = \theta_{vT} - \theta_{iT}$.

The following example illustrates the simplicity of the *power factor correction scheme,* which is a favorite type of question on the fundamentals of engineering (FE) examination taken in preparation for obtaining a professional engineer's license.

Example 5.7

An industrial load consisting of a bank of induction motors consumes 50 kW at a PF of 0.8 lagging from a 220 $\angle 0°$ V rms, 60 Hz line. We wish to raise the PF to 0.95 lagging by placing a bank of capacitors in parallel with the load.

The circuit diagram for this problem is shown in Figure 5.10. $P = 50$ kW and since $\cos^{-1} 0.8 = 36.87°$, $\theta_{old} = 36.87°$. Therefore,

$$Q_{old} = P_{old}\tan\theta_{old} = (50)(10^3)(0.75) = 37.5 \text{ kvar}$$

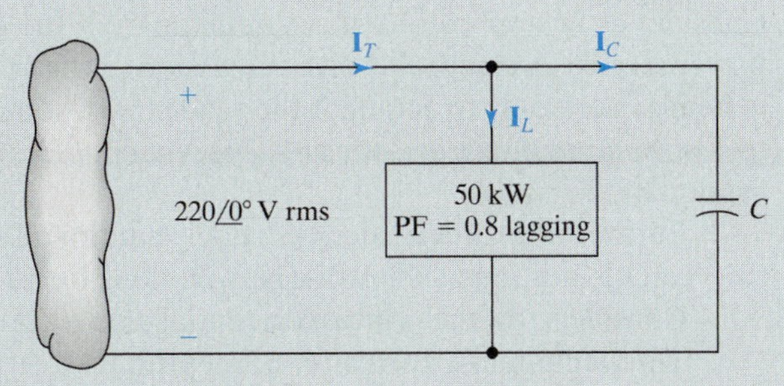

FIGURE 5.10 Example circuit for power factor correction.

Hence

$$\mathbf{S}_{old} = 50{,}000 + j37{,}500$$

Since the required power factor is 0.95, $\theta_{new} = 18.19°$. Then

$$\mathbf{S}_{new} = 50{,}000 + j50{,}000 \tan 18.19°$$

$$= 50{,}000 + j16{,}430$$

and therefore,

$$\mathbf{S}_{cap} = \mathbf{S}_{new} - \mathbf{S}_{old}$$

$$= -j21{,}070 \text{ VA}$$

Hence

$$C = \frac{21{,}070}{(377)(220)^2}$$
$$= 1155\ \mu\text{F}$$

By using a capacitor of this magnitude in parallel with the industrial load, we create, from the utility's perspective, a load with a PF of 0.95 lagging. However, the parameters of the actual load remain unchanged.

Drill Exercise

D5.7. Compute the value of the capacitor necessary to change the power factor in Drill Exercise D5.5 to 0.95 lagging.

Ans: $C = 773\ \mu\text{F}$.

5-8 Typical Residential AC Power Circuits

Consider as an application of ac circuit analysis the standard American residential electrical power service. A comprehensive discussion of the subject is beyond the scope of this book; it is treated here only to acquaint the reader with some basic principles. The reader is referred to *The National Electric Code* and *The National Electric Safety Code* for an authoritative discussion of the issues.

Furthermore, the reader is strongly cautioned that working with residential power circuits can be fatal, and such work may be done *only* by persons properly licensed to do so.

Consider now the typical residential electric power service illustrated in Figure 5.11(a). The single-phase two-wire utility primary distribution line serves as a 7200 V rms voltage source. Note that one, typically the bottom, conductor is grounded via a bare conductor running down the pole and connected to a ground rod, which is a copperclad steel rod driven into the earth close to the base of the pole. This voltage is applied to the primary winding of a distribution transformer—a device that will be described in some detail in Chapter 6. The transformer steps the input voltage down to a three-wire 240/120 V rms level represented by the circuit diagram shown in Figure 5.11(b). Typically, lights or small appliances are connected from one line to neutral n and operate at 120 V rms: large appliances—for example, hot water heaters—are connected line to line and operate at approximately 240 V rms.

As indicated in Figure 5.11(a), a "surge arrester" is typically connected at the high-voltage transformer terminals. The surge arrester is basically a nonlinear resistor, offering high (ideally infinite) resistance at normal operating voltage, and low (ideally zero) resistance at abnormally high system voltage, typically caused by lightning.

"Grounding" means to connect a part, or parts, of an electrical circuit to the local earth, its purpose being primarily for safety (i.e., to minimize shock hazards), and to suppress lightning and switching-induced transient overvoltages. The "service drop" to the residence typi-

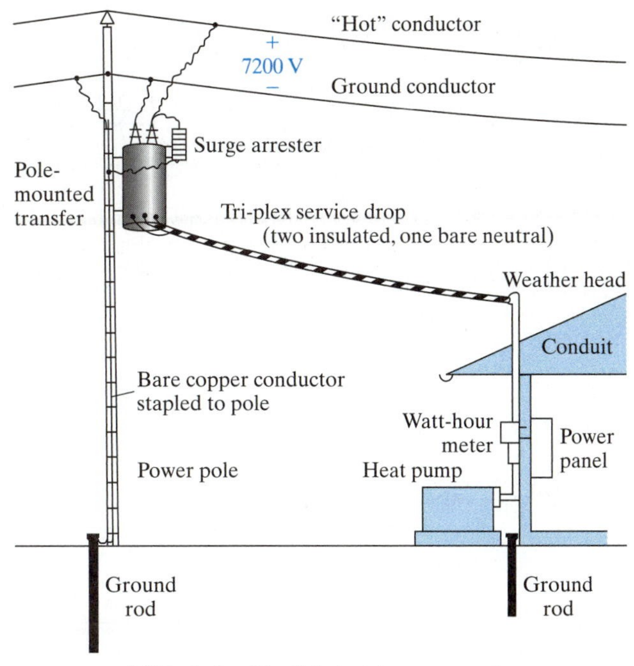

(a) Typical residential electric power service

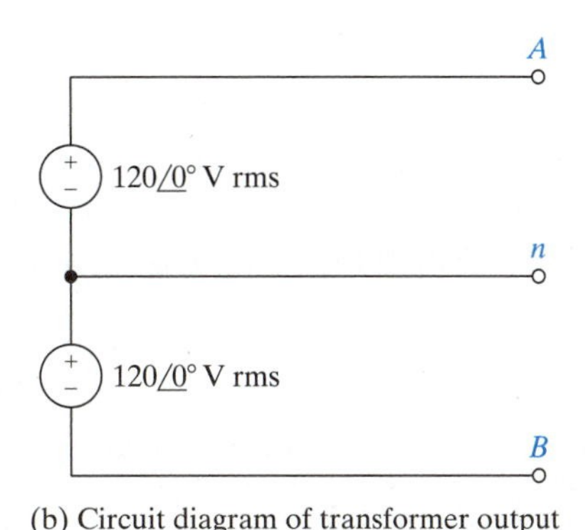

(b) Circuit diagram of transformer output

FIGURE 5.11 Diagrams for residential electric power service.

cally consists of triplex cable, made up of three conductors: one bare aluminum neutral, which is grounded at both ends, and two insulated, spiraled about the neutral. The cable enters "conduit," a metallic pipe used for mechanical support and protection, through a "weather head," and enters a "watthour meter." The watthour meter is basically an integrating wattmeter, which records the total electrical energy flow from the service drop into the residence. If it is read at time t_1, and subsequently at time t_2, the difference in the readings represents the electrical energy supplied in the interval $t_2 - t_1$. Typical units used are "kW-hrs" (1 kW-hr = 3.6 MJ).

The "electrical panel" is basically a metal box containing circuit breakers (switches that automatically open if the current through them is excessive), thermal devices (fuses, which melt when the current in them is excessive, thus breaking a closed circuit), and terminals for all elec-

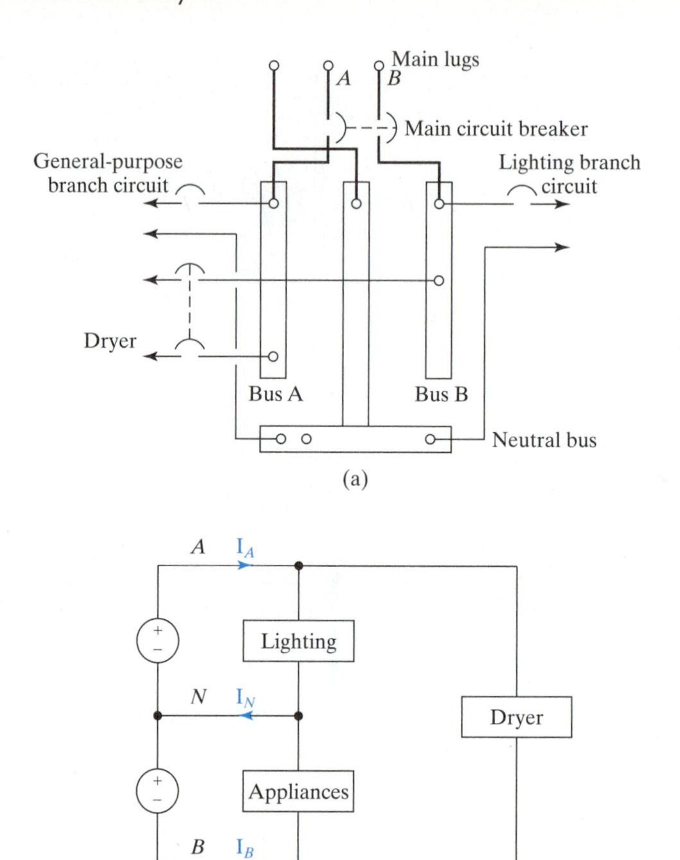

FIGURE 5.12 Diagrams used to explain a residential power circuit.

trical conductors. Figure 5.12(a) illustrates three typical branch circuits that might be found in a residence, and Figure 5.12(b) illustrates the corresponding equivalent circuit diagram.

Consider the following example, which describes some of the practical aspects of residential power circuits.

Example 5.8

Suppose that three residential power circuits are composed of a lighting branch, appliance branch, and an electric dryer circuit, as shown in Figure 5.12(b). The lighting branch circuit must illuminate an area of 640 sq. ft., the appliance circuit must serve 10 electrical receptacles, and the dryer is rated at 5 kVA. We wish to determine (a) the size of circuit breaker required for each individual circuit, (b) the currents in all parts of the power network in Figure 5.12(b), and (c) the monthly cost, at $0.075 per kW-hr, for operating the lights, appliances, and dryer 40%, 8%, and 3% of the time, respectively.

(a) For general residential illumination, electrical distribution designers use a general "rule of thumb" of 3 watts per sq. ft. Therefore, the power required for lighting is $P = (3)(640) = 1920$ W. Assuming unity power factor, $S = 1920$ VA, and since the lighting voltage is 120 V rms, the current is $I = 1920/120 = 16$ A rms. For this current, an AWG (American Wire Gauge) #12 copper conductor with a typical polyethelene insulation such as RH or RHW (these are standard wiring insulation designations found in the National Electric Code) would typically be used. Since circuit breakers come in 15 A, 20 A, 25 A, and 30 A rms sizes, a 20 A rms circuit breaker would be used to protect the lighting branch circuit.

For the appliance branch circuit, when the actual load is unknown, the figure frequently used is 180 VA per receptacle. For 10 receptacles the apparent power is $S = (10)(180) = 1800$ VA. At 120 V rms, the current would be $1800/120 = 15$ A rms, and therefore once again #12 conductors protected by a 20 A rms breaker would serve this circuit.

The 5 kVA electric dryer operates at 240 V rms, and therefore the current is $5000/240 = 20.83$ A rms. However, for this higher power circuit the National Electric Code specifies #10 copper conductors, protected by a two-pole (breaks both lines as shown in Figure 5.12(a)) 30 A rms breaker.

(b) Rigorously speaking, the load should be summed as complex power. However, power factors (PF) are frequently unknown; also they are typically between 0.9 and 1.0. Conservatively, then, we may assume unity PF for loads, that is, currents computed by this method will be slightly higher than is actually the case. The magnitude of the current $\mathbf{I}_A$ shown in Figure 5.12(b) is the lighting current plus the dryer current or

$$\begin{aligned} I_A &= 20.83 + 16 \\ &= 36.83 \text{ A rms} \end{aligned}$$

The magnitude of the current $\mathbf{I}_B$ shown in Figure 5.12(b) is the sum of the appliance current and the dryer current or

$$\begin{aligned} I_B &= 20.83 + 15 \\ &= 35.83 \text{ A rms} \end{aligned}$$

Assuming that the phase angle for the two voltage sources in Figure 5.12(b) is 0°, the magnitude of the current $\mathbf{I}_N$ is the difference between I_A and I_B or 1 A.

(c) Assuming a 30-day month, the total number of hours in the month is $(24)(30) = 720$ hours. Then at \$0.075 per kW-hr, the operation of the lights, appliances, and dryer 40%, 8%, and 3% of the time, respectively, would cost

$$\text{Cost} = 0.075[(0.4)(1.92) + (0.08)(1.8) + (0.03)(5.0)] = \$57.35$$

In the basic single-phase 120 V rms branch circuit, three conductors are normally used: one with black insulation, that is, connected to Bus A or B in Example 5.8; one with white insulation that is connected to the neutral bus, which serves as the return path for the load current; and one bare conductor, also connected to the neutral bus, which is not intended to carry load current. These conductors are illustrated in Figure 5.13. The bare conductor serves to maintain the potential of the receptacle metal enclosure, and exposed metal parts of connected appliances, at ground level, for safety purposes. Carefully examine a common three-wire plug. Note the three blades: one small-ended spade connector, the black wire; one large-ended spade connector, the white wire; and one round connector, the bare wire.

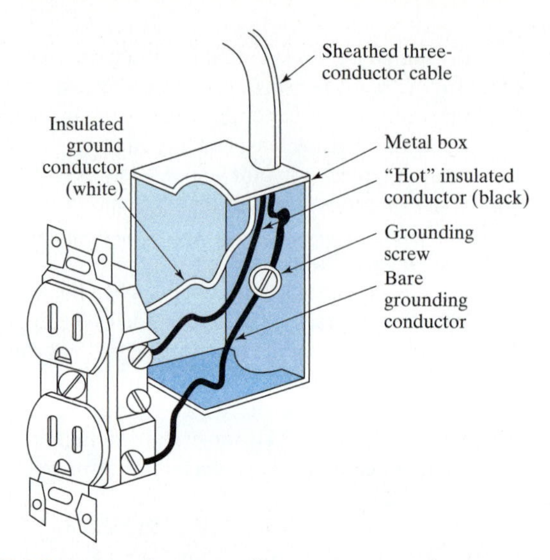

FIGURE 5.13 Typical general-purpose appliance receptacle.

5-9 Three-Phase Circuits

Up to this point we have dealt with what we refer to as single-phase circuits. Now we extend our analysis techniques to *three-phase circuits,* that is, circuits containing three voltage sources that are one-third of a cycle apart in time.

The study of three-phase circuits is important because it is more advantageous and economical to transmit electric power in the three-phase mode. That is why we find that all the very high voltage transmission lines have three conductors, that is, three phases.

As the name implies, three-phase circuits are those in which the forcing function is a three-phase system of voltages. If the three sinusoidal voltages have the same magnitude and frequency and each voltage is 120° out of phase with the other two, the voltages are said to be *balanced.* If the loads are such that the currents produced by the voltages are also balanced, the entire circuit is referred to as a *balanced three-phase circuit.*

A balanced set of three-phase voltages can be represented in the frequency domain as shown in Figure 5.14(a), where we have assumed that their magnitudes are 120 V rms. From the figure we note that

$$\begin{aligned} \mathbf{V}_{an} &= 120\underline{/0^\circ} \text{ V rms} \\ \mathbf{V}_{bn} &= 120\underline{/-120^\circ} \text{ V rms} \\ \mathbf{V}_{cn} &= 120\underline{/-240^\circ} \text{ V rms} \end{aligned} \tag{5.27}$$

Note that our double-subscript notation is exactly the same as that employed in the earlier chapters.

The phasor voltages, which can be expressed in the time domain as

$$\begin{aligned} v_{an}(t) &= 120\sqrt{2} \cos \omega t \text{ V} \\ v_{bn}(t) &= 120\sqrt{2} \cos(\omega t - 120^\circ) \text{ V} \\ v_{cn}(t) &= 120\sqrt{2} \cos(\omega t - 240^\circ) \text{ V} \end{aligned} \tag{5.28}$$

are shown in Figure 5.14(b).

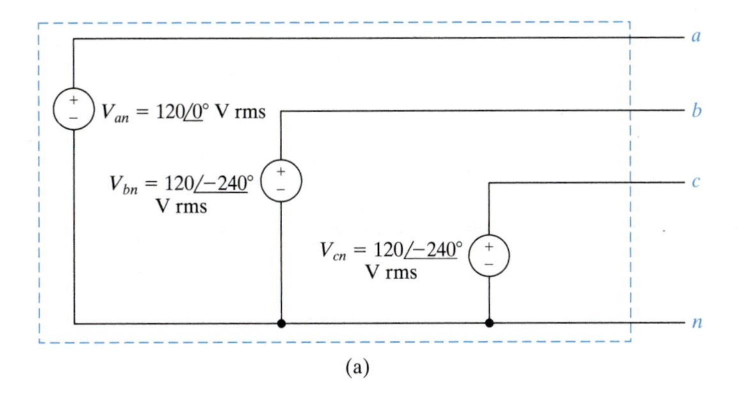

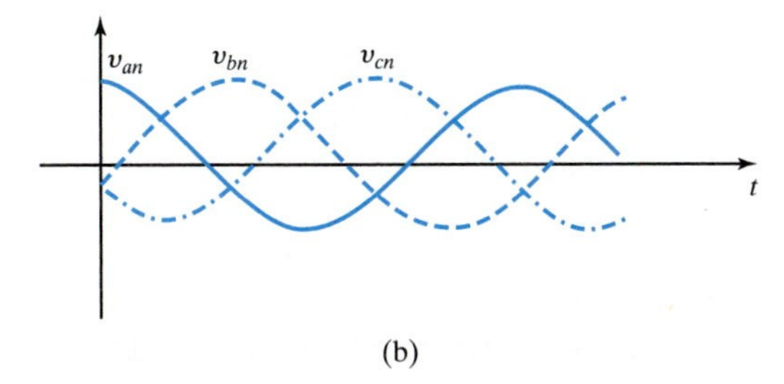

FIGURE 5.14 Balanced three-phase voltages.

Let us examine the instantaneous power generated by a three-phase system. Assume that the voltages are given by Eq. (5.28).

If the load is balanced, the currents produced by the sources are

$$\begin{aligned} i_a(t) &= I_M \cos(\omega t - \theta) \text{ A} \\ i_b(t) &= I_M \cos(\omega t - \theta - 120°) \text{ A} \\ i_c(t) &= I_M \cos(\omega t - \theta - 240°) \text{ A} \end{aligned} \tag{5.29}$$

where θ is the angle between the voltage and the current. The instantaneous power produced by the system is

$$\begin{aligned} p(t) &= p_a(t) + p_b(t) + p_c(t) \\ &= V_M I_M[\cos\omega t \cos(\omega t - \theta) + \cos(\omega t - 120°)\cos(\omega t - \theta - 120°) \\ &\quad + \cos(\omega t - 240°)\cos(\omega t - \theta - 240°)] \end{aligned} \tag{5.30}$$

Using the two trigonometric identities

$$\cos\alpha\cos\beta = \frac{1}{2}[\cos(\alpha - \beta) + \cos(\alpha + \beta)] \tag{5.31}$$

and

$$\cos\phi + \cos(\phi - 120°) + \cos(\phi + 120°) = 0 \tag{5.32}$$

We can show that the expression for the power reduces to

$$p(t) = 3\frac{V_M I_M}{2}\cos\theta \text{ W} \tag{5.33}$$

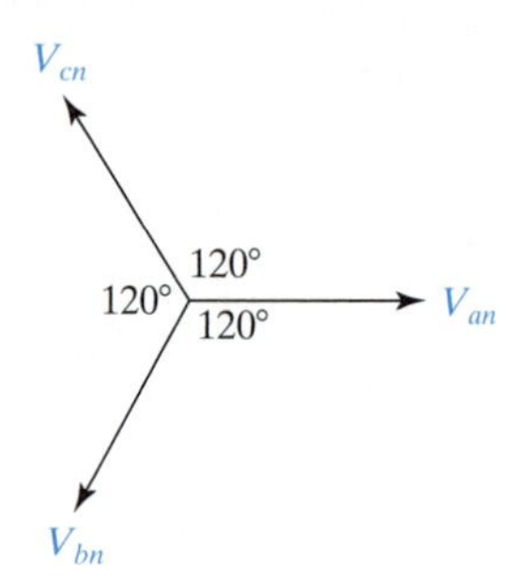

FIGURE 5.15 Phasor diagram for a balanced three-phase voltage source.

This equation is very interesting. It states that the *instantaneous* power is *independent of time.* Recall that in the single-phase case, described by Eq. (5.5) and illustrated in Figure 5.2, the power is pulsating at twice the excitation frequency. However, in the three-phase case the power is always *constant,* which reduces wear on the generators and is therefore a good reason to generate power in three-phase form.

The use of three-phase circuits results in smooth power delivery

The phasor diagram for the three-phase voltages is shown in Figure 5.15. The phase sequence of this set is said to be *abc,* meaning that V_{bn} lags V_{an} by 120°.

We will standardize our notation so that we always label the voltages $\mathbf{V}_{an}$, $\mathbf{V}_{bn}$, and $\mathbf{V}_{cn}$ and observe them in the order *abc,* which will be referred to as a *positive phase sequence.* Furthermore, we will normally assume with no loss of generality that $\angle \mathbf{V}_{an} = 0°$.

An important property of the balanced voltage set is that

$$\mathbf{V}_{an} + \mathbf{V}_{bn} + \mathbf{V}_{cn} = 0 \tag{5.34}$$

This property can easily be seen by resolving the voltage phasors into components along the real and imaginary axes. It can also be demonstrated via Eq. (5.32).

Balanced three-phase systems are always connected in either delta or wye

From the standpoint of the user who connects a load to the balanced three-phase voltage source, it is not important how the voltages are generated. It is important to note, however, that if the load currents generated by connecting a load to the power source are also *balanced,* there are two possible equivalent configurations for the load. The equivalent load can be considered as being connected in either a *wye* (Y) or a *delta* (Δ) configuration. The balanced wye configuration is shown in Figure 5.16(a) and equivalently in Figure 5.16(b). The delta configuration is shown in Figure 5.17(a) and equivalently in Figure 5.17(b). Note that in the case of the delta connection, there is no neutral line. The actual function of the neutral line in the wye connection will be examined and it will be shown that in a balanced system the neutral line carries no current and, for purposes of analysis, may be omitted.

5.9.1 Balanced Wye–Wye Connection

Suppose now that the source and load are both connected in a wye, as shown in Figure 5.18. The phase voltages with positive phase sequence are

$$\begin{aligned} \mathbf{V}_{an} &= V_P\angle 0° \\ \mathbf{V}_{bn} &= V_P\angle -120° \\ \mathbf{V}_{cn} &= V_P\angle +120° \end{aligned} \tag{5.35}$$

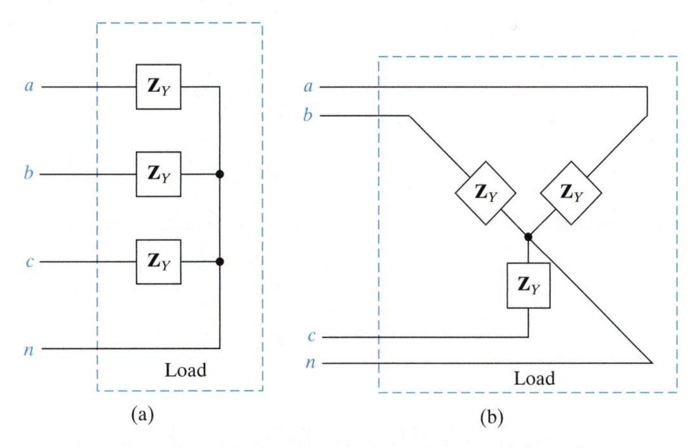

FIGURE 5.16 Wye (Y)-connected loads.

The difference between line voltage and phase voltage

where V_P, the *phase voltage,* is the magnitude of the phasor voltage from the neutral to any line. The *line-to-line* or simply, *line voltages* V_L, can be calculated using KVL; for example,

$$\begin{aligned}\mathbf{V}_{ab} &= \mathbf{V}_{an} - \mathbf{V}_{bn} \\ &= V_P\underline{/0^\circ} - V_P\underline{/-120^\circ} \\ &= V_P - V_P\left[-\frac{1}{2} - j\frac{\sqrt{3}}{2}\right] \\ &= V_P\left[\frac{3}{2} + j\frac{\sqrt{3}}{2}\right] \\ &= \sqrt{3}\,V_P\underline{/30^\circ}\end{aligned} \tag{5.36}$$

The phasor addition is shown graphically in Figure 5.19(a). In a similar manner, we obtain the set of line-to-line voltages as

$$\begin{aligned}\mathbf{V}_{ab} &= \sqrt{3}\,V_P\underline{/30^\circ} \\ \mathbf{V}_{bc} &= \sqrt{3}\,V_P\underline{/-90^\circ} \\ \mathbf{V}_{ca} &= \sqrt{3}\,V_P\underline{/-210^\circ}\end{aligned}$$

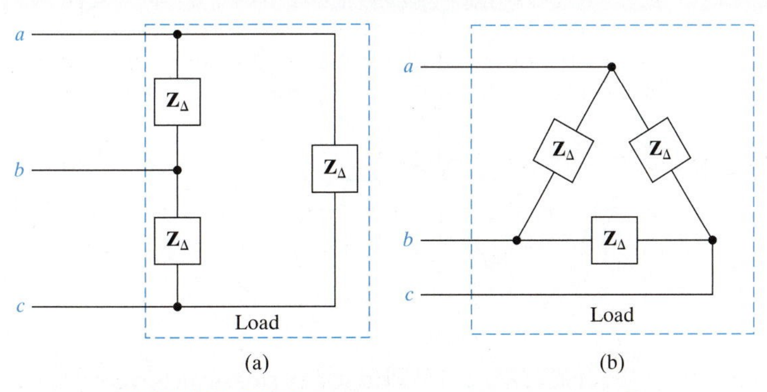

FIGURE 5.17 Delta (Δ)-connected loads.

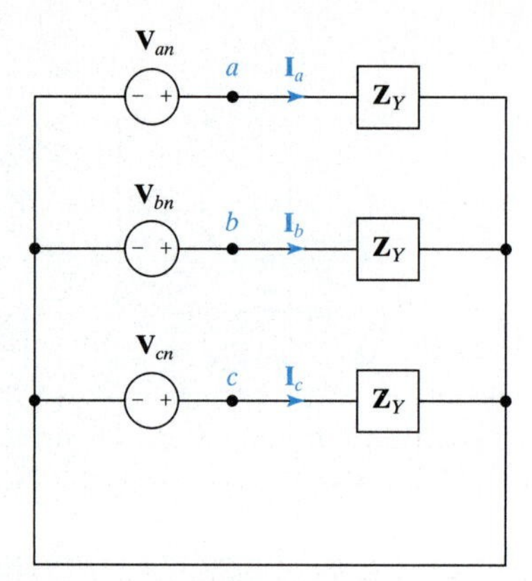

FIGURE 5.18 Balanced three-phase wye–wye connection.

All the line voltages together with the phase voltages are shown in Figure 5.19(b).

Note carefully that the phase voltages are multiplied by $\sqrt{3}$ and shifted by 30° to obtain the line voltages. Furthermore, if V_L, I_L, V_P, and I_P represent the line voltage, line current, phase voltage, and phase current, respectively, then for a balanced wye–wye system

$$\begin{aligned} V_L &= \sqrt{3}\,V_P \\ I_L &= I_P \end{aligned} \tag{5.37}$$

As shown in Figure 5.18, the line currents are

$$\begin{aligned} \mathbf{I}_a &= \frac{\mathbf{V}_{an}}{\mathbf{Z}_Y} = \frac{V_P\angle 0^\circ}{\mathbf{Z}_Y} \\ \mathbf{I}_b &= \frac{\mathbf{V}_{bn}}{\mathbf{Z}_Y} = \frac{V_P\angle -120^\circ}{\mathbf{Z}_Y} \\ \mathbf{I}_c &= \frac{\mathbf{V}_{cn}}{\mathbf{Z}_Y} = \frac{V_P\angle +120^\circ}{\mathbf{Z}_Y} \end{aligned} \tag{5.38}$$

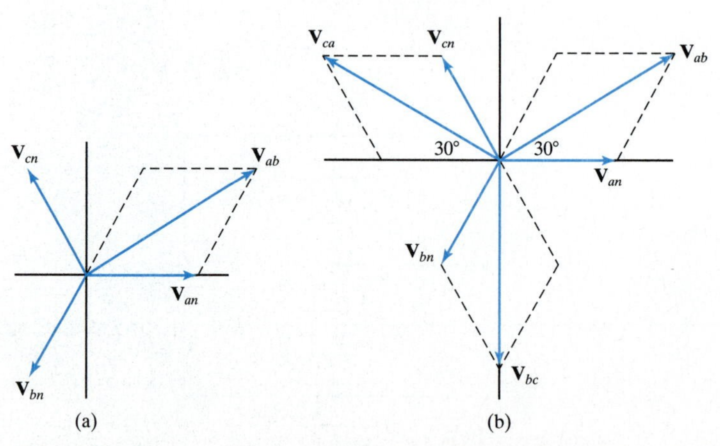

FIGURE 5.19 Phasor representation of phase and line voltages in a balanced wye–wye system.

In balanced three-phase wye-connected systems there is no neutral current

The neutral current $\mathbf{I}_n$ is then

$$\mathbf{I}_n = (\mathbf{I}_a + \mathbf{I}_b + \mathbf{I}_c) = 0 \tag{5.39}$$

Since there is no current in the neutral, this conductor could contain any impedance or it could be an open or a short circuit, without changing the results found above. Therefore, for simplicity, we will assume that the neutral line is not present, that is, an open circuit.

It is important to note that although we have a three-phase system composed of three sources and three loads, Eq. (5.38) illustrates that we can compute the currents and voltages in each phase independent of the other phases. Therefore, in a balanced three-phase system, we can analyze only one phase and use the phase sequence to obtain the voltages and currents in the other phases. This is, of course, a direct result of the balanced condition. We may even have impedances present in the lines; however, as long as the system remains balanced, we need analyze only one phase.

Example 5.9

A three-phase wye-connected load is supplied by an *abc* sequence balanced three-phase wye-connected source, as shown in Figure 5.20(a). Note that we employ lowercase letters to represent the generator end of the network and uppercase letters to represent the load end. If the phase voltage of the source is 120 V rms, the line impedance and load impedance per phase are $1 + j1\ \Omega$ and $20 + j10\ \Omega$, respectively, we wish to determine the value of the line currents and the load voltages. The phase voltages are

$$\mathbf{V}_{an} = 120\angle 0^\circ \text{ V rms}$$

$$\mathbf{V}_{bn} = 120\angle -120^\circ \text{ V rms}$$

$$\mathbf{V}_{cn} = 120\angle +120^\circ \text{ V rms}$$

For a balanced system, we need only analyze the a phase, since the results for the b and c phases are displaced by 120° and 240°, respectively. The per-phase circuit diagram is shown in Figure 5.20(b). The line current for the a phase is

$$\mathbf{I}_{aA} = \frac{120\angle 0^\circ}{21 + j11}$$

$$= 5.06\angle -27.65^\circ \text{ A rms}$$

where $\mathbf{I}_{aA}$ represents the current from point a to point A. The load voltage for the a phase, which we call $\mathbf{V}_{AN}$, is

$$\mathbf{V}_{AN} = (5.06\angle -27.65^\circ)(20 + j10)$$

$$= 113.15\angle -1.08^\circ \text{ V rms}$$

The corresponding line currents and load voltages for the b and c phases are

$$\mathbf{I}_{bB} = 5.06\angle -147.65^\circ \text{ A rms} \qquad \mathbf{V}_{BN} = 113.15\angle -121.08^\circ \text{ V rms}$$

$$\mathbf{I}_{cC} = 5.06\angle -267.65^\circ \text{ A rms} \qquad \mathbf{V}_{CN} = 113.15\angle -241.08^\circ \text{ V rms}$$

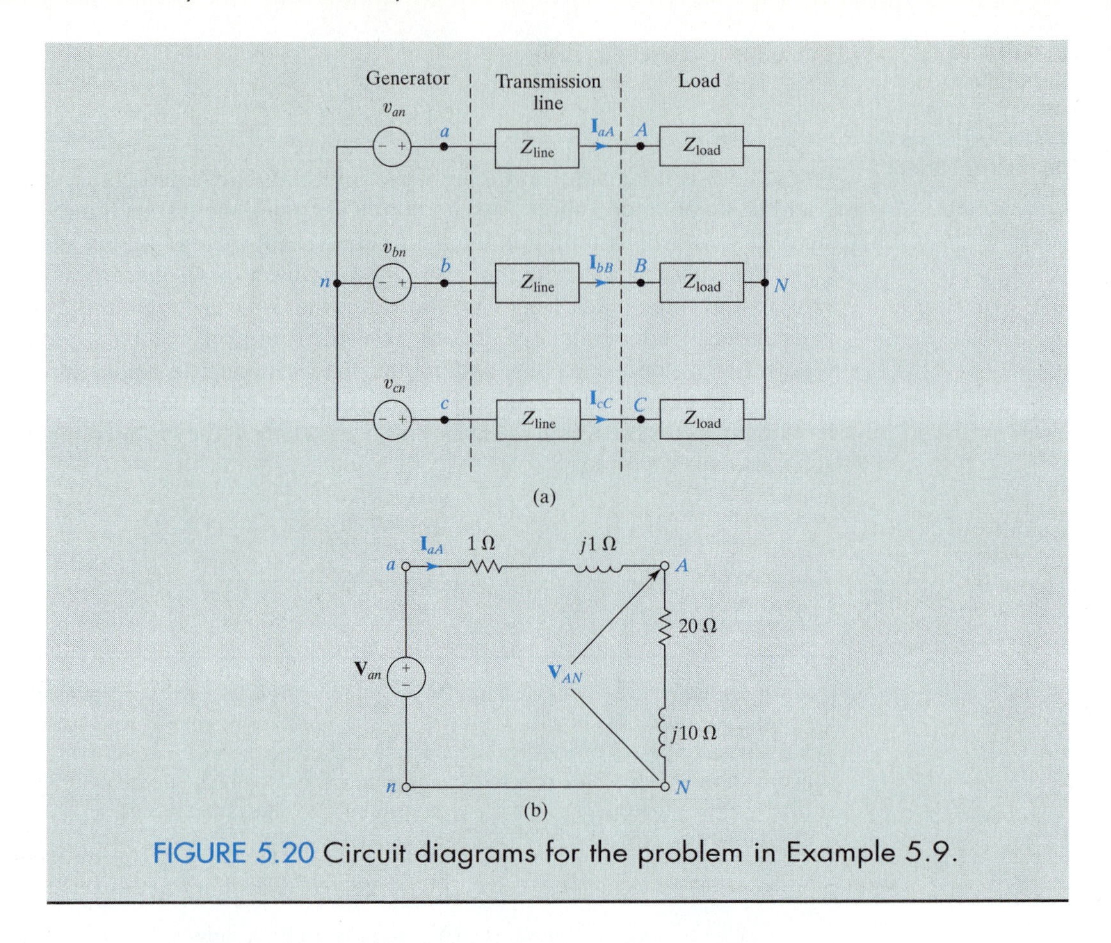

FIGURE 5.20 Circuit diagrams for the problem in Example 5.9.

To reemphasize and clarify our terminology, phase voltage, V_P, is the magnitude of the phasor voltage from the neutral to any line, while line voltage, V_L, is the magnitude of the phasor voltage between any two lines. Thus, the values of V_L and V_P will depend on the point at which they are calculated in the system.

Drill Exercises

D5.8. The voltage for the *a* phase of an *abc*-phase-sequence–balanced wye-connected source is $\mathbf{V}_{an} = 120\angle 90°$ V rms. Determine the line voltages for this source.

Ans: $\mathbf{V}_{ab} = 208\angle 120°$ V rms, $\mathbf{V}_{bc} = 208\angle 0°$ V rms, $\mathbf{V}_{ca} = 208\angle -120°$ V rms.

D5.9. A three-phase wye load is supplied by an *abc*-sequence–balanced three-phase wye-connected source through a transmission line with an impedance of $1 + j1$ ohms per phase. The load impedance is $8 + j3$ ohms per phase. If the load voltage for the *a* phase is $104.02\angle 26.6°$ V rms (i.e., $V_P = 104.02$ V rms at the load end), determine the phase voltages of the source.

Ans: $\mathbf{V}_{an} = 120\angle 30°$ V rms, $\mathbf{V}_{bn} = 120\angle -90°$ V rms, $\mathbf{V}_{cn} = 120\angle -210°$ V rms.

5.9.2 Balanced Wye–Delta Connection

Another important three-phase circuit is the balanced wye–delta system; that is, a wye-connected source and a delta-connected load, as shown in Figure 5.21. From Figure 5.21 note that the line-to-line voltage is the voltage across each load impedance in the delta-connected load. Therefore, if the phase voltages of the source are

$$\begin{aligned} \mathbf{V}_{an} &= V_P\underline{/0^\circ} \\ \mathbf{V}_{bn} &= V_P\underline{/-120^\circ} \\ \mathbf{V}_{cn} &= V_P\underline{/+120^\circ} \end{aligned} \tag{5.40}$$

then the line voltages are

$$\begin{aligned} \mathbf{V}_{ab} &= \sqrt{3}\,V_P\underline{/30^\circ} \\ \mathbf{V}_{bc} &= \sqrt{3}\,V_P\underline{/-90^\circ} \\ \mathbf{V}_{ca} &= \sqrt{3}\,V_P\underline{/+150^\circ} \end{aligned} \tag{5.41}$$

Knowing the voltage across each phase of the Δ, we can easily compute the phase currents in the Δ. KCL can then be employed in conjunction with the phase currents to determine the line currents. For example,

$$\begin{aligned} \mathbf{I}_{aA} &= \mathbf{I}_{AB} + \mathbf{I}_{AC} \\ &= \mathbf{I}_{AB} - \mathbf{I}_{CA} \end{aligned}$$

Following a development similar to that which led to Eq. (5.36), we can show that the magnitudes of the line and phase voltages and currents for the delta-connected load are related by the equations

$$\begin{aligned} V_L &= V_P \\ I_L &= \sqrt{3}\,I_P \end{aligned} \tag{5.42}$$

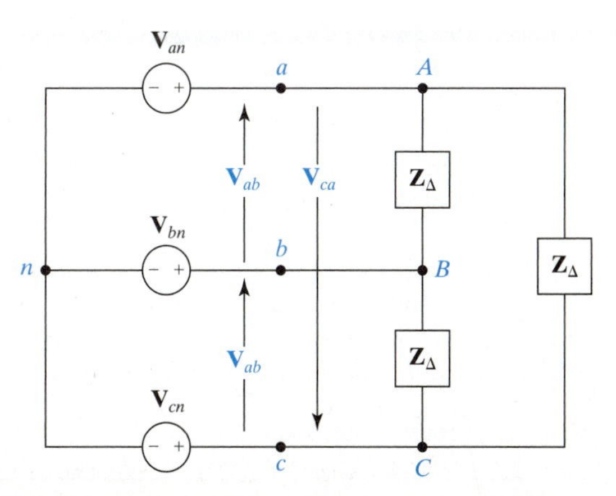

FIGURE 5.21 Balanced three-phase wye–delta system.

Example 5.10

The balanced three-phase wye–delta system shown in Figure 5.21 has the following parameters: the voltage source has an *abc* sequence and $\mathbf{V}_{an} = 120\angle 30°$ V rms, and the impedance per phase in the delta load is $\mathbf{Z}_\Delta = 6 + j6\ \Omega$. We wish to determine the currents in the delta and the line currents.

At the generator, $\mathbf{V}_{an} = 120\angle 30°$ V rms, and therefore the line voltage is $\mathbf{V}_{ab} = 120\sqrt{3}\angle 60°$ V rms. Since there is no line impedance, the line voltage at the delta load is

$$\mathbf{V}_{AB} = \mathbf{V}_{ab} = 120\sqrt{3}\angle 60° \text{ V rms}$$

and hence

$$\mathbf{I}_{AB} = \frac{120\sqrt{3}\angle 60°}{6 + j6}$$

$$= 24.50\angle 15° \text{ A rms}$$

Recall that the line voltages at the load are 120° out of phase with one another and the load impedance is balanced. Therefore, the phase currents at the load differ by 120° and hence

$$\mathbf{I}_{BC} = 24.50\angle -105° \text{A rms}$$

$$\mathbf{I}_{CA} = 24.50\angle 135° \text{A rms}$$

The line current can be computed using KCL at the node labeled *A*.

$$\mathbf{I}_{aA} = \mathbf{I}_{AB} - \mathbf{I}_{CA}$$

$$= 24.50\angle 15° - 24.50\angle 135°$$

$$= 42.44\angle -15° \text{ A rms}$$

and hence

$$\mathbf{I}_{bB} = 42.44\angle -135° \text{ A rms}$$

$$\mathbf{I}_{cC} = 42.44\angle 105° \text{ A rms}$$

It is interesting to note that from the standpoint of determining the line currents we could simply employ the $Y \rightleftarrows \Delta$ transformation to the delta-connected load and compute the line currents directly. For the balanced impedance case, the transformation Eqs. (4.41) and (4.42) reduce to

$$\mathbf{Z}_Y = \frac{1}{3}\mathbf{Z}_\Delta$$

Therefore, the delta load can be replaced by the equivalent wye load, which would then produce an equivalent balanced wye–wye system in which the phase voltage at the generator is $\mathbf{V}_{an} = 120\angle 30°$ V rms and the impedance in one branch of the wye load is $2 + j2\ \Omega$. Hence, the line current

$$\mathbf{I}_{aA} = \frac{120\angle 30°}{2 + j2}$$

$$= 42.44\angle -15° \text{A rms}$$

which is, of course, identical to that obtained by applying KCL at the delta load.

The wye/delta transformation relationships are also useful in solving three-phase systems with multiple loads. The following example, which for simplicity has only resistive loads, illustrates their use.

Example 5.11

Consider the network shown in Figure 5.22(a). We wish to determine all the line currents. Note that the 30 Ω resistors are connected in wye and the 60 Ω resistors are connected in delta. If we convert the delta to an equivalent wye, the impedance of each branch of the equivalent wye would contain a 20 Ω resistor. The two wye loads are now in parallel and the equivalent circuit for the *a* phase is shown in Figure 5.22(b). The line current $\mathbf{I}_{aA}$ is then

$$\begin{aligned}\mathbf{I}_{aA} &= \frac{120\angle 0^\circ}{4 + 30\|20} \\ &= \frac{120\angle 0^\circ}{16} \\ &= 7.5\angle 0^\circ \text{ A rms}\end{aligned}$$

and hence $\mathbf{I}_{bB} = 7.5\angle -120^\circ$ A rms and $\mathbf{I}_{cC} = 7.5\angle +120^\circ$ A rms.

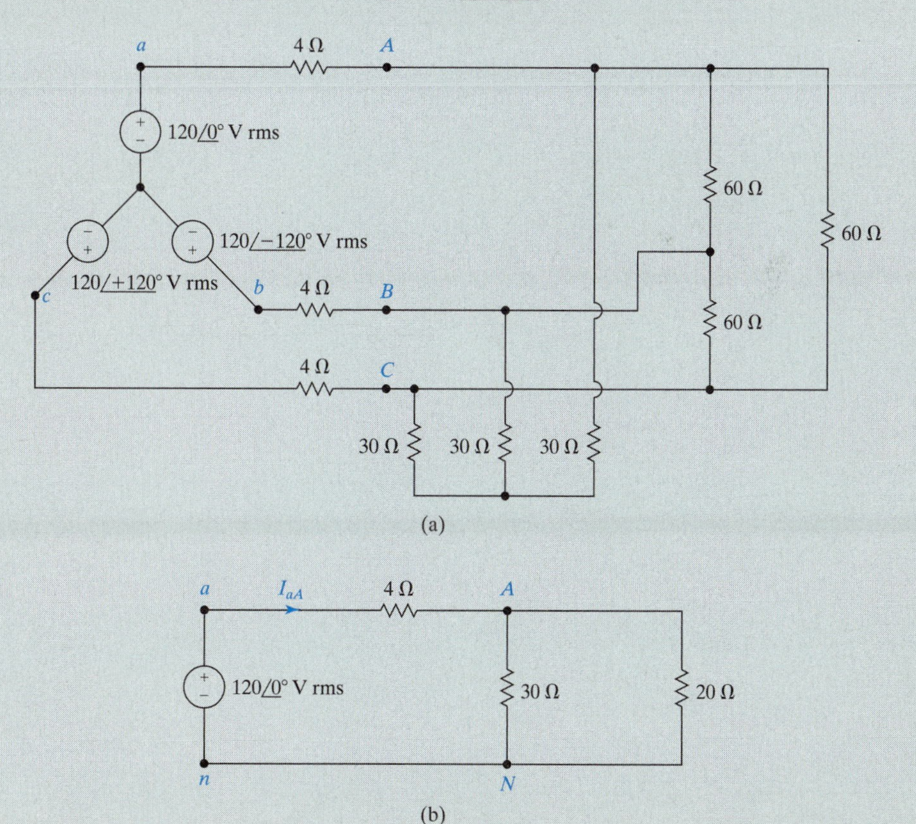

FIGURE 5.22 Networks used in Example 5.11: (a) original network; (b) a-phase equivalent network.

Drill Exercises

D5.10. A balanced three-phase wye-connected source has a line voltage of $\mathbf{V}_{ab} = 208\underline{/50^\circ}$ V rms. Compute the phase voltages of the source.

Ans: $\mathbf{V}_{an} = 120\underline{/20^\circ}$ V rms, $\mathbf{V}_{bn} = 120\underline{/-100^\circ}$ V rms, $\mathbf{V}_{cn} = 120\underline{/+140^\circ}$ V rms.

D5.11. In a balanced three-phase wye–delta system, the delta-connected load consists of a 20 Ω resistor in series with a 20 mH inductor. If the system frequency is 60 Hz, find the impedance per phase of an equivalent wye load.

Ans: $\mathbf{Z}_Y = 6.67 + j2.51\ \Omega$.

5.9.3 Delta-Connected Source

Up to this point we have concentrated our discussion on circuits that have wye-connected sources. However, our analysis of the wye–wye and wye–delta connections provides us with the information necessary to handle a delta-connected source.

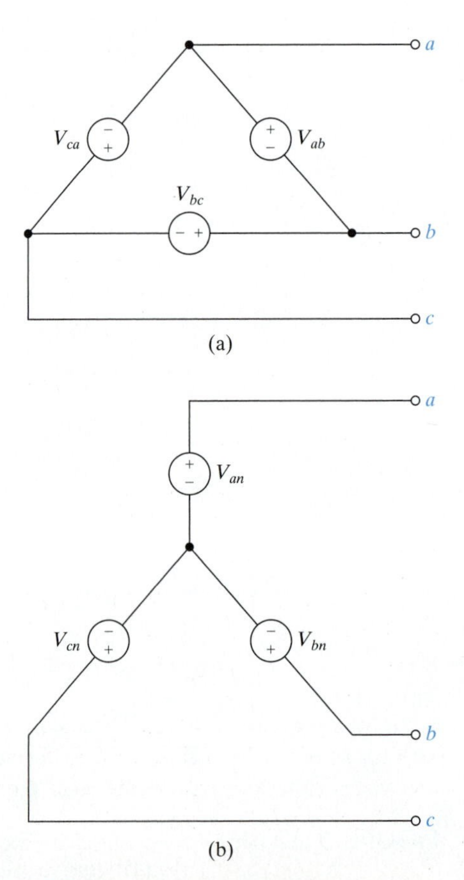

FIGURE 5.23 Sources connected in delta and wye.

Consider the delta-connected source shown in Figure 5.23(a). Note that the sources are connected line to line. We found earlier that the relationship between line-to-line and line-to-neutral voltages was given by Eq. (5.36) and illustrated in Figure 5.19 for an *abc* phase sequence of voltages. Therefore, if the delta sources are

$$\begin{aligned} \mathbf{V}_{ab} &= V_L\angle 0^\circ \\ \mathbf{V}_{bc} &= V_L\angle -120^\circ \\ \mathbf{V}_{ca} &= V_L\angle +120^\circ \end{aligned} \tag{5.43}$$

where V_L is the magnitude of the voltage sources connected in delta, the equivalent wye sources shown in Figure 5.23(b) are

$$\begin{aligned} \mathbf{V}_{an} &= \frac{V_L}{\sqrt{3}}\angle -30^\circ \\ \mathbf{V}_{bn} &= \frac{V_L}{\sqrt{3}}\angle -150^\circ \\ \mathbf{V}_{cn} &= \frac{V_L}{\sqrt{3}}\angle -270^\circ \end{aligned} \tag{5.44}$$

Therefore, if we encounter a network containing a delta-connected source, we can easily convert the source from delta to wye so that all the techniques we have discussed previously can be applied in an analysis.

Drill Exercise

D5.12. A delta-connected source has the following values: $\mathbf{V}_{ab} = 440\angle 60^\circ$ V rms, $\mathbf{V}_{bc} = 440\angle -60^\circ$ V rms, and $\mathbf{V}_{ca} = 440\angle -180^\circ$ V rms. Find the values of the equivalent wye-connected source.

Ans: $\mathbf{V}_{an} = 254\angle 30^\circ$ V rms, $\mathbf{V}_{bn} = 254\angle -90^\circ$ V rms, and $\mathbf{V}_{cn} = 254\angle -210^\circ$ V rms.

5.9.4 Power Relationships

It is interesting to note that the complex power for a single phase of a three-phase system can be expressed using Eq. (5.17) as

$$\mathbf{S}_{1\phi} = V_P I_P \angle \theta_z \tag{5.45}$$

where θ_z is the impedance angle of the load. Since the line current and line voltage are the quantities most easily measured, we wish to express the total complex power $\mathbf{S}_T$ in terms of these quantities. For a wye-connected load, Eqs. (5.37) indicate that the complex power for a single phase can be expressed as

$$\mathbf{S}_{1\phi} = \frac{V_L I_L}{\sqrt{3}} \angle \theta_z \tag{5.46}$$

The total complex power is the same for wye- and delta-connected loads

The same results are obtained from Eq. (5.42) if the load is delta-connected.

The total complex power for all three phases is then

$$\mathbf{S}_T = \sqrt{3}\, V_L I_L \angle \theta_z \tag{5.47}$$

where

$$\begin{aligned} S_T &= P_T + jQ_T \\ P_T &= \sqrt{3}\, V_L I_L \cos\theta_z \\ Q_T &= \sqrt{3}\, V_L I_L \sin\theta_z \end{aligned} \tag{5.48}$$

and

$$\begin{aligned} |\mathbf{S}_T| &= \sqrt{P_T^2 + Q_T^2} \\ &= \sqrt{3}\, V_L I_L \end{aligned} \tag{5.49}$$

Example 5.12

A balanced three-phase source serves two small industrial plants, which are located at the intersection of two major country roads. Each plant represents a load, and the characteristics of the loads are as follows.

Load 1: 28 kW at 0.85 lagging power factor

Load 2: 18 kW at unity power factor

If the line voltage at the loads is 208 V rms at 60 Hz, we wish to determine the total line current and the combined power factor for the total load.

The power factor angle for load 1 is

$$\theta_1 = \cos^{-1} 0.85 = 31.79°$$

The power triangle for this load is shown in Figure 5.24. The magnitude of the complex power for load 1 is then

$$\begin{aligned} |\mathbf{S}_1| &= \frac{P_1}{\cos\theta_1} = \frac{28{,}000}{0.85} \\ &= 32.941 \text{ kVA} \end{aligned}$$

and

$$\begin{aligned} \mathbf{S}_1 &= 32{,}941 \angle 31.79° \text{ VA} \\ &= 28{,}000 + j17{,}354 \text{ VA} \end{aligned}$$

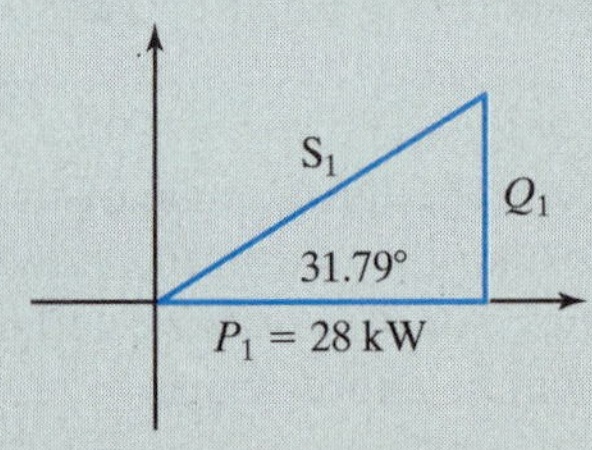

FIGURE 5.24 Power triangle used in Example 5.12.

The power angle for load 2 is 0° and hence

$$\mathbf{S}_2 = 18{,}000 \text{ VA}$$

The total load is

$$\begin{aligned}\mathbf{S}_T &= \mathbf{S}_1 + \mathbf{S}_2 \\ &= 46{,}000 + j17{,}354 \text{ VA} \\ &= 49{,}165\underline{/20.67^\circ} \text{ VA}\end{aligned}$$

The line current that serves both loads is

$$I_L = \frac{|\mathbf{S}_T|}{\sqrt{3}\,V_L}$$

$$I_L = 136.47 \text{ A rms}$$

and the combined power factor is

$$\begin{aligned}\text{PF}_T &= \cos 20.67^\circ \\ &= 0.936 \text{ lagging}\end{aligned}$$

Summary

- Given the circuit in Figure 5.25, the average power is $P = \frac{1}{2}V_M I_M \cos(\theta_v - \theta_i)$. If the network is purely resistive, $P = \frac{1}{2}V_M I_M$, and if the network is purely reactive, $P = 0$.

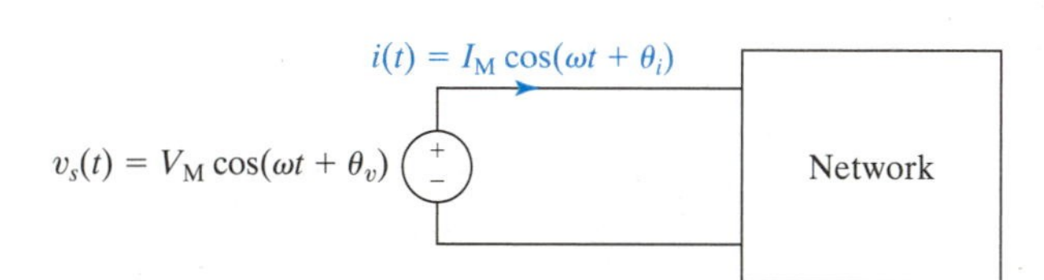

FIGURE 5.25 Network for description of power relationships.

- The root-mean-square (rms) or effective value of a periodic current is a constant, that is, dc value, which delivers the same average power to a resistor, R. The average power delivered to a resistor R is $P = I_{\text{rms}}^2 R$

  where

$$I_{\text{rms}} = \left[\frac{1}{T}\int_{t_0}^{t_0+T} i^2(t)\,dt\right]^{\frac{1}{2}}$$

- The power relationships are specified in the diagram shown in Figure 5.26 where

  S = Apparent power measured in volt amperes

  Q = Quadrature power measured in vars

  P = Real power measured in watts

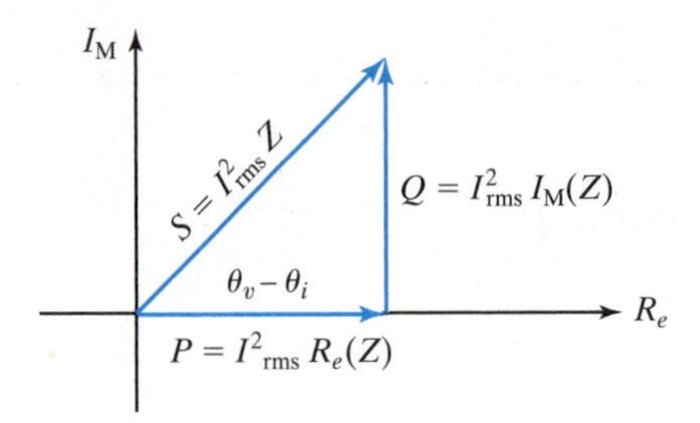

FIGURE 5.26 The power triangle.

$$PF = \text{Power factor} = \cos(\theta_v - \theta_i) = \frac{P}{V_{rms}I_{rms}} \text{ and } \theta_v - \theta_i = \text{power factor angle}$$

- In a RL network, the current lags the voltage and the power factor is lagging.
  In a RC network, the current leads the voltage and the power factor is leading.
- Power factor correction can typically be accomplished by connecting a bank of capacitors in parallel with the load. The effect of this addition is shown in Figure 5.27.
  By adding Q_C to Q_L, $\theta_2 < \theta_1$ and since $PF = \cos\theta$, the PF is raised by adding the capacitor bank.
- A balanced three-phase network
  - is always connected in either delta or wye.
  - exhibits smooth power delivery since the *instantaneous* power is *constant.*
  - can be analyzed by examining a single phase and then shifting the results 120° and 240° to obtain the results for the other two phases.
  - has the same total complex power whether connected in delta or wye.

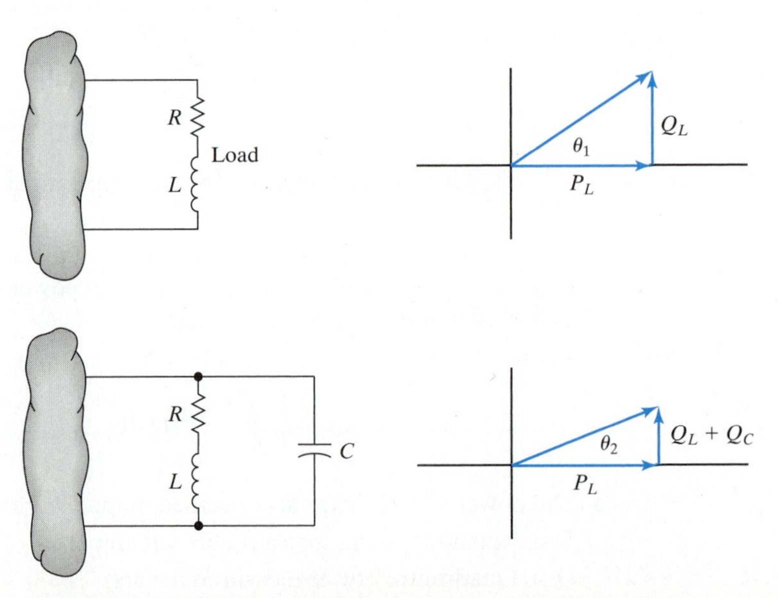

FIGURE 5.27 Power factor correction illustration.

Problems

5.1. In the circuit in Figure P5.1, $v_1(t) = 12 \cos (377t - 40°)$ V. Determine the equations for the current and instantaneous power as a function of time.

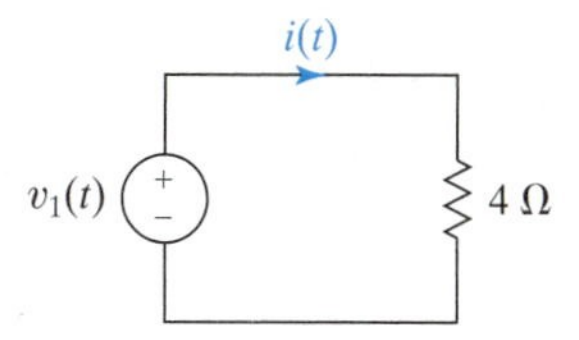

FIGURE P5.1

5.2. In the network in Figure P5.2, $v_1(t) = 24 \cos (377t + 20°)$ V. Find the equations for the current and instantaneous power as a function of time.

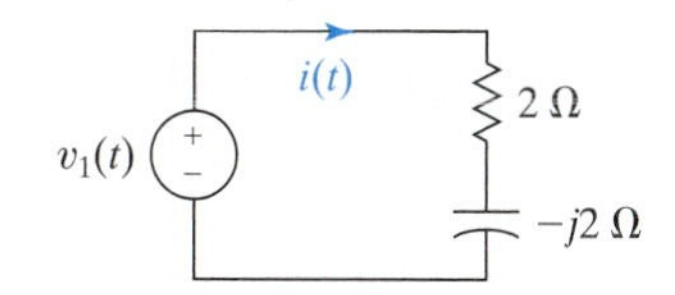

FIGURE P5.2

5.3. Determine the total average power absorbed and supplied in the network in Figure P5.3.

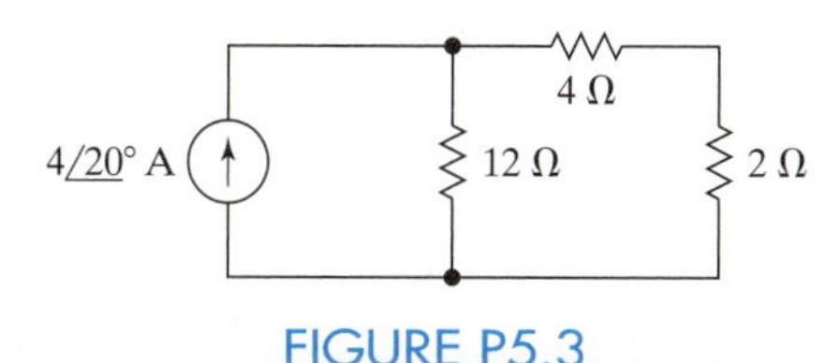

FIGURE P5.3

5.4. Determine the total average power absorbed and supplied in the network in Figure P5.4.

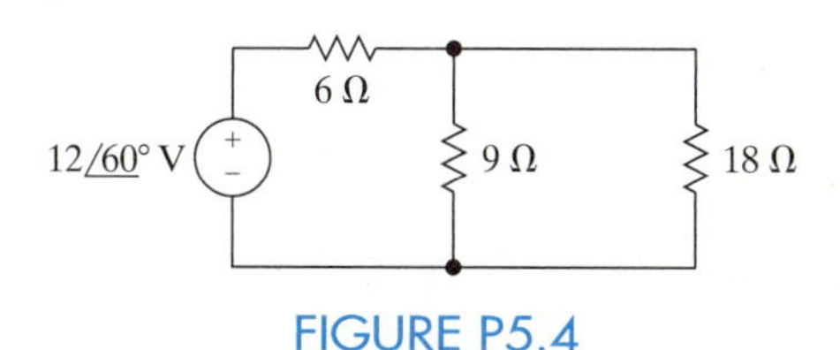

FIGURE P5.4

5.5. Determine the average power absorbed in the 4 Ω resistor in the circuit in Figure P5.5.

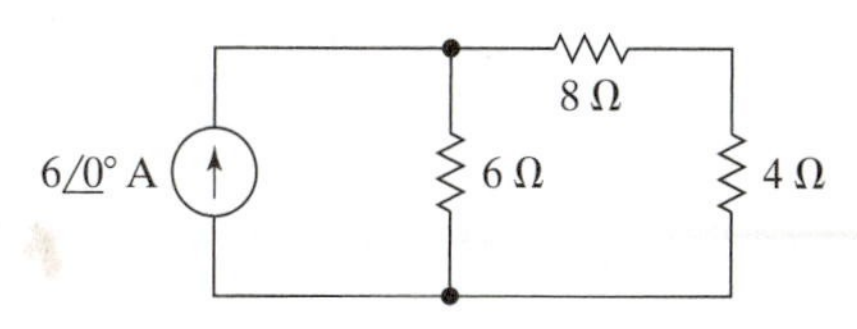

FIGURE P5.5

5.6. Determine the average power absorbed in the 6 Ω resistor in the network in Figure P5.6.

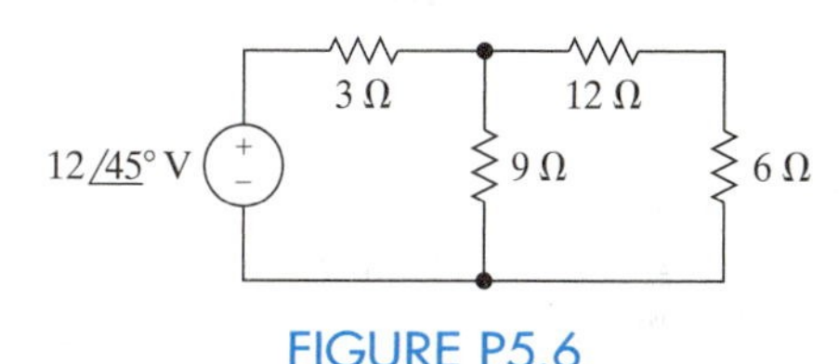

FIGURE P5.6

5.7. Find the total average power absorbed and supplied in the circuit in Figure P5.7.

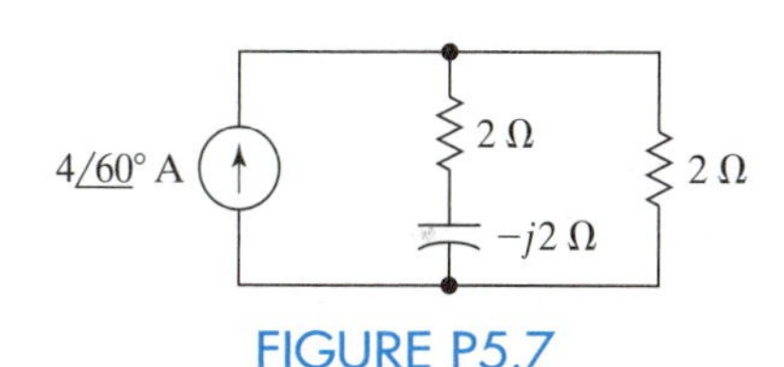

FIGURE P5.7

5.8. Find the total average power absorbed and supplied in the network in Figure P5.8.

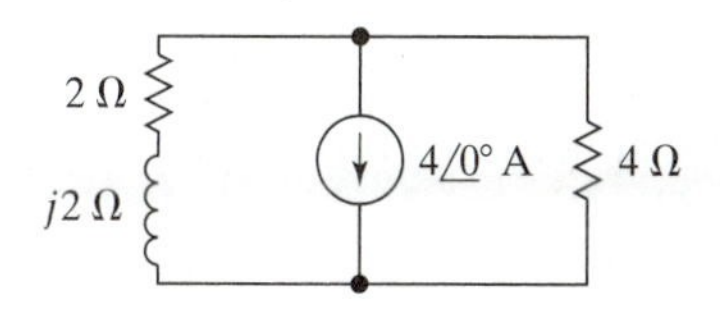

FIGURE P5.8

5.9. Find the total average power absorbed and supplied in the circuit in Figure P5.9.

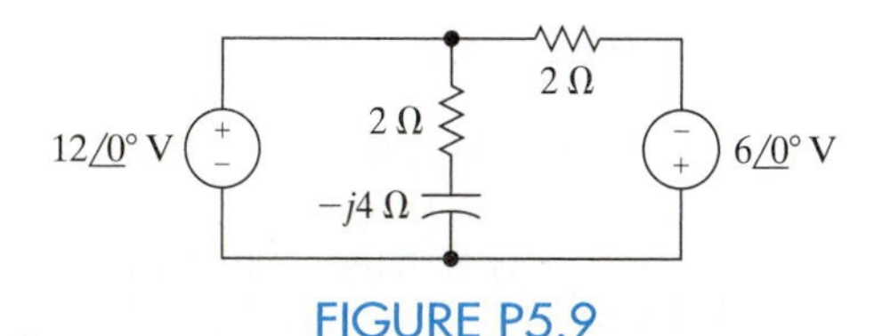

FIGURE P5.9

5.10. Show that the conservation of power holds for the network shown in Figure P5.10.

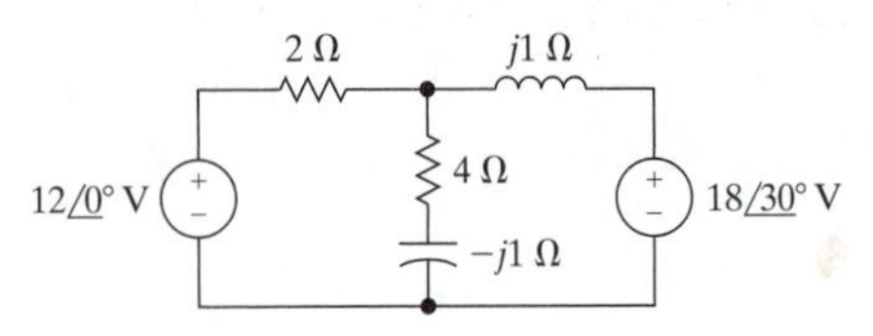

FIGURE P5.10

5.11. Given the network in Figure P5.11, determine the average power absorbed or supplied by each element.

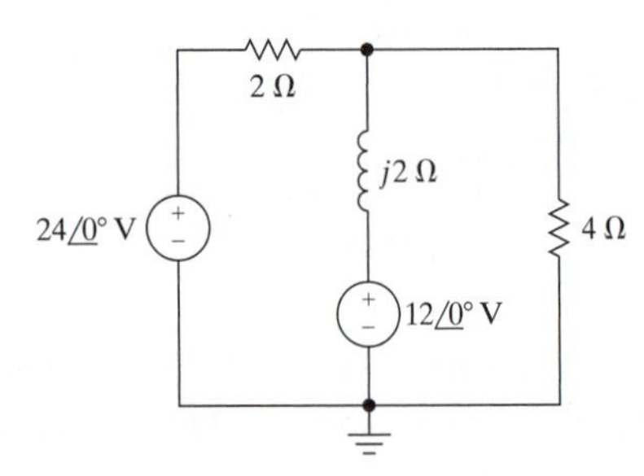

FIGURE P5.11

5.12. Find the total average power absorbed and supplied in the circuit in Figure P5.12.

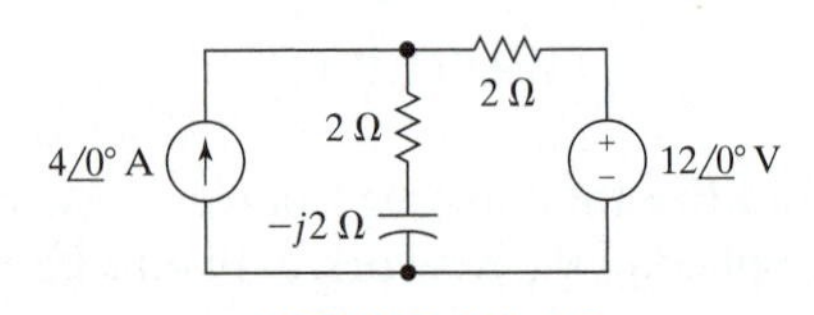

FIGURE P5.12

5.13. Determine the average power absorbed and supplied by each element in the network in Figure P5.13.

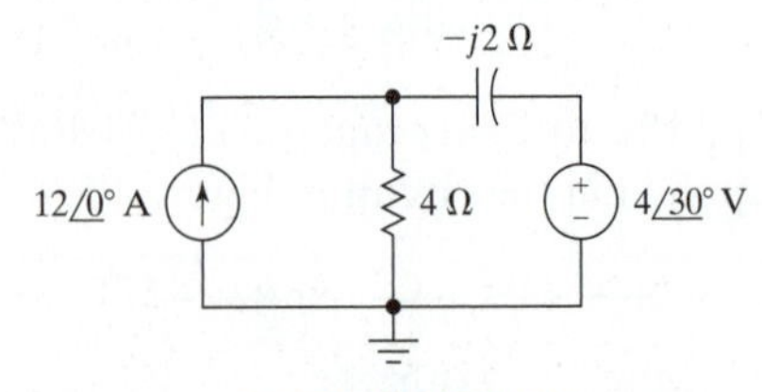

FIGURE P5.13

5.14. Determine the rms value of the waveform in Figure P5.14

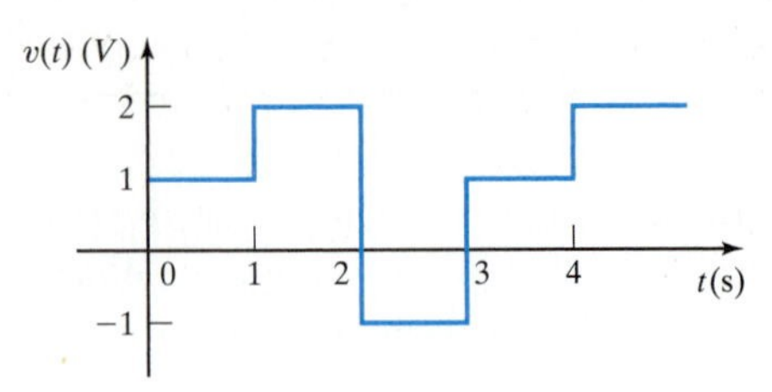

FIGURE P5.14

5.15. Calculate the rms value of the waveform shown in Figure P5.15.

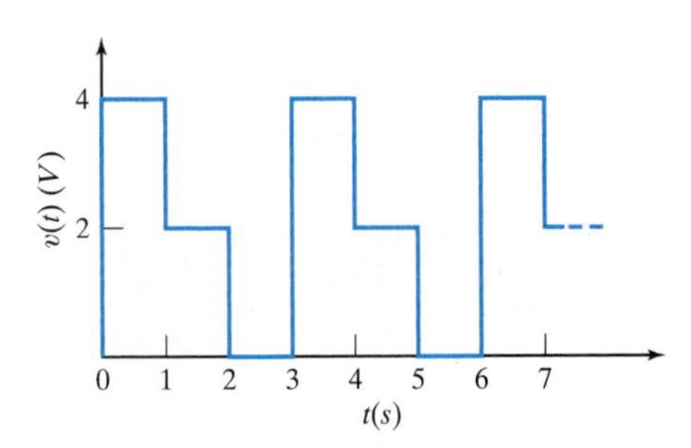

FIGURE P5.15

5.16. Determine the rms value of the waveform shown in Figure P5.16.

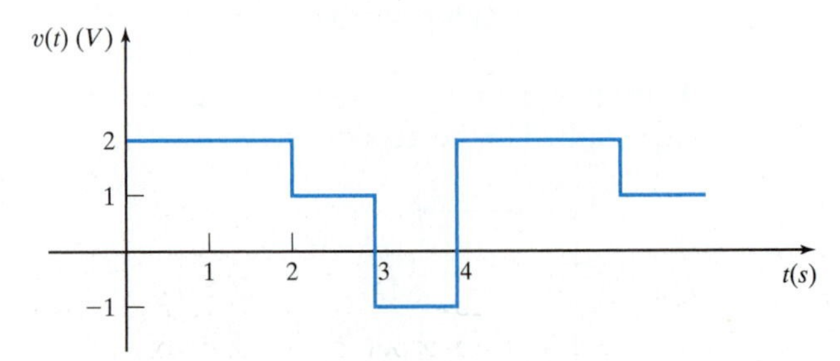

FIGURE P5.16

5.17. Compute the rms value of the voltage waveform shown in Figure P5.17.

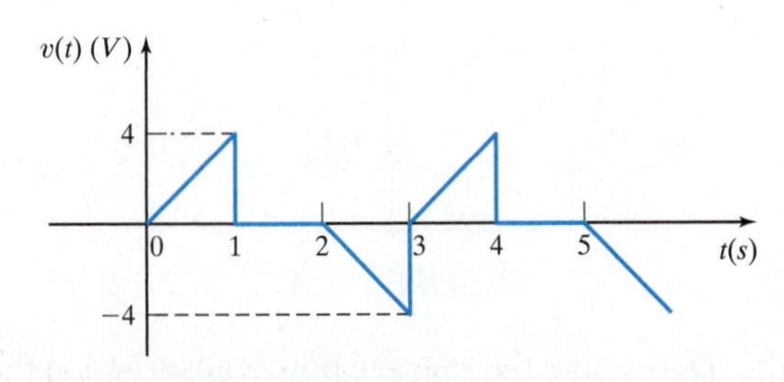

FIGURE P5.17

5.18. The current waveform in Figure P5.18 exists in a 10 Ω resistor. Determine the average power delivered to the resistor.

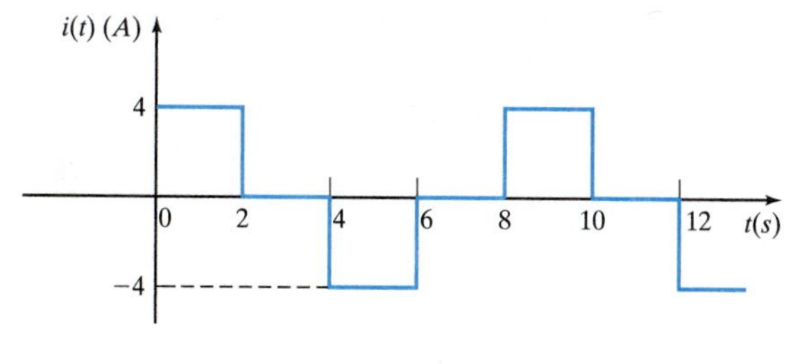

FIGURE P5.18

5.19. The current in a 4 Ω resistor is given by the waveform in Figure P5.19. Find the average power absorbed by the resistor.

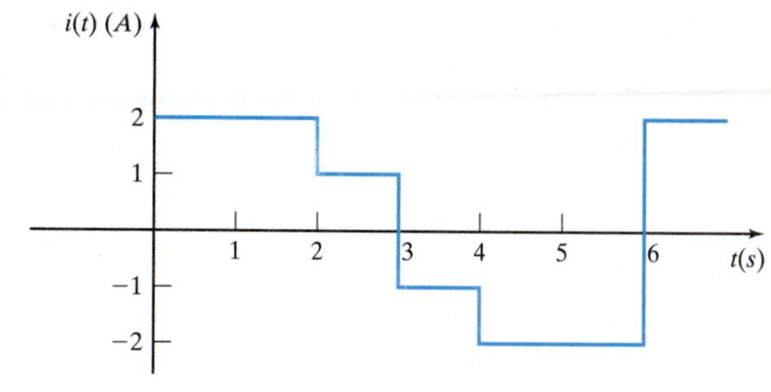

FIGURE P5.19

5.20. The current in a 2 Ω resistor is given by the waveform shown in Figure P5.20. Find the average power absorbed by the resistor.

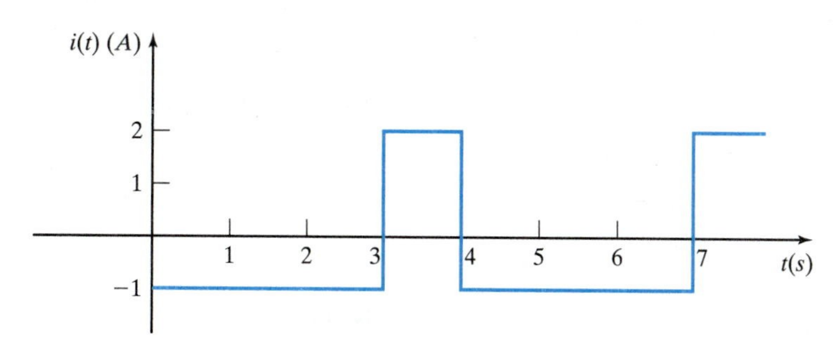

FIGURE P5.20

5.21. The voltage across a 4 Ω resistor is given by the waveform shown in Figure P5.21. Find the average power absorbed by the resistor.

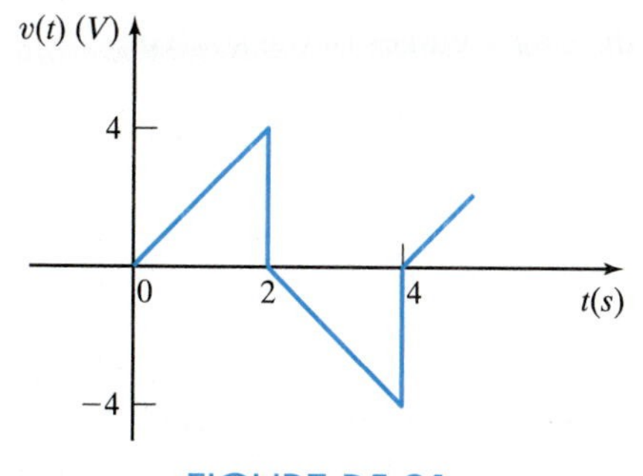

FIGURE P5.21

5.22. The power consumed by an industrial load is 120 kW at 0.70 PF lagging from a 480 V rms line. If the transmission line resistance between the generator and the load is 0.14 Ω, find the power that must be supplied by the power company.

5.23. An industrial load consumes 100 kW at 0.8 PF lagging. The line voltage is 480 V rms. If the line resistance between the generator and load is 0.1 Ω, find the transmission line losses.

5.24. If the power factor in problem 5.23 is changed to 0.92 lagging, determine the effect on the line losses.

5.25. A load operates at 20 kW, 0.8 PF lagging. The load voltage is $220\angle 0°$ V rms at 60 Hz. The impedance of the line is $0.09 + j0.3\ \Omega$. Determine the voltage and power factor at the input to the line.

5.26. A particular load has a PF of 0.8 lagging. The power delivered to the load is 40 kW from a 220 V rms 60 Hz line. If the transmission line resistance is $0.085\ \Omega$, determine the real power that must be generated at the supply.

5.27. The line voltage at an industrial load is 220 V rms The load consumes 50 kW at 0.75 PF lagging. The line resistance from the power company's transformer to the load is $0.1\ \Omega$. Determine the savings in line losses if the PF is somehow changed to 0.92 lagging.

5.28. Calculate the voltage $\mathbf{V}_s$ that must be supplied to obtain 2 kW, $240\angle 0°$ V rms, and a power factor of 0.8 leading at the load $\mathbf{Z}_L$ in the network in Figure P5.28.

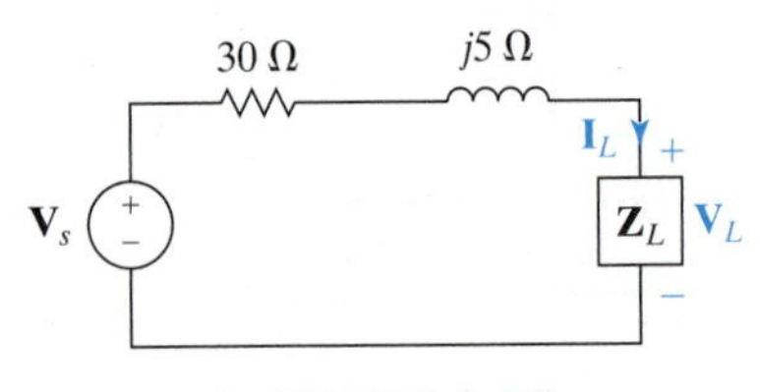

FIGURE P5.28

5.29. An industrial plant at the end of a transmission line consumes 144 kW at 0.88 PF lagging. The line voltage at the plant is $480\angle 0°$ V rms. The resistance of the transmission line is $0.13\ \Omega$. Determine the voltage and power factor at the input of the transmission line.

5.30. A plant, representing the load on a transmission line, consumes 110 kW at 0.88 PF lagging. The load line voltage is $480\angle 0°$ V rms. If the transmission line resistance is $0.15\ \Omega$, determine the complex power at both ends of the line.

5.31. An industrial plant consumes 160 kW at 0.9 PF lagging. The line voltage at the plant is $480\angle 0°$ V rms. The transmission line feeding the plant is 2 miles long. If the impedance of the line is $0.1 + j0.2\ \Omega$, find the power factor at the sending end of the line.

5.32. A small plant has a bank of induction motors that consume 64 kW at a PF of 0.68 lagging. The 60 Hz line voltage across the motors is $220\ \angle 0°$ V rms. The local power company has told the plant to raise the PF to 0.92 lagging. What value of capacitance is required?

5.33. What value of capacitance, placed in parallel with the load in problem 5.26, will raise the PF to 0.9 lagging?

5.34. An industrial plant consumes 75 kW at 0.84 PF lagging when connected to a $220\ \angle 0°$ V rms, 60 Hz line. Determine the value of the capacitance, which, when placed in parallel with the load, will raise the power factor to 0.94 lagging.

5.35. An industrial load is connected to a 60 Hz line and the load voltage is $480\ \angle 0°$ V rms. The load consumes 120 kW at 0.77 PF lagging. Select the capacitor value needed to raise the power factor to 0.9 lagging.

5.36. An industrial plant draws 100 kW at 0.7 PF lagging from a $480\ \angle 0°$ V rms, 60 Hz line. If a 500 μF capacitor bank is placed in parallel with the load, what is the new power factor?

5.37. An abc-sequence three-phase voltage source connected in a balanced wye has a phase voltage of $\mathbf{V}_{an} = 120\ \angle -45°$ V rms. Determine the line voltages of the source.

5.38. An abc-sequence three-phase voltage source connected in a balanced wye has a line voltage of $\mathbf{V}_{ab} = 208\ \angle 175°$ V rms. Find the phase voltages of the source.

5.39. A three-phase, abc-sequence, balanced wye-connected source is connected to a balanced wye-connected load. The phase voltage of the source is 120 V rms, the load impedance is $16 + j8\ \Omega$, and the line impedance is negligible. Determine the line currents.

5.40. If the line impedance in problem 5.39 is $0.8 + j0.6\ \Omega$, determine the line currents and the load voltages.

5.41. An abc-sequence balanced three-phase wye-connected source with a phase voltage of 100 V rms supplies power to a balanced wye-connected load. The per-phase load impedance is $40 + j10\ \Omega$. Determine the line currents in the circuit if $\angle \mathbf{V}_{an} = 0°$.

5.42. An abc-sequence balanced three-phase wye-connected source supplies power to a balanced wye-connected load. The line impedance per phase is $1 + j0\ \Omega$, and the load impedance per phase is $20 + j20\ \Omega$. If the source line voltage $\mathbf{V}_{ab}$ is $100\ \angle 0°$ V rms, find the line currents.

5.43. An abc-sequence balanced wye-connected source supplies a balanced wye-connected load. If the line voltage at the source is $\mathbf{V}_{ab} = 240\ \angle 0°$ V rms, the load impedance is $18 + j12\ \Omega$, and the line impedance is $1.2 + j1\ \Omega$, determine the line currents and the load voltages.

5.44. An abc-sequence balanced wye-connected source supplies a balanced wye-connected load. If the line impedance is $1 + j1\ \Omega$, the load impedance is $12 + j8\ \Omega$, and the load voltage is $\mathbf{V}_{AN} = 109.46\ \angle 18.99°$ V rms, determine the source voltages.

5.45. In a balanced three-phase wye–delta system, the line current is $\mathbf{I}_{aA} = 8\ \angle 13.13°$ A rms. If the impedance per phase of the delta load is $36 + j27\ \Omega$, find the source voltage if the line impedance can be ignored.

5.46. In a balanced three-phase wye–delta system, the phase voltage of the source is $\mathbf{V}_{an} = 120\ \angle 10°$ V rms, and the load impedance per phase in the Δ is $24 + j18\ \Omega$. If the line impedance is negligible, determine the line currents in the system.

5.47. In a balanced three-phase wye–delta system, the line voltage is $\mathbf{V}_{ab} = 120\sqrt{3}\ \angle 70°$ V rms and the line current is $\mathbf{I}_{aA} = 24\ \angle 3.13°$ A rms. If the line impedance is negligible, find the impedance per phase of the delta load.

5.48. In a balanced three-phase wye–delta system, the source has an abc phase sequence. The load impedance is $12 + j8\ \Omega$. If the phase voltage at the load is $\mathbf{V}_{AB} = 260\ \angle 45°$ V rms, find the line currents and the phase voltages of the source.

5.49. In a balanced three-phase wye–delta system, the impedance per phase of the load is $21 + j9\ \Omega$ and the source voltage is $\mathbf{V}_{ab} = 120\sqrt{3}\ \angle 60°$ V rms. If the line impedance is $1 + j1\ \Omega$, determine the line currents.

5.50. A balanced three-phase system has a load that consists of a balanced wye in parallel with a balanced delta. The impedance per phase of the wye is $10 + j8\ \Omega$ and the impedance per phase of the delta is $24 + j12\ \Omega$. Determine both the equivalent wye load and the equivalent delta load.

5.51. A three-phase load impedance consists of a balanced wye in parallel with a balanced delta, as shown in Figure P5.51. Determine the equivalent delta load.

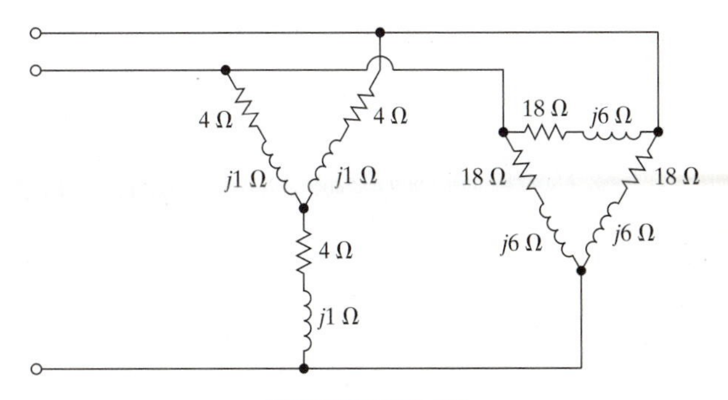

FIGURE P5.51

5.52. An abc-phase-sequence three-phase voltage source connected in a balanced wye supplies power to a balanced delta-connected load. The load current $\mathbf{I}_{AB} = 4\ \angle 20°$ A rms. Determine the line currents.

5.53. An abc-sequence balanced three-phase wye-connected source supplies power to a balanced delta-connected load. The load impedance per phase is $12 + j8\ \Omega$. If the current $\mathbf{I}_{AB}$ in one phase of the delta is $14.42 \angle 86.31°$ A rms, determine the line currents and phase voltages at the source.

5.54. Find I_{ay} in the circuit shown in Figure P5.54.

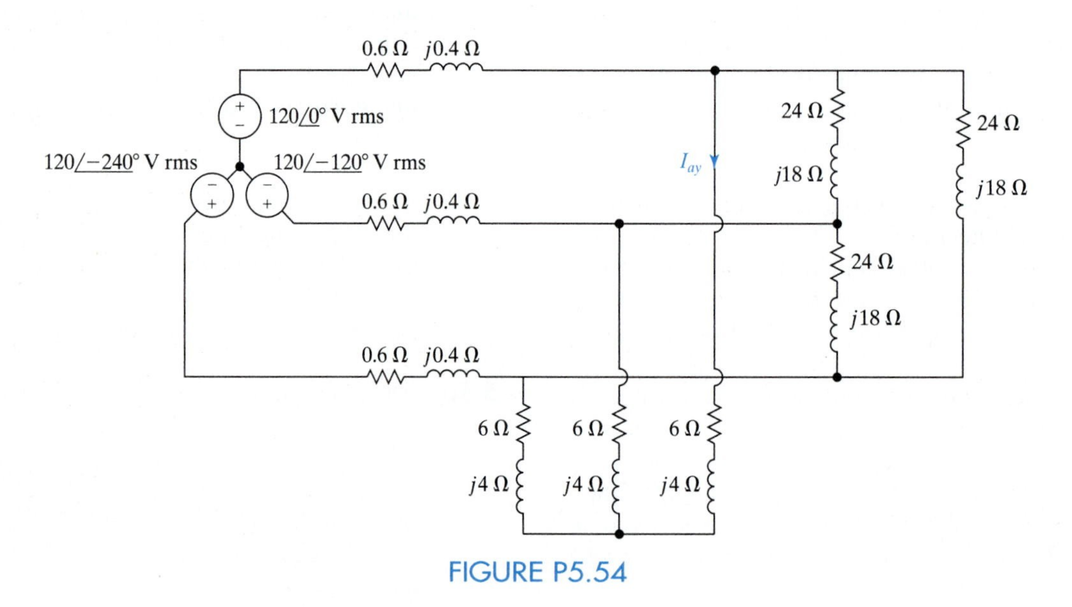

FIGURE P5.54

5.55. Consider the network shown in Figure P5.55. Compute the magnitude of the line voltages at the load and the magnitude of the phase currents in the delta-connected source.

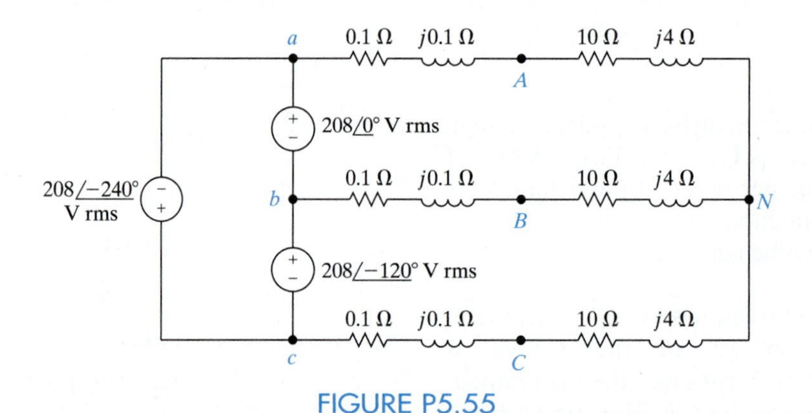

FIGURE P5.55

5.56. A balanced three-phase delta–delta system has the following parameters: $\mathbf{V}_{ab} = 207.84 \angle -20°\ V$ rms, $\mathbf{Z}_{\text{Line}} = 1 + j1.2\ \Omega$, and $\mathbf{Z}_{Load} = 18 + j12\ \Omega$. Find the line currents.

5.57. Two small industries located side-by-side are fed from a three-phase balanced 60 Hz source with a line voltage of 208 V rms. Load #1 consumes 24kW at 0.75 PF lagging and load #2 consumes 16kW at 0.88 PF lagging. Determine the current in the line that serves both loads.

5.58. A 480 V rms line feeds two balanced three-phase loads. If the two loads are rated as follows:

Load 1: 5kVA at 0.8 PF lagging

Load 2: 10kVA at 0.9 PF lagging

determine the magnitude of the line current from the 480 V rms source.

5.59. A balanced three-phase source serves the following loads:

Load 1: 48kVA at 0.9 PF lagging

Load 2: 24kVA at 0.75 PF lagging

The line voltage at the load is 208 V rms at 60 Hz. Determine the line currents and the combined power factor at the load.

5.60. Three industrial loads are supplied by a balanced three-phase source. The line voltage at the loads is 208 V rms at 60 Hz. The characteristics of the loads are

Load 1: 20kW at 0.8 PF lagging

Load 2: 26kW at 0.85 PF leading

Load 3: 18kW at 0.9 PF lagging

determine the total complex power and power factor of the load.

5.61. A balanced three-phase wye–wye system has, two parallel loads. Load 1 is rated at 3000 VA, 0.7 PF lagging, and load 2 is rated at 2000 VA, 0.75 PF leading. If the line voltage is 208 V rms, find the magnitude of the line current.

5.62. Two industrial plants represent balanced three-phase loads. The plants receive their power from a balanced three-phase source with a line voltage of 4.6kV rms. Plant 1 is rated at 300kVA, 0.8 PF lagging, and plant 2 is rated at 350kVA, 0.84 PF lagging. Determine the power line current.

6–1 Introduction

In this chapter some of the basic concepts of magnetic fields are introduced. It is shown that these concepts form the basis for the development of magnetic circuits, which are fundamental building blocks in transformers and electric machinery.

In order to provide a basis for understanding the operation of a transformer, we first examine two coils that are placed in close proximity to one another. Because they are physically located close to one another, they share a common magnetic flux. The magnetic coupling between the coils is the vehicle by which energy is transmitted.

Once the coupled inductors have been introduced, the concepts are extended to the development of transformers. First, linear transformers are presented, and then coils that are coupled with ferromagnetic material are examined and used to derive an approximation for ideal coupling, called the ideal transformer.

Finally, some of the practical considerations of the use of transformers in modern technology are presented and discussed.

6–2 Magnetic Circuits

Magnetic circuits are a fundamental component of the study of electrical engineering. Their importance stems from the fact that they form the basis for the operation of transformers, generators, and motors. In this chapter, we introduce magnetic circuits and illustrate their use in transformers. In the following chapters, we will show that an electromagnetic field is the basic mechanism by which generators and motors transform mechanical energy into electrical energy, and vice versa.

We begin our discussion by considering the permanent magnet shown in Figure 6.1. This device creates a magnetic field between the north (N) and south (S) poles. A *magnetic flux;* ϕ or simply flux, emanates from the north pole and returns through the south pole in a closed path. The flux is measured in webers (Wb), named after the German physicist Wilhelm Weber (1804–1891). The existence of the flux lines is dramatically illustrated in Figure 6.2, where a bar magnet is placed under a sheet of paper and iron filing are sprinkled on the paper. A compass needle placed near the iron filings will align itself tangential to the flux lines, just as it would align itself with the magnetic field lines of the earth.

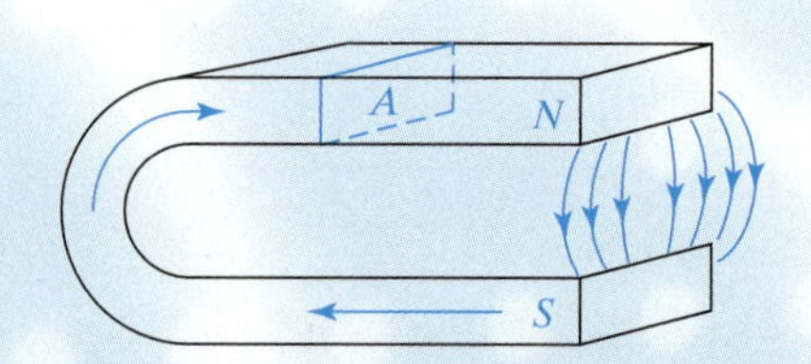

FIGURE 6.1 Permanent magnet.

Magnetically Coupled Circuits and Transformers

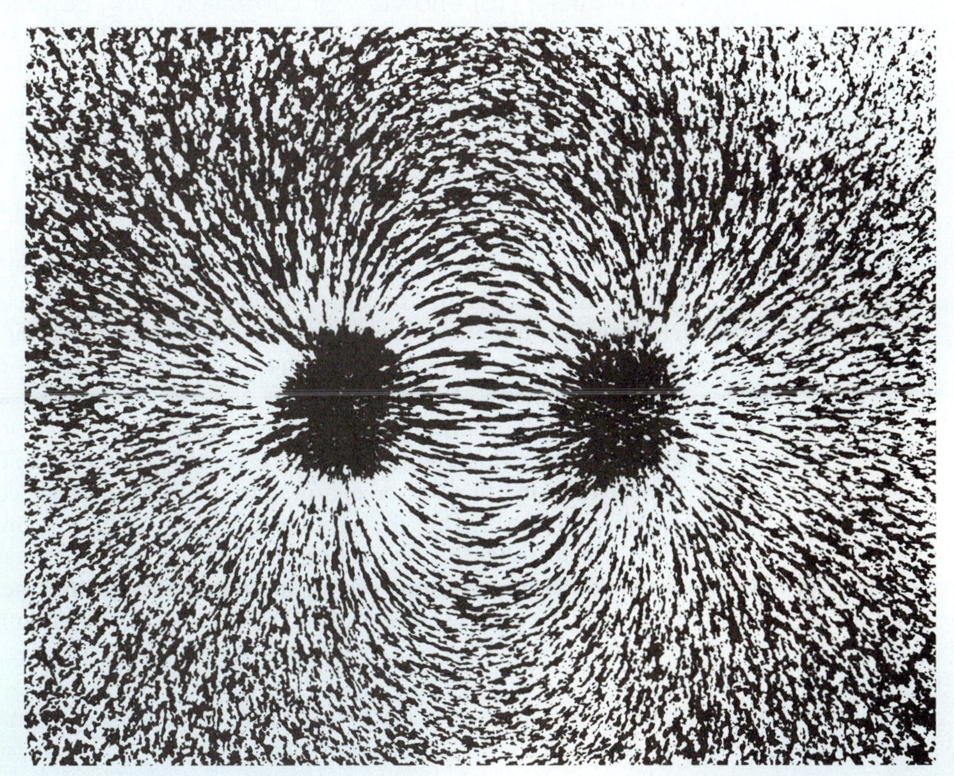

FIGURE 6.2 Illustration of flux paths around a bar magnet.

The basic components of a magnetic circuit

If we examine a cross-sectional area A of the magnet shown in Figure 6.1 and assume that the flux is uniformly distributed over the area, the *magnetic flux density, B,* is defined by the equation

$$B = \phi A \tag{6.1}$$

where the units of flux density are Wb/m^2, or Tesla, after Nikola Tesla (1856–1943).

Furthermore, it is important to note that the flux will pass through anything, including air. However, ferromagnetic materials such as iron and steel have flux densities that are typically one thousand times greater than that obtained in air. In essence, ferromagnetic materials form a superhighway for the flux.

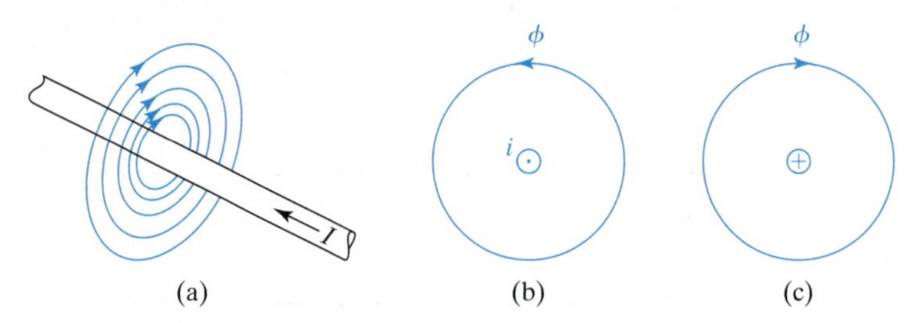

FIGURE 6.3 (a) Magnetic field surrounding a current-carrying conductor; (b) end view of current-carrying conductor. Current is coming out of page; (c) current into the page.

A magnetic field can also be created by a current flowing through a conductor as shown in Figure 6.3. The flux lines encircle the current-carrying conductor and the direction of the magnetic field is determined by a right-hand rule, which states that if the thumb on the right hand points in the direction of positive current, then the fingers of the right hand curl in the direction of the magnetic field.

It is interesting to note that the creation of a magnetic field by a current-carrying conductor is the reason people are concerned about the biological effects of using electronic devices such as cellular telephones as well as living or working near high-voltage lines.

Consider now the magnetic circuit shown in Figure 6.4(a). It consists of an iron core and an electrical winding of N turns carrying a current of I amperes. As Figure 6.3 demonstrates, the current will produce a magnetic flux, which circulates in the core. While there may be some small leakage flux that circulates around the conductor and through the surrounding air, almost all of the flux will be confined to the ferromagnetic core. The flux is not only dependent upon the current but the number N of turns of the wire around the core. Thus, the driving force, which pushes the flux around the magnetic circuit, is the number of ampere-turns NI just as the voltage source is the driving mechanism that forces the current in an electrical circuit. This magnetic driving force is called *magnetomotive force* (mmf), $\mathcal{F}$, and defined as

$$\mathcal{F} = NI \tag{6.2}$$

where I is the current in amperes in an N-turn coil, and therefore $\mathcal{F}$ is measured in ampere-turns.

A linearized relationship between the flux and the mmf for the magnetic circuit shown in Figure 6.4(a) is demonstrated by the curve in Figure 6.4(b). As indicated in the

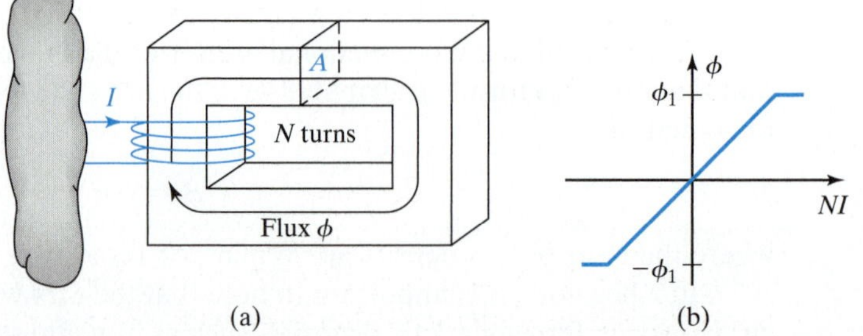

FIGURE 6.4 (a) Magnetic circuit consisting of an iron core excited by NI amp-turns; (b) relationship between flux and amp-turns. ϕ_1 is the saturation flux.

TABLE 6.1 Electric/Magnetic Circuits Analogies

Electric Circuit	**Magnetic Circuit**
$V = IR$	$\mathscr{F} = \phi\mathscr{R}$
V = voltage in volts	$\mathscr{F} = NI$ = mmf, in ampere-turns
I = current in amperes	ϕ = flux in webers
R = resistance in ohms	$\mathscr{R}$ = reluctance in amp-turns/Wb
$G = \dfrac{1}{\mathscr{R}}$ = conductance in siemens	$\mathscr{P} = \dfrac{1}{\mathscr{R}}$ = permeance in Wb/amp-turns

figure, for small values of ϕ, doubling either the current I or the number of turns N will double ϕ. In other words, the relationship between ϕ and NI is linear until the iron begins to saturate, at which point further increases in the driving force NI yield little or no increase in the flux ϕ.

Although the mmf produces a flux that penetrates some medium such as the iron core, this flux is limited by the magnetic resistance, which is called *reluctance.* Reluctance is defined by the equation

$$\mathscr{R} = \frac{\mathscr{F}}{\phi} \tag{6.3}$$

and the units for reluctance are ampere-turns/wb. Similarly, *magnetic permeance* is defined as:

$$\mathscr{P} = \frac{1}{\mathscr{R}} \tag{6.4}$$

Examples of high reluctance materials, or magnetic resistance, are free space, teflon, and wood. Furthermore, materials such as iron and steel have low reluctance. While reluctance is a useful concept, its applicability is limited by the fact that the ϕ vs NI curve is nonlinear as shown in Figure 6.4(b), and therefore the reluctance is not constant.

Equation (6.3) is often called Ohm's law for the magnetic circuit. Table 6.1 lists analogous relationships between electric and magnetic circuits.

Having described some of the basic concepts of magnetic circuits, we now turn our attention to their application. We demonstrate that when two current-carrying conductors are in close proximity, their magnetic fields interact. It is through the interactive coupling of the magnetic fields that we transfer energy.

6–3 Mutual Inductance

Consider the situation illustrated in Figure 6.5. To simplify our discussion, consider all conductor resistance to be negligible. Now recall *Faraday's law,* which can be stated as follows: The induced voltage in a coil is proportional to the time rate of change of *flux linkage* ($\lambda = N\phi$), where N is the number of turns in the coil. Two coupled coils are shown in Figure 6.5 together with the following flux components.

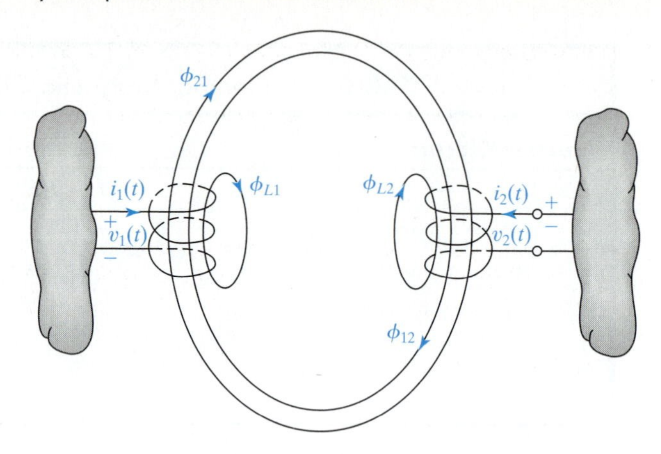

FIGURE 6.5 Flux relationships for mutually coupled coils.

ϕ_{L1}	The flux in coil 1, which does not link coil 2, that is produced by the current in coil 1.
ϕ_{L2}	The flux in coil 2, which does not link coil 1, that is produced by the current in coil 2.
ϕ_{12}	The flux in coil 1 produced by the current in coil 2.
ϕ_{21}	The flux in coil 2 produced by the current in coil 1.
$\phi_{11} = \phi_{L1} + \phi_{21}$	The flux in coil 1 produced by the current in coil 1.
$\phi_{22} = \phi_{L2} + \phi_{12}$	The flux in coil 2 produced by the current in coil 2.
ϕ_1	The total flux in coil 1.
ϕ_2	The total flux in coil 2.

In order to write the equations that describe the coupled coils, we define the voltages and currents, using the passive sign convention, at each pair of terminals as shown in Figure 6.5.

Mathematically, Faraday's law can be written as

$$v_1(t) = N_1 \frac{d\phi_1}{dt} \tag{6.5}$$

The flux ϕ_1 will be equal to the algebraic sum of ϕ_{11}, the flux in coil 1 caused by current coil 1, and ϕ_{12}, the flux in coil 1 caused by current in coil 2; that is,

$$\phi_1 = \phi_{11} + \phi_{12} \tag{6.6}$$

The equation for the voltage can be written

$$\begin{aligned} v_1(t) &= N_1 \frac{d\phi_1}{dt} \\ &= N_1 \frac{d\phi_{11}}{dt} + N_1 \frac{d\phi_{12}}{dt} \end{aligned} \tag{6.7}$$

where N_1 is the number of turns in coil 1. For magnetically linear situations, the flux is proportional to the current and Eq. (6.7) reduces to

$$v_1(t) = L_{11} \frac{di_1}{dt} + L_{12} \frac{di_2}{dt} \tag{6.8a}$$

Where the constant L_{11} is now called the *self-inductance,* and the constant L_{12} is called the *mutual inductance.*

Using the same technique, we can write

$$= L_{21}\frac{di_1}{dt} + L_{22}\frac{di_2}{dt} \tag{6.8b}$$

If the media through which the magnetic flux passes its linear, then $L_{12} = L_{21} = M$. For convenience, let us define $L_1 = L_{11}$ and $L_2 = L_{22}$. Thus

The voltage/current equations for mutually coupled coils

$$\begin{aligned} v_1(t) &= L_1\frac{di_1}{dt} + M\frac{di_2}{dt} \\ v_2(t) &= L_2\frac{di_2}{dt} + M\frac{di_1}{dt} \end{aligned} \tag{6.9}$$

In order to indicate the physical relationship of the coils, we employ what is commonly called the *dot convention.* Dots are placed beside each coil so that if currents are entering both dotted terminals or leaving both dotted terminals, the mutual fluxes produced by these currents will add. The dots have been correctly placed on the two coupled circuits in Figure 6.6(a). The corresponding circuit symbol is shown in Figure 6.6(b).

Note carefully that the mathematical equations are written for the circuit diagram in Figure 6.6(b), and hence changing a voltage polarity or current direction will reverse the sign of the appropriate variable in the equations. It is interesting to note that this procedure is directly analogous to the use of Ohm's law. For sinusoidal steady-state analysis, the following transformations are appropriate:

$$v \rightarrow \mathbf{V}$$

$$i \rightarrow \mathbf{I}$$

$$L\frac{d}{dt}() \rightarrow j\omega\mathbf{L}$$

Thus, Eq. 6.9 becomes

$$\begin{aligned} \mathbf{V}_1 &= j\omega L_1\mathbf{I}_1 + j\omega M\mathbf{I}_2 \\ \mathbf{V}_2 &= j\omega L_2\mathbf{I}_2 + j\omega M\mathbf{I}_1 \end{aligned} \tag{6.10}$$

The symbology of the coupled circuit in the frequency domain is identical to that in the time domain except for the way the elements and variables are labeled.

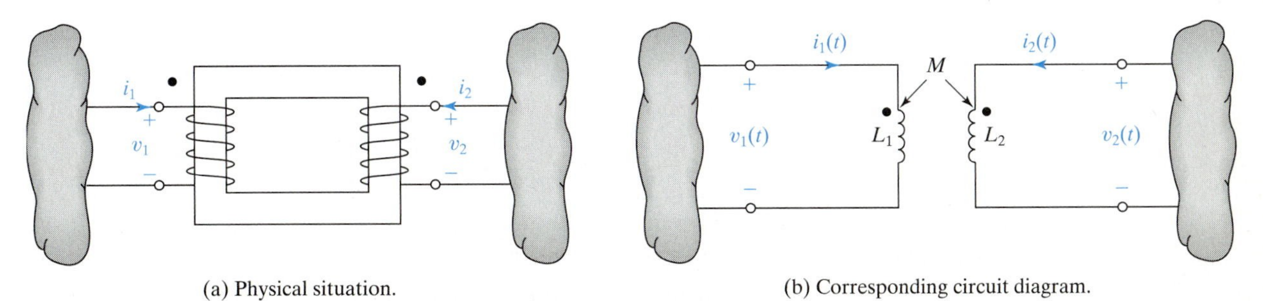

(a) Physical situation.

(b) Corresponding circuit diagram.

FIGURE 6.6 Two strongly coupled coils.

Example 6.1

We wish to determine the output voltage $\mathbf{V}_o$ in the circuit in Figure 6.7.

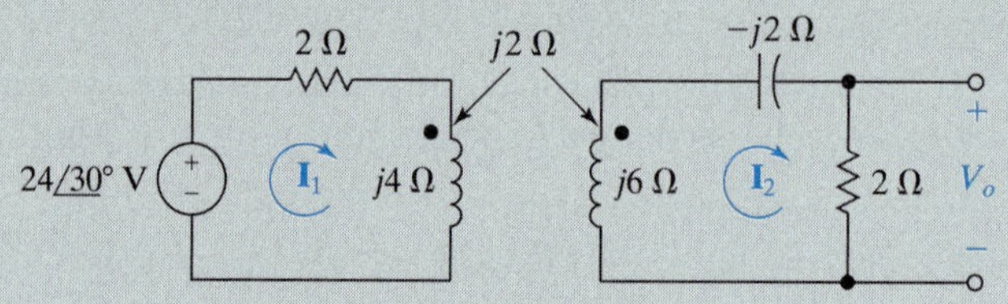

FIGURE 6.7 Example of a magnetically coupled circuit.

The two KVL equations for the network are

$$24\angle 30^\circ = (2 + j4)\mathbf{I}_1 - j2\mathbf{I}_2$$

$$0 = -j2\mathbf{I}_1 + (j6 - j2 + 2)\mathbf{I}_2$$

Note that the negative sign on the mutual term that results from the fact that the direction of the current $\mathbf{I}_2$ with respect to the dot is opposite that shown in Figure 6.6b. Rearranging the terms in the equation yields

$$(2 + j4)\mathbf{I}_1 - j2\mathbf{I}_2 = 24\angle 30^\circ$$

$$-j2\mathbf{I}_1 + (2 + j6 - j2)\mathbf{I}_2 = 0$$

Solving the equations yields

$$\mathbf{I}_2 = 2.68\angle 3.43^\circ \text{ A}$$

Therefore,

$$\mathbf{V}_0 = 2\mathbf{I}_2 = 5.36\angle 3.43^\circ \text{ V}$$

Drill Exercise

D6.1. Find the currents $\mathbf{I}_1$ and $\mathbf{I}_2$ and the output voltage $\mathbf{V}_0$ in the network in Figure D6.1

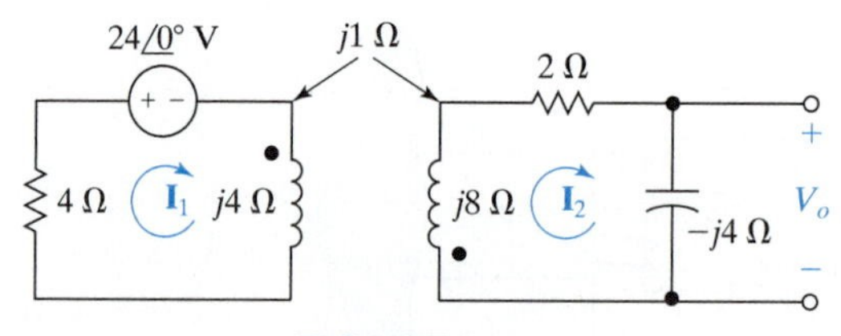

FIGURE D6.1

Ans: $\mathbf{I}_1 = -4.29\angle -42.8^\circ$ A, $\mathbf{I}_2 = 0.96\angle -16.26^\circ$ A, $\mathbf{V}_0 = 3.84\angle -106.26^\circ$ V.

Definition of a coupling coefficient

A quantity that is useful in dealing with magnetically coupled circuits is the coefficient of coupling.

We define the *coefficient of coupling* between two coils as

$$k = \frac{M}{\sqrt{L_1 L_2}} \tag{6.11}$$

and its range is

$$0 \le k \le 1 \tag{6.12}$$

This coefficient is an indication of how tightly the coils are magnetically coupled; that is, if all the flux in one coil links the other coil, then we have 100% coupling and $k = 1$. The previous equations indicate that the value for the mutual inductance is confined to the range

$$0 \le M \le \sqrt{L_1 L_2} \tag{6.13}$$

6-4 The Linear Transformer

A transformer is a device that exploits the properties of two magnetically coupled coils. A typical transformer network is shown in Figure 6.8. The source is connected to what is called the *primary* of the transformer, and the load is connected to the *secondary.* Thus, R_1 and L_1 refer to the resistance and self-inductance of the primary, and R_2 and L_2 refer to the secondary's resistance and self-inductance. The transformer is said to be *linear* if the magnetic permeance (μ) of the paths through which the fluxes pass is constant, as discussed earlier. Without the use of low reluctance material, the coefficient of coupling, k, may be very small. Transformers of this type find wide application in such products as radio and TV receivers.

With reference to Figure 6.8, let us compute the input impedance to the transformer as seen by the source. The network equations are

$$\mathbf{V}_s = \mathbf{I}_1 (R_1 + j\omega L_1) - j\omega M \mathbf{I}_2$$

$$0 = -j\omega M \mathbf{I}_1 + (R_2 + j\omega L_2 + Z_L)\mathbf{I}_2$$

Solving the second equation for $\mathbf{I}_2$ and substituting it into the first equation yields

$$\mathbf{V}_s = \left(R_1 + j\omega L_1 + \frac{\omega^2 M^2}{R_2 + j\omega L_2 + \mathbf{Z}_L} \right) \mathbf{I}_1$$

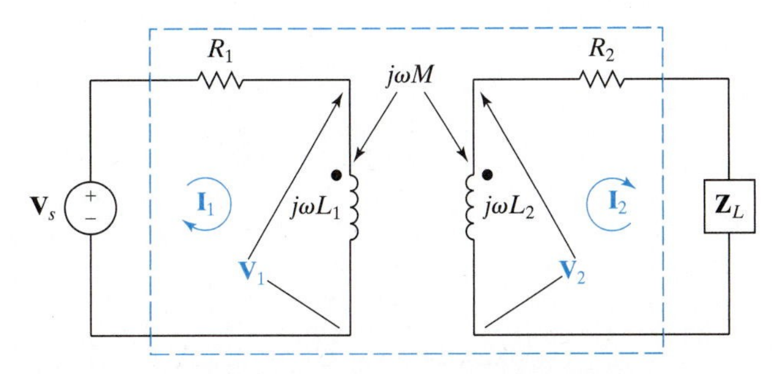

FIGURE 6.8 Transformer network.

Therefore, the *input impedance* is

$$\mathbf{Z}_i = \frac{\mathbf{V}_s}{\mathbf{I}_I} = R_1 + j\omega L_1 + \frac{\omega^2 M^2}{R_2 + j\omega L_2 + \mathbf{Z}_L} \tag{6.14}$$

Impedance relationships for the linear transformer

As we look from the source into the network to determine $\mathbf{Z}_i$, we see the impedance of the primary (i.e., $R_1 + j\omega L_1$) plus an impedance that the secondary of the transformer reflects, due to mutual coupling, into the primary. This *reflected impedance* is

$$\mathbf{Z}_R = \frac{\omega^2 M^2}{R_2 + j\omega L_2 + \mathbf{Z}_L} \tag{6.15}$$

Note that this reflected impedance is independent of the dot locations.

If $\mathbf{Z}_L$ in Eq. (6.15) is written as

$$\mathbf{Z}_L = R_L + jX_L \tag{6.16}$$

then

$$\mathbf{Z}_R = \frac{\omega^2 M^2}{R_2 + R_L + j(\omega L_2 + X_L)}$$

which can be written as

$$\mathbf{Z}_R = \frac{\omega^2 M^2[(R_2 + R_L) - j(\omega L_2 + X_L)]}{(R_2 + R_L)^2 + (\omega L_2 + X_L)^2} \tag{6.17}$$

Note that if $\omega L_2 > X_L$, then the reflected reactance is capacitive. If $\omega L_2 + X_L = 0$ (i.e., the secondary is in resonance), $\mathbf{Z}_R$ is purely resistive and

$$\mathbf{Z}_R = \frac{\omega^2 M^2}{R_2 + R_L} \tag{6.18}$$

Example 6.2

For the network shown in Figure 6.9, we wish to determine the input impedance. Following the development that led to Eq. (6.14), we find that the input impedance is

$$\begin{aligned}\mathbf{Z}_i &= 12 + j10 + \frac{(1)^2}{16 + j8 - j4 + 4 + j6} \\ &= 12.04 + j9.98 \\ &= 15.64\underline{/39.65^\circ}\ \Omega\end{aligned}$$

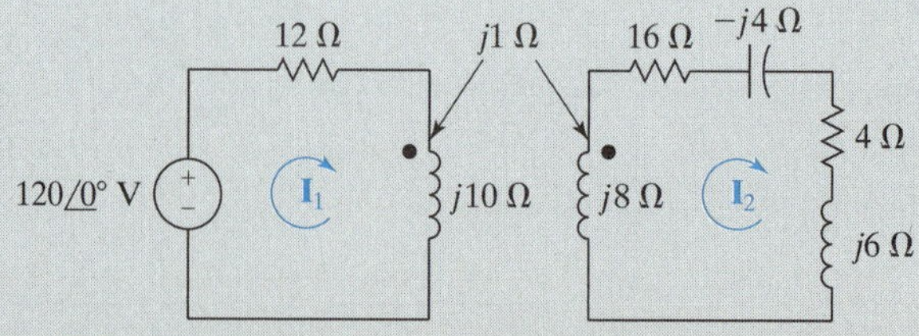

FIGURE 6.9 Example transformer circuit.

Drill Exercise

D6.2. Given the network in Figure D6.2, find the input impedance of the network and the current in the voltage source.

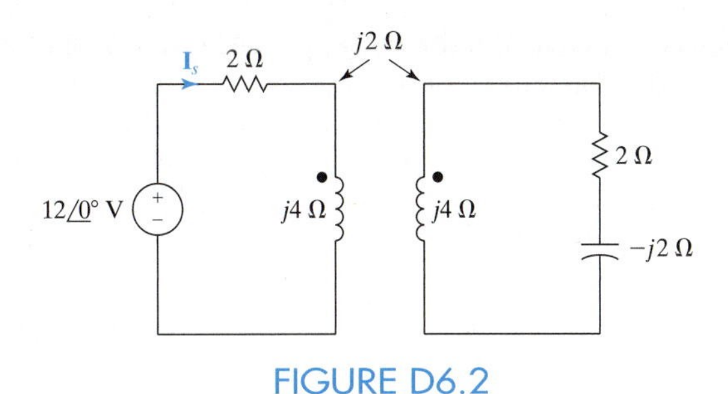

FIGURE D6.2

Ans: $\mathbf{Z}_i = 3 + j3\ \Omega, \mathbf{I}_s = 2 - j2$ A.

A *perfect transformer* is a linear transformer for which $R_1 = R_2 = 0$, and $k =$ unity.

6–5 The Ideal Transformer

An *ideal transformer* is a linear transformer for which $L_1 \rightarrow \infty$, $L_2 \rightarrow \infty$, $k \rightarrow 1$, $R_1 \rightarrow 0$, and $R_2 \rightarrow 0$. Consider the situation illustrated in Figure 6.10, showing two coils of wire wound on a single closed magnetic core. The magnetic core flux links all the turns of both coils. Therefore,

$$v_1 = N_1 \frac{d\phi}{dt}$$

$$v_2 = N_2 \frac{d\phi}{dt}$$

and therefore,

$$\frac{v_1}{v_2} = \frac{N_1 \dfrac{d\phi}{dt}}{N_2 \dfrac{d\phi}{dt}} = \frac{N_1}{N_2} \tag{6.19}$$

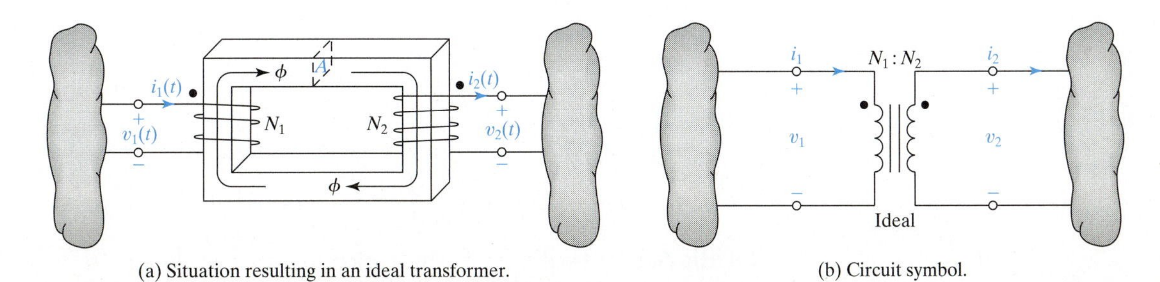

(a) Situation resulting in an ideal transformer. (b) Circuit symbol.

FIGURE 6.10 The ideal transformer.

Another relationship can be developed between the currents $i_1(t)$ and $i_2(t)$ and the number of turns in each coil.

If the transformer is constructed of ideal core material, that is, the reluctance is zero, then we can employ what is known as Ampere's law to show that

$$N_1 i_1 \pm N_2 i_2 = 0 \tag{6.20}$$

Where, once again, the + sign is employed if the relationship of the currents with respect to the dots is as shown in the diagram in Figure 6.6b. Since the current i_2 in Figure 6.10b is in the opposite direction, the proper equation is

$$N_1 i_1 - N_2 i_2 = 0 \tag{6.21}$$

or

$$\frac{i_1}{i_2} = \frac{N_2}{N_1} \tag{6.22}$$

Note that if we divide Eq. (6.21) by N_1 and multiply it by v_1 we obtain

$$v_1 i_1 - \frac{N_2}{N_1} v_1 i_2 = 0$$

However, since $v_1 = (N_1/N_2)v_2$, then

$$v_1 i_1 = v_2 i_2$$

and hence the power *into* the device equals the *output* power, which means that an ideal transformer is *lossless.*

Consider now the circuit shown in Figure 6.11. The phasor voltages $\mathbf{V}_1$ and $\mathbf{V}_2$ are related by the expression

$$\frac{\mathbf{V}_1}{\mathbf{V}_2} = \frac{N_1}{N_2}$$

and the phasor currents, from Eq. (6.22), are related by

$$\frac{\mathbf{I}_1}{\mathbf{I}_2} = \frac{N_2}{N_1}$$

These two equations above can be rewritten as

$$\mathbf{V}_1 = \frac{N_1}{N_2} \mathbf{V}_2$$

$$\mathbf{I}_1 = \frac{N_2}{N_1} \mathbf{I}_2$$

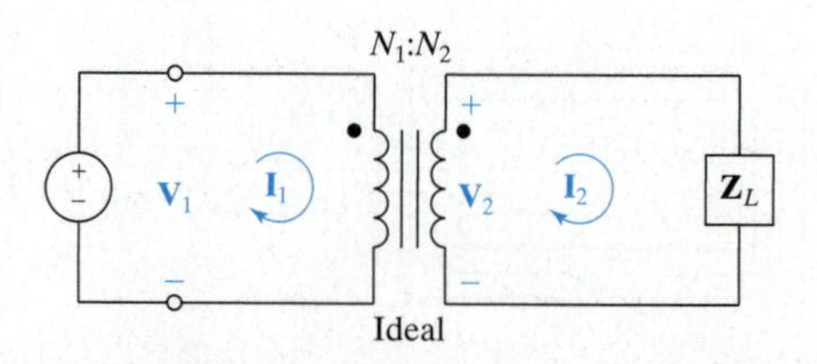

FIGURE 6.11 Ideal transformer circuit used to illustrate input impedance.

Also note that

$$\mathbf{S}_1 = \mathbf{V}_1\mathbf{I}_1^* = \left(\frac{N_1}{N_2}\mathbf{V}_2\right)\left(\frac{N_2}{N_1}\mathbf{I}_2\right)^*$$
$$= \mathbf{V}_2\mathbf{I}_2^* = \mathbf{S}_2$$

From the figure we note that $\mathbf{Z}_L = \mathbf{V}_2/\mathbf{I}_2$, and therefore the input impedance

$$\mathbf{Z}_i = \frac{\mathbf{V}_1}{\mathbf{I}_1} = \left(\frac{N_1}{N_2}\right)^2 \mathbf{Z}_L \tag{6.23}$$

If we now define the turns ratio as

$$n = \frac{N_2}{N_1} \tag{6.24}$$

then the defining equations for the *ideal transformer* are

A summary of the defining equations for the ideal transformer

$$\mathbf{V}_1 = \frac{\mathbf{V}_2}{n}$$
$$\mathbf{I}_1 = n\mathbf{I}_2 \tag{6.25}$$
$$\mathbf{S}_1 = \mathbf{S}_2$$
$$\mathbf{Z}_i = \frac{\mathbf{Z}_L}{n^2}$$

Equations (6.25) define the important relationships for an ideal transformer, where the signs on the voltages and currents are dependent on the assigned references defined in Figure 6.10.

Example 6.3

Given the circuit shown in Figure 6.12, we wish to determine all indicated voltages and currents.

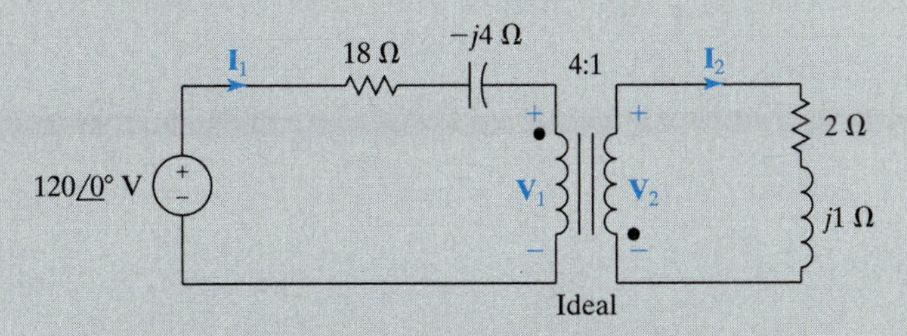

FIGURE 6.12 Ideal transformer circuit.

Because of the relationships between the dots and the currents and voltages, the transformer equations are

$$\mathbf{V}_1 = -\frac{\mathbf{V}_2}{n} \text{ and } \mathbf{I}_1 = -n\mathbf{I}_2$$

where $n = 1/4$. The reflected impedance at the input to the transformer is

$$\mathbf{Z}_i = 16(2 + j1) = 32 + j16\ \Omega$$

Therefore, the current in the source is

$$\mathbf{I}_1 = \frac{120\angle 0^\circ}{18 - j4 + 32 + j16} = 2.23\angle -13.5^\circ\ \text{A}$$

The voltage across the input to the transformer is then

$$\begin{aligned}\mathbf{V}_1 &= \mathbf{I}_1\mathbf{Z}_1 \\ &= (2.33\angle -13.5^\circ)(32 + j16) \\ &= 83.50\angle 13.07^\circ\ \text{V}\end{aligned}$$

Hence, $\mathbf{V}_2$ is

$$\begin{aligned}\mathbf{V}_2 &= -n\mathbf{V}_1 \\ &= -(1/4)(83.50\angle 13.07^\circ) \\ &= 20.88\angle 193.07^\circ\ \text{V}\end{aligned}$$

The current $\mathbf{I}_2$ is

$$\begin{aligned}\mathbf{I}_2 &= -\frac{\mathbf{I}_1}{n} \\ &= -4(2.33\angle -13.5^\circ) \\ &= 9.32\angle 166.50^\circ\ \text{A}\end{aligned}$$

Example 6.4

In the transformer network shown in Figure 6.13, the commercial load is 1 kW at 0.85 pf lagging. We wish to determine the required source voltage $\mathbf{V}_s$.

Using the relationship $P = |\mathbf{V}||\mathbf{I}|\cos\theta$, we can compute the magnitude of $\mathbf{I}_2$ as

$$\begin{aligned}I_2 &= \frac{1000}{(120)(0.85)} \\ &= 9.8\ \text{A}\end{aligned}$$

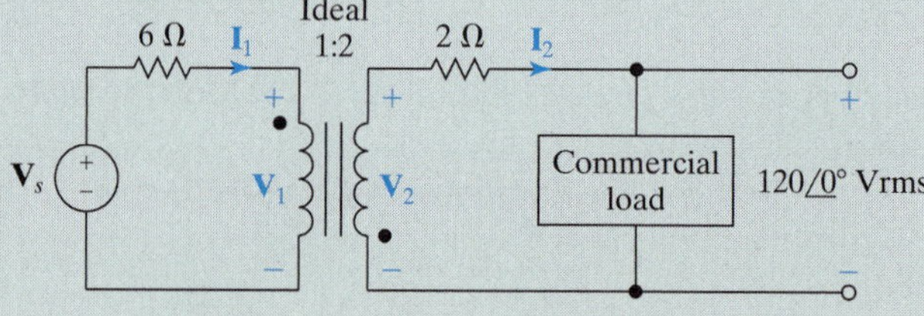

FIGURE 6.13 Ideal transformer feeding a commercial load.

The phase angle is

$$\begin{aligned}\theta &= \cos^{-1} 0.85\\ &= 31.79^\circ\end{aligned}$$

Hence

$$\mathbf{I}_2 = 9.8\underline{/-31.79^\circ}\text{ A}$$

Therefore,

$$\begin{aligned}\mathbf{V}_2 &= 2\mathbf{I}_2 + 120\underline{/0^\circ}\\ &= 19.6\underline{/-31.79^\circ} + 120\,\underline{/0^\circ}\\ &= 137.05\underline{/-4.32^\circ}\text{ V}\end{aligned}$$

Given the transformer ratio $n = 2$ and the dot locations, we obtain

$$\mathbf{V}_1 = \frac{-\mathbf{V}_2}{n} = -68.52\underline{/-4.32^\circ}\text{ V}$$

and

$$\mathbf{I}_1 = -n\mathbf{I}_2 = -19.6\underline{/-31.79^\circ}\text{ A}$$

then

$$\begin{aligned}\mathbf{V}_s &= 6\mathbf{I}_1 + \mathbf{V}_1\\ &= 6(-19.6\underline{/31.79^\circ}) + (-68.52\underline{/-4.32^\circ})\\ &= 181.18\underline{/158.26^\circ}\text{ V}\end{aligned}$$

Drill Exercises

D6.3. Compute the current $\mathbf{I}_1$ in the network in Figure D6.3.

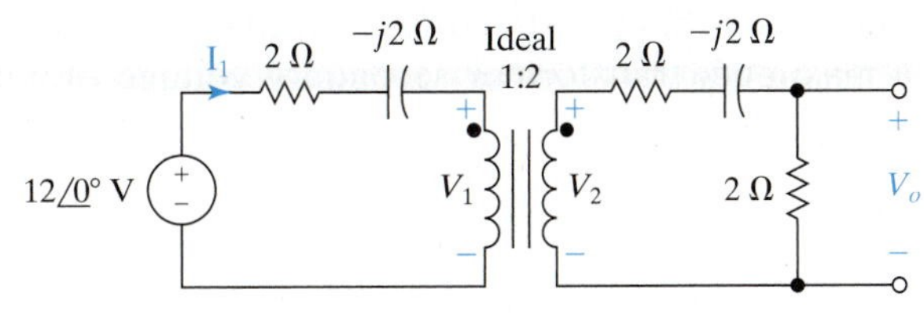

FIGURE D6.3

Ans: $\mathbf{I}_1 = 3.07\underline{/39.81^\circ}$ A.

D6.4. Find $\mathbf{V}_0$ in the network in Figure D6.3

Ans: $\mathbf{V}_0 = 3.07\underline{/39.82^\circ}$ V.

6-6 Transformer Applications

As we have noted, transformers can be used in applications that require the conversion of transient or ac voltage from one level to another. Practical transformers have "ratings," that is, values at which they are designed to operate. Typically, ratings are interpreted as upper limits of operation, although this is not true in general, since sometimes it is potentially harmful to operate the device below its ratings. The two basic ratings of transformers involve rms voltage and apparent power, that is, the voltage level(s) at which the transformer was designed to operate, and the power it was designed to process. A very common engineering problem is to determine appropriate transformer ratings for a specific application.

There are two broad categories of use: "electronic" transformers, which operate at the microwatt, milliwatt, or watt level, and "power" transformers, which process kilowatts or megawatts. We discuss two common applications of electronic and power transformers here.

Electronic Transformers. Consumer electronic equipment includes radios, television sets, VCRs, compact disk players, personal computers, and dozens of other devices. These devices contain electronic circuits designed for many functions such as amplification, signal processing, encoding, and decoding. All such circuits require a source of electrical energy to properly operate, typically in the dc form. If the power requirements are very small, that is, in the micro or milliwatt range, batteries may serve this function. However at larger power levels, the appropriate batteries may be too large, heavy, and/or expensive; in addition, batteries need to be replaced periodically.

Another option is to connect the device to the residential ac 120 V system. There are two obvious problems: first, most electronic circuits operate at a much lower voltage level and second, the required source is typically dc. A circuit designed to accept 120 V ac as input and convert power to different voltage levels is called an electronic "power supply," and will be introduced in more detail in Chapter 10. The transformer frequently is used to solve the voltage conversion problem.

Consider the circuit in Figure 6.14. Suppose that electronic loads require 5 volts dc and a maximum of 17.3 watts to operate properly. The filter capacitor will smooth the voltage to the peak secondary value, and the zener diode (diodes are discussed in Chapter 10) will "regulate," or clamp, the voltage to 5 volts, as long as the capacitor voltage is ≥ 5 V (with the zener disconnected). It is good design to provide a little more than 5 volts to accommodate low ac input voltage, the internal transformer voltage drop, and the forward voltage drop in the rectifier diodes. Suppose the total forward voltage drop, is estimated at 2.0 V. This would produce a maximum transformer secondary voltage of $5.0 + 2.0 = 7.0$ volts for a 120 V ac rms

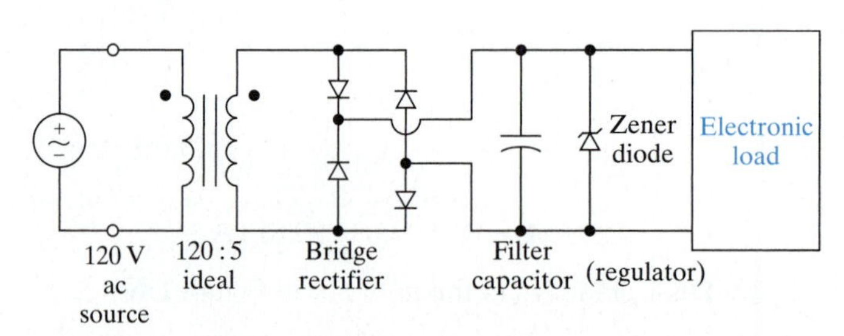

FIGURE 6.14 A typical electronic power supply employing a transformer.

transformer primary input voltage. Thus, V_2 rms $= 7.00/\sqrt{2} = 4.950$ V. An appropriate transformer rating would be 120 V; 5 V; 20 VA.

Consider the engineering issues even in this simple situation. If we undersize the transformer, it will get too hot, damaging itself and nearby components. If we oversize it, it will be too big, too heavy, and too expensive. If we are confused about conversion between rms and maximum values we will produce the wrong output voltage, possibly destroying the zener diode and damaging the circuits it supplies. Finally, we had to consider that the transformer was approximately a power-invariant device. In a practical design we would need more precise data about low voltage operation and transformer series voltage drop.

Power Transformers. Bulk electrical power is optimally generated at "medium" ac voltage levels of from about 7 to 25 kV; whereas it is transmitted from generation to load points at "high" ac voltage levels, ranging from 115 to 800 kV. Thus, it is required to convert large amounts of power from medium voltage to high voltage at high efficiency. The power transformer is admirably suited for this purpose. Power at this level is always processed in the balanced polyphase form. Typically, but not always, the transformer itself is a three-phase device; for our purposes we will use three single-phase transformers.

Example 6.5

The specific application we will consider in this example is connecting a 17 kV, 800 MVA, 0.866 power factor (PF) lagging, three-phase generator into a 500 kV transmission system. Our job is to determine appropriate ratings and compute the currents everywhere. See Figure 6.15. Note that we have elected to use a delta–wye transformer connection. We shall model the transformers as ideal.

Operating at rated conditions, the magnitudes of the generator voltages are:

$$V_{AB} = V_{BC} = V_{CA} = 17 \text{ kV}$$

See the phasor diagram for phase angles for all quantities. The generator currents are

$$I_A = I_B = I_C = \frac{800 \times 10^6}{\sqrt{3} \times 17 \text{ k}} = 27.17 \text{ kA}$$

Also

$$I_{AB} = I_{BC} = I_{CA} = 27.17 \text{ k}/\sqrt{3} = 15.69 \text{ kA}$$

It is desired to make

$$V_{ab} = V_{bc} = V_{ca} = 500 \text{ kV}$$

Therefore,

$$V_{an} = V_{bn} = V_{cn} = 500/\sqrt{3} = 288.7 \text{ kV}$$

The high-side currents will be

$$I_A = I_B = I_C = 800 \times 10^6/(\sqrt{3} \cdot 500 \text{ k}) = 923.8 \text{ A}$$

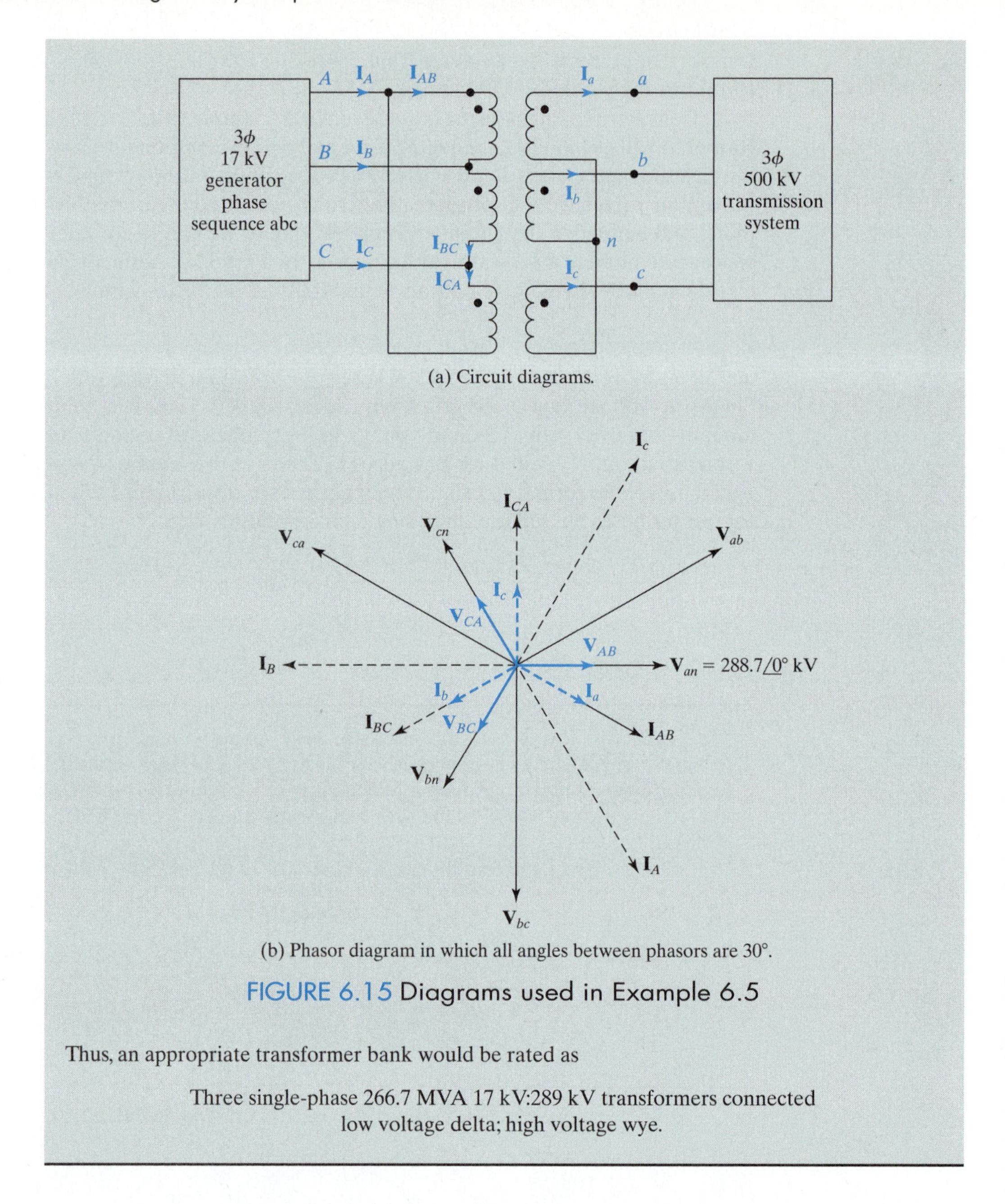

(a) Circuit diagrams.

(b) Phasor diagram in which all angles between phasors are 30°.

FIGURE 6.15 Diagrams used in Example 6.5

Thus, an appropriate transformer bank would be rated as

Three single-phase 266.7 MVA 17 kV:289 kV transformers connected
low voltage delta; high voltage wye.

The foregoing examples should give the reader an appreciation for the dozens of applications of transformers in electrical systems. Advantages of transformers include simplicity, high efficiency, and electrical isolation between primary and secondary. Disadvantages include bulk, weight, and fairly high cost. Advances in power electronics have enabled electronic circuits to replace transformers in some cases; however, the transformer remains an important component in many practical situations, particularly for high-power applications.

Summary

- Magnetic circuits form the basis for transformers, generators, and motors.
- Magnetic fields are produced by magnets or current passing through a conductor.
- The analogies between electric and magnetic circuits are illustrated in Figure 6.16, where

$$V = IR \qquad \text{and} \qquad \mathcal{F} = \phi\mathcal{R}$$

V = voltage in volts	$\mathcal{F}$ = mmf in amp-turns
I = current in amps	ϕ = flux in webers
R = resistance in volts/amps	$\mathcal{R}$ = reluctance in amp-turns/wb

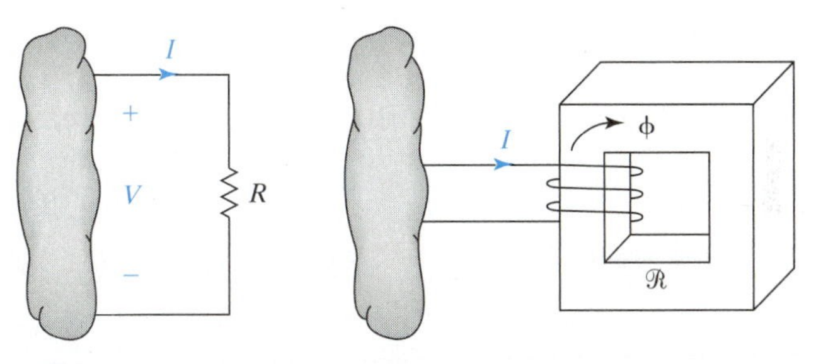

FIGURE 6.16 Analogous electric and magnetic circuits.

- The defining equations for the coupled coils shown in Figure 6.17 are

$$\mathbf{V}_1 = j\omega L_1 \mathbf{I}_1 + j\omega M \mathbf{I}_2$$
$$\mathbf{V}_2 = j\omega L_2 \mathbf{I}_2 + j\omega M \mathbf{I}_1$$

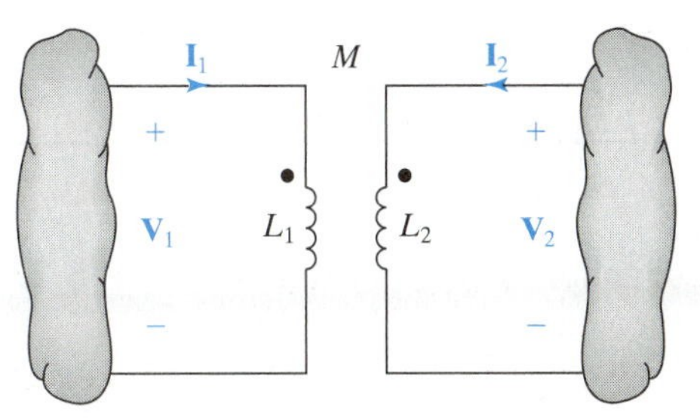

FIGURE 6.17 A pair of mutually coupled coils.

If any voltage or current in this network changes direction, the sign on the corresponding term must change in the equations.

If a dot location is reversed, for example, moved from top to bottom in the network, then the sign on the voltage and current on this specific coil must be changed.

- The coefficient of coupling between two coils is defined as $k = \dfrac{M}{\sqrt{L_1 L_2}}$ and the range of k is $0 \leq k \leq 1$.

- The circuit symbol for an ideal transformer is shown in Figure 6.18.

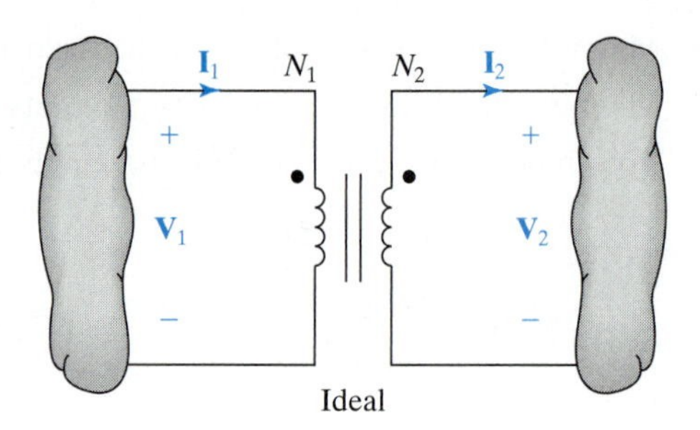

FIGURE 6.18 Ideal transformer representation.

The equations that relate voltages and currents on each side of the transformer are

$$\frac{V_1}{V_2} = \frac{N_1}{N_2}$$

$$\frac{I_1}{I_2} = \frac{N_2}{N_1}$$

Ideal transformers are lossless devices and thus $S_1 = S_2$.

- Transformers are widely used in electronic systems and electric power apparatus.

Problems

6.1. Write the circuit equations necessary to find $\mathbf{I}_2$ in the network shown in Figure P6.1.

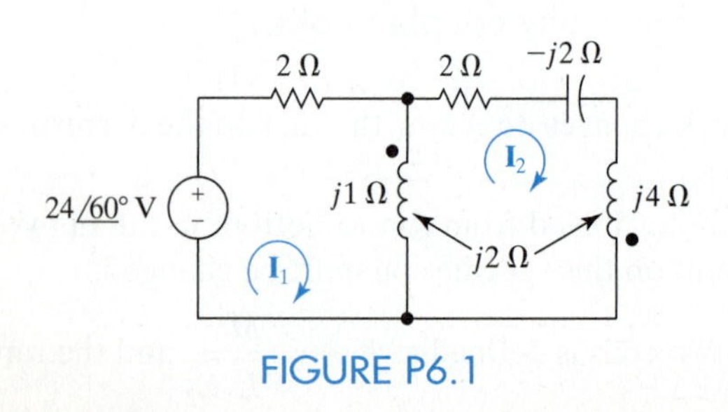

FIGURE P6.1

6.2. Write the circuit equations necessary to find $\mathbf{I}_1$ and $\mathbf{I}_2$ in the circuit in Figure P6.2.

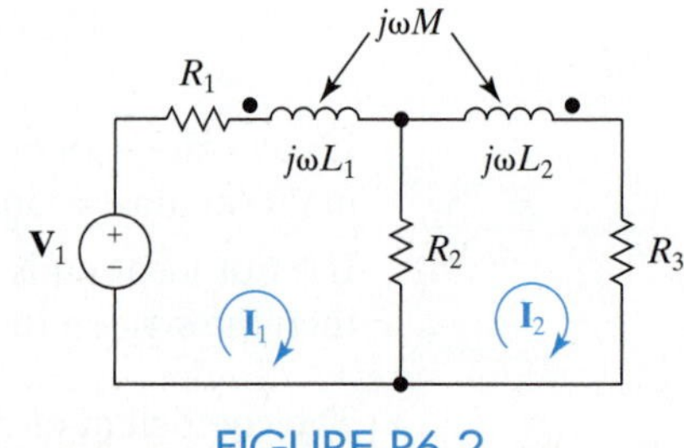

FIGURE P6.2

6.3. Write the circuit equations necessary to determine the loop currents $\mathbf{I}_1$ and $\mathbf{I}_2$ in the network in Figure P6.3.

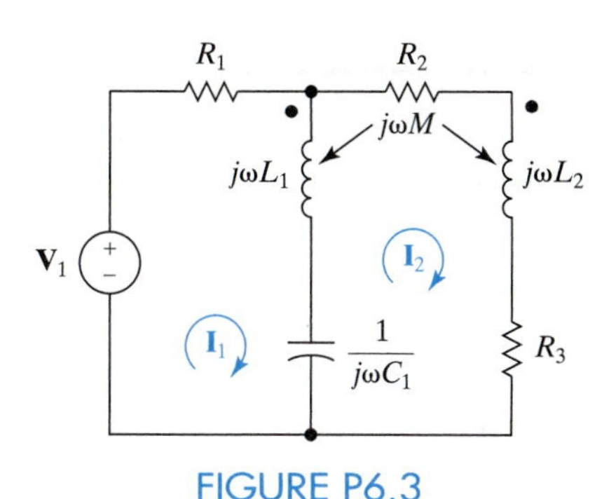

FIGURE P6.3

6.4. Find the current $\mathbf{I}_1$ in the circuit in Figure P6.4.

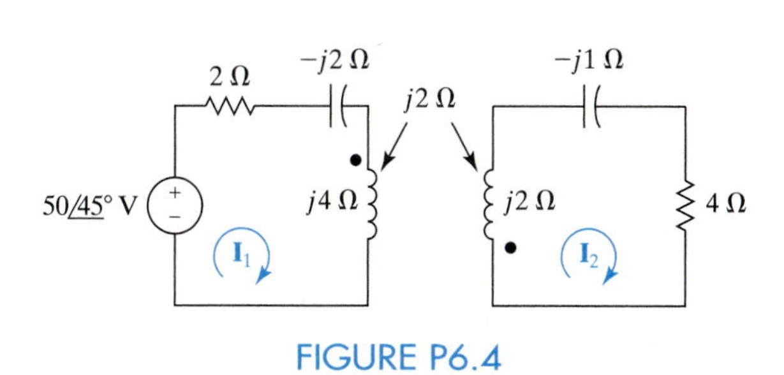

FIGURE P6.4

6.5. Find the current $\mathbf{I}_2$ in the network shown in Figure P6.5.

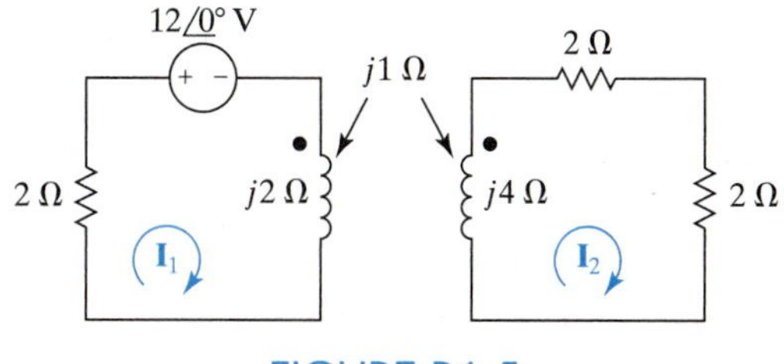

FIGURE P6.5

6.6. Determine the two loop currents shown in the network in Figure P6.6.

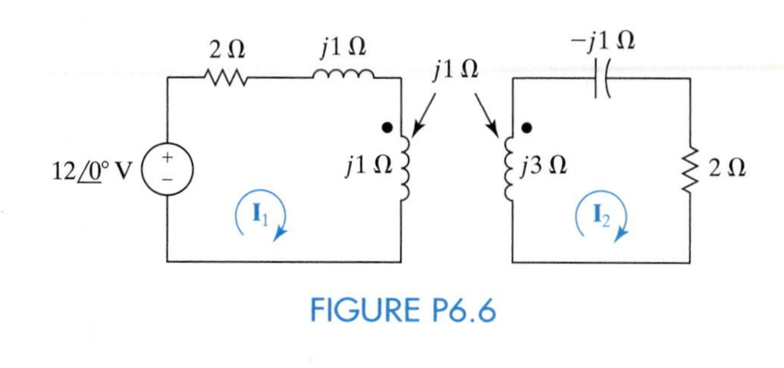

FIGURE P6.6

6.7. Find $\mathbf{I}_2$ in the circuit shown in Figure P6.7.

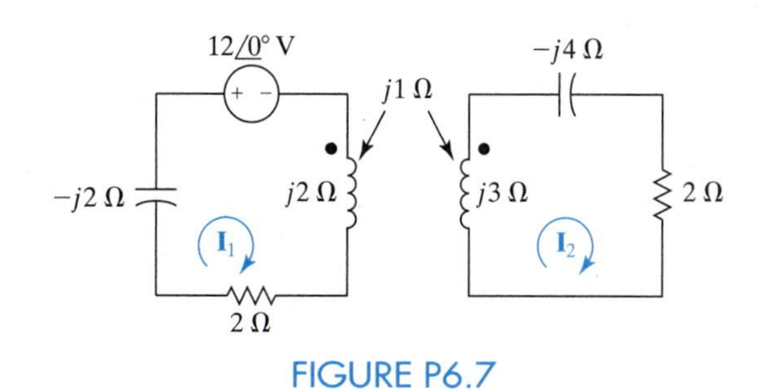

FIGURE P6.7

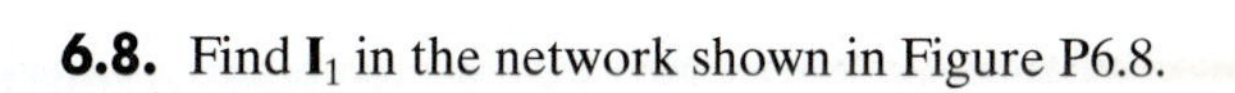

6.8. Find $\mathbf{I}_1$ in the network shown in Figure P6.8.

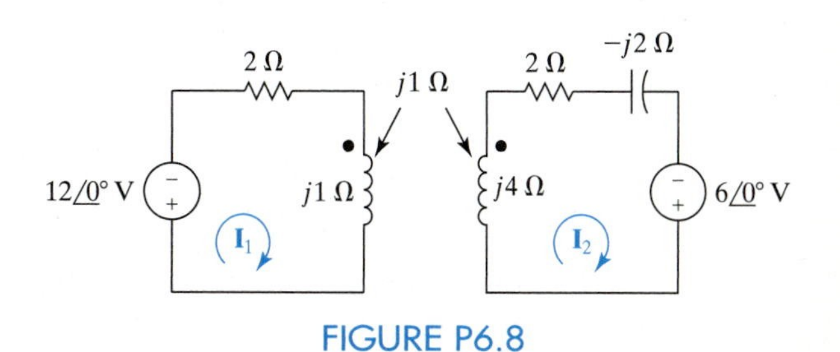

FIGURE P6.8

6.9. Find $\mathbf{V}_0$ in the circuit shown in Figure P6.9.

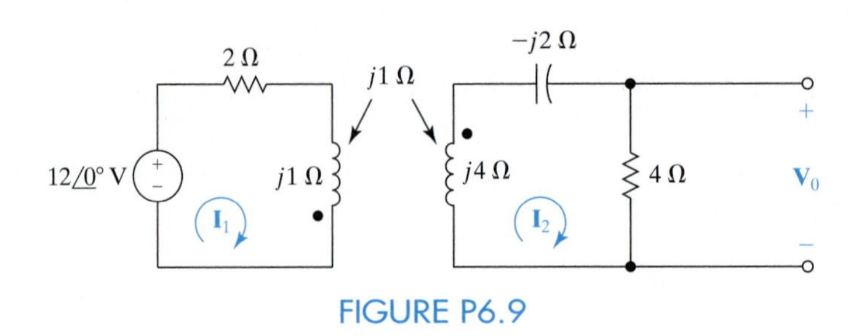

FIGURE P6.9

6.10. Find $\mathbf{V}_X$ in the circuit shown in Figure P6.10.

6.11. Find $\mathbf{V}_X$ in the network shown in Figure P6.11.

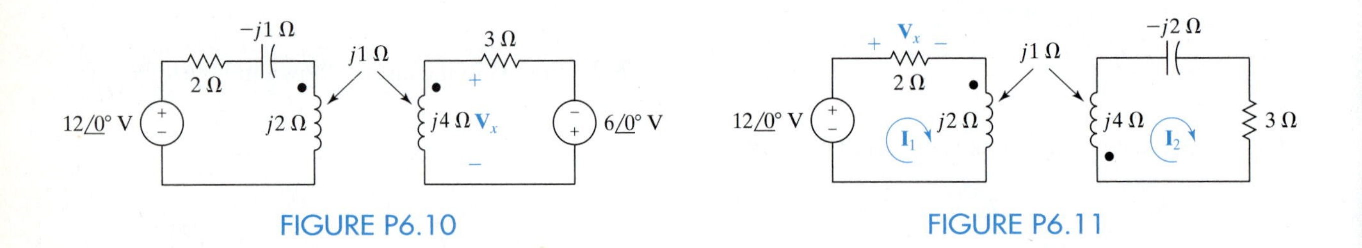

FIGURE P6.10

FIGURE P6.11

6.12. Find $\mathbf{I}_A$ in the network in Figure P6.12.

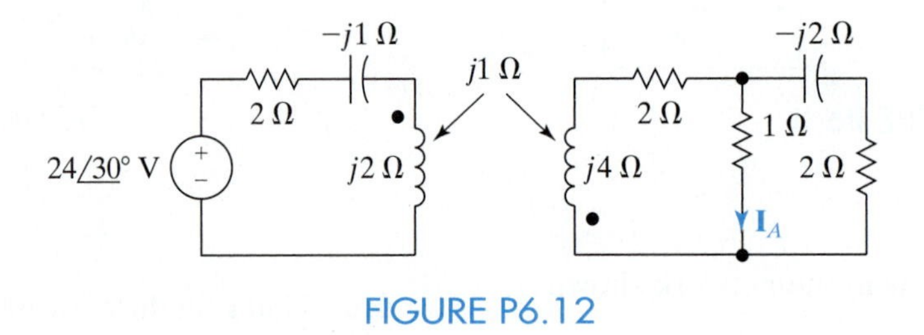

FIGURE P6.12

6.13. Find $\mathbf{V}_A$ in the network shown in Figure P6.13.

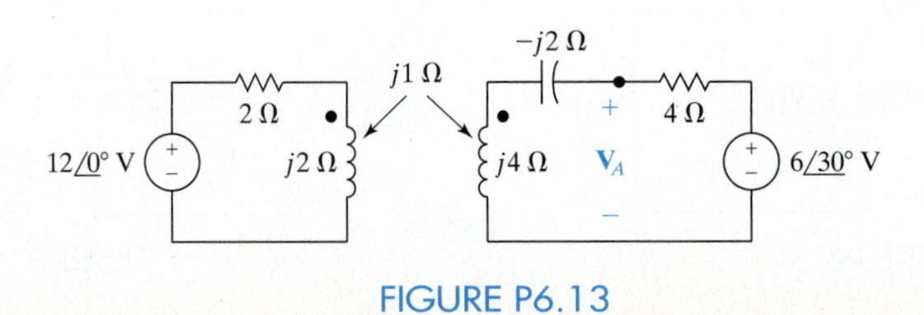

FIGURE P6.13

6.14. Find $\mathbf{V}_0$ in the circuit shown in Figure P6.14.

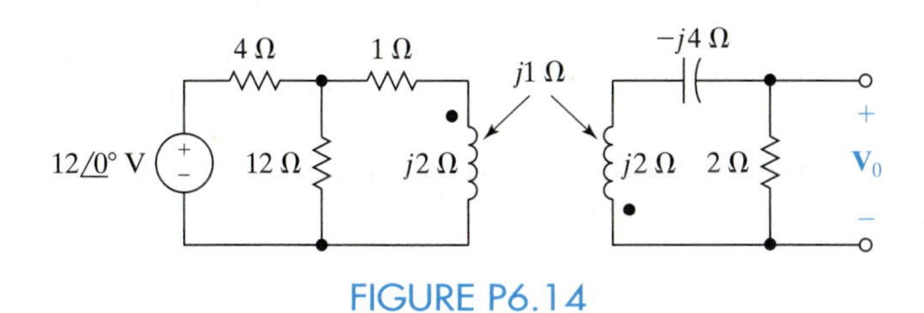

FIGURE P6.14

6.15. Find $\mathbf{I}_2$ in the network shown in Figure P6.15.

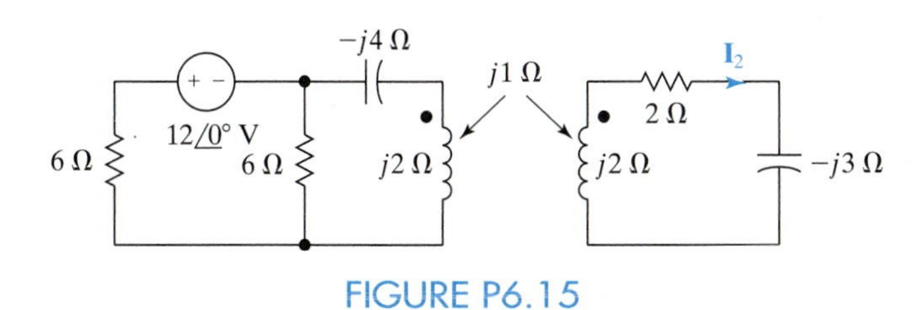

FIGURE P6.15

6.16. Find the voltage gain $\mathbf{V}_0/\mathbf{V}_S$ of the network shown in Figure P6.16.

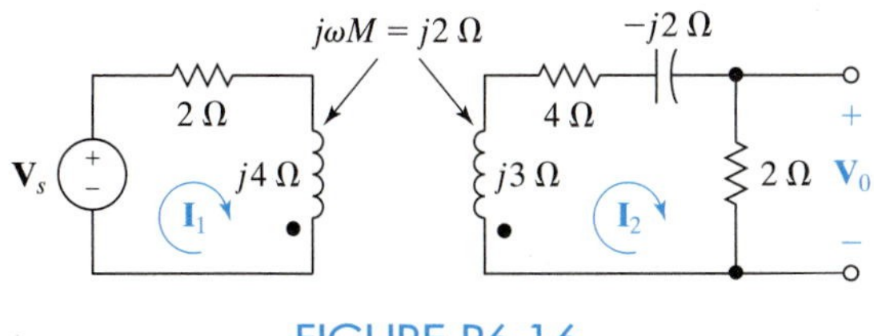

FIGURE P6.16

6.17. Find the voltage gain $\mathbf{V}_0/\mathbf{V}_S$ for the network shown in Figure P6.17.

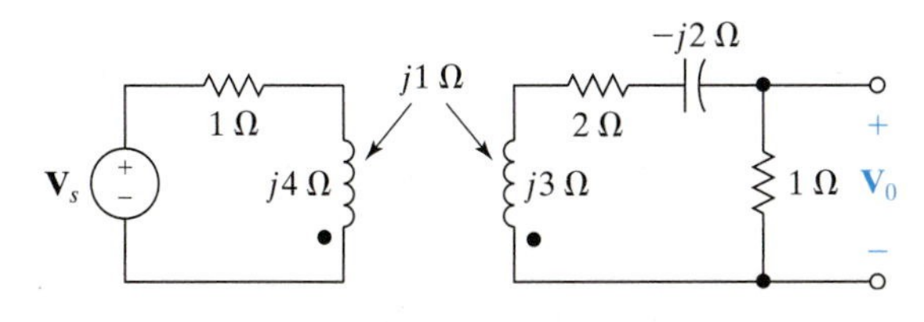

FIGURE P6.17

6.18. Determine the voltage gain $\mathbf{V}_0/\mathbf{V}_1$ of the network shown in Figure P6.18.

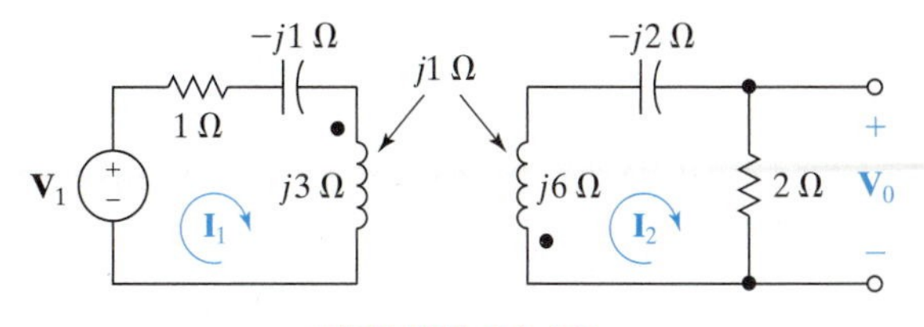

FIGURE P6.18

6.19. Determine the impedance seen by the source $\mathbf{V}_1$ in the circuit shown in Figure P6.19.

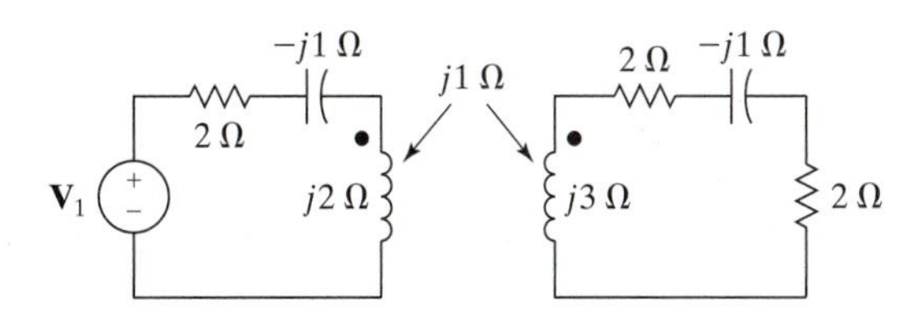

FIGURE P6.19

6.20. Determine the impedance seen by the source $\mathbf{V}_1$ in the network shown in Figure P6.20.

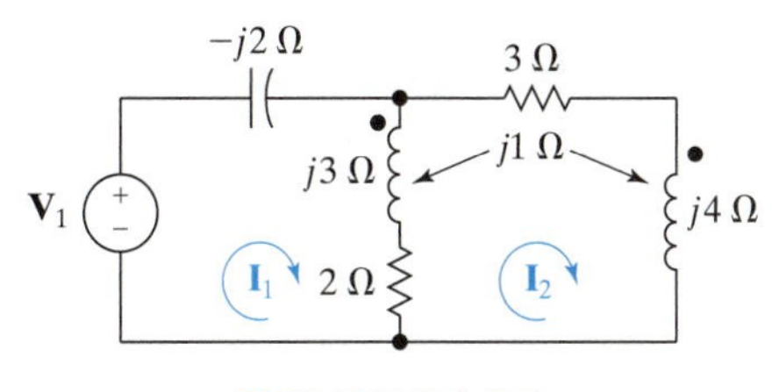

FIGURE P6.20

6.21. Given the network shown in Figure P6.21, determine the value of the capacitor C that will cause the reflected impedance to the primary to be purely resistive.

12 Ω $\quad j\omega M = j2\ \Omega \quad \dfrac{1}{j\omega C}$

4 Ω $\quad$ 10 Ω

24/0° V, $f = 60$ Hz $\quad j10\ \Omega \quad j10\ \Omega \quad j6\ \Omega$

FIGURE P6.21

6.22. Analyze the network in Figure P6.22 and determine if a value of X_C can be found such that the output voltage is equal to twice the input voltage.

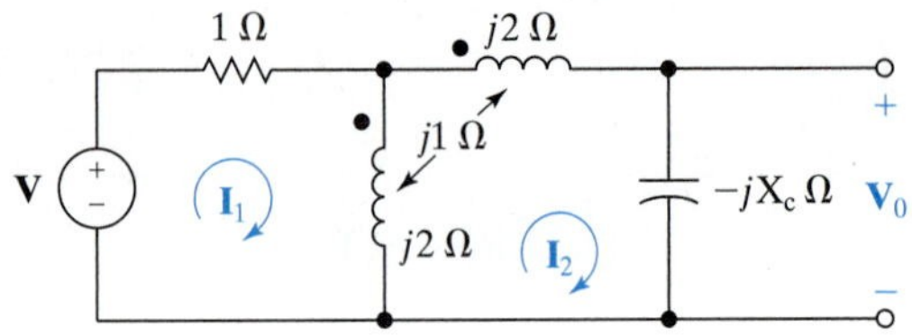

FIGURE P6.22

6.23. Find $\mathbf{I}_1$ and $\mathbf{I}_2$ in the circuit shown in Figure P6.23.

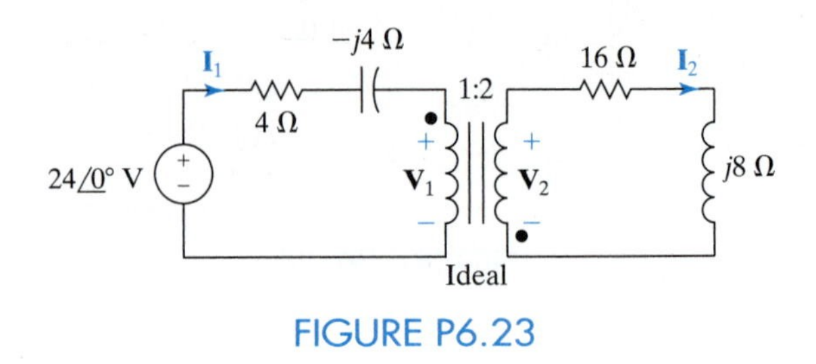

FIGURE P6.23

6.24. Find all voltages and currents in the circuit shown in Figure P6.24

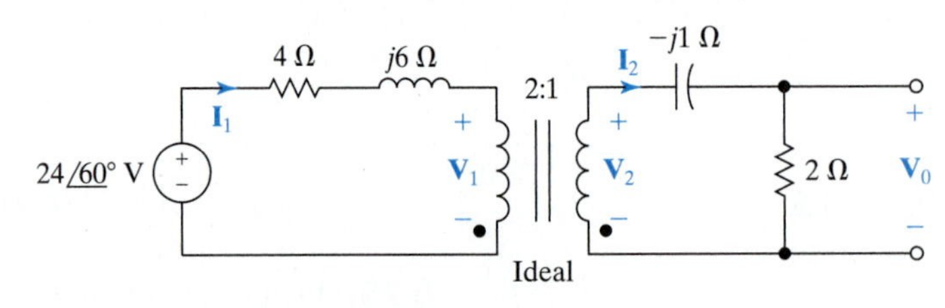

FIGURE P6.24

6.25. Find $\mathbf{V}_0$ in the network in Figure P6.25.

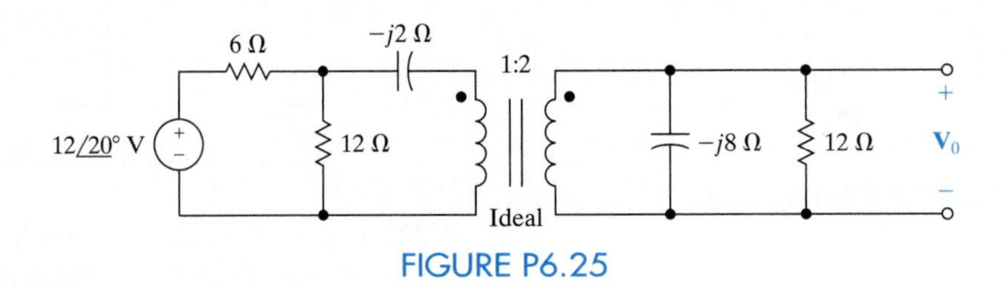

FIGURE P6.25

6.26. Find $\mathbf{V}_0$ in the circuit shown in Figure P6.26.

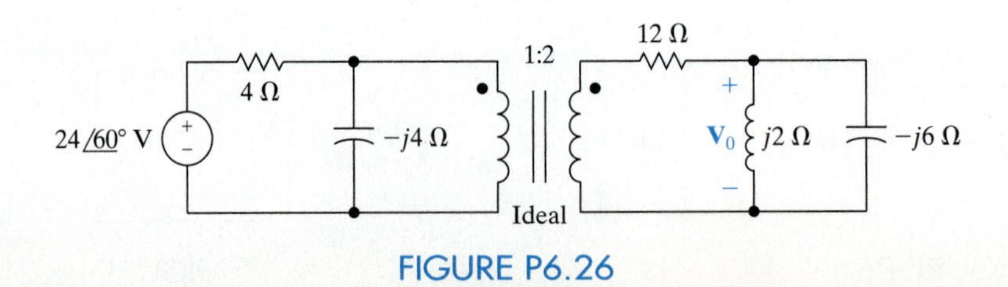

FIGURE P6.26

6.27. In the network in Figure P6.27 the voltage $\mathbf{V}_0 = 10\underline{/0°}$ V. Find the input voltage $\mathbf{V}_S$.

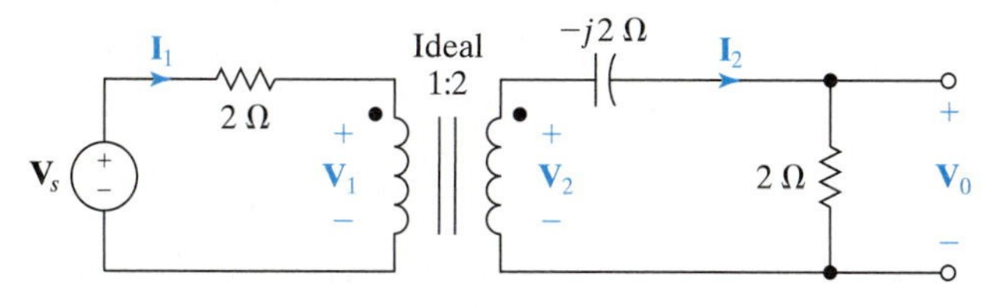

FIGURE P6.27

6.28. In the network in Figure P6.28 $\mathbf{I}_2 = 4\underline{/0°}$ A. Find $\mathbf{V}_S$.

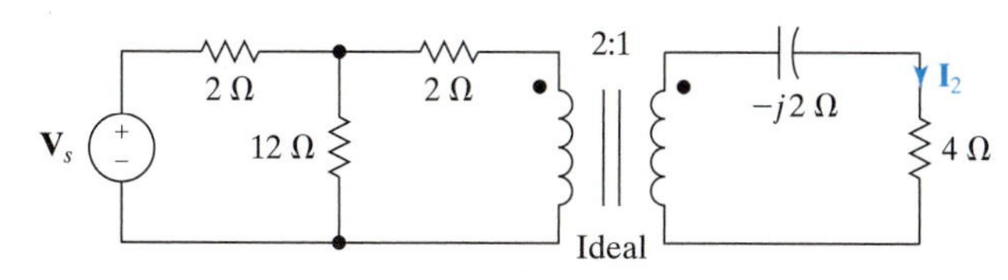

FIGURE P6.28

6.29. In the circuit in Figure P6.29 $\mathbf{V}_0$ is known to be $12\underline{/0°}$ V. Find $\mathbf{I}_S$.

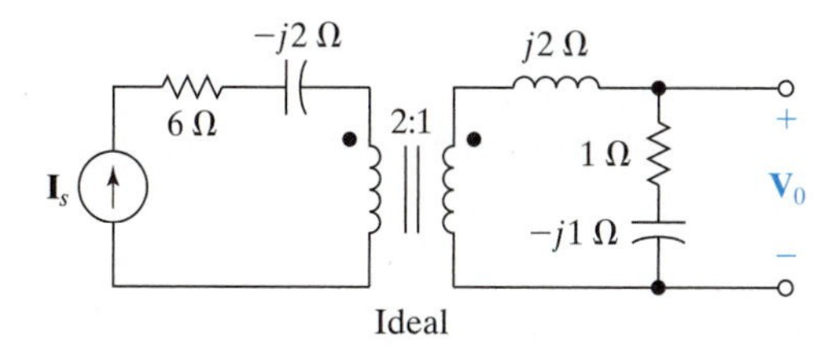

FIGURE P6.29

6.30. In the network in Figure P6.30 it is known that $\mathbf{V}_0 = 4\underline{/30°}$ V. Find $\mathbf{I}_S$.

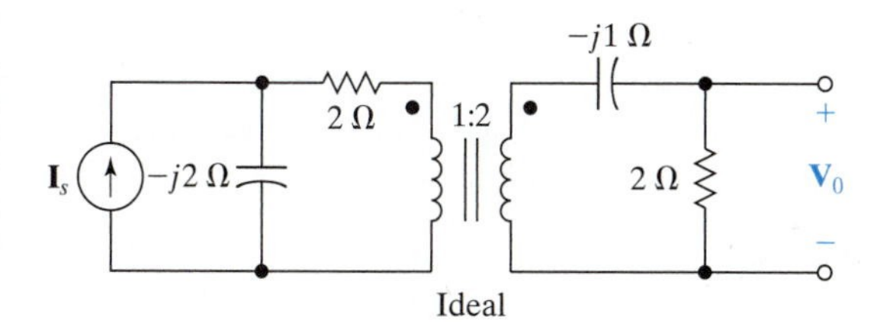

FIGURE P6.30

6.31. The output stage of an amplifier is to be matched to the impedance of a speaker as shown Figure P6.31. If the impedance of the speaker is 8 Ωand the amplifier requires a load impedance of 3.2 kΩ, determine the turns ratio of the ideal transformer.

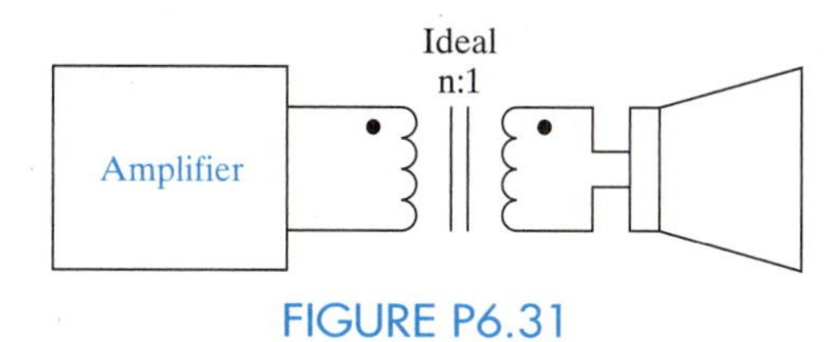

FIGURE P6.31

6.32. If the load voltage in the network shown in Figure P6.32 is $100\underline{/0°}$ V rms, determine the input voltage $\mathbf{V}_S$.

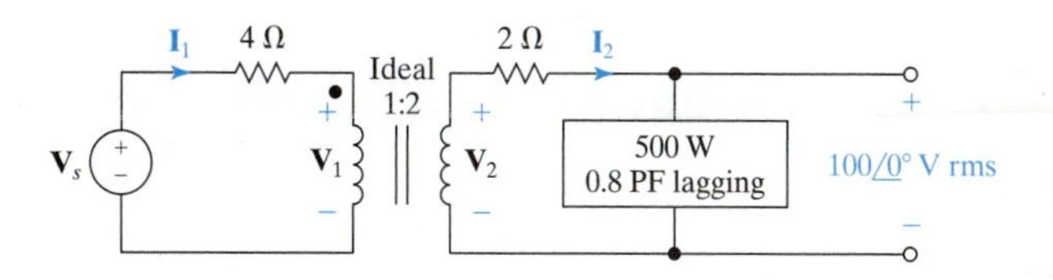

FIGURE P6.32

6.33. In the network shown in Figure P6.33, if $\mathbf{V}_L = 120\underline{/0°}$ V rms and the load Z_L absorbs 500 W at 0.85 PF lagging, compute the voltage $\mathbf{V}_S$.

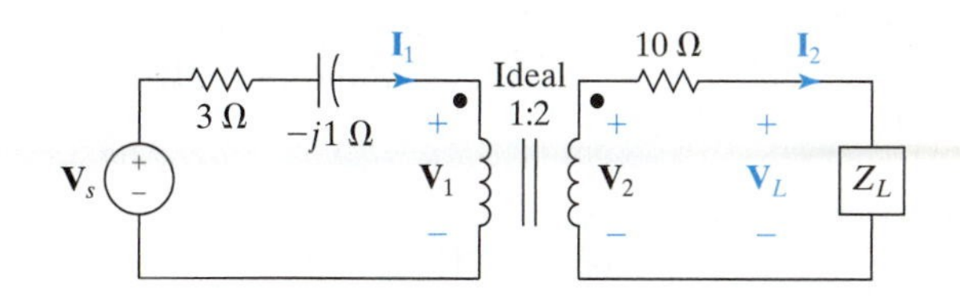

FIGURE P6.33

7-1 Introduction

In this chapter we examine the frequency characteristics of electrical networks. Of particular interest to us will be the effect of the source frequency on a network. Techniques for determining the frequency response of a network are presented, and standard plots that display the network's performance as a function of frequency are discussed.

The concept of resonance is examined. The various parameters used to define the frequency selectivity of a network, such as bandwidth, cutoff frequency, and quality factor, are discussed.

Networks with special filtering properties are examined. Specifically, low-pass, high-pass, band-pass, and band-elimination filters are discussed.

Networks that exhibit particular filtering characteristics have wide application in numerous types of communication and control systems where it is necessary to pass certain frequencies and reject others.

7-2 Sinusoidal Frequency Analysis

Many dynamic systems display phenomena that are frequency dependent. An example is a tuning fork; regardless of how the fork is pulsed, it will vibrate at only one frequency. In addition, electrical networks are designed to operate at a single frequency, for example, the power grid that includes the ac outlets in our homes and offices. However, as a general rule, circuits will respond differently to sinusoidal signals of different frequency. Recall from Example 4.5 that the network characteristics were quite different at the frequency used in aircraft power systems than at the U.S. power grid frequency. In this section we add a new dimension to our analysis of electric circuits by examining the performance of a network as a function of frequency. We are typically interested in the *sinusoidal frequency response,* or what we simply call the *frequency response,* of a circuit. The frequency response defines the behavior of the network as a function of frequency. Consider the following example, which demonstrates that networks respond differently at different frequencies.

Definition of frequency response

Example 7.1

Let us determine the transfer function, that is, the ratio of output voltage to input voltage, for the circuit in Figure 7.1(a), and sketch the magnitude and phase of this function over the frequency range 0 to 8 rad/sec.

Using voltage division, the output voltage can be expressed as

$$\mathbf{V}_0 = \left(\frac{R}{j\omega L + \dfrac{1}{j\omega C} + R} \right) \mathbf{V}_1$$

Network Frequency Characteristics

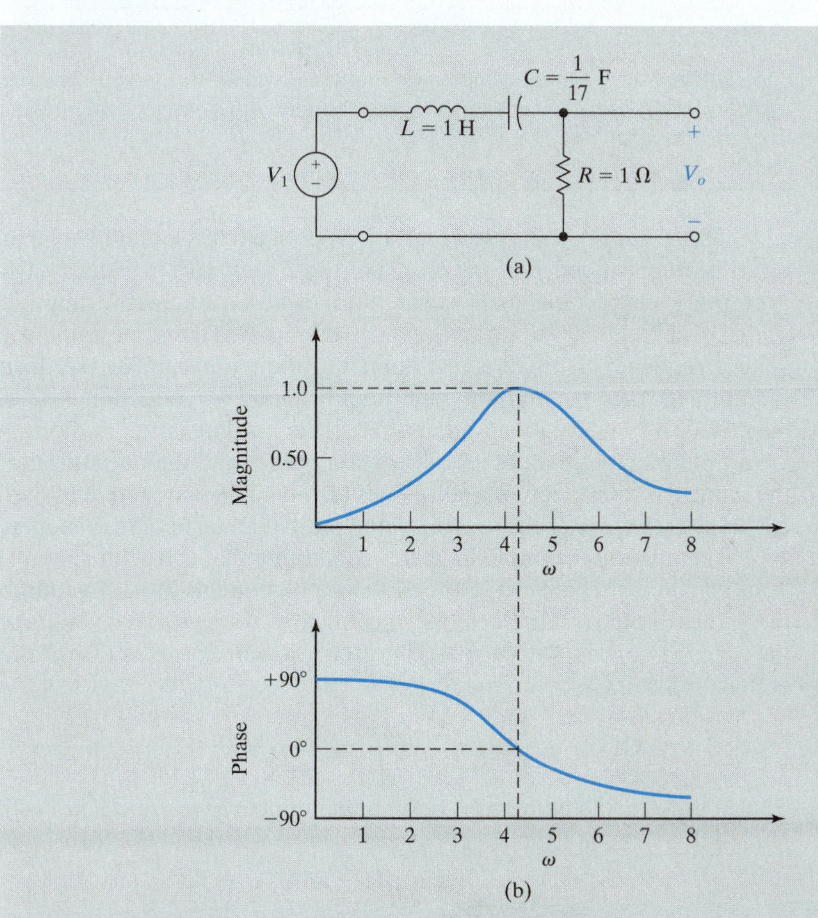

FIGURE 7.1 Circuit and graphs used in Example 7.1.

and therefore the transfer function is

$$\frac{\mathbf{V}_0}{\mathbf{V}_1}(j\omega) = \frac{j\omega \frac{R}{L}}{(j\omega)^2 + j\omega \frac{R}{L} + \frac{1}{LC}}$$

which with the parameter values is

$$\frac{\mathbf{V}_0}{\mathbf{V}_1}(j\omega) = \frac{2j\omega}{(j\omega)^2 + 2j\omega + 17}$$

If we now evaluate this function at $\omega = 0, 1, 2, \ldots 8$, we obtain the following values of the magnitude and phase as a function of frequency.

ω	0	1	2	3	4	$\sqrt{17}$	5	6	7	8
Magnitude	0	0.12	0.29	0.60	0.99	1.0	0.78	0.53	0.40	0.32
Phase	90°	83°	73°	53°	7°	0°	−39°	−58°	−66°	−71°

A sketch of the magnitude and phase characteristics for the network transfer function is shown in Figure 7.1(b). Thus, the network response is quite different depending upon the frequency of the input voltage source.

The frequency response of certain types of circuits is extremely important, and enormous effort is often expended in the design of these networks in order to achieve certain frequency response characteristics. For example, in a stereo system the amplifiers are often designed so that each frequency in the audio range is amplified the same amount, that is, the magnitude-versus-frequency characteristic is flat in the audio range. If each frequency in the audio range is amplified the same amount, high-fidelity sound reproduction is achieved. However, if the magnitude-versus-frequency characteristic is not flat in the audio range, some frequencies are amplified more than others, distortion occurs, and the output is not an exact duplicate of the input. An "equalizer" is a component in an audio system that allows the user to adjust the frequency response of the system to the individual taste of the listener.

General form of a transfer function

The previous example indicates something that is true in general, that is, transfer functions can be expressed as the ratio of two polynomials in $j\omega$. In addition, we note that since the values of our circuit elements, or controlled sources, are real numbers, the coefficients of the two polynomials will be real. Therefore, we will express a transfer function, which in general we will call $\mathbf{G}(j\omega)$, in the form

$$\mathbf{G}(j\omega) = \frac{N(j\omega)}{D(j\omega)} = \frac{a_m(j\omega)^m + a_{m-1}(j\omega)^{m-1} + \cdots + a_1 j\omega + a_0}{b_n(j\omega)^n + b_{n-1}(j\omega)^{n-1} + \cdots + b_1 j\omega + b_0} \tag{7.1}$$

where $N(j\omega)$ is the numerator polynomial of degree m and $D(j\omega)$ is the denominator polynomial of degree n. Equation (7.1) can also be written in the form

$$\mathbf{G}(j\omega) = \frac{K_0(j\omega - z_1)(j\omega - z_2)\ldots(j\omega - z_m)}{(j\omega - p_1)(j\omega - p_2)\ldots(j\omega - p_n)} \tag{7.2}$$

Poles and zeros defined

where K_0 is a constant, $z_1 \ldots z_m$ are the roots of $N(j\omega)$, and $p_1, \ldots p_n$ are the roots of $D(j\omega)$. Note that if $j\omega = z_1$ or $z_2 \ldots z_m$, then $\mathbf{G}(j\omega)$ becomes zero and hence $z_1 \ldots z_m$ are called *zeros* of the function. Similarly, if $j\omega = p_1$ or $p_2 \ldots p_n$, then $\mathbf{G}(j\omega)$ becomes infinite and therefore $p_1 \ldots p_n$ are called *poles* of the function. The zeros or poles may actually be complex. However, if they are complex, they must occur in conjugate pairs since the coefficients of the polynomial are real. The importance of this form (Eq. 7.2) stems from the fact that the dynamic properties of a system can be gleaned from an examination of the system poles. For example, recall that the transient performance of circuits with a second-order characteristic equation could be overdamped, underdamped, or critically damped depending upon the values of the circuit's poles.

Drill Exercise

D7.1. Determine the transfer function $\frac{\mathbf{V}_0}{\mathbf{V}_1}(j\omega)$ for the circuit in Figure D7.1 and locate the poles and zeros of the function.

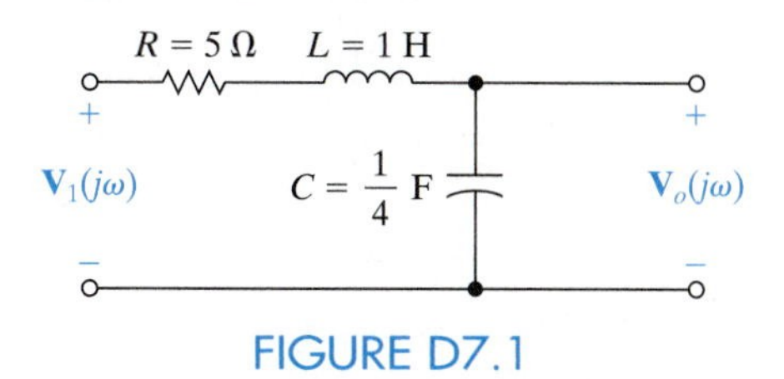

FIGURE D7.1

Ans: $\frac{\mathbf{V}_0}{\mathbf{V}_1}(j\omega) = \frac{4}{(j\omega)^2 + 5j\omega + 4}$, there are no zeros and the pole locations are $j\omega = -1$ and $j\omega = -4$.

7-3 Passive Filter Networks

Standard passive filter networks

A filter network is generally designed to pass signals with a specific frequency range and reject or attenuate signals whose frequency spectrum is outside this passband. The most common filters are *low-pass filters,* which pass low frequencies and reject high frequencies; *high-pass filters,* which pass high frequencies and block low frequencies; *band-pass filters,* which pass some particular band of frequencies and reject all frequencies outside the range; and *band-rejection filters,* which are specifically designed to reject a particular band of frequencies and pass all other frequencies.

The ideal frequency characteristic for a low-pass filter is shown in Figure 7.2(a). Also shown is a typical or physically realizable characteristic. Ideally, we would like the low-pass filter to pass all frequencies up to some frequency ω_0 and pass no frequency above that value; however, it is not possible to design such a filter with linear circuit elements. Hence, we must be content to employ filters that we can actually build in the laboratory, and these filters have frequency characteristics that are simply not ideal.

A simple low-pass filter network is shown in Figure 7.2(b). The voltage gain for the network is

$$\frac{\mathbf{V}_0}{\mathbf{V}_1}(j\omega) = \frac{\dfrac{1}{j\omega C}}{R + \dfrac{1}{j\omega C}}$$

This transfer function can be expressed as $\mathbf{G}_v(j\omega)$ in the form

$$\mathbf{G}_v(j\omega) = \frac{1}{1 + j\omega RC} \tag{7.3}$$

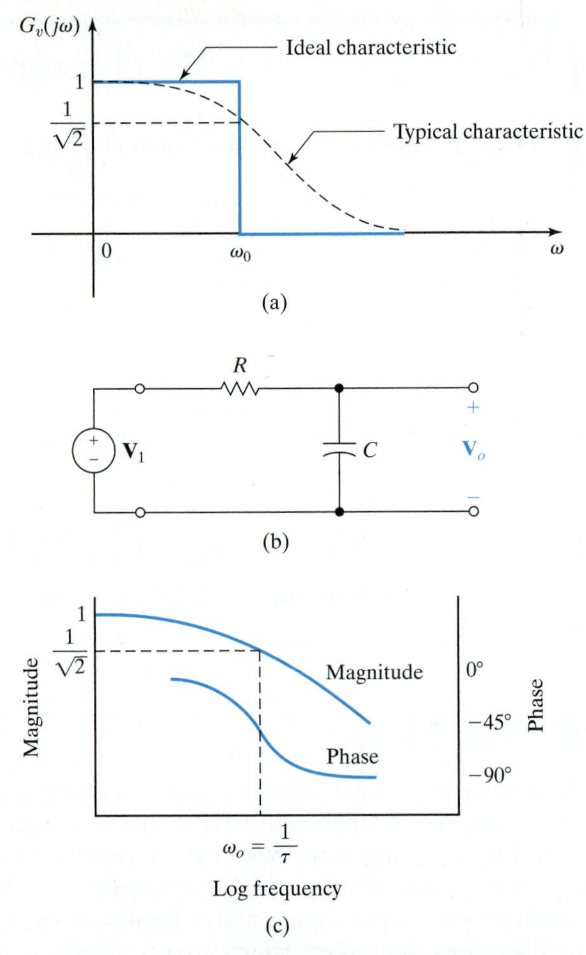

FIGURE 7.2 Low-pass filter circuit and its frequency characteristics.

which can be written as

$$\mathbf{G}_v(j\omega) = \frac{1}{1 + j\omega\tau} \tag{7.4}$$

where $\tau = RC$, the *time constant.*

In general, in a sinusoidal steady-state analysis the transfer function can be expressed as

$$\mathbf{G}(j\omega) = M(\omega)e^{j\phi(\omega)}$$

where $M(\omega) = |\mathbf{G}(j\omega)|$ is the magnitude function and $\phi(\omega)$ is the phase. For the low-pass filter, the magnitude function is

$$\mathbf{M}(\omega) = \frac{1}{[1 + (\omega\tau)^2]^{1/2}} \tag{7.5}$$

and the phase characteristic is

$$\phi(\omega) = -\tan^{-1} \omega\tau \tag{7.6}$$

Half-power (break) frequency defined

The magnitude and phase curves for this simple low-pass circuit are shown in Figure 7.2(c). Note that the magnitude curve is flat for low frequencies and rolls off at high frequencies. The phase shifts from 0° at low frequencies to −90° at high frequencies. Note that at the frequency $\omega = 1/\tau$, which we call the *break frequency,* the amplitude is

$$\mathbf{M}(\omega = 1/\tau) = \frac{1}{\sqrt{2}} \tag{7.7}$$

The break frequency is also commonly called the *half-power frequency.* This name is derived from the fact that if the voltage or current is $1/\sqrt{2}$ of its maximum value, then the power, which is proportional to the square of the voltage or current, is one-half its maximum value. The phase angle at the break frequency is −45°.

The ideal frequency characteristic for a high-pass filter is shown in Figure 7.3(a) together with a typical characteristic that we could achieve with linear circuit components. Ideally, the high-pass filter passes all frequencies above some frequency ω_0 and no frequencies below that value.

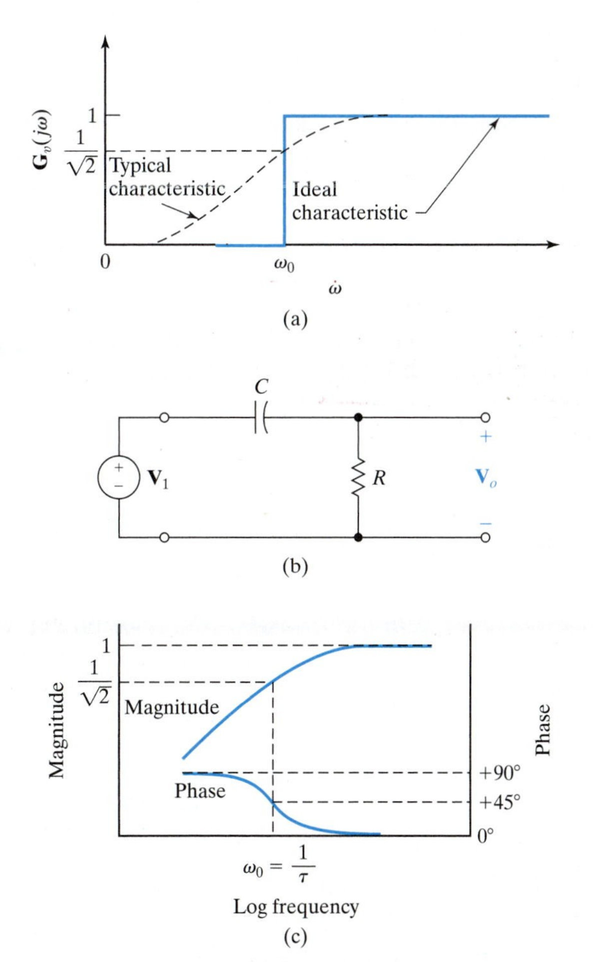

FIGURE 7.3 High-pass filter circuit and its frequency characteristics.

A simple high-pass filter network is shown in Figure 7.3(b). This is a network similar to that shown in Figure 7.2(b) with the output voltage taken across the resistor. The voltage gain for this network is

$$\mathbf{G}_v(j\omega) = \frac{j\omega\tau}{1 + j\omega\tau} \tag{7.8}$$

where once again $\tau = RC$. The magnitude of this function is

$$M(\omega) = \frac{\omega\tau}{[1 + (\omega\tau)^2]^{1/2}} \tag{7.9}$$

and the phase is

$$\phi(\omega) = \frac{\pi}{2} - \tan^{-1}\omega\tau \tag{7.10}$$

The half-power frequency is $\omega = 1/\tau$, and the phase at this frequency is 45°.

The magnitude and phase curves for this high-pass filter are shown in Figure 7.3(c). At low frequencies the magnitude curve has a positive slope due to the term $\omega\tau$ in the numerator of Eq. (7.9). Then at the break frequency the curve begins to flatten out. The phase curve is derived from Eq. (7.10).

Note that since we know the basic form of the low-pass and high-pass filters shown in Figures 7.2 and 7.3, we can select parameters to *design* a filter with certain characteristics.

Example 7.2

A source generates a low-frequency signal that contains noise. It appears that the noise could be eliminated with a simple low-pass filter with a half-power frequency of 1 kHz. If a 1.6 μF capacitor is available, select a resistor that, when used with the capacitor in the network in Figure 7.2, will eliminate the noise.

At the half-power frequency, $\omega\tau = 1$. Therefore,

$$\omega RC = 1$$

or

$$R = \frac{1}{2\pi(10)^3(1.6)(10)^{-6}}$$

$$\cong 100\ \Omega$$

Drill Exercise

D7.2. Design a simple *RC* high-pass filter with a break frequency of 20 kHz. Use a resistor value of 1 kΩ.

Ans: $C = 8\ nF$.

Ideal and typical amplitude characteristics for simple band-pass and band-rejection filters are shown in Figures 7.4(a) and (b), respectively. Simple networks that are capable of realizing the band-pass and band-rejection filters are shown in Figures 7.4(c) and (d), respectively. ω_0 is the *center frequency* of the pass or rejection band and the frequency at which the maximum or minimum amplitude occurs. ω_{LO} and ω_{HI} are the *lower* and *upper break frequencies* or *cutoff frequencies,* where the amplitude is $1/\sqrt{2}$ of the maximum value. The width of the pass or rejection band is called the *bandwidth,* and hence

Filter bandwidth defined

$$BW = \omega_{HI} - \omega_{LO} \tag{7.11}$$

To illustrate these points, let us consider the band-pass filter in Figure 7.4(c). Note carefully that this is the same network examined in Example 7.1. The voltage transfer function is

$$\mathbf{G}_v(j\omega) = \frac{R}{R + j(\omega L - 1/\omega C)}$$

and therefore the amplitude characteristic is

$$M(\omega) = \frac{RC\omega}{\sqrt{(RC\omega)^2 + (\omega^2 LC - 1)^2}} \tag{7.12}$$

It is tedious but straightforward to show that the center frequency obtained from the expression

$$\frac{dM(\omega)}{d\omega} = 0$$

yields

$$\omega_0 = \frac{1}{\sqrt{LC}}$$

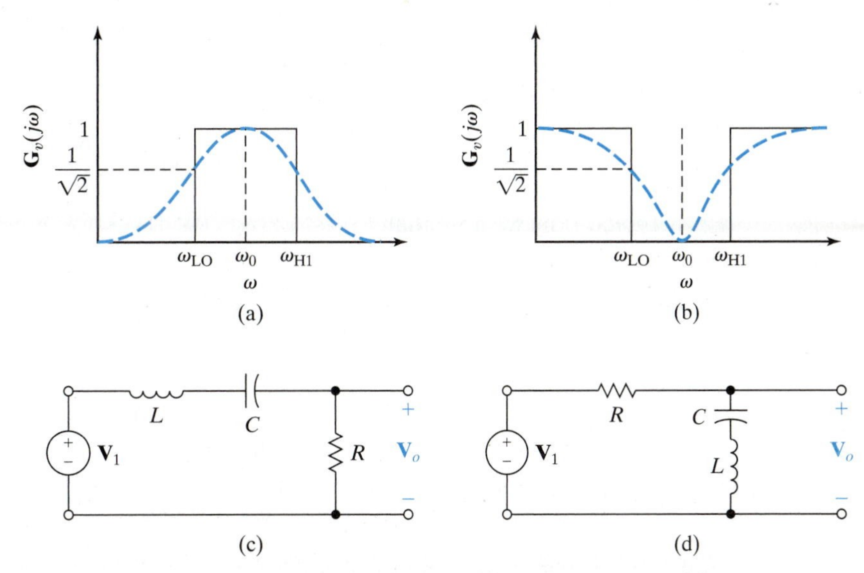

FIGURE 7.4 Band-pass and band-rejection filters and characteristics.

At the upper and lower cutoff frequencies, the magnitude characteristic is

$$M(\omega) = \frac{1}{\sqrt{2}} \tag{7.13}$$

Substituting this value into Eq. (7.12) and simplifying the resulting expression yields the equation

$$\omega^2 LC - 1 = \pm RC\omega \tag{7.14}$$

At the lower cutoff frequency

$$\omega^2 LC - 1 = -RC\omega \tag{7.15}$$

and using the fact that $\omega_0 = 1/\sqrt{LC}$, Eq. (7.15) can be expressed in the form

$$\omega^2 + \frac{R}{L}\omega - \omega_0^2 = 0 \tag{7.16}$$

Solving this expression for ω_{LO}, we obtain

$$\omega_{LO} = \frac{-(R/L) + \sqrt{(R/L)^2 + 4\omega_0^2}}{2}$$

At the upper cutoff frequency

$$\omega^2 LC - 1 = +RC\omega$$

or

$$\omega^2 - \frac{R}{L}\omega - \omega_0^2 = 0$$

Solving this expression for ω_{HI}, we obtain

$$\omega_{HI} = \frac{+(R/L) + \sqrt{(R/L)^2 + 4\omega_0^2}}{2}$$

Therefore, the bandwidth of the filter is

$$BW = \omega_{HI} - \omega_{LO} = \frac{R}{L} \tag{7.17}$$

In addition, we note that

$$\omega_{LO}\omega_{HI} = \frac{-R^2}{4L^2} + \frac{(R/L)^2 + \dfrac{4}{LC}}{4}$$

$$= \frac{1}{LC} \tag{7.18}$$

$$= \omega_0^2$$

which illustrates that *the center frequency is the geometric mean of the two half-power frequencies.*

Example 7.3

Consider the band-pass filter network shown in Figure 7.5. Let us determine the filter's center frequency, half-power frequencies, and bandwidth.

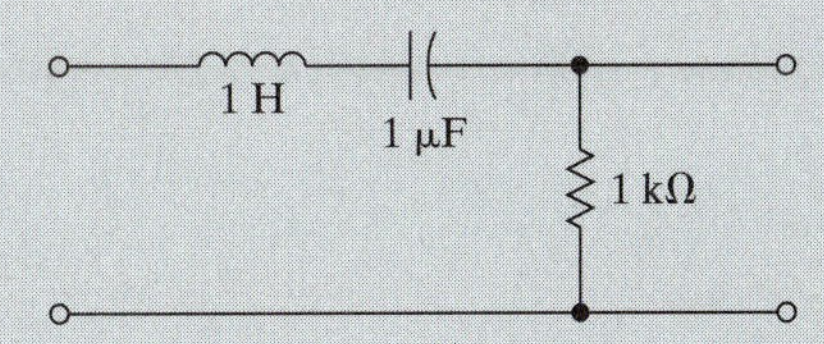

FIGURE 7.5 A band-pass filter network.

The center frequency is

$$\omega_0 = \frac{1}{\sqrt{LC}} = \frac{1}{\sqrt{(1)(10)^{-6}}}$$
$$= 1 \text{ k rad/s}$$

The half-power frequencies are

$$\omega_{LO} = \frac{-\left(\frac{R}{L}\right) + \sqrt{\left(\frac{R}{L}\right)^2 + 4\omega_0^2}}{2}$$
$$= \frac{-1000 + \sqrt{10^6 + 4(10)^6}}{2}$$
$$= \frac{-1000 + 10^3\sqrt{5}}{2}$$
$$= 618 \text{ rad/s}$$

and

$$\omega_{HI} = \frac{1000 + 10^3\sqrt{5}}{2}$$
$$= 1618 \text{ rad/s}$$

The bandwidth, obtained from either Eq. (7.17) or (7.18), is $BW = 1000$ rad/s.

Example 7.4

The internal communication system on a small plane is "picking up" interference from the power cables. The frequency for the aircraft power system is 400Hz. If the speaker system is modeled as a 4 kΩ resistor, design a band-rejection filter to be placed at the input of the speaker system to eliminate this 400Hz frequency component.

The model for the network is shown in Figure 7.6. The voltage transfer function for this circuit is

$$\mathbf{G}(j\omega) = \frac{\mathbf{V}_o(j\omega)}{\mathbf{V}_i(j\omega)} = \frac{R}{R + j\omega L // \dfrac{1}{j\omega C}}$$

$$= \frac{R}{R + \dfrac{L/C}{j\omega L + \dfrac{1}{j\omega C}}}$$

$$= \frac{R}{R - \dfrac{j\omega L}{\omega^2 LC - 1}}$$

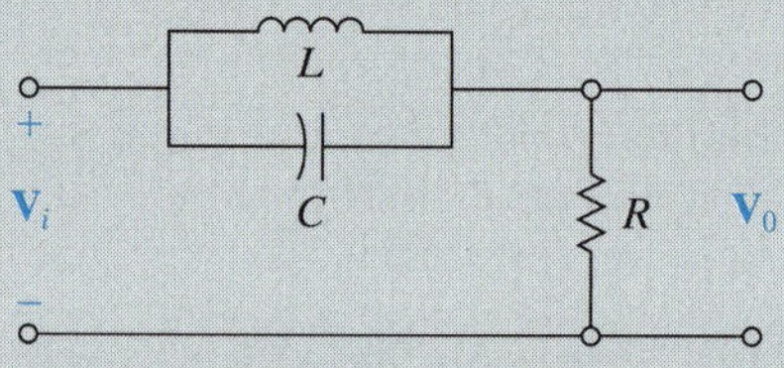

FIGURE 7.6 Band-rejection filter and input to speaker system modeled as R = 4 kΩ.

This transfer function indicates that if $\omega = \dfrac{1}{\sqrt{LC}}$, $\mathbf{G}(j\omega) = 0$, that is, the gain of the band-rejection filter, or what is typically called a "notch" filter, is zero. Thus, if we arbitrarily select $C = 200\ \mu\text{F}$, then for a frequency of 400Hz

$$L = \frac{1}{\omega^2 C}$$

$$= \frac{1}{[(2\pi)(400)]^2(200)(10^{-6})}$$

$$= 791.6\ \mu\text{H}$$

Substituting all the component values into the transfer function yields

$$\mathbf{G}(f) = \frac{4000}{4000 - j\dfrac{(4.974 \times 10^{-3})f}{(6.25)(10^{-6})f^2 - 1}}$$

A magnitude plot of this function is shown in Figure 7.7.

Note that the notch occurs at exactly 400Hz, and thus this frequency is completely eliminated in the speaker system.

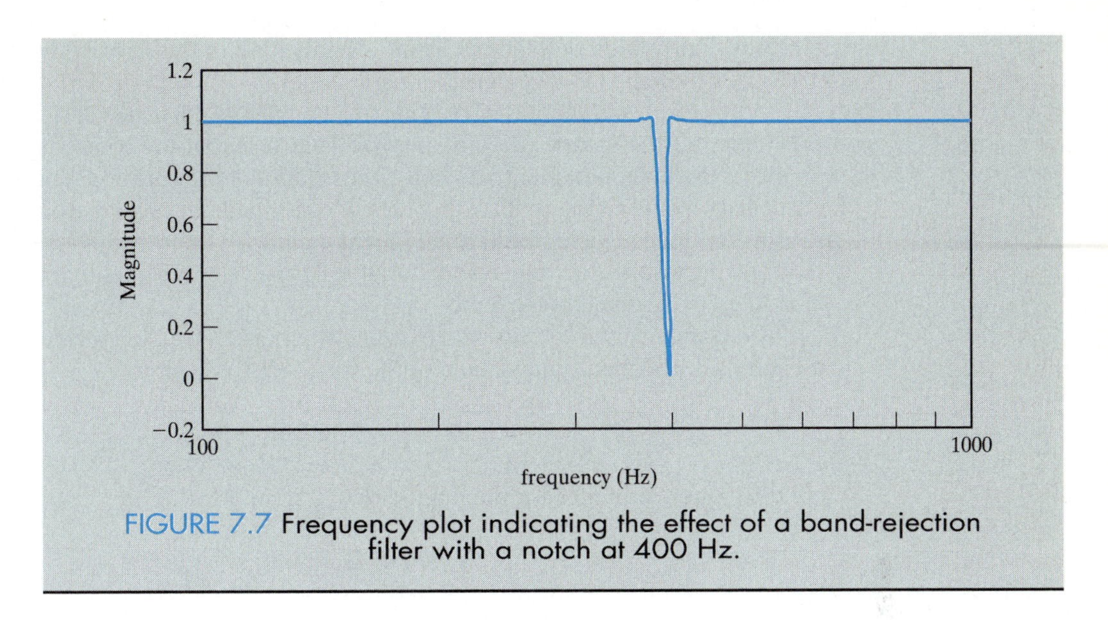

FIGURE 7.7 Frequency plot indicating the effect of a band-rejection filter with a notch at 400 Hz.

Drill Exercise

D7.3. Determine the half-power frequency for each of the filters in Figure D7.3 and identify the type of filter.

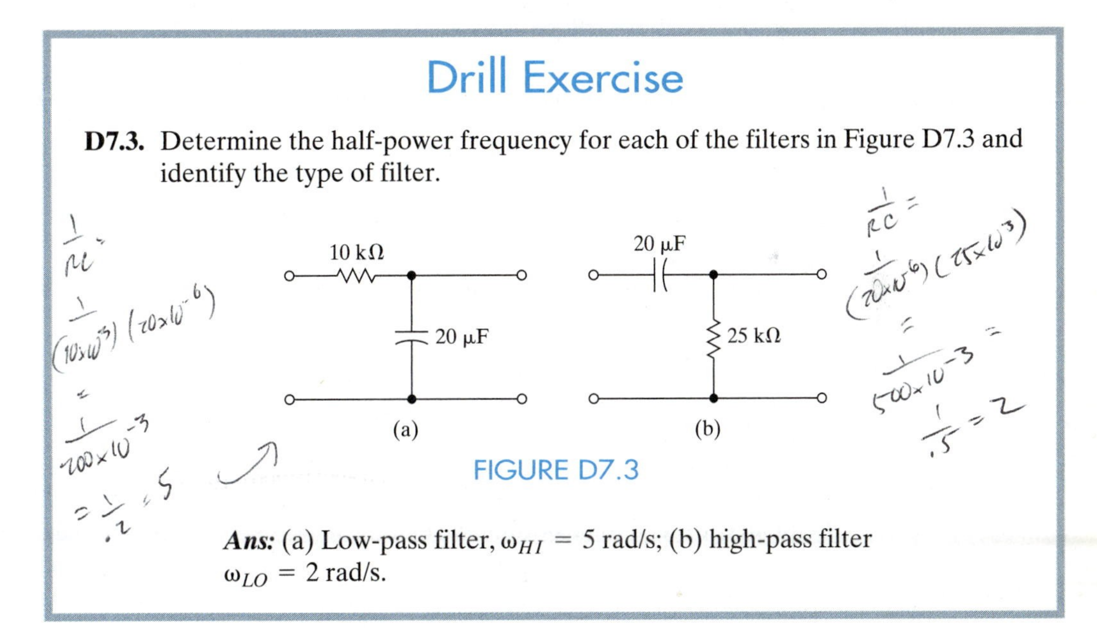

FIGURE D7.3

Ans: (a) Low-pass filter, $\omega_{HI} = 5$ rad/s; (b) high-pass filter $\omega_{LO} = 2$ rad/s.

7–4 Resonant Circuits

Resonance is a fascinating phenomenon that exists in a wide variety of engineering systems. For example, consider an old automobile with weak shock absorbers such that the suspension system can be approximated by a second-order underdamped system. If we press down on the front end of the car, we find that it is difficult to do so. However, if we push the front end down in a repetitive mode with the proper rhythm, that is, at the proper frequency, we find that the front end of the automobile will begin to oscillate and we will not have to use as much force to achieve fairly wide deflections. What is happening in this case is that we are forcing the mechanical system at its resonant frequency.

As another example, it is interesting to note that the engineers designing the attitude control system for the Saturn moon rocket had to ensure that the control system frequency did not excite the body-bending (resonant) frequencies of the rocket. Excitation of the bending frequencies would cause oscillation, which, if continued unchecked, would result in a buildup of stress until the vehicle would finally break apart.

Having briefly mentioned some practical aspects of resonance, let us now examine the phenomenon in some basic circuits.

Two fundamental circuits with extremely important frequency characteristics are shown in Figure 7.8. The input impedance for the series RLC circuit is

$$\mathbf{Z}(j\omega) = R + j\omega L + \frac{1}{j\omega C} \tag{7.19}$$

and the input admittance for the parallel RLC circuit is

$$\mathbf{Y}(j\omega) = G + j\omega C + \frac{1}{j\omega L} \tag{7.20}$$

Note that these two equations have the same general form. The imaginary terms in both of the equations above will be zero if

$$\omega L = \frac{1}{\omega C}$$

The value of ω that satisfies this equation is

$$\omega_0 = \frac{1}{\sqrt{LC}} \tag{7.21}$$

and at this value of ω the impedance of the series circuit becomes

$$\mathbf{Z}(j\omega_0) = \mathrm{R} \tag{7.22}$$

and the admittance of the parallel circuit is

$$\mathbf{Y}(j\omega_0) = G \tag{7.23}$$

This frequency ω_0, at which the impedance of the series circuit or the admittance of the parallel circuit is purely real, is called the *resonant frequency,* and the circuits themselves, at this frequency, are said to be *in resonance.*

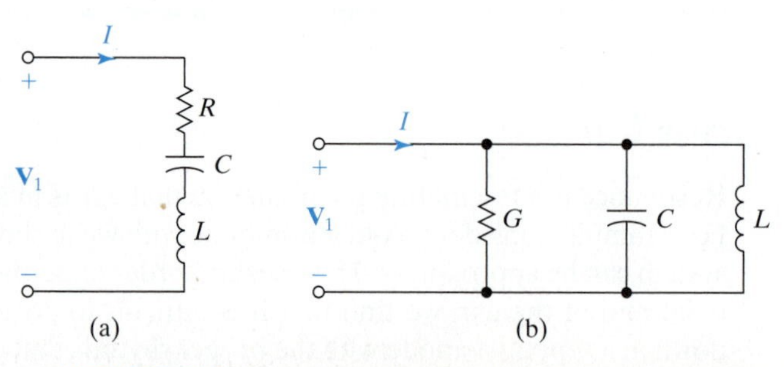

FIGURE 7.8 Series and parallel *RLC* circuits.

The definition of resonance for series or parallel circuits

At resonance the voltage and current are in phase, and therefore the phase angle is zero and the power factor is unity. In the series case, at resonance the impedance is a minimum, and therefore the current is maximum for a given voltage. At low frequencies, the impedance of the series circuit is dominated by the capacitive term and the admittance of the parallel circuit is dominated by the inductive term. At high frequencies, the impedance of the series circuit is dominated by the inductive term and the admittance of the parallel circuit is dominated by the capacitive term.

Resonance can be viewed from another perspective—that of the phasor diagram. Once again we will consider the series and parallel cases together in order to illustrate the similarities between them. In the series case the current is common to every element, and in the parallel case the voltage is a common variable. Therefore, the current in the series circuit and the voltage in the parallel circuit are employed as references. Phasor diagrams for both circuits are shown in Figure 7.9 for the three frequency values $\omega < \omega_0$, $\omega = \omega_0$, and $\omega > \omega_0$.

In the series case when $\omega < \omega_0$, $\mathbf{V}_C > \mathbf{V}_L$, θ_Z is negative, and the voltage $\mathbf{V}_1$ lags the current. If $\omega = \omega_0$, $\mathbf{V}_L = \mathbf{V}_C$, θ_Z is zero, and the voltage $\mathbf{V}_1$ is in phase with the current. If $\omega > \omega_0$, $\mathbf{V}_L > \mathbf{V}_C$, θ_Z is positive, and the voltage $\mathbf{V}_1$ leads the current. Similar statements can be made for the parallel case in Figure 7.9(b). Because of the close relationship between series and parallel resonance, as illustrated by the preceding material, we will concentrate most of our discussion on the series case in the following developments.

For the series circuit we define what is commonly called the *quality factor* Q as

$$Q = \frac{\omega_0 L}{R} \tag{7.24}$$

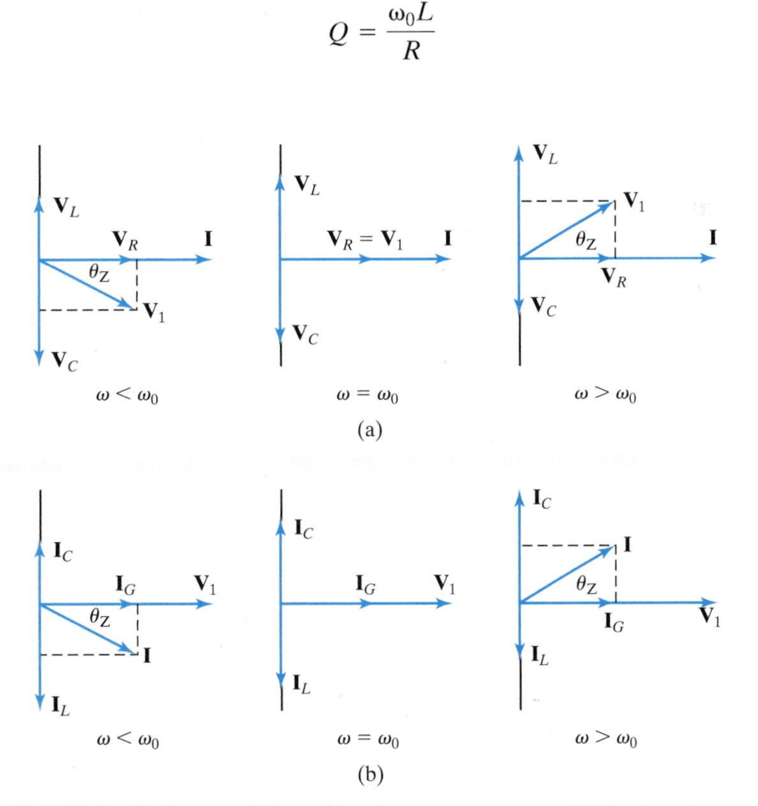

FIGURE 7.9 Phasor diagrams for (a) a series *RLC* circuit, and (b) a parallel *GLC* circuit.

The quality factor, Q, and its impact

Using Eq. (7.21), the quality factor can be expressed in the alternate forms.

$$Q = \frac{1}{\omega_0 CR} = \frac{1}{R}\sqrt{\frac{L}{C}} \tag{7.25}$$

Q is a very important factor in resonant circuits, and its ramifications will be illustrated throughout the remainder of this section.

Example 7.5

Consider the network shown in Figure 7.10. Let us determine the resonant frequency, the voltage across each element at resonance, and the value of the quality factor.

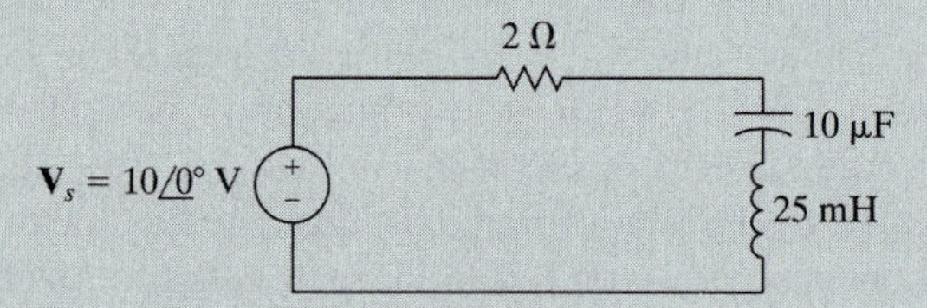

FIGURE 7.10 Series circuit.

The resonant frequency is obtained from the expression

$$\begin{aligned}\omega_0 &= \frac{1}{\sqrt{LC}}\\ &= \frac{1}{\sqrt{(25)(10^{-3})(10)(10^{-6})}}\\ &= 2000 \text{ rad/s}\end{aligned}$$

At this resonant frequency

$$\mathbf{I} = \frac{\mathbf{V}}{\mathbf{Z}} = \frac{\mathbf{V}}{R} = 5\angle 0^\circ \text{ A}$$

Therefore,

$$\begin{aligned}\mathbf{V}_R &= (5\angle 0^\circ)(2) = 10\angle 0^\circ \text{ V}\\ \mathbf{V}_L &= j\omega_0 L\mathbf{I} = 250\angle 90^\circ \text{ V}\\ \mathbf{V}_C &= \frac{\mathbf{I}}{j\omega_0 \mathbf{C}} = 250\angle -90^\circ \text{ V}\end{aligned}$$

Note the magnitude of the voltages across the inductor and capacitor with respect to the input voltage. Note also that these voltages are equal and 180° out of phase with one another. Therefore, the phasor diagram for this condition is shown in Figure 7.9 for $\omega = \omega_0$. The quality factor Q derived from Eq. (7.24) is

$$Q = \frac{\omega_0 L}{R} = \frac{(2)(10^3)(25)(10^{-3})}{2} = 25$$

It is interesting to note that the voltages across the inductor and capacitor can be written in terms of Q as

$$|\mathbf{V}_L| = \omega_0 L|\mathbf{I}| = \frac{\omega_0 L}{R}|\mathbf{V}_s| = Q|\mathbf{V}_s|$$

and

$$|\mathbf{V}_c| = \frac{|\mathbf{I}|}{\omega_0 C} = \frac{1}{\omega_0 CR}|\mathbf{V}_s| = Q|\mathbf{V}_s|$$

This analysis indicates that for a given current there is a resonant voltage rise across the inductor and capacitor that is equal to the product of Q and the applied voltage.

Drill Exercises

D7.4. Given the network in Figure D7.4, find the value of C that will place the circuit in resonance at 1800 rad/s.

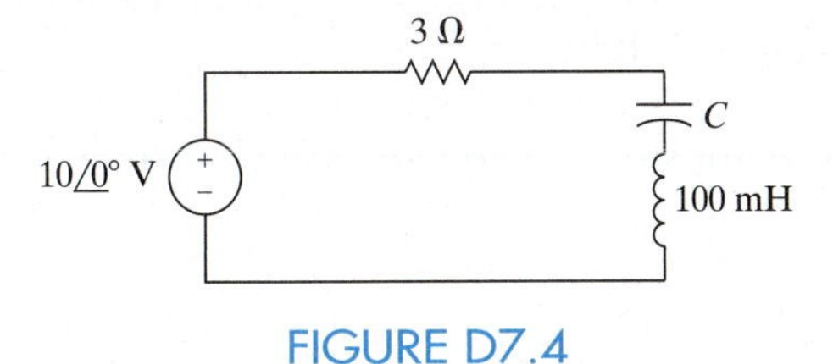

FIGURE D7.4

Ans: $C = 3.09\ \mu\text{F}$.

D7.5. Given the network in D7.4, determine the Q of the network and the magnitude of the voltage across the capacitor.

Ans: $Q = 60$, $|\mathbf{V}_c| = 600$ V.

Equation (7.24) indicates the dependence of Q on R. A high-Q series circuit has a small value of R, and as we will illustrate later, a high-Q parallel circuit has a relatively large value of R.

In the previous section we showed that the circuit bandwidth could be expressed as

$$BW = \omega_{HI} - \omega_{LO} = \frac{R}{L}$$

which can be written as

$$\begin{aligned} BW &= \frac{R\omega_0}{L\omega_0} \\ &= \frac{\omega_0}{Q} \end{aligned} \tag{7.26}$$

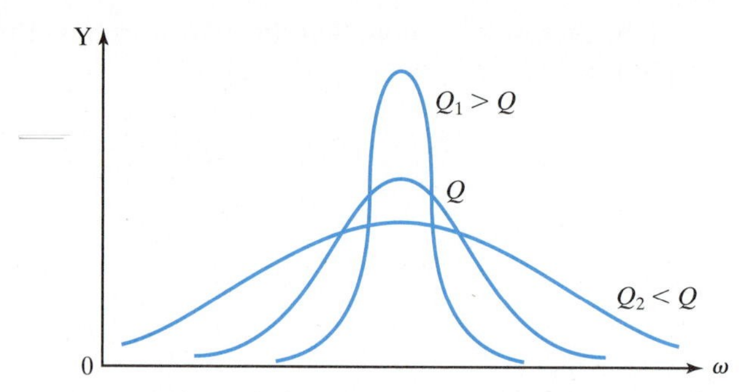

FIGURE 7.11 Network frequency response as a function of Q.

This equation illustrates that the bandwidth is inversely proportional to Q. Therefore, the *frequency selectivity* of the circuit is determined by the value of Q. A high-Q circuit has a small bandwidth, and therefore the circuit is very selective. The manner in which Q affects the frequency selectivity of the network is graphically illustrated in Figure 7.11. Hence, if we pass a signal with a wide frequency range through a high-Q circuit, only the frequency components within the bandwidth of the network will not be attenuated; that is, the network acts like a band-pass filter.

From an energy standpoint, recall that an inductor stores energy in its magnetic field and a capacitor stores energy in its electric field. When a network is in resonance, there is a continuous exchange of energy between the magnetic field of the inductor and the electric field of the capacitor. During each half-cycle, the energy stored in the inductor's magnetic field will vary from zero to a maximum value and back to zero again. The capacitor operates in a similar manner. The energy exchange takes place in the following way. During one quarter-cycle, the capacitor absorbs energy as quickly as the inductor gives it up, and during the following one quarter-cycle, the inductor absorbs energy as fast as it is released by the capacitor. Energy is exchanged back and forth between the two reactive elements.

Example 7.6

Given a series RLC circuit with $R = 2\ \Omega$, $L = 2$ mH, and $C = 5\ \mu$F, we wish to determine the resonant frequency, the quality factor, and the bandwidth for the circuit. Then we wish to determine the change in Q and the BW if R is changed from 2 to 0.2 Ω.

Using Eq. (7.21), we have

$$\omega_0 = \frac{1}{\sqrt{LC}} = \frac{1}{[(2)(10^{-3})(5)(10^{-6})]^{1/2}}$$
$$= 10^4 \text{ rad/s}$$

and therefore the resonant frequency is $10^4/2\pi = 1592$ Hz. The quality factor is

$$Q = \frac{\omega_0 L}{R} = \frac{(10^4)(2)(10^{-3})}{2}$$
$$= 10$$

and the bandwidth is

$$BW = \frac{\omega_0}{Q} = \frac{10^4}{10}$$

$$= 10^3 \text{ rad/s}$$

If R is changed to $R = 0.2\ \Omega$, the new value of Q is 100, and therefore the new BW is 10^2 rad/s.

Example 7.7

We wish to determine the parameters R, L, and C so that the circuit shown in Figure 7.12 operates as a band-pass filter with an ω_0 of 1000 rad/s and a bandwidth of 100 rad/s.

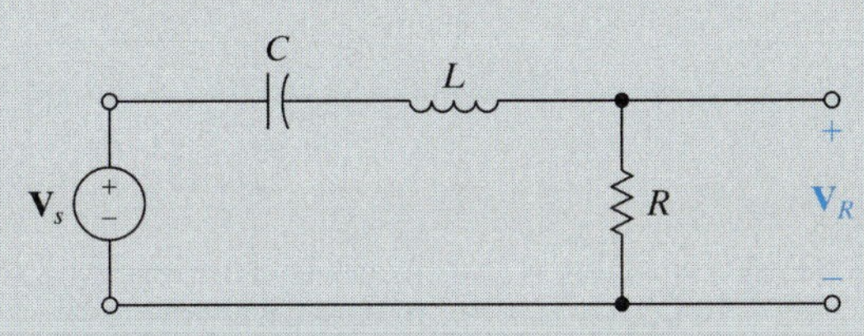

FIGURE 7.12 Series *RLC* circuit.

The resonant frequency for the circuit is

$$\omega_0 = \frac{1}{\sqrt{LC}}$$

and since $\omega_0 = 10^3$,

$$\frac{1}{LC} = 10^6$$

The bandwidth is

$$BW = \frac{\omega_0}{Q}$$

and hence

$$Q = \frac{\omega_0}{BW} = \frac{1000}{100}$$

$$= 10$$

However,

$$Q = \frac{\omega_0 L}{R}$$

and therefore,

$$\frac{1000L}{R} = 10$$

This equation, together with the equation for the resonant frequency, represents *two* equations in the *three* unknown circuit parameters R, L, and C. Hence, if we select $C = 1\ \mu\text{F}$, then

$$L = \frac{1}{10^6\, C} = 1\ \text{H}$$

and

$$\frac{1000(1)}{R} = 10$$

yields

$$R = 100\ \Omega$$

Therefore, the parameters $R = 100\ \Omega$, $L = 1\ \text{H}$, and $C = 1\ \mu\text{F}$ are one set of parameters that will produce the proper filter characteristics.

Drill Exercises

D7.6. A series RLC circuit is composed of $R = 2\ \Omega$, $L = 40\ \text{mH}$, and $C = 100\ \mu\text{F}$. Determine the bandwidth of this circuit about its resonant frequency.

Ans: $BW = 50\ \text{rad/s}$, $\omega_0 = 500\ \text{rad/s}$.

D7.7. A series RLC circuit has the following properties: $R = 4\ \Omega$, $\omega_0 = 4000\ \text{rad/s}$, and $BW = 100\ \text{rad/s}$. Determine the values of L and C.

Ans: $L = 40\ \text{mH}$, $C = 1.56\ \mu\text{F}$.

In our presentation of resonance thus far, we have focused most of our discussion on the series resonant circuit. We should recall, however, that the equations for the impedance of the series circuit and the admittance of the parallel circuit are similar. Therefore, the networks possess similar properties.

Consider the network shown in Figure 7.13. The source current $\mathbf{I}_s$ can be expressed as

$$\begin{aligned}\mathbf{I}_s &= \mathbf{I}_G + \mathbf{I}_C + \mathbf{I}_L \\ &= \mathbf{V}_s G + j\omega C \mathbf{V}_s + \frac{\mathbf{V}_s}{j\omega L} \\ &= \mathbf{V}_s\left[G + j\left(\omega C - \frac{1}{\omega L}\right)\right]\end{aligned}$$

When the network is in resonance,

$$\mathbf{I}_s = G\mathbf{V}_s$$

that is, all the source current flows through the conductance G. Does this mean that there is no current in L or C? Definitely not! $\mathbf{I}_c$ and $\mathbf{I}_L$ are equal in magnitude but 180° out of phase

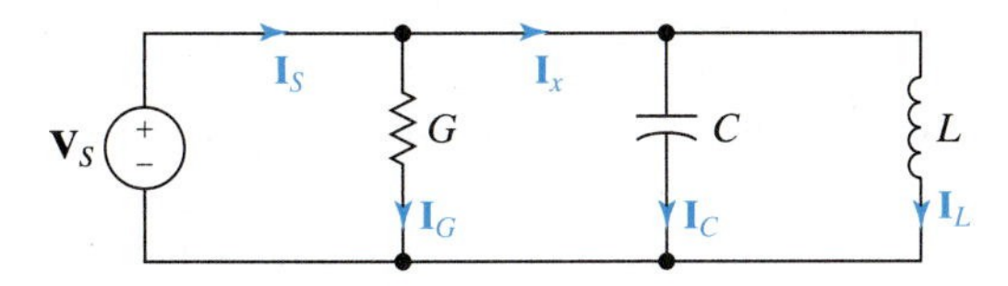

FIGURE 7.13 Parallel *RLC* circuit.

with one another and there is an energy exchange between the electric field of the capacitor and the magnetic field of the inductor. As one increases, the other decreases, and vice versa.

Example 7.8

The network in Figure 7.13 has the following parameters:

$$\mathbf{V}_s = 120\angle 0^\circ \text{ V}, G = 0.01 \text{ S}, C = 600 \text{ } \mu\text{F, and } L = 120 \text{ mH.}$$

If the source operates at the resonant frequency of the network, compute all the branch currents.

The resonant frequency for the network is

$$\begin{aligned}\omega_0 &= \frac{1}{\sqrt{LC}} \\ &= \frac{1}{\sqrt{(120)(10^{-3})(600)(10^{-6})}} \\ &= 117.85 \text{ rad/s}\end{aligned}$$

At this frequency

$$\mathbf{Y}_C = j\omega_0 C = j7.07 \times 10^{-2} \text{ S}$$

and

$$\mathbf{Y}_L = -j\left(\frac{1}{\omega_0 L}\right) = -j7.07 \times 10^{-2} \text{ S}$$

The branch currents are then

$$\begin{aligned}\mathbf{I}_G &= G\mathbf{V}_s = 1.2\angle 0^\circ \text{ A} \\ \mathbf{I}_C &= Y_C\mathbf{V}_s = 8.49\angle 90^\circ \text{ A} \\ \mathbf{I}_L &= Y_L\mathbf{V}_s = 8.49\angle -90^\circ \text{ A}\end{aligned}$$

and

$$\mathbf{I}_s = \mathbf{I}_G + \mathbf{I}_C + \mathbf{I}_L = 1.2\angle 0^\circ \text{ A}$$

As the analysis indicates, the source supplies only the losses in the resistive element. In addition, the source voltage and current are in phase and, therefore, the power factor is unity.

Consider the network in Figure 7.14. The output voltage can be written as

$$\mathbf{V}_{out} = \frac{\mathbf{I}_{in}}{\mathbf{Y}_t}$$

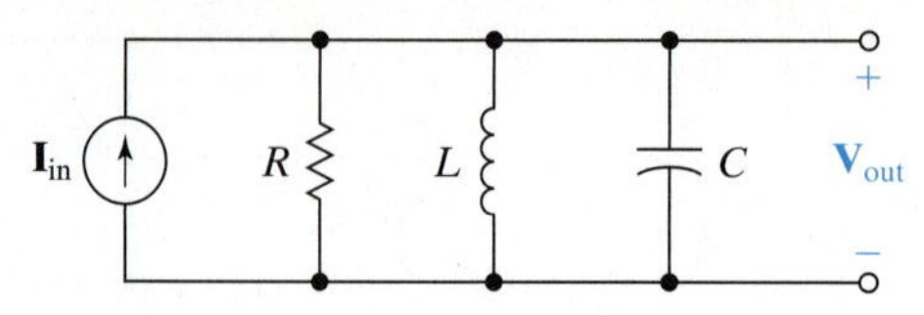

FIGURE 7.14 A parallel *RLC* circuit.

and, therefore, the magnitude of the transfer characteristic can be expressed as

$$\left|\frac{\mathbf{V}_{out}}{\mathbf{I}_{in}}\right| = \frac{1}{\sqrt{(1/R^2) + (\omega C - 1/\omega L)^2}} \tag{7.27}$$

$$\omega_0 = \frac{1}{\sqrt{LC}} \tag{7.28}$$

and at this frequency

$$\left|\frac{\mathbf{V}_{out}}{\mathbf{I}_{in}}\right|_{\max} = R \tag{7.29}$$

As demonstrated earlier, at the half-power frequencies the magnitude is equal to $1/\sqrt{2}$ of its maximum value, and hence the half-power frequencies can be obtained from the expression

$$\frac{1}{\sqrt{(1/R^2) + (\omega C - 1/\omega L)^2}} = \frac{R}{\sqrt{2}} \tag{7.30}$$

Solving this equation and taking only the positive values of ω yields

$$\omega_{LO} = -\frac{1}{2RC} + \sqrt{\frac{1}{(2RC)^2} + \frac{1}{LC}} \tag{7.31}$$

and

$$\omega_{HI} = \frac{1}{2RC} + \sqrt{\frac{1}{(2RC)^2} + \frac{1}{LC}} \tag{7.32}$$

Subtracting these two half-power frequencies yields the bandwidth

$$\begin{aligned} BW &= \omega_{HI} - \omega_{LO} \\ &= \frac{1}{RC} \end{aligned} \tag{7.33}$$

Therefore, the quality factor is

$$\begin{aligned} Q &= \frac{\omega_0}{BW} \\ &= \frac{RC}{\sqrt{LC}} \\ &= R\sqrt{\frac{C}{L}} \end{aligned} \tag{7.34}$$

Example 7.9

A stereo receiver is tuned to 98 MHz on the FM band. The tuning knob controls a variable capacitor in a parallel resonant circuit: If the inductance of the circuit is 0.1 μH and the Q is 120, determine the values of C and G.

Using the expression for the resonant frequency, we obtain

$$C = \frac{1}{\omega_0^2 L}$$

$$= \frac{1}{(2\pi \times 98 \times 10^6)^2(0.1 \times 10^{-6})}$$

$$= 26.4 \text{ PF}$$

The conductance is obtained from Eq. (7.34) where

$$Q = \frac{RC}{\sqrt{LC}}$$

which can be expressed using the equation for the resonant frequency as

$$Q = RC\omega_0$$

If C is expressed in terms of the resonant frequency, we obtain

$$Q = \frac{R}{\omega_0 L}$$

and since $G = 1/R$, the conductance is

$$\mathbf{G} = \frac{1}{\omega_0 L Q}$$

$$= \frac{1}{(2\pi \times 98 \times 10^6)(10^{-7})(120)}$$

$$= 135 \ \mu\text{S}$$

Prior to the adoption of digital technology in modern radios, the selection of a particular frequency was performed with what is commonly known as a "tank" circuit consisting of an inductor in parallel with a variable capacitor, as shown in Figure 7.15a. This tank circuit acts as a band-pass filter, and the center frequency of the filter is changed by varying the value of the capacitor. For example, Figure 7.15b illustrates the movement of the filter's center frequency across the AM (amplitude modulation) radio band as the capacitance value changes. However, the bandwidth of the filter must be narrow enough so that when the radio is tuned to one frequency (station) there is no interference from a station operating at a nearby frequency. The following example illustrates this issue.

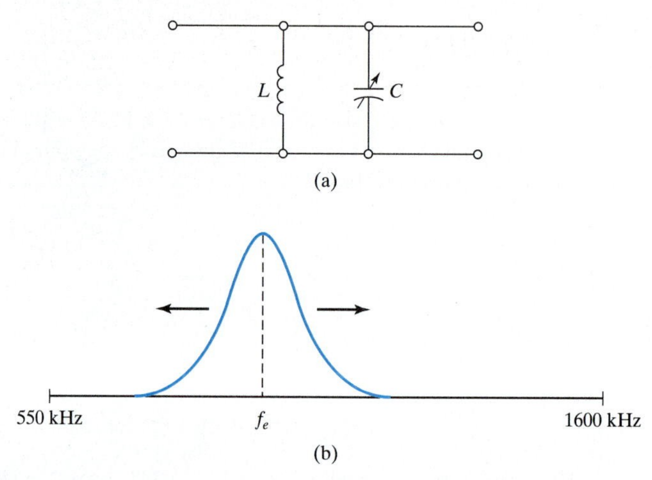

FIGURE 7.15 (a) A band-pass filter and (b) an illustration of the movement of its center frequency across the AM radio band.

Example 7.10

Consider the simplified block diagram of an AM radio shown in Figure 7.16a. We will model this network with the circuit shown in Figure 7.16b where we have modeled the antenna current I_a as a current source. The tank circuit is placed between the current source and input stage of the radio, which has been modeled by its Thevenin equivalent resistance R_i; assumed to be 1 kΩ. We wish to select values for the tank circuit so that a station broadcasting at 1000 kHz will not be "picked up" when the radio is tuned to a signal at 1200 kHz.

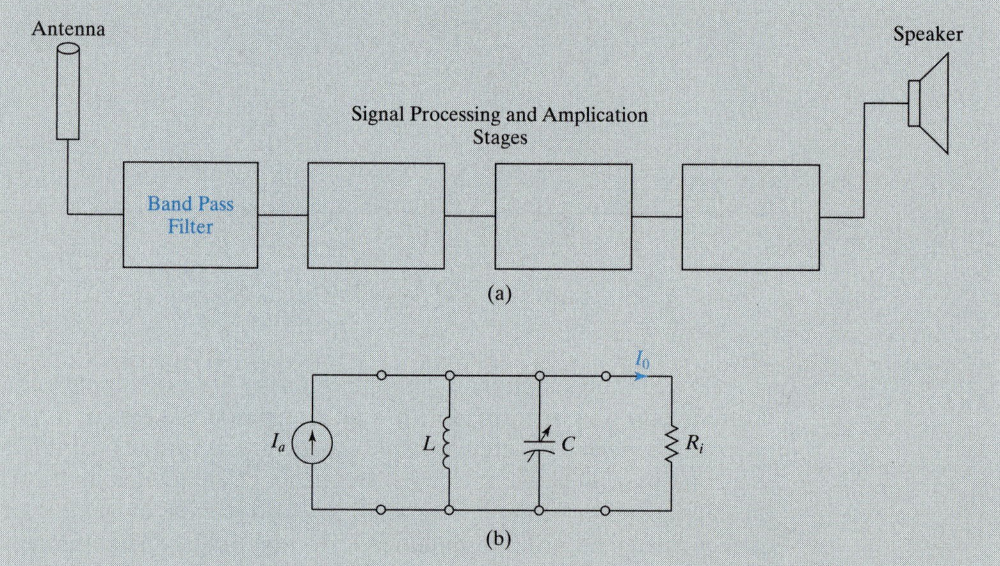

FIGURE 7.16 (a) Simplified block diagram for an AM radio and (b) a simple circuit used to model the radio's performance.

The impedance of the tank circuit is

$$\mathbf{Z}_T(j\omega) = \frac{j\omega L / j\omega C}{j\omega L + \dfrac{1}{j\omega C}}$$

$$= \frac{j\omega L}{-\omega^2 LC + 1}$$

The output current of the filter is then

$$\mathbf{I}_o = \mathbf{I}_a \frac{Z_T}{Z_T + R_i}$$

and

$$\frac{\mathbf{I}_o}{\mathbf{I}_a} = \frac{\dfrac{j\omega L}{-\omega^2 LC + 1}}{\dfrac{j\omega L}{-\omega^2 LC + 1} + R_i}$$

which can be expressed as

$$\frac{\mathbf{I}_o}{\mathbf{I}_a} = \frac{\dfrac{j\omega}{R_i C}}{-\omega^2 + \dfrac{j\omega}{R_i C} + \dfrac{1}{LC}}$$

The center frequency of the filter and BW expressed in radians per second are

$$\omega_o = \frac{1}{LC}$$

$$BW = \frac{1}{R_i C}$$

or in Hz, the variables are

$$f_o = \frac{1}{2\pi\sqrt{LC}}$$

$$BW = \frac{1}{2\pi R_i C}$$

Assuming the radio is tuned to 1200 kHz and assuming an inductor value of 100 μH, the value of the capacitor at 1200 kHz is derived from the expression

$$f_o = \frac{1}{2\pi\sqrt{LC}}$$

or, solving for C yields

$$C = \frac{1}{(2\pi f_o)^2 L}$$

$$= \frac{1}{[(2\pi)(12)(10^2)(10^3)]^2(10^{-4})}$$

$$= 176\text{pF}$$

The bandwidth of the tank circuit is then

$$BW = \frac{1}{2\pi R_i C}$$

$$= \frac{1}{(2\pi)(4000)(176)(10^{-12})}$$

$$= 226 \text{ kHz}$$

and the Q of the circuit is

$$Q = \frac{\omega_o}{\text{BW}}$$

$$= \frac{1200}{22.6}$$

$$= 5.3$$

If we now substitute all the component values into the transfer function expression, we obtain

$$\frac{\mathbf{I}_o}{\mathbf{I}_a}(f) = \frac{j(8.92)(10^6)f}{-39.48f^2 + j(8.92)(10^6)f + (56.82)(10^{12})}$$

A magnitude plot of this characteristic is shown in Figure 7.17. Clearly, a station operating at 1000kHz will be picked up by the radio when tuned to 1200kHz.

Since the bandwidth is inversely proportional to the capacitance, let us increase the capacitance value by a factor of 10 and decrease the inductor value by the same amount, thus maintaining the center frequency. Under this condition $C = 1.76\text{nF}$ and $L = 10\ \mu\text{H}$. The new bandwidth and Q will be 22.6kHz and 53, respectively. Obviously, this is a much more selective circuit. The transfer characteristic in this case is

$$\frac{\mathbf{I}_o}{\mathbf{I}_a}(f) = \frac{j(0.8925)(10^6)f}{-39.84f^2 + j(0.8925)(10^6)f + (56.82)(10^{12})}$$

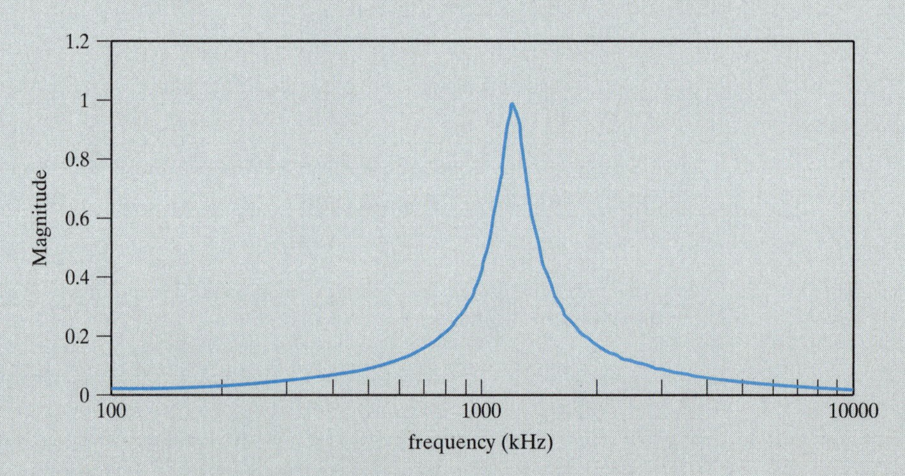

FIGURE 7.17 A plot of a band-pass filter with a center frequency of 1200 kHz and a bandwidth of 226 kHz.

A plot of this new characteristic is shown, together with the one in Figure 7.17 for comparison, in Figure 7.18. In this latter case, the station operating at 1000 kHz will have little, if any, impact when the radio is tuned to 1200 kHz.

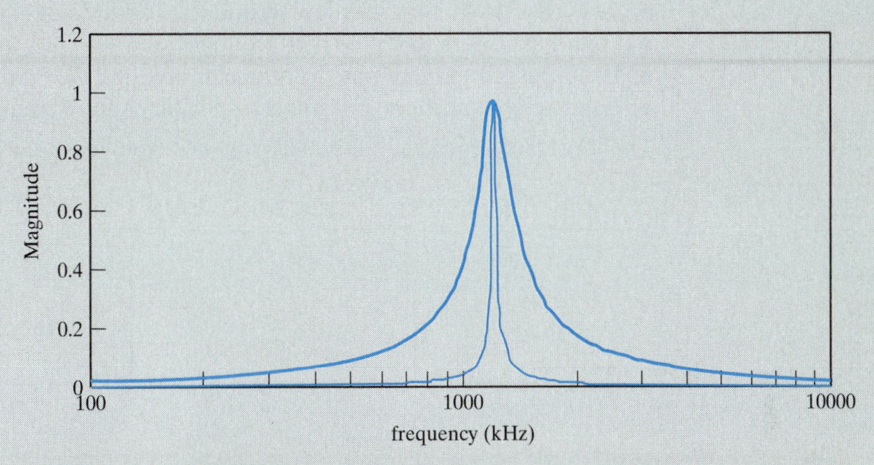

FIGURE 7.18 A comparison of two band-pass filters with bandwidths of 226 kHz and 22.6 kHz.

Drill Exercises

D7.8. A parallel *RLC* circuit has the following parameters: $R = 2\ \text{k}\Omega$, $L = 20$ mH, and $C = 150\ \mu\text{F}$. Determine the resonant frequency, the Q, and the bandwidth of the circuit.

Ans: $\omega_0 = 577$ rad/s, $BW = 3.33$ rad/s, $Q = 173$.

D7.9. A parallel *RLC* circuit has the following parameters: $R = 6\ \text{k}\Omega$, $BW = 1000$ rad/s, and $Q = 120$. Determine the values of L, C, and ω_0.

Ans: $C = 0.167\ \mu\text{F}$, $L = 416.7\ \mu\text{H}$, $\omega_0 = 119760$ rad/s.

Summary

- The frequency response of a network defines the behavior of the network as a function of frequency.
- Network transfer functions, for example, the ratio of the output voltage of a network to its input voltage, can be expressed in the form

$$\mathbf{G}(j\omega) = \frac{N(j\omega)}{D(j\omega)} = \frac{a_m(j\omega)^m + \cdots a_1 j\omega + a_0}{b_n(j\omega)^n + \cdots b_1 j\omega + b_0} = \frac{k_0(j\omega - z_1)\cdots(j\omega - z_m)}{(j\omega - p_1)\cdots(j\omega - p_n)}$$

where k_0 is a constant, $z_j, j = 1 \cdots m$ are called zeros of the network, and $p_j, j = 1 \cdots n$ are called poles.

The network poles determine the dynamic properties of the network.

- The most common types of passive filters are:
  - Low-pass filters that pass low frequencies and reject high frequencies.
  - High-pass filters that pass high frequencies and reject low frequencies.
  - Band-pass filters that pass frequencies in a specific band and reject all others.
  - Band-rejection filters that reject a specific band of frequencies and pass all others.

  The ideal frequency characteristics for these networks are shown in Figure 7.19.

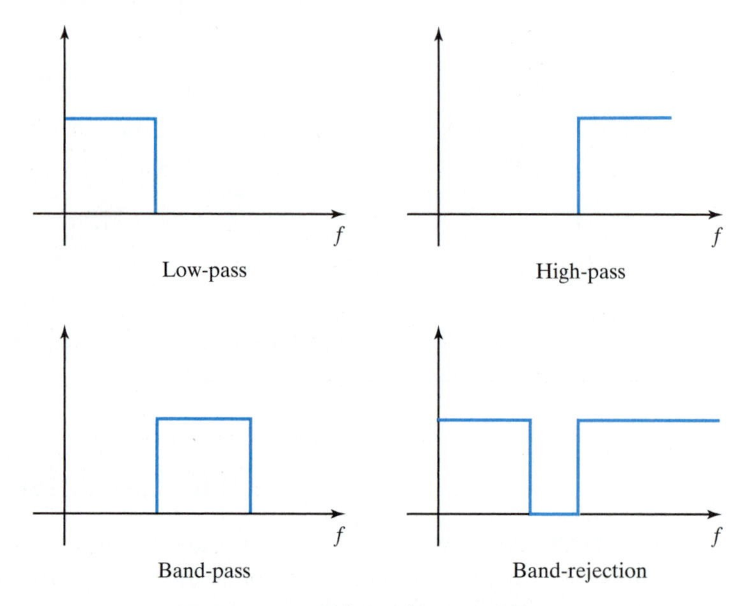

FIGURE 7.19 Filter characteristics.

- The half-power frequency, also known as the break frequency or cut-off frequency, is the frequency at which the magnitude characteristic is $\frac{1}{\sqrt{2}}$ of its maximum value.
- The width of the pass-band in a band-pass filter or the rejection-band in a band-rejection filter is called the bandwidth, and is defined as the frequency range between the upper and lower half-power frequencies, as shown in Figure 7.20.

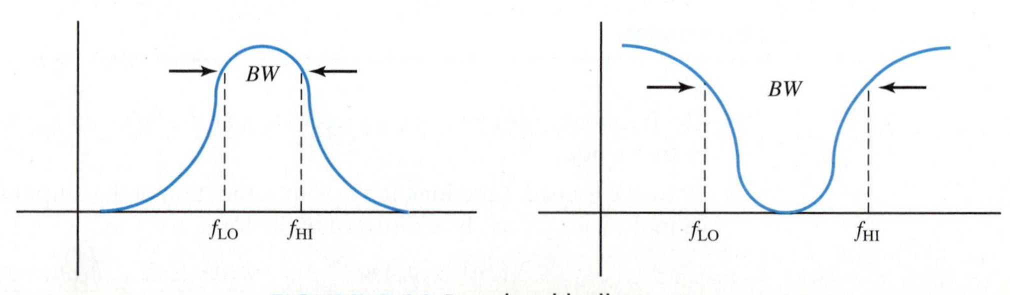

FIGURE 7.20 Bandwidth illustrations.

- The frequency at which the impedance of a series RLC circuit or the admittance of a parallel RLC circuit is purely real is called the resonant frequency. For the networks in Figure 7.21,

$$\mathbf{Z}(j\omega) = R + j\omega L + \frac{1}{j\omega C}$$

and

$$\mathbf{Y}(j\omega) = G + j\omega C + \frac{1}{j\omega L}$$

and at the resonant frequency $\omega_0 = \dfrac{1}{\sqrt{LC}}$,

$$\mathbf{Z}(j\omega_0) = R$$
$$\mathbf{Y}(j\omega_0) = G$$

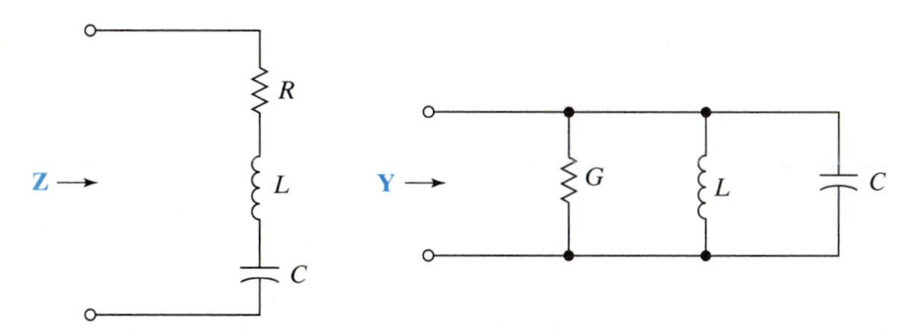

FIGURE 7.21 Series and parallel RLC networks.

- The quality factor, Q, for a network specifies the network's frequency selectivity. High Q circuits are very selective and low Q circuits are not selective. Figure 7.11 illustrates this issue.

Problems

7.1. Find the transfer function $\dfrac{\mathbf{V}_0}{\mathbf{V}_s}(j\omega)$ for the network in Figure P7.1.

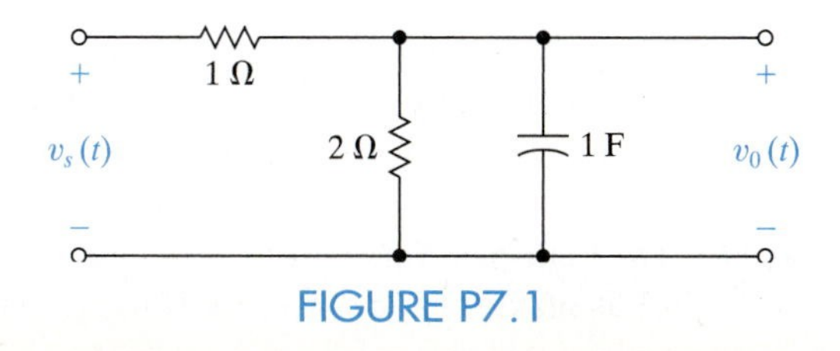

FIGURE P7.1

7.2. Find the transfer function $\dfrac{\mathbf{I}_0}{\mathbf{V}_s}(j\omega)$ for the network in Figure P7.2.

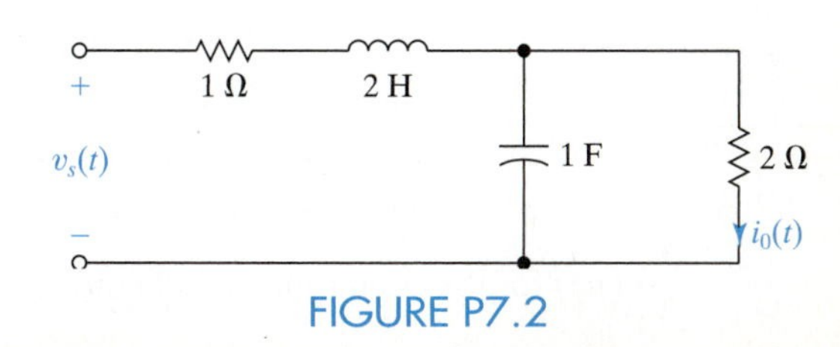

FIGURE P7.2

7.3. Determine the poles and zeros of the transfer function $\frac{\mathbf{V}_0}{\mathbf{V}_1}(j\omega)$ for the network in Figure P7.3.

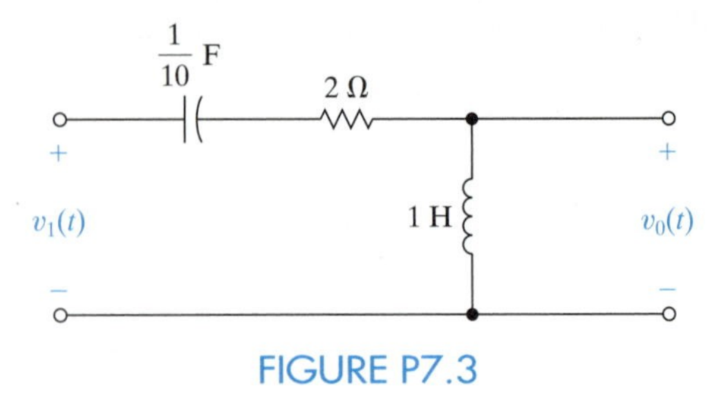

FIGURE P7.3

7.4. Find the poles and zeros of the transfer function $\frac{\mathbf{V}_0}{\mathbf{V}_1}(j\omega)$ for the network in Figure P7.4.

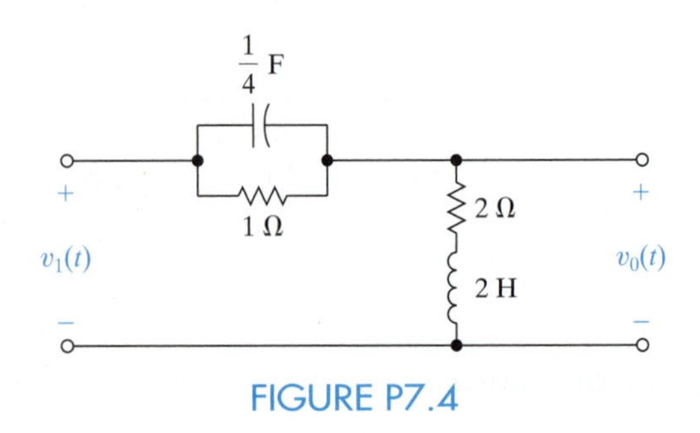

FIGURE P7.4

7.5. Determine the poles and zeros of the transfer function $\frac{\mathbf{V}_0}{\mathbf{V}_1}(j\omega)$ for the circuit shown in Figure P7.5.

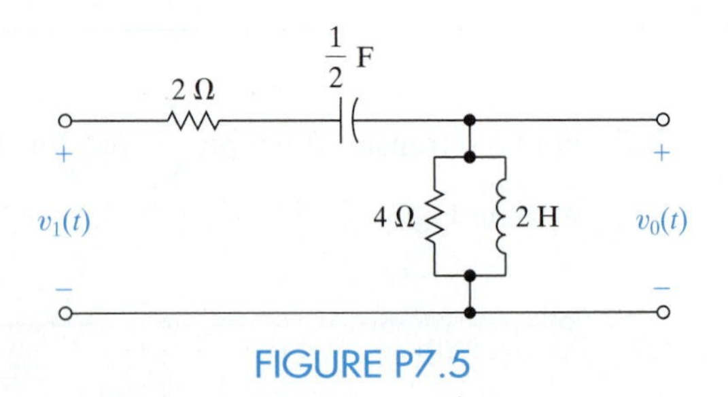

FIGURE P7.5

7.6. Find the poles and zeros of the transfer function $\frac{\mathbf{V}_0}{\mathbf{V}_1}(j\omega)$ for the circuit shown in Figure P7.6.

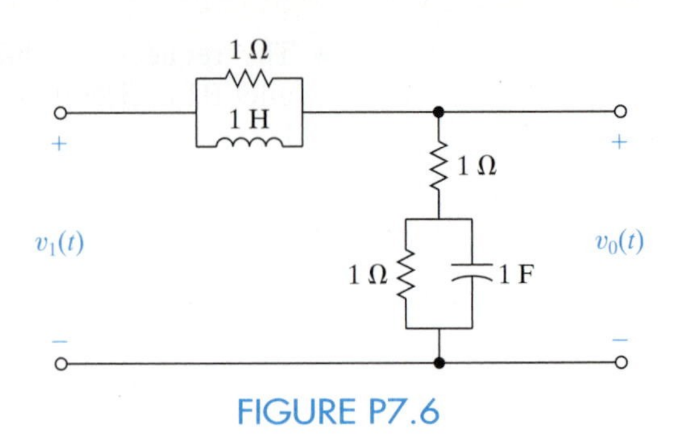

FIGURE P7.6

7.7. Plot the magnitude and phase of the transfer function $\frac{\mathbf{V}_0}{\mathbf{V}_1}(j\omega)$ in increments of 0.1 r/s from 0.5 r/s to 1.5 r/s for the circuit shown in Figure P7.7.

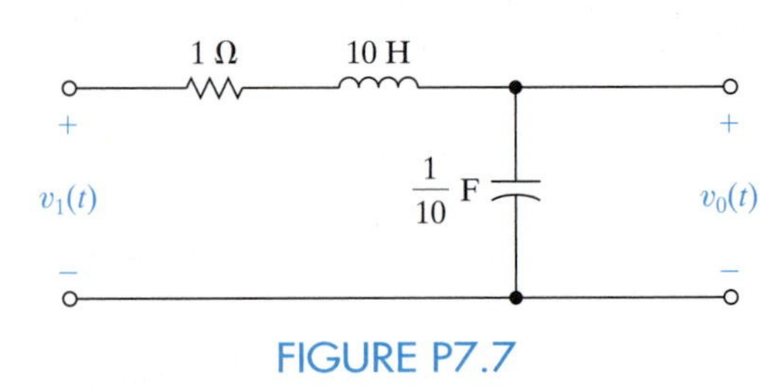

FIGURE P7.7

7.8. A simple low-pass filter is shown in Figure P7.8. If $R = 2\ \text{k}\Omega$ and $C = 75\ \mu\text{F}$, determine the half-power frequency of the filter.

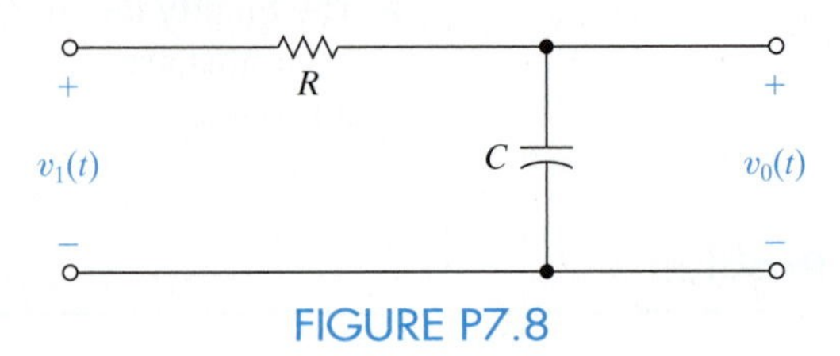

FIGURE P7.8

7.9. We wish to design a low-pass filter of the form shown in Figure P7.8 to have a break frequency of 50 Hz. If a 2 kΩ resistor is available, determine the required value of the capacitor.

7.10. An RC low-pass filter has the following parameters: $R = 1\ \text{k}\Omega$ and $C = 50\ \mu\text{F}$. Determine the half-power frequency of the filter.

7.11. The high-pass filter shown in Figure P7.11 has a cut-off frequency of 75 r/s. If the resistor has a value of 4 kΩ, determine the value of the capacitor.

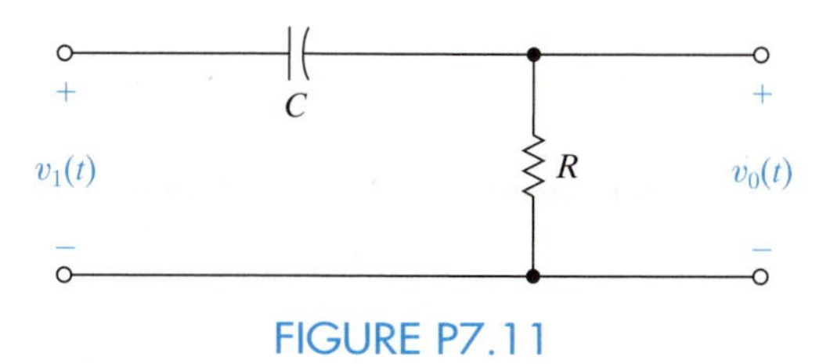

FIGURE P7.11

7.12. An RC high-pass filter has the following parameters: $R = 10\ \text{k}\Omega$ and $C = 200\ \mu\text{F}$. Determine the half-power frequency of the filter and the phase angle of the magnitude transfer function at this frequency.

7.13. A high-pass filter with a cut-off frequency of 500 Hz is needed. If a 2 μF capacitor is available, determine the value of the resistor for the network in Figure P7.11 that will produce the desired filter.

7.14. Determine the center frequency and bandwidth of the band-pass filter shown in Figure P7.14.

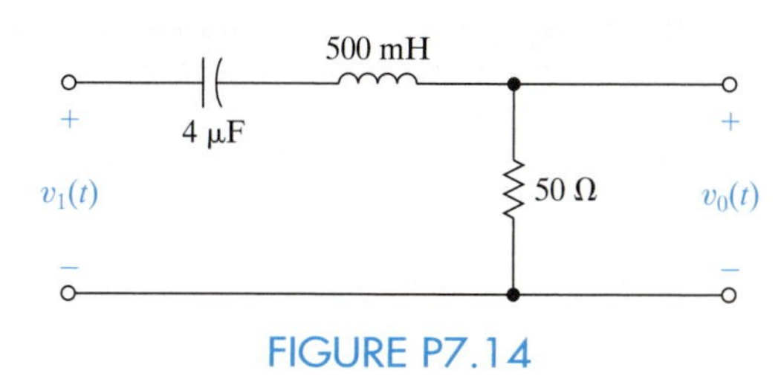

FIGURE P7.14

7.15. A band-pass filter has a center frequency of 924 rad/s. If the upper half-power frequency is 1132 rad/s, determine the bandwidth of the filter.

7.16. Given the band-pass filter shown in Figure P7.14 with $C = 2\ \mu\text{F}$ and $L = 2$ H, determine the center frequency and find the value of R that will yield a bandwidth of 100 r/s.

7.17. Determine the cut-off frequencies of the band-pass filter in problem 7.16.

7.18. Compute the voltage transfer function for the network shown in Figure P7.18 and tell what type of filter the network represents.

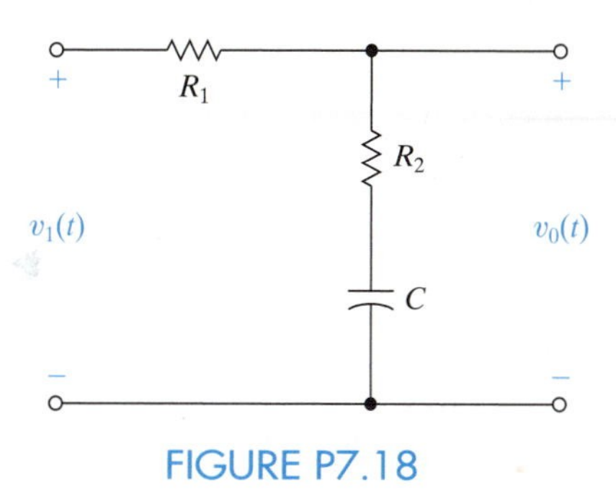

FIGURE P7.18

7.19. Determine what type of filter the network in Figure P7.19 represents by determining the voltage transfer function.

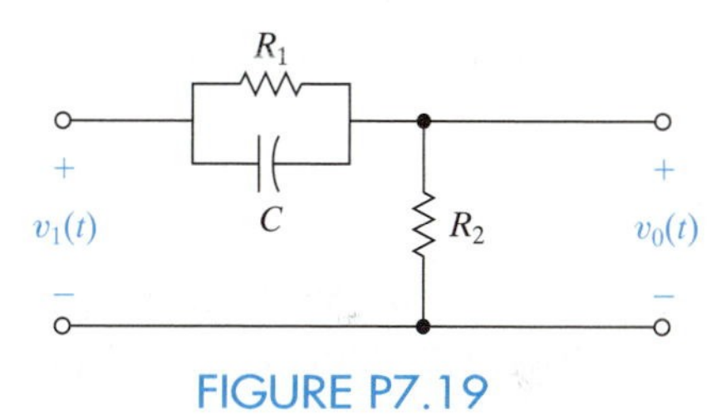

FIGURE P7.19

7.20. Given the lattice network shown in Figure P7.20, determine what type of filter this network represents by determining the voltage transfer function.

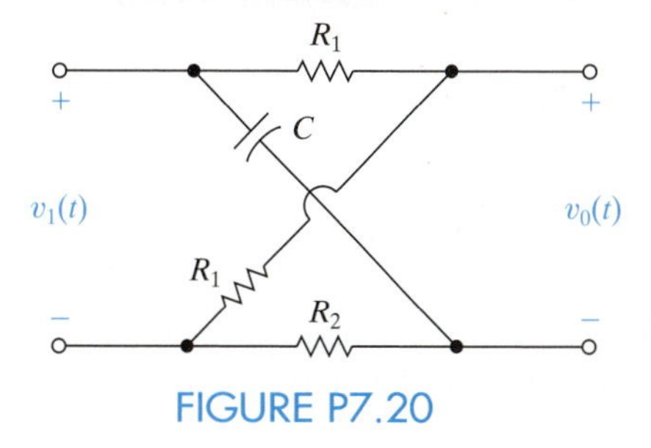

FIGURE P7.20

7.21. Determine the type of filter that is represented by the network in Figure P7.21.

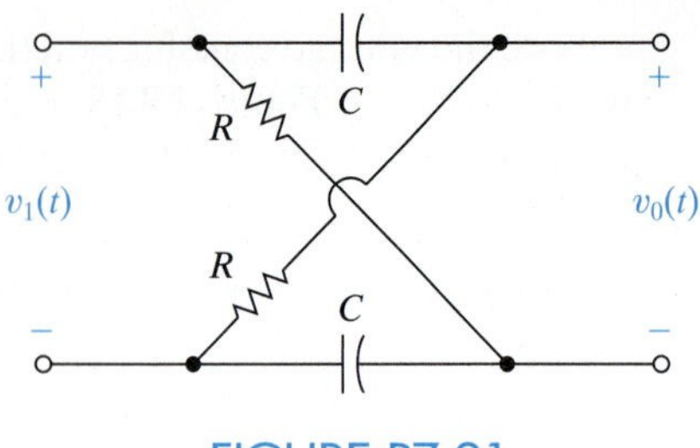

FIGURE P7.21

7.22. In the network in Figure P7.22 the component values are $R = 4\ \Omega, C = 2\ \mu\text{F}$, and $L = 50$ mH. Determine the resonant frequency of the network.

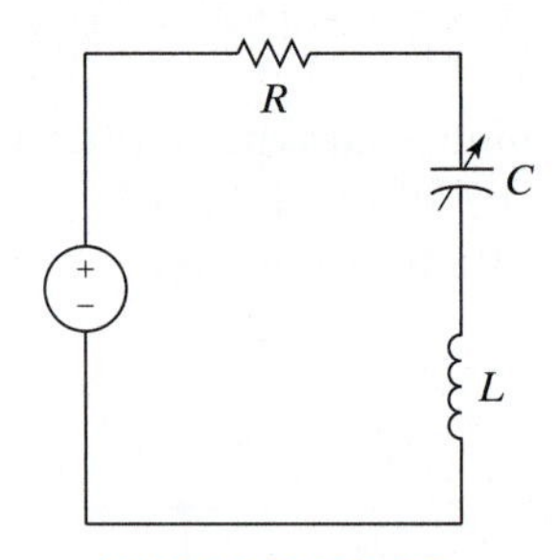

FIGURE P7.22

7.23. Select a value for the variable capacitor in the network in Figure P7.22 that will place the circuit in resonance at 2000 r/s.

7.24. Find the value of C that will place the circuit in Figure P7.24 in resonance at 1800 r/s. Then determine the Q of the network and the magnitude of the voltage across the capacitor.

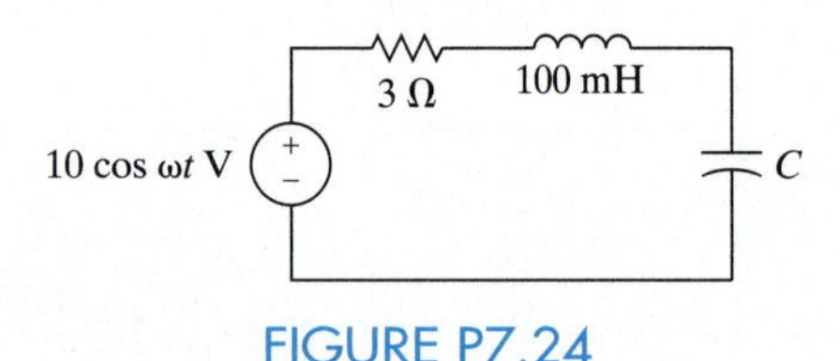

FIGURE P7.24

7.25. Determine the bandwidth and half-power frequencies of the network in problem 7.24.

7.26. Given the network in Figure P7.26, find the resonant frequency, the Q, and the magnitude of the voltage across the capacitor at resonance.

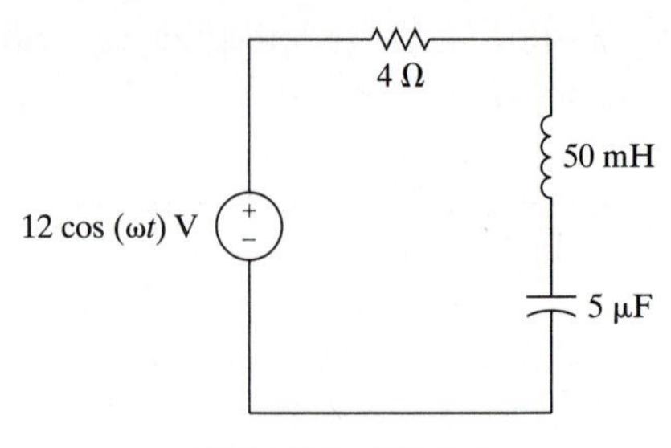

FIGURE P7.26

7.27. In the network in Figure P7.27, at resonance the magnitude of the voltage across the capacitor is 120 V. Determine the value of the resistor R.

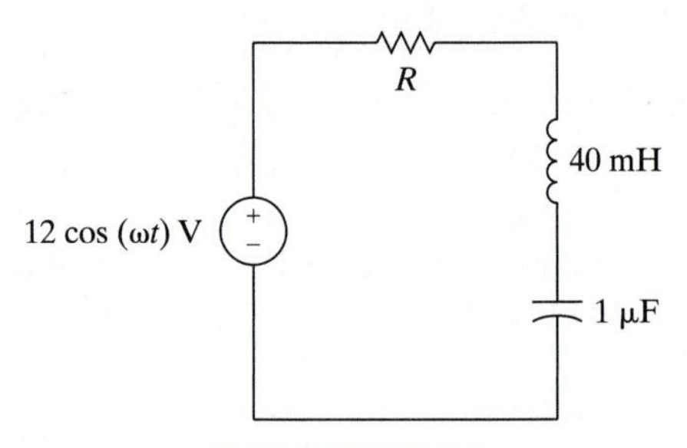

FIGURE P7.27

7.28. The Q and resonant frequency of a series RLC circuit are known to be 40 and 6000 r/s, respectively. If the value of the resistor is 4 Ω, determine the values of the inductor and capacitor.

7.29. Given the series RLC circuit in Figure P7.29, if $R = 10\ \Omega$, find the values of L and C such that the network will have a resonant frequency of 100 kHz and a bandwidth of 1 kHz.

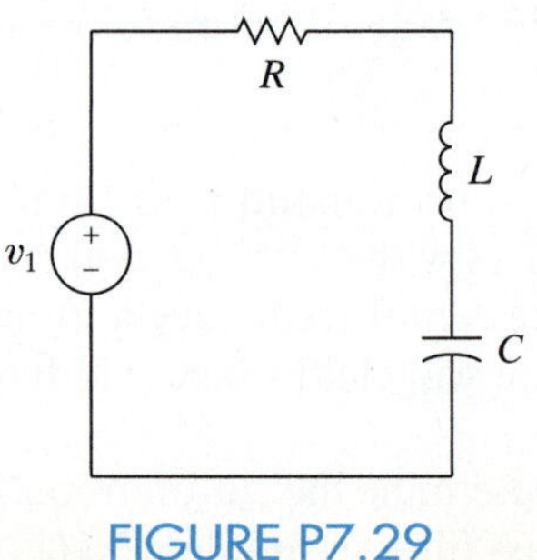

FIGURE P7.29

7.30. A series RLC circuit has a resistance at resonance of 3.2 Ω. The network has a bandwidth of 200 r/s and a resonant frequency of 2000 r/s. Determine the circuit parameters.

7.31. A series resonant circuit has a Q of 120 and a resonant frequency of 60,000 rad/s. Determine the half-power frequencies and the bandwidth of the circuit.

7.32. Given the series RLC circuit in Figure P7.32,

(a) Derive the expression for the half-power frequencies, the resonant frequency, the bandwidth, and the quality factor for the transfer characteristic $\mathbf{I}/\mathbf{V}_{in}$ in terms of R, L, and C.

(b) Compute the quantities in part (a) if $R = 10\ \Omega$, $L = 100$ mH, and $C = 10\ \mu$F.

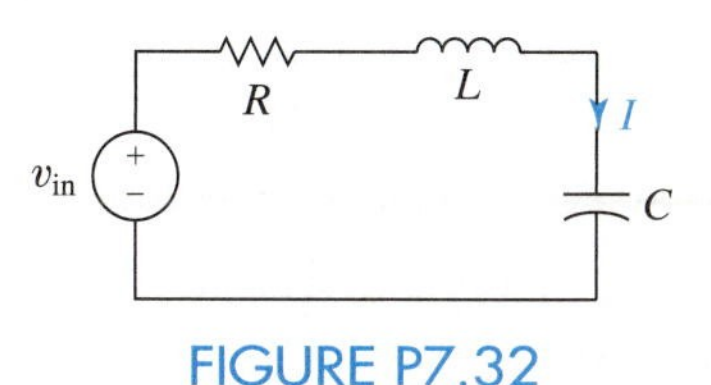

FIGURE P7.32

7.33. A parallel RLC circuit consists of the following elements: $R = 4$ kΩ, C = 100 μF, and $L = 40$ mH. Compute the resonant frequency and bandwidth of the circuit.

7.34. Given the parallel RLC circuit shown in Figure P7.34, determine the resonant frequency and the voltage across the elements at resonance.

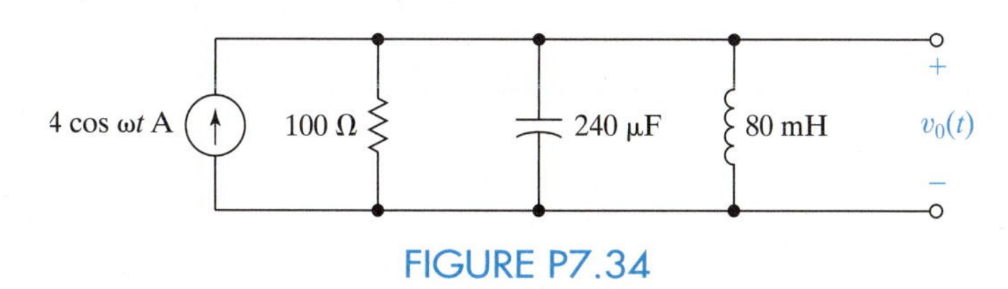

FIGURE P7.34

7.35. Determine the Q and the bandwidth of the network shown in Figure P7.35.

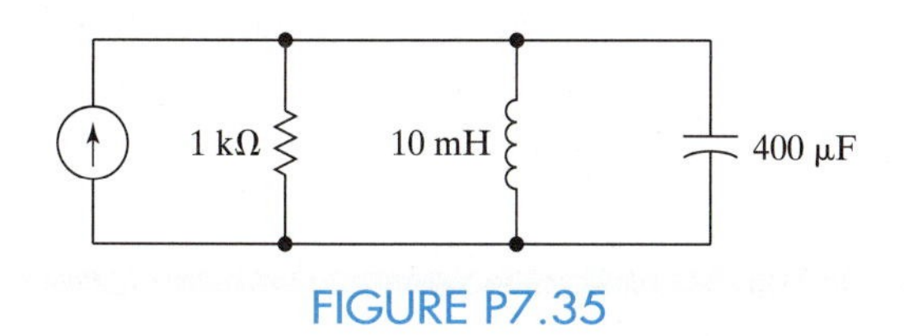

FIGURE P7.35

7.36. The network in Figure P7.36 has a $Q = 80$ and a $BW = 800$ r/s. Determine the resonant frequency and the unknown circuit parameters.

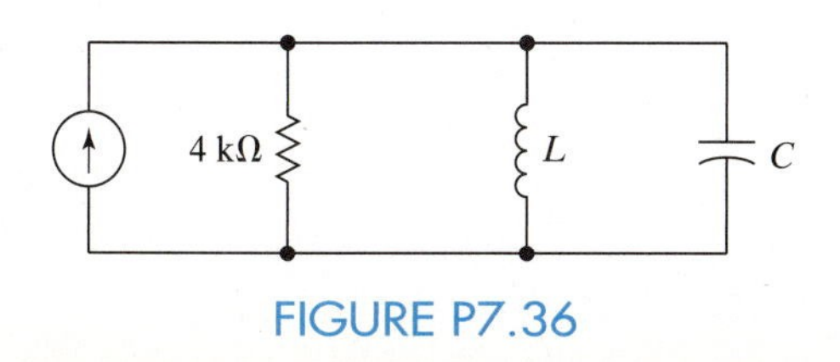

FIGURE P7.36

7.37. A variable frequency current source supplies the parallel RLC circuit shown in Figure P7.37. Determine the BW, Q, and the half-power frequencies of the network.

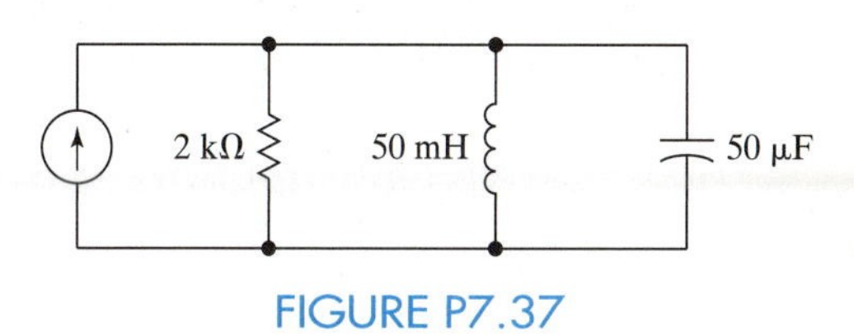

FIGURE P7.37

7.38. Given the parallel RLC circuit in Figure P7.38,

(a) Derive the expression for the resonant frequency, the half-power frequencies, the bandwidth, and the quality factor for the transfer characteristic $\mathbf{V}_{out}/\mathbf{I}_{in}$ in terms of the circuit parameters R, L, and C.

(b) Compute the quantities in part (a) if $R = 1$ kΩ, $L = 10$ mH, and $C = 100\ \mu$F.

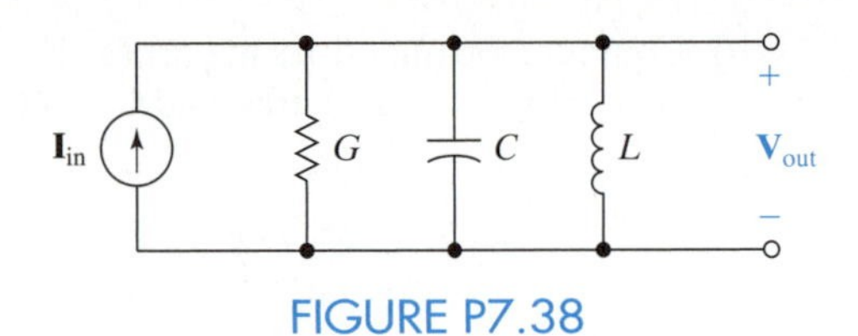

FIGURE P7.38

7.39. A stereo receiver is tuned to 98 mHz on the FM band. The tuning knob controls a variable capacitor in a parallel resonant circuit. If the inductance of the circuit is 2 μH and the Q is 100, determine the values of C and G.

7.40. Given the data in problem 7.39, suppose that another FM station in the vicinity is broadcasting at 98.1 mHz. Let us determine the relative value of the voltage across the resonant circuit at this frequency compared with that at 98 mHz, assuming that the current produced by both signals has the same amplitude.

7.41. Determine the value of C in the network shown in Figure P7.41 in order for the circuit to be in resonance.

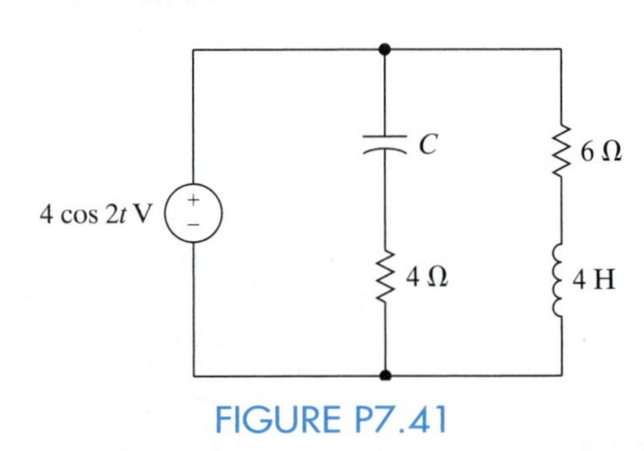

FIGURE P7.41

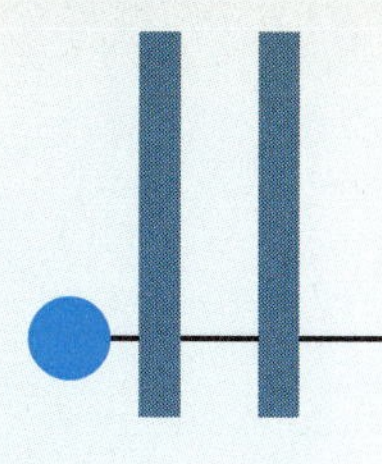

Electronics

8–1 Introduction

The field of *electronics* involves the use of devices and circuits that specifically control the flow of electric current to achieve some purpose. All electronic systems involve circuits, and therefore this section of the text builds heavily on the first. Electronic circuits often contain resistors, capacitors, and inductors; however, they also utilize "electronic devices" such as transistors or diodes. These latter nonlinear elements are used to control or direct the current into desired paths in the circuit. Most modern electronic devices are termed *solid state,* because the current flow is achieved through solid materials called *semiconductors.*

Electronic circuits may have a wide variety of functions such as operational amplifiers (see Chapter 9), power supplies (see Chapter 10), logic gates (the building blocks of computers; see Chapter 14), and amplifiers (see Chapter 11). This chapter will provide an introduction to basic concepts in electronics, many of which will be further developed in the chapters that follow.

8–2 Energy and Power

Power can be transferred from its point of generation to its point of use as either ac or dc, or first one and then the other. Alternating current (ac) is almost universally used for distributing power to households throughout the world.

An automobile typically utilizes a dc power distribution system at approximately 12 volts. The electrical power, however, is created at the alternator as ac and converted to dc by a process called rectification using electronic devices called diodes. This dc voltage is used to maintain the battery in the vehicle in a charged condition.

Most electronic circuits require dc as a source of power for operation

Most electronic circuits require dc as a source of power in order to operate. Therefore, these circuits obtain their operating power from either batteries, which always produce dc, or from an ac source (such as a wall socket), which is subsequently rectified or converted to dc. The solar cell, which directly converts light into electricity, is being used more frequently as a power source, particularly in remote locations. A solar cell produces a dc current approximately proportional to the intensity of the illumination on the cell.

8–3 Analog and Digital Systems; Signals and Pulses

There are two major types of electronic circuits or systems, classified by which signal type they process: analog or digital.

Analog and digital signals defined

The "bit" defined

A voltage or current that, in some manner, is varied over time in order to encode and transmit information is called a *signal.* Typically, signals are termed either *analog* if they vary continuously with time, or *digital* if they switch between discrete levels. In a digital signal there are typically two such levels, a "high" level and a "low" level, which are arbitrarily termed a "1" and a "0," respectively. The information conveyed by the single presentation of a high or low is called a *bit.* In the analog signal in Figure 8.1(a), the amplitude of the signal represents the information at every point in time. For the digital signal in Figure 8.1(b), the information is conveyed by the presence or absence of a pulse.

A *positive pulse* is a single rectangular-shaped waveform representing a change of voltage or current, which goes from a low level to a high level and returns. The waveform for both a positive and a negative pulse is shown in Figure 8.2. A rectangular pulse always has two edges—one positive going and the other negative going. The digital signal of Figure 8.1(b) conveys information as a result of the signal being high or low at sequential points in time. Such a digital signal is termed *serial* because on a single conductor, the pulses must all follow one after the other in time. This approach is viable; however, it is also time consuming.

Serial and parallel data buses defined

In order to increase the rate of data transmission, many digital systems convey information by simultaneously presenting 1s or 0s on a number of parallel conductors. Such an arrangement is termed a *parallel* digital data bus, and the input or output (I/O) of such a bus is termed a parallel input or output port.

By operating at the same pulse transmission speed, an 8-bit parallel data bus can deliver information eight times faster than a single conductor in a serial mode. Most modern personal computers have both serial and parallel ports for connecting the computer to different types of peripheral equipment.

Since digital systems operate using 1s and 0s, the data in these signals is encoded in the *binary number system.* Therefore, prior to a detailed study of digital systems, a review of the binary system and basic logic will be presented in Chapter 13.

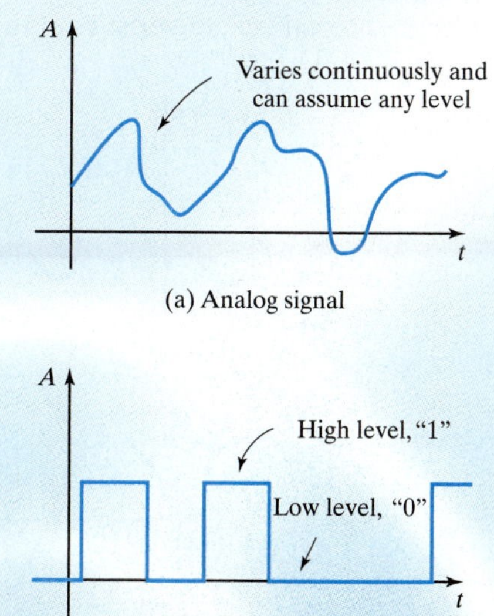

FIGURE 8.1 Analog and digital signals.

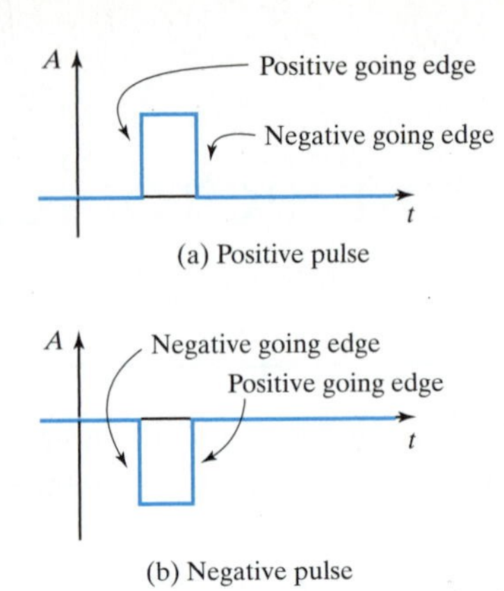

(a) Positive pulse

(b) Negative pulse

FIGURE 8.2 Positive and negative pulses.

8-4 Analog Systems; Amplifiers and Gain

An analog signal can be a complex waveform such as that shown in Figure 8.3(a), or it can be repetitive or periodic, like the sinusoidal signal shown in Figure 8.3(b). The sinusoidal signal response is fundamental to understanding the performance of many electronic circuits and systems. First, as shown in Chapter 4, a complex waveform can be shown to be composed of the sum of a number of sinusoidal signals using Fourier analysis techniques. In addition, the waveform normally produced by an ac generator is sinusoidal.

Recall that a voltage that varies sinusoidally with time can be represented by the function

$$v(t) = A \sin(\omega t + \theta) \tag{8.1}$$

(Compare the above equation to equation 4.5.)

In such a sinusoidally varying signal there are three parameters that can be varied: the amplitude A, the angular frequency ω, and the phase angle θ. The value of each of these parameters determines certain characteristics of the sinusoidal signal.

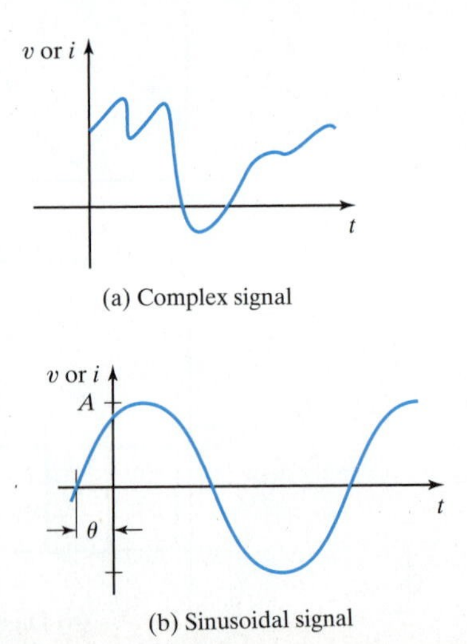

(a) Complex signal

(b) Sinusoidal signal

FIGURE 8.3 Complex and sinusoidal analog signals.

JUST IN TIME

REFERENCE CARD: ELECTRONICS

ELECTRONIC SIGNALS:

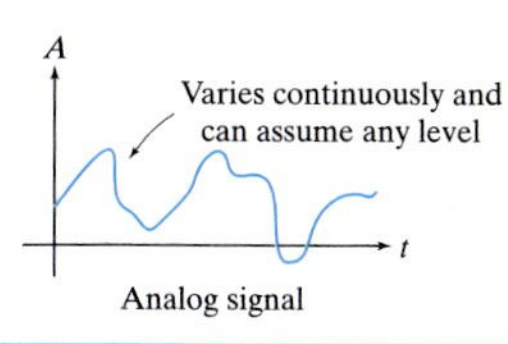

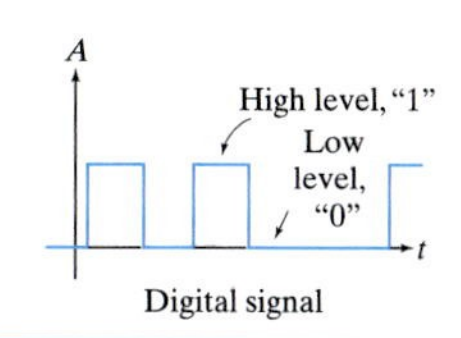

AN AMPLIFIER INCREASES A SIGNAL'S MAGNITUDE:

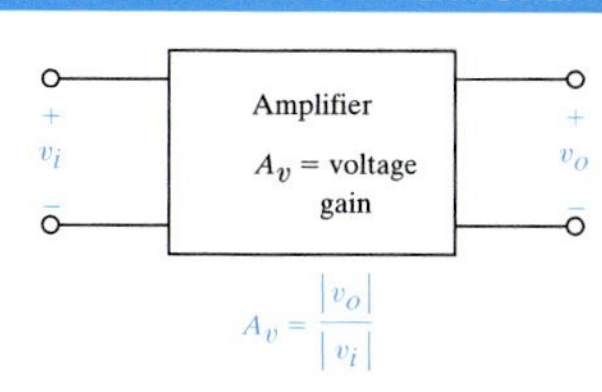

$$A_v = \frac{|v_o|}{|v_i|}$$

GAIN EXPRESSED IN DECIBELS (DB):

$$A_V(\text{db}) = 20 \log Av$$

AMPLIFIERS GAIN OVER A RANGE OF FREQUENCIES:

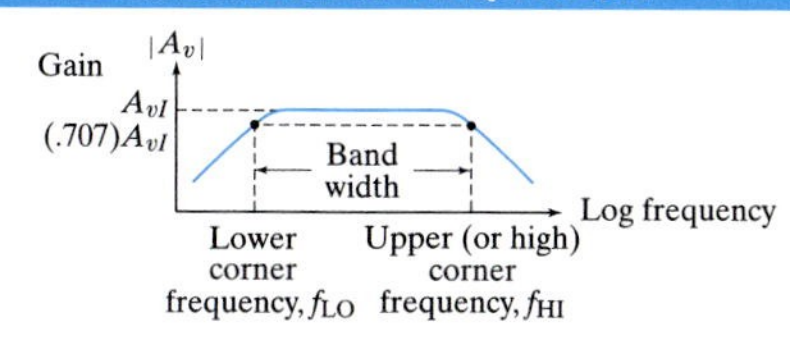

COMMUNICATIONS:

Amplitude Modulation:

$$v_{AM}(t) = V_c sin\omega_c t + m\frac{V_c}{2}\cos(\omega_c - \omega_m)t - m\frac{V_c}{2}\cos(\omega_c + \omega_m)t$$

Number of Zones of Resolution Obtained by Digitizing:

$$Z = 2^n$$

Nyquist Frequency:

$$2(f_m)$$

OP AMPS:

An ideal Op Amp has infinite voltage gain, and no current flowing into its inputs. For an ideal Op Amp with feedback network, we may assume:

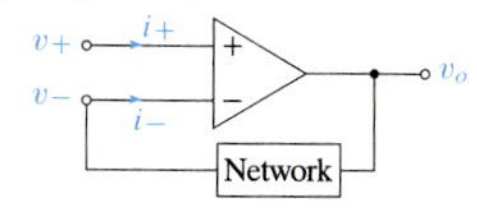

$$i_+ = i_- = 0$$
$$v_- = v_+$$

FOR THE NONINVERTING AMPLIFIER:

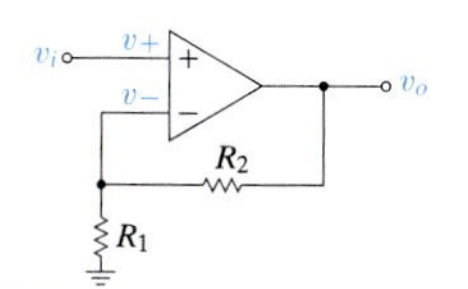

$$A_F = \frac{v_o}{v_i} = 1 + \frac{R_2}{R_1}$$

FOR THE INVERTING AMPLIFIER:

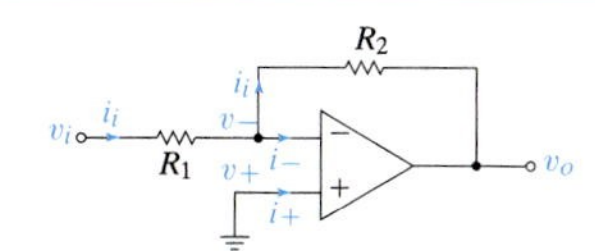

$$A_F = \frac{v_o}{v_i} = -\frac{R_2}{R_1}$$

FOR THE DIFFERENTIAL AMPLIFIER:

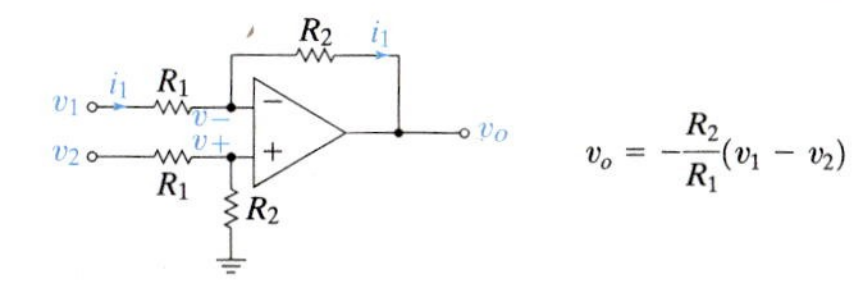

$$v_o = -\frac{R_2}{R_1}(v_1 - v_2)$$

FOR THE UNITY GAIN BUFFER AMPLIFIER:

$$A_F = \frac{v_o}{v_i} = 1$$

FOR THE SUMMING AMPLIFIER:

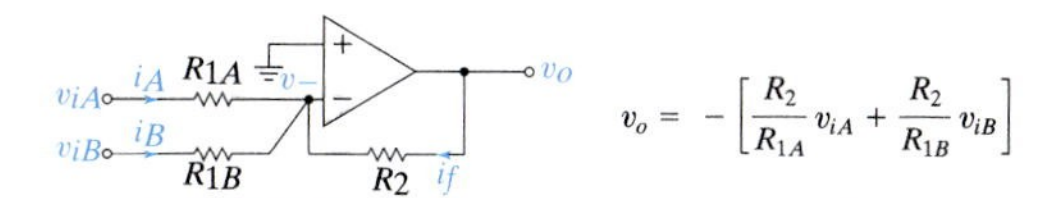

$$v_o = -\left[\frac{R_2}{R_{1A}}v_{iA} + \frac{R_2}{R_{1B}}v_{iB}\right]$$

THE DIODE:

The diode allows current to pass in only one direction. The ideal diode behaves like an open switch (zero current) if V_D is negative, and like a closed switch (passing any amount of current) if the circuit applies a positive V_D.

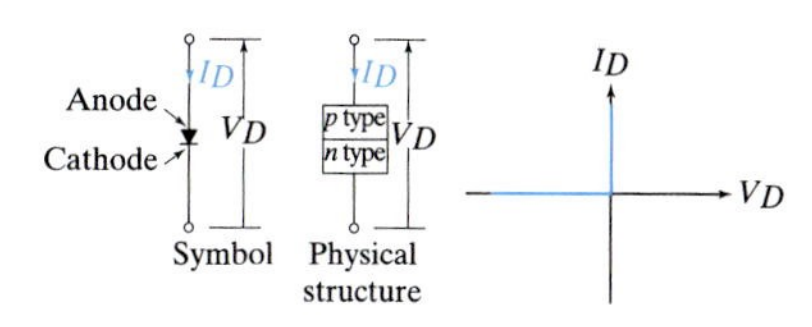

THE DIODE EQUATION:

$$I_D = I_o(e^{\frac{qV_D}{kT}} - 1)$$

THE PIECEWISE LINEAR DIODE MODEL:

(ideal diode)
V_F
r_S
=
PL

THE HALF-WAVE RECTIFIER CIRCUIT:

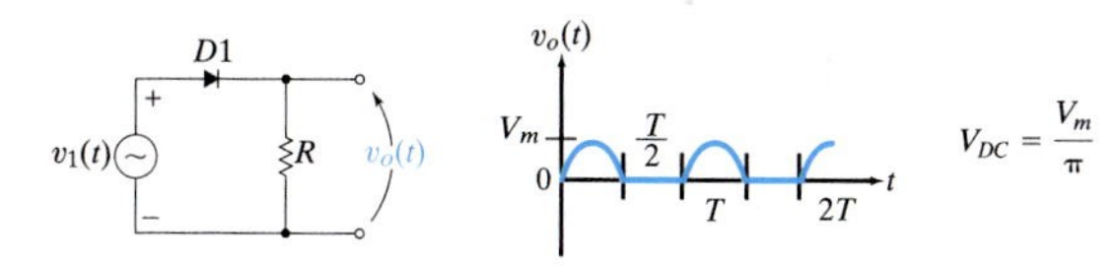

$$V_{DC} = \frac{V_m}{\pi}$$

THE FULL-WAVE BRIDGE RECTIFIER CIRCUIT:

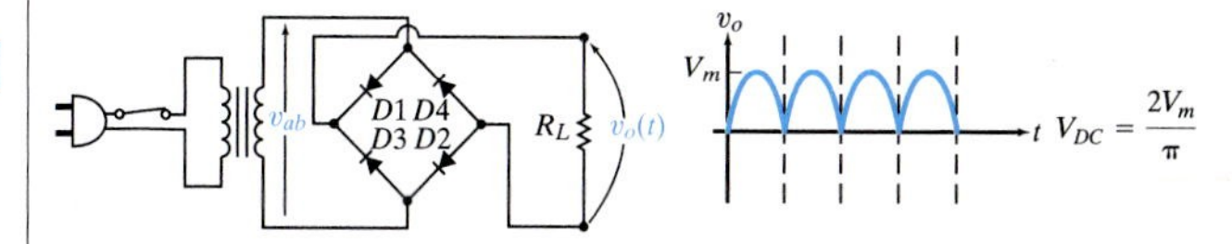

$$V_{DC} = \frac{2V_m}{\pi}$$

THE TRANSISTOR:

Transistors perform one of two functions:

1. an electronically controlled switch,
2. an electronic amplifier.

There are two basic types of transistors: FETs (Field-Effect Transistors) and BJTs (Bipolar- Junction Transistors)

MOSFETs are either enhancement-mode or depletion-mode, and either n-channel or p-channel. Symbols for n-channel devices are shown. The arrow is reversed for p-channel devices.

Enhancement-Mode MOSFET Depletion-Mode MOSFET

The *Threshold Voltage*, V_T, is the minimum voltage applied from gate to source (V_{GS}) in a MOSFET that initiates current conduction.

For the Active Region: $I_D = K(V_{GS} - V_T)^2$

For the Ohmic Region: $I_D = K[2(V_{GS} - V_T)V_{DS} - V_{DS}^2]$

A MOSFET INVERTER (NOT GATE) CIRCUIT WITH A LOAD LINE ANALYSIS:

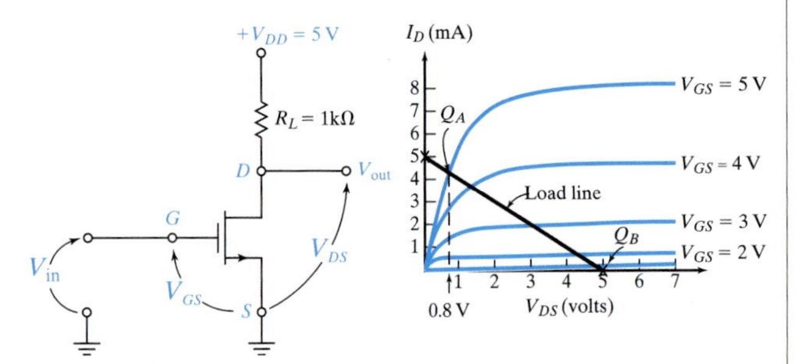

COMMON SOURCE AMPLIFIER

For the inverter circuit, often the MOSET is modeled as a switch:

- when $V_{in} = V_{GS} < V_T$, the MOSFET an open switch, $V_{out} = V_{DD}$
- when $V_{in} = V_{GS} < V_T$, the MOSFET a closed switch, $V_{out} = 0$

The Common Source amplifier circuit is analyzed by superimposing the load line (dashed curve) on the transistor's output curves. In this example, $R_D = 2\,k\Omega$, $R_1 = 7\Omega$, $R_2 = 3\,k\Omega$.

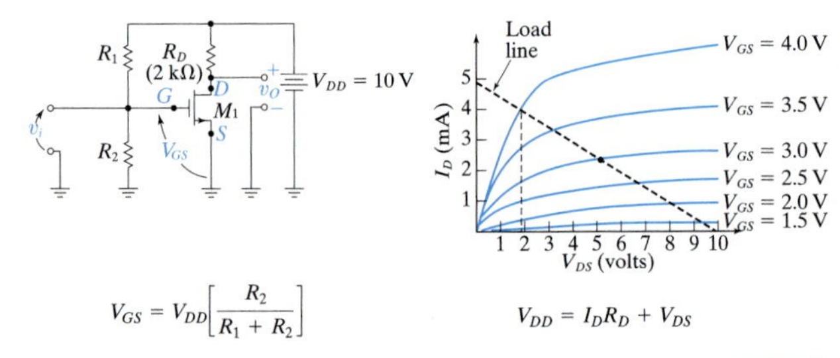

$$V_{GS} = V_{DD}\left[\frac{R_2}{R_1 + R_2}\right] \qquad V_{DD} = I_D R_D + V_{DS}$$

THE BJT:

The BJT (Bipolar Junction Transistor) is either NPN or PNP depending on structure.

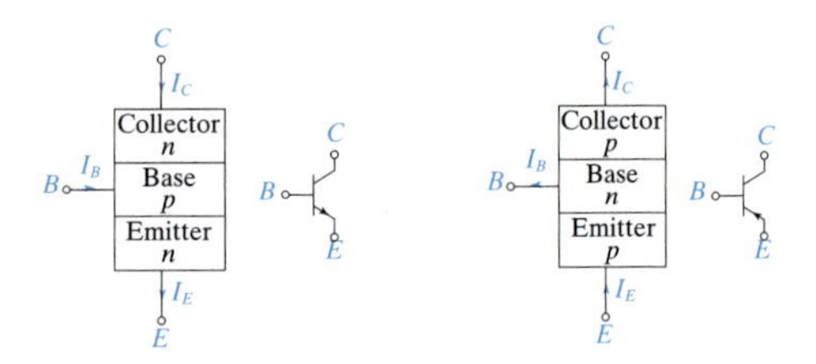

NPN BJT Output Curves:

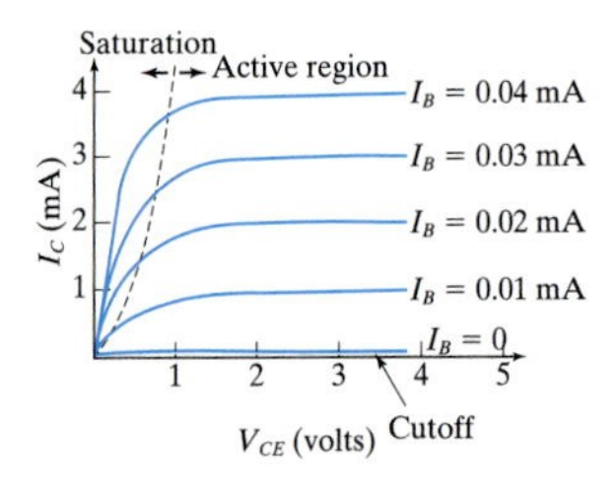

- For the BJT, $I_E = I_B + I_C$; α_F or β_F can be used to relate BJT terminal currents in the forward active region: $I_C = \beta_F I_B$, and $\beta_F = \alpha_F/(I - \alpha_F)$.

BJT EQUIVALENT CIRCUIT FOR THE ACTIVE REGION:

BJT EQUIVALENT CIRCUIT FOR CUTOFF AND SATURATION:

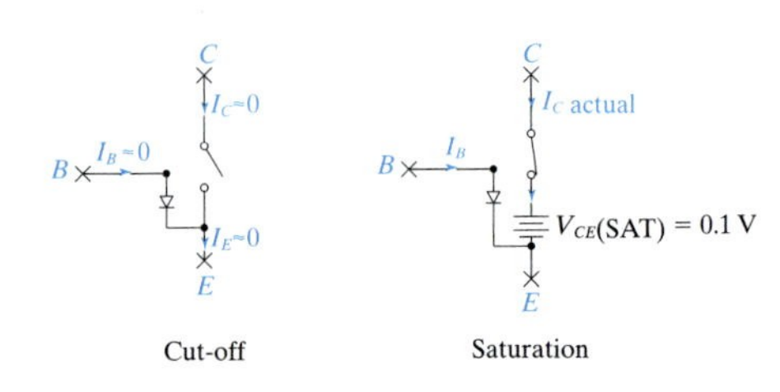

COMMON EMITTER AMPLIFIER CIRCUIT:

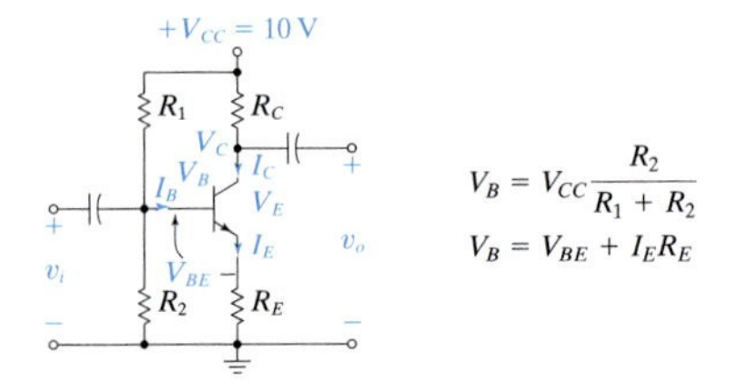

$$V_B = V_{CC}\frac{R_2}{R_1 + R_2}$$

$$V_B = V_{BE} + I_E R_E$$

MOSFET SMALL-SIGNAL MODEL IN COMMON-SOURCE AMPLIFIER CIRCUIT:

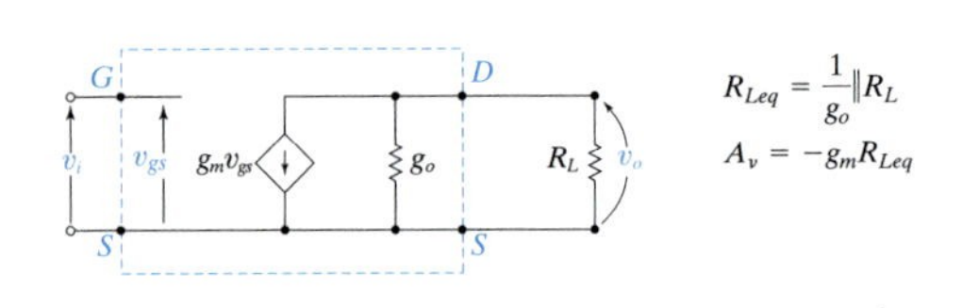

$$R_{Leq} = \frac{1}{g_o} \| R_L$$

$$A_v = -g_m R_{Leq}$$

BJT SMALL-SIGNAL MODEL IN COMMON-EMITTER AMPLIFIER CIRCUIT:

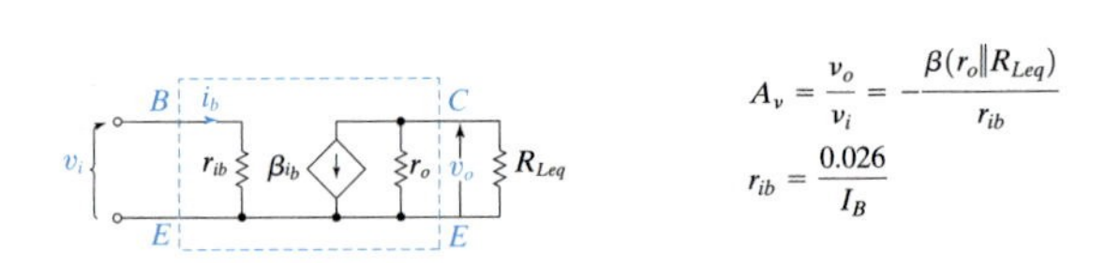

$$A_v = \frac{v_o}{v_i} = -\frac{\beta(r_o \| R_{Leq})}{r_{ib}}$$

$$r_{ib} = \frac{0.026}{I_B}$$

THE GAIN OF A MULTIPLE STAGE AMPLIFIER:

$$A_{v(total)} = A_{v1}A_{v2} \ldots A_{vN}$$

Recall the angular frequency, ω, in radians per second, is related to f, the frequency in hertz by the relation

$$\omega = 2\pi f \tag{8.2}$$

The standard frequency for the transmission of electric power in the United States and Canada is 60 hertz, whereas 50 hertz is used in Europe and in other parts of the world.

The audio frequency range, or the range of frequencies the human ear can detect, is from approximately 30 hertz to 15,000 hertz, which is the frequency range of the electronic signal observed from the output of a high-quality microphone. The entire frequency spectrum was presented in Figure 1.6.

The amplitude, A, of a signal is an extremely important parameter and can vary over many orders of magnitude. The voltage received on the antenna of a television set may be in the order of microvolts (10^{-6} volts), whereas the voltage applied to the picture tube in the same set may be 20,000 volts (2×10^4 volts). This represents a voltage range of some 10 orders of magnitude.

In many applications, an exact replica of a particular signal is needed, but with a larger amplitude. Consider the following example.

Example 8.1

Assume the voltage signal from an electric guitar is 20 millivolts in amplitude, and this signal must be amplified or increased in amplitude in order to provide 100 watts of power to an 8-ohm speaker. Let us first determine the required *rms* sinusoidal voltage across the speaker.

For this case, the voltage and power are related by the expression

$$P = \frac{V_{rms}^2}{R}$$

and therefore,

$$V_{rms} = \sqrt{PR} = \sqrt{(100)(8)} = 28 \text{ volts}$$

Assuming this signal is sinusoidal, the amplitude is

$$V_m = \sqrt{2}\,V_{rms} \doteq (1.41)(28) = 40 \text{ volts}$$

Since the guitar's output amplitude is 20 millivolts, the signal voltage must be increased by a factor of

$$\frac{40}{20 \times 10^{-3}} = 2000$$

Amplifier and gain defined

An *amplifier*, shown symbolically in Figure 8.4, is an electronic circuit that is used to increase the amplitude of a signal. The magnitude of the amplifier's *voltage gain*, A_v, is defined as the ratio of the amplitude of the output voltage, v_o, to the amplitude of the input voltage, v_i, or

$$A_v = \frac{|v_o|}{|v_i|} \tag{8.3}$$

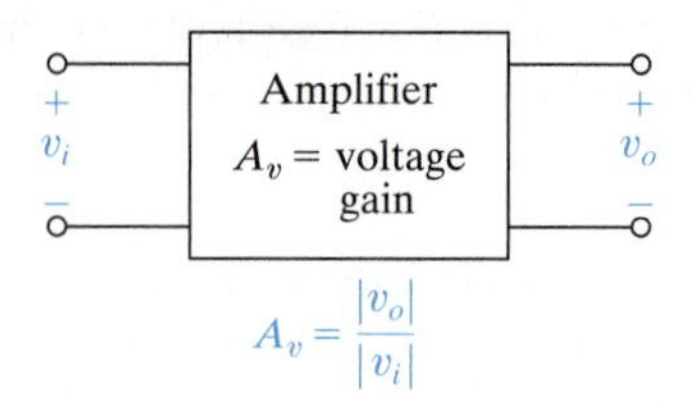

FIGURE 8.4 A voltage amplifier.

In the example just described, the voltage gain, A_v, of the required amplifier is 2000.

Thus far we have discussed only the magnitude of the gain; however, there is also a phase relation between the input and output signal. Thus, the voltage gain is more accurately represented as a complex quantity.

The complex voltage gain, $\mathbf{A}_v$, is the ratio of the phasor transform of the output voltage to that of the input voltage, assuming the signals are sinusoidal,

$$\mathbf{A}_v = \frac{\mathbf{V}_o}{\mathbf{V}_i} \tag{8.4}$$

Most electronic circuits are designed to operate in what is called the *midband frequency region*, and in this range the phase shift of amplifiers is either zero or 180°, that is, noninverting or inverting. For this reason, in the basic analysis of electronic amplifiers we most often speak only of the magnitude of the voltage gain and include a plus sign if the amplifier is noninverting and a minus sign if it is inverting.

There are also current amplifiers, which produce an output current that is larger than its input current by a constant factor called the *current gain*.

Example 8.2

A current of 3×10^{-5} amperes, dc, is derived from a solar cell illuminated by the sun. Let us determine the current gain required in order to activate a small electric motor requiring 5×10^{-2} amperes. The current gain, A_i, needed is

$$A_i = \frac{5.00 \times 10^{-2}}{3.00 \times 10^{-5}} = 1670$$

Drill Exercise

D8.1. Determine the voltage gain required in Example 7.1 if a 4 Ω speaker is used.

Ans: 1410.

Decibels defined

The voltage gain (or current gain) of an amplifier is sometimes expressed in decibels (db), where the gain in *decibels*, A_v(db), is defined by

$$A_v(\text{db}) = 20 \log A_v \tag{8.5}$$

Note that a gain of 0 db represents a voltage gain of 1 (unity), while 20 db represents a gain of 10, 40 db a gain of 100, and so on. Therefore, factors of 10 increase in gain are expressed as a linear increase in A_v(db), each additional 20 db representing another factor of 10.

Drill Exercise

D8.2. What is the current gain, A_i (expressed as a ratio), of an amplifier if we are told the gain is 60 db?

Ans: 1000

Drill Exercise

D8.3. An amplifier has an output signal amplitude of 1.7 volts when the input is attached to a signal source with an amplitude of 30 mV. What is the voltage gain expressed as a ratio, and what is the voltage gain expressed in decibels?

Ans: 56.7; 35.1 db

Frequency response and corner (half-power) frequencies

Another important characteristic of an amplifier is its *frequency response*, that is, the way in which the gain varies as the frequency of a sinusoidal input signal is changed. No real amplifier can amplify an input signal over an infinite range of frequencies. At some high frequency the amplifier will no longer be able to produce the same amplitude of output signal as it could at a lower frequency, and hence the gain is said to "roll off." Many amplifiers also roll off as frequency is decreased below some particular low-frequency value. The high frequency at which the gain is reduced by a factor of 0.707 from the midband value is termed the *upper* or *high-corner frequency,* f_{HI}, and the low frequency at which the gain has dropped by a factor of 0.707 is termed the *low-corner frequency*, f_{LO}.

Note that $1/\sqrt{2} = 0.707$; expressed in decibels, $20 \log(0.707) = 3$ db. f_{HI} and f_{LO} are analogous to the cutoff frequencies expressed by equation 7.13. These corner (or cutoff) frequencies are also called *half-power frequencies.*

Bandwidth defined

The difference in frequency between the high-corner frequency and the low-corner frequency is called the *bandwidth, BW*. This is illustrated in the plot in Figure 8.5.

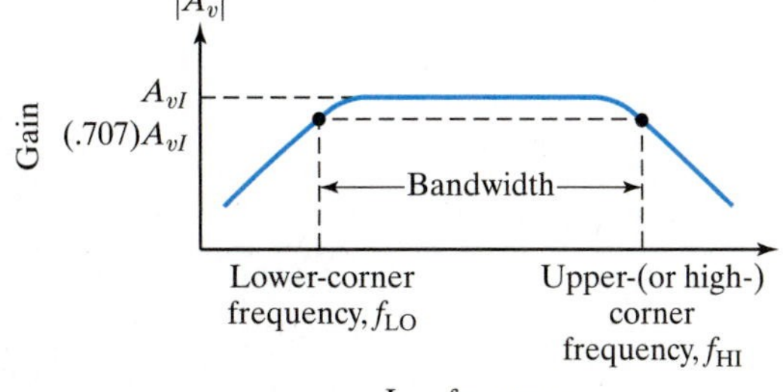

FIGURE 8.5 Frequency response of amplifier.

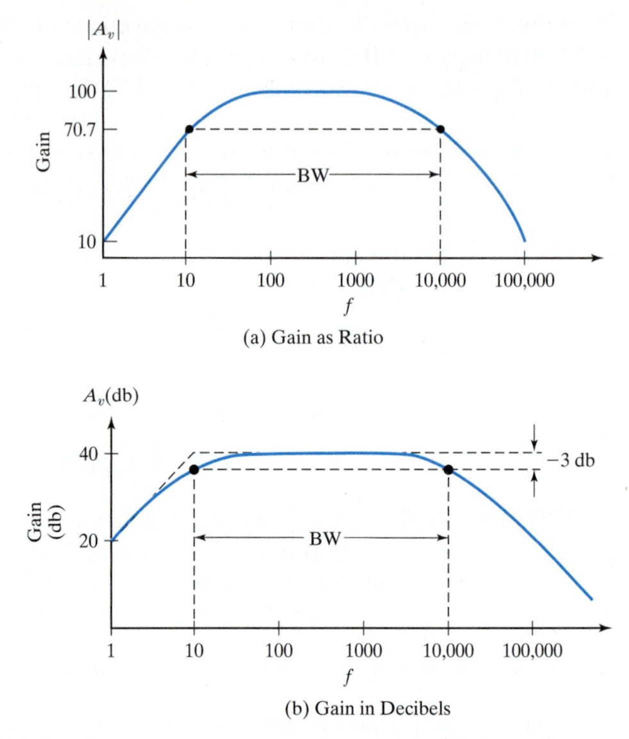

FIGURE 8.6 Frequency response of amplifier with gain of 100.

Plots of frequency response are almost always done on a logarithmic frequency scale. To further clarify, let's take a specific example of an amplifier with a midband gain of 100, an upper-corner frequency of 10 kHz, and a bandwidth of 9990 Hz. The gain can be plotted on the vertical axis as the voltage ratio, as shown in Figure 8.6(a). However, it is more common for the gain to be plotted in decibels, as shown in Figure 8.6 (b); in this case the half-power points or corner frequencies at which the gain is reduced by 0.707 correspond to a gain reduction of 3 db. The use of decibels effectively provides a logarithmic scale for gain, and plots for real circuits often result in straight-line segments.

Some amplifiers do not have a lower-corner frequency, and will amplify signals all the way down to dc or zero frequency. These amplifiers are called *dc amplifiers.* A plot of such an amplifier's frequency response is shown in Figure 8.7.

For a dc amplifier the bandwidth is the same as the high-corner frequency, since the low-corner frequency is zero.

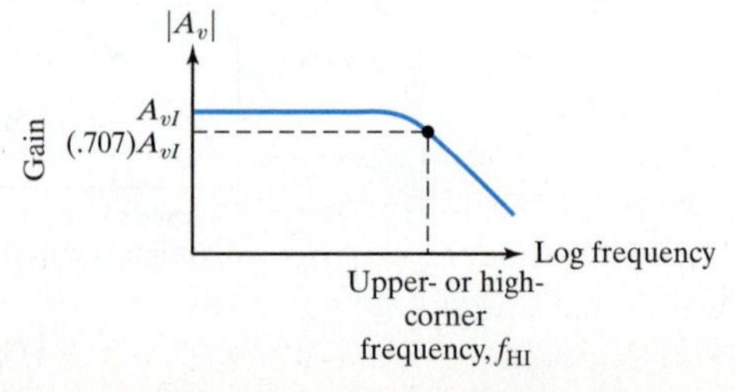

FIGURE 8.7 Frequency response of dc amplifier.

Example 8.3

The midband gain of a voltage amplifier is 20. If the gain drops to 14.1 at a high frequency of 11 MHz, and the amplifier has a bandwidth of 3 MHz, let us determine the low-frequency half-power point.

Since the voltage gain drops to 0.707 of its midband value at 11 MHz, this frequency is the high-frequency half-power point. The bandwidth is the difference between the high-and the low-corner frequencies, and therefore, the low-frequency half-power point is

$$11\text{ MHz} - 3\text{ MHz} = 8\text{ MHz}$$

Drill Exercise

D8.4. An ac amplifier has a lower-corner frequency of 0.5 MHz and a bandwidth of 1.0 MHz. (a) Determine the amplifier's upper-corner frequency. (b) Determine the upper-corner frequency of a dc amplifier with the same bandwidth.

Ans: (a) 1.5 MHz (b) 1.0 MHz.

8–5 Modulation and Demodulation; Encoding and Decoding

Three forms of modulation

Modulation is the process used to encode, or "attach and carry," information on an analog signal. *Demodulation* is the reverse process in which the information is extracted from an analog signal.

Recall that there are three basic ways of carrying information via a sinusoidal signal: by varying the amplitude, the frequency, or the phase. Assume, for example, the information we wish to send is represented by the "voltage ramp" shown in Figure 8.8(a); this is called the *baseband signal.*

The sinusoidal wave, called the carrier wave, which is amplitude modulated with this information, would appear as shown in Figure 8.8(b). Note that the amplitude of the sinusoidal signal varies in relation to the information desired to be transmitted. *Amplitude modulation* (AM) is commonly used for transmission of radio signals. For example, in the United States the Federal Communications Commission has established a range of frequencies for the commercial broadcast of AM signals. The AM band is available on most home and automobile radios.

Frequency modulation, used, for example, on the commercial FM radio band, employs changes in frequency to represent the desired information. The same wave transmitted by FM would appear as shown in Figure 8.8(c). Note that the frequency of the sinusoidal signal changes in proportion to the information to be transmitted.

Phase modulation is similar to frequency modulation; however, rather than varying the frequency, the phase of the sinusoidal signal is varied relative to some fixed reference.

The telephone was designed as an instrument to transmit analog signals, primarily the tones of the human voice. With the advent of the computer, a need developed to transmit digital signals via phone lines. To accomplish this, a modulation system was designed that

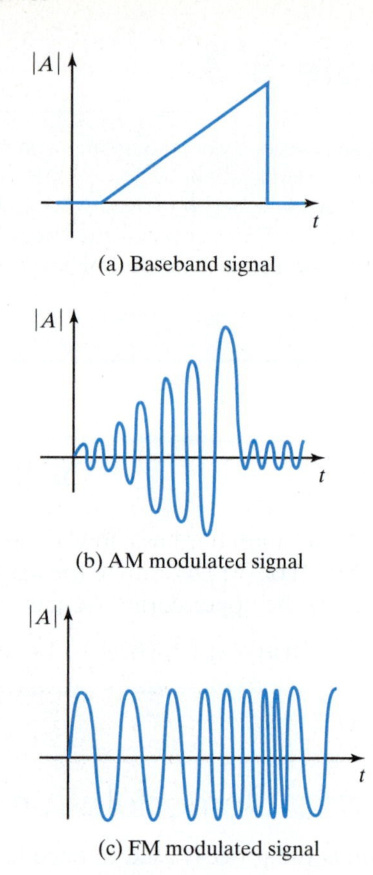

FIGURE 8.8 (a) Baseband signal. (b) AM modulated signal. (c) FM modulated signal.

translated the digital information into analog tones that could be sent over the phone lines and reconstructed at the other end. Such a system is called a *modem,* an abbreviation for "*mo*dulator–*dem*odulator."

The process of modifying information so that it is suitable for transmission by a digital signal and constructing the digital signal to represent the information is called simply *encoding.* The opposite process, in which the encoded information is extracted from a digital signal, is termed *decoding.*

8.5.1 Amplitude Modulation

Amplitude modulation is an important form of modulation, and gives us insight into how the modulation of a carrier signal affects the resulting frequency spectrum.

In amplitude modulation (AM) the amplitude of a "carrier wave" is changed in accordance with the information to be transmitted.

Figure 8.9(a) shows a continuous sinusoidal carrier wave of frequency, f_c. Figure 8.9(b) shows the information that we wish to transmit, $v_m(t)$; for illustration, we will consider a sinusoidal signal of frequency, f_m. Finally, Figure 8.9(c) shows the high-frequency wave, f_c, amplitude modulated with the information at a frequency of f_m.

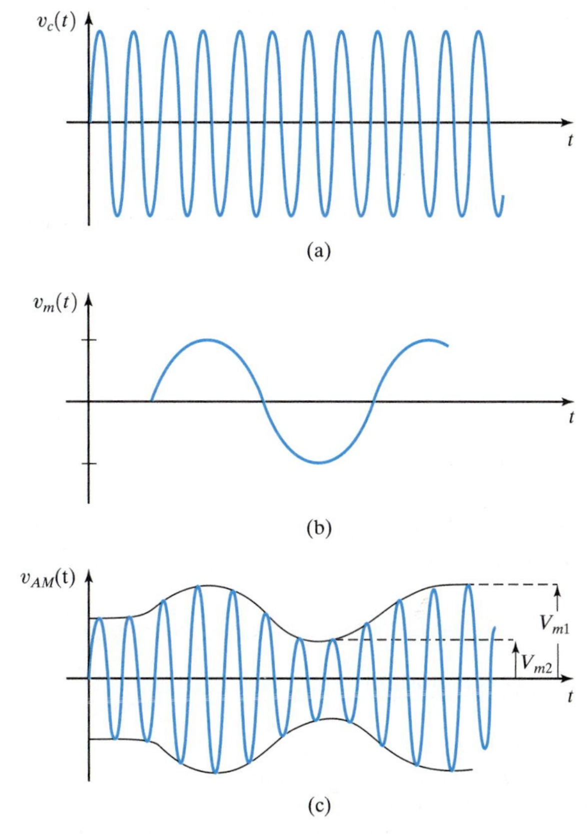

FIGURE 8.9 (a) Carrier wave of frequency f_c; (b) message signal of frequency, f_m ($f_m < f_c$); (c) amplitude modulated signal.

Mathematically, we let the carrier wave be represented as

$$v_c(t) = V_c \sin(\omega_c t) \tag{8.6}$$

where V_c is the peak amplitude of the carrier signal in volts and ω_c is the carrier frequency in radians/second.

For convenience we will initially assume that the message signal is a single frequency (a tone) expressed as a sinusoid of a much lower frequency; that is, $\omega_m << \omega_c$. Hence

$$v_m(t) = V_m \sin(\omega_m t) \tag{8.7}$$

where V_m is the peak amplitude of the modulating signal in volts and ω_m is the angular frequency of the message signal in radians/second.

To construct an expression for amplitude modulation, we let the carrier signal amplitude be changed by that of the message. Thus

$$v_{AM}(t) = [V_c + V_m \sin \omega_m t] \sin(\omega_c t) \tag{8.8}$$

This expression can be written as

$$v_{AM}(t) = V_c\left[1 + \frac{V_m}{V_c}\sin(\omega_m t)\right]\sin \omega_c t \tag{8.9}$$

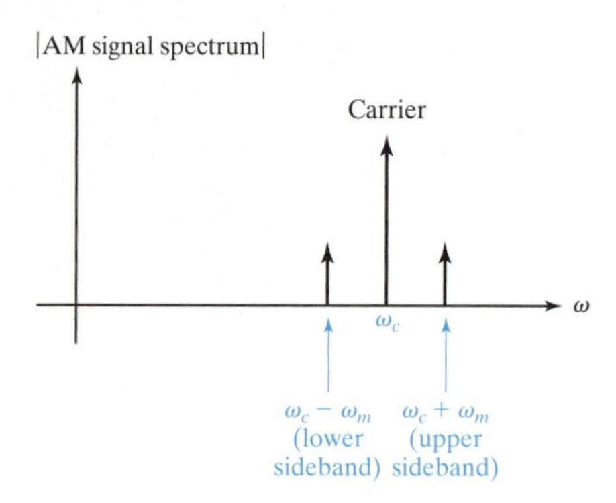

FIGURE 8.10 Spectrum of AM signal with sinusoidal message.

letting m = the modulation index = V_m/V_c, which should be <1

$$v_{AM}(t) = V_c \sin\omega_c t + V_c m\,(\sin\omega_m t)(\sin\omega_c t) \tag{8.10}$$

Using a trigonometric identity for the product of the two sine functions, this equation can be written with the last term expressed as a "sum" and a "difference" frequency, as

Expression for amplitude modulation

$$v_{AM}(t) = V_c \sin\omega_c t + m\frac{V_c}{2}\cos(\omega_c - \omega_m)t - m\frac{V_c}{2}\cos(\omega_c + \omega_m)t \tag{8.11}$$

This important result shows that an AM modulated signal has a frequency component at the carrier frequency, but, in addition, there are two components with the information, one at a frequency of $(\omega_c - \omega_m)$ and another at $(\omega_c + \omega_m)$. These frequency components are called the *lower* and *upper sidebands*, respectively. A frequency spectrum of this AM modulated signal is shown in Figure 8.10.

Example 8.4

Let us plot the anticipated frequency spectrum of a carrier signal with an amplitude of unity and frequency f_c = 10 MHz that is AM modulated (m = 1) with a signal, $v_m(t)$, where

$$v_m(t) = .8\sin(2\pi 10000\,t) + .4\sin(2\pi\,22000\,t).$$

There is a carrier present with a magnitude of unity; each sinusoidal signal produces an upper and a lower sideband at half the magnitude of the message signal; therefore, the frequency spectrum appears as in Figure 8.11.

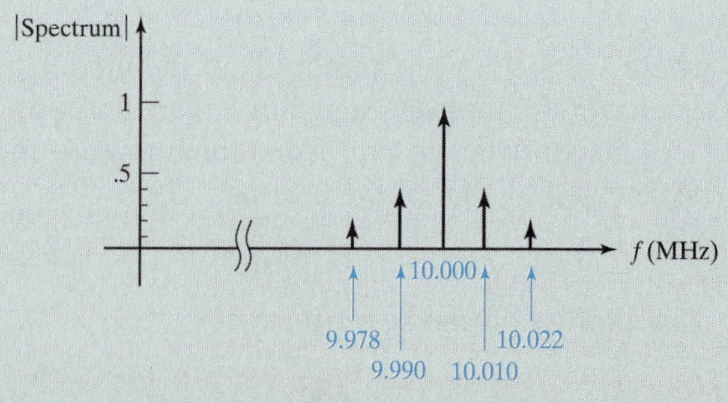

FIGURE 8.11 Spectrum for signal described in Example 8.4.

Example 8.5

A 10 MHz carrier is AM modulated with a sinusoidal message signal of 20 kHz. What is the bandwidth of a bandpass filter centered at 10 MHz required to transmit this AM signal?

The AM signal will contain the carrier at 10 MHz, and an upper and lower sideband at the sum and difference frequencies, respectively.

Therefore, the upper sideband,

$$f_{\text{upper}} = 10\text{ MHz} + 20\text{ kHz} = 10.02\text{ MHz}$$

The lower sideband,

$$f_{\text{lower}} = 10\text{ MHz} - 20\text{ kHz} = 9.980\text{ MHz}$$

The minimum bandwidth of the filter must be sufficiently wide to include both sidebands, therefore,

$$\text{BW}_{\text{min}} = f_{\text{upper}} - f_{\text{lower}} = 10.02 - 9.980 = 40\text{ kHz}$$

Example 8.6

A square wave has harmonic frequency components at odd multiples of the fundamental frequency. Consider a 5 MHz carrier that is AM modulated by a square wave with a period of 10 msec. A filter with a center at 5 MHz requires what bandwidth to transmit the carrier and the first two nonzero harmonics? (three and five times the fundamental frequency)?

The message signal has a frequency, f_m, where

$$f_m = 1/\text{T} = 1/10\text{ msec} = 100\text{ Hz}$$

There is a nonzero harmonic at $3 f_m = 300$ Hz; the next nonzero harmonic is at $5 f_m = 500$ Hz. Therefore, the highest required frequency component in the message signal is 500 Hz.

The bandwidth required to include the upper and lower sideband is twice the highest frequency in the message signal, or

$$BW = 2(500) = 1\text{ kHz}$$

8–6 Digital Systems: Information, Sampling, and Logic Gates

Almost all digital systems utilize circuits with *binary logic*. In binary digital logic, data is represented by a voltage (or occasionally a current) switching between one of two possible levels, a low level called a logic 0, and a high level called a logic 1. This process is termed "asserted positive logic." The system could be implemented using the opposite convention where the high level is considered a logic 0 and the low level a logic 1, and such a system is said to use "asserted negative logic." Positive logic is by far the most common.

The single unit of digital information, the *bit*, is represented by the transmission of a 1 or a 0. The bit has been found to be a very useful means of quantizing information. Information theory, a subspecialty within the field of communications, has developed expressions for calculating the number of equivalent bits of information contained in various signals. (See Figure 8.1(b).)

The series of bits that represent a particular piece of information, or value such as an analog level, is termed a digital *word*. If this series of bits is presented at the same time via parallel conductors, that is, a parallel bus, we receive a parallel word; if they appear one after the other via a single conductor, that is, a serial data bus, then we receive a serial word. Eight-bit word segments are normally referred to as a *byte*.

We will now discuss the digitizing of an analog signal. The *most significant bit* in the word conveys to us whether the information or value is in the top half or lower half of its possible range. For example, if we consider a signal, v, which we know has values in the range $0 < v < 2$, one bit of information would tell us the following: if the voltage is in the range $0 < v < 1$, then the bit status could be 0, and if the voltage is in the range $1 < v < 2$, the bit status would be 1.

This is very coarse information about this signal, v. We originally knew its value was between zero and two, and now we have started to "pin it down" by breaking the total range into two zones. We use this first bit, the *most significant bit* (MSB), to tell us whether we are in the upper 50% or lower 50% of the entire range.

We can add a second bit to tell us whether we are in the top half or lower half of the smaller range just selected by the previous bit. We are now capable of quantifying the signal to within four possible "zones" using the following correspondence:

Range	**Bit status**	
	MSB	LSB
$0.0 < v < 0.5$	0	0
$0.5 < v < 1.0$	0	1
$1.0 < v < 1.5$	1	0
$1.5 < v < 2.0$	1	1

Where MSB = most significant bit and LSB = least significant bit.

Number of zones as a function of number of bits

We could now add a third bit, which would give us a resolution of eight possible ranges, or zones. Note that in the binary system, the number of zones of resolution, Z, is related to the number of bits, n, by the expression

$$Z = 2^n \tag{8.12}$$

Example 8.7

Let us determine the voltage resolution that can be achieved if a signal with a maximum value of 12 volts and minimum value of 0 volts is represented by 10 bits.

The number of zones defined by 10 bits is:

$$Z = 2^n = 2^{10} = 1024 \text{ zones}$$

$$\textit{Resolution} = \frac{12.0}{1024} = 0.0117 \text{ volts/zone}$$

Drill Exercises

D8.5. A 4-bit parallel data bus can transmit 8 bits of information in 40 microseconds. If the same technology were used to transmit data serially over a single conductor, how many bits could be transmitted in the same 40 microseconds?

Ans: 2 bits.

D8.6. A signal that can have values between −10 to +10 volts is represented by a 12-bit digital word; what is the voltage resolution obtainable with this system?

Ans: 4.9 mV.

8.6.1 A/D and D/A Converters: Sampling and Aliasing

Electronic circuits, which are designed to automatically convert an analog voltage into a digital or binary representation of that voltage, are called *analog to digital converters*, or A/D converters. Circuits that convert a digital word into an analog voltage level are called *digital to analog converters*, or D/A converters. Both converters are shown symbolically in Figure 8.12. A timing signal is used to specify the point in time at which a sample is taken.

An 8-bit A/D converter, for example, converts a continuously variable voltage within a specified range at its input into an 8-bit digital word at its output, which represents the quantized value of the input voltage at a specific point in time. Therefore, we are told which of 256 zones the input voltage is contained within ($2^8 = 256$) at the time of the sample. A/D and D/A converters are available from many manufacturers integrated on a single IC chip.

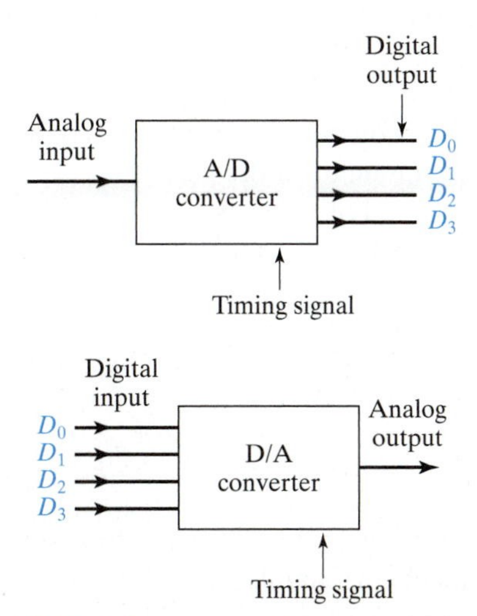

FIGURE 8.12 A/D and D/A converters.

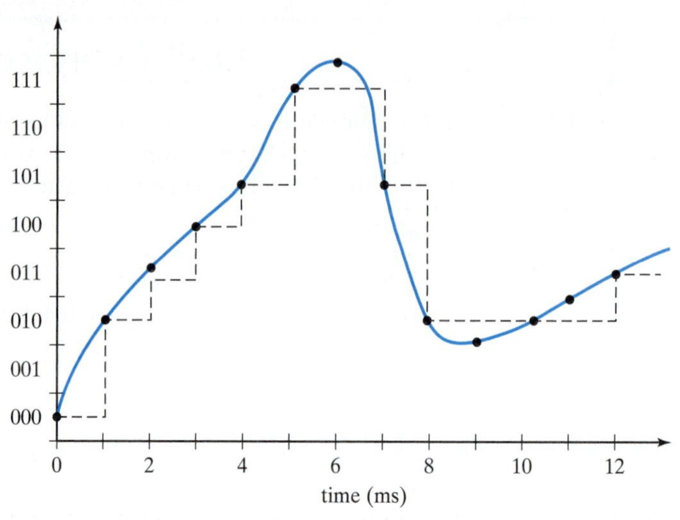

FIGURE 8.13 Digitizing of analog signal with 3-bit resolution.

To illustrate sampling, consider the analog signal shown in Figure 8.13. We will assume we have a three bit A/D converter, which provides eight possible zones for quantization. We will assume that we sample every millisecond. Also shown in the same figure is the digitized signal. Note that it closely resembles the original analog signal.

You can also easily see that if you don't sample often enough, you would lose an accurate representation of the signal. For example, if you sampled every 8 ms, you would miss the entire peak of the analog signal that occurs at about 6 ms. One form of this signal distortion is known as aliasing. Aliasing occurs when sampling a periodic signal too slowly, and an artifact at a lower frequency is observed.

Most modern digital systems that input analog data use an A/D converter to sample the analog signal at discrete points in time. A digital representation of the continuously changing analog signal is constructed by storing each of these sampled values in its memory as a digital word. The question naturally arises, how often must one sample and store a value of the analog signal in order to completely represent it in sampled digital form? Of course, the answer depends on how fast the analog signal is changing, and that is related to the highest frequency components in the signal.

If the analog signal is changing values rapidly, it will have high-frequency components and a large bandwidth, and therefore it will require a high *sampling rate.*

Consider an analog baseband signal, *f(t)*, and let f_m be the highest or maximum frequency component in this signal. Then the signal can be uniquely determined by samples taken at evenly spaced time intervals separated in time by no more than T_s where

$$T_s = \frac{1}{f_s} \leq \frac{1}{2f_m} \text{ seconds} \tag{8.13}$$

Nyquist frequency, minimum sampling rate defined

Stated alternatively, the sampling frequency, f_s, must be at least twice the highest frequency of the signal being sampled; the *minimum sampling rate* is known as the *Nyquist frequency*, $2f_m$.

$$f_s \geq 2\,f_m \tag{8.14}$$

Example 8.8

If the audio signal in a telephone line has a maximum frequency of 2 kHz, let us determine the rate at which an A/D converter must sample this signal in order to capture an accurate record of it.

The Nyquist frequency is $2f_m$, therefore, the sampling rate must be a minimum of 2×2 kHz or 4 kHz.

Drill Exercise

D8.7. A signal is bandlimited with a maximum frequency of 25 kHz. It is to be sampled at a rate 50% higher than the minimum allowed rate to ensure margin. These samples will be used by the system to reconstruct the original signal at a later time. Determine the time interval to be used between samples.

Ans: 13.3 μs.

8.6.2 Logic Gates

Information represented as 1s and 0s in a digital system is processed primarily by elements called *logic gates.*

A practical *logic gate* is an electronic circuit that has a digital output that can assume voltage levels which correspond to a 1 or a 0 state, and one or more digital inputs, which determine the state of the output.

Three simple logic gates will be described here: the *inverter*, the *AND-gate*, and the *OR-gate.* Later, further details of these and more complex logical functions will be described.

The simplest logic gate is the inverter. The inverter has only one input and one output, and its output is always the opposite or *complement* of its input. *Truth tables* are often used in order to describe logic gate operation. A truth table is a chart showing the logical state of the output for every possible input combination. The truth table for the *inverter* is relatively simple since it has only one input. If A is the input and B is the output, then the truth table is

A (input)	*B* (output)
0	1
1	0

Inverter, AND, OR gates defined

There are sets of standard symbols for the basic logic gates. The symbol for the inverter is shown in Figure 8.14(a).

The *AND-gate* has a single output and can have any number of inputs greater than 1. The output of this gate is high only when all the inputs are high, and for any other combina-

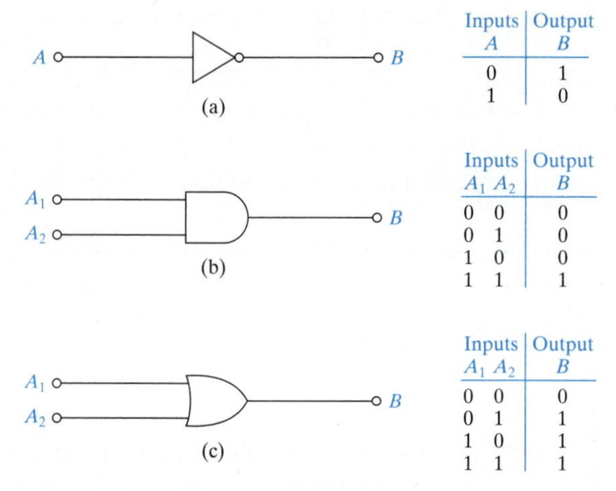

Inputs A	Output B
0	1
1	0

Inputs A_1	A_2	Output B
0	0	0
0	1	0
1	0	0
1	1	1

Inputs A_1	A_2	Output B
0	0	0
0	1	1
1	0	1
1	1	1

FIGURE 8.14 (a) Inverter or NOT-gate. (b) AND-gate. (c) OR-gate.

tion of inputs, the output is low. The logic symbol and truth table for a two-input AND-gate are shown in Figure 8.14(b).

The *OR-gate* has a single output and can have any number of inputs greater than 1. This gate produces a high level at its output if *any* of its inputs are high, and the output is low only if none of the inputs are high. The truth table and logic symbol for a two-input OR-gate are shown in Figure 8.14(c).

NAND and NOR gates defined

In order to implement certain logic functions, it often becomes necessary to use an AND-gate followed by an inverter. This combination produces an output that is the exact complement of the AND-gate, and the combination is defined as a *NAND-gate.* Similarly, a gate that produces an output that is the complement of the OR-gate is called the *NOR-gate.* The logic symbols and truth tables for three input NAND and NOR gates are given in Figure 8.15.

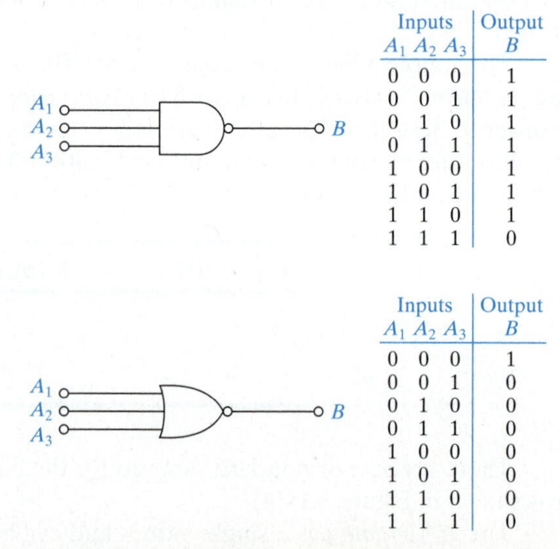

Inputs A_1	A_2	A_3	Output B
0	0	0	1
0	0	1	1
0	1	0	1
0	1	1	1
1	0	0	1
1	0	1	1
1	1	0	1
1	1	1	0

Inputs A_1	A_2	A_3	Output B
0	0	0	1
0	0	1	0
0	1	0	0
0	1	1	0
1	0	0	0
1	0	1	0
1	1	0	0
1	1	1	0

FIGURE 8.15 NAND and NOR logic gates.

Many electronic circuits utilized for implementing logic inherently invert the signal while performing the logic function, and therefore, NAND/NOR logic is quite common in practical electronic systems.

It is straightforward to develop a truth table from a combination of logic gates, a logic circuit. First, identify the inputs and construct the left column of the truth table so all binary input combinations are included (e.g., if there are three inputs, there are $2^3 = 8$ possible combinations; for four inputs, there are 16 different input possibilities). For each input combination, determine the output of each gate, and use that output as the input to a subsequent gate. It is helpful to label intermediate nodes; in the example we label the single intermediate node, B. Using this process an output state for each possible input can be determined. This is illustrated below in Example 8.9.

The reverse process of generating a set of logic gates that will produce a given truth table is more difficult, and is the essence of logic design; a common design goal is to achieve the function with the fewest number of gates. This will be covered in Chapter 13.

Example 8.9

Construct a truth table for the combination of logic gates given in Figure 8.16. That is, what is the logic state of C for every possible combination of inputs, A_1, A_2, and A_3?

(Assume A_1 is the MSB.)

(MSB) A_1
A_2
A_3
B
C

FIGURE 8.16 A combination of logic gates.

Ans: B is only a 1 if *both* A_1 and A_2 are a 1; C is a 1 if *either* A_3 or B is a 1.

A_1	A_2	A_3	**B**	**C**
0	0	0	0	0
0	0	1	0	1
0	1	0	0	0
0	1	1	0	1
1	0	0	0	0
1	0	1	0	1
1	1	0	1	1
1	1	1	1	1

8–7 Electronic Instrumentation and Measurement Systems

Electronic instrumentation and measurement systems are comprised of a number of elements or components, as will be described in this section. These systems are capable of electronically measuring a desired physical quantity, and electronically entering that information into the memory of a computer. The data can then be displayed to the user, or in measurement and control systems, the data is analyzed and used to issue a command that effects a particular process based on the new data. The device that senses physical quantities and generates a corresponding electronic signal is called a sensor; the opposite device, which receives an electronic signal and causes a physical action, is called an actuator. Actuators can close valves, move objects, and turn shafts by electronic control.

8.7.1 Sensors (or Transducers)

In almost every electronic instrumentation or measurement system, at least one (and often many) physical quantity must be measured, such as force, temperature, stress, acceleration, and so on. A sensor or transducer is a device that performs the measurement and converts the value to an electronic signal. Most sensors convert the change in value of the physical quantity to a change in an electrical quantity, such as resistance, voltage, or current. Often, the relationship in the physical change to the electrical change is proportional or linear.

There are sensors commercially available to measure a very wide range of quantities. Table 8.1 shows a partial list of quantities that can be measured by electronic sensors.

As an example of a sensor, consider the accelerometer, a device that measures acceleration in two axes, manufactured by Analog Devices, Incorporated (ADI). The model shown in the block diagram of Figure 8.17 is the AD-XL202E. This device has a maximum acceleration measurement range of +/− 2 g's. The outputs are analog signals whose duty cycles (ratio of pulsewidth to period) are proportional to acceleration. This feature makes it possible to directly interface the sensor with a digital system without the use of an A/D converter.

TABLE 8.1 Analog Parameters Measurable by Electronic Sensors

Pressure	Temperature
Light Intensity	Magnetic Fields
Electric Fields	Proximity
Position	Acoustic Waves
Seismic Vibrations	Humidity/Dew Point
Acceleration/Vibration	Force
Rotation	Radiation
Gas Concentrations	Gas Flow
Acidity (pH)	Imaging (visible/IR)
Biopotentials	Ion Concentrations
Gas Composition	Torque
Tactile/Touch	

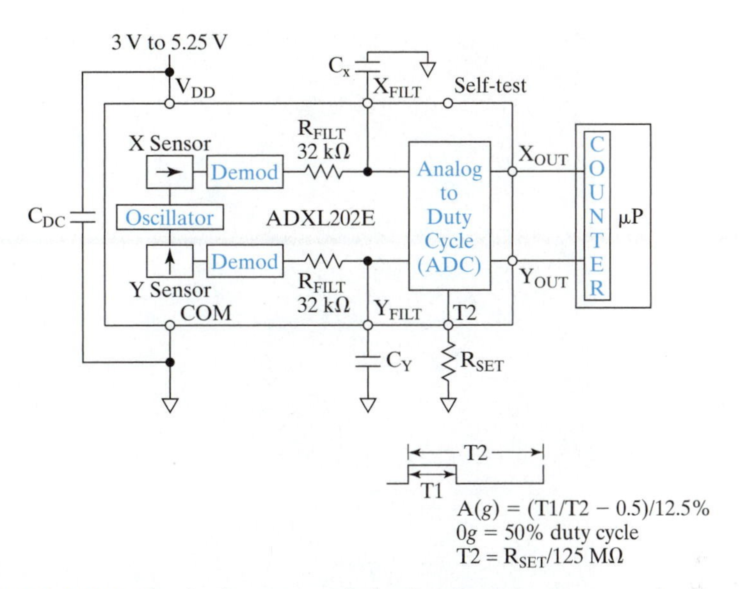

FIGURE 8.17 Block diagram of dual-axis +/− 2 g accelerometer, ADXL202E (courtesy of Analog Devices, Incorporated).

The ADI dual-axis accelerometer is an example of a class of sensors using MEMS (microelectromechanical systems technologies). This device includes the mechanical motion-sensing structure and the processing electronics integrated on a single silicon chip. Figure 8.18 shows a scanning electron microscope image of a corner of this device. In the foreground the mechanical springs are etched into a suspended polysilicon membrane. On the left and right sides are differential capacitors, which appear as interdigitated fingers. As acceleration is sensed the mass suspended at the top moves relative to the fingers attached at the edges. The change in capacitance between these fingers is sensed electronically, and converted into a voltage proportional to acceleration. Note the scale in the photograph at the bottom center, which designates a length of 100 micrometers.

8.7.2 Signal Conditioning

Signal conditioning is generally required to convert the signal from the sensor to a voltage of the appropriate range that can be sampled by an A/D converter. In some cases it may be that the signal from the sensor must be increased in amplitude, by the use of a voltage amplifier. In other cases, such as a sensor in which its resistance changes with the change in the physical quantity being measured, then additional signal conditioning is required. In this latter case, a Wheatstone Bridge circuit, as described in section 2.12 of Chapter 2, may be useful. The signal from a bridge circuit is typically small, and the instrumentation differential amplifier, which will be described in the next chapter (see Figure 9.9 or Figure D9.2), is often used.

Signal conditioning may also include appropriate filtering of the analog signal, using frequency selective circuits similar to those described in Chapter 7. For example, if the vibration of a motor is being sensed by placing an accelerometer on the motor, then the fundamental frequency of the vibration is related to the rpm (revolutions per minute) of the motor shaft. A filter can be used to pass the frequency of the desired signal, and reject unwanted signals at other frequencies.

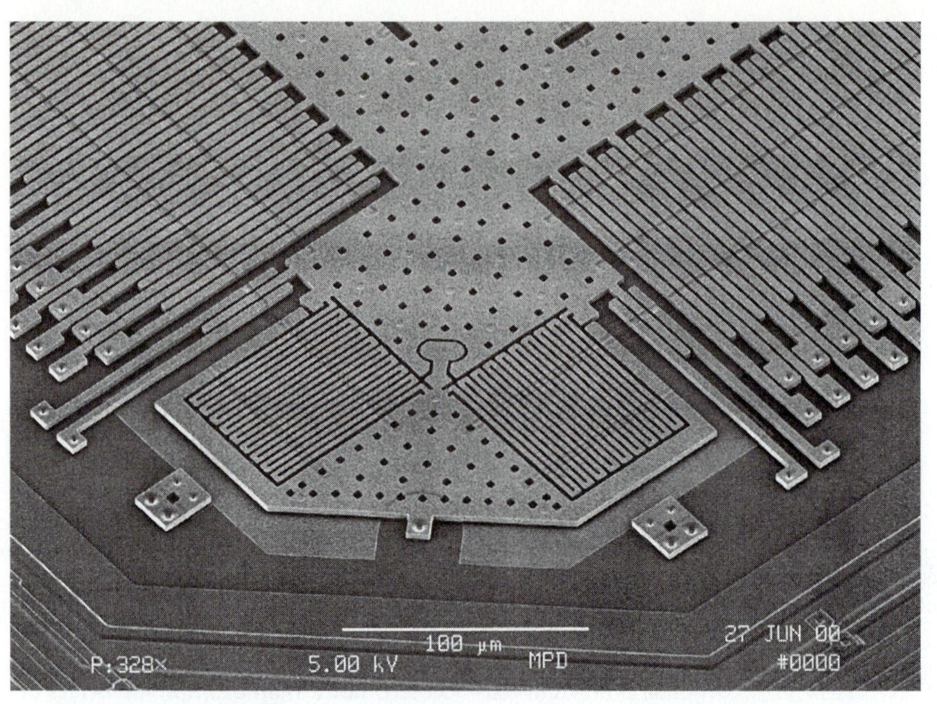

FIGURE 8.18 Scanning electron microscope image of dual-axis accelerometer chip (courtesy of Analog Devices, Inc.).

Example 8.10

A motor turning at 1000 rpm has an accelerometer attached to measure vibration. What is the fundamental frequency of vibration and at what cutoff frequency would we use in a filter to reject stray 60 Hz signals from surrounding power lines?

The number of revolutions per minute is converted to revolutions per second by dividing by 60. This is the fundamental vibration frequency in Hertz.

$$\frac{1000}{60} = 16.6Hz$$

To ensure that we measure the signal at 16.6 Hz, and reject the power-line interference at 60 Hz, we would use a low-pass filter with a cutoff frequency between these values. Since we may be interested in measuring some harmonics of the vibration, we note that the second harmonic is at $2 \times 16.6 = 33.2$ Hz, and the third harmonic is at $3 \times 16.6 = 49.8$ Hz. Therefore, we could place the cutoff frequency at 50 Hz, if the filter has a slope steep enough to reject sufficient signal at 60 Hz.

8.7.3 A/D Conversion

After appropriate signal conditioning the analog signal is sampled and converted to a digital signal by an analog-to-digital converter (A/D converter), as described in section 8.6. The frequency of sampling is related to the highest frequency component desired in the data, as shown in Eq. 8.14.

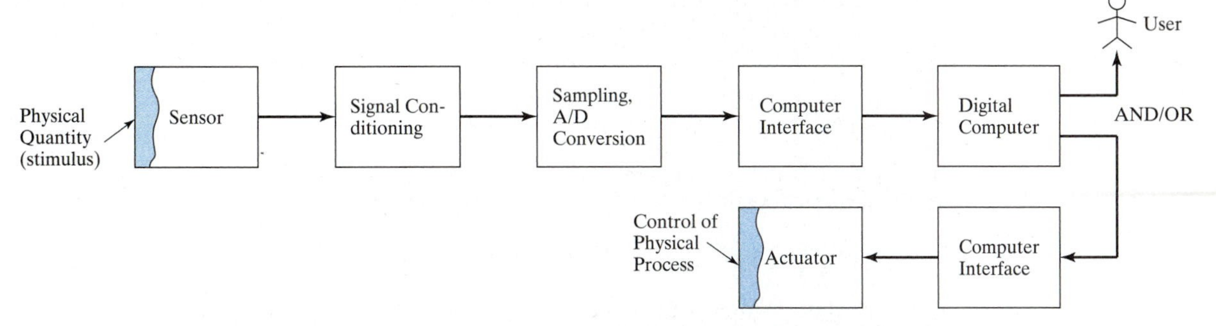

FIGURE 8.19 Electronic measurement system.

8.7.4 Systems

The digital signal from the A/D converter is then provided as input to a digital processor or computer for computation. There is often an interface card required to properly connect the digital signal from the A/D converter to the computer. Therefore, a complete electronic measurement system is shown in Figure 8.19.

Electronic measurement system

This system can become an electronic control system with the addition of an output interface so the computer can send signals to an actuator to affect changes in the system being measured.

Summary

- Electronic circuits generally utilize passive linear circuit elements (resistors, capacitors, and inductors) and also nonlinear components such as diodes and active devices such as transistors. Electronic circuits can be configured to create amplifiers, logic gates (building blocks of computers), power supplies, and complex electronic systems.
- Electronic circuits generally require dc power to operate. This power can be supplied from a dc source, such as a battery or solar cell, or from ac, which has been rectified (by a diode circuit) to create dc.
- A signal is a voltage or current that is varied in some manner over time in order to encode and transmit information.
- Signals are either analog if they vary continuously or digital if they switch between discrete levels. Figure 8.20 shows an example of an analog and digital voltage signal. Digital signals typically have two levels, a high called a one, and a low called a zero. The single presentation of a 1 or a 0 is called a bit.

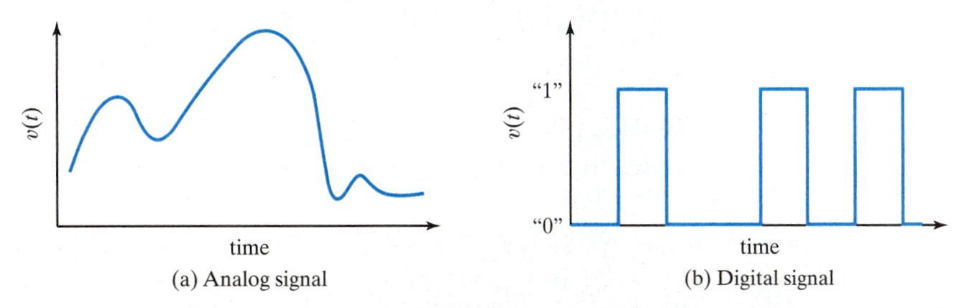

FIGURE 8.20 Example of analog signal and digital signal. (a) Analog signal (b) Digital signal

- An voltage amplifier produces an output voltage, v_o, which is a factor of A_v (the voltage gain) larger than the input voltage, v_i.

  Therefore,

  $$A_v = v_o/v_i$$

  The voltage (or current) gain is often expressed in decibels. The voltage gain in decibels is given by the relation

  $$A_v\,(\text{db}) = 20 \log A_v$$

  Similar relationships hold for current amplifiers.
- Modulation is the process of attaching information to an analog signal; demodulation is the reverse process of extracting the information from an analog signal. There are three main types of modulation: amplitude modulation (AM), frequency modulation (FM), and phase modulation.
- Amplitude modulation is an important type of modulation, and it provides insight into the frequency spectrum produced by modulation of a carrier signal. The modulation of a carrier signal at a frequency of f_c by a message signal with a frequency of f_m produces a frequency spectrum with a carrier at a frequency of f_c, an upper sideband at $f_c + f_m$, and a lower sideband at $f_c - f_m$.
- A passband filter centered at the carrier frequency must have a bandwidth, BW, of at least $2(f_m)$ to transmit the modulated signal.
- Digital representation of an analog signal is achieved by sampling the analog signal at points in time. The value of the analog signal when sampled is quantized and represented by a binary word; this word describes one of Z zones. The more bits in the word, the more zones, and the better the resolution. The number of zones, Z, is given by

  $$Z = 2^n$$

  where n is the number of bits.
- An analog-to-digital converter (A/D) is a circuit that samples an analog signal and creates a digital output. A digital-to-analog converter (D/A) performs the reverse task of converting a digital word into an analog voltage or current. The resolution of an A/D converter (or D/A) can be obtained by dividing the full input voltage range by the number of zones computed (using the above relationship) from the number of bits the converter uses.
- To accurately digitize an analog signal, $f(t)$, which has a highest frequency component of f_m, the sampling frequency, f_s, must be greater than two times f_m. That is, the minimum sampling rate is known as the Nyquist frequency, or $2f_m$.

  $$f_s > 2f_m$$

- Practical logic gates are electronic circuits that have a digital output and one or more digital inputs; the logic state of the output is uniquely determined by the logic values of the inputs. Three common types of logic gates are:
  - The inverter: the output is the opposite of the input.
  - The AND-gate: the output is a 1 only if *all* inputs are a 1.
  - The OR-gate: the output is a 1 if *any* input is a 1.

- Electronic circuits are often configured as a:
  - NAND-gate: an AND gate followed by an inverter.
  - NOR-gate: an OR gate followed by an inverter
- Combinations of logic gates make logic circuits. The truth table for a combination of logic gates can be generated by assigning labels to intermediate nodes, constructing a truth table that includes all possible input combinations, a column(s) for intermediate node(s), and a column for the final output. Consider the behavior of each gate and work through the circuit from input to output.

Problems

8.1. For each of the following, decide if it is most analogous to digital information or analog information.
(a) the result of a coin toss
(b) the sound of a slide trombone
(c) the beat of a drum
(d) a human voice
(e) the ticking of a clock
(f) the sound of a siren
(g) the motion of a cat
(h) the motion of a frog

8.2. A solar-cell is placed outdoors on a clear day and has an output current of 2 mA at peak sun intensity (noon), and 0.01 mA when exposed to moonlight. Plot the approximate current output expected versus time over a 24-hour period, assuming:
(a) The solar cell is unobstructed.
(b) A cat stands over the solar cell for one hour beginning at noon (assume an opaque cat).
(c) A cloud cover comes in at 3:00 PM, reducing the sun's intensity on the solar cell by one-half.

8.3. Plot serial digital signals representing the following sequences of bits, using pulses with a duration of 50 ns.
(a) 1 0 1 1 0 0 1 0 1 0 1 1
(b) 0 1 0 1 1 0 0 0 1 0 0 1
(c) 0 0 1 1 0 1 0 1 0 1 1 1

8.4. Construct plots of digital voltage signals by drawing the pulse waveforms based on the following descriptions: high level = 5 V; low level = 0.2 V.
(a) High at $t = 0$, negative going edge at $t = 1$, positive going edge at $t = 1.5$, negative going edge at $t = 2.5$, positive going edge at $t = 3$.
(b) Low at $t = 0$, positive going edge at $t = 2$, negative going edge at $t = 3$, positive going edge at $t = 4$.
(c) Assuming each bit requires the same time to transmit, what's the minimum number of bits represented by the pulse sequence in (a).
(d) Assuming each bit requires the same time to transmit, what's the minimum number of bits represented by the pulse sequence in (b).

8.5. A 16-bit parallel data bus is used to transmit 1280 bits in 4 microseconds.
(a) How many bits are transmitted over one of the lines in the bus?
(b) If the same technology was used to transmit data over a single serial data line, how many bits could be transmitted in 1 second?

8.6. In a particular system, 50 megabits is transmitted on a single serial data line in 1 second.
(a) What is the time required to transmit 1 bit?
(b) If this system utilized the same technology with an 8-bit parallel data bus, how long would it take to transmit 50 megabits?

8.7. A modem connects to a phone line with a data rate of 56.6 k bits per second. How long does it take to download

(a) 2 megabits of information?
(b) 2 megabytes of information?

8.8. The PCI bus found in many desktop computers transmits 64 bits per clock cycle at a 33 MHz clock rate. How does the bandwidth of the PCI bus compare to the serial FireWire (IEEE 1394) serial bus specification, which is 400 Mbits/s?

8.9. Assume a computer is copying an entire 100-Gigabyte disk drive's worth of information over a 100 Mbit/s Ethernet connection, and that a protocol is utilized over the Ethernet that utilizes 50% of the available bandwidth of the connection. How long will the disk copy operation take?

8.10. A PC133 SDRAM supplies 64 bits (8 bytes) in parallel. It has the following timing specifications:

Clock frequency: 133 MHz

Delay for transfer of the first 8-byte word: 7 clock cycles

Delay for transfer of successive adjacent 8-byte word: 1 clock cycle

(a) If a computer without a cache fetches 64 bit words at random, what is the effective average bandwidth (in bytes/s) of the memory?
(b) If a computer with a cache fetches successive 64 bit words 95% of the time, and random words 5% of the time, what is the effective average bandwidth (in bytes/s) of the memory?

8.11. An amplifier has a voltage gain $A_v = 300$ and a load resistor connected between its output terminals of 2k. If the input to the amplifier, $v_i = 75$ mV,
(a) what is the output voltage, v_o?
(b) what power is delivered to the load resistor?

8.12. The output of an amplifier drives an 8 Ω speaker with a signal of 3 V in amplitude.
(a) What is the amplitude of the input voltage, assuming the voltage gain of the amplifier is 150?
(b) What is the power delivered to the speaker?

8.13. A radio receives a signal on its antenna of 2 μV, and we want to deliver 20 watts of power to an 8-ohm speaker. What is the voltage gain of the entire system?

8.14. Consider an amplifier in which the input voltage is sinusoidal with an amplitude of 100 mV and $\omega = 500$. The complex gain is given by $20\,\angle 30°$. Write an expression for the output voltage as a function of time.

8.15. The input and the output signals of four different amplifiers are given below. Obtain the voltage gain and the phase shift for each of the amplifiers.
(a) $v_{in}(t) = 3\cos(\omega t)$ $\quad v_{out}(t) = 27\cos(\omega t)$
(b) $v_{in}(t) = 5\sin(10t)$ $\quad v_{out}(t) = 15\cos(10t)$
(c) $v_{in}(t) = 4\sin(\omega t)$ $\quad v_{out}(t) = 20\sin(\omega t + \pi/2)$
(d) $v_{in}(t) = 7\,e^{20jt}$ $\quad v_{out}(t) = j5\,e^{20jt}$

8.16. An electronic thermometer generates a voltage signal of 6 mV for every 1°C rise in temperature. This signal is used to activate a switch, which requires an input signal of 5 V to operate. What is the voltage gain of the amplifier that will allow one to operate the switch at the boiling point of water (100° C) if the thermometer generates 0 V at 0° C?

8.17. A solar cell is used to electronically detect when sunrise occurs. It is determined that the light at dawn produces 0.05 mA, and the cell is connected to a current amplifier. The amplifier is used to increase the current to produce 3 V across a 1 k resistor. What current gain is required for the amplifier?

8.18. A voltage of 35 mV is applied to the input of a voltage amplifier. What gain is required to produce an output voltage of 10 V,
(a) expressed as a voltage ratio.
(b) expressed in decibels.

8.19. If a voltage amplifier has a gain of 60 db and an output voltage of 5 V, what is the input voltage?

8.20. A current amplifier has a gain of 100 db, however, a stray leakage path at the output reduces

the effective gain by 20 db. What is the effective current gain of the amplifier
(a) as a current ratio?
(b) in decibels?

8.21. Calculate the upper-and lower-corner frequencies and the bandwidth of the amplifier whose frequency response is given in Figure P8.2.

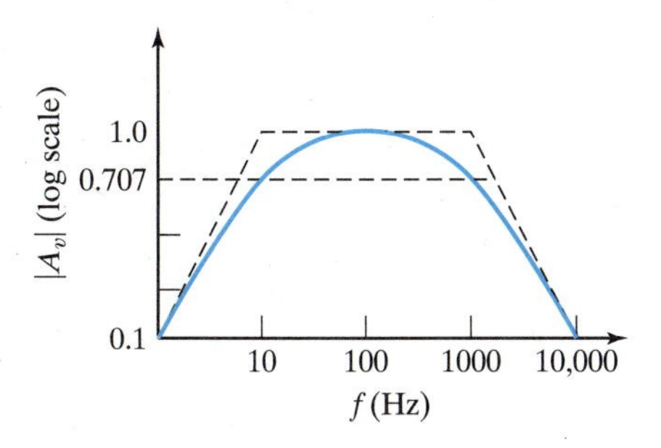

FIGURE P8.21

8.22. An audio amplifier has a low-corner frequency, f_{LO}, of 100 Hz, and a bandwidth of 15 kHz. The amplifier has an input voltage of 20 mV and an output voltage of 6 volts. Plot the frequency response (frequency on a log scale) of this amplifier showing the midband gain in decibels, the two corner frequencies, and the bandwidth.

8.23. A dc amplifier has a voltage gain of 100 and this gain is down 3 db at 10 MHz. What is the amplifier's bandwidth?

8.24. In a particular current amplifier the half-power frequencies are separated by 10^3 Hz. If the gain is reduced from its midband value by 3 db at 100 Hz, what is the
(a) high corner frequency?
(b) bandwidth?

8.25. A dc current amplifier has an output current that is 40 db larger than its input current. Plot the frequency response of the amplifier in decibels, assuming it has a bandwidth of 20 kHz.

8.26. A sinusoidal carrier signal of 1 MHz is modulated with a message signal of 100 kHz. Sketch the resulting waveform for two cycles of the message signal for
(a) amplitude modulation
(b) frequency modulation

8.27. The message signal shown in Figure P8.27 modulates a sinusoidal carrier that has a period one-tenth that of the message signal. Sketch the resulting waveform for
(a) amplitude modulation
(b) frequency modulation

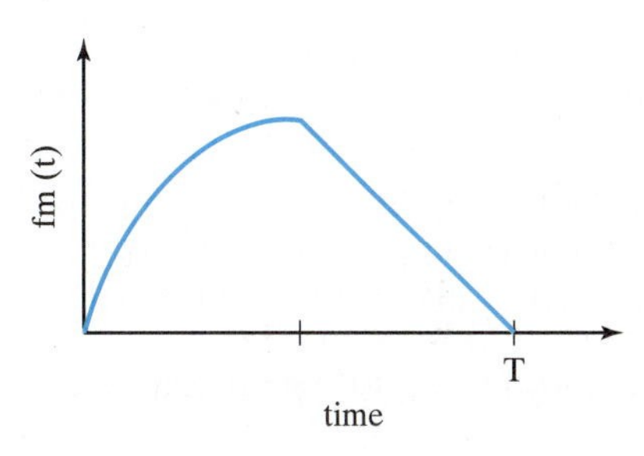

FIGURE P8.27

8.28. The frequency spectrum of an AM-modulated signal has a carrier at 1 MHz and an upper sideband at 1.01 MHz.
(a) What is the frequency of the message signal?
(b) What is the frequency of the lower sideband?

8.29. If the highest frequency component of message signal is 15 kHz and this AM modulates a carrier signal of 500 kHz, what is the minimum bandwidth of a filter centered at the carrier frequency that will transmit the signal?

8.30. A message signal has frequency components at 400 Hz and 800 Hz. This is used to AM modulate a 30 kHz carrier signal. Plot the frequency spectrum of the AM-modulated signal.

8.31. A square wave (which contains frequency components at odd multiples of the fundamental frequency) is used to AM modulate a sinusoidal carrier. If the carrier frequency is 4 MHz, and the square wave has a frequency of 10 kHz, plot the frequency spectrum, and clearly designate the frequency of the carrier and all sidebands up to the third nonzero harmonic.

8.32. Find the minimum number of bits necessary to represent a 6 V analog signal with a resolution greater than 2 mV.

8.33. An analog signal having values from −4 to +4 volts is represented using 8 bits.
(a) Calculate the voltage resolution.
(b) If you wished to increase the resolution by at least a factor of 5, what's the minimum number of additional bits needed?

8.34. An analog signal has values between 0 and 5 V and is represented using a 7-bit digital word. Due to a fault in the digital circuit, the middle bit is incorrect. Find the magnitude of the error in the analog representation of the signal.

8.35. An analog-to-digital converter (A/D) has 10 bits and samples an analog signal with a range from −5 to +5 V and a maximum frequency of 3 kHz.
(a) What is the voltage resolution of the sampling?
(b) What is the minimum sampling frequency?

8.36. An analog-to-digital converter (A/D) samples an analog signal at a sampling rate of 10 kHz. To ensure accurate sampling, the signal should not have frequency components higher than what frequency?

8.37. A digital-to-analog converter (D/A) has 12 bits and an output analog voltage range of 0 to 10 volts.
(a) What is the voltage resolution of the analog output?
(b) If the most significant input bit changes, by what amount does the output voltage change?

8.38. Obtain the digital words corresponding to the indicated analog signal levels, a through j, as shown in Figure P8.38, that would be assigned by an A/D system with:
(a) 2 bits
(b) 3 bits
(c) 4 bits

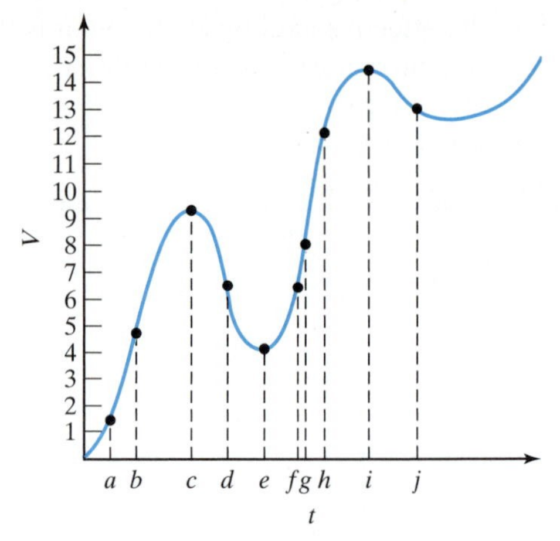

FIGURE P8.38

8.39. An analog signal with a maximum amplitude of 5 volts is sampled 15 times at intervals of 1 ms by a 4-bit A/D converter. The values are shown below. Reconstruct the analog signal and comment on the accuracy of the plot. Identify two ways of obtaining a better digital representation of the original analog signal.

Sample	4-bit digital word
1	0000
2	0010
3	0011
4	0001
5	0100
6	0101
7	0110
8	1010
9	1101
10	1111
11	1000
12	0110
13	0111
14	1011
15	1111

8.40. An Exclusive OR gate (XOR) is a logic gate with an output that is high only when all its inputs are at the same logic value. (Either all inputs high, or all inputs low.) Construct the truth table for a two-input XOR gate.

8.41. Construct the truth table for the logic circuit shown in Figure P8.41 (assume A_1 is the MSB).

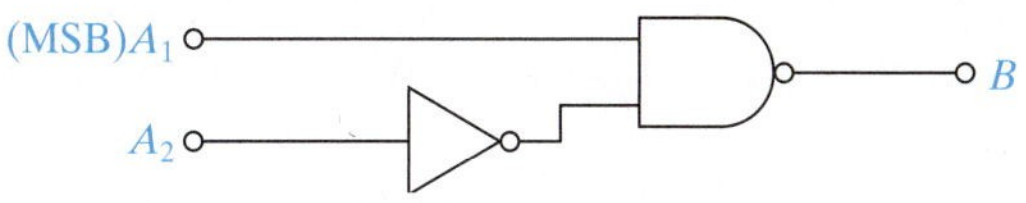

(MSB)A_1

A_2

B

FIGURE P8.41

8.42. Construct the truth table for the logic circuit shown in Figure P8.42 (assume A_1 is the MSB).

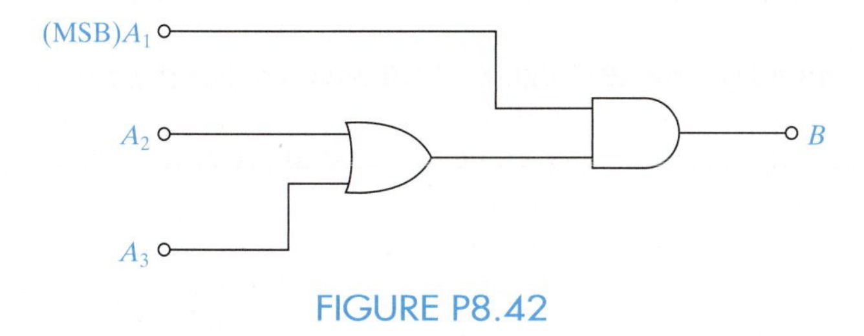

FIGURE P8.42

8.43. Construct the truth table for the logic circuit shown in Figure P8.43 (assume A_1 is the MSB).

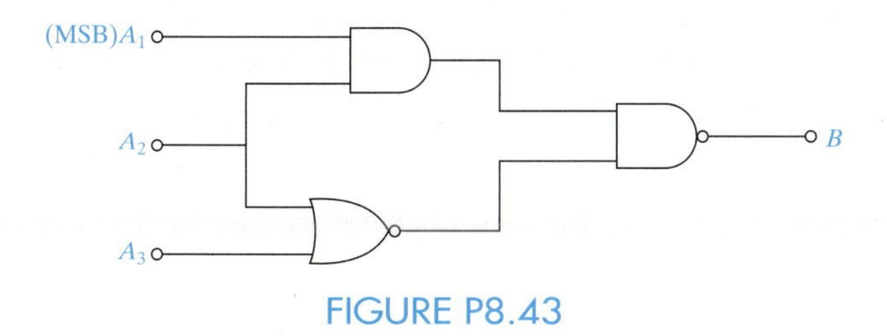

FIGURE P8.43

8.44. (a) What is the purpose of a sensor?

(b) What is the purpose of an actuator?

8.45. A temperature measurement system is designed to measure the temperature range of 50 to 100 degrees C°, and uses a temperature transducer that changes resistance in proportion to temperature. The resistance is 1 kΩ at 50 degrees, and increases 1 Ω per degree. Assume this device is placed in a Wheatstone Bridge circuit with three other resistors, each of 1 kΩ, and the bridge is supplied by a voltage source of 5 V.

(a) What is the output voltage of the bridge at 50 degrees?

(b) What is the output voltage of the bridge at 100 degrees?

(c) What signal conditioning is needed to provide this signal to an A/D converter with an input voltage range of 0 to 3 V?

8.46. An accelerometer is used as the sensor in a computer measurement system to measure the vibration of a motor turning at 2500 rpm.

(a) What is the fundamental frequency of vibration in Hz?

(b) Is it possible to use a low-pass filter as signal conditioning to suppress interference from 60 Hz power lines?

(c) If so, what cutoff frequency would be appropriate for the low-pass filter?

(d) What is the minimum sampling frequency required of the A/D converter to ensure that the fundamental frequency is captured?

9–1 Introduction

General definition of op amp

The *operational amplifier* (op amp) described in this chapter is one of the basic building blocks for constructing analog electronic systems. It can be used in combination with various external components for a wide variety of purposes. A basic knowledge of op amps is essential for understanding modern instrumentation and measurement systems. Also, op amp questions also frequently appear on the FE and PE exams.

An op amp is essentially a voltage amplifier with an extremely high voltage gain. Op amp circuits use external components to provide negative feedback, and thereby control the output or set the gain at reasonable levels.

Operational amplifiers are typically purchased as an integrated circuit (IC), an array of transistors, resistors, and capacitors all fabricated as a circuit on a single silicon chip. These chips are packaged in various ways to make them easy to connect to other "external" circuit components. The most common package is the dual in-line package (DIP).

Modern integrated circuit technology provides high-performance single op amps or multiple op amps (e.g., a quad, or four op amps) on a single chip.

As introduced in Chapter 8, an *amplifier* is an electronic device that produces an output signal that is an exact copy or replica of the input signal increased in amplitude, as illustrated in Figure 9.1.

An ideal linear *voltage amplifier* has an output voltage, v_{out}, given by Eq. (9.1), where v_{in} is the input voltage and A_v is the voltage gain.

$$v_{out} = A_v v_{in} \tag{9.1}$$

An op amp is a special type of amplifier, called a *differential amplifier,* in which the output voltage is a factor of A_v times the voltage **difference** between the two inputs. This is explained in more detail in the next section, where we will consider the *ideal* op amp. This effect is useful, because signals that appear on both inputs (such as stray noise) are cancelled, and only the voltage difference is amplified.

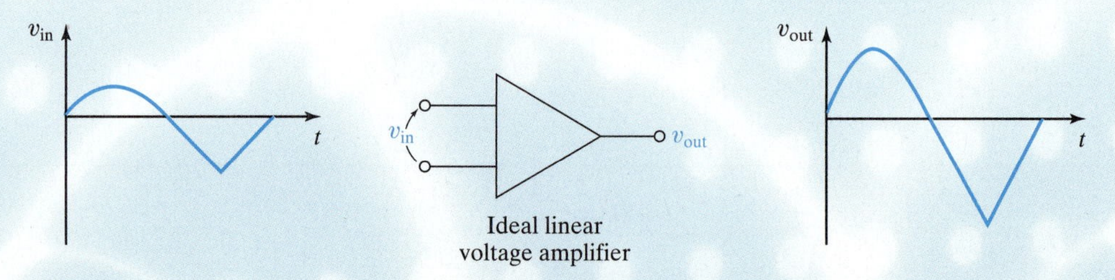

FIGURE 9.1 A linear amplifier and its characteristics.

Operational Amplifiers (Op Amps)

9-2 The Ideal Op Amp

The ideal op amp is illustrated in Figure 9.2. It has two inputs, one labeled with a "+" (the noninverting input) and the other labeled with a "−" (the inverting input). The voltage applied to the "+" input is designated as v_+, and the voltage at the "−" input is designated v_-.

The currents into the inputs (i_+ and i_-) are zero, because an ideal op amp has infinite input resistance.

The output voltage, v_o, is given by the open loop gain, A_v, times the difference in voltage between v_+ and v_-, with $A_v \to \infty$.

In summary, an ideal op amp has the following characteristics:

1.
$$v_o = A_v\,(v_+ - v_-) \tag{9.2}$$

where A_v (the open-loop gain) is assumed extremely large, approaching infinity.

2. The current into the inputs are zero, or

$$i_+ = i_- = 0 \tag{9.3}$$

Based on the above, a circuit model for the ideal op amp can be provided, as shown in Figure 9.3.

Negative feedback makes useful circuits

Negative feedback is required to make a large class of useful circuits with op amps. Negative feedback is achieved when the output terminal, v_o, is connected through a component (or network of components) to the inverting input.

The negative feedback and the provision that the open-loop gain, A_v, approaches infinity allow us to make the following assumption:

The voltage at the "−" input terminal is driven to the same voltage as that applied at the "+" input terminal. In other words,

Important result of negative feedback

$$v_- = v_+ \tag{9.4}$$

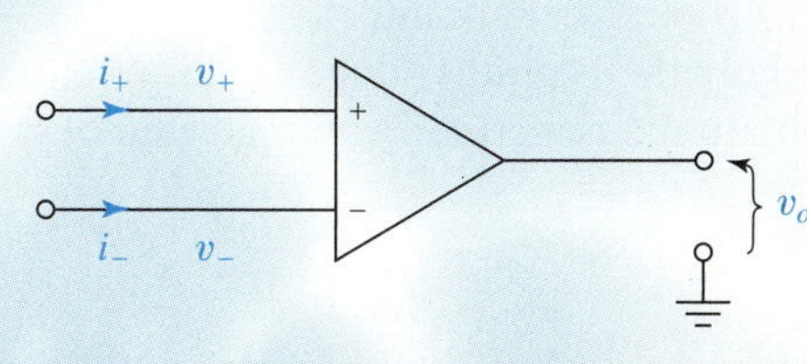

The ideal op amp

FIGURE 9.2 The ideal op amp.

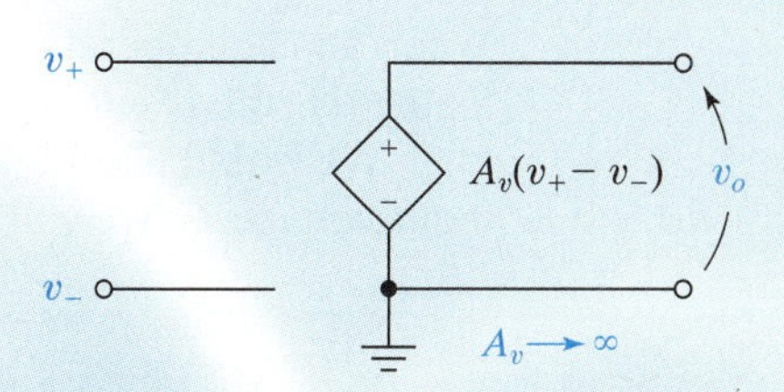

FIGURE 9.3 Circuit model for ideal op amp.

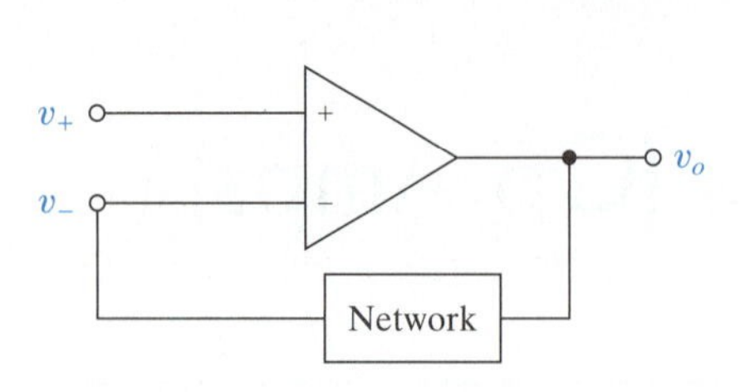

FIGURE 9.4 An ideal op amp with negative feedback through external network.

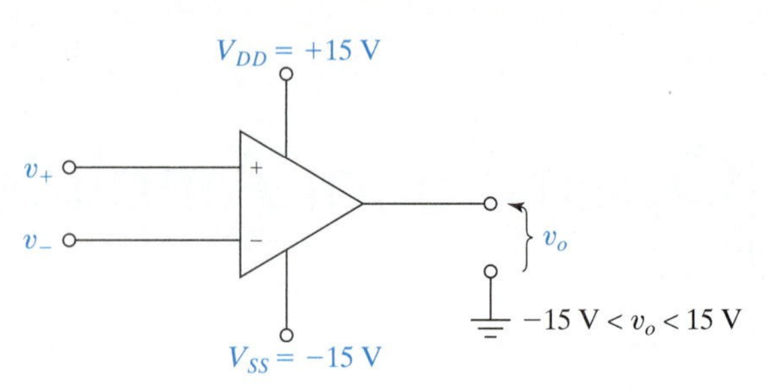

FIGURE 9.5 Ideal op amp with real voltage supply limits.

Equation 9.4 is illustrated in Figure 9.4, in which a network connects the output to the inverting input, and v_- becomes equal to v_+. The way in which negative feedback operates and allows us to assume Equation 9.4 is valid will be explained in Section 9.6.

Closed-loop gain

The connection of negative feedback "closes the loop," and in future sections we will compute the ***closed-loop gain, A_F,*** of circuits containing such feedback.

One additional rule is provided now. When using the ideal op amp model to analyze circuits, one "real" constraint may sometimes become important:

> The output voltage of an op amp cannot exceed the supply voltage applied to operate the op amp.

Output voltage is constrained by power supply voltage

This is illustrated in Figure 9.5 where an ideal op amp is shown with real voltage supply limits. In the example in Figure 9.5, the amplifier is operated with dual power supplies of $V_{DD} = +15V$ and $V_{SS} = -15$ V; therefore, v_o is constrained between $+V_{DD}$ and $-V_{SS}$, or,

$$V_{SS} < v_o < +V_{DD} \tag{9.5}$$

Summary of characteristics of ideal op amp

> In summary, for an ideal op amp circuit with feedback, assume:
>
> 1. $i_+ = i_- = 0$
> 2. $v_- = v_+$
> 3. v_o is bounded by the power supply voltage.

9-3 The Noninverting Amplifier

When an ideal operational amplifier is combined with two resistors in the manner shown in Figure 9.6, the result is a *noninverting amplifier* circuit.

We would like to determine how the output voltage of this circuit, v_o, depends on the input voltage, v_i. We will now calculate the closed-loop voltage gain of the circuit, A_F, where

$$A_F = \frac{v_o}{v_i} \tag{9.6}$$

In Figure 9.6, the input voltage, v_i, equals the voltage at the "+" input, or

$$v_i = v_+.$$

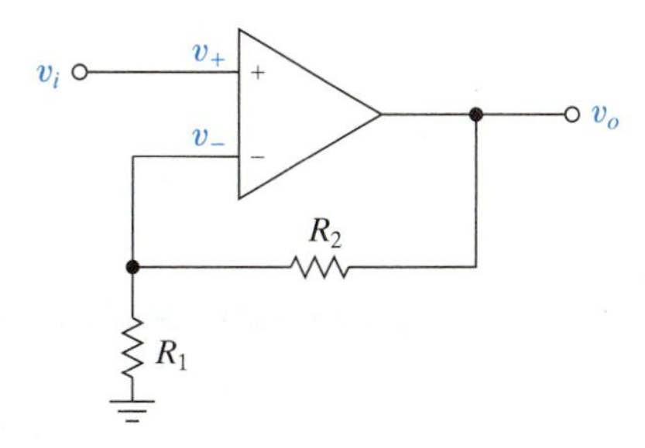

FIGURE 9.6 Noninverting op amp circuit.

The negative feedback causes,

$$v_- = v_+ = v_i$$

Since no current flows into the v_- input, the voltage at v_- can be related to v_o by simple voltage division,

$$v_+ = v_- = v_i = \frac{R_1}{R_1 + R_2} v_o$$

and therefore, the closed-loop gain, A_F, is given by

Gain of noninverting amplifier

$$A_F = \frac{v_o}{v_i} = 1 + \frac{R_2}{R_1} \tag{9.7}$$

Note that the voltage gain for this circuit configuration has a positive sign, and, therefore, does not invert the input signal. The magnitude of the voltage gain, A_F, is set by the ratio of the two external resistors. This configuration provides cancellation of the effect of variations in resistor values, which are common to both resistors. Finally, the minimum value of voltage gain for the circuit configuration is unity, which is achieved when $R_2 = 0$.

Example 9.1

Given the circuit in Figure 9.6, if R_1 is 10 kΩ, what value of R_2 is required to produce a circuit with a voltage gain of 25?

Substituting the known values in Eq. (9.7) yields

$$25 = 1 + \frac{R_2}{10\text{ k}}$$

Solving for R_2, we obtain $R_2 = 240$ kΩ.

9–4 The Unity-Gain Buffer

The *unity-gain buffer* is a circuit that has a voltage gain of unity; that is, the output voltage is the same as the input voltage. While this may seem strange, there is an important use for this type of circuit, as will be explained at the end of this section.

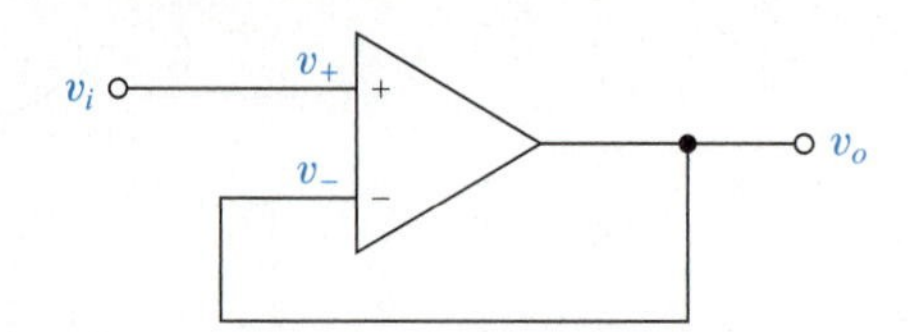

FIGURE 9.7 Unity-gain buffer op amp circuit.

Gain of unity-gain buffer

The noninverting amplifier circuit configuration described in the previous section will produce unity gain when R_2 is set to zero. This is the equivalent of a short between the output and the inverting input, and, therefore, the resistor R_1 becomes inconsequential and can be dropped from the circuit. We are left with the unity-gain buffer circuit shown in Figure 9.7.

The closed-loop gain of this circuit can be easily derived using the basic rules of section 9.2.

$$v_i = v_+, \quad \text{and} \quad v_- = v_+$$

Since v_o is connected to v_- by the direct feedback, $v_o = v_-$. Combining these equations leads to $v_o = v_i$, or

$$A_F = \frac{v_o}{v_i} = 1 \tag{9.8}$$

Since the voltage gain of this circuit is unity, its primary function is an impedance converter or transformer that can receive a voltage from a high-impedance source, and provide an output of the same voltage at a very low output impedance level; this circuit provides substantial current gain. Circuits such as this are often used for "line drivers," which send the signal down a long length of wire or cable.

9–5 The Inverting Amplifier

The connection of two external resistors in the manner shown in Figure 9.8 creates a circuit known as the *inverting amplifier.* As you will see, the closed-loop gain of this circuit has a "negative sign," and this signifies that the output voltage has the opposite polarity of the input voltage. For example, if the closed-loop gain is -10 and the input voltage is 0.5 V, the output voltage would be -5 V.

This circuit connects the "+" input to ground, or zero volts; therefore, $v_+ = 0$ V. The feedback drives $v_- = v_+ = 0$ V. Therefore, v_- is also always at zero volts and this node is termed a "virtual ground."

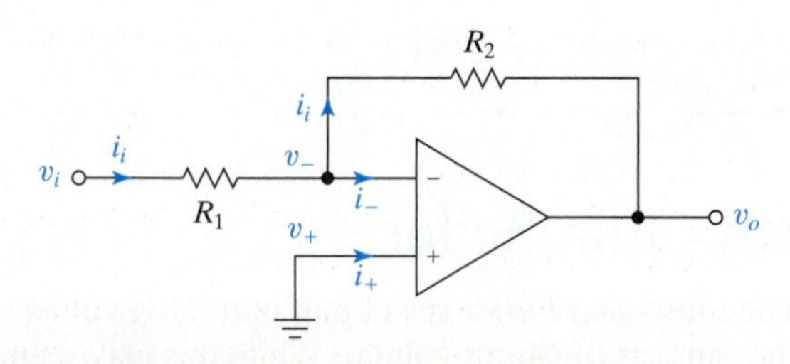

FIGURE 9.8 The inverting op amp circuit.

We can now compute the current through R_1, or the circuit input current, i_i, as

$$i_i = \frac{v_i - 0}{R_1} = \frac{v_i}{R_1} \tag{9.9}$$

Since the current into the op amp input is zero (Equation 9.3 states $i_- = 0$), by Kirchhoff's current law, i_i must flow through R_2. Therefore, i_i can also be expressed as

$$i_i = \frac{0 - v_o}{R_2} = -\frac{v_o}{R_2} \tag{9.10}$$

Equating Equations 9.9 and 9.10,

$$\frac{v_i}{R_1} = \frac{-v_o}{R_2}$$

$$v_o = \frac{-R_2}{R_1} v_i$$

Gain of inverting amplifier

and the closed-loop gain, A_F, is given by,

$$A_F = \frac{v_o}{v_i} = -\frac{R_2}{R_1} \tag{9.11}$$

Example 9.2

Let us assume an ideal op amp is used in the circuit of Figure 9.8, with $R_1 = 2\ \text{k}\Omega$ and $R_2 = 80\ \text{k}\Omega$. For this network let us determine the *closed loop* voltage gain A_F.

$$A_F = -\frac{R_2}{R_1} = -\frac{80\ \text{k}}{2\ \text{k}} = -40$$

9–6 The Principle of Negative Feedback

The operation of negative feedback will be illustrated using the inverting amplifier of Figure 9.8. Recall that an op amp is a differential amplifier and hence the output is proportional to the difference between v_+ and v_-. Because the gain is extremely high, or for purposes of discussion here, infinite, if v_+ is slightly greater than v_- the output of the amplifier will attempt to approach a very large positive voltage. Conversely, if v_+ is slightly less than v_-, the output voltage will attempt to approach a large negative voltage. It is the resistors in the circuit that provide negative feedback and control the output response in a predictable and manageable way as illustrated in the next paragraph.

Suppose a positive voltage is applied to the input, v_i. This places a positive voltage on the v_- input. Since the v_+ input is connected to zero volts, the v_- input becomes more positive than the v_+ input. This condition drives the output voltage toward a large negative value. However, this output voltage is coupled back to the v_- input through the network of R_2 and R_1 and lowers the voltage at that node until it just reaches zero—or exactly the same voltage as is connected to the v_+ input. If the output voltage attempted to go more negative, the voltages at the input would reverse in polarity, and halt or reverse the negative voltage swing of the output. *Therefore, the output voltage stabilizes at a value that exactly feeds back the proper voltage level to place the v_- input at the same voltage as the v_+ input.*

Drill Exercise

D9.1. Find the value of I_o in the network of Figure D9.1; assume an ideal op amp.

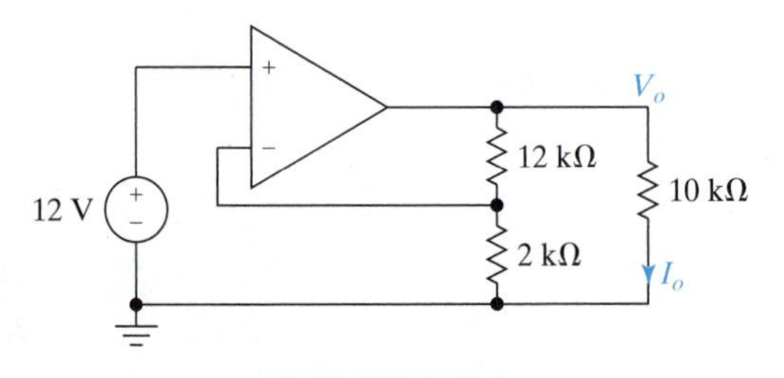

FIGURE D9.1

Ans: $I_o = 8.4$ mA.

9-7 The Differential Amplifier

The op amp circuit shown in Figure 9.9 is a differential amplifier. It has two inputs and the output voltage responds only to the difference between the two input voltages, v_1 and v_2.

The analysis of this circuit is performed by the same process as in previous circuits, although the algebra becomes tedious. Assume an ideal op amp.

$$v_+ = \frac{R_2}{R_1 + R_2} v_2$$

$$v_- = v_+$$

$$i_1 = \frac{v_1 - v_-}{R_1} = -\frac{v_o - v_-}{R_2}$$

Combining the above three equations and solving for v_o yields

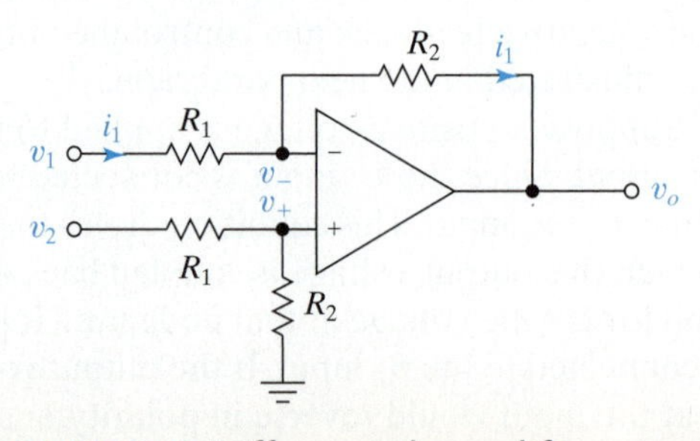

FIGURE 9.9 Differential amplifier circuit.

Gain of differential amplifier

$$v_o = -\frac{R_2}{R_1}(v_1 - v_2) \tag{9.12}$$

Because the differential amplifier responds to the difference of the input voltages, any voltage applied in common to both inputs is rejected. This feature makes this type of circuit useful in a variety of instrumentation applications where we wish to measure a small voltage difference between two points. Any interference, for example, from stray electric or magnetic fields, is likely to be picked up on both input leads, and being common to both inputs is therefore cancelled. The quality of a differential amplifier to reject common-mode signals is measured by the *common mode rejection ratio (CMRR),* usually expressed in decibels. The CMRR is the ratio of the differential mode gain to the common mode gain; it should be large.

Examples of applications appropriate for a differential amplifier include the measurement of the output of a Wheatstone Bridge circuit (see Figures 2.42 to 2.45 in Chapter 2), electrocardiogram (EKG) measurements (measuring the voltage difference generated by the heart on the chest of a patient), and electroencephalography (EEG, the measurement of brain waves by electrodes attached to the scalp).

One of the most common types of interference in instrumentation systems is stray radiation from 60 Hz power lines. The interference signal is picked up on both input leads, and cancelled while the desired signal is amplified.

Drill Exercise

D9.2 Figure D9.2 is a differential voltage amplifier, often called an instrumentation amplifier, which has a high input resistance, and therefore more appropriate for applications with a high source resistance (like the medical applications previously mentioned). It is also commonly used to measure sensor outputs from bridge circuits. Assuming ideal op amps; what is an expression for the output voltage in terms of the two inputs?

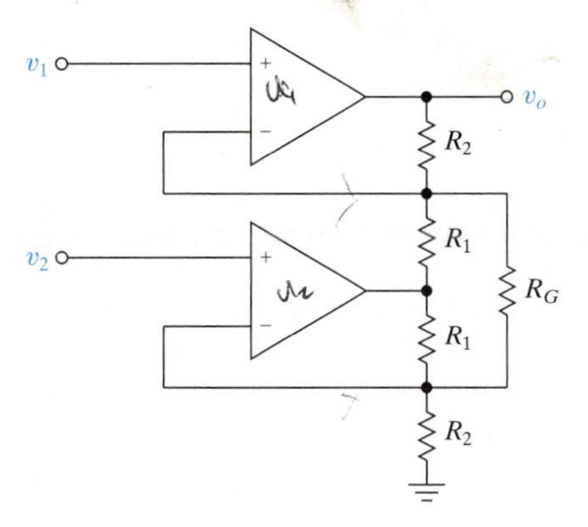

FIGURE D9.2

Ans:

$$v_o = (v_1 - v_2)\left[1 + \frac{R_2}{R_1} + \frac{2R_2}{R_G}\right]$$

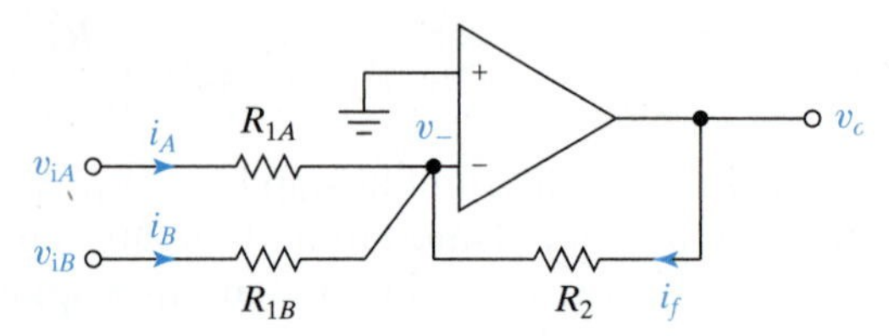

FIGURE 9.10 Summing op amp circuit.

9-8 The Summing Circuit

The circuit shown in Figure 9.10 is similar to the circuit for the inverting amplifier shown in Figure 9.8. The primary difference is that this circuit has two input voltages, v_{iA} and v_{iB}, and two corresponding input resistors, R_{1A} and R_{1B}.

This circuit acts as a *summing circuit* and will provide an output voltage that is related to the sum, or the addition, of the values of the two input voltages. This circuit has the same basic topology as the inverting amplifier circuit and retains a -1 multiplier (inverting) factor in the expression for voltage gain. Furthermore, as we shall see, each input voltage is weighted in the sum by a resistor ratio.

In analyzing this circuit we will again assume the op amp is ideal, and, therefore, v_- is forced to zero ($v_- = v_+ = 0$). With this assumption, we can easily write expressions for i_A, i_B, and i_f as follows.

$$i_A = \frac{v_{iA}}{R_{1A}}; i_B = \frac{v_{iB}}{R_{1B}}; i_f = \frac{v_o}{R_2}$$

Applying Kirchhoff's law at the inverting input node results in the following expression:

$$i_A + i_B = -i_f$$

Combining the above equations leads to the following result:

$$\frac{v_{iA}}{R_{1A}} + \frac{v_{iB}}{R_{1B}} = -\frac{v_o}{R_2}$$

Therefore,

Output of a summing circuit

$$v_o = -\left[\frac{R_2}{R_{1A}}v_{iA} + \frac{R_2}{R_{1B}}v_{iB}\right] \tag{9.13}$$

This equation defines the output of a summing circuit with two input voltages and two corresponding input resistors. Summing circuits with three or more input voltages and resistors can be designed by a straightforward extension of these results. Once again, notice that the relative gain of each of the inputs to the sum is controlled by the ratio of two resistor values.

9-9 The Integrator

In the circuit of Figure 9.11, a capacitor is placed in the feedback position of an inverting op amp circuit. This circuit will provide an output voltage proportional to the integral of the input voltage. To illustrate this fact, we again assume an ideal op amp, and v_- is made zero by the feedback. Then

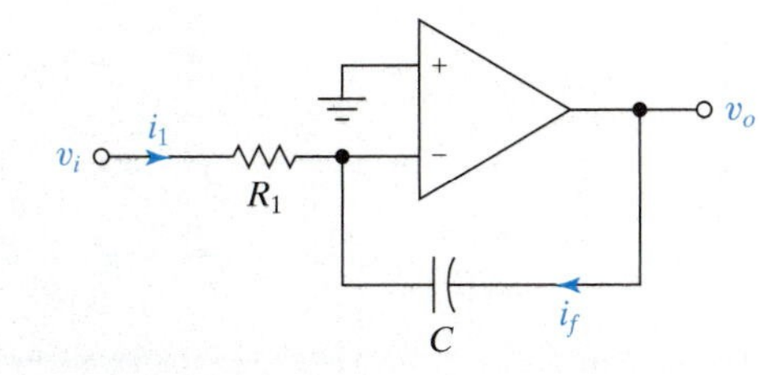

FIGURE 9.11 Op amp integrator circuit.

$$i_f = C\frac{dv_o}{dt}; i_1 = \frac{v_i}{R_1}; i_f = -i_1$$

Combining these equations leads to the expression

$$\frac{v_i}{R_1} = -C\frac{dv_o}{dt}$$

Solving this equation for v_o yields

Output of an integrating circuit

$$v_o = -\frac{1}{R_1 C}\int_0^t v_i \, dt + v_o(0) \tag{9.14}$$

The term $v_o(0)$ is the output voltage at time zero resulting from any initial charge on the capacitor.

Example 9.3

An *integrator circuit* of the type shown in Figure 9.11 has the following component values: $C = 100\ \mu\text{F}$ and $R_1 = 30\ \text{k}\Omega$. If the voltage, v_i, at the input of this circuit is given by the plot shown in Figure 9.12(a), derive an expression for, and construct a plot of, the output voltage, v_o. Assume $v_o(0) = 0$.

Using Eq. (9.14),

$$v_o(t) = -\frac{1}{3}2t \text{ for } 0 < t < 2 \text{ seconds}$$

At $t = 2$ seconds, $v_o(2) = -1.33$ volts.
For the next interval,

$$v_o(t) = -\frac{1}{3}[-4(t - 2)] - 1.33 \text{ for } 2 < t < 3 \text{ seconds}$$

A plot of the output voltage is given in Figure 9.12(b).

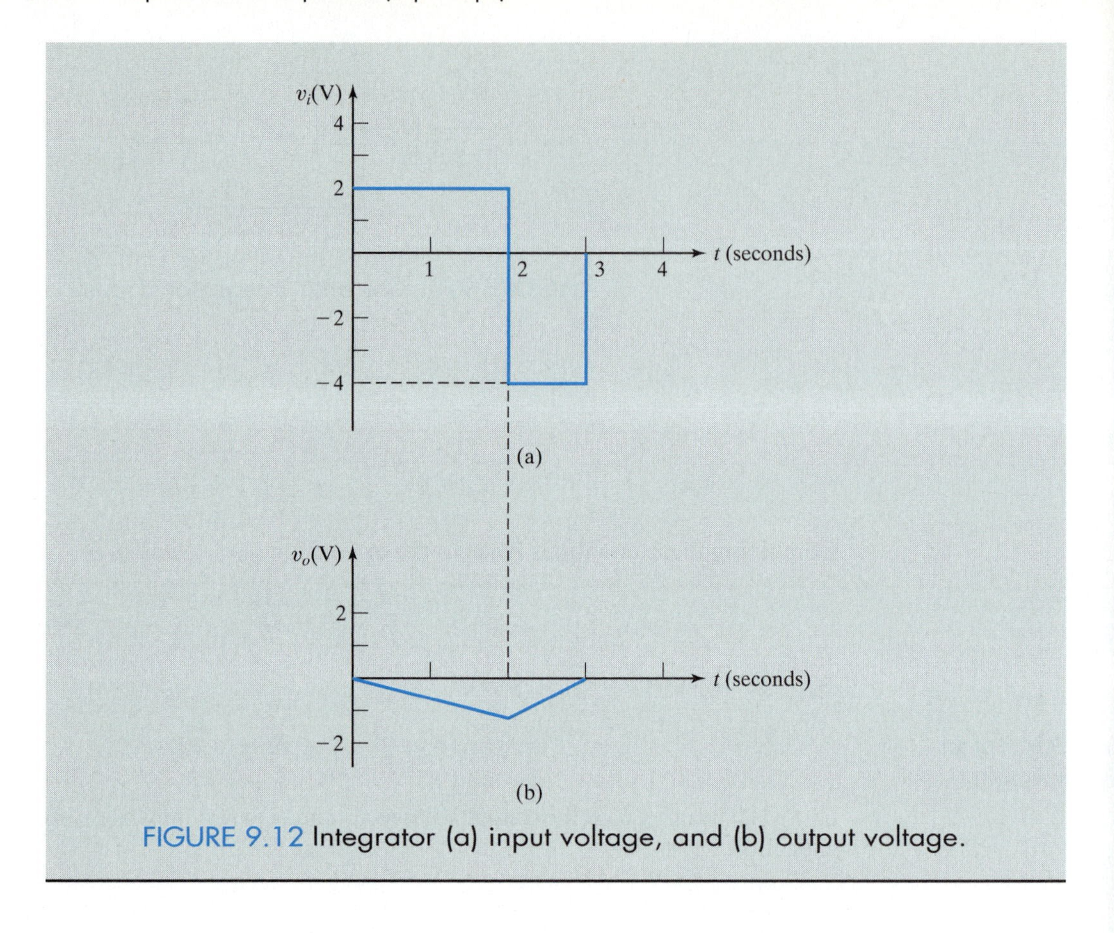

FIGURE 9.12 Integrator (a) input voltage, and (b) output voltage.

9–10 The Active Filter

As indicated in Chapter 7, a filter is a network that is frequency-selective in that it responds to certain signal frequencies differently than others. While a passive filter uses only passive components, such as capacitors, resistors, and inductors, an active filter utilizes amplifiers, usually op amps, and by doing so can often eliminate the need for costly and bulky inductors and simultaneously achieve higher performance.

When considering only resistive elements in the feedback and input signal paths, and an ideal op amp, the closed loop voltage gain, A_F, is real. With capacitors and/or inductors in op amp circuits we can, in an analogous way, consider the impedance of circuit elements, and obtain a complex voltage gain, $\mathbf{A}_F$.

As a simple example, consider the low-pass active filter circuit in Figure 9.13.

The circuit is an inverting op amp configuration, however, the RC network in the feedback path is frequency-selective.

The complex voltage gain of this circuit, $\mathbf{A}_F$, can be computed by taking the ratio of two impedances, the impedance of the feedback branch to that of the input branch. The complex voltage gain is the ratio of the phasor transforms of the output to the input voltage. That is,

$$\mathbf{A}_F = \frac{\mathbf{v}_o}{\mathbf{v}_i} = -\frac{\mathbf{Z}_2}{\mathbf{Z}_1} \tag{9.15}$$

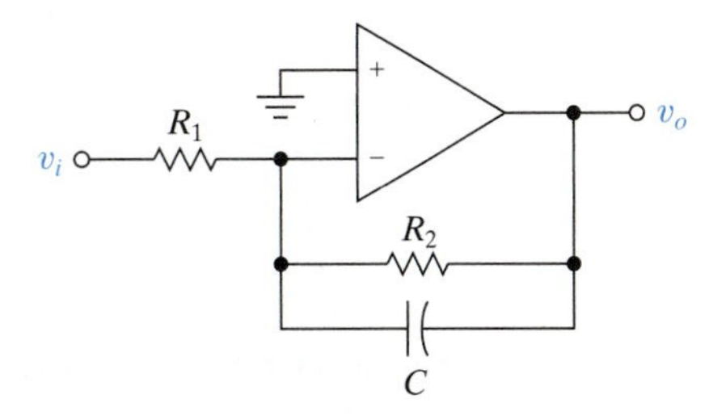

FIGURE 9.13 Low-pass filter circuit.

where

$$\mathbf{Z}_2 = \frac{1}{j\omega C + \left(\dfrac{1}{R_2}\right)} \tag{9.16}$$

and

$$\mathbf{Z}_1 = R_1 \tag{9.17}$$

Therefore,

Gain of a single-pole active filter

$$\mathbf{A}_F = -\frac{\left[\dfrac{R_2}{R_1}\right]}{1 + j\omega R_2 C} \tag{9.18}$$

The frequency response of this circuit is plotted in Figure 9.14. At low frequencies the gain of the circuit is constant at R_2/R_1. The high cutoff frequency is the value at which the magnitude of the voltage gain is reduced to 0.707 of its maximum. This value corresponds to a reduction in power by one-half, that is, the half-power point. For this circuit, ω_{HI} is

$$\omega_{HI} = \frac{1}{R_2 C} \tag{9.19}$$

This simple circuit does not produce a very sharp rolloff in gain with frequency, since it has a single-pole response. However, more complex circuits with multiple op amps can produce filter responses with very accurate and sharp response characteristics. By placing frequency-selective circuits in the input path, and/or feedback path, low-pass, high-pass, and band-pass filters can be created.

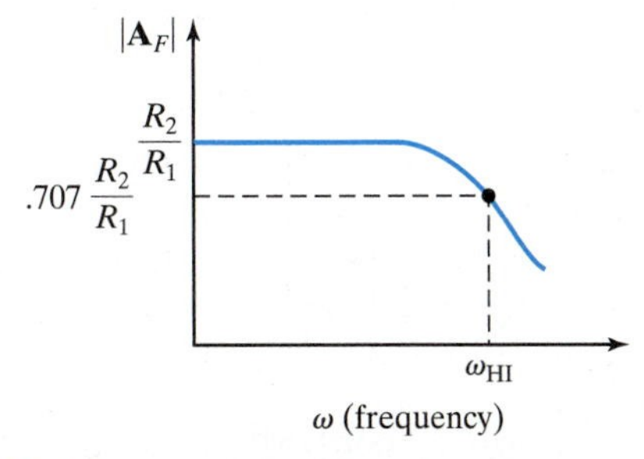

FIGURE 9.14 Low-pass filter frequency response.

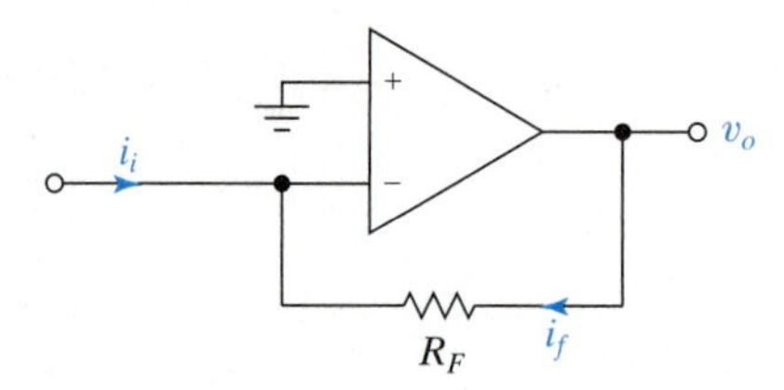

FIGURE 9.15 Current-to-voltage converter circuit.

9-11 The Current-to-Voltage Converter

There are some applications for which a circuit is needed that will transform an input current to an output voltage. To accomplish this, a simple op amp circuit can be used with a resistor in the feedback path, as shown in Figure 9.15.

The input current i_i cannot flow into the op amp since its input resistance is infinite; therefore, this current flows entirely through R_F. Hence

$$i_i = -i_f$$

The voltage at v_- is zero, and therefore,

$$v_o = -i_i R_F \tag{9.20}$$

It is impossible to refer to the "voltage gain" or "current gain" of this circuit because the input is a current and the output is a voltage. The parameter that describes how much the output voltage changes for a given change in input current is the *transresistance. Trans* means the voltage and current are not measured at the same place.

Output of a current-to-voltage converter

One such use of this type of circuit is in an electronic illumination (light) intensity meter. Photodiodes are devices that generate an output current approximately proportional to the incident radiation, such as light, on them. If a photodiode is connected to the input of a *current-to-voltage converter* circuit, the output voltage will be proportional to incident light intensity.

Example 9.4

A photodiode designed for visible light has a sensitivity of 25 μA per milliwatt of incident radiation. If this diode is used in the light meter circuit in Figure 9.16, calculate the value of R_F needed to make the magnitude of the output voltage equal 4 volts when the incident radiation deposits 50 milliwatts at the detector.

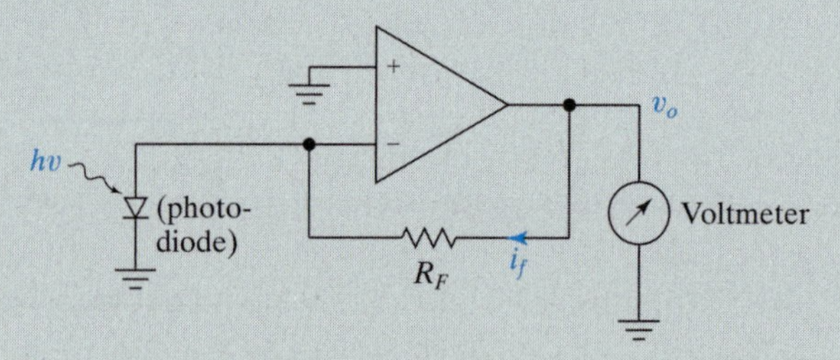

FIGURE 9.16 Circuit used in Example 9.4.

The detector photodiode produces 25 μA per milliwatt of radiation; therefore, at 50 milliwatts, it produces:

$$i_{PH} = (50)(25 \times 10^{-6}) = 1.25 \text{ mA}$$

In order to produce a magnitude of 4 volts at the output of the circuit,

$$R_F = \frac{4}{1.25 \times 10^{-3}} = 3.2 \text{ k}\Omega$$

The photodiode produces positive current flow from the anode, and therefore, in this circuit, positive current flows inward and opposite to the assumed direction of i_f. Therefore, in operation, the output voltage goes more negative as light intensity is increased, reaching −4 volts with 50 milliwatts of incident radiation. The photodiode could be reversed end-for-end, and the output voltage would go positive with increasing light intensity.

9–12 The Nonideal Op Amp

Real op amps have limitations not described by the ideal op amp model. These real limitations include:

- Output voltage is limited by power supply voltage(s)
- Finite gain
- Limited frequency response
- Finite input resistance
- Finite output resistance
- Finite slew rate
- Input bias currents
- Input bias current offset
- Input offset voltage
- Finite common mode rejection ratio (CMRR)

In many applications these limitations are not significant, and do not substantially affect the performance of the circuit compared to that anticipated using an ideal op amp model. However, it is important to be aware of these limitations, and consider them when they are important.

In this section we will briefly describe each of these limitations, with special attention to the effect of finite open-loop voltage gain. Further details can be obtained from op amp data sheets available from op amp manufacturers.

The *output voltage limitation* has already been described, and is summarized by equation 9.5. Basically, the output voltage of an op amp can not exceed the voltage of the power source applied to operate the op amp.

If the *open-loop gain* of the op amp is *finite,* the effect is to lower the closed loop gain over that value computed assuming infinite open-loop gain. Most practical op amps have open-loop gains approaching 10^5, and as long as the anticipated closed-loop gain is much lower, the effect is minimal. We can calculate the magnitude of this limitation by substituting

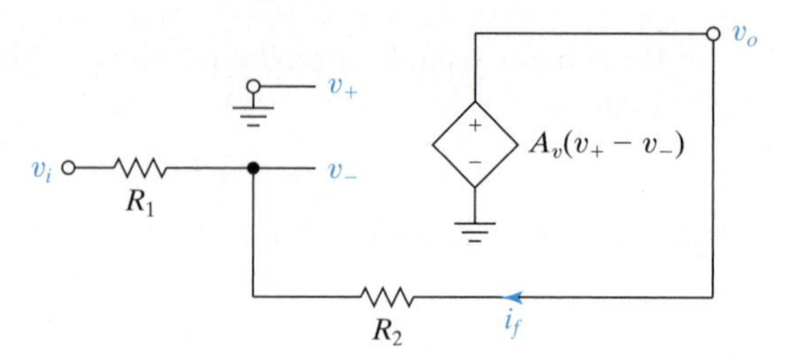

FIGURE 9.17 Inverting op amp equivalent circuit with finite gain.

the circuit model for the ideal op amp shown in Figure 9.3 into the inverting op amp circuit configuration shown in Figure 9.8. The resulting circuit is shown in Figure 9.17.

From the circuit in Figure 9.17, we note that the current through the feedback resistor, i_f, can be expressed as

$$i_f = \frac{(v_o - v_i)}{R_2 + R_1}$$

Likewise, the voltage at the inverting input, v_-, can be written as

$$v_- = v_i + R_1 i_f$$

Combining these two equations yields the expression

$$v_- = v_i + R_1\left[\frac{v_o - v_i}{R_2 + R_1}\right]$$

Since v_+ is connected directly to ground, that is, $v_+ = 0$ V, the output voltage, v_o, is

$$v_o = -A_v v_-$$

$$v_o = -A_v\left[v_i + R_1\left[\frac{v_o - v_i}{R_2 + R_1}\right]\right]$$

The voltage gain of this circuit, A_F, is equal to the ratio, v_o/v_i, and hence

Expression for closed-loop gain of nonideal (real) op amp

$$A_F = \frac{v_o}{v_i} = -\frac{1 - \left[\dfrac{R_1}{R_1 + R_2}\right]}{\dfrac{1}{A_v} + \left[\dfrac{R_1}{R_1 + R_2}\right]} \tag{9.21}$$

It is worth noting that Equation 9.21, in the limit as A_v goes to infinity, reduces to Equation 9.11, as expected.

Example 9.5

Consider again Example 9.2 in which an inverting amplifier circuit utilizes an ideal op amp, and has external resistor values of $R_1 = 2\text{ k}\Omega$ and $R_2 = 80\text{ k}\Omega$. The closed-loop gain was calculated to be -40. Now let $A_v = 100$.

For the case when A_v cannot be considered infinitely large, the simpler expression Eq. (9.11) is not valid, and Eq. (9.21) must be used. Substituting the circuit values into this equation yields

$$A_F = -\frac{1 - \dfrac{2\text{ k}}{82\text{ k}}}{\dfrac{1}{100} + \dfrac{2\text{ k}}{82\text{ k}}} = -28.4$$

Notice that in this latter case, A_F was reduced substantially—from 40 to 28.4 when A_v was reduced from infinity to 100.

The *frequency response* of a real op amp is limited, and most op amps are dominated by a single pole response over most of their frequency range. This means the gain decreases by a factor of 10 for each factor of 10 increase in frequency. (The "roll-off" is 20 db per decade.) Over this range the gain-bandwidth product is a constant for any particular op amp. Generally, op amp circuits are operated at closed-loop gains substantially less than the open-loop gain, and the bandwidth of the closed-loop circuit is found by dividing the gain-bandwidth product by the closed-loop gain.

Real op amps have a very high but *finite input resistance.* Therefore, the assumption that i_- and i_+ are zero must sometimes be reconsidered. This is generally only a problem if one is sensing signals from a very high impedance source. Similarly, the *output resistance* of real op amps is finite; the output does not behave like a perfect voltage source, but rather a voltage source in series with an output resistance. This may be an issue in circuits with a very low value of load resistance (or high load currents).

Slew rate (SR) is a parameter that specifies how fast the op amp can change its output voltage. Due to finite currents in the output circuitry, there is a limit to how fast the output node can change voltage. If you apply a step input to the op amp, and measure the slope of the output voltage versus time, you can determine the slew rate.

Slew rate defined

$$\text{slew rate} = \frac{dv_o(t)}{dt}_{\text{MAX}} \tag{9.22}$$

Drill Exercise

D9.3. If an op amp has a slew rate, SR, of 10 V/μs and a step increase in voltage is applied to the input, how long will it take for the output to move from 0 to 6 V?

Ans:

$$\text{time required} = \frac{6}{10} = 0.6\ \mu\text{s}$$

The input stage of an ideal op amp is a perfectly balanced differential amplifier, so that if exactly zero volts is applied between the two inputs, the output is exactly zero. Real op amps have manufacturing variations that make this not quite true. The *input offset voltage* is the very small input voltage required to drive the output to zero. The effect of this is minimal in most circuits. The *input bias current* is the average of the currents, i_- and i_+ (resulting from finite input resistance); these currents are very small and depend greatly on the type and quality of the op amp. The *input offset current* is the difference in these small input currents.

The *common mode rejection ratio (CMRR)* has already been discussed in section 9.7. It is a measure of the op amp's ability to amplify the difference signal between the two inputs (expressed by the differential mode or open-loop gain, A_v) and reject the signals common to both inputs (expressed by the common-mode gain, A_c). The CMRR expressed in decibels is

Common mode rejection ratio (CMRR) defined

$$CMRR = 20 \log \left| \frac{A_v}{A_c} \right| \qquad (9.23)$$

Summary

- The operational amplifier (op amp) is a basic building block for analog electronic circuits. Op amps are differential voltage amplifiers with very high gain. Differential amplifiers amplify only the *difference* in voltage between two inputs. The symbol commonly used for the op amp is shown in Figure 9.18.

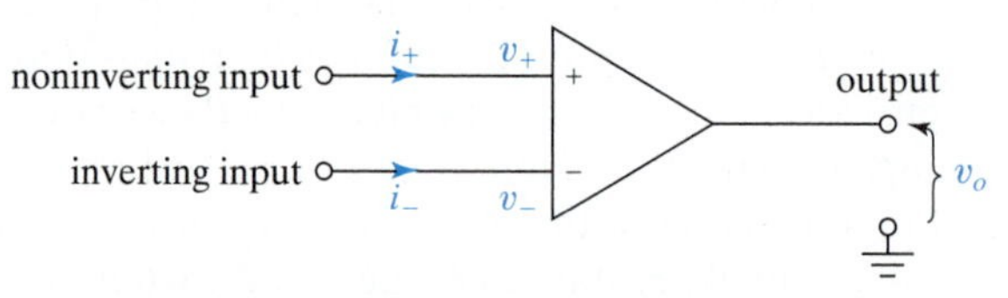

FIGURE 9.18 Op amp symbol.

- A linear voltage amplifier produces an output voltage that is a replica of the input voltage multiplied by a constant called the voltage gain, A_v.

$$v_{out} = A_v\, v_{in}$$

- The ideal op amp is a differential amplifier with: (1) infinite voltage gain, (2) infinite input resistance (and hence zero input currents, i_+ and i_-), and (3) zero output resistance. The circuit model of the ideal op amp is shown in Figure 9.19.

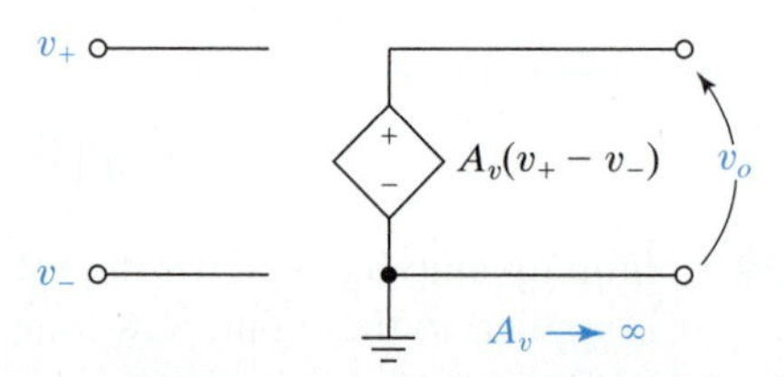

FIGURE 9.19 Circuit model for ideal op amp.

- Negative feedback is used in a large class of circuits using op amps. The connection from the output to the inverting input causes

$$v_- = v_+$$

- The op amp can be combined with external components to construct a wide variety of practical circuits. The availability of inexpensive IC op amps makes these circuits inexpensive and simple to implement.
- The noninverting amplifier circuit shown in Figure 9.20 has a voltage gain of

$$A_F = \frac{v_o}{v_i} = 1 + \frac{R_2}{R_1}$$

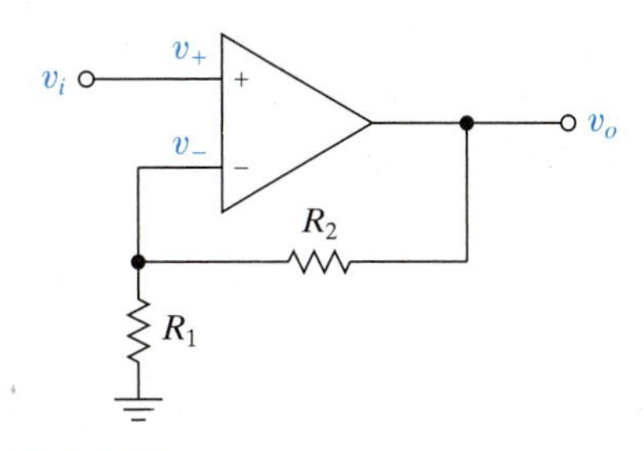

FIGURE 9.20 Noninverting op amp circuit.

- The inverting amplifier circuit shown in Figure 9.21 has a voltage gain of

$$A_F = \frac{v_o}{v_i} = -\frac{R_2}{R_1}$$

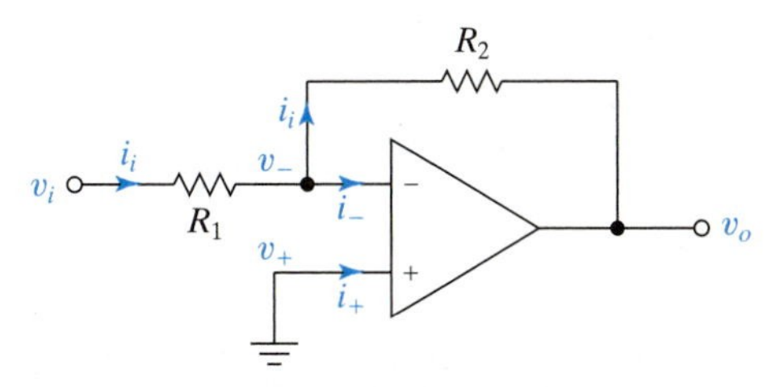

FIGURE 9.21 Inverting amplifier circuit.

- The differential amplifier circuit shown in Figure 9.22 has a voltage gain of

$$v_o = -\frac{R_2}{R_1}(v_1 - v_2)$$

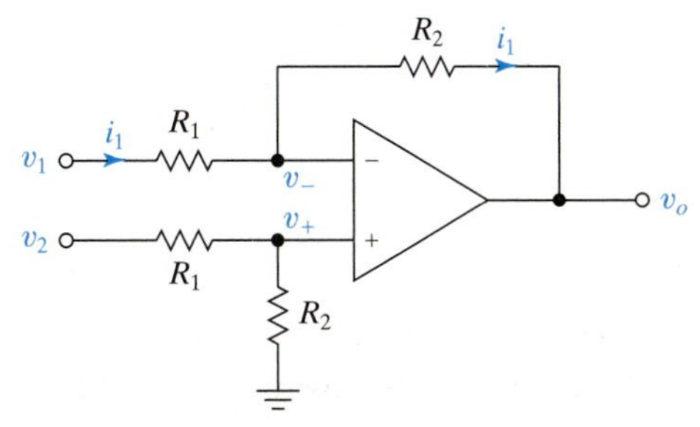

FIGURE 9.22 Differential amplifier circuit.

- Other op amp circuit configurations are capable of implementing a voltage-summing circuit, an integrator, an active filter, and the current-to-voltage converter circuit.
- Real op amps have physical limitations not described by the ideal op amp model. The ideal op amp model often works well, however, the limitations of real circuits must be considered when appropriate.

Problems

9.1. The input and output signals of an amplifier are shown in Figure P9.1. (a) Find the voltage gain of the amplifier. (b) Is it a linear amplifier? Explain your answer.

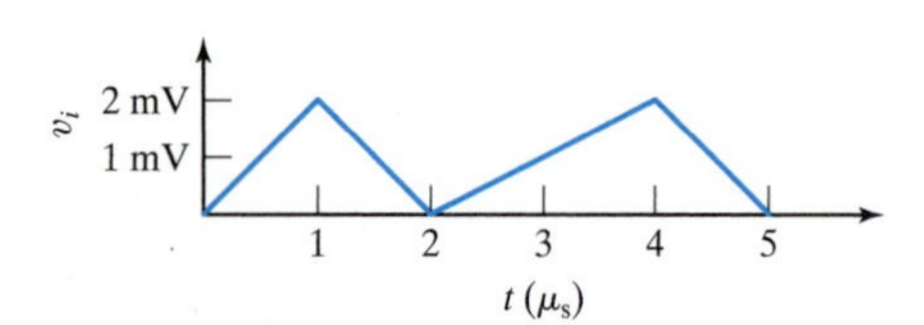

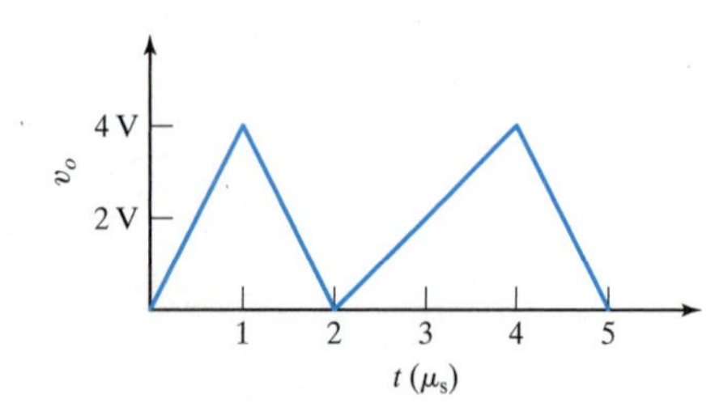

FIGURE P9.1

9.2. The input and output signals of an amplifier are shown in Figure P9.2. (a) Find the voltage gain of the amplifier. (b) Is it a linear amplifier? Explain your answer.

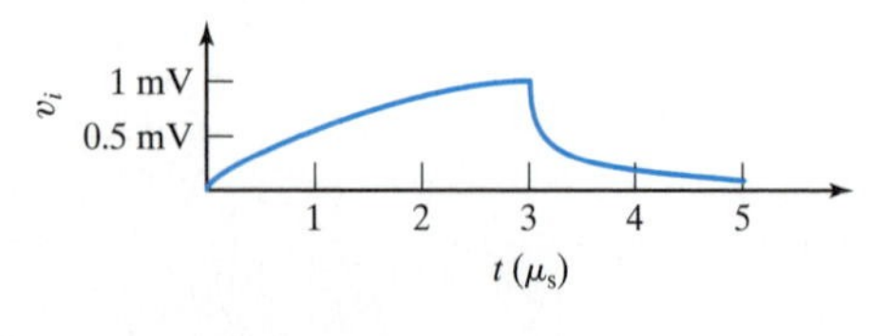

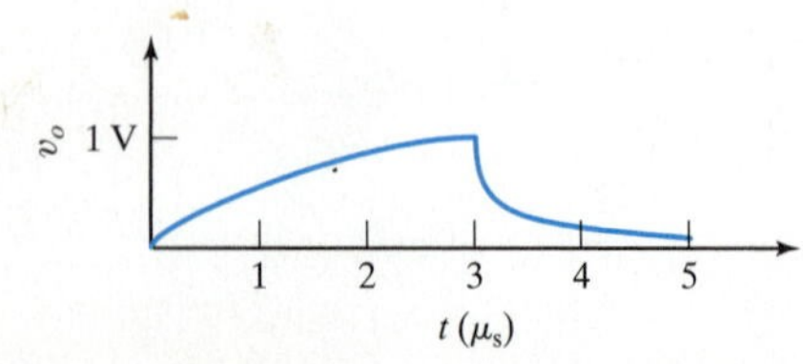

FIGURE P9.2

9.3. Given an ideal op amp, what assumptions are normally made regarding
(a) the voltage gain of the op amp?
(b) the current into each of the inputs?
(c) the resistance between the input terminals

9.4. When negative feedback is established in an op amp circuit by connecting the output terminal through a network to the inverting input terminal, what is the value of the voltage at the inverting input?

9.5. An op amp is powered by dual power supplies, $V_{DD} = +5$ V and $V_{SS} = -5$ V. The op amp is placed in an inverting op amp circuit with a closed-loop gain of 30. What would be a reasonable estimate of the voltage at the output if
(a) 0.3 V is applied to the input?
(b) 0.1 V is applied to the input?
(c) -0.17 V is applied to the input?

9.6. A noninverting op amp circuit is operated with $V_{DD} = 5$ V and $V_{SS} = 0$ V, and the input signal ranges from 0.3 V to 0.6 V. What is the largest value of the closed-loop gain for which the circuit will perform as a linear amplifier?

9.7. Determine the voltage gain, A_F, for the circuit in Figure P9.7, assuming an ideal op amp.

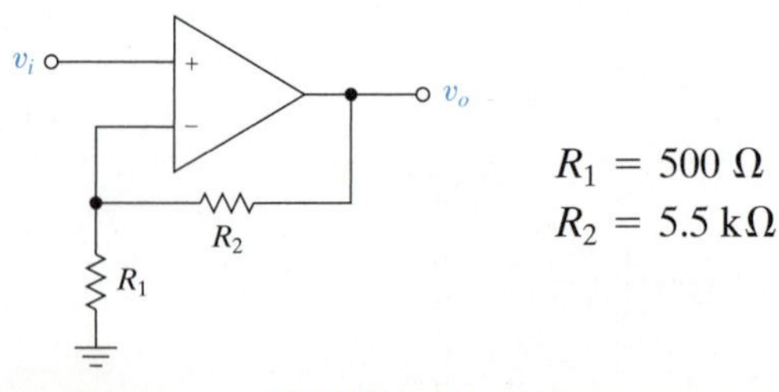

FIGURE P9.7

9.8. Determine the voltage gain, A_F, for the circuit in Figure P9.8, assuming an ideal op amp.

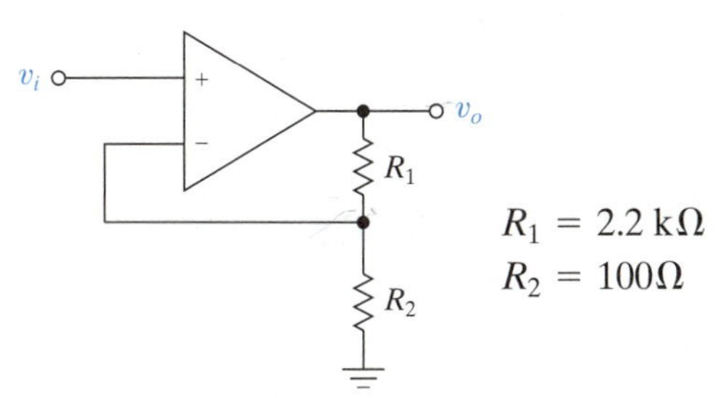

FIGURE P9.8

9.9. Determine the voltage gain, A_F, for the circuit in Figure P9.9, assuming an ideal op amp.

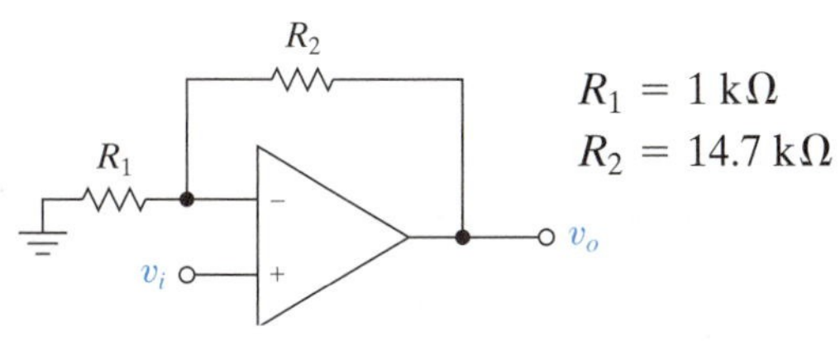

FIGURE P9.9

9.10. Determine the voltage gain, A_F, for the circuit in Figure P9.7, assuming an ideal op amp, if $R_1 = 3\ \mathrm{k\Omega}$ and $R_2 = 3\ \mathrm{k\Omega}$.

9.11. Determine the voltage gain, A_F, for the circuit in Figure P9.8, assuming an ideal op amp, if $R_1 = 500\ \Omega$ and $R_2 = 1\ \mathrm{k\Omega}$.

9.12. Determine the voltage gain, A_F, for the circuit in Figure P9.9, assuming an ideal op amp, if $R_1 = 1.5\ \mathrm{k\Omega}$ and $R_2 = 100\ \mathrm{k\Omega}$.

9.13. Determine the voltage gain, A_F, for the circuit in Figure P9.13, assuming an ideal op amp.

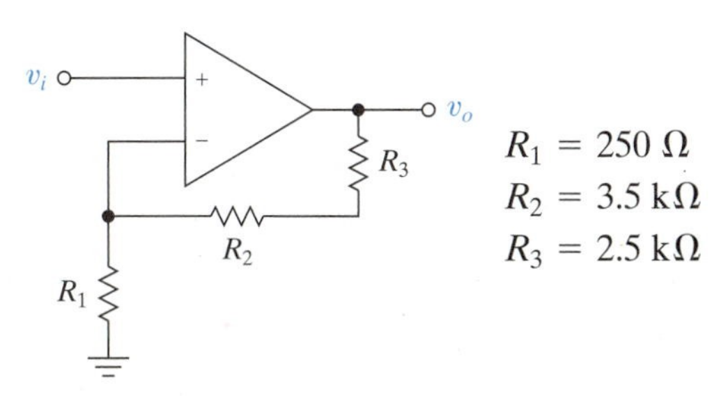

FIGURE P9.13

9.14. For the circuit shown in Figure P9.14, assume the voltage source is given by $v_s = 0.1 \cos(2000\,t)\ V$.

(a) Write an expression for v_o, the output voltage across the load resistor, R_L?
(b) What is the maximum current through R_L?
(c) What is the maximum current from the output of the op amp?

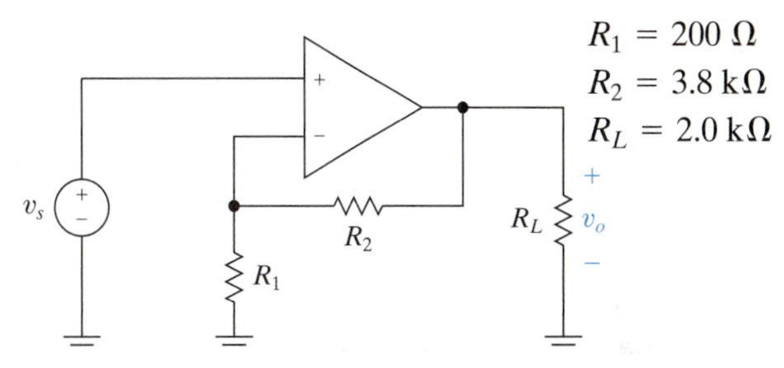

FIGURE P9.14

9.15. Repeat problem 9.14 for the case where $v_s = 0.2 + 0.1 \cos(2000t)\ V$.

9.16. Determine the value of R_2 required to establish the voltage gain of the circuit in Figure P9.16 at $A_F = 25$; assume an ideal op amp and $R_1 = 3.0\ \mathrm{k\Omega}$.

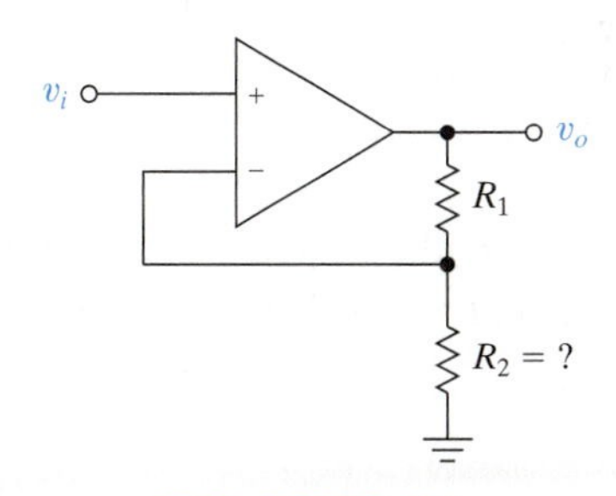

FIGURE P9.16

9.17. For the circuit shown in Figure P9.17, determine the voltage, v_o, across R_L.

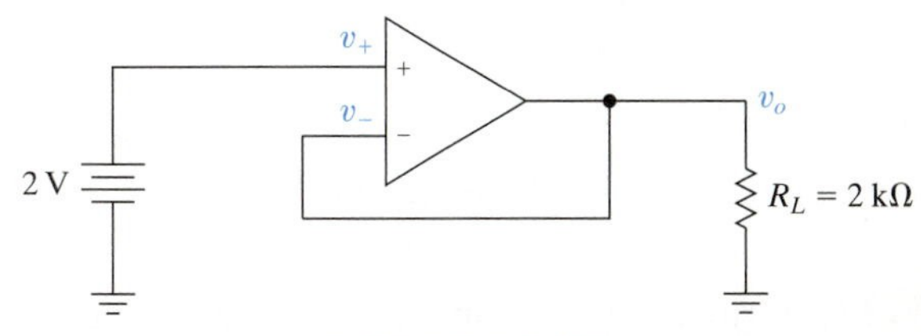

FIGURE P9.17

9.18. Determine the voltage gain, A_F, for the circuit in Figure P9.18, assuming an ideal op amp.

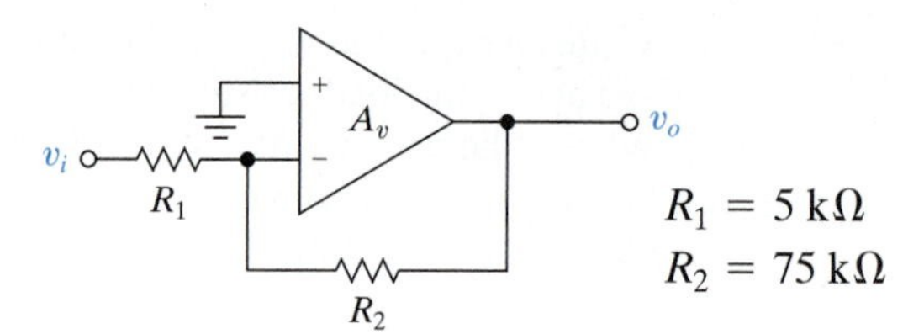

FIGURE P9.18

9.19. Determine the voltage gain, A_F, for the circuit in Figure P9.18, assuming $R_1 = 3.3\ \mathrm{k}\Omega$ $R_2 = 70\ \mathrm{k}\Omega$ and the op amp is ideal.

9.20. Determine the voltage gain, A_F, for the circuit in Figure P9.18, assuming an ideal op amp.

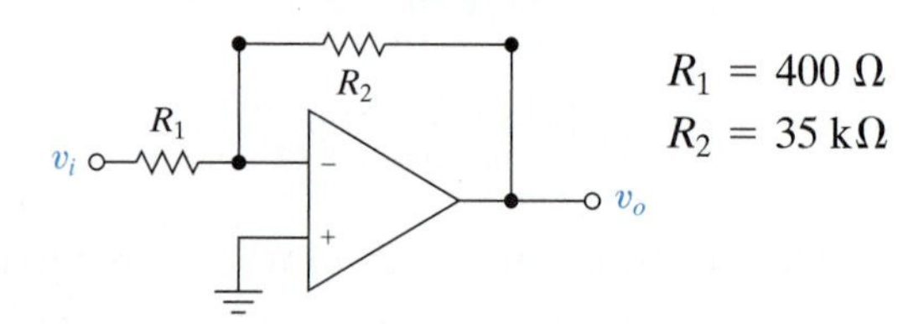

FIGURE P9.20

9.21. For the circuit shown in Figure P.20, find the voltage gain assuming an ideal op amp, $R_1 = 1\ \mathrm{k}\Omega$ and $R_2 = 65\ \mathrm{k}\Omega$.

9.22. Determine the voltage gain, A_F, for the circuit in Figure P9.22, assuming an ideal op amp.

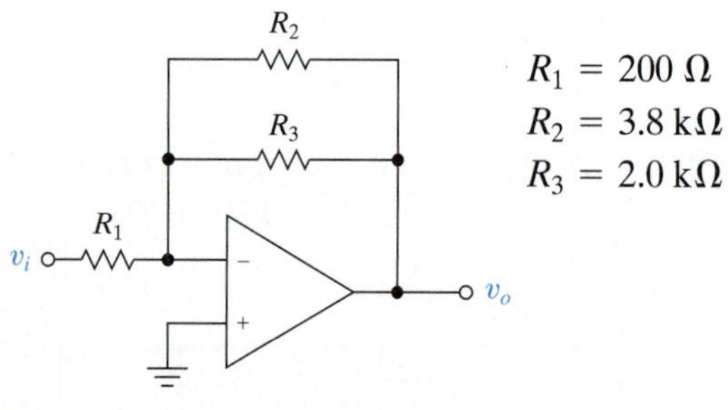

FIGURE P9.22

9.23. Write an expression for the output voltage, v_o, across R_L given that $v_s = 2\sin(\omega t)$.

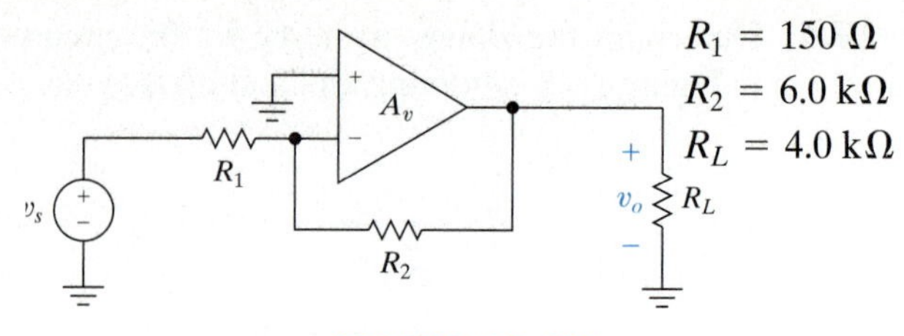

FIGURE P9.23

9.24. Determine the output voltage, v_o, across R_L in Figure P9.24, assuming an ideal op amp.

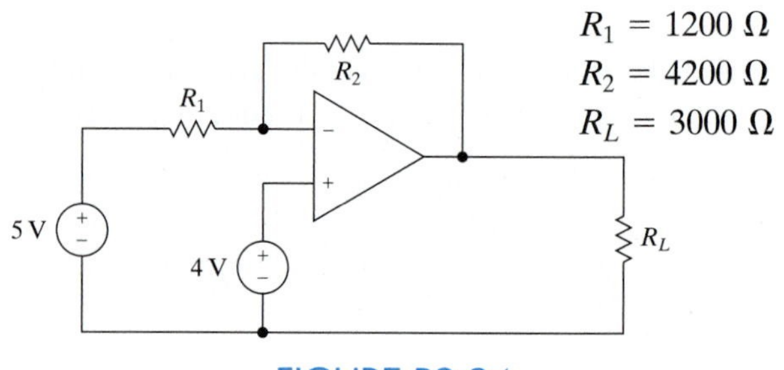

FIGURE P9.24

9.25. The signal from an electronic pressure transducer (sensor) has a maximum value of 10 mV, corresponding to maximum pressure. We would like to amplify this signal to a maximum of 3 volts. If an op amp circuit similar to that in Figure P9.8 is used, and $R_2 = 750\ \Omega$, what is the proper value for R_1? (Assume an ideal op amp.)

9.26. Repeat problem 9.25 using an op amp circuit similar to Figure P9.18 with $R_2 = 750\ \Omega$.

9.27. For the circuit shown in Figure P9.27, determine the value of the output voltage, v_o.

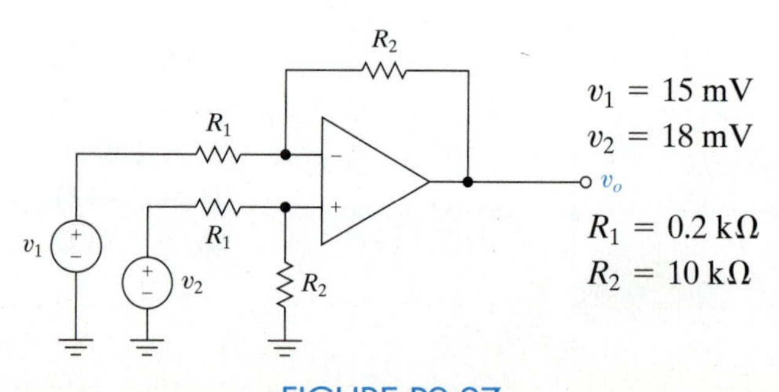

FIGURE P9.27

9.28. For the circuit shown in Figure P9.28, show that if $R_1/R_2 = R_3/R_4$, then $v_o = (R_2/R_1)(v_1 - v_2)$, assuming an ideal op amp.

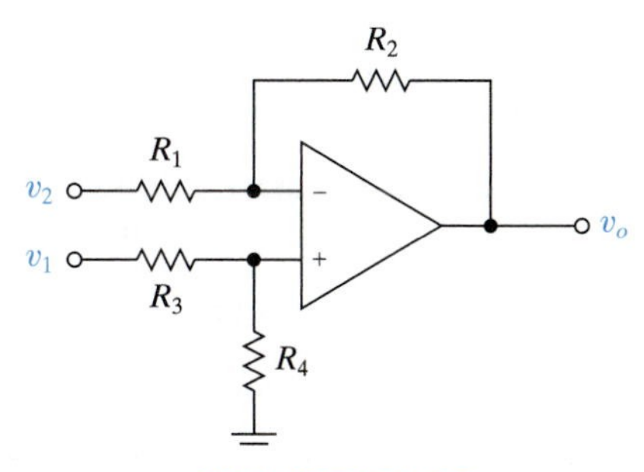

FIGURE P9.28

9.29. In the circuit shown in Figure P9.29, the Wheatstone Bridge is part of a temperature sensing system, in which R_a is nominally 100 Ω, and increases 1 ohm for every 1° C temperature increase. Choose the value of R_2 that will provide a 2 volt change at the output, v_o, for every degree temperature change at the sensor.

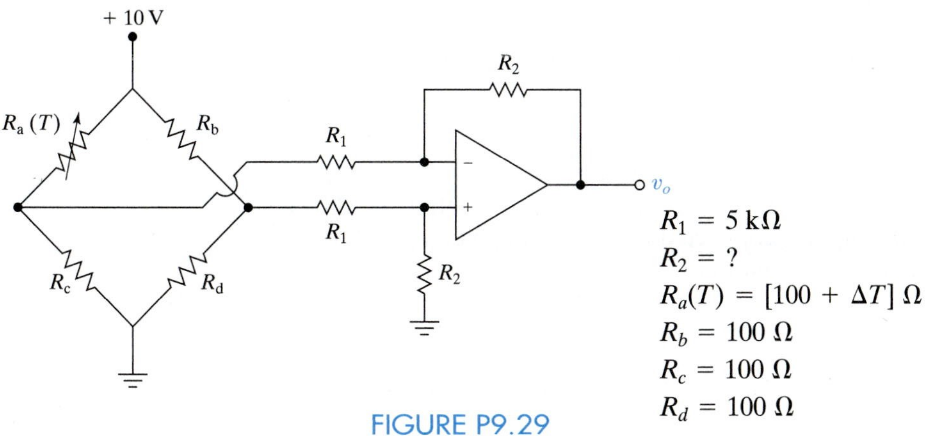

FIGURE P9.29

9.30. Calculate the voltage gain of the circuit shown in Figure P9.30, assuming an ideal op amp. Are there values of R that should be avoided?

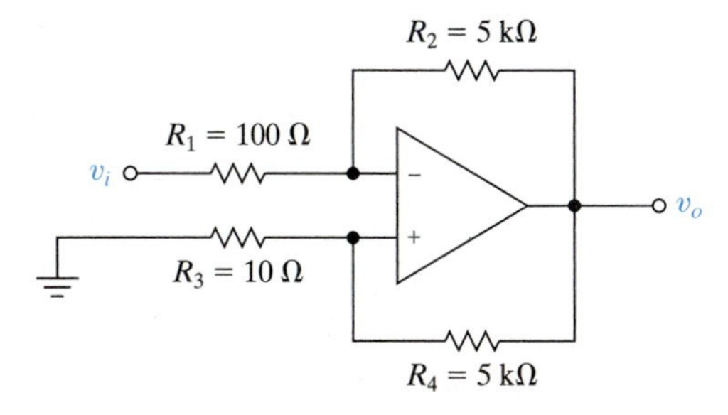

FIGURE P9.30

9.31. For the circuit in Figure P9.31, determine an expression for the output voltage, v_o, in terms of the input voltages, v_A, v_B, and v_C; assume an ideal op amp.

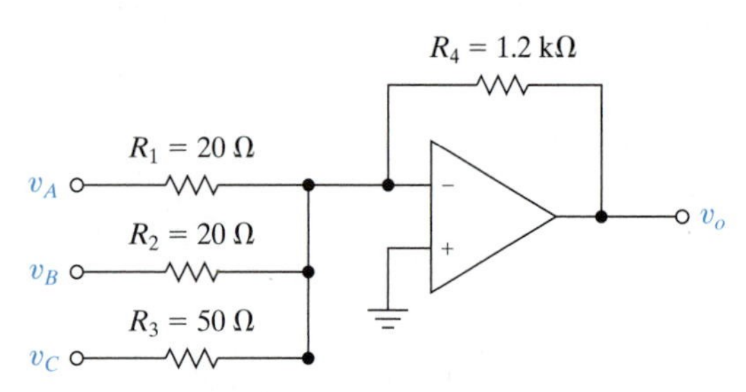

FIGURE P9.31

9.32. Using an ideal op amp, draw a circuit to implement the following function: $v_o = -[2v_A + 8v_B]$.

9.33. Using a summing amplifier, construct a circuit that will provide an output voltage that is the average of three input signals, $v_1(t)$, $v_2(t)$, and $v_3(t)$, inverted (with a negative sign). Following the topology of the circuit in Figure 9.10, let $R_2 = 10\ k\Omega$, and find the appropriate values for R_{1A}, R_{1B}, and R_{1C}.

9.34. Given the circuit in Figure P9.34, carefully plot the input and output voltage if the input voltage is defined as follows (time is in seconds, and the output is 0 at $t = 0$.)

From $t = 0$ to $t = 1$, the input is at +1 V

From $t = 1$ to $t = 3$, the input is at −0.5 V

From $t = 3$ to $t = 5$, the input is at +0.5 V.

Assume $R_1 = 4\ k\Omega$, $C = 20\ \mu F$, and an ideal op amp.

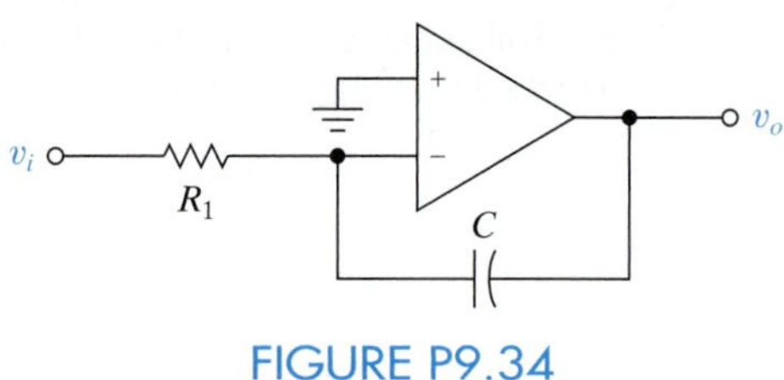

FIGURE P9.34

9.35. A circuit with an ideal op amp is shown in Figure P9.35(a); let $C = 180\ \mu F$ and $R = 5\ k\Omega$. (a) Plot the input waveform, v_i versus time, for the output, v_0, shown in Figure P9.35(b). (b) If the input is connected to a constant voltage, V_1, show that the output is the solution of the equation:

$$C\frac{d\,v_o(t)}{dt} + \frac{V_1}{R} = 0$$

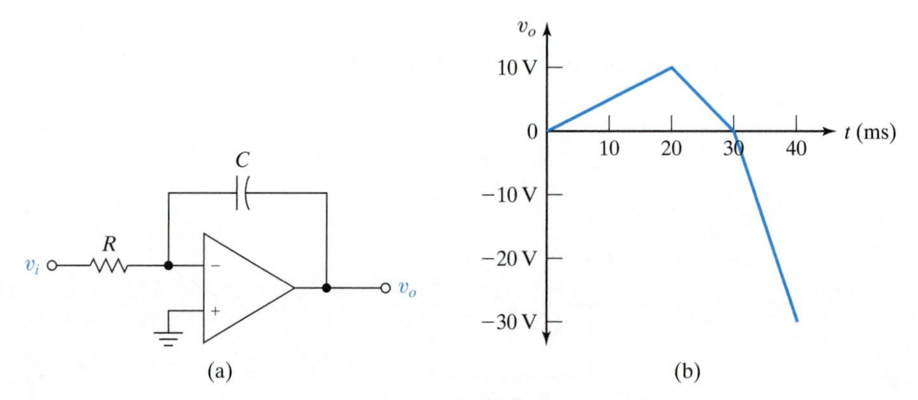

FIGURE P9.35

9.36. The circuit shown in Figure P9.36(a) is obtained by interchanging the capacitor and resistor in an integrator circuit. (a) Show that the circuit acts as a differentiator, that is,

$$v_o(t) = -RC\frac{d\,v_i(t)}{dt}$$

(b) Sketch the output voltage for the circuit, $v_o(t)$, as a function of time if the input voltage, $v_i(t)$, is given in Figure P9.36(b); assume $R = 10\text{ k}\Omega$, $C = 0.22\ \mu\text{F}$, and an ideal op amp.

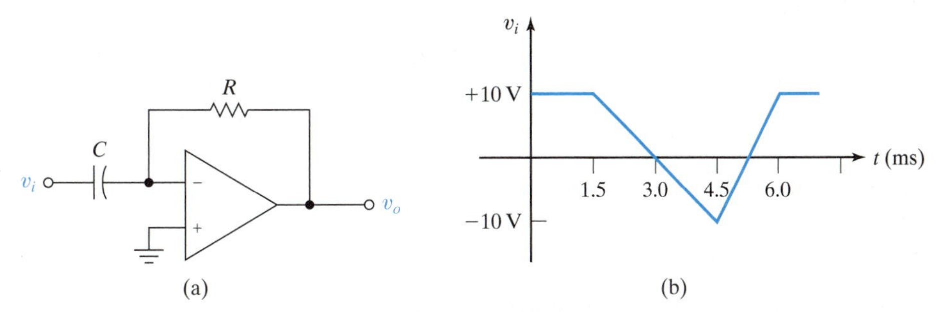

FIGURE P9.36

9.37. Design a circuit to obtain the solution of the following differential equation:

$$20\frac{dv(t)}{dt} + \frac{5}{7} = 0$$

9.38. The waveforms shown in Figure P9.38(a) are the input and output voltages of the op amp circuit of Figure P9.38(b). Specify the components and their values that should be placed in the boxes labeled A and B in order to obtain the given performance. (Assume the desired circuit input resistance is $2\text{ k}\Omega$.)

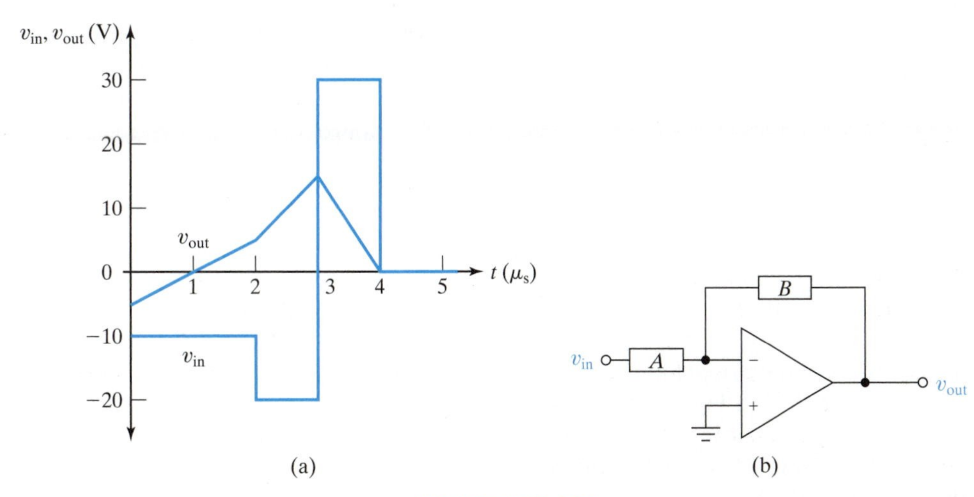

FIGURE P9.38

9.39. Plot the magnitude of the closed loop gain, A_F, of the circuit presented in Figure P9.39 as a function of frequency; let $R_1 = 1\ \text{k}\Omega$, $R_2 = 5\ \text{k}\Omega$, $C = 20\ \mu\text{F}$, and assume the op amp is ideal.

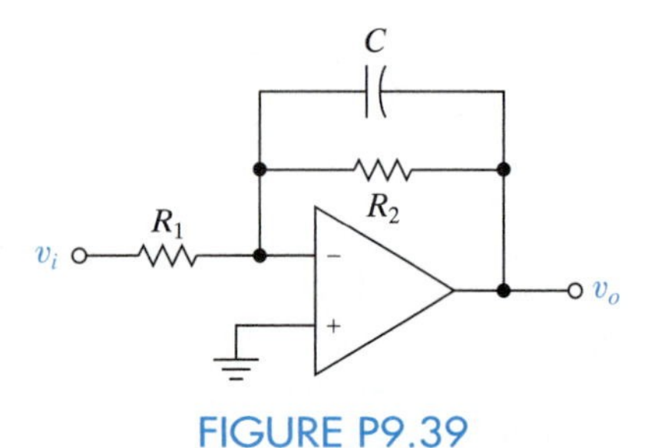

FIGURE P9.39

9.40. Repeat Problem 9.39, assuming $C = 35\mu\text{F}$, $R_2 = 10\ \text{k}\Omega$, and $R_1 = 2\ \text{k}\Omega$.

9.41. Determine the maximum gain and bandwidth of the filter shown in Figure P9.41; assume an ideal op amp.

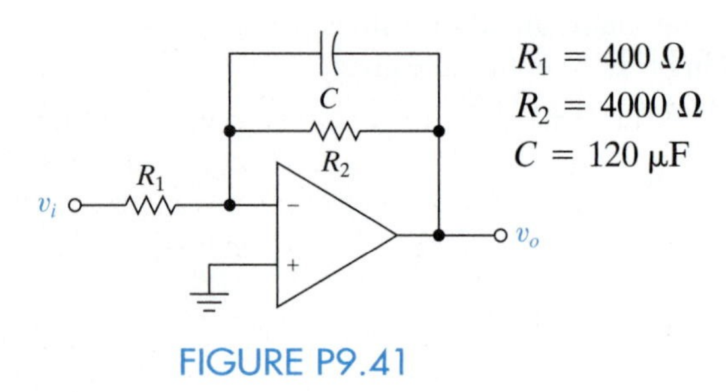

FIGURE P9.41

9.42. Repeat Problem 9.41, assuming $R_1 = 600\ \Omega$, $R_2 = 6\ \text{k}\Omega$, and $C = 80\ \mu\text{F}$.

9.43. Plot the magnitude of the closed loop gain, A_F, of the circuit presented in Figure P9.43 as a function of frequency; let $R_1 = 2\ \text{k}\Omega$, $C_1 = 30\ \mu\text{F}$, $R_2 = 3\ \text{k}\Omega$, $C_2 = 2\ \mu\text{F}$, and assume the op amp is ideal.

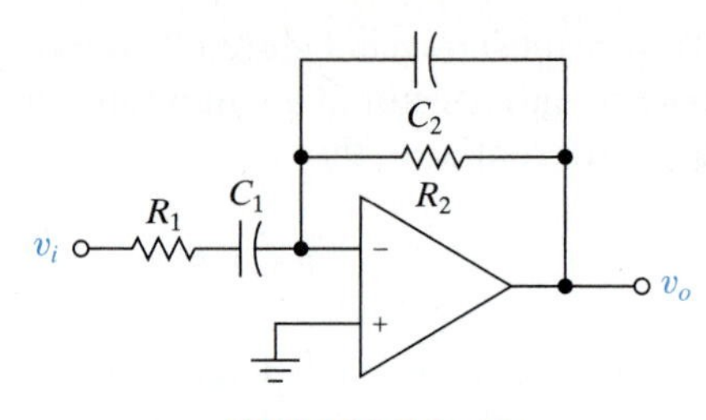

FIGURE P9.43

9.44. The circuit shown in Figure P9.44 is an amplifier circuit that has a closed loop gain that can be controlled by the position of a switch. Obtain the gain (a) when the switch, S_1, is closed and (b) when the switch, S_1, is open.

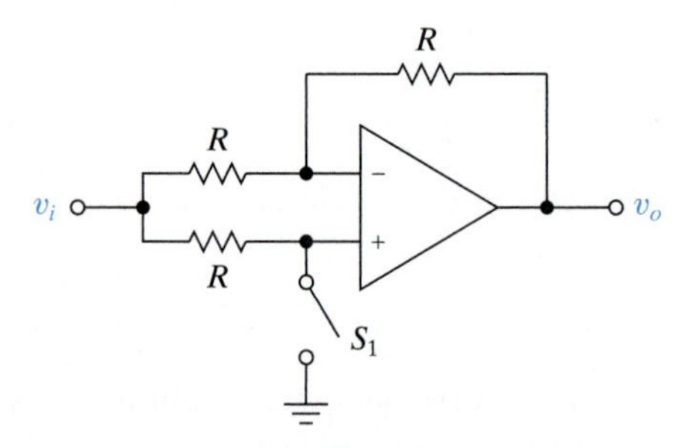

FIGURE P9.44

9.45. The circuit given in Figure P9.45 is a current-to-voltage converter. Determine the transresistance of this circuit; assume an ideal op amp.

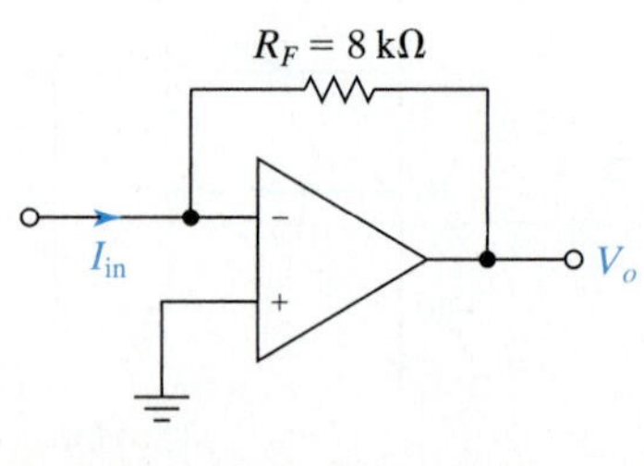

FIGURE P9.45

9.46. The circuit of Figure P9.46 is an electronic radiation detector. The photodiode has a sensitivity of 10 μA/mW of incident radiation. If the voltmeter reads 8 V, determine the power being deposited by the radiation.

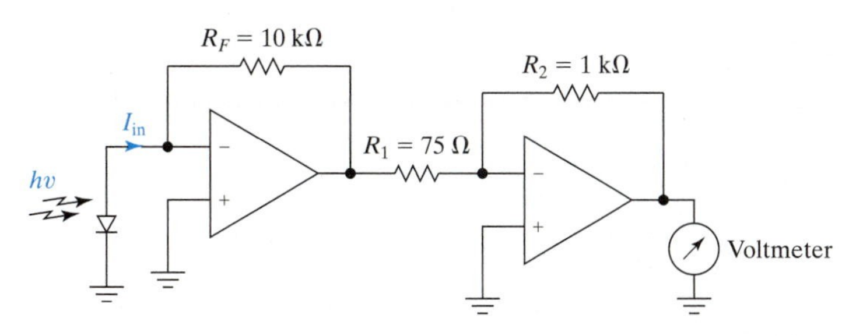

FIGURE P9.46

9.47. (a) Determine the voltage gain of the inverting amplifier circuit shown in Figure P9.47 using the op amp model of Figure 9.3. Assume $A_v = 50$, $R_2 = 10\ \text{k}\Omega$, $R_1 = 1\ \text{k}\Omega$. (b) Repeat (a) with $A_v = 500$. (c) Repeat (a) taking the limit as $A_v \to \infty$.

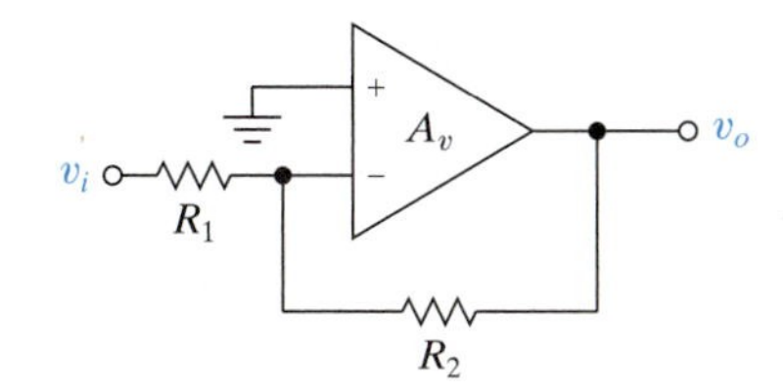

FIGURE P9.47

9.48. For the circuit shown in Figure P9.47, find the voltage gain if $A_v = 500$, $R_1 = 200\ \Omega$, and $R_2 = 3.0\ \text{k}\Omega$.

9.49. For the circuit shown in Figure P9.47, assume $R_2 = 15\ \text{k}\Omega$ and $R_1 = 800\ \Omega$. What is the closed-loop gain of the circuit if

(a) A_v = infinity
(b) $A_v = 200$
(c) $A_v = 60$

9.50. An op amp with a slew rate of 30 V/μs has a step change in the input voltage. Approximately how long will it take the output voltage to move from −5 V to +5 V?

9.51. With a step input voltage change applied to the input of an op amp, the output voltage changes from 0 to 10 V in 0.27 μs. What is the slew rate for this amplifier?

9.52. An op amp with an open loop gain, A_v, of 10,000 also has a common mode gain, A_c, of 0.1. What is the common mode rejection ratio, CMRR, expressed in decibels?

9.53. If an op amp is a factor of 1000 more responsive to differential mode signals than common mode signals, what is the op amp's common mode rejection ratio, CMRR, expressed in decibels?

10–1 Introduction

Diode operation described

One of the most basic and yet remarkable effects in solid-state science is the electronic behavior of the solid-state *diode.*

A *diode* is a two-terminal electronic device that conducts current if a voltage source is applied in one direction, and refuses to conduct significant current when the voltage is applied with the opposite polarity.

A diode with a voltage applied so that the diode is conducting a current is said to be *forward biased;* a diode with a voltage applied in the opposite direction such that no current flows is said to be *reverse biased.*

The schematic symbol for the diode and a photograph of a common semiconductor diode installed on a circuit board is shown in Figure 10.1. The direction of the "arrow" contained in the symbol indicates the direction of positive current flow that is allowed, in this case top to bottom. Current will not flow in the opposite direction.

The fundamental characteristics of a diode can be illustrated by an analogous fluid system component—a valve that allows fluid to flow only in one direction. Usually these valves are called "check" valves or "flapper" valves. Such valves allow flow in one direction, but close and restrict fluid flow if the fluid attempts to move in the other direction.

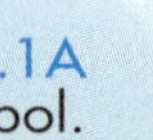

FIGURE 10.1A Diode symbol.

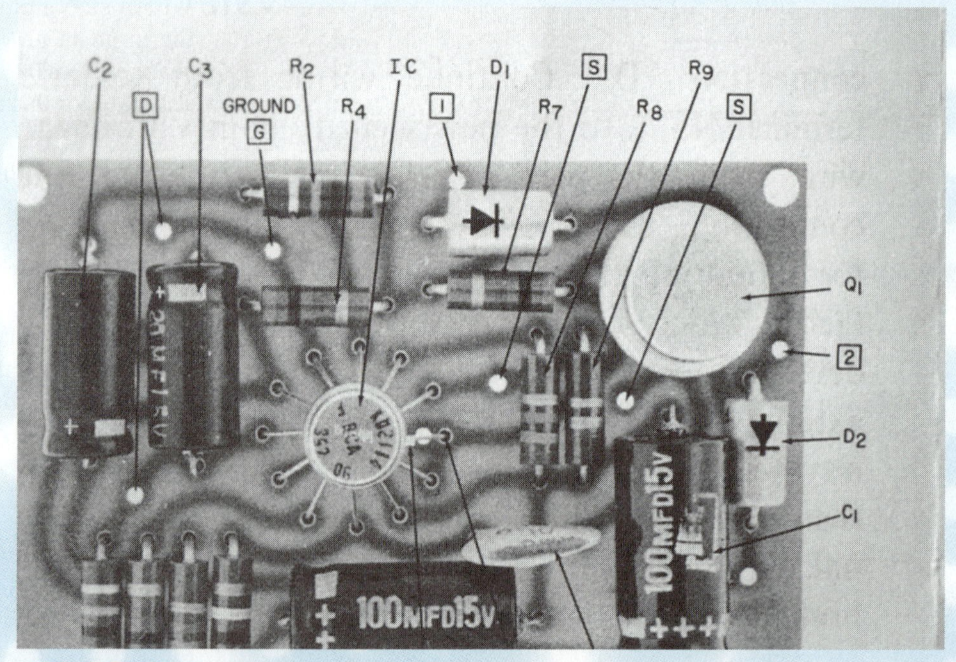

FIGURE 10.1B Photograph of diodes (D_1 and D_2) on circuit board with other components.

An illustration of such a valve is shown in Figure 10.2. In this analogy remember that fluid flow is analogous to current, and pressure is analogous to voltage. Part (a) of this figure illustrates that if a pressure (voltage) difference is applied so the left side is at a higher pressure than the right, then this pressure attempts to move fluid to the right and the valve opens and fluid (current) flows. The application of a pressure difference of opposite polarity, as shown in part (b) of the figure, attempts to force fluid to the left; the valve closes and no fluid flows. Figure 10.2(c) shows by analogy a diode; only if V_D is positive (the voltage on the left higher than that on the right), then current I_D flows. The terminal on the left is called the anode; the other, the cathode.

10–2 *p*- and *n*-Type Semiconductors

A semiconductor material can be made either *n-type* or *p-type.* We will now describe what is meant by these terms as well as how these critical material properties are created. This information will be important for understanding how diodes, transistors, and other solid-state devices operate.

In the present discussion, attention will be focused on the semiconductor material, *silicon.* Most modern devices are fabricated in silicon; however, the basic principles present-

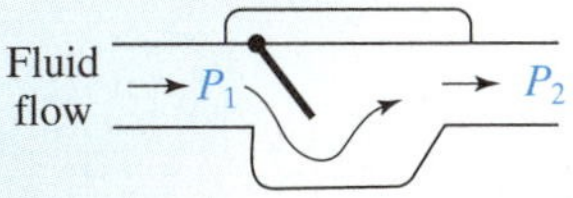

(a) $P_1 > P_2$

FIGURE 10.2(a) Fluid passes through from left to right—valve forced open.

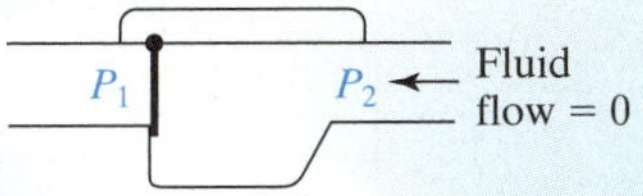

(b) $P_1 < P_2$

FIGURE 10.2(b) No fluid flows from right to left—valve forced closed.

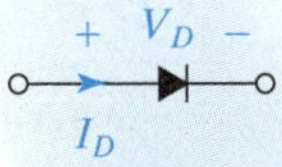

(c)

FIGURE 10.2(c) Diode allows current to flow in only one direction.

ed could be applied to germanium, gallium arsenide, or any other semiconductor material used for making such devices.

Recall the Periodic Table of the Elements and note the position of silicon. Silicon is in the fourth column of the table and has a valence of four. A portion of this table surrounding silicon is shown in Figure 10.3. As illustrated in Figure 10.4(a), a single isolated neutral silicon atom has four electrons in its outer shell, each represented by a "dash" in the figure.

When millions of atoms are joined together in a lattice to form "single crystal" silicon material, each silicon atom contributes four electrons to the covalent bonds, which connect it with its four nearest neighboring atoms. Each of the nearest neighbors also contributes an electron to each bond, making four completely filled bonds (two electrons each) surrounding each atom—a very stable condition. The term "single crystal" means the atoms are stacked in a regular three-dimensional pattern forming a perfectly ordered structure called a *crystal lattice.* A two-dimensional representation of this is shown in Figure. 10.4(b).

This pure silicon semiconductor lattice is neutral in total charge. There is as much positive charge contributed by protons in each silicon nucleus as there is negative charge contributed by the electrons surrounding the nuclei. This is as expected since combining charge-neutral atoms to make a lattice should produce a charge-neutral lattice.

This silicon lattice is a relatively poor conductor of electric current. Current requires movement of charge. All the electrons in the material are tightly bound in covalent bonds, so there aren't any free electrons available that could move and create a current. Semiconductor material in this situation is termed *intrinsic.*

Doping; *n*-type or *p*-type semiconductors

To create semiconductor material that can more easily conduct, it must be "doped"—yes, that's what it's called. *Doping* is the process of adding very precise amounts of a very small concentration of certain so-called impurities termed *dopants.* Actually, dopants are elements from columns in the periodic table adjacent to silicon. There are two types of dopants, *donor* and *acceptor impurities;* the first is used to create *n*-type silicon, and the latter, *p*-type.

Donor impurities are so named because they *donate* extra electrons to the silicon lattice. One of the most common donors is phosphorus, an atom with a valence of 5. If we add a small

Valence:	III (+3)	IV (+4)	V (+5)
	5 B Boron 10.811	6 C Carbon 12.011	7 N Nitrogen 14.0067
	13 Al Aluminum 26.98154	14 Si Silicon 28.0855	15 P Phosphorus 30.97376
	31 Ga Gallium 69.723	32 Ge Germanium 72.59	33 As Arsenic 74.9216
	49 In Indium 114.82	50 Sn Tin 118.710	51 Sb Antimony 121.75

FIGURE 10.3 Elements surrounding silicon in periodic table.

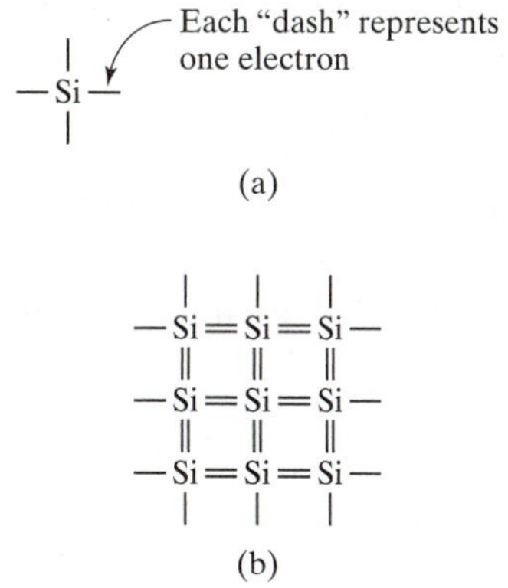

Each "dash" represents one electron

—Si—

(a)

—Si=Si=Si—
—Si=Si=Si—
—Si=Si=Si—

(b)

FIGURE 10.4 (a) Individual silicon atom (valence = 4).
(b) Silicon atoms in lattice.

portion of phosphorus to the silicon lattice, it will bind into one of the *lattice sites* in place of a silicon atom. It has five outer-shell electrons, four of which are used for covalent bonding with the four neighboring silicon atoms. However, the fifth electron is not used in bonding and is easily freed from the original atom by thermal energy even at room temperature. This creates a free electron in the lattice, which is easily moved when a voltage is applied across the material, and the material can therefore conduct a current. The more the material is doped with phosphorus, the more free electrons are created and the more easily the material conducts, that is, its resistance is lowered. Since this doped material has free electrons, each with a *n*egative charge, the material is now considered *n-type.* Recall that the entire charge in the total material is still neutral, because each phosphorus atom originally has one more unit of positive charge in its nucleus than silicon and for each atom an extra electron has been contributed.

An example of a silicon lattice with extra electrons as a result of phosphorus doping is shown in Figure 10.5.

Similarly, *p*-type material can be created by doping with atoms that have a valence of three, so-called acceptor impurities, in which free positive charge is added to the lattice. One of the most common such impurities is boron, and an example of a silicon lattice doped with boron is shown in Figure 10.6. Notice that the trivalent boron does not have enough electrons to fill all the orbitals around it, and there remains a place (bond site) where there is an electron absent; this is called a *hole.* A hole can be shown to behave like a positively charged particle and can move through the crystal lattice by a process of "musical chairs." Hole conduction occurs by an adjacent electron jumping over and filling the original hole, but leaving a hole in the place from which it came. Then another electron near the new hole moves over and fills that hole, but leaves a new hole, and so on. Electrons and holes are the *particles* that conduct current in solid-state electronic devices.

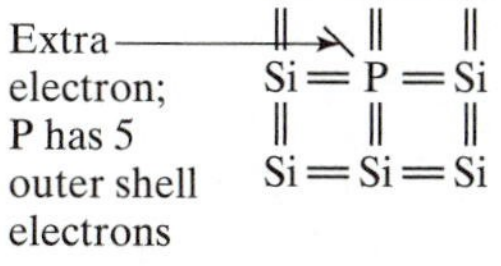

Si=Si=Si
Si=P=Si
Si=Si=Si

Extra electron; P has 5 outer shell electrons

FIGURE 10.5 Silicon doped with phosphorus.

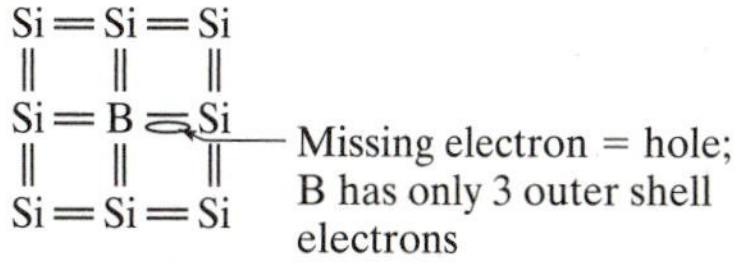

Si=Si=Si
Si=B=Si
Si=Si=Si

Missing electron = hole; B has only 3 outer shell electrons

FIGURE 10.6 Silicon doped with boron.

Since each ionized dopant atom in the lattice contributes one charge carrier at moderate doping levels, we find that in n-type material the free electron concentration, n, in electrons/cm^3 is approximately equal to the donor atom doping density, N_D, in donor atoms/cm^3, or

$$n \approx N_D \qquad (10.1a)$$

Similarly, in p-type material,

$$p \approx N_A \qquad (10.1b)$$

where p is the free hole concentration in holes/cm^3 and N_A is the acceptor atom doping concentration in acceptor atoms/cm^3.

If $N_D > N_A$, the material is n-type and $n > p$; if $N_A > N_D$, the material is p-type and $p > n$. The free carrier concentrations also depend on temperature.

As stated earlier, a pure semiconductor with no dopant impurities is termed intrinsic and the free carrier concentrations are very low. In a pure silicon lattice where every atom has a valence of 4, free electrons and holes are only created in pairs; therefore, the free electron density, n, equals the free hole density, p. This special density is called the *intrinsic carrier concentration*, and designated n_i. For an intrinsic material,

$$n_i = n = p$$

For silicon at 300° K, $n_i \approx 1.6 \times 10^{10}$ electrons/cm^3.

10–3 Current Conduction in Semiconductors

In a semiconductor material, there are therefore two types of mobile charge carriers that contribute to current flow. The electron is negatively charged, and the hole behaves as a positively charged particle. At temperatures above absolute zero, these free carriers are in constant random motion as a result of their thermal energy—however, their *net* motion in any particular direction is zero. An electron may start off in one direction, collide with the lattice, go off in another direction and collide again, and then repeat this process over and over. The mean-free-path, the average distance traveled before a collision, for an electron in silicon is of the order of 10^{-7} cm. This random motion is illustrated in Figure 10.7. Although the holes and electrons are in constant motion, because there is no net motion in any specific direction, there is no net current flow.

There are two principle mechanisms by which charge carriers are forced to move, on average, in a particular direction and thus create an electric current: *drift* and *diffusion*.

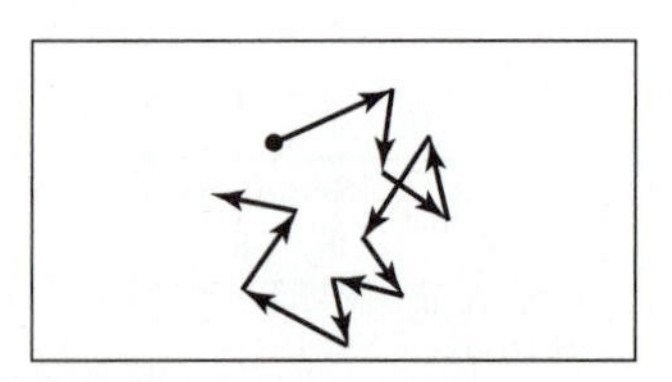

FIGURE 10.7 Random path of carrier in semiconductor (due to thermal energy).

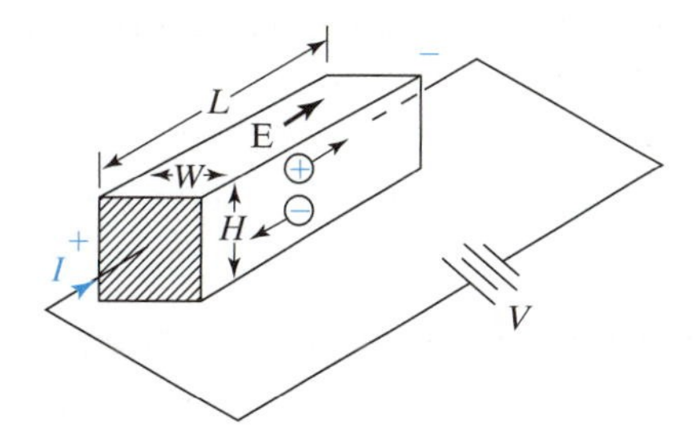

FIGURE 10.8 Rectangular block of semiconductor material with E-field applied.

10.3.1 Drift

Recall that a single electron carries a negative charge of 1.6×10^{-19} coulombs; a hole effectively carries a positive charge of the same magnitude. When an electric field is applied across a material, the resulting current is carried by both types of carriers, each moving in opposite directions. If, for example, in the block of material shown in Figure 10.8, a voltage, V, is applied as shown from one end to the other, then an electric field vector **E** is established in the material. The magnitude of the electric field is the applied voltage divided by the distance, L, between the parallel end plates at the terminals.

Electric field between parallel plates

$$|\mathbf{E}| = \frac{V}{L} \text{ volts/cm} \qquad (10.2)$$

The direction of the electric field vector, **E**, is defined to be the direction a small positive charge would be pushed if placed in the field. The E-field in the previous figure moves positive charge (holes) away from the "+" end and toward the "−" end; simultaneously negatively charged electrons are moved in the opposite direction.

The carriers begin drifting toward one of the end terminals and then collide with atoms in the lattice along the way and are deflected or scattered. However, the action of the field is continuous and they again start moving toward the terminal by a very indirect path yet with a net motion toward the goal. The motion of such a carrier is illustrated in Figure 10.9.

Electron drift velocity defined

The effective velocity of a carrier moving by the drift action of an applied electric field is proportional to the magnitude of the field over a wide range of field magnitudes. Therefore, the magnitude of the electron drift velocity, υ_n, is

$$\upsilon_n = \mu_n |\mathbf{E}| \qquad (10.3a)$$

where μ_n is the electron mobility constant.

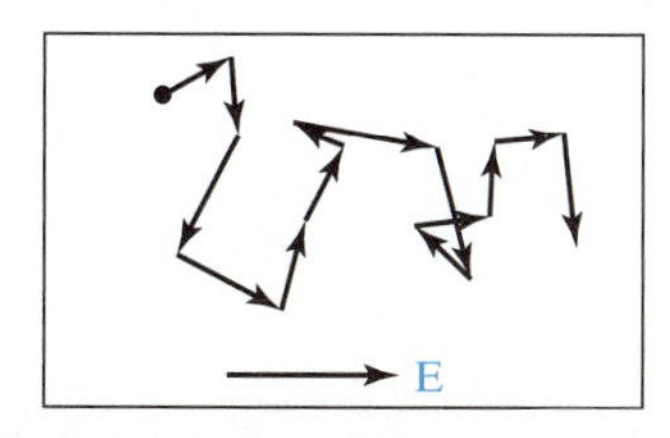

FIGURE 10.9 Net motion of "hole" to right due to E-field.

There is an analogous expression for holes:

$$\upsilon_p = \mu_p|\mathbf{E}| \tag{10.3b}$$

For silicon, $\mu_n = 1350\ \text{cm}^2/\text{V-s}$ and $\mu_p = 480\ \text{cm}^2/\text{V-s}$

Drill Exercise

D10.1. A cube of semiconductor material 1 cm on each side has 20 volts applied across two opposite faces. The mobility of holes in the material is $480\ \text{cm}^2/\text{V-s}$. Find the magnitude of the electric field in the cube, and the average drift velocity of holes.

Ans: $E = 20\ \text{V/cm};\ \upsilon_p = 9600\ \text{cm/s}$.

Conductivity of a semiconductor

The *conductivity* of a material is a property of the material and is a measure of the material's ability or propensity to carry electric current. The conductivity of a semiconductor is proportional to the density of electrons and holes and their respective mobilities. That is, if n is the density of electrons in electrons/cm^3 and p is the hole density in holes/cm^3, then

$$\sigma = \text{conductivity} = q(n\,\mu_n + p\,\mu_p) \tag{10.4}$$

Resistivity of a semiconductor

Resistivity, ρ generally measured in ohm-cm, is the reciprocal of conductivity.

$$\rho = \frac{1}{\sigma} \tag{10.5}$$

Resistance of a bar

The resistance, R, of a material with a constant cross-section can be calculated by knowing its resistivity and physical dimensions using the following relation:

$$R = \rho\frac{L}{A} \tag{10.6}$$

where A is the cross-sectional area normal to the direction of current flow and L is the length in the direction of the current.

Example 10.1

Let us calculate the resistance from end-to-end of the rectangular bar shown in Figure 10.8 assuming that the bar is made of a material with a resistivity of 4 ohm-cm, and its dimensions are: length, $L = 2$ cm; height, $H = 0.5$ cm; and width, $W = 0.2$ cm. Using Eq. (10.6),

$$R = \rho\frac{L}{A} = \rho\frac{L}{WH}$$

$$R = (4)\frac{2}{(0.5)(0.2)} = 80\ \text{ohms}$$

Drill Exercise

D10.2. The semiconductor cube in drill exercise 10.1 is determined to be *p*-type silicon with a hole concentration of 3×10^{15} holes/cm^3; the electron concentration is so low it can be ignored. Find the resistivity of the material and the resistance from one face of the cube to the other. Are these numbers always the same for any shape semiconductor?

> ***Ans:*** $\rho = 4.3\ \Omega$-cm; $R = 4.3\ \Omega$; No, these answers are only the same for a cube 1 cm on a side. The resistivity is a property of the material and is independent of the shape of the bar; the resistance depends on the shape of the bar, that is, length and cross-sectional area.

Current density defined

The *current density*, J, in a material is defined as the current per unit cross-sectional area, and is expressed in amperes per cm^2.

The current density is directly related to the applied field by a constant, the conductivity. Therefore,

$$\mathbf{J} = \sigma \mathbf{E} \tag{10.7}$$

The direction of current flow, indicated by the direction of the current density vector, is in the same direction as the electric field vector. Equation (10.7) is an alternate expression of Ohm's law.

Example 10.2

In the rectangular bar of Figure 10.8, assume that the material has the same properties described in Example 10.1, and that the voltage, V, applied across the bar is 12 volts. Let us determine the magnitude of the current density in the bar.

Since we have already calculated the total resistance in Example 10.1, the current, *I*, is

$$I = \frac{V}{R} = \frac{12}{80} = 0.15 \text{ amperes}$$

The current density is determined as the current per unit of cross-sectional area. Since the direction of current flow is parallel to the long axis of the bar, which is the same direction as the electric field, **E**, the cross-section through which the current flows is simply the cross-section of the bar. Therefore,

$$J = \frac{I}{A} = \frac{0.15}{(0.5)(0.2)} = \frac{0.15}{0.1} = 1.5 \text{ amperes/cm}^2$$

Drill Exercise

D10.3. Verify that the same answer obtained in Example 8.2 can be obtained using Eq. (10.7) directly.

10.3.2 Diffusion

The second mechanism by which charge carriers move in a solid is diffusion. A *diffusion current* occurs because of the physical principle that over time particles undergoing random motion will show a net movement from a region of high concentration to a region of lower concentration. Simple examples include the diffusion of smoke particles in the air, and the diffusion of gas molecules away from regions of high concentration. Heat flow from regions of high temperature to regions of low temperature follows the same law.

In a semiconductor with no electric field applied, holes and electrons move about randomly due to thermal energy. In Figure 10.10 the diffusion process is illustrated. Suppose at time zero, $t = 0$, a large concentration of electrons is established at the left end of the rectangular bar shown in Figure 10.10(a). At a later time, $t = t_1$, the carriers have begun to spread out, and some have passed through "plane A," creating a net current through this plane as shown in Figure 10.10(b). At an even later time, as illustrated in Figure 10.10(c), the carriers will have dispersed uniformly throughout the semiconductor and the concentration difference that was the driving force behind the net movement of carriers will have been equalized; the current through plane A will have returned to zero.

The diffusion equation simply states that the diffusion current density J is directly proportional to the gradient of carrier concentration. The proportionality constant consists of two terms, the charge per carrier and a constant that describes how easily a particular carrier type diffuses in its host material, which in this case is the *diffusion constant for electrons, D_n*.

For illustration, consider again the rectangular bar. Current flow is parallel to the long axis of the bar, which we define as the x direction. Therefore, the one-dimensional diffusion equation for electrons states that the current density for electrons, J_n, at any cross-section in the bar is given by:

Electron diffusion current defined

$$J_n = q\, D_n \left[\frac{dn}{dx} \right] \tag{10.8}$$

where dn/dx is the electron concentration gradient at the plane under consideration.

For silicon at 300° K, $D_n = 35\ \text{cm}^2/\text{sec}$; there is an analogous diffusion constant for holes, $D_p = 12\ \text{cm}^2/\text{sec}$.

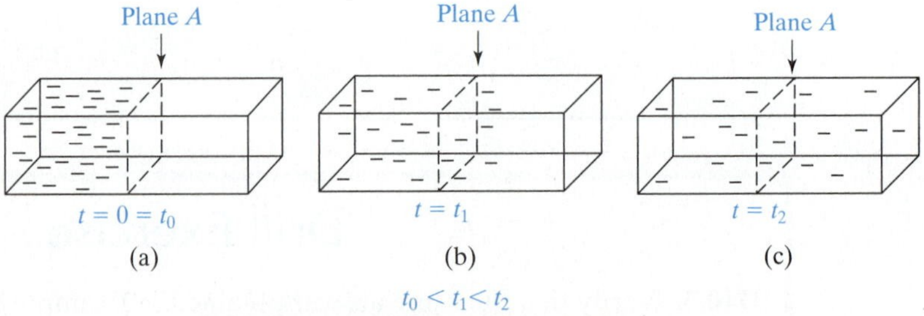

Plane A Plane A Plane A

$t = 0 = t_0$ (a) $t = t_1$ (b) $t = t_2$ (c)

$t_0 < t_1 < t_2$

FIGURE 10.10 Diffusion of electrons.

Example 10.3

Let us determine the magnitude of the current resulting from diffusion in a region of a rectangular semiconductor bar where the electron concentration changes linearly from $3 \times 10^{16}/\text{cm}^3$ to $3 \times 10^{18}/\text{cm}^3$ over a distance of 0.02 cm. Assume the bar has the same physical dimensions as in Example 10.1.

The electron concentration gradient is constant over the region of interest and

$$\frac{dn}{dx} = \frac{\Delta n}{\Delta x} = \frac{(3 \times 10^{18}) - (3 \times 10^{16})}{0.02}$$

$$\frac{dn}{dx} = 1.49 \times 10^{20}/\text{cm}^4$$

Thus, the current density according to Eq. (10.8) is

$$J_n = q\,D_n\left[\frac{dn}{dx}\right] = (1.6 \times 10^{-19})(35)(1.49 \times 10^{20}) =$$

$$8.32 \times 10^2\ \text{A/cm}^2$$

Recall that the cross-sectional area of the bar was $0.1\ \text{cm}^2$. Therefore, the current in amperes is

$$I = JA = (8.32 \times 10^2)(0.1) = 83.2\ \text{amperes}$$

Although carrier diffusion was illustrated for electrons, there is an analogous diffusion equation for holes based on the *hole diffusion constant* D_p and the hole concentration gradient. In a semiconductor we can simultaneously have holes and electrons diffusing, each according to its own diffusion constant and concentration gradient.

10–4 The *p–n* Junction Diode

A p–n junction diode can be created by bringing together a *p*- and *n*-type region within the same semiconductor lattice, as shown in Figure 10.11. Imagine that at the instant this junction is created, there's an *n*-type region with many free electrons joined to a *p*-type region with an abundance of free holes.

What happens? The electrons diffuse from their region of high concentration into the *p* material where their concentration is low. Simultaneously, the high density of holes in the

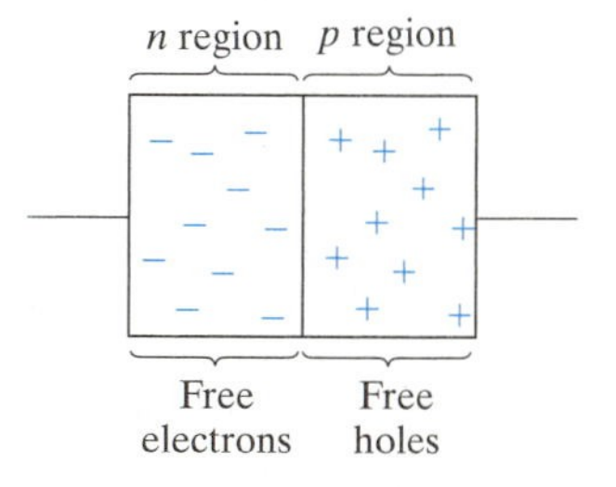

FIGURE 10.11 *p–n* junction at instant of formation.

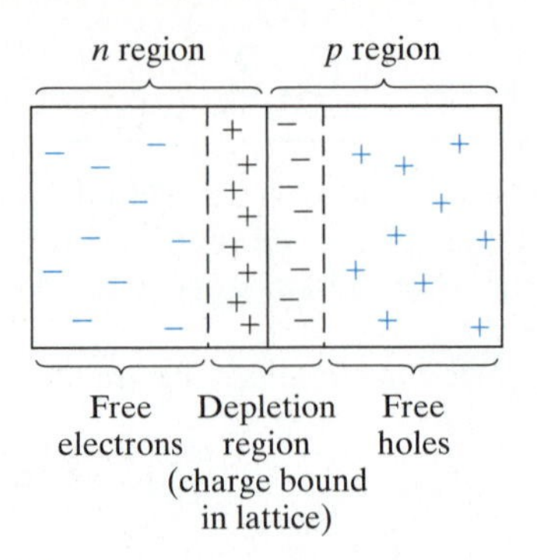

FIGURE 10.12 *p–n* junction with depletion region.

p-region drives the diffusion of holes into the *n*-region. But this initial diffusion is quickly stopped by the following fact: Every time an electron diffuses into the *p*-region it leaves behind an uncovered positive charge bound in the nucleus of the dopant atom on the *n*-side; similarly, negative charge is bound in the lattice of the *p*-side as hole diffusion occurs. This process builds up charge layers, as shown in Figure 10.12 in the so-called *depletion region*—a region that is depleted of carriers. These charge layers prevent further diffusion.

This charge barrier creates a state of balance with the diffusion process; any attempt for the diffusion to increase uncovers more bound charge, which increases the barrier and reduces the diffusion. This barrier can be represented as a voltage or potential barrier.

The height of the potential barrier for a *p–n* junction in equilibrium is shown in Figure 10.13. Because electron energy is plotted as increasing upward in this figure, hole energy (opposite sign) is downward—therefore, the upper curve shows the energy barrier to electrons moving from the *n*-region to the *p*-region, and the lower curve shows the energy barrier to holes moving from the *p*-region to the *n*-region.

It is very important to note that the height of the potential barrier across a *p–n* junction can be changed by applying a voltage across the junction from an external source. The diffusion of carriers across the junction is exponentially related to the barrier height, so as the barrier height is changed by an external voltage source, V, large (exponential) changes in current, I, due to carrier diffusion are observed.

If an external voltage source is applied and

Diode forward and reverse bias defined

1. the *p*-region is made more *positive* than the *n*-region, the barrier height is reduced, and carriers can easily diffuse across and the diode readily conducts a current—this is called *forward bias*, as shown in Figure 10.14(a).

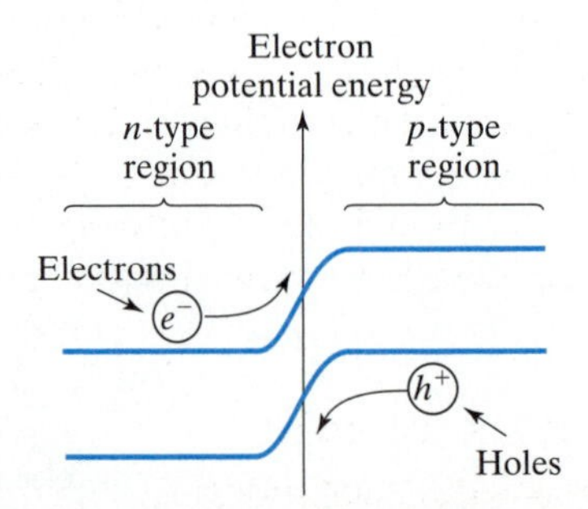

FIGURE 10.13 *p–n* junction potential barrier.

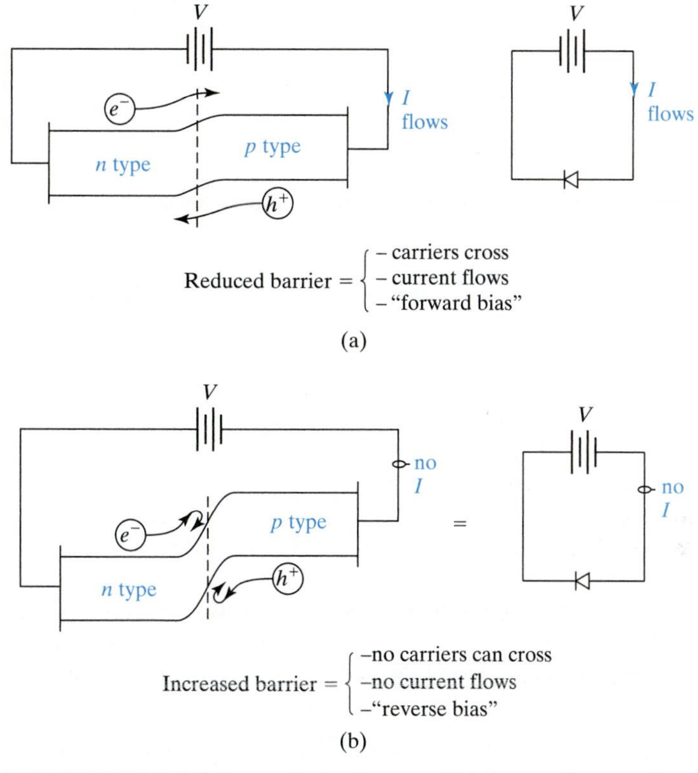

FIGURE 10.14 (a) p–n junction with externally applied forward bias. (b) p–n junction with externally applied reverse bias.

2. the p-region is made more *negative* than the n-region, the barrier height is increased, and very few carriers can cross, and virtually no current flows—this is called *reverse bias*, as shown in Figure 10.14(b).

10–5 Diode Circuit Models

There are several circuit models commonly used to describe the electronic characteristics of a real diode. The primary purpose of such models is to provide an equivalent circuit and quantitative relationships describing the key parameters. These models can then be used in analyzing circuits containing diodes in order to predict the performance of the circuits.

In this section three diode models will be described that predict the relation between the dc voltage across a diode, V_D, and the current through the diode, I_D. The three models are:

1. The ideal diode model
2. The diode equation model
3. The piecewise linear diode model

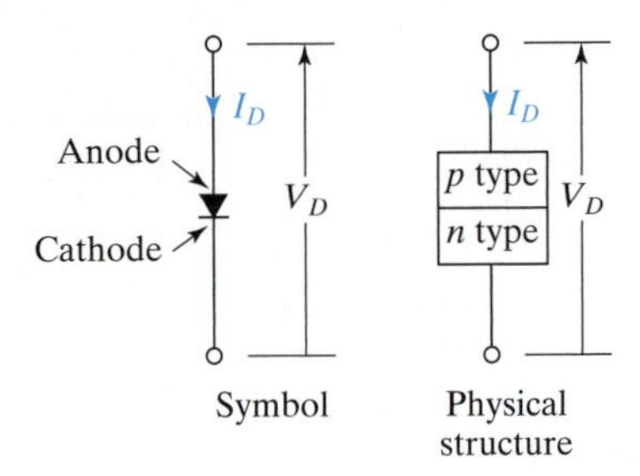

FIGURE 10.15 Ideal diode symbol and real diode physical structure.

10.5.1 The Ideal Diode

The *ideal diode* is simply an idealized two-terminal electronic device that performs the process of rectification perfectly; that is, an ideal diode passes current perfectly in one direction (zero resistance), and passes no current in the opposite direction (infinite resistance). Real diodes differ from this idealization slightly, as we'll see later; however, this model works well for analysis of many circuits.

The symbol for the ideal diode is given by the solid (filled) symbol as shown in Figure 10.15.

The *p*-side of the diode is called the *anode*, and the *n*-side designated in the symbol by the straight line is called the *cathode*.

The "ideal diode"

For an ideal diode:

Rule 1. If the voltage on the *p*-side (anode) is made more positive than the voltage on the *n*-side (forward bias)

then

the ideal diode conducts current as a closed switch.

Rule 2. If the voltage on the *n*-side (cathode) is made more positive than the voltage on the *p*-side (reverse bias)

then

the ideal diode will not conduct, and appears as an open switch.

A result of Rules 1 and 2 is that:

If the circuit attempts to force positive current from the *p*-side through to the *n*-side (in the direction of the arrow in the diode symbol)

then

The ideal diode conducts as a closed switch (forward bias). Otherwise, the ideal diode behaves as an open switch.

If a plot is made of the voltage applied across an ideal diode versus the resulting current, the curve lies on the negative voltage axis and the positive current axis, as shown in Figure 10.16. Any applied positive voltage results in infinite currents since the device has zero

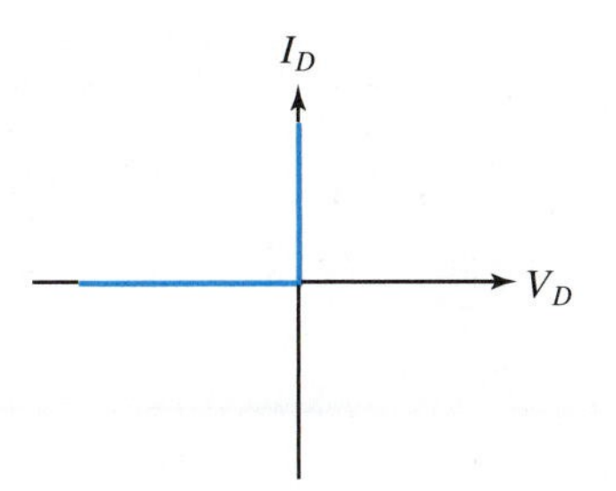

FIGURE 10.16 Plot of current through diode, I_D, versus voltage across diode, V_D, for an "ideal" diode.

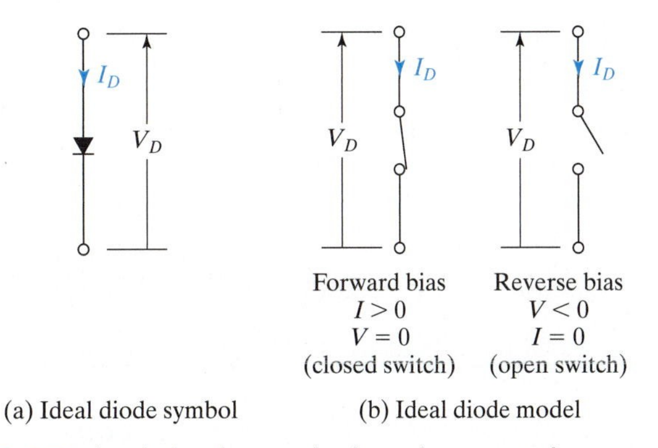

FIGURE 10.17 Ideal diode symbol and its switch circuit model.

resistance under this condition; any applied negative voltage results in zero current since the device has infinite resistance in this condition. Notice that the direction of positive current conduction is the same as that of the arrow in the diode symbol.

The diode symbol and circuit model

In summary, the circuit model of the ideal diode is shown in Figure 10.17. It behaves as a closed switch under forward bias, and an open switch under reverse bias.

In solving circuit problems, it is necessary to determine which voltage polarity the circuit is attempting to place on the diode terminals. This can be easily done by replacing the diode with an extremely small finite "test" resistance, δR. Then if the voltage across δR is in such a direction to establish forward bias, replace the resistor with a closed switch or a short; otherwise, replace it with an open circuit. We illustrate the use of the ideal diode model with some examples.

Example 10.4

In Figure 10.18(a), let us compute the current; I_1, through the resistor, R, assuming an ideal diode.

First, we determine the polarity of the voltage that the circuit will establish across the diode; or equivalently, the direction that the circuit wishes to drive positive current through the diode. To examine this, the diode is replaced with a small test resistor, δR, such that the circuit becomes that shown in Figure 10.18(b).

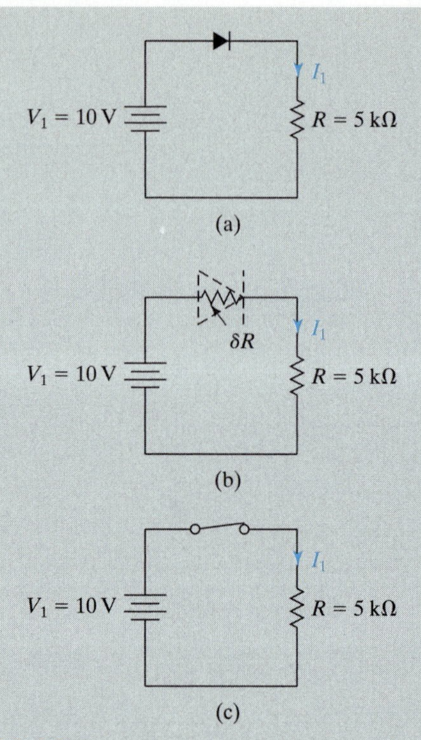

FIGURE 10.18 Ideal diode current in simple circuit.

It is clear in this simple circuit that the left side of the diode, *p*-side or anode in this case, is at a higher or more positive voltage than the other side. Therefore, the diode is forward biased and it can be replaced with a closed switch, as illustrated in Figure 10.18(c).

We can arrive at the same conclusion by evaluating the current the circuit forces through the test resistor. From Figure 10.18(b), the polarity of I_1 through the diode can be determined

$$I_1 = +\frac{V_1}{R + \delta R} = (+\text{ value})$$

All terms above are positive, and the resulting direction of I_1 is from left to right; or from *p*-side to *n*-side—the direction in which a diode conducts positive current.

The above analysis has indicated, in two different ways, the diode is *forward biased*, and, therefore, can be replaced with a closed switch.

Now with the closed switch replacing the diode, I_1 is

$$I_1 = +\frac{V_1}{R} = \frac{10}{5\text{ k}} = 2\text{ mA}$$

Drill Exercise

D10.4. In Figure D10.4(a), if V_1 is -10 V, find the current, I_1, through the resistor, R.

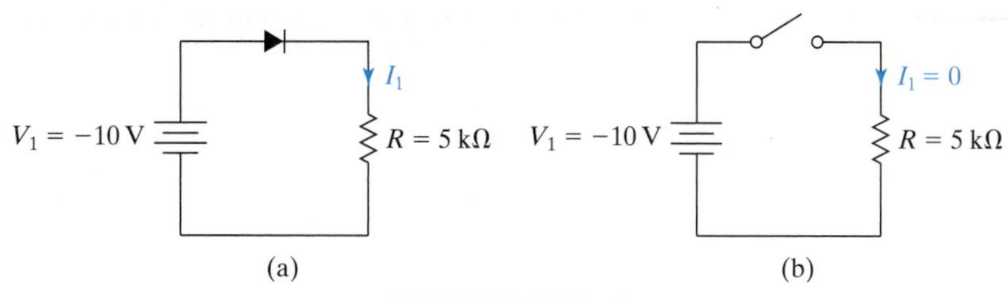

FIGURE D10.4

Ans: In this case, $I_1 = 0$; the single loop has been opened by the reverse-biased diode. This is illustrated in Figures D10.4(a) and (b).

Example 10.5

In Figure 10.19, if the voltage source, V_1, can be varied from 0 to 10 volts, (a) sketch a plot of the voltage at node A, V_A, as a function of V_1 for $0 < V_1 < 10$ V, and (b) calculate the current through $D2$ for two cases: (1) for $V_1 = 2$ V and (2) for $V_1 = 4$ V.

(a) The cathode of $D2$ is set at 3 volts, relative to ground, by V_2. If node A is less than 3 volts, then $D2$ is open. Thus, for any value of V_1 below 3 volts, $D1$ is conducting as a closed switch and $V_A = V_1$. For values of V_1 above 3 volts, $D2$ conducts as a closed switch, and D1 becomes an open switch. Therefore, node A is set by V_2 at 3 V; in this range $D1$ remains reverse biased, and node A stays "pinned" at 3 V. A plot of V_A as a function of V_1 is shown in Figure 10.20.

(b) For case 1, where $V_1 = 2$ V, $D2$ is reverse biased, and, therefore, the current through $D2$ is zero.

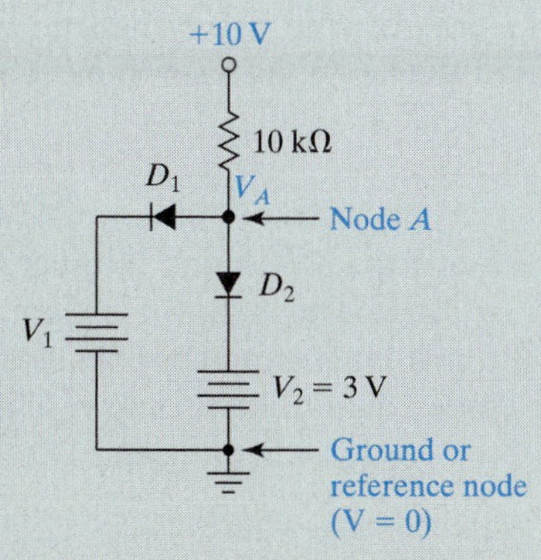

FIGURE 10.19 Circuit for Example 10.5.

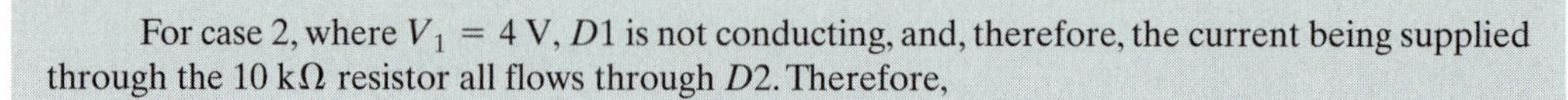

For case 2, where $V_1 = 4$ V, $D1$ is not conducting, and, therefore, the current being supplied through the 10 kΩ resistor all flows through $D2$. Therefore,

$$I_{D2} = \frac{10 - 3}{10\text{k}} = 0.7 \text{ mA}$$

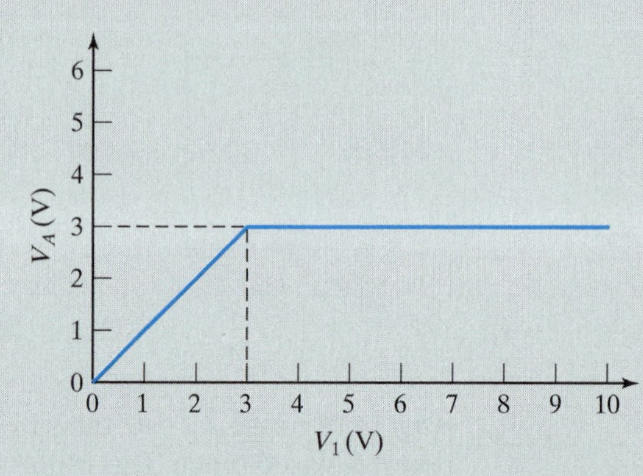

FIGURE 10.20 Plot of V_A versus V_1 from Example 10.5.

10.5.2 The Diode Equation and Model

A *real p–n junction diode* does not behave exactly like an open or closed switch; it can be shown to have a voltage–current (*V-I*) relationship over its range of normal operation, which follows closely to the so-called *diode equation* given as Eq. (10.9). This equation can be derived based on the assumption that carriers move by diffusion, as described in section 10.3.

The diode equation—an important relationship

$$I_D = I_o\left(e^{\frac{qV_D}{kT}} - 1\right) \tag{10.9}$$

In this equation, V_D is the externally applied voltage across the diode, I_D is the current through the diode, q is the electronic charge, T is temperature in degrees Kelvin, k is Boltzmann's constant, and I_o is called the *reverse saturation current* and equals a constant that depends on the properties of the diode. At room temperature, the constants

$$\frac{q}{kT} \cong 39 \tag{10.10}$$

A plot of Eq. (10.9) using a linear current scale at room temperature and a value of $I_o = 1 \times 10^{-16}$ amperes is shown in Figure 10.21. Notice that for applied voltages below about 0.6 volts, the current is imperceptibly close to zero.

The diode equation has some very interesting features:

For $V_D = 0$, $I_D = 0$, as expected.

For *forward bias*, where

$$V_D \gg \frac{kT}{q} (0.026\, V \text{at room temperature})$$

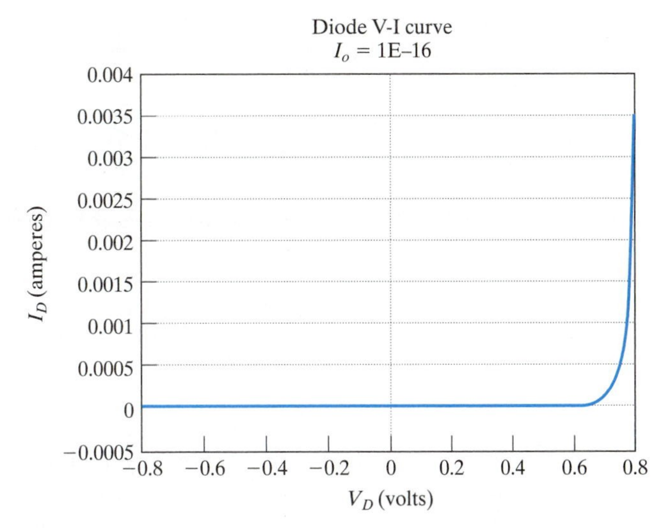

FIGURE 10.21 Plot of diode equation for $I_o = 1 \times 10^{-16}$A.

the exponential term dominates, and

$$I_D \approx I_o e^{\frac{qV_D}{kT}} = I_o e^{39V_D} \tag{10.11}$$

When a diode is conducting (forward bias) the current depends exponentially on voltage

In this forward bias condition the voltage–current relationship follows the exponential function over a current range of many decades. It is often convenient to plot the forward characteristics of the diode on a plot of log I_D versus V_D, since in this region the resulting curve follows a straight line, as illustrated in Figure 10.22.

For *reverse bias*, where

$$-V_D \ll -kT/q$$

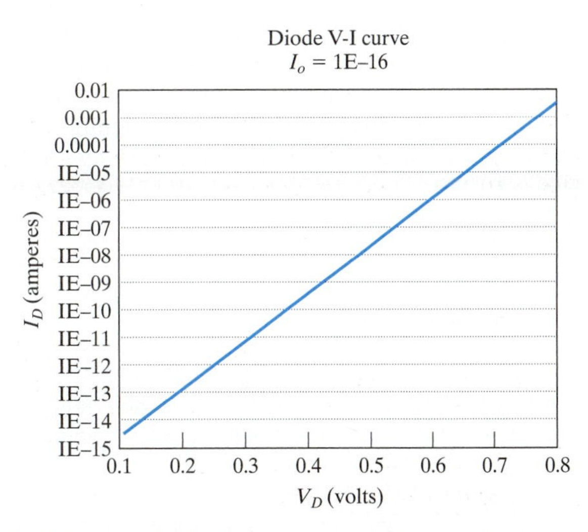

FIGURE 10.22 Plot of diode equation (forward bias) on semilog scale ($I_o = 1 \times 10^{-16}$A).

FIGURE 10.23 Resistor, r_s, used to model diode series resistance.

the exponential term is negligible compared to unity and

$$I_D \approx -I_o \tag{10.12}$$

Typical silicon diodes have a value for I_o in the range of 10^{-14}A for large area junctions to 10^{-18}A for very small junctions. Schottky junctions have I_o's that depend on the materials used, but typically are in the range of 10^{-11} to 10^{-14}A.

The reverse saturation current, I_o, increases rapidly with temperature. An often-used rule of thumb is that I_o approximately doubles for every 10°C rise in temperature.

Notice the primary differences between a real diode described by Eq. (10.9) and the ideal diode. In a real diode:

1. For positive applied voltage, forward bias, the bias current increases exponentially; however, some small positive voltage is required before the diode conducts reasonable current. In a silicon diode this *turn-on voltage*, V_F, is about 0.5 to 0.7 volts and is the value of V_D at which I_D reaches the microampere range. By contrast, the ideal diode has a discontinuity that occurs precisely at $V_D = 0$. This difference in modeling is very important in some circuits, where voltage changes of 0.5 to 0.7 volts make a significant difference in circuit performance.
2. For negative applied voltage, reverse bias, there is a small finite reverse current that flows and it is temperature dependent. The ideal diode had zero current for $V_D < 0$.

Series Resistance. All practical diodes also have some series resistance due to the bulk semiconductor material on either side of the junction and the resistance of the contacts made to the semiconductor material. Series resistance is only a concern in circuit analysis when the diode is forward biased and conducting significant current. To model series resistance, a resistor of the proper value, r_s, is placed in series with the diode model being used, as illustrated in Figure 10.23.

Example 10.6

If a diode has an I_o of 2×10^{-15} A, let us determine (a) the voltage across this diode when it is forward biased and carrying 2 mA and (b) the change in voltage across the diode when the current is changed from 2 to 1 mA.

(a) From Eq. (10.11)

$$I_D = I_o e^{39V_D}$$

or

$$e^{39V_D} = \frac{I_D}{I_o}$$

Solving the equation for V_D yields

$$V_D = \frac{1}{39}\, ln\frac{I_D}{I_o} = \frac{1}{39}\, ln\frac{2 \times 10^{-3}}{2 \times 10^{-15}}\text{V} \tag{10.13}$$

or

$$V_D = 0.026\, ln(10^{12}) = 0.718 \text{ V}$$

(b) Using the results of part (a)

$$V_D = \frac{1}{39}\, ln\frac{I_D}{I_o} = 0.026\, ln\frac{1 \times 10^{-3}}{2 \times 10^{-15}}\text{V}$$

and therefore,

$$V_D = 0.026\, ln(5 \times 10^{11}) = 0.700 \text{ V}$$

Notice that reducing the current by a factor of two only changed the voltage across the diode from 0.718 V to 0.700 V, a change of 18 millivolts.

It is interesting that in such diodes the voltage across the diode always changes by 18 mV when the current is changed by a factor of two.

Drill Exercise

D10.5. (a) Prove for the general case that if the forward bias current of a diode is doubled, the voltage will increase by 18 mV. (b) Find the voltage change if the current is changed by a factor of 10.

Ans: (a) Hint: Use Eq. (10.13) (b) 60 mV.

Example 10.7

A diode is rated at 100 milliwatts, which is its maximum allowed power dissipation. This limitation is generally imposed as a result of the ability of the diode's mechanical structure and packaging to remove the heat generated in the diode. If the diode is forward biased from a 5-volt dc source through a 1 kΩ resistor and the voltage across the diode is 0.65 volts, let us determine (a) the power being dissipated in the diode and (b) if the power rating would be exceeded if the same diode were put in another circuit and the forward voltage across it were measured as 0.75 V.

(a) The circuit described is shown in Figure 10.24. The current through the resistor is

$$I_R = \frac{5 - 0.65}{1\text{ k}} = 4.35 \times 10^{-3}\text{A} = 4.35 \text{ mA}$$

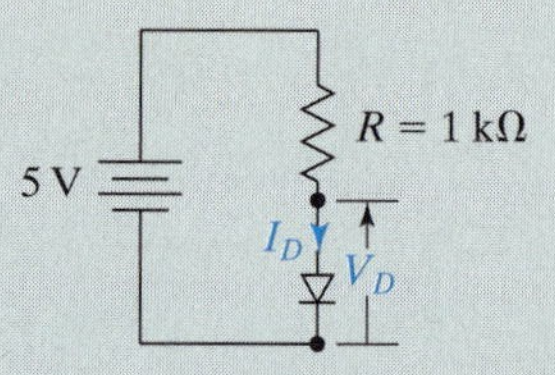

FIGURE 10.24 Circuit for Example 10.7.

This same current flows through the diode, so $I_D = 4.35$ mA. The power dissipated is then

$$P = V_D I_D = (0.65)(4.35 \times 10^{-3}) = 2.83 \text{ milliwatts}$$

(b) In order to calculate the power dissipated when the voltage is increased to 0.75 volts, we must first determine the new current.

From the data in part (a) we can calculate I_o using Eq. (10.11).

$$I_o = I_D e^{\frac{-qV_D}{kT}} = 4.35 \times 10^{-3}\, e^{-39(0.65)}$$

and

$$I_o = 4.26 \times 10^{-14} \text{A}$$

We now use this value of I_o to calculate the new current, I'_D, when the voltage across this diode is 0.75 V, that is,

$$I'_D = I_o e^{\frac{qV_D}{kT}} = (4.26 \times 10^{-14})e^{39(0.75)} = 0.215 \text{ A}$$

The power dissipated under these new conditions is

$$P = V_D I_D = (0.75)(0.215) = 161 \text{ milliwatts}$$

which exceeds the maximum power dissipation allowed. If this diode were connected in a circuit under these conditions, it would burn up.

Virtually every electronic component has a maximum allowed power dissipation and a maximum voltage and/or maximum current rating. They should not be exceeded.

Drill Exercise

D10.6. Given the circuit shown in Figure 10.25 and assuming the diode characteristics are represented by the diode equation, let us find (a) the maximum (peak) instantaneous voltage appearing across the diode if the peak current through R is measured to be 1.8 mA, and (b) I_o for this diode.

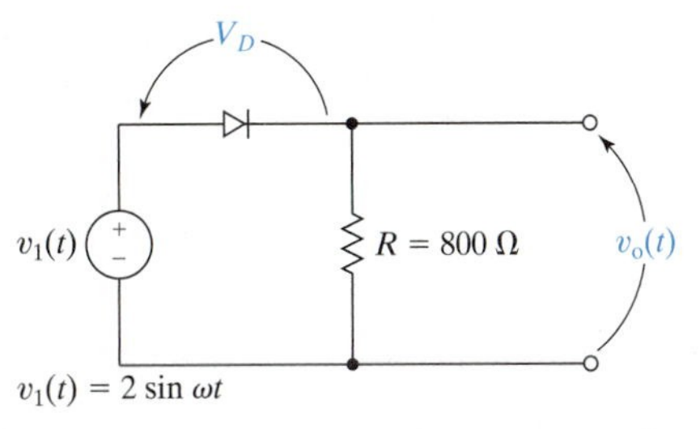

FIGURE 10.25 Circuit for finding peak current.

Ans: (a) $V_D(\text{peak}) = 0.56$ V (b) $I_o = 5.89 \times 10^{-13}$A.

10.5.3 The Piecewise Linear Diode Model

A real *p–n* junction requires a small but finite foward-bias voltage to be externally applied to sufficiently lower the barrier height to initiate the onset of reasonable conduction.

Recall the plot of I_D as a function of V_D on a linear scale as shown in Figure 10.21 for a real diode. Notice that the diode conducts a negligibly small current until the turn-on voltage, V_F, of the junction is reached, which is generally at about 0.7 V in silicon devices.

Many diode manufacturers arbitrarily choose 1 microampere as the threshold of conduction and define the externally applied forward bias required to obtain 1 microampere as the diode's *turn-on voltage, V_F*.

The real diode characteristic curve can be approximated by a model that uses two connected straight line segments. Such a model is called a piecewise linear (PL) model.

Figure 10.26 shows a real diode curve and a piecewise linear approximation to that curve. The turn-on voltage, V_F, marks the voltage at which the two line segments meet, and at which the slope is discontinuous. Modeling of the finite voltage, V_F, requires including a voltage source of value V_F in the model. The portion of the characteristics that represents diode conduction has a large finite positive slope and can be modeled by including a resistor in the model.

A circuit model that will reproduce this curve can be created using linear circuit elements and an ideal diode; such a model is shown in Figure 10.27 and is known as the *piecewise linear circuit model.* In this piecewise linear diode equivalent circuit, the ideal diode internal to

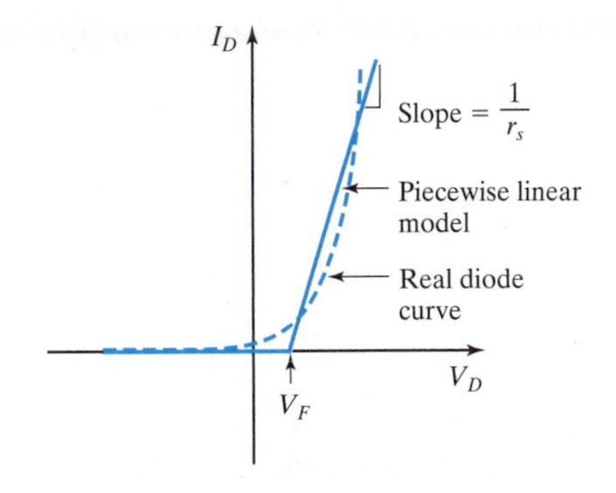

FIGURE 10.26 *V–I* curves for real diode and piecewise linear model.

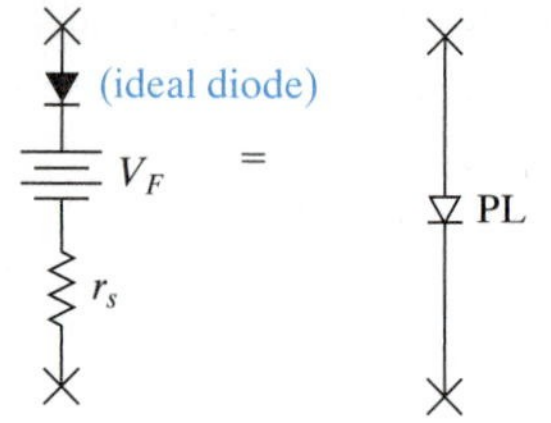

FIGURE 10.27 Piecewise linear diode circuit model and symbol.

The piecewise linear diode model

the model has infinite resistance until it becomes forward biased; this occurs when the externally applied voltage is enough to overcome V_F. Therefore, the "break" to initiate diode conduction occurs at $V_D = V_F$; we will assume $V_F = 0.7$ V unless specified otherwise.

The device has a series resistance, r_s, which gives the plot of the voltage–current characteristics a finite slope of $1/r_s$ in the forward-biased region. The use of the PL model will be illustrated with several examples.

Example 10.8

Let us calculate the current through the 400 Ω resistor in the circuit shown in Figure 10.28, assuming a piecewise linear model for the diode with $V_F = 0.7$ V and $r_s = 10$ Ω.

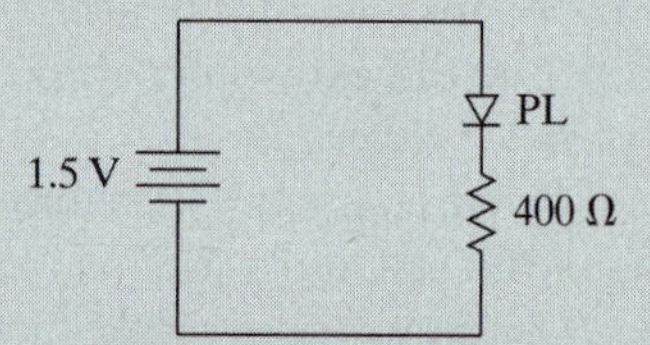

FIGURE 10.28 Circuit for Example 10.8.

The diode is replaced with the piecewise linear circuit model, as shown in Figure 10.29(a). Note that the ideal diode in the model is forward biased and becomes a short, or closed switch. Therefore, this circuit reduces to that shown in Figure 10.29(b). Writing a loop equation for this circuit, we obtain

$$0 = -1.5 + 0.7 + I(10) + I(400)$$

or

$$I = (0.8)/(410) = 1.95 \text{ mA}$$

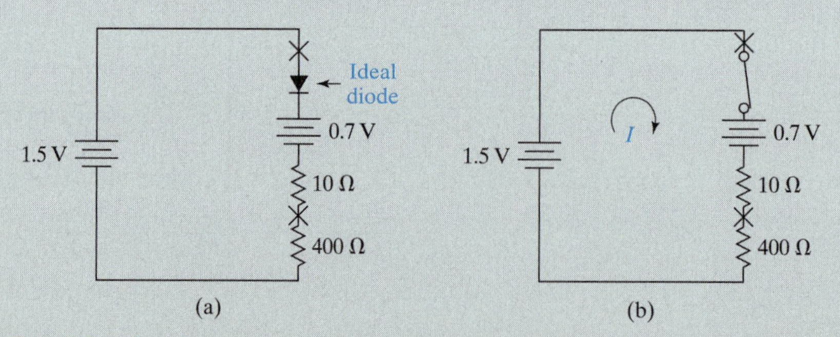

FIGURE 10.29 Piecewise linear circuit model for Example 10.8.

The piecewise linear model greatly simplifies circuit calculations in that it approximates the exponential relationship of the diode equation with linear line segments, which can be modeled with linear circuit elements. It provides a significantly more accurate representation of the real diode than the ideal diode model, particularly if circuit voltages are relatively low, and the turn-on voltage, V_F, becomes a significant factor in the calculation.

Example 10.9

If the voltage $v_x(t)$, as shown in Figure 10.30, is applied to the circuit of Figure 10.31(a) and the diode has a V_F of 0.7 V and an $r_s = 10\ \Omega$, let us plot the current through the diode in the time interval $0 \leq t \leq 2T$.

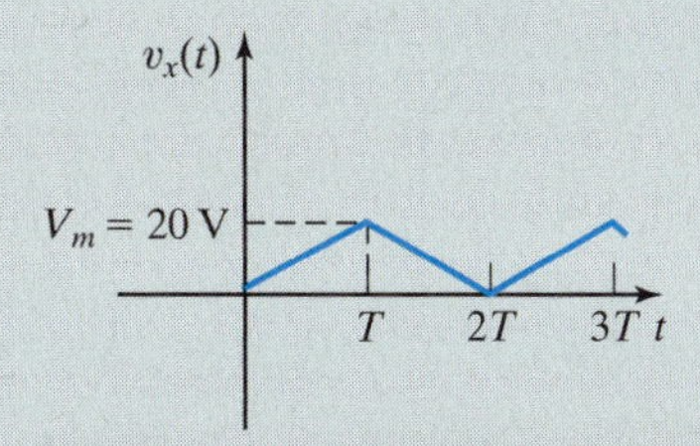

FIGURE 10.30 Input voltage for Example 10.9.

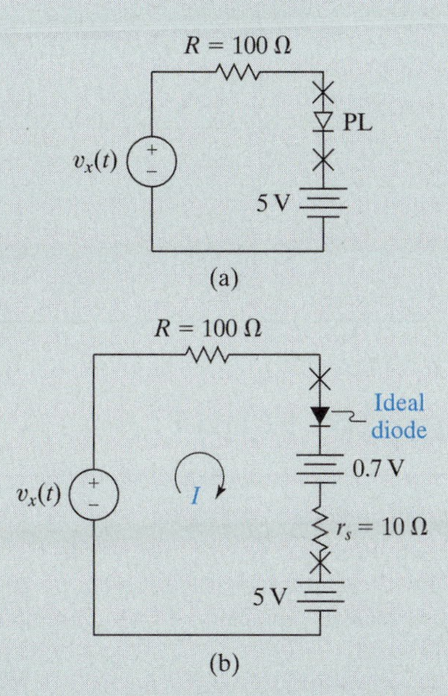

FIGURE 10.31 Piecewise linear circuit models for Example 10.9.

First, we replace the diode with its piecewise linear equivalent circuit as shown in Figure 10.31(b). Note that the ideal diode in the model will remain reverse biased until $v_x(t)$ reaches a value of 5.7 volts; the current I will remain zero during this time. When $v_x(t)$ exceeds 5.7 volts, positive current will begin to flow, and will increase to a maximum at time T when $v_x(t)$ is maximum. At this point, the loop equation used to determine I_{max} is

$$20 - 0.7 - 5.0 = I_{max}\,(100 + 10)$$

and

$$I_{max} = 130 \text{ mA}$$

After the diode initiates conduction, $v_x(t)$ increases linearly and all other elements in the circuit are linear and resistive. Hence, we expect I to increase linearly from zero to I_{max}, and, therefore, the plot of applied voltage $v_x(t)$ and current, I, appear as shown in Figure 10.32.

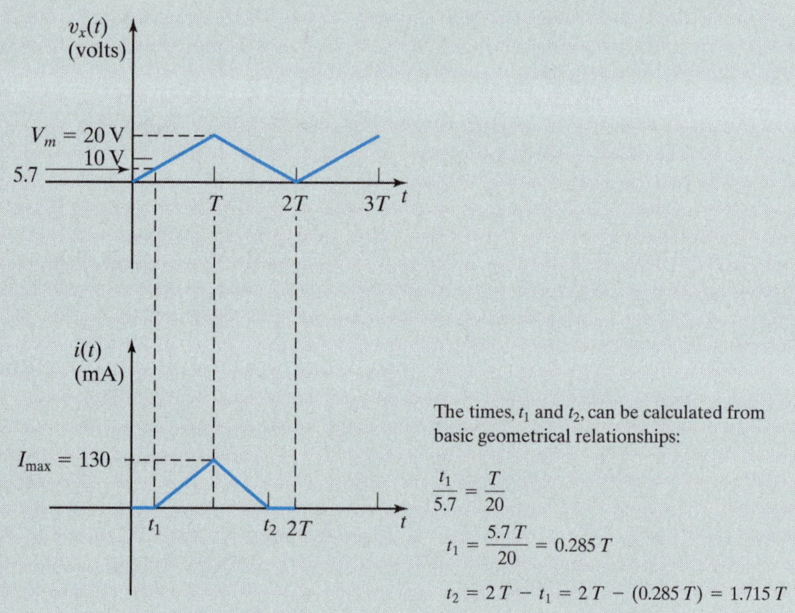

FIGURE 10.32 Answers for Example 10.9.

Example 10.10

If diode $D1$ in Figure 10.33(a) is modeled by a piecewise linear model with $V_F = 0.7$ V and $r_s = 0$, let us determine (a) the current through $R1$ and (b) the current through $D1$.

The direction of positive current is in a direction to forward bias the diode $D1$. Replacing $D1$ with the piecewise linear model assuming forward bias and $r_s = 0$ results in the circuit of Figure 10.33(b).

The current through $R1$, I_{R1}, is

$$I_{R1} = \frac{V1 - 0.7}{R1} = \frac{7.3}{1\text{k}} = 7.3 \text{ mA}$$

The current through $R2$, I_{R2}, is

$$I_{R2} = \frac{0.7}{R2} = \frac{0.7}{1\text{k}} = 0.7 \text{ mA}$$

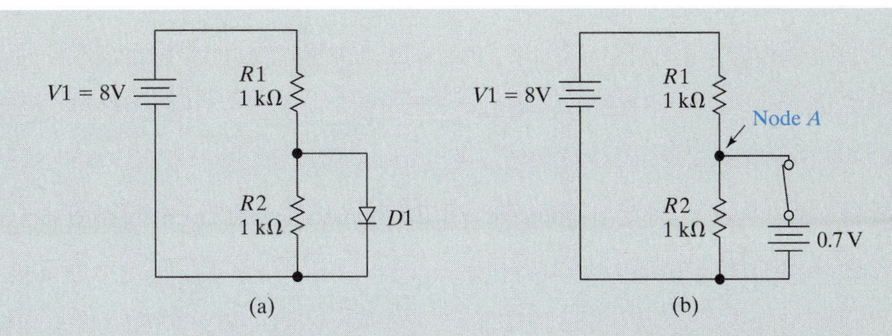

FIGURE 10.33 Circuit models for Example 10.10.

The current into node A is 7.3 mA; the current out through $R2$ is 0.7 mA; therefore, by Kirchhoff's current law, the current through $D1$ is

$$I_{D1} = 7.3\text{ mA} - 0.7\text{ mA} = 6.6\text{ mA}$$

Drill Exercise

D10.7. In Example 10.10, find the values of I_{R2} and I_{D1} if $V1$ is doubled.

Ans: $I_{R2} = 0.7$ mA; $I_{D1} = 14.6$ mA.

10-6 Power Supply Circuits

A power supply provides voltage and current for operating an electronic circuit

Diodes are widely used in *power supply* circuits, which convert ac into dc for the purpose of operating electronic equipment. Recall that residential ac power distribution is typically done at either 110–120 volts or 220–240 V ac.

These voltages are substantially larger than the voltage required to operate most solid-state electronic equipment. Digital electronic systems typically require 5 volts dc, although some new circuits require lower voltages, such as 3.3 volts. Analog electronic systems operate over a wide range of power supply voltages, but a common practice is to utilize two dc voltage supplies, one +15 volts, and a second at −15 volts, as shown in Figure. 10.34.

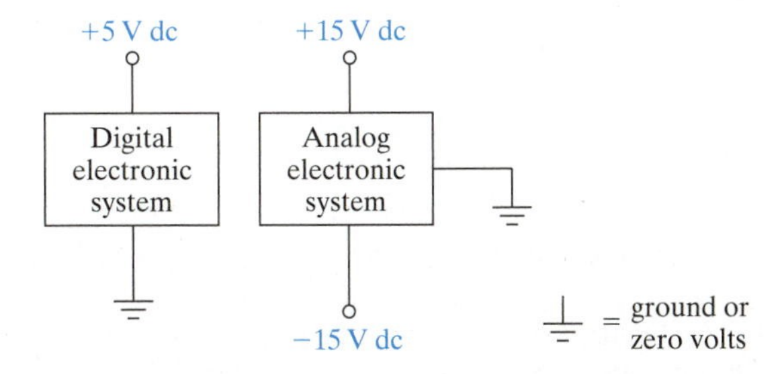

FIGURE 10.34 Typical dc operating voltage requirements.

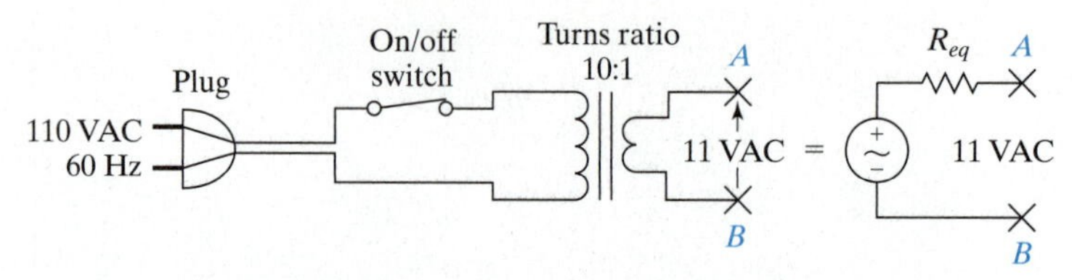

FIGURE 10.35 Typical input section of a power supply.

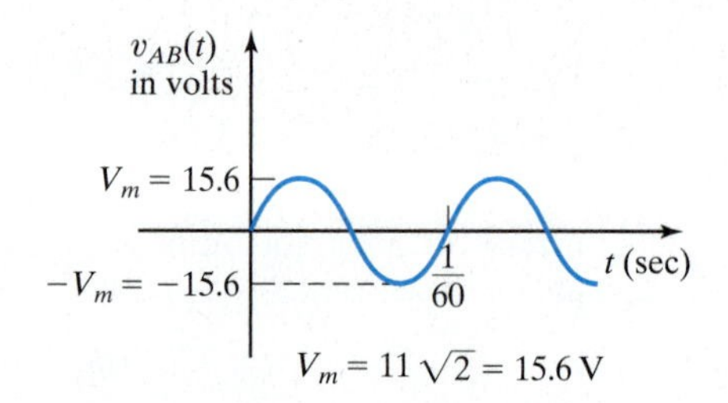

FIGURE 10.36 Plot of $V_{AB}(t)$.

In designing circuits to convert household ac power into power for use in electronic circuits, the first step is generally to reduce the magnitude of the voltage from the wall receptacle, and thus a *transformer* (a device described in detail in Chapter 6) is commonly used to step down the voltage. A transformer, which consists of two separate coils of wire on a common iron core, produces an ac output voltage (across the secondary) proportional to the input voltage (across the primary); the constant of proportionality is the ratio of the number of turns of wire in the secondary coil to that in the primary coil, or the *turns ratio*. Therefore, the input part of such a circuit might look like that in Figure 10.35, where 110 V ac is stepped down by a factor of 10 to 11 V ac. Therefore, the turns ratio for the transformer is 10 to 1. These are *rms* values, so the actual amplitude of the sinusoidal wave form is a factor of $\sqrt{2}$ larger. The output of this ideal transformer can be modeled as a Thevenin's equivalent circuit with an open-circuit sinusoidal voltage source of 11 V ac, and a small equivalent resistance, R_{eq}. A plot of the voltage between A and B is shown in Figure 10.36; it is 11 V *rms*, 60 Hz.

10.6.1 Half-Wave Rectification

Half-wave rectification is the simplest process in which ac can be converted to dc. It is performed by a circuit in which a diode is used to clip the input ac signal excursions of one polarity to zero, while passing those of the other polarity. The following example illustrates the half-wave rectifier circuit.

Example 10.11

If a sinusoidal voltage source, $v_1(t)$, of amplitude V_m is applied to the circuit shown in Figure 10.37, let us draw the waveform of the voltage, $v_o(t)$. Assume an ideal diode.

Figure 10.38(a) shows the input waveform, $v_1(t)$. Figure 10.38(b) shows the calculated output waveform, $v_o(t)$.

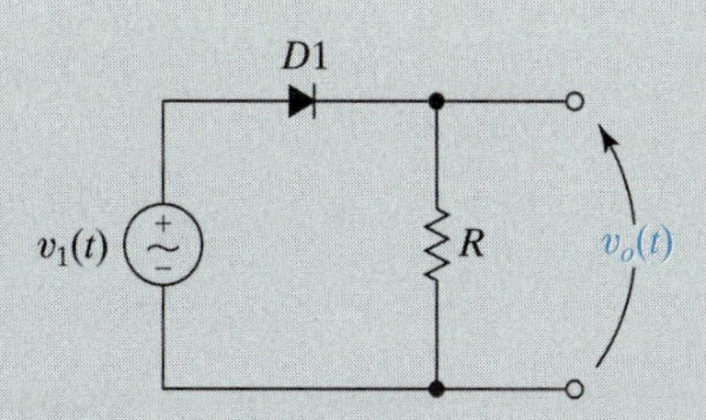

Illustration of half-wave rectification

FIGURE 10.37 Half-wave rectifier circuit from Example 10.11.

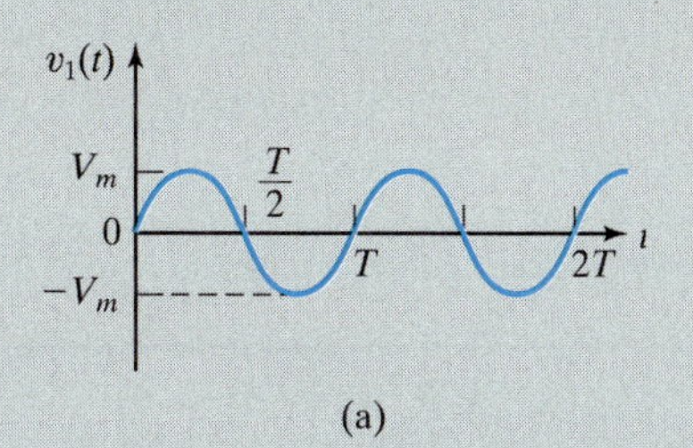

(a)

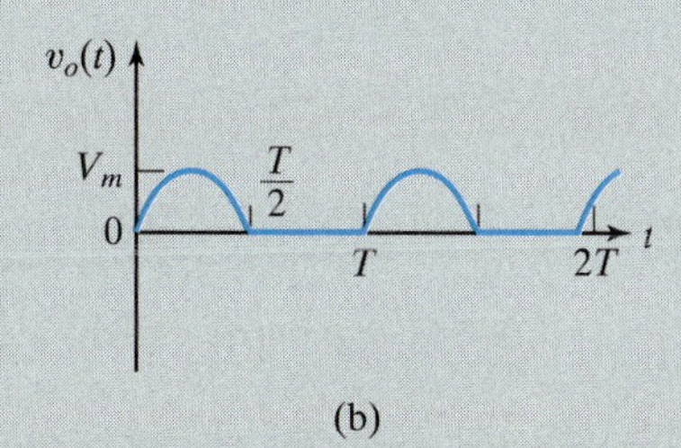

(b)

FIGURE 10.38 Voltage waveforms from Example 10.11.

During the positive half-cycle from time 0 to $\frac{1}{2}T$, the polarity of v_1 makes $D1$ forward biased and conducting as a closed switch, and, therefore, $v_o(t)$ is identical to $v_1(t)$ during this time.

During the negative half-cycle, from $\frac{1}{2}T$, to T, the diode $D1$ is reverse biased, and acts as an open switch. Since there is no current through the resistor R, v_o remains zero during this entire half-cycle.

It is important to notice (1) the *average* value of the input ac waveform v_1 is zero, (2) the output v_o is positive since the waveform is always greater than or equal to zero, and (3) this circuit is a simple example of a half-wave rectifier circuit, which is one type of circuit to convert ac to dc.

The voltage waveform of the shape of $v_o(t)$ in Figure 10.38(b) is termed a half-wave rectified signal. The ac voltage v_1 has been changed into an all-positive dc voltage by rectification.

The dc value of a waveform is defined as its average value; therefore, for a periodic signal of period, T

$$V_{DC} = \frac{1}{T}\int_0^T v(t)\,dt \tag{10.14}$$

The dc value of the output voltage, $v_o(t)$, in the previous example can be calculated from Eq. (10.14)

$$V_{DC} = \frac{1}{T}\int_0^T V_m \sin\omega t \, dt$$

$$V_{DC} = \frac{1}{T}\left\{\int_0^{T/2} V_m \sin\omega t \, dt + \int_{T/2}^{T} 0 \, dt\right\}$$

dc value of half-wave rectified signal

Letting $T = 2\pi$

$$V_{DC} = \frac{V_m}{2\pi}\int_0^{\pi} \sin x \, dx = \frac{V_m}{2\pi}[-\cos x]|_0^{\pi}$$

$$V_{DC} = \frac{V_m}{\pi} \qquad (10.15)$$

Example 10.12

Consider the half-wave rectifier circuit containing an ideal diode as shown in Figure 10.39. We wish to find the dc value of the output voltage.

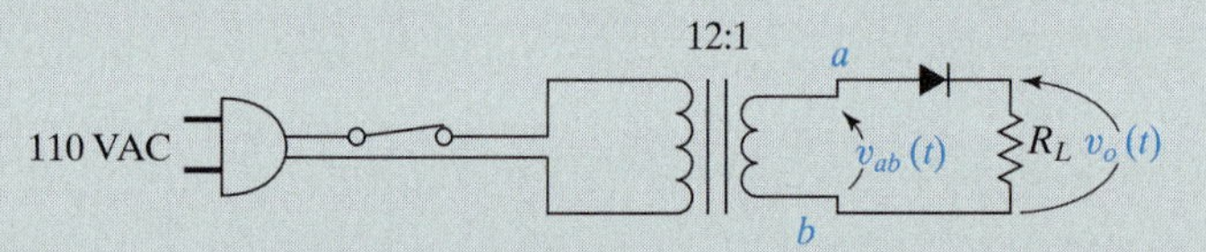

FIGURE 10.39 Half-wave rectifier circuit.

The load, R_L, represents whatever is connected to the power supply circuit. The voltage from nodes a to b is sinusoidal and has been reduced by a transformer with a turns ratio of 12:1 to 1/12 of the input value of 110 V ac.

Thus

$$V_{ab} = 110\left(\frac{1}{12}\right) = 9.17 \text{ V rms}$$

The amplitude of this voltage, V_m, is $\sqrt{2}(9.17) = 13$ V. The voltage across R_L, designated $v_o(t)$, follows the input voltage on the positive half-cycle, and is zero when the input voltage is on a negative half-cycle. Therefore, a plot of $v_{ab}(t)$ and $v_o(t)$ appears as shown in Figure 10.38(a) and (b), respectively.

Therefore, since $V_m = 13$ V,

$$V_{DC} = \frac{13}{\pi} = 4.14 \text{ V}$$

Drill Exercise

D10.8. A 115 V ac line is connected to a step-down transformer with a turns ratio of 18:4; if the secondary of the transformer is connected to a half-wave rectifier circuit, what is the dc voltage output of the circuit? (Assume ideal diode.)

Ans: 11.5 V dc.

Example 10.13

Consider the circuit shown in Figure 10.40 and assume the diode can be modeled with a piecewise linear model in which $V_F = 0.7$ V and $r_s = 10\ \Omega$. If we also assume that $v_1(t)$ is a sinusoid with an amplitude of 2 volts, as shown in Figure 10.41(a), we wish to carefully plot $v_o(t)$.

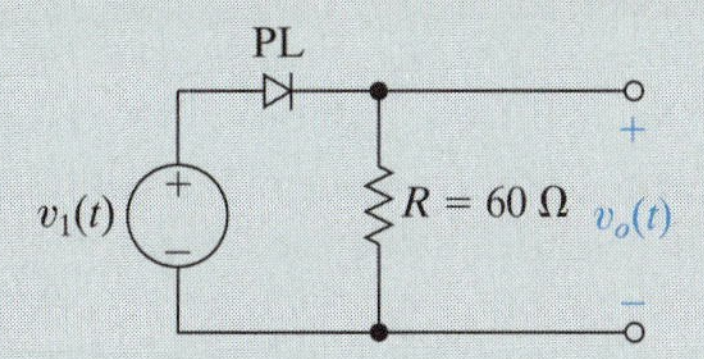

FIGURE 10.40 Half-wave rectifier circuit for Example 10.13 (with PL diode model).

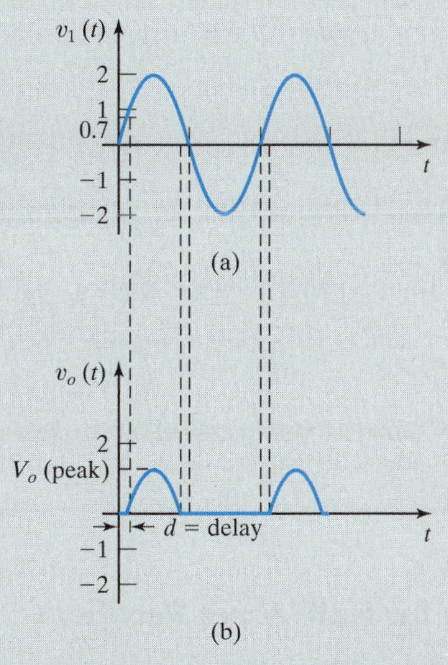

FIGURE 10.41 Voltage waveforms for Example 10.13.

The plot of $v_o(t)$ is shown in Figure 10.41(b), and is derived as follows. Replacing the diode with its piecewise linear model yields the circuit shown in Figure 10.42. The voltage source, $v_1(t)$, supplies a voltage at its peak of 2 volts. At the time this peak occurs, the appropriate loop equation is

$$2.0 - 0.7 = I_{peak}\,(10 + 60)$$

Therefore,

$$I_{peak} = 18.6 \text{ mA}$$

The peak or maximum value of the voltage $v_o(t)$ is the same as the peak voltage across R. Therefore,

$$V_{o(peak)} = (I_{peak})(60) = (18.6)(60) = 1.11 \text{ V}$$

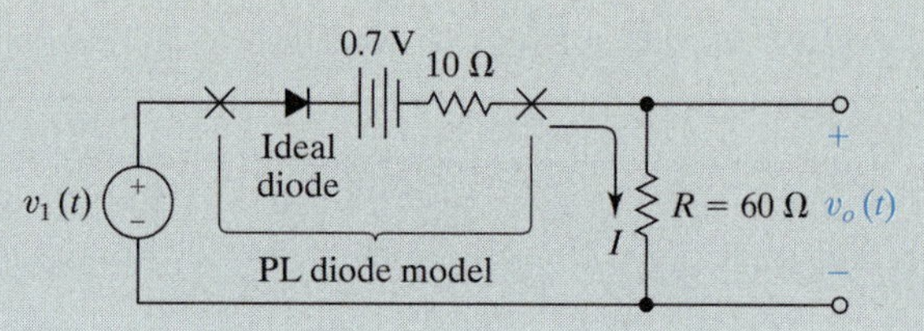

FIGURE 10.42 Piecewise linear circuit model for Example 10.13.

This is the peak positive value of the sinusoidally varying voltage, $v_o(t)$, during the positive half-cycle. During the negative half cycle, I is zero.

Finally, in order for the diode to conduct, v_1 must be sufficiently positive to offset $V_F = 0.7$ volts; in fact, v_1 must reach 0.7 volts before the circuit forward biases the diode, and positive current can begin to flow. Therefore, there is an *offset* or *time delay* from the point where $v_1(t)$ turns positive, to the point where $v_o(t)$ becomes nonzero. Similarly, there is the same offset when $v_1(t)$ is decreasing at the end of the positive half-cycle.

Trigonometric relationships can be used to calculate the duration of this delay, d. Setting the value of v_1 equal to 0.7 volts and solving for the time d, we obtain

$$0.7 = 2\sin(\omega d) \tag{10.16}$$

and hence

$$d = \frac{1}{\omega}\sin^{-1}(0.35)$$

If, for example, the input sinusoid had a frequency of 60 Hz, or 377 radians/second, then

$$d = \frac{1}{377}\sin^{-1}(0.35) = 9.5 \times 10^{-4} \text{ sec}$$

During the portion of the half-cycle when the diode is conducting the waveform, v_o follows a sinusoidal function.

10.6.2 Filter Circuits for Half-Wave Rectifiers

The voltage at the output of the half-wave rectifier is dc, but if the ac signal is 60 Hz, it rises and falls to zero 60 times a second. While this may be acceptable for some applications, such as some battery charger circuits, it is not very useful for powering most electronic systems. These systems require a dc voltage similar to the voltage supplied by a battery, that is, a constant voltage that has little or no variations with time. Real power supply systems operating from ac inputs usually do not produce completely smooth dc; however, with the addition of a *filter,* a dc signal can be closely approximated. The small variations in voltage from the filter output are called *ripple,* and good power supply circuits produce as little ripple as possible.

The output of the half-wave rectifier circuit, such as the waveform shown in Figure 10.43(a), can be smoothed to something like that in Figure 10.43(b) by a filter circuit, and the dc value increased toward the ideal value of V_m. The ideal dc output is shown in Figure 10.43(c). One of the most commonly used filter circuits is the *RC* network, low-pass filter described in Chapter 7. A power supply circuit using such a network appears in Figure 10.44.

Illustration of ripple

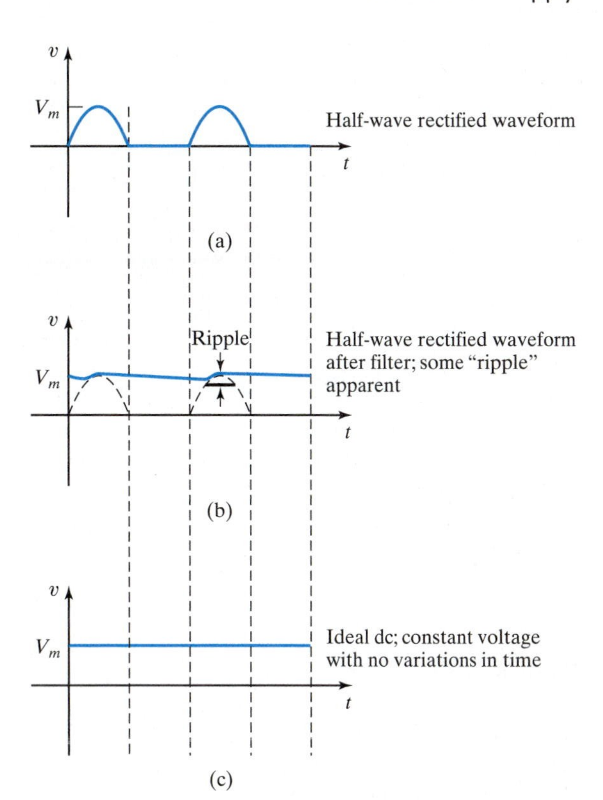

FIGURE 10.43 Voltage waveforms for half-wave rectifier with filter.

During positive half-cycles the diode conducts and charges the capacitor to a value of approximately V_m. R_1 is generally negligibly small and used only to prevent diode burnout due to large current transients experienced while initially charging the capacitor; it is ignored in the following analysis. When C is charged to V_m, the capacitor holds the voltage at the output high until the next charging cycle. When v_{ab} falls below the voltage across C, the diode reverse biases and disconnects from the circuit until the next cycle when v_{ab} exceeds the voltage on C. With a finite load resistance, R_L, current is supplied to the load only from C between charging cycles, and so v_o falls slightly between cycles. The fall in voltage is the exponential decay of an RC circuit of the type studied in Part I.

Therefore, the amount of *sag* in voltage between charging cycles depends on the time constant, τ where

Calculation of ripple magnitude

$$\tau = R_L C \tag{10.17}$$

The charging voltage, $v_{ab}(t)$, and the power supply output voltage, $v_o(t)$, are shown in Figure 10.45.

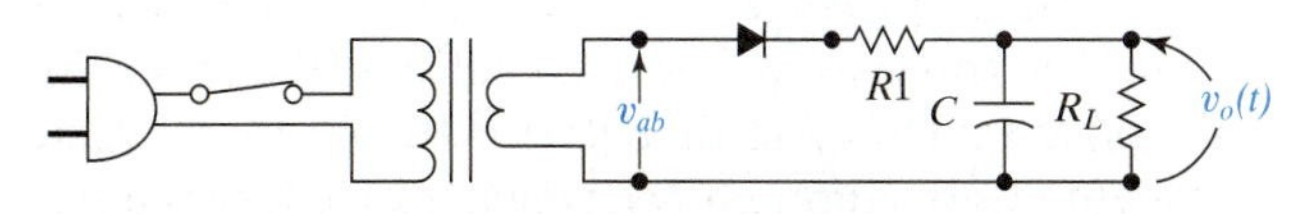

FIGURE 10.44 Half-wave rectifier circuit with filter.

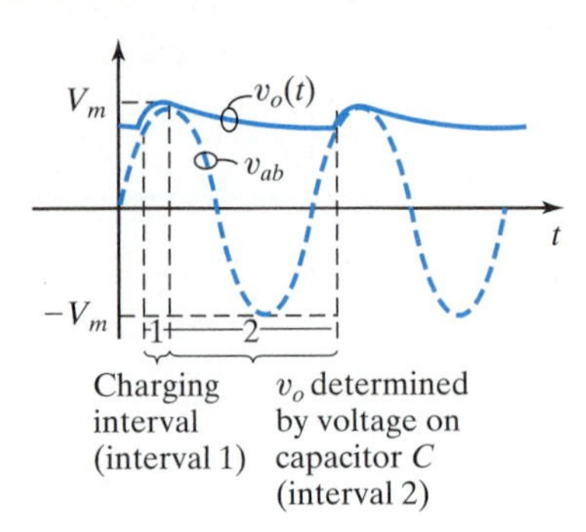

FIGURE 10.45 Filtered output of half-wave rectifier.

The amount of ripple can be approximated by straightforward transient circuit calculations as done in Part I, Chapter 3. Assume, for example, in this circuit that $C = 10\ \mu\text{F}$, $R_L = 10\ \text{k}\Omega$, and $T = 16.7$ ms, which corresponds to 60 Hz ac. If v_o is charged to V_m, the expression for the decay of voltage across the capacitor is

$$v(t) = V_m e^{-\frac{t}{\tau}} \tag{10.18}$$

where

$$\tau = R_L C = (10^4)(10 \times 10^{-6}) = 100\ \text{ms}$$

Evaluating the above expression at the end of a full cycle, that is, 16.7 ms, results in only a small error if the ripple is small, because interval 2 is much longer than interval 1. Therefore,

$$\frac{v_o(16.7)}{V_m} = e^{\frac{-16.7}{100}} = 0.846 = 84.6\% \tag{10.19}$$

The voltage at the end of a full cycle is 84.6% of its original value, V_m. Therefore, if V_m was 13 volts, as in Example 10.12, with the above filter it would only sag to $(13)(0.846) = 11$ volts during a full cycle. This cyclic variation from a peak of 13 volts to a minimum of 11 volts would be a 2-volt peak-to-peak ripple. Peak-to-peak means the voltage difference of the extremes. A 2-volt peak-to-peak ripple is very poor for electronic power supplies, and is presented for illustration only; good supplies can produce ripple measured in millivolts.

Often ripple is specified by the *ripple factor, RF*, which compares the *rms* value of the ripple to the magnitude of the dc voltage.

$$RF = \frac{rms\ value\ of\ ripple}{dc\ value} \tag{10.20}$$

10.6.3 Full-Wave Rectification

In half-wave rectifier circuits, the output is driven by the sinusodial input *only* during the positive half-cycle. A circuit using four diodes provides for charging of the output on both the positive and negative input cycles, essentially constructing the absolute value of the input wave. This circuit, called a *full-wave bridge rectifier circuit*, is shown in Figure 10.46.

The voltage $v_{ab}(t)$ is sinusoidal with equal positive and negative voltage swings. During the positive half-cycle, diode $D1$ is forward biased and supplies current to the top of R_L; the current returns through $D2$, which also is forward biased. The other two diodes are not conducting.

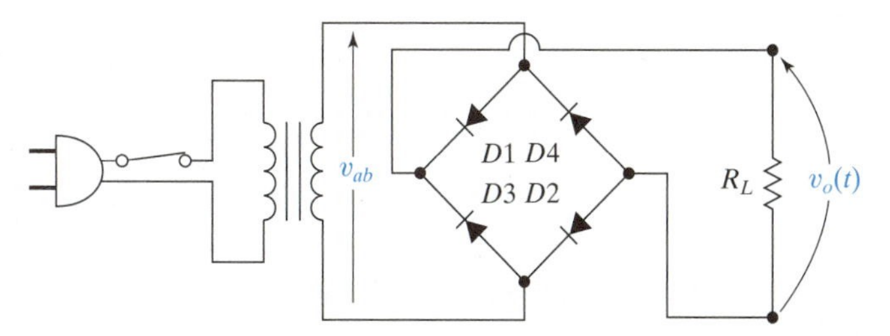

FIGURE 10.46 Full-wave bridge rectifier circuit.

During the negative half-cycle the bottom of the bridge is more positive than the top; therefore, positive current is supplied through $D3$ to the top of R_L, and returns through forward-biased $D4$. During this half-cycle, $D1$ and $D2$ are reverse biased. As a result, the plots of $v_{ab}(t)$ and $v_o(t)$ for this circuit are shown in Figures 10.47(a) and (b), respectively.

Another circuit that is sometimes used for full-wave rectification utilizes a transformer with a center tap on the output or secondary. If the center tap is taken as the ground reference, the transformer then supplies on each half-cycle a positive and a negative output, and two diodes are used to ensure that only the positive voltage swings are connected to the output. Such a circuit is shown in Figure 10.48.

During the positive half-cycle, v_{ab1} indicates the polarity of the sinusoidal peak on each of the windings. The diode $D1$ conducts and positive current is supplied to the top of R_L. $D2$ is not conducting. During the negative half-cycle, the polarity is such that v_{ab2} represents the direction of the positive peak; during this time $D2$ conducts current to the top of R_L and $D1$ is not conducting.

It can be shown that the dc value of a full-wave rectified sinusoid, as illustrated in Figure 10.47(b), is twice the value previously calculated for half-wave rectification. Thus

dc value of full-wave rectified signal

$$V_{DC} = \frac{2V_m}{\pi} \tag{10.21}$$

Illustration of full-wave rectification

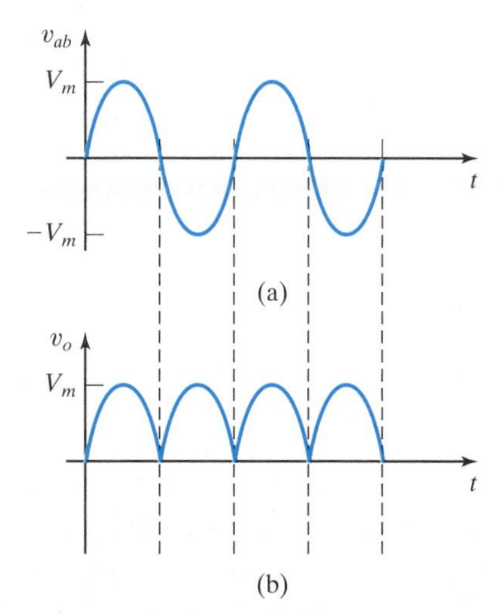

FIGURE 10.47 Voltage waveforms for full-wave rectifier.

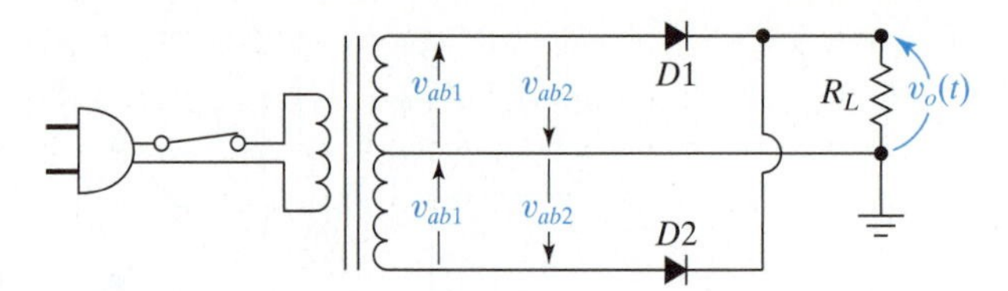

FIGURE 10.48 Alternate full-wave rectifier circuit.

Capacitive filtering of the output of the full-wave rectifier circuit is much like that of the half-wave rectifier circuit. The full-wave rectifier circuit provides less ripple for the same value of filter capacitance and load resistance.

Drill Exercise

D10.9. A full-wave rectifier circuit is used to rectify an ac voltage of 20 V *rms*. Find the dc output voltage of the circuit. Assume no filter and ideal diodes.

Ans: 18 V.

10–7 Wave Shaping: Clippers and Clampers

There are a number of very useful circuits utilizing diodes that can be employed to alter the shape of a waveform for a particular purpose, or shift the dc level of a signal. Several of these type circuits are described in the following sections.

10.7.1 Clipper Circuits

Clipper circuits are used to limit the voltage excursions of a signal at some particular positive value, at a particular negative value, or both.

The operation of a clipper circuit defined

A simple clipper circuit is illustrated in Figure 10.49. The voltage source v_i provides the input voltage to this circuit. The output voltage follows the input voltage exactly in this circuit, except when v_i exceeds V_A; for this latter case, $v_o = V_A$, that is,

$$v_o = v_i \text{ for } v_i < V_A$$

$$v_o = V_A \text{ for } v_i \geq V_A$$

where V_A is a constant voltage.

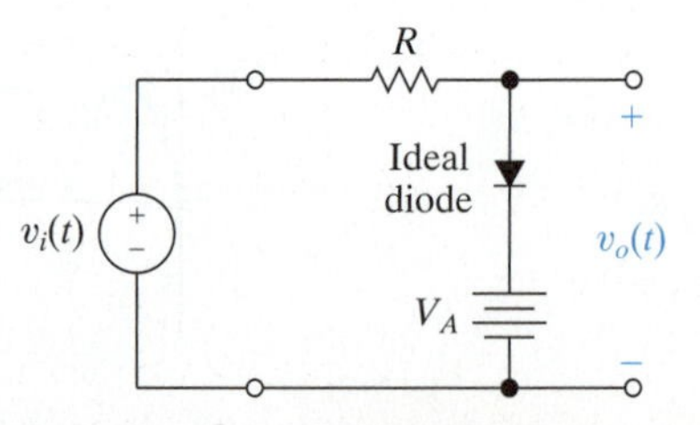

FIGURE 10.49 Simple clipper circuit.

If $v_i < V_A$, the diode is reverse biased and acts like an open switch. For this case, the input voltage, v_i, is connected directly through R to the output. Therefore, $v_o = v_i$, since there is no current through R, and, therefore, no voltage drop across R.

When $v_i > V_A$, the ideal diode is forward biased and the voltage source V_A is connected directly to the output, which effectively sets the output voltage at V_A.

Example 10.14

Given the circuit in Figure 10.49, with a sinusoidal input of amplitude 10 volts, and $V_A = 8$ V, we wish to plot the output voltage, $v_o(t)$.

The sinusoidal input voltage is shown in Figure 10.50(a), and the circuit's output voltage, $v_o(t)$, is illustrated in Figure 10.50(b). Notice that for all periods of time where the input exceeds 8 volts, the output is clipped at 8 volts.

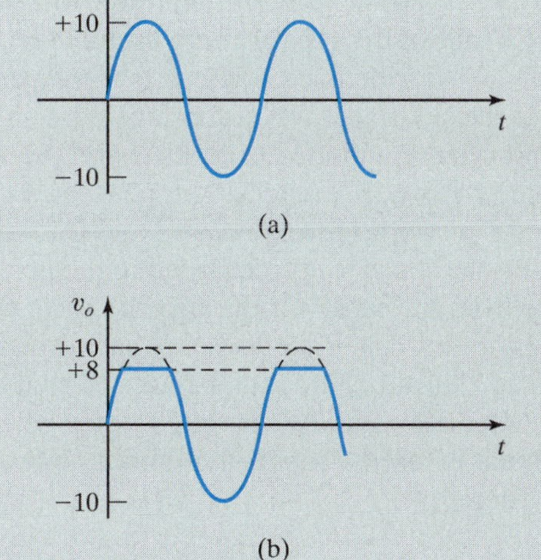

FIGURE 10.50 Voltage waveforms from Example 10.14 illustrating clipping.

The diode and voltage-source combination in the previous example can be placed in a similar circuit, but switched end-for-end, and used to limit the negative excursions of an input voltage. It is also possible to combine in one circuit a diode-source configuration for positive limiting with one for negative limiting; this circuit will clip the input at both positive and negative limits, each set independently by the appropriate constant voltage source. An example of this type of circuit is shown schematically in Figure 10.51. This circuit will clip positive input voltage swings at +5 volts and negative input voltage excursions at −7 volts.

10.7.2 Clamping Circuits

The operation of a clamping circuit defined

A *clamping circuit* is a circuit that produces an output that appears just as the input with one exception—the dc level or average voltage is shifted positively or negatively. Clamping circuits are also called dc restorer circuits or level shifter circuits.

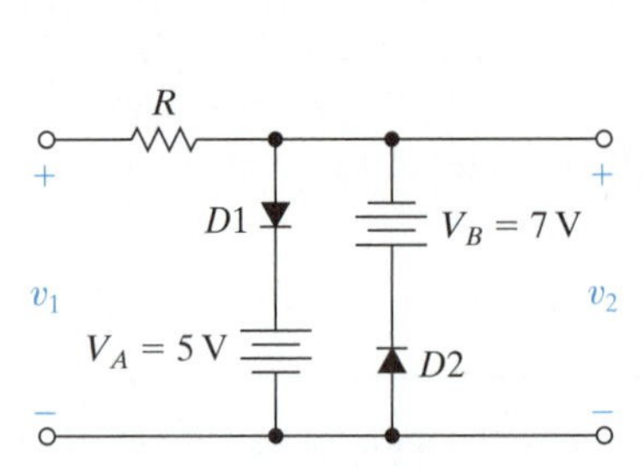

FIGURE 10.51 Clipper circuit.

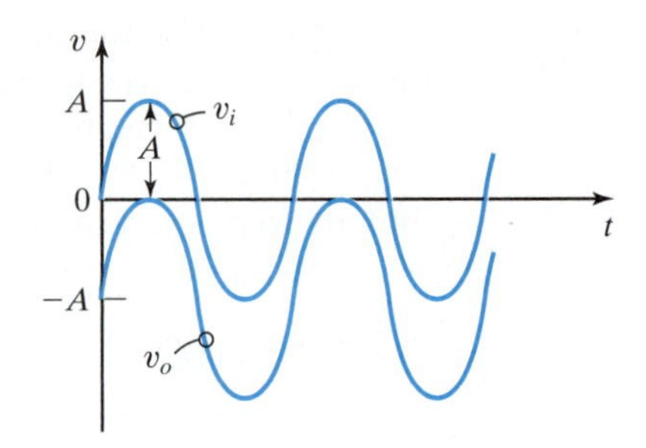

FIGURE 10.52 Voltage waveforms illustrating clamping.

For example, if the voltage waveform shown in Figure 10.52 identified as v_i is applied to a simple clamping circuit, it might appear at the output of such a circuit as the voltage v_o shown in the same figure. In this example, the input has a dc or average value of zero; the output, v_o, has its dc level shifted lower to a new value, −A.

Circuits of this type are very useful in reestablishing a known dc level in a signal that has an unknown dc reference. A circuit that can perform this operation is shown in Figure 10.53(a).

If the sinusoidal waveform labeled v_i in Figure 10.52 is the input to this circuit, during the first cycle, the diode *D* conducts and the voltage across capacitor *C* charges to +A. The voltage across *C*, v_C, reaches the peak of the input voltage, and then as the voltage v_i decreases, *D* becomes reverse biased and *C* is left charged at its peak value. If this waveform is periodic, the capacitor is recharged to the peak value on every cycle, and any slow leakage of charge from the capacitor during each cycle will be ignored for now.

In this circuit, the charged capacitor acts like a dc voltage source, and the equivalent circuit of Figure 10.53(b) can be used to analyze the circuit performance.

After a few initial "charging" cycles, when v_C has stabilized at the peak value, the diode *D* remains essentially open at all times.

Therefore,

$$v_o = v_i - v_C = v_i - \text{A}$$

This is the waveform plotted as v_o in Figure 10.52.

Using the same basic circuit configuration and reversing the polarity of the diode will create a dc level shift, which clamps the output with the minimum of v_i at zero (instead of the maximum as in the first case). In addition, a dc voltage source placed in series with the diode can create clamping levels at any arbitrary voltage.

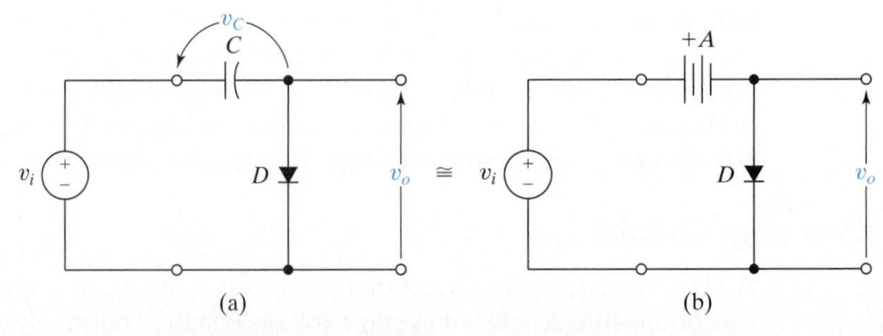

FIGURE 10.53 Clamper circuit and model.

Example 10.15

If the clamper circuit, shown in Figure 10.53, has an input voltage, $v_i(t) = 12 \sin \omega t$, let us write an expression for the voltage, $v_o(t)$.

D conducts on positive swings of v_i and charges the capacitor *C* to a value of $v_C = 12$. The polarity is such that the positive side is on the left of the capacitor. Therefore, the output is shifted 12 volts negative relative to v_i, and $v_o(t) = [12 \sin \omega t] - 12$ V.

10–8 The Zener or Avalanche Diode

For real semiconductor diodes, *in the reverse bias region*, the reverse current remains essentially constant and extremely small until the reverse bias voltage reaches the *breakdown voltage*, called the *avalanche* or *zener breakdown voltage*, V_Z.

At this value of applied reverse voltage the diode is said to break down and it conducts a large current in the reverse direction with the voltage across the diode essentially clamped at the voltage, V_Z. As reverse bias is increased further, the increasing negative current plotted as a function of reverse voltage shows a finite slope. The inverse of this slope is a small resistance called the equivalent zener resistance, r_Z. Figure 10.54 shows a typical diode voltage–current curve including the region of zener breakdown.

In most applications a diode is biased such that it never experiences a voltage large enough to cause breakdown. This section discusses a very important exception, *voltage regulation circuits*. The zener diode provides an effective way of clamping or limiting the voltage of a circuit at a relatively constant value to create a voltage regulation capability. Zener diodes can be purchased for this purpose, each of which has a specified breakdown voltage. Such diodes are available over a wide range of breakdown voltage values.

The symbol and characteristics of a zener diode

A piecewise linear model, similar to that used for forward-bias characteristics, can be employed for zener breakdown diode characteristics. In Figure 10.55, the zener diode symbol is shown on the left and the circuit model on the right; although all diodes will break down at some voltage, the special symbol is often used for diodes specifically designed to be used in zener breakdown.

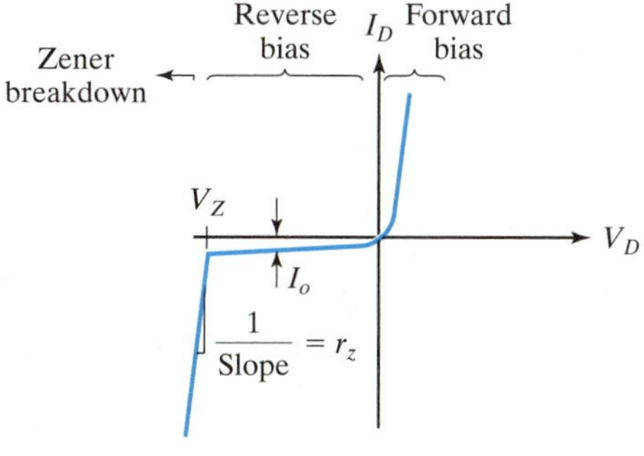

FIGURE 10.54 *V—I* curve for zener diode.

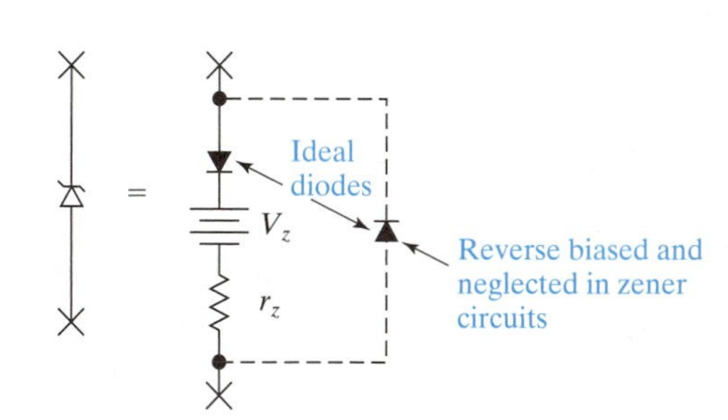

FIGURE 10.55 Zener diode symbol and circuit model.

Example 10.16

If a zener diode with a zener breakdown voltage, $V_Z = 5.0$ V and $r_Z = 100\ \Omega$, is connected as shown in Figure 10.56(a), let us find the voltage from A to B and the current through the zener diode.

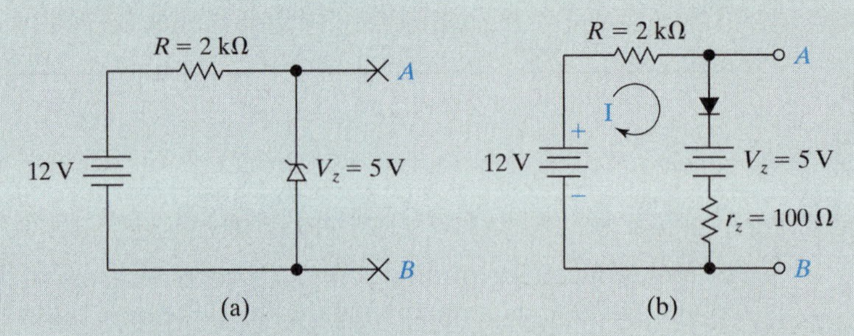

FIGURE 10.56 Zener diode circuit and circuit model.

If we replace the zener diode with its equivalent circuit, we obtain the circuit shown in Figure 10.56(b). The loop equation for this circuit is

$$12 - V_Z = (12 - 5) = I(2\text{k} + 100)$$

and therefore,

$$I = \frac{7}{2.1\text{k}} = 3.33 \text{ mA}$$

The current, I, is positive and in the direction that would cause the diode to be in zener breakdown. The ideal diode in the zener diode model acts as a closed switch.

The voltage from A to B is the sum of the voltage across r_Z and V_Z:

$$V_{AB} = I(r_Z) + V_Z$$

hence

$$V_{AB} = (3.33 \times 10^{-3})100 + 5 = 5.33 \text{ V}$$

The above circuit could be used, for example, in an automobile to provide the required 5 V dc operating voltage for electronic circuitry from a 12 V automobile battery.

Drill Exercise

D10.10. If a current source of 10 mA replaces the 12 V dc source in the circuit of Example 10.16, let us find the voltage from A to B and the power dissipated in the zener diode.

Ans: $V_{AB} = 6$ V. $P = 60$ milliwatts.

10–9 Load Lines and Graphical Solutions

In solving circuit problems with a nonlinear element, such as a diode, a useful technique in many cases is a graphical approach. If the characteristics of the nonlinear element are well charted, then one can superimpose a plot of the circuit response, excluding the nonlinear element, with a plot of the nonlinear characteristics of the element; where these plots intersect is the desired solution.

Example 10.17

If a silicon diode with a forward-bias voltage–current curve as shown in Figure 10.57(a) is placed in the circuit shown in Figure 10.58, let us find the current in this circuit.

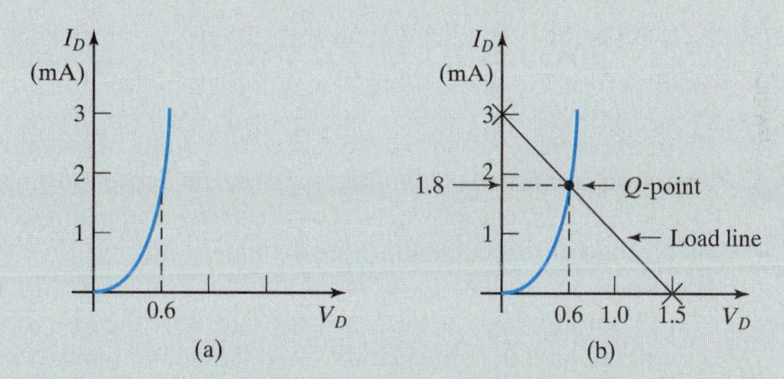

FIGURE 10.57 Diode V-I curve and load line analysis for Example 10.17.

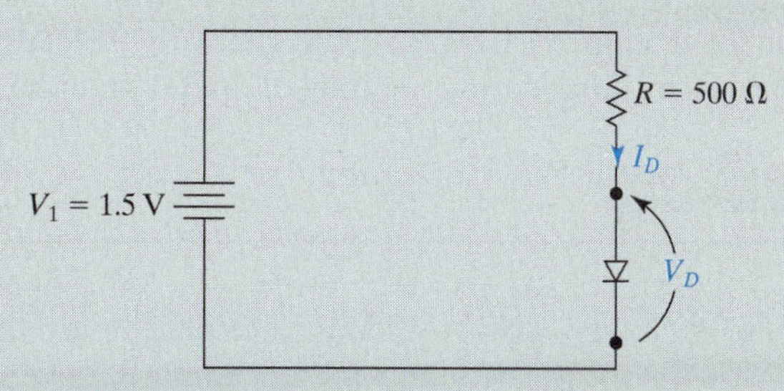

FIGURE 10.58 Circuit for Example 10.17.

The loop equation for this network is

$$V_D = V_1 - I_D R \tag{10.22}$$

which is the equation of a straight line on the V_D, I_D curve.

Because the constant voltage source and the resistor are linear circuit elements, the collection of possible solutions falls on this straight line. The end points of the line are easy to find. Imagine the nonlinear element acting at its two extremes. If the diode is shorted and $V_D = 0$, I_D is

$$I_D = \frac{V_1}{R} = \frac{1.5}{500} = 3\text{ mA} \tag{10.23}$$

The graphical solution for diode current and voltage (the Q-point) uses a load line superimposed on the diode V-I curve

The point, $\{V_D = 0, I_D = 3 \text{ mA}\}$, specifies one end of a line, as shown on Figure 10.57(b).

The other extreme occurs when the nonlinear element is an open circuit and $I_D = 0$. For this case, no current flows, the voltage V_D is simply V_1, and there is no voltage drop across R. Therefore, the other end of the line is at $\{V_D = 1.5 \text{ V}, I_D = 0\}$.

These two end points specify a straight line, sometimes called a *load line*. The intersection of the nonlinear device characteristic, in this case the diode curve, and the load line is the actual *quiescent bias point*, called the *Q-point*. In this circuit the current is 1.8 mA and the voltage across the diode is 0.6 V—the bias values at the *Q*-point, as shown in Figure 10.57(b).

This graphical technique is often used to establish the dc bias points of transistors operating as amplifiers and will be discussed in Chapter 11.

10–10 Photodiodes and Light Emitting Diodes

Certain types of diodes can be used to transform light into current or current into light

Semiconductor diodes are often used to convert incident radiation to electrical current—these are called *photodiodes. Solar cells* are one of the most common applications. The sun's radiation creates electron–hole pairs in the depletion region of a large *p–n* diode. The electric field in this region sweeps the carriers to the terminals and a current is thus generated; the magnitude of this current is approximately proportional to the intensity of light incident on the diode.

Photodiodes are also used for light intensity meters in cameras, for sensing an interrupted light beam in burglar alarm systems, and many other applications.

Light emitting diodes (LEDs) are *p–n* junctions generally fabricated from special semiconductor materials; gallium-arsenide is one of the more common materials. They are useful because they allow the direct recombination of electrons and holes, thus releasing energy in the form of light. LEDs have become very useful as indicator lights on electronic display panels and for illuminating sections of digital or alphanumeric displays.

Summary

- A diode is a two-terminal electronic device that conducts current if a voltage is applied with one polarity, and will not conduct current when the voltage is applied with the opposite polarity.
- The terminal of the diode that must be positive relative to the other for conduction is called the anode; the other terminal is the cathode.
- A diode biased for conduction is said to be forward biased; a diode biased for nonconduction is said to be reverse biased.
- *n*-type semiconductors have an excess of free electrons. In silicon, they are created by doping with impurities called donor atoms, which have a valence of 5, such as phosphorus. *p*-type semiconductors have an excess of free holes, and are created with acceptor dopants (valence $= 3$), such as boron.
- Current in a semiconductor is the result of both electron (negative charge) and hole (positive charge) movement. These carriers move by drift or diffusion.

- Carriers move by *drift* under the influence of an electric field, E. The magnitude of the electron drift velocity is given by

$$v_n = \mu_n|\mathbf{E}|$$

There is a similar expression for the drift velocity of holes

- Resistivity, ρ, is the reciprocal of conductivity, σ.

$$\sigma = q(n\mu_n + p\mu_p)$$

- Current density is expressed as the current per unit of cross-sectional area; $J = I/A$.
- The resistance from end-to-end of a bar of known length and cross-sectional area is given by

$$R = p\frac{L}{A}$$

- Carriers move by diffusion as a result of a concentration gradient. The expression for the electron current density is

$$J_n = q\,D_n\left[\frac{dn}{dx}\right]$$

- The *p*-*n* junction of a diode forms a potential barrier. If an external voltage is applied making the anode (*p* region) more positive than the cathode (*n* region), the barrier is reduced and current flows. If the external voltage is applied making the anode more negative than the cathode, the barrier increases and no current flows.
- The ideal diode has the solid symbol shown in Figure 10.59(a). The ideal diode acts like a closed switch under forward bias, and an open switch if reverse biased (see Figure 10.59(b).

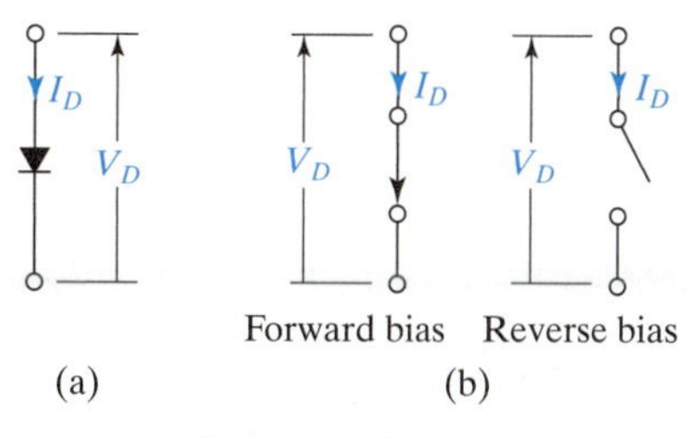

FIGURE 10.59

- Real diodes have V-I curves similar to that predicted by the diode equation

$$I_D = I_o(e^{\frac{qV_D}{kT}} - 1)$$

- The piecewise linear diode model approximates the characteristics of a real diode with two straight-line segments, as shown in Figure 10.60(a). Figure 10.60(b) shows the piecewise linear circuit model and the symbol.

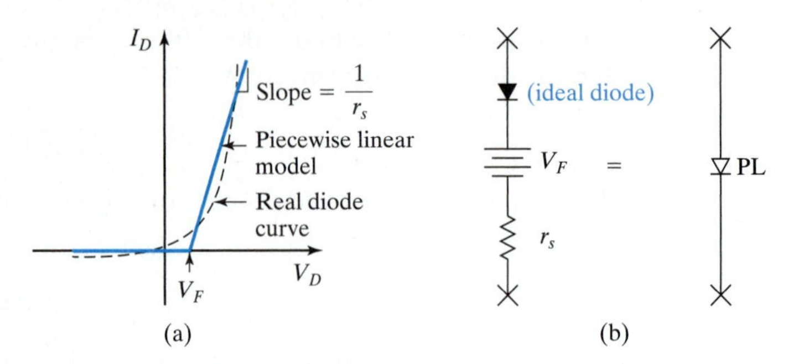

FIGURE 10.60

- A half-wave rectifier circuit, shown in Figure 10.61(a) uses a single diode to convert ac to "half-wave rectified" dc, shown in Figure 10.61(b).

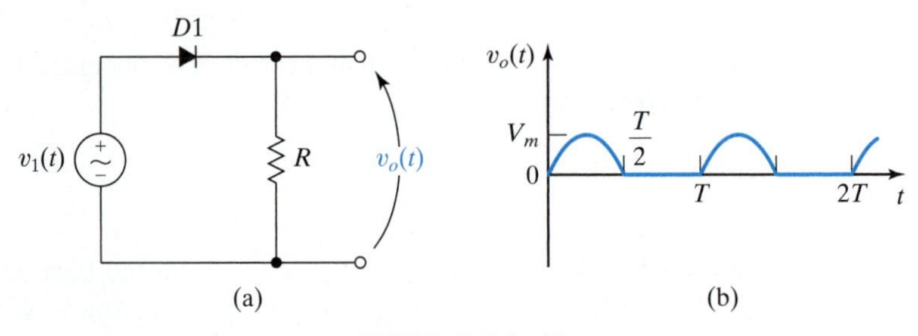

FIGURE 10.61

- A full-wave bridge rectifier circuit, shown in Figure 10.62(a) uses four diodes to convert ac to "full-wave rectified" dc, shown in Figure 10.62(b).

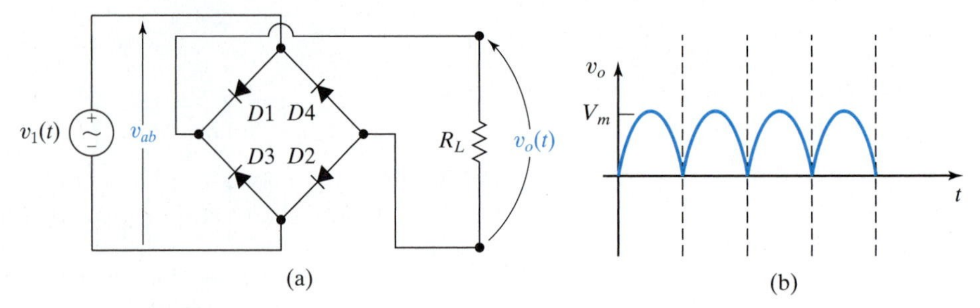

FIGURE 10.62

- A low-pass filter can be used at the output of a rectifier circuit to "smooth" the rectified ac to approximately a constant voltage. The small variation in the output of the filter is called ripple.
- A clipper circuit limits the output voltage excursions of the circuit at a level set by the circuit. A clamper circuit shifts the dc level of a signal by an amount set by the circuit.
- A zener diode is operated in breakdown to provide a constant voltage reference. The reverse bias voltage at which zener breakdown occurs is called V_Z. Figure 10.63 shows the zener diode symbol and the circuit model.

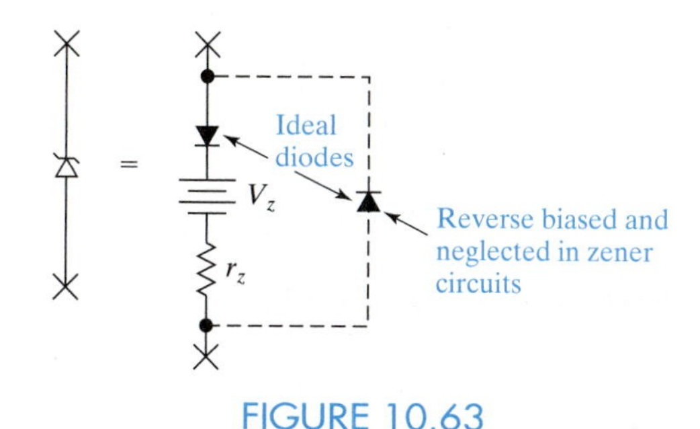

FIGURE 10.63

Problems

10.1. Please answer true or false to the following:
(a) A diode passes current in one direction and not in the other.
(b) A diode is a nonlinear device.
(c) A diode conducts more current when reverse biased than when forward biased.
(d) A diode conducts more current when its anode is more positive than the cathode.
(e) A diode is analogous to a check valve in fluid flow.

10.2. (a) Why must the linear network analysis techniques discussed in previous chapters be applied judiciously with diode circuits?
(b) In the "check valve" fluid analogy of a diode discussed in section 10.1, the case of the open valve (fluid flowing) corresponds to forward or reverse bias?

10.3. From what column in the periodic table of the elements do we get:
(a) *n*-type dopants?
(b) *p*-type dopants?

10.4. True or False: *n*-type dopants cause the conductivity of intrinsic silicon to increase and *p*-type dopants cause the conductivity of intrinsic silicon to decrease.

10.5. Classify the following as *n*-type dopant, *p*-type dopant, or cat.
(a) Aluminum
(b) Arsenic
(c) Boron
(d) Tin
(e) Indium
(f) Persian

10.6. Identify the samples shown in Figure P10.6 as *p*-type or *n*-type.

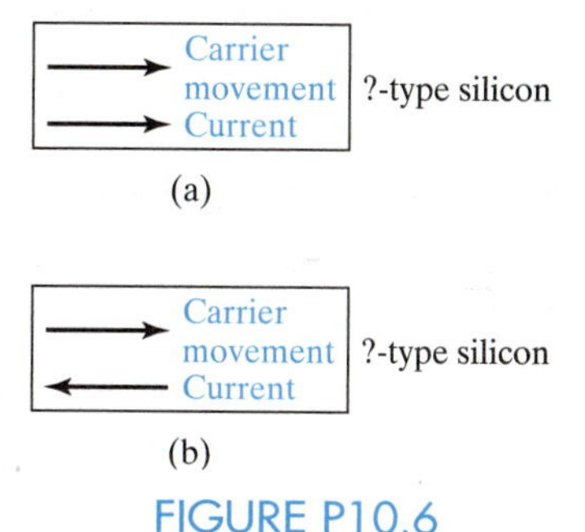

FIGURE P10.6

10.7. Doping is a process of adding certain impurities to pure silicon.
(a) Adding donor impurities creates what type of silicon?
(b) Adding acceptor impurities creates what type of silicon?

10.8. Assuming all impurities are ionized,
(a) if pure silicon material is doped with phosphorus at a density of 3×10^{18}atoms/cm^3, what is the density of free electrons in this material?
(b) if this material is subsequently doped with boron at the same concentration, what is the density of free electrons?

10.9. The rectangular bar in Figure P10.9 has a resistance from end to end of 300 Ω and has a voltage applied that establishes an electric field in the bar of 5 V/cm as shown.

(a) If the bar is *n*-type material, what type of carrier is carrying the majority of the current and in which direction are these carriers moving? How many carriers pass through a cross-sectional plane per second? What is the current density? What is the current?

(b) Same questions as in (a) if we assume the bar is *p*-type material.

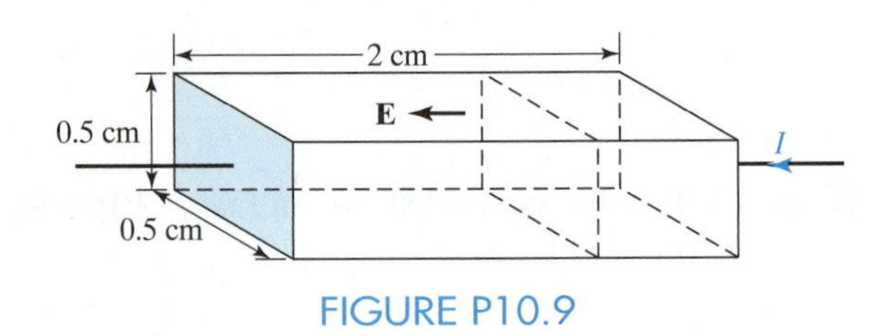

FIGURE P10.9

10.10. There is an electric field of 6 V/cm in a silicon material. Find the magnitude of the resulting electron and hole drift velocities.

10.11. Calculate the intrinsic conductivity of Si at room temperature (300°K). Assuming each dopant atom creates one free carrier, what is the conductivity of silicon when doped with 10^{18}atoms/cm^3 of arsenic?

10.12. (a) If the conductivity of *p*-type silicon material is 8 Ω-cm, what is the hole concentration?

(b) A wire that is round in cross-section has a diameter of 1 mm, and carries 25 amperes of current. What is the current density?

10.13. What's the drift velocity of an electron in an *n*-type silicon cube, 1 cm on a side, with a voltage of 25 V applied between two opposite faces?

10.14. A current of 1 mA flows through a rectangular solid of *n*-type silicon doped at a density of 10^{16}atoms/cm^3, as shown in Figure P10.14. Calculate:

(a) the magnitude of the current density,

(b) the resistance of the solid from one end to the other, and

(c) the magnitude and direction of the applied electric field.

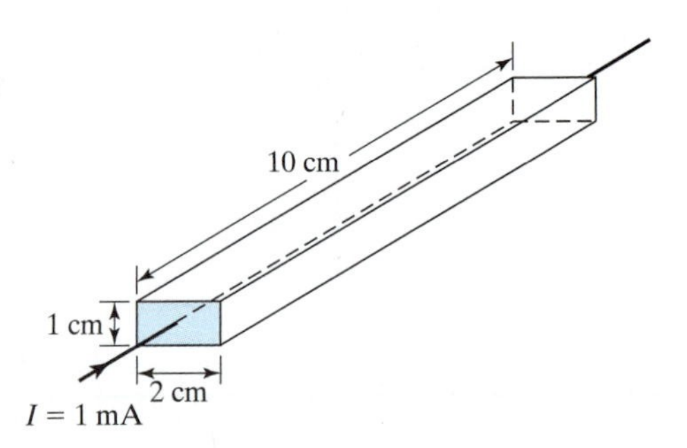

FIGURE P10.14

10.15. (a) Write the one-dimensional diffusion equation for holes.

(b) Consider a rectangular bar of silicon with a distribution of electrons and holes as shown in Figure P10.15(a). Find the diffusion current due to electrons, that due to holes, and the total current.

(c) Repeat (b) for the distribution in Figure P10.15(b).

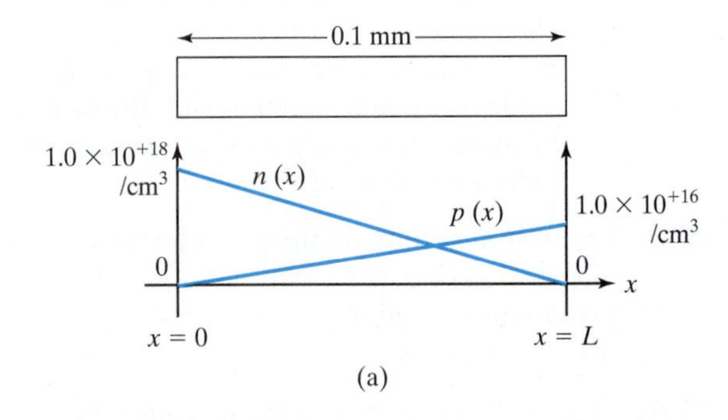

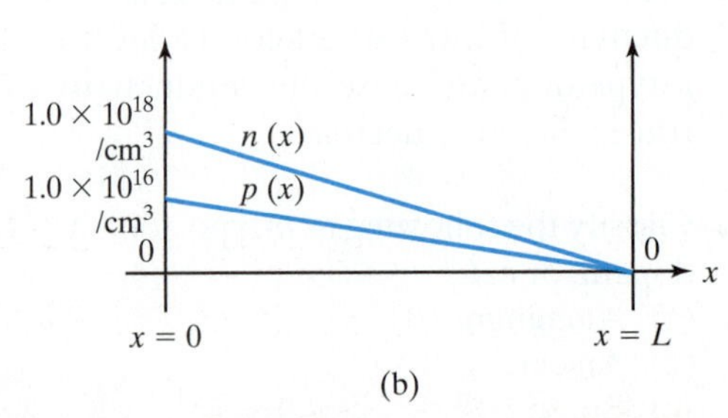

FIGURE P10.15

10.16. Assuming all diodes are ideal, calculate the current through R for each of the circuits shown in Figure P10.16.

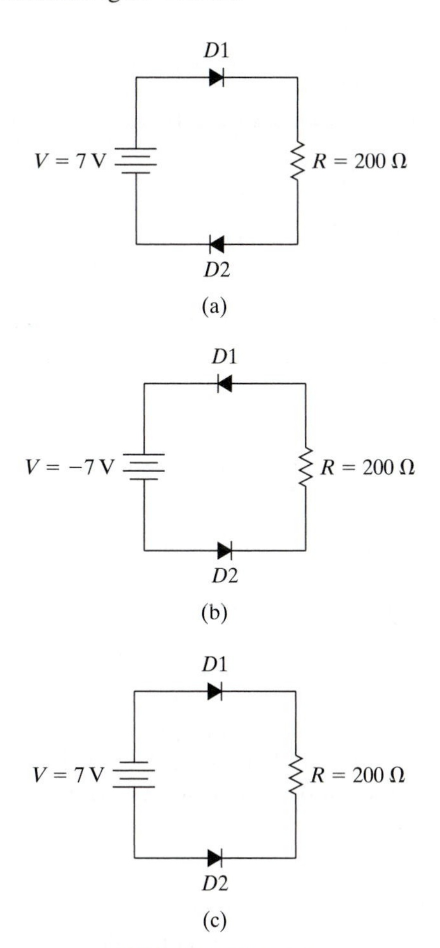

FIGURE P10.16

10.17. Assuming an ideal diode, in the circuit in Figure P10.17 (a) what is the voltage across R_2? and (b) what is the current through D?

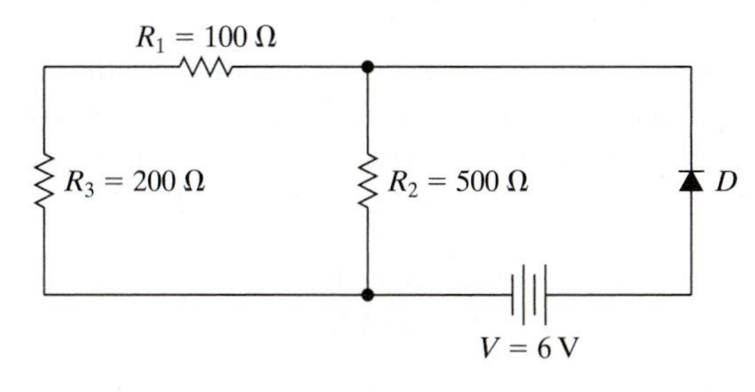

FIGURE P10.17

10.18. Calculate the current through R_1 in Figure P10.18 if:

(a) $V = 3$ V
(b) $V = 6$ V
(c) $V = -6$ V

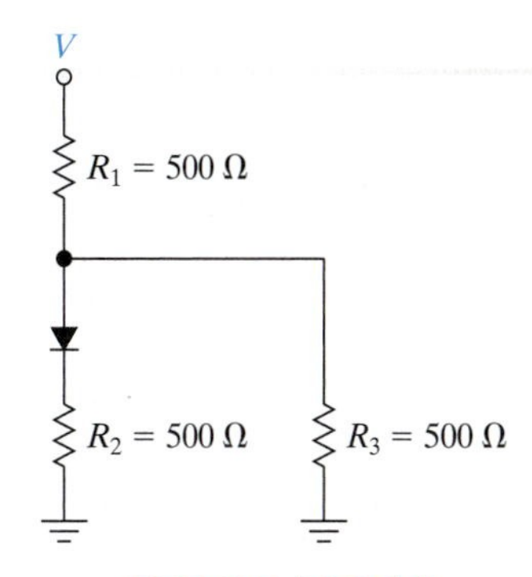

FIGURE P10.18

10.19. Plot V_o and a function of V_i, for V_i from 0 V to 10 V in the circuit of Figure 10.19.

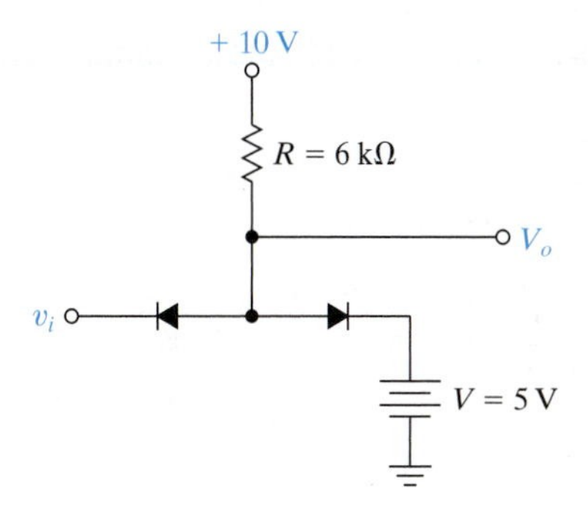

FIGURE P10.19

10.20. Assuming ideal diodes, in the network of Figure P10.20, (a) what is the current through $D1$? (b) what is the current through $D2$?

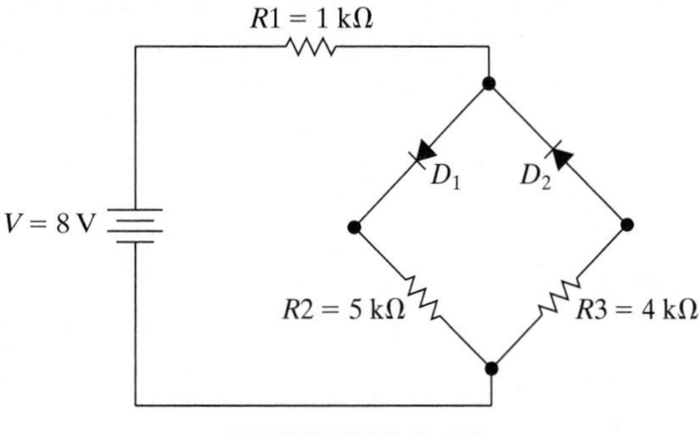

FIGURE P10.20

10.21. Assuming ideal diodes, (a) plot the transfer characteristics of the curcuit shown in Figure P10.21 for $0 \text{ V} \leq V_i \leq 6 \text{ V}$. (b) Plot the current in D_1 and that in D_2 over the same range of V_i.

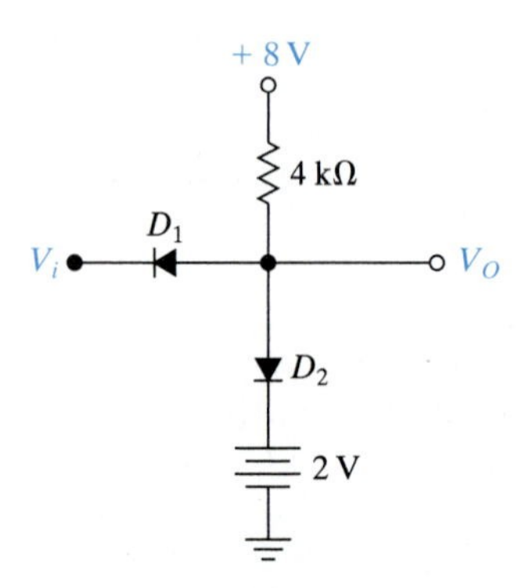

FIGURE P10.21

10.22. Sketch the *V–I* characteristics of each of the circuits in Figure P10.22 assuming ideal diodes.

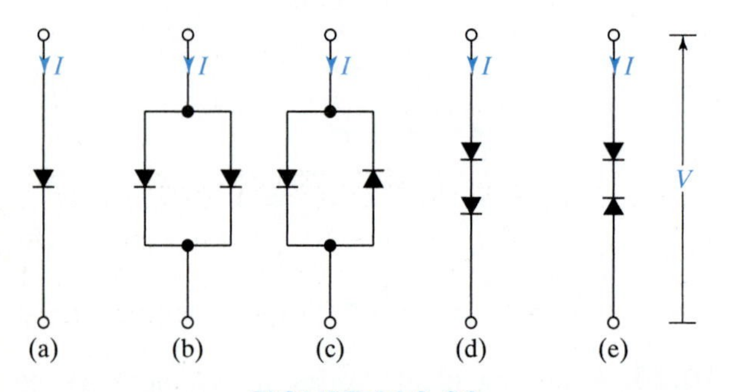

FIGURE P10.22

10.23. In the network in Figure P10.23, assuming ideal diodes, calculate the current through (a) D_1, (b) D_2, (c) V_1, the source.

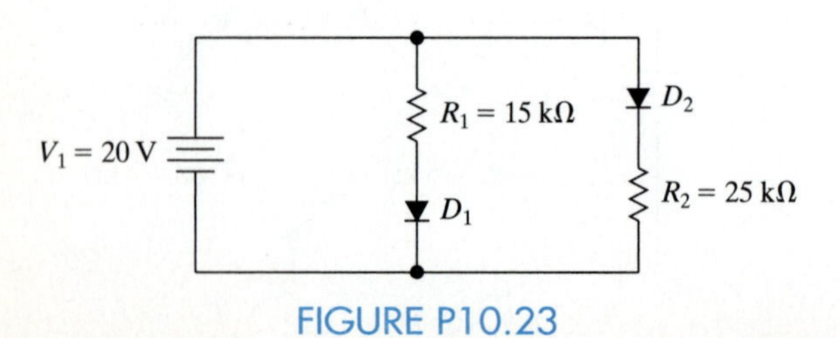

FIGURE P10.23

10.24. In the circuit in Figure P10.24, assuming an ideal diode, (a) find the voltage across resistor R_1. (b) What is the current through diode D?

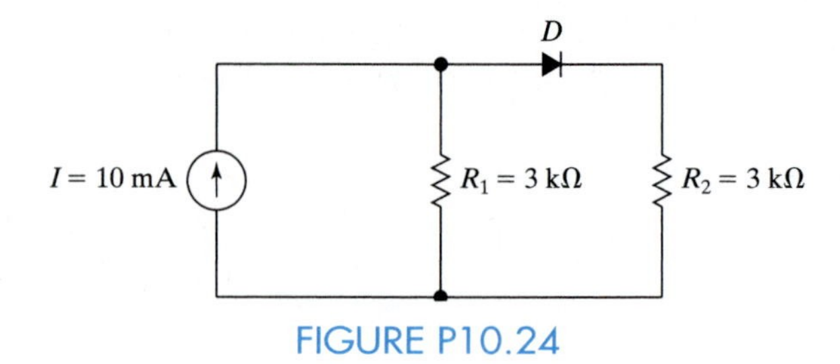

FIGURE P10.24

10.25. In Figure P10.25, for $V_1 = 3$ V, (a) calculate the current through D, (b) find the voltage across resistor R_2, (c) repeat (a) and (b) for $V_1 = 10$ V.

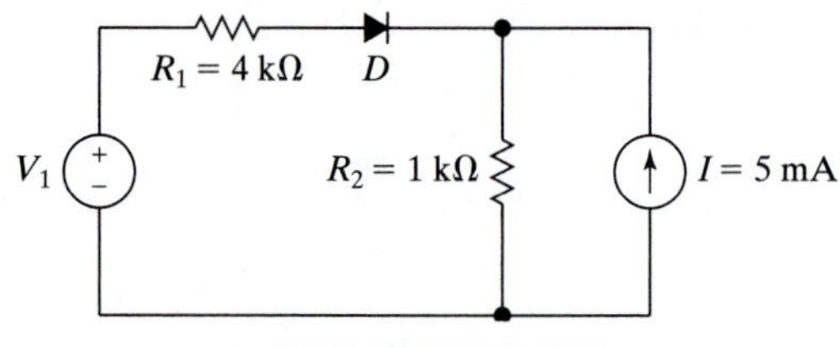

FIGURE P10.25

10.26. A semiconductor diode had a reverse saturation current, I_o of 3×10^{-14} A. Using the diode equation, determine and plot on a linear scale the diode current for $-3 < V_D < 0.8$ V.

10.27. A forward bias of 0.7 V causes a current of 2 mA to flow through a diode. What is the reverse saturation current, I_o, of the diode?

10.28. A diode conducts 5 mA with a forward bias of 0.6 V. What is the current through the diode at a forward bias of 0.9 V? Assume the diode equation can be used to represent the diode.

10.29. A diode that can be represented by the diode equation has a forward bias of 0.55 V and is conductiong 0.5 mA. If the voltage, V_D, is increased to 0.60 V, what is the new diode current?

10.30. A diode is considered ideal except that it has a series resistance of 8 Ω.

(a) If a current source is connected across the diode such that positive current enters the anode, how much power is dissipated in the diode?

(b) If the polarity of the current source is reversed, how much power is dissipated in the diode?

10.31. Obtain the voltage transfer characteristics (v_o versus v_i) for the circuit shown in Figure P10.31 for $-2\text{ V} \leq v_i \leq +2\text{ V}$, using a piecewise linear diode model with $V_F = 0.6$ V and zero forward resistance.

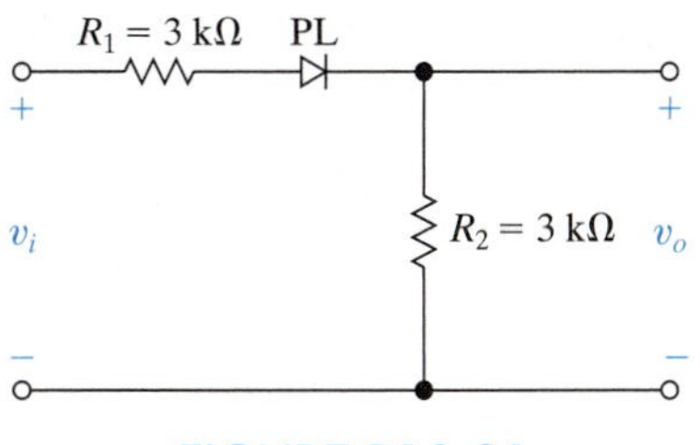

FIGURE P10.31

10.32. Sketch the output voltage, $v_o(t)$, for the circuit shown in Figure P10.32 for $0 \leq t \leq 10$ ms; $v_i(t)$ is given in the same figure. Assume that the diode has: (a) ideal V–I characteristics, (b) piecewise linear V–I characteristics with $V_F = 0.6$ V, and $r_s = 50\ \Omega$.

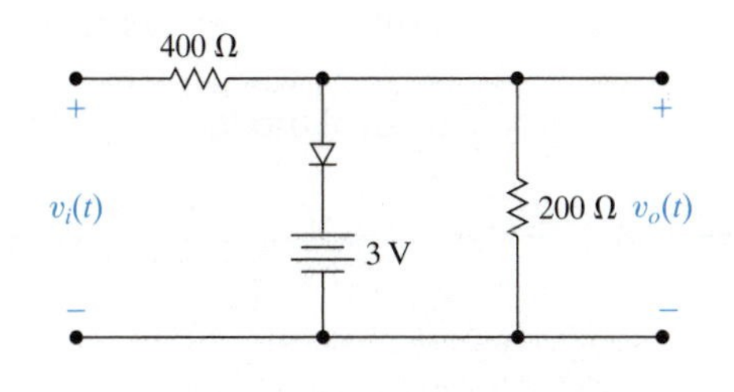

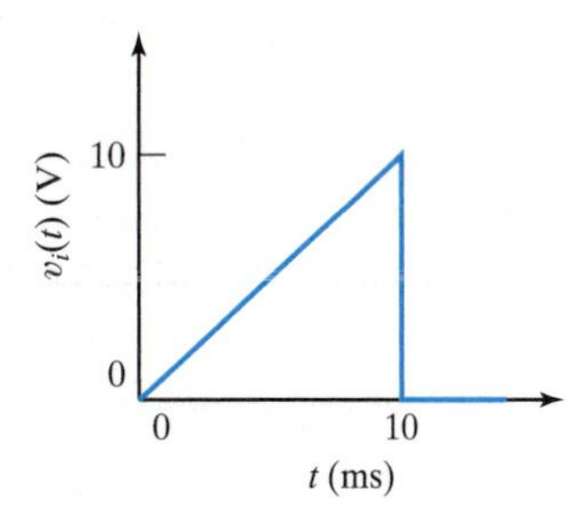

FIGURE P10.32

10.33. Use the piecewise linear diode model to find V_o for the following combinations of V_1 and V_2 as shown in Figure P10.33. Assume $V_F = 0.6$ V, $r_s = 30\ \Omega$.

(a) $V_1 = 0, V_2 = 0$
(b) $V_1 = 0, V_2 = 5$
(c) $V_1 = 5, V_2 = 0$
(d) $V_1 = 5, V_2 = 5$

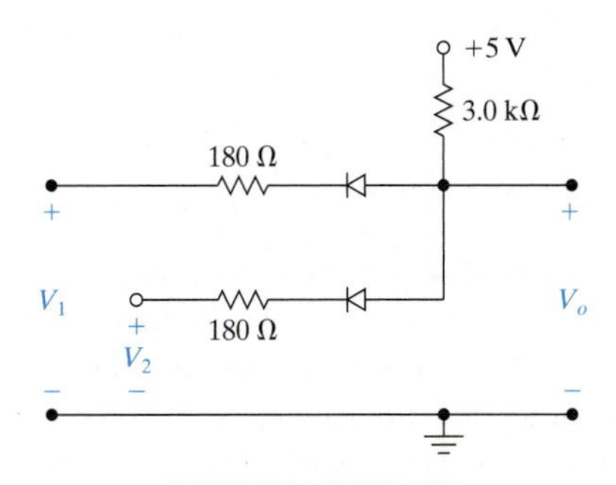

FIGURE P10.33

10.34. The circuit shown in Figure P10.34 includes a diode that can be modeled with a piecewise linear model, $V_F = 0.65$ V, $r_s = 40\ \Omega$. Plot the waveform of the voltage, v_o, at the output of the circuit.

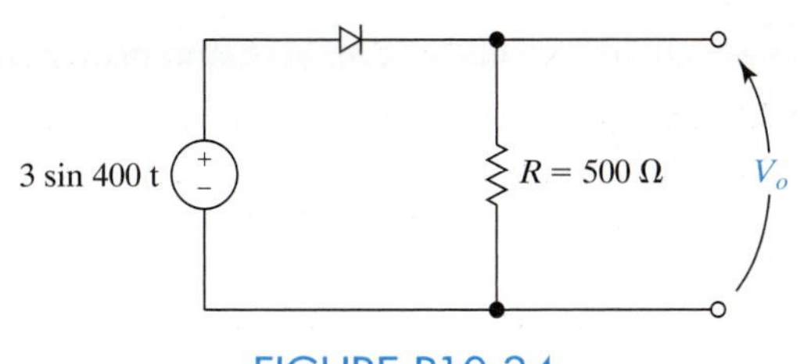

FIGURE P10.34

10.35. Plot the voltage across and the current through the load resistance, R_L, in the circuit shown in Figure P10.35(a). Use the diode model shown in Figure P10.35(b).

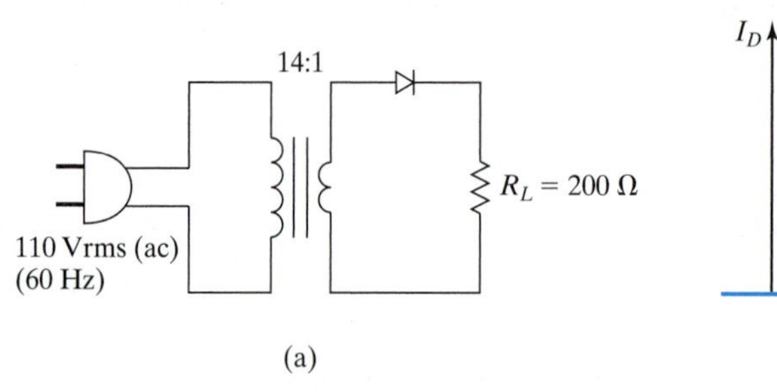

FIGURE P10.35

10.36. The circuit shown in Figure P10.36 has a diode that can be modeled with a piecewise linear model in which $V_F = 0.6$ V and $r_s = 0$. (a) Plot the voltage transfer characteristics of this circuit (v_o versus v_i) for $-5 < v_i < +5$ V. (b) If a sinusoidal voltage of amplitude 5 V and frequency 60 Hz is applied as the input, plot the output voltage $v_o(t)$ and the current $i_R(t)$. (c) What is the dc voltage output in (b)?

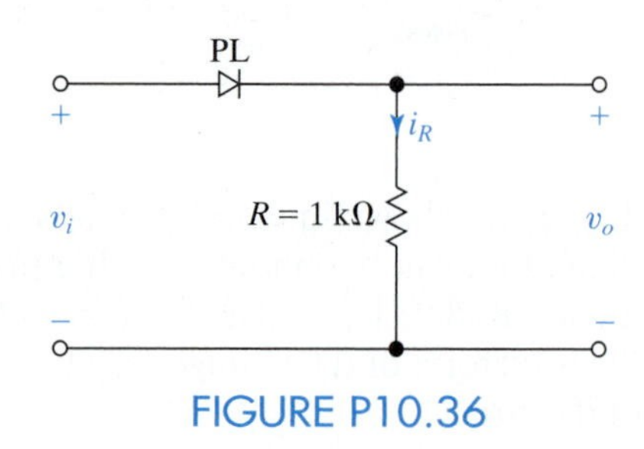

FIGURE P10.36

10.37. The waveform shown in Figure P10.37 is applied as an input to the circuit in Figure P10.36. (a) Plot the output waveform, $v_o(t)$. (b) What is the dc voltage output?

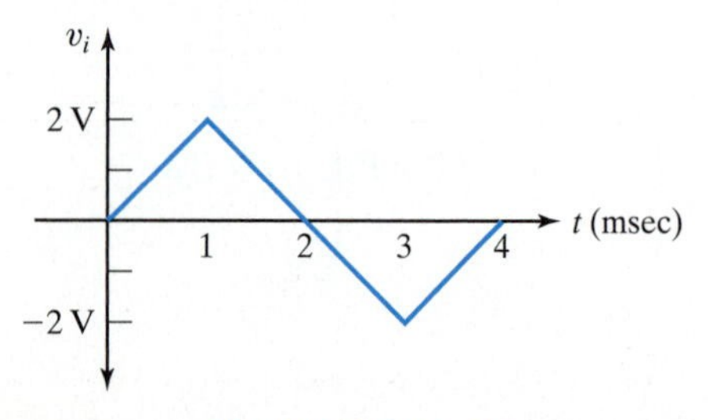

FIGURE P10.37

10.38. A half-wave rectifier circuit with a filter is shown in Figure P10.38. Plot the output waveform and estimate the peak-to-peak ripple for (a) $C = 150\ \mu$F and (b) $C = 1.5\ \mu$F. Assume an ideal diode.

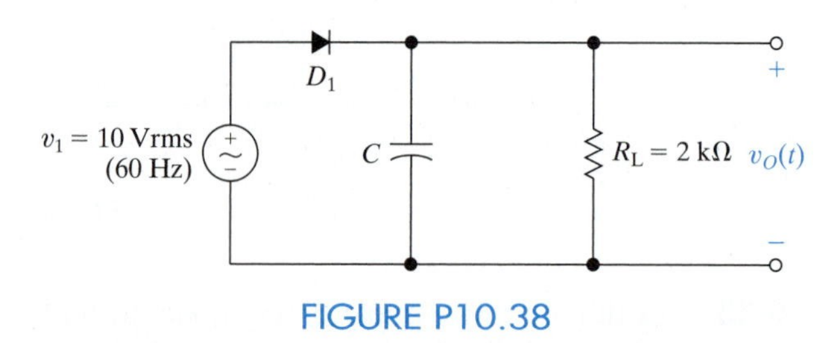

FIGURE P10.38

10.39. An electronic calculator operates on a dc supply of 6 V. This supply is obtained from a half-wave rectifier with an RC filter. If the calculator can be modeled as a 10 kΩ resistance and it can tolerate a maximum peak-to-peak variation of 0.1 V around the dc value, calculate the minimum value of capacitor that can be used in the filter. Use a piecewise linear diode model with $r_s = 50\ \Omega$, and $V_F = 0.7$ V. Assume ac input is 60 Hz.

10.40. A four-diode full-wave rectifier circuit is shown in Figure P10.40. Assuming the diodes are ideal, (a) plot the output voltage $v_o(t)$ and the output current $i_o(t)$. (b) Determine the maximum reverse bias on any diode in this circuit. (c) What is the dc output voltage?

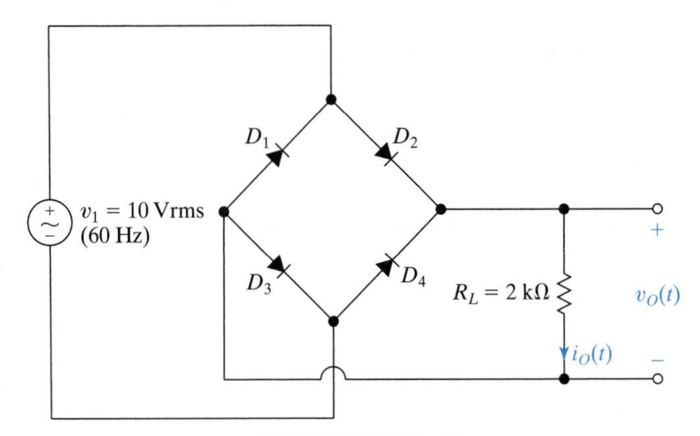

FIGURE P10.40

10.41. Repeat problem 10.40 using the diode model of problem 10.39.

10.42. Repeat problem 10.40 assuming ideal diodes, if the input voltage is:
(a) 5 Vrms (60 Hz)
(b) 30 Vrms (60 Hz)
(c) 8 Vrms (50 Hz)

10.43. A two-diode full-wave rectifier circuit is shown in Figure P10.43; assume ideal diodes.
(a) If $C = 0$, plot the output voltage and determine its dc value.
(b) If C and R_L are the values given in Figure P10.43, plot the output voltage waveform, and estimate the peak-to-peak ripple.
(c) What is the maximum reverse bias on either diode?

10.44. Repeat problem 10.43 assuming the diodes are modeled by the piecewise linear model given in problem 10.39.

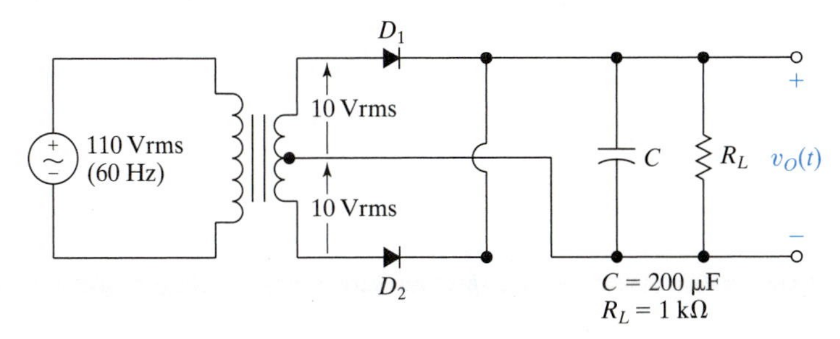

FIGURE P10.43

10.45. A clipping circuit is shown in Figure P10.45. If the diode is ideal, sketch voltage transfer characteristics (v_o versus v_i) for this circuit for $-5 < v_i < +5$ V.

10.46. Repeat problem 10.45 assuming a piecewise linear diode model with $V_F = 0.6$ V, $r_l = \infty$ and $r_s = 40\ \Omega$.

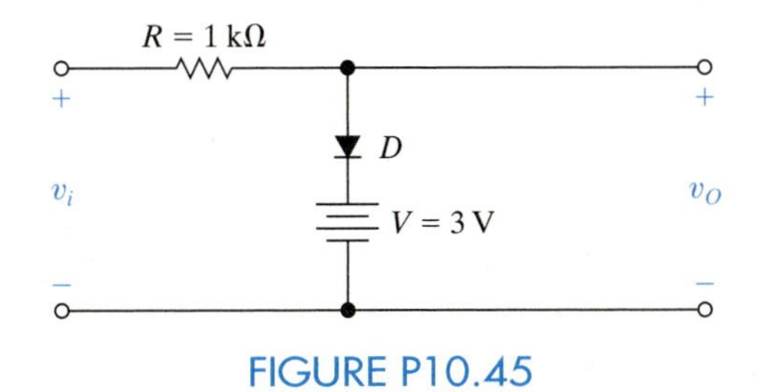

FIGURE P10.45

10.47. The input voltage, $v_i(t) = 5\sin(\omega t)$V, is applied to the circuit shown in Figure P10.47. Assuming the diodes are ideal, sketch the output voltage $v_o(t)$ as a function of time.

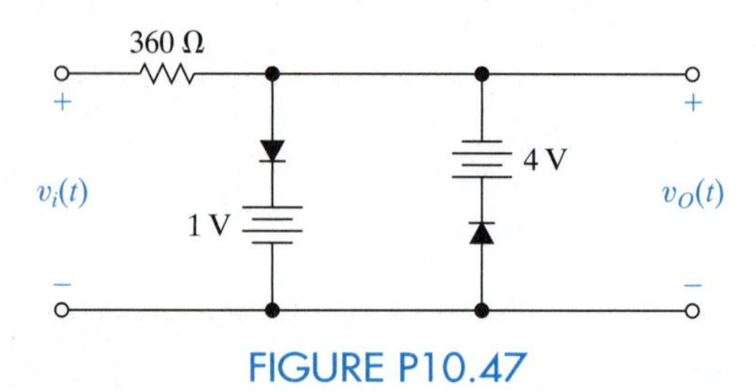

FIGURE P10.47

10.48. Repeat problem 10.47 using the diode model of problem 10.46.

10.49. A clamping circuit is given in Figure P10.49; assume the diode is ideal and $v_i = 1 + 5\sin(\omega t)$ V. (a) Sketch the output waveform, and (b) determine the dc level of the output signal.

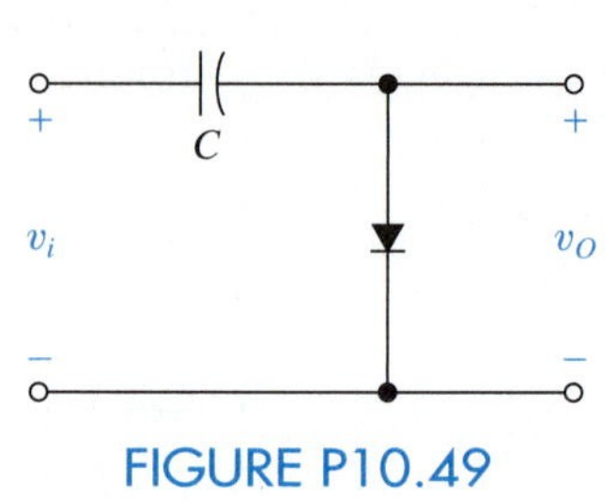

FIGURE P10.49

10.50. Repeat problem 10.49 with the diode polarity reversed (i.e., redraw Figure P10.49 with the diode "upside down" from that drawn).

10.51. Figure P10.51(a) shows a zener diode voltage regulator circuit. Using the zener diode with the V–I curve shown in Figure P10.51(b), (a) determine the zener diode model parameters, V_Z and r_Z, (b) obtain the voltage transfer characteristics of the circuit for $0 < v_i < 15$ V, (c) determine the power dissipated in the zener diode if $v_i = 10$ V, and (d) determine the output voltage in (c).

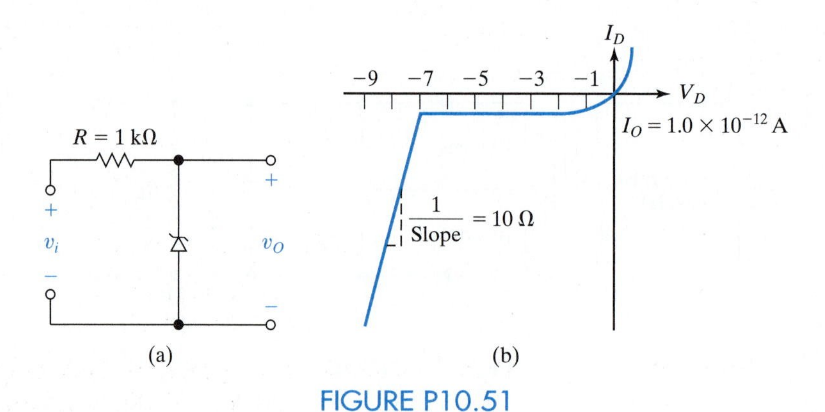

FIGURE P10.51

10.52. In the circuit in Figure P10.52, determine the value of the output voltage, v_o. Use the zener diode characteristics given in Figure 10.51(b).

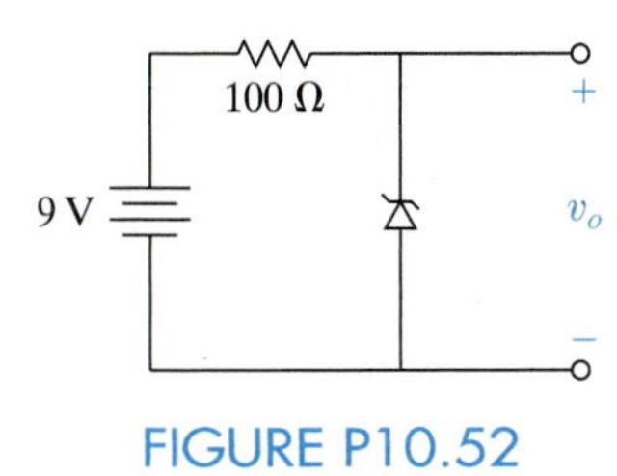

FIGURE P10.52

10.53. The zener diode with $V_Z = 12$ V and $r_Z = 0$ is placed in the circuit in Figure P10.51(a). If v_i is 20 V dc, (a) what is the current through the zener diode? and (b) if a 6 kΩ load resistance is attached at the output, what is the current through the zener diode?

10.54. A diode that follows the diode equation conducts 30 mA with a forward bias of 0.8 V. (a) Determine I_o. (b) Plot the V–I characteristics of this diode. (c) This diode is placed in the circuit in Figure P8.41; using the plot from (b), obtain the diode current and voltage graphically.

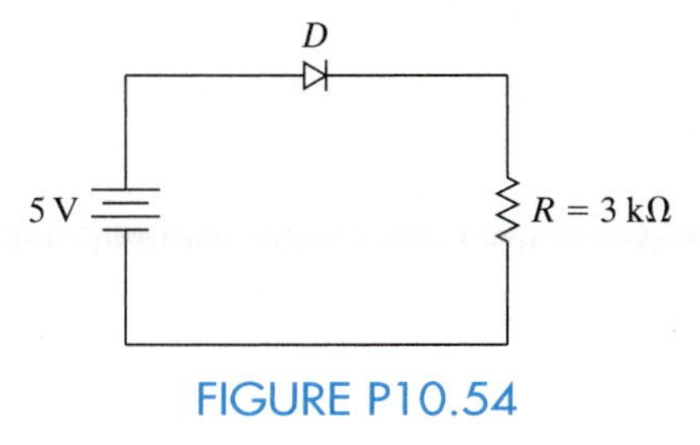

FIGURE P10.54

10.55. The diode in Figure P10.55(a) has V–I characteristics shown in Figure 10.55(b). Use a graphical method to solve the diode current and voltage in this circuit. Plot the load line on the same graph as the diode curve and clearly identify the Q-point.

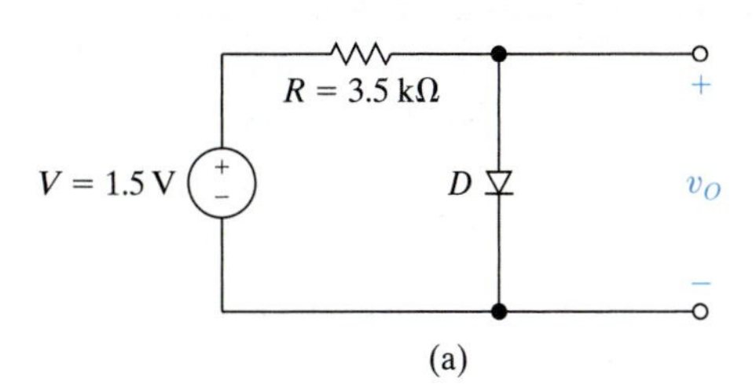

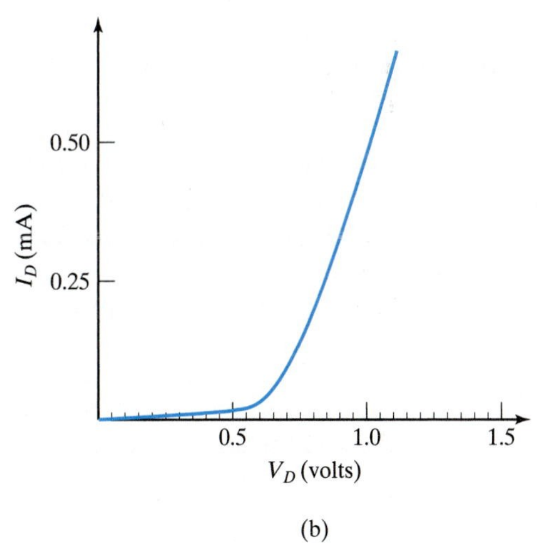

FIGURE P10.55

10.56. Repeat problem 10.55 if

(a) $R = 3.0$ kΩ
(b) $R = 2.5$ kΩ

10.57 Briefly describe the difference between a photodiode and a light emitting diode (LED).

11-1 Introduction

Transistors are electronic devices that are critical to the operation of most electronic circuits. Transistors are three terminal devices that perform one of two functions:

The functions of a transistor

1. In digital circuits the transistor acts as an electronically controlled switch.
2. In analog circuits the transistor acts as an electronic amplifier.

Modern electronic systems often utilize digital circuitry to achieve the myriad of new capabilities and functions available. Digital signals toggle between a high and a low voltage level representing a "1" and a "0," respectively. The transistor can operate as an electronic switch in a circuit to create an output at the high or low level. These circuits are called logic gates. A single microprocessor chip may contain millions of transistor switching devices.

The simplest generic model of a transistor as an electronically controlled switch is shown in Figure 11.1. A voltage or a current is applied at the control terminal, which determines whether the switch (connected between the other two terminals) is open or closed.

Transistors are also the devices that perform amplification of electronic signals in modern analog circuits. Recall from Chapter 9 (see Figure 9.1) that an amplifier is an electronic circuit that produces an output signal that is a copy of the input signal, but increased in amplitude. The op amps described in Chapter 9 are fabricated with transistors to amplify the input signal.

There are two basic types of transistors: FETs (field effect transistors) and BJTs (bipolar junction transistors). The physical structure and operating mechanisms of the two types are completely different. In this chapter we will study both types, and evaluate their application as switches and amplifiers.

A simple circuit model of a transistor makes use of dependent current sources. An FET is controlled by input voltage; it has a high (almost infinite) input resistance and functions over much of its operating range as a voltage-controlled current source, as shown in Figure 11.2(a). A BJT is controlled by input current, and functions much like a current-controlled current source; see Figure 11.2(b). (Refer to Chapter 1, Figure 1.15.)

We will use circuit models similar to Figure 11.2 in Chapter 12 when we examine in detail small-signal amplifier circuits. In this chapter we will use large-signal amplifier techniques, which depend on graphical representation, or plots, of a transistor's current versus voltage characteristics for analysis.

The transistor can act as an electronically controlled switch

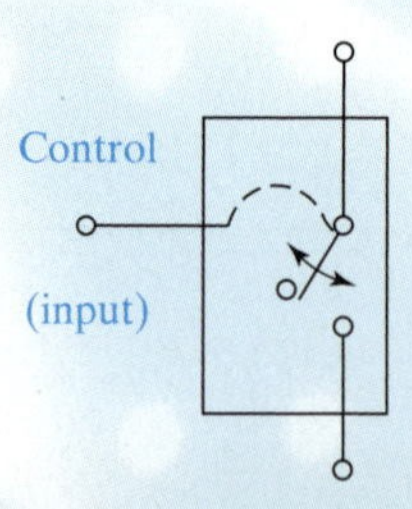

FIGURE 11.1 Electronically controlled switching device.

Transistor Fundamentals: Switches, Large-Signal Amplifiers, and Power Electronics

Small-signal and large-signal amplifiers defined

A *small-signal amplifier* is one in which the signal voltage variations are reasonably small, and over this small range the nonlinearities of the transistor can be approximated by linear circuit models. From a practical standpoint, this generally requires that the voltage swings not exceed the range of a few hundreds of millivolts, unless feed-back is used to linearize the response as is done in many op amp circuits.

A *large-signal amplifier* is one in which the voltage swings are large, that is, several volts or more, and the device nonlinearities cannot be ignored. Typically these circuits are used to provide high levels of signal output, such as a power amplifier driving a stereo speaker. The design and analysis of these circuits is often done graphically, using plots of the voltage–current characteristics of the transistor over their entire operating voltage range. The transistor output curves provide such graphical information for large-signal analysis.

Large-signal amplifiers are somewhat similar to switching circuits in that both require the output voltage and current to swing over a wide range. For example, as an electronic switch transitions from the closed to the open state, the current must decrease from a high value to zero. Many of the same transistor analysis techniques in this chapter may be applied to both digital logic circuits and large-signal amplifiers.

11-2 MOSFET Fundamentals

There are two primary types of field effect transistors: the *JFET (junction FET)* and the *MOSFET (metal-oxide-semiconductor FET)*. The latter is most commonly used in modern digital electronic circuits, and, therefore, we will concentrate here on this device. JFETs will, however, be discussed in section 11.6. MOSFETs are sometimes referred to as MOS transistors.

MOS transistors can be either *n-channel* or *p-channel,* each of which can be further subdivided into either *enhancement mode* or *depletion mode,* as shown in Figure 11.3. All of these

The transistor can amplify signals by acting like either a voltage-controlled or current-controlled (depending on transistor type) current source

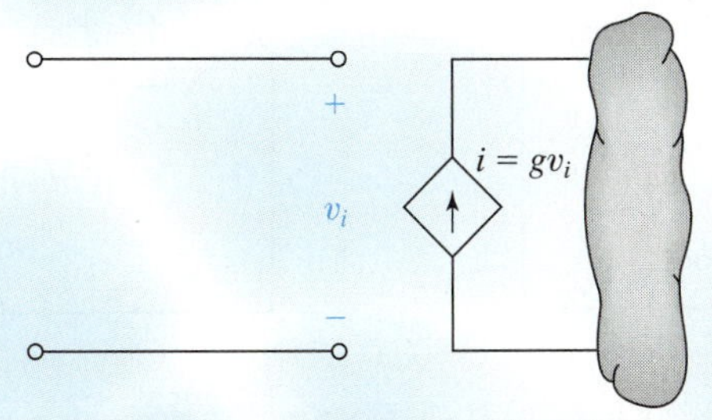

(a) Voltage-controlled current source (FET)

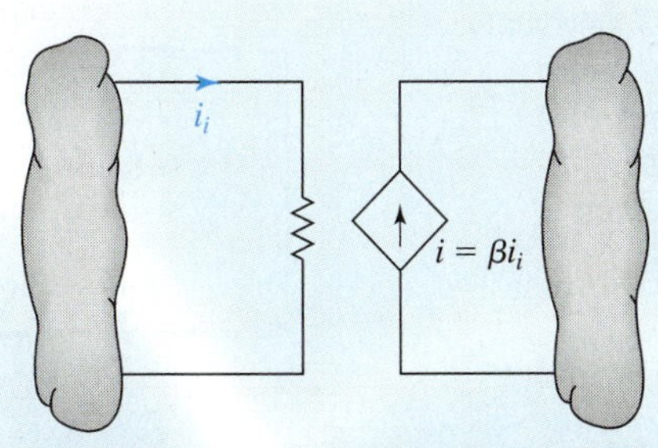

(b) Current-controlled current source (BJT)

FIGURE 11.2 Controlled current sources.

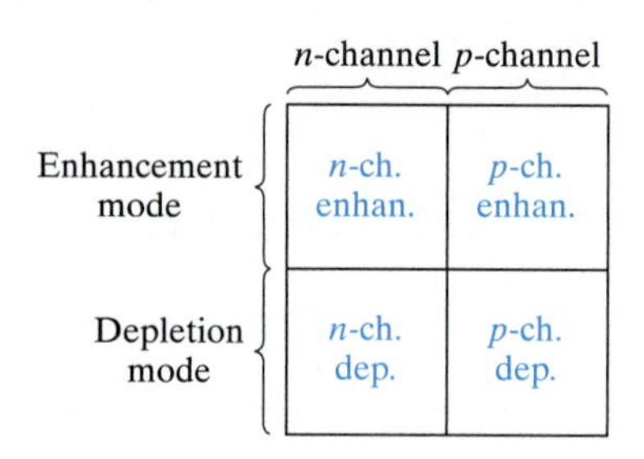

FIGURE 11.3 MOS transistor types.

The most common field-effect transistor, the MOSFET, has four types; the *n*-channel enhancement mode is the most common of these

transistors can operate as electronically controlled switches. For purposes of illustration, we will look first at an *n-channel, enhancement-mode device,* which is probably the most commonly used device. The definition of these terms will be made clear in the following sections. The other types of devices and their corresponding structure can be easily understood later by analogy. MOS transistors are the key switching elements in popular digital technologies such as NMOS and CMOS—described in Chapter 14.

11.2.1 MOSFET Structure and Symbols

Metal-oxide-semiconductor is a description of a structure comprised of layers: metal on top, silicon dioxide in the middle, and a semiconductor, generally silicon, underneath. This is, however, of historical origin and not representative of modern structures. New technologies generally use a film of polysilicon instead of metal for the top layer, but the old designation, MOS, has been retained.

The basic structure of a silicon *n*-channel enhancement-mode MOS transistor is shown in Figure 11.4.

The cross-section drawing in Figure 11.4(a) shows a *substrate* of *p*-type silicon (the *body*) into which an *n*-type *source* region and an *n*-type *drain* region have been placed. Electrical connections are made to the source region, labeled *S,* and the drain region, labeled *D.* Covering the gap between the source and drain is a very thin layer of silicon dioxide—basically

MOSFET physical structure for an *n*-channel enhancement mode device

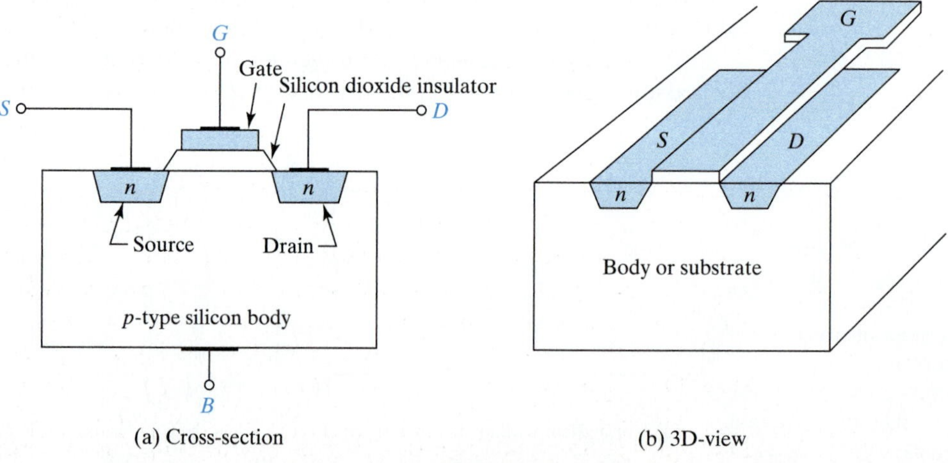

FIGURE 11.4 Basic structure of *n*-channel MOS transistor.

MOSFET schematic symbols defined

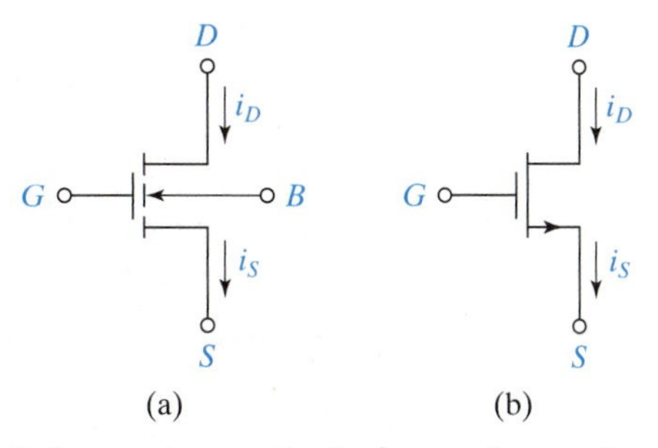

FIGURE 11.5 Schematic symbols for *n*-channel, enhancement-mode MOSFET.

glass and a superb insulator. On top of this glass layer (called the *gate oxide* or *gate dielectric*) is a ribbon of conducting material to which the gate electrode is attached, labeled *G*. The *p*-type substrate also has an electrical contact that is labeled *B,* for body. In most digital circuits the body is electrically connected to the source and its primary purpose is to isolate one transistor from another on the same silicon chip. As shown in Figure 11.4(a), a capacitor-like structure is formed with the gate oxide (an insulator), and the *gate* as the top electrode and the semiconductor material (body) as the bottom electrode.

The schematic symbol used for this device is shown in Figure 11.5(a). Sometimes the alternate symbol, shown in Figure 11.5(b) is used.

The arrow designating the body connection in the symbol is in the opposite direction for a *p*-channel device; the structure of a *p*-channel device is similar, with the *n* and *p* regions interchanged.

11.2.2 MOSFET Device Operation

Threshold voltage, V_T, described

Consider that the *n*-channel MOSFET is now connected in a circuit with a voltage V_{DS} applied from drain (D) to source (S), as shown in Figure 11.6. Current flows, or does not flow, through the device in the S-D loop, by the control of the gate-to-source voltage, V_{GS}.

In Figure 11.6(a) the $V_{GS} = 0$. In this situation electrons at the source cannot cross the gap to the drain, even as V_{DS} is increased. The drain current, I_D, remains zero, and the device is in *cutoff* mode. The circuit path from source to drain appear as "back-to-back" diodes, a circuit combination that will not pass current in either direction.

In Figure 11.6(b) we see the effect of increasing V_{GS} above a critical value known as the *threshold voltage,* V_T. If the gate is made sufficiently positive, then sufficient electrons are attracted to the silicon surface under the gate oxide to temporarily invert the surface from *p*-type to *n*-type. This inversion layer, or *n-channel,* between the source and drain allows electrons to flow through a single *n*-type region from source to drain and current flows. The current $I_D > 0$, and the device is conducting either in the *linear* or *saturation* mode, terms that will be defined in the next section.

Note that the gate is separated from the device by an insulator, and no dc current ever flows in the gate terminal.

The way in which I_D varies as V_{GS} and V_{DS} are varied is captured by the MOSFET's *output curves.* These are plots of I_D versus V_{DS}, for different values of V_{GS}. Output curves and the *modes* or *regions* of MOSFET operation are described in the next section.

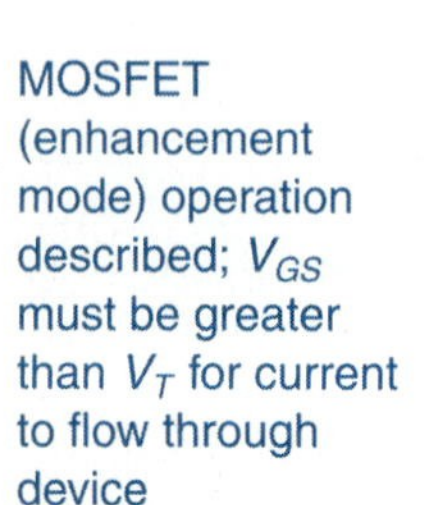
MOSFET (enhancement mode) operation described; V_{GS} must be greater than V_T for current to flow through device

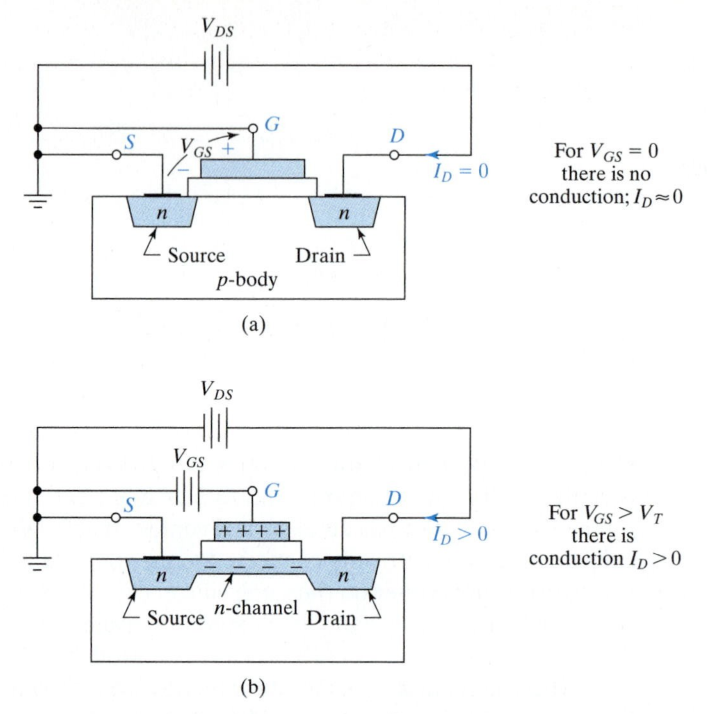

FIGURE 11.6 The operation of an *n*-channel MOSFET.

11–3 MOSFET Output Curves and Regions of Operation

Transistor output curves defined

The V-I curves of transistors are often displayed by a family of curves on a simple graph, referred to as the *output curves.* In general these curves plot the current through the device versus the voltage across the device for several values of the input value (voltage for FETs and current for BJTs).

Therefore, for an enhancement-mode MOSFET, the circuit used to test the device and construct the output curves appears in Figure 11.7. This is the same circuit as shown in Figure 11.6(b), except the transistor symbol is used in place of the cross-section drawing. One curve

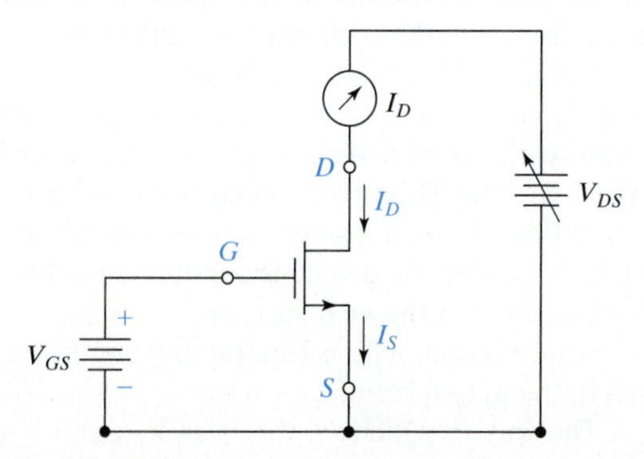

FIGURE 11.7 Circuit for generating output curves for *n*-channel enhancement-mode MOSFET.

in the family of output curves is generated by setting the value of V_{GS}, and sweeping V_{DS} from 0 to its maximum value while recording I_D. V_{GS} is changed to several other values to generate the set of curves.

Note that for a MOSFET, I_D always equals I_S, by Kirchhoff's current law, since the gate current is always zero.

11.3.1 Output Curves

The output curves for an *n*-channel enhancement-mode MOSFET are plots of drain current, I_D, as a function of drain-to-source voltage, V_{DS}, for several different values of V_{GS}. There are no curves for $|V_{GS}| < |V_T|$, because there is no current flow for that case, and thus the bottom curve occurs for $V_{GS} = V_T$, the threshold of conduction. Figure 11.8 shows an example of the output curves for such a device with a threshold voltage of 1 volt. In this figure, V_{GS} is increased in one-volt steps to form the family of curves.

Notice that as the magnitude of V_{DS} is increased, the current, I_D, levels off, and becomes nearly constant for a given V_{GS}. This is a result of the field increasing at the drain end of the channel and pinching off the current flow.

11.3.2 Regions of Operation

Regions of operation defined

Figure 11.8 clearly illustrates three important regions of operation for the MOSFET. They are:

1. The ohmic region, on the left where drain current, I_D, rises with increasing V_{DS}.
2. The active or saturation region where the drain current, I_D, remains almost constant with increasing V_{DS}.
3. The cutoff region, which lies along the horizontal axis. This is the region where the drain current is zero ($V_{GS} < V_T$).

The ohmic and saturation regions are separated by the locus of points where

$$V_{DS} = V_{GS} - V_T \tag{11.1}$$

Theoretical analysis of the MOSFET has provided expressions for the drain current, I_D. There is a different expression applicable for each region:

In the ohmic region, where $|V_{DS}| < |V_{GS} - V_T|$,

MOSFET output curves with three regions of operation illustrated: ohmic region, active region, and cutoff

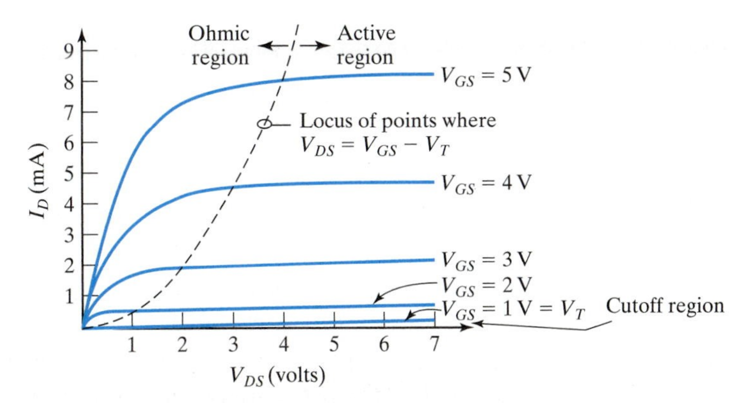

FIGURE 11.8 MOSFET output curves.

Equation for enhancement-mode MOSFET current in the ohmic region

$$I_D = K[2(V_{GS} - V_T)V_{DS} - V_{DS}^2] \quad (11.2)$$

In the saturation region, where $|V_{DS}| > |V_{GS} - V_T|$:

This equation provides the saturated current level, where the current curve is horizontal and independent of V_{DS},

Equation for enhancement-mode MOSFET current in the active (or saturation) region

$$I_D = K(V_{GS} - V_T)^2 \quad (11.3)$$

And in the cutoff region, where $|V_{GS}| < |V_T|$,

$$I_D = 0 \quad (11.4)$$

The constant, *K*, is a device parameter that is the product of two terms, one dependent on device processing and cross-section, and the other dependent only on device layout or topology and in particular the channel width-to-length ratio.

The parameter, K, can be easily measured experimentally.

Figure 11.9 shows a typical plot of drain current as a function of V_{GS}, for a given value of V_{DS}. Note that the onset of conduction occurs at $V_{GS} = V_T$, approximately 0.4 volts in this case. Typical modern enhancement-mode devices have threshold voltages in the range of 0.2 to 0.6 volts.

Example 11.1

Let us determine the value of the parameter *K* for the device characteristic plotted in Figure 11.9.

The parameter, *K*, can be easily determined from experimentally measured device curves such as that of Figure 11.9. For this device, the threshold voltage V_T, that is, the value of V_{GS} where current becomes nonzero, is 0.4 volts. In addition, note that at $V_{GS} = 0.6$ V, $I_D = 0.3$ mA. Therefore, evaluating *K* using this data point, we find that

$$K = \frac{I_D}{(V_{GS} - V_T)^2} = \frac{0.3 \text{ mA}}{(0.6 - 0.4)^2} = 7.5 \times 10^{-3} \text{ A/V}^2$$

Note that a more accurate determination of V_T can be obtained by plotting the square root of I_D versus V_{GS}. This plot is a straight line, and its intercept on the V_{GS} axis is V_T.

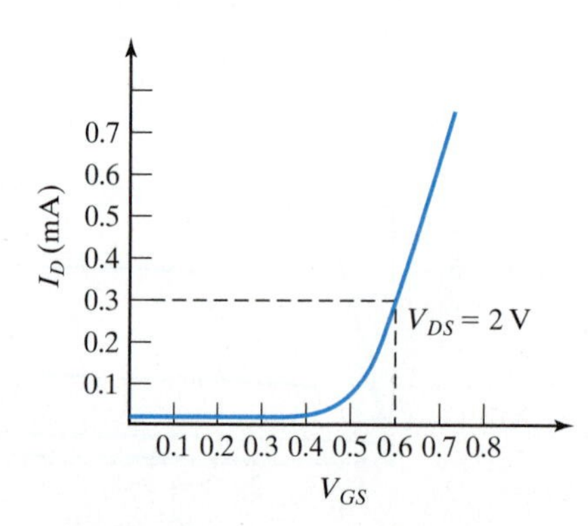

FIGURE 11.9 Drain current as a function of V_{GS} for *n*-channel device ($V_{DS} > V_{GS} - V_T$).

11-4 The NOT Gate: MOSFET Implementation

The inverter, sometimes called a NOT gate, defined

The inverter or NOT gate is a digital circuit that inverts the signal:

Low input → High output
High input → Low output

The circuit of Figure 11.10 uses an n-channel enhancement-mode MOSFET to create an inverter circuit. Let $V_{DD} = +5$ V (the power supply voltage) and $R_L = 5$ kΩ.

Assume that the transistor in Figure 11.10 is characterized by the output curves already presented in Figure 11.8. The circuit contains two linear circuit elements (the supply V_{DD} and the resistor R_L) and a nonlinear device (the transistor) with characteristics described by the output curves. We can analyze these types of problems graphically using the load-line technique described in Chapter 10, section 10.9. In this method the behavior of the linear elements is represented by a straight line (the load line) and superimposed on the nonlinear device characteristics. The point where the two curves intersect is the actual operating point, called the quiescent bias point, or Q-point.

To analyze this problem, we will overlay a load line on the output curves, as illustrated in Figure 11.11.

Recall that the load line is established by first assuming the nonlinear device is a short and computing one end-point of the line:

$$I_D\Big|_{V_{DS}=0} = \frac{V_{DD}}{R_L} = \frac{5}{1\text{ k}} = 5\text{ mA}$$

The other load line end-point is fixed by computing the voltage V_{DS} when the device is open, that is, $I_D = 0$.

$$V_{DS}\Big|_{I_D=0} = V_{DD} = 5\text{ V}$$

The load line is drawn superimposed on the transistor's output curves by connecting the two end-points.

As the input to the gate is increased to 5 volts, the Q-point (bias point) moves along the load line to the intersection of the $V_{GS} = 5$ V curve, labeled as point Q_A. At this point the output voltage, V_{DS}, reaches a lower limit of 0.8 volts. This point represents the logic "low" state.

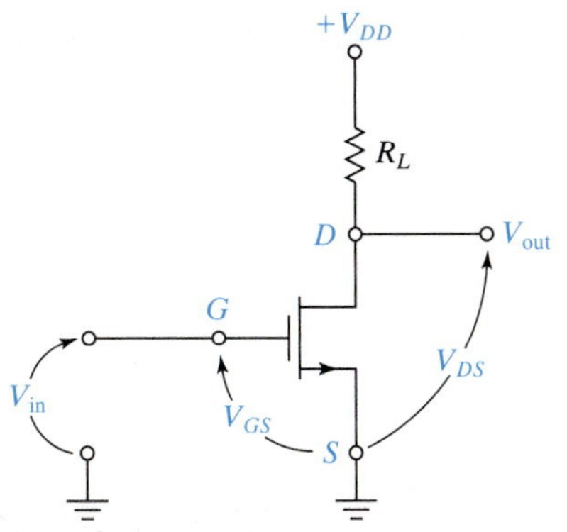

FIGURE 11.10 Inverter circuit using a MOSFET.

Using the load line technique to predict the high and low output voltage of the inverter circuit

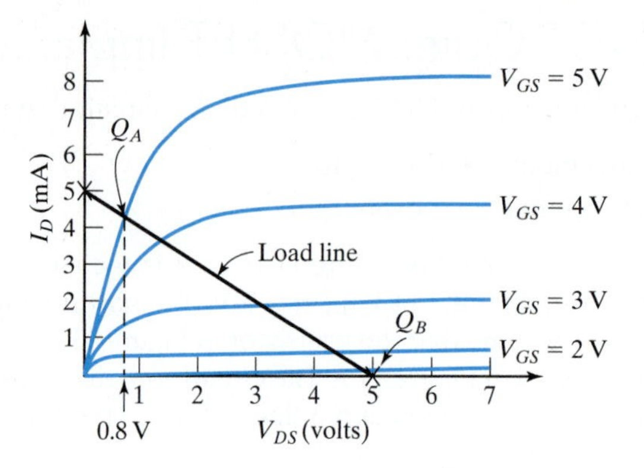

FIGURE 11.11 MOSFET output curves (from Figure 11.8) with load line for circuit in Figure 11.10.

The "logic high" state is determined by assuming the input to the gate is "low," that is, below the threshold voltage. At this input level, the transistor ceases to conduct moving the Q-point along the load line to the point Q_B on the V_{DS} axis where the output voltage is V_{DD}.

11.4.1 MOSFET Circuit Model for Switching

In digital applications, the n-channel, enhancement-mode MOSFET is in the nonconducting state when $V_{GS} \ll V_T$ and is switched to the conducting state when $V_{GS} \gg V_T$, and the Q-point is moved to the ohmic region.

In digital MOS circuits, the MOS transistor can be modeled as a device with a switch between source and drain, in series with an *on resistance,* r_{on}. The state of the switch is controlled by the magnitude of V_{GS}.

The symbol for the n-channel enhancement-mode MOS transistor is repeated in Figure 11.12(a) and its circuit model for digital switching is given in Figure 11.12(b), assuming it is biased in the ohmic region.

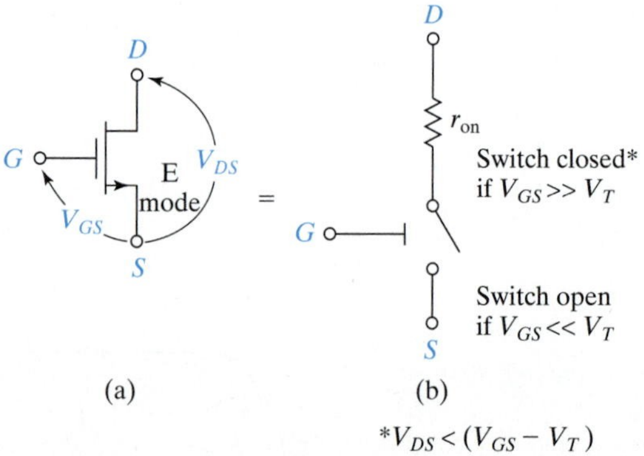

D, G, S, E mode, V_{DS}, V_{GS} = D, r_{on}, G, S

Switch closed* if $V_{GS} >> V_T$

Switch open if $V_{GS} << V_T$

(a) (b)

*$V_{DS} < (V_{GS} - V_T)$

FIGURE 11.12 Enhancement mode (E-mode) n-channel transistor switch model.

The *on resistance*, r_{on}, is the internal resistance of the "on" transistor conducting in the ohmic region. The *on resistance* is the inverse of the slope of the output curve at its Q-point at the left side.

An analytic expression for r_{on} can be obtained by first differentiating Eq. (11.2) to obtain g_{on}, the on conductance, that is,

$$g_{on} = \left.\frac{\partial I_D}{\partial V_{DS}}\right|_{V_{DS}=0} = K2(V_{GS} - V_T)$$

therefore,

r_{on} defined

$$r_{on} = \frac{1}{g_{on}} = \frac{1}{K2(V_{GS} - V_T)} \tag{11.5}$$

Substituting the transistor switch model in Figure 11.12 into the inverter (NOT gate) circuit of Figure 11.10 yields the circuits shown in Figure 11.13, (a) for input low and (b) for input high.

In Figure 11.13(a), when the input is low, $V_{in} \ll V_T$ and the transistor appears as an open switch. With zero current through the transistor, there is no current through R_L, and $V_{out} = +V_{DD}$.

For the case in which the input is high, as shown in Figure 11.13(b), the transistor is conducting with an internal resistance from source to drain of r_{on}, and V_{out} is given by

$$V_{out} = \left[\frac{r_{on}}{r_{on} + R_L}\right](+V_{DD}) \tag{11.6}$$

Using a switch model to predict the high and low output voltage of the inverter circuit

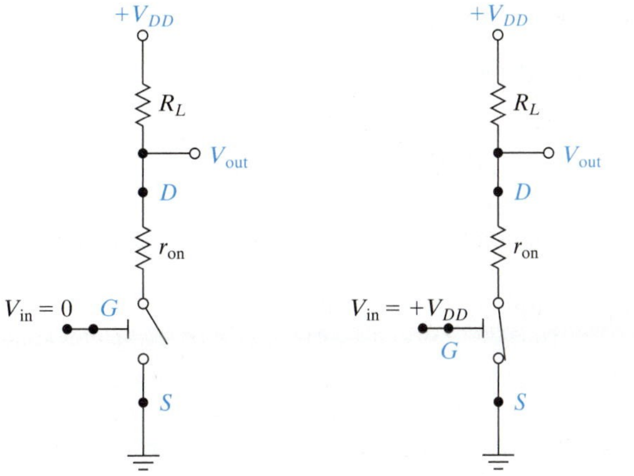

For $V_{in} = 0$,
$V_{in} = V_{GS} = 0$
$0 << V_T$
The switch is open
(a)

For $V_{in} = +V_{DD}$
$V_{in} = V_{GS} = V_{DD}$
$V_{DD} >> V_T$
The switch is closed*
(b)

*and $V_{DS} < V_{GS} - V_T$

FIGURE 11.13 MOSFET inverter (NOT gate) with transistor switch model.

Since the desired output is low, proper design requires that $r_{on} \ll R_L$. Furthermore, in order to ensure that this output low level is low enough to be interpreted by the next gate as a low,

$$V_{out} \ll V_T$$

and therefore,

$$\left[\frac{r_{on}}{r_{on} + R_L}\right] V_{DD} \ll V_T$$

Example 11.2

In an inverter circuit with $V_{DD} = 5$ V, an n-channel enhancement-mode transistor has the following parameters: $r_{on} = 100\ \Omega$, and $V_T = 1$ volt. Let us determine the value of R_L required to make V_{out} in the low state 10% of V_{DD}.

From Eq. (11.6)

$$(0.1)V_{DD} = V_{out} = \left[\frac{r_{on}}{r_{on} + R_L}\right] V_{DD}$$

Solving for R_L yields

$$R_L = 900\ \Omega$$

11–5 Other FET Types

11.5.1 The *p*-Channel MOSFET

The *p*-channel MOSFET described

The *p-channel MOSFET* is the exact complement of the n-channel device already described. The p-channel device is fabricated by placing two p-type regions for the source and drain into an n-type substrate or body.

Analogous to the n-channel device, forcing $V_{GS} = 0$ creates a device with a nonconducting channel; however, the conducting state in a p-channel device requires the application of a complementary set of voltages.

Therefore, the sign of V_{DS} and V_{GS} must be negative. In addition, the threshold voltage for an E-mode p-channel MOSFET is generally given as a negative value, for example, $V_T = -0.4$ V.

In order to induce a conducting p-type channel, the gate is made negative relative to the source to attract sufficient holes to invert the surface and create a p-type conducting channel as shown in Figure 11.14.

The symbols commonly used for the p-channel enhancement mode MOSFET are shown in Figure 11.15.

11.5.2 Depletion-Mode MOSFETS

Depletion-mode MOSFETS differ in structure in that a conducting channel region is deliberately created by doping the surface under the gate during device fabrication. With such a device, current can be made to flow between source and drain even with zero gate voltage ($V_{GS} = 0$).

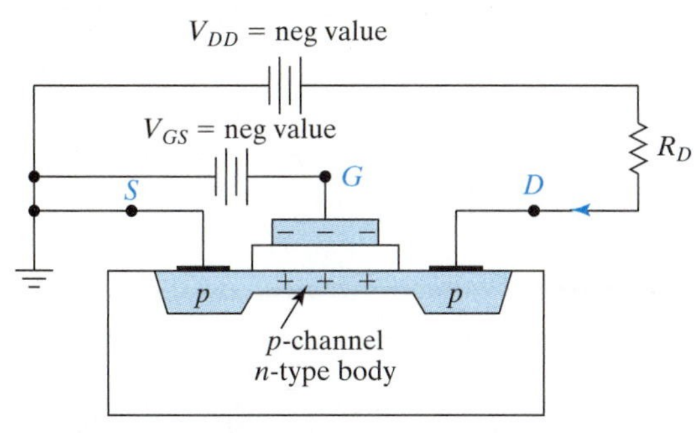

FIGURE 11.14 A *p*-channel MOSFET.

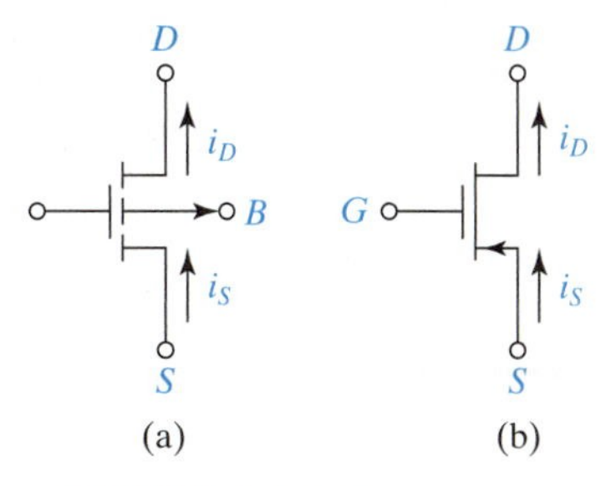

FIGURE 11.15 Schematic symbols for *p*-channel, enhancement-mode MOSFET.

The depletion-mode MOSFET conducts current even with $V_{GS} = 0$, and is characterized by a "pinch-off voltage," V_P

A set of typical output curves for an *n*-channel depletion-mode device is shown in Figure 11.16. Notice that there is significant current flow for $V_{GS} = 0$. This device can be operated in the depletion mode by making the gate region more negative, further depleting the channel of carriers and further reducing the level of current I_D. This action is illustrated in the figure for negative values of V_{GS}. The negative value of V_{GS} required to reduce I_D to zero is defined as the *pinch-off voltage,* V_p. This is analogous to a negative threshold voltage and is an indicator of a depletion-mode device. A plot of I_D versus V_{GS} for a fixed V_{DS} is shown in Figure 11.17.

The device can also be operated in the enhancement mode, where the application of a positive V_{GS} increases channel conduction, and I_D increases.

The schematic symbols commonly used for (a) *n*-channel and (b) *p*-channel, depletion-mode MOSFETs are illustrated in Figure 11.18.

11.5.3 The JFET-Junction Field Effect Transistor

The *Junction Field Effect Transistor* (JFET) is a depletion-mode FET, but with a different structure than that of the MOSFET. JFETs have been used primarily in special circuit applications, such as analog circuits, where very high input resistance is required.

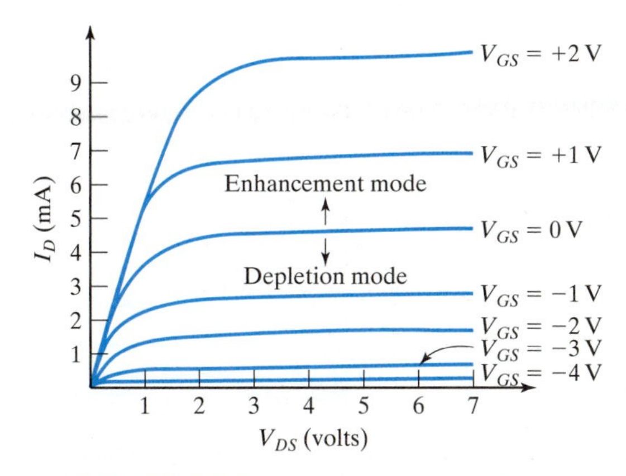

FIGURE 11.16 Output curves for a depletion-mode device.

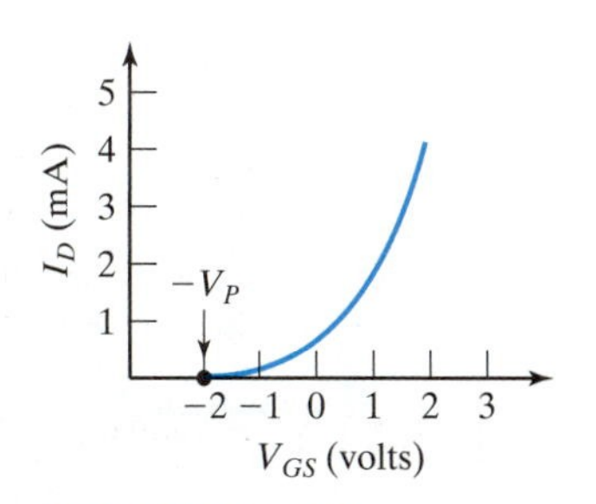

FIGURE 11.17 A plot of I_D-vs-V_{GS} for an *n*-channel depletion mode MOSFET.

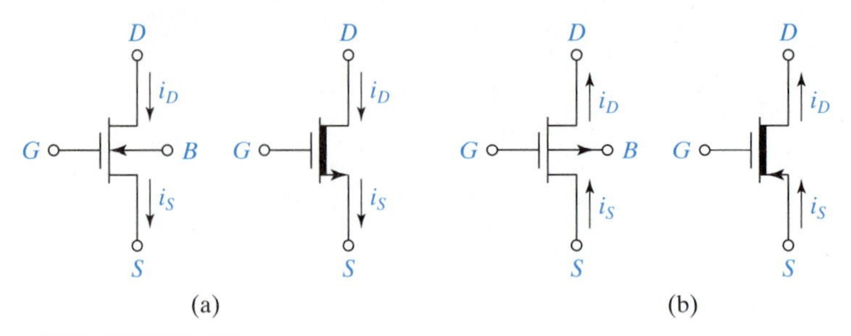

FIGURE 11.18 Schematic symbols commonly used for (a) n-channel and (b) p-channel, depletion-mode MOSFETs.

The cross-section of a typical JFET device appears as shown in Figure 11.19. The n-channel in this structure is fabricated in a "U" shape beneath the surface of the silicon. The channel is sandwiched between two p-type layers, and the top one is connected to the gate terminal. In some instances the top and bottom p-regions are connected to the gate terminal.

In the previous figure, if the gate is made more negative with respect to the source, the width of the depletion region grows and further blocks off a part of the conducting channel region. Therefore, current flow through the channel can be regulated by the magnitude of the applied voltage V_{GS}.

An example of a typical output curve for such a device is shown in Figure 11.20. The value of V_{GS} required to just reduce the curve to $I_D = 0$ is defined as the pinch-off voltage, V_P. In this example, $V_P = -4$ volts.

For an n-channel JFET, the drain is biased positive with respect to the source, as is done with an n-channel MOSFET. The symbol for such a JFET together with the bias voltages are shown in Figure 11.21.

The example just described is for an n-channel JFET; there is a complementary device, the p-channel JFET, which has the same structure with p and n regions and bias voltages reversed. A p-channel JFET has a positive pinch-off voltage. For JFETs and other depletion-mode devices, in the saturation region,

Equation for current of depletion-mode MOSFET or JFET in the active (or saturation) region

$$I_D = I_{DSS}\left(1 - \frac{V_{GS}}{V_P}\right)^2 \tag{11.7}$$

where I_{DSS} is the drain current when $V_{GS} = 0$.

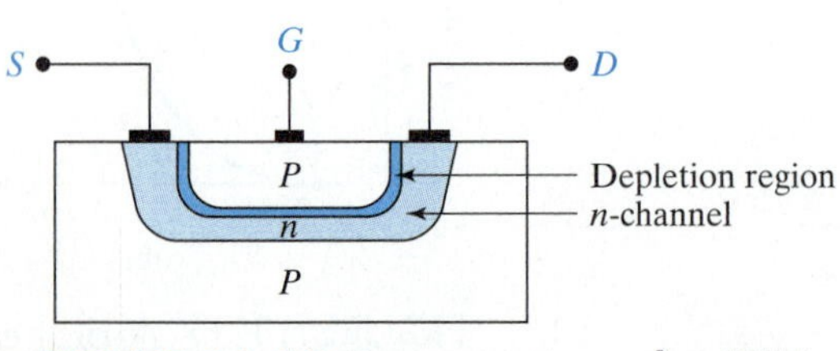

FIGURE 11.19 Cross-section of a JFET device.

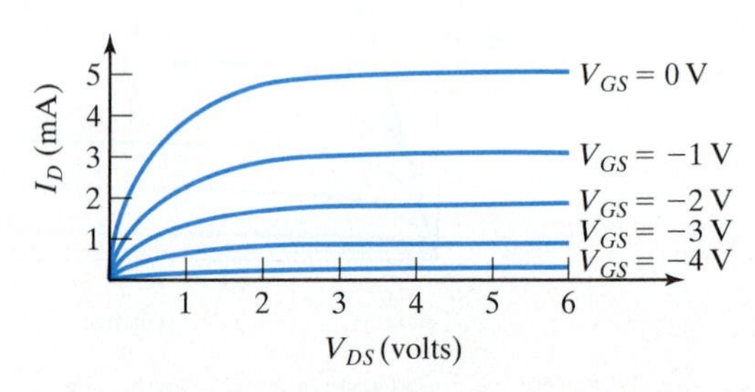

FIGURE 11.20 JFET output curves.

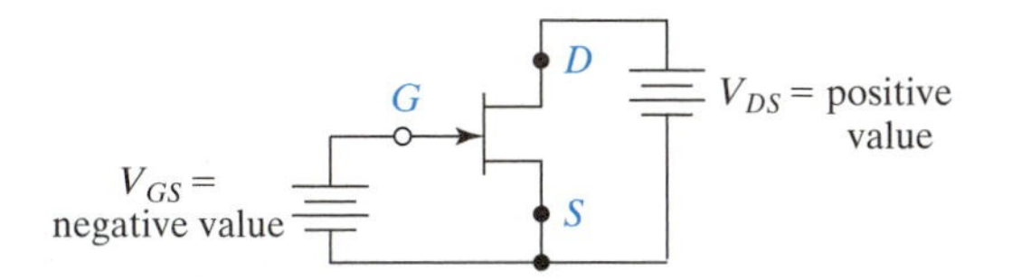

FIGURE 11.21 A typical JFET bias circuit.

11-6 Large-Signal Amplifiers: Using the MOSFET

Transistors are the devices that perform the amplification of electronic signals in most modern systems, and as such are critical elements in analog circuits. In this section we will explore how transistors are biased and how they can be used to make amplifiers and other circuits for processing analog signals.

11.6.1 DC Biasing

The first step in designing or analyzing any amplifier is to consider the biasing. The biasing network is comprised of the power supply and the passive circuit elements surrounding the transistor that provide the correct dc levels at the terminals. This is termed setting the Q-point or quiescent operating bias point, that is, the terminal voltages and currents with NO signal applied. Much of this chapter addresses methods for establishing proper dc bias.

A good bias circuit must not only establish the correct dc levels, but must maintain them even when confronted with sources of variation, such as changes in temperature, and spread in component values due to manufacturing inconsistency.

Consider a transistor with the output characteristics measured and plotted as shown in Figure 11.22. This device is an enhancement-mode MOSFET with a threshold voltage of 1.5 volts. The transistor's response is represented by a family of output curves. There are actually an infinite number of curves since V_{GS} can vary continuously—one for each possible value of V_{GS}. For convenience, we only plot a curve for incremental values of V_{GS}; however, one can interpolate curves between those plotted.

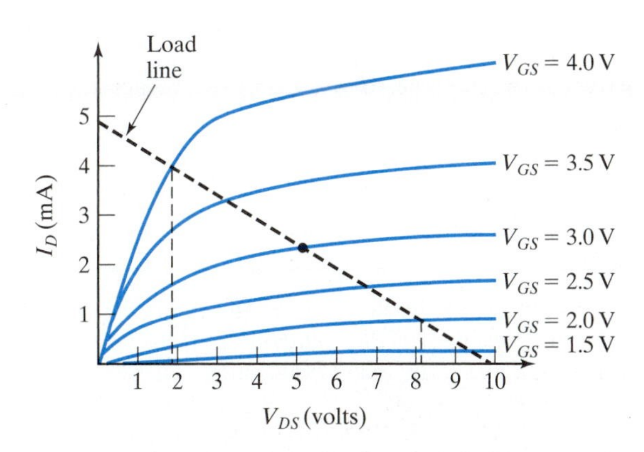

FIGURE 11.22 Enhancement-mode MOSFET transistor output characteristics.

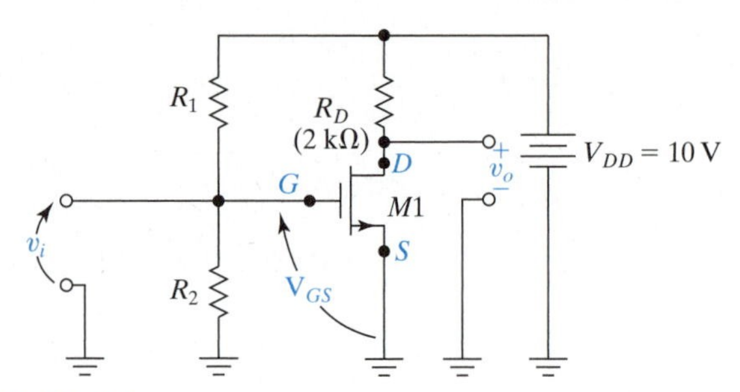

FIGURE 11.23 MOSFET in a common source bias circuit.

11.6.2 The Common Source Amplifier

Let us now place the transistor with characteristics shown in Figure 11.22 in a *common source bias circuit* as illustrated in Figure 11.23. Note that the total resistance in series with the transistor from source to drain is $R_D = 2\ \text{k}\Omega$. A dc load line is therefore established, which connects the following two points: $V_{DS} = 10$ V, which is the value of V_{DD} on the horizontal axis, and $I_D = 10\ \text{V}/2\ \text{k}\Omega = 5$ mA on the vertical axis. The load line is sketched on the output curves of Figure 11.22 as a dashed line.

This circuit is called a *fixed bias circuit* because the gate-to-source voltage is fixed by the resistor network consisting of R_1 and R_2. Since no dc current flows into the gate of a MOSFET,

$$V_{GS} = V_{DD}\left[\frac{R_2}{R_1 + R_2}\right] \tag{11.8}$$

A loop equation, including R_D and the transistor from drain to source, is

$$V_{DD} = I_D R_D + V_{DS} \tag{11.9}$$

Conditions for establishing the Q-point of a MOSFET amplifier

The use of the load line, which is a plot of R_D's characteristics, superimposed on the transistor's curves, can provide a graphical solution to Eq. (11.9). The solution satisfies the following conditions:

- In order to satisfy the load resistor's *V–I* characteristics, the bias point must fall somewhere on the load line.
- In order to satisfy the transistor requirements, the bias point must be located on an output curve corresponding to the appropriate value of V_{GS}.
- The intersection of the two curves provides the solution.

Example 11.3

Given the transistor network in Figure 11.23 and the transistor characteristics shown in Figure 11.22, let us determine (a) the value of V_{DS} if $V_{GS} = 2.0$ V, (b) the value of V_{DS} if $V_{GS} = 4.0$ V, (c) the best place to locate the *Q*-point, and (d) the values of R_1 and R_2 required for the *Q*-point selected.

(a) From Figure 11.22 a V_{GS} of 2.0 V yields a V_{DS} of 8.2 V.

(b) Figure 11.22 illustrates that a V_{GS} of 4.0 V yields a V_{DS} of 1.9 V. The results for (a) and (b) are obtained by locating the intersection of the appropriate output curve and the load line.

(c) Since this circuit is an amplifier, we would like for the output signal to swing equal voltage excursions on either side of the Q-point. We have tacitly assumed that our input signal will have equal positive and negative voltage swings. Therefore, placing the Q-point near the center of the range where the load line intersects the operating curves is generally best. For this example, let's place the Q-point at the point indicated, where $V_{GS} = 3.0$ V.

(d) Now, using Eq. (11.8), we can compute values for the resistor network, R_1 and R_2.

$$3.0 = \left[\frac{R_2}{R_1 + R_2}\right]10$$

If we choose one of the values, for example, $R_2 = 10\ \text{k}\Omega$, then solving for R_1 yields $R_1 = 23\ \text{k}\Omega$.

The operation of this circuit as a large-signal amplifier can be easily seen from Figure 11.24. The same output curves are reproduced with the $2\ \text{k}\Omega$ load line and the Q-point set at $V_{GS} = 3$ V. Observe what happens if the input voltage to the circuit, v_i, is changed: the voltage v_i, which is applied directly gate to source, that is, $v_i = V_{GS}$, is increased sinusoidally from 3 volts up to a peak of 4 volts and back to 3 volts again. The actual bias point moves up and down the load line following the movement of V_{GS}. In a similar manner, the output voltage of this circuit, v_o, which is the same as V_{DS}, moves from just over 5 volts down to 1.9 volts, and back up again. On the figure, we refer to the gate-to-source and drain-to-source voltages during these *swings* as v_{GS} and v_{DS}, respectively, indicating that the *total* instantaneous value is the dc bias plus the signal.

During the second half-cycle, the input change continues sinusoidally, symmetrically down to 2 volts and back up to 3 volts again, while the output voltage swings positively to a peak of 8.2 volts, and then returns to its quiescent value of just over 5 volts.

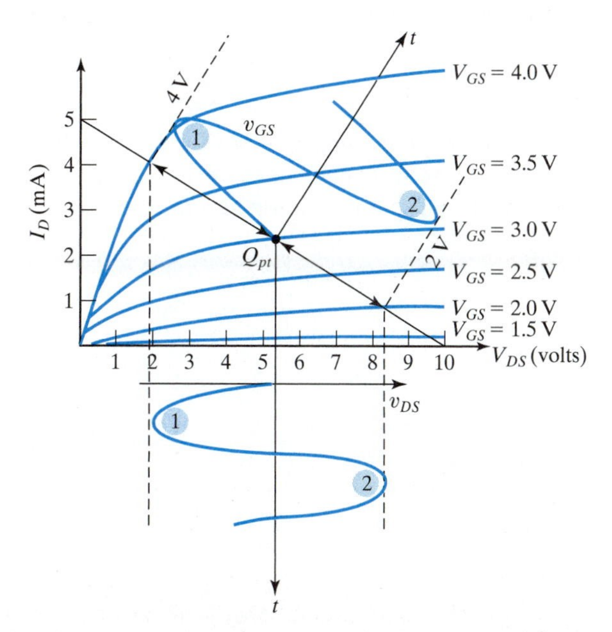

FIGURE 11.24 Large-signal common source amplifier operation.

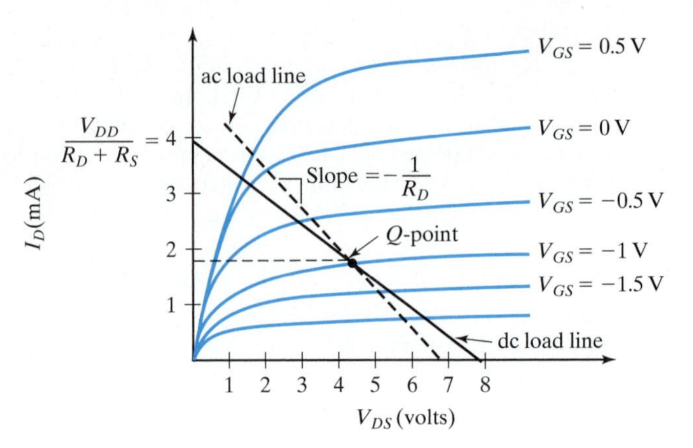

FIGURE 11.25 Output curves for depletion-mode MOSFET transistor.

Notice that this circuit provides signal gain. The input voltage changed 2 volts peak-to-peak, while the output of the circuit changed from a low of 1.9 volts to a high of 8.2 volts, or a difference of 6.3 volts peak-to-peak. Therefore, the *large-signal voltage gain* of the circuit is

$$A_v = \frac{\Delta v_o}{\Delta v_i} = \frac{-6.3}{2} = -3.15$$

The common source amplifier inverts the signal

The *negative sign* indicates that the amplifier inverts the signal so that an increase in v_i produces a decrease in v_o.

11.6.3 The Self-Bias Circuit

Another bias circuit configuration often used is called the *self-bias* circuit. This circuit is useful for devices that require a negative gate-to-source bias voltage, such as a depletion-mode *n*-channel device. The circuit achieves a negative gate-to-source voltage by raising the source voltage higher than that at the gate.

As an example, consider the MOSFET transistor with the output curves shown in Figure 11.25. The circuit in Figure 11.26 will self-bias this transistor.

First the Q-point will be placed on the $V_{GS} = -1$ V curve at its intersection with a 2 kΩ load line. The Q-point location and the dc load line are also shown in Figure 11.25.

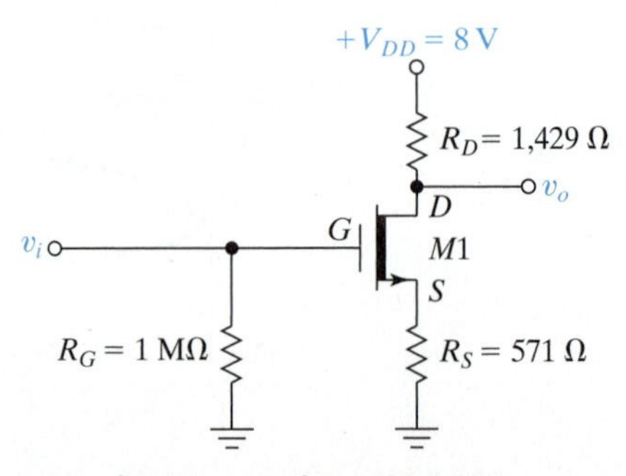

FIGURE 11.26 Depletion-mode MOSFET transistor amplifier using self-bias circuit.

The quiescent dc voltage on the gate of the device is zero, since there is no dc current flow through R_G. The voltage across R_S is given by the expression

$$V_S = I_D R_S$$

and thus

$$V_{GS} = -I_D R_S \tag{11.10}$$

Since the resistor R_S has been added in the drain-source current loop, the dc load line now has a slope of $-1/(R_D + R_S)$ and the loop equation becomes

$$V_{DD} = I_D(R_D + R_S) + V_{DS} \tag{11.11}$$

The desired Q-point is located at a quiescent drain current of 1.75 mA. Therefore, Eq. (11.10) yields

$$V_{GS} = -1 = -R_S(1.75 \times 10^{-3})$$

and hence

$$R_S = 571\ \Omega$$

To obtain the load line shown in the figure, we note that

$$R_D + R_S = 2\ \text{k}\Omega$$

and therefore,

$$R_D = 2\ \text{k} - 571 = 1429\ \Omega$$

Note that there is a potential problem with the circuit in Figure 11.26. The addition of R_S tends to lower the voltage gain of the circuit. The output voltage is the sum of V_{DS} and the voltage across R_S. As V_{DS} decreases and thus I_D increases, the voltage drop across R_S increases, thus canceling some of the output change.

This problem can be avoided by adding a *bypass capacitor* across R_S, as shown in Figure 11.27. Bypass capacitors are assumed to be large enough in value to have a very low reactance at the minimum signal frequency, and therefore are considered to be a short circuit to ac. The capacitor C_S effectively shorts R_S and, therefore, we can construct an *ac load line* that has a slope of $-1/R_D$, and passes through the Q-point. This ac load line is labeled as such in Figure 11.25. Furthermore, this new circuit has *coupling capacitors,* C_1 and C_2, which couple the ac signal in and out of the circuit but block the dc levels. Coupling capacitors also are cho-

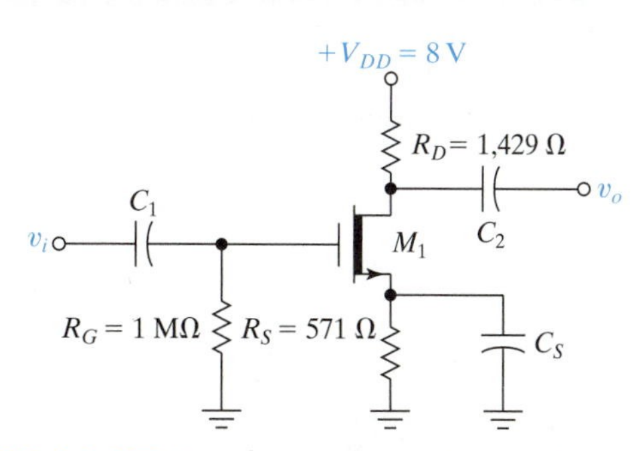

FIGURE 11.27 Transistor amplifier with a source bypass capacitor.

sen to act as ac shorts at the minimum signal frequency. The input signal, v_i, moves the bias point on the ac load line. The computed voltage gain is -1.8.

Summary of procedure for large-signal analysis of MOSFET circuits

Therefore, the procedure for large-signal analysis of MOSFET circuits can be summarized as follows.

1. Draw the dc load line on the output curves of the transistor. This load line intersects the voltage axis at V_{DD}, and intersects the current axis at V_{DD} divided by the total resistance in series with the S and D terminals of the transistor.
2. Locate the Q-point on this load line. This is done by calculating the gate-to-source voltage, V_{GS}, applied by the bias circuit. The Q-point is the intersection of the dc load line with the appropriate V_{GS} curve.
3. If there is a bypass capacitor in the circuit shunting an element in the S-D loop, then construct an ac load line. The ac load line passes through the Q-point and has a slope given by

$$slope = -\frac{1}{\textit{total resistance within S-D loop not shorted by C}}$$

   In most cases, this will be simply $-1/R_D$.

   If there are no bypass capacitors, then the ac load line is the same as the dc load line.
4. Calculate the large-signal voltage gain. This is done by first assuming reasonable variations in the input signal, that is, use variations in V_{GS} that fit the output curves. Now graphically determine the extent of the resulting output signal excursion, that is, maximum and minimum voltages, or deviations from the initial Q-point, as the bias point moves up and down the ac load line. The large-signal voltage gain is then

$$A_v = \frac{\Delta v_o}{\Delta v_i} \tag{11.12}$$

Note that in this section we used n-channel transistors. A p-channel transistor can be used in an analogous manner and the same analysis techniques applied. The only difference is the polarity of the required bias voltages.

11.6.4 Other FET Amplifier Configurations

Other amplifier configurations: common source, common gate, and common drain

There are three basic circuit configurations for FET amplifiers: common source (CS), common gate (CG), and common drain (CD).

The MOSFET circuits discussed in the previous section were configured so that the input signal was applied between the gate and source, and the output connected between drain and source. The source was the common terminal. These are all common source amplifiers. There are, however, two other possibilities: common gate and common drain. All three circuit configurations are illustrated in Figure 11.28.

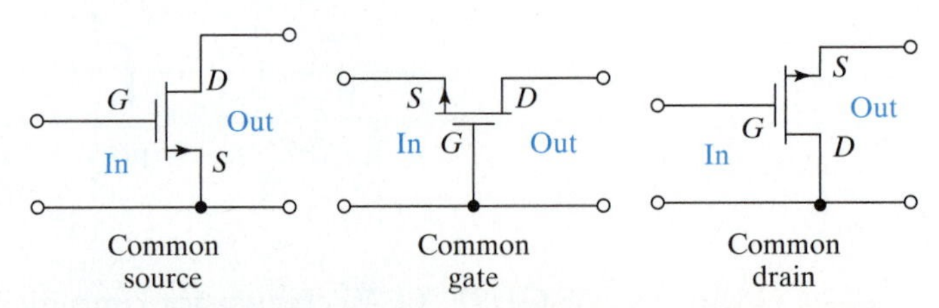

FIGURE 11.28 Transistor amplifier configurations.

The large-signal analysis of these two remaining circuit configurations follows the same procedure as that outlined for the common source configuration in the previous section.

All three amplifier configurations will be discussed in detail in Chapter 12.

11-7 BJT Fundamentals

The *bipolar junction transistor* (BJT) is the solid-state transistor that first revolutionized the field of electronics. Invented in 1947 at Bell Laboratories, its introduction into electronic systems in the late 1950s and early 1960s replaced the large, inefficient, and unreliable vacuum tube in almost every application.

11.7.1 BJT Structure

The structure of a bipolar transistor consists of essentially two *p–n* junction diodes fabricated very close to each other; in fact, they are so close together that they share a common region. Therefore, a bipolar transistor is a three-layer sandwich of alternating semiconductor material types. There are two possible variations, the *PNP transistor* and the *NPN transistor,* where these designations describe the order of the two types of materials in the device. The structure and the standard symbols for the BJT are shown in Figure 11.29. Basic principles will be illustrated using primarily the NPN transistor; the PNP transistor will be addressed by symmetry later.

The center region of the BJT is called the *base,* labeled (B), and in modern bipolar transistors it is fabricated as thin as possible. One of the end regions is called the *emitter* (E) and has the primary purpose of emitting carriers, which travel through the base and are collected at the opposite end of the transistor in the *collector* (C).

In modern silicon planar processing, the bipolar transistor is generally fabricated with the emitter on top of the collector with a thin base between, as illustrated in Figure 11.30 for

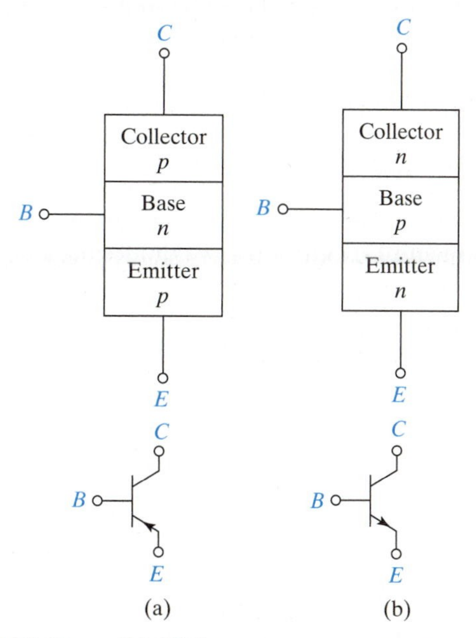

FIGURE 11.29 PNP and NPN transistors; structure and symbols.

Physical structure of BJT (bipolar junction transistor); there are two types, NPN and PNP

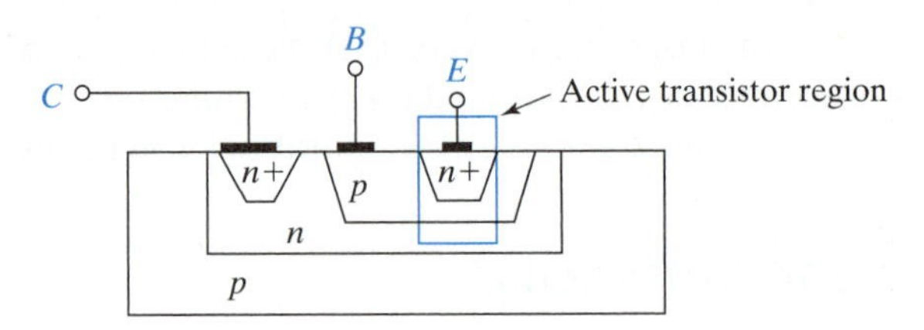

FIGURE 11.30 Cross-section of planar-processed bipolar transistor (BJT).

an NPN device. The primary carrier flow is downward from emitter to collector in the area labeled "active device." The lateral part of the structure serves only to make electrical connections from the surface to the layers in the vertical transistor structure.

11.7.2 BJT Modes of Operation: Saturation, Active, and Cutoff

Since the bipolar transistor has two junctions, and either junction can be forward or reverse biased, there are four possible bias conditions, as shown in Figure 11.31. The junction between emitter and base is commonly called the *emitter junction;* that between collector and base, the *collector junction.*

For the case in which both junctions are reverse biased, no terminal conducts any significant current, and the transistor is said to be in *cutoff* or "off." In this condition, the transistor appears as an *open switch.* When both junctions are forward biased, there is a direct *conducting path from collector to emitter,* and the transistor is said to be "on" or *saturated.* This condition corresponds to a *closed switch.* In contrast to FETs, it will be shown that a continuous supply of base current, I_B, is required to keep the switch closed.

These two bias conditions, shaded in Figure 11.31, are of primary importance for bipolar devices in digital circuits, because they represent the "on" and "off" states of the bipolar switch.

For the case in which the emitter junction is forward biased and the collector junction is reverse biased, the transistor is in the *active* region. This is the region of operation used for amplifiers, and is important in understanding how a BJT operates. Therefore, we will examine the active region first.

11.7.3 The BJT in the Active Region

Consider an NPN transistor. A circuit model of this device might first be imagined to appear as in Figure 11.32(a), with two diodes back to back. Since the collector junction is reverse bi-

BJT regions of operation defined

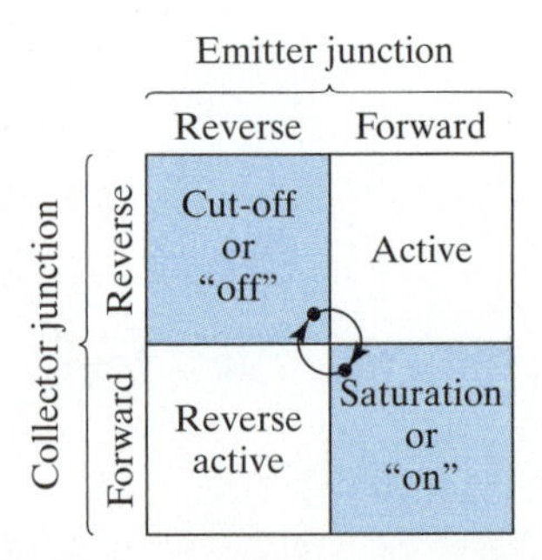

FIGURE 11.31 BJT bias conditions.

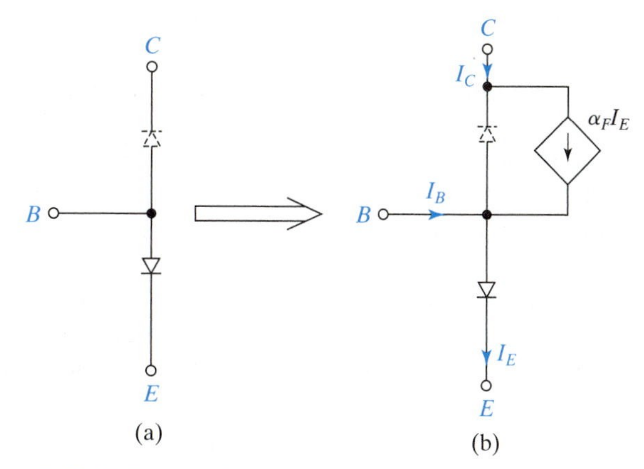

FIGURE 11.32 BJT model in active region.

ased in the active region, that diode is dashed, indicating it's not conducting. One might incorrectly predict that the only current flow is from base to emitter; however, this is an incomplete picture.

In addition to the separate action of the two diodes, the fact that they are extremely close together and separated by only a thin base region allows an interaction between the two diodes, which is the basis of transistor action.

In this active region the emitter junction is forward biased and electrons from the n-type emitter diffuse into the base. The base is made very thin, and few of the injected electrons recombine with holes in the base. Most of the carriers survive the trip by diffusion across the base and they are swept into the collector region by the field at the collector junction.

These carriers contribute to the collector current even though the collector junction is reverse biased. As illustrated in Figure 11.33, only a small portion of the injected electrons recombine and contribute to base current.

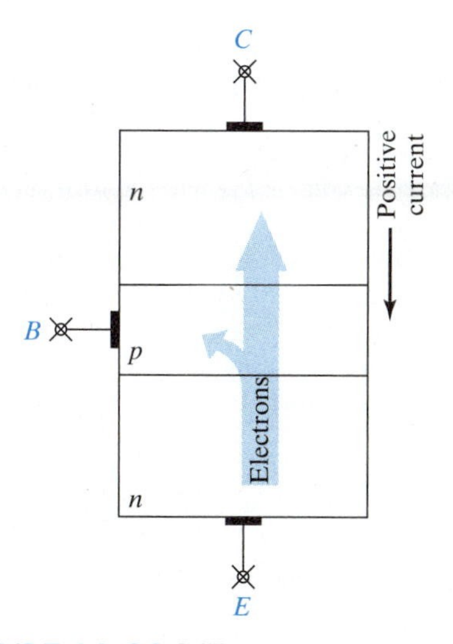

FIGURE 11.33 BJT carrier movement.

"Transistor action" explained

In an NPN device, the dominant component of current is the electrons moving from emitter to collector, which is equivalent to positive current moving from collector to emitter.

To model this new component of collector current we add to the circuit model of Figure 11.32(a) a dependent current source, as illustrated in Figure 11.32(b). The magnitude of this current source is some fraction, less than unity, of the emitter current, representing the portion of the carriers that make it across the base. This source is defined as α_F times the emitter current, I_E. The *forward alpha,* α_F, is an important parameter of the transistor; it can be measured for a given device as the ratio of the collector current to emitter current for an emitter junction that is forward biased, and a collector junction that is not. Generally, $V_{CB} = 0$ for this measurement. The term α_F is sometimes called the *forward common base (CB) current transfer ratio.* It is always less than unity and has a typical value in the range of 0.97 to 0.995.

$$\alpha_F = \left.\frac{I_C}{I_E}\right|_{\text{active region}} \tag{11.13}$$

This phenomenon of *transistor action* is very important. Under the bias conditions just described, the current at the collector terminal of the BJT is independent of the applied collector voltage, and depends only upon the injected emitter current, which is set by the current through the emitter *p–n* junction.

In order to forward bias the emitter junction, the voltage applied must be equal to the turn-on voltage of the junction diode, V_F. For the base emitter junction of a silicon transistor, we often assume that this value of $V_{BE} = V_F = 0.7$ V.

The application of Kirchhoff's current law to the three terminals of a transistor yields an important equation:

$$I_E = I_B + I_C \tag{11.14}$$

where the current directions are referenced as in Figure 11.32(b).

Example 11.4

Consider the NPN transistor and bias circuit shown in Figure 11.34(a). If this transistor has $\alpha_F = 0.99$, the emitter junction forward biased at $V_{BE} \approx 0.7$ V, and $I_E = 2$ mA, let us determine (a) the collector current, (b) the collector voltage, and (c) the base current.

The emitter voltage $V_E = 0$, since this terminal is grounded.

The base voltage V_B is at the turn-on voltage of the emitter junction, which is approximately 0.7 volts in this case. The emitter junction is forward biased. A voltage source is connected directly from collector to ground, setting the collector voltage, V_C, equal to 2 volts. Since $V_C = 2$ V and $V_B \approx 0.7$ V, the collector junction is clearly reverse biased by 1.3 volts. The transistor is in the active bias condition.

Therefore, replacing the transistor symbol with the equivalent circuit for the transistor in the active region, as shown in Figure 11.34(b), yields the following.

(a) The collector current $I_C = \alpha_F I_E$ is

$$I_C = (.99)(2 \times 10^{-3}) = 1.98 \text{ mA}$$

(b) The collector voltage = 2 V

and

(c) The base current $I_B = I_E - I_C$ is

$$I_B = 2 \times 10^{-3} - 1.98 \times 10^{-3} = 0.02 \text{ mA}$$

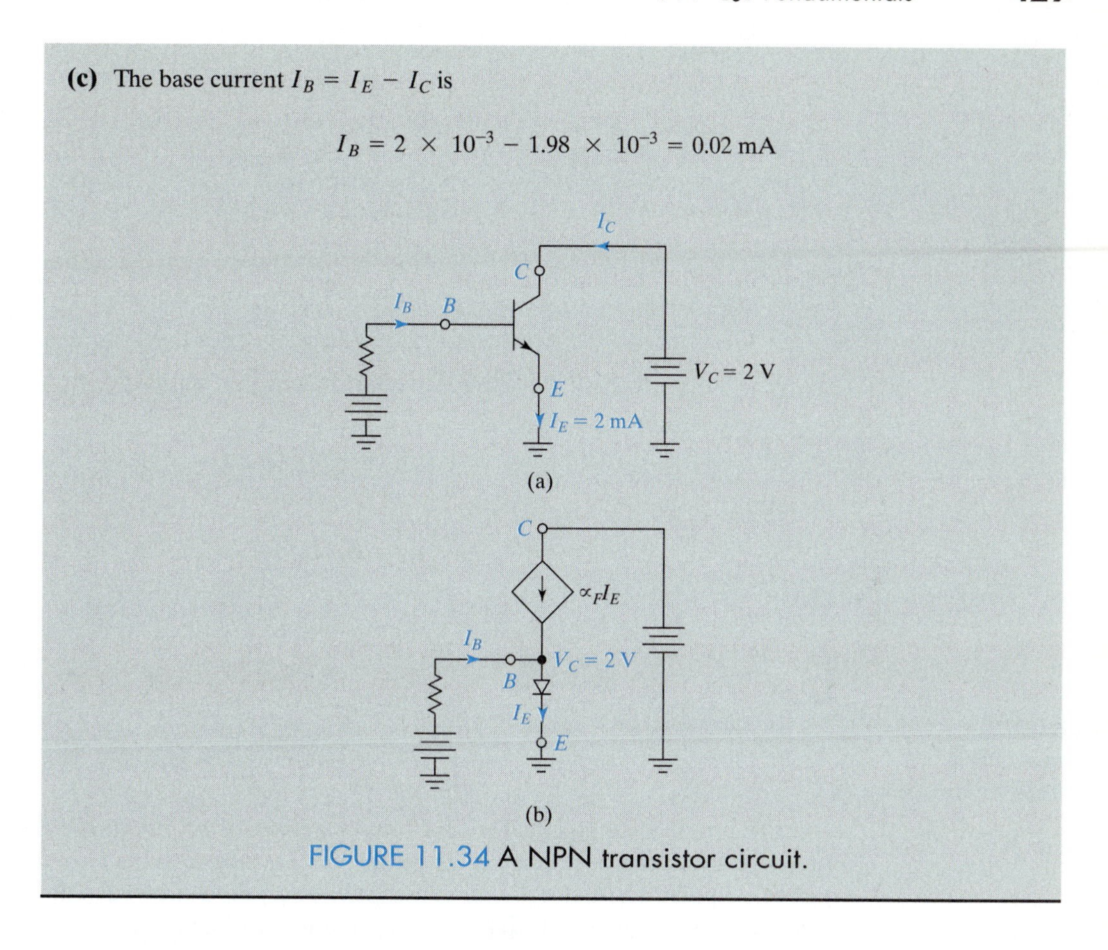

FIGURE 11.34 A NPN transistor circuit.

11.7.4 The Common Emitter (CE) Configuration

Most applications make use of the bipolar transistor in the common emitter configuration. This is the circuit configuration with the emitter grounded, the input or control signal applied to the device at the base, and the output taken from the collector, as illustrated in Figure 11.35.

For this case it is convenient to develop an equivalent circuit that represents the output current, I_C, in terms of I_B rather than I_E. Recall that for the active bias region:

C
Out
I_C
B I_B
In
I_E
E

FIGURE 11.35 BJT common emitter configuration.

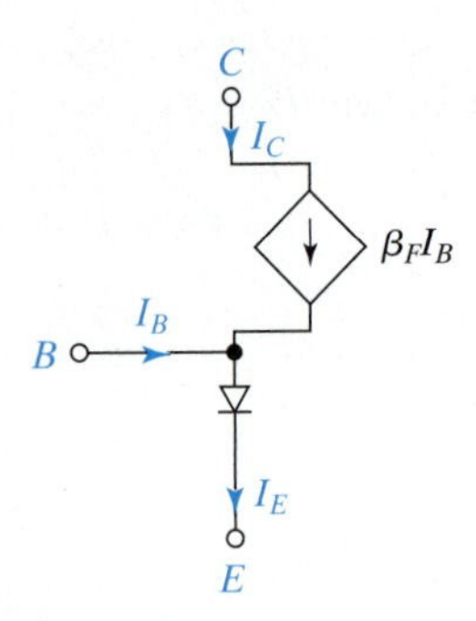

FIGURE 11.36 BJT common emitter equivalent circuit.

$$I_C = \alpha_F I_E \tag{11.15}$$

therefore,

$$I_C = \alpha_F (I_B + I_C) \tag{11.16}$$

and

$$I_C(1 - \alpha_F) = \alpha_F I_B \tag{11.17}$$

hence

Important relationship between α_F and β_F

$$\left.\frac{I_C}{I_B}\right|_{\text{active region}} = \frac{\alpha_F}{1 - \alpha_F} = \beta_F \tag{11.18}$$

The parameter, β_F, the *forward common emitter current transfer ratio,* is defined as the ratio of collector to base current for active bias. This forward beta is one of the key parameters of a bipolar transistor. A common emitter equivalent circuit can now be developed analogous to that of Figure 11.32(b), and is presented in Figure 11.36. It can be seen from this model that for the active bias region:

$$I_C = \beta_F I_B \tag{11.19}$$

Drill Exercise

D11.1. Determine the value of β_F for the transistor in Example 11.4.

Ans: $\beta_F = 99$

11.7.5 The PNP Transistor

The PNP transistor is the complement of the NPN transistor. It operates in a completely analogous manner, but rather with the *p*-type emitter providing holes, which traverse the base, and are collected by the *p*-type collector. To forward bias the emitter junction, the base must be made about 0.7 volts more *negative* than the emitter. Normally the collector is connected through a load resistance to the terminal of a dc voltage source more negative than the voltage at the emitter.

Considering equally sized devices, an NPN transistor generally outperforms the PNP device because the primary carriers in an NPN transistor, electrons, have a mobility higher than that of holes. Consequently, most bipolar circuits utilize NPN devices; however, some integrated circuits utilize both NPN and PNP devices in the same circuit.

11-8 BJT Output Curves

The output curves for a bipolar junction transistor (BJT) is a family of curves that display the voltage–current relationships for the device over a wide range. (Output curves for the MOSFET were presented in section 11.3.)

The test circuit used to measure a BJT's characteristics and plot the output curves is shown in Figure 11.37. One curve in the family of curves is generated by setting the value if I_B, and sweeping V_{CE} from 0 to its maximum value while recording the value of I_C. I_B is then changed to several other values to generate the set of curves.

The output curves for a BJT in the common emitter configuration is a plot of I_C versus V_{CE}, for a set of different values of I_B. An example of such a set of curves is shown in Figure 11.38.

Notice that in the active region the collector current is almost constant for a given I_B value; the ratio of I_C/I_B is β_F, which is about 100 for this example. There is generally a small but finite slope to the output curves, which will be discussed in Chapter 12.

The active region occupies the majority of the central portion of the output curves, and is the region in which we bias a transistor as an amplifier.

As the saturation region on the left side of the plot is approached, the value of I_C falls for a given I_B value, indicating a β_F^*, or forward *forced beta,* of less than β_F.

In the saturation region the collector junction is forward biased (in addition to the emitter junction, which is already forward biased). With both junctions forward biased the transistor's behavior in a circuit will resemble that of a closed switch.

Note: The choice of the word "saturation" for the ohmic region on the left of the BJT curve is unfortunate because the active region for FET curves (where the curves are horizontal) is sometimes called the FET "saturation region"; this is the opposite of a BJT. There is no connection in the meaning of "saturation" for the two cases, so one must be careful and keep it straight.

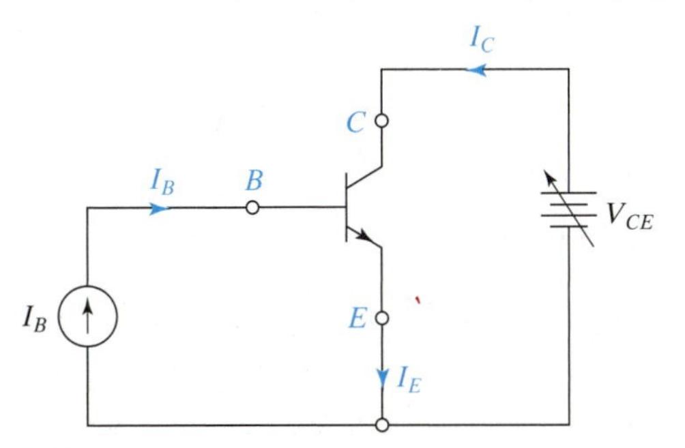

FIGURE 11.37 Circuit for generating output curves for NPN bipolar transistor.

BJT output curves with three regions of operation illustrated: saturation region, active region, and cutoff. (Note: In the MOSFET, saturation and active regions are the same. With the BJT the saturation region is analogous with the ohmic region in a MOSFET.)

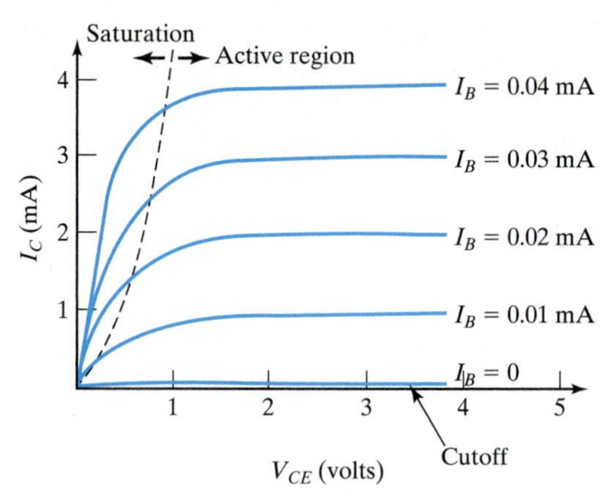

FIGURE 11.38 Output curves for a BJT.

The cutoff region is along the horizontal axis for $I_B = 0$. In this latter region, the collector current is essentially zero.

In the cutoff region the transistor is not conducting and can be modeled as an open switch. We will develop models for the saturation and cutoff regions in the next section. These are the regions of importance for digital circuits.

The load line approach for analysis can be used for BJTs in a similar manner to that already demonstrated for other devices, as illustrated in the following example.

Example 11.5

The circuit shown in Figure 11.39 has a transistor with the output characteristics of Figure 11.38.

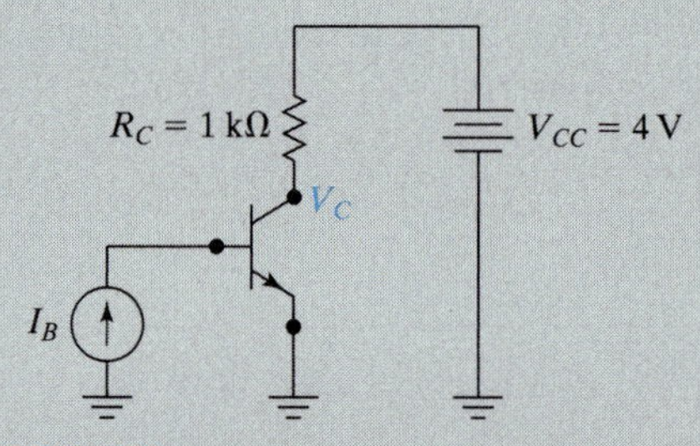

FIGURE 11.39 Circuit used in Example 11.5.

Figure 11.40 shows the output curves with the load line for this circuit superimposed. The horizontal axis intercept occurs at the voltage across the device when $I_C = 0$; this is the open circuit voltage of 4 volts. The intercept on the vertical axis is the short-circuit current, the current through the device if the device acts as a perfect short; this is determined by the circuit as

$$I_{C(MAX)} = \frac{V_{CC}}{R_C} = \frac{4}{1\ \text{k}} = 4\ \text{mA}$$

Now, with the load line constructed, let us determine (a) the value of I_B required to drive the transistor into saturation, and (b) the value of V_C when $I_B = 0.02$ mA.

(a) From the load line, $I_B \approx 0.03$ mA is required to move the Q-point along the load line into the saturation region on the far left.

(b) The load line intercepts the $I_B = 0.02$ mA curve at $V_C = 2$ V.

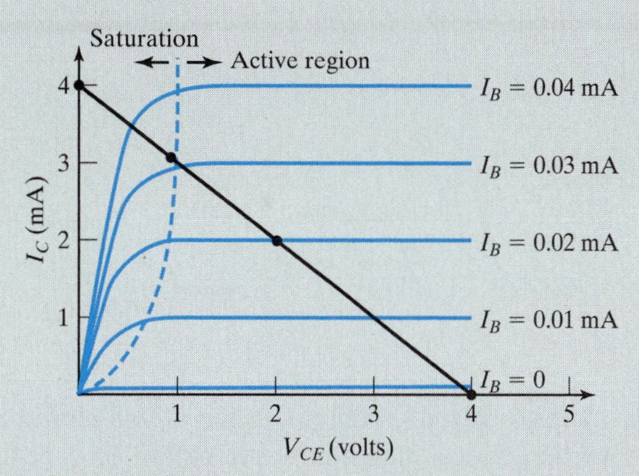

FIGURE 11.40 Transistor characteristics used in Example 11.5.

11-9 The NOT Gate: BJT Implementation

The inverter or NOT gate was described in section 11.4 using a MOSFET. In this section we will illustrate the implementation of this digital circuit with an NPN BJT. Recall the NOT gate inverts the signal, creating a high at the output if the input is low, and vice versa.

For digital applications, typically a BJT's operation alternates between saturation and cutoff. It will be useful to have a better understanding of transistor operation in these regions, and develop circuit models appropriate for each. Therefore, before describing the NOT gate, we will consider appropriate circuit models for the BJT specifically in these bias regions that occur the extreme ends of the load line. We will then apply these models to the NOT gate circuit.

11.9.1 BJT Circuit Models for Switching

The conditions for biasing an NPN transistor in cutoff (open switch) and saturation (closed switch) will now be described, and a circuit model for each of these situations presented.

The Open Switch: BJT in Cutoff. If the emitter junction and the collector junction of a BJT are *not* forward biased, the base current is approximately zero. Under this condition, there is no collector current. The transistor's equivalent circuit is simply an open circuit between collector and emitter, analogous to an open switch as shown in Figure 11.41(a).

The Closed Switch: BJT in Saturation. The conditions required to establish a BJT in saturation are more complex than other bias conditions in that both device junctions must be

"Cut-off"
Make $I_B = 0 \Longrightarrow$ other terminal currents ≈ 0
Both junctions reverse biased

FIGURE 11.41(a) BJT in cutoff.

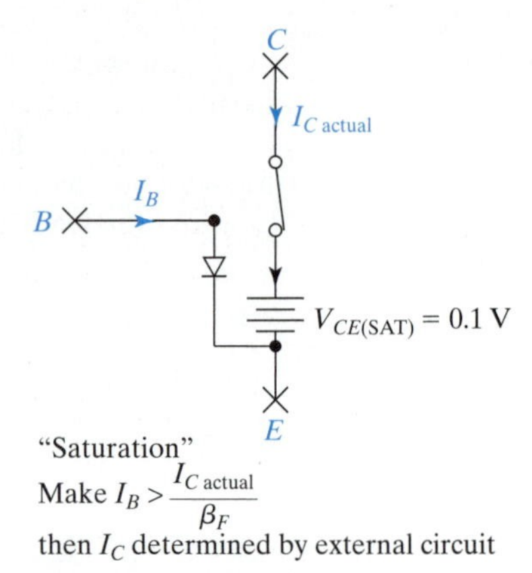

FIGURE 11.41(b) BJT in saturation.

forward biased. Maintaining the switch closed requires a constant base current exceeding a certain critical minimum value, called $I_{B(SAT)}$; the value of $I_{B(SAT)}$ depends on parameters of the transistor and the circuit in which the transistor is connected.

The BJT switch model

In saturation, the collector current of the BJT becomes limited by the circuit in which the device is connected in the same manner as the current through a real switch is controlled by the external circuit. If insufficient base current is provided, the device moves out of saturation and into the active region where the collector current is β_F times the supplied base current.

The critical minimum base current, $I_{B(SAT)}$, is:

$$I_{B(SAT)} = \frac{I_{C\ actual}}{\beta_F} \tag{11.20}$$

where $I_{C\ actual}$ is the collector current that would flow if the transistor were saturated (closed switch) and is determined primarily by the external circuit and bias voltages. To ensure saturation, the circuit should supply a base current larger than $I_{B(SAT)}$, that is, $I_B > I_{B(SAT)}$.

The ratio of the actual I_C to the actual I_B for a transistor in saturation is defined as the normal forced beta, β_F^*.

$$\beta_F^* = \frac{I_{C\ actual}}{I_{B\ actual}} \tag{11.21}$$

where

$$\beta_F^* < \beta_F, \qquad \textit{for saturated BJT}$$

A BJT in saturation appears to the circuit as a closed switch in series with a small voltage source, typically less than 0.1 volts, called $V_{CE(SAT)}$. For purposes of the present discussion, we will assume $V_{CE(SAT)} = 0.1$ V.

A circuit model of the BJT in saturation is presented in Figure 11.41(b).

Example 11.6

A BJT is used in the circuit in Figure 11.42 to switch a small light bulb on and off. The bulb has a resistance of 1 kΩ and will be modeled as a 1 kΩ resistor. Assuming the transistor has a $B_F = 50$, and the turn-on voltage of the emitter junction is 0.7 volts, let us determine the circuit's response to base currents of 0, 40, 100, and 200 μA.

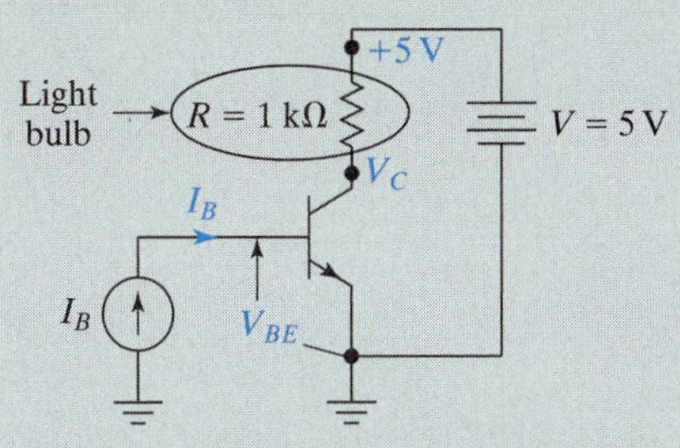

FIGURE 11.42 Circuit used in Example 11.6.

To illustrate this circuit's behavior, the circuit voltages, V_C and V_R, are plotted in Figure 11.43, for $0 \leq I_B \leq 200$ μA.

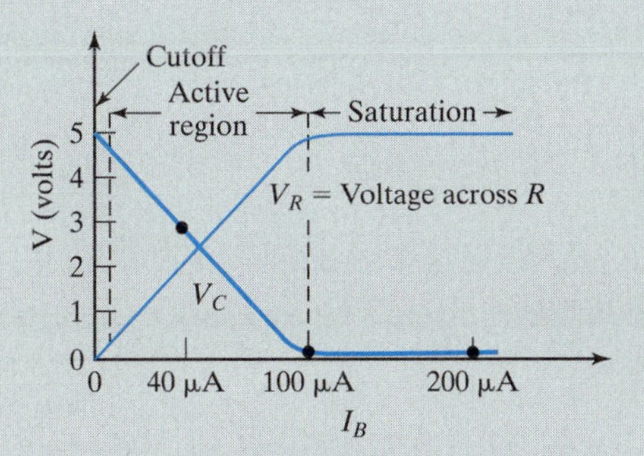

FIGURE 11.43 Characteristics of the BJT circuit used in Example 11.6.

For: $I_B = 0$, $I_C = 0$, and there is no current through the resistor *R;* therefore, $V_C = 5$ V; since $I_C = 0$, the voltage across *R* is zero, and the transistor is in cutoff.

For: $I_B = 40$ μA

$$I_C = \beta_F(40\ \mu\text{A}) = 50(40\ \mu\text{A}) = 2\ \text{mA}$$

$$V_C = 5 - I_C R = 5 - (2\ \text{mA})(1\ \text{k}) = 3\ \text{V}$$

At this point, the voltage across *R* is $5 - V_C = 5 - 3 = 2$ V.
The collector junction is still reverse biased.

$$V_{CB} = V_C - V_B = 3 - 0.7 = 2.3\ \text{V}$$

and the transistor is in the active region.

For: $I_B = 100$ μA

$$I_C = \beta_F I_B = 50(100\ \mu\text{A}) = 5\ \text{mA}$$

$$V_C = 5 - I_C R = 5 - (5\ \text{mA})1\ \text{k} = 5 - 5 = 0$$

$$V_{CB} = V_C - V_B = 0 - 0.7 = -0.7\ \text{V}$$

The collector junction has just reached forward bias and the transistor is at the edge of saturation. The bulb, *R*, has the full 5 volts across it.

$I_{C(actual)} = I_{C(max)}$ and occurs when the transistor is a short; therefore,

$$I_{C\ actual} = I_{C\ max} = \frac{5}{1\ \text{k}} = 5\ \text{mA}$$

and

$$I_{B(SAT)} = \frac{I_{C\ actual}}{\beta_F} = \frac{5 \times 10^{-3}}{50} = 100\ \mu A$$

That is, 100 μA is the value of I_B required to place the device at the edge of saturation.

For $I_B = 200\ \mu\text{A}$: This base current will drive the transistor deeper into saturation. I_C cannot exceed 5 mA, since this current is determined by the circuit when the transistor acts as a closed switch.

Therefore, $I_C = 5\ \text{mA}$, $I_B = 200\ \mu\text{A}$, and

Calculation of BJT forced beta, $\beta_F{}^*$

$$\beta_F^* = \text{forced } \beta = \frac{I_{C\ actual}}{I_{B\ actual}} = \frac{5 \times 10^{-3}}{200 \times 10^{-6}} = 25$$

The *forced beta* β_F^* is always less than β_F for a BJT in saturation. The ratio

$$0 < \frac{\beta_F^*}{\beta_F} < 1$$

is an indicator of how deeply the device is driven into saturation. In this example, the ratio of forced beta to beta is 25/50 = 0.5.

11.9.2 The NOT Gate Circuit

For the circuit shown in Figure 11.44, we assume the transistor has the following parameters: $\beta_F = 75$ and $V_{BE} = 0.7$ V.

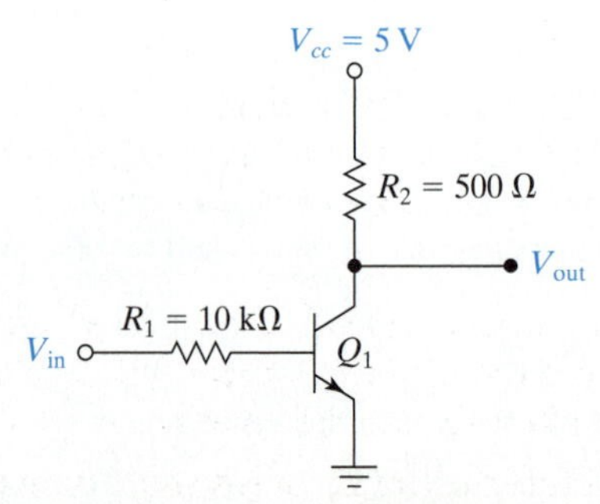

FIGURE 11.44 NOT gate implemented with a BJT.

When $V_{in} < 0.7$ V, that is, an input "low" level, the emitter junction is not forward biased; $I_B = 0$, $I_C \approx 0$, and the transistor is in cutoff. Since $I_C \approx 0$, $V_C = V_{CC} = 5$ V, the output is at a "high" level. See the circuit model in Figure 11.41(a)

When $V_{in} = 5$ V, an input "high" level

$$I_B = \frac{V_{in} - V_{BE}}{R_1} = \frac{5 - 0.7}{10\text{ k}} = 0.43\text{ mA}$$

and using the circuit model in Figure 11.41(b),

$$I_{C(actual)} = \frac{V_{CC} - V_{CE(SAT)}}{R_2} = \frac{5 - 0.1}{500} = 9.8\text{ mA}$$

We assume $V_{CE(SAT)} = 0.1$ V unless information is given to determine it more accurately.

Therefore,

$$\beta_F^* = \frac{I_{C\,actual}}{I_{B\,actual}} = \frac{9.8 \times 10^{-3}}{0.43 \times 10^{-3}} = 23$$

$$\beta_F^* \ll \beta_F;$$

and

$$\frac{\beta_F^*}{\beta_F} = \frac{23}{75} = 0.3$$

This indicates a transistor in saturation since the base current supplied by the circuit is well in excess of that required to saturate the transistor. A good design rule of thumb is $\beta_F^*/\beta_F < 0.7$ to ensure saturation with margin. Therefore, for this circuit, $V_{out} = V_{CE(SAT)} \approx 0.1$ volt, a low level.

This circuit operates as an inverter or NOT gate with logic levels switching between 0.1 volt and 5 volts.

A transistor in saturation has a lot of charge stored in its base region. The NOT gate circuit in Figure 11.44 could be improved by adding an additional resistor from the base of the BJT to ground. During the transition from "on" to "off" this would provide a path for the stored base charge to exit the device and speed up the process.

11-10 Large-Signal Amplifiers: Using the BJT

As was described in, section 11.8, the output curves of the common emitter (CE) bipolar junction transistor are very useful in predicting the large-signal behavior of such devices in circuits. The analysis of BJT circuits follows a similar procedure to that illustrated earlier in this chapter for MOSFETs. The analysis techniques will be illustrated with examples.

In order to construct dc load lines for BJT circuits, we proceed in a manner that is analogous to that previously described for MOSFETs. Reference to Figures 11.38 to 11.40 may be useful.

1. Imagine the transistor is an open circuit such that $I_C = 0$. Then determine the voltage across the device. Generally, this voltage will be the supply voltage. This voltage is the intercept on the V_{CE} axis.
2. Imagine the transistor is a short from C to E such that $V_{CE} = 0$. Then determine the current through the short. Generally, this current will be the supply voltage divided by the

total resistance in series with the collector emitter loop. This is the current value, which is the intercept on the I_C axis.

3. Connect the two intercepts with a straight line to form the dc load line. This approach is viable for any circuit configuration.

11.10.1 The Common Emitter Amplifier

Large-signal analysis of common emitter amplifier

Consider the following example for a *common emitter amplifier.*

Example 11.7

An NPN transistor has the output characteristics shown in Figure 11.45. This device is placed in the common emitter circuit in Figure 11.46.

The output curves do not provide information about the input characteristics of a device; however, for a BJT in the active region we can generally make a simplifying assumption. The input is applied across the base emitter junction, and in the active region this junction is forward biased. For silicon devices, the dc voltage across the base emitter junction is approximated by the condition

$$V_{BE} = \text{turn-on voltage} = 0.7 \text{ volts}$$

The dc load line has been drawn on the BJT output curves, with an intercept on the V_{CE} axis at 5 volts, and an intercept on the current axis at $V_{CC}/R_C = 5$ mA.

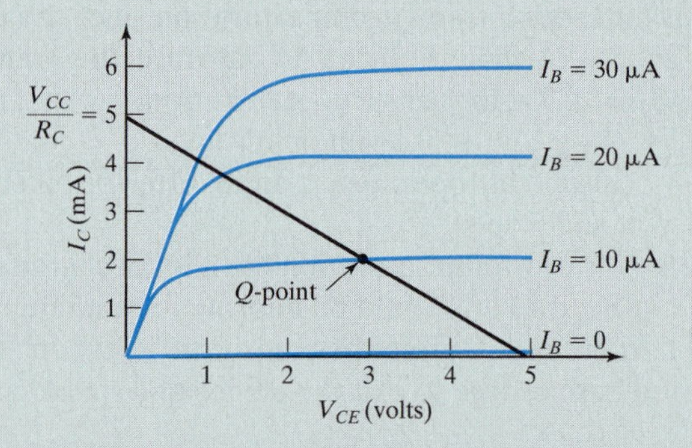

FIGURE 11.45 NPN transistor common emitter output characteristics.

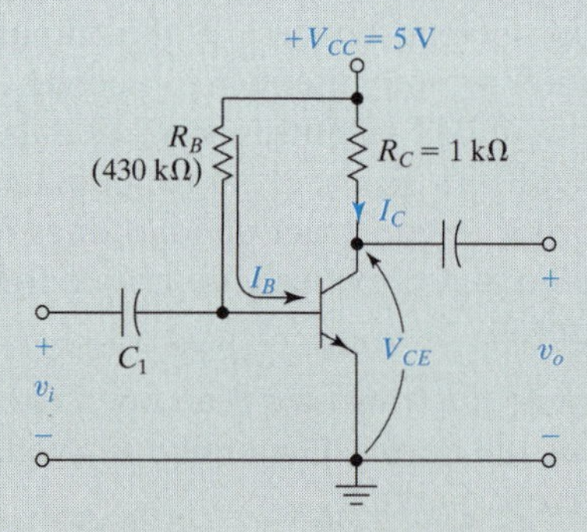

FIGURE 11.46 A common emitter NPN BJT amplifier circuit.

We can determine the location of the Q-point by a simple calculation of the base current. The dc base current for this device, I_B, flows from V_{CC} through R_B and into the base of the device. Since $V_B = V_{BE} = 0.7$ V,

$$I_B = \frac{V_{CC} - V_{BE}}{R_B} = \frac{5 - 0.7}{430\text{ k}} = 10\ \mu\text{A}$$

Therefore, the Q-point lies on the intersection of the dc load line and the $I_B = 10\ \mu$A output curve. From the curve, all the dc bias conditions are now known, that is, $V_{CE} = 3$ volts and $I_C = 2$ mA.

In amplifiers, the BJTs are always biased in the forward active region in which the collector junction is reverse biased. For this case, it is common convention to refer to just β for β_F. Therefore, $\beta \equiv \beta_F$.

Example 11.8

Let us determine the beta (β) of the transistor in Example 11.7. The beta at the Q-point is defined as the ratio of collector current to emitter current, that is,

$$\beta = \frac{I_C}{I_B} \text{ at the } Q\text{-point; } V_{CE} = \text{constant}$$

$$\beta = \frac{2 \times 10^{-3}}{10 \times 10^{-6}} = 200$$

The spacing between the output curves for a given family of I_B's indicates the beta. The beta in real transistors has some bias current dependence; however, for convenience in calculations, beta is often assumed to be a constant for a given transistor. It is often measured at $V_{CB} = 0$.

We can make the following additional observations about the above example:

1. As a large-signal amplifier, the output voltage can swing positively all the way up to 5 volts when $I_B = 0$, and down to about 1 volt with a base drive current of 30 μA.
2. Note that both the output voltage and the current I_C change approximately linearly with changes in the input CURRENT, I_B. However, the input is applied across the emitter base p–n junction and recall that I_B increases exponentially as V_B increases. In addition, the voltage V_B changes directly with v_i since coupling capacitor C_1 acts as an ac short. Therefore, as a large-signal VOLTAGE amplifier, this circuit would be highly nonlinear.
3. Bipolar transistors manufactured on the same line can have relatively large variations in beta from one batch to another, sometimes as much as 50% to 100%. Imagine the problem of trying to manufacture the circuit of Example 11.7 if the transistors varied in beta from 100 to 400. The circuit provides a specific base current, 10 μA; however,

   if $\beta = 100$, $I_C = 100\ (10\ \mu\text{A}) = 1$ mA, and

   if $\beta = 400$, $I_C = 400\ (10\ \mu\text{A}) = 4$ mA

   With this circuit the Q-point is very sensitive to the value of β and in this example, β variations can move the Q-point from near cutoff to near saturation. This is unacceptable for a circuit intended to be manufactured in quantity.

4. *Thermal runaway* could affect this circuit. Thermal runaway is a catastrophic cycle that can ultimately destroy a transistor. The power dissipated in a device during operation increases the device's temperature. This temperature increase can cause an increase in base leakage current, which gets multiplied by β and appears as a larger increase in collector current. The increased current, in turn, increases the power dissipated in the device and increases the heating, and the cycle continues, increasing the temperature further. If left unchecked, the device can self-destruct.

In summary, the bias circuit of Figure 11.46 is simple, but has many limitations.

11.10.2 The BJT Self-Bias Circuit

BJT self-bias circuit, a very important bias circuit

The use of a bias circuit, which is designed to stabilize the collector current instead of the base current, will solve the problems outlined above. The *BJT self-bias circuit* of Figure 11.47 greatly reduces the effects of β variations and temperature on the quiescent operating point. In this circuit, the collector current is determined by the voltage across a resistor, R_E, which is placed in series with the emitter.

To analyze this circuit, first consider the voltage divider, R_1 and R_2. Its purpose is to establish a known dc voltage, V_B, at the base of the transistor. For simplicity, we will now assume that the value of $(R_1 + R_2)$ is small enough that the current down through the divider is much greater than I_B. That is,

$$\frac{V_{CC}}{R_1 + R_2} \gg I_B \tag{11.22}$$

This condition ensures that changes in I_B will not significantly change the value of V_B, and, therefore,

$$V_B = V_{CC}\frac{R_2}{R_1 + R_2} \tag{11.23}$$

In addition, note that

$$V_B = V_{BE} + I_E R_E \tag{11.24}$$

Equations (11.22–11.24) provide a simple solution to many problems using the self-bias circuit.

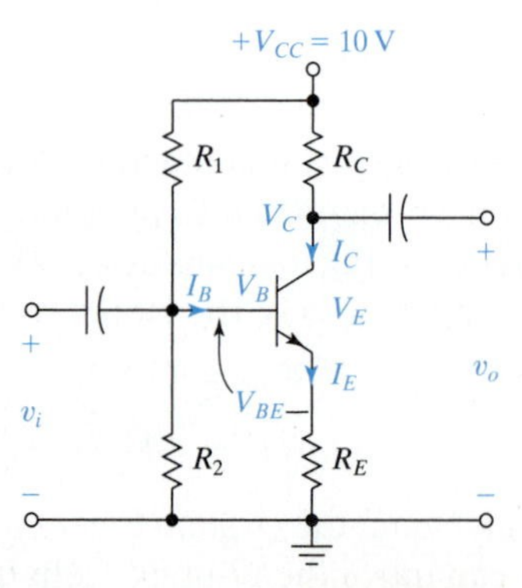

FIGURE 11.47 A BJT self-bias circuit.

Example 11.9

Consider the circuit in Figure 11.47. We wish to find the value of I_E assuming the following component values:

$$R_1 = 3\ \text{k}\Omega \qquad R_C = 4\ \text{k}\Omega$$
$$R_2 = 1\ \text{k}\Omega \qquad R_E = 1.5\ \text{k}\Omega$$

First, let us consider the voltage divider circuit comprised of R_1 and R_2. Using Eq. (11.23),

$$V_B = V_{CC}\frac{R_2}{R_1 + R_2} = 10\frac{1\ \text{k}}{1\ \text{k} + 3\ \text{k}} = 2.5\ \text{volts}$$

Then from Eq. (11.24) we find that

$$V_B = 2.5 = V_{BE} + I_E\,(1.5\ \text{k})$$

The value of V_{BE} for a BJT in the active region is assumed to be the junction turn-on voltage, $V_{BE} = 0.7$ volts. Therefore,

$$I_E = \frac{2.5 - 0.7}{1.5\ \text{k}} = 1.2\ \text{mA}$$

Note that the value of β never entered this calculation; this is because the assumption expressed in Eq. (11.22) indicates that I_B does not affect the value of V_B. Let's now arbitrarily assume a β value of 100 and check to see if this assumption was justified.

The current through the voltage divider is approximately

$$I_{R1} = I_{R2} = \frac{V_{CC}}{R_1 + R_2} = \frac{10}{1\ \text{k} + 3\ \text{k}} = 2.5\ \text{mA}$$

And the base current is approximately

$$I_B = \frac{I_E}{\beta + 1} = \frac{1.2 \times 10^{-3}}{101} = 0.012\ \text{mA}$$

Therefore, the original assumption, expressed in Eq. (11.22), is a justifiable one.

11.10.3 BJT Self-Bias Circuit—Complete Analysis

If the assumption made in Eq. (11.22) is not valid, then the calculations become more cumbersome, but not difficult. First, consider the voltage divider consisting of R_1 and R_2, as shown in Figure 11.48(a). A Thevenin equivalent for this circuit is shown in Figure 11.48(b). The expressions for the Thevenin equivalent voltage and resistance are

$$V_{BT} = V_{CC}\frac{R_2}{R_1 + R_2} \tag{11.25}$$

$$R_{BT} = R_1 || R_2 = \frac{R_1 R_2}{R_1 + R_2} \tag{11.26}$$

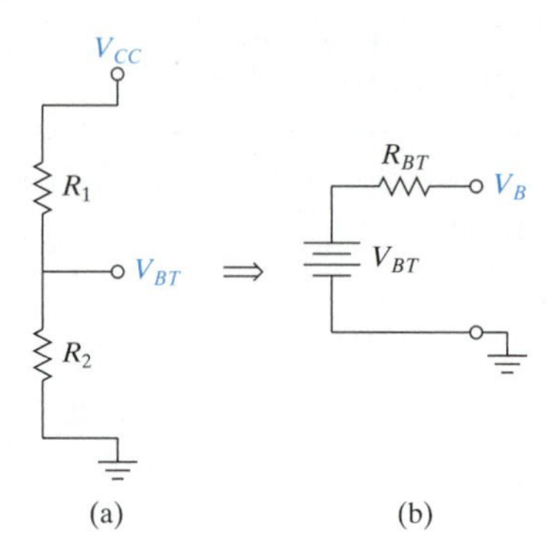

FIGURE 11.48 Base bias circuit and its Thevenin equivalent.

Using the Thevenin equivalent circuit in Figure 11.48(b), the bias circuit in Figure 11.47 can be redrawn as shown in Figure 15.18. The loop equation around the base emitter loop is

$$V_{BT} - I_B R_{BT} - V_{BE} - I_E R_E = 0 \tag{11.27}$$

The equation for I_B is

$$I_B = \frac{I_E}{\beta + 1} \tag{11.28}$$

and combining Eqs. (11.27) and (11.28) produces one equation with one unknown. This approach can be used to determine the bias conditions for any BJT self-bias circuit.

Example 11.10

Consider the self-bias circuit in Figure 11.47. The transistor has a $\beta = 25$ and the resistors have the following values:

$$R_1 = 45\ \text{k}\Omega \qquad R_C = 3\ \text{k}\Omega$$
$$R_2 = 30\ \text{k}\Omega \qquad R_E = 2\ \text{k}\Omega$$

Let us determine both I_C and V_C.

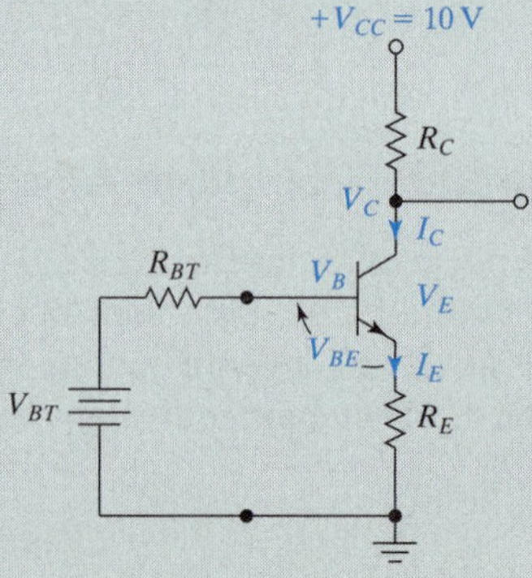

FIGURE 11.49 An equivalent circuit for the network in Figure 11.47.

Since the condition of Eq. (11.22) may not be met, we will perform the analysis by developing a Thevenin equivalent of the input circuit. This approach is always valid.

From Eqs. (11.25) and (11.26), we find that

$$V_{BT} = V_{CC}\frac{R_2}{R_1 + R_2} = 10\left[\frac{30\text{ k}}{30\text{ k} + 45\text{ k}}\right] = 4\text{ V}$$

and

$$R_{BT} = \frac{(30\text{ k})(45\text{ k})}{30\text{ k} + 45\text{ k}} = 18\text{ k}\Omega$$

The KVL equation around the base emitter loop is

$$V_{BT} - \frac{I_E}{\beta + 1}R_{BT} - V_{BE} - R_E I_E = 0$$

Using a value of $V_{BE} = 0.7$ V and solving for I_E yields the value

$$I_E = 1.23\text{ mA}$$

Knowing I_E, we can now compute I_C as

$$I_C = \frac{\beta}{\beta + 1}I_E = \left[\frac{25}{26}\right]1.23 \times 10^{-3} = 1.18\text{ mA}$$

and then

$$V_C = V_{CC} - I_C R_C = 10 - (1.18 \times 10^{-3})(3\text{ k}) = 6.46\text{ V}$$

Example 11.11

Consider the circuit shown in Figure 11.50(a). The transistor in this network is a PNP device described by the output curves shown in Figure 11.50(b).

Illustration of dc and ac load lines

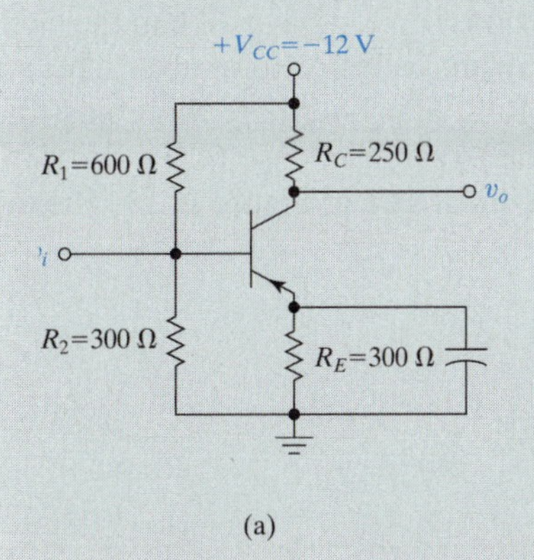

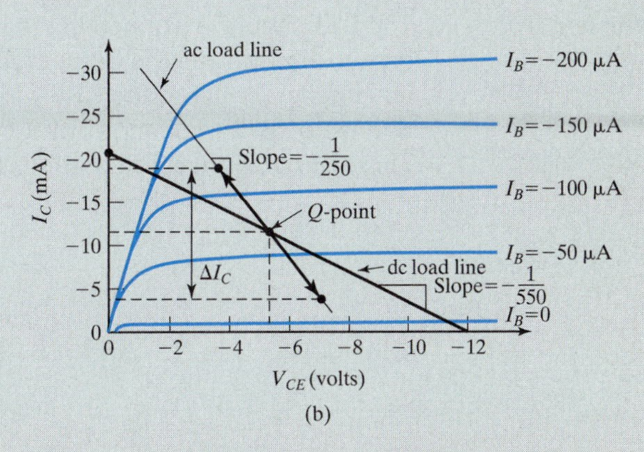

FIGURE 11.50 (a) A PNP common emitter transistor amplifier circuit. (b) Output curves and load lines for the transistor in the network in Figure 11.50(a).

Let us identify the Q-point, construct both the dc and the ac load lines on the output curves, and determine the current gain.

The dc load line is constructed as shown. The reader can verify that the condition of Eq. (11.22) is satisfied and, therefore, V_B can be determined by Eq. (11.23) as $V_B = -4$ volts; therefore, $V_E = -4 - (-0.7) = -3.3$ volts and

$$I_E = \frac{-3.3}{300} = -11 \text{ mA} \approx I_C$$

Interpolating, one can judge that the value of I_B at the Q-point is approximately $-75\ \mu$A; having located the Q-point, the ac load line with the slope shown in the figure is constructed.

The large-signal current gain of this circuit can be determined by

$$A_i = \frac{\Delta I_{out}}{\Delta I_{in}} = \frac{\Delta I_C}{\Delta I_B}$$

If we assume the input signal changes the base current $\pm$ 50 μA, the bias point moves up and down the ac load line to the extremes shown in Figure 11.50(b). The corresponding total change in output current is determined from the plot as

$$\Delta I_C = (18 - 4) \times 10^{-3} = 14 \text{ mA}$$

Therefore,

$$A_i = \frac{14 \times 10^{-3}}{100 \times 10^{-6}} = 140$$

The voltage gain calculation for BJTs requires the input resistance of the device in order to determine input current changes from input voltage changes. For this reason, a detailed discussion of ac voltage gain for BJT circuits will be deferred until Chapter 12.

11.10.4 Other BJT Amplifier Configurations

Other amplifier configurations: common emitter, common base, and common collector

The BJT circuits examined in the previous section have all had the signal input applied from base to emitter, and the output taken from collector to emitter. These are all common emitter circuits. Similar to the case with MOSFETs, there are three possible bias circuit configurations for BJTs: common emitter (CE), common base (CB), and common collector (CC). These three circuit configurations are illustrated in Figure 11.51. The methods for calculating

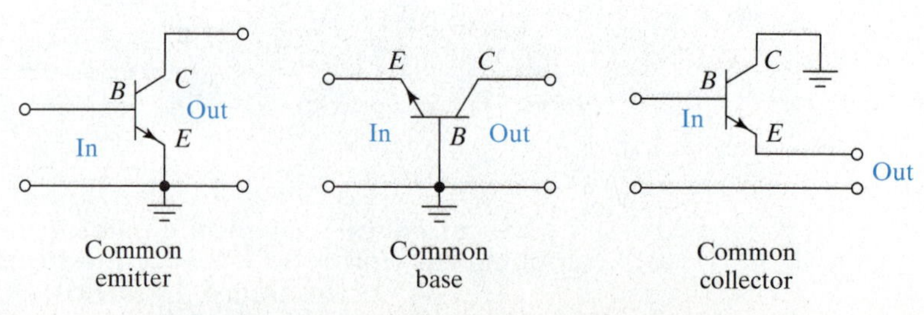

FIGURE 11.51 BJT circuit configurations.

dc bias for the other configurations follow the same principles as those outlined for the common emitter.

All three BJT amplifier configurations will be discussed in Chapter 12.

11-11 Power and Voltage Limits of MOSFETs and BJTs

Large-signal amplifiers generally have large voltage and/or current swings.

For MOSFETs, there are physical limits on the ability of actual MOSFETs to withstand high voltages and currents, and, therefore, real devices typically have the following parameters specified:

Physical limits of applied voltage, current, and power for the MOSFET

1. Maximum drain current, I_{Dmax}
2. Maximum D–S voltage, V_{DSmax}
3. Maximum power dissipation, P_{max}
4. Maximum G–S voltage, V_{gsmax}

The drain current safe operating area is designated on a transistor's output curve as everything below I_{Dmax}, as illustrated in Figure 11.52.

Similarly, there is a maximum safe operating voltage, V_{DSmax}, also illustrated in Figure 11.52.

Finally, there is an upper limit on power dissipation due to the finite ability of the transistor, its substrate, and package to remove heat from the device. Power dissipated is the product of voltage and current so that

$$P = I_D V_{DS} \text{ watts} \tag{11.29}$$

This is a hyperbolic function. As an example, the contour for a maximum power of 80 milliwatts is also plotted on the curve in Figure 11.52.

Therefore, for the device described by the curves in Figure 11.52,

$$I_{Dmax} = 80 \text{ mA}; V_{DSmax} = 8 \text{ volts}; P_{max} = 80 \text{ mW}$$

The safe operating area is the clear area under the maximum power contour. The Q-point and the load lines should all be designed to fall in the safe operating area.

For a bipolar junction transistor (BJT), typically the following maximum operating conditions will be specified:

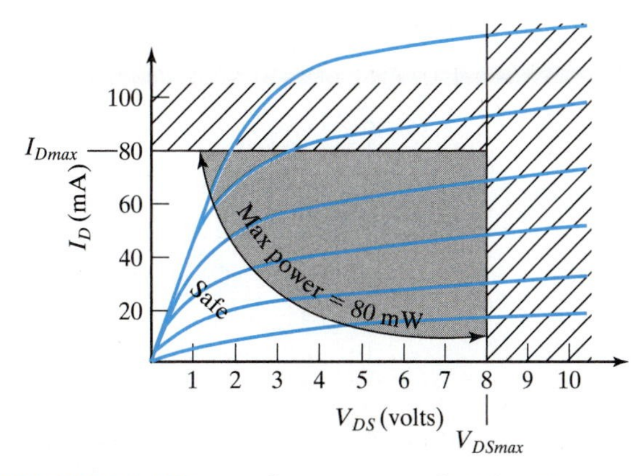

FIGURE 11.52 An illustration of MOSFET's safe region of operation.

Physical limits of applied voltage, current, and power for the BJT

1. Maximum collector current
2. Maximum *C-E* voltage
3. Maximum power dissipation, and often
4. Maximum base current

These real physical limitations of a device place restrictions on the safe operating area of the output curves. For example, there is a *do not exceed* limit on V_{CE}, designated as V_{CEmax}, imposed by the breakdown voltage limit of the device. The maximum current, I_{Cmax}, is a limit imposed by the size of the device and the connections to it. The power dissipated in a BJT is

$$P = I_C V_{CE} \tag{11.30}$$

The maximum power allowed, P_{max}, is determined by the ability of the device to effectively dissipate heat. The safe region is restricted to a similar-shaped area as that illustrated in Figure 11.52 for MOSFETs, but on axes labeled I_C and V_{CE}.

11-12 Thyristors, Silicon-Controlled Rectifiers (SCRs), and Motor Control

Both the thyristor and the SCR are *four-layer* structures consisting of alternating semiconductor types (*pnpn*). These devices can control large amounts of power with only a small amount of control energy. Once these devices are switched *on* they can hold themselves in the *on* state until the applied voltage being switched is reversed or removed. For this reason they are often used in applications that require switching power from a few watts to many kilowatts, such as sophisticated power supply circuits and motor speed control circuits.

The cross-section of a *pnpn* device is shown in Figure 11.53(a). The operation of this device is best understood by considering it to be two transistors (an NPN and a PNP) merged together and connected as shown in Figure 11.53(b). A schematic circuit drawing of this configuration is shown in Figure 11.53(c).

From the circuit drawing, we note that if Q_1 is *off*, that is, not conducting, then there is no base current for Q_2 and it is also *off*. Likewise, if Q_2 is *off* there is no base current for Q_1, and it is *off*. If both transistors are *off* there is no conduction from anode (A) to cathode (K).

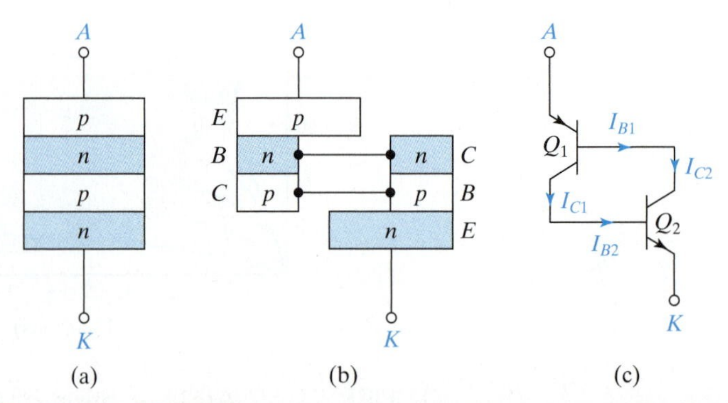

FIGURE 11.53 Model of a *pnpn* device as two transistors.

However, the introduction of any significant base current in either device creates a snowball effect and positive feedback proceeds to lock the device in a full conducting mode. For example, if I_{B2} is the base current of Q_2, then $\beta_2 I_{B2}$ flows in the collector of Q_2, which is the same as the base current of Q_1. The collector current of Q_1, which is the same as I_{B2}, is $\beta_1 I_{C2}$. Therefore, note that when the product of the two betas exceeds unity, that is, $\beta_1 \beta_2 > 1$, and there is any available base current, a regenerative process occurs, which turns *on* both transistors and current can readily flow from A to K.

11.12.1 Thyristors

The symbol for a *thyristor* is shown in Figure 11.54(a) and a typical V–I curve for the device is shown in Figure 11.54(b). Notice that when V_{AK} is negative, the device behaves much like a reverse-biased diode. It conducts minimal current until V_B, the breakdown voltage, is exceeded. However, for positive values of V_{AK}, there is minimal conduction until V_{BO}, the *breakover voltage,* is reached. At this point, there is an avalanche breakdown of the *center* junction, which supplies base current to both *transistors* in the model; both transistors are switched to the *on* state and the device conducts readily from A to K. Conduction will continue until either the current is reduced below the holding current, I_H, or the polarity of V_{AK} is reversed.

11.12.2 Silicon-Controlled Rectifiers

Silicon-controlled rectifiers, or SCRs, are similar to thyristors, with the exception that a control connection, called the gate, G (NOT to be confused with the gate of an FET), is added, as shown in Figure 11.55(a). The terminal G provides an external path through which base current can be added to initiate switching the device to the *on* state. The equivalent circuit for an SCR is shown in Figure 11.55(b).

The symbol used for the SCR is given in Figure 11.56(a) and typical $V-I$ curves for the device are shown in Figure 11.56(b). Note that if $I_G = 0$, the SCR and the thyristor have the same characteristics. Increasing the value of I_G simply lowers the value of V_{AK} at which the device switches *on.*

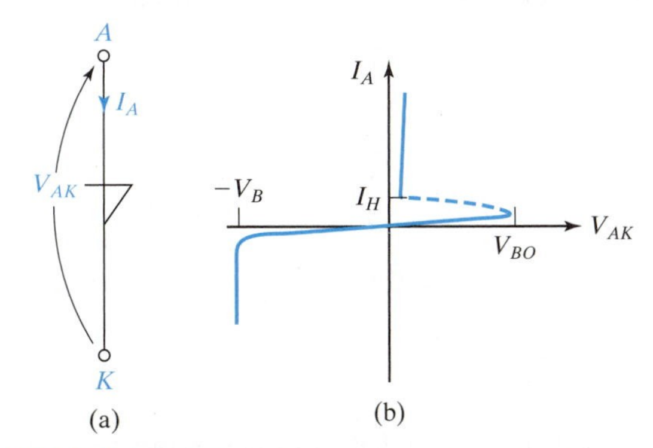

FIGURE 11.54 A thyristor and its V–I curve.

Structure and circuit model used for analysis of thyristor and SCR

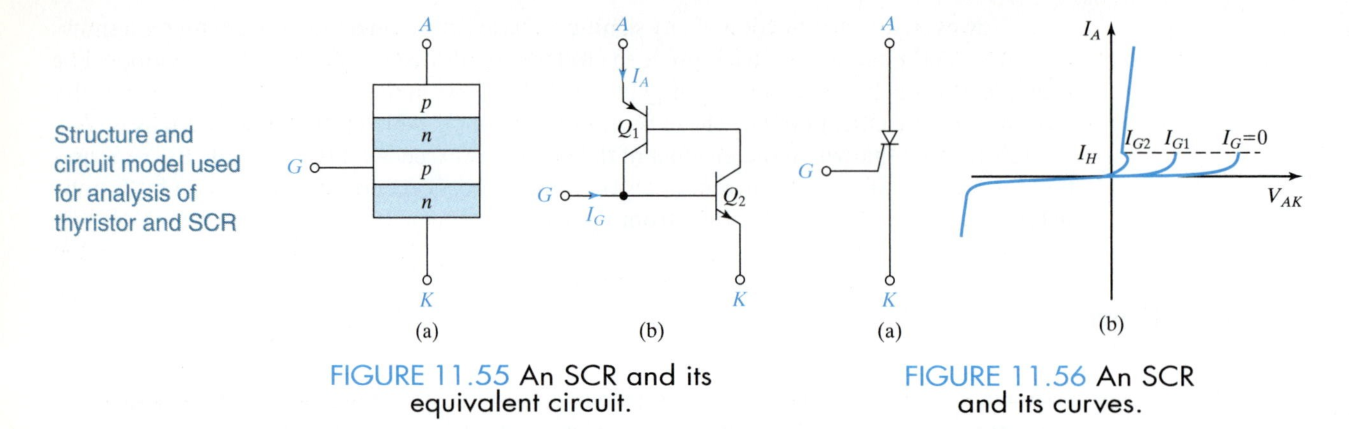

FIGURE 11.55 An SCR and its equivalent circuit.

FIGURE 11.56 An SCR and its curves.

11.12.3 Motor Speed Control

Motor speed control achieved by adjusting firing angle in SRC circuit

One of the most common applications of the SCR is in *motor speed control.* In this simple example a sinusoidal supply voltage is applied to a dc motor through an SCR, as shown in the circuit in Figure 11.57(a). The SCR provides rectification, that is, conversion to dc, by only allowing current to flow in one direction. However, more importantly, the average current through the motor can be regulated by the fraction of time that the SCR is switched *on* during the positive cycle of the current waveform. This time fraction is usually expressed as a phase angle, called the *conduction angle,* θ. The *firing angle,* ϕ, is 180° − θ.

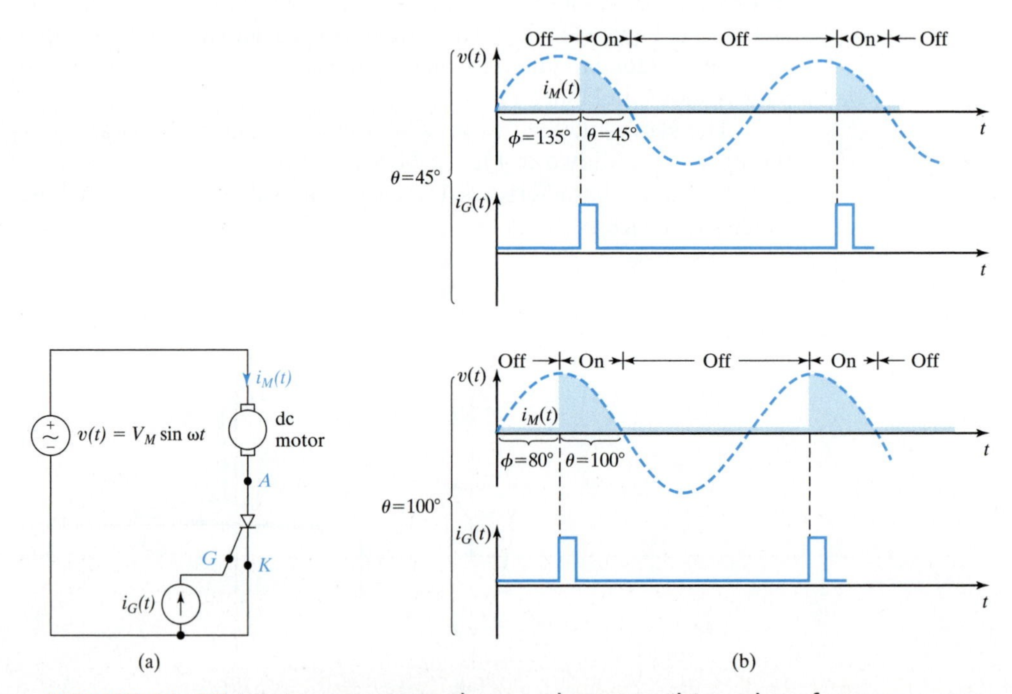

FIGURE 11.57 (a) A motor speed control circuit; (b) a plot of gate current for two different firing angles.

The SCR can be switched *on* via a firing pulse of gate current, $i_G(t)$. The pulse length is not important because the SCR will remain in the conducting state until the polarity of the applied voltage reverses.

Figure 11.57(b) plots the applied voltage, $v(t)$, the motor current, $i_M(t)$, and the gate current, $i_G(t)$, for two different *firing angles*. The average current delivered to the motor is proportional to the area under the $i_M(t)$ curve. Notice that the average current delivered to the motor is much larger for a conduction angle of 100 degrees than for one of 45 degrees. By varying the phase, or the time of the gate firing pulse relative to the sinusoidal supply voltage, the average current and hence the speed of the motor can be controlled.

Summary

- Transistors are three terminal devices that perform one of two functions:
  - In digital circuits the transistor acts as an electronically controlled switch
  - In analog circuits the transistor acts as an electronic amplifier
- There are two basic types of transistors: FETs (field effect transistors) and BJTs (bipolar junction transistors).
- Over much of their operating range FETs act like a voltage-controlled current source, and BJTs act like a current-controlled current source.
- A large-signal amplifier has large-signal voltage swings and the nonlinearities of the transistor must be considered. Typically, this analysis is done by graphical techniques such as plotting the load line on the output curves.
- There are two primary types of FETs: MOSFETs and JFETs. MOSFETs are one of four types: either n-channel or p-channel, and each of these can be either enhancement-mode or depletion-mode.

  Shown below are symbols used for the n-channel enhancement-mode MOSFET, depletion mode MOSFET, and JFET. For p-channel devices the direction of the arrow is reversed in the symbol.

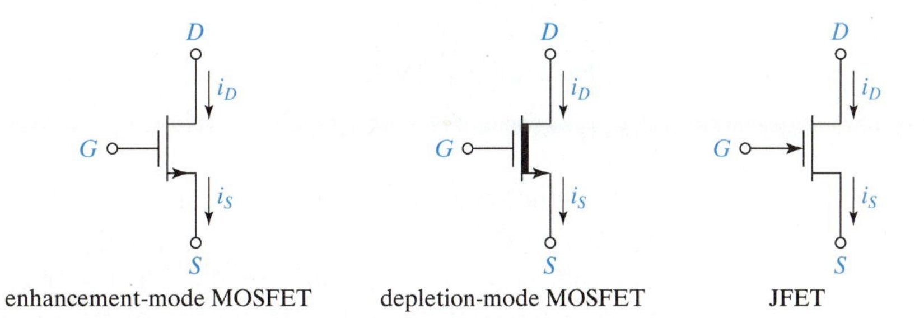

- The *threshold voltage*, V_T, is the minimum voltage that must be applied from gate to source (V_{GS}) in a MOSFET to form a channel and initiate current conduction from drain to source (I_D).
- MOSFET output curves are a plot of I_D versus V_{DS} for a family of V_{GS} values, as shown in Figure 11.58. The output curves display the important regions of operation for a MOSFET: the ohmic region, the active (or saturation) region, and the cutoff region.

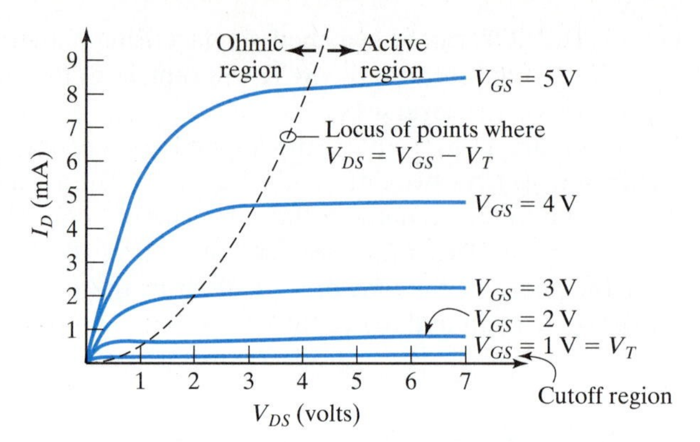

FIGURE 11.58 MOSFET output curves for an *n*-channel, enhancement-mode transistor.

- The load line technique is used with the MOSFET output curves to characterize the switching of an MOSFET inverter, as shown in Figure 11.59(a). Figure 11.59(b) shows the transistor's output curves with the load line for the circuit superimposed. The two output states of the inverter are shown as Q_A and Q_B.

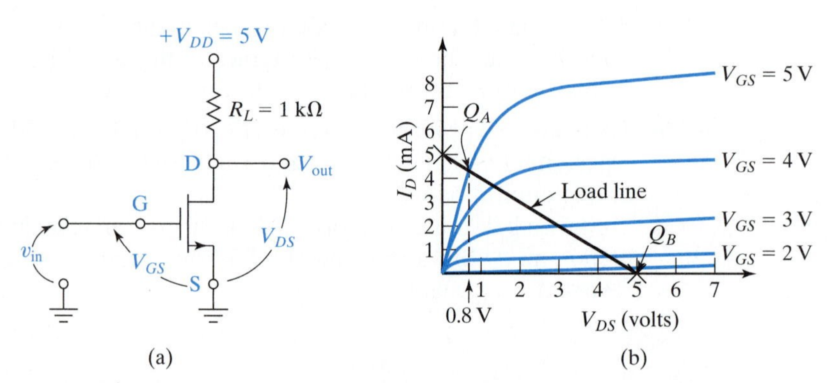

FIGURE 11.59 MOSFET inverter (NOT gate) circuit, (b) output curves with load line.

- The performance of an inverter circuit using a MOSFET can be calculated using the switch model.
- The enhancement-model MOSFET acts like an open switch if $|V_{GS}| < |V_T|$, where V_T is the threshold voltage. It conducts in one of two ways if $|V_{GS}| > |V_T|$: (1) If $|V_{DS}| < |V_{GS} - V_T|$, it acts like a closed switch in series with a resistance, r_{on}; this is the ohmic region that is used in digital circuits. (2) In the other case it acts like a dependent current source controlled by V_{GS}; this is the active or saturated region that is used in amplifier circuits.
- A *p*-channel MOSFET has the same structure as an *n*-channel device but with the *n* and *p* regions interchanged. The *p*-channel device requires a complementary set of bias voltages: V_{GS} and V_{DS} are negative for normal operation.

- Depletion-mode MOSFETs have a channel fabricated in the device structure and conduct with $V_{GS} = 0$. They are used in digital MOS circuits primarily as load devices.
- The JFET is a depletion-mode FET fabricated with a *p–n* junction as the gate.
- Transistors are the key element in circuits called *amplifiers* that provide voltage and/or current gain.
- The first step in the analysis of any amplifier circuit is to determine the dc bias conditions at the *Q*-point—the transistor's terminal voltages and currents with no signal applied.
- For a common source MOSFET amplifier, the *Q*-point is located on the output curves at the intersection of the dc load line and the appropriate V_{GS} curve. The output voltage swing can then be determined by plotting the movement of the bias point up and down the load line (deviations from the *Q*-point) as the input signal changes V_{GS}.
- If a bypass capacitor is used, then an ac load line must be plotted, and the signal excursions determined by movement of the bias point up and down the ac load line.
- There are three amplifier circuit configurations using FETs: common source, common gate, and common drain. The common source is used more than the others.
- There are two basic types of BJTs (bipolar junction transistors): NPN and PNP. The structure and the symbol for each is shown in Figure 11.60.

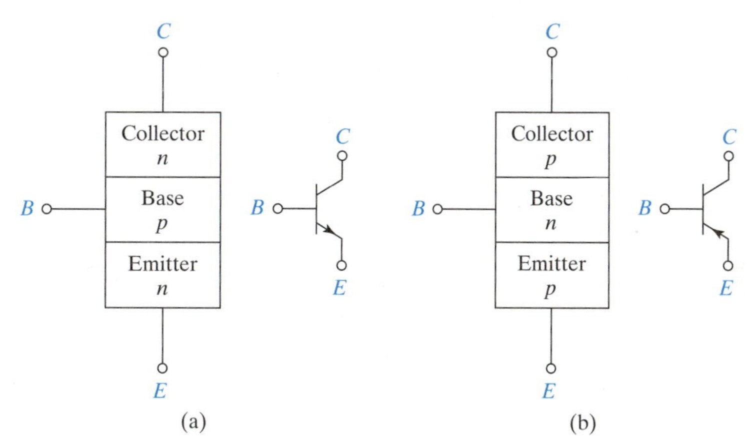

FIGURE 11.60 Structure and symbols for (a) NPN and (b) PNP bipolar transistors.

- The BJT is biased in the active region (emitter junction forward biased; collector junction reverse biased) for amplifier applications.
- For the BJT, $I_E = I_B + I_C$; α_F or β_F can be used to relate BJT terminal currents in the forward active region: $I_C = \beta_F I_B$, and $\beta_F = \alpha_F/(1 - \alpha_F)$.
- BJT output curves plot I_C versus V_{CE} for a family of values of I_B, as shown in Figure 11.61.
- If the base current, $I_B = 0$, the BJT is in cutoff, and it acts like an open switch. If $|I_B| > 0$, the BJT conducts current in one of two possible ways depending on other bias conditions: (1) In saturation the transistor acts like a closed switch with a small voltage drop called $V_{CE(SAT)}$; this is the case most used in digital circuits. (2) In the active region it conducts like a dependent current source controlled by the base current; this is the bias condition used in amplifier circuits.

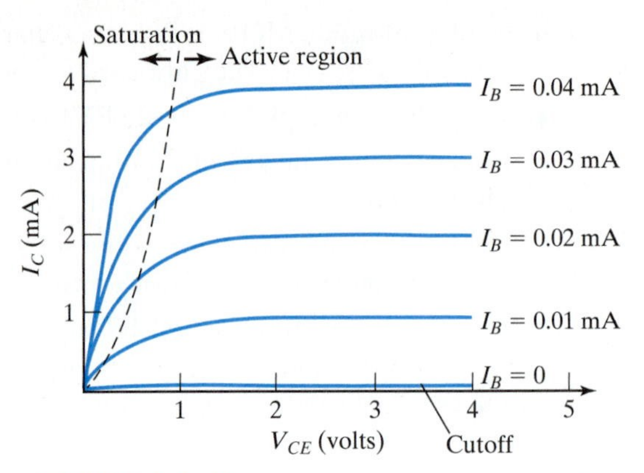

FIGURE 11.61 Output curves for a BJT.

- The BJT can be used as a switch in digital applications.
- The circuit model describing the BJT in the cutoff (open switch) and saturation (closed switch) regions is presented in Figure 11.62.

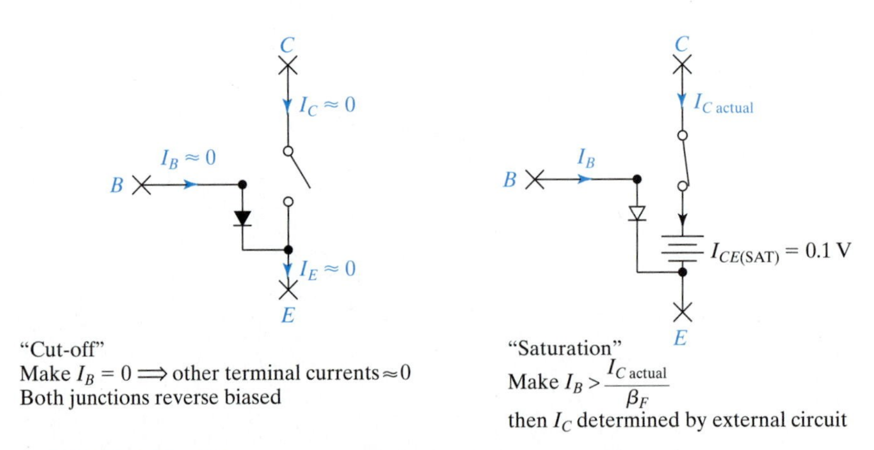

FIGURE 11.62 Circuit models for BJT in cutoff and saturation.

- The BJT differs from the MOSFET in that the input terminal to the BJT connects to a *p–n* diode; a constant input current is required to maintain the switch closed; a MOSFET gate has a high (essentially infinite) input resistance.
- For a BJT in the active region, I_C is controlled by I_B; once saturated, I_C is controlled by the external bias circuit.
- The large-signal analysis of BJT circuits follows a similar procedure to that for MOSFETs. For a common emitter amplifier the *Q*-point is located on the output curves at the intersection of the dc load line and the appropriate base current curve. The output voltage swing is determined by plotting the movement of the bias point up and down the load line, that is, plotting the deviations from the *Q*-point, as the input signal changes I_B.
- If a bypass capacitor is used, an ac load line must be plotted and the bias point moved on the ac load line.

- The common emitter self-bias circuit is often used, as shown in Figure 11.63.

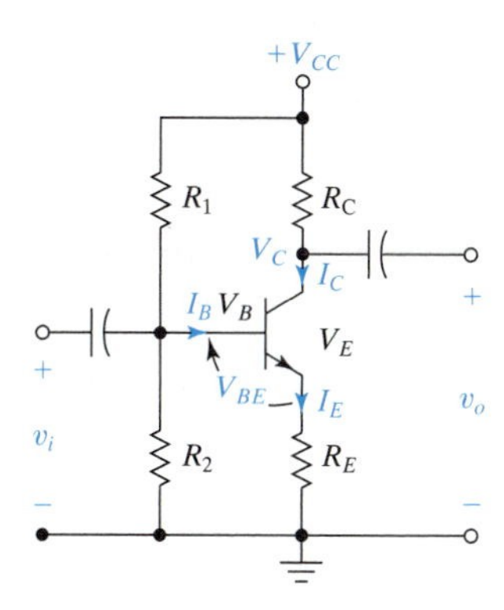

FIGURE 11.63 Common emitter self-bias circuit.

- There are three amplifier circuit configurations using BJTs: common emitter, common base, and common collector. The common emitter is used more than the others.
- Real MOSFETs and BJTs have finite limits for applied voltages, currents, and power; circuits should be designed to operate well within these limits.
- Thyristors and silicon-controlled rectifiers (SCRs) are four-layer structures (*pnpn*) that can control large currents with small input (control) power. These devices are commonly used in power control circuits, such as setting the speed of a motor.

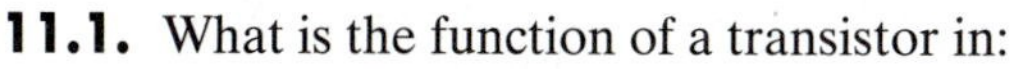

Problems

11.1. What is the function of a transistor in:
(a) a digital circuit?
(b) an analog circuit?

11.2. What are the two basic types of transistors?

11.3. What type transistor functions most closely as
(a) a voltage-controlled current source?
(b) a current-controlled current source?

11.4. Define a small-signal amplifier and a large-signal amplifier and highlight the important differences between them.

11.5. A digital switching circuit is most closely related to what type of amplifier?

11.6. Identify the device structures shown in Figure P11.6 as *n*-channel enhancement-mode, *n*-channel depletion-mode, *p*-channel enhancement-mode, *p*-channel depletion-mode, or none of the above.

11.7. Match each characteristic, listed (a) through (n), with the appropriate structure(s), listed I through V. More than one structure may apply to each.
(a) conducts when V_{GS} is positive
(b) hole current flows when transistor is ON
(c) electron current flows when transistor is ON
(d) conducts when $V_{GS} = 0$
(e) conducts when V_{GS} is negative
(f) turns OFF through the repulsion of electrons
(g) turns OFF through the repulsion of holes
(h) conducting channel formed during fabrication
(i) conducting channel formed by biasing the gate
(j) turns ON through the attraction of electrons
(k) turns ON through the attraction of holes
(l) the body is *p*-type

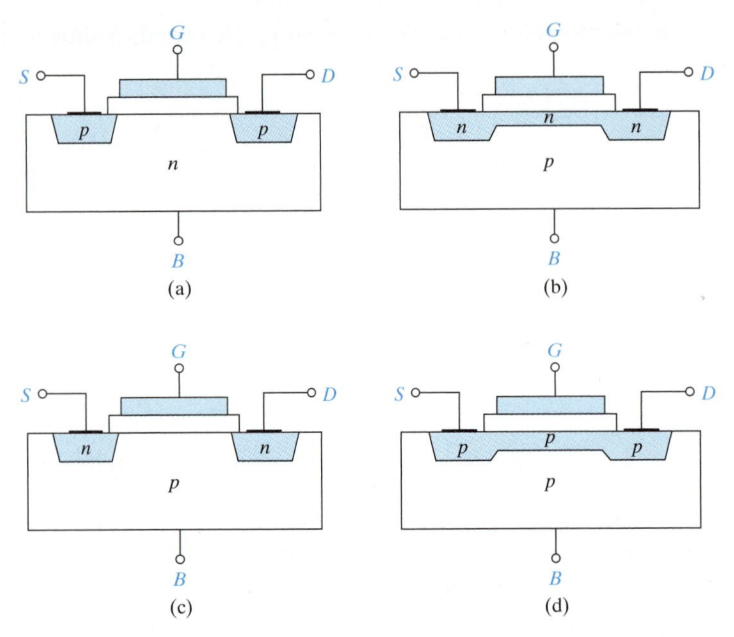

FIGURE P11.6

(m) the body is n-type
(n) the body is furry

I. n-channel enhancement
II. n-channel depletion
III. p-channel enhancement
IV. p-channel depletion
V. cat

11.8. Sketch the cross-section of a p-channel enhancement-mode transistor and label the source, drain, gate, and substrate contacts.

11.9. Sketch the cross-section and two common symbols for an n-channel enhancement-mode MOSFET.

11.10. For an enhancement-mode MOSFET, the gate-to-source voltage must be increased in magnitude above a critical value to initiate current conduction from source-to-drain. What is the name of this critical voltage and its symbol? If the gate-to-source voltage is below this level, the transistor is said to be in what mode?

11.11. a) What are the three important regions of operation (or modes) of the output curves for a MOSFET? b) Sketch a hypothetical set of output curves for an n-channel enhancement-mode MOSFET with a threshold voltage of 1.5 V and a current of 6 mA in the active region when V_{GS} is 4 V.

11.12. Determine the values of the parameter K and V_T for the MOSFET characteristics plotted in Figure P11.12.

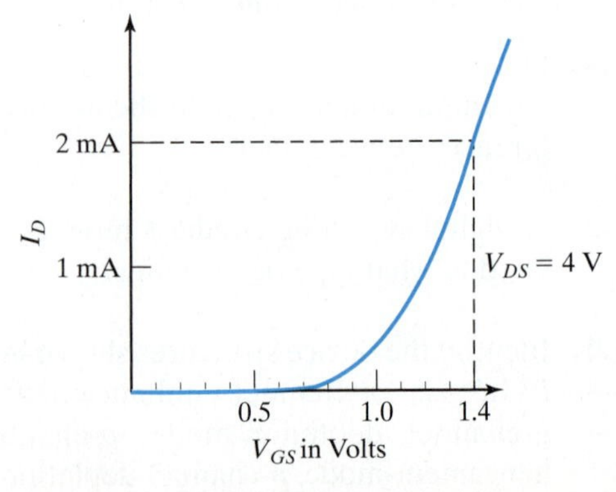

FIGURE P11.12

11.13. The threshold voltage of an n-channel enhancement mode MOSFET is 0.8 V. The MOSFET conducts a current of 2 mA with a $V_{GS} = 2$ V and $V_{DS} = 5$ V. What is the drain current when V_{GS} is doubled?

11.14. The drain currents of an n-channel MOSFET biased in the saturated (active) region for two values of V_{GS} are given in Table P11.14. Plot the square root of I_D versus V_{GS} to obtain the threshold voltage and parameter K for the transistor.

TABLE P11.14

V_{GS} (V)	I_D (A)
1.0	3.2×10^{-4}
2.0	1.15×10^{-2}

11.15. A particular n-channel MOSFET has $V_T = 0.4$ V and conducts in the active region a current of 2.5 mA when $V_{GS} = 3$ V.
(a) What is the value of K?
(b) What current does this same device conduct when $V_{DS} = 1$ V?

11.16. From the transistor output curves and the load line for an inverter plotted in Figure P11.16, determine the values of V_{DD} and R_L.

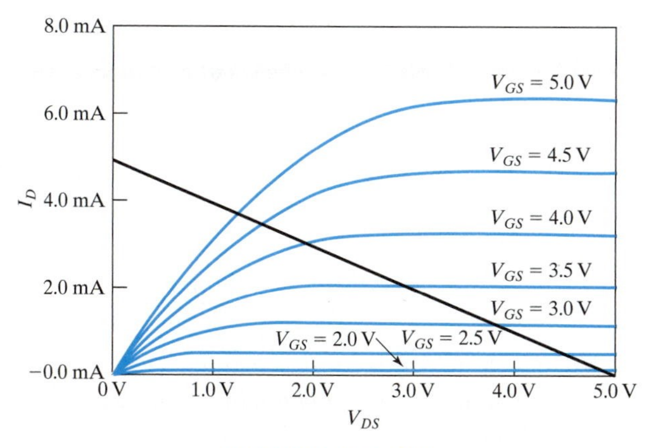

FIGURE P11.16

11.17. (a) On the MOSFET output curve of Figure P11.16, sketch the curve of drain current, I_D, versus V_D for the circuit shown in Figure P11.17(a). (b) What other two-terminal device has a V–I characteristic that resembles a transistor connected this way? (c) In what region of operation is the transistor biased? (d) Repeat 11.17(a) for the circuit in Figure P11.17(b).

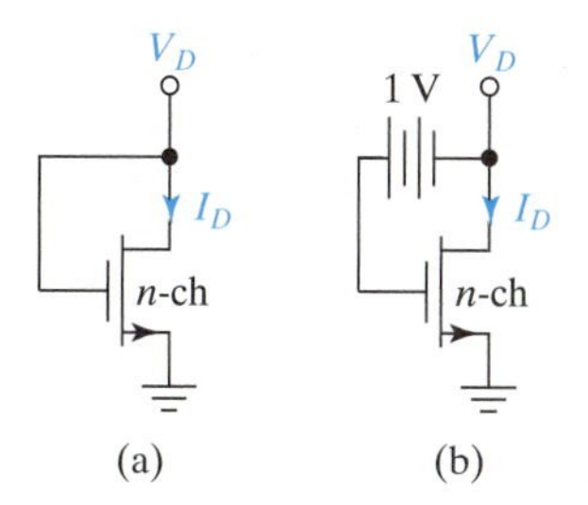

FIGURE P11.17

11.18. Draw the appropriate load line on the output curves shown in Figure P11.16 if the inverter had a supply voltage, V_{DD}, of 3.5 V and a load resistance of 475 Ω.

11.19. A simple inverter using an n-channel enhancement-mode MOSFET is shown in Figure P11.19(a). Use the transistor model shown in

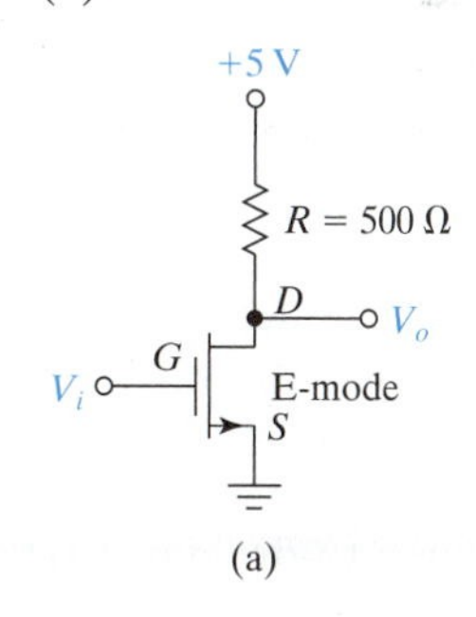

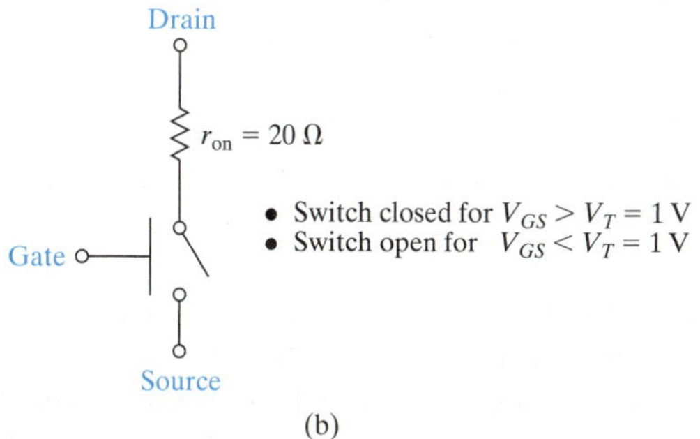

FIGURE P11.19

Figure P11.19(b) to obtain the transfer characteristics of this inverter, a plot of V_o versus V_i.

11.20. A NOT gate is implemented using an n-channel enhancement-mode MOSFET as shown in Figure P11.20 with $V_{DD} = 5$ V, $V_T = 0.9$ V, and $R_L = 1$ kΩ.

(a) If $V_{in} = 5$ V, and $r_{on} = 100$ Ω; calculate V_{out}.

(b) Find R_L if $V_{out} = 0.1$ V.

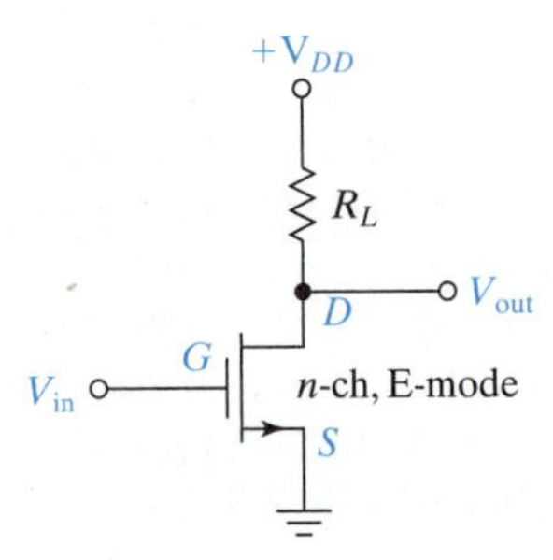

FIGURE P11.20

11.21. For the NOT gate and transistor described in problem 11.20(a), determine the value of K required to make $r_{on} = 100$ Ω.

11.22. A NOT gate is modeled using an inverter similar to that shown in Figure P11.20. For $V_{in} = V_{DD} = 5$ V and $V_{out} = 0.2$ V, determine the load resistance, R_L, and the n-channel ON source-to-drain resistance (r_{on}) if the power dissipated in the load resistance during ON state is 0.48 mW.

11.23. Sketch the cross-section and two common symbols for the p-channel enhancement-mode MOSFET.

11.24. The drain current of an n-channel depletion-mode MOSFET is plotted as a function of the gate voltage in Figure P11.24. Obtain the value of the "pinch-off" voltage for the MOSFET.

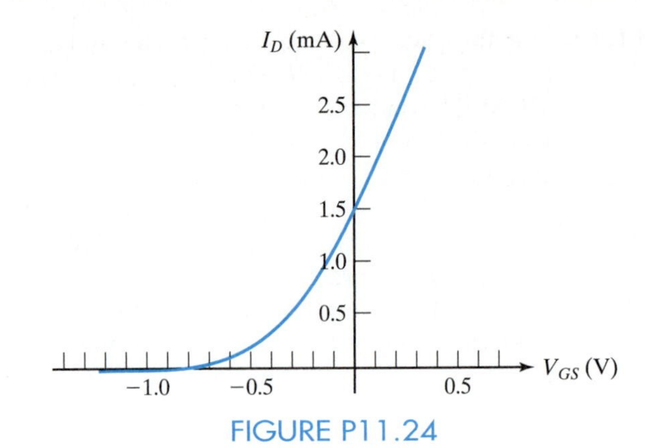

FIGURE P11.24

11.25. The I_D–V_{DS} characteristics of a JFET are shown in Figure P11.25(a). Using the load line concept, compute the Q-point of the circuit in Figure 11.25(b).

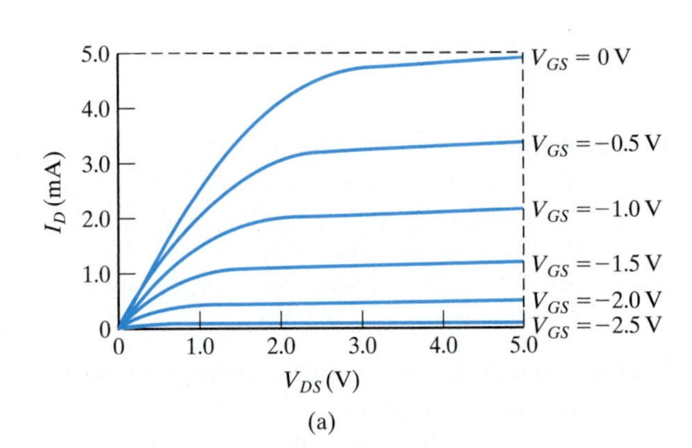

(a)

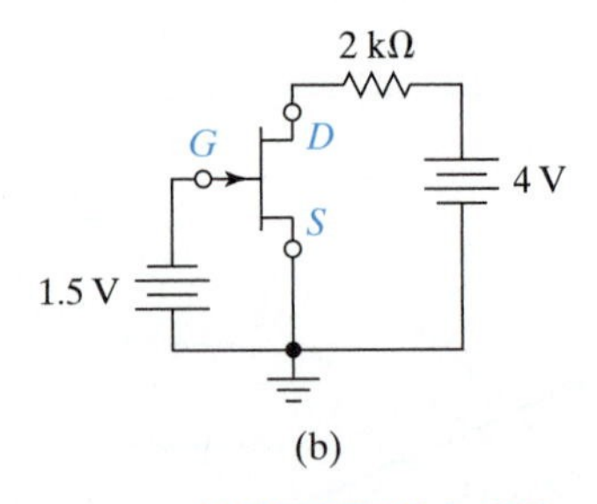

(b)

FIGURE P11.25

11.26. Draw two schematic symbols each for the n-channel and p-channel depletion-mode MOSFET.

11.27. For switching applications, which device terminal is usually used as the control terminal for (a) MOSFETs? (b) BJTs?

11.28. The circuit of an n-channel enhancement-mode MOSFET amplifier is shown in Figure P11.28. (a) If we wish to establish $V_{GS} = 2$ V, find R_2 if $R_1 = 150$ kΩ. (b) For this circuit would we expect V_T to be more or less than 2 V?

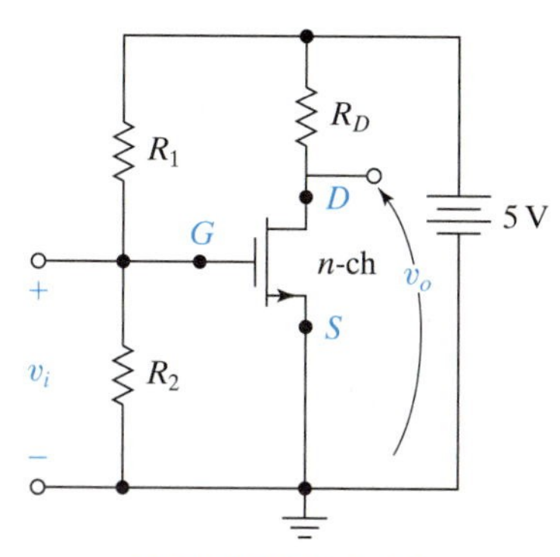

FIGURE P11.28

11.29. The output curves of an n-channel enhancement-mode MOSFET are shown in Figure P11.29. This transistor is placed in the common source amplifier in Figure P11.28 with $R_1 = 100$ kΩ, $R_2 = 30$ kΩ, and $R_D =$ 1.25 kΩ. (a) Construct the load line for this circuit. (b) Obtain the quiescent operating point, that is, Q-point. (c) If v_i is a sinusoidal signal of amplitude 1 V, sketch the variation of the output voltage v_o about the operating point. (d) Find the large-signal voltage gain. (e) Describe any possible distortion of the output signal. If we reduce the amplitude of the input signal, would there be less distortion?

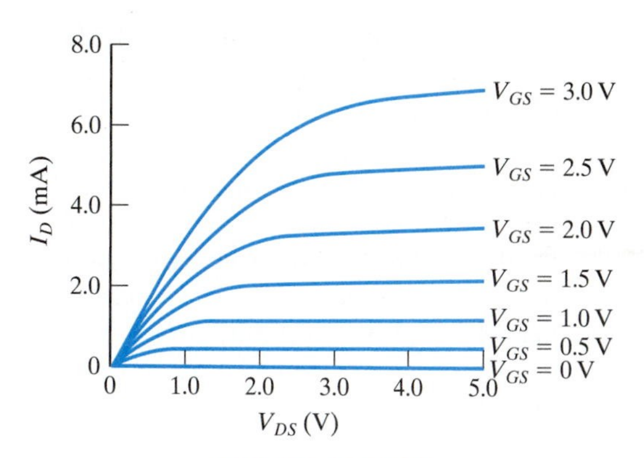

FIGURE P11.29

11.30. Describe the function of the following in an amplifier circuit: (a) coupling capacitor, (b) bypass capacitor.

11.31. What is the difference between an ac load line and a dc load line? Under what conditions are the two identical?

11.32. The output curves of an n-channel MOSFET are shown in Figure P11.32(a). This transistor is

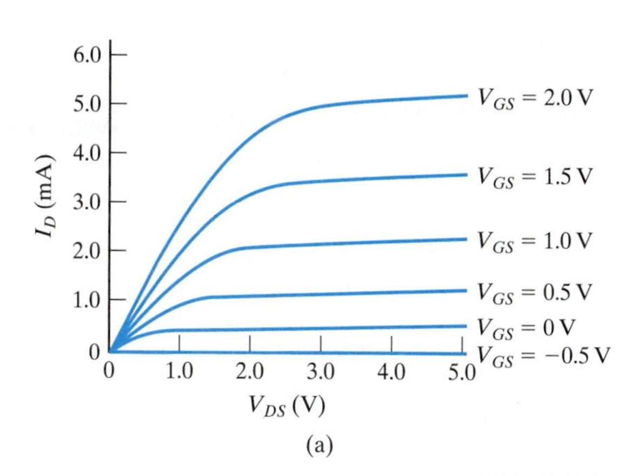

(a)

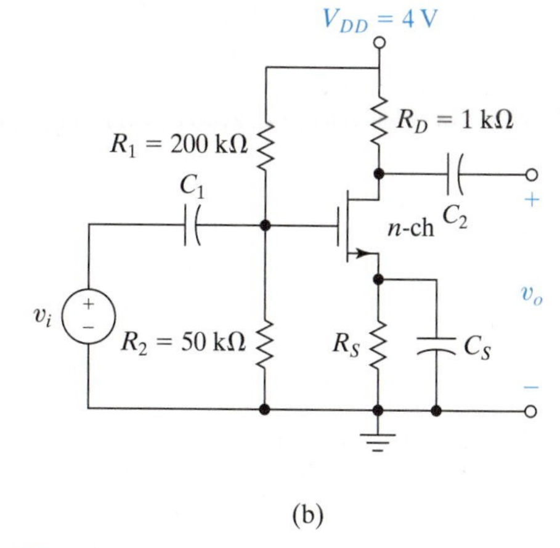

(b)

FIGURE P11.32

placed in the circuit in Figure P11.32(b). (a) What mode device is this MOSFET? (b) If we wish to put the Q-point on the $V_{GS} = 0.5$ V curve, what value of R_S should be selected? Hint: First compute V_G; then write an equation for V_{GS} and use it to solve for R_S. (c) Construct the dc load line on the output curves. (d) Obtain the Q-point of the circuit. (e) Construct the ac load line. (f) Sketch the output voltage for a triangular input voltage of 1 V peak-to-peak. (g) Find the large-signal voltage gain.

11.33. Figure P11.33 shows a common source amplifier circuit using an n-channel depletion-mode MOSFET in a self-biasing configuration. (a) Why is this configuration self-biasing? If I_D is measured to be 1.2 mA, determine V_{GS}. (b) Calculate the slope of the dc load line. (c) Calculate the slope of the ac load line.

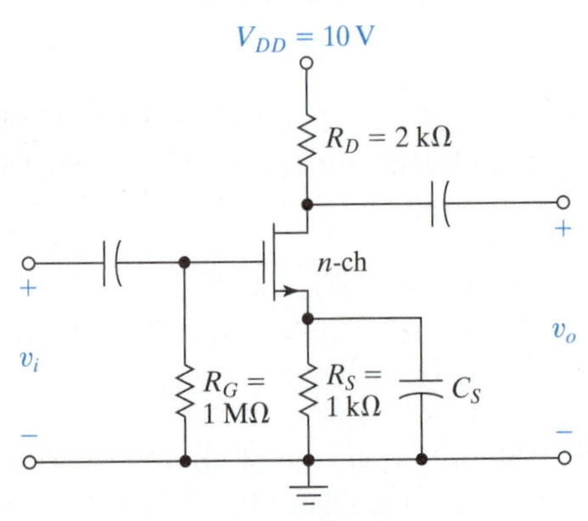

FIGURE P11.33

11.34. Figure P11.34 shows a common gate amplifier configuration using an n-channel depletion-mode transistor. The Q-point for this circuit is chosen to be $I_D = 5$ mA, $V_{DS} = 5$ V, and $V_{GS} = -2$ V. (a) Calculate the values of resistances R_S and R_D. (b) What is the slope of the dc load line? (c) What is the slope of the ac load line?

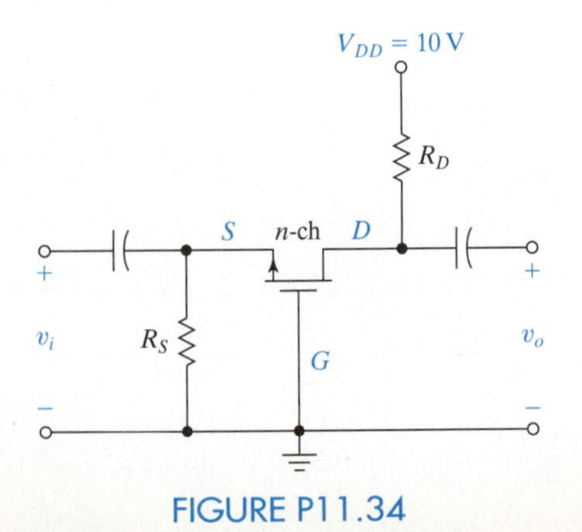

FIGURE P11.34

11.35. The circuit for a common drain amplifier is shown in Figure P11.35 with $R_S = 750\ \Omega$ and $R_G = 2\ \text{M}\Omega$. If the Q-point is chosen to be $I_D = 2$ mA, find V_{GS}.

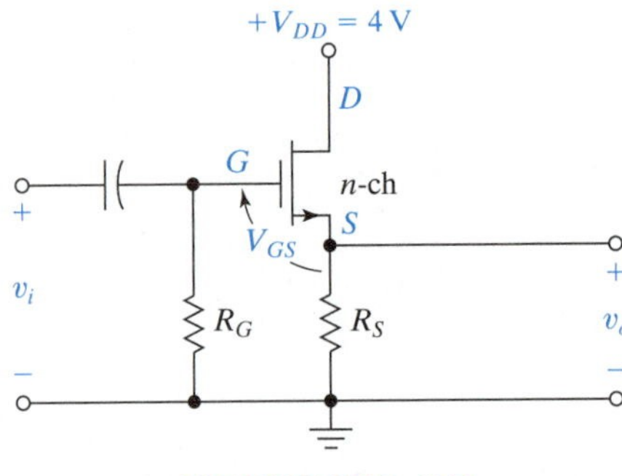

FIGURE P11.35

11.36. a) What does BJT stand for? b) What are the two basic types of BJTs?

11.37. The direction of the arrow in the symbol for the PNP and NPN transistors has what significance?

11.38. Sketch the cross-section of a planar-processed PNP transistor clearly showing the three terminals of the BJT.

11.39. Indicate the direction of positive current (net positive charge movement) in or out of each terminal of the transistors in Figure P11.39 assuming that both the transistors are biased in the active region of operation.

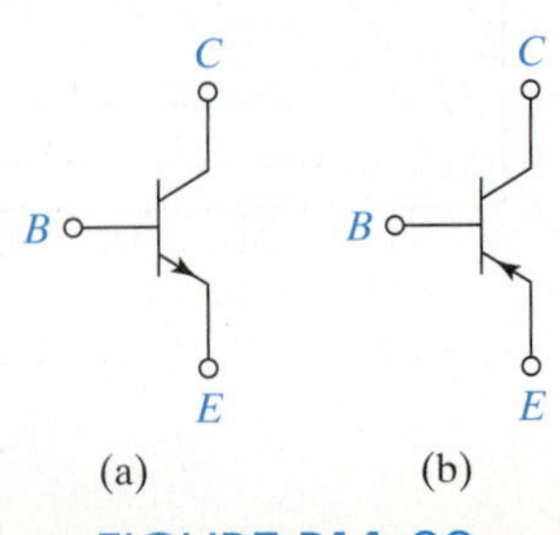

FIGURE P11.39

11.40. Figures P11.40 (a–f) illustrate NPN and PNP BJTs with biased junctions. For each case identify each of the junctions as forward or reverse biased. Also identify the mode of operation of the BJT, that is, cutoff, saturation, active, or reverse-active, and redraw each circuit with the proper transistor symbol.

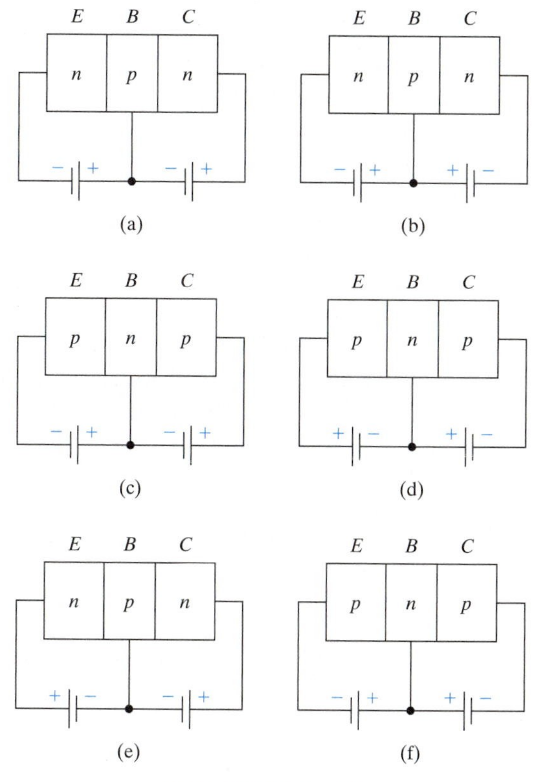

FIGURE P11.40

11.41. The NPN transistor in Figure P11.41 has $\beta_F = 100$ and the emitter junction is forward biased at $V_{BE} = 0.6$ V.

(a) What is the mode of operation of the transistor?

(b) Calculate the base, emitter, and collector currents.

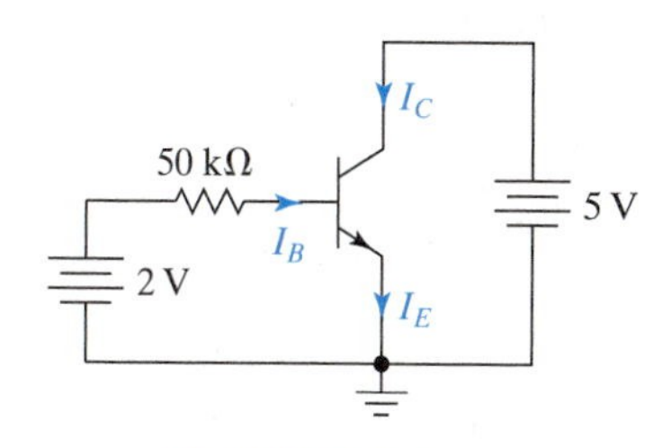

FIGURE P11.41

11.42. Figure P11.42 (a) shows a BJT common emitter amplifier circuit; Figure P11.42 (b) shows the output curves for the transistor. Assuming $V_{BE} = 0.7$ V, (a) draw the dc load line. (b) Determine the Q-point. (c) At the Q-point, what is the value of V_{CE} and I_C? (d) Determine the transistor's β.

11.43. The values for α_F are measured for three transistors as $\alpha_F = 0.97$, $\alpha_F = 0.98$, and $\alpha_F = 0.99$. Calculate the corresponding values of β_F for each.

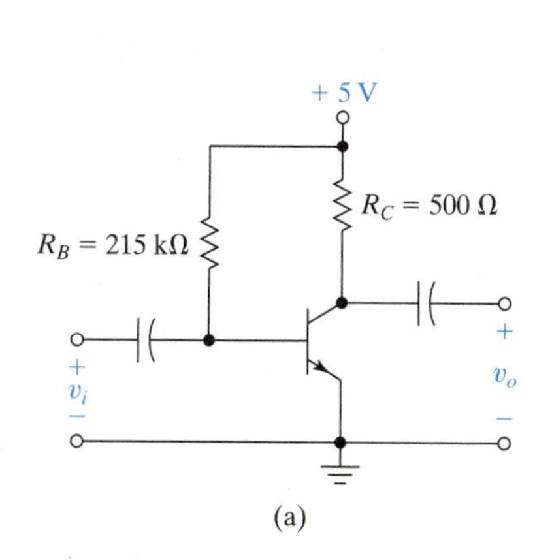

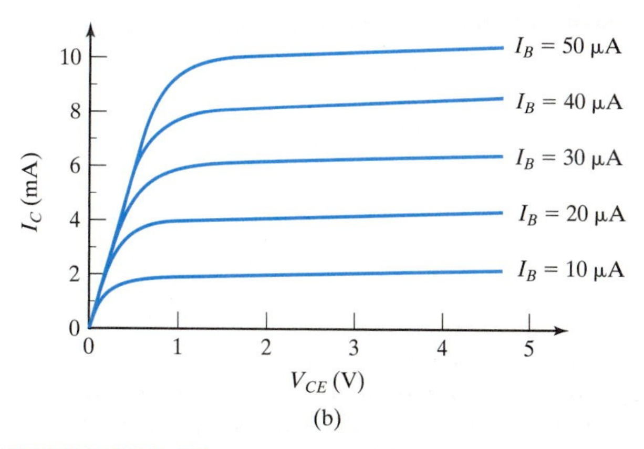

FIGURE P11.42

11.44. The PNP transistor in the circuit shown in Figure P11.44 has the following characteristics: $\beta_F = 75$, and assume $V_{CE(SAT)} = -0.1$ V. (a) What value of collector current flows when the transistor is saturated? (b) If $V_{BE} = -0.6$ V, what value of V_1 is required to saturate the transistor?

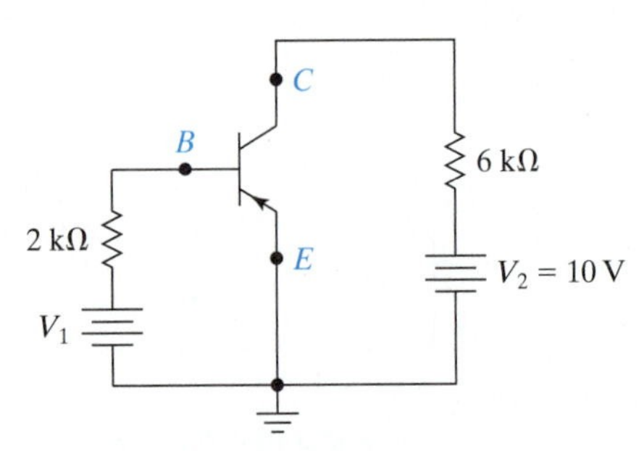

FIGURE P11.44

11.45. Figure P11.45 shows an NPN transistor connected in a way that it looks like a diode from the terminals the transistor is operating in the active region. Given $V_{BE} = 0.7$ V and $\beta_F = 60$, calculate the base and collector currents.

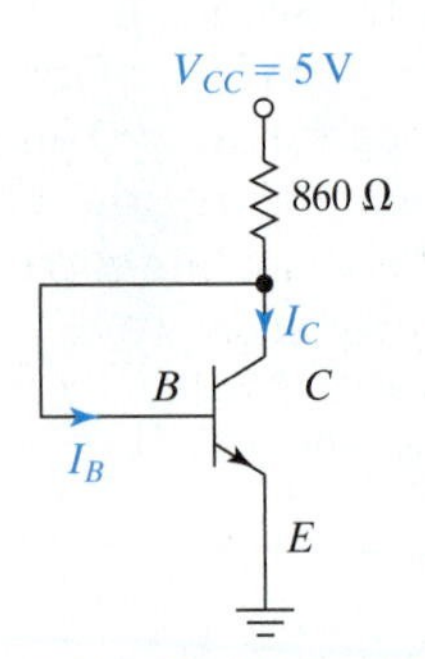

FIGURE P11.45

11.46. For the circuit given in Figure P11.46, assuming $\beta_F = 100$ and $V_{BE} = 0.7$ V, (a) find V_o for $V_i = 0.8, 1.5, 2.0,$ and 2.5 V. (b) At approximately what value of V_i will the collector current be determined by the circuit bias conditions rather than the β_F relationship? What mode of operation is this? (c) For $V_i = 2.5$ V, what is the forced beta, β_F^*?

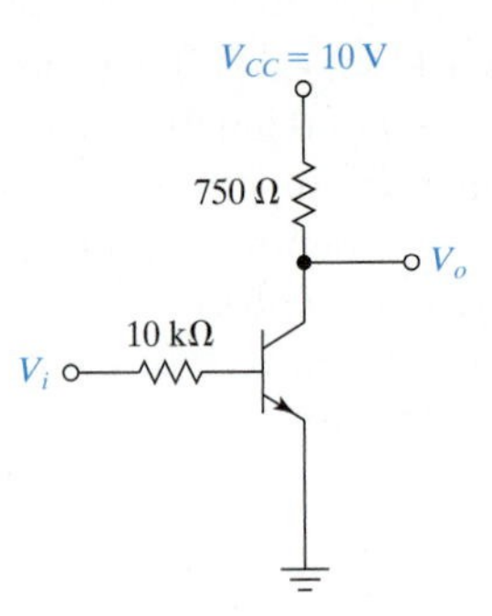

FIGURE P11.46

11.47. Repeat problem 11.42
(a) with $R_C = 1$ kΩ
(b) with $R_C = 2$ kΩ

11.48. Figure P11.48 shows a BJT common emitter circuit and curves. The Q-point is chosen to be $I_C = 30$ mA and $V_{CE} = 5$ V; assume $V_{BE} = 0.7$ V. (a) Draw the dc load line. (b) Calculate the value of R_C. (c) Calculate the value of R_B. (d) Calculate the value of transistor's β. (e) If $v_s(t)$ is sinusoidal with an amplitude of 2.5 V, show on the load line the range of movement of the bias point, and sketch a plot of $v_{CE}(t)$. (f) Calculate the value of the large-signal voltage gain.

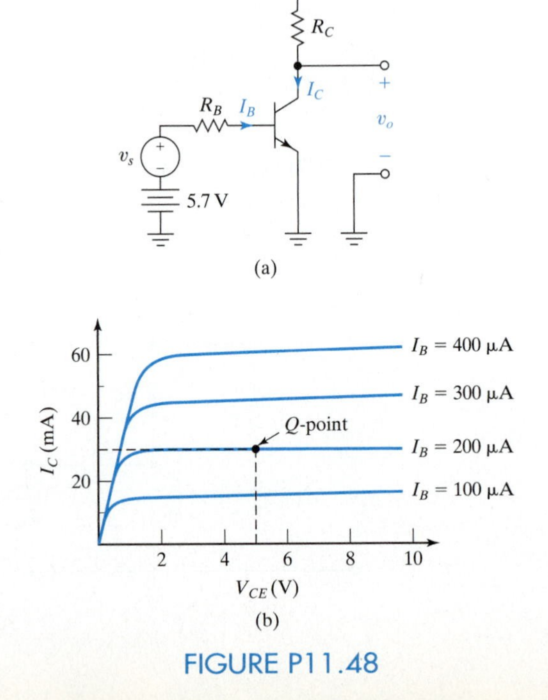

FIGURE P11.48

11.49. In Figure P11.49, determine I_C and V_C for the following values of I_B and designate the mode of transistor operation. (a) $I_B = 0$, (b) $I_B = 20\ \mu A$, (c) $I_B = 60\ \mu A$, (d) $I_B = 100\ \mu A$.

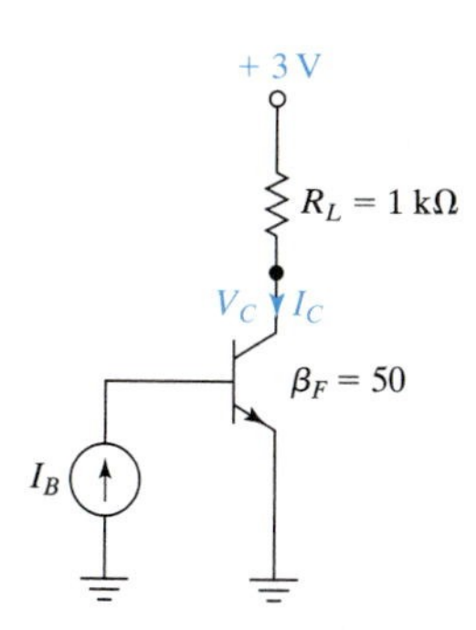

FIGURE P11.49

11.50. In the circuit shown in Figure P11.50, assume the base emitter turn-on voltage, V_{BE}, is 0.7 V, $V_{CE(SAT)}$ is 0.1 V, and β_F is 200. Obtain the value of the output voltage for $V_i = 0.5$ V, 0.8 V, 1.0 V, and 3.5 V.

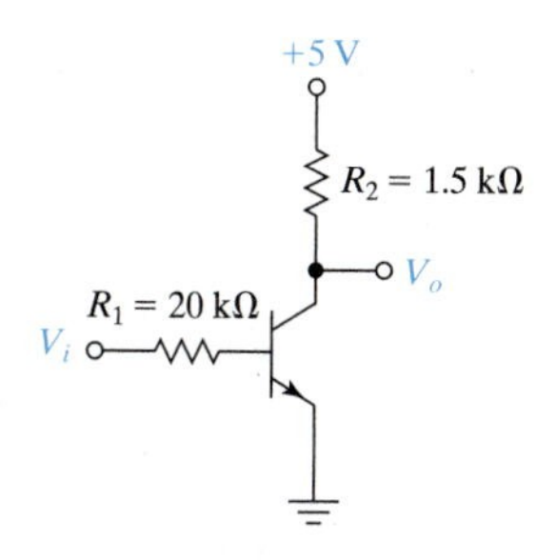

FIGURE P11.50

11.51. A transistor with output curves, shown in Figure P11.51, is used in the circuit in Figure P11.50. Use a graphical approach (plot the load line) to find the value of V_o if $V_i = 1.1$ V.

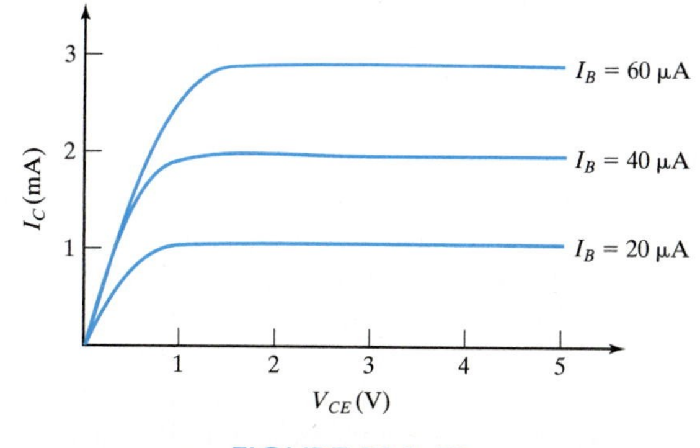

FIGURE P11.51

11.52. Figure P11.52 shows a BJT common emitter self-bias circuit. Assuming $I_B \ll I_1$, $\beta = 200$, and $V_{BE} = 0.7$ V, (a) calculate the values of I_E, I_C, and I_B. (b) Calculate the value of V_{CE}. (c) If v_i is increased by 0.1 V, what's the effect on v_o?

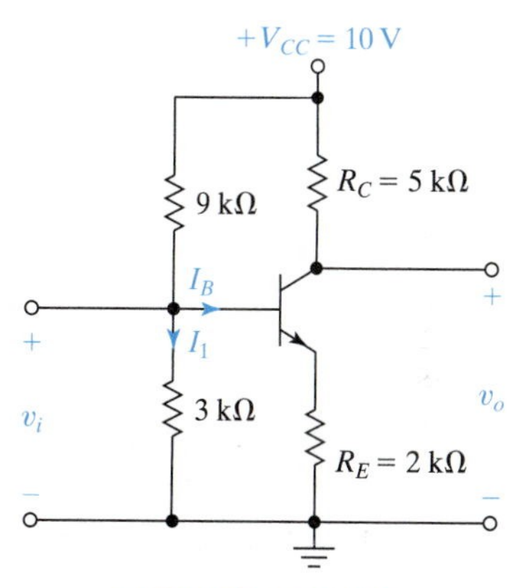

FIGURE P11.52

11.53. Assume that the circuit of Figure P11.53 utilizes the transistor characterized by the output curves in Figure P11.51(b). $V_{BE} = 0.7$ V. (a) Draw the dc load line. (b) Find the Q-point and draw the ac load line. (c) Estimate the voltage gain by determining how a small change in v_i changes the collector current, and track this change on the ac load line.

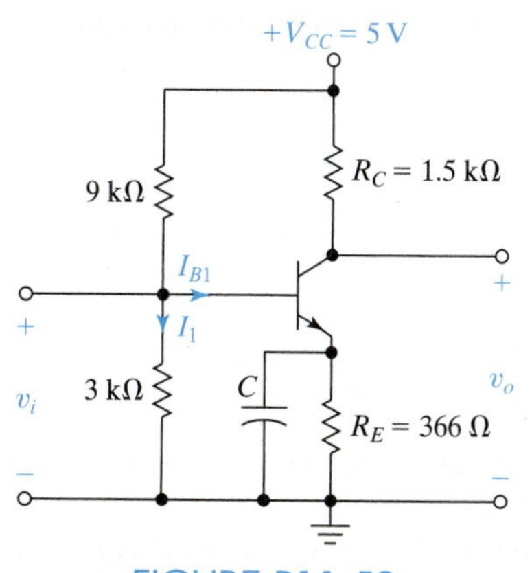

FIGURE P11.53

11.54. Figure P11.54 shows a BJT common emitter self-bias amplifier circuit with a PNP transistor. Assuming $V_{BE} = -0.7$ V and $\beta = 120$, (a) find the value for R_1 that makes $I_E = -1.2$ mA. (b) Find the value for R_C that will make $V_C = -6$ V. (c) Determine the slope of the dc load line. (d) Where would we place a bypass capacitor in this circuit, and why?

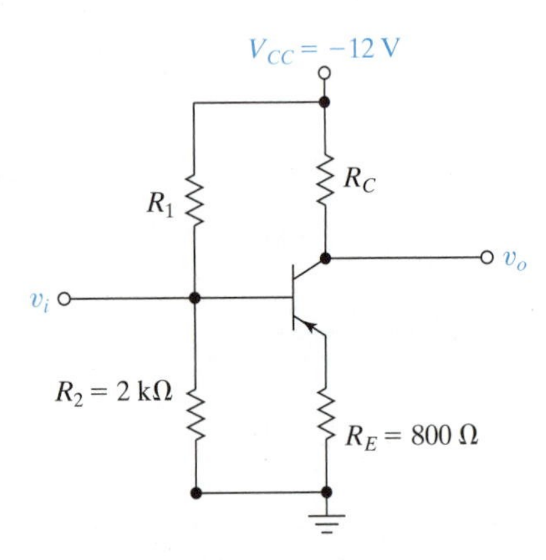

FIGURE P11.54

11.55. Given the common base BJT bias circuit shown in Figure P11.55, let us calculate the location of the Q-point, assuming β is large, if

$R_1 = 6$ kΩ $\quad$ $R_C = 4.5$ kΩ

$R_2 = 1$ kΩ $\quad$ $R_E = 1.5$ kΩ

Note that this is exactly the same dc circuit as that previously discussed in the common emitter circuit configuration.

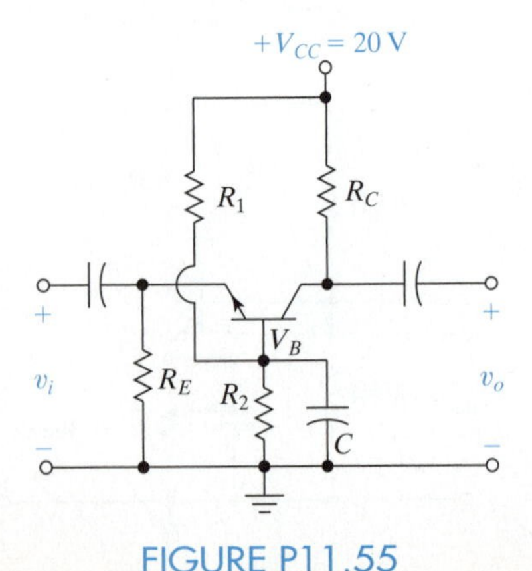

FIGURE P11.55

11.56. Calculate the dc value of I_C for the common collector amplifier in Figure P11.56 assuming the following values:

$R_1 = 4$ kΩ

$R_2 = 2$ kΩ $\quad$ $R_E = 1.0$ kΩ

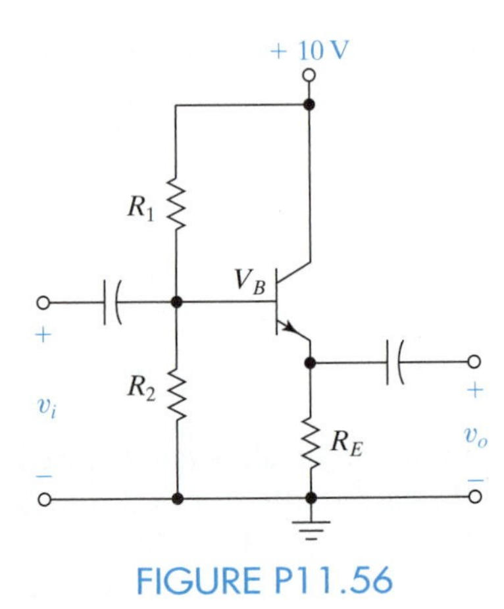

FIGURE P11.56

11.57. List the factors that impose limits on a MOSFET's region of safe operation. How would you expect each of these to be related to the physical size or structure of the MOSFET?

11.58. Plot the constant power contour for 1 mW and 4 mW on the MOSFET output curves in Figure P11.32(a).

11.59. (a) On the transistor output curves shown in Figure P11.42(b), plot three constant power contours: 4 mW, 10 mW, and 30 mW. (b) If we wish to limit the power dissipated in this device to 10 mW, draw an acceptable load line that would give large swings in V_{CE}. (c) If we wished to obtain large output current swings, would you design a different load line?

11.60. Draw a constant power curve for $P = 200$ mW on the output curves for the transistor shown in Figure P11.48(b). If this is the maximum specified value for power dissipation, is the Q-point selected in problem 11.48 acceptable?

11.61. A thyristor with $V_{BO} = 5$ V and $I_H = 10$ mA is placed in the circuit in Figure P11.61(a). The voltage source $v_1(t)$ ramps up to 10 volts over 10 seconds and back down again, as shown in Figure 11.61(b). Plot the current $i(t)$ over the same 20 seconds.

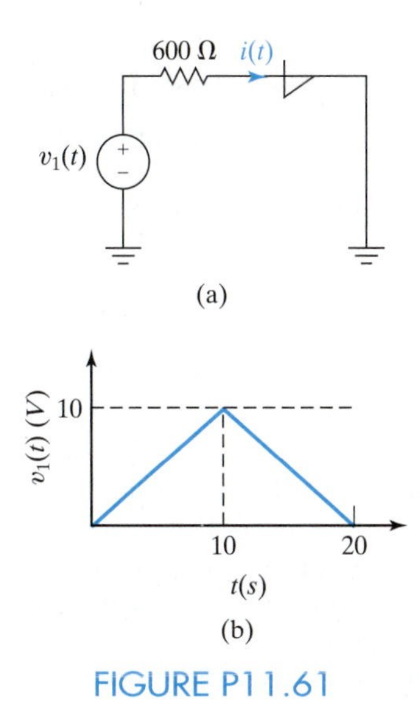

FIGURE P11.61

11.62. The circuit shown in Figure P11.62 can be used as a timer circuit. Switch S_1 is closed at $t = 0$ and the capacitor is initially uncharged; at time t_1 the thyristor will fire and turn on the small indicator light, which has a resistance of 100 Ω. The thyristor has $V_{BO} = 20$ V and $I_H = 30$ mA. Find time t_1.

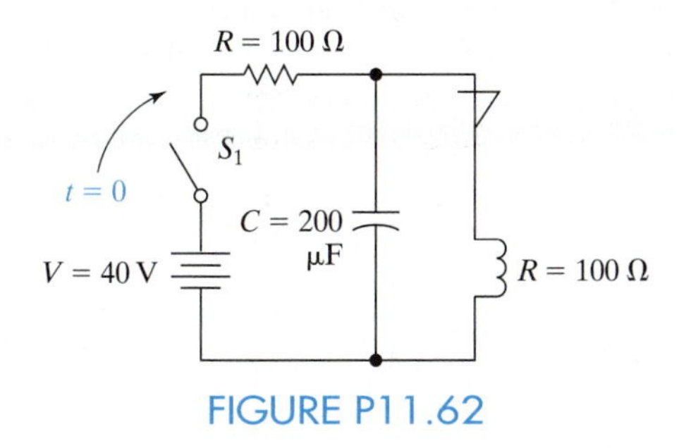

FIGURE P11.62

11.63. For the SCR motor speed controller shown in Figure 11.57, sketch the waveforms for the gate current and the motor current as a function of time for firing angles of 30° and 160°.

11.64. Figure P11.64 is a circuit in which switch S_1 is used in the normal mode of operation to control Q_1, which switches a large current in load R_L. If there is an accidental short across the load (simulated by closing S_2), the increased current in Q_1 and R_{sense} causes the SCR to fire, and this lowers the base voltage of Q_1, turning it off. Assume the SCR fires at $V_G = 0.7$ V, $V_{BE} = 0.7$ V, and $\beta = 500$. (a) Determine the normal current through R_L (and Q_1) when S_1 closes. (b) If there is a short across R_L, at what load current will the circuit "shut down" (turn off) Q_1? (c) What must be done to reactivate the circuit?

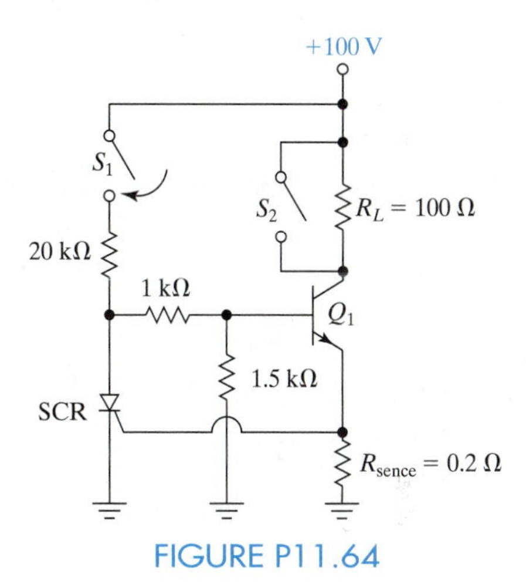

FIGURE P11.64

12

12–1 Introduction

Small-signal model and midband frequency range defined

In this chapter we will develop small-signal models for MOSFETs and BJTs and apply them in the solution of transistor circuit problems. The purpose of a small-signal model is to simplify the calculations involved in determining the ac response of a circuit.

A *small-signal model* is a *linearized model,* which presumes that the signal variations about the *Q*-point are sufficiently small so that all nonlinearities can be ignored. This assumption enables us to use a model with normal linear circuit elements, such as resistors, and dependent sources.

We will also assume in this chapter that these circuits operate in the *midband frequency range.* This range of signal frequencies is high enough that all coupling capacitors and bypass capacitors have sufficiently low impedance to be considered as ac shorts. In addition, the impedance of all device junction capacitances and parasitic capacitances are sufficiently high so that they can be considered as open circuits and ignored. It is in this *midband range* that most amplifiers are designed to operate. The ac gain of the circuit is generally constant over this range of frequencies, and is at its maximum value. The gain will generally decrease or "roll off" at both ends of the midband frequency region.

The signal input to a BJT is normally applied to the base-emitter *pn* junction. Therefore, we must develop a large and small signal model of the diode, which we will then apply to modeling the transistor.

12.1.1 Diode DC Resistance

Recall that we considered a *pn* junction diode's large-signal *V–I* characteristics as described by a nonlinear relationship, expressed by the diode equation presented in Chapter 10 as Eq. (10.9),

$$I_D = I_o[e^{\frac{qV_D}{kT}} - 1] \tag{12.1}$$

A plot of the *V–I* characteristic predicted by this equation is shown in Figure 12.1. Now assume there is a dc bias established so the diode conducts a current, I_1. The diode curve then enables us to determine the diode dc voltage, V_1. The pair of coordinates V_1 and I_1 identifies

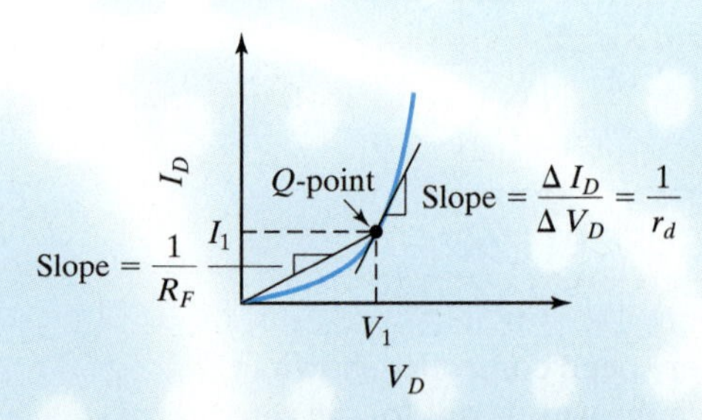

FIGURE 12.1 Illustration of dc and ac resistance on the *V–I* characteristic of a diode.

the Q-point, and the *static forward resistance,* R_F, is a dc resistance that is obtained from the expression

$$R_F = \frac{V_1}{I_1} \tag{12.2}$$

12.1.2 Diode Small-Signal (Dynamic or AC) Resistance

We can now consider the effect of a small signal applied to the diode. If we allow the voltage across the diode to vary up and down a small amount about the Q-point, the resulting current will also vary a small amount approximately *following a line tangent to the curve at the Q-point.* The relationship between the voltage variations, ΔV_D, and the current variations, ΔI_D, can be expressed as a ratio, which we call the incremental or *small-signal resistance,* r_d.

The slope of a line tangent to the V–I curve at the Q-point is proportional to the inverse of r_d, that is,

$$r_d \approx \left.\frac{\Delta V_D}{\Delta I_D}\right|_{\text{at the Q-point}} \tag{12.3}$$

and the slope at the Q-point is

$$slope = \frac{1}{r_d} = \frac{i_d}{v_d} \tag{12.4}$$

where v_d and i_d are the small-signal or incremental changes in voltage and current, which are by definition changes from the Q-point.

An expression for r_d was developed in Chapter 10 by differentiating the diode equation. This important result is

$$r_d = \frac{1}{\frac{\partial I_D}{\partial V_D}} = \frac{kT}{qI_D} \tag{12.5}$$

which at room temperature becomes

Equation for small-signal resistance of a diode at room temperature

$$r_d = \frac{0.026}{I_D}\,\Omega \tag{12.6}$$

Example 12.1

Let us determine the ac resistance of a silicon diode carrying 3.5 mA at room temperature.
From Eq. (12.6) the resistance is

$$r_d = \frac{0.026}{I_D} = \frac{0.026}{3.5 \times 10^{-3}} = 7.43\ \Omega$$

The dc bias circuits, such as those described in the previous chapter, establish the desired dc quiescent operating condition, or Q-point, of transistor amplifier circuits. If the applied signal causes small variations from this bias point, then small-signal linear models can be used for analysis, as will be illustrated in this chapter.

12.1.3 Nomenclature Review

The following table briefly reviews the meaning of uppercase and lowercase letters in describing the voltages and currents in small-signal analysis.

	Diode	MOSFET	BJT
Instantaneous total value	v_D, i_D	v_{GS}, i_D	v_{BE}, i_C
Instantaneous signal component	v_d, i_d	v_{gs}, i_d	v_{be}, i_c
Quiescent or dc value	V_D, I_D	V_{GS}, I_D	V_{BE}, I_C
Supply voltage (dc magnitude)	V, I	V_{DD}, V_{GG}	V_{CC}, V_{BB}

12–2 General Linear Two-Port Models

Transistors, both MOSFETs and BJTs, can be modeled as special cases of general two-port linear networks. A *port* is defined as a pair of connections, and thus a two-port network has a pair of wires (connections) for the input and another pair for the output, as shown in Figure 12.2(a).

y, z, and h parameters defined

The mathematical description of a two-port network can be accomplished in several fully equivalent forms. These are commonly referred to as models using *y parameters* (admittance parameters), *z parameters* (impedance parameters), or *h parameters* (hybrid parameters).

Illustration of two-port network using y parameters

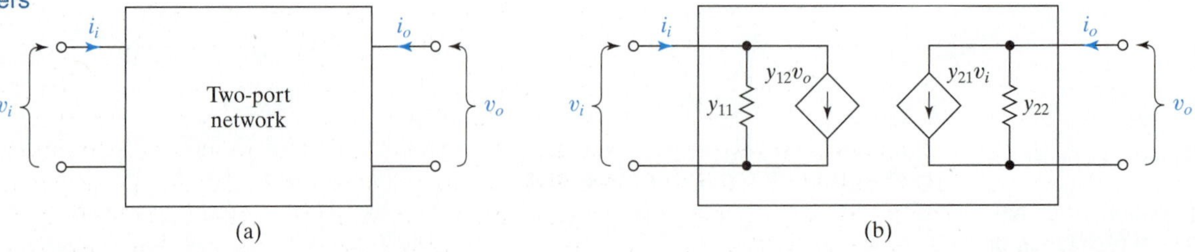

FIGURE 12.2 (a) A two-port network, and (b) two-port network using y parameters.

In each case, two equations can be used to relate the input voltage and current to the output voltage and current using four parameters.

Using y parameters:

$$\begin{aligned} i_i &= v_i y_{11} + v_o y_{12} \\ i_o &= v_i y_{21} + v_o y_{22} \end{aligned} \tag{12.7}$$

Using z parameters:

$$\begin{aligned} v_i &= i_i z_{11} + i_o z_{12} \\ v_o &= i_i z_{21} + i_o z_{22} \end{aligned} \tag{12.8}$$

Using h parameters:

$$\begin{aligned} v_i &= i_i h_{11} + v_o h_{12} \\ i_o &= i_i h_{21} + v_o h_{22} \end{aligned} \tag{12.9}$$

A dimensional analysis will confirm that all the y parameters have units of admittance and all the z parameters have units of impedance. The units for the hybrid parameters are as follows: h_{11}—impedance, h_{12}—voltage transfer ratio, h_{21}—current transfer ratio, and h_{22}—admittance.

Notice that the parameters with the same subscript, for example, y_{11} and y_{22}, relate change in voltage to the change in current at the same pair of terminals. The other two parameters, for example, y_{12} and y_{21}, relate the change in voltage at one pair of terminals to the change in current at the other, and, therefore, they are termed transadmittances or transconductances. For example, y_{21} relates the change in output current to the change in input voltage, for the case when v_o is zero, that is, shorted.

Consider, for illustration, the set of admittance equations given in Eq. (12.7). Note that each of the currents, i_i and i_o, are composed of two components represented by the two terms on the right side of each equation. The term that relates current and voltage at the same port can be modeled by an admittance, while the remaining term is modeled by a dependent current source with a magnitude expressed by that y-parameter term. Thus, an equivalent circuit for the transistor can be constructed in which the input and output are each represented by an admittance in parallel with a dependent current source, as shown in Figure 12.2(b). A similar circuit model could be developed for each of the other parameter sets.

Figure 12.3 illustrates all the possible circuit configurations for the MOSFET and the BJT, and a two-port network analysis approach may be applied to each of these. For each circuit configuration and for every dc bias condition, a different set of small-signal parameters must be obtained and used for analysis. The process of determining the small-signal parameters can be cumbersome. In actual practice these parameters are often measured directly by computer-controlled instrumentation that applies a dc bias to the transistor and then superimposes upon it small-signal variations in order to measure the small-signal ac parameters. One can also calculate these small-signal parameters from the large-signal output curves. This approach will be illustrated later. In the following example, the small-signal parameters are assumed to be known.

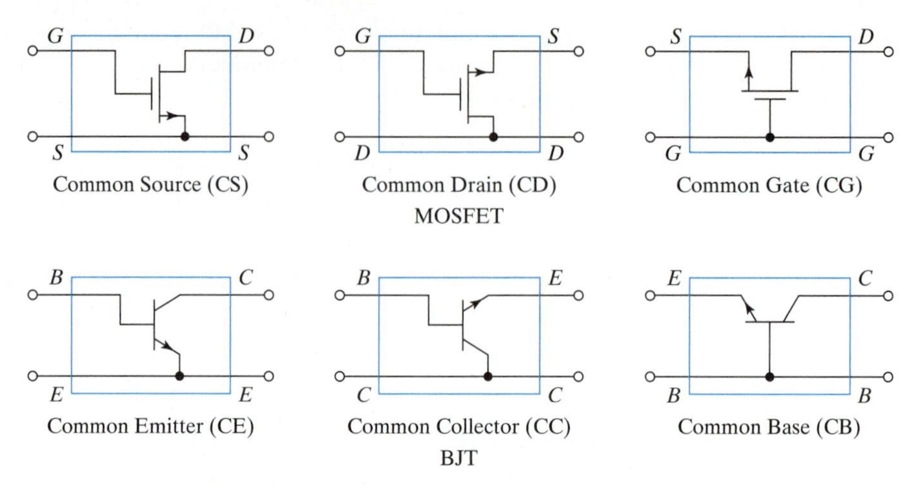

FIGURE 12.3 Two-port configurations for MOSFET and BJT transistor circuits.

Example 12.2

A MOSFET is placed in a common source amplifier circuit with an equivalent load resistance of $R_L = 10\ \text{k}\Omega$. Let us determine the small-signal voltage gain of the circuit if the y parameters of the MOSFET are known to be $y_{11} = 0$ S, $y_{12} = 0$ S, $y_{21} = 1 \times 10^{-3}$ S, and $y_{22} = 0$ S, where S is the unit of siemens.

This network configuration can be represented by the circuit shown in Figure 12.4. Since $y_{22} = 0$, the second part of Eq. (12.7) reduces to

$$i_o = y_{21}\, v_i$$

In addition, we note from Figure 12.4 that

$$v_o = -i_o\, R_L$$

Therefore, the small-signal voltage gain is

$$A_v = \frac{v_o}{v_i} = -\frac{i_o\, R_L}{\dfrac{i_o}{y_{21}}} = -y_{21}\, R_L = -10$$

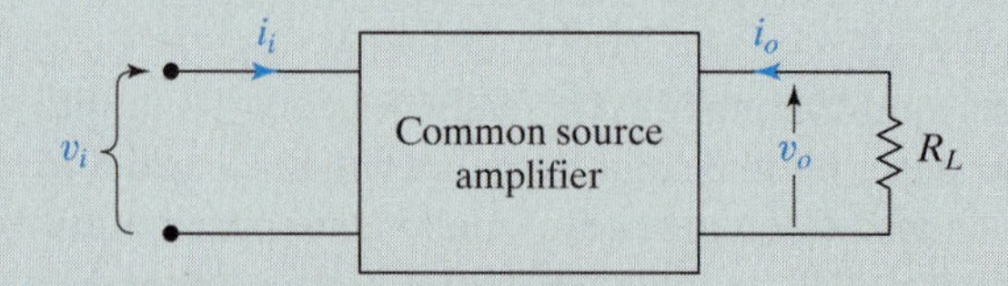

FIGURE 12.4 Circuit used in Example 12.2.

Circuit for simplified small-signal transistor model

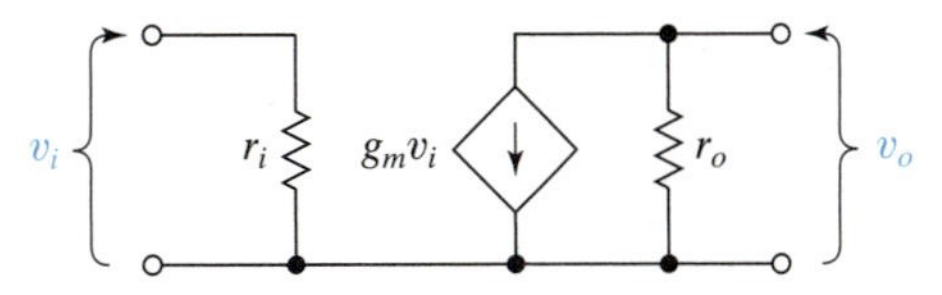

FIGURE 12.5 Simplified small-signal transistor model.

It is common practice to use two-port network theory to describe small-signal transistor characteristics. However, as the previous example indicates, it is often not necessary to use all four parameters to obtain reasonably accurate transistor modeling. For example, in the midband frequency region, the input impedance of a MOSFET is typically so large that z_{11} can generally be assumed to be infinite. For the same reason, we may often assume that $y_{11} = 0$. The parameter y_{12}, which models the signal coupling from the output back to the input, is generally negligible. Therefore, small-signal linear circuit models that simplify the parameter measurement and analysis process are very useful, especially at low and moderate frequencies.

In the midband frequency range, where device capacitances and inductances are ignored, the admittance and impedance parameters are reduced to their "real" components, or simply, conductance and resistance.

The general small-signal equivalent circuit of such a model is shown in Figure 12.5 where

$$\begin{aligned} r_i &= \text{input resistance} = v_i/i_i \\ g_m &= \text{transconductance} = i_o/v_i|\text{output shorted; } v_o = 0 \\ r_o &= \text{output resistance} = v_o/i_o|\text{input shorted; } v_i = 0 \end{aligned}$$

These parameters can be related to any other set of parameters through algebraic manipulation of the parameter equations.

In the following sections, we apply this simplified small-signal model to the MOSFET and the BJT.

12–3 The MOSFET Small-Signal Model

Typical output characteristic curves for a common source MOSFET are shown in Figure 12.6. The small-signal model is developed to describe the device's behavior for *small excursions of voltage and current about the* Q*-point* in the active region where the output curves are almost

Determining small-signal parameters from transistor output curves

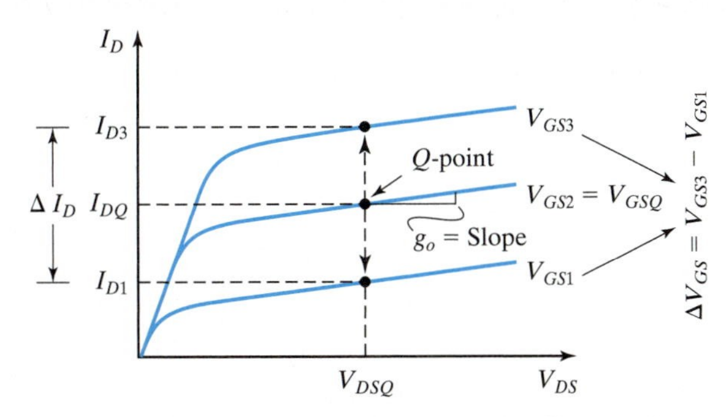

FIGURE 12.6 Illustration of estimating small-signal parameters from common source output curves.

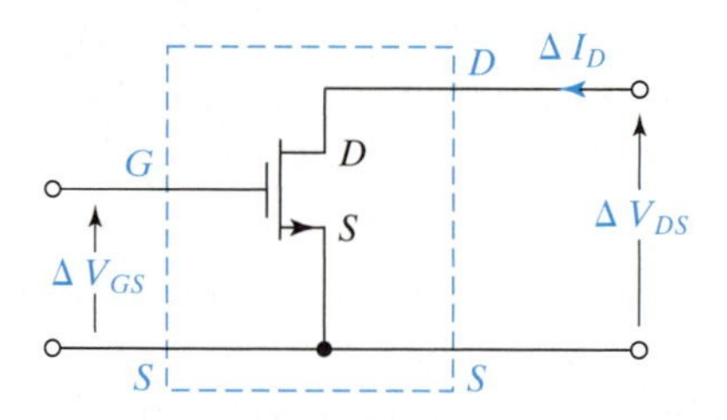

FIGURE 12.7 Common source amplifier configuration.

horizontal. A dc bias is applied to the transistor by a bias circuit, which establishes its Q-point at the point defined by V_{DSQ} and I_{DQ}.

The common source amplifier configuration is illustrated in Figure 12.7. The input voltage is applied from gate to source, and the output is taken from drain to source. An examination of the output curve about the Q-point reveals that only slight changes in the output current I_D occur as V_{DS} is changed. I_D is primarily affected by changes in input voltage, V_{GS}.

Therefore, a small-signal model representing the *output* of the device consists of both a dependent current source and a conductance, as shown in Figure 12.8.

The dependent current source has a value of $g_m v_{gs}$, where g_m is the transconductance of the device and is defined as:

$$g_m = \left.\frac{\partial I_D}{\partial V_{GS}}\right|_{V_{DS}=V_{DSQ}} \approx \left.\frac{\Delta I_D}{\Delta V_{GS}}\right|_{V_{DS}=constant=V_{DSQ}} \tag{12.10}$$

Note that the parameter g_m is the same as the parameter y_{21} in the two-port admittance model. Recall that when determining y_{21} or equivalently the transconductance g_m, the output is ac shorted, that is, $v_{ds} = 0$ or $V_{DS} =$ constant. The appropriate small-signal model parameter is determined at the Q-point.

The value of g_m can be estimated from the output curves of the device by drawing a vertical line ($\Delta V_{DS} = 0$) through the Q-point, which intersects V_{GS} curves above and below the Q-point. Assuming that a change in V_{GS} is the difference between these neighboring curves, and calculating the ratio of that change to the resulting change in output current, yields an approximate value for g_m. With reference to Figure 12.6, this calculation is

$$g_m \approx \frac{\Delta I_D}{\Delta V_{GS}} = \left.\frac{I_{D3} - I_{D1}}{V_{GS3} - V_{GS1}}\right|_{V_{DS}=constant=V_{DSQ}} \tag{12.11}$$

We have purposely exaggerated the variations in voltages and currents in this illustration. In general, small-signal variations about the Q-point are quite small.

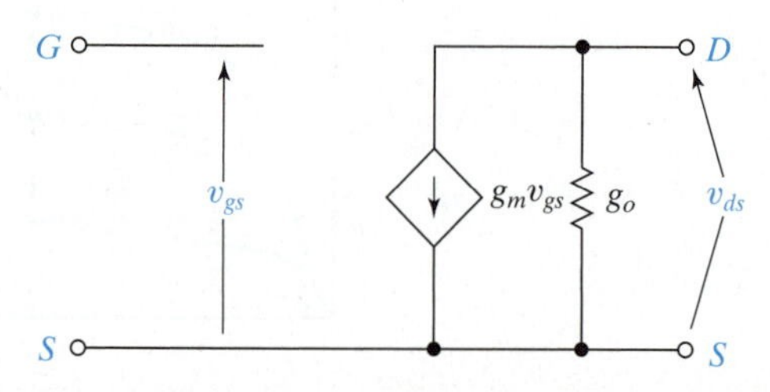

FIGURE 12.8 Small-signal model for a common source configuration.

The output conductance, g_o, is included in the model to provide the small change in output current resulting from changes in output voltage. This conductance accounts for the small but finite slope of the output curves in the active region.

$$g_o = \left.\frac{\partial I_D}{\partial V_{DS}}\right|_{\text{at the Q-point}} \approx \left.\frac{\Delta I_D}{\Delta V_{DS}}\right|_{\text{at the Q-point}} = \textit{slope of curve at Q-point} \quad (12.12)$$

It is interesting to note that g_o is the same as y_{22} in the two-port admittance model.

As illustrated in Figure 12.7, the *input* to the gate of a MOSFET is electrically insulated from the remainder of the device. Furthermore, since device capacitances are small and need not be considered unless we are performing high-frequency analyses, the MOSFET circuit model for the input is simply an open circuit, as shown in Figure 12.8. Once again, note that this assumption is equivalent to setting y_{12} and y_{11} to zero in the two-port admittance model. The resulting model is quite useful for solving circuit problems.

Example 12.3

Consider a MOSFET with output curves as shown in Figure 12.9. Using the procedures described above, let us determine the small-signal parameters, g_m and g_o, and then use them to calculate the small-signal voltage gain of a common source circuit utilizing this device with a total external load resistance of 8 kΩ.

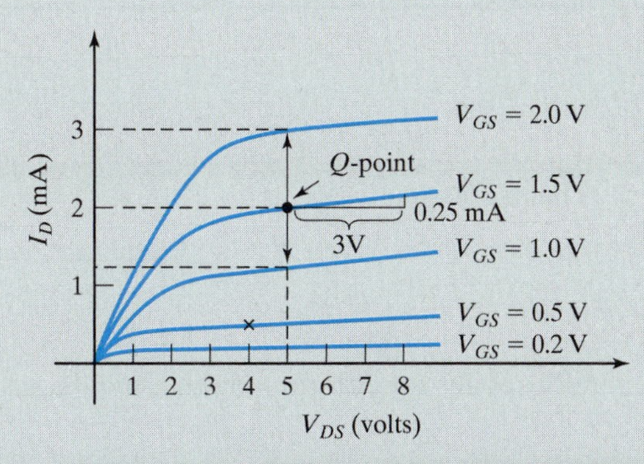

FIGURE 12.9 MOSFET output curves used in Examples 12.3 and 12.4.

Figure 12.9 indicates that for V_{GS}, changes of ± one-half volt ($\Delta V_{GS} = 1$ V), the current change ΔI_D is 1.75 mA. Therefore, using Eq. (12.11), g_m becomes:

$$g_m \approx \frac{\Delta I_D}{\Delta V_{GS}} = \frac{1.75 \times 10^{-3}}{1} = 1.75 \text{ mS}$$

From the figure, we also note that the output conductance, g_o, is

$$g_o \approx \frac{\Delta I_D}{\Delta V_{DS}} = \frac{0.25 \times 10^{-3}}{3} = 83.3\ \mu\text{S}$$

In order to calculate the voltage gain of the CS circuit represented by this model, we must first determine the total equivalent load resistance, R_{Leq}. This equivalent load is the parallel combination of g_o and the external load resistance of 8 kΩ, as illustrated in Figure 12.10.

Hence

$$R_{Leq} = \frac{1}{g_o} \| R_L = \left[\frac{1}{83.3\ \mu\text{S}}\right] \| 8\text{ k} = 4.8\text{ k}\Omega$$

And, therefore, the voltage gain, A_v, is

$$A_v = \frac{v_o}{v_i} = -\frac{v_{gs} g_m R_{Leq}}{v_{gs}} = -g_m R_{Leq} = -(1.75 \times 10^{-3})(4.8\text{ k}) = -8.4$$

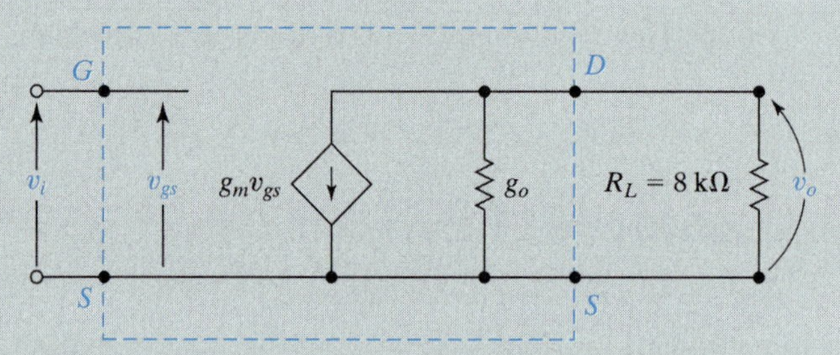

FIGURE 12.10 MOSFET small-signal model used in Example 12.3.

Equation for small-signal voltage gain of common source amplifier

The expression

$$\boxed{A_v = -g_m R_{Leq}} \tag{12.13}$$

generally applies for determining the small-signal voltage gain of a CS amplifier.

12-4 MOSFET Amplifier Circuits—Small-Signal Analysis

12.4.1 The Common Source Amplifier

In this section, a complete amplifier circuit will be analyzed using small-signal analysis. First, the dc circuit is analyzed to determine the dc bias condition. At this specific bias point, the small-signal parameters appropriate for the particular bias condition are determined. Then a small-signal circuit model of the transistor and the circuit in which it operates are constructed. And finally, small-signal calculations are performed to determine the ac midband circuit performance.

The principles inherent in the analysis will be presented through the use of several examples.

Example 12.4

The complete schematic diagram of a common source amplifier utilizing an n-channel MOSFET is shown in Figure 12.11(a). The MOSFET has the output curves illustrated in Figure 12.9. Let us determine the dc bias condition (Q-point) and the small-signal parameters, g_m and g_o, for this device at that Q-point.

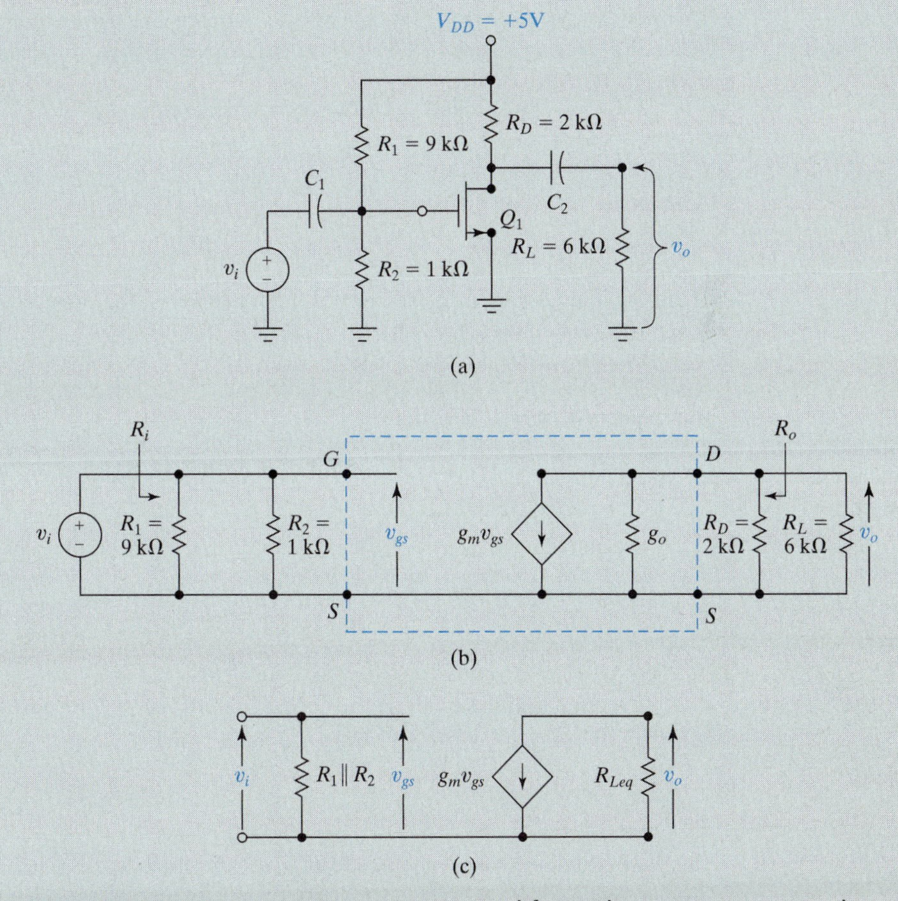

FIGURE 12.11 A common source amplifier schematic circuit and its small-signal equivalent circuits.

We will first determine the dc drain current, I_D, and the drain-to-source voltage, V_{DS}. Since a capacitor is a dc open circuit, the coupling capacitors, C_1 and C_2, block dc current and, therefore, nothing to the left of C_1 or to the right of C_2 in the circuit need be considered for the dc calculations.

Calculation of dc voltages and currents (Q-point)

In the active region, the gate-to-source voltage will set the drain current. Therefore, we must first determine V_{GS}. The source voltage is

$$V_s = 0$$

The gate voltage determined by the voltage divider is

$$V_G = V_{DD}\left[\frac{R_2}{R_1 + R_2}\right] = 5[0.1] = 0.5 \text{ V}$$

Therefore,

$$V_{GS} = V_G - V_S = 0.5 - 0 = 0.5 \text{ V}$$

We now know that the Q-point will lie somewhere along the curve corresponding to $V_{GS} = 0.5$ Volts in Figure 12.9. This curve is at a level of approximately $I_D = 0.5$ mA throughout the active region.

If $I_D = 0.5$ mA, then V_{DS} can be determined as follows.

$$V_D = V_{DD} - R_D I_D = 5 - (2\text{ k})(0.5 \times 10^{-3}) = 4 \text{ V}$$

And hence

$$V_{DS} = V_D - V_S = 4 - 0 = 4 \text{ V}$$

Therefore, the Q-point is located on the output curves at the point defined by $I_D = 0.5$ mA and $V_{DS} = 4$ V and marked with an x.

The small-signal transconductance, g_m, will now be determined at the specified Q-point. From Figure 12.9, note that a variation in V_{GS} of 0.8 volts (+0.5, −0.3) yields a drain current variation of approximately 1.0 mA. Therefore,

Calculation of small-signal parameters

$$g_m \approx \frac{\Delta I_D}{\Delta V_{GS}} = \frac{1.0 \times 10^{-3}}{0.8} = 1.25 \times 10^{-3} \text{ S}$$

The output conductance is often difficult to determine graphically when the slopes are small. However, for this device g_o can be approximated as

$$g_o \approx \frac{\Delta I_D}{\Delta V_{DS}} \approx \frac{0.1 \times 10^{-3}}{4} = 2.5 \times 10^{-5} \text{ S}$$

It is often useful to convert the output conductance to an equivalent resistance value, and hence for this case the output resistance of the transistor is

$$r_o = \frac{1}{g_o} = 40 \text{ k}\Omega \qquad (12.14)$$

This value, which we have computed to illustrate the procedure, is relatively low. Typical output resistance values for MOSFETs in the active region are normally much higher.

In general, a small-signal equivalent circuit for an amplifier operating in the midband frequency region can be constructed from a schematic drawing of a circuit using the following procedure.

1. Consider all bypass and coupling capacitors as ac shorts.
2. Consider all independent dc voltage sources as ac shorts. If the instantaneous voltage between two nodes is not allowed to vary, then there is no ac voltage component possible and it acts as if there were an ac short. Thus, the supply (V_{DD}) becomes the same node as ground.

3. Consider all independent dc current sources as ac open circuits.
4. Insert the small-signal transistor model into the circuit in place of the transistor.

This procedure is illustrated by the following example.

Example 12.5

Once again we consider the amplifier circuit shown in Figure 12.11(a). For this network, we wish to (a) construct the small-signal equivalent circuit, assuming the amplifier is operating in the mid-band frequency region, and (b) use this equivalent circuit to calculate the small-signal voltage gain.

(a) Using the procedure outlined above, the schematic circuit for this amplifier is reduced to the small-signal equivalent circuit shown in Figure 12.11(b). Both capacitors act as ac shorts and since the supply node V_{DD} is also an ac ground, R_1 and R_2 are in parallel.

The small-signal MOSFET model is then substituted for the transistor symbol in the circuit drawing. Note that the model representing the transistor is outlined with a box.

Finally, since C_2 is an ac short, the output of this circuit consists of the dc load resistance, R_D, in parallel with the external load, R_L.

The ac gain can now be calculated from this small-signal model of the amplifier. From this equivalent circuit, we note that the input voltage, v_i, is the same as v_{gs}.

The three resistors in the output of this circuit are all in parallel and can be reduced to an equivalent load resistance, R_{Leq}. Thus, the circuit can be simplified to that shown in Figure 12.11(c), where

Calculation of R_{Leq}–the equivalent load resistance

$$R_{Leq} = r_o \| R_D \| R_L = \frac{1}{\dfrac{1}{r_o} + \dfrac{1}{R_D} + \dfrac{1}{R_L}} = 1.45\ \text{k}\Omega \qquad (12.15)$$

The output voltage can be expressed as

$$v_o = -g_m v_{gs} R_{Leq} = -g_m v_i R_{Leq}$$

And therefore, the voltage gain, A_v

Calculation of small-signal voltage gain

$$A_v = \frac{v_o}{v_i} = -g_m R_{Leq} = -(1.25 \times 10^{-3})(1.45\ \text{k}) = -1.81$$

Two other commonly used terms can be defined with the aid of the previous example: (1) amplifier input resistance, R_i, and (2) amplifier output resistance, R_o.

Amplifier input resistance and output resistance

1. The *input resistance of an amplifier,* R_i, is the total equivalent resistance seen looking into the input of the amplifier. In the previous example,

$$R_i = R_1 \| R_2 = 1\ \text{k} \| 9\ \text{k} = 900\ \Omega$$

2. The *output resistance of the amplifier,* R_o, is the total resistance seen looking back into the output terminals of the amplifier, not including any external load resistance. In the previous example,

$$R_o = r_o \| R_D = 40\ \text{k} \| 2\ \text{k} = 1.90\ \text{k}\Omega$$

The arrows in Figure 12.11(b) provide a reference for measuring both R_i and R_o.

12.4.2 The Common Gate Amplifier

The dc bias techniques for the common gate amplifier are similar to those for the common source. However, in this case the gate is connected to ac ground, the input is applied from source to gate, and the output is taken from drain to gate.

Example 12.6

Consider the common gate MOSFET circuit shown in Figure 12.12(a). If the dc drain current is measured to be 1 mA, let us determine the value of V_{GG} required to establish V_{GS} at +1 volt.

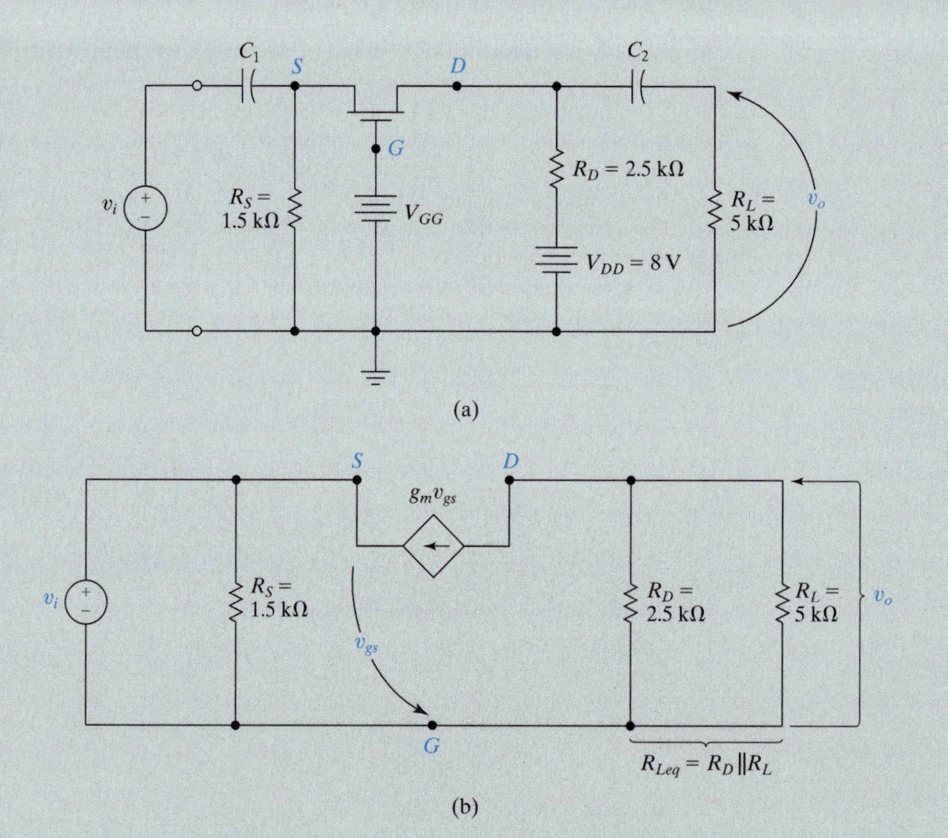

FIGURE 12.12 (a) Common gate MOSFET amplifier schematic circuit. (b) Common gate MOSFET amplifier small-signal equivalent circuit.

The path of the dc drain current includes V_{DD}, R_D, the transistor (D-to-S), and R_S. Therefore,

$$V_S = I_D R_S = (1 \times 10^{-3})(1.5\text{ k}) = 1.5\text{ V}$$

And since V_{GS} must be 1 V

$$V_{GG} = V_G = V_{GS} + V_S = 1 + 1.5 = 2.5\text{ V}$$

Example 12.7

Let us determine (a) the small-signal equivalent circuit for the amplifier shown in Figure 12.12(a), and (b) the small-signal voltage gain of this common gate circuit, assuming the transistor parameters are

$$g_o = 0$$

$$g_m = 5 \times 10^{-3}\ \text{S}$$

(a) The small-signal equivalent circuit is shown in Figure 12.12(b). Since $g_o = 0$, it does not appear in the equivalent circuit.

(b) Note that the only ac current through R_{Leq} is $g_m v_{gs}$; therefore, with reference to Figure 12.12(b),

$$v_i = -v_{gs}$$

$$v_o = -g_m v_{gs} R_{Leq}$$

Equation for small-signal voltage gain of common gate amplifier

and, therefore, the voltage gain is

$$A_v = \frac{v_o}{v_i} = g_m R_{Leq} = 8.33 \tag{12.16}$$

Example 12.8

Let us determine the input resistance, R_i, of the amplifier described in Example 12.7.

The input signal to the transistor is applied at the source terminal, NOT the gate. Therefore, in this case, the resistance looking into the transistor is not infinite.

The equivalent circuit in Figure 12.12(b) indicates that because of the presence of the dependent source, a change in the input voltage $(-v_{gs})$ at the input terminals of the transistor will result in a change in input current. The input resistance of the transistor is the ratio of the change in input voltage to the change in input current at the terminals S–G. Therefore,

Equation for resistance looking into the source of a MOSFET

$$r_{i(source)} = -\frac{v_{gs}}{-g_m v_{gs}} = \frac{1}{g_m} \tag{12.17}$$

The input resistance of the amplifier is then the parallel combination of R_S and $1/g_m$,

$$R_i = R_S \| \frac{1}{g_m} = (1.5\ \text{k}) \| (200) = 176\ \Omega$$

Several general comments can be made about the common gate circuit. The input resistance to this circuit is not high as it is in both the common source and the common drain configurations. The voltage gain is positive, that is, the circuit does NOT invert the signal, and the magnitude of the voltage gain can be quite large. The circuit is also useful for matching a low impedance input to a high impedance output.

It is important to note that Eq. (12.17) can be used to express the resistance looking into the source for any properly biased MOSFET.

12.4.3 The Common Drain Amplifier

The *common drain* (CD) amplifier is sometimes called a *source follower,* a typical example of which is shown in Figure D12.1. A calculation of the voltage gain of this circuit will reveal that it is slightly less than unity, and the approximation is often made that it is simply "one." This circuit is, therefore, not useful for providing increased signal voltage levels, but is primarily used for impedance conversion. The input resistance of this circuit can be made quite high, and its output resistance can be made quite low.

The exact expression for this amplifier's small-signal voltage gain, A_v, can be obtained by inserting the MOSFET model into the small-signal equivalent circuit—a procedure described in this chapter. The result obtained is

Equation for small-signal voltage gain of common drain amplifier

$$A_v = \frac{v_o}{v_i} = \frac{g_m R_{Leq}}{1 + g_m R_{Leq}} \qquad (12.18)$$

where R_{Leq} is defined as the parallel combination of R_S and any other external load resistance. This amplifier configuration has a very high input resistance, low output resistance, and does not invert the signal.

Drill Exercise

D12.1. Consider the common drain amplifier circuit shown in Figure D12.1. Note that the drain is connected directly to the supply, that is, an ac ground. The calculation of dc bias conditions for this circuit is similar to methods previously described.

Determine the voltage gain assuming $g_m = 7 \times 10^{-3}$ S, $R_S = 2\ \text{k}\Omega$ and $R_L = 5\ \text{k}\Omega$.

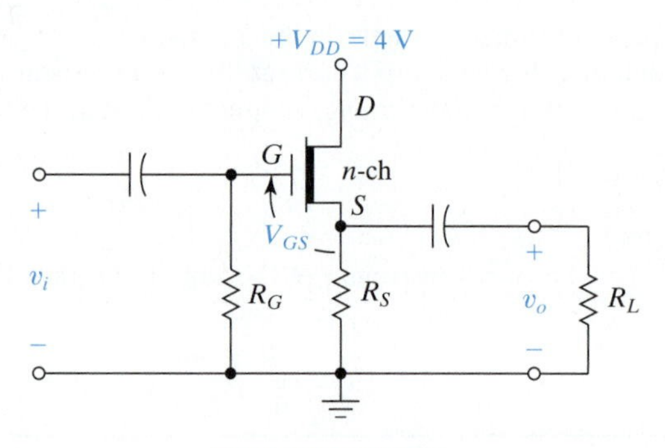

FIGURE D12.1

Ans: $A_v = 0.909$

12.4.4 Summary of Important MOSFET Relationships

Table 12.1 summarizes the important relationships for small-signal circuit analyses of MOSFETs in the midband frequency region.

TABLE 12.1 Important MOSFET Relationships for Small-Signal Analysis

Configuration	Notes	Voltage Gain, A_v	Input Resistance: To Transistor	Input Resistance: To Circuit	Output Resistance: Transistor	Output Resistance: Circuit
COMMON SOURCE	$R_{Leq} = R_D \| R_L \| r_o$ R_G = equivalent resistance of gate bias resistance (voltage signal inverted)	$A_v = \frac{v_o}{v_i}$ $A_v = -g_m R_{Leq}$	$r_i \approx \infty$	$R_i \approx R_G$	$r_o \approx \frac{1}{g_o}$	$R_o \approx R_D \| \frac{1}{g_o}$
COMMON GATE	$R_{Leq} = R_D \| R_L$ R_G (as above) Assume $r_o = \infty$ (voltage signal not inverted)	$A_v = g_m R_{Leq}$	$r_i \approx \frac{1}{g_m}$	$R_i \approx R_S \| \frac{1}{g_m}$	$r_o > \frac{1}{g_o}$	$R_o \approx R_D$
COMMON DRAIN	$R_{Leq} = R_S \| R_L$ R_G (as above) (voltage signal not inverted)	$A_v = \frac{g_m R_{Leq}}{1 + g_m R_{Leq}}$	$r_i \approx \infty$	$R_i \approx R_G$	$r_o \approx \frac{1}{g_m}$	$R_o \approx R_S \| \frac{1}{g_m}$

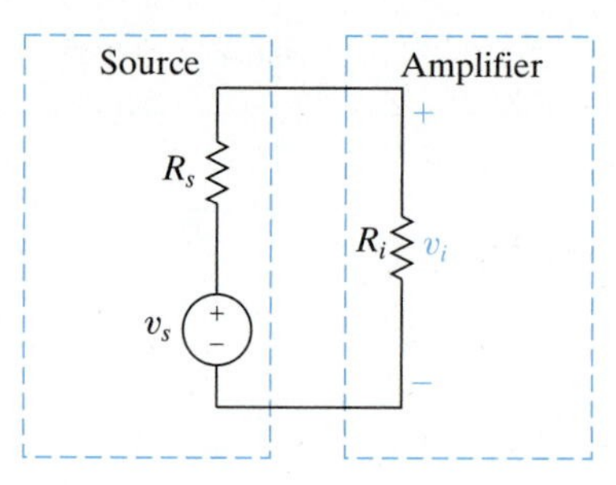

FIGURE 12.13 Equivalent circuit of the input of an amplifier.

An analytic expression for g_m derived from Eq. (11.3) is $g_m = 2K(V_{GS} - V_T)$; similarly, for depletion-mode devices, from Eq. (11.7) $g_m = 2I_{DSS}V_P^{-2}(V_{GS} - V_P)$.

12-5 Voltage Gain Loss at the Input

In our calculations of small-signal voltage gain thus far, we have only considered the gain of the transistor stage, that is, v_o/v_i, where v_i is the signal voltage at the INPUT of the transistor. If the transistor stage is driven by a voltage source, v_s, with finite internal resistance, R_s, some gain will be lost in the input circuit. The input circuit of an amplifier stage can be represented by the circuit shown in Figure 12.13, where R_i represents the input resistance to the amplifier stage.

From this circuit,

$$v_i = v_s\left[\frac{R_i}{R_i + R_s}\right] \tag{12.19}$$

Normally, R_i is designed to be large compared to R_s, so that

$$v_i \approx v_s \tag{12.20}$$

Equation for small-signal voltage loss at the input; this gain is less than one

We often speak of the voltage gain of the input circuit, which is always <1, as A_{vs}, where

$$A_{vs} = \frac{v_i}{v_s} = \frac{R_i}{R_i + R_s} \tag{12.21}$$

The gain of the entire circuit from v_s to v_o is the product of the two gains

$$\frac{v_o}{v_s} = \left[\frac{v_i}{v_s}\right]\left[\frac{v_o}{v_i}\right] = A_{vs}A_v \tag{12.22}$$

These same input circuit considerations also apply to the bipolar transistor circuits described in the next section.

12-6 The BJT Small-Signal Model

There are two major differences between the BJT and the MOSFET that affect small-signal modeling: (1) the input connection to the BJT is always attached to one end of a forward biased base emitter junction, which is not an extremely large impedance as was assumed for the

MOSFET gate; and (2) since output current for the BJT is most conveniently modeled as if it were controlled by input current, the output curves for a BJT are constructed by plotting a separate curve for different input currents, NOT voltage, as was the case for a MOSFET.

12.6.1 The Common Emitter Model

We will consider first the most common bipolar circuit configuration, the common emitter. Figure 12.14(a) shows the two-port representation of this configuration, with the input applied between base and emitter and output taken from collector to emitter.

Applying the small-signal model of Figure 12.5 to this configuration, we obtain the circuit of Figure 12.14(b). Note the introduction of the term r_{ib}, which represents the input resistance of the device looking into the base terminal. In a similar manner, we will later define another term, r_{ie}, which we use to designate the input resistance looking into the emitter terminal for the common base circuit.

The magnitude of r_{ib} can be easily calculated. This resistance represents the small-signal resistance of the forward biased base emitter diode seen from the base side of the device. In the first section of this chapter, we reviewed the expression for determining the small-signal resistance of a diode and found that it is inversely related to the dc bias current, which in this case is the dc base current, I_B. Therefore, r_{ib} can be determined by extension from Eq. (12.5) as

Equation for calculating the BJT small-signal parameter, r_{ib}

$$r_{ib} = \frac{kT}{qI_B} \tag{12.23}$$

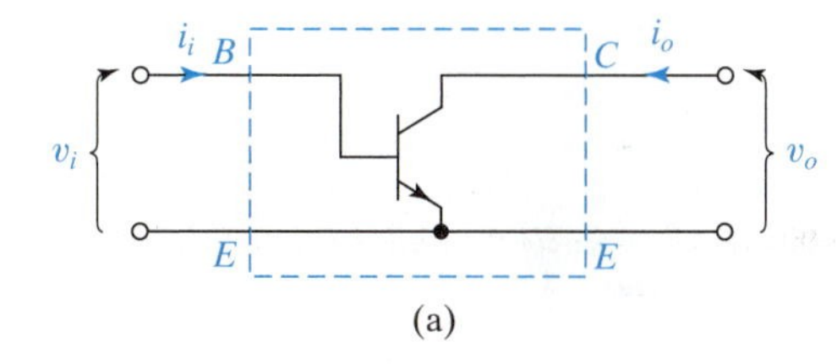

(a)

Drawing of small-signal model for BJT

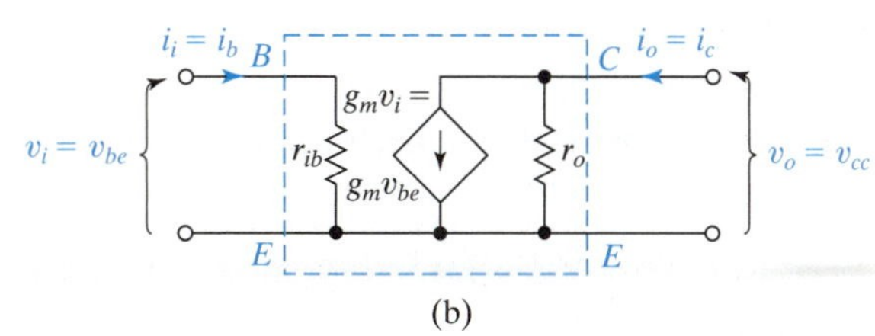

(b)

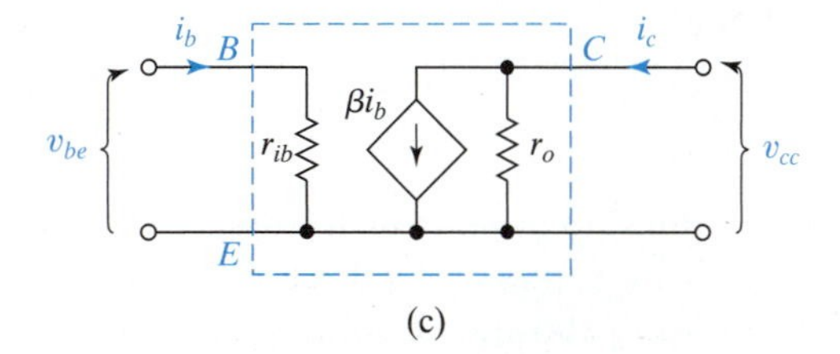

(c)

FIGURE 12.14 (a) Final BJT common emitter circuit configuration; (b) BJT common emitter small-signal model; (c) final BJT common emitter small-signal model.

Example 12.9

We wish to determine the input resistance, r_{ib}, for a transistor that is biased in the common emitter configuration, assuming it has a dc collector current of 1 mA and a beta of 50 at room temperature.

In order to determine r_{ib}, we must first determine I_B. Recall that β relates I_C to I_B in the active region, that is,

$$\beta = \frac{I_C}{I_B}$$

From the data we obtain

$$I_B = \frac{I_C}{\beta} = \frac{1 \times 10^{-3}}{50} = 20\ \mu\text{A}$$

Therefore, at room temperature,

$$r_{ib} = \frac{0.026}{I_B} = \frac{0.026}{20 \times 10^{-6}} = 1.3\ \text{k}\Omega \qquad (12.24)$$

The output section of this *CE* model has a dependent current source, $g_m v_i$, and an output resistance, r_o. The "short-circuit output current" is the ac current that flows through a short placed across the output from *C* to *E*. For this case all the current from the current source flows in the short and

$$i_o = g_m v_i$$

or equivalently,

$$i_c = g_m v_{be} \qquad (12.25)$$

Furthermore, we can assume, for purposes of this discussion, that beta represents the ratio of the collector current to base current, for both dc current and ac current. Therefore,

$$i_c = \beta i_b \qquad (12.26)$$

And hence

$$g_m v_{be} = \beta i_b \qquad (12.27)$$

This relationship permits us to replace the current source in the output of the small-signal model with a dependent source proportional to the input current, i_b, as shown in Figure 12.14(c). While the models shown in Figures 12.14(b) and (c) are equivalent and either can be used for circuit calculations, the model in Figure 12.14(c) has found widespread acceptance due to its ease of use, and is called a simplified hybrid -π model.

Example 12.10

A BJT is biased in the common emitter configuration with a dc base current of 10 microamperes and has an external equivalent load resistance of 10 kΩ. Let us determine the small-signal voltage gain of this circuit assuming the transistor has a beta of 100 and an output resistance, r_o, of 30 kΩ at the Q-point.

The small-signal model for this configuration is shown in Figure 12.15. From this model we note that the output voltage is

$$v_o = -(\beta i_b)(r_o \| R_{Leq})$$

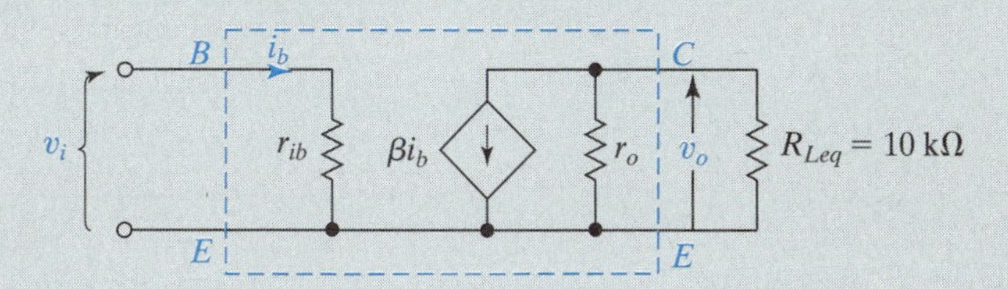

FIGURE 12.15 Equivalent circuit used in Example 12.10.

and the input current i_b is

$$i_b = \frac{v_i}{r_{ib}}$$

Equation for calculating small-signal voltage gain of common emitter amplifier

Therefore,

$$A_v = \frac{v_o}{v_i} = -\frac{\beta(r_o \| R_{Leq})}{r_{ib}} \tag{12.28}$$

Recall that at room temperature,

$$r_{ib} = \frac{0.026}{I_B} = \frac{0.026}{10 \times 10^{-6}} = 2.6 \text{ k}\Omega$$

and, therefore, from Eq. (12.28),

$$A_v = -\frac{(100)(7.5 \text{ k})}{2.6 \text{ k}} = -288$$

In many practical circuits we find that $r_o \gg R_{Leq}$, and hence r_o is often ignored in the calculation of A_v.

The values of the BJT small-signal parameters can be determined by direct measurement on an actual device, or from calculations using the output curves. The input resistance, r_{ib}, can be calculated using Eq. (12.23), in which only the dc base current is a variable. The parameters on the output side of the model, β and r_o, can be determined from the output curves, as illustrated in the following example.

Example 12.11

Consider the typical output curves for a common emitter device as shown in Figure 12.16. If the transistor is biased with the Q-point at $I_C = 2$ mA and $V_{CE} = 6$ volts, let us calculate approximate values for β and r_o at this Q-point.

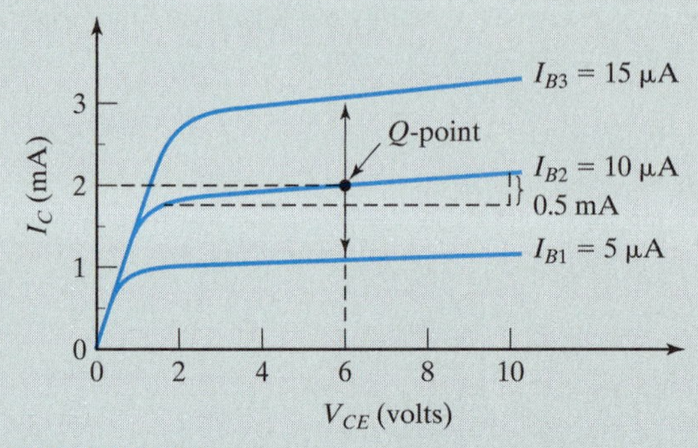

FIGURE 12.16 Common emitter output curves used in Example 12.11.

In order to determine β, we construct a vertical line through the Q-point that intersects the curve above and below the Q-point. These intersections determine the change in collector current that results from the given change in base current. Performing this analysis for the curves in Figure 12.16 yields

$$\beta \approx \frac{\Delta I_C}{\Delta I_B} = \frac{(3.2 - 1)10^{-3}}{(15 - 5)10^{-6}} = 220$$

The output resistance, r_o, is determined by computing the inverse of the slope of the I_C curve at the Q-point, that is,

$$r_o \approx \frac{1}{\dfrac{\Delta I_C}{\Delta V_{CE}}} = \frac{1}{\dfrac{0.5 \times 10^{-3}}{10 - 2}} = 16\ \text{k}\Omega$$

12.6.2 The Common Base Model

For small-signal analysis of BJT circuits in the common base configuration, the previously developed small-signal model can be used directly, although the calculations are somewhat awkward. However, a more useful *common base small-signal model* can be readily developed directly from the common emitter model. Figure 12.17(a) shows a simplified common emitter small-signal model with the output resistance omitted. The common base configuration has a very high output resistance, and thus ignoring the output resistance is often easily justified in practice.

Figure 12.17(b) shows the same circuit model redrawn so that the base is the common node in the circuit. In this model, the input is from emitter to base, and the output from collector to base. The use of this model complicates the analysis because there is now a current

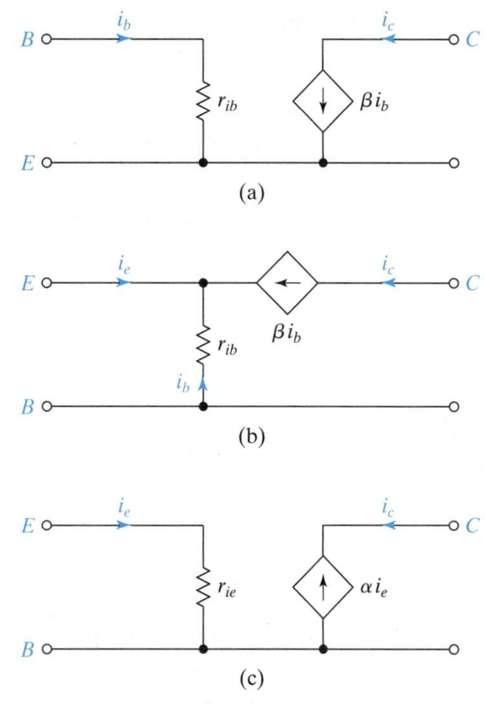

FIGURE 12.17 (a) Simplified common emitter BJT small-signal model; (b) simplified common base BJT small-signal model; (c) final simplified common base BJT small-signal model.

source appearing directly from output to input. However, this circuit can be reconfigured into an equivalent circuit similar to the common emitter circuit shown in Figure 12.17(c) by changing the circuit parameters as follows.

The input resistance r_{ie} for the common base model in Figure 12.17(b) is

$$r_{ie} = \frac{v_{eb}}{i_e} = \frac{-v_{be}}{-i_b - \beta i_b} = \frac{1}{\beta + 1}\frac{v_{be}}{i_b} \tag{12.29}$$

Now since

$$\frac{v_{be}}{i_b} = r_{ib}$$

$$r_{ib} = \frac{kT}{qI_B}$$

and

$$(\beta + 1)I_B = I_E$$

Then

$$r_{ie} = \frac{1}{\beta + 1} r_{ib} = \frac{1}{\beta + 1}\frac{kT}{qI_B} = \frac{kT}{qI_E} \tag{12.30}$$

Thus, the input resistance seen looking into the emitter is a factor of $1/(\beta + 1)$ less than that seen looking into the base. Similarly, just as the dc currents between emitter and base are related by the factor $(\beta + 1)$, so are the ac currents, and so are the ac resistances seen looking into the base and emitter terminals.

From Figure 12.17(b), the value of ac current at the collector is given by

$$i_c = \beta i_b = \beta\left[\frac{-i_e}{\beta + 1}\right] = \left[\frac{\beta}{\beta + 1}\right](-i_e) = -\alpha i_e \tag{12.31}$$

Where

Important relationship between α and β

$$\alpha = \frac{\beta}{\beta + 1} \tag{12.32}$$

is the *common base current gain.*

The result of Eq. 12.31 can be made positive by reversing the polarity of the dependent current source, as shown in Figure 12.17(c).

12-7 BJT Amplifier Circuits—Small-Signal Analysis

As was our approach with MOSFETs, the small-signal analysis of BJT circuits will be illustrated with a series of examples.

12.7.1 The Common Emitter Amplifier

Consider the following example of a common emitter amplifier.

Example 12.12

Consider the common emitter amplifier circuit shown in Figure 12.18(a). The transistor is an NPN BJT described by the output curves shown in Figure 12.16. Assuming that the dc voltage across the forward biased base emitter junction, V_{BE}, is 0.7 volts, let us determine the values of R_E and R_C that are required to place the Q-point at the position shown in Figure 12.16.

Recall that when biasing BJT circuits, the coupling capacitors C_1 and C_2 block dc current and nothing to the left of C_1 or to the right of C_2 need be considered in calculating the dc bias. In addition, bias circuits of this type set the base voltage by the resistor divider, R_1 and R_2. The dc emitter voltage is then fixed at 0.7 volts below the dc base voltage, and this resultant voltage across R_E determines the dc emitter current. It is important to note that once any one current for a BJT in the active region is known, the others can be easily found by the following simple relations:

$$\text{If } I_B = x\text{, then } I_C = (\beta)\,x\text{, and } I_E = (\beta + 1)\,x$$

Recall that if the current I_B is negligible compared to the current flowing down through the voltage divider composed of R_1 and R_2, then the dc base voltage is set by the resistors R_1 and R_2. From Example 12.11 we know that at the required Q-point, $I_c = 2$ mA and $\beta = 220$.

Setting the dc voltages and currents (Q-point) for common emitter amplifier

Therefore, the dc base current is

$$I_B = \frac{I_C}{\beta} = \frac{2 \times 10^{-3}}{220} = 9.1\ \mu\text{A}$$

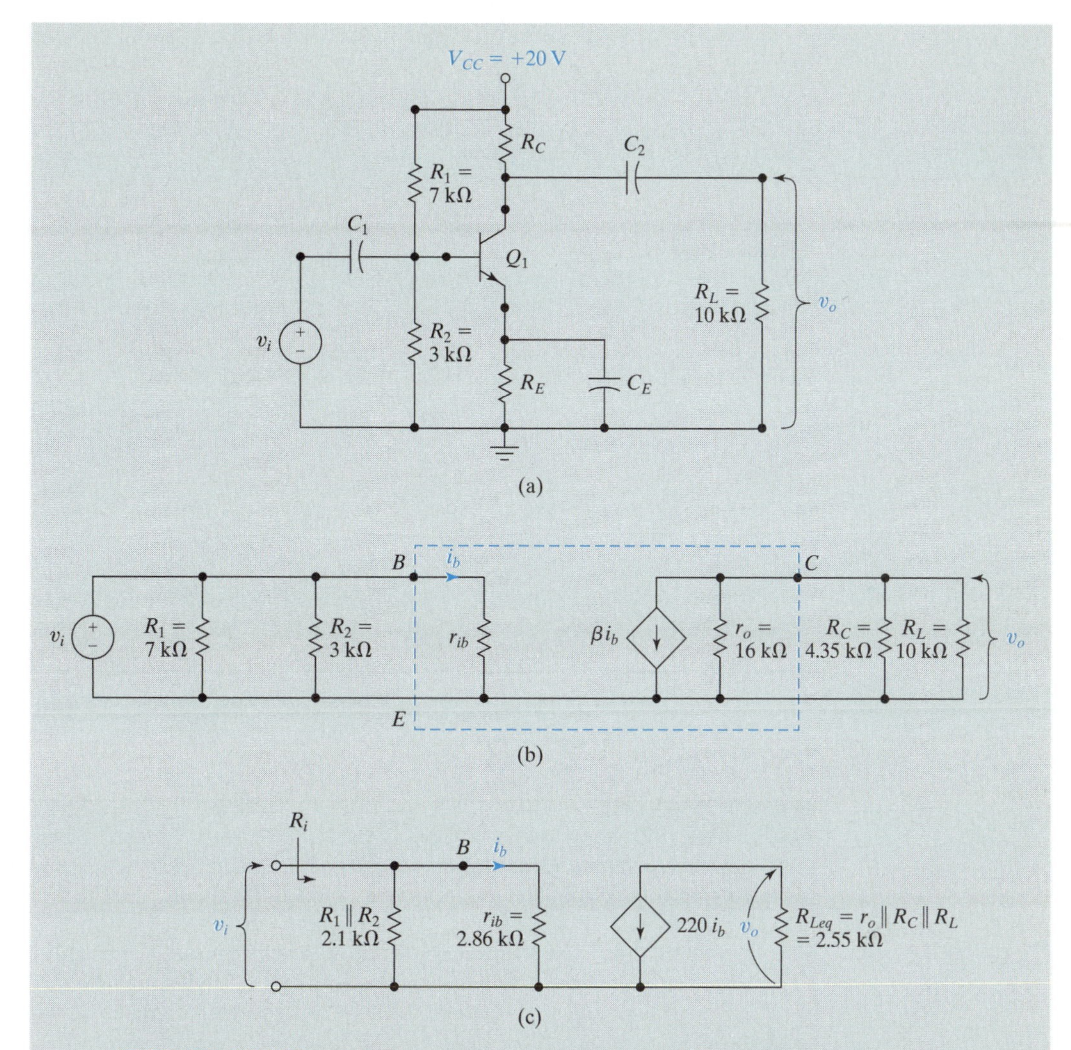

FIGURE 12.18 (a) BJT common emitter amplifier schematic circuit. (b) BJT common emitter amplifier small-signal equivalent circuit. (c) Simplified BJT common emitter amplifier small-signal equivalent circuit.

Ignoring I_B, the current in the voltage divider R_1 and R_2 is

$$I_{R1} \approx I_{R2} \approx \frac{V_{CC}}{R_1 + R_2} = \frac{20}{7\text{ k} + 3\text{ k}} = 2\text{ mA}$$

Clearly,

$$I_{R1} \approx I_{R2} > > I_B$$

and, therefore, I_B can be ignored in calculating the voltage, V_B. V_B is derived from the expression

$$V_B = 20\left[\frac{R_2}{R_1 + R_2}\right] = 6\text{ V}$$

and

$$V_E = V_B - V_{BE} = 6 - 0.7 = 5.3 \text{ V}$$

Since I_C must be set at 2 mA, then

$$I_E = I_C + I_B = 2 \times 10^{-3} + 9.1 \times 10^{-6} \approx 2 \text{ mA}$$

And hence

$$R_E = \frac{V_E}{I_E} = \frac{5.3}{2 \times 10^{-3}} = 2.65 \text{ k}\Omega$$

Finally, we must select the proper value of R_C to set the Q-point at $V_{CE} = 6$ volts. Since

$$V_C = V_E + V_{CE} = 5.3 + 6 = 11.3 \text{ V}$$

Then

$$R_C = \frac{V_{CC} - V_C}{I_C} = \frac{20 - 11.3}{2 \times 10^{-3}} = 4.35 \text{ k}\Omega$$

The resistors R_E and R_C have now been determined to set the Q-point to satisfy the specified bias conditions.

Example 12.13

Given the circuit shown in Figure 12.18(a), we wish to construct a small-signal equivalent circuit for the amplifier, compute values for all necessary small-signal parameters, and finally, calculate the small-signal voltage gain and the input resistance of the circuit. Use the transistor from Example 12.11.

Note that the bypass capacitor, C_E, provides an ac ground connection to the emitter, effectively shorting R_E. Therefore, the ac equivalent circuit is shown in Figure 12.18(b).

Every parameter in this circuit is known except the parameter r_{ib}, which can be easily calculated as

$$r_{ib} = \frac{0.026}{I_B} = \frac{0.026}{9.1 \times 10^{-6}} = 2.86 \text{ k}\Omega$$

By combining parallel resistances at both the input and output, this circuit can be simplified to that shown in Figure 12.18(c).

From this equivalent circuit, we note that

$$v_o = -\beta i_b R_{Leq}$$

and

$$v_i = i_b r_{ib}$$

The small-signal voltage gain expression; also see Eq 12.28

From these two equations we obtain the result previously expressed in Eq. (12.28).

$$A_v = \frac{v_o}{v_i} = -\frac{\beta R_{Leq}}{r_{ib}} \tag{12.33}$$

This equation specifies the gain for any common emitter circuit in which the emitter is grounded. Using the values for this example,

$$A_v = -\frac{(220)2.55\text{ k}}{2.86\text{ k}} = -196$$

The input resistance of the circuit, R_i, is given by

$$R_i = [R_1\|R_2]\|r_{ib} = 2.1\text{ k}\|2.86\text{ k} = 1.21\text{ k}\Omega$$

12.7.2 The Common Collector Amplifier

The common collector amplifier configuration is often called the *emitter follower* and either term refers to the circuit shown in Figure 12.19(a). In this circuit, the input is applied to the base, the output is taken from the emitter, and the collector is at ac ground potential. This circuit is analogous to the common drain FET circuit, and thus has a voltage gain less than unity.

Example 12.14

Let us determine the general expression for the voltage gain of the *CC* circuit shown in Figure 12.19(a). The small-signal equivalent circuit for the amplifier is shown in Figure 12.19(b). If we define the parallel combination of R_E and R_L as R_{Leq}, the loop equation for the input loop is

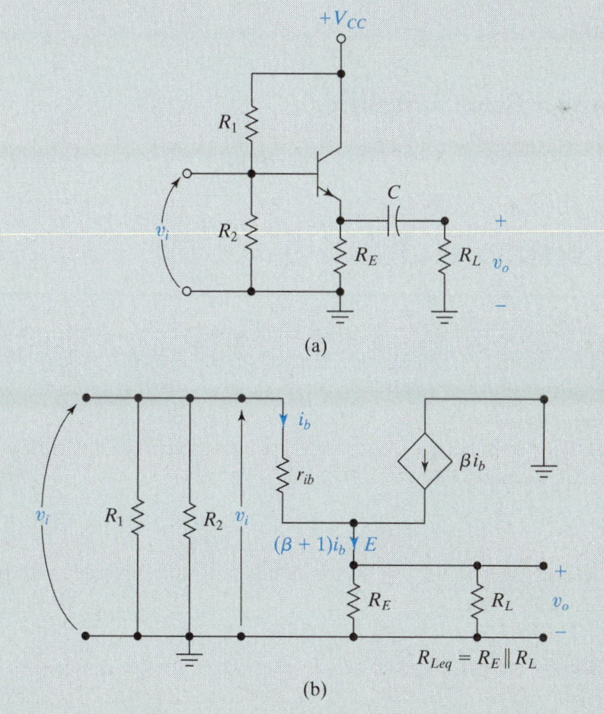

FIGURE 12.19 (a) BJT common collector amplifier schematic circuit. (b) BJT common collector small-signal equivalent circuit.

$$v_i = i_b(r_{ib}) + (\beta + 1)\, i_b R_{Leq}$$

and the expression for the output voltage is

$$v_o = (\beta + 1)\, i_b\, R_{Leq}$$

Equation for small-signal voltage gain of common collector amplifier

Dividing these two equations, we obtain the voltage gain A_v as

$$A_v = \frac{v_o}{v_i} = \frac{R_{Leq}}{R_{Leq} + \dfrac{r_{ib}}{\beta + 1}} = \frac{R_{Leq}}{R_{Leq} + r_{ie}} \tag{12.34}$$

This value is always less than unity; however, since R_{Leq} is generally large compared to r_{ie}, the voltage gain of this circuit is often assumed to be approximately one. Recall r_{ie} is defined by Eq. 12.30.

Drill Exercise

D12.2. If the dc emitter current in the *CC* circuit is 2 mA and R_{Leq} is given as 1 kΩ, what is the value of r_{ie} and the voltage gain?

Ans: $r_{ie} = 13\ \Omega$ and $A_v = \dfrac{1000}{1013} = 0.99$

12.7.3 The Common Base Amplifier

The analysis of a common base amplifier is illustrated in the following example.

Example 12.15

Assuming the PNP transistor has a beta of 50 and a V_{BE} of −0.7 V, let us determine (a) the dc collector current and the dc voltages on the emitter and collector, (b) the small-signal equivalent circuit, and (c) the small-signal voltage gain and the input resistance for the amplifier shown in Figure 12.20(a).

(a) Since the capacitor C_1 blocks dc current, the dc loop equation around the emitter base circuit shown in Figure 12.20(a) is

$$V_{EE} = I_E R_E + V_{EB}$$

Using the known parameter values and solving for I_E yields

$$I_E = 0.46 \text{ mA}$$

Since $\beta = 50$,

$$\alpha = \frac{\beta}{\beta + 1} = \frac{50}{51} = 0.98$$

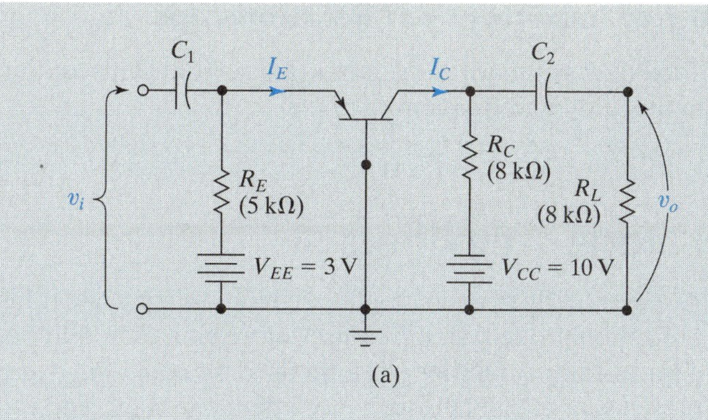

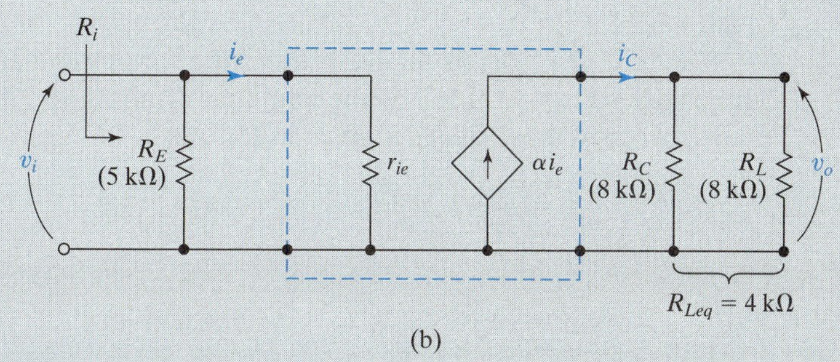

FIGURE 12.20 (a) BJT common base amplifier schematic circuit. (b) BJT common base amplifier small-signal equivalent circuit.

and then

$$I_C = \alpha I_E = 0.98\,(0.46 \times 10^{-3}) = 0.45\text{ mA}$$

Since the capacitor C_2 also blocks dc current, the collector voltage can be found from the equation

$$V_C = V_{CC} - R_C I_C = -10 - 8\text{ k}(-0.45 \times 10^{-3}) = -6.4\text{ V}$$

And, of course, the voltage on the emitter, V_E, is 0.7 V.

(b) The small-signal equivalent circuit for the amplifier is shown in Figure 12.20(b), where the value of r_{ie} is

$$r_{ie} = \frac{0.026}{I_E} = \frac{0.026}{0.46 \times 10^{-3}} = 57\ \Omega$$

(c) The model indicates that the equations for the input and output are

$$v_i = i_e r_{ie}; \qquad v_o = \alpha i_e R_{Leq}$$

Dividing these two equations yields the voltage gain

Equation for small-signal voltage gain of common base amplifier

$$A_v = \frac{\alpha R_{Leq}}{r_{ie}} = \frac{(0.98)(4\text{ k})}{57} = 69 \qquad (12.35)$$

The input resistance to the amplifier, R_i, is dominated by r_{ie}

$$R_i = R_E \| r_{ie} = 5000 \| 57 \approx 57\Omega \qquad (12.36)$$

Eq. (12.35) may be used in general for *CB* circuits.

12.7.4 Summary of Important BJT Relationships

Table 12.2 summarizes the important relationships for the small-signal analysis of BJT circuits in the mid-band frequency region.

12-8 Multi-Stage Amplifiers

A *stage* is defined as an amplifier circuit utilizing one transistor, or other gain element, for amplification. If the system requires more gain than that possible from a single-stage amplifier, a multi-stage amplifier must be used. A *multi-stage amplifier* is one in which the signal is passed sequentially through more than one stage, and each stage, in turn, increases the signal gain.

Figure 12.21 shows an illustration of a three-stage amplifier circuit where each of the three stages is represented by the amplifier symbols, A_1, A_2, and A_3. If the midband voltage gain of each of these stages is given as follows:

$$A_{v1} = 20$$

$$A_{v2} = 30$$

$$A_{v3} = 40$$

then the midband voltage gain of the entire circuit is the product of the voltage gains of each of the stages, and hence

$$A_{v(total)} = A_{v1}A_{v2}A_{v3} = (20)(30)(40) = 24{,}000$$

This relationship is easily derived since

$$A_{v(total)} = \frac{v_{out}}{v_{in}} = \frac{v_{out}}{v_b}\frac{v_b}{v_a}\frac{v_a}{v_{in}} = A_{v3}A_{v2}A_{v1}$$

The total voltage gain of a multi-stage amplifier, or a series of cascaded gain stages, is the product of the gains of each stage.

In general, the total voltage gain of a multi-stage amplifier is the product of the individual voltage gains of each of the stages. Therefore,

$$A_{v(total)} = A_{v1}\, A_{v2} \ldots \ldots \ldots \ldots A_{vN} \tag{12.37}$$

where N is the total number of stages in the multi-stage amplifier. An analogous relation applies for current gain, A_i.

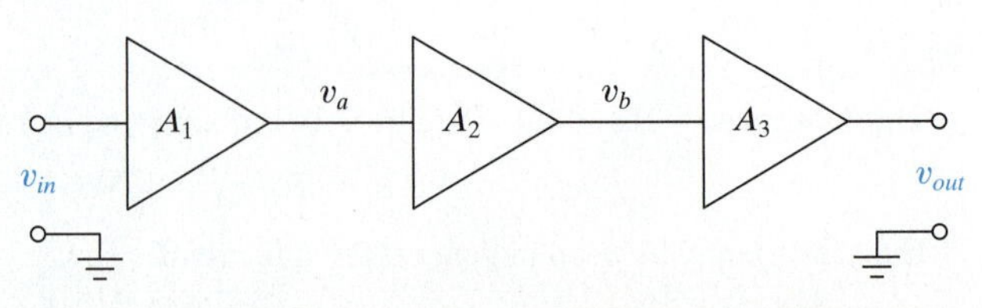

FIGURE 12.21 A three-stage amplifier.

TABLE 12.2 Important BJT Relationships for Small-Signal Analysis

Configuration	Notes	Current Gain, A_i	Voltage Gain, A_v	Input Resistance To Transistor	Input Resistance To Circuit	Output Resistance Transistor	Output Resistance Circuit
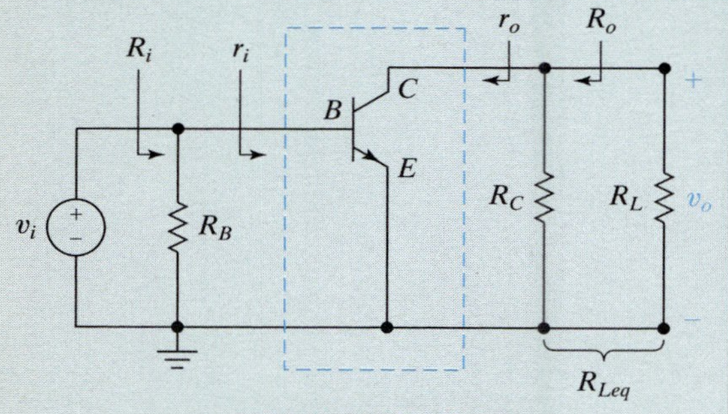 COMMON EMITTER	$R_{Leq} = R_C \| R_L \| r_o$ R_B = equivalent resistance of base bias resistors	$A_i = \frac{i_c}{i_b} = \beta$	$A_v = \frac{v_o}{v_i}$ $A_v = -\frac{\beta R_{Leq}}{r_{ib}}$	$r_i = r_{ib}$ $= \frac{kT}{qI_B}$ $= \frac{0.026}{I_B}$ (room temp)	$R_i = R_B \| r_{ib}$	$r_o = \frac{1}{g_o}$	$R_o = R_C \| \frac{1}{g_o}$
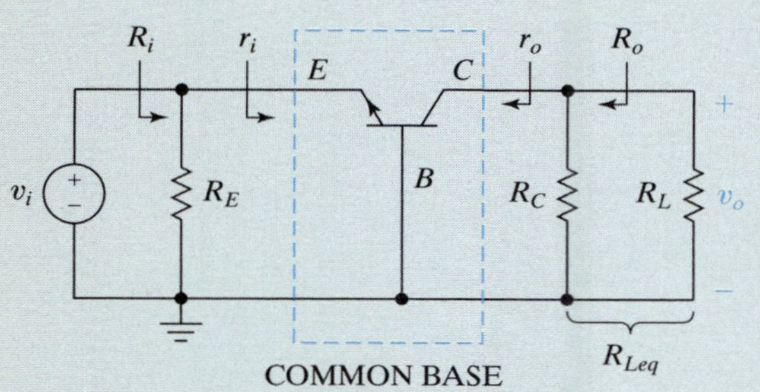 COMMON BASE	$R_{Leq} = R_C \| R_L$ Assume $r_o \approx \infty$	$A_i = \frac{i_c}{i_e} = \alpha$ $\alpha = \frac{\beta}{\beta + 1}$	$A_v = \frac{\alpha R_{Leq}}{r_{ie}}$	$r_i = r_{ie}$ $= \frac{kT}{qI_E}$ $= \frac{0.026}{I_E}$ (room temp) Also $r_{ie} = \frac{r_{ib}}{(\beta + 1)}$	$R_i = R_E \| r_{ie}$	$r_o \approx \infty$	$R_o \approx R_C$
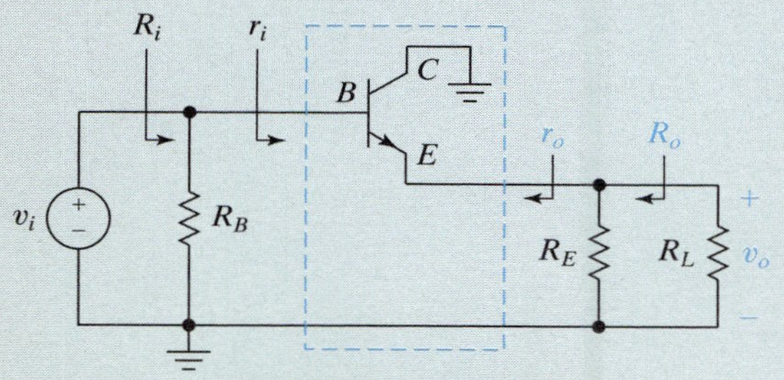 COMMON COLLECTOR	$R_{Leq} = R_E \| R_L$	$A_i = \frac{i_e}{i_b} =$ $A_i = (\beta + 1)$	$A_v = \frac{R_{Leq}}{R_{Leq} + r_{ie}}$	$r_i = r_{ib} +$ $(\beta + 1) R_{Leq}$	$R_i = R_B \| r_i$	$r_o = r_{ie} +$ $\frac{R_B \| R_S^*}{\beta + 1}$	$R_o \approx R_E \| r_o$

*R_S = resistance associated with source, v_i

Example 12.16

A two-stage voltage amplifier is designed to have a total voltage gain of 1,000. Let us determine the gain of the second stage if the first stage has a gain of 25.

The total voltage gain of 1,000 is the product of 25 and the unknown gain of the second stage. Therefore,

$$1{,}000 = 25A_{v2}$$

Solving for A_{v2} we obtain

$$A_{v2} = 40$$

Drill Exercise

D12.3. If the voltage gain of the first stage of a three-stage amplifier is doubled and that of the third stage is tripled, by what factor is the total voltage gain of the amplifier changed?

Ans: 6.

The gain of amplifiers is often a large number, especially in multi-stage amplifiers. Therefore, it becomes convenient to express the voltage gain in *decibels* (db), using the following relation:

Definition of a decibel

$$\textit{gain in decibels} = 20\log\left[\frac{v_o}{v_i}\right] = 20\log[A_v] \qquad (12.38)$$

This expression provides a logarithmic measure of amplifier gain. Thus, for multi-stage amplifiers, the gain of the entire amplifier is the sum (in db) of the gains of each stage.

Current gain can also be expressed in decibels using an analogous equation.

Example 12.17

If a two-stage amplifier has a first-stage voltage gain of 100 and a second-stage gain of 1,000, let us express the gains of each stage in decibels and find the total gain.

$$A_{v1} = 100;\ 20\log(100) = 40 \text{ db}$$
$$A_{v2} = 1{,}000;\ 20\log(1{,}000) = 60 \text{ db}$$

And hence the gain of the entire amplifier is the SUM of the gains expressed in db:

$$A_{v(total)} = 40 + 60 = 100 \text{ db}$$

As a check, let us calculate the total gain as the PRODUCT of the gains expressed as voltage ratios:

$$A_{v(total)} = (100)(1{,}000) = 100{,}000$$

Note that 100,000 expressed in db is 100 db, as expected.

Summary

- A small-signal model is used when the signal magnitude is sufficiently small that nonlinearities in the circuit can be approximated by linear elements.
- The midband frequency region is a range of frequencies high enough that all coupling and bypass capacitors may be considered as ac shorts, and NOT high enough for small device and parasitic capacitances to be a factor, that is, they are considered open.
- The ac gain is generally constant and at its maximum over the midband frequency range.
- A *p–n* diode has a dynamic or ac resistance, r_d; it is the inverse of the slope of a line tangent to the *Q*-point on the diode curve.
- At room temperature,

$$r_d = \frac{0.026}{I_D}\,\Omega$$

- Two-port linear networks may be used to model small-signal amplifiers. The voltage and current for both the input and output are related by a set of two equations and four parameters. There are several parameter sets commonly used, for example, *y* parameters, *z* parameters, and *h* parameters.
- A simplified small-signal model can be used effectively for modeling transistors in the midband range.
- The MOSFET small-signal model at midband frequencies has two dominant parameters, g_m and g_o.
- The small-signal voltage gain of a common source MOSFET amplifier is $A_v = -g_m R_{Leq}$, where R_{Leq} is the total effective load resistance including g_o.
- Small-signal analysis begins with a dc bias analysis in order to calculate values for the transistor's small-signal parameters; then a small-signal equivalent circuit is developed and the parameter values are used in the model.
- The small-signal voltage gains and other amplifier characteristics for all three MOSFET circuit configurations, that is, common source, common gate, and common drain, are developed and summarized in Table 12.1.
- If an amplifier has input resistance R_i and is driven from a voltage source with an internal resistance R_s, then if $R_i \gg R_s$ we avoid significant loss of voltage gain at the input.
- Two small-signal models for the BJT are developed, one more appropriate for common emitter and common collector configurations, and the other for common base configurations.
- The BJT small-signal model for midband frequencies contains three parameters: input resistance, current gain, and output resistance. Output resistance can be ignored when it is high compared to the external load resistances.
- The small-signal voltage gain of a common emitter BJT amplifier is

$$A_v = -\frac{\beta R_{Leq}}{r_{ib}}$$

where

$$r_{ib} = \frac{0.026}{I_B} \quad \text{at room temperature.}$$

- The small-signal voltage gains and other amplifier characteristics for all three BJT circuit configurations, that is, common emitter, common base, and common collector, are developed and summarized in Table 12.2.
- The voltage gain of a multi-stage amplifier is the product of the voltage gains of each of the stages, that is,

$$A_{v(total)} = A_{v1}A_{v2}A_{v3}\ldots A_{vN}$$

Problems

12.1. What is a small-signal transistor model?

12.2. Define the midband frequency region. In this region what can be said about an amplifier's voltage gain?

12.3. A p–n junction diode has a forward bias applied of 0.68 V and is conducting 2 mA. (a) Determine I_o. (b) Determine the static forward resistance. (c) Determine the ac small-signal resistance of the diode at room temperature.

12.4. Determine the ac resistance of a silicon diode at room temperature that is conducting 4 μA.

12.5. Two silicon diodes are connected in series and are conducting a dc current of 2 mA; what is the ac resistance of the combination?

12.6. The dc current through a silicon diode is doubled. What is the effect of this on the ac resistance of the diode?

12.7. At room temperature, what is the ac resistance of a diode conducting 0.5 A?

12.8. A two-port network as illustrated in Figure 12.2 has the following parameters: $y_{11} = 0$; $y_{12} = 0$; $y_{21} = 3.5 \times 10^{-3}$ S; $y_{22} = 1 \times 10^{-4}$ S. If an external load resistance of 12 kΩ is connected to the output, what is the voltage gain of this network?

12.9. A set of h parameters are provided as follows:, $h_{11} = 20$ kΩ; $h_{12} = 0$; $h_{21} = 100$; and $h_{22} = 1 \times 10^{-5}$. If the output is connected to an external load resistance of 50 kΩ, determine: (a) the network's input resistance, (b) the network's current gain, (c) the network's voltage gain, (d) the network's output resistance.

12.10. A MOSFET in the common source configuration is modeled as a two-port network as illustrated in Figure 12.4. If $R_L = 6$ kΩ, and $y_{11} = 0$; $y_{12} = 0$; $y_{21} = 2 \times 10^{-3}$ S; and $y_{22} = 0$, determine the small-signal voltage gain of the amplifier.

12.11. (a) Assume the simplified small-signal model for transistors shown in Figure 12.5 has $r_i = \infty$, $g_m = 1.8 \times 10^{-3}$ S, and $r_o = 100$ kΩ. This device is placed in the circuit as shown in Figure P12.11. Calculate the small-signal voltage gain.
(b) In the amplifier circuit shown in Figure P12.11, calculate the small-signal voltage gain assuming $r_1 = 200$ kΩ, $g_m = 2.5 \times 10^{-3}$ S, and $r_o = 120$ kΩ.

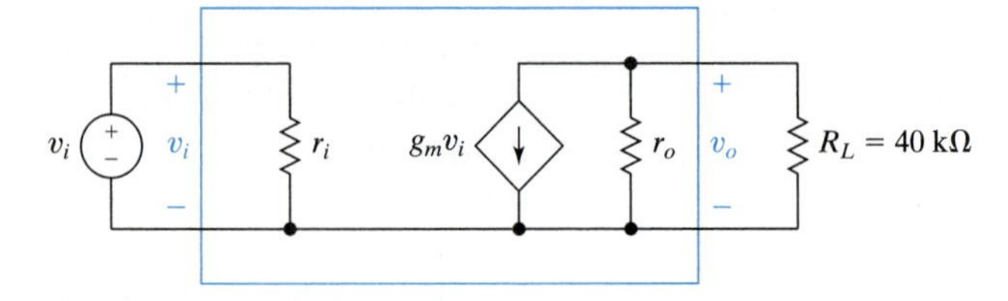

FIGURE P12.11

12.12. For the n-channel enhancement-mode MOSFET with output curves of Figure P12.12, determine an approximate value for g_m at (1) Q-point Q_{P1}, and (2) Q-point Q_{P2}.

12.13. For the MOSFET with output curves in Figure P12.12 (a) Determine the approximate value

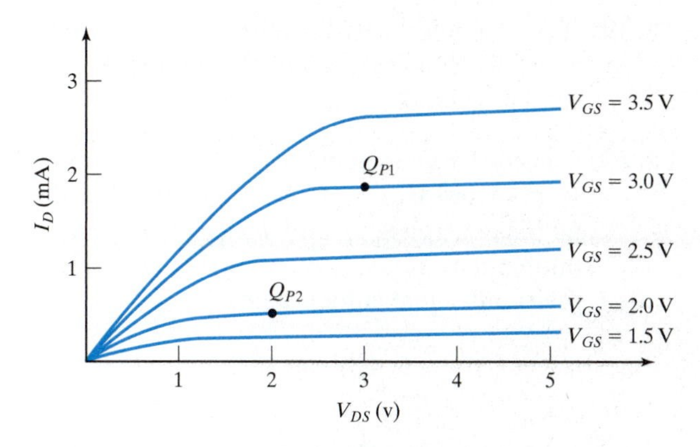

FIGURE P12.12

of g_o for each Q-point. (b) Redraw the output curves of Figure P12.12 for a device with approximately the same g_m values, but $g_o = 1 \times 10^{-4}$ S.

12.14. Consider the common source circuit shown in Figure 12.11(a) with a transistor that has output curves in Figure P12.12, and (a) determine a new value for R_2 that will place the Q-point on the $V_{GS} = 2.5$ V curve. (b) Plot the dc load line to locate the Q-point. (c) Compute an approximate value for g_m at this Q-point. (d) Draw a small-signal equivalent circuit for this amplifier. (e) Using the equivalent circuit, calculate the small-signal voltage gain.

12.15. In the common source amplifier circuit in Figure P12.15, (a) draw a small signal equivalent circuit, (b) calculate the voltage gain. Assume that for this transistor, $g_m = 3.0 \times 10^{-3}$ S and $g_o = 1.66 \times 10^{-5}$ S.

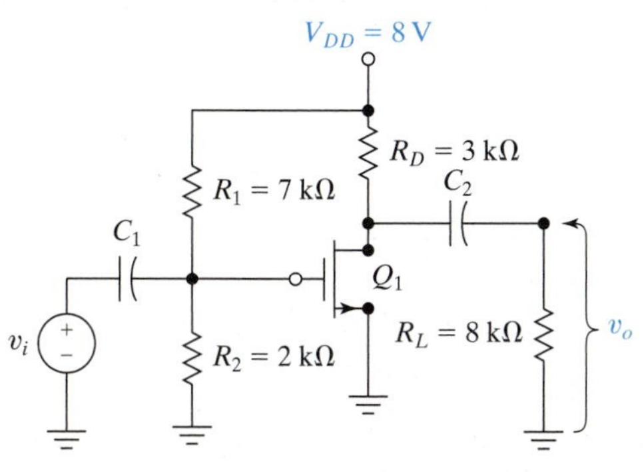

FIGURE P12.15

12.16. In the circuit in Figure P12.15, what value of g_m would be required for the circuit to have a voltage gain of magnitude 10?

12.17. The common gate n-channel enhancement mode MOSFET circuit shown in Figure 12.12(a) has new component values as follows: $R_S = 1\ \text{k}\Omega$, $R_D = 3\ \text{k}\Omega$, and g_m for the transistor is determined to be 2×10^{-3} S; assume r_o is infinite. (a) Draw a small-signal equivalent circuit. (b) Compute the small-signal voltage gain. (c) Determine the amplifier input resistance, R_i.

12.18. If the value of R_D is doubled in problem 12.17, what is the new value of the small signal voltage gain?

12.19. The common drain amplifier circuit shown in Figure P12.19 utilizes a transistor with $g_m = 3.8$ mS and $R_S = 4\ \text{k}\Omega$. (a) Compute the small-signal voltage gain. (b) If a different transistor is used with $g_m = 10$ mS, what is the new value of the voltage gain?

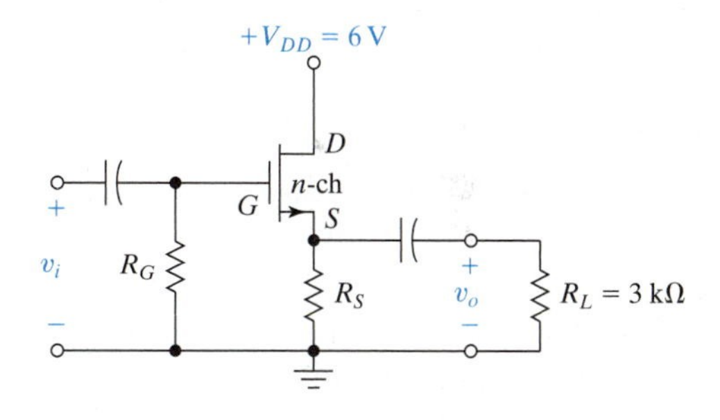

FIGURE P12.19

12.20. As shown in Figure 12.20, an amplifier has a voltage gain of 10, and is driven by an input voltage source with an internal resistance of

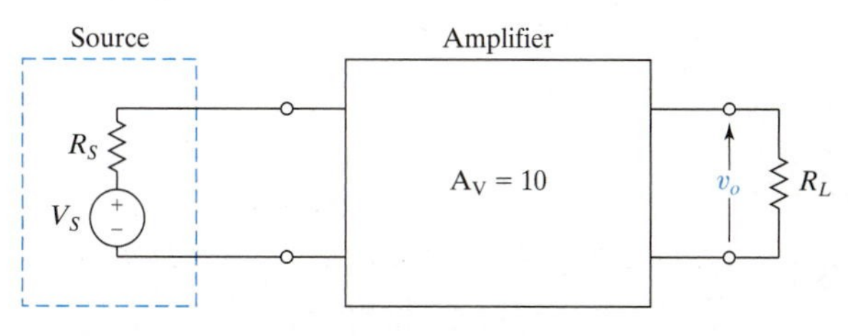

FIGURE P12.20

20 kΩ. Calculate the voltage gain of the entire circuit if the input resistance to the amplifier is (a) 50 kΩ, (b) 100 kΩ, (c) 1 MΩ.

12.21. In order to maximize the voltage gain of an amplifier circuit, state whether each of these should be made high or low in value:
(a) Source resistance
(b) Amplifier input resistance

12.22. If the internal resistance of a voltage source is 50 Ω, what is the required input resistance of the amplifier in order to only lose 10% of the signal amplitude at the input?

12.23. An amplifier using a BJT common emitter configuration is shown in Figure P12.23. If the following parameters apply, calculate (a) the input resistance of the amplifier and (b) the small-signal voltage gain.

$$r_{ib} = 10\text{ k}\Omega, \beta = 120, r_o = 200\text{ k}\Omega.$$

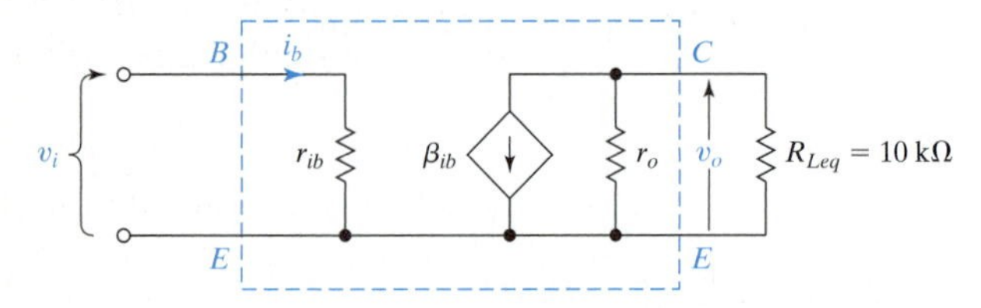

FIGURE P12.23

12.24. A BJT in a common emitter amplifier circuit is biased in the active region. The measured dc currents are $I_C = 3$ mA, $I_B = 15$ μA; when V_{CE} is increased 5 V, I_C increases 0.2 mA. (a) Determine the small-signal model parameters for this transistor. (b) Construct a small-signal equivalent circuit for the amplifier assuming $R_{Leq} = 8$ kΩ. (c) Calculate the small-signal voltage gain. (d) Calculate the amplifier's input resistance.

12.25. Repeat problem 12.23 if $R_{Leq} = 100$ kΩ.

12.26. Repeat problem 12.24 if $I_B = 10$ μA.

12.27. If the common emitter current gain of a BJT, β, is 150, calculate the value of the common base current gain, α.

12.28. If the common base current gain, α, of a BJT is 0.97, calculate the value of common emitter current gain, β.

12.29. Consider the circuit in Figure P12.29, assuming $\beta = 80$ and $V_{BE} = 0.7$ V. (a) Determine the dc bias currents, I_C and I_B. (b) Construct a midband ac equivalent circuit. (c) Determine the small-signal voltage gain.

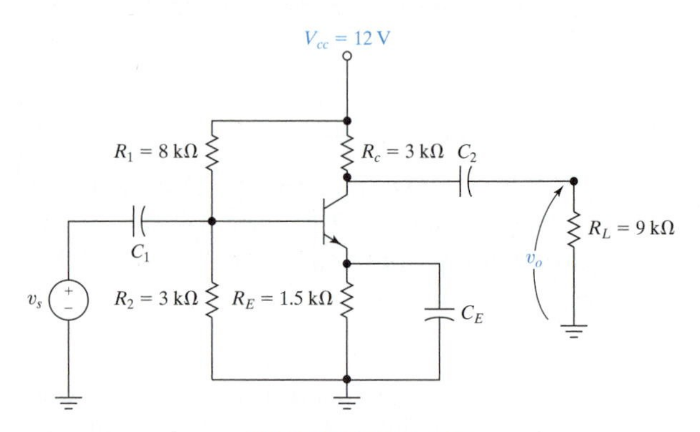

FIGURE P12.29

12.30. Repeat problem 12.29 with $\beta = 180$ and $R_C = 4$ kΩ.

12.31. Repeat problem 12.29 with $R_2 = 4$ kΩ.

12.32. In the circuit in Figure P12.32, the external load resistance is considered infinite. For the case where $\beta = 50$, (a) Calculate the dc bias currents, I_C and I_B. (b) Calculate the value of V_{CE}. (c) Construct a midband ac equivalent circuit. (d) Determine the small-signal voltage gain. (Assume $V_{BE} = 0.7$ V.)

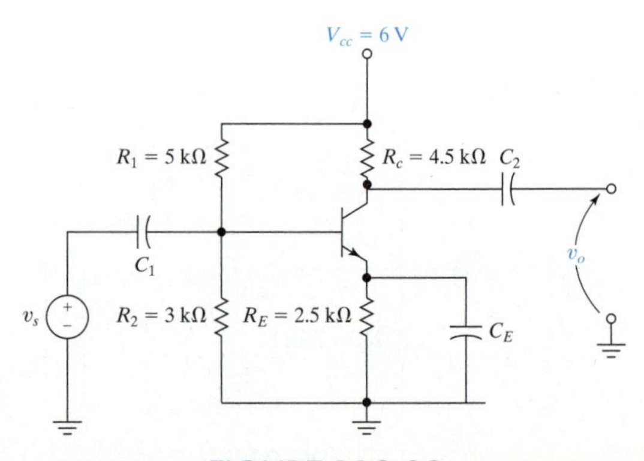

FIGURE P12.32

12.33. Repeat problem 12.32 if $V_{CC} = 10$ V.

12.34. A common emitter amplifier circuit has a transistor with $\beta = 100$ and $r_{ib} = 2$ kΩ. If the circuit provides $R_{Leq} = 6$ kΩ, what is the small-signal voltage gain?

12.35. A transistor with $\beta = 50$ is placed in a common base amplifier circuit with $I_E = 1$ mA and $R_{Leq} = 5$ kΩ. (a) What is the small-signal voltage gain? (b) Does this circuit invert the signal?

12.36. Sketch the small-signal common base BJT model, assuming the output resistance is high enough to be ignored. If $r_{ie} = 45\Omega$ and $\alpha = 0.98$, (a) determine the dc emitter current, I_E, in the bias circuit. (b) Find the dc base current, I_B. (c) Construct a small-signal equivalent circuit for an amplifier using this model and with v_s as the voltage input source, $R_s = 50\ \Omega$, $R_{Leq} = 2$ kΩ, and assume $R_i = r_{ie}$. (d) Determine the small-signal voltage gain, including any loss in the input circuit; that is, find v_o/v_s.

12.37. The circuit in Figure P12.37 uses a transistor with $\beta = 120$ and $V_{BE} = -0.6$ V. Find the small-signal voltage gain.

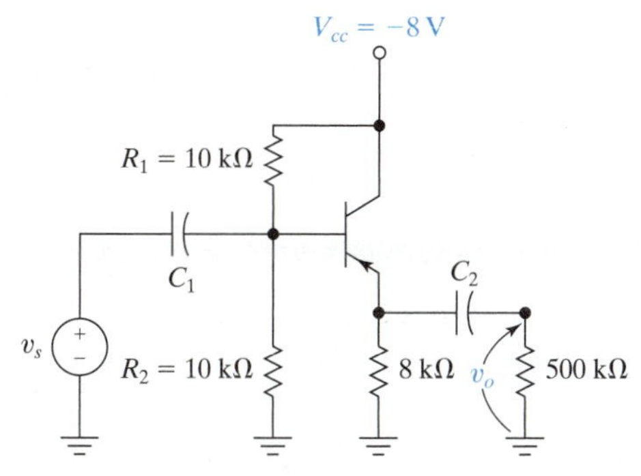

FIGURE P12.37

12.38. A transistor is placed in a common collector circuit with $I_E = 2$ mA and $R_{Leq} = 500\ \Omega$. Find the small-signal voltage gain.

12.39. A transistor with a measured $\beta = 60$ is placed in the circuit in Figure P12.39; assume $V_{BE} = 0.7$ V. (a) Construct an ac equivalent circuit. (b) Determine the small-signal voltage gain.

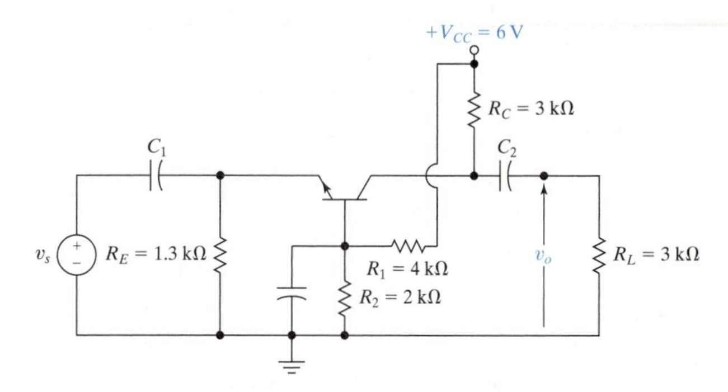

FIGURE P12.39

12.40. A common base amplifier uses a transistor with $\alpha = 0.97$. If I_E is measured to be 1.3 mA, and the total effective load resistance $R_{Leq} = 2.5$ kΩ, what is the small-signal voltage gain?

12.41. Determine the composite voltage gain of three voltage amplifiers cascaded together as shown in Figure 12.21 and with gains as follows: $A_{v1} = 40$, $A_{v2} = 50$, and $A_{v3} = -20$.

12.42. Repeat problem 12.41 if the voltage gains are: $A_{v1} = 30$, $A_{v2} = 80$, and $A_{v3} = 0.9$.

12.43. Determine the current gain of the multi-stage current amplifier comprised of two stages, $A_{i1} = 30$, $A_{i2} = -15$.

12.44. (a) Express the voltage gains of each of the stages in problem 12.41 in decibels. (b) Compute the gain for the multi-stage amplifier in db.

12.45. The voltage gain of a multi-stage amplifier is measured to be 100 db. The gain of the first stage was calculated as $A_{v1} = 8$. Determine the total gain of the remaining stages.

13

13-1 Introduction

The world is going digital! As strange as that may sound, there is a great deal of truth to that statement. Today, digital technology permeates a very large segment of our lives. Essentially all long-distance communication is digital. Over the past ten years, the Internet and its attendant technologies have grown in size, complexity, and speed. Companies are now at work on hardware and software for data transfer rates in excess of 1 Tbps, or one terabit per second, via optical fibers. That's 10^{12} bits per second as compared to a standard 56.6k phone modem rate of only 56,600 bps. Processing within and among computers is all done digitally. Many modern control systems employ a computer, and instruments of all types, for example, voltmeters, oscilloscopes, and the like, use digital circuits and digital readouts. In fact, if the trend toward digital watches continues, the terms *clockwise* and *counterclockwise* may not be generally understood.

Digital circuits operate in one of two discrete states: the logic 1 state or the logic 0 state. These two states are generated by the electronics. In one case the transistor circuit's output voltage is high and in the other case the output voltage is low. Furthermore, these two cases correspond to a transistor being turned off or turned on. As we have seen earlier, initially relays were used as the basic building blocks; however, at the present time, the electronic switching devices are very small, very fast, and are crammed into VLSI chips by the millions. As of early 2002, the commercially available Pentium 4 microprocessor, the size of a dime, contains 55 million transistors, has over 400 external connections, and operates at 3.2 GHz clock speed. Research-grade processors contain more than 300 million transistors!

13-2 Number Systems

The base or radix of a number system defined

The number system that we typically use is the decimal system. This system employs 10 digits and is certainly convenient for us as humans since we have 10 fingers. The total number of digits allowed in a number system is called the *base* or *radix* of the system, and thus the decimal system has a base of 10.

In digital logic circuits the output is either a 0 or a 1. Therefore, it is most convenient to use the binary number system, which uses the binary digits or bits 0 and 1 and has a base of 2. A short table illustrating the relationship between decimal and binary numbers is shown in Table 13.1.

As children, we learned to add and multiply in base 10 by memorizing addition and multiplication tables. Since the decimal number system has 10 digits, we memorized a 10-by-10 array of numbers for both addition and multiplication. The binary number system, however, contains only two digits, and, therefore, binary arithmetic is much simpler. The tables for binary addition and multiplication are shown in Table 13.2. Let us illustrate the use of these tables via the following examples.

Digital Logic Circuits

TABLE 13.1 Relationship between Base 10 and Base 2 Number Systems

Base 10	Base 2
0	0
1	1
2	10
3	11
4	100
5	101
6	110
7	111
8	1000
9	1001
10	1010
11	1011
12	1100
13	1101
14	1110
15	1111

TABLE 13.2

+	0	1
0	0	1
1	1	10

×	0	1
0	0	0
1	0	1

Example 13.1

Let us add the decimal numbers 7 and 9 in binary. Performing the addition with the aid of Tables 13.1 and 13.2, we obtain

Decimal	Binary	
	1111	Carries
7	0111	
9	1001	
16	10000	Sum

Note that in binary arithmetic, $1 + 1 = 0$ with 1 to carry.

Binary multiplication is also a very simple operation. It is performed in the same manner as decimal multiplication. However, since the only digits are 0 and 1, it is essentially a shift and add operation, as the following example illustrates.

Example 13.2

Let us multiply the decimal number 7 by the decimal number 5. The multiplication is

Decimal	Binary	
7	111	Multiplicand
× 5	× 101	Multiplier
35	111	
	000	
	111	
	100011	Product

Note that for every 1 digit in the multiplier, the multiplicand is copied as a partial product. A 0 digit in the multiplier simply shifts the partial product one digit, but otherwise adds nothing.

Drill Exercise

D13.1. Given the decimal numbers 5 and 6, (a) add the two numbers in binary, and (b) multiply the two numbers in binary.

Ans: (a) 1011; (b) 11110.

Number system conversion techniques

In general, we can convert a number in base $r = \alpha$ to the number in base $r = \beta$. One of the popular techniques for performing *base conversion* is the *series substitution method*. Any number in base r can be written in the format.

$$N = \sum_{j=-m}^{n-1} a_j r^j \tag{13.1}$$
$$= a_{n-1}r^{n-1} + a_{n-2}r^{n-2} + \ldots a_0 r^0 + a_{-1}r^{-1} \ldots + a_{-m}r^{-m}$$

Base conversion using the series substitution method is performed as follows: When the terms of the series are expressed in base α, each factor of each term is converted to base β and then the series is evaluated using arithmetic in base β. The following examples illustrate the technique.

Example 13.3

Let us convert 10011 in binary to decimal. Using the series substitution method, we obtain

$$\begin{aligned} 10011 &= 1(2)^4 + 0(2)^3 + 0(2)^2 + 1(2)^1 + 1(2)^0 \\ &= 16 + 0 + 0 + 2 + 1 \\ &= 19 \end{aligned}$$

Therefore, 10011 in binary is equivalent to 19 in decimal.

Example 13.4

Using the series substitution method we will convert 35 in decimal to binary. The number 35 can be written as

$$\begin{aligned} 35 &= 3(10)^1 + 5(10)^0 \\ &= 11(1010) + 101(1) \\ &= 100011 \end{aligned}$$

Hence, 35 in decimal is equivalent to 100011 in binary.

Drill Exercises

D13.2. Convert 1010101 in binary to decimal.

Ans: 85.

D13.3. Convert 28 in decimal to binary.

Ans: 11100.

13–3 Boolean Algebra

Boolean algebra provides the mathematical foundation for the analysis and design of digital systems. It is essentially the mathematics of logic circuits even though it was formulated by George Boole, an English mathematician, in 1849, many decades before digital computers were even a figment of anyone's imagination. The fundamental concepts of Boolean algebra are set forth in the following *postulates*.

The seven postulates of Boolean algebra

P1. The algebraic system, which contains two or more elements and the operators $\cdot$(AND) and $+$ (OR), is closed.*

P2. Two algebraic expressions are equal ($=$) if one can be replaced by the other.

P3. The unique elements 1 and 0 exist such that
1. $A + 0 = A$
2. $A \cdot 1 = A$

P4. A unique element $\overline{A}$ (the complement of A) exists such that
1. $A + \overline{A} = 1$
2. $A \cdot \overline{A} = 0$

P5. The commutative law is
1. $A + B = B + A$
2. $A \cdot B = B \cdot A$

P6. The associative law is
1. $A + (B + C) = (A + B) + C$
2. $A \cdot (B \cdot C) = (A \cdot B) \cdot C$

P7. The distributive law is
1. $A + (B \cdot C) = (A + B) \cdot (A + C)$
2. $A \cdot (B + C) = (A \cdot B) + (A \cdot C)$

The reader is cautioned to note that some of these algebraic rules are quite different than those we normally apply in real variable analysis.

The postulates that have been presented can be used to develop a number of useful theorems, which further enhance our ability to manipulate logic expressions. These *theorems* are summarized in Table 13.3.

The postulates and theorems given above have all been stated in a (1), (2) format. These expressions are said to be *duals* of one another. The dual of an expression is found by replacing all $+$ operators with $\cdot$, all $\cdot$ operators with $+$, all 0s with 1, and all 1s with 0. This *principle of duality* is very important in Boolean algebra.

Theorem T6 is called *DeMorgan's Theorem* and its importance stems from the fact that it is a general technique for complementing Boolean expressions.

Boolean function minimization involves reducing the number of literals

In the manipulation of Boolean functions, we typically have one goal: minimize the number of literals. A *literal* is any occurrence of a variable in either complemented or uncomplemented form. For example, the Boolean function

$$f(A, B, C, D) = \overline{A}BC + A(B + C + \overline{D}) + \overline{C}\,\overline{D}$$

has 9 literals.

*An algebraic system is closed when the result of a function is a subset of the allowable members. For example, let A represent all women in the classroom and B represent everyone over 20 years old in the classroom. The result of the function $A \cdot B$ (A AND B) is all women over age 20 in the classroom. Note that the members of $A \cdot B$ are ALSO IN THE CLASSROOM! This is consistent with the statement that Boolean algebra is closed.

TABLE 13.3 Theorems of Boolean Algebra

T1	(1)	$A + A = A$	(2)	$A \cdot A = A$
T2	(1)	$1 + A = 1$	(2)	$A \cdot 0 = 0$
T3	(1)	$A + AB = A$	(2)	$A(A + B) = A$
T4	(1)	$A + \overline{A}B = A + B$	(2)	$A(\overline{A} + B) = AB$
T5	(1)	$AB + \overline{A}C + BC = AB + \overline{A}C$	(2)	$(A + B)(\overline{A} + C)(B + C) = (A + B)(\overline{A} + C)$
T6	(1)	$\overline{A + B} = \overline{A}\,\overline{B}$	(2)	$\overline{AB} = \overline{A} + \overline{B}$
T7	(1)	$\overline{A}B + AB = B$	(2)	$(\overline{A} + B)(A + B) = B$

Example 13.5

Let us minimize the following function of four variables with 10 literals.

$$
\begin{aligned}
f(A, B, C, D) &= AB + \overline{AB}\,\overline{C} + \overline{C}\,\overline{D} + B\overline{CD} \\
&= AB + \overline{C} + \overline{C}\,\overline{D} + B\overline{CD} && \text{(T4)} \\
&= AB + \overline{C} + B\overline{CD} && \text{(T3)} \\
&= AB + \overline{C} + B(\overline{C} + \overline{D}) && \text{(T6)} \\
&= AB + \overline{C} + B\overline{C} + B\overline{D} && \text{(P7)} \\
&= AB + \overline{C} + B\overline{D} && \text{(P5,T3)} \\
&= BA + B\overline{D} + \overline{C} && \text{(P5)} \\
&= B(A + \overline{D}) + \overline{C} && \text{(P7)}
\end{aligned}
$$

This minimum form of the function has only four literals.

As we will illustrate later, electronic circuits will be employed to realize these Boolean functions in hardware. Therefore, the fewer the number of literals in the function, the simpler the hardware realization.

Drill Exercise

D13.4. Find the minimum realization of the function $f(A, B, C) = \overline{A + B} + A\overline{B} + B\overline{C}$

Ans: $f(A, B, C) = \overline{BC}$.

13-4 Truth Tables

Another method of describing Boolean functions is the *truth table*, which displays the value of the Boolean function for all values of the variables.

Example 13.6

Let us compute the truth table of the Boolean function

$$f(A, B, C) = AB + \overline{B}C$$

Since there are three variables, there are eight combinations, which range from 000 to 111. For example, if $A = 0, B = 0, C = 0$, the function is

$$\begin{aligned} f(0, 0, 0) &= 0 \cdot 0 + 1 \cdot 0 \\ &= 0 \end{aligned}$$

Truth table definition

The truth table, which lists all combinations, is shown in Table 13.4.

TABLE 13.4

A	B	C	f(A, B, C)
0	0	0	0
0	0	1	1
0	1	0	0
0	1	1	0
1	0	0	0
1	0	1	1
1	1	0	1
1	1	1	1

The truth table gets its name from the fact that in the context of a truth function the 0s are replaced with Fs (False) and the 1s are replaced by Ts (True).

Truth tables play an important role in Boolean algebra for the simple reason that although there are an infinite number of ways in which to write a Boolean function, each function has one and only one truth table.

Drill Exercise

D13.5. Derive the truth table for the function $f(A, B) = A\overline{B} + \overline{A}B$

Ans:

A	B	f(A, B)
0	0	0
0	1	1
1	0	1
1	1	0

0·0 + 1·1

0 + 1

1

The standard logic gates

TABLE 13.5 Switching Devices

Operator	Symbol	Input/output relationship
AND	A_1, A_2 → $f(A_1, A_2)$	$f(A_1, A_2) = A_1A_2$
OR	A_1, A_2 → $f(A_1, A_2)$	$f(A_1, A_2) = A_1 + A_2$
NOT	A → $f(A)$	$f(A) = \overline{A}$
NAND	A_1, A_2 → $f(A_1, A_2)$	$f(A_1, A_2) = \overline{A_1A_2}$
NOR	A_1, A_2 → $f(A_1, A_2)$	$f(A_1, A_2) = \overline{A_1 + A_2}$

13-5 Switching Networks

The electronic devices that are used to construct the logic functions in hardware were discussed in Chapter 10. These *gates*, as they are called, realized the following functions: AND, OR, NOT, NAND, and NOR. Table 13.5 provides a listing of the gates, which include the operator, the symbol used to represent the gate, and the mathematical relationship between the gate's inputs and its output.

At this point it is important to note that any Boolean function can be written in terms of the operators AND, OR, and NOT. Furthermore, these three operators can be completely expressed in terms of either NAND or NOR. Thus, in realizing logic functions with gates, we can use AND, OR, and NOT, or only NAND, or only NOR.

Specific logic functions within a digital system are derived through an interconnection of these gates. The gate outputs are Boolean functions, and, therefore, can be manipulated using Boolean algebra. In fact, it may be possible via Boolean algebra to simplify the gate structure and thus realize the desired function with fewer gates.

Example 13.7

Consider the gate structure in Figure 13.1(a). Note that these gates realize the logic function

$$
\begin{aligned}
f(A, B, C, D) &= B_1 + B_2 + B_3 + B_4 + B_5 \\
&= BC\overline{D} + \overline{B}D + \overline{AC}D + BC + A\overline{C}D \\
&= BC + \overline{B}D + \overline{AC}D + A\overline{C}D && \text{(T3)} \\
&= BC + \overline{B}D + \overline{C}D && \text{(P7, P4)} \\
&= BC + (\overline{B} + \overline{C})D && \text{(P7)} \\
&= BC + \overline{BC}D && \text{(T6)} \\
&= BC + D && \text{(T4)}
\end{aligned}
$$

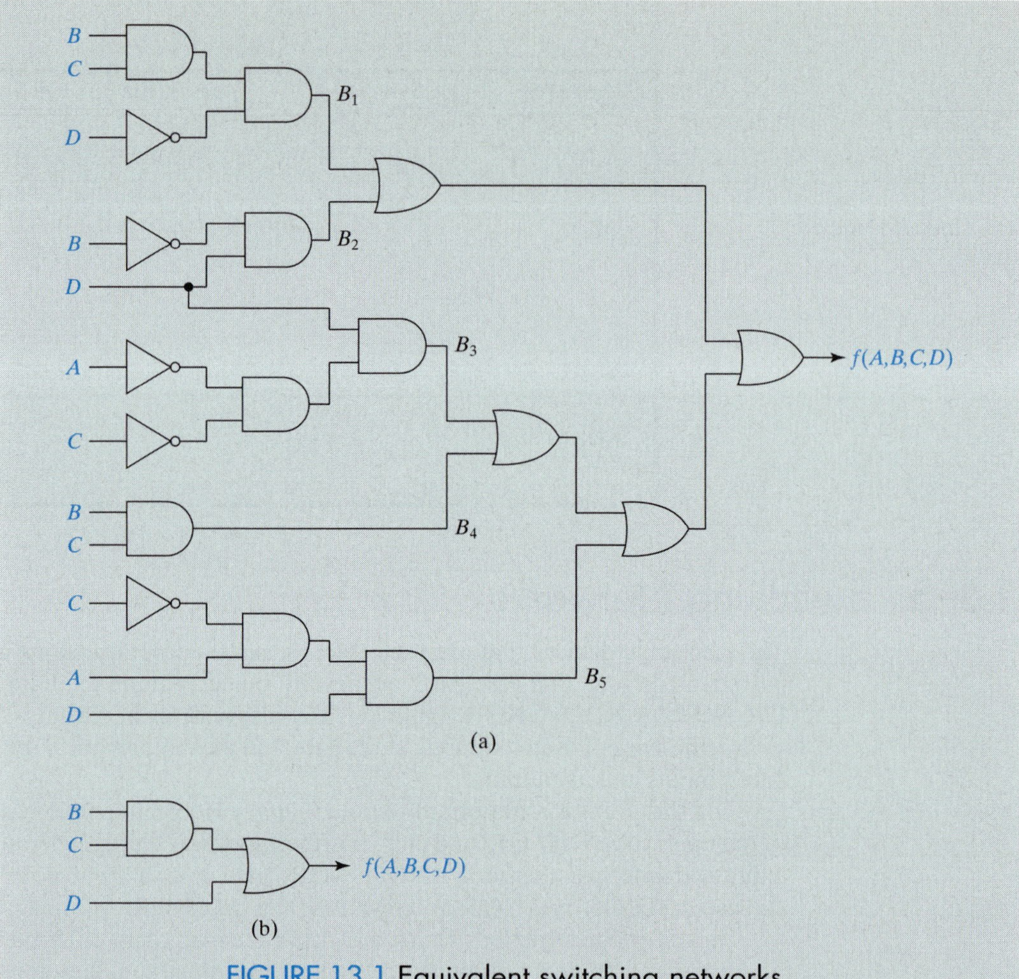

FIGURE 13.1 Equivalent switching networks.

Therefore, the two gates in Figure 13.1(b) realize the same function as do those in Figure 13.1(a). Both gate structures have the same truth table; however, the switching network in Figure 13.1(b) is much simpler and thus much easier to construct with electronic hardware. Note that the output of this logic circuit is independent of A.

13-6 Canonical Forms

Although we have listed Boolean functions in a number of ways, there are several specific forms that are of special importance. Two such forms are SOP (*sum of products*) and POS (*product of sums*). The following examples illustrate these two forms.

Example 13.8

The following switching functions are in SOP form:

$$f_1(A, B, C) = AB + \overline{A}B\overline{C} + AC + BC$$

$$f_2(A, B, C, D) = A\overline{B}CD + \overline{A}BC\overline{D} + AB\overline{C}\,\overline{D} + \overline{A}\,\overline{B}\,\overline{C}\,\overline{D}$$

Example 13.9

The following switching functions are in POS form:

$$f_3(A, B, C) = (A + B)(A + \overline{B} + C)(\overline{A} + \overline{B} + \overline{C})$$

$$f_4(A, B, C, D) = (A + B + \overline{C} + D)(\overline{A} + \overline{B} + C + \overline{D})(A + \overline{B} + \overline{C} + \overline{D})$$

Minterm and maxterm definitions

It is important to note that the switching functions $f_2(A, B, C, D)$ and $f_4(A, B, C, D)$ in Examples 13.8 and 13.9, respectively, have a special form, that is, every variable is present in each term in either complemented or uncomplemented form. This form is called *canonical* form. Therefore, the functions $f_2(A, B, C, D)$ and $f_4(A, B, C, D)$ are said to be in canonical SOP form and canonical POS form, respectively. Each term in canonical SOP form is called a *minterm* and each term in canonical POS form is called a *maxterm*.

The description of Boolean functions in terms of minterms and maxterms can be further simplified by coding the variables. In the minterm case, if variables are coded as 1 and complements as 0, then for the resulting input values, one and only one minterm will be true. For example, in $f_2(A, B, C, D)$ let the inputs $ABCD = 1011$, which is 11 in binary. The only true minterm is $A\overline{B}CD$— all other minterms are false. Thus, we can uniquely and *meaningfully* define $A\overline{B}CD$ as minterm 11, or m_{11}.

Therefore, the function $f_2(A, B, C, D)$ can be expressed in the form

$$f_2(A, B, C, D) = m_{11} + m_6 + m_{12} + m_0 = \Sigma_m(0, 6, 11, 12)$$

where m_i is the minterm and i is the decimal integer for the corresponding binary code.

In the maxterm case, variables are coded as 0 and complements as 1, then for the resulting input values, one and only one maxterm will be false. Again, in $f_2(A, B, C, D)$ let the inputs $ABCD = 1011$. The only false maxterm is $\overline{A} + B + \overline{C} + \overline{D}$— all other maxterms are true. Thus, we define $\overline{A} + B + \overline{C} + \overline{D}$ as maxterm 11, or M_{11}. The coding scheme for minterms and maxterms of three variables is listed in Table 13.6.

Therefore, the function $f_4(A, B, C, D)$ is written as

$$f_4(A, B, C, D) = (A + B + \overline{C} + D)(\overline{A} + \overline{B} + C + \overline{D})(A + \overline{B} + \overline{C} + \overline{D})$$

The maxterm code for $(A + B + \overline{C} + D)$ is 0010, for $(\overline{A} + \overline{B} + C + \overline{D})$ is 1101, and so on, and, therefore, the function can be expressed as

$$f_4(A, B, C, D) = (M_2)\,(M_{13})\,(M_7)$$

An alternate expression is $\Pi M(2, 7, 13)$, where Π represents a product,

TABLE 13.6 Coding Schemes for Minterms and Maxterms

Minterm	True if abc	Code #
$\bar{a}\,\bar{b}\,\bar{c}$	000	m_0
$\bar{a}\,\bar{b}\,c$	001	m_1
$\bar{a}\,b\,\bar{c}$	010	m_2
$\bar{a}\,b\,c$	011	m_3
$a\,\bar{b}\,\bar{c}$	100	m_4
$a\,\bar{b}\,c$	101	m_5
$a\,b\,\bar{c}$	110	m_6
$a\,b\,c$	111	m_7

Maxterm	False if abc	Code #
$a + b + c$	000	M_0
$a + b + \bar{c}$	001	M_1
$a + \bar{b} + c$	010	M_2
$a + \bar{b} + \bar{c}$	011	M_3
$\bar{a} + b + c$	100	M_4
$\bar{a} + b + \bar{c}$	101	M_5
$\bar{a} + \bar{b} + c$	110	M_6
$\bar{a} + \bar{b} + \bar{c}$	111	M_7

M_i is the maxterm and i is the decimal integer for the corresponding binary code.

The order of the variables in the coding process is very important, that is, $f_2(A, B, C, D) = \Sigma m(0, 6, 11, 12)$ is *not* the same as $f(D, C, B, A) = \Sigma m(0, 6, 11, 12)$.

It is instructive to examine the relationship among truth tables, minterms, and maxterms. The following example serves to illustrate the connection.

Example 13.10

Given the switching function $f(A, B, C) = \overline{A}BC + A\overline{B}C + ABC$, the minterm list form is $f(A, B, C) = \Sigma m(3, 5, 7)$ and the truth table is shown in Table 13.7

TABLE 13.7

A	B	C	f(A, B, C)	$\bar{f}$(A, B, C)
0	0	0	0	1
0	0	1	0	1
0	1	0	0	1
0	1	1	1	0
1	0	0	0	1
1	0	1	1	0
1	1	0	0	1
1	1	1	1	0

The truth table for $\overline{f}(A, B, C)$ is also shown and can be expressed as $\overline{f}(A, B, C) = \Sigma m(0, 1, 2, 4, 6)$. Since the maxterms produce a 0 in the truth table listing, the function can also be expressed as $f(A, B, C) = \Sigma m(3, 5, 7) = \Pi M(0, 1, 2, 4, 6)$, and, of course, $\overline{f}(A, B, C) = \Sigma m(0, 1, 2, 4, 6) = \Pi M(3, 5, 7)$.

The previous example illustrates that a switching function can be immediately written in canonical form from the truth table; however, Boolean algebra can also be used to generate a canonical form.

Example 13.11

We wish to find the canonical SOP form of the function $f(A, B, C) = A\overline{B} + B\overline{C} + A\overline{C}$. This function can be written as

$$
\begin{aligned}
f(A, B, C) &= A\overline{B}(C + \overline{C}) + (A + \overline{A})\, B\overline{C} + A(B + \overline{B})\,\overline{C} \\
&= A\overline{B}C + A\overline{B}\,\overline{C} + AB\overline{C} + \overline{A}B\overline{C} + AB\overline{C} + A\overline{B}\,\overline{C} \\
&= A\overline{B}C + A\overline{B}\,\overline{C} + AB\overline{C} + \overline{A}B\overline{C} \\
&= \Sigma m(2, 4, 5, 6)
\end{aligned}
$$

Drill Exercise

D13.6. Express the following switching function in both minterm and maxterm form.

$$f(A, B, C) = AB + \overline{A}\,\overline{C}$$

Ans: $f(A, B, C) = \Sigma m(0, 2, 6, 7) = \Pi M(1, 3, 4, 5)$.

Thus far our manipulation of Boolean functions has been done algebraically. It is possible, however, to graphically display the mathematical operations using *Venn diagrams*. This possibility exists because the *algebra of sets* is also a Boolean algebra in which the sets correspond to the elements and the set operations of union and intersection correspond to the Boolean operations of + and $\cdot$, respectively. Sets are represented by some type of closed contour, and several basic sets together with the operations + and $\cdot$ are shown in Figure 13.2.

Venn diagrams can be used to visually demonstrate the postulates and theorems we have presented earlier. Consider, for example, the Boolean expression

$$A_1(A_2 + A_3) = A_1A_2 + A_1A_3$$

Figure 13.3 displays this expression in Venn diagrams. Note that the set $A_1(A_2 + A_3)$ is identical to the set $A_1A_2 + A_1A_3$.

Although Venn diagrams can be employed to visualize Boolean mathematical operations, much of their importance stems from the fact that they provide the basis for the minimization

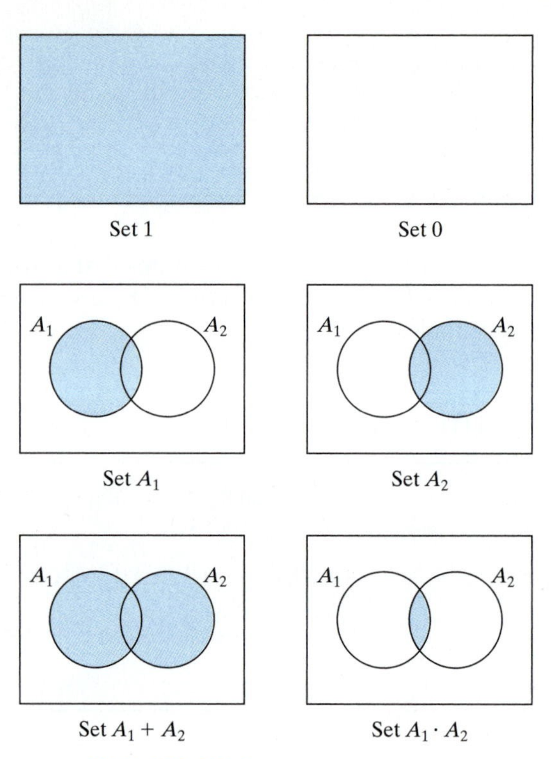

FIGURE 13.2 Set operations.

The Venn diagram as a graphical display tool

of switching circuits using what is called a *Karnaugh map* (K-map). We transform the Venn diagram into a K-map using Figure 13.4 in the following manner. The Venn diagram for the three variables *A, B*, and *C* is shown in Figure 13.4(a). Each area of the diagram within the universal set corresponds to one of the eight minterms as shown in Figures 13.4(b) and 13.4(c). Since one minterm is of no more importance than another, the diagram is reshaped to give equal area to each minterm as shown in Figure 13.4(d). The final form of the map is shown in Figure 13.4(e) where the *m*'s have been dropped, but the minterm number is retained in each block.

The crucial step in this transformation is the specific format of Figure 13.4(d). If we examine m_6 in Figure 13.4(c), we note that it is physically adjacent to m_2, m_4, and m_7. This condition has been maintained in the transformation to Figure 13.4(d). Next consider m_4 in Figure 13.4(c). In addition to m_5 and m_6, we find that m_4 is physically adjacent to m_0. This adjacent condition can be satisfied by folding the map into a cylinder so that the left and right edges are connected. Then m_5 is adjacent to m_4, m_7, and m_1, m_0 is adjacent to m_1, m_2, and m_4, and so on.

The K-map–Venn diagram–Truth table interconnection

The four-variable K-map is shown in Figure 13.5. Once again, in order to satisfy the minterm adjacent conditions, the left and right edges of the K-map are considered to be the same line as are the top and bottom edges.

Finally, it is interesting to note that there exists a direct correspondence between the K-map and the truth table. The former has one block per minterm while the latter has one row per minterm.

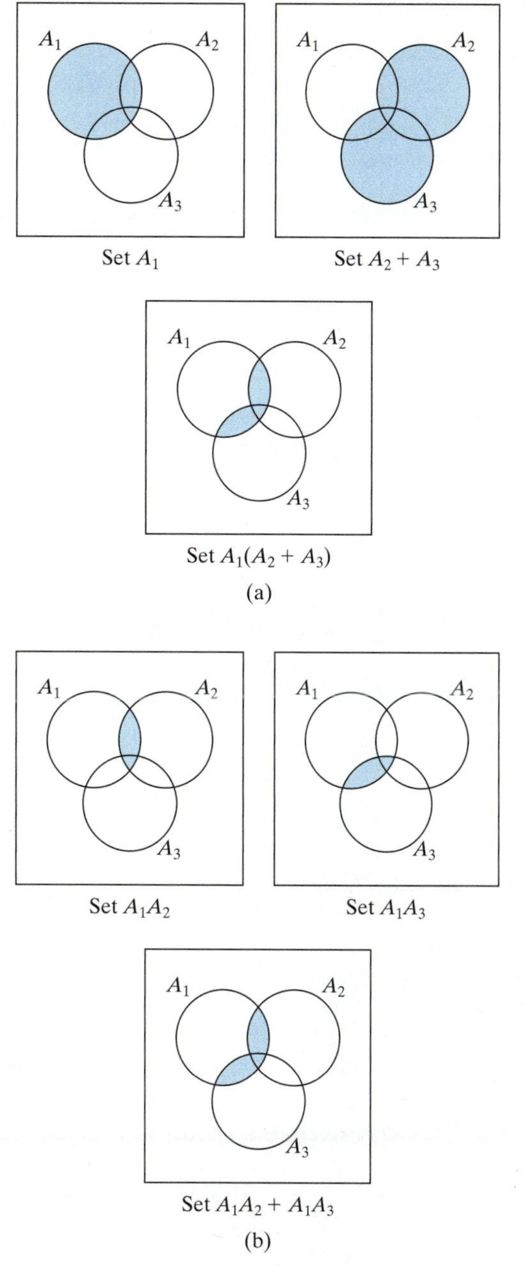

FIGURE 13.3 The use of Venn diagrams.

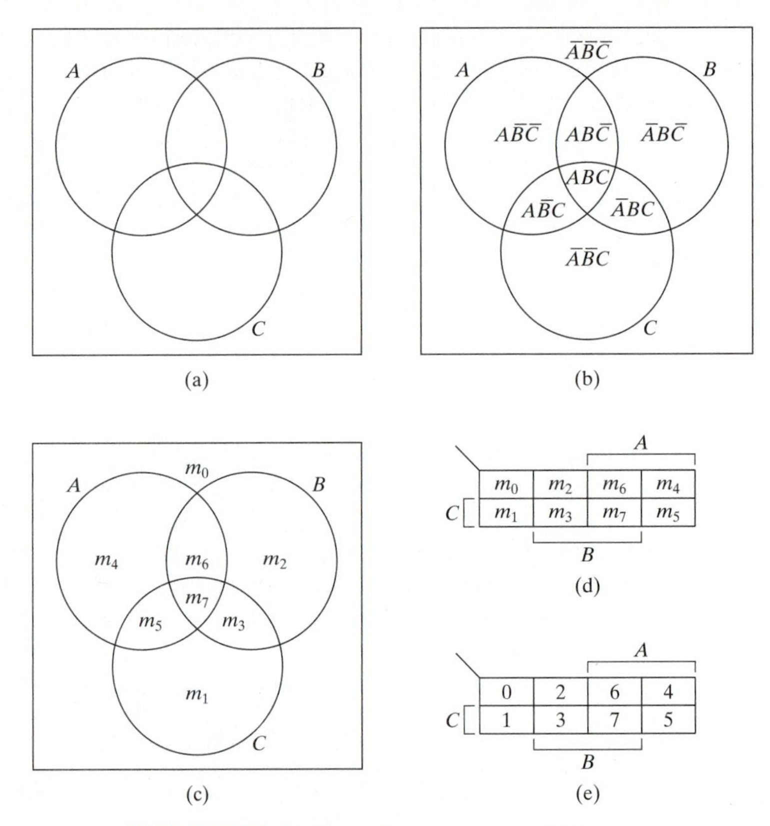

FIGURE 13.4 Venn diagrams and K-maps for three-variable functions.

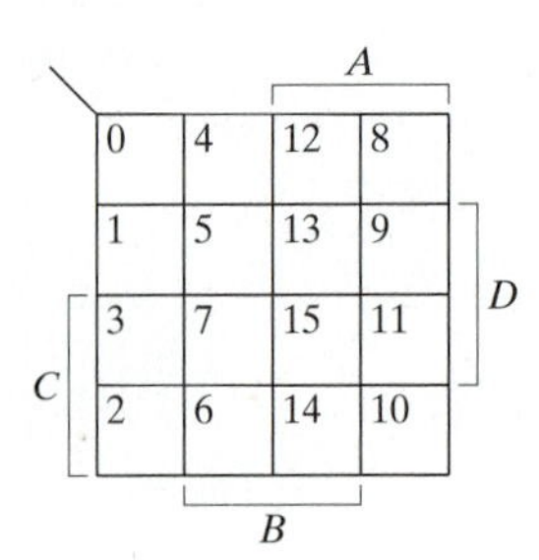

FIGURE 13.5 A four-variable K-map.

13-7 Function Minimization

The basis of using the Karnaugh map for function reduction is Theorem 7 in Table 11.3, which states

$$\overline{A}B + AB = B$$

Terms $\overline{A}B$ and AB are said to be logically adjacent since the only difference between them is that one variable, A, is complemented in one term but uncomplemented in the other. From

Theorem 7 the changing variable can be eliminated. In a K-map, cells that share a boundary are said to be physically adjacent and are defined by products terms that differ by only one variable changing from complemented to uncomplemented form. Therefore, physically adjacent cells in a K-map are also logically adjacent and can be combined and represented by a smaller product term through Theorem 7. This forms the basis for a graphical function reduction scheme using the K-map rather than Boolean algebra. Therefore the K-map can be used as a graphical tool for Boolean function minimization, as illustrated in the following example.

Example 13.12

Use of the K-map in Boolean function minimization

We wish to determine the minimum form of the switching function

$$f(A, B, C, D) = \Sigma m(3, 4, 5, 11, 15)$$

The function is shown listed on the map in Figure 13.6(a) where, in accordance with the correspondence that exists between the map and the truth table, we have placed a 1 in the listed minterm blocks and ignored the 0s, which would appear in the remaining blocks. The function in variable form is

$$\begin{aligned} f(A, B, C, D) &= m_3 + m_4 + m_5 + m_{11} + m_{15} \\ &= \overline{A}\overline{B}CD + \overline{A}B\overline{C}\overline{D} + \overline{A}B\overline{C}D + A\overline{B}CD + ABCD \end{aligned}$$

where, for example, m_3 corresponds to 0011 and thus $\overline{A}\overline{B}CD$. Furthermore, on the map m_3 is outside of both A and B and inside both C and D. The remaining terms can be visualized in a similar manner.

Note that minterms 4 and 5 differ in only a single literal, and, therefore, they can be combined to yield the term $\overline{A}B\overline{C}$. Similarly, minterms 3 and 11 and minterms 11 and 15 can be combined to yield $\overline{B}CD$ and ACD, respectively. Note that minterm 11 was used twice; however, that is the rule rather than the exception, since $A = A + A + A + \ldots$.

On the map, the logically adjacent terms are also physically adjacent, and are combined by drawing a loop around the minterms to be combined, as shown in Figure 13.6(b). We note, for example, that the combination of minterms 4 and 5 is outside A, inside B, and outside C; therefore, this combination yields $\overline{A}B\overline{C}$. The function representing the two remaining combinations is determined in a similar manner, and, therefore, the minimum function is

$$f(A, B, C, D) = \overline{A}B\overline{C} + \overline{B}CD + ACD.$$

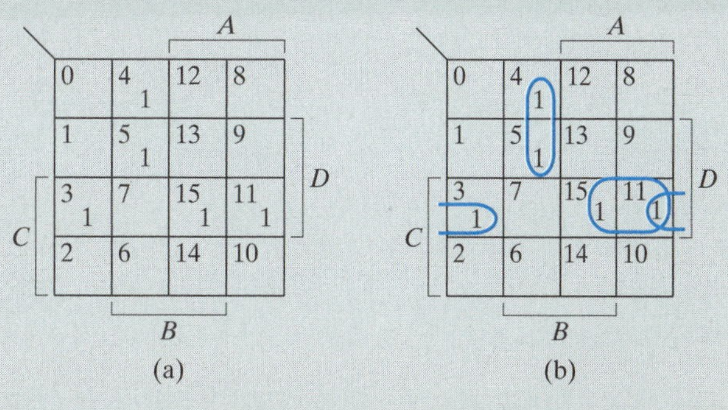

FIGURE 13.6 K-maps used in Example 13.12.

In the minimization procedure, we should "cover" each minterm at least once, and then group the minterms into the largest possible blocks. When combining minterms we group them in powers of 2. A group of 2 minterms eliminates 1 literal, a group of 4 minterms eliminates 2 literals, and so on.

Example 13.13

We wish to find the minimum form for the function

$$f(A, B, C) = \Sigma m(0, 2, 3, 7)$$

The map for this function is shown in Figure 13.7 and the minimum function is

$$f(A, B, C) = \overline{A}\,\overline{C} + BC$$

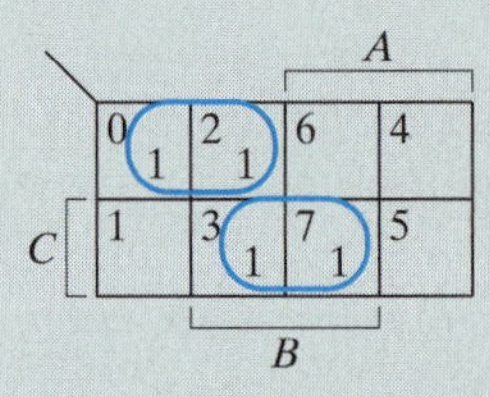

FIGURE 13.7 K-map for Example 13.13.

Example 13.14

The map for the following function is shown in Figure 13.8.

$$f(A, B, C, D) = \Sigma m(1, 3, 9, 11, 12, 13, 14)$$

Note that minterm 13 could be combined with either minterms 9 or 12. Combining minterm 13 with minterm 12 yields

$$f(A, B, C, D) = AB\overline{C} + AB\overline{D} + \overline{B}D$$

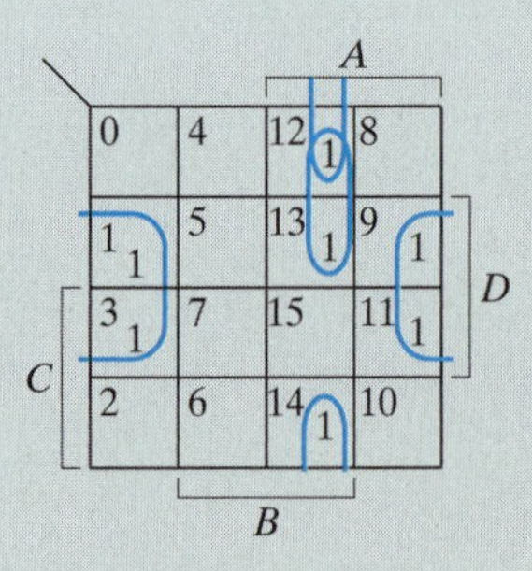

FIGURE 13.8 K-map for Example 13.14.

Drill Exercises

D13.7. Find the minimum form for the function $f(A, B, C) = \Sigma m(1, 5, 6, 7)$

Ans: $f(A, B, C) = AB + \overline{B}C$.

D13.8. Find the minimum form for the function $f(A, B, C, D) = \Sigma m(0, 1, 4, 5, 7, 9, 15)$

Ans: $f(A, B, C, D) = \overline{A}\,\overline{C} + \overline{B}\,\overline{C}D + BCD$

13–8 Combinational Logic Design

At this point we begin to apply what we have just learned to logic circuit design. Luckily, the design process for a minimum sum-of-products solution is rather procedural. The steps listed below will always yield a minimum SOP solution and a corresponding minimum AND-OR circuit.

Logic design strategy

1. **Create a design statement.** The design statement is a written description of what the circuit should do. A clear design statement solidly specifies the required circuit performance and facilitates the remaining steps.
2. **Determine the I/O requirements.** From the design statement, determine the number of input and output bits, and name each bit.
3. **Construct the truth table.** The truth table, listing the I/O values bit by bit, converts the design statement to a table of ones and zeros.
4. **Extract minterm lists.** Circuit outputs are expressed in minterm list form because minterm lists are easily mapped into K-maps.
5. **Reduce functions using K-maps.** Using K-maps for function reduction is easier than using Boolean algebra. If the K-maps are properly used, the results are guaranteed to be in minimum SOP format.
6. **Draw the corresponding circuit diagram.**

The following examples will serve to illustrate the manner in which the latter can be employed in a variety of applications.

Example 13.15

We wish to design a logic circuit with the following conditions: The input is a 4-bit binary coded decimal (BCD); there is a single output line; and the circuit should produce a 1 at the output (detect) if the input is divisible by 2.

The *BCD code* is listed as follows:

0	0000	5	0101
1	0001	6	0110
2	0010	7	0111
3	0011	8	1000
4	0100	9	1001

TABLE 13.8

Input *ABCD*	Output f	Minterm Listing
0000	0	0
0001	0	1
0010	1	2
0011	0	3
0100	1	4
0101	0	5
0110	1	6
0111	0	7
1000	1	8
1001	0	9
1010	d	10
1011	d	11
1100	d	12
1101	d	13
1110	d	14
1111	d	15

Since the output should be 1 if the input is either 2, 4, 6, or 8, the truth table for the network is shown in Table 13.8.

The definition and importance of don't care terms

An examination of this table prompts an immediate question—what are the *d*'s? *d* stands for *don't care*. The BCD input can only range from 0 to 9. Therefore, the numbers 10–15 cannot occur. Since these numbers cannot occur, we "don't care" whether the output is a 1 or a 0, and, therefore, we use a *d*. When we place the function on the K-map, the *d*'s can be 1's if they simplify the output function and 0 if they do not. The output function that results from the truth table is

$$f(A, B, C, D) = \Sigma m(2, 4, 6, 8) + d(10, 11, 12, 13, 14, 15)$$

The K-map for the function is shown in Figure 13.9.

The simplified logic function is then

$$f(A, B, C, D) = C\overline{D} + B\overline{D} + A\overline{D}$$

This Boolean function can be written in the form

$$f(A, B, C, D) = \overline{\overline{C\overline{D} + B\overline{D} + A\overline{D}}}$$

now applying DeMorgan's Theorem, the function becomes

$$f(A, B, C, D) = \overline{\overline{A\overline{D}} \cdot \overline{B\overline{D}} \cdot \overline{C\overline{D}}}$$

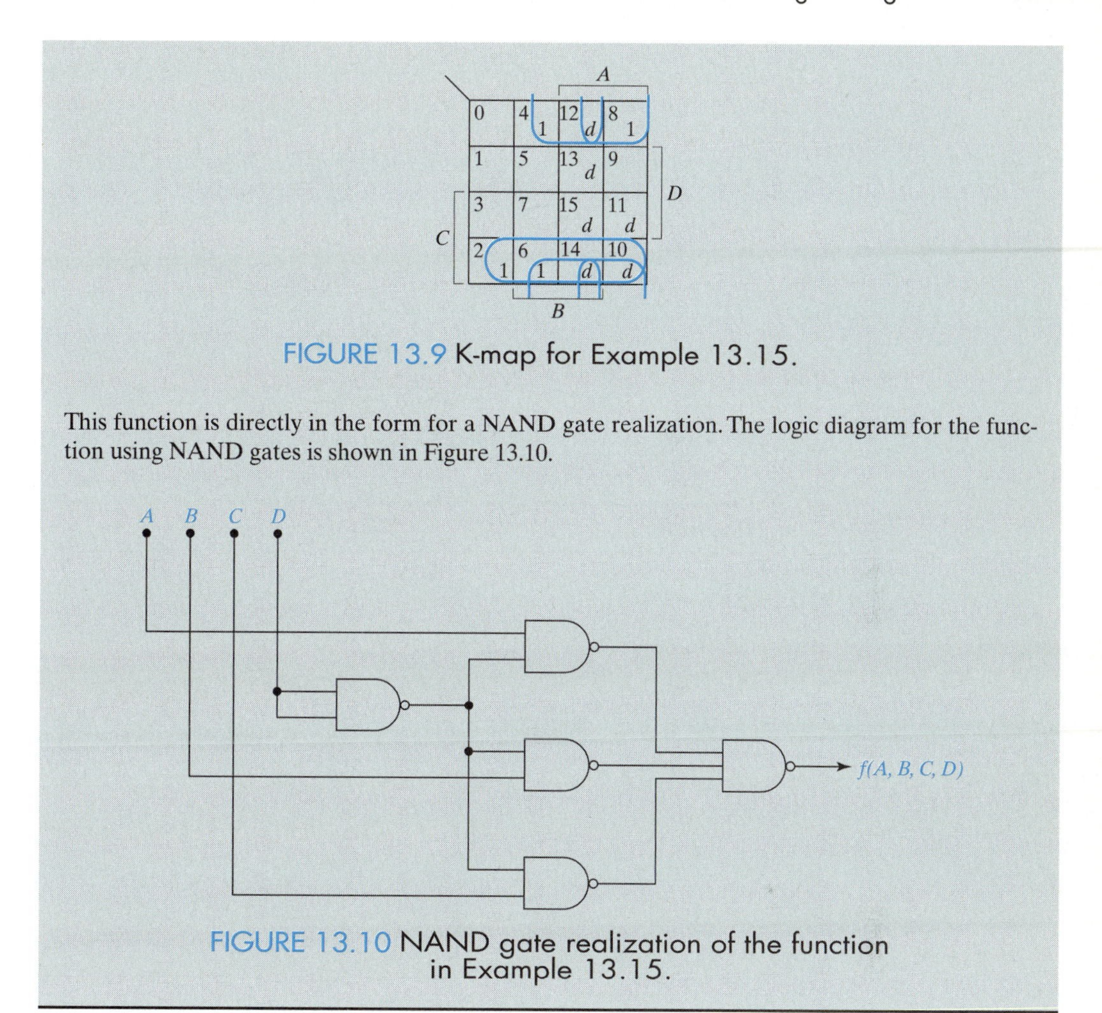

FIGURE 13.9 K-map for Example 13.15.

This function is directly in the form for a NAND gate realization. The logic diagram for the function using NAND gates is shown in Figure 13.10.

FIGURE 13.10 NAND gate realization of the function in Example 13.15.

A code converter is a multiple input, multiple output combinational logic network, which translates an input codeword into a bit pattern that represents the new codeword. The following example illustrates the design of such a device.

Example 13.16

The *EXCESS-3 code* is a code that is obtained by adding the decimal number 3 or 0011 in binary to the corresponding BCD code. This code is listed as follows:

0	0011	5	1000
1	0100	6	1001
2	0101	7	1010
3	0110	8	1011
4	0111	9	1100

This code is *self-complementing*, for example, the complement of 9(1100) is 0(0011), the complement of 8(1011) is 1(0100), and so on. We wish to obtain the logic equations for the code converter, which will convert the BCD code to EXCESS-3.

The truth table for the code converter is shown in Figure 13.11. The K-maps for the four bits in the EXCESS-3 code are shown in Figure 13.12. The logic equations for each bit in the EXCESS-3 code are

$$B_1 = A_1 + A_2A_3 + A_2A_4$$

$$B_2 = \overline{A_2}A_3 + \overline{A_2}A_4 + A_2\overline{A_3}\,\overline{A_4}$$

$$B_3 = A_3A_4 + \overline{A_3}\,\overline{A_4}$$

$$B_4 = \overline{A_4}$$

These equations represent the 4-input, 4-output logic circuit, which performs the code conversion.

Decimal	**BCD**				**Excess-3**			
	A₁	**A₂**	**A₃**	**A₄**	**B₁**	**B₂**	**B₃**	**B₄**
0	0	0	0	0	0	0	1	1
1	0	0	0	1	0	1	0	0
2	0	0	1	0	0	1	0	1
3	0	0	1	1	0	1	1	0
4	0	1	0	0	0	1	1	1
5	0	1	0	1	1	0	0	0
6	0	1	1	0	1	0	0	1
7	0	1	1	1	1	0	1	0
8	1	0	0	0	1	0	1	1
9	1	0	0	1	1	1	0	0
10	d	d	d	d	d	d	d	d
11	d	d	d	d	d	d	d	d
12	d	d	d	d	d	d	d	d
13	d	d	d	d	d	d	d	d
14	d	d	d	d	d	d	d	d
15	d	d	d	d	d	d	d	d

FIGURE 13.11 Truth table for BCD to Excess-3 code converter.

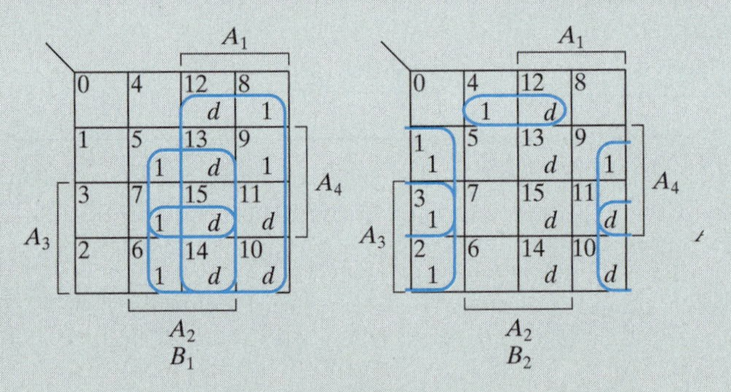

FIGURE 13.12 K-maps for Example 13.16.

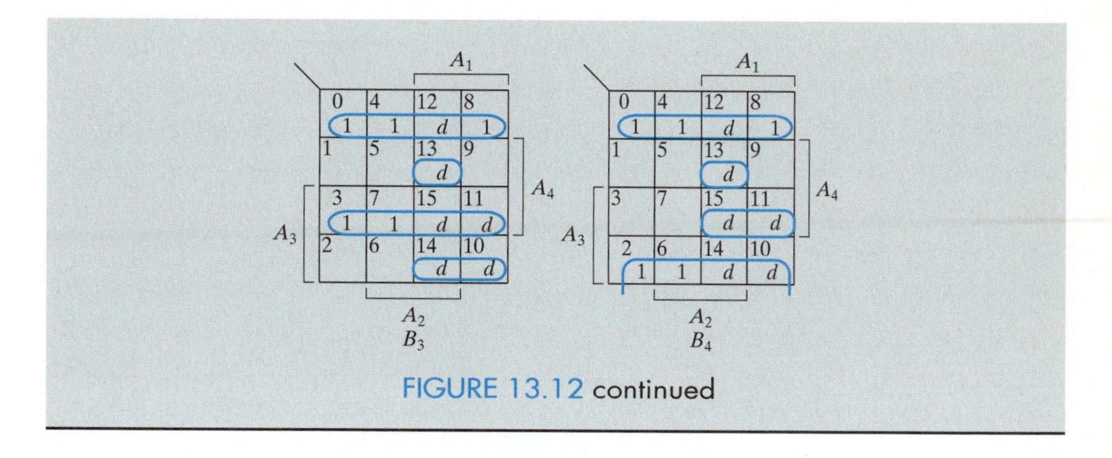

FIGURE 13.12 continued

Drill Exercise

D13.9. Design a logic circuit with a BCD input that detects the odd numbers 1, 3, 5, 7, and 9.

Ans: If the BCD inputs are labeled $A_1A_2A_3A_4$, then $f(A_1, A_2, A_3, A_4) = A_4$.

Example 13.17

A factory employs two engines and each is equipped with two identical sensors. One sensor measures output speed and the other measures engine temperature. If speed and temperature are normal, the sensor outputs are low. If the speed is too fast or the temperature too high, the sensor outputs are high. We wish to design a logic circuit that will detect whenever the speed of either or both engines is too fast and the temperature of either or both engines is too high.

The logic variables are defined as follows:

A = speed of engine 1

B = speed of engine 2

C = temperature of engine 1

D = temperature of engine 2

The truth table for this example is listed in Figure 13.13.

The minterms for the function are plotted in the K-map in Figure 13.14. The minimized logic function that defines the logic network is

$$f(A, B, C, D) = AC + BC + AD + BD$$

A	B	C	D	f
0	0	0	0	0
0	0	0	1	0
0	0	1	0	0
0	0	1	1	0
0	1	0	0	0
0	1	0	1	1
0	1	1	0	1
0	1	1	1	1
1	0	0	0	0
1	0	0	1	1
1	0	1	0	1
1	0	1	1	1
1	1	0	0	0
1	1	0	1	1
1	1	1	0	1
1	1	1	1	1

FIGURE 13.13 Truth table used in Example 13.17.

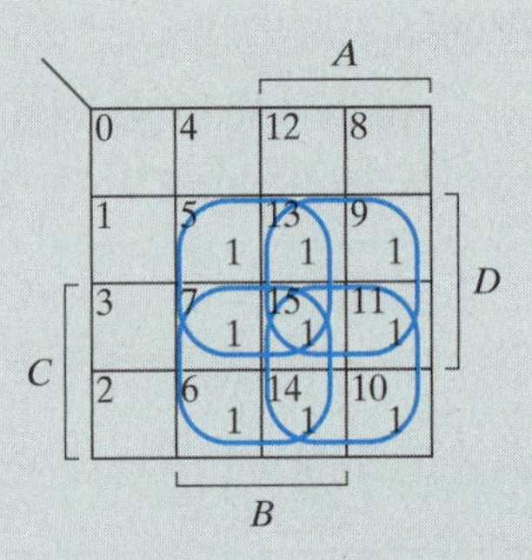

FIGURE 13.14 K-map for Example 13.17.

Drill Exercise

D13.10. Design a logic circuit with three inputs *A, B,* and *C,* such that the output is to be high only when exactly two of the inputs are high.

Ans: $f(A, B, C) = AB\overline{C} + A\overline{B}C + \overline{A}BC.$

Example 13.18

A low-budget sci-fi movie needs a countdown sequence (9,8,7, ... 1, 0) for an alien missile launch. Of course, aliens do not use our Arabic numerals. The alien numerals are shown in Figure 13.15(a) and can be displayed on the standard 7-segment display seen in Figure 13.15(b). A countdown circuit already exists where the outputs, WXYZ, are the BCD representation of the count. We need a circuit to convert BCD to alien seven-segment code. Write minimum SOP functions for a through g in terms of W, X, Y, and Z. Assume that a segment turns on when a 1 is applied to it.

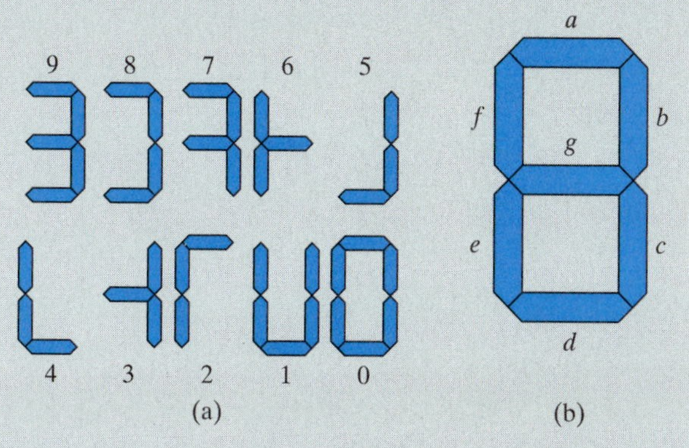

FIGURE 13.15 Alien font set and seven-segment map for Example 13.18.

The circuit has a four-bit BCD input, WXYZ, and seven outputs, $a - g$. Figure 13.16 shows the corresponding truth table. From the truth table we see that segments b and c are the same function. The same is true for segments e and f. As a result, we only need minterm lists and K-maps for five of the seven segments. The minterm lists are extracted from the truth table.

WXYZ	abcdefg
0 0 0 0	1 1 1 1 1 1 0
0 0 0 1	0 1 1 1 1 1 0
0 0 1 0	1 0 0 0 1 1 0
0 0 1 1	0 1 1 0 0 0 1
0 1 0 0	0 0 0 1 1 1 0
0 1 0 1	0 1 1 1 0 0 0
0 1 1 0	0 0 0 0 1 1 1
0 1 1 1	1 1 1 0 0 0 1
1 0 0 0	1 1 1 1 0 0 0
1 0 0 1	1 1 1 1 0 0 1
1 0 1 0	x x x x x x x
1 0 1 1	x x x x x x x
1 1 0 0	x x x x x x x
1 1 0 1	x x x x x x x
1 1 1 0	x x x x x x x
1 1 1 1	x x x x x x x

FIGURE 13.16 Truth table for Example 13.18.

$$a(W,X,Y,Z) = \Sigma m(0,2,7,8,9) + d(10 - 15)$$
$$b(W,X,Y,Z) = \Sigma m(0,1,3,5,7,8,9) + d(10 - 15)$$
$$d(W,X,Y,Z) = \Sigma m(0,1,4,5,8,9) + d(10 - 15)$$
$$e(W,X,Y,Z) = \Sigma m(0,1,2,4,6) + d(10 - 15)$$
$$g(W,X,Y,Z) = \Sigma m(3,6,7,9) + d(10 - 15)$$
$$c = b \quad \text{and} \quad f = e$$

The corresponding K-maps, shown in Figure 13.17, yield the following minimum SOP functions.

$$a = W + \overline{X}\,\overline{Z} + XYZ \qquad b = c = W + \overline{X}\,\overline{Y} \qquad d = \overline{Y}$$
$$e = f = \overline{W}\,\overline{X}\,\overline{Y} + \overline{W}\,\overline{Z} \qquad g = WZ + YZ + XY$$

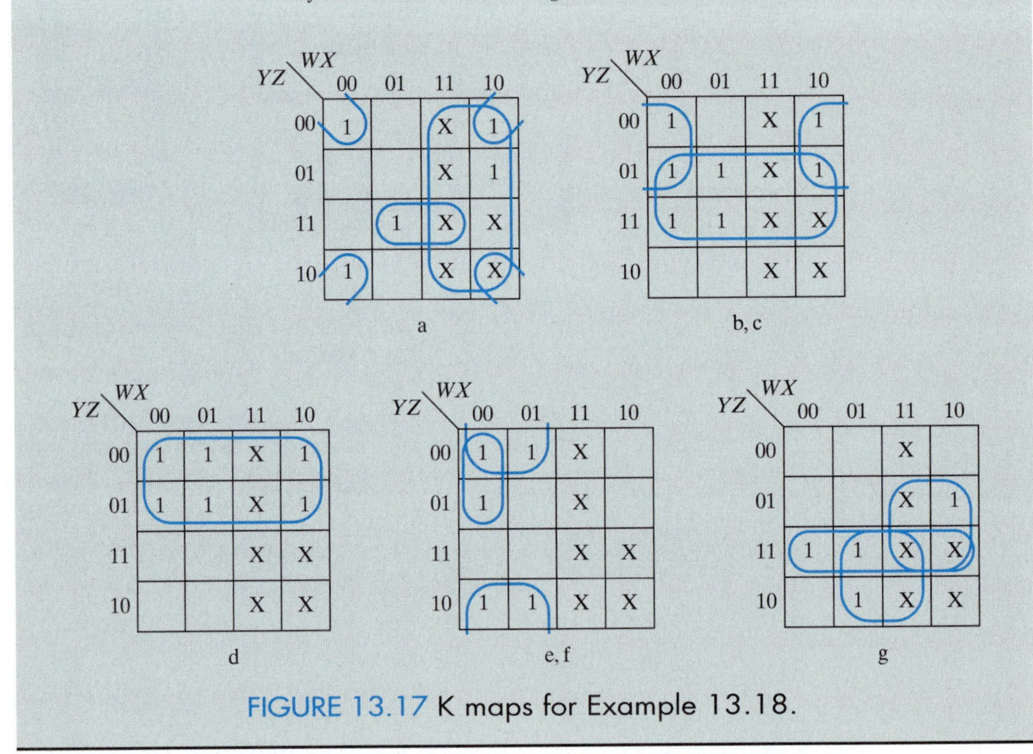

FIGURE 13.17 K maps for Example 13.18.

13-9 Sequential Logic Circuits

We have shown that in combinational logic circuits the output is a function of only the current input, that is, what has happened in the past has absolutely no bearing on the current output.

The use of memory in logic circuits

Sequential circuits, with their inherent *memory*, provide us with a whole new dimension in the design of logic circuits. This memory provides us with the capability to remember the past, and, therefore, the current output can be a function of not only the current input but prior inputs as well.

Although there are numerous examples of sequential devices, one example that we regularly encounter is the washing machine. This device has several *states*, for example, wash, rinse, and spin dry, and they are performed in a specific order. The *output* of the machine, that is, the specific task that the machine performs, is a function of not only the machine's *present state* but its input as well. The input also transitions the machine from its present state to the *next state*.

The use of memory is clearly the key to the added capability that exists in sequential circuits. Let us now examine a general model for this new type of circuit.

13.9.1 The Structure of Sequential Logic Circuits

Sequential circuits can be modeled as shown in Figure 13.18. This block diagram clearly illustrates the difference between sequential and combinational logic circuits.

As the model indicates, both the outputs, z_i, and the next states, Y_j, are functions of the inputs, x_k, and the present state, y_l. Mathematically, the relationships can be expressed as follows:

$$\begin{aligned} z_i &= f_1(x_1 x_2 \ldots x_n, y_1, \ldots y_p) \qquad i = 1,2, \ldots m \\ Y_j &= f_2(x_1 x_2 \ldots x_n, y_1, y_2 \ldots y_p) \qquad j = 1,2, \ldots p \end{aligned} \tag{13.2}$$

The equations can be written in vector notation as

$$\begin{aligned} \mathbf{z} &= f_1(\mathbf{x},\mathbf{y}) \\ \mathbf{Y} &= f_2(\mathbf{x},\mathbf{y}) \end{aligned} \tag{13.3}$$

We will later explore the exact forms of the input and output signals, as well as the different types of memory devices that are typically employed in sequential circuits.

13.9.2 State Tables and Diagrams

State tables and *diagrams* illustrate in tabular and graphical form, respectively, the functional relationship that exists among input, present state, output, and next state. These two equivalent forms are shown in Figure 13.19. In each case, for input x, the circuit will transition from present state y to next state Y with an output z. The following example explicitly illustrates the connection between these two equivalent forms.

Techniques for describing sequential circuit operations

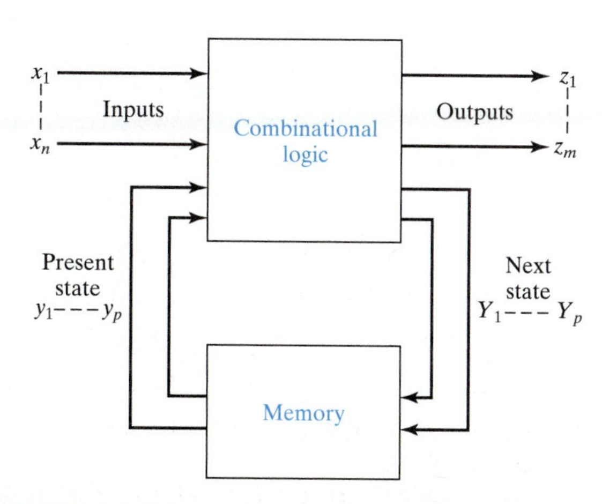

FIGURE 13.18 A model for a sequential circuit.

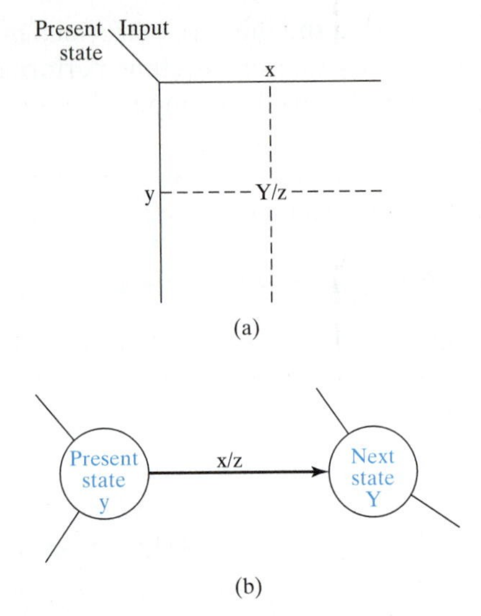

FIGURE 13.19 State table and equivalent state diagram.

Example 13.19

The state table and equivalent state diagram for a specific sequential circuit are shown in Figure 13.20. These equivalent descriptions indicate that if the circuit is in state *A* and the input is a 1, the circuit will transition to state *B* and produce an output of 0. Note that if the circuit is initially in state *A* and the input sequence 1001 is applied, the circuit will move from state *A* to *B* to *D* to *C* to *A* and produce an output sequence 0101. The same input applied to the circuit when it is initially in state *C* would produce the output string 1000.

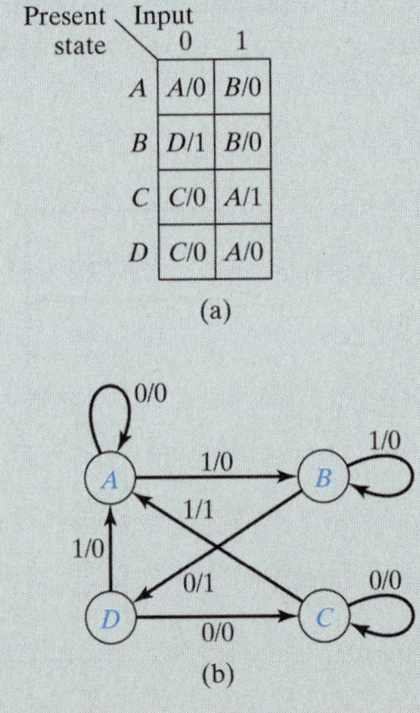

Present state \ Input	0	1
A	*A*/0	*B*/0
B	*D*/1	*B*/0
C	*C*/0	*A*/1
D	*C*/0	*A*/0

(a)

FIGURE 13.20 Equivalent descriptions of a sequential circuit.

Drill Exercise

D13.11. A sequential circuit is described by the state table in Figure D13.11. If the circuit is initially in state B and the input sequence is $x = 010110$, determine the output sequence.

PS \ x	0	1
A	$A/0$	$B/1$
B	$B/0$	$A/1$

FIGURE D13.11

Ans: $z = 010110$.

13.9.3 Clocked Memory

In general, sequential circuits may operate in a variety of modes. For example, the memory elements may be clocked or unclocked. Furthermore, the circuit's input signals may be synchronous pulses, synchronous levels, asynchronous pulses, or asynchronous levels. In the material that follows, we will consider only those circuits that function under the control of a clock signal that is normally zero and contains periodic pulses defined by a $0 \rightarrow 1 \rightarrow 0$ transition. The clock signal serves to synchronize the operation of all memory elements. Therefore, when the memory elements change state, they do so in response to the *clock pulse* rather than some other input.

Common memory elements for sequential circuits

Devices called *flip-flops* are normally employed as memory elements in *synchronous sequential circuits.* These devices will store either a 0 or a 1. The flip-flop typically has two outputs, one of which is the normal state Q and the other is the complement $\overline{Q}$. In addition to the clock signal, clocked flip-flops have one or more control inputs. However, the effects of these control inputs are controlled by the clock signal, that is, the control inputs prepare the flip-flop for a state transition, but it is the clock pulse that actually *triggers* the change.

There are a number of *different types of flip-flops,* for example, S–R or set–reset, D or delay, T or trigger, and J–K. Each has its own operating characteristics. Since their operations are similar, we will confine our discussion here to one of them—the J–K flip-flop.

The block diagram for a clocked J–K flip-flop is shown in Figure 13.21(a). C is the clock signal, J and K are the control signals, and Q and $\overline{Q}$ are the outputs. The state table that defines the transitions under clock control is shown in Figure 13.21(b). The operation can be summarized in the table in Figure 13.21(c). Under the control of the clock pulse, that is, $C = 1$, $J = 0$, and $K = 0$ causes no change in the present output Q_p. $J = 0$ and $K = 1$ will *reset* the output to $Q = 0$. $J = 1$ and $K = 0$ will *set* the output to $Q = 1$. $J = 1$ and $K = 1$ *toggles* the output, that is, the output will change states from Q_p to $\overline{Q_p}$. This operation is also illustrated by the timing diagram shown in Figure 13.22. In this diagram we assume that the transition of the flip-flop is triggered by the leading edge of the clock pulse, and we ignore all nuances associated with the timing of the signals. Note that initially the flip-flop is set, that is,

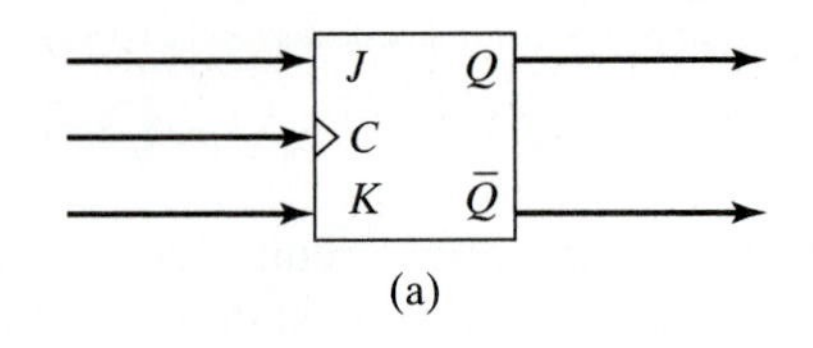

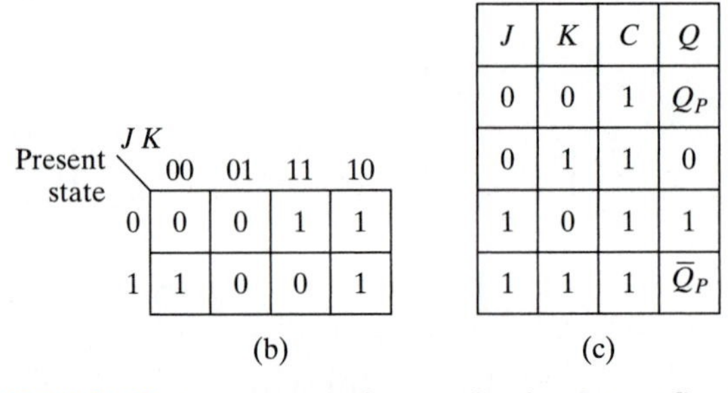

Present state \ JK	00	01	11	10
0	0	0	1	1
1	1	0	0	1

(b)

J	K	C	Q
0	0	1	Q_P
0	1	1	0
1	0	1	1
1	1	1	$\bar{Q}_P$

(c)

FIGURE 13.21 Diagrams for a clocked *J–K* flip-flop.

$Q = 1$ (high) and at the time of the first clock pulse $J = 0$ and $K = 0$, and, therefore, Q remains at 1. When the second clock pulse arrives, J is still 0 but $K = 1$, and, therefore, the flip-flop resets to $Q = 0$ (low). At the time of the third clock pulse $J = 1$ and $K = 0$, and, therefore, the flip-flop is set to $Q = 1$. When the fourth clock pulse arrives, $J = 1$ and $K = 1$, and hence the flip-flop is toggled to the opposite state $Q = 0$. Finally, during the last clock pulse $J = 0$, and $K = 1$, and, therefore, the flip-flop is reset to $Q = 0$. Since the flip-flop is already in this state, it simply remains there.

13.9.4 Analysis of Synchronous Sequential Circuits

Given a synchronous sequential circuit, we wish to determine the functional relationship that exists among the input x_k, the present state y_k, the next state Y_k, and the output, z_k. The condition of the flip-flops defines the present state of the circuit. This information, when combined with the input, yields the next state and output. Recall from our earlier discussion that a state table or state diagram completely defines this relationship. In addition, since each flip-flop has two states, a circuit containing n flip-flop can be described by a state table with 2^n rows.

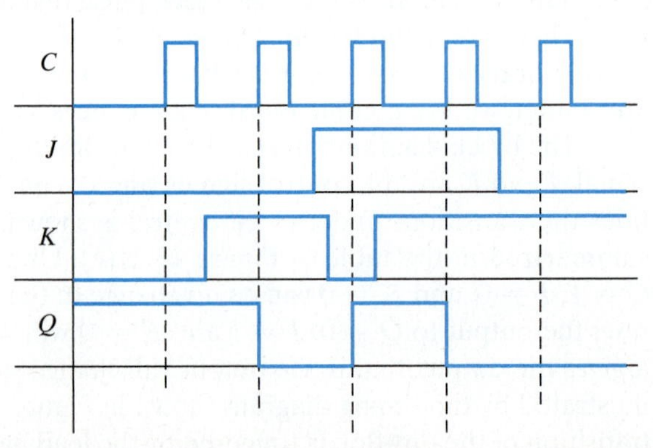

FIGURE 13.22 Timing diagram for a *J–K* flip-flop.

The following example illustrates two approaches to the *analysis procedure* and illuminates many of the facets that exist between them.

Example 13.20

Consider the network shown in Figure 13.23(a). This synchronous sequential circuit contains one *J–K* flip-flop, and, therefore, has two states. Furthermore, since there is a single input, the state table for this network is of the form shown in Figure 13.23(b). Assuming a combination of present states and inputs, we can complete this state table. For example, by tracing the various signals through the circuit we find that if the present state is $y_k = 0$ and the input is $x = 0$, the output is $z = 0$ and the next state, determined by $J = 0$ and $K = 1$, is $Y_k = 0$. Therefore, the entry in the upper left-hand corner of the state table is $Y_k/z_k = 0/0$. Also, if the present state is $y_k = 0$ and the input is $x = 1$, the output is $z = 0$ and the next state, determined by $J = 1$ and $K = 1$, is $Y_k = 1$. Therefore, the entry in the upper right-hand corner of the state table is $Y_k/z_k = 1/0$. The completed state table is shown in Figure 13.23(c). Once this completed state table is known, given an initial state, the output sequence can be determined for any input string.

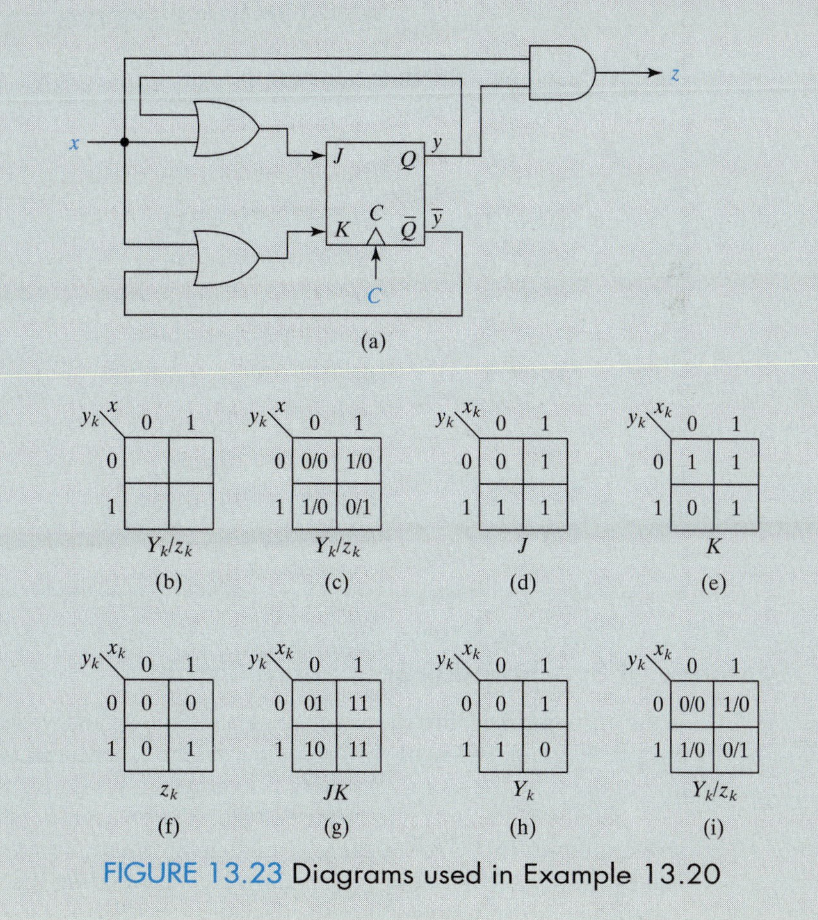

FIGURE 13.23 Diagrams used in Example 13.20

The analysis can also be performed from a different perspective. The logic equations that describe the network are

$$z_k = x_k y_k$$
$$J = x_k + y_k$$
$$K = x_k + \overline{y_k}$$

The K-maps for these functions are shown in Figures 13.23(d), (e), and (f), respectively. If we transpose the data in Figures 13.23(d) and (e), we obtain the table in Figure 13.23(g).

This latter table defines the control inputs to the flip-flop, which govern the state transition during the clock pulse. For example, if the present state is $y_k = 0$, the input is $x_k = 0$, and the control signals are $J = 0$ and $K = 0$, the next state is $Y_k = 0$. Likewise, if the present state is $y_k = 0$, the input is $x_k = 1$, and the control signals are $J = 1$ and $K = 1$, the next state is $Y_k = 1$. The table in Figure 13.23(h) is completed in this manner. Finally, combining the table in Figure 13.23(f) with that in Figure 13.23(h) yields the state table in Figure 13.23(i), which is identical to that in Figure 13.23(c).

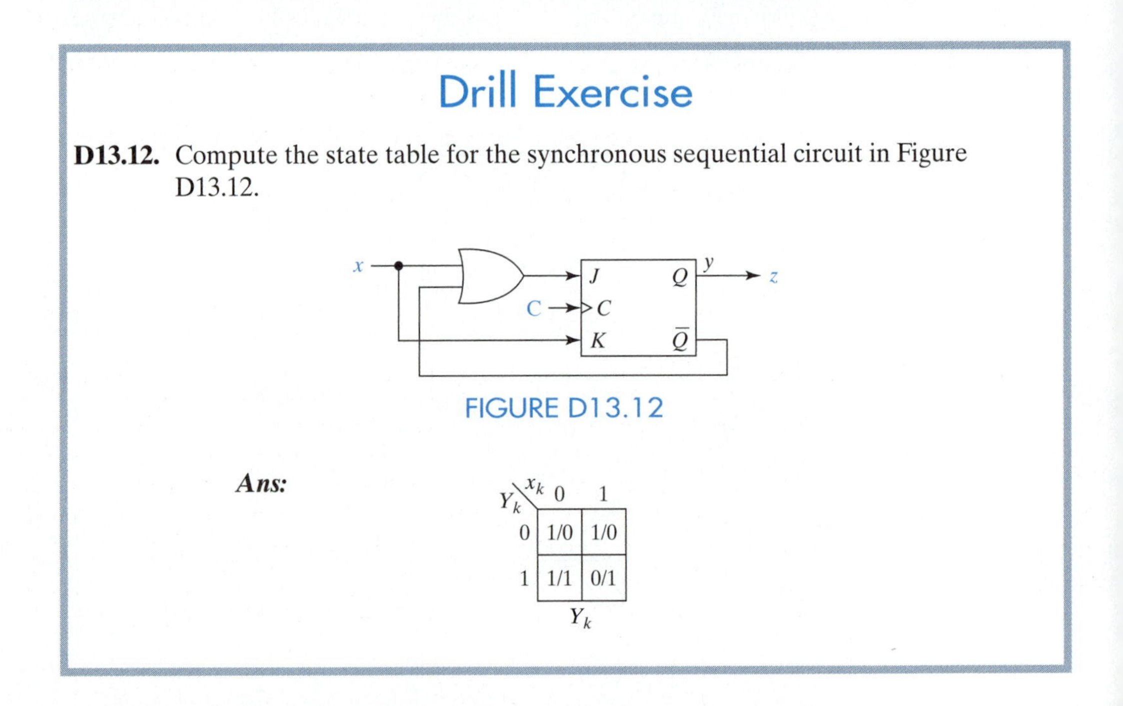

Drill Exercise

D13.12. Compute the state table for the synchronous sequential circuit in Figure D13.12.

FIGURE D13.12

Ans:

$Y_k \backslash x_k$	0	1
0	1/0	1/0
1	1/1	0/1

Y_k

13.9.5 Synthesis of Synchronous Sequential Circuits

In the analysis procedure, the circuit diagram is known and we wish to determine the state table or state diagram. The *synthesis procedure,* on the other hand, typically starts with a specification of the state table or state diagram, and from it we derive the circuit.

Sequential circuits must be used when the present inputs are insufficient to produce a proper output. That is to say there is missing information we require to complete the design. The following 10-step design procedure aids in isolating the missing information and systematically incorporating it into the design.

1. **Create a design statement.** The design statement is a written description of what the circuit should do.
2. **Determine the I/O requirements.** Determine the number of input and output bits, and name each bit.
3. **Identify the missing information and its possible scenarios.** Succinctly define the additional information we require as well as its possible scenarios.
4. **Draw the state diagram.** In the state diagram, the different scenarios for the missing information are assigned to states. Being in a particular state means that the present missing information scenario is the one assigned to that state. Thus, knowing the present state is identical to knowing the present missing information scenario. In this way, the state diagram converts the design statement to a "flowchart-like" diagram where the states remember the missing information.
5. **Make state assignments.** The state assignments give each state in the diagram a unique code number made of flip-flop output bits.
6. **Assemble the state table.** The state table combines the diagram and assignment into a table of ones and zeros.
7. **Choose a flip-flop type.** Most designers choose D or J-K flip-flops.
8. **Minimize flip-flop inputs using K-maps.** Circuit outputs are expressed in minterm list form because minterm lists are easily mapped into K-maps.
9. **Minimize output functions using K-maps.** The output K-maps yield the minimum forms for the overall circuit outputs.
10. **Draw the corresponding circuit diagram.**

Example 13.21

We wish to design a synchronous sequential circuit with a single input and a single output that *recognizes* or *detects* the input sequence $x = 10$. Recognition of a particular input string can be accomplished by producing a 1 at the output whenever the specific string occurs. The importance of this example stems from the fact that this type of circuit is very useful in detecting the handshake signal sent by a printer to a computer for the purpose of acknowledging the receipt of a byte of message. As soon as the computer detects the acknowledge signal from the printer, the next byte of message can be sent. Similar applications can be found in communication systems. The circuit should be designed so that if the input string is

$$x = 001001100$$
$$\longrightarrow TIME$$

the output will be

$$z = 000100010$$

Referring to our design procedures, we already have a design statement that clearly indicates that the circuit has one input, x, and one output, z. Next, we identify the missing information. If we knew exactly how many bits in the sequence have been received in the correct order, we could produce the proper output for any input. Therefore, the missing information is "how many bits have been received correctly thus far." There are two possible scenarios: no bits are correct and one bit is correct. Let us assign the duty of remembering the "no bits" scenario to a state called A and the "one bit" case to state B. This is shown in Figure 13.24(a), which is the beginning of our state

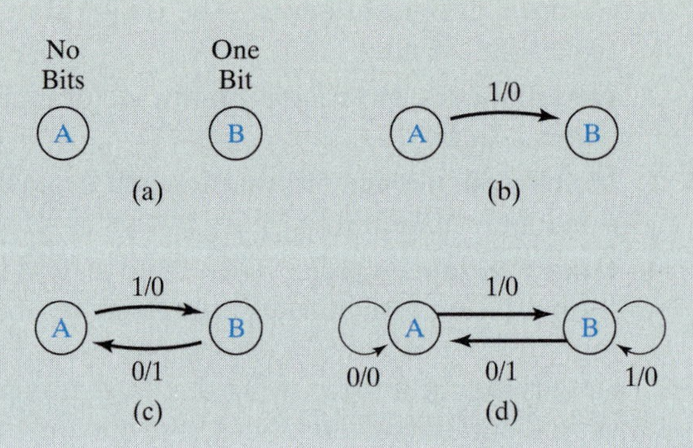

FIGURE 13.24 State diagram development for a 10 detector.

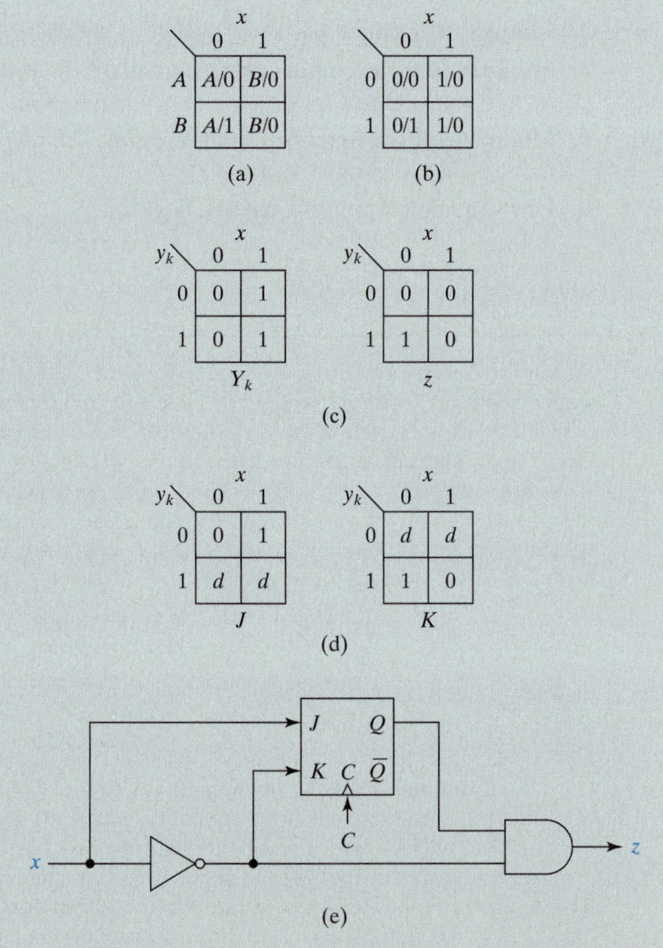

FIGURE 13.25 Diagrams employed in Example 13.21

diagram. Now we consider the various inputs that might occur. Suppose, starting in state A, that a 1 is received. Since this is the first bit in our 10 sequence, we now have one bit correct and transition to state B with an output of 0, as shown in Figure 13.24(b). If a 0 is received next, our sequence is complete. We return to state A to start searching for the next 10 sequence and the output value is 1, as seen in Figure 13.24(c). Now suppose, in state A, that a 0 is received. Since this is not the first bit in our sequence, there are still no bits correct and we stay in state A with $z = 0$. Finally, if we are in state B and a 1 is received, we do not have the desired sequence, however, the most recent input, a 1, is indeed the first bit in the 10 sequence. Therefore, we go to the "one bit correct" state (state B) with an output of 0. The completed state diagram is shown in Figure 13.24(d).

The state table that corresponds to the state diagram in Figure 13.24(d) is shown in Figure 13.25(a). If we make the *state assignment* $A = 0$ and $B = 1$, the state table is changed to that shown in Figure 13.25(b). Note that we could have made the assignment $A = 1$ and $B = 0$, which will also result in a valid circuit. Methods for making state assignments that minimize the amount of hardware are known but will not be addressed here.

The state table in Figure 13.25(b) is split into the two tables in Figure 13.25(c). The first table specifies the state transitions, that is, given a present state y_k and an input x, the next state Y_k is known. The second table is simply a K-map for the output z. In order to realize state transitions specified in Figure 13.25(c) using a clocked J–K flip-flop, we must now determine the proper control signals on the J and K input lines. Note that since the state table has two states, only one J–K flip-flop is required. Let us examine the upper left-hand corner of the state transition table in Figure 13.25(c). If $y_k = 0$ and $x = 0$, the next state is $Y_k = 0$. In order to affect this transition, J must be 0; however, K may be 0 or 1, and, therefore, we simply specify it as a don't care, d. Next consider the upper right-hand corner of the table, that is, $y_k = 0$, $x = 1$, and $Y_k = 1$. In this latter case J must be 1; however, once again K may be 0 or 1, and, therefore, is a d. The complete tables are shown in Figure 13.25(d). These tables are K-maps and, together with the K-map for z, yield the following logic equations.

$$J = x$$
$$K = \overline{x}$$
$$z = \overline{x}y_k$$

Therefore, the actual circuit derived from the equations is shown in Figure 13.25(e).

The final example will not only indicate the versatility of synchronous sequential circuits but will illustrate some additional features of the synthesis process.

Example 13.22

We wish to design an up/down counter using clocked J–K flip-flops that counts in the range of 0, 1, 2, and 3. When $x = 0$, the circuit should count up, and when $x = 1$, the circuit should count down. The output should be designed so that it indicates the current count, that is, is the count 0, 1, 2, or 3. The design statement clearly indicates that the circuit has one input, x, and two outputs, z_1z_0, which should be viewed as a two-bit number. The input, x, identifies only the direction of the count. To know the next count value, we must know the present count value. That is the missing information. Also, since the count should cycle over and over, there are four scenarios for the present count: 00, 01, 10, and 11. The state diagram, shown in Figure 13.26(a), is very simple. If we are cunning, we should choose state assignments that match the count sequence as listed below:

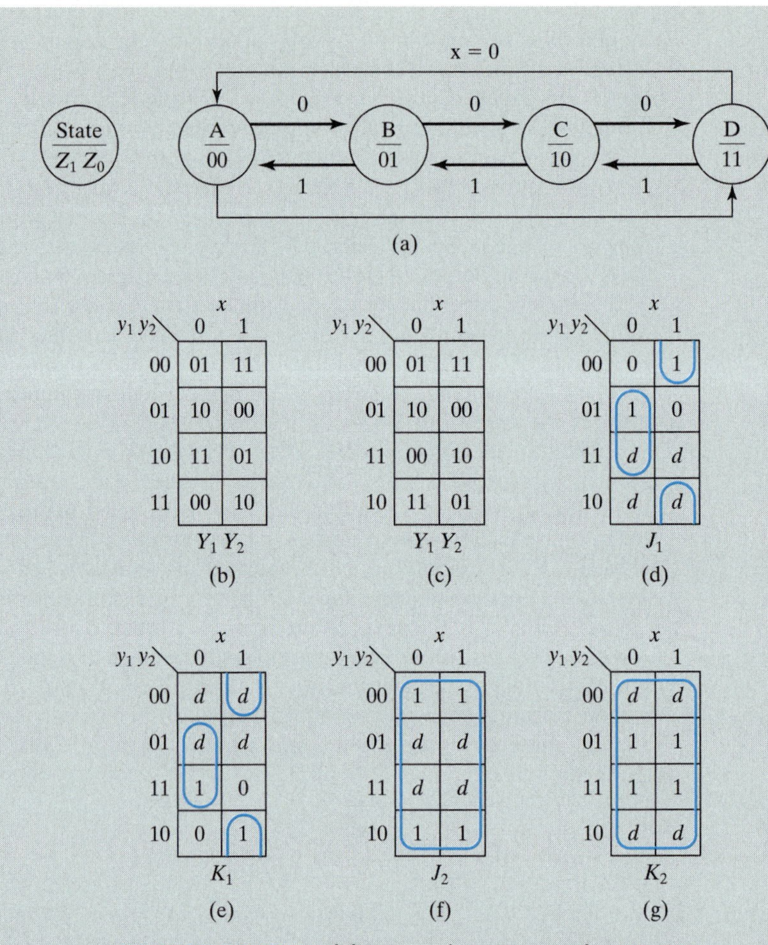

FIGURE 13.26 Tables used in Example 13.22

State	y_1	y_0	z_1	z_0
A	0	0	0	0
B	0	1	0	1
C	1	0	1	0
D	1	1	1	1

Note that the state assignments are the same as the output values. Therefore, we can state that $z_1 = y_1$ and $z_0 = y_0$, completing step 9 in our design procedure. Using this state assignment, the state transition table is shown in Figure 13.26(b). The table in Figure 13.26(b) is rearranged to form the K-map in Figure 13.26(c). The K-maps for the two *J–K* flip-flops are shown in Figures 13.26(d), (e), (f), and (g). The logic equations derived from the K-maps are

$$J_1 = \bar{x}y_2 + x\overline{y_2} = K_1$$
$$J_2 = 1 = K_2$$

Since the present state indicates the count, the circuit output can display the count by using two lights, which are connected to the flip-flop outputs. In this manner, as the circuit counts from $0 \rightarrow 1 \rightarrow 2 \rightarrow 3$, the lights will indicate off off $\rightarrow$ off on $\rightarrow$ on off $\rightarrow$ on on.

Drill Exercise

D13.13. We wish to find the logic circuit for the state table shown in Figure D13.13. Derive the logic equations for J, K, and z using the state assignment $A = 0$ and $B = 1$.

x	0	1
A	$B/1$	$A/0$
B	$A/0$	$B/1$

FIGURE D13.13

Ans: $z = \overline{x}\,\overline{y} + xy, J = k = \overline{x}$.

Summary

- The base or radix of a number system is the total number of digits allowed in the system, for example, the binary system has two digits and the decimal system has 10.
- Converting a number in base $r = \alpha$ to the number in base $r = \beta$ can be done using what is called the series substitution method.
- Boolean algebra provides the mathematical foundation for the analysis and design of logic circuits and are set forth in seven postulates.
- In addition to the postulates, there are seven theorems that are useful in the manipulation of logic functions. These theorems are outlined in Table 13.3.
- A truth table is a method of describing Boolean functions, and each Boolean function has one and only one truth table.
- Logic functions can be realized using either AND, OR, and NOT, or NAND or NOR gates. These gates, together with their input/output relationships, are shown in Table 13.5.
- Logic functions can be expressed in either a canonical sum-of-products (SOP) form or a canonical product-of-sums (POS) form. Each term in canonical SOP form is called a minterm and each term in a canonical POS form is called a maxterm.

  For example, the switching function:

  $$f_1(A, B, C) = \overline{A}\,\overline{B}C + \overline{A}BC + ABC = \Sigma m(1, 3, 7)$$

  is in SOP form and the minterms are 1, 3, and 7.

  The switching function:

  $$f_2(A, B, C) = (A + \overline{B} + C)(\overline{A} + B + C)(\overline{A} + \overline{B} + C) = \Pi M(2, 4, 6)$$

  is in a POS form and the maxterms are 2, 4, and 6.

- Venn diagrams can be used to visually demonstrate Boolean postulates and theorems. Furthermore, they provide the basis for the development of the Karnaugh map used in the minimization of switching functions.
- Switching function minimization via the K-map is based upon the fact that terms that are logically adjacent are physically adjacent on the map.

  For example, given the function:

$$f_1(A, B, C) = \Sigma m(1, 3, 7) = \overline{A}\,\overline{B}C + \overline{A}BC + ABC$$

  and the three-variable K-map shown in Figure 13.27,

  we note that minterms 1 and 3 differ in only a single variable, that is, B, and thus can be

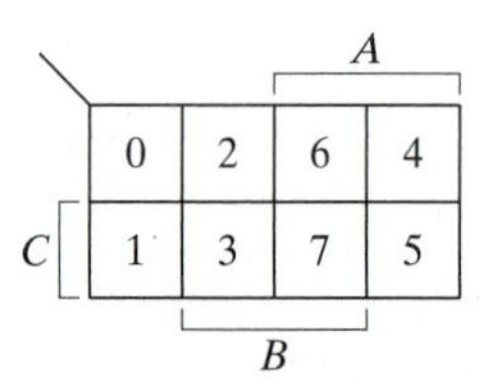

FIGURE 13.27 Three-variable K-map.

  combined as $\overline{A}\,\overline{B}C + \overline{A}BC = \overline{A}C$. Note that these two terms are adjacent on the K-map, that is, m_1 is next to m_3 and the variable that changes between the two terms is B.
- Sequential circuits, modeled as shown in Figure 13.18, provide a new dimension to the development of logic circuits, as a result of the inherent *memory* capability.
- Sequential logic circuits are described by state tables or state diagrams. These equivalent forms specify the manner in which the circuit transitions from the present state, as a result of an input, to the next state and produces an output.
- Memory in sequential circuits is provided by different types of flip-flops. Four standard types of flip-flops are set–reset (SR), delay (D), trigger (T), and J-K.
- If the memory elements in a sequential circuit are unclocked, the circuit operates in an asynchronous mode. If the memory elements operate under control of a clock, the circuit operates in a synchronous mode.

Problems

13.1. If $A = 0111$, $B = 1010$, $C = 0101$, and $D = 1011$, find
(a) $A + B$
(b) $C + D$

13.2. Given the data in problem 13.1, find
(a) $A + C$
(b) $B + D$

13.3. Using the data in problem 13.1, find
(a) $B + C$
(b) $A + D$

13.4. If $A = 111$, $B = 011$, $C = 110$, and $D = 010$, find
(a) $A \times D$
(b) $C \times D$

13.5. Given the data in problem 13.4, find
(a) $B \times D$
(b) $B \times C$

13.6. Using the data in problem 13.4, determine
(a) $A \times C$
(b) $A \times B$

13.7. Given the data in problem 13.1, find
(a) $A \times B$
(b) $C \times D$

13.8. Using the data in problem 13.1, compute
(a) $A \times C$
(b) $B \times D$

13.9. Using the data in problem 13.1, find
(a) $B \times C$
(b) $A \times D$

13.10. Convert the following numbers in base 2 to base 10:
(a) 1100
(b) 10101
(c) 1010
(d) 11111111

13.11. Convert the following numbers in binary to decimal:
(a) 1111
(b) 10010
(c) 100001
(d) 101011

13.12. Convert the following numbers from base 2 to base 10:
(a) 101010
(b) 110111
(c) 11101
(d) 1110001111

13.13. Convert the following numbers in binary to decimal:
(a) 1100011
(b) 110110111
(c) 10000001
(d) 11111000000

13.14. Convert the following numbers from decimal to binary:
(a) 7
(b) 13
(c) 15
(d) 27

13.15. Convert the following numbers from base 10 to base 2:
(a) 19
(b) 25
(c) 33
(d) 72

13.16. Convert the following numbers from decimal to binary:
(a) 48
(b) 57
(c) 99
(d) 100

13.17. Convert the following numbers from base 10 to base 2:
(a) 101
(b) 172
(c) 210
(d) 255

13.18. Use the Boolean postulates and theorems to simplify the following expressions:
(a) $f(A, B, C) = \overline{A}\,\overline{B} + \overline{B}C + A\overline{B}$
(b) $f(A, B, C) = \overline{A}B\overline{C} + ABD + \overline{A}BC$

13.19. Compute the truth table for the following functions:
(a) $f(A, B, C) = B\overline{C} + \overline{B}C$
(b) $f(A, B, C) = \overline{B} + C$

13.20. Compute the truth table for the following functions:
(a) $f(A, B, C) = \overline{A}\,\overline{B} + C$
(b) $f(A, B, C) = \overline{A}\,\overline{B} + \overline{B}C + A\overline{B}$

13.21. Use a Venn diagram, show that $f(A, B, C) = \Sigma m(1, 2, 5, 6) = B\overline{C} + \overline{B}C$

13.22. Using a Venn diagram, show that $f(A, B, C) = \Sigma m(0, 1, 3, 4, 5, 7) = C + \overline{B}$

13.23. Use a Venn diagram to demonstrate that $f(A, B, C) = BC + \overline{A}\,\overline{B} + A\overline{B}C = C + \overline{A}\,\overline{B}$

13.24. Find the minimum form for the Boolean functions
(a) $f(A, B, C) = \Sigma m(0, 1, 3, 4, 5, 7)$
(b) $f(A, B, C) = \Sigma m(1, 2, 5, 6)$

13.25. Find the minimum form for the Boolean functions
(a) $f(A, B, C) = \Sigma m(1, 2, 5, 7)$
(b) $f(A, B, C) = \Sigma m(0, 1, 3, 6, 7)$

13.26. Expand the following function into a set of minterms and then use the K-map to find a minimum SOP form.

$$f(A, B, C) = \overline{A}\,\overline{B} + \overline{B}C + A\overline{B}$$

13.27. Expand the following function into a set of minterms and then use the K-map to find the minimum SOP realization.

$$f(A, B, C) = BC + \overline{A}\,\overline{B} + A\overline{B}C$$

13.28. Expand the following function into a set of minterms and then use the K-map to find the minimum SOP realization.

$$f(A, B, C, D) = \overline{A}B\overline{C} + ABD + \overline{A}BC$$

13.29. Expand the following function into a set of minterms and then use the K-map to find the minimum SOP realization.

$$f(A, B, C, D) = \overline{A}\,\overline{B}D + \overline{A}B\overline{C}D + AB\overline{C} + A\overline{B}D$$

13.30. Expand the following function into a set of minterms and then use the K-map to find the minimum SOP realization.

$$f(A, B, C, D) = \overline{B}\,\overline{C}D + \overline{A}B\overline{C}D + A\overline{C}D + \overline{B}CD + BCD$$

13.31. Find a minimum SOP form for the switching functions
(a) $f(A, B, C, D) = \Sigma m(1, 4, 7, 9, 12, 15)$
(b) $f(A, B, C, D) = \Sigma m(4, 6, 7, 12, 14, 15)$

13.32. Find the minimum SOP form for the switching functions
(a) $f(A, B, C, D) = \Sigma m(2, 3, 11, 13, 14, 15)$
(b) $f(A, B, C, D) = \Sigma m(0, 2, 3, 7, 9, 13)$

13.33. 13.33. Find the minimum SOP form for the switching functions
(a) $f(A, B, C, D) = \Sigma m(0, 2, 4, 10, 12, 14)$
(b) $f(A, B, C, D) = \Sigma m(3, 4, 6, 7, 11, 12, 13, 15)$

13.34. Find the minimum SOP form for the switching functions
(a) $f(A, B, C, D) = \Sigma m(1, 4, 5, 7, 9, 15)$
(b) $f(A, B, C, D) = \Sigma m(0, 2, 5, 7, 8, 10, 13, 15)$

13.35. Design a logic circuit with a BCD input that detects all numbers that are greater than or equal to 7.

13.36. Design a logic circuit with a BCD input that detects the decimal numbers 3, 4, and 5.

13.37. In the network in Figure P13.37, circuit *A* inputs certain bit patterns to circuit *B*. A bit pattern containing exactly two 1's is an error and should trigger the alarm circuit. Design an alarm circuit that produces a 1 if exactly two 1's appear in the input bit pattern to circuit B.

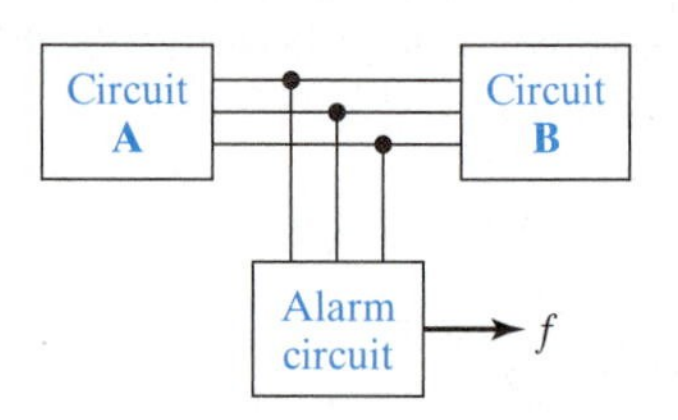

FIGURE P13.37

13.38. A half adder circuit has two input bits, a_i and b_i. The output is a sum bit, s_i, and a carry bit, c_{i+1}. Derive the logic equations for the sum and carry bits that are necessary for designing a half adder circuit.

13.39. The 4221 code is a weighted code in which the four bit positions are assigned the weights (4221). The code is listed below.

0 – 0000	5 – 0111
1 – 0001	6 – 1100
2 – 0010	7 – 1101
3 – 0011	8 – 1110
4 – 1000	9 – 1111

Design a BCD to 4221 code converter.

13.40. Design a logic circuit with three inputs *A*, *B*, and *C*, such that the output will be high when at least two of the inputs are high.

13.41. Design a logic circuit with four inputs *A*, *B*, *C*, and *D*, such that the output will be high only when an even number of the inputs, greater than zero, are high.

13.42. A logic circuit has four input lines, A, B, C, and D; A represents the MSB and D represents the LSB. Design a logic circuit in such a way that the output is high if the input signal is outside the midrange of the input numbers, that is, in the range $(0)_{10}$ to $(3)_{10}$ or $(12)_{10}$ to $(15)_{10}$.

13.43. Three sensors are strategically placed along a production line. The sensor outputs are low if all measurements are in the normal range. Measurements outside the normal range produce a high output. The sensors are used to trigger an alarm if any two of the measurements are simultaneously high. Design a logic circuit that will produce a high signal for the alarm.

13.44. A tank of fluid employed in a chemical process is being monitored with three sensors. The sensors measure temperature, pressure, and fluid level. If all the sensor measurements are in the normal range, the sensor outputs are low. If the measurements are outside the normal range, the sensor outputs are high. Design a logic circuit that will produce a high signal for an alarm under the following conditions:

- pressure and temperature are too high
- fluid level is too high and either pressure or temperature or both are too high

13.45. An industrial plant has two reservoirs that are used to temporarily store fluid A and fluid B. Each reservoir is equipped with two sensors: one detects the incoming flow rate and the other detects the fluid level. Assume the flow rate sensor outputs are low when the flow rate is satisfactory and high when the flow rate is too high. In addition, assume the fluid level sensor outputs are low when the fluid level is satisfactory and high when the level is too high. Design a detector circuit that will produce a high output whenever the fluid level in either or both reservoirs is too high and the flow rate for either of both reservoirs is too high.

13.46. A circuit that displays voting results is required. There are three voters who can vote yea or nay. The circuit output should be high if the majority of the votes are yea. Produce the smallest possible circuit.

13.47. A circuit is needed that identifies prime numbers between 0 and 9. The input to the circuit is in BCD format. The output is low if the input is prime. Draw the minimum possible circuit.

13.48. Unfortunately, Alice, Bob, and Carol own a .com company. They have decided to hire David, a shrewd business major, to guide them through these perilous business times. However, they must decide whether to offer David significant stock options or just compensation. Each person votes STOCKS or CASH. Draw a truth table for this voting scenario where votes and the resulting decision are encoded in ones and zeros. Create your own code scheme.

13.49. Compute the state table for the synchronous sequential circuit shown in Figure P13.49.

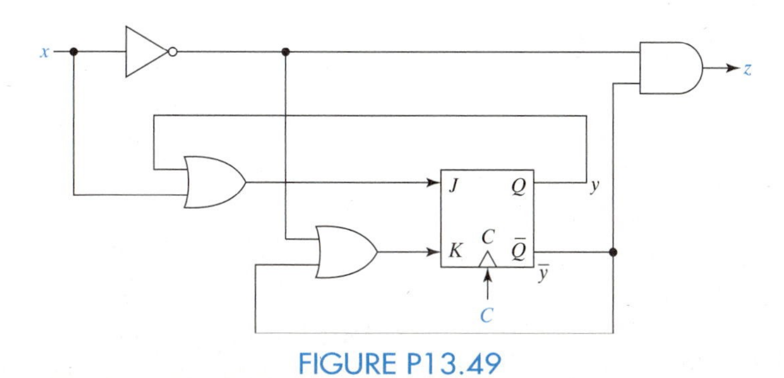

FIGURE P13.49

13.50. Compute the state table for the synchronous sequential circuit shown in Figure P13.50.

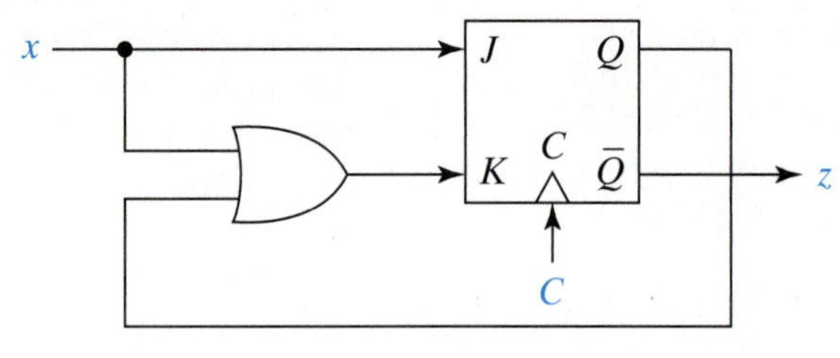

FIGURE P13.50

13.51. Determine the state table for the synchronous sequential circuit shown in Figure P13.51.

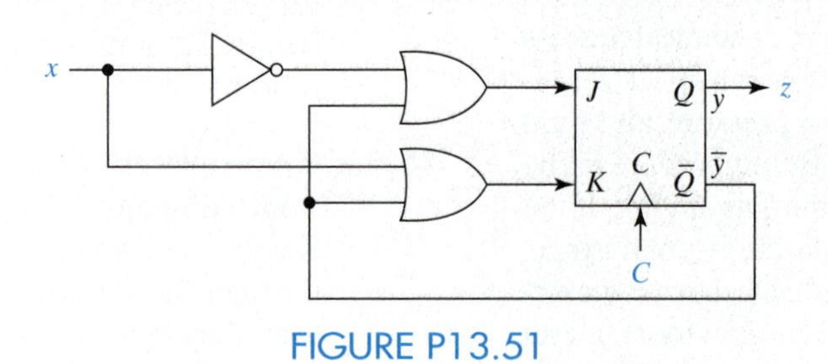

FIGURE P13.51

13.52. Determine the state table for the synchronous sequential circuit shown in Figure P13.52.

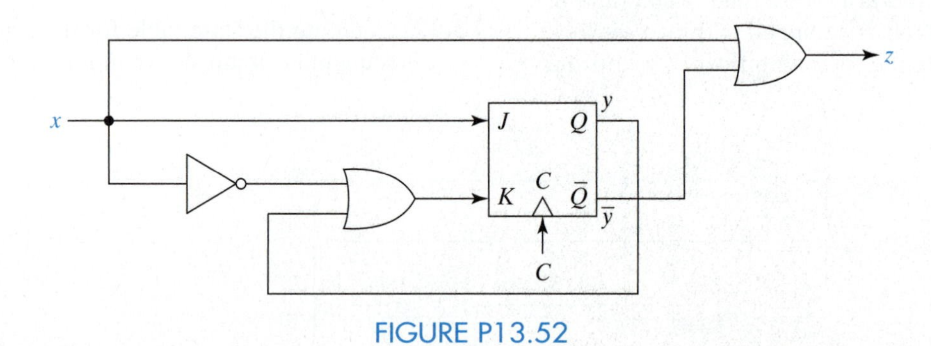

FIGURE P13.52

13.53. Compute the state table for the synchronous sequential circuit shown in Figure P13.53.

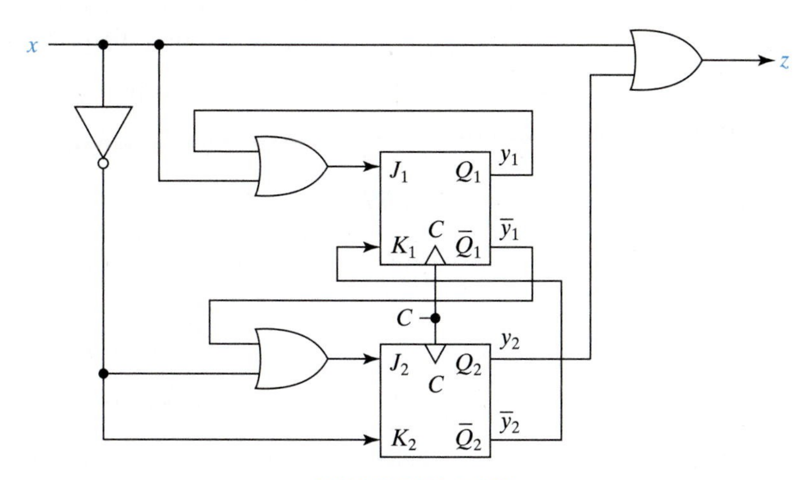

FIGURE P13.53

13.54. Compute the state table for the synchronous sequential circuit shown in Figure P13.54.

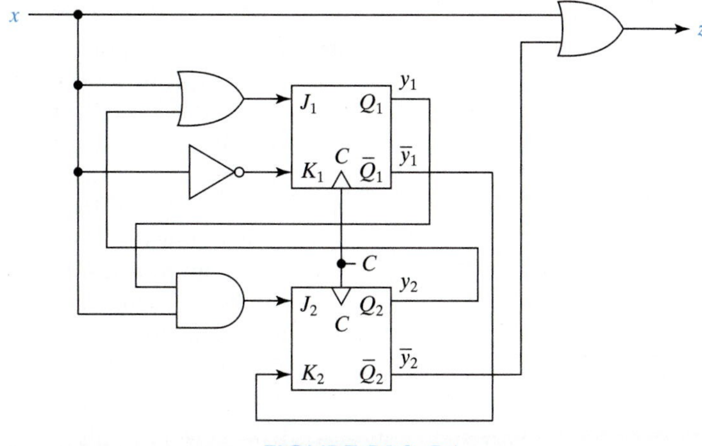

FIGURE P13.54

13.55. Find the logic equations for a J–K flip-flop realization of the state table in Figure P13.55 using the state assignment $A = 00$, $B = 01$, $C = 11$, and $D = 10$.

	x = 0	1
A	$A/0$	$B/0$
B	$C/0$	$B/0$
C	$D/0$	$B/0$
D	$A/0$	$B/1$

FIGURE P13.55

13.56. Find the logic equations for a J–K flip-flop realization of the state table in Figure P13.56 using the state assignment $A = 00$, $B = 01$, $C = 11$, and $D = 10$.

	x = 0	1
A	$A/0$	$B/0$
B	$C/0$	$D/0$
C	$A/1$	$B/0$
D	$A/0$	$D/0$

FIGURE P13.56

13.57. Determine the state diagram for a synchronous sequential circuit that has a single input and single output that will recognize the input string 0000 with overlap, that is, if

$$x = 0000010000$$

$$z = 0001100001$$

13.58. Determine the state diagram for a synchronous sequential circuit that has a single input and single output that will recognize the input string 0110 with overlap, that is, if

$$x = 101101100$$

$$z = 000010010$$

13.59. Determine the state diagram for the synchronous sequential circuit that has a single input and a single output that will recognize the input string 1001 with overlap, that is, if

$$x = 10100100100$$

$$z = 00000100100$$

13.60. Determine the state diagram for the synchronous sequential circuit that has a single input and single output that will recognize the input string of exactly one 1 followed by two 0s.

13.61. A PC's serial port transfers data in byte-size units. Typically, several additional bits are exchanged between transmitter and receiver to coordinate the transfer. This is called handshaking. A part of handshaking is a short bit sequence called the stop bits, which immediately follow the data byte. In a particular serial communication protocol the stop bits are the four-bit sequence 1111. This sequence does not occur elsewhere in the transmission. Using J–K flip-flops, design a detection circuit that will recognize the stop bits sequence. The output, STOP, is high when the sequence is detected.

13.62. Design a serial adder where inputs A and B arrive least significant bit first. Call the output Σ. Draw the circuit using J–K flip-flops.

13.63. Design a serial subtractor where inputs A and B arrive least significant bit first. Call the output Δ. Draw the circuit using J–K flip-flops.

13.64. Design a serial comparator that compares two inputs X and Y, which arrive LSB first. There are three outputs: L, G, and E. L is high if $X < Y$, G is high if $X > Y$, and E is high if $X = Y$.

13.65. Draw a state diagram for a serial circuit that performs the mathematical operation $Z = 2X - Y$ where X and Y are serial inputs arriving least significant bit first and Z is the result exiting the circuit least significant bit first.

14

14–1 Introduction

As described at the beginning of the previous chapter, the "electronics revolution" has produced a stream of new products enabled by advancements in digital electronic circuits. The logic circuits described in Chapter 13 are typically fabricated using silicon integrated circuit technology. Individual logic gates are constructed by connecting transistors to form logic gate circuits that perform basic logic functions. These gates are then interconnected to create complex digital systems.

This chapter describes the way both MOS transistors or BJTs can be connected to create a circuit that will perform the basic logic functions: NAND, NOR, Exclusive OR, etc. These logic functions were described in detail in Chapter 13. The next section of this chapter presents a brief review of these gates for those who may have skipped Chapter 13.

14–2 Review of Ideal Logic Gates

This section presents a brief review of basic logic gates. For more details and other problems, refer to section 8–6 and Chapter 13. The basic *logic gate* is a device whose output is binary (one or a zero) and predictable depending on the states of one or more inputs. Since each output or input can have only two possible values (one or zero), a logic gate with two inputs can have four possible input combinations, four inputs would have 16 combinations, and so on. In general, the number of input combinations Z is given by the following equation, where n is the number of inputs.

$$Z = 2^n \qquad (14.1)$$

Truth table defined

We generally make a *truth table* to describe the state of the output for a given set of inputs. Recall a truth table is a chart that lists on the left all the possible input combinations and has a column on the right that shows the output that occurs for each combination of inputs. The next sections show truth tables for several of the most common gates, the NAND gate, the NOR gate, the EXCLUSIVE OR (XOR) gate, and the NOT (inverter) gate.

Also given in each of the following sections is the Boolean algebraic expression for each type of gate. For purposes of this discussion recall that the sum (+) represents OR, the product (•) represents AND, and the bar over the top of a symbol represents the NOT or complement operator.

14.2.1 The NAND Gate

Four fundamental logic gates defined: NAND, NOR, Exclusive-OR, NOT (inverter)

The *NAND gate* is a logic gate whose output is zero only if all of its inputs are one. The standard logic symbol and the truth table for a three-input NAND gate are shown in Figure 14.1. Note that the output is the complement or exact opposite of the truth table for the AND gate, as is apparent in the symbol, which looks like that for an AND gate, followed by a small circle, which is the symbol for inversion. Also shown in the figure is the Boolean algebraic expression for the NAND gate.

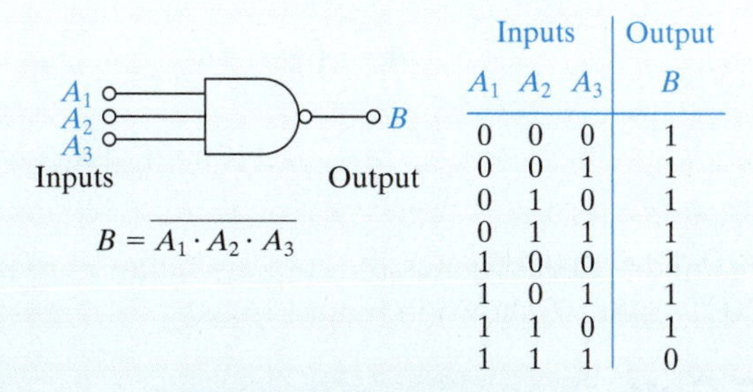

Inputs			Output
A_1	A_2	A_3	B
0	0	0	1
0	0	1	1
0	1	0	1
0	1	1	1
1	0	0	1
1	0	1	1
1	1	0	1
1	1	1	0

FIGURE 14.1 NAND gate.

14.2.2 The NOR Gate

The *NOR gate* has an output of zero if any one of its inputs is a one. Therefore, the only input condition in which the NOR gate has a one output occurs when all of its inputs are zero. The logic symbol, Boolean expression, and the truth table for the NOR gate are shown in Figure 14.2. Note that this gate has an output that is the exact complement of the OR gate.

14.2.3 The Exclusive-OR Gate

The *Exclusive-OR* function (or XOR) can be constructed from more fundamental logic gates, that is, a combination of an OR gate, a NAND gate, and an AND gate. It is a circuit, however, often used with digital systems, and for convenience has been given its own logic symbol. The Exclusive-OR function is used as an "inequality comparator" because its output is high only if the inputs are not equal. An example of how a two-input XOR circuit can be imple-

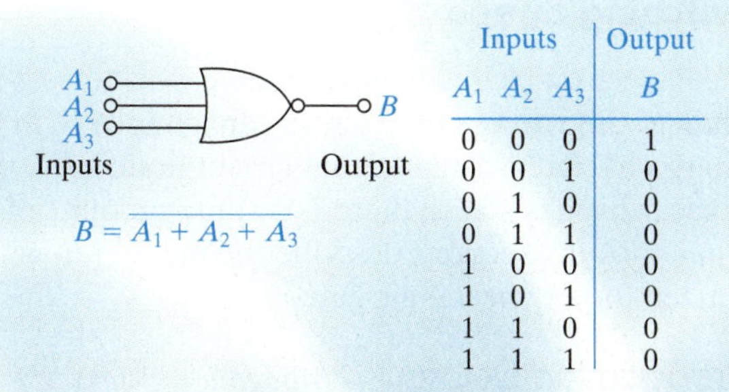

Inputs			Output
A_1	A_2	A_3	B
0	0	0	1
0	0	1	0
0	1	0	0
0	1	1	0
1	0	0	0
1	0	1	0
1	1	0	0
1	1	1	0

FIGURE 14.2 NOR gate.

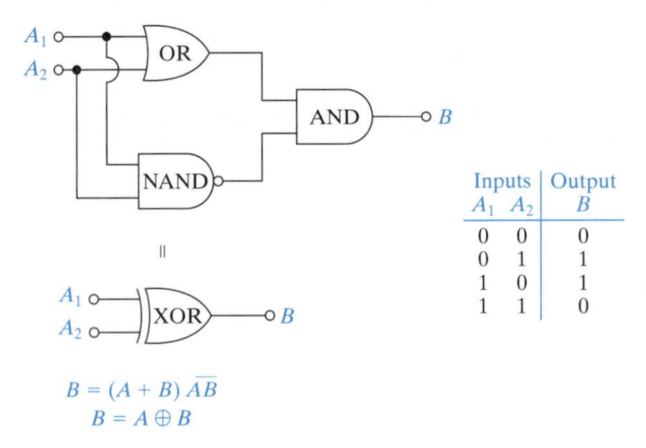

Inputs		Output
A_1	A_2	B
0	0	0
0	1	1
1	0	1
1	1	0

FIGURE 14.3 XOR gate.

mented with basic gates, the corresponding truth table, and the special symbol adopted for the XOR gate are shown in Figure 14.3.

14.2.4 The NOT Gate

The *NOT gate* was introduced in Chapter 8 and is often called the inverter. It is unusual in that it always has only one input and one output, and its output is the inverse or opposite of the logic state presented at its input. Therefore, the truth table for the NOT gate, or inverter, has only two lines and appears with its symbol as Figure 8.14(a).

14–3 Real Logic Gates: Speed, Noise Margin, and Fanout

The logic gates described in the previous section were described as ideal logic elements; however, when actual electronic hardware is used to implement real gates, there are limitations in performance that must be recognized. There are, first, the limitations associated with time; that is, it takes a finite amount of time for a real gate to respond to changes at its input. This affects the operation of the gate in several ways, which will be described in this section.

Second, there are limitations associated with how the logic levels may deviate from the desired levels. Excessive loading, usually a result of too many gates connected to the output of a single gate, may adversely affect the logic levels. The concept of *noise margin* is introduced to describe the margin designed into the circuit to protect against unwanted level changes.

14.3.1 Finite Switching Speed

Real electronic circuits have finite capacitance, voltage, and current at each circuit node. To change the voltage on a finite capacitance with finite current requires a charging (or discharging) time related to that circuit node's *RC* time constant. Therefore, when the input to a gate changes states, there is a finite amount of time before the output actually responds. The following sections describe the manner in which these time delays are generally characterized for a typical logic gate.

Propagation Delays. *Propagation delays* are measures of how long it takes the output of a gate to respond to a transition at the input of the gate. Three parameters will be defined:

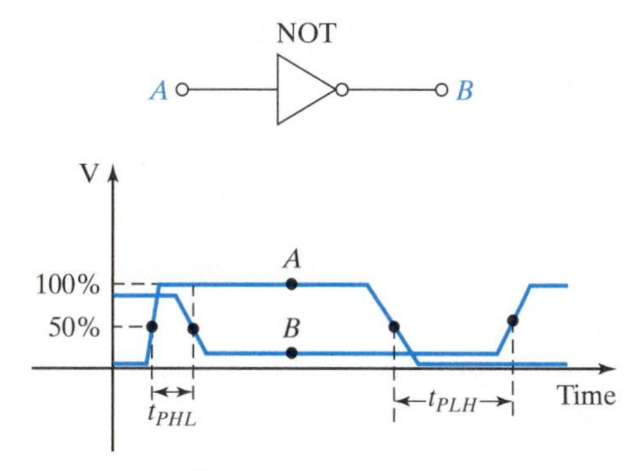

FIGURE 14.4 An illustration of propagation delays.

Propagation delays defined

$$t_{PHL} = \text{the propagation delay high-to-low,}$$
$$t_{PLH} = \text{the propagation delay low-to-high, and}$$
$$t_P = \text{the average propagation delay.}$$

Assume for simplicity that the gate under consideration is a NOT gate, although this discussion may be applied to any gate where an input logic state change causes an output state change. When the input to a gate is given a transition from a low state to a high state, the output, after some time delay, transitions from high to low. This time difference is defined as the *propagation delay, high-to-low,* t_{PHL}. Generally, propagation delay times are measured from the 50% point, or middle, of any given transition.

Similarly, if the input transition is from a high state to a low state, the output transition from low to high occurs at a time, t_{PLH}, after the input transition. These time delays are illustrated in Figure 14.4. In general, t_{PHL} is not equal to t_{PLH} because a circuit is usually not symmetric in its response to inputs of opposite polarity.

For convenience we often define the average propagation delay, t_p, as:

$$t_P = \frac{t_{PHL} + t_{PLH}}{2} \tag{14.2}$$

Rise time and fall time defined

Rise Times and Fall Times. The *rise time* t_r and the *fall time* t_f are measures of how fast the output voltage of the gate moves between the two allowed output levels (or states). This is generally measured from the 10% point to the 90% point of the full transition.

Figure 14.5 shows the output waveform for a logic gate with t_r and t_f defined. In general, t_r is not equal to t_f because most circuits are not symmetric in their ability to drive the voltage at the output node either positive or negative.

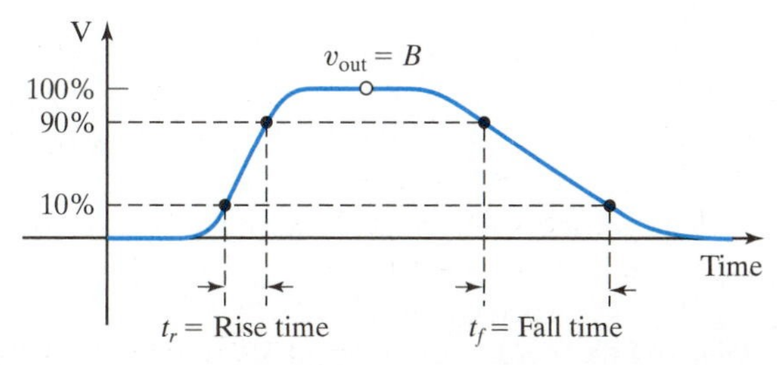

FIGURE 14.5 An illustration of rise time and fall time.

Timing and Race Conditions. In most digital systems, a signal (for illustration consider one particular pulse) must propagate through a number of gates one after the other before it reaches its destination. Since each gate introduces a propagation delay time, if too many such gates are strung together the total delay of the signal, that is, the sum of the average propagation delays for each of the individual gates in the string, may be excessive. Excessive delays can be disastrous to the system's performance. First, the system may not perform the desired application if it responds too slowly. However, also disastrous is the possibility of a *race condition.* This is a condition in which two pulses are intended to arrive at a destination gate in some specific order (or simultaneously), but due to each one racing through different paths in the logic with different numbers of gates, the delays stack up differently and the timing order is lost. The circuit malfunctions. Avoiding race conditions requires careful analysis of the timing delays through all critical paths, that is, the ones that can make a difference in the logic.

The *clock signal* in digital logic circuits is generally a continuous square wave, switching alternately from a high level to a low level, and is used to time and sequence the flow of digital data through a sequential digital system (see Chapter 13). In many cases, for example, every time the clock signal goes from low to high, new data are presented at the inputs of various logic circuits. Therefore, the higher the clock frequency the faster data move through the system. Computer manufacturers spend great effort to develop circuits that operate at as high a clock frequency as possible. For a given logic circuit, the upper limit, or *maximum clock frequency,* is usually determined by the accumulation of propagation delays through strings of gates in the logic. To avoid timing problems, the gate inputs should not be presented with new data before the output of the circuit has changed from the data presented in the previous clock cycle. If new data are assumed to be presented every clock cycle, then determing the total delay through the longest path in the logic will yield the maximum allowed clock frequency. The following examples illustrate these points.

Example 14.1

Seven NOT gates, each with an average propagation delay of 7 ns, are connected as shown in Figure 14.6. Let us determine

(a) the total propagation delay from A to $B1$.

(b) the total propagation delay from A to $B2$.

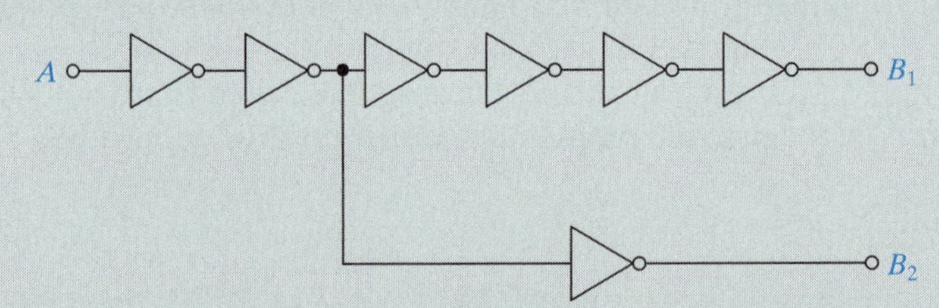

FIGURE 14.6 Circuit used in Example 14.1.

In addition, if the input, A, makes a logic state change, we wish to determine (c) which output changes first, and the elapsed time before the other output change.

(a) The logic path from A to $B1$ goes through six identical gates, each with a propagation delay of 7 ns. Therefore, the total delay is 6×7 ns, or 42 ns.

(b) Similarly, the path from A to $B2$ includes three gates, and, therefore, the total delay through that path is 21 ns.

(c) Clearly, $B2$ changes first, and $B1$ changes $42 - 21 = 21$ ns later.

Example 14.2

A digital switching circuit operates at a clock frequency of 50 MHz. New data is presented to the circuit input on the leading edge of every clock cycle. If each gate in the network has an average propogation delay of 1.5 ns, let us determine (a) how often new data is clocked through the system, and (b) how many gates can be connected in a serial string.

(a) The leading edge of a clock signal is defined to be the transition from a low level to a high level, and this occurs once each cycle. Therefore, the clock period, which is the inverse of frequency, tells us how often this occurs. It occurs every

$$T = \frac{1}{f} = \frac{1}{50 \text{ MHz}} = 20 \text{ ns} \tag{14.3}$$

(b) If we require the output of a serial string of gates, each with a delay of 1.5 ns, not to exceed 20 ns, then we may only use 13 such gates, that is, 20 ns/1.5 ns, rounded down to the next integer.

14.3.2 Real Logic Levels—Noise Margin

The output of a real logic gate must produce an output signal that is unambiguous to the input of the next gate. That is, if the output is intended to be a logic 1 (high level), it must be interpreted as such by the next input. To ensure this, the minimum voltage at the output of a gate that is intended to represent a high must exceed the minimum voltage level at the input of a gate that guarantees a high will be perceived. An analogous situation applies, of course, for logic low levels as well.

The formalization of this concept is straightforward, and is illustrated in Figure 14.7. The left side of the figure addresses the voltage levels at the input of a gate. Two specific levels are defined:

Four important voltage levels defined: V_{IL}, V_{IH}, V_{OL}, V_{OH}

V_{IL} = the input low level = the HIGHEST voltage at the input that is always recognized by the input as a logic low.

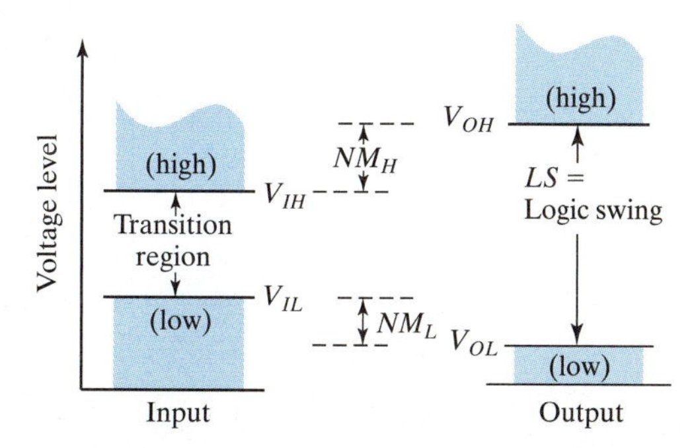

FIGURE 14.7 Illustration of logic levels and noise margin.

V_{IH} = the input high level = the LOWEST voltage at the input that is always recognized by the input as a logic high.

The voltage region between these levels is the input transition region, where the input voltage is not permitted except during the brief times of transition from one level to the other. If an input voltage is applied to the gate in this transition region, the gate cannot guarantee whether it will be interpreted as a high or a low.

At the output, two voltage levels are defined:

V_{OL} = the output low level = the HIGHEST voltage level at the output that can occur when the output is intended to be low.

V_{OH} = the output high level = the LOWEST voltage level at the output that can occur when the output is intended to be high.

The above four parameters can be determined from the voltage transfer characteristics of a logic gate such as an inverter. This is illustrated in Figure 14.8, where V_i is the input voltage to the inverter and V_o is the output voltage.

The *transition width, TW,* is defined as

$$TW = V_{IH} - V_{IL} \tag{14.4}$$

An important concept is that of *noise margin.* The high and low noise margins will now be defined:

Two important noise margins defined: NM_H and NM_L

$$NM_H = \text{the high noise margin} = V_{OH} - V_{IH} \tag{14.5}$$

$$NM_L = \text{the low noise margin} = V_{IL} - V_{OL} \tag{14.6}$$

The high noise margin and the low noise margin measure the ability of the gate to properly distinguish low and high levels. In general, digital circuits with higher noise margins are more resistant to spurious interference and are more reliable in noisy environments such as automobiles and industrial applications.

The *logic swing* is the difference between the output high and low levels and is defined as:

$$LS = V_{OH} - V_{OL} \tag{14.7}$$

Logic swing and fanout defined

To be generally useful, a digital logic gate must be capable of driving more than one subsequent gate. *Fanout* is generally a specification of a digital logic gate, which indicates the maximum number of similar gates that can simultaneously be connected to the output of the gate and still maintain proper operation. Fanout is an integer number, *n,* and if more than *n* gates are connected to the output of a particular gate, the circuit may not function properly.

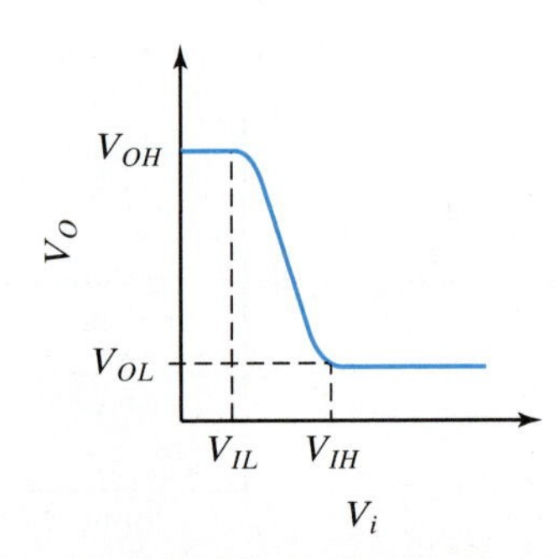

FIGURE 14.8 Voltage transfer characteristic.

Sometimes the term *fanout* is used merely to describe the number of gates connected to the output of a particular gate, such as "the fanout of this gate is two." This means its output is connected directly to the input of two other gates.

Logic gates in general must accept one or more inputs from other gates. *Fanin* is a term for an integer that describes how many independent inputs a particular logic gate receives.

14-4 Basic Logic Gates Using Relays

Early computers used electromechanical relays to implement the basic logic functions. Until relatively recently, relay switching was used in some telephone applications and in the controls of many electric appliances. Relay logic is still used occasionally for simple logic control systems, and is useful to understand for its tutorial value. MOS transistor logic circuits are analogous to the relay circuits, with the relay switch replaced by a transistor switch.

Recall a relay consists of a coil of wire forming an electromagnet and contacts (a switch) that is closed when the magnet is energized. The letters "NO" by the contacts indicate "normally open"; this means the contacts are configured to be an open circuit with no magnetic field, and when the magnet is activated, the contacts close.

In the following examples we will define that a one is represented by a positive voltage, V, and a zero represented by ground or zero volts.

14.4.1 The NAND Gate: Using Relays

If we consider a two-input NAND gate, the truth table requires that both inputs be high for the output to be low; otherwise, the output is high. Figure 14.9 shows that each of the two inputs, when high, energizes a coil in a relay. The energized coil closes the contacts associated with that relay. Both relays must be energized, that is, both sets of contacts must be closed, before ground (zero volts) is connected to the output. Otherwise, the output remains high since it is connected to +V through a resistor.

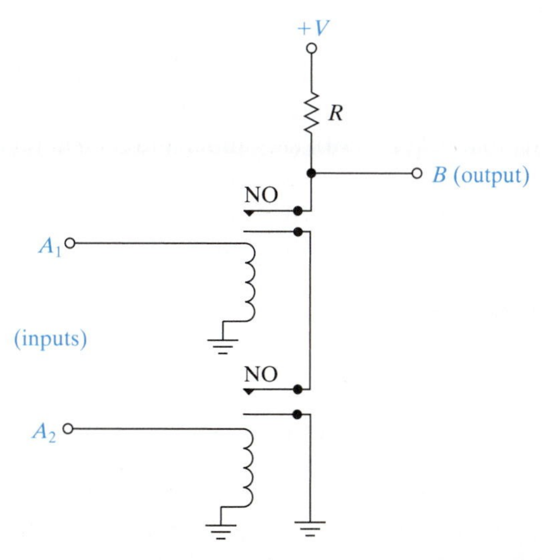

FIGURE 14.9 Relay implementation of a NAND gate.

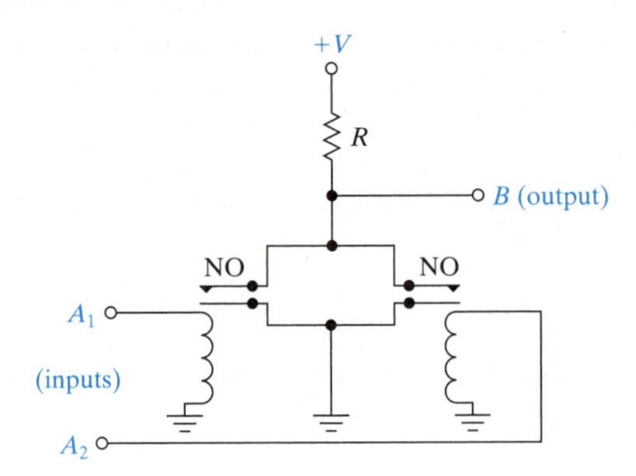

FIGURE 14.10 Relay implementation of a NOR gate.

Note carefully that any load connected to B must not pull enough current through R to drop the voltage at the output too much when B is supposed to be high.

14.4.2 The NOR Gate: Using Relays

The truth table of the two-input NOR gate requires that the output be low if either of the inputs is high. The circuit described in Figure 14.10 accomplishes this. Since the relay contacts are connected in parallel, if either relay is energized, ground is connected to the output and the output is, therefore, low; the only case when the output is high occurs when both inputs are low—neither relay is engaged.

14–5 Basic Logic Gates Using MOSFETS

The majority of today's digital electronic circuitry is implemented using MOSFET switching elements.

The first commercial digital MOS-integrated circuits were fabricated in *PMOS technology*—circuits that utilized all *p-channel MOSFETs.* This rather quickly was replaced by *NMOS* or *n-channel technologies* during the 1970s.

NMOS circuits are still utilized; however, during the early 1980s, CMOS emerged as the dominant MOS technology and remains so today. *CMOS* stands for *complementary MOS*—circuits that require both *n*-channel and *p*-channel devices to implement each logic gate.

CMOS has one very important advantage over other technologies: when the logic is not switching, that is, quiescent, it requires no dc current to retain the information in the gate—and hence no power is used or dissipated.

14.5.1 NMOS with Passive Loads

The NMOS inverter, or NOT gate, with a passive or resistive load and the voltage transfer characteristics for this gate are shown in Figure 14.11. This circuit utilizes an *n*-channel, enhancement-mode MOSFET as the switching element, and a resistor, R_D, as the load. The high and low output voltage levels are calculated using the MOSFET switching circuit model.

Referring to Figure 14.11, if the input voltage to the gate is increased from zero, nothing happens to move the output from its value of V_{DD} until $V_i = V_T$. At this point the transistor begins to conduct, and the input level is V_{IL}.

Basic circuit for inverter (NOT gate)

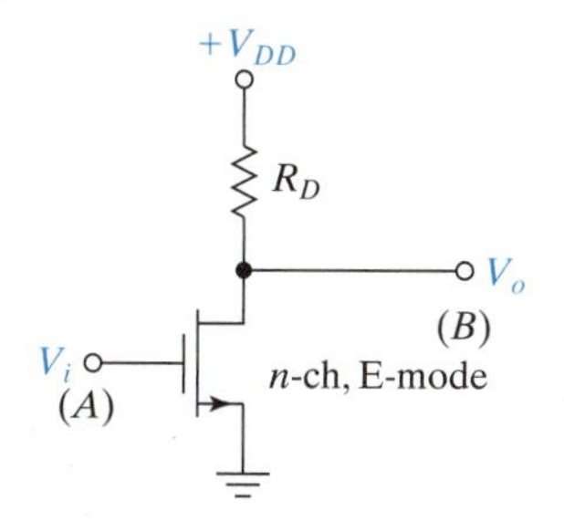

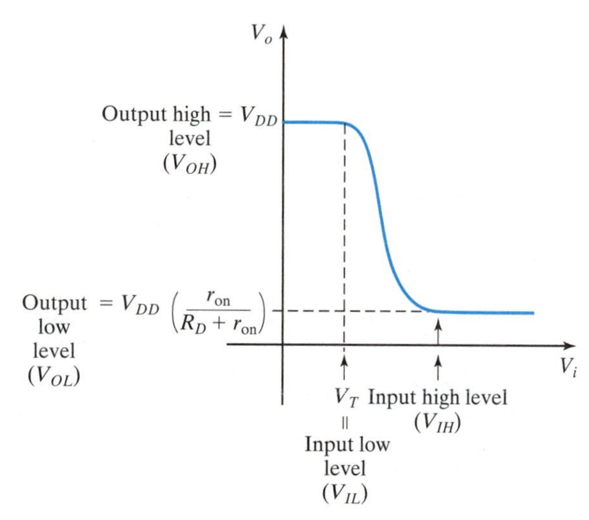

FIGURE 14.11 An NMOS NOT gate and its transfer characteristic.

As V_i is further increased, the drain current increases, and V_o begins to fall. When the transistor enters the ohmic region, the output voltage is set by the voltage division between r_{on} of the device and the load resistance R_D.

A voltage transfer curve of V_o versus V_i, similar to that shown in Figure 14.11, can be created by mapping point by point from the output curves and loadline (as shown in section 11.4) as the Q-point moves from the OFF region to the ohmic region.

The implementation of a NAND gate using n-channel MOSFET switches follows exactly the same circuit topology as that used with relay switches.

The circuits for an NMOS NAND gate and NMOS NOR gate, with resistive loads, are shown in Figure 14.12.

The NAND function requires stacking n-channel devices in series. For the output to be low, *both* devices must be on, and the r_{on}'s of each device are in series. These resistances in series add, and the resulting large equivalent resistance degrades the output low level. This large value of resistance must be accounted for in the gate design. Three-in-put NAND gates stack three transistors, and so as the number of inputs increase, this resistance can become a problem.

The NOR function has n-channel devices in parallel, and if *either* device is on, the output is low. Either device must be independently capable of pulling the output to an appropriately low level. For NOR gates with more than two inputs, additional devices are placed in parallel.

Basic circuits for NAND gate and NOR gate

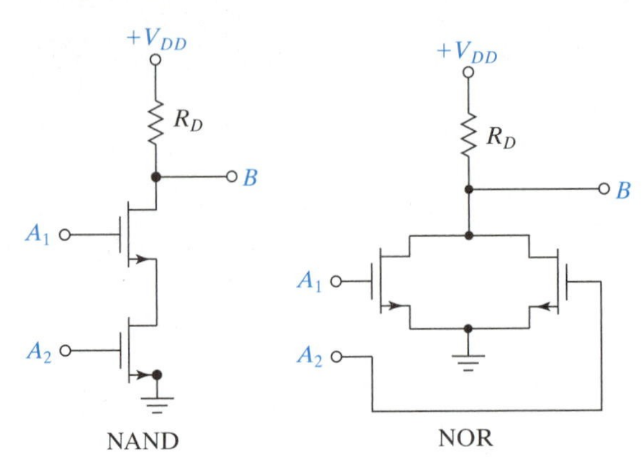

FIGURE 14.12 (a) NMOS NAND gate. (b) NMOS NOR gate.

You may recall that fanout is the maximum number of gates that can be successfully driven from the output of the gate under consideration. In these MOS technologies, the input to each gate is a very high resistance, that is, the insulated gate terminal of the MOSFET. Therefore, the loading caused by additional gates is primarily capacitive, and this increased loading does not change the dc levels. Fanout limitations for MOS technologies occur primarily because of degraded switching speeds resulting from too high a load capacitance being driven with a finite transistor output current.

14.5.2 NMOS with Active (Enhancement-Mode) Loads

All the digital circuits described in this chapter can be constructed using the integrated circuit fabrication techniques. The fabrication of the load resistor in NMOS circuits with passive loads presents a small problem; the resistor consumes a lot of chip area. However, a MOS transistor can be biased in such a way that it electrically looks like a resistor, and as such uses less chip area than an equivalent resistor. Furthermore, it's easier to make a chip with just MOS devices than one containing both devices and resistors. Therefore, most NMOS circuitry uses active loads, or another *n*-channel device, properly biased, as the load resistance.

The simplest way of biasing an *n*-channel, enhancement-mode device as a resistive element is to connect the gate to the drain as illustrated in Figure 14.13. The value of the resistance varies somewhat depending on the value of dc bias applied. Therefore, it's shown in the figure with an arrow through it to indicate that its value can vary. In addition, it must have at least a threshold voltage, V_T, across it before it conducts at all. These deviations from the per-

The MOSFET with gate connected to drain can act like a resistor

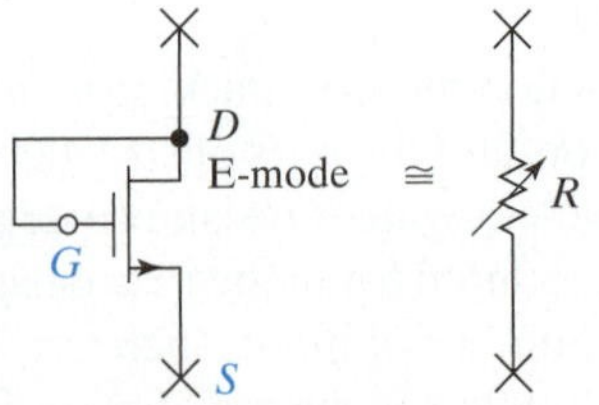

FIGURE 14.13 *n*-channel enhancement-mode device as a resistive element.

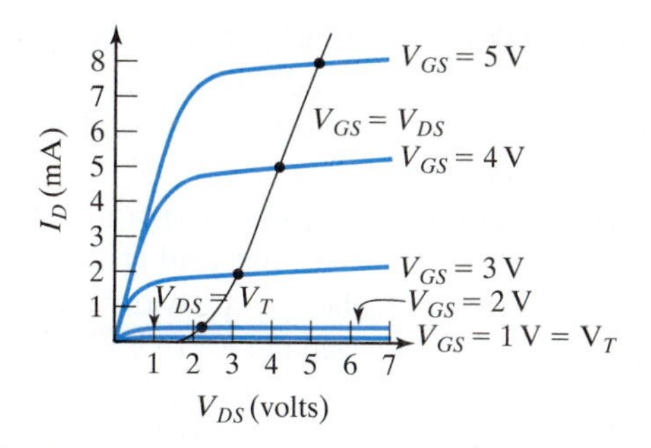

FIGURE 14.14 Output curves for an *n*-channel device.

formance of a pure resistor are not sufficient to prohibit the active load being very effectively used in NMOS logic circuits.

First, let's look in more detail at why connecting the gate to the drain creates a resistance between the terminals indicated. To illustrate this, refer to the typical output curve of the *n*-channel device shown in Figure 14.14. With this connection, V_{GS} always equals V_{DS}.

The new curve on the figure is the locus of all points where $V_{GS} = V_{DS}$. Notice that this curve has a positive slope for voltages above V_T, and the device corresponds to some equivalent, although variable, resistance. Using this approach, the inverter circuit and its voltage transfer characteristics appear as shown in Figure 14.15.

Basic circuit for inverter with MOSFET load

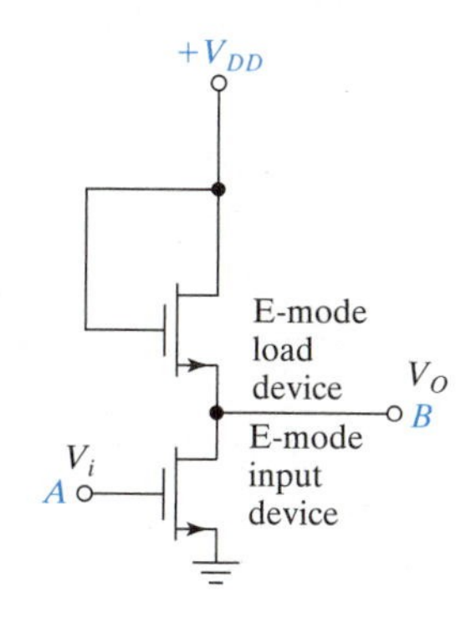

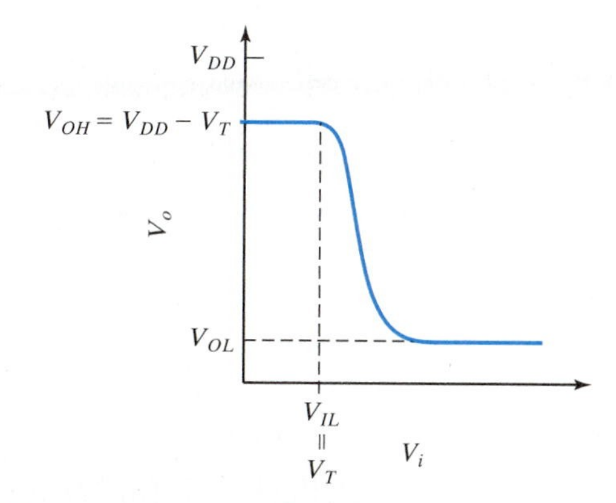

FIGURE 14.15 NMOS inverter with active load and its voltage transfer characteristic.

Notice that the output high level, V_{OH}, is now a threshold voltage below V_{DD} because the output voltage is pulled up toward V_{DD} by the load device. When the voltage reaches a value of $V_{DD} - V_T$, the voltage across the active load is reduced to V_T and no further conduction occurs.

The output low level, V_{OL}, is again determined by the voltage division between the on-resistance of the input device, and the equivalent resistance of the load device. The on-resistance can be controlled by the width-to-length ratio (W/L) of each MOSFET. For this type of circuit, we want the load device to have substantially higher equivalent resistance than the r_{on} of the input device. Therefore, in the layout of the inverter, the load device is typically made long and narrow (large L; small W), and the input device is made just the opposite (minimum size L; large W). The layout of such an inverter is illustrated in Figure 14.16.

The implementation of NAND and NOR functions using active loads is analogous to the circuits with resistive loads, that is, each resistor replaced by an active enhancement-mode load as shown in Figure 14.17.

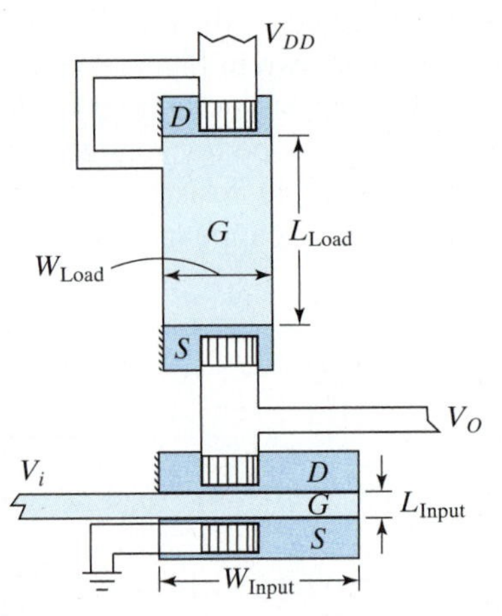

FIGURE 14.16 Layout of an inverter.

Basic circuits for NAND gate and NOR gate with MOSFET enhancement-mode load

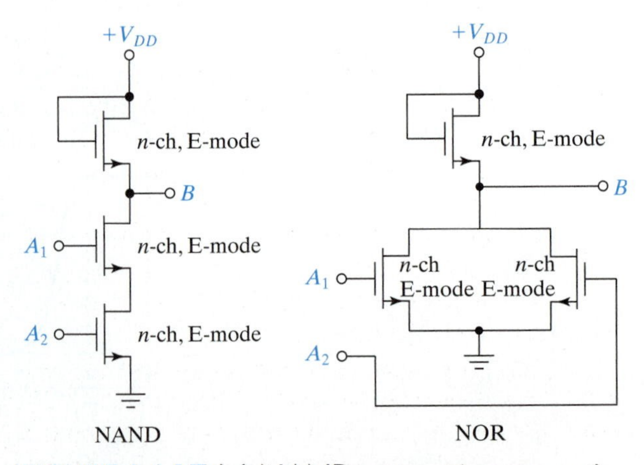

FIGURE 14.17 (a) NAND gate using an active enhancement-mode load; (b) NOR gate using an active enhancement-mode load.

Example 14.3

The input device to an NMOS (active load) inverter has an on-resistance, $r_{on} = 100\ \Omega$, and $V_T = 1$ V. If the power supply is 5 V, let us determine (a) the output high level, V_{OH}; (b) the input low level, V_{IL}; (c) the low level noise margin, NM_L, if the output low level is $V_{OL} = 0.5$ V; and (d) the effective resistance of the load device.

For an NMOS inverter circuit,

a. $V_{OH} = V_{DD} - V_T = 5 - 1 = 4$ V
b. $V_{IL} = V_T = 1$ V
c. $NM_L = V_{IL} - V_{OL} = 1 - 0.5 = 0.5$ V
d. If we let r_{load} = effective resistance of load device, by voltage division

$$V_{OL} = V_{DD}\left[\frac{100\ \Omega}{100\ \Omega + r_{load}}\right]$$

Substituting into the above equation, and solving for r_{load}, we obtain

$$r_{load} = 900\ \Omega$$

14.5.3 CMOS: Complementary MOS

CMOS digital logic circuits utilize both n-channel and p-channel devices, both of which are enhancement-mode devices. In CMOS logic circuits, the output voltage is either pulled high (toward V_{DD}) by one or more p-channel devices, or low (toward ground) by one or more n-channel devices. Consider a CMOS inverter as an example. The basic CMOS inverter circuit is shown in Figure 14.18(a). The n-channel and p-channel devices are connected in series between the supply voltage, V_{DD}, and ground. The output is taken from the center point and hence only one of the devices is on at a time. The gates of both devices are connected together at the input. The supply voltage, V_{DD}, is often 5 V; the threshold voltages of both devices are typically about a volt or less in magnitude.

Now consider two cases. In the first case the input is high, $V_i = V_{DD}$. The switch model equivalent circuit for this case is shown in Figure 14.18(b). The high voltage V_{DD} on the input is much larger than the threshold voltage of the n-channel device, and, therefore, it is on. Simultaneously, the gate and source terminals on the p-channel gate are at V_{DD} ($V_{GS} = 0$) and, therefore, it is off. In this situation, the output, *B,* is connected directly to ground through the n-channel device and V_o is zero volts.

Consider now the second case, when $V_i = 0$. For this case, V_{GS} for the n-channel device is zero, therefore, it's off, and the p-channel device is on. The switch level equivalent circuit for this situation is shown in Figure 14.18(c). The output is connected directly to $+V_{DD}$ through the p-channel device and thus $V_o = V_{DD}$.

In both the equivalent circuits just considered, notice that there is no dc path for current from the voltage supply source, $+V_{DD}$, to ground. Therefore, as stated earlier, current only flows in a CMOS gate during a transition from one logic state to the other.

Figure 14.19 shows the voltage transfer characteristics for the CMOS inverter. It has an output high level (V_{OH}) equal to V_{DD} and an output low level (V_{OL}) at ground or zero volts. This arrangement provides maximum possible voltage swing at the output. The transition be-

CMOS inverter circuit and switch model

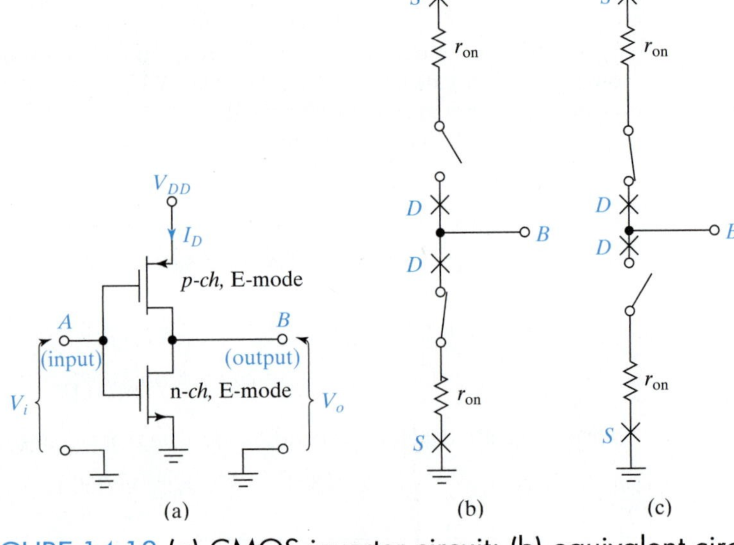

FIGURE 14.18 (a) CMOS inverter circuit; (b) equivalent circuit $V_{in} = V_{DD}$; (c) equivalent circuit $V_{in} = 0$.

tween states in a well-designed CMOS gate is steep and switches at approximately one-half of V_{DD}. These factors result in a gate with a very high noise margin.

Also plotted on this figure is the current from the supply, I_D. It peaks near the center of the transition and, as already shown, is essentially zero at either end of the transition.

The NAND function is implemented in CMOS by stacking in series the n-channel devices and connecting in parallel the p-channel devices. Each input is connected simultaneously to one n-channel device and one p-channel device. A two-input NAND gate is illustrated in Figure 14.20. Constructing a switch model equivalent circuit of this gate should convince the reader that it produces the NAND function at the output.

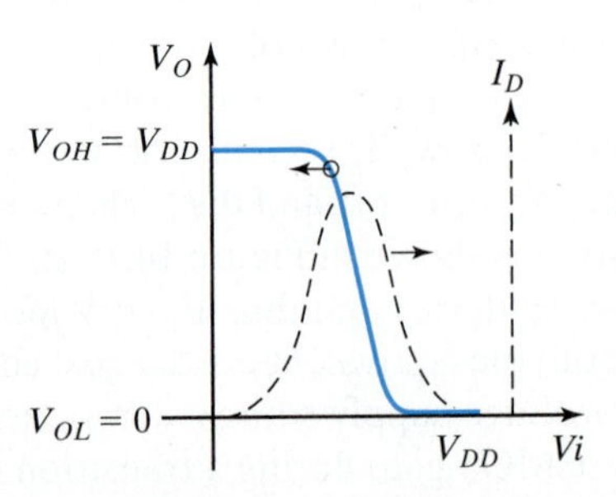

FIGURE 14.19 Voltage transfer characteristic for a CMOS inverter.

Basic CMOS logic circuits

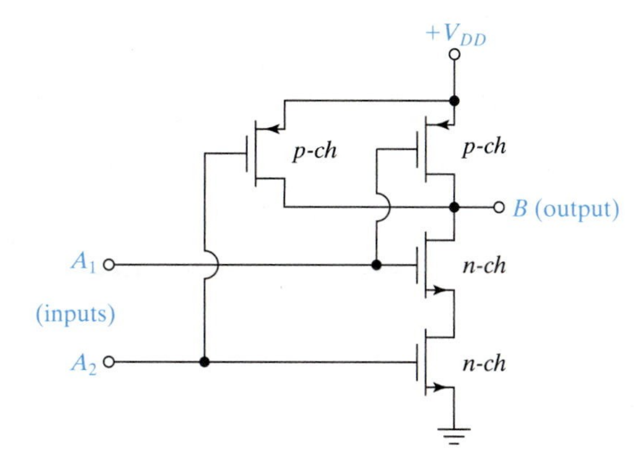

FIGURE 14.20 CMOS NAND gate.

The NOR function can be produced by the opposite procedure, that is, stacking the *p*-channel devices in series, and placing the *n*-channel devices in parallel. The CMOS circuit required to implement a two-input NOR gate is shown in Figure 14.21.

The CMOS technology also offers the possibility of implementing a special gate not easily accomplished with other technologies, the so-called *transmission gate*. The transmission gate is used as a switch that can be turned off or on to stop or pass a logic signal from one circuit to another. It is controlled by the state of a control input, labeled *C*.

The transmission gate is made by connecting an *n*-channel device in parallel with a *p*-channel device and also by constructing control logic such that both devices are simultaneously biased either off or on. Figure 14.22 shows the circuit implementation of a transmission gate, its logic symbol, and the equivalent circuit, which is merely a switch under the control of the signal at *C*.

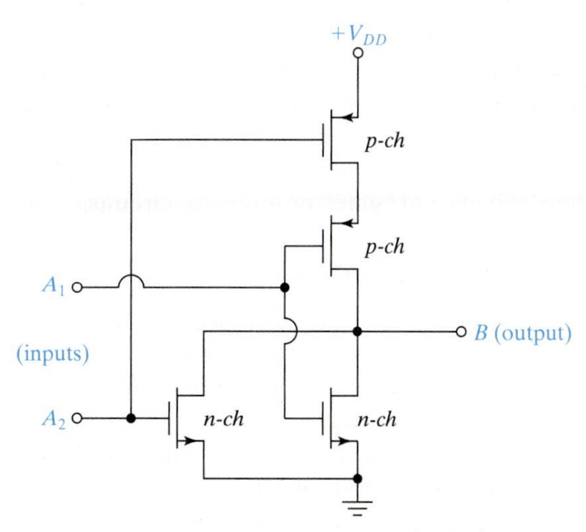

FIGURE 14.21 CMOS NOR gate.

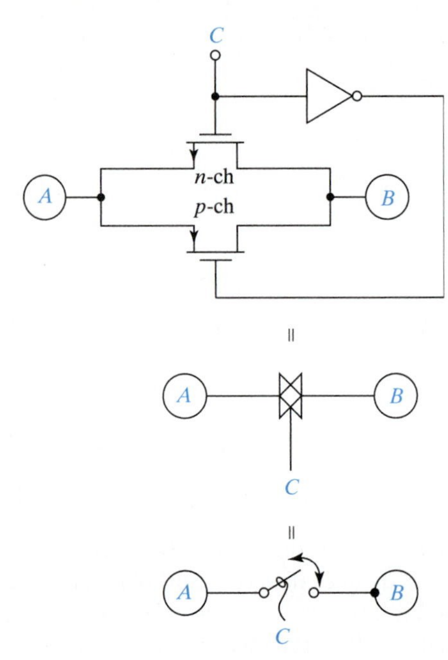

FIGURE 14.22 The CMOS transmission gate.

14–6 Basic Logic Gates Using BJTs

One of the most common logic gate families that utilize bipolar transistors is called TTL (transistor–transistor logic). This technology was first introduced in the 1970s and is still very common today. There have been refinements over time to increase its speed and reduce its power consumption, however, the basic circuit approach remains unchanged. TTL is a "saturating" logic family because the output transistor goes in the saturation mode. Schottky TTL is a small variation of the standard TTL circuit that operates faster by avoiding saturation. ECL (emitter coupled logic) is a different approach in which the BJTs operate in the active mode, again avoiding saturation to achieve higher switching speed. Modern CMOS circuit technology exceeds TTL and ECL in achieving a higher circuit density, lower power consumption, faster switching speeds, and better noise margins. The latter are now used primarily for custom circuits and "glue" or interface circuits.

14.6.1 TTL: Transistor–Transistor Logic

The use of TTL has been common for over two decades and remains a very popular bipolar logic technology. It has become a standard for implementation of many digital systems, and it is not unusual for complex logic chips implemented in CMOS circuitry to have special input and output circuits that mimic the logic levels of TTL at the external connections so that these chips can be directly interfaced to other TTL chips.

The basic circuit for TTL is illustrated by the circuit schematic drawing for a TTL two-input NAND gate, shown in Figure 14.23.

There is an unusual component in this circuit, the two-emitter transistor, labeled as Q1. Figure 14.24(a) shows this circuit symbol, and the cross-section of the multi-emitter transis-

Basic circuit for TTL NAND gate uses BJTs

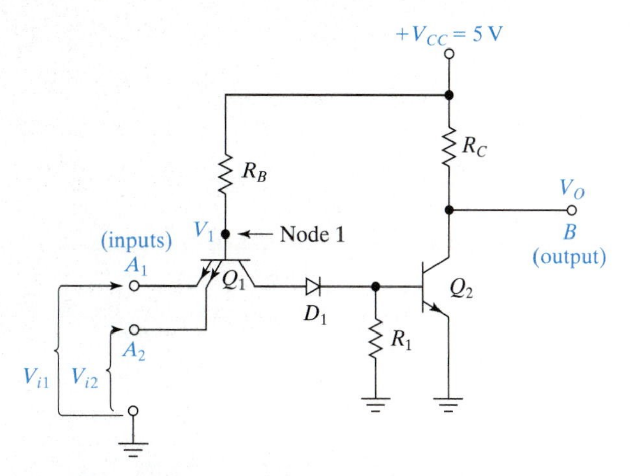

FIGURE 14.23 Two-input TTL NAND gate.

tor. Note that this structure is actually a simple way to make the multi-diode circuit shown in Figure 14.24(b).

In order to understand the operation of the circuit, let's substitute the multi-diode circuit in place of Q1 in Figure 14.23. This results in a circuit like Figure 14.25.

Recall that the output of a NAND gate is high for every set of inputs except the case in which all inputs are high. In this latter case, the output is low. Assume the logic levels for this gate are zero volts (logic low) and five volts (logic high) and that silicon junctions can be represented by the piecewise linear model with $V_F = 0.7$.

Consider the following two cases with reference to Figure 14.25:

Case 1. If EITHER or BOTH of the inputs are placed at zero volts, or grounded (logic low), then there is a path for current from $+V_{CC}$ though R_B and one (or both) of the diodes (D_2, D_3) to ground. Node 1 is then established at V_F or 0.7 volts. In order for current to flow through D_4 and D_1 and into the base of Q_2, the voltage at node 1 would have to be increased to $3 \times V_F$, or $3 \times 0.7 = 2.1$ volts, which is not possible with a grounded input. Therefore, for

The multi-emitter transistor functions as a diode network

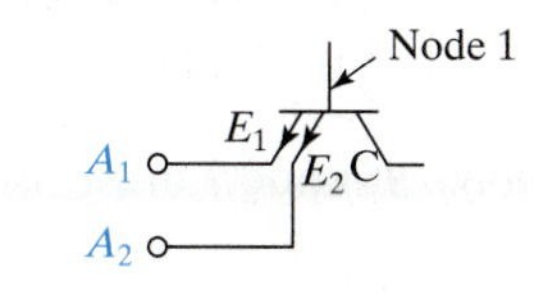

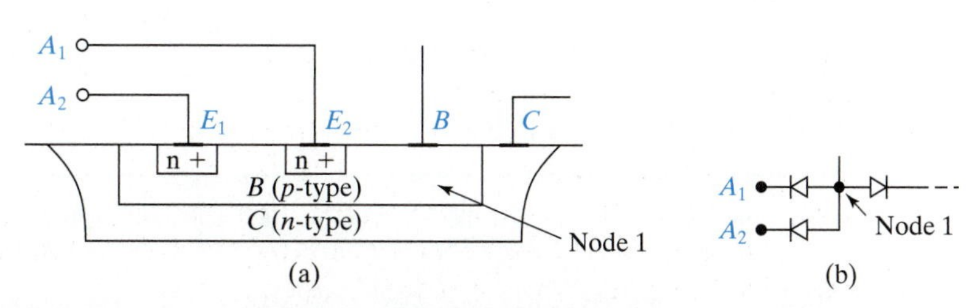

FIGURE 14.24 Multi-emitter NPN transistor (a) circuit symbol and cross-section, (b) diode equivalent circuit.

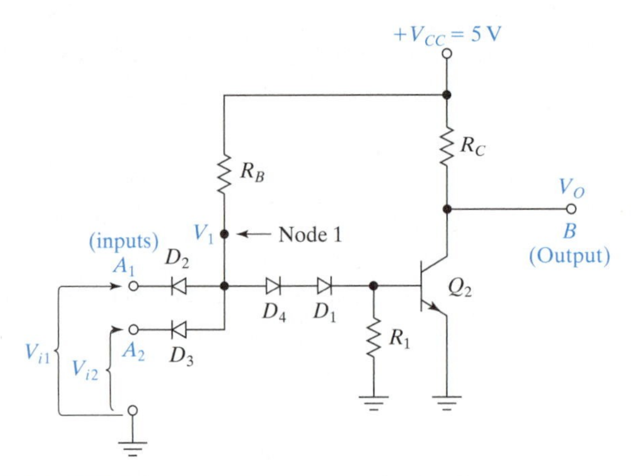

FIGURE 14.25 TTL NAND gate with diode equivalent circuit replacing multi-emitter transistor.

this case $I_{BQ2} = 0$, and Q_2 is cutoff. With Q_2 off, there is no current through R_C, and V_O is +5 volts (logic high).

Case 2. If BOTH inputs are high (+5 volts), then both D_2 and D_3 are reversed biased. Current flows from the source V_{CC} through R_B, and the voltage at node 1 increases to $3 \times V_F$, or 2.1 volts. This current flows into the base of Q_2 and also through R_1. In a properly designed TTL circuit, there is sufficient base current to place Q_2 in saturation. Therefore, V_O is $V_{CE(sat)}$, or approximately 0.1 volts.

As expected for a NAND gate, the only condition in which the output is low is when all the inputs are high.

Consider again the original two-input TTL NAND gate circuit in Figure 14.23. Understanding the operation of this circuit is straightforward by analogy with the circuit including the diode model for Q_1 just presented.

If either or both inputs are pulled low, that is, to zero volts, there is a current path through R_B and a base-emitter junction of Q_1 to the grounded input. This places node 1 at 0.7 volts. As was the case with the diode equivalent circuit, there is a series connection of three diodes in the base circuit of Q_2: the collector junction of Q_1, diode D_1, and the base-emitter junction of Q_2. Therefore, Q_2 is off, V_o is high, and the 0.7 volts at node 1 is insufficient to forward bias three diodes in series.

For Q_2 to turn on, the voltage at node 1 must rise to 2.1 volts ($3 \times V_F$). The voltage at node 1 tracks the *lowest* input voltage (A_1 or A_2) at a level of V_F higher than the input voltage. Therefore, node 1 reaches 2.1 volts when V_{i1} or V_{i2} rises to 1.4 volts. Thus, $V_i = 1.4$ volts is considered to be the input low level, V_{IL}, for TTL technology.

Example 14.4

In the circuit in Figure 14.23, assume $R_1 = R_B = 5\text{k}\Omega$, $R_C = 4\,\text{k}\Omega$, and $\beta_F = 60$ for all transistors.

(a) If A_1 is low (zero volts), how does the voltage at A_2 affect a change in the output?

(b) If A_1 is low, what is the value of current flowing through the connection at A_1 to ground?

(c) If BOTH A_1 and A_2 are high, what is the base current at Q_2?

(d) Is Q_2 in saturation? What is V_O?

(e) What is the forced beta of Q_2?

(a) If A_1 is low, at zero volts, then the voltage on A_2 doesn't matter. If A_2 is zero volts (ground) then the current through R_B is shared between the two diodes, but the voltage at Node 1 remains at 0.7 volts. If A_2 increases in voltage, then the *p-n* junction to which it is attached becomes more reverse biased, and isolated from the remaining circuit.

(b) If A_1 is low (connected to ground), the current through that connection can be calculated as:

$$I_B = \frac{V_{CC} - V_F}{R_B} = \frac{5 - 0.7}{5\ k} = 0.85\ mA$$

(c) If both inputs are high, both input diodes are reversed biased. The current through R_B flows through the base-collector junction of Q_1, through D_1, and is split between the input of Q_2 and that flowing through R_1.

$$I_{BQ2} = \frac{V_{CC} - 3(0.7)}{R_B} - \frac{0.7}{R_1} = 0.58\ mA - 0.14\ mA = 0.44\ mA$$

(d) and (e) If Q_2 is saturated, $V_{CE(SAT)} = 0.1$ V; therefore, $I_{C\,(MAX)}$ is;

$$I_{CQ2} = \frac{V_{CC} - 0.1}{R_C} = \frac{4.9}{4\ k} = 1.23\ mA$$

The forced beta is

$$\beta^* = \frac{1.23\ mA}{0.44\ mA} = 2.8$$

The forced beta is substantially less than the forward beta given of 60. Therefore, the device is in saturation, and the output voltage, V_O, is $V_{CE(SAT)} = 0.1$ V.

The simplified TTL NAND gate circuit shown in Figure 14.23 has several deficiencies. The base current for the transistor that saturates (to pull the output voltage low) comes directly through R_B, Q_1, and D_1. This current must be large enough to saturate the output transistor, and this requires a lower value for R_B. When an input to this circuit is low, the current through R_B must be sunk through the device at its input. The input stage would perform better if the currents were reduced. This problem can be addressed by adding another stage of current amplification. This is shown in Figure 14.26 with the addition of transistor Q_2, which serves as a current amplifier to increase the current available to the base of Q_3.

In addition, the circuit in Figure 14.23 does not perform very well for positive output transitions. Current to the output is supplied only by the resistor, R_C. Resistive pull-up is a relatively ineffective way of supplying positive load current. It would be better to provide a transistor from $+V_{CC}$ to the output which supplied current for positive transitions.

Changing the output circuit to a so-called "totem pole" output provides this current as shown in Figure 14.26. This schematic of a modern two-input TTL NAND gate is the actual circuit implemented on silicon chips by many manufacturers.

Modern TTL NAND gate with totem pole output

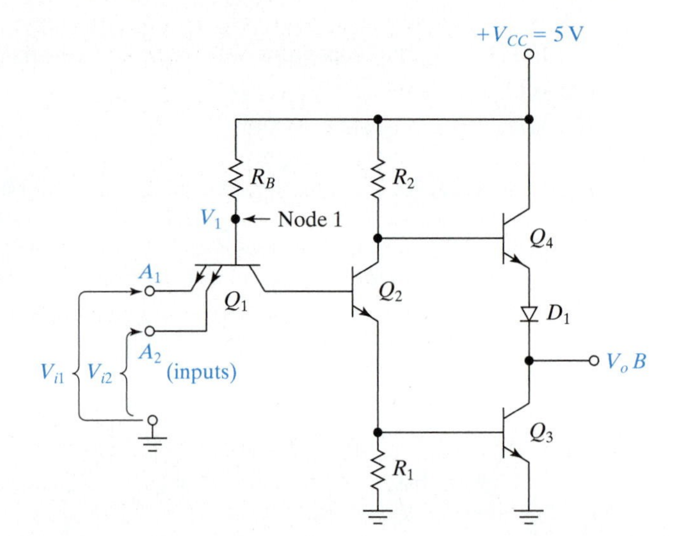

FIGURE 14.26 Totem pole TTL gate configuration.

To understand the operation of this circuit, consider the two cases that follow:

Case 1. If either or both of the inputs are grounded (logic low), then the voltage at node 1 is 0.7 volts. From node 1, there are still three silicon junctions in series: the collector base of Q_1, the emitter base of Q_2, and the base emitter junction of Q_3. Current cannot flow in this string unless node 1 reaches 2.1 volts. Therefore, $I_{BQ2} = 0$ and $I_{BQ3} = 0$ and thus, both Q_2 and Q_3 are off. Under these conditions, the output circuit reduces to that shown in Figure 14.27. Note that current is supplied to the output load resistance and capacitance (R_L and C_L) by the transistor Q_4, and the voltage at the output, V_o, rises to the high level, V_{OH}, that is,

$$V_{OH} = V_{CC} - I_{BQ4} R_2 - V_{BEQ4} - V_{FD1}$$

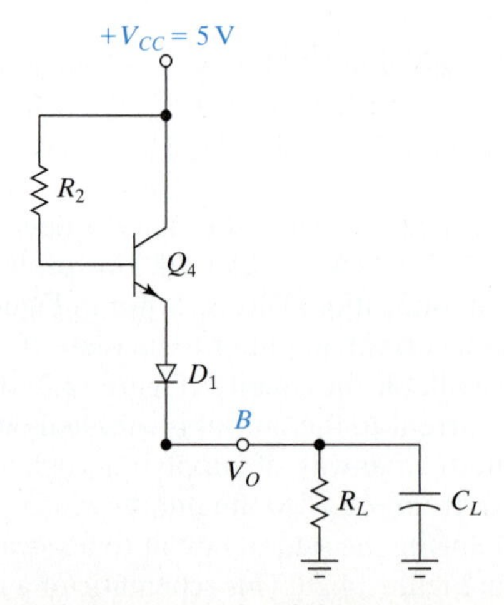

FIGURE 14.27 Output network of the circuit in Figure 14.26.

The transistor Q_4 remains in the active region because its collector base junction can never be forward biased. The collector is at V_{CC} and, therefore, if the load current is not excessive and β_F is large,

$$I_{BQ4} = \frac{I_{CQ4}}{\beta_F}$$

and the term $I_{BQ4} R_2$ is small.
Thus

$$V_{OH} \approx V_{CC} - V_{BEQ4} - V_{FD1}$$

$$V_{OH} \approx 5 - 0.7 - 0.7 = 3.6 \text{ V}.$$

Case 2. If both inputs-to this circuit are connected high, then node 1 rises to 2.1 volts and current through R_B flows into the base of Q_2, saturating Q_2. Current also flows into the base of Q_3, saturating Q_3. Hence, the output voltage is low at a value of $V_o = V_{CE(SAT)} \approx 0.1$ V.

For this case, we would like to ensure that Q_4 is off, so that the gate is not simultaneously trying to pull the output voltage both down and up. Note that when Q_3 is on, the voltage on the base of Q_3 is $V_{FQ3} = 0.7$ V. If Q_2 is saturated and $V_{CE(SAT)} = 0.1$ V, then the voltage on the base of Q_4 is $V_{BQ4} = 0.7 + 0.1 \approx 0.8$ volts.

The output voltage is 0.1 volts. Thus, if diode $D1$ were not in the circuit, Q_4 would turn on. *But* diode $D1$ has been inserted in the circuit to add another $V_F = 0.7$ V in series with the emitter junction of Q_4. With $D1$ in the circuit, if $V_o = 0.1$ volts, the base of Q_4 must reach 1.5 volts before Q_4 is turned on, and this can't happen while Q_2 is saturated.

Thus, *either* Q_3 is on, Q_4 is off, and the output is low, *or* when Q_3 is off, Q_4 conducts current to the output. From this analysis of the TTL gate shown in Figure 14.26, a voltage transfer plot can be developed and is shown in Figure 14.28. Note that all the key break points are determined except V_{IH}, which would require a more thorough analysis of the circuit.

14.6.2 Schottky TTL—A Nonsaturating Bipolar Logic Family

Schottky TTL and so-called "low-power" Schottky TTL circuits are families of integrated circuit logic chips that have evolved from the original TTL circuits. The circuits utilized are almost identical to those discussed in the previous section on TTL. The primary difference is the addition of Schottky diodes placed in parallel with the base collector junctions of the transistors.

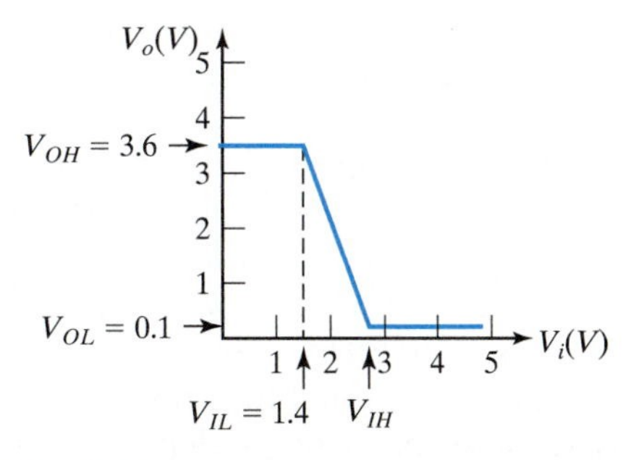

FIGURE 14.28 TTL gate transfer characteristic.

The addition of a Schottky diode prevents the BJT from entering the saturation mode

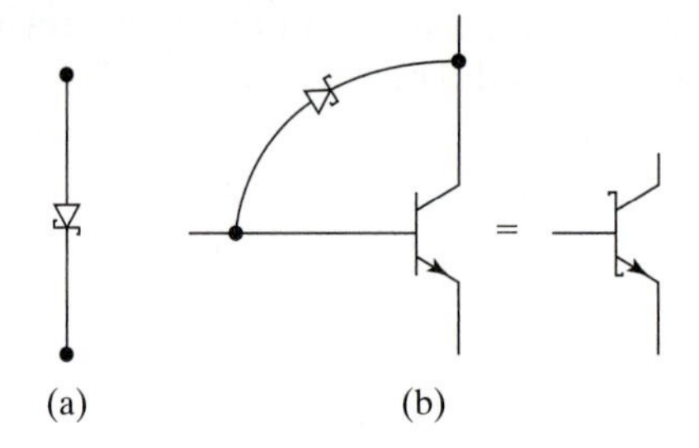

FIGURE 14.29 (a) Schottky diode; (b) Schottky transistor.

Schottky diodes are rectifying junctions fabricated by joining a metal with a semiconductor material. The Schottky diode has a symbol shown in Figure 14.29(a). By the proper choice of metal, these diodes can be made to turn on or conduct current at forward bias voltages in the range of 0.3 volts. This turn-on voltage is relatively small ($V_F \approx 0.3$ V), which is significantly less than the turn-on voltage of a silicon junction ($V_F = 0.7$ V). Therefore, a transistor with a Schottky diode attached, as shown in Figure 14.29(b), can never have its base collector junction forward biased. This arrangement makes it impossible for the transistor to enter the saturation region. The transistor fabricated with this Schottky diode is called a Schottky transistor.

The improved performance of circuits that employ these devices is derived primarily from the increased switching speed of the transistors, which are not allowed to saturate. Recall that a saturated transistors, which is modeled as a closed switch, stores a lot of charge in its base region. A relatively long time, usually measured in nanoseconds, is required to remove this charge and to switch an on transistor to the off condition. Therefore, saturating logic, in general, operates at a slower speed than comparable nonsaturating logic.

A typical Schottky TTL NAND gate from the 54S/74S logic family is shown in Figure 14.30.

14.6.3 ECL—Emitter-Coupled Logic

Another bipolar nonsaturating logic family is ECL, or emitter-coupled logic. This logic is often used when extremely fast logic is required. ECL gates can have propagation delay times of less than a nanosecond and clock rates that extend up to hundreds of megahertz. The primary disadvantage of ECL logic is that these gates are power hungry and they use significantly more power per gate than most other technologies. This limits their general application in several ways. First, not as many gates can be put on a single chip as with other technologies because of the buildup of heat in the chip. Thermal managment is critical in ECL designs. Second, with reduced gate counts per chip, it takes more chips to implement a system, which means larger boards and a larger and more costly system. There are applications where the speed advantage is worth this additional cost, but generally these are special situations.

The basis of all ECL circuits is the emitter-coupled pair or as it is sometimes called, the nonsaturating current switch. This circuit configuration is basically symmetric, with two inputs and two possible outputs, as illustrated in Figure 14.31. Note that the emitters of the NPN transistors are connected together at one of the critical nodes in the circuit. Current is pulled from this node to ground by a resistor, R_E. The current comes down to this node through EITHER transistor Q_1 or Q_2, depending on which one is conducting, since only one will be conducting at a time. *The transistor with the higher base voltage will be the one conducting*. In

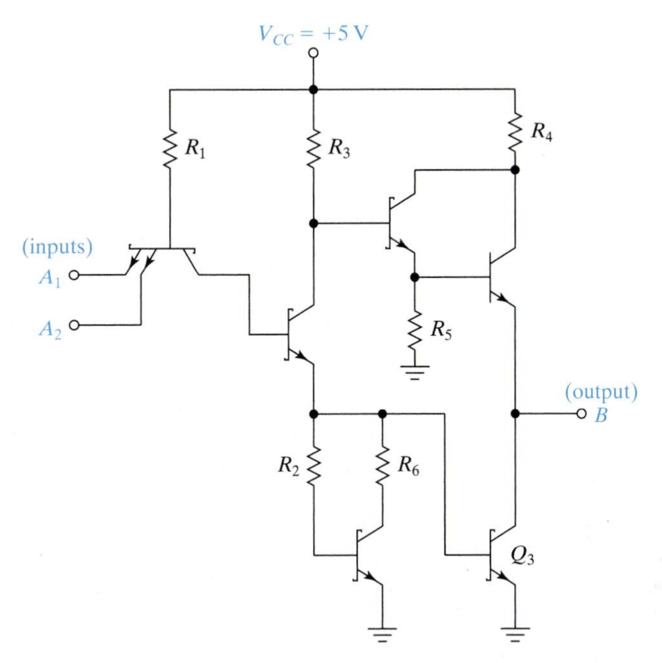

FIGURE 14.30 A typical Schottky TTL NAND gate.

a properly designed ECL gate, the conducting transistor remains in the active region in order to maintain the speed advantage, and the off transistor is cut off; neither device ever saturates. An equivalent circuit can be constructed by substituting the model for the bipolar transistor in the active region (from Chapter 11), resulting in the equivalent circuit in Figure 14.32 for the case where $V_{i1} > V_{i2}$. In general, the voltage at the critical node at the top of R_E will be controlled by the higher of the V_{i1} or V_{i2}. This voltage will be one diode voltage drop, that is, $V_{BE} = 0.7$ volts, below the higher of the two input voltages. Notice that the other base emitter diode, that is, the one attached to the lower input voltage, will then have less than 0.7 volts across it; this results in zero base current and, therefore, zero collector current, and hence the device will be off. This transistor appears as an open switch. Therefore, there are two possible cases:

Circuit used in ECL logic is "emitter-coupled pair"

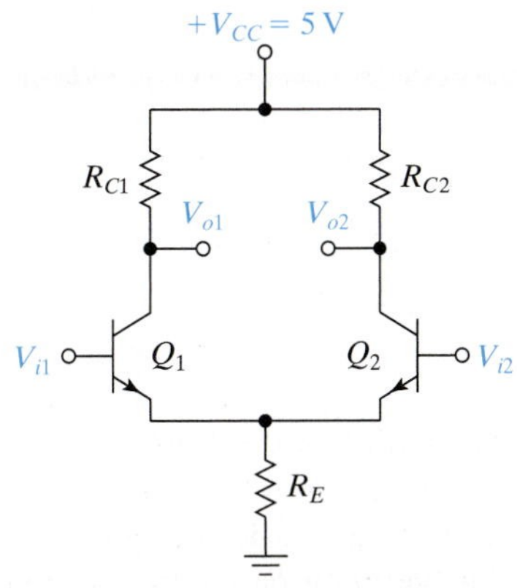

FIGURE 14.31 An emitter-coupled pair.

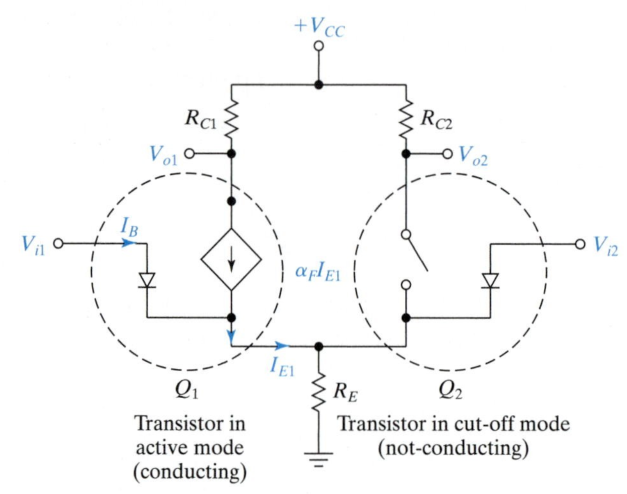

FIGURE 14.32 Equivalent circuit used with the network in Figure 14.31.

case 1: If $V_{i1} > V_{i2}$, then Q_1 is conducting; Q_2 is off.
case 2: If $V_{i1} < V_{i2}$, then Q_1 is off; Q_2 is conducting.

The equivalent circuit for case 1 was previously shown; the equivalent circuit for case 2 is similar, but with the transistor models exchanged.

As shown in Figure 14.32, for case 1, the output voltage, V_{o1}, is pulled low by the voltage drop from current through R_{C1}. This current can be calculated by computing the transistor collector current, which is $\alpha_F I_E$. The current I_E is set by the voltage at the top of R_E, that is, $V_{i1} - 0.7$, which is the voltage across R_E. On the right side, $I_{E2} = 0$. The voltage V_{o2} rises to the supply voltage, V_{CC}, because there is no current through R_{C2}, and hence no voltage drop across it.

Therefore, the current through R_E is given by:

$$I_{RE} = \frac{[V_{i1} - 0.7]}{R_E} = I_E$$

and

$$I_{C1} = \alpha_F I_E$$

Therefore,

$$V_{o1} = V_{CC} - I_{C1}R_{C1} = V_{CC} - \alpha_F I_E R_{C1}$$

For case 2, just the opposite situation occurs, with V_{o1} at a voltage of V_{CC}, and V_{o2} pulled lower.

Therefore, the emitter-coupled pair acts as a current switch, steering or directing the current by providing a path for it to come down the left or the right side of the circuit depending on the relative values of the input voltages, V_{i1} and V_{i2}.

In ECL logic applications, one input of the emitter-coupled pair is permanently connected internally to a voltage reference, that is, a constant voltage derived from a special circuit on the chip. The other input is the logic input to the circuit and this voltage is compared to the reference voltage, and the state of the current switch is determined by whether the input voltage is above or below the reference voltage. This is illustrated in the following example.

Example 14.5

If the silicon transistors in the ECL circuit shown in Figure 14.33 have betas of 100, let us plot the output voltages, V_{o1} and V_{o2} as a function of the input voltage, V_{i1}, as it is swept from 0 to +5 volts.

Basic ECL inverter circuit

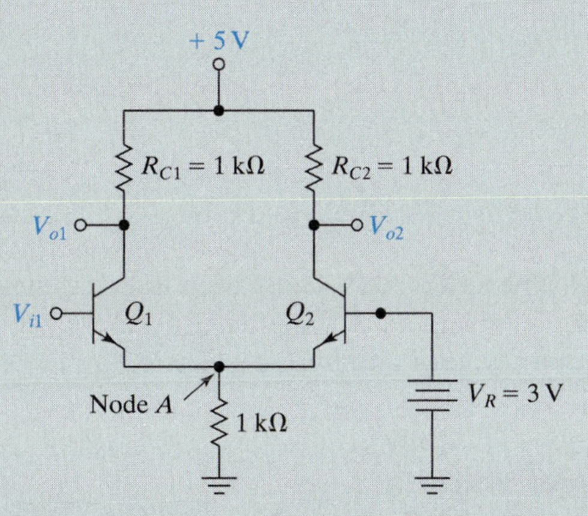

FIGURE 14.33 An example ECL inverter circuit.

For $V_{i1} < 3$ volts, Q_1 is open and, therefore, there is no current flow through the resistor, R_{C1}, and V_{o1} is +5 volts. The voltage V_{o2} is determined by replacing Q_2 with the model for the transistor in the active region.

The voltage at the critical node "A" can be determined by applying KVL to the input loop and assuming the silicon transistor has a junction turn-on voltage of 0.7 volts.

The voltage at node $A = 3 - 0.7\text{ V} = 2.3\text{ V}$. Therefore,

$$I_E = \frac{2.3}{1\text{ k}} = 2.3\text{ mA}$$

$$\alpha_F = \frac{\beta_F}{\beta_F + 1} = \frac{100}{101} = 0.99$$

$$I_C = \alpha_F I_E = (0.99)(2.3 \times 10^{-3}) \approx 2.3\text{ mA}$$

and

$$V_{o2} = 5 - I_C R_{C2} = 5 - [2.3 \times 10^{-3} \times 10^3] = 2.7\text{ V}$$

For $V_{i1} > 3$ volts, the voltages at V_{o1} and V_{o2} exchange values, as Q_1 turns on and Q_2 goes into cutoff.

Therefore, the output voltages cross at the point where the input voltage, V_{i1}, reaches 3 volts, as shown in Figure 14.34.

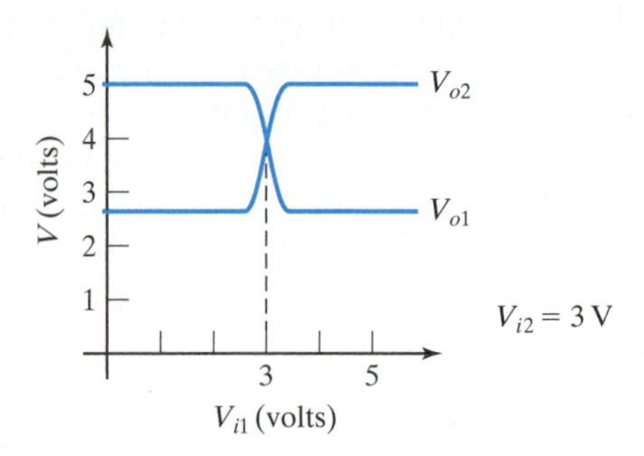

FIGURE 14.34 Plots used in Example 14.5.

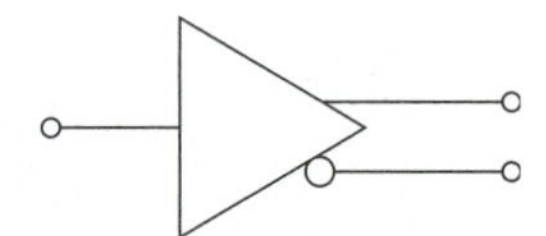

FIGURE 14.35 ECL inverter symbol.

The ECL gate, because of its circuit symmetry, easily provides two outputs, one of which is the complement of the other. Therefore, the logic symbol used for ECL gates often shows complementary outputs, as indicated by the symbol for an ECL inverter shown in Figure 14.35.

14.6.4 Output Level Shifting

In the previous example, the output low level, V_{o1}, is calculated to be 2.7 volts. This is lower than the switching threshold of the gate (3 volts), which is set, in this circuit, by the reference voltage, and does not allow a great deal of margin. The low-level output of the gate must fall below 3 volts for all conditions in order to ensure that a similar gate connected to the output of this one would always perceive the logic level to be low.

In order to improve the noise margin of ECL circuits, a level shifter stage is usually added to the basic ECL circuit previously shown. This addition is a bipolar transistor connected in a common collector configuration, that is, an emitter follower, which basically serves to shift the output voltage down by the voltage drop of one silicon diode and provide additional current gain.

Example 14.6

We wish to calculate the logic levels and noise margins of the ECL circuit, with level shifter, shown in Figure 14.36. Assume the β_F's of the transistors are large.

This circuit is typical of a very popular ECL family, 10K ECL. In this logic family the common convention is to establish ground, that is, zero volt reference, at the top and use a supply voltage of -5.2 V at the bottom node in the circuit.

If $V_i < V_{Ref}$, then Q_1 is off and Q_2 is conducting. The voltage at node A is a diode drop below V_{ref}, or

ECL inverter with output level shifting

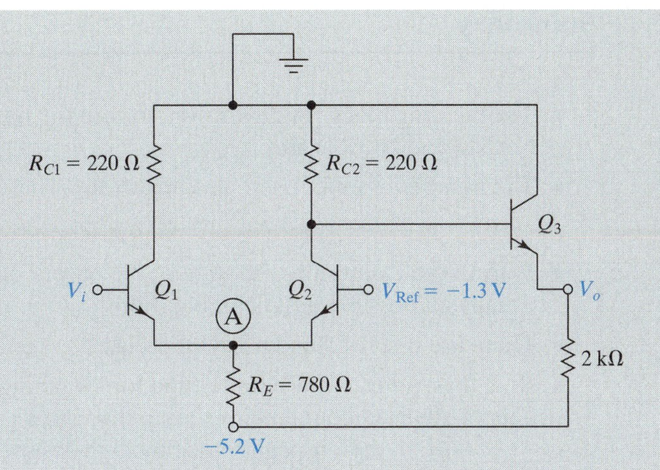

FIGURE 14.36 Circuit used in Example 14.6

$$V_A = -1.3\text{ V} - 0.7\text{ V} = -2.0\text{ V}$$

Therefore, the current through R_E is

$$I_{RE} = \frac{[-2.0 - (-5.2)]}{780} = 4.1\text{ mA}$$

Since $I_{E1} = 0$, then $I_{E2} = I_{RE} = 4.1$ mA.

Assuming the β_F's are large, $I_{C2} \sim I_{E2} = 4.1$ mA, and I_{B3} is negligibly small. Therefore, the current through R_{C2} is approximately I_{C2} and

$$V_{C2} = 0 - I_{C2}R_{C2} = 0 - (4.1 \times 10^{-3})(220) = -0.90\text{ V}$$

$$V_o = V_{C2} - 0.70 = -0.90 - 0.70 = -1.60\text{ V}$$

or

$$V_{OL} = -1.60\text{ V}$$

When $V_i > V_{Ref}$, Q_2 is off, and since there is negligible current through R_{C2}, $V_{C2} \approx 0$, and

$$V_o = 0 - 0.70 = -0.70\text{ V}$$

or

$$V_{OH} = -0.70\text{ V}$$

If input switching occurs exactly at V_{Ref}, then

$$V_{IH} = V_{IL} = -1.3\text{ V}$$

Therefore, the low-level noise margin, NM_L, and the high-level noise margin, NM_H, are given by

$$NM_L = V_{IL} - V_{OL} = -1.30 - (-1.60) = 0.30\text{ V}$$

and

$$NM_H = V_{OH} - V_{IH} = -0.70 - (-1.30) = 0.60\text{ V}$$

Summary

- The building blocks of digital systems are the basic logic gates: AND, OR, and NOT (or NAND and NOR) gates.
- The number of input combinations, Z, for n inputs is:

$$Z = 2^n$$

- A truth table describes the state of the output of a logic circuit for a given set of inputs, usually all possible input combinations.
- There are a set of standard symbols used to represent each of the basic gates.
- Real logic gates require finite time for switching. Propagation delay describes the time delay a signal encounters in passing through a gate.

  t_{PHL} = the propagation delay high-to-low,
  t_{PLH} = the propagation delay low-to-high, and
  t_P = the average propagation delay.

  These parameters are described in Figure 14.37.

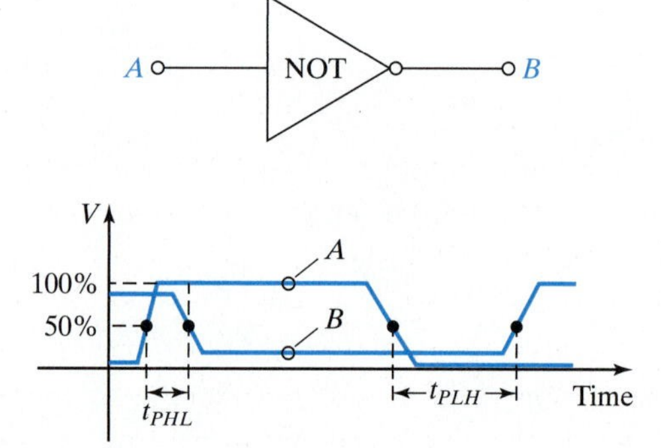

FIGURE 14.37 An illustration of propagation delays.

- The *rise time* t_r and the *fall time* t_f are measures of how fast the output voltage of the gate moves between the two allowed output levels (or states). This is generally measured from the 10% point to the 90% point of the full transition.

  These parameters are illustrated in Figure 14.38.

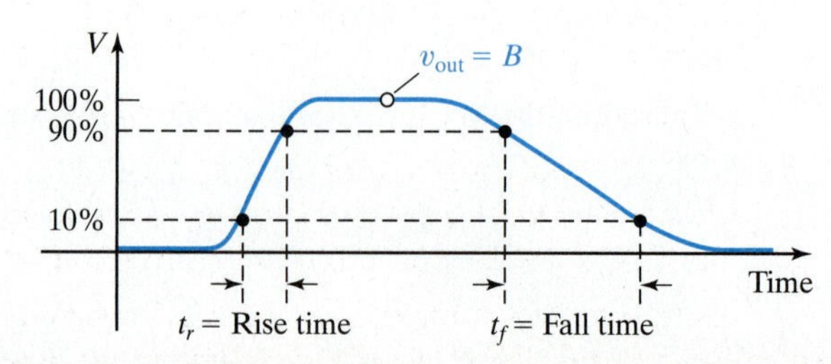

FIGURE 14.38 An Illustration of rise time and fall time.

- A race condition is an abnormal situation in which one signal arrives at its intended destination delayed enough relative to another signal so as to cause an error; this delay is generally a result of accumulated circuit propagation delays.
- Real logic gates are designed to unambiguously recognize input voltage levels as a high or a low, specified by V_{IH} and V_{IL}, respectively; they produce output levels specified by V_{OH} and V_{OL}. Noise margins are defined that indicate the magnitude of tolerance the design has for incorrectly recognizing a bit (see Figure 14.39).

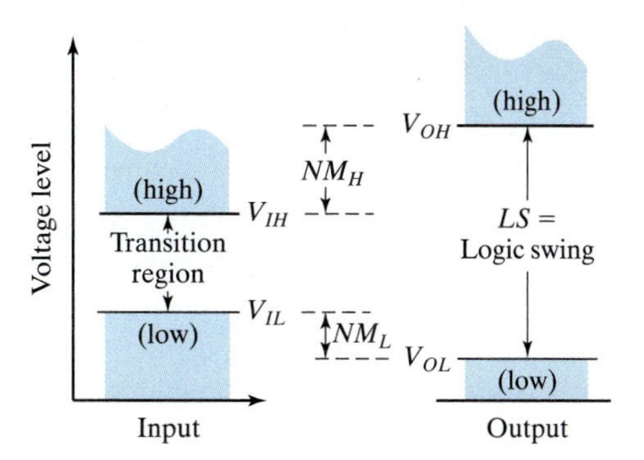

FIGURE 14.39 Illustration of logic levels and noise margin.

- Fanout is an integer that describes the maximum number of gates that can be connected to the output of a similar gate and ensure proper operation.
- Relays can be used to illustrate basic logic circuit functions.
- NMOS (circuits using *n*-channel enhancement-mode transistors) circuits are analogous to those introduced with relays, and can have resistive loads or active loads; an active load is the use of a transistor biased in a way that it can be used as a load resistor.
- Active loads can use an enhancement-mode transistor (enhancement-mode load).
- CMOS (complementary MOS) logic circuits use a combination of *n*-channel and *p*-channel enhancement-mode MOS transistors in each gate. CMOS circuits only conduct dc current during switching; thus, they use less power on average per logic function and are used in most high-density integrated circuits.

  An example of a CMOS two-input NAND gate is shown in Figure 14.40.
- BJTs can be used to implement logic circuits; the NPN transistor is dominant because an NPN device performs better than an equivalent PNP. (This is primarily because electron mobility is higher than hole mobility in silicon.)
- TTL (transistor–transistor logic) circuits use a multi-emitter transistor in the input section of the circuit. TTL is a very popular bipolar logic family and has been common for several decades.

  An example of a TTL two-input NAND gate is shown in Figure 14.41.
- TTL circuits use BJTs, which are allowed to saturate. Saturated BJTs store significant charge, and switch slowly. Schottky TTL is similar to TTL but with the addition of Schottky diodes to keep all transistors out of the saturation region and speed the operation.
- ECL (emitter-coupled logic) uses BJTs, which remain biased in the active region in both logic states. These circuits consume more power and are less dense, but are extremely fast.

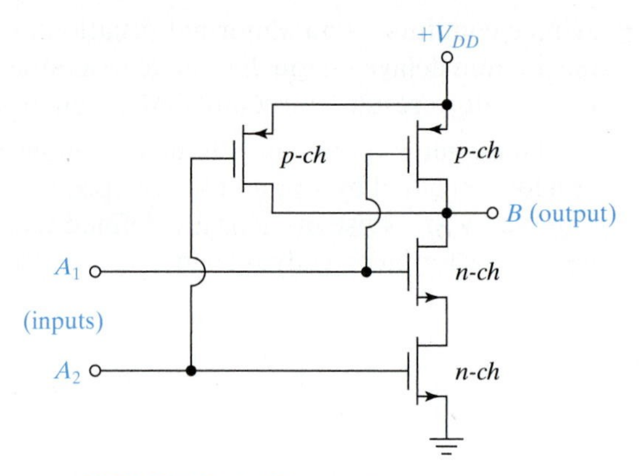

FIGURE 14.40 CMOS NAND gate.

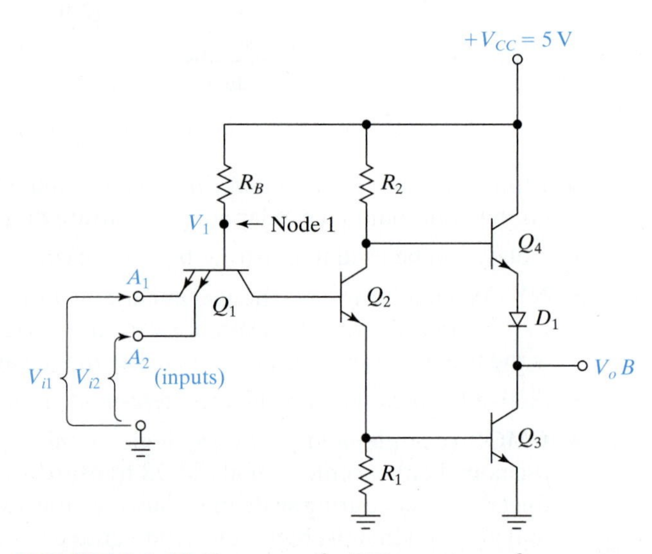

FIGURE 14.41 Totem pole TTL gate configuration.

Problems

14.1. (a) A logic gate has three input terminals. What is the number of possible input combinations to this logic circuit? (b) How does this change if one more input is added to the circuit?

14.2. Determine the truth table for the logic circuit shown in (a) Figure P14.2(a), (b) Figure P14.2(b).

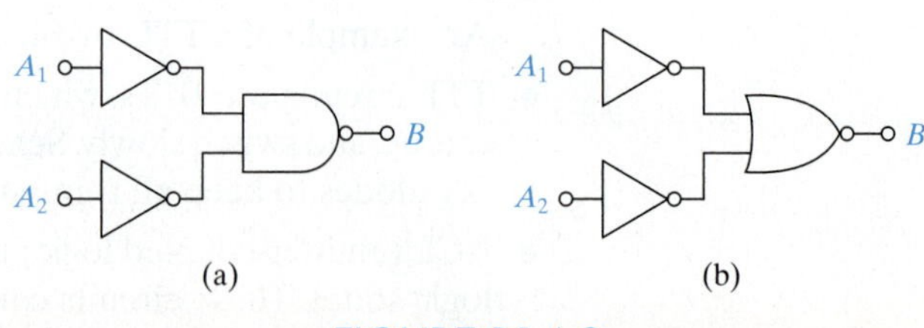

FIGURE P14.2

14.3. Determine the truth table for the logic circuit shown in (a) Figure P14.3(a), (b) Figure P14.3(b).

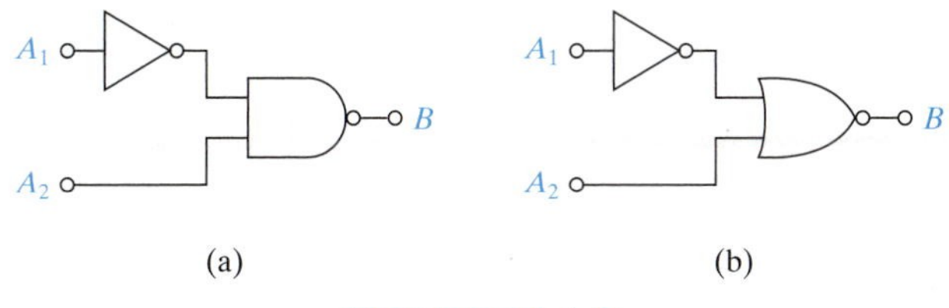

FIGURE P14.3

14.4. (a) Construct the truth table for the circuit obtained by connecting together as a single input the two inputs of a NAND gate, as shown in Figure P14.4 (a). (b) Repeat (a) for a NOR gate, as shown in Figure P14.4(b).

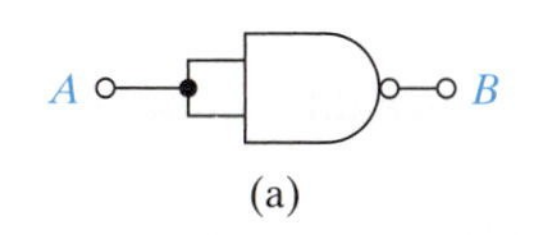

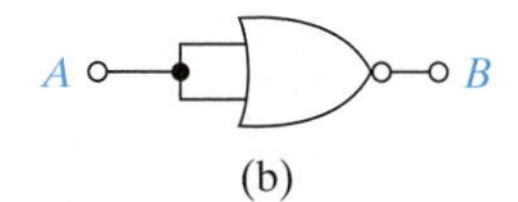

FIGURE P14.4

14.5. Construct the truth table for a three-input XOR-gate.

14.6. The input and output waveforms of an inverter are shown in Figure P14.6. Obtain the values of t_{PHL}, t_{PLH}, and t_P for the inverter.

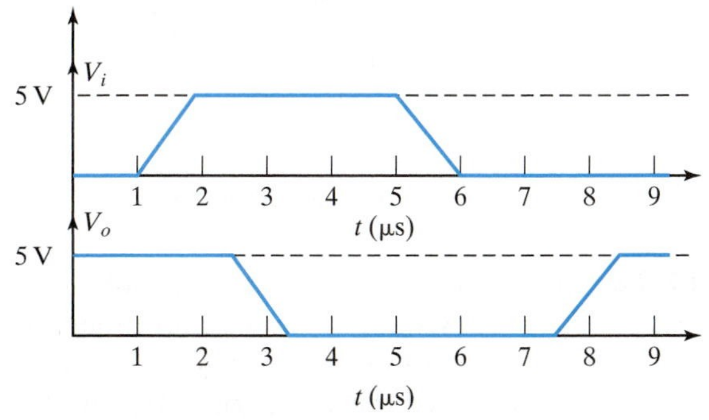

FIGURE P14.6

14.7. If two inverters identical to the one in problem 14.6 are cascaded, what are the values of t_{PLH}, t_{PHL}, and t_P for the combined circuit?

14.8. (a) Construct a plot of the input and output waveform of an inverter similar to that in problem 14.6, but with $t_{PHL} = 3\ \mu s$ and $t_P = 5\ \mu s$. (b) What is the value of t_{PLH}?

14.9. (a) Determine the rise and fall time of the signals shown in Figure P14.9 (a). (b) Repeat (a) for Figure P14.9 (b).

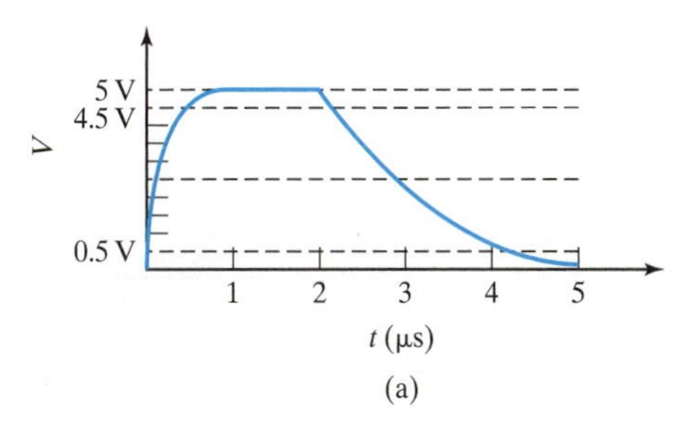

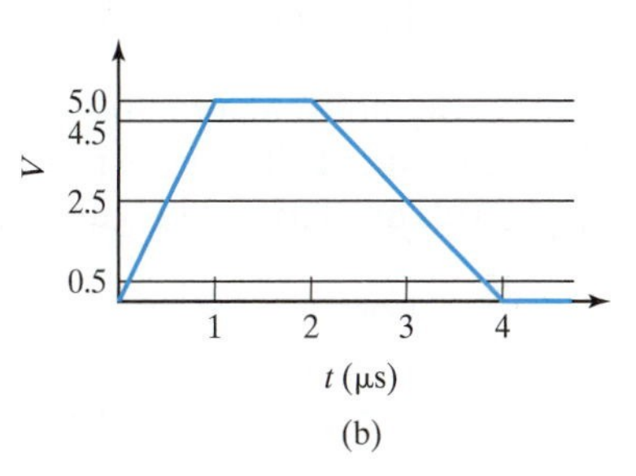

FIGURE P14.9

14.10. a) Construct a plot of the output waveform of an inverter similar to that in problem 14.9(a), with a rise time of 2 ns and a fall time of 0.5 ns.

14.11. a) Construct a plot of the output waveform of an inverter similar to that in problem 14.9(b), with a rise time of 4 ns and a fall time of 1 ns.

14.12. If four NAND gates each with an average propagation delay of 5 ns are connected in a serial path with three NOR gates each with a propagation delay of 4 ns, what is the propagation delay of the entire circuit?

14.13. A digital circuit has a clock frequency of 25 MHz. The circuit uses gates with propogation delays $t_{PHL} = t_{PLH} = t_P = 2$ ns. If data are presented at the input of a cascaded string of these gates at the leading edge of each clock cycle, what is the maximum number of gates that can be connected in series?

14.14. Repeat problem 14.13 if the clock frequency is 100 MHz.

14.15. Obtain the noise margins NM_L and NM_H for the gate whose transfer characteristic is shown in Figure P14.15

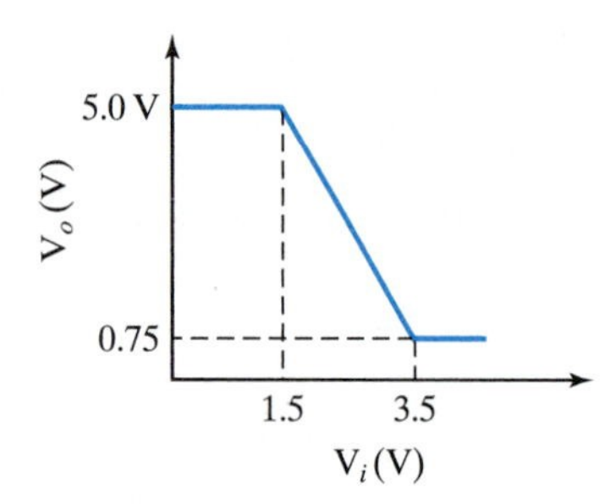

FIGURE P14.15

14.16. Calculate the noise margin, transition width, and logic swing of the gate whose input and output levels are shown in Figure P14.16

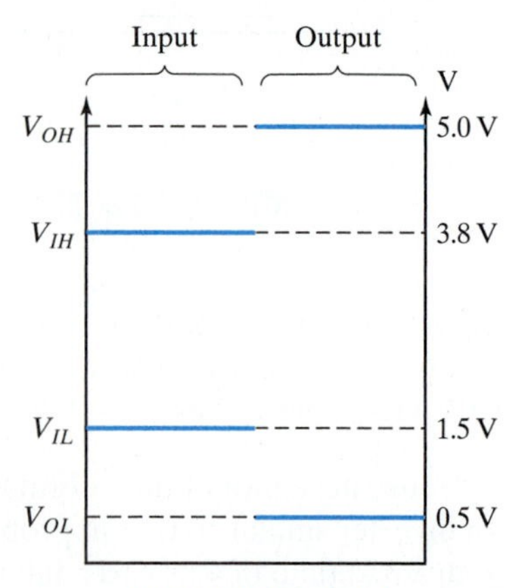

FIGURE P14.16

14.17. An NMOS inverter with a resistive load of $R_D = 1.5\ \text{k}\Omega$ is shown in Figure P14.17. If $V_T = 1.0$ V and $r_{on} = 100\ \Omega$ in the ohmic region of MOSFET operation, obtain the values of V_{OH}, V_{OL}, V_{IL}, V_{IH}, NM_L, and NM_H for the inverter. Assume $V_{IL} = V_{IH}$.

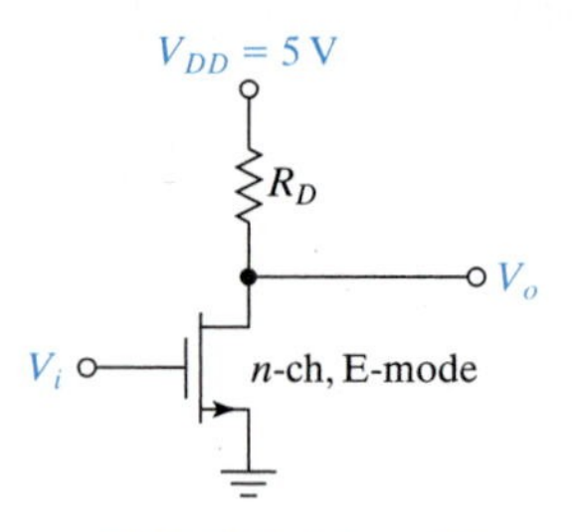

FIGURE P14.17

14.18. Repeat problem 14.17 if $r_{on} = 50\ \Omega$.

14.19. (a) Construct a circuit drawing using *n*-channel MOSFETs and resistive loads for a two-input AND gate. (b) Repeat (a) for a two-input OR gate.

14.20. (a) Design a three-input NAND gate with passive loads; show the circuit drawing including all transistors and other elements. (b) Repeat (a) for a three-input NOR gate.

14.21. An NMOS inverter with an enhancement-mode active load is shown in Figure P14.21. (a) If $V_T = 0.8$ V for both devices, determine V_{OH} and V_{IL}. (b) If the resistance of the load device is $1.5\ \text{k}\Omega$, what value of r_{on} for the input device is required to obtain $V_{OL} = .3$ V?

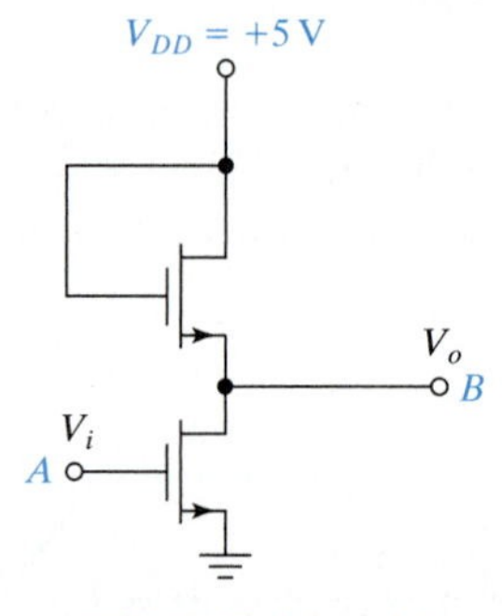

FIGURE P14.21

14.22. For the inverter circuit in problem 14.21, $V_T = 0.7$ V and V_{OL} is determined to be 0.2 V. If the value of r_{on} for the input transistor is $120\ \Omega$, find the values of NM_L and the effective resistance of the load device.

14.23. For the NMOS inverter circuit given in Figure P14.21, sketch the voltage transfer curve, V_o versus V_i. (Assume $V_T = 0.8$ V and $V_{IH} = 2.1$ V.)

14.24. (a) Draw the circuit diagram of a three-input NAND gate with enhancement-mode active loads and NMOS transistors. (b) Repeat (a) for a three-input NOR gate.

14.25. The voltage transfer characteristics of an inverter are shown in Figure P14.25. (a) Draw the transfer characteristics of a circuit obtained by cascading two of these inverters. (b) Compare the noise margins of the cascade and a single inverter.

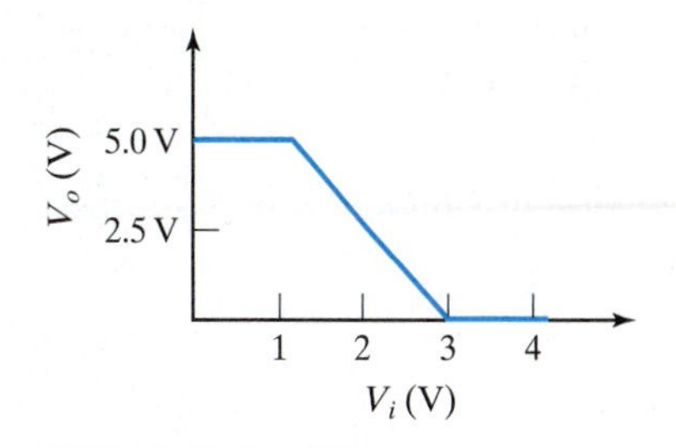

FIGURE P14.25

14.26. (a) Construct the truth table for the circuit shown in Figure P14.26(a). (b) Construct the truth table of the logic circuit shown in Figure P14.26(b). (c) Compare the results in (a) and (b).

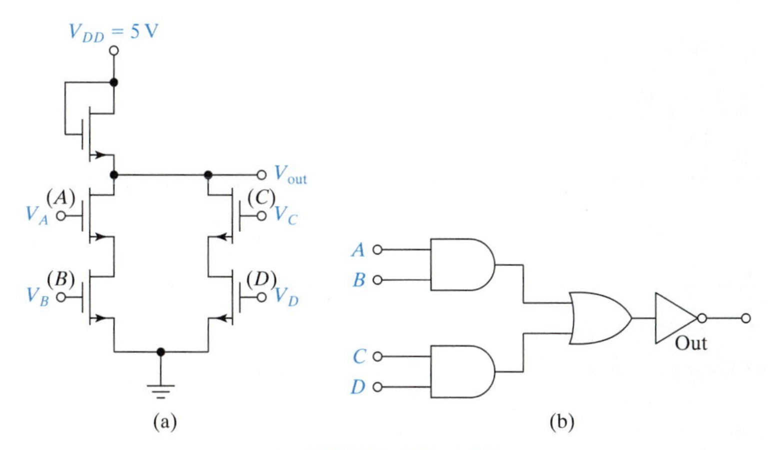

FIGURE P14.26

14.27. (a) Draw the circuit diagram of a three-input CMOS NAND gate. (b) Repeat (a) for a three-input CMOS NOR gate.

14.28. Construct the truth table for the CMOS logic circuit given in Figure 14.28.

14.29. (a) Draw the complete circuit diagram for a CMOS AND gate. (b) Repeat (a) for a CMOS OR gate.

14.30. Consider the CMOS inverter with transfer characteristics shown in Figure 14.19. Assuming $V_{DD} = 5$ V, (a) determine approximate values for the noise margins in this circuit. (b) Compare the CMOS noise margins to those of

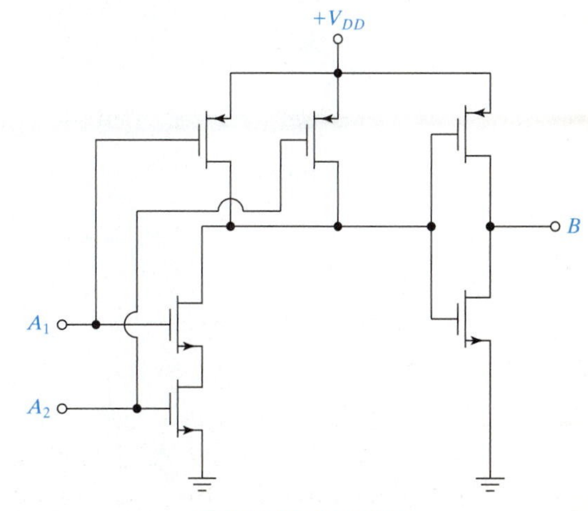

FIGURE P14.28

the enhancement-mode load inverter shown in Figure 14.15.

14.31. Compare and contrast the performance of TTL bipolar logic with CMOS logic based on the following criteria:
(a) logic levels
(b) switching speeds
(c) circuit density
(d) power consumption

14.32. For the NPN transistor circuit shown in Figure P14.32, assume $V_{CE(SAT)} = 0.2$ V,$V_{BE} = 0.7$ V, $\beta_F = 50$. (a) Determine the minimum value of V_i that saturates the transistor. (b) Determine the fanout when the output is high.

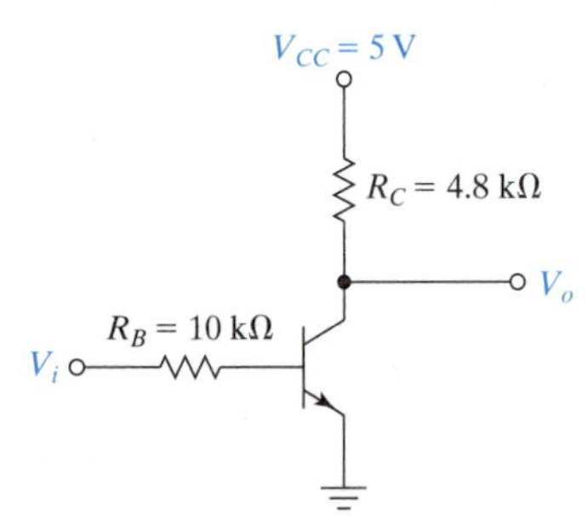

FIGURE P14.32

14.33. Assume the transistors in Figure P14.33 have $\beta_F = 100$, $V_{BE} = 0.6$ V, and $V_{CE(SAT)} = 0.1$ V; the diode has $V_F = 0.6$ V. (a) Calculate V_{IL}, V_{OL}, and V_{OH}. (b) What is the forced beta, β^*, for Q_2 when the output is low? (c) Construct a truth table for this circuit.

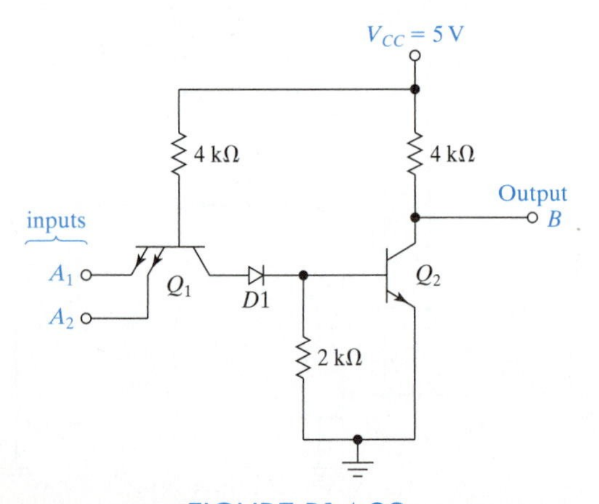

FIGURE P14.33

14.34. Repeat problem 14.33 for the case where the 2 kΩ resistor is removed from the circuit.

14.35. For the circuit in Figure P14.33, (a) calculate the current that flows to ground through an input when a single input is at a logic low state. (b) Calculate the base current into Q2 when the output is in a logic low state.

14.36. The transistor in the circuit in Figure P14.36 has $\beta_F = 50$, and $V_{BE} = 0.6$ V. Determine V_o, the collector, base, and diode currents for $V_i = 4$ V. Assume a Schottky turn-on voltage $V_F = 0.3$ V.

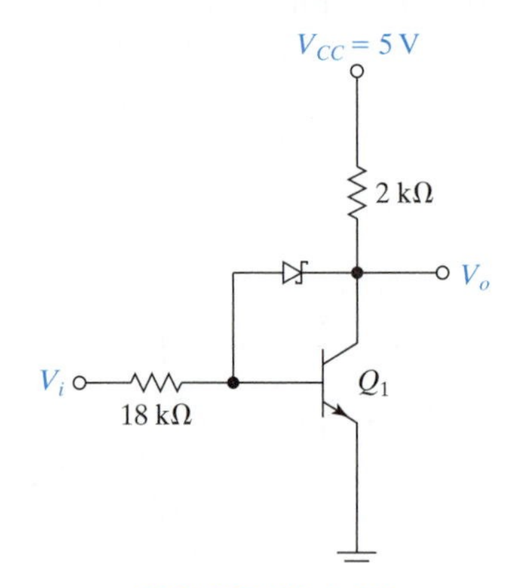

FIGURE P14.36

14.37. Figure P14.37 shows a two-input TTL NAND gate. The transistors are identical with high betas, $V_{BE} = 0.7$ V and assume $V_{CE(SAT)} = 0.25$ V; for the diode, assume $V_F = 0.6$ V. Calculate V_{OL}, V_{OH}, and V_{IL} for this circuit. Sketch the transfer characteristics of the circuit.

14.38. For the circuit in problem 14.37, calculate the forced beta, β^*, for Q_3 if the output is in a low state, and β_F for all transistors is assumed to be 100.

14.39. Construct a truth table for the logic circuit in Figure P14.37.

14.40. Repeat problem 14.37 if a load resistance of 300 Ω is attached from the output to ground.

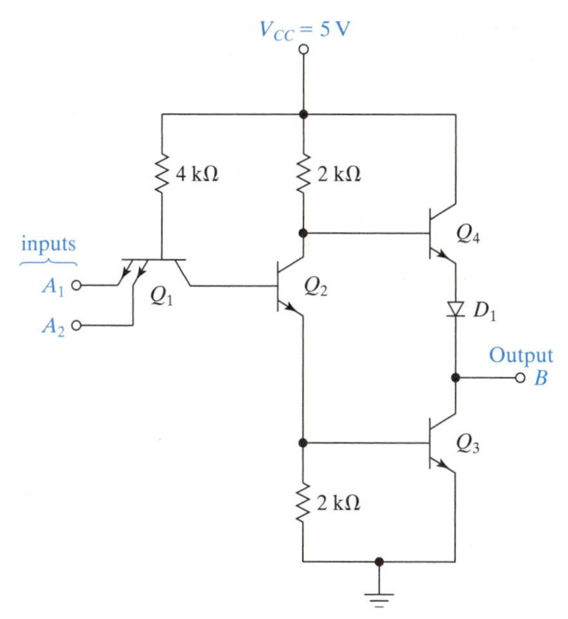

FIGURE P14.37

14.41. For the ECL circuit shown in Figure P14.41, plot the output voltages V_{o1} and V_{o2} as a function of the input voltage V_i as it is swept from 0 to 5 volts. Assume $\beta_F = 125$ and $V_{BE} = 0.6$ V for the transistors.

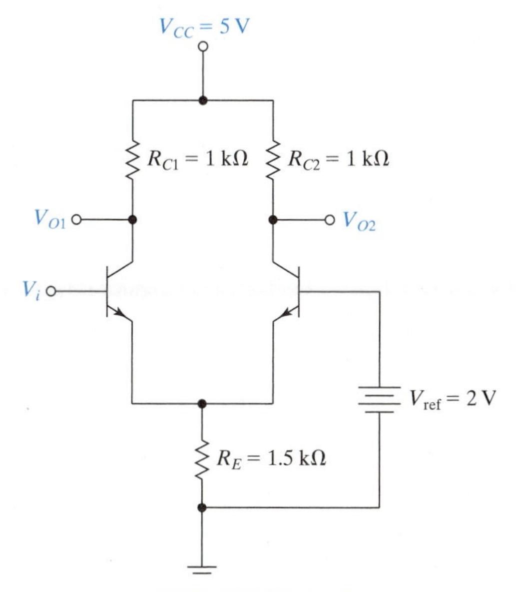

FIGURE P14.41

14.42. Calculate the logic levels and noise margins of the ECL circuit with level shifter shown in Figure P14.42. Assume that the β_F's of the transistors are large, $V_{BE} = 0.7$ V, and that $V_{IH} = V_{IL}$.

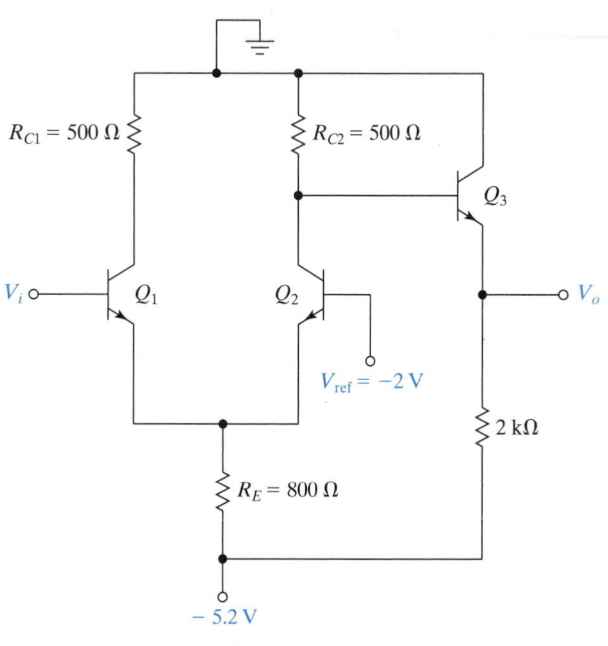

FIGURE P14.42

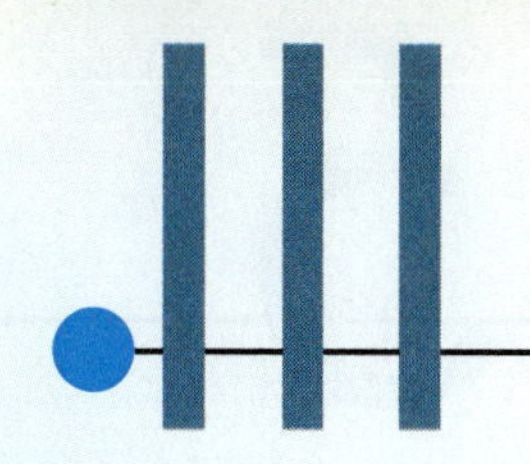

Electromechanical Systems

15

15-1 Introduction

In this chapter we discuss the fundamentals and some applications of dc machines. First, we describe the basic physical principles that govern their operation. We then show how these concepts can be employed to construct a dc machine. The equivalent circuits for dc motors and generators are presented and analyzed to exhibit some of their operating characteristics. Finally, we describe some applications, which demonstrate the use of dc machines in industry.

15-2 Fundamental Concepts

Perhaps the easiest method of describing the fundamentals that govern the operation of a dc machine is to first examine what is called a linear machine. A simple linear machine is shown in Figure 15.1. In this figure, a voltage source is connected through a switch to a pair of electrical conducting rails. A conducting bar, which makes electrical contact with the rails, is free to move along the rails in the x direction. The rails and bar are present in a constant magnetic **B** field that is directed into the page, that is, in the negative z direction. Let us now examine the operation of this machine in three separate time intervals, that is, $t < t_0$, $t = t_0$, and $t > t_0$. Prior to the time $t = t_0$, no current exists in the rails.

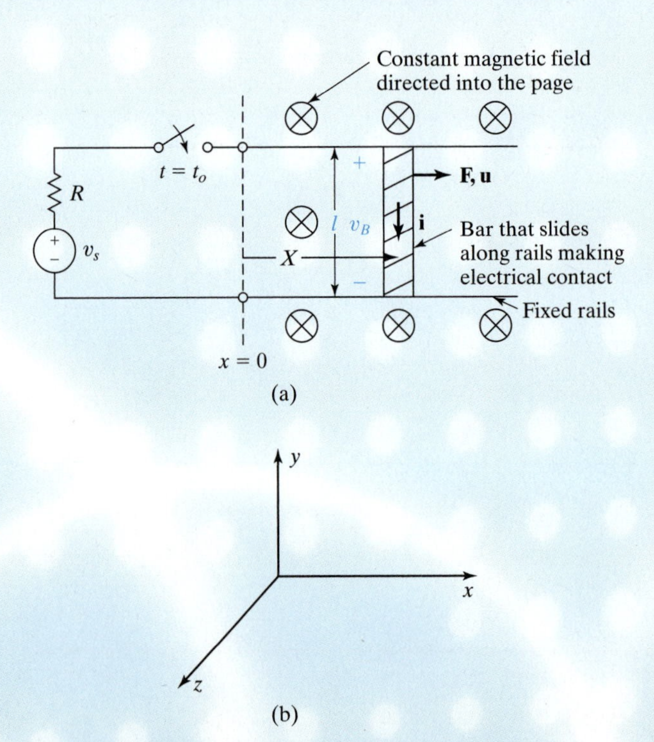

FIGURE 15.1 (a) Linear machine; (b) coordinates used in discussing the linear machine.

According to the Lorentz force equation, the vector force on the sliding bar is

$$\mathbf{F} = (\mathbf{i} \times \mathbf{B})\,\ell \tag{15.1a}$$

where $\times$ represents the *vector cross product,* **F** is measured in the positive x direction, and the vector **i** is measured in the direction of the positive current flow. Since there is no force acting on the bar, the velocity **u** of the bar is zero. Therefore, in view of Faraday's law, we find that

$$\begin{aligned} \mathbf{v}_B &= |(\mathbf{u} \times \mathbf{B})\ell| \\ &= 0 \end{aligned} \tag{15.2a}$$

and hence the induced voltage across the bar is zero.

At time t_0, the magnitude of the current is $i(t_0) = v_s/R$ assuming that the impedance of the loop is dominated by "R," the loop resistance.

This current produces a force (**F**) on the bar. The direction of the force defined by the vector cross product is obtained using the *right-hand rule,* as illustrated in Figure 15.2. If we rotate the vector **i** into the vector **B,** the force is in the direction as shown. Note that this is the direction of motion of a right-hand screw. The force on the bar causes the bar to accelerate in the $+x$ direction. This is actually the principle behind the rail gun. As the bar gains speed, the voltage across the bar begins to increase in accordance with the expression in Eq. (15.2). The polarity of the induced voltage $\mathbf{v}_B$ is obtained by the right-hand rule in which the vector cross product points to the positive terminal.

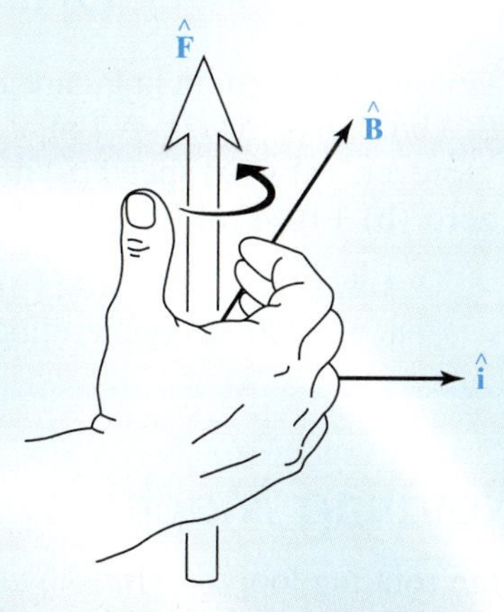

FIGURE 15.2 Right-hand rule for determining the direction of **F** (perpendicular to the **i, B** plane).

Since **F**, **B**, and **i** (and correspondingly, **u** and **B**) are perpendicular, the scalar versions of Eqs. (15.1a) and (15.2a) are

$$F = iB\ell \tag{15.1b}$$

and

$$v_B = uB\ell \tag{15.2b}$$

For time $t > t_0$, the magnitude of the current is given by the expression

$$i(t) = [v_s - v_B(t)]/R \tag{15.3}$$

and the bar continues to accelerate until

$$v_B(t) = uB\ell = v_s \quad \text{and} \quad u = u_o = \frac{v_s}{B\ell}$$

At this point the current is zero, the force is then zero, the bar moves at constant speed, and the machine is in an equilibrium state. Conversion of energy from electrical to mechanical form is the action of a *motor.*

Now suppose that by some means we increase the speed of the bar beyond v_s. This reverses the direction of the current. Using the Lorentz force equation, we find that reversing the direction of the current also reverses the direction of the force on the bar. Since the bar tries to move in the negative x direction, we must apply force in the positive x direction in order to keep the bar moving in this direction at a constant speed, which is greater than the equilibrium speed. The application of this external force produces a voltage at the input terminals, and, therefore, in this mode the linear machine acts like a *generator.*

Note that the key factor that determines whether the machine operates as a motor or generator is the velocity of the bar with respect to the equilibrium speed.

That is,

$u < u_o$ ------motor operation

$u > u_o$ ------generator operation

Drill Exercise

D15.1. Consider the system in Figure 15.1. Suppose the **B** field into the page is 2 Wb/m^2, $R = 5\ \Omega$, $\ell = 1$ m, $v_s = 150$ V, and the switch has been closed "forever." At what speed (u) must the bar move for the current (i) to be (a) zero, (b) +10 A, or (c) −10 A?

Ans: (a) $u = +75$ m/s, (b) $u = +50$ m/s (motoring), and (c) $u = +100$ m/s (generating).

15-3 A Simple Rotating Machine

Consider the rotating loop of wire shown in Figure 15.3(a). The loop rotates in a counterclockwise direction around the z axis, and is immersed in a constant magnetic **B** field that is directed along the negative x axis. θ is used to measure the angular position of the loop and

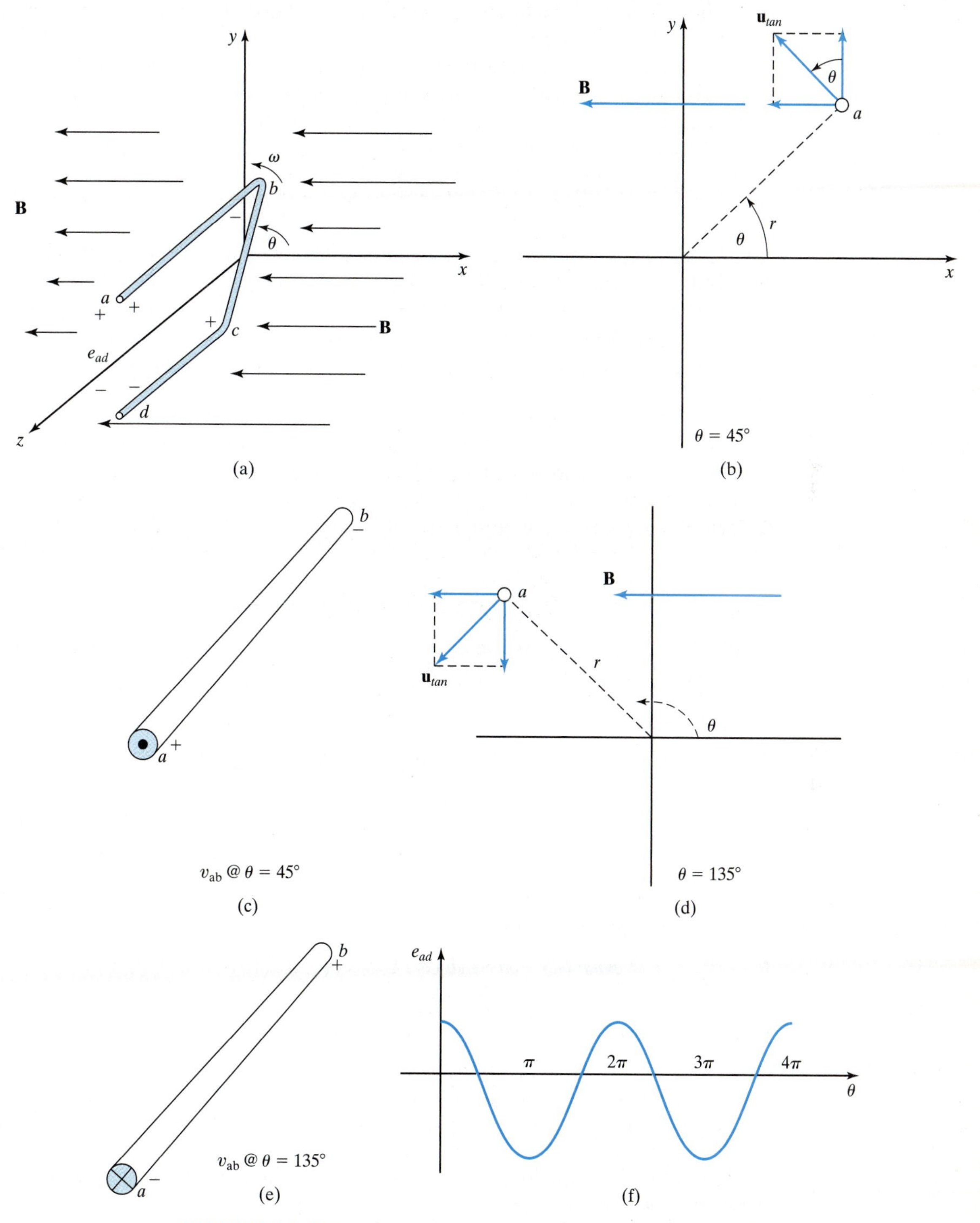

FIGURE 15.3 Fundamentals of a simple rotating machine.

is positive in the counterclockwise direction. In addition, we define $\theta = 0$ when the rotating loop lies in the xz plane.

With reference to Figure 15.3(a), let us consider the conductor *ab,* that is, the top side of the rectangular loop *abcd.* A two-dimensional "free body diagram" of the conductor immersed in the **B** field is shown in Figure 15.3(b). The magnitude of the tangential velocity of the conductor $\mathbf{u}_{tan}$ is $r\omega$ where r is the radius of the loop and ω is the angular velocity. The induced voltage along the conductor *ab,* which we will call e_{ab}, is then

$$e_{\mathbf{ab}} = |(\mathbf{u}_{tan} \times \mathbf{B})\, \ell| \tag{15.4}$$

The velocity $\mathbf{u}_{tan}$ can be split into two components; one tangential to the **B** field and one perpendicular to it. The cross product of the component of $\mathbf{u}_{tan}$ along the **B** field, with the **B** field, is zero. However, the cross product of the velocity component perpendicular to the **B** field with the **B** field produces an induced voltage (out of the page), as shown in Figure 15.3(c). If the **B** field is constant, then, as shown in Figure 15.3(b), Eq. (15.4) can be expanded as

$$e_{ab} = (r\omega \cos\theta)\, B\ell \tag{15.5}$$

Voltage induced in a rotating conductor in a magnetic field

Suppose now that the conductor *ab* is in the position shown in Figure 15.3(d). Once again, only the velocity component perpendicular to the **B** field yields a nonzero cross product. However, in this case the cross product produces an induced voltage (into the page), as shown in Figure 15.3(e). A similar argument follows for the conductor *cd* and hence

$$\begin{aligned} e_{ad} &= e_{ab} + e_{cd} \\ &= 2Br\ell\omega \cos\theta \end{aligned} \tag{15.6}$$

Note that the voltage e_{ad} is a maximum at $\theta = 0°$. Furthermore, the analysis illustrates that the induced voltage as a function of the angle θ is of the form shown in Figure 15.3(f).

Drill Exercise

D15.2. Consider the U-shaped coil shown in Figure 15.3(a). Its dimensions are $ab = cd = 50$ cm and $bc = 20$ cm. $B = 2$ Wb/m^2 and $\omega = 100$ rad/s. Evaluate the voltage e_{ad} at the following coil positions: (a) $\theta = 0°$, (b) $\theta = 45°$, (c) $\theta = 90°$, (d) $\theta = 135°$, (e) $\theta = 180°$, (f) $\theta = 225°$, (g) $\theta = 270°$, and (h) $\theta = 315°$.

Ans: (a) +20 V, (b) +14.14 V, (c) 0 V, (d) −14.14 V, (e) −20 V, (f) −14.14 V, (g) 0 V, (h) +14.14 V.

Now suppose that our loop of wire *abcd* in Figure 15.3(a) is connected to what is called a segmented ring, which is composed of two semicircular pieces of metal, as shown in Figure 15.4. These segments are in constant contact with *brushes,* which are the connection points for the loop voltage. As the loop rotates, the segments slide under the brushes. This mechanism is called a *commutator.*

This commutator is essentially a mechanical switch that reverses the direction of the currents and fluxes so that the magnetic field of the armature currents is stationary in space while the armature is rotating. The result is the production of a net torque in one direction.

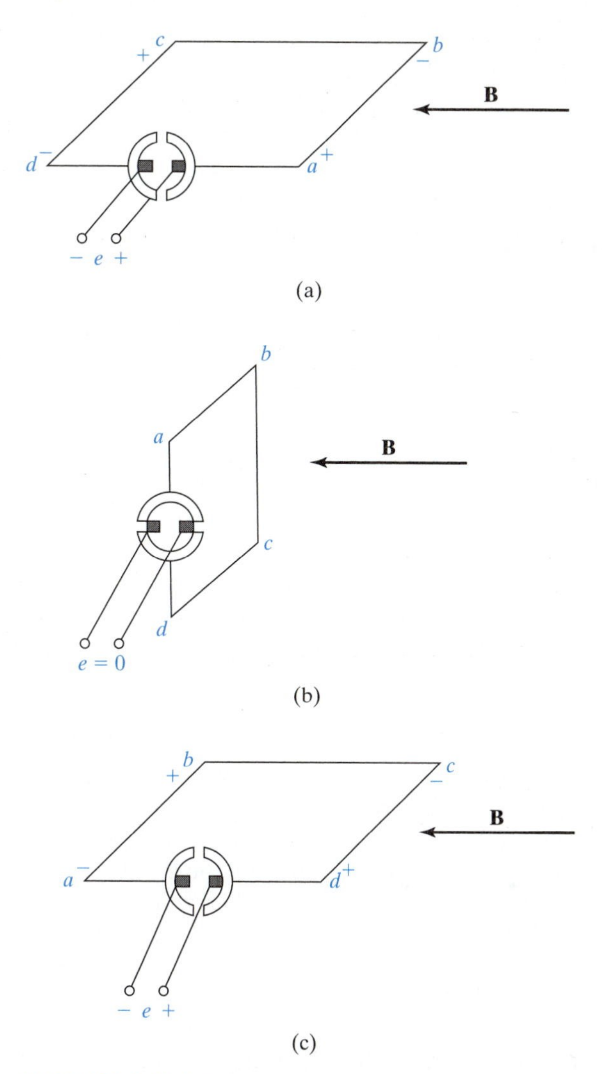

FIGURE 15.4 Demonstration of commutator action for a single loop.

When the loop is in the position shown in Figure 15.4(a), the voltage e is positive and decreasing as the loop rotates to the position shown in Figure 15.4(b). When the loop is in the position shown in Figure 15.4(b), note that the loop voltage is zero. As the loop rotates beyond the position shown in Figure 15.4(b), the voltage e is positive and increasing as the loop rotates to the position shown in Figure 15.4(c). Therefore, while the voltage between the commutator segments, that is, e_{ad}, is as shown in Figure 15.5(a), the voltage at the brushes, that is, e, is as shown in Figure 15.5(b). Note that this voltage shown in Figure 15.5(b) is a rectified version of the voltage shown in Figure 15.5(a).

The importance of commutator action

The previous analysis illustrates the basic principles of a rotating machine. However, in an actual machine, there are numerous coils of wire and commutator sections, as shown in Figure 15.6.

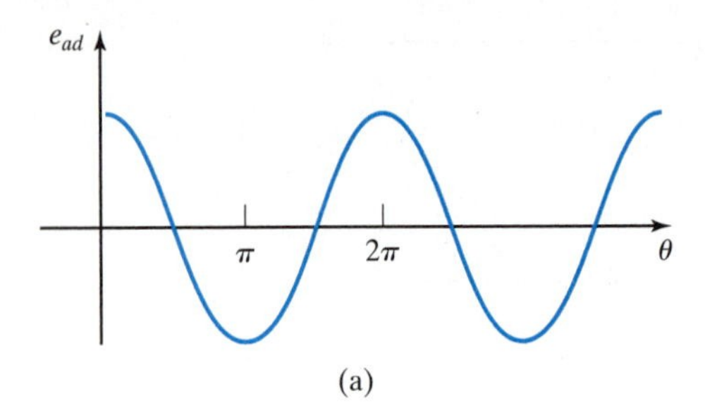

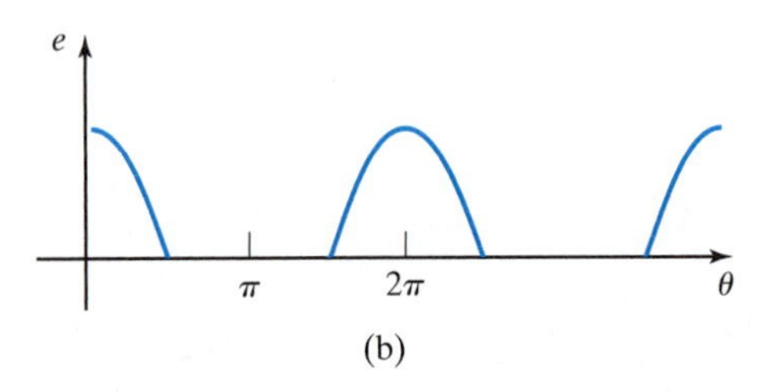

FIGURE 15.5 (a) Loop voltage and (b) brush voltage for the rotating wire in Figure 15.4.

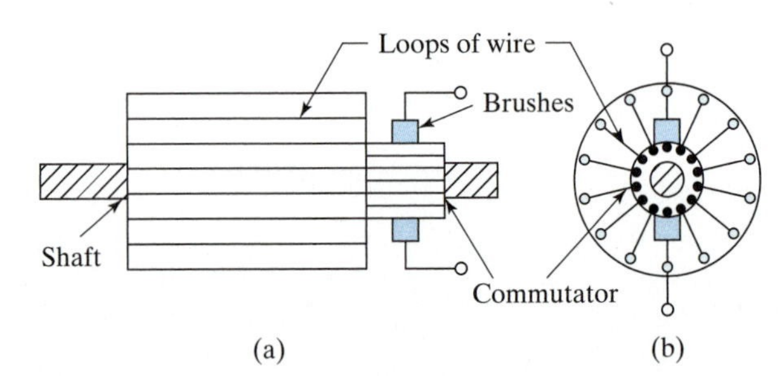

FIGURE 15.6 Multiple loops and commutator sections built on a shaft.

Also, the windings are interconnected in a much more complicated manner, and referred to as the armature winding. Both the armature winding and the commutator are mounted on a structure referred to as the *armature* or *rotor,* as shown in Figure 15.6. The brushes are mounted on the stationary (stator) frame, which encloses this rotating structure and contains the items necessary to construct the B field. The terminal voltage will resemble that shown in Figure 15.7, which when smoothed will yield a constant dc voltage. It is important to note that while the geometry of the coils and commutator are represented as shown in Figure 15.6, the actual electrical connections are more complex.

15-4 The Basic DC Machine

At this point let us try to relate the concepts we have just discussed to an actual machine. The diagram in Figure 15.8(a) illustrates the basic design of a *dc machine.* For simplicity, we assume that the rotor has a single coil (loop), as shown in both Figures 15.8(a) and (b). The rotor and the two field poles that surround it are made of iron. The voltage V_f establishes the current

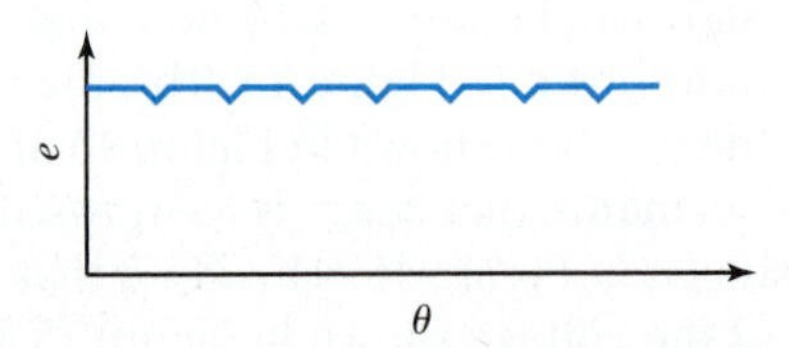

FIGURE 15.7 Terminal voltage of a rotating machine with multiple loops and commutator sections.

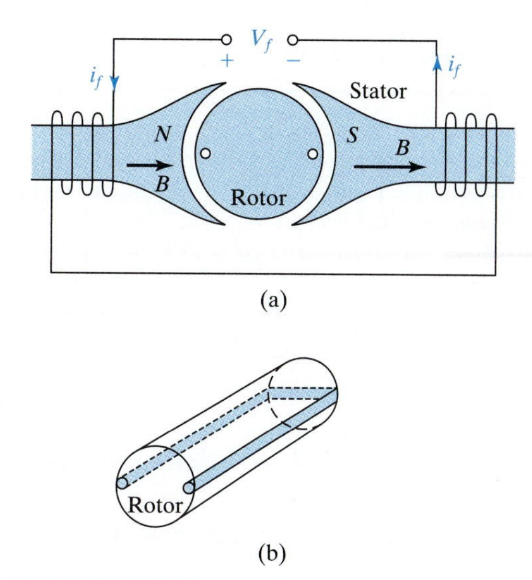

FIGURE 15.8 (a) A basic dc machine; (b) rotor displaying a single coil.

i_f. Because of Ampere's rule, this current creates a constant magnetic field, as shown in Figure 15.8(a). Figure 15.9 indicates that flux lines of the magnetic field are perpendicular to the rotor at every point except in the two small gaps where the rotor is not covered by a field pole. The flux will follow the path of least reluctance, crossing the air gap approximately radially. This path is the shortest possible distance from one piece of iron to another through the least amount of air. Therefore, the B field is essentially always perpendicular to the velocity vectors of the loop of wire except in the interpolar regions.

Note that the basic dc machine we have described satisfies the conditions that the conducting loop rotates in the constant magnetic field in such a way that the conductor's velocity vector is always perpendicular to the field except in the interpolar regions. The use of multiple conducting loops and commutator sections will then generate a voltage at the brushes, which is of the form shown in Figure 15.7.

Thus far we have described the basics features of a *dc machine.* As noted, the machine can be operated either as a motor or a generator. In the *motor mode* the input is electrical power and the output is mechanical power. When operated in the *generator mode,* mechanical power is the input and electrical power is the output. The following example illustrates the dual modes of a dc machine.

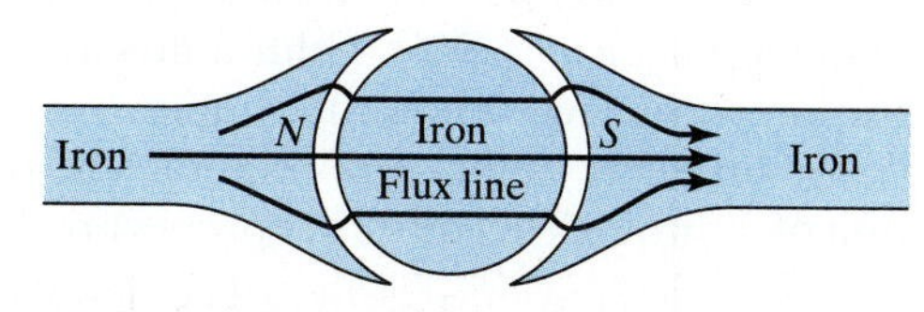

FIGURE 15.9 Illustration of the flux paths in a dc machine.

Example 15.1

The basic dc machine can be operated as either a motor or a generator

A permanent magnet field dc machine is connected as shown in Figure 15.10, and may be assumed to be 100% efficient, that is, $P_{in} = P_{out} = 40$ kW. The speed is $\omega = 100$ rad/s. We wish to find the directions and magnitude of the current and torques if the dc machine is operating in (a) the motor mode and (b) the generator mode.

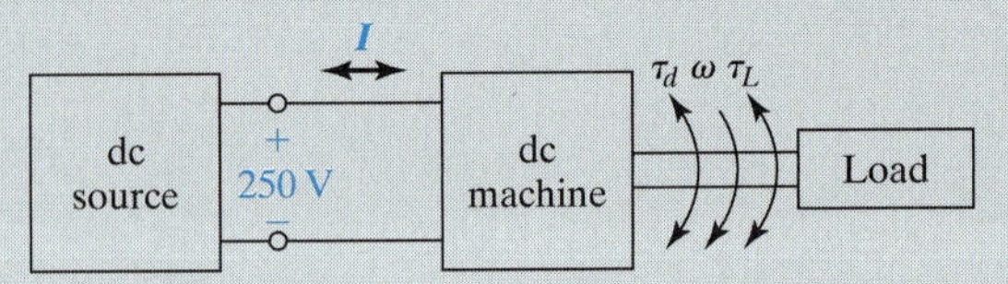

FIGURE 15.10 Schematic diagram used in Example 15.1.

(a) In the motor operating mode the current I shown in Figure 15.10 is

$$
\begin{aligned}
I &= \frac{P_{in}}{250} \\
&= 160 \text{ A}
\end{aligned}
$$

and is directed *into* the machine.

The developed torque, τ_d, is given by the fundamental relationship

$$
\begin{aligned}
\tau_d &= \frac{P_{out}}{\omega} \\
&= \frac{40000}{100} \\
&= 400 \text{ Nm}
\end{aligned}
$$

and is *in* the direction of rotation. τ_L, the load torque, is always equal and opposite to τ_d for steady-state operation.

(b) In the generator mode the current is $I = 160$ A, as calculated in part (a); however, the current is directed *out of* the machine. In addition, the torque $\tau_d = 400$ Nm is in the direction *opposite to* that of rotation.

In the more general case we can illustrate the motoring action of a dc machine via Figure 15.11. The voltage V_1 causes a current I to exist in the loops, which are embedded in the rotor. The current enters the upper brush and through commutator action, is directed into the loops under the S pole. The current goes around the loops on the rotor and out of the loops under the N pole. The dotted line in the figure illustrates the current path for a single loop. Applying the Lorentz force equation to the single loop, we find that for the portion of the single loop under the S pole, $F = (B\ell I)$ yields a downward force producing a clockwise rotation. For the portion of the loop under the N pole, $F = (B\ell I)$ yields a force in the upward direction, which also produces a clockwise rotation. The result of the force produced by all loops is the creation of a torque. This torque is proportional to the force, that is,

$$
\begin{aligned}
\tau &\propto F \\
&\propto I\ell B
\end{aligned}
$$

REFERENCE CARD: DIGITAL SYSTEMS & MACHINES

ARITHMETIC:

Base $r = \alpha$ to Base $r = \beta$ conversion

$$N = \sum_{j=-m}^{n-1} a_j r^j = a_{n-1} r^{n-1} + \cdots + a_0 r^0 + \cdots a_{-m} r^{-m}$$

series expressed in Base α, each term converted to Base β, series evaluated using arithmetic in Base β.

SOME IMPORTANT BOOLEAN ALGEBRA POSTULATES:

The unique elements 1 and 0 exist such that

(1) $A + 0 = A$
(2) $A \cdot 1 = A$

A unique element $\overline{A}$ (the complement of A) exists such that

(1) $A + \overline{A} = 1$
(2) $A \cdot \overline{A} = 0$

The commutative law is

(1) $A + B = B + A$
(2) $A \cdot B = B \cdot A$

The associative law is

(1) $A + (B + C) = (A + B) + C$
(2) $A \cdot (B \cdot C) = (A \cdot B) \cdot C$

The distributive law is

(1) $A + (B \cdot C) = (A + B) \cdot (A + C)$
(2) $A \cdot (B + C) = (A \cdot B) + (A \cdot C)$

SOME IMPORTANT BOOLEAN ALGEBRA THEOREMS:

T1	(1)	$A + A = A$	(2)	$A \cdot A = A$
T2	(1)	$1 + A = 1$	(2)	$A \cdot 0 = 0$
T3	(1)	$A + AB = A$	(2)	$A(A + B) = A$
T4	(1)	$A + \overline{A}B = A + B$	(2)	$A(\overline{A} + B) = AB$
T5	(1)	$AB + \overline{A}C + BC = AB + \overline{A}C$	(2)	$(A + B)(\overline{A} + C)(B + C) = (A + B)(\overline{A} + C)$
T6	(1)	$\overline{A + B} = \overline{A}\,\overline{B}$	(2)	$\overline{AB} = \overline{A} + \overline{B}$

A *Truth table* lists the value of the Boolean function for all values of the variables. The following electronic devices (gates) are used to construct logic functions in hardware.

Switching Devices

Operator	Symbol	Input/output relationship
AND	A_1, A_2 → $f(A_1, A_2)$	$f(A_1, A_2) = A_1 A_2$
OR	A_1, A_2 → $f(A_1, A_2)$	$f(A_1, A_2) = A_1 + A_2$
NOT	A → $f(A)$	$f(A) = \overline{A}$
NAND	A_1, A_2 → $f(A_1, A_2)$	$f(A_1, A_2) = \overline{A_1 A_2}$
NOR	A_1, A_2 → $f(A_1, A_2)$	$f(A_1, A_2) = \overline{A_1 + A_2}$

We can realize logic functions with either AND-OR-NOT or NAND or NOR.

Boolean functions can be expressed as a sum of products (SOP) or a product of sums (POS). If every variable is present in every term, the terms in SOP are called minterms and the terms in POS are called Maxterms.

K-maps are used in Boolean function minimization because terms that are logically adjacent, e.g., $AB + A\overline{B}$ are physically adjacent on the map and can be combined, i.e., $AB + A\overline{B} = A$.

SEQUENTIAL LOGIC:

Sequential circuits use *memory*. The output and next state are functions of the input and present state, i.e.,

$$z_i = f_1(x_1\ x_2 \ldots x_n, y_1, \ldots y_p) \qquad i = 1, 2, \ldots m$$
$$Y_j = f_2(x_1\ x_2 \ldots x_n, y_1, y_2 \ldots y_p) \qquad j = 1, 2, \ldots p$$

The following sequential logic diagram illustrates the contrast with combinational logic:

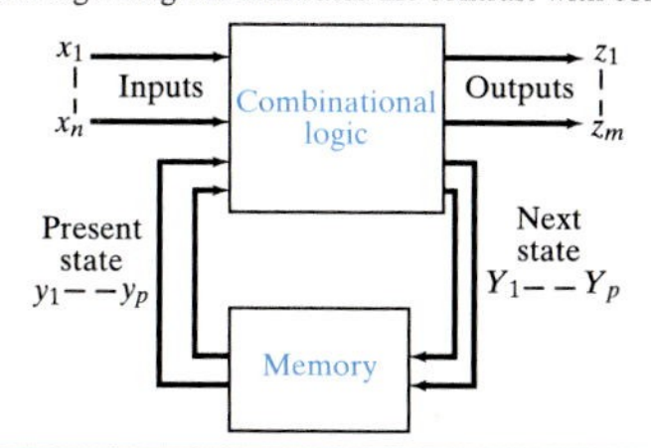

State tables and state diagrams of the form

Present state / Input: x; row y: Y/z — Present state y —x/z→ Next state Y

define the relationship among input, present state, output, and next state. A popular memory device is the J-K Flip-Flop.

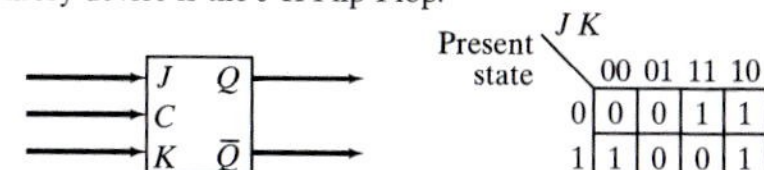

Present state \ JK	00	01	11	10
0	0	0	1	1
1	1	0	0	1

REAL LOGIC GATES:

Propagation delay describes the time delay a signal encounters in passing through a gate.

t_{PHL} = the propagation delay high-to-low,
t_{PLH} = the propagation delay low-to-high, and
t_P = the average propagation delay.

Consider the following figure:

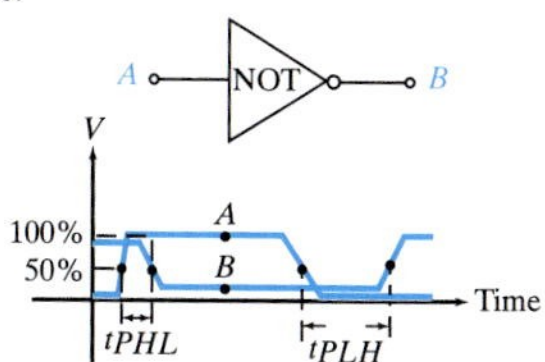

The average propagation delay, t_p, is

$$t_p = \frac{t_{PHL} + t_{PLH}}{2}$$

The *rise time* t_r and the *fall time* t_f are measures of how fast the output voltage of the gate moves between the two allowed output levels (or states).

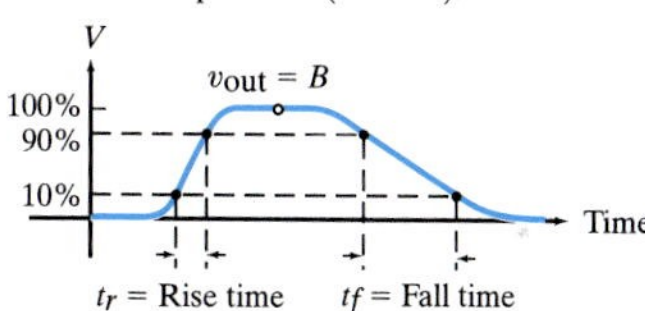

A race condition is an abnormal situation in which one signal arrives at its intended destination delayed enough relative to another signal so as to cause an error; this delay is generally a result of accumulated circuit propagation delays.

Real logic gates are designed to unambiguously recognize input voltage levels as a high or a low, specified by V_{IH} and V_{IL} respectively; they produce output levels specified by V_{OH} and V_{OL}. Noise margins are defined that indicate the magnitude of tolerance the design has for incorrectly recognizing a bit (see below).

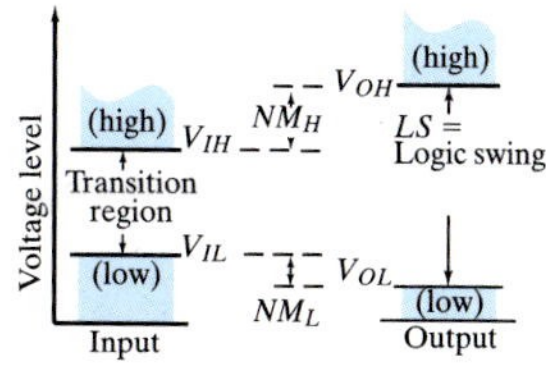

V_{IL} = the input low level = the HIGHEST voltage at the input that is always recognized by the input as a logic low.

V_{IH} = the input high level = the LOWEST voltage at the input that is always recognized by the input as a logic high.

V_{OL} = the output low level = the HIGHESTvoltage level at the output that can occur when the output is intended to be low.

V_{OH} = the output high level = the LOWEST voltage level at the output that can occur when the output is intended to be high.

The *transition width*, *TW*, is

$$TW = V_{IH} - V_{IL}$$

The high and low noise margins are:

$$NM_H = \text{the high noise margin} = V_{OH} - V_{IH}$$
$$NM_L = \text{the low noise margin} = V_{IL} - V_{OL}$$

The logic swing is the difference between the output high and low levels

$$LS = V_{OH} - V_{OL}$$

NMOS NOT GATE AND TRANSFER CURVE:

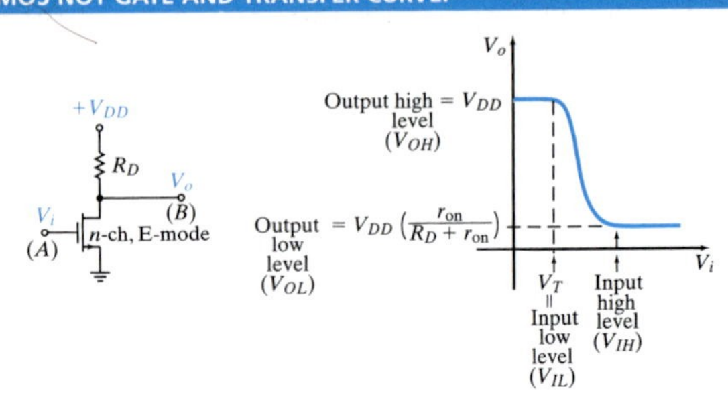

NMOS NAND GATE AND NOR GATE:

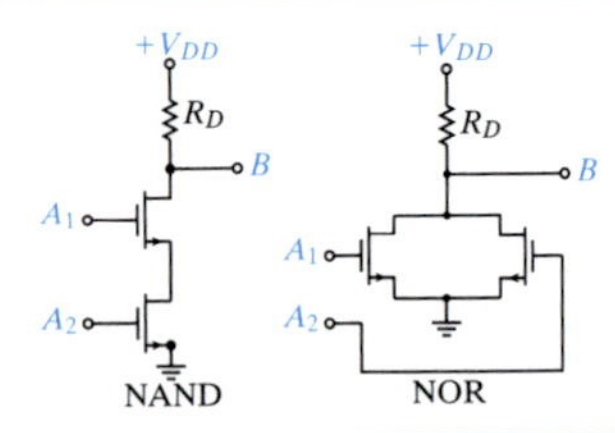

CMOS NOT GATE AND VOLTAGE TRANSFER CURVE:

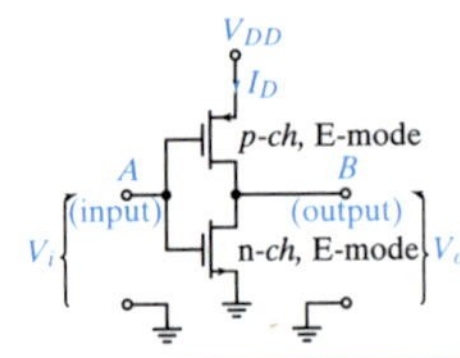

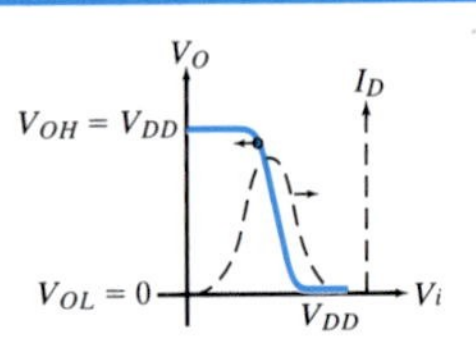

CMOS NAND GATE AND NOR GATE:

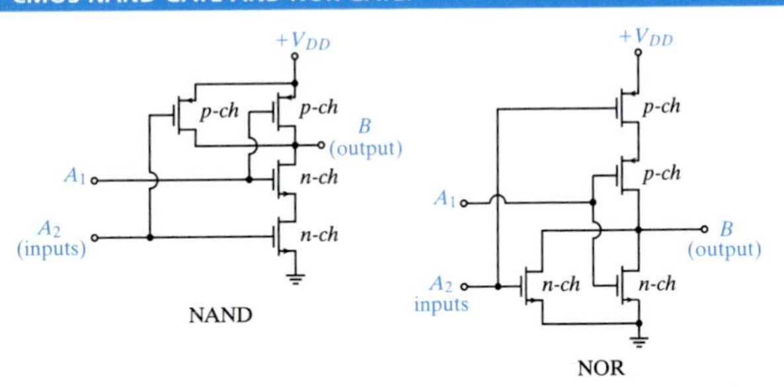

DC MACHINES:

dc machines can operate as a motor-input electrical, output mechanical or as a generator-input mechanical, output electrical. However, dc machines are primarily used as motors. The equivalent circuit and equations for a *separately excited motor* are

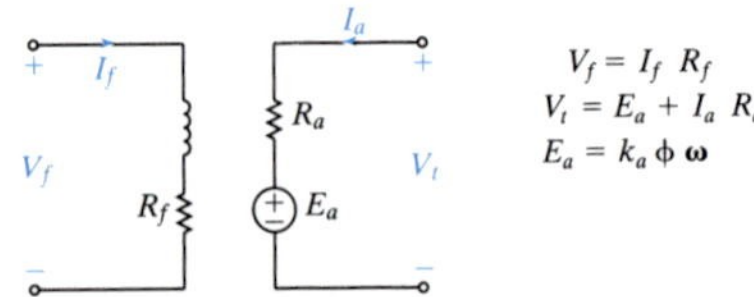

$$V_f = I_f\, R_f$$
$$V_t = E_a + I_a\, R_a$$
$$E_a = k_a\, \phi\, \omega$$

subscript f refers to field circuit, subscript a refers to armature circuit, ϕ is the flux/pole and ω is the rotational speed. The magnetization curve provides information on $k_a\,\phi$ vs. I_f.

The electromagnetic torque is $T_d = k_a\, \phi\, I_a$.

The mechanical power developed is $P_d = E_a\, I_a = T_d\, \omega$.

Self-excited dc motors are connected in shunt or series. The *shunt* connection is

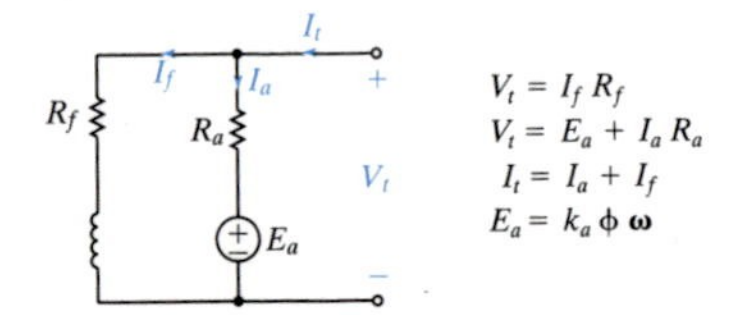

$$V_t = I_f\, R_f$$
$$V_t = E_a + I_a\, R_a$$
$$I_t = I_a + I_f$$
$$E_a = k_a\, \phi\, \omega$$

The *series* connection is

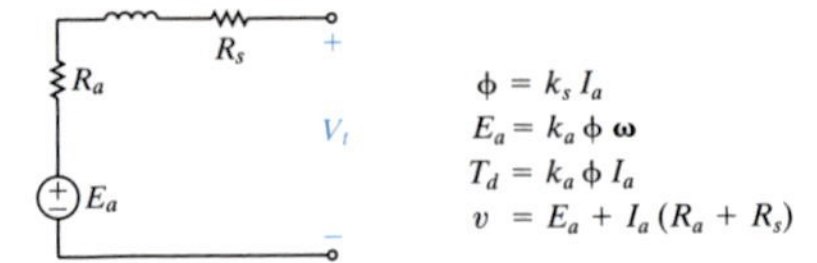

$$\phi = k_s\, I_a$$
$$E_a = k_a\, \phi\, \omega$$
$$T_d = k_a\, \phi\, I_a$$
$$v = E_a + I_a\,(R_a + R_s)$$

dc machines can also be compound-connected.

POLY PHASE MACHINES:

Induction machine per phase Y equivalent circuit

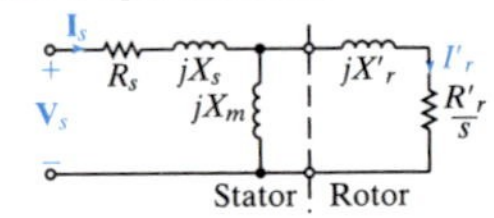

$\mathbf{V}_s$ = Line-to-neutral stator phase-*a* phasor voltage applied at the terminals, usually used as phase reference in volts.
$\mathbf{I}_s$ = Stator phase-*a* current in amperes.
R_s = Phase-*a* winding resistance of the stator in ohms.
X_s = Leakage reactance associated with the stator flux that does not link rotor windings in ohms.
X_m = Magnetizing reactance in ohms.
I'_r = Rotor phase-*a* current reflected into the stator in amperes.
X'_r = Leakage rotor reactance, reflected into the stator, associated with the rotor flux that does not link stator windings in ohms.
R'_r = Rotor resistance reflected into stator, in ohms.
s = Refers to the slip that is a measure of rotor speed. It is defined as

$$s = \frac{\omega_s - \omega_r}{\omega_s}$$

The power flow diagram for all three phases is

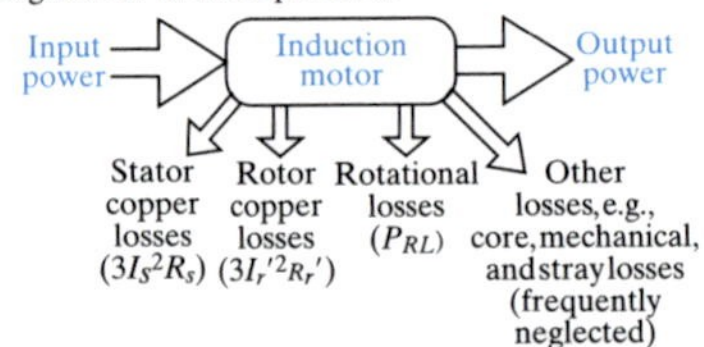

$R'_r\,(1 - s)/s$ accounts for the mechanical power developed.

The three-phase power $P_d = 3(I'_r)^2\, R'_r\left(\frac{1 - s}{s}\right)$. Torque developed $\tau_d = \frac{P_d}{\omega_r}$.

SYNCHRONOUS MACHINE:

Operation as a generator:

(a) Rotor equivalent circuit

(b) Magnetization characteristic

$\mathbf{E}_f = E_f\angle\delta$, jXd, Ra (negligible), $\mathbf{I}_s = I_s\angle\theta$, $\mathbf{V}_s = V_s\angle 0°$

(c) Stator equivalent circuit

(d) Mechanical considerations

The key equations are $\mathbf{E}_f = \mathbf{V}_S + jX_d\mathbf{I}_S$

$P_{1\phi} = V_sI_s\cos(\theta) = E_fI_s\cos(\delta - \theta)$

Power Factor = PF = $\cos(\theta)$

$X_d >> R_a$
δ = Angle of E_f relative to V_s
θ = Power factor angle
ϕ = Phase angle of I_s

Also, $P_{3\phi} = 3P_{1\phi}$, $\tau_m = \tau_d$, $P_m = P_d$ and $\omega_r = \omega_s$

Operation as a motor:

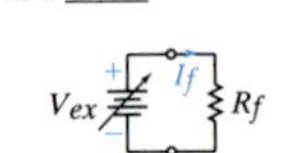

(a) Rotor equivalent circuit

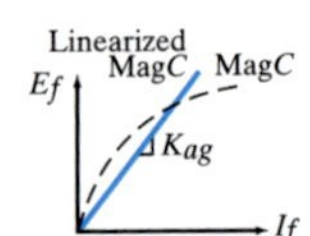

(b) Magnetization characteristic

$Ef = Ef\angle\delta$, jXd, Ra (negligible), $\mathbf{I}_s = I_s\angle\theta$, $\mathbf{V}_s = V_s\angle 0°$

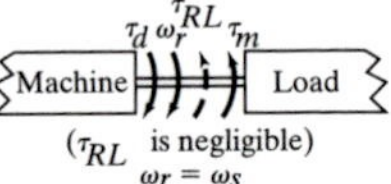

The machine equations for the motor are $\mathbf{V}_s = \mathbf{E}_f + jX_d\,\mathbf{I}_s$. Power flow into the machine is $P_{1\phi} = V_sI_s\cos(\theta) = E_fI_s\cos(\delta - \theta)$. The power factor is PF = $\cos(\theta)$. And $P_{1\phi} = (E_fV_s/X_d)\sin(\delta)$.

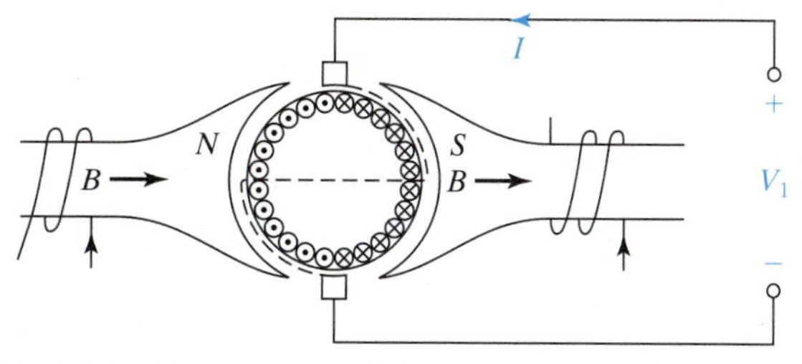

FIGURE 15.11 Illustration of the current path in a dc motor.

Thus, we find that the current produced by V_1 produces a torque that causes the rotor to rotate. The rotor speed will continue to increase until the induced voltage (i.e., $(u \times B)\,\ell$) is equal to the applied voltage V_1. This equality defines the stable operating speed of the motor.

Our previous discussion has employed a boldface notation for the variables because our description of the physical phenomena required the use of vectors. At this point in our analysis, however, we recognize that the machine is designed in such a way that all quantities are mutually perpendicular and hence the same equations hold for scalar magnitudes. Thus, we can simplify the analysis by the subsequent use of scalar notation.

15-5 Equivalent Circuits and Analysis

Direct current machines can be connected to operate as either a generator or a motor. However, solid-state rectifiers have essentially replaced the dc generator in most applications. Thus, dc machines are typically used in industrial drives requiring accurate speed control. For example, their applications include such things as, rolling mills, cranes, and electric trains. Because of their universal utility, we will concentrate our discussion primarily on the operation of the dc machine as a motor.

A dc machine has several field windings and the exciting-field circuit connections determine the type of machine. Machines may be either *separately excited* or *self-excited.* Consider the circuit representation shown in Figure 15.12 for a separately excited machine. The equations for the circuits in steady state are

The two types of dc machines

$$V_f = I_f R_f$$

$$V_t = E_a \pm I_a R_a \qquad (15.7)$$

In these equations, V_f and I_f represent the field voltage and current and R_f represents the winding resistance of the field circuit that establishes the magnetic **B** field of the machine. V_t is the terminal voltage at the commutator terminals, E_a is the generated electromotive force (also known as the back emf) and is the total voltage induced between brushes, I_a is the armature current and R_a is the armature resistance.

In the second expression in Eq. (15.7), the + sign is used for a motor and the − sign is used for a generator. In other words, the input to the motor is electric power and the output is shaft power, and the input to a generator is shaft power and the output is electric power. Since the focus of our discussion is primarily confined to the operation of the dc machine as a motor, we employ the + sign in Eq. (15.7). In addition to the above equations, from Faraday's Law we know that the generated electromotive force is given by the expression

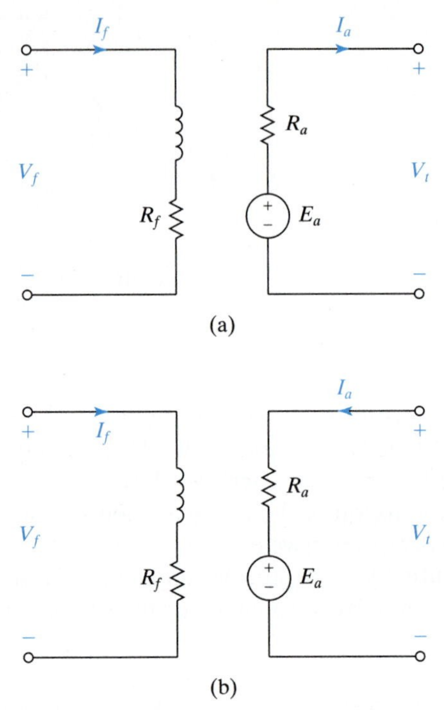

FIGURE 15.12 (a) Generator and (b) motor circuit representation.

$$E_a = K_a\phi\omega \qquad (15.8)$$

The equivalent circuits and the magnetization curve form the basis for machine analysis

Where K_a is an armature constant, ϕ is the flux per pole due to the field current and ω is the rotational speed.

Information on $K_a\phi$ versus I_f is available from the manufacturer in the form of a *magnetization curve* such as that shown in Figure 15.13. The curve is generated by running the machine at some reference rated speed (ω_0) under open-circuit armature conditions ($I_a = 0$), and measuring $V_t = E_a$ versus I_f. The relationship exhibited in the figure occurs because ϕ is proportional to the **B** field and, in turn, the **B** field is created by I_f. Therefore, E_a is "caused by" I_f.

It is desirable to operate close to the knee of the magnetization curve for maximum utilization of the iron. Note that machine weight depends on the size and density of the field poles, which determine the **B** field.

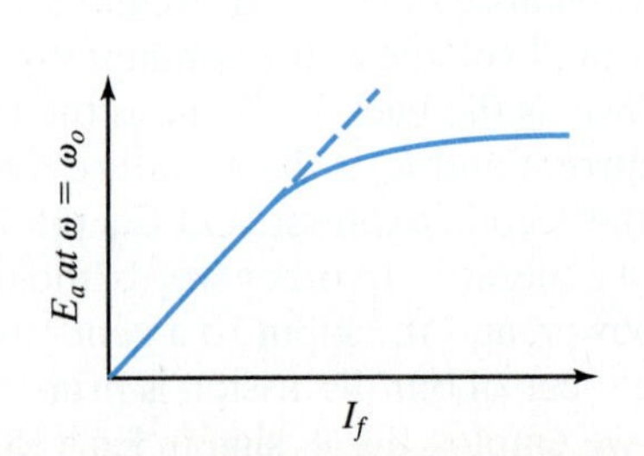

FIGURE 15.13 dc Machine magnetization curve.

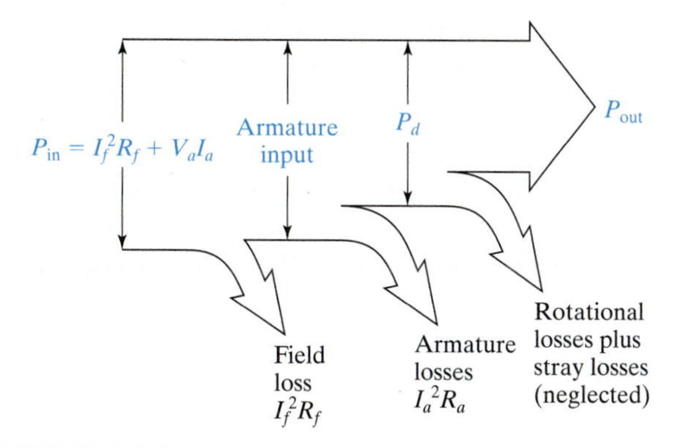

FIGURE 15.14 dc Machine power flow analysis.

The electromagnetic torque is given by the equation

$$\tau_d = K_a\phi I_a \tag{15.9}$$

And the electromagnetic/mechanical power balance can be expressed as

$$P_d = E_aI_a = \tau_d\omega \tag{15.10}$$

Where this developed power, that is, the power converted from electrical to mechanical form, is shown in Figure 15.14.

Given these general equations, let us now consider two self-excited dc motor arrangements: the *shunt* motor and the *series* motor. A dc machine is called a shunt motor when the field winding is connected in shunt, or parallel, with the armature, as shown in Figure 15.15. For this configuration, the defining equations are

Self-excited dc motors are classified by the field winding connections, that is, series or shunt

$$\begin{aligned} V_t &= I_fR_f \\ V_t &= E_a + I_aR_a \\ I_t &= I_a + I_f \end{aligned} \tag{15.11}$$

Since the electromotive force can be expressed as

$$E_a = K_a\phi\omega \tag{15.12}$$

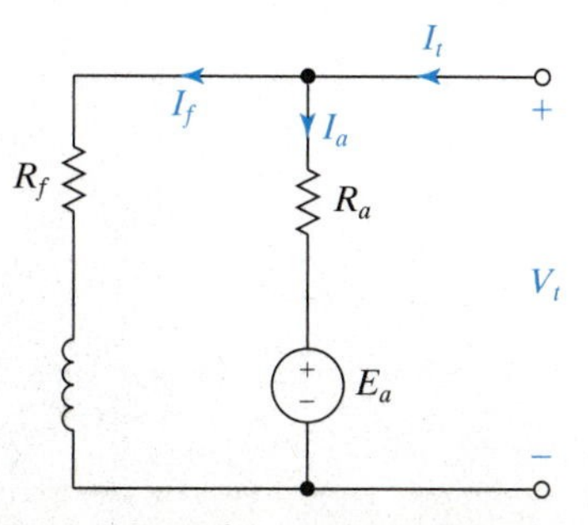

FIGURE 15.15 Shunt-connected motor.

The angular velocity can be written as

$$\omega = \frac{V_t - I_a R_a}{K_a \phi} \tag{15.13}$$

This equation indicates that the speed is inversely proportional to flux in the field. If the field flux is very small, the speed can be very high. Furthermore, it is dangerous to open-circuit the field since the speed would theoretically become infinite. This fact is well-known and machines are designed with small stabilizing winding to prevent problems of this type.

Since the armature current is related to the torque by equation (15.9), equation (15.13) can be rewritten in the form

$$\omega = \frac{V_t}{K_a \phi} - \frac{R_a \tau_d}{(K_a \phi)^2} \tag{15.14}$$

This equation describes the steady-state torque-speed characteristic for a shunt-connected motor.

The series motor configuration is shown in Figure 15.16. Since the field is in series with the armature, the armature current determines the field flux. If we assume that the motor operates in the linear region of the magnetization curve, then the relationship between the flux and the armature current is of the form

$$\phi = K_s I_a \tag{15.15}$$

Then the pertinent equations for this motor become

$$\begin{aligned} E_a &= K_a \phi \omega = K_a K_s I_a \omega \\ \tau_d &= K_a \phi I_a = K_a K_s I_a^2 \\ V_t &= E_a + I_a(R_a + R_s) = (K_a K_s \omega + R_a + R_s) I_a \end{aligned} \tag{15.16}$$

where R_s is the series field winding resistance.

In a situation similar to that exhibited by the shunt motor, we note that the speed of a series motor can be quite large if the motor is operated at no load. This is why this motor is designed with a shunt field winding, and/or is mechanically coupled to the load, to limit the no-load speed. This motor is typically used in situations where large torques at low speed are required.

Finally, another type of dc machine is the *compound-connected* machine. Its name is derived from the fact that it is a combination of the shunt and series configurations, that is, it has both series and shunt windings. Figure 15.17 illustrates the four types of compound-connect-

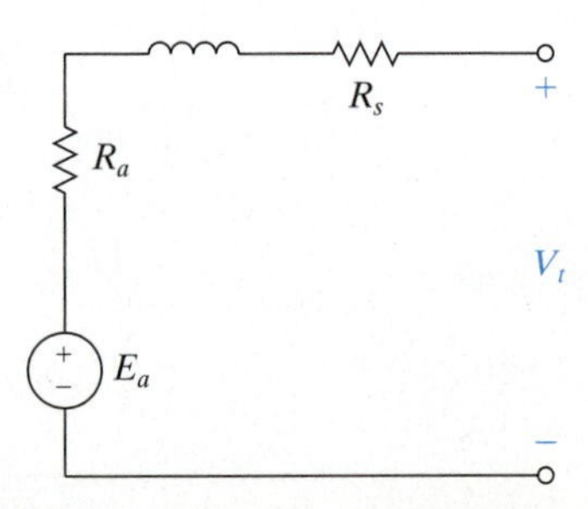

FIGURE 15.16 Series-connected motor.

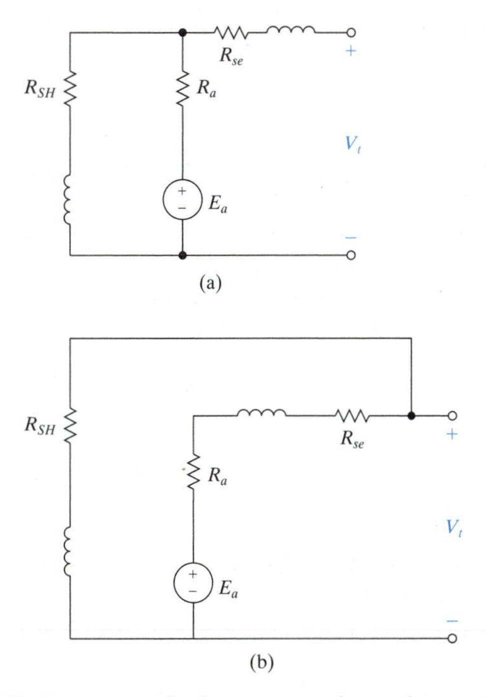

FIGURE 15.17 Compounded-connected machines (a) short-shunt, (b) long shunt.

ed machines. The machines may be either *long shunt* or *short shunt* and each of those types can be either *cumulative-compounded* or *differential-compounded.* The latter designation indicates whether the fields add or subtract, respectively. The circuit equations for these machines are straightforward and written in the same manner as those for the shunt and series machines.

Example 15.2

A dc machine with the following parameters has the schematic diagram shown in Figure 15.18(a) and the magnetization curve shown in Figure 15.18(b).

dc Machine Parameters

Ratings

Arm. voltage = 400.0 V;	Horsepower = 60.0 hp
Arm. current = 119.7 A;	No. of poles = 4
Field current = 4.27 A;	Rated speed = 1800 rpm = 188.5 rad/s
Base speed = 1200 rpm	J motor = 0.581 kg-m sq.

*****Equivalent Circuit Values*****

Ra = 0.0669 *ohms*;	*Rf* = 93.60 *ohms*

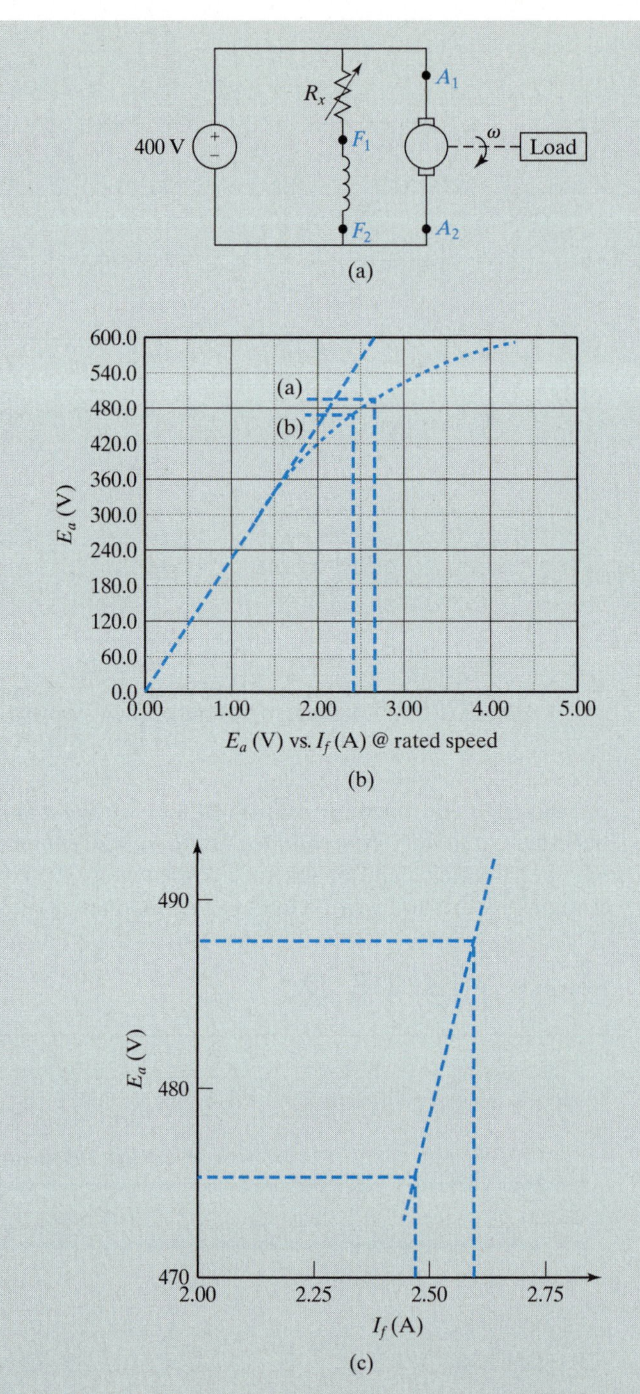

FIGURE 15.18 (a) Schematic diagram and (b) and (c) magnetization curves employed in Example 15.2.

We wish to find the field current, the armature current, the operating mode, and the developed torque and power if the shaft speed is 1500 rpm and the field rheostat (variable resistor) is set to (a) 60.4 Ω and (b) 68.4 Ω.

(a) If the field rheostat is set to 60.4 Ω, then by Ohm's Law,

$$I_f = \frac{400}{93.6 + 60.4}$$
$$= 2.597 \text{ A}$$

From the expanded version of the magnetization curve in the region of interest (Figure 15.18c), Eq. (15.8) yields

$$K_a\phi = \frac{488.2}{188.5}$$
$$= 2.590 \text{ Wb}$$

Since

$$\omega = \frac{2\pi \times 1500}{60}$$
$$= 157.1 \text{ rad/s}$$

Then

$$E_a = K_a\phi\omega$$
$$= 406.9 \text{ V}$$

Since $E_a > V_a$, current is directed *out of* the machine

And the value of the current, calculated by Ohm's law, is

$$I_a = \frac{E_a - V_t}{R_a}$$
$$= 103.5 \text{ A}$$

and the machine operates as a *generator.* Using Eq (15.9) the developed torque and power are then determined as

$$\tau_d = K_a\phi I_a$$
$$= 268.1 \text{ Nm}$$

and

$$P_d = \tau_d\,\omega$$
$$= 42.12 \text{ kW}$$

and since 746 watts = 1 hp

$$P_d = 56.46 \text{ hp}$$

(b) If the field rheostat is set to 68.4 Ω, then

$$I_f = \frac{400}{93.6 + 68.4}$$
$$= 2.469 \text{ A}$$

From the magnetization curve Figure (15.18c) we find that

$$K_a\phi = \frac{475.6}{188.5}$$
$$= 2.523 \text{ Wb}$$

And since $\omega = 157.1$ rad/s,

$$E_a = K_a \phi\omega$$
$$= 396.3 \text{ V}$$

In this case, $E_a < V_a$, and hence current is directed *into* the machine and

$$I_a = \frac{V_t - E_a}{R_a}$$
$$= 54.7 \text{ A}$$

and the machine operates as a *motor.*

The developed torque and power are

$$\tau_d = K_a \phi I_a$$
$$= 137.9 \text{ Nm}$$

and

$$P_d = \tau_d \omega$$
$$= 21.66 \text{ kW}$$
$$= 29.03 \text{ hp}$$

Example 15.3

A separately excited dc generator supplies 120 kW at 600 V. If the armature resistance is 0.2 ohms and the field current is fixed to provide a $K_a\phi = 1.3$ Wb, determine the shaft speed of the generator in rpm and the mechanical torque required to turn the generator. Assume all losses are negligible.

The generator is modeled as shown in Figure 15.19.

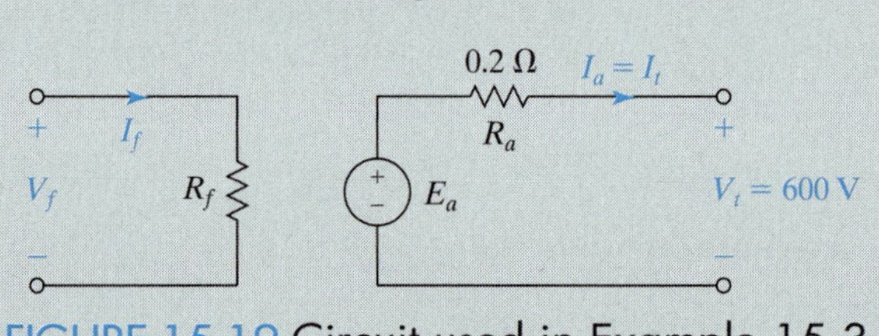

FIGURE 15.19 Circuit used in Example 15.3.

The power developed is expressed as

$$P_d = V_t I_a$$
$$120{,}000 = 600\, I_a$$
$$I_a = 200 \text{ A}$$

Then from KVL,

$$\begin{aligned} E_a &= V_t + I_a R_a \\ &= 600 + (200)(0.2) \\ &= 640 \text{ V} \end{aligned}$$

Since

$$\begin{aligned} E_a &= K_a \phi \omega \\ \omega &= \frac{640}{1.3} \\ &= 492.31 \text{ r/s} \end{aligned}$$

or

$$\begin{aligned} \omega &= (492.31)\left(\frac{60}{2\pi}\right) \\ &= 470.19 \text{ rpm} \end{aligned}$$

where the factor $\frac{60}{2\pi}$ converts radians/second to rpm. Finally,

$$\begin{aligned} \tau_d &= K_a \phi I_a \\ &= (1.3)(200) \\ &= 260 \text{ N-m} \end{aligned}$$

Example 15.4

A dc shunt motor develops 13.41 hp. Under this condition $E_a = 250$ V and the armature resistance is $R_a = 0.1\ \Omega$. We wish to determine the motor's terminal voltage.

The circuit diagram for the motor is shown in Figure 15.20. The power developed is 13.41 hp or (13.41)(746) W where the factor 746 converts horsepower to watts. The armature current can be found from the expression

$$P_d = E_a I_a$$

or

$$\begin{aligned} (13.41)(746) &= 250\ \text{I}_a \\ I_a &= 40.015 \text{ A} \end{aligned}$$

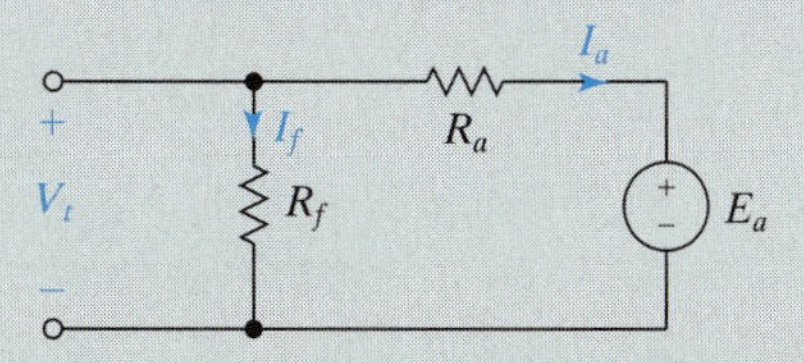

FIGURE 15.20 Circuit used in Example 15.4.

Then applying KVL to the circuit in Figure 15.20 yields

$$\begin{aligned} V_t &= I_a R_a + E_a \\ &= (40.015)(0.1) + 250 \\ &= 254 \text{ V} \end{aligned}$$

Example 15.5

A 250 V, 25 hp dc series motor operates at full load at 750 rpm. The armature resistance is 0.11 Ω and the series field resistance is 0.03 Ω. If the motor draws 80 A at full load, find (a) the back emf at full load, (b) the developed power and torque, and (c) the new speed if the load change causes the line current to drop to 60 A.

(a) The circuit diagram for the machine is shown in Figure 15.21.

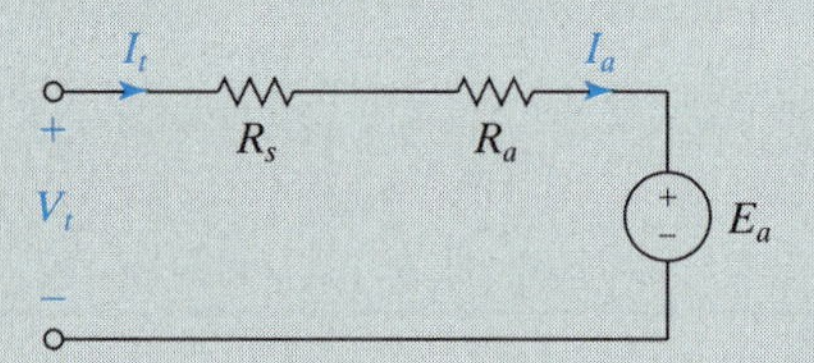

FIGURE 15.21 Circuit used in Example 15.5.

The KVL equations for the circuit are

$$\begin{aligned} E_a &= V_t - I_a(R_s + R_a) \\ &= 250 - 80\,(0.03 + 0.11) \\ &= 238.8 \text{ V} \end{aligned}$$

(b) The developed power is obtained by the expression

$$\begin{aligned} P_d &= E_a I_a \\ &= (238.8)(80) \\ &= 19.104 \text{ kW} \end{aligned}$$

Then

$$\begin{aligned} \tau_d &= \frac{P_d}{\omega} \\ &= \frac{19104}{(750)\left(\dfrac{2\pi}{60}\right)} \\ &= 243.24 \text{ N-m} \end{aligned}$$

(c) The new value of the back emf corresponding to the new line current is

$$E_{a2} = 250 - 60(0.03 + 0.11)$$
$$= 241.6 \text{ V}$$

Then since $E_a = K_a\phi\omega$, we can form the ratio

$$\frac{E_{a1}}{E_{a2}} = \frac{K_a K_s I_{a1}\omega_1}{K_a K_s I_{a2}\omega_2}$$

And thus

$$\omega_2 = \frac{E_{a2} I_{a1} W_1}{E_{a1} I_{a2}}$$
$$= \frac{(241.6)(80)(750)}{(238.8)(60)}$$
$$= 1011.73 \text{ rpm}$$

At this point let us investigate speed control under varying load conditions. In order to do this, we need a relationship between the output torque and the shaft speed. From equation

$$\tau_d = K_a\phi I_a,$$

recall that the circuit equation for the armature is

$$V_t = I_a R_a + E_a$$

Therefore, the armature current can be written as

$$I_a = (V_t - E_a)/R_a$$

and since

$$E_a = K_a\phi\omega$$

I_a can be expressed as

$$I_a = [V_t - K_a\phi\omega]/R_a$$

and then the developed torque is

$$\tau_d = \frac{V_t K_a\phi}{R_a} - \frac{(K_a\phi)^2}{R_a}\omega \tag{15.17}$$

The torque/speed curve represented by this equation is shown in Figure 15.22. Note that V_t and R_a are known constants, and $K_a\phi$ for the separately excited machine is dependent only upon the field current. Note that this torque/speed characteristic permits us to determine the changes that will occur in speed as a result of varying load conditions, that is, changes in torque.

Machine manufacturers may provide multiple windings, which can be employed to create the constant magnetic field. The different methods in which these windings are used lead to machines operating as motors or generators with different torque-speed characteristics.

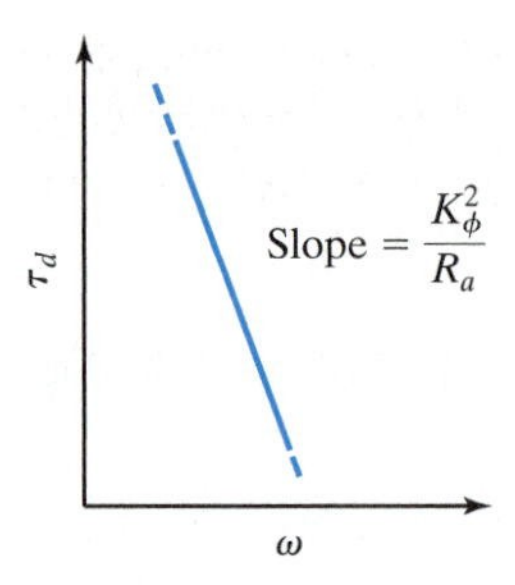

FIGURE 15.22 Torque/speed curve for the dc machine.

The steady-state performance of a dc machine can be modeled with reasonable accuracy using the simple circuits, graphs, and equations summarized earlier. Hence, at least in part, dc machine analysis reduces to dc circuit analysis. The key point to note is that the machine is an electrical–magnetic–mechanical device, and its operation can only be understood when the interaction between these EMM phenomena is properly accounted for.

In addition to the machines described above, there also exists a *brushless dc machine.* However, this device is discussed in the following chapter on ac machines, since it employs what is traditionally called a three-phase synchronous machine.

Summary

- DC machines can be operated as motors or generators. In motor operation, the input is electrical and the output is mechanical. In generator operation, the input is mechanical and the output is electrical.
- Motor operation in a dc machine is based upon the principle that a force is produced on a conductor that is carrying current when immersed in a magnetic field.
- Generator operation in a dc machine is based upon the principle that a voltage is induced in a conductor that is moving in a magnetic field.
- The dc machine consists of a stator, or stationary frame, and a rotor or armature, cylindrical in shape, that rotates within the stator. The electrical connection between stator and rotor is made by brushes on the stator that slide over the commutator that is attached to the rotor. The commutator ensures that the magnetic field of the armature currents remains stationary in space while the armature rotates.
- The exciting-field circuit determines the type of dc machine, and machines are either separately excited or self-excited.
- dc machines are modeled with equivalent circuits that are used in conjunction with the machines' magnetization curve. For example, the models for a separately excited motor and two self-excited motors (shunt and series) are shown in Figures 15.12, 15.15, and 15.16, respectively. A typical magnetization curve is shown in Figure 15.15. The current equations for the models and the magnetization curve can be used to analyze machine performance.

- dc machines may be compound-connected. This configuration uses both series and shunt windings. The machine is said to be cumulative-compounded if fields add and differentially compounded if the fields subtract.

Problems

15.1. A separately excited dc generator develops 100 N-m of torque. Find the terminal voltage V_a if $E_a = 320$ V, $R_a = 0.3\ \Omega$, and $K_a\phi = 1.5$ Wb.

15.2. A separately excited dc generator develops 90 N-m of torque and 18 kW of power. Compute the generator speed.

15.3. A separately excited dc generator develops 100 N-m of torque, 20 kW of power, and has a armature resistance of 0.25 Ω. If $K_a\phi = 1.5$ Wb, calculate the terminal voltage.

15.4. If the generator described in problem 15.2 is operated as a self-excited generator, determine the field resistance R_f if the field current $I_f = 3.0$ A.

15.5. A separately excited dc generator has the following characteristics: $\tau_d = 120$ N-m, $P_d = 24$ kW, $R_a = 0.12\ \Omega$, and $K_a\phi = 1.5$ Wb. Calculate the terminal voltage.

15.6. A separately excited dc generator has a terminal voltage at no load of 360 V with the shaft rotating at 1600 rpm. If both I_a and I_f remain unchanged, what is the new terminal voltage if the shaft speed drops to 1600 rpm?

15.7. A 300 V self-excited dc generator is used to supply power to a 300 V dc power distribution grid in an underground coal mine. Note that this application requires a constant terminal voltage of 300 V. If the torque developed by the machine is 100.4 N-m, $R_a = 1\ \Omega$, $R_f = 85\ \Omega$, and $\omega = 1800$ rpm, find the machine's terminal output power.

15.8. Find the armature current in a dc shunt motor if $E_a = 300$ V and the motor develops 4 kW of power.

15.9. If $K_a\phi = 1.1$ Wb, determine the speed of the motor in problem 15.8.

15.10. Determine the torque that is developed by the motor described in problems 15.8 and 15.9.

15.11. A dc shunt motor develops 30 N-m of torque with $K_a\phi = 1.4$ Wb. Find E_a if $V_t = 280$ V and $R_a = 0.16\ \Omega$.

15.12. Determine the speed of the motor in problem 15.11.

15.13. A dc shunt motor develops 30 hp with $V_a = 350$ V and $E_a = 340$ V. Find the value of the armature resistance R_a.

15.14. If the motor in problem 15.13 operates at 1423 rpm, find the values of $K_a\phi$ and τ_{dev}.

15.15. A dc shunt motor has the following characteristics: $I_a = 180$ A, $R_a = 0.14\ \Omega$, and $E_a = 340$ V. Find the terminal voltage of the motor.

15.16. A shunt-connected dc motor has the following characteristics: $V_t = 240$ V, $R_a = 0.22\ \Omega$, and $I_a = 40$ A. Determine the induced voltage.

15.17. Determine the armature and field currents in a dc motor if $V_t = 380$ V, $E_a = 330$ V, $R_a = 0.1\ \Omega$, and $R_f = 120\ \Omega$.

15.18. A separately excited dc shunt motor is operated at constant terminal voltage and constant developed power. Assuming the armature resistance is zero, if the field current (and therefore $K_a\phi$) is decreased, will the speed of the machine increase or decrease, and why?

15.19. Given the motor and operating conditions described in problem 15.18, will the armature current increase, decrease, or remain the same, and why?

15.20. Find the terminal current I_a in a dc shunt motor if $V_a = 250$ V, $R_f = 100\ \Omega$, $R_a = 0.1\ \Omega$ $K_a\phi = 1.25$ Wb, and the shaft speed is 1800 rpm.

15.21. A dc shunt motor has the following characteristics: $V_a = 400$ V, $R_f = 110\ \Omega$, and $R_a = 0.3\ \Omega$. The magnetization curve for the machine running at a speed of $\omega = 3476$ rpm is shown in Figure P15.21. Find the machine's armature current and developed shaft torque at $\omega = 3476$ rpm.

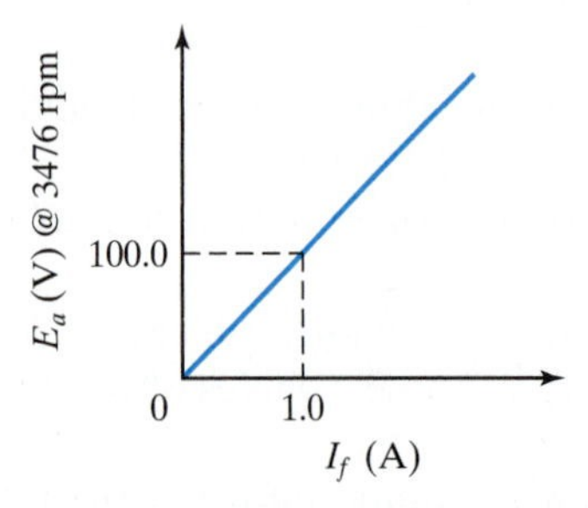

FIGURE P15.21

15.22. Determine the input power that must be supplied to the machine in problem 15.21.

15.23. If shaft rotational losses are neglected, determine the efficiency of the dc motor described in problem 15.21.

15.24. A dc shunt motor has the following characteristics: $V_a = 250$ V, $R_a = 0.2\ \Omega$, $R_f = 100\ \Omega$, and $\omega = 1800$ rpm. Use the magnetization curve in Figure P15.24 to find the torque developed by the machine.

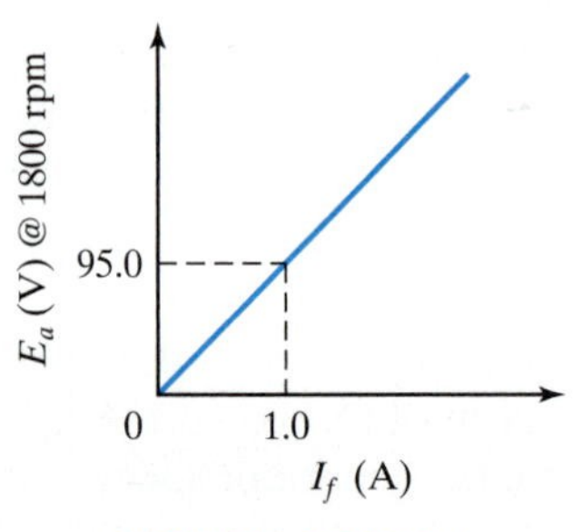

FIGURE P15.24

15.25. Given all the data for the machine in problem 15.24, derive a torque-speed curve for this motor and use it to find the developed torque if the shaft speed drops to 1200 rpm.

15.26. A shunt dc motor has the following characteristics: $V_t = 640$ V, $R_a = 0.6\ \Omega$, $R_f = 120\ \Omega$, and $K_a\phi = 0.46\ I_f$. If the motor is used to drive the wheels of a subway train, find the torque available for starting if a 20 Ω resistor is connected in series with the armature.

15.27. A dc series motor operates at full load at a speed of 640 rpm with a terminal voltage of 280 V. $E_a = 236.4V$ at a I_t of 36 A. If $R_s = 0.24\ \Omega$, find R_a. In addition, if $I_t = 1.2$ A at no load, find the no-load speed.

15.28. A 480 V, 120 hp dc series motor has an armature plus field resistance of 0.12 Ω and operates at 600 rpm. If the full-load current is 180 A, determine E_a, P_d, and τ_d at full load.

15.29. A 20 hp, 230 V dc series motor draws 64 A when the speed is 56 r/s. If $R_a = 0.12\ \Omega$ and $R_s = 0.06\ \Omega$, determine the speed when the line current is 84 A.

15.30. A 230 V dc series motor draws a line current of 60 A when running at a rated speed of 600 rpm. $R_a = 0.12\ \Omega$ and $R_s = 0.08\ \Omega$. Determine the speed of the motor when the line current drops to 30 A and the no-load speed of the machine for a line current of 3.2 A.

.16

16–1 Introduction

In this chapter we examine the two most important types of ac polyphase machines: induction and synchronous. In each case we examine the basic characteristics, present the equivalent circuits for the machines, and discuss the operational modes through a number of examples.

16.2 The Revolving Magnetic Field

Consider a stator structure on which are mounted two identical N-turn sinusoidally distributed windings (a-a' and b-b'), as illustrated in Figure 16.1(a). Suppose we supply two balanced currents to the windings, so that

$$i_a = I_m \cos(\omega t)$$
$$i_b = I_m \sin(\omega t) \tag{16.1}$$

and

$$\omega = 2\pi f$$

which is the stator radian frequency, in rad/s. These currents are plotted in Figure 16.1(b). Note the spatial angle θ, measured positive CCW, referenced from the winding a-a' magnetic axis, which is coincident with the positive x axis. The mmf's produced by these windings are

$$\mathscr{F}_a(\theta,t) = Ni_a \cos(\theta) = NI_m \cos(\omega t)\cos(\theta)$$
$$\mathscr{F}_b(\theta,t) = Ni_b \sin(\theta) = NI_m \sin(\omega t)\sin(\theta) \tag{16.2}$$

Hence, the total mmf, $\mathscr{F}(\theta,t)$, inside the stator is

$$\begin{aligned}\mathscr{F}(\theta,t) &= \mathscr{F}_a(\theta,t) + \mathscr{F}_b(\theta,t)\\ &= NI_m[\cos(\omega t)\cos(\theta) + \sin(\omega t)\sin(\theta)]\\ &= NI_m \cos(\omega t - \theta)\end{aligned} \tag{16.3}$$

This mmf varies sinusoidally in space and time and may be visualized as follows. Suppose we draw an arrow in the direction of maximum field intensity with magnetic flux lines flowing in the direction of the arrow. From Eq. (16.3), this orients the arrow such that

$$\omega t - \theta = 0$$

or equivalently

$$\theta = \omega t$$

Figure 16.1(c) shows the spatial orientation of the mmf at four different ωt values $(0, \pi/2, \pi, 3\pi/2)$. The overall effect is that $\mathscr{F}(\theta, t)$ appears to be revolving, or spatially rotating, at angular velocity ω, which is also the radian frequency of the currents. This angular velocity is called the *synchronous speed* and is given the symbol ω_s.

AC Polyphase Machines

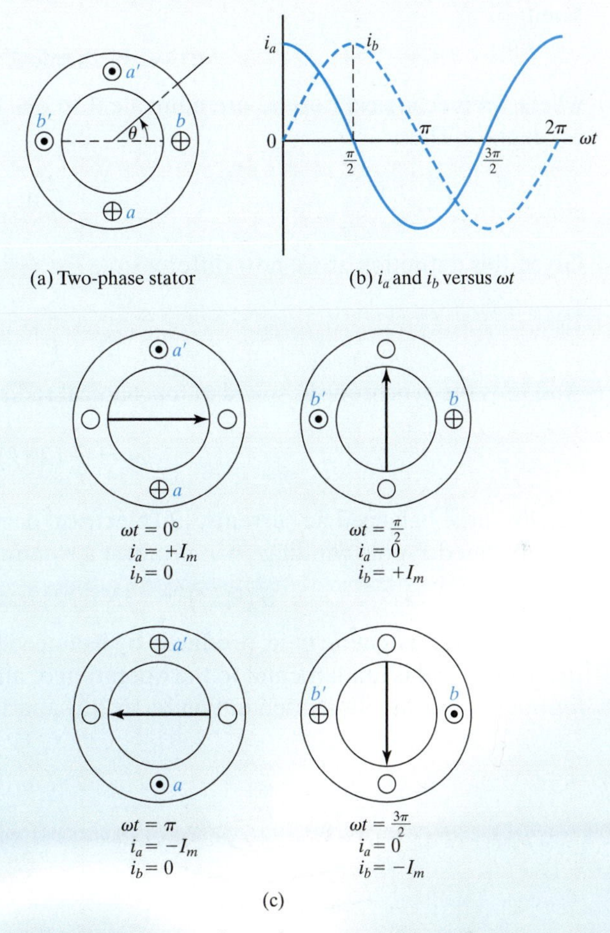

FIGURE 16.1 Figures used to describe a revolving magnetic field.

The operation of ac polyphase machines is based upon the existence of a rotating magnetic field

We have investigated the mmf $\mathcal{F}(\theta, t)$ produced by two balanced ac currents, 90° apart in *phase,* in two sinusoidally distributed windings, positioned 90° apart in *space.* In general, "n" balanced ac currents, $360°/n$ apart in phase, which exist in n sinusoidally distributed windings, positioned $360°/n$ apart in space, will also produce a rotating mmf $\mathcal{F}(\theta,t)$, for all integers $n \geq 3$. For this more general case,

$$\mathcal{F}(\theta,t) = (nNI_m/2)\cos(\omega t - \theta) \qquad (16.4)$$

In machine terminology, these "windings" are also called "phases" and collectively the "n-windings" configuration, the "n-phase" case. Commonly $n = 3$, producing a "three-phase" stator winding configuration, and we shall limit our discussion to this case. Also, the foregoing discussion is relevant to a so-called "two-pole" field geometry. The winding locations may be modified to form, in general, a "P-pole" field, where P is any even integer. To deal with the P-pole situation, it is convenient to define two different units of angular measure. We define:

$$\theta_e = \text{electrical angle} \tag{16.5}$$

where electrical radian is equal to one electrical cycle/2π and electrical degree is equal to one electrical cycle/360.
Then

$$\theta_m = \text{mechanical angle} \tag{16.6}$$

where 2π mechanical radians are equivalent to one mechanical revolution or 360 mechanical degrees. Thus,

$$\theta_m = \frac{2}{P}\theta_e \tag{16.7}$$

Given this definition, if we now differentiate Eq. (16.7), we obtain

$$\omega_m = \frac{2}{P}\omega_e \tag{16.8}$$

And thus the synchronous speed in mechanical rad/s is

$$\omega_s = \frac{2}{P}(2\pi f) \tag{16.9}$$

Finally, three balanced ac currents, 120 electrical degrees apart in phase, in three sinusoidally distributed P-pole windings, will produce a rotating mmf $\mathcal{F}(\theta_m, t)$ of the form

$$\mathcal{F}(\theta_m, t) = (3NI_m/2)\cos(\omega_s t - \theta_m) \tag{16.10}$$

This revolving magnetic field, produced by balanced three-phase stator currents, is called the *stator field,* and is fundamental to the operation of all ac three-phase machines. The two- and four-pole cases are illustrated in Figure 16.2(a) and 16.2(b), respectively.

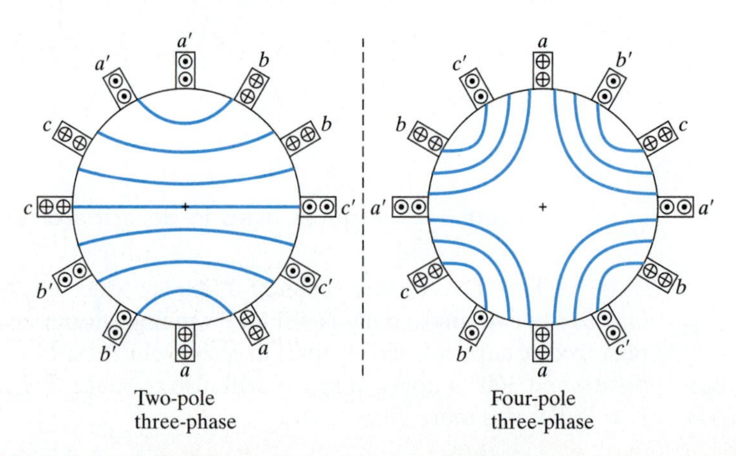

FIGURE 16.2 Field patterns in ac polyphase machine stators.

Drill Exercise

D16.1. Consider the two-phase stator shown in Figure 16.1. Note that the direction of field rotation is counterclockwise (ccw). Determine the direction of field rotation if (a) $i_a = +I_m \cos\omega t$ and $i_b = -I_m \sin\omega t$, (b) $i_a = -I_m \cos\omega t$ and $i_b = +I_m \sin\omega t$, (c) $i_a = -I_m \cos\omega t$ and $i_b = -I_m \sin\omega t$, and (d) $i_a = +I_m \cos\omega t$ and $i_b = +I_m \sin\omega t$.

Ans: (a) cw, (b) cw, (c) ccw, and (d) ccw.

16–3 The Polyphase Induction Machine: Balanced Operation

16.3.1 Basic Principles of Operation

The induction motor is an important example of a polyphase machine

We shall next discuss the first of the two basic types of ac machines, namely the *three-phase induction machine* operating at constant speed under balanced three-phase conditions. The stator is designed as discussed in previous sections, and produces a sinusoidally distributed P-pole revolving field, revolving at speed ω_s. To simplify things, all further diagrams and discussion will be restricted to the two-pole case; however, the mathematics will be valid for the P-pole case unless specifically stated otherwise.

Consider a cylindrical rotor structure on which are mounted three sinusoidally distributed windings (A-A', B-B', C-C'), separated 120° (electrical) apart, which for the moment we shall consider to be open-circuited. We further consider this *wound rotor* to be rotating at speed ω_r, which we shall assume is less than ω_s. The situation is illustrated in Figure 16.3(a).

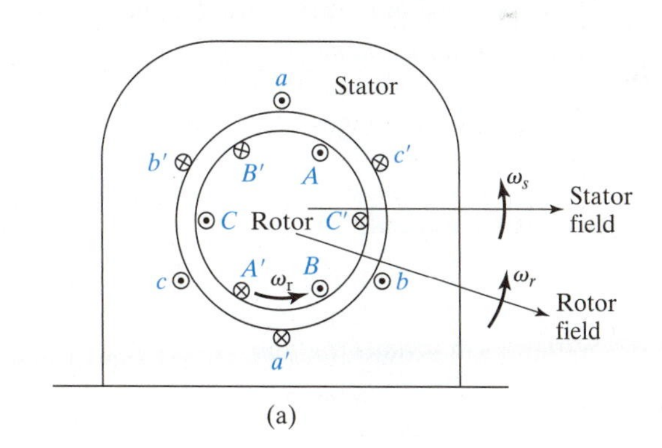

(a)

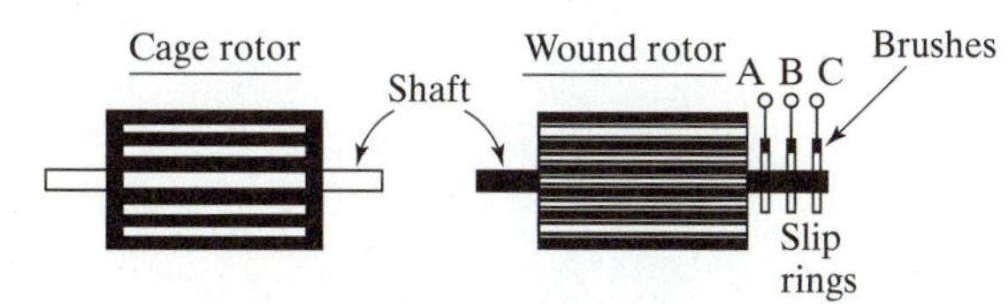

Both behave as "P" pole 3-phase wye connected ac windings.

(b)

FIGURE 16.3 Induction machine details.

From the rotor's perspective, the *stator field* sweeps over the rotor surface at a speed of $(\omega_s - \omega_r)$. If we define $s = slip$ as follows:

$$s = slip = \frac{\omega_s - \omega_r}{\omega_s} \tag{16.11a}$$

then the stator field rotates at speed $s\omega_s$ (in **mechanical** rad/s) relative to the rotor.

The stator Eq (16.11a) indicates that the rotor speed in mechanical radian per second is

$$\omega_r = \omega_s (1 - \text{s}) \tag{16.11b}$$

This field will induce balanced three-phase voltages in the rotor windings at radian frequency $s\omega_s$ (in **electrical** rad/s); likewise, the rotor cyclic frequency in Hz is $f_r = sf$, where f = stator frequency, in Hz.

Torque production results from the interaction of the rotor and stator fields

If we now connect the rotor windings in a balanced three-phase passive termination, a balanced pattern of ac three-phase currents will flow in the rotor with frequency f_r. Therefore, the rotor currents will produce a second sinusoidally distributed *P*-pole revolving field, revolving at speed $s\omega_s = (\omega_s - \omega_r)$. This *rotor field* rotates at $(\omega_s - \omega_r) + \omega_r = \omega_s$, and thus turns synchronously with the stator field. It is the interaction of these two synchronized fields that is the mechanism of torque production, and thus power conversion, in the polyphase induction machine.

The above discussion is valid for all conceivable balanced rotor terminations, including a short circuit. In fact, a short circuit is the best possible termination for many operating conditions, since it maximizes the rotor current, and hence the rotor field and torque. Since the number of rotor winding turns is irrelevant, consider a one-turn case. A short circuit would, in effect, short out each rotor conductor. For this case, we don't need a rotor winding at all, simply provision for appropriate conducting paths on the rotor structure. Such a rotor design is called a *squirrel cage* or *cage rotor,* because of the conductor arrangement resemblance to the exercise cage used for pet gerbils, hamsters, or other small rodents. The two rotor designs are illustrated in Figure 16.3(b).

16.3.2 The Equivalent Circuit

Balanced constant speed operation of the induction machine may be modeled by the ac per-phase wye equivalent circuit shown in Figure 16.4. The parameters shown on the circuit are defined as follows:

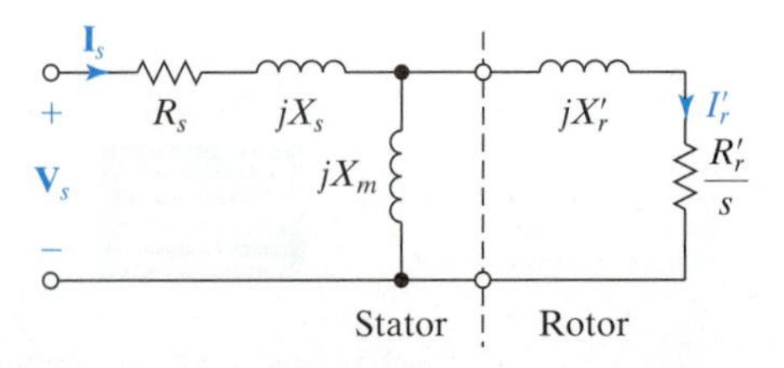

FIGURE 16.4 Per-phase wye equivalent circuit for an induction machine.

$\mathbf{V}_s$ = Line-to-neutral stator phase-*a* phasor voltage applied at the terminals, usually used as phase reference in volts.

$\mathbf{I}_s$ = Stator phase-*a* current in amperes.

R_s = Phase-*a* winding resistance of the stator in ohms.

X_s = Leakage reactance associated with the stator flux that does not link rotor windings in ohms.

X_m = Magnetizing reactance in ohms.

I_r' = Rotor phase-*a* current reflected into the stator in amperes.

X_r' = Leakage rotor reactance, reflected into the stator, associated with the rotor flux that does not link stator windings in ohms.

R_r' = Rotor resistance reflected into stator, in ohms.

s = Refers to the slip, which is a measure of rotor speed. It is defined as

$$s = \frac{\omega_s - \omega_r}{\omega_s}$$

It is important to note that the rotor components are reflected to the stator circuit in the same manner in which the secondary circuit of a transformer is reflected to the primary, and are indicated by primes.

The power flow diagram for an induction motor is shown in Figure 16.5(a). The per-phase circuit diagram can be redrawn as shown in Figure 16.5(b) in order to account for

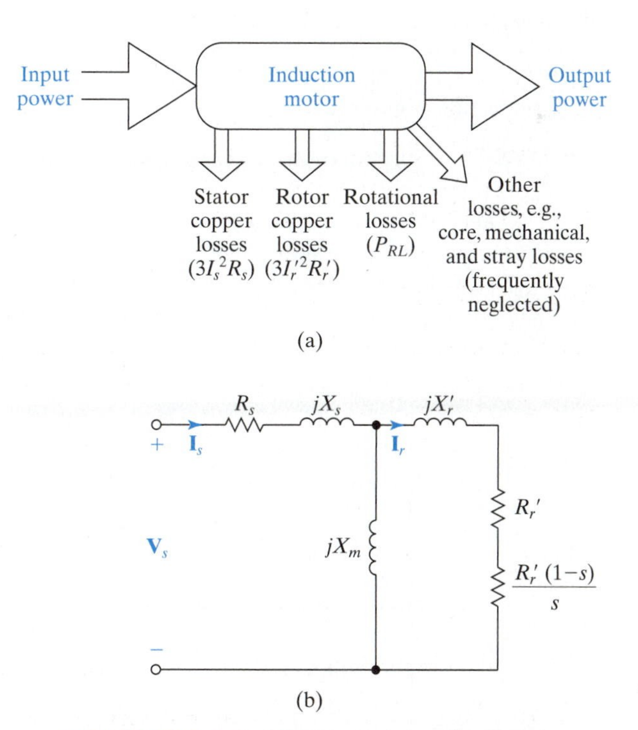

FIGURE 16.5 Induction motor diagrams.

some of these terms. In this new circuit, R_s represents the element that accounts for the stator copper losses, R_r the rotor copper losses, and $R'_r\,(1 - s)/s$ accounts for the mechanical power developed. Other losses noted in Figure 16.5(a) will be neglected in our calculations.

Since the circuit in Figure 16.5(b) is a per-phase equivalent circuit, and the induction motor is a 3ϕ machine, the 3ϕ power developed is

$$P_d = 3(I'_r)^2 R'_r \frac{(1 - s)}{s} \tag{16.12}$$

where $I'_r = |\mathbf{I}'_r|$. The torque developed is

$$\tau_d = \frac{P_d}{\omega_r} \tag{16.13}$$

which after some algebraic manipulation can be expressed as

$$\tau_d = \frac{3(I'_r)^2(R'_r/s)}{\omega_s} \tag{16.14}$$

Given the equivalent circuit and the equations that have been developed, many induction motor problems may be reduced to circuit problems.

Example 16.1

An induction motor is to be used to drive a conveyer belt by turning the main drive roller at an angular velocity of 120 rad/s. We wish to determine (a) the maximum number of pole pairs that the motor can possess, and (b) the slip at which the motor is running when operating under the conditions in (a).

Table 16.1, calculated from Eq. (16.9), indicates the relationship between the number of poles and the speed of the stator magnetic field where 377 rad/s corresponds to the standard power frequency of 60 Hz. The table indicates that the machine should have six poles. Note that eight poles would result in a speed that is too slow. Since $\omega_s = 125.67$ rad/s and $\omega_r = 120$ rad/s, the slip is

$$s = \frac{125.67 - 120}{125.67} = 0.0451$$

TABLE 16.1

# of Poles	ω_s
4	377/2 = 188.5 mechanical rad/s
6	377/3 = 125.67 mechanical rad/s
8	377/4 = 94.25 mechanical rad/s

Example 16.2

Consider the three-phase wound rotor induction machine described by Table 16.2.

TABLE 16.2 Three-Phase Induction Motor Data

Ratings	
Line Voltage = 460 Volts;	Horsepower = 75 hp
Stator Frequency = 60 Hz	No. of Poles = 4
Rotor Type: Wound	Synchronous Speed = 1800.0 rpm
Equivalent Circuit Values (in stator ohms)	
$R_s = 0.0564$;	$X_s = 0.2539$; $X_m = 9.875$
$R'_r = 0.0564$;	$X'_r = 0.2539$
Rotational Loss Torque = $\tau_{RL} = 0.03149\,\omega_r$ N-m	

For a shorted rotor termination, and a slip of 0.015, compute; rotor speed in rpm and rad/s; rotor frequency; currents (I_s, I'_r); developed, rotational, and output torques; stator copper, rotor copper, and rotational losses; input and output powers; power factor, and efficiency.

The synchronous speed in mechanical rad/s is

$$\begin{aligned}\omega_s &= 2\pi(60)/2\\ &= 188.5 \text{ rad/s}\\ &= 1800 \text{ rpm}\end{aligned}$$

The rotor speed in mechanical rad/s is

$$\begin{aligned}\omega_r &= (1 - \text{s})1800\\ &= (0.985)188.5\\ &= 185.7 \text{ rad/s}\\ &= 1773.0 \text{ rpm}\end{aligned}$$

The a-phase equivalent circuit is shown in Figure 16.6. The mesh currents for the circuit are

$$\begin{aligned}\mathbf{V}_s &= (0.056 + j10.129)\mathbf{I}_s + (0.000 - j9.875)\mathbf{I}'_r\\ 0 &= (0.000 - j9.875)\mathbf{I}_s + (3.762 + j10.129)\mathbf{I}_r'\end{aligned}$$

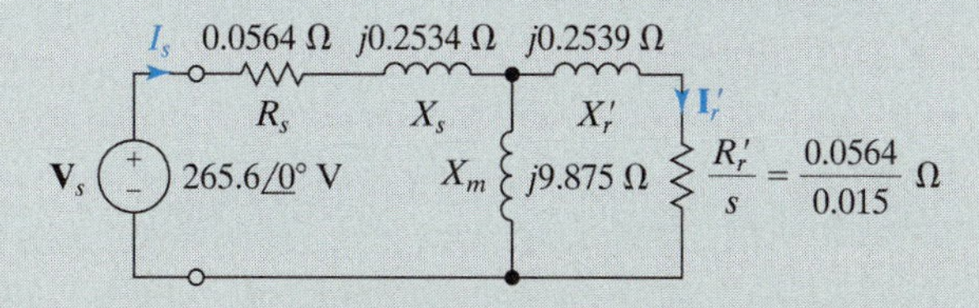

FIGURE 16.6 Circuit for the machine in Example 16.2.

Solving these equations yields

$$\mathbf{I}_s = 73.62\underline{/-27.55^\circ}\text{A}$$
$$\mathbf{I}'_r = 67.28\underline{/-7.17^\circ}\text{A}$$

The developed torque is

$$\begin{aligned}\tau_d &= 3(I'_r)^2(R'_r/s)/\omega_s \\ &= \frac{3(67.28)^2(0.0564/0.015)}{188.5} \\ &= 271.0\text{ N-m}\end{aligned}$$

The rotational loss torque is

$$\begin{aligned}\tau_{RL} &= 0.03149(185.7) \\ &= 5.85\text{ N-m}\end{aligned}$$

And the load torque is

$$\begin{aligned}\tau_{load} &= \tau_d - \tau_{RL} \\ &= 271.0 - 5.8 \\ &= 265.2\text{ N-m}\end{aligned}$$

The input power to the machine is

$$\begin{aligned}P_{in} &= 3V_sI_s\cos\theta \\ &= 3(265.6)(73.62)\cos(-27.55^\circ) \\ &= 52.00\text{ kW}\end{aligned}$$

The stator copper loss (SCL) is

$$\begin{aligned}SCL &= 3I_S^2R_S \\ &= 0.917\text{ kW}\end{aligned}$$

The rotor copper loss (RCL) is

$$\begin{aligned}RCL &= 3(I'_r)^2R'_r \\ &= 0.766\text{ kW}\end{aligned}$$

The power developed by the machine is

$$\begin{aligned}P_d &= P_{in} - SCL - RCL \\ &= 50.32\text{ kW}\end{aligned}$$

And the rotational losses are

$$\begin{aligned}P_{RL} &= \tau_{RL}\omega_r \\ &= 5.85(185.7) \\ &= 1.086\text{ kW}\end{aligned}$$

The total losses are then

$$\begin{aligned}Total\ loss &= SCL + RCL + P_{RL} \\ &= 2.769\text{ kW}\end{aligned}$$

And hence the output power is

$$P_{out} = P_{in} - Total\ Loss$$
$$= 49.24 \text{ kW}$$
$$= 66.00 \text{ hp}$$

The machine's power factor is

$$Power\ factor = \cos(-27.55^\circ)$$
$$= 0.8866\ lagging$$

And hence the efficiency is

$$Efficiency = P_{out}/P_{in}$$
$$= 94.67\%$$

Drill Exercise

D16.2. A three-phase, four-pole, 60Hz cage rotor induction motor runs at 1746 rpm, drawing a rotor current $I_r' = 100$ A. The rotational loss of the machine is 4 kW. Find the developed power, rotor copper losses, and output power if $R_r' = 0.09\ \Omega$.

Ans: $P_d = 87.3$ kW, $RCL = 2.7$ kW, and $P_{out} = 83.3$ kW.

16–4 The Polyphase Synchronous Machine: Balanced Operation

16.4.1 Basic Principles of Operation

The second major type of ac machine is the *three-phase synchronous machine.* Note that the stator structure is essentially identical to the three-phase induction machine, that is, a cylindrical ferromagnetic structure inside which are mounted balanced three-phase P-pole windings as discussed in section 16.2. Like the induction device, the fundamental purpose of the stator is to produce a revolving P-pole magnetic field, revolving at speed ω_s. Recall that

$$\omega_s = \frac{2\pi f}{P/2}\ mechanical\ rad/s$$

Synchronous machines are important examples of polyphase machines

Like the three-phase induction machine, the synchronous machine can operate in both the generator and motor modes and has important applications when used both ways.

The difference between synchronous and induction machines is in the design of the rotor. There are two types: *salient* and *nonsalient,* as illustrated in Figure 16.7. The number of stator and rotor poles must always be the same, that is, a P-pole stator always requires a

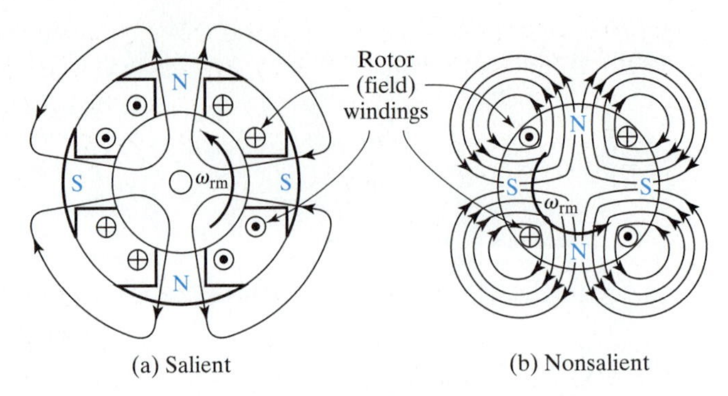

FIGURE 16.7 Two four-pole synchronous machine rotor types.

P-pole rotor for proper operation. Another basic difference is that the synchronous machine rotor is always synchronized with the stator field in the steady state. That is,

$$\omega_r = \omega_s$$

And hence

$$s = 0$$

Because there is no relative motion between the rotor and stator field, there are no induced rotor voltages and currents, and hence the rotor field cannot be produced by induction processes. The rotor field is produced by dc currents in windings provided for that purpose, called the "field" windings, as shown in Figure 16.7.

The mechanism of torque production is illustrated in Figure 16.8. In Figure 16.8(a), note that the stator field south pole ("SS") would attract the rotor north pole ("RN"), producing a torque in the direction of rotor rotation. In a similar manner, "SN" attracts "RS." We observed earlier that developed electromagnetic torque on the rotor in the direction of motion was a

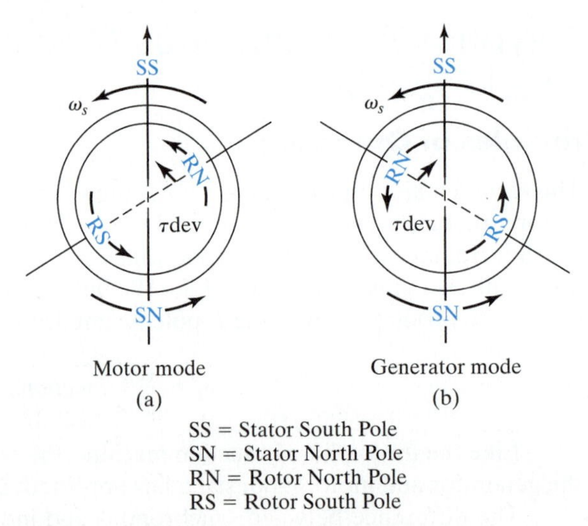

FIGURE 16.8 Basic synchronous machine operation.

The relative angular position of the rotor and stator fields determines the machine operation, that is, motor or generator

positive indication of *motor* operation. Now consider the situation in Figure 16.8(b). Again, the stator field south pole ("SS") would attract the rotor north pole ("RN"), and likewise, "SN" attracts "RS." However, this time the torque on the rotor **opposes** rotation, a sure sign of *generator* operation. Thus, it appears that the relative angular **position** of the stator and rotor fields determines the machine operating mode. Remember that both fields rotate at the same speed $\omega_r = \omega_s$.

16-4.2 The Nonsalient Synchronous Machine Equivalent Circuit

Balanced three-phase ac constant speed nonsalient synchronous machine operation can be predicted with reasonable accuracy using the equivalent circuits shown in Figure 16.9. Consider the rotor field circuit illustrated in Figure 16.9(a). The adjustable dc source, called the *exciter,* provides the dc field current I_f needed to create the rotor field. The rotor field circuit may be modeled electrically by its resistance R_f. The ac stator voltage E_f is created by the rotor field sweeping over the stator conductors at $\omega_r = \omega_s$, which also determines the frequency of E_f. Since E_f is directly proportional to the rotor field, E_f is functionally related to I_f. This function is called the *magnetization characteristic* of the machine, and is shown in Figure 16.9(b). It will be sufficiently accurate for our purposes to use a linearized approximation to the magnetization characteristic in our calculations. The key equations are

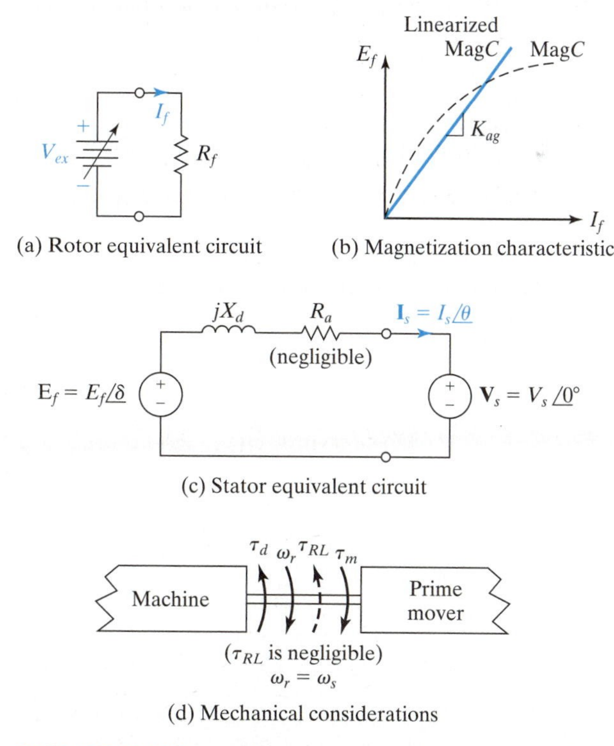

FIGURE 16.9 Synchronous machine equivalent circuits generator convention.

$$I_f = V_{ex}/R_f$$

$$E_f = K_{ag}I_f$$

where K_{ag} is the slope of the magnetization characteristic. The per-phase stator ac wye-equivalent circuit is shown in Figure 16.9(c). The source E_f models rotor field effects. The reactance X_d accounts for two basic phenomena: "armature reaction," that is, the voltages induced into the stator windings caused by the rotating stator magnetic field, which is produced by the balanced three-phase stator currents, and the "leakage field," that is, that portion of the stator field that does not cross the air gap. The circuit also has resistance R_a, which we shall neglect since $X_d >> R_a$. We shall limit our study to the case where the machine is always connected to a large external balanced three-phase ac system, modeled with an ideal voltage source $\mathbf{V}_s$, which shall always be our phase reference; that is, $\mathbf{V}_s = |\mathbf{V}_s|\angle 0°$. The stator current $\mathbf{I}_s$ represents the a-phase line current. The angle δ is the phase angle of $\mathbf{E}_f$ relative to $\mathbf{V}_s$; the angle θ is the phase angle of $\mathbf{I}_s$, relative to $\mathbf{V}_s$, and hence, θ is the power factor angle. The key equations are

$$\mathbf{E}_f = \mathbf{V}_s + jX_d\mathbf{I}_s \quad (16.15)$$

$$P_{1\phi} = V_s I_s \cos(\theta) = E_f I_s \cos(\delta - \theta) \quad (16.16)$$

$$Power\ Factor = \text{PF} = \cos(\theta) \quad (16.17)$$

Assume the machine is operating at a rated voltage of 440 V and draws a current of 50 A.

An alternate expression for $P_{1\phi}$ is

$$P_{1\phi} = (E_f V_s / X_d)\sin(\delta) \quad (16.18)$$

See problem 16.30 for a discussion of this equation. Furthermore, remember that

$$P_{3\phi} = 3P_{1\phi} \quad (16.19)$$

Finally, consider the mechanical issues at the shaft, as shown in Figure 16.9(d). Neglecting rotational losses, and for constant speed operation, the torque, τ_m, of the prime mover (for example, a steam turbine), is equal to the electromagnetic torque, that is,

$$\tau_m = \tau_d \quad (16.20)$$

Likewise, the prime mover power is equal to the electromagnetic power, that is,

$$P_m = P_d$$

or

$$\begin{aligned} P_m &= \tau_m\omega_r \\ &= \tau_d\omega_r \quad (16.21) \\ &= P_d \end{aligned}$$

and

$$\omega_r = \omega_s \quad (16.22)$$

Consider the following example.

Example 16.3

A 3ϕ 2300 V 4-pole 1000 kVA 60 Hz synchronous machine has $X_d = 5\ \Omega, R_f = 10\ \Omega$, and $K_{ag} = 200\ \Omega$; it is to be used as a generator connected to a balanced three-phase ac system.

We wish to find (a) the rated stator current, (b) the exciter setting, V_{ex}, for operation at rated conditions for a power factor of 0.866 lagging, (c) V_{ex} in part (b) if the power factor is 0.866 leading, (d) V_{ex} in part (b) for unity power factor and the same real power output as in parts (b) and (c), and (e) the complex power delivered by the generator to the system for parts (b) and (c).

(a) The rated stator current is found from the complex power as follows:

$$S_{1\phi rated} = 1000\text{ k}/3$$
$$= 333.3\text{ kVA}$$

and

$$V_{srated} = 2.3\text{ k}/\sqrt{3}$$
$$= 1.328\text{ kV}$$

then

$$I_{srated} = S_{1\phi rated}/V_{srated}$$
$$= 333.3\text{ k}/1.328\text{ k}$$
$$= 251.0\text{ A}$$

(b) In order to find the exciter setting V_{ex} for operation at rated conditions for a power factor of 0.8666 lagging, we first determine

$$\theta = \cos^{-1}(0.866)$$
$$= -30°$$

then

$$\mathbf{E}_f = 1328\underline{/0°} + j5(251\underline{/-30°})$$
$$= 2495\underline{/14.6°}\text{ V}$$

and since

$$I_f = E_f/K_{ag}$$
$$= 2495/200$$
$$= 12.48\text{ A}$$

Therefore,

$$V_{ex} = I_f R_f$$
$$= 12.48(10)$$
$$= 124.8\text{ V}$$

(c) For a power factor of 0.8666 leading we find that

$$\theta = \cos^{-1}(0.866)$$
$$= +30°$$

Then

$$\mathbf{E}_f = 1328\angle 0^\circ + j5(251\angle +30^\circ)$$
$$= 1293\angle 57.2^\circ \text{ V}$$

Since

$$I_f = E_f/K_{ag}$$
$$= 1293/200$$
$$= 6.465 \text{ A}$$

Then

$$V_{ex} = I_f R_f$$
$$= 6.465(10)$$
$$= 64.65 \text{ V}$$

(d) V_{ex} for operation at rated voltage unity power factor, for the same real power output as in parts (b) and (c), is derived as follows:
From parts (b) and (c),

$$P_{1\phi} = V_s I_s \cos(\theta)$$
$$= 1328(251)(0.866)$$
$$= 288.7 \text{ kW}$$

Therefore, at unity PF,

$$I_s = P_{1\phi}/V_s$$
$$= 288.7 \text{ k}/1.328 \text{ k}$$
$$= 217.4 \text{ A}$$

Since

$$\theta = \cos^{-1}(1.000)$$
$$= 0^\circ$$

Then

$$\mathbf{E}_f = 1328\angle 0^\circ + j5(217.4\angle 0^\circ)$$
$$= 1716\angle 39.3^\circ \text{ V}$$

And

$$I_f = E_f/K_{ag}$$
$$= 1716/200$$
$$= 8.580 \text{ A}$$

Therefore,

$$V_{ex} = I_f R_f$$
$$= 8.580(10)$$
$$= 85.80 \text{ V}$$

(e) For parts (b), (c), and (d), the complex power delivered by the generator to the system is derived from the equation

$$\mathbf{S}_{3\phi} = 3\mathbf{V}_s\mathbf{I}_s^*$$

Thus, for part (b),

$$\begin{aligned}\mathbf{S}_{3\phi} &= 3(1.328)(251\angle{+30^\circ}) \\ &= 866 \text{ kW} + j500 \text{ kvar}\end{aligned}$$

For part (c),

$$\begin{aligned}\mathbf{S}_{3\phi} &= 3(1.328)(251\angle{-30^\circ}) \\ &= 866 \text{ kW} - j500 \text{ kvar}\end{aligned}$$

And for part (d),

$$\begin{aligned}\mathbf{S}_{3\phi} &= 3(1.328 \text{ k})(217.4) \\ &= 866 \text{ kW} + j0 \text{ kvar}\end{aligned}$$

Example 16.3 demonstrates some general points about synchronous generator operation. Lagging, unity, and leading generator power factor operation is associated with high, medium, and low excitation levels called "over, normal, and under" excitation. Note that the *generator lagging* mode is associated with reactive power Q **delivery,** and *generator leading* operation means that Q is **absorbed** by the machine. The point is that field control can be used to control Q flow into and out of the machine regardless of motor or generator operation.

For the machine operating in the motor mode, the current $\mathbf{I}_s$ would be phase-positioned in the 2nd or 3rd quadrants. Likewise, the powers $P_{1\phi}$ and $P_{3\phi}$ would be negative. To avoid this correct, but awkward, situation, we reverse the positive definition of $\mathbf{I}_s$ and δ, as shown in Figure 16.10, that is, $\mathbf{I}_s$ now is defined positive **into** the machine, and δ is defined positive when $\mathbf{E}_f$ **lags** $\mathbf{V}_s$. The *motor convention* machine equations are

$$\mathbf{V}_s = \mathbf{E}_f + jX_d\,\mathbf{I}_s \tag{16.23}$$

Power flow into the machine is

$$\begin{aligned}P_{1\phi} &= V_sI_s\cos(\theta) \\ &= E_fI_s\cos(\delta - \theta)\end{aligned} \tag{16.24}$$

The power factor is

$$PF = \cos(\theta) \tag{16.25}$$

And

$$P_{1\phi} = (E_fV_s/X_d)\sin(\delta) \tag{16.26}$$

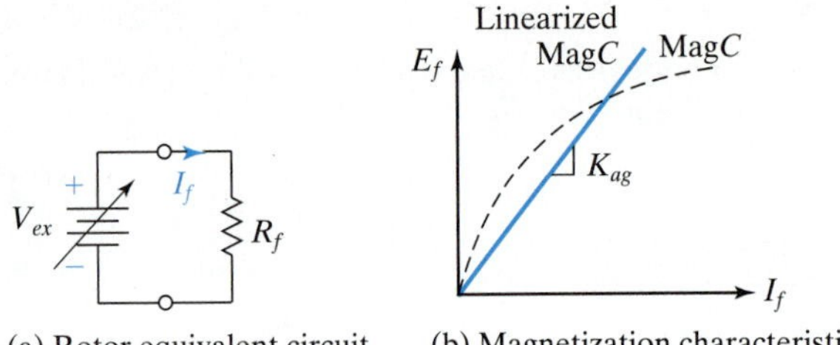

(a) Rotor equivalent circuit (b) Magnetization characteristic

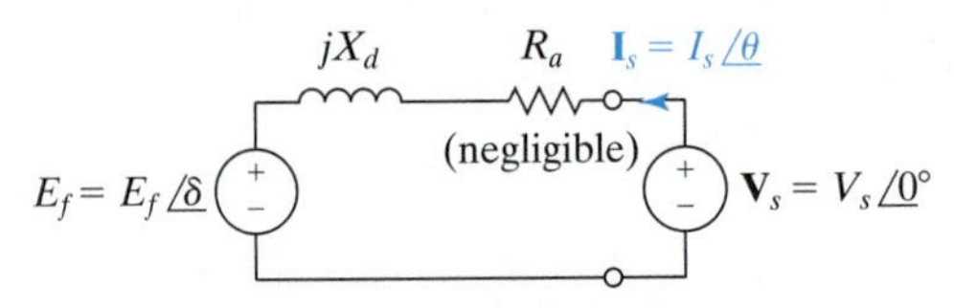

(c) Stator equivalent circuit

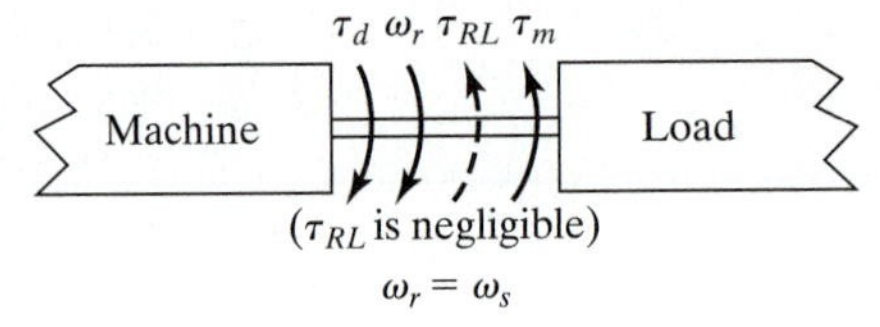

(d) Mechanical considerations

FIGURE 16.10 Synchronous machine equivalent circuits *motor* convention.

Example 16.4

A 3ϕ 2300 V four-pole 1000 kVA 60 Hz synchronous machine has $X_d = 5\ \Omega$; $R_f = 10\ \Omega$; and $K_{ag} = 200\ \Omega$, that is, the machine in Example 16.3, and is to be used as a motor.

We wish to find (a) the exciter setting, V_{ex}, for operation at rated conditions for a power factor of 0.866 lagging, (b) V_{ex} in part (a) if the power factor is 0.866 leading, (c) V_{ex} in part (a) for unity power factor and the same real power as in parts (a) and (b), and (d) the complex power absorbed by the machine in parts (a), (b), and (c).

(a) In order to find the exciter setting V_{ex} for operation at rated conditions for a power factor of 0.866 lagging, we first determine

$$\theta = \cos^{-1}(0.866) = -30°$$

Then

$$\begin{aligned}\mathbf{E}_f &= 1328\angle 0° - j5(251\angle -30°)\\ &= 1293\angle -57.2°\ \text{V}\end{aligned}$$

And since

$$\begin{aligned}I_f &= E_f/K_{ag}\\ &= 1293/200\\ &= 6.465\ \text{A}\end{aligned}$$

Therefore,

$$V_{ex} = I_f R_f$$
$$= 6.465(10)$$
$$= 64.65 \text{ V}$$

(b) For a power factor of 0.866 leading, we find that

$$\theta = \cos^{-1}(0.866)$$
$$= +30°$$

Then

$$\mathbf{E}_f = 1328\underline{/0°} - j5(251\underline{/+30°})$$
$$= 2237\underline{/-29.1°} \text{ V}$$

Since

$$I_f = E_f/K_{ag}$$
$$= 2237/200$$
$$= 11.19 \text{ A}$$

Hence

$$V_{ex} = I_f R_f$$
$$= 11.19(10)$$
$$= 111.9 \text{ V}$$

(c) V_{ex} for operation at rated voltage, unity power factor, and the same real power input as in parts (a) and (b) is derived as follows:
From parts (a) and (b)

$$P_{1\phi} = V_s I_s \cos(\theta)$$
$$= 1328(251)(0.866)$$
$$= 288.7 \text{ kW}$$

Therefore, at unity PF,

$$I_s = P_{1\phi}/V_s$$
$$= 288.7 \text{ k}/1.328 \text{ k}$$
$$= 217.4 \text{ A}$$

Since

$$\theta = \cos^{-1}(1.000) = 0°$$

Then

$$\mathbf{E}_f = 1328\underline{/0°} - j5(217.4\underline{/0°})$$
$$= 1716\underline{/-39.3°} \text{ V}$$

And

$$\begin{aligned} I_f &= E_f/K_{ag} \\ &= 1716/200 \\ &= 8.580 \text{ A} \end{aligned}$$

Therefore,

$$\begin{aligned} V_{ex} &= I_f R_f \\ &= 8.580(10) \\ &= 85.80 \text{ V} \end{aligned}$$

(d) For parts (a), (b), and (c), the complex power absorbed by the machine is as follows: For part (a),

$$\begin{aligned} \mathbf{S}_{3\phi} &= 3(1.328 \text{ k})(251\underline{/+30^\circ}) \\ &= 866 \text{ kW} + j500 \text{ kvar} \end{aligned}$$

For part (b),

$$\begin{aligned} \mathbf{S}_{3\phi} &= 3(1.328 \text{ k})(251\underline{/-30^\circ}) \\ &= 866 \text{ kW} - j500 \text{ kvar} \end{aligned}$$

And for part (c),

$$\begin{aligned} \mathbf{S}_{3\phi} &= 3(1.328 \text{ k})(217.4) \\ &= 866 \text{ kW} + j0 \text{ kvar} \end{aligned}$$

Example 16.4 demonstrates some general points about synchronous motor operation. Leading, unity, and lagging motor power factor operation is associated with high, medium, and low excitation levels called "over, normal, and under" excitation. Note that the *motor leading* mode is associated with reactive power Q flow from motor to system; *motor lagging* operation means that Q is absorbed by the machine.

Drill Exercise

D16.3. A medium head hydroelectric power plant in Europe employs a hydraulic turbine that produces peak efficiency at 635 rpm. The European power frequency is 50 Hz. Select an appropriate number of poles for the generator.

Ans: $P = 10$.

16–5 AC Machine Applications

The overwhelming majority of industrial motor applications utilize ac three-phase cage rotor induction motors, particularly where speed control is noncritical. Included are pumps, fans, compressors, and drives for industrial processes. Where speed control is important, both induction and synchronous machines, with electronic controllers, called *drives,* compete with dc machines. The speed is controlled by varying stator applied voltage magnitude and frequency such that V/f = constant. As ac drive technology advances, dc machines are becoming less common.

Applications that utilize ac three-phase wound induction motors are less common because of their much greater cost; however, a significant number are still being used in situations that demand unusually large starting torque and moderate speed control. Very few induction devices are used as generators.

The importance of three-phase synchronous generators

The overwhelming majority of bulk electric energy production in the world utilizes the ac three-phase synchronous machine as the generator. The two main types of electric energy-producing plants, that is, power plants, are thermal and hydro, where the former accounts for better than 80% of the U.S. production and most of the balance is produced by the latter. Thermal plants use either fossil fuels such as coal, oil, gas, and biomass, or nuclear fuel such as enriched uranium. Emerging technologies, such as wind energy, solar thermal, and solar electric, also show promise for making significant contributions. The nonsalient rotor design is typically used for thermal plant generators, whereas the salient pole type is used in slower speed hydro applications. For applications that require constant speed and few starts, synchronous motors are ideal. As we have observed, the ac three-phase synchronous machine also provides the capability of reactive power control in both motor and generator modes.

Another machine that oddly enough falls into the category of machines described in this chapter is the *brushless dc machine.* Recall that ac three-phase synchronous machines operate at a speed determined by the applied stator voltage frequency; indeed, the term *synchronous* means that the stator and rotor permanent magnet fields, and the rotor structure, are synchronized, that is, turn at the same speed. Hence, if you control the frequency, you control the speed. Suppose we start from a constant voltage constant frequency balanced three-phase ac source. This 3ϕ ac source can be rectified to dc, and inverted back to variable voltage magnitude and frequency, balanced three-phase ac, which serves as the input stator voltage to a three-phase synchronous machine. This integrated system-rectifier, inverter, synchronous machine, is called a "brushless dc" machine, since its speed controllability is comparable to the dc machine.

Finally, the most common type of electric motor is the ac single-phase type, which, although more complicated, can be analyzed using the same principles. These are the motors found in household appliances, including mixers, dryers, washing machines, refrigerators, blenders, rotisseries, garage door openers, and many other low-power applications.

Summary

- Induction and synchronous machines are the two major types of polyphase machines.
- A revolving magnetic field that is produced by the three-phase stator currents forms the basis for the operation of all ac polyphase machines.
- In a three-phase induction machine, both the stator field and rotor field rotate at ω_s with respect to some stationary point. The rotor rotates at ω_r. It is the interaction of the two synchronous fields (stator and rotor) that produces torque.
- A balanced constant speed induction machine can be modeled by the per-phase wye equivalent circuit shown in Figure 16.4 (with its attendant definitions).
- The various losses in an induction motor are outlined in the power flow diagram in Figure 16.5(a).

- The difference between induction machines and synchronous machines lies in the design of the rotor. There are two types of rotors used in synchronous machines: salient and nonsalient.
- Both induction and synchronous machines can be operated in either the generator or motor mode. The operating mode for a synchronous machine is determined by the relative angular position of the stator and rotor fields.
- Like the induction machines, equivalent circuits for synchronous machines can be used to analyze machine performance. The equivalent circuits using both generator and motor conventions are shown in Figures 16.9 and 16.10, respectively.
- Three-phase induction motors are the overwhelming choice for industrial motor applications, and the ac three-phase synchronous machine, operating in the generator mode, is the primary element used for bulk electric energy production in the world.

Problems

16.1. A three-phase 6 hp induction motor is rated at 220 V, 50 Hz, and 1410 rpm. Find the number of poles, the slip, and the frequency of the rotor currents.

16.2. A three-phase 4 hp induction motor is rated at 120 V, 400 Hz, and 3840 rpm. Find the number of poles, the slip, and the frequency of the rotor currents.

16.3. A 50 Hz induction motor has a full-load speed of 460 rpm. If the no-load speed is 476 rpm, determine the slip at full load.

16.4. A 3ϕ, 440 V, 60 Hz, eight-pole, Y-connected induction motor has the following parameters: $R_s = 0.29\ \Omega$, $X_s = 1.25\ \Omega$, $X_r' = 1.25\ \Omega$, $R_r' = 0.1\ \Omega$, and $X_m = 18.5\ \Omega$. Find the terminal current for a slip of 10%.

16.5. An often-used simplified equivalent circuit for an induction motor is shown in Figure P16.5, where the shunt branch has been moved to the voltage source side.

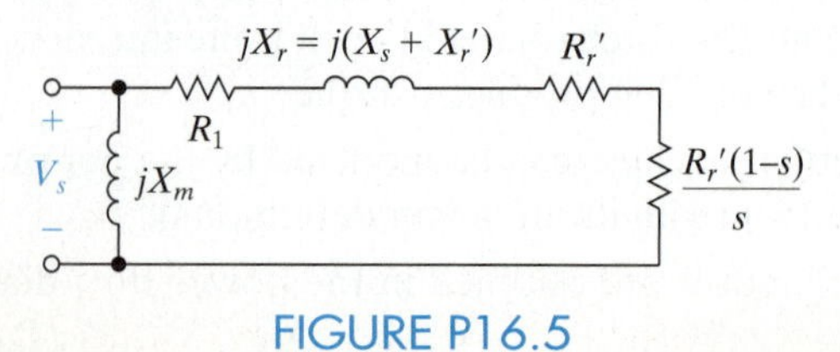

FIGURE P16.5

Using this simplified equivalent circuit, determine the rotor speed and torque of a 40 hp, 440 V, three-phase, 60 Hz, four-pole, Y-connected induction motor with the following parameters: $R_r' = 0.13\ \Omega$, $R_i = 0.12\ \Omega$, $X_i = 0.7\ \Omega$, $X_m = \infty$, and a slip of 4%.

16.6. A three-phase 20 hp, 220 V, 60 Hz, six-pole, Y-connected induction motor has the following parameters: $R_1 = 0.15\ \Omega$, $R_2 = 0.1\ \Omega$, $X_1 = 0.2\ \Omega$, $X_2 = 0.3\ \Omega$, and $X_m = j10\ \Omega$. Using the approximate equivalent circuit in problem 16.5, determine the input line current and the input power factor if the slip is 3%.

16.7. A 3ϕ, six-pole, 60 Hz, Y-connected induction motor has the following parameters: $R_S = 0.21\ \Omega$, $X_s = 1.01\ \Omega$, $X_r' = 1.01\ \Omega$, $R_r' = 0.11\ \Omega$ and $X_m = \infty$. The motor is used to drive a fan. The fan must turn at 1145 rpm and 10 hp of shaft power is required to run the fan at this speed. Find the magnitude of the terminal voltage required to achieve this operating condition.

16.8. A 3ϕ, four-pole, 60 Hz, Y-connected induction motor rated at 440 V and 1750 rpm has the following per-phase model parameters: $R_S = 0.35\ \Omega$, $X_s = 1.1\ \Omega$. $X_r' = 1.1\ \Omega$, $R_r' = 0.15\ \Omega$, and $X_m >> |R_r'/s + jX_r'|$ and can, therefore, be neglected. If the motor is operated at rated voltage and shaft speed, find the magnitude of the line current if the motor is used in a hoist that requires a torque of 146.29 N-m to drive a load.

16.9. A three-phase, four-pole, 230 V, 60 Hz induction motor has the following parameters: $R_1 = 0.2\ \Omega$, $R_2 = 0.1\ \Omega$, $(X_1 + X_2) = 0.3\ \Omega$, and X_m is infinite. Find the output power and torque for a slip of 4%.

16.10. A 3ϕ, four-pole, 440 V, 60 Hz, Y-connected induction motor has the following parameters: $R_s = 0.22\ \Omega$, $X_s = 1.3\ \Omega$, $X'_r = 1.0\ \Omega$, $R'_r = 0.1\ \Omega$, and it is assumed that $X_m = \infty$. Find the torque developed at starting if rated voltage is applied to the machine terminals.

16.11. A 3ϕ, four-pole, 60 Hz, 550 V, Y-connected induction motor has the following parameters: $R_s = 1.0\ \Omega$, $X_s = 3.0\ \Omega$, $X'_r = 4.5\ \Omega$, $R'_r = 0.9\ \Omega$, and $X_m = 35\ \Omega$. When the motor is running at rated speed, the frequency of the rotor currents is measured to be 5 Hz. (a) Find the rated speed. (b) Find the torque developed.

16.12. A three-phase, 50 hp, 440 V, four-pole, 60 Hz induction motor has a stator resistance of 0.05 Ω, a rotor resistance of 0.072 Ω, and a combined $(X_1 + X_2)$ reactance of 0.06 Ω. Find the horsepower and output torque for a speed of 1746 rpm.

16.13. A 3ϕ, two-pole, 60 Hz, 550 V, Y-connected induction motor has the following parameters: $R_s = 0.3\ \Omega$, $X_s = 0.75\ \Omega$, $X'_r = 0.75\ \Omega$, $R'_r = 0.17\ \Omega$, and $X_m = \infty$. The motor is used to drive a centrifugal pump. When the pump is primed and running, the motor slip is 0.1. Neglecting rotational and stray losses, find the efficiency of the motor at this slip.

16.14. A 3ϕ, eight-pole, 60 Hz, 440 V, Y-connected induction machine has the following parameters: $R_s = 0.5\ \Omega$, $X_s = 1.0\ \Omega$, $X'_r = 1.0\ \Omega$, $R'_r = 0.4\ \Omega$, and $X_m = \infty$. If the motor draws a line current of 29.09 A, find the shaft speed.

16.15. A local power company charges \$0.08 per kW-hr of energy used and pays \$0.02 kW-hr that a customer supplies back to the power company's system. A 3ϕ, four-pole, 60 Hz, 440 V, Y-connected motor with the following parameters: $R_s = 0.8\ \Omega$, $X_s = 1.9\ \Omega$, $X'_r = 1.9\ \Omega$, $R'_r = 0.45\ \Omega$, and $X_m = \infty$, is employed at a local construction site to raise and lower a hoist. The motor speed in the "raise" mode is 1600 rpm and the speed in the "lower" mode is 2000 rpm, and the shaft always turns in the same direction because of a mechanical gearbox. If it takes 10 seconds to raise the loaded hoist and 5 seconds to lower the hoist, find the total cost to operate the hoist through one complete raise-and-lower cycle. Neglect rotational losses.

16.16. A three-phase, 220 V, 60 Hz, six-pole induction motor has the following parameters: $R_1 = 0.18\ \Omega$, $R_2 = 0.1\ \Omega$, $X_1 = 0.4\ \Omega$, $X_2 = 0.24\ \Omega$, and $X_m = j20\ \Omega$. Find the input power and output power and the efficiency if the fixed losses are 300 W and the slip is 2%.

16.17. In parts of South America, the frequency of the power system is 50 Hz. If a three-phase, eight-pole synchronous machine is used as a generator, determine the speed of the rotor.

16.18. A 1000 kVA, three-phase, Y-connected, 4160 V, 60 Hz synchronous gererator has an armature resistance and synchronous reactance of 0.14 Ω and 2.5 Ω per phase, respectively. If the power factor is 0.77 lagging, determine the full load generated voltage per phase.

16.19. A 960 hp synchronous motor is fed by a 2300 V, three-phase supply at 0.75 pf lagging. If the rotational losses are known to be 20 kW, the armature resistance is negligible and the synchronous reactance is 2.2 Ω, determine the excitation voltage at full load.

16.20. A 3ϕ, six-pole, Y-connected synchronous machine is operating as a motor. The machine is rated at 2080 volts and $X_s = 4.0\ \Omega$. If the magnitude of the induced voltage $\mathbf{E}_f$ is 1500 volts, find the maximum three-phase power that the motor can develop without losing synchronism.

16.21. A three-phase, 4160 V synchronous motor has a X_s value of 6 Ω. If the motor supplies 600 kW of shaft power and 360 kvars of reactive power, determine the induced voltage E_f.

16.22. A 3ϕ, four-pole, Y-connected synchronous motor is operating at a rated voltage of 550 V and the input current is $\mathbf{I}_s = 45\angle{-25°}A$. Find the three-phase power developed by the machine.

16.23. A 10,000 kVA, three-phase, Y-connected, 60 Hz synchronous generator is fed by a 13.8 kV line. If the armature resistance and synchronous reactance are 0.8 Ω and 2 Ω, respectively, find the full-load generated voltage if the PF is (a) 0.85 lagging, and (b) 0.85 leading.

16.24. A 3ϕ, six-pole, Y-connected synchronous generator is rated at 550 volts and has a synchronous reactance of $X_d = 2.0\ \Omega$. If the generator supplies 50 kVA at a rated voltage and a power factor of 0.95 lagging, find $\mathbf{I}_s$ and $\mathbf{E}_f$ and sketch the phasor diagram for $\mathbf{V}_s$, $\mathbf{I}_s$, and $\mathbf{E}_f$.

16.25. A 3ϕ, six-pole, Y-connected synchronous generator with a synchronous reactance of $X_d = 12\ \Omega$ is rated at 4160 V. If the dc field current is adjusted to produce an induced voltage of 5000 V and the rotor angle delta is known to be 35°, find the three-phase complex power output at the generator terminals.

16.26. For the machine in problem 16.25, if the three-phase real power output does not change, find the new rotor angle if the field current is adjusted to produce an $E_f = 4000$ V while the terminal voltage is held constant.

16.27. A 3ϕ, eight-pole, 4160 V, Y-connected synchronous generator is operated at a rated terminal voltage to supply a terminal current of 100 A at 0.9 power factor lagging. If $X_d = 12.0\ \Omega$ and the dc field current in the rotor is related to E_f by the equation $I_f = 0.15\ E_f$, find the dc field current required to operate the generator.

16.28. Repeat problem 16.27 if the machine is operated as a motor and draws a current of $75.0\angle{15°}$A.

16.29. A 3ϕ, six-pole, 2080 V, Y-connected synchronous machine is operated as a generator. The generator delivers 300 kVA at a power factor of 0.75 lagging. Find the induced voltage, E_f, and rotor angle, δ, if the per-phase stator impedance is $\mathbf{Z}_s = 0.1 + j8\ \Omega$. Note that in this case we are simply including the effects of stator winding resistance.

Appendicies

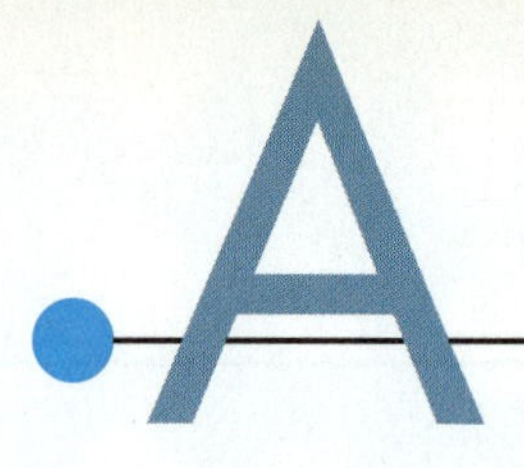

Complex numbers are typically represented in three forms: exponential, polar, or rectangular. In the exponential form a complex number **A** is written as

$$\mathbf{A} = Ae^{j\theta}$$

The real quantity A is known as the amplitude or magnitude, the real quantity θ is called the *angle,* and j is the imaginary operator $j = \sqrt{-1}$. θ is expressed in radians or degrees. The polar form of a complex number **A,** which is symbolically equivalent to the exponential form, is written as

$$\mathbf{A} = A \underline{/\theta}$$

and the rectangular representation of a complex number is written as

$$\mathbf{A} = x + jy$$

where x is the real part of **A** and y is the imaginary part of **A.**

The connection between the various representations of **A** can be seen via Euler's identity, which is

$$e^{j\theta} = \cos\theta + j\sin\theta$$

Using this identity, the complex number **A** can be written as

$$\mathbf{A} = Ae^{j\theta} = A\cos\theta + jA\sin\theta$$

which can be written as

$$\mathbf{A} = x + jy$$

Equating the real and imaginary parts of these two equations yields

$$x = A\cos\theta$$
$$y = A\sin\theta$$

From these equations we obtain

$$x^2 + y^2 = A^2\cos^2\theta + A^2\sin^2\theta = A^2$$

Therefore,

$$A = \sqrt{x^2 + y^2}$$

Additionally,

$$\frac{A\sin\theta}{A\cos\theta} = \tan\theta = \frac{y}{x}$$

and hence

$$\theta = \tan^{-1}\frac{y}{x}$$

The interrelationships among the three representations of a complex number are as follows.

Complex Numbers

Exponential	Polar	Rectangular
$Ae^{j\theta}$	$A \angle \theta$	$x + jy$
$\theta = \tan^{-1} y/x$	$\theta = \tan^{-1} y/x$	$x = A\cos\theta$
$A = \sqrt{x^2 + y^2}$	$A = \sqrt{x^2 + y^2}$	$y = A\sin\theta$

We will now show that the operations of addition, subtraction, multiplication, and division apply to complex numbers in the same manner that they apply to real numbers. The sum of two complex numbers $\mathbf{A} = x_1 + jy_1$ and $\mathbf{B} = x_2 + jy_2$ is

$$\begin{aligned}\mathbf{A} + \mathbf{B} &= x_1 + jy_1 + x_2 + jy_2 \\ &= (x_1 + x_2) + j(y_1 + y_2)\end{aligned}$$

that is, we simply add the individual real parts, and we add the individual imaginary parts to obtain the components of the resultant complex number.

Suppose we wish to calculate the sum $\mathbf{A} + \mathbf{B}$ if $\mathbf{A} = 5 \angle 36.9^\circ$ and $\mathbf{B} = 5 \angle 53.1^\circ$. We must first convert from polar to rectangular form.

$$\begin{aligned}\mathbf{A} &= 5 \angle 36.9^\circ = 4 + j3 \\ \mathbf{B} &= 5 \angle 53.1^\circ = 3 + j4\end{aligned}$$

Therefore,

$$\begin{aligned}\mathbf{A} + \mathbf{B} &= 4 + j3 + 3 + j4 = 7 + j7 \\ &= 9.9 \angle 45^\circ\end{aligned}$$

The difference of two complex numbers $\mathbf{A} = x_1 + jy_1$ and $\mathbf{B} = x_2 + jy_2$ *is*

$$\begin{aligned}\mathbf{A} - \mathbf{B} &= (x_1 + jy_1) - (x_2 + jy_2) \\ &= (x_1 - x_2) + j(y_1 - y_2)\end{aligned}$$

that is, we simply subtract the individual real parts and we subtract the individual imaginary parts to obtain the components of the resultant complex number.

Let us calculate the difference $\mathbf{A} - \mathbf{B}$ if $\mathbf{A} = 5 \angle 36.9^\circ$ and $\mathbf{B} = 5 \angle 53.1^\circ$. Converting both numbers from polar to rectangular form

$$\begin{aligned}\mathbf{A} &= 5 \angle 36.9^\circ = 4 + j3 \\ \mathbf{B} &= 5 \angle 53.1^\circ = 3 + j4\end{aligned}$$

then

$$\mathbf{A} - \mathbf{B} = (4 + j3) - (3 + j4) = 1 - j1 = \sqrt{2}\,\underline{/-45^\circ}$$

The product of two complex numbers $\mathbf{A} = A_1\,\underline{/\theta_1} = x_1 + jy_1$ and $\mathbf{B} = B_2\,\underline{/\theta_2} = x_2 + jy_2$ is

$$\mathbf{AB} = (A_1 e^{j\theta_1})(B_2 e^{j\theta_2}) = A_1 B_2\,\underline{/\theta_1 + \theta_2}$$

Given $\mathbf{A} = 5\,\underline{/36.9^\circ}$ and $\mathbf{B} = 5\,\underline{/53.1^\circ}$, we wish to calculate the product in both polar and rectangular forms.

$$\begin{aligned}\mathbf{AB} &= (5\,\underline{/36.9^\circ})(5\,\underline{/53.1^\circ}) = 25\,\underline{/90^\circ}\\ &= (4 + j3)(3 + j4)\\ &= (12 + j16 + j9 + j^2 12)\\ &= 25j\\ &= 25\,\underline{/90^\circ}\end{aligned}$$

The quotient of two complex numbers $\mathbf{A} = A_1\,\underline{/\theta_1} = x_1 + jy_1$ and $\mathbf{B} = B_2\,\underline{/\theta_2} = x_2 + jy_2$ is

$$\frac{\mathbf{A}}{\mathbf{B}} = \frac{A_1 e^{j\theta_1}}{B_2 e^{j\theta_2}} = \frac{A_1}{B_2} e^{j(\theta_1 - \theta_2)} = \frac{A_1}{B_2}\,\underline{/\theta_1 - \theta_2}$$

If $\mathbf{A} = 10\,\underline{/30^\circ}$ and $\mathbf{B} = 5\,\underline{/53.1^\circ}$, we wish to determine the quotient $\mathbf{A/B}$ in both polar and rectangular forms.

$$\begin{aligned}\frac{\mathbf{A}}{\mathbf{B}} &= \frac{10\,\underline{/30^\circ}}{5\,\underline{/53.1^\circ}}\\ &= 2\,\underline{/-23.1^\circ}\\ &= 1.84 - j0.79\end{aligned}$$

B

In solving circuits and electronics problems we are often presented with a set of simultaneous equations. We require as many equations as there are unknowns. For purposes of illustration we first focus on equations with two unknowns, however, the technique can be generalized to higher orders.

Following is a typical set of equations with two unknowns:

$$a_{11}x_1 + a_{12}x_2 = b_1$$

$$a_{21}x_1 + a_{22}x_2 = b_2$$

In the equations above x_1 and x_2 are the two unknowns (typically voltage or current), the coefficients a_{11}, a_{12}, a_{21}, and a_{22} are known quantities (typically a combination of circuit component values), and the two quantities on the right-hand side, b_1 and b_2, are also known. The b's in a circuits problem are typically the supply voltages or currents.

This set of equations can be written in matrix form as:

$$\begin{bmatrix} a_{11} & a_{12} \\ a_{21} & a_{22} \end{bmatrix} \begin{bmatrix} x_1 \\ x_2 \end{bmatrix} = \begin{bmatrix} b_1 \\ b_2 \end{bmatrix}$$

Cramer's rule utilizes determinants to compute a solution to a set of simultaneous equations. The determinant of the coefficients, Δ is defined as:

$$\Delta = \begin{vmatrix} a_{11} & a_{12} \\ a_{21} & a_{22} \end{vmatrix} = a_{11}\,a_{22} - a_{21}\,a_{12}$$

The value of the second order (2×2) determinant is computed as the product of the down diagonal minus the product of the up diagonal, as illustrated in the following:

$$\begin{vmatrix} a_{11} & a_{12} \\ a_{21} & a_{22} \end{vmatrix}$$

We now define two more determinants, Δx_1, and Δx_2. The first of these, Δx_1, is obtained by replacing the first column of Δ with the column from the right side of the equation (the b's). Likewise, Δx_2 is obtained by replacing the second column with the b's.

Therefore,

$$\Delta_{x1} = \begin{vmatrix} b_1 & a_{12} \\ b_2 & a_{22} \end{vmatrix} = b_1\,a_{22} - b_2\,a_{12}$$

and

$$\Delta_{x2} = \begin{vmatrix} a_{11} & b_1 \\ a_{21} & b_2 \end{vmatrix} = a_{11}\,b_2 - a_{21}\,b_1$$

Cramer's rule states that the unknowns, x_1 and x_2, can be determined by the ratio of two determinants. The denominator is always the same, Δ.

$$x_1 = \frac{\Delta_{x1}}{\Delta} \qquad \text{and} \qquad x_2 = \frac{\Delta_{x2}}{\Delta}$$

Linear Algebra and Cramer's Rule

For a system of three equations and three unknowns (or for higher order systems) the same procedure can be applied. The only difference is that the determinants will be larger. To apply Cramer's rule to a third order system, we must learn to evaluate a 3×3 determinant.

The value of a 3×3 determinant can be determined calculating the sum of the product of the down diagonals to the right, minus the sum of the product of the up diagonal to the right. That is,

$$\Delta = \begin{vmatrix} a_{11} & a_{12} & a_{13} \\ a_{21} & a_{22} & a_{23} \\ a_{31} & a_{32} & a_{33} \end{vmatrix} =$$

$$(a_{11}a_{22}a_{33} + a_{12}a_{23}a_{31} + a_{13}a_{21}a_{32}) - (a_{31}a_{22}a_{13} + a_{32}a_{23}a_{11} + a_{33}a_{21}a_{12})$$

The determination of the value of determinants of higher order can also be done by a system of cofactors and minors. If we expand the above determinant on the top row, the cofactors are alternating signs, or alternating $+1$ and -1. The minors are the determinants remaining if the row and column of the selected element is eliminated. For example, the minor of a_{11} is

$$\begin{vmatrix} a_{22} & a_{23} \\ a_{32} & a_{33} \end{vmatrix}$$

and

$$\Delta = (+1)a_{11}\begin{vmatrix} a_{22} & a_{23} \\ a_{32} & a_{33} \end{vmatrix} + (-1)a_{12}\begin{vmatrix} a_{21} & a_{23} \\ a_{31} & a_{33} \end{vmatrix} + (+1)a_{13}\begin{vmatrix} a_{21} & a_{22} \\ a_{31} & a_{32} \end{vmatrix}$$

The above expression is a_{11} times its minor, minus a_{12} times its minor, plus a_{13} times its minor.

The expansion of the 2×2 determinants above will produce the same equation as that presented earlier for a 3×3 determinant. This process can be applied to the evaluation of determinants larger than 3×3. However, in practice, MATLAB or other computer programs are generally used to solve for the unknowns in such higher order systems of equations.

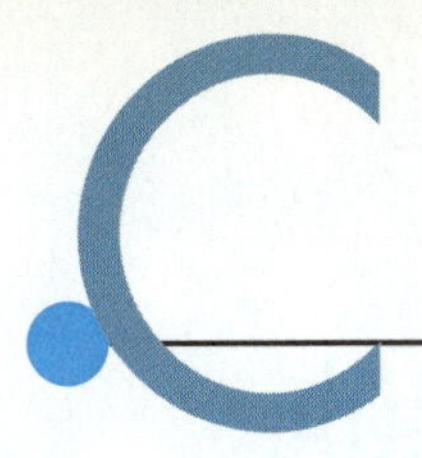

Introduction

The engineering profession is regulated by boards in each of the 50 states and jurisdictions. Any individual who wishes to practice the profession of engineering by offering their professional services to the public must become registered as a professional engineer (PE).

The process of becoming a registered or licensed professional engineer is a multi-step process. First, one must obtain the necessary education to be allowed to take the Fundamentals of Engineering (FE) examination; this was formerly called the Engineer-in-Training (EIT) exam. Engineering programs accredited by the Engineering Accreditation Commission (EAC) of the Accreditation Board for Engineering and Technology (ABET) are acceptable to all boards as qualifying education. Graduates of other programs should contact their appropriate registration board for the required education and experience prior to applying to take the FE examination. The FE exam is offered twice a year and is usually taken as a college senior or just following graduation. Those that successfully pass the FE exam are called an "Engineer-Intern" (EI), and are admitted to preprofessional status as a newly trained engineer.

After passing the FE exam the EI must obtain a minimum of 4 years acceptable experience before being qualified to take the Professional Engineering (PE) examination. This text serves as an excellent reference for both of these examinations; however, its use as a study guide for the FE exam will be emphasized here.

The FE examination is 8 hours long, with one 4-hour session in the morning and another in the afternoon. Examinees must participate in both sessions on the same day. The exam consists of 180 multiple-choice questions. During the morning session, all examinees take a general exam of 120 questions common to all disciplines. During the afternoon session, examinees can opt to take a general exam or a discipline-specific (chemical, civil, electrical, environmental, industrial, or mechanical) exam consisting of 60 questions.

In the morning session, 10% of the questions relate to electric circuits (12 questions) and 6% to computers (seven questions). In the afternoon general session, 10% of the questions relate to electrical circuits (six questions) and 5% to computers (three questions).

The exam is prepared by the National Council of Examiners for Engineering and Surveying (NCEES). Both the morning and afternoon sessions are "closed book," however, some reference material is provided by a booklet called the "Supplied-Reference Handbook." The materials on the Reference Charts in this text provide similar information to that in the handbook, such as relevant tables, formulae, drawings, and so on.

In this appendix we will outline the electrical engineering topics covered on the FE exam and identify the location of these topics in this text to facilitate study and review. In addition we will note important equations and concepts that are included in the FE Reference Handbook, which you will be provided at the examination.

Examination Topics

Presented here is a topic list for the morning session of the FE exam. Each of these areas will be addressed in the following sections.

Fundamentals of Engineering [FE] Exam Review

1. **1.** DC Circuits
2. **2.** AC Circuits
3. **3.** Capacitance and Inductance
4. **4.** Fourier and Laplace Transforms
5. **5.** Diode Applications
6. **6.** Operational Amplifiers (Ideal)
7. **7.** Electric and Magnetic Fields
8. **8.** Ideal Transformers

The afternoon session in electrical includes more detailed topics such as analog electronic circuits, communications theory, computer and numerical methods, computer hardware engineering, computer software engineering, control systems theory and analysis, digital systems, electromagnetic theory and applications, instrumentation, network analysis, power systems, signal processing, and solid-state electronics and devices.

1. DC Circuits. Chapter 1 in this text provides an important introduction and definitions of quantities used in all subsequent chapters; quantities such as charge, voltage, current and so on, are defined in section 1.2. Basic concepts are illustrated with examples and drill exercises. Your time invested in thoroughly understanding these fundamental quantities will prove well worth the effort. This chapter uses numerous analogies to assist the newcomer in developing such understanding.

Equation (1.1) expresses the electrostatically induced force between two point charges; this equation is one of the first given in the Reference Handbook (the constant $k = 1/4\pi\epsilon$). Chapter 2 is titled "DC Circuits." This chapter develops Ohm's law, explains Kirchhoff's laws in section 2.3, and illustrates their application with numerous examples to single loop circuits in section 2.4.

Resistor combinations in series and parallel are given in section 2.6; these equations appear directly in the Reference Handbook DC nodal analysis presented in section 2.7 and loop and mesh analysis presented in section 2.8 provide a study of essential material for the systematic analysis of dc circuits. Thevenin's and Norton's theorems, explained in section 2.11, are provided in the Reference Handbook under the title *Source Equivalents.*

2. AC Circuits. Chapter 4 of this text provides a complete introduction to ac steady-state analysis. Central to the analysis of ac circuits is the transformation of a sinusoidal time-varying quantity into the frequency domain as a phasor consisting of a magnitude and an angle. The phasor transformation defined by Eq. (4.17) shows that the amplitude of the time-varying function is equal to the magnitude of the phasor. One must use the same convention for the reverse transformation, that is, the magnitude of the phasor transforms to the amplitude of the time-varying function.

The magnitude in the phasor transform can be defined alternatively as $1/\sqrt{2}$ times the amplitude of the time function, and thus the rms phasor can be expressed as

$$A\cos(\omega t \pm \theta) \leftrightarrow \frac{A}{\sqrt{2}} \angle \pm \theta \qquad (AC.1)$$

We can easily illustrate that consistent application of this alternative phasor definition results in exactly the same answers as when the phasor definition of Eq. (4.17) is utilized. For example, let us rework the first part of Example 4.5 with the phasor definition of Eq. (AC.1).

The impedance $\mathbf{Z}$ is calculated exactly the same; therefore, at $f = 60$ Hz, $\mathbf{Z} = 25 - j45.51\ \Omega$. We are given that $v(t) = 50\cos(377t + 30°)$ V. Therefore, using Eq. (AC.1), the *rms* phasor transform,

$$\mathbf{V} = \frac{50}{\sqrt{2}} \angle 30° = 35.4 \angle 30°$$

$$\mathbf{I} = \frac{\mathbf{V}}{\mathbf{Z}} = \frac{35.4 \angle 30°}{51.92 \angle -61.22°} = 0.679 \angle 91.22°\ A$$

Converting, this back into the time domain again using Eq. (AC.1),

$$i(t) = \sqrt{2}(0.679)\cos(377t + 91.22°) = 0.96\cos(377t + 91.22°)\ \text{A}$$

This is the same result as originally given in Example 4.5. The Reference Handbook provides the *rms* phasor definition given in Eq. (AC.1).

The important concepts of impedance and admittance are defined in section 4.5 with several numerical examples. The important concept of effective or *rms* value is introduced in section 5.4, the power factor in section 5.5, and complex power in section 5.6. The power factor (PF) is described in more detail in section 5.7, titled "Power Factor Correction"; this section describes an important practical example of ac circuits and a common type of exam question.

The algebraic manipulation of complex algebra, which is necessary for calculations involving phasors, impedance, admittance, and complex power, can be assisted by the review of complex algebra; such a review is provided in Appendix A of this text. There is a brief review of the algebra of complex numbers in the Reference Handbook.

The formulae for resonance, including series resonance, quality factor, bandwidth, and parallel resonance, are described in Chapter 7 with a number of examples and drill exercises. Eqs. (7.21), (7.24), (7.26), and other relevant expressions are repeated in the Reference Handbook.

3. Capacitance and Inductance. The basic concepts of capacitance and inductance are first introduced in Chapter 1 and summarized in Figure 1.12. The beginning of Chapter 3 reviews these concepts in more detail and describes the series and parallel connection of capacitors in Eqs. (3.8) and (3.9), and the series and parallel combination of inductors in Eqs. (3.15) and (3.16). These equations are repeated in the Reference Handbook.

4. Transients. "Transient Analysis" is the title of Chapter 3. The transient analysis of RC and RL circuits is presented in section 3.3 with four worked examples and three drill exercises. The Reference Handbook summarizes the response of a single loop series *RC* circuit such as that illustrated in Figure 3.9(a); equations similar to the following are presented:

$$v_C(t) = v_C(0)e^{-t/r} + V_s(1 - e^{-t/\tau})$$
$$i(t) = \{[V_s - v_C(0)]/R\}e^{-t/\tau}$$
$$v_R(t) = i(t)R = [V_s - v_C(0)]e^{-t/\tau}$$

where $v_C(0)$ is the initial voltage on the capacitor, and τ is the time constant, RC.

The set of analogous equations for a series RL circuit such as that presented in Figure 3.9(b) are also given; these include expressions for $i(t)$, $v_R(t)$, and $v_L(t)$ with the initial current expressed as $i(0)$ and the time constant τ as L/R.

5. Diode Applications. Chapter 10 provides a comprehensive review of the fundamentals of diode applications. The study of these applications begins in section 10.5 with the diode circuit models; the ideal diode, the diode equation, and the piece-wise linear model. These basic diode circuit models are used in a wide variety of circuit applications in sections 10.6 through 10.10. These applications include power supply circuits including half-wave and full-wave rectification, filter circuits, clipper circuits, clamping circuits, zener diodes, photo diodes and LEDs.

6. Operational Amplifiers. Chapter 9 in this text reviews the fundamentals of operational amplifiers. The ideal op-amp is described in section 9.2. In sections 9.3 through 9.11 an array of ideal op-amp applications are discussed including the inverting amplifier, the noninverting amplifier, the unity-gain buffer, the summing circuit, the integrator, the active filter, and the current-to-voltage converter. This chapter is independent and may be studied at any point after dc circuits.

7. Electric and Magnetic Fields. The definition of a uniform electric field between parallel plates is presented in Eq. 10.2. Chapter 6 is titled "Magnetically Coupled Circuits and Transformers" and introduces the fundamental definitions required for analysis of magnetic fields, magnetic circuits, and transformers. Faraday's law is illustrated by the expression (6.5) and other related equations in Chapter 6. Chapters 15 and 16 discuss the application of these principles to dc and ac machines (motors and generators).

8. Additional Topics. The Reference Handbook presents an expression for the resistance of a bar of cross-sectional area, A; this equation is given in the text as Eq. (10.6). The handbook also describes the change in resistance resulting from temperature changes, which is described by a temperature coefficient, alpha; these concepts are illustrated by problem 8.45 in the text.

For additional or updated information regarding the FE examination, contact directly the NCEES, PO Box 1686, Clemson, SC, 29633-1686.

Answers to Selected Problems

CHAPTER 1

1.1 2.08×10^{-13} C
1.4 8.19×10^{-8} N
1.7 (a) wet aluminum, (b) salt water, (c) copper
1.10 0.96 A
1.11 2 A (away from node)
1.15 12 V
1.19 1800 J
1.23 (a) $V = -15$ V; $I = 1$ A
(b) $V = 2$ V; $I = 2$ A
(c) $V = 1$ V; $I = -1$ A
1.26 (a) A absorbing; B supplying; 64,800 J
(b) A supplying; B absorbing; 151,200 J
1.30 $V_o = -144$ V
1.34 (a) 25 mA
(b) -150 mA

CHAPTER 2

2.1 $I_1 = 6$ mA
2.5 $V_1 = 8$ V and $V_{bd} = 4$ V
2.9 $I = 2$ mA
2.13 $I = 2$ mA, $V_1 = 8$ V, and $V_2 = 16$ V
2.17 $V_0 = -12$ V
2.21 $V_S = -36$ V
2.25 $V_0 = 24$ V and $I_1 = 4$ mA
2.29 $I_0 = 6$ mA
2.33 $V_0 = 16$ V
2.37 $I_S = 6$ mA
2.41 $R_{AB} = 4$ k
2.45 $I_0 = 2.5$ mA
2.49 $I_0 = \frac{6}{5}$ mA
2.53 $V_0 = 2.8$ V
2.57 $V_0 = -\frac{6}{5}$ V
2.61 $V_0 = -2.5$ V
2.65 $V_0 = \frac{3}{2}$ V
2.69 $V_0 = \frac{14}{5}$ V
2.73 $I_0 = \frac{20}{9}$ mA
2.77 $V_0 = -12$ V

CHAPTER 3

3.1 $i(t) = 12$ mA $\quad 0 \le t \le 1$ ms
$= -12$ mA $\quad 3 \le t \le 4$ ms
$= 0$ elsewhere
3.5 $C = 9$ F
3.8 $C_{AB} = \frac{3}{5}$ F
3.11 $v(t) = -40$ V $\quad 0 \le t \le 1$ ms
$= 20$ V $\quad 2 \le t \le 4$ ms
$= 0$ elsewhere
3.16 $L_{AB} = 12$ mH
3.21 $v_0(t) = 6e^{-t/1.2}$ V
3.25 $v_c(t) = 6e^{-t/0.6}$ V
3.29 $v_0(t) = -8e^{-t/8}$ V
3.34 $v_c(t) = 12 - 3e^{-t/0.9}$ V
3.38 $i_1(t) = 1e^{-9t}$ A
3.42 $v_0(t) = -6e^{-4t}$ V
3.46 Underdamped circuit
3.49 Critically damped circuit
3.55 $v(t) = -10e^{-t} + 2e^{-5t} + 8$ V

CHAPTER 4

4.1 $i_1(t)$ leads $i_2(t)$ by $-80°$
4.5 $V = 53\angle -30°$ V
4.9 $\mathbf{Z}_{AB} = 4.79\angle -7.33°\ \Omega$
4.13 $I = 33.5\angle 18.43°$ A
4.17 $\mathbf{V}_0 = 12\angle -53.1°$ V
4.21 $\mathbf{V}_0 = -5.66\angle 45°$ V
4.26 $\mathbf{I}_1 = 3.38\angle -17.64°$ A
$\mathbf{I}_2 = 2.095\angle -24.77°$ A
$\mathbf{I}_3 = 1.33\angle -6.33°$ A
4.30 $\mathbf{V}_S = 17.89\angle -18.46°$ V
4.34 $\mathbf{I}_0 = 3.954\angle -30.36°$ A
4.38 $\mathbf{I}_1 = 3.78\angle 18.44°$ A
$\mathbf{I}_2 = 2.68\angle -116.56°$ A
4.42 $\mathbf{V}_1 = 3 + j3$ V
$\mathbf{V}_2 = -3 + j5$ V
4.46 $\mathbf{V}_0 = 4.48\angle 26.57°$ V
4.52 $\mathbf{I}_0 = 1\angle -90°$ A
4.57 $\mathbf{I}_0 = 2.61\angle -32.47°$ A
4.61 $\mathbf{I}_0 = 1\angle -90°$ A

4.65 $C_0 = 2$

$$C_n = \frac{2}{n\pi}\left(2\sin\frac{2\pi n}{3} - \sin\frac{n\pi}{3}\right)$$

CHAPTER 5

5.1 $p(t) = 18 + 18\cos(754t - 80°)$ W

5.5 $P = 8$ W

5.9 $P_{sup} = P_{ABS} = 88.2$ W

5.14 $V_{rms} = 1.29$ V

5.18 $P = 80$ W

5.22 $P_s = 137.857$ kW

5.26 $P_s = 44.39$ kW

5.31 $\theta_S = 5.29°$; $\text{pf}_S = 0.996$

5.35 $C = 510.2$ F

5.39 $\mathbf{I}_{aA} = 6.71 \angle -26.57°$ A rms
$\mathbf{I}_{bB} = 6.71 \angle -146.57°$ A rms
$\mathbf{I}_{cC} = 6.71 \angle -266.57°$ A rms

5.44 $\mathbf{V}_{an} = 120 \angle 20°$ V rms
$\mathbf{V}_{bn} = 120 \angle -100°$ V rms
$\mathbf{V}_{cn} = 120 \angle -220°$ V rms

5.49 $\mathbf{I}_{aA} = 13.42 \angle 3.43°$ A rms
$\mathbf{I}_{bB} = 13.42 \angle -116.57°$ A rms
$\mathbf{I}_{cC} = 13.42 \angle -236.57°$ A rms

5.54 $\mathbf{I}_{ay} = 14.21 \angle -33.46°$ A rms

5.58 $\mathbf{I}_L = 17.97$ A rms

CHAPTER 6

6.1 $(2 + j)\mathbf{I}_1 - j3\mathbf{I}_2 = 24 \angle 60°$
$-j3\mathbf{I}_1 + (2 + j7)\mathbf{I}_2 = 0$

6.5 $\mathbf{I}_2 = 0.749 \angle -176.42°$ A

6.10 $\mathbf{V}_x = -1.9 \angle 71.57°$ V

6.15 $\mathbf{I}_2 = 0.697 \angle -144.46°$ A

6.19 $\mathbf{Z} = 2.377 \angle 22.24°$ Ω

6.23 $\mathbf{I}_1 = 2.91 \angle 14.04°$ A
$\mathbf{I}_2 = -1.46 \angle 14.04°$ A

6.27 $\mathbf{V}_S = 25.5 \angle -11.31°$ V

6.32 $\mathbf{V}_S = -100.8 \angle -19.6°$ V

CHAPTER 7

7.1 $\dfrac{\mathbf{V}_0}{\mathbf{V}_S} = \dfrac{2}{3 + j\omega}$

7.5 Double zero at $j = 0$
Poles at $-\dfrac{2}{5} \pm j\dfrac{4}{5}$

7.9 $C = 1.6$ F

7.13 $R = 159.2$

7.17 $\omega_{LO} = 452.49$ r/s
$\omega_{HI} = 552.49$ r/s

7.21 All pass filter
$\dfrac{\mathbf{V}_0}{\mathbf{V}_1} = \dfrac{1 - j\omega CR}{1 + j\omega CR}$

7.25 BW = 30 r/s
$\omega_{LO} = 1785$ r/s
$\omega_{HI} = 1815$ r/s

7.29 $C = 1.59$ nF
$L = 1.59$ mH

7.33 $\omega_0 = 500$ r/s
BW = 2.5 r/s

7.37 BW = 10 r/s
Q = 63.25
$\omega_{LO} = 627.475$ r/s
$\omega_{HI} = 637.475$ r/s

7.41 $C = 45.2$ mF or 345.4 mF

CHAPTER 8

8.1 (a) D; (b) A; (c) D; (d) A; (e) D; (f) A; (g) A; (h) D

8.5 (a) 80 bits per line; (b) 2×10^7 bits per second

8.9 2×10^8 s

8.11 (a) 22.5 V; (b) 0.253 W

8.13 6.32×10^6

8.15 (a) $9 \angle 0°$; b) $3 \angle 90°$

8.18 (a) 286; (b) 49.1 db

8.21 $f_{HI} = 1000$ Hz; $f_{LO} = 10$ Hz; BW = 990 Hz

8.28 (a) 10 kHz ; (b) 0.99 MHz

8.32 12

8.35 (a) 9.8 mV; (b) 6 kHz

8.41

A_1	A_2	B
0	0	1
0	1	1
1	0	0
1	1	1

8.45 (a) 0; (b) 61 mV; (c) Amplifier with $A_v = 49.2$

CHAPTER 9

9.1 (a) 2000; (b) yes; $v_o = A_v v_i$, where A_v = constant

9.5 (a) v_o −5 V; (b) $v_o = -3$ V; (c) v_o + 5 V

9.8 23

9.12 67.7

9.17 2 V
9.20 −87.5
9.24 0.5 V
9.27 0.15 V
9.31 $v_o = -60\,(v_A + v_B) - 24\,v_C$
9.38 Element A = resistor, $R = 2$ k
Element B = capacitor,
$C = 1 \times 10^{-9}$ F
9.41 $A_{F(\max)} = -10$
BW = 0.33 Hz
9.45 −8 kΩ
9.48 −14.5
9.51 37 V/μs

CHAPTER 10

10.3 (a) Fifth column; (b) Third column
10.9 (a) Electrons to the right (opposite of the direction of electric field); 2.0×10^{17} carriers/s; $J = 0.133$ A/cm^2; $I = -0.0333$ A
(b) holes to the left (same direction as electric field); all other answers same as in (a).
10.11 $\sigma_i = 4.69 \times 10^{-6}$ S/cm; $\sigma =$ 216 S/cm
10.15 (b) $J_n = -560$ A/cm^2; $J_p = -1.9$ A/cm^2; $J = -561.9$ A/cm^2
10.20 (a) 1.33 mA; (b) 0
10.24 (a) 15 V; (b) 5 mA
10.28 603 A
10.33 (a) 0.749 V; (b) 0.888 V; (c) 0.888 V; (d) 5 V
10.36 (c) 1.40 V
10.40 (c) 8.98 V
10.45 The voltage transfer plot shows that
For $-5 < v_i + 3$ V, then $v_o = v_i$
For $v_i > +3$ V, then $v_o = V = +3$ V, because D becomes forward biased (closed switch)
10.49 (b) −5.0 V
10.52 7.182 V

CHAPTER 11

11.2 Field Effect Transistor (FET); Bipolar Junction Transistor (BJT)
11.6 (a) p-channel enhancement mode
(b) n-channel depletion mode
(c) n-channel enhancement mode
(d) p-channel depletion mode
11.10 Threshold voltage, V_T; cutoff
11.13 14.2 mA
11.15 (a) 3.7×10^{-4}
11.20 (a) 0.455 V
11.27 (a) gate; (b) base
11.33 (a) −1.2 V; (b) -3.33×10^{-4}; (c) -5.0×10^{-4}
11.37 The arrow (emitter terminal) indicates the direction of positive current flow, and also designates transistor type: "arrow-out" = NPN; "arrow-in" = PNP
11.41 (a) active; (b) $I_B = 28$ μA; $I_C = 2.8$ mA; $I_E = 2.83$ mA
11.45 $I_B = 82$ μA; $I_C = 4.92$ mA
11.50 For $V_i = 0.8$ V, $V_o = 3.5$ V; For $V_i =$ 3.5 V, $V_o = 0.1$ V
11.55 $I_C = 1.44$ mA; $V_C = 13.53$ V

CHAPTER 12

12.4 6.5 kΩ
12.8 −19.1
12.12 1.3×10^{-3} S; 7.5×10^{-4} S
12.16 4.74×10^{-3} S
12.20 (a) 7.14; (b) 8.33
12.24 (a) $r_{ib} = 1.733$ kΩ; $\beta = 200$; $r_o = 25$ kΩ
(c) −699
(d) 1.722 kΩ
12.28 32.3
12.34 −300
12.38 0.975
12.42 2160
12.45 1.25×10^4

CHAPTER 13

13.1 (a) 10001
(b) 10000
13.5 (a) 110
(b) 10010
13.9 (a) 110010
(b) 1001101
13.14 (a) 111
(b) 1101
(c) 1111
(d) 11011
13.18 (a) $\bar{B}$
(b) $\bar{A}B + BD$
13.24 (a) $\bar{B} + C$
(b) $B\bar{C} + \bar{B}C$

13.26 $f(A, B, C) = \bar{B}$

13.31 (a) $B\bar{C}\bar{D} + \bar{B}\bar{C}D + BCD$

(b) $BC + B\bar{D}$

13.35 $f(A_1, A_2, A_3, A_4) = A_1 + A_2A_3A_4$

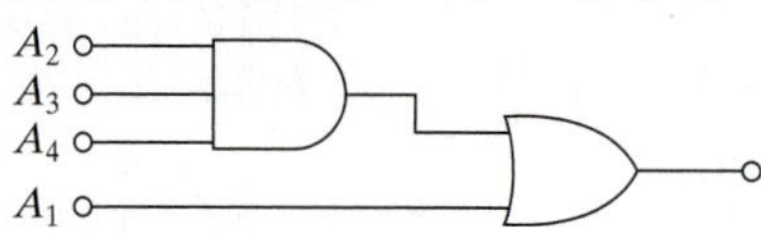

13.39 (BCD) = $(A_1A_2A_3A_4)$

(4221) = $(B_1B_2B_3B_4)$

$B_1 = A_1 + A_2A_4 + A_2\bar{A}_3$

$B_2 = A_1 + A_2A_3 + A_2A_4$

$B_3 = A_1 + \bar{A}_2A_4 + A_2A_3\bar{A}_4$

$B_4 = A_3$

13.44 A – Alarm

P – Pressure

F – Fluid Level

T – Temperature

$A = PF + FT + PT$

13.49

y \ x		
	0/1	1/0
	0/0	1/0

y_k+1/z_k

13.53

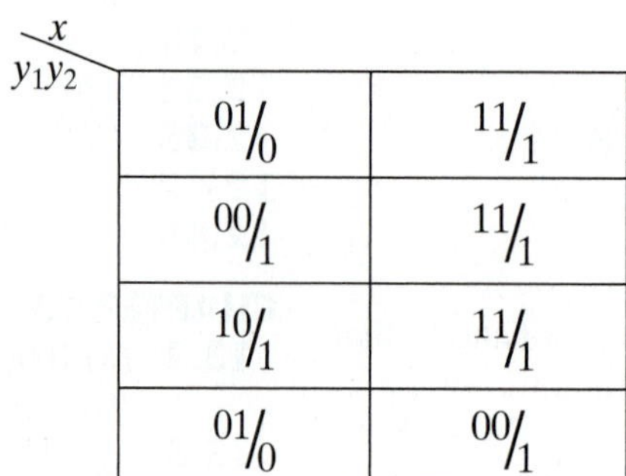

y_1y_2 \ x		
	01/0	11/1
	00/1	11/1
	10/1	11/1
	01/0	00/1

13.57

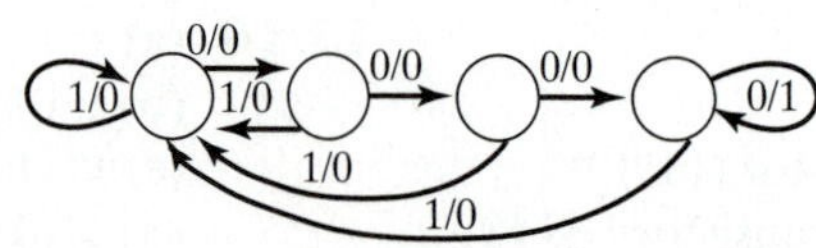

13.62

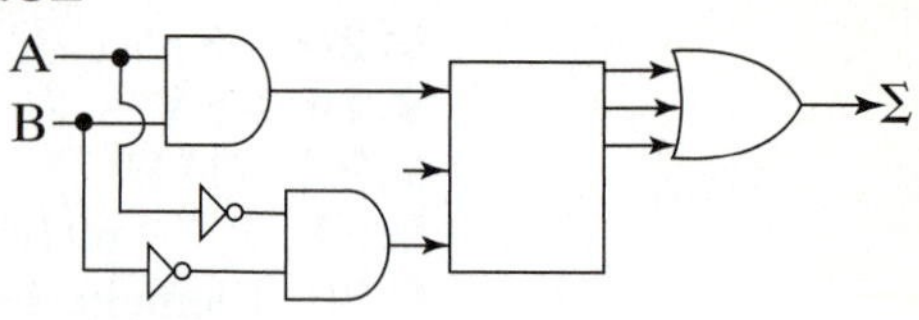

CHAPTER 14

14.1 8; 16

14.5 Output "1" except in cases: (a) when all inputs "0", and (b) when all inputs "1." For these two cases, output is "1."

14.6 $t_{PHL} = 1.5$ μs; $t_{PLH} = 2.5$ μs; $t_P = 2$ μs

14.12 32 ns

14.16 $NM_H = 1.2$ V; $NM_L = 1.0$ V; $TW = 2.3$ V; $LS = 4.5$ V

14.21 a) $V_{OH} = 4.2$ V; $V_{IL} = 0.8$ V

b) $r_{on} = 96\ \Omega$

14.25 (a) Plot shows steeper transition than single inverter

(b) For single inverter $NM_L = 1$ V; cascaded $NM_L = 1.75$ V; thus, NM_L improved

14.30 (a) $NM_H\ NM_L$ 2.5 V; (sharp transition occurs at 1/2 V_{DD})

(b) CMOS noise margins are higher

14.34 (a) $V_{IL} = 1.2$ V; $V_{OL} = 0.1$; $V_{OH} = 5$ V

(b) $\beta^* = 1.54$

14.39

A_1	A_2	B
0	0	1
0	1	1
1	0	1
1	1	0

CHAPTER 15

15.1 $V_t = 400$ V

15.3 $V_t = 300$ V

15.5 $V_t = 290.4$ V

15.9 $\omega = 272.73$ r/s

15.13 $R_a = 0.152$

15.18 If $K_a\ \phi$ decreases, ω increases

15.22 $P_{in} = 66.3$ Hp

15.26 $T = 76.2$ N-m

15.30 $\omega = 616.5$ rpm

$\omega_{(no\ load)} = 631.3$ rpm

CHAPTER 16

16.1 $P = 4$, slip = 0.06 and $f_r = 1.5$ Hz
16.4 $I_s = 93.17\ \underline{/-64.7°}$ A
16.8 $I_s = 41.26$ A
16.13 Eff = 76.5%
16.17 $\omega_s = 78.54$ r/s
16.21 $E_f = 2754.9\ \underline{/-10.49°}$ V
16.25 $S_{3\phi} = 1.722 + j1.017$ MVA
16.29 $E_f = 1720.37\ \underline{/16.7°}$ V

Index